The Routledge Handbook of Tourism and the Environment

The Routledge Handbook of Tourism and the Environment explores and critically evaluate the debates and controversies inherent to tourism's relationship with nature, especially pertinent at a time of major re-evaluation of our relationship with the environment as a consequence of the environmental problems we now face. It brings together leading specialists from range of disciplinary backgrounds and geographical regions, to provide state-of-the-art theoretical reflection and empirical research on this complex relationship and future direction.

The book is divided into five inter-related parts. Part 1 evaluates the philosophical basis, rationale and complexity of what is meant by the term 'environment' considering the major influences in the construction of how we understand our surroundings and the types of values we place upon them. Part 2 evaluates the types of ecosystems that are used as natural resources for tourism and the negative and positive impacts upon them. Part 3 evaluates relevant environmental policy and management mechanisms for the impacts of tourism on the natural environment. Part 4 focuses on the changing tourism–environment relationship, and types of tourism that have become established in the tourism industry, market and policy. Part 5 analyses contemporary and future issues of the tourism–environment relationship, based on themes of environmental and social welfare.

This timely book will provide an invaluable resource for all those with an interest in tourism's relationship with the natural environment, encouraging dialogue across disciplinary boundaries and areas of study. The book is international in its focus, emphasising that issues of tourism and the natural environment are not only localised but transcend national boundaries that sometimes require both international and global responses.

This is essential reading for students, researchers and academics of Tourism as well as those of Geography, Environmental Studies and Development Studies.

Andrew Holden is Professor in Environment and Tourism at Bedfordshire University, UK.

David Fennell teaches and researches in the areas of ecotourism and tourism ethics at Brock University, St Catharines, Ontario, Canada.

The Routledge Handbook of Tourism and the Environment

Edited by Andrew Holden and David Fennell

Routledge
Taylor & Francis Group

LONDON AND NEW YORK

First published 2013
by Routledge
2 Park Square, Milton Park, Abingdon, Oxon OX14 4RN

Simultaneously published in the USA and Canada
by Routledge
711 Third Avenue, New York, NY 10017

Routledge is an imprint of the Taylor & Francis Group, an informa business

British Library Cataloguing in Publication Data
A catalogue record for this book is available from the British Library

Library of Congress Cataloging in Publication Data
Holden, Andrew.
  The Routledge handbook of tourism and the environment / Andrew Holden and David
Fennell.
     p. cm.
  Includes bibliographical references and index.
  1. Tourism–Environmental aspects–Handbooks, manuals, etc. 2. Sustainable tourism–
Handbooks, manuals, etc. 3. Ecotourism–Handbooks, manuals, etc. I. Fennell, David A.,
1963- II. Title.
  G155.A1H65 2012
  338.4'791–dc23
                                                    2011044795

ISBN: 978-0-415-58207-0 (hbk)
ISBN: 978-0-203-12110-8 (ebk)

Typeset in Bembo
by Taylor & Francis Books

Printed and bound by CPI Group (UK) Ltd, Croydon, CR0 4YY

Contents

Contents

Contents

Illustrations

Tables

Figures

List of Contributors

Theodosia Anthopoulou is Associated Professor of Social and Rural Geography, Department of Social Policy, Panteion University, Athens, Greece. Her research interests and publications centre on rural restructuring and multifunctionality, social and spatial recomposition, localised agrifood systems, territorial development and Euromediterranean cooperation.

Adama Bah has many years of experience in The Gambia working with small producers to improve their livelihoods through tourism. He has played a major role in developing ASSET, a trade association for small scale producers in tourism, the Gambia is Good initiative which has enabled small farmers to sell fruit and vegetables to the hotels, increasing their incomes and Guaranteed Gambian which improves market access for craft producers.

Godfrey Baldacchino is Canada Research Chair (Island Studies), University of Prince Edward Island, Canada; Visiting Professor of Sociology, University of Malta, Malta; and Executive Editor, *Island Studies Journal*. His doctoral thesis – published as *Global Tourism & Informal Labour Relations* (Mansell 1997) – explored value collisions between indigenous culture and the corporate ethos of multinational hospitality forms.

Mark Ballantyne is commencing his PhD research in the Environment Futures Research Centre at Griffith University in Queensland, Australia. He has a Bachelor of Science in Ecology with Honours from Lancaster University. During his undergraduate degree he undertook a year of study at Griffith University, where he completed a study of orchid tourism and the impacts of tourism on orchids. Some of this research has already been published including in the *Journal of Ecotourism*. He will be continuing this research during his PhD as part of developing the field of plant-based tourism.

Agustina Barros is a PhD student in the Environment Futures Research Centre at Griffith University in Queensland, Australia. Her Master's thesis examined visitor impacts on vegetation, soil and water in Aconcagua Provincial Park in Argentina. She has worked in international non-profit organisations on issues relating to mountain conservation and sustainable mountain development. Her current PhD research is examining the range of ecological impacts from tourism in high mountain protected areas using Aconcagua, the highest mountain in the Southern Hemisphere as a case study.

Diana Barsham was formerly Head of English & Creative Writing at the University of Chichester, having worked previously at NYUiL, and the Universities of Warwick, Derby and

Birmingham City. She is now a full-time writer, with a special interest in poetry and biography. She has published monographs on the life, work and travels of Sir Arthur Conan Doyle (Arthur Conan Doyle and the Meaning of Masculinity, Ashgate 2000) and on Victorian women writers, travellers and occultists (The Trial of Woman, Macmillan 1992). Other publications include essays on the Sherlock Holmes stories and an edition of the poetry of Ted Walker.

Lyn Bibbings (Oxford Brookes University) is a planner and a designer who has been working in tourism and tourism education for over 30 years. Her special interest and expertise lie with the interactions between government policy, tourism governance, society and culture, including issues around tourism and climate change. She is a director of Tourism South East and of the Tourism Society. She also works in supporting academics who teach tourism through her role as Discipline Lead for Hospitality, Leisure, Sport, Tourism and Events in the social science cluster at the Higher Education Academy.

Erin Bohensky is a social-ecological systems scientist with the Commonwealth Scientific and Industrial Research Organisation (CSIRO) based in Townsville, Australia. Her research focuses on societal framing and perceptions of environmental change and their underlying drivers. She works in the Great Barrier Reef region and elsewhere in the Asia-Pacific region.

David T. Brown is a founding faculty member of the Department of Tourism and Environment at Brock University in St. Catharines, Ontario, Canada. He has been active in domestic and international waste management research since the mid 1990s. Dr. Brown's diverse academic background in ecology, urban and environmental studies, systems theory, sustainability, and environmental policy informs his current work, which also includes heritage mapping, sustainable tourism, and the use of mobile digital technologies in tourism and educational interpretation. He has lived, worked, and lectured in many parts of the world including Thailand, New Zealand, Hong Kong, and China, and represented Brock University internationally as Brock's Associate Vice-President for International Cooperation for five years. He holds a PhD from McGill University and a B.Sc. from Macdonald College.

Ralf Buckley is Director of the International Centre for Ecotourism Research at Griffith University, and Director of the university's strategic research initiative in sustainable tourism. He has 750 publications including 200 journal articles and a dozen books, about half in ecotourism, and has worked in 40 countries.

Peter Burns (University of Brighton) is an applied social scientist with special interest in the interactions between tourism, society, and culture. He is founding director of the Centre for Tourism Policy Studies (CENTOPS), University of Brighton, specialising in researching sustainable tourism in its broadest sense. In 2010 he wrote 'Climate Change Policy Recommendations' for the World Travel and Tourism Council.

Carl Cater is a lecturer in tourism at Aberystwyth University, Wales, and his research centres on the experiential turn in tourism and the subsequent growth of special interest sectors. He is a fellow of the Royal Geographical Society, a qualified pilot, diver, lifesaver, mountain and tropical forest leader, and maintains an interest in both the practice and pursuit of sustainable outdoor tourism activity. He is co-author (with Dr Erlet Cater) of *Marine Ecotourism: Between the Devil and the Deep Blue Sea* (CABI 2007), and is an editorial board member of *Tourism Geographies*, *Journal of Ecotourism* and *Tourism in Marine Environments*.

Jonathan Chenoweth is a senior lecturer in the Centre for Environmental Strategy at the University of Surrey, where he teaches issues relating to environment and sustainable development. Jonathan is a natural resources management specialist whose research is focused upon the institutional and policy dimensions of water management. He researches on water policy and sustainable development in developed and developing regions, including in the UK and elsewhere in Europe, the Middle East and Africa.

Alan Clarke moved to the University of Pannonia, Hungary, to develop tourism courses at undergraduate and postgraduate levels in English. An active believer in partnership working, he is actively engaged in research projects seeking to share and embed knowledge within and around tourism developments, such as the cross border developments between Hungary and Croatia and with RECULTIVATUR framing best practice guidelines. He has recently returned from Istria, Croatia, where he was advising on the development of cultural tourism. Before moving to Hungary, he had been actively engaged in the Wirksworth consultancy project and was the first chair of the Peak District Sustainable Tourism Partnership. He was also one of the researchers in the DETOUR project, which continues to inspire his approach to strategic development in partnerships.

Alexandra Coghlan is a Research Fellow at Griffith University's International Centre for Ecotourism Research. She has a BSc (Honours) in Environmental and Marine Biology from the University of St Andrews, and a PhD from James Cook University, Townsville, Australia. Her primary research interests focus on change processes facilitated through alternative and nature-based tourism, including transformative travel experiences, environmental education/interpretation, governance issues and tourism partnerships.

Janet Dickinson is a Senior Lecturer in the School of Tourism, Bournemouth University, UK. Her research interests include sustainable tourism and transport.

Kay Dimmock has research interests and publications in several areas related to water-based leisure and tourism including scuba divers' experiences in water with comfort, constraint and negotiation, marine leisure, risk in diving, whale watching, marine conservation and visitor interpretation. She has guest edited (with G. Musa) a special edition of the journal *Tourism in Marine Environments*. Kay currently lectures in management, special interest tourism and marine tourism at the School of Tourism and Hospitality Management at Southern Cross University.

Trisia Farrelly is a Lecturer in the Social Anthropology Programme, School of People, Environment and Planning, Massey University, Palmerston North, New Zealand. Her research interests are based in the South Pacific and include indigenous community-based ecotourism as indigenous entrepreneurship, indigenous decision-making, and indigenous epistemologies. Recently, her work has turned to more broadly address negotiations occurring at the nexus of notions of 'environmental sustainability' and human–environment relationships in general.

David Fennell teaches and researches in the areas of ecotourism and tourism ethics at Brock University, St Catharines, Ontario, Canada.

Xavier Font is an expert in responsible tourism marketing, with extensive experience in industry and government training on all aspects of sustainable tourism production and consumption. He is the most published academic in the world in sustainable tourism certification, having consulted on this subject for UNEP, UNCTAD, UNWTO, IFC, EC, VisitEngland, Fáilte Ireland, WWF and the Travel Foundation among others. Since 2008, he administers the validation process for sustainable tourism certification programmes for VisitEngland, VisitWales and the Northern Ireland Tourist Board.

Adrian Franklin is Professor of Sociology at the University of Tasmania, Hobart, Australia, and has held professorial positions at the University of Bristol, UK, and the University of Oslo, Norway. He is a Founding Editor of *Tourist Studies* and has written widely in the areas of tourism theory, the sociology of travel and tourism, nature and social theory and human–animal relations. He is the author of many books including *Tourism* (London: Sage), *Animals and Modern Cultures* (London: Sage), *Nature and Social Theory* (London: Sage) and *City Life* (London: Sage).

Harold Goodwin is Professor of Responsible Tourism in the International Centre for Research on Events, Tourism and Hospitality at Leeds Metropolitan University. He was a founding partner in the Pro-Poor Tourism Partnership and is a Member of the International Centre for Responsible Tourism.

Stefan Gössling is a Professor at the School of Business and Economics at Linnaeus University, Kalmar, and the Department of Service Management, Lund University, both Sweden. He is also the Research Coordinator of the Research Centre for Sustainable Tourism at the Western Norway Research Institute. Stefan has worked with climate change since 1992, focusing primarily on aviation-related emissions and tourism. He has also worked extensively in islands, particularly in the Western Indian Ocean and Caribbean.

Bryan Grimwood is an Assistant Professor in the Department of Recreation and Leisure Studies at the University of Waterloo, Canada. His PhD dissertation engaged case study research of the Thelon River to explore the intersecting the geographies of nature, ethics, and travel.

Danuta de Grosbois, Associate Professor of Tourism and Environment, Brock University, St Catherines, Ontario, Canada.

Michalis Hadjikakou is a PhD student at the Centre for Environmental Strategy, based in the University of Surrey, UK. His research aims to quantify, through the use of input–output modelling, the economic productivity of water use for a range of tourism products in a semi-arid Mediterranean setting. Michalis holds a BA in Physical Geography from the University of Cambridge, UK, a matrise in hydrology from Grenoble I (Joseph Fourier) and an MSc in Water Science, Policy and Management from the University of Oxford, UK. In addition to his academic work, Michalis has also been involved in Tourism Concern's Water Equity for Tourism (WET) programme.

Michael Hall is Professor in the Department of Management, University of Canterbury, New Zealand; Docent, Department of Geography, Oulu University, Finland; and Visiting Professor, Linneaus University, Kalmar, and Lund University, Helsingborg, Sweden and the University of Eastern Finland, Savonlinna. Co-editor of *Current Issues in Tourism*, he has wide-ranging interests in tourism and mobility, environmental history and gastronomy.

Kevin Hannam is Associate Dean of Research, Head of the Department of Tourism, Hospitality and Events, Professor of Tourism Development and Director of the Centre for Research into the Experience Economy (CREE) at the University of Sunderland and a research affiliate at the University of Johannesburg, South Africa. He is founding co-editor of the journal *Mobilities* (Routledge), co-author of the recent text *Understanding Tourism* (Sage) and monograph *Tourism and India* (Routledge). He is co-chair of the ATLAS Backpacker Research Group, chair of the World Leisure Commission on Tourism. He has published research on aspects of cultural, heritage and nature-based tourism development in India and Scandinavia. He holds a PhD in geography from the University of Portsmouth.

James Higham is Professor of Tourism in the Department of Tourism (School of Business), University of Otago, New Zealand, and Visiting Professor of Sustainable Tourism at the University of Stavanger, Norway. His research interests address tourism, environmental change and sustainable development

Michael Hitchcock has written and edited 14 books, as well as 40 refereed articles and other papers. He holds a doctorate from the University of Oxford and was appointed Professor of Tourism at the University of North London (London Metropolitan University) in 1995. He was made a Centenary Professor in the same institution the following year. He also taught anthropology and sociology at the University of Hull, and was appointed Deputy Dean of External Relations and Research at the University of Chichester in 2008. For two years he was Academic Director of IMI Switzerland, and is currently working as a consultant and freelance writer.

Andrew Holden is Professor of Environment and Tourism and Director of the Institute for Tourism Research (INTOUR) at the University of Bedfordshire.

Keith Hollinshead analyses issues of cultural selection/cultural production from *transdisciplinary* or *postdisciplinary* (or even *adisciplinary*) outlooks. Specialising in the understandings/misunderstandings that course through the representational repertoires of tourism, he critically inspects the claimed traditions and the emergent transitionalities of populations. Currently, he is Professor of Public Culture at the University of Bedfordshire.

Debbie Hopkins is a PhD candidate at the University of Otago, New Zealand. Her research explores the human–environment relationship, climate governance, narratives of climate change, socio-scientific knowledge and climate change adaptation and mitigation in New Zealand's ski industry.

Tazim Jamal is an Associate Professor in the Department of Recreation, Park and Tourism Sciences, Texas A&M University, College Station, Texas. Her research areas are community-based tourism, collaborative planning, integrated heritage management, and theoretical/methodological issues related to tourism and sustainability.

John Jenkins is Professor of Tourism and Chair of Academic Board at Southern Cross University (SCU), Australia. John was previously (2007–11) Head of the School of Tourism and Hospitality Management at SCU. John has published several books, including *Tourism and Public Policy* (with C.M. Hall, 2003), *Tourism Planning and Policy* (with D. Dredge, 2007) and *Outdoor Recreation Management* (with J.J. Pigram, 2006). His most recent book, *Stories of Practice: Tourism Policy and Planning* (with D. Dredge), was published by Ashgate in 2011. John is currently managing editor of *Annals of Leisure Research*, and his research interests are mainly in the fields of leisure and tourism planning and policy, outdoor recreation management, and leisure and recreation in rural areas.

Angela Kalisch is Senior Lecturer in Tourism Management at the University of Gloucestershire, UK. She teaches on tourism impacts, sustainable tourism, managing across cultures and tourism ethics. Her PhD research centres on equitable and sustainable trade in tourism and is based on her research on Fair Trade in Tourism with the UK based non-governmental organisation Tourism Concern, before joining academia. This work has informed various academic and non-academic publications. Her interest in these topics emerged from her practical experience as adventure travel operator to destinations in South Asia.

Christopher Lemieux is a Postdoctoral Fellow in the Department of Geography and Environmental Management at the University of Waterloo. His research interests primarily focus on climate change and protected areas management, and nature-based tourism and recreation.

Michael Lück, Associate professor and head of the Department of Tourism and Events, Auckland University of Technology, New Zealand.

Les Lumsdon is Emeritus Professor of Tourism at the University of Central Lancashire, UK. He researches the interfaces between transport and tourism.

Stephen McCool is Professor Emeritus with the Department of Society and Conservation, the College of Forestry and Conservation at The University of Montana in the USA. Dr. McCool's research interests encompass management of tourism and visitation in protected areas, public engagement processes and frameworks for protected area planning, and developing new paradigms of protected area planning.

Peter Mason is currently Visiting Professor of Tourism at South Bank University, London and Adjunct Professor of Tourism at Victoria University, Melbourne. He was previously Head of the School of Hospitality, Tourism and Marketing at Victoria University, Melbourne, and prior to that Head of Tourism, Leisure and Sport at Bedfordshire University, UK. His first degree is in Geography, he obtained his PhD at the University of Plymouth and has taught and researched at universities in the UK, Australia and New Zealand since 1989.

Yorgos Melissourgos has recently completed his PhD on geography at Harokopio University, Athens, Greece, where he is currently a part-time lecturer. His research interests include the analysis of the supply-side of tourism, the relationship between tourism and local/regional development, and special forms of tourism.

David Mercer is currently Associate Professor in the School of Global Studies, Social Science & Planning at RMIT University in Melbourne, Australia, where he is Director of the post-graduate program in International Urban and Environmental Management. A geographer by training, he has degrees from Cambridge, UK, and Monash Universities, Melbourne, Australia. He has served on the editorial boards of a number of journals including the *Journal of Leisure Research, The Australasian Journal of Natural Resources Law and Policy, The Open Environmental Journal* and *The Annals of Leisure Research*. His most recent research has been on food security and alternative food networks in Australia, as well as human responses to natural disasters with a particular focus on post-tsunami reconstruction in Sri Lanka and Tamil Nadu and bushfires in southeastern Australia.

Graham Miller is Head of the School of Hospitality and Tourism Management at the University of Surrey, UK, where he teaches issues relating to business ethics, sustainability and the tourism industry. Graham's main research interest is in the forces that enable and prevent the drive towards a more sustainable tourism industry, publishing the first book to address the monitoring of sustainable tourism in 2005. Graham sits on the editorial board of the *Journal of Sustainable Tourism*, is a co-ordinating editor for the *Annals of Tourism Research* and is the Tourism editor of the journal *Tourism and Hospitality Research*.

Patrizia Modica is an Associate Professor of Business Economics in the Department of Economics and Business Studies at the University of Cagliari, Italy.

David Newsome's research interests span many areas of natural area tourism including wildlife tourism, the biophysical impacts of recreation in protected areas, evaluation of the quality of ecotourism operations, sustainable trail management and geotourism. In recent years he has co-ordinated several significant research projects for the Australian Government funded Sustainable Tourism Cooperative Research Centre including projects relating to understanding the importance of wildlife icons, investigating the nature of impact creep and the development of a wildlife tourism auditing framework. Significant publications include the books *Natural Area Tourism: ecology, impacts and management* and *Wildlife Tourism*. David is also a member of the Conservation Commission of Western Australia. He is a member of the Shark Bay advisory Committee and Coral Coast Advisory Committee in Western Australia and holds membership of the IUCN World Commission on Protected Areas. He has experience of ecotourism development in southeast Asia and has acted as advisor to the ASEAN Centre for Biodiversity (Regional Training on Ecotourism Workshop for Protected Area Managers) in Malaysia.

Mark Orams, Professor at the School of Hospitality and Tourism, Auckland University of Technology, New Zealand.

Catherine Pickering is an Associate Professor in the Environment Futures Research Centre at Griffith University, Australia. She has undertaken a wide range of research including on plant-based tourism, examining the impacts of tourism on plants including direct impacts from a range of activities, such as hiking, camping and mountain biking and indirect impacts including tourists as seed vectors. More recently, she has focused on plants as tourism attractions—a parallel field to wildlife tourism. She has over 200 publications, including over 70 papers published in international referred academic journals.

Ryan Plummer is a Professor in the Department of Tourism and Environment and Director of the Environmental Sustainability Research Centre at Brock University, Canada. He is also a Senior Research Fellow at the Stockholm Resilience Centre, Sweden. His programme of research concerns the governance of social-ecological systems.

Ágnes Raffay is a Docens/Senior Lecturer in the Department of Tourism at the University of Pannonia in Veszprém, Hungary, following a career in destination management with Tourinform and acting as the tourism referent for Veszprém City Council. Her PhD at the University of Derby, UK, unpacked the dynamics of stakeholder relations in two historic cities, successfully demonstrating the impact of several different discourses of power on tourism developments. She is currently Vice-President of the Veszprém Tourism Association. Her recent research has focused on the implementation of new policies for tourism management through the introduction of Tourism Destination Management Organisations. She is a reviewer for funding bids for new tourism development submitted to the regional development agency in Central Transdanubia.

Kate Rodger has extensive experience in collaborating closely with the tourism industry, in particular park agencies, and has produced technical reports on management planning, improving the sustainability of wildlife tourism, and using visitor data more effectively. Her research has been published in leading international journals such as *Society and Natural Resources*, *Journal of Sustainable Tourism* and the *Annals of Tourism Research*. Current research interests include human–wildlife interactions in the marine and terrestrial environment, identifying and minimising visitor impacts through visitor management techniques in protected areas, improving links between science and policy, and integrating ecological and social sciences in nature tourism research.

Jarkko Saarinen is Professor of Human Geography at the University of Oulu, Finland, and Research Affiliate, School of Tourism and Hospitality, Faculty of Management, University of Johannesburg, South Africa. He is also External Program Leader in the International Tourism Research Centre (ITRC), University of Botswana. His research interests include tourism development and sustainability and the use and transformations of nature and culture in tourism.

Daniel Scott is a Canada Research Chair in Global Change and Tourism at the University of Waterloo, Ontario, Canada. He has been a contributing author to the IPCC and is a member of the Advisory Committee for the UN co-ordinated Global Partnership for Sustainable Tourism.

Tony Seaton is Emeritus Professor of Tourism Behaviour at the University of Bedfordshire, UK, and MacAnally Professor of Travel and Tourism History and Behaviour at the University of Limerick. He has lectured and researched in 65 different countries in Europe, America and Australia, and produced almost 100 articles, papers and presentations, and written/edited six books. He recently completed an MA in Theology (with distinction) at Lampeter, Ireland, specialising in Monastic Studies, and research on Godstow Monastery, and Mary-Anne Schimmelpenninck's monastic writings on La Grande Chartreuse, La Trappe and the two Jansenist Port Royals.

Richard Sharpley is Professor of Tourism and Development at the University of Central Lancashire, UK. He has previously held positions at a number of other institutions, including the University of Northumbria (Reader in Tourism) and the University of Lincoln, where he was professor of Tourism and Head of Department, Tourism and Recreation Management. His principal research interests are within the fields of tourism and development, island tourism, rural tourism and the sociology of tourism. He has published numerous journal articles on these subjects and his books include *Tourism and Development in the Developing World* (2008), *Tourism, Tourists and Society*, 4th Edn (2008) and *Tourism, Development and Environment: Beyond Sustainability* (2009).

Nancy Stevenson is the Undergraduate Programme Leader for Tourism at the University of Westminster, UK. Her research is focused on the experience and practice of cultural and tourism policy making and draws from complexity theory. Current projects are focused on the 2012 Games and include an investigation of the cultural Olympiad and an evaluation of Post Games Legacies.

Samantha Stone-Jovicich is a social scientist with the Commonwealth Scientific and Industrial Research Organisation (CSIRO). Based in Townsville, Australia, her research examines the role of social processes and structures (social learning, worldviews, institutions) in shaping natural resource management decisions and actions, from primary producers to policy makers.

Jessica Taplin has worked as a research assistant with the School of Tourism and Hospitality Management at Southern Cross University, Australia, and her research interests include the impacts of tourism and recreation on local communities and environments. Jessica was recently awarded a national/Commonwealth scholarship and is currently undertaking a PhD focused on volunteer tourism.

David Telfer is Associate Professor in the Department of Tourism and Environment at Brock University, Canada. His research interests include the linkages between tourism and development theory, rural tourism and the linkages between tourism and agriculture.

Dallen Timothy is Professor of Community Resources and Development at Arizona State University, USA, and Senior Sustainability Scientist in the Global Institute of Sustainability at the same university. He is also Visiting Professor of Heritage Tourism at the University of Sunderland, and Adjunct Professor of Geography at Indiana University. His tourism-oriented research focuses on geopolitics and borders, tangible and intangible heritage, tourism and religion, and community-based development. He is editor-in-chief of the *Journal of Heritage Tourism* and serves on the editorial boards of twelve international journals. Professor Timothy is also co-commissioning editor of Channel View Publications' *Aspects of Tourism* book series, and has ongoing research projects in Asia, the Middle East, Europe and Latin America.

Cain S. Todd is Lecturer in Philosophy at Lancaster University, UK. Specialising in aesthetics and value theory, he has written various articles in these areas, focusing on fiction, emotion, imagination and the objectivity of aesthetic judgment. He has also written on the nature and appreciation of tourism, sport and wine.

Fernanda de Vasconcellos Pegas is an anthropologist who hails originally from the ranchlands of Brazil. She gained her PhD from Texas A&M University, USA, on turtle tourism and conservation. She is currently a Research Fellow in the International Centre for Ecotourism Research at Griffith University, Australia, and has ongoing research programmes, collaborations and publications in Brazil, the Pacific and elsewhere.

Peter Wiltshier is Senior Lecturer and Programme Leader for travel and tourism management at the University of Derby, UK, and aims to ensure that the public and private sectors work together to develop resources and skills for communities to take charge of their own destinies. He is currently researching small business and lifestyles in the Peak District, and also working with the Diocese of Derby to identify how tourism can benefit churches and through local government offices evaluating the impact of tourism on host communities.

Acknowledgements

Pulling this book together has taken a great deal to trust, time and effort from a variety of people. The editors would especially like to begin by thanking the anonymous reviewers of the proposal for their guiding comments and advice. We would also like to especially thank all the contributors to agreeing to be willing to participate in this book. You have demonstrated a great deal of faith in the project, without which it could not have happened. We hope that your efforts will be rewarded in the future as this tomb is widely read and its words of wisdom contained in all its chapters are acted upon.

Co-ordinating nearly 50 independent contributors is an enormous organisational and administrative task requiring a lot of skill and patience. The editors would like to thank the support they have had from Routledge in doing this, including the support of Emma Travis, Carol Barber, the proofreading of Eildh McGregor and the final pulling together of Paola Celli. We are also especially grateful to Dr. Carol Tie of the University of Bedfordshire for all the co-ordination and liaison work she has undertaken between the editors, authors and Routledge. These efforts have pulled together what the editors believe to be a major reference text for multitude of issues that relate to this complex relationship of the environment and tourism. We hope you enjoy the readings.

Part 1
Scientific realities and cultural constructs of the environment

1

Introduction

Andrew Holden

The term 'environment' is now embedded in the global vernacular and since the 1960s has progressively become synonymous with concern and political controversy. The conscious and deliberate use of the term is symbolic of an increased re-awareness of human interaction with the surroundings, an interaction that had been up to the Industrial Revolution implicit to our own survival and welfare. A combination of Enlightenment rationality, scientific endorsement and industrial development had, until the latter part of the twentieth century, created a generalised perception that nature could be 'mastered' and controlled for our own benefit. However, the emergent realisation that human endeavour could affect our surroundings, an awareness created by research endeavour in the environmental sciences alongside political and ethical green discourses has caused a re-evaluation of our interaction with the 'environment'. This process of re-evaluation is politically and economically contentious, we need look no further than the issue of climate change to exemplify divergent interests and stakes in the environment. However, in many debates, issues of spatial scale, ecological composition and ecosystem changes, 'rights' of non-human species vis-á-vis anthropocentric interests, reflect disparate constructions and interpretations of our surroundings.

The focus of the opening section of this handbook is to subsequently reflect on and critically evaluate the paradigms and constructs of the term environment, utilising approaches from the national and social sciences. Underpinning how philosophical paradigms have influence on our understanding of the environment, a natural science ontology of the environment that attempts to organise the knowledge of material aspects of existence is analysed by Hall. Drawing on the ontological traditions of classical empiricism, transcendental idealism and transcendental realism, he illustrates how ontological differences lead to different paradigms and awareness of the environment, incorporating reductionist and constructivist perspectives. Utilising the example of climate change, Hall highlights how ontologies of environment influence knowledge creation and policy. It is argued that a dominant paradigm of reductionism has led to knowledge creation in a business-as-usual scenario on a global scale, emphasising the physical properties of greenhouse gases in isolation of the surrounding social relations.

In contrast to the natural science ontology presented by Hall, Grimwood presents and evaluates social science ontology of the environment that challenges human exceptionalism, the construct that emphasises that humanity is different from and superior to all other species. His chosen four theoretical moments that present this challenge are critical realism, phenomenology of perception, social nature and ontological multiplicity, all of which are applied to the analysis of the ecological impact of tourism on the Thelon River in Canada. The application of these ontologies to the case study illustrates how our interpretation of environment as social scientists generates different research questions to the 'same' situation. Thus it can be argued, as in the case of critical realism, of the primacy of ontology over epistemology.

Although both the natural and social sciences lend understanding to the scientific 'reality' of environment, central to the evaluation of human constructs comprehending our relationship to our surroundings have been the influences of spirituality and religion. Developing the theme of religious and spiritual influences on the understanding of nature, Dallen Timothy's chapter evaluates the primary interfaces between religion and nature and spirituality and nature. Contrasting spiritual belief systems with organised religion, he cites the research of Owen and Videras (2007), which found that people with spiritual belief systems who are not part of an organised religion are more likely to exhibit pro-environmental attitudes than people who belong to organised religion. This derives from an ontological construct of environment that explains the oneness of humans and nature. He proceeds to explore how these influences play out in the realm of tourism, including the context of pilgrimage tourism, cultural tourism and the introduction of geomantic design in tourist settings. Hollinshead also stresses the sacred belief in living things of the surrounding environment in the Indigenous Worldview.

Transcending the spiritual and religious to incorporate the cultural, the theme of 'wonderment' of aspects of nature is developed in Basham and Hitchcock's chapter, which continues to evaluate the influence of the Romantic movement in the cultural framing of why certain landscapes are attractive. The Romantic era, approximately dated to the time between the end of the eighteenth century and the mid-nineteenth century, emphasised the imaginative gaze through poetry, pose or landscape painting of the traveller. Critically in terms of making what had been unattractive landscapes attractive, the emphasis of observation changed from the material objects of environments to emphasise the emotions of landscape. As Barsham and Hitchcock observe, the Romantics believed they had found an interpretive key to nature, formulated in a transcendent language that embraced human life.

Continuing the theme of Romanticism, Seaton's chapter explores the construct of nature from the time of classical and pagan cultures through to the epoch of Romanticism, considering as part the influence of Christianity upon the nature construct as it was transferred into an understanding of the human condition, a position that was subsequently challenged by Romanticism. As Seaton comments, 'nature' has always been a construct, shaped by centuries of human interaction, manipulation and agency. Recognising three key discursive orientations in the writings of the Romantics: the rational-scientific, transcendental religious, and the sublime, he exemplifies how they have influenced contemporary tourism.

A constitute part of the Romantic is the concept of the 'aesthetic'. An in-depth analysis of the aesthetic and the role of the aesthetic in tourism is the theme of Todd's chapter. Utilising a primarily normative approach to understanding the role of the aesthetic in tourism, Todd explores the relevance of Kant's distinctiveness of the aesthetic appreciation of tourism, distinctiveness of type of appreciation, and issues of authenticity and well-being.

Stressing the role of inter-disciplinary and trans-disciplinary approaches to understanding the relationships between tourism and the environment, Stevenson investigates and reviews approaches to the use of complexity theory to challenge positivism and linear thinking and to offer a holistic approach to comprehending the relationship between society and environment. Taking a conceptually different perspective, Franklin finishes the first section of the tome with an analysis of how nature has and continues to transpose political interpretations. In the context of Romanticism, Franklin points out that not only was the movement a precursor to contemporary tourism but also involved a politic of protection and conservation, which sat uneasily with a democratising culture over 200 years ago, just as it does today. He also highlights the outstanding and indeed political involvement with society in presenting a new way to live with nature.

Reference

Owen, A.L. and Videras, J.R. (2007) 'Culture and public goods: the case of religion and voluntary provision of environmental quality', *Journal of Environmental Economics and Management*, 54(2), 162–80.

2

The natural science ontology of environment

Michael Hall

Introduction

Whether explicitly recognised or not, humankind's and hence tourism's relationship to the environment is underlain by philosophy. Philosophy affects how we understand the environment, our positionality and our ethics. For some commentators the present global environmental crisis characterised by biodiversity loss, deforestation and desertification, and climate change, is more than a crisis of policy, economics and governance but also extends to philosophy itself (Stott 1998; Demeritt 2006; Stables 2010). As Weston (1999: vii) commented, it is 'a crisis of the senses, of imagination, and of our tools for thinking – our concepts and theories – themselves'.

The sciences

The natural sciences are distinguished academically, philosophically and, to an extent, methodologically, from the formal, behavioural and social sciences as well as from the humanities (Weyl 2009). The term 'natural sciences' generally refers to those areas of organised knowledge that utilise a naturalistic approach and are concerned with the material aspects of existence. Such an approach posits an understanding of reality, existence and being that excludes supernatural theological knowledge (Balashov and Rosenberg 2002; Weyl 2009). Natural science is a term also used to describe natural history, the scientific study of plants and animals (Mayr 1982; Worster 1994), but this chapter will use the term natural science in its broader sense.

The formal sciences are those areas of knowledge that are concerned with formal systems – pure deductive systems consisting of a formal language and a set of inference rules in which no meaning can be ascribed to the expressions of the system other than that explicitly assigned by the formation rules of the system. The formal sciences, including mathematics, statistics, computer science and logic, are not necessarily concerned with the validity of theories based on observations in the real world as are the natural sciences. Nevertheless, formal science methods are extremely important for the methods and frameworks used in the natural sciences (Balashov and Rosenberg 2002; Weyl 2009).

Social science refers to a range of fields, usually also including tourism studies (Hall 2005; Holden 2005; Coles *et al.* 2006; Tribe 2009), that are primarily concerned with the study of society and the individuals, institutions and social structures within it. According to Bhaskar (2008: 195), 'the trouble with social science … is not that it has no (or too many) paradigms or research programmes; but rather that it lacks an adequate general conceptual scheme'. Arguing that for science to be possible, 'society must consist of an ensemble of powers irreducible to but present only in the intentional actions of men; and men must be causal agents capable of acting self-consciously on the world' (Bhaskar 2008: 20). The natural sciences have had considerable influence within the social sciences with respect to research philosophies, particularly positivism, as well as method, primarily quantitative. However, the social sciences are also characterised by an extremely significant interpretive tradition that tends to be qualitative, or at least a combination of qualitative and quantitative methodologies, and an understanding of society and the environment as being socially constructed. Much of the criticism of natural science ontologies and associated epistemologies and methods stems from research on the history and philosophy of science (Kuhn 1970, 1977; Feyerabend 1993; Galison and Stump 1996; Greenberg 1999; Henry 2002). Such criticisms shed light on the implications of how natural science ontologies, particularly with respect to environmental change and impact analysis (Demeritt, 2001a), are interpreted and utilised by tourism researchers (Gössling and Hall 2006a; Hall 2008a; Hall and Lew 2009).

Ontologies of the environment

Understanding ontologies of the environment is significant at a number of levels. Different ontologies lead to different paradigms and assumptions. Ontologies can be regarded as meta-theories, which 'presupposes a schematic answer to the question of what the world must be like for science to be possible' (Bhaskar 2008: 18). Different fields of knowledge have different ontologies.

> Every account of science presupposes an ontology … Thus suppose a philosopher holds, as both empiricists and transcendental idealists do, that a constant conjunction of events apprehended in sense-experience is at least a necessary condition for the ascription of a causal law and that it is an essential part of the job of science to discover them. Such a philosopher is then committed to the belief that, given that science occurs, there are such conjunctions.
>
> *(Bhaskar 2008: 18–19)*

Ontologies frame the ways of seeing, creating and understanding not only different forms of knowledge but also their acceptability. As Castree (2005: 16) comments,

> without knowledges of nature we can never really come to know the nature to which these knowledges refer … we use tacit and explicit knowledges to organise our engagements with those phenomenon we classify as "natural". There is, in short, no unmediated access to the natural world free from frameworks of understanding.

Ontologies are therefore not just academic concerns. Such a situation is directly related to: how the environment is defined and understood (Merchant 1980; Humphrey 2000; Keller 2009); the difficulties that can exist in legal and institutional decision-making systems in recognising the validity and standing of different environmental knowledge claims; the ways in which different institutions, interest groups, individuals and researchers define environmental management problems and issues (Alm and Burkhart 2006); and the difficulties that exist in getting different groups of researchers to work together on environmental problems (Hines 1991; Hinchliffe 2007; Jerneck *et al.* 2010). Indeed, these issues have been long recognised as a concern in trying to address environmental problems. For example, in commenting on the inter-relationships between human and physical geography, Gregory (1978) noted the integration of human and physical systems:

> ... is not so much an epistemological problem as an ontological one. In these terms it is resolved every day that men [sic] appropriate their material universe in order to survive. The two worlds are necessarily connected by social practice, and there is nothing in this which requires them to be connected through a formal system of common properties and universal constructs. In reifying this sort of system, human geography must inevitably represent social structures and space economies as parts of the fabric of nature, which man [sic] can regulate only within limits which he transcends at his peril.
>
> *(Gregory 1978: 75)*

Nevertheless, attempts to provide a unity of method between the natural and social sciences remain. Bhaskar (2008) has suggested that there are three main ontological traditions within science: classical empiricism, transcendental idealism and transcendental realism. *Classical empiricism* recognises 'the ultimate objects of knowledge' as 'atomistic events' in which 'knowledge and the world may be viewed as surfaces whose points are in isomorphic correspondence or, in the case of phenomenalism, actually fused' (Bhaskar 2008: 14, 15). The positivist account, which is usually associated with the scientific method of the natural sciences, presupposes an ontology of empirical realism, whereby the world consists of 'experience and atomistic events constantly conjoined' (Bhaskar 2008: 221–22) in which there is a dichotomous and oppositional division between humans (or the individual) and the environment. Such an approach has a strong relationship to the role of reductionism and mechanism as distinguishing features of Western natural science. Ontological reduction is the notion that the universe is a composite built out of smaller, simpler units – once molecules and atoms but now a range of exotic sub-atomic particles. 'Ontological reduction is the thesis that the properties of any entity may be understood by knowing the properties of its parts, because nothing can be explained about the entity without reference to its parts' (Keller and Golley 2000: 172).

The classical empiricist approach has been extremely significant in research on tourism and the environment but the framework it provides is often taken for granted without consideration of the 'assumptions that organise and, importantly, circumscribe the field of analysis' (Castree 2002: 116–17). For example, consider the use of the metaphor of tourism or tourist impact on the environment, which has become strongly embedded in tourism and wider discourse (Hall and Lew 2009), so much so that 'the metaphor of human impacts has come to frame our thinking and circumscribe debate about what constitutes explanation' (Head 2008: 374). This metaphor is derived from the material realist ontology of classical empiricism and has several features.

1 The emphasis on *the moment(s) of collision between two separate entities* (e.g. the 'impact' between tourism and the environment) has favoured explanations that depend on correlation in time and space (Weyl 2009), and methodologies that are fully focused on dating and/or particular moments in time, to the detriment of the search for mechanisms of connection and causation rather than simple correlation (Head 2008).
2 The emphasis on the moment(s) of impact also *assumes a stable natural, social or economic baseline* (Hall and Lew 2009), *and an experimental method in which only one variable is changed* (Head 2008). Such an approach is also inappropriate for understanding complex and dynamic

socio-environmental systems (Farrell and Twinning-Ward 2004; Hall 2008a; Head 2008; Hall and Lew 2009).

3 Third, and perhaps most profoundly influential (Head 2007, 2008), is the way the terms 'tourism impacts' or 'tourist impacts' ontologically *position tourism and tourists as 'outside' the system under analysis*, as outside of nature (or whatever it is that is being impacted) (Hall and Lew 2009). This is ironic given that research on global environmental change demonstrates just how deeply entangled tourism is in environmental systems (Gössling and Hall 2006a; Gössling *et al.* 2010; Hall 2010; Hall and Saarinen 2010), yet the metaphor remains in widespread use.

4 Putting a significant explanatory divide between humans and nature requires the *conflation of bundles of variable processes* under such headings as 'human', 'climate', 'environment' and 'nature' (Head 2007, 2008).

5 A further characteristic of dichotomous explanations is their *veneer of simplicity and elegance*. Yet, 'The principle that preference should be given to explanations that require the fewest number of assumptions has been incorrectly conflated with the idea that simpler explanations are more likely to be true than complex ones … In fact, the view that causality is simple takes many more assumptions than the view that it is complex' (Head 2008: 374).

In contrast, *transcendental idealism* suggests that 'the objects of scientific knowledge … models, ideals of natural order etc. … are artificial constructs and though they may be independent of particular [individuals], they are not independent of … human activity in general' (Bhaskar 2008: 15). From this perspective 'Knowledge is seen as a structure rather than a surface. But the natural world becomes a construction of the human mind, or, in its modern versions, of the scientific community' (Bhaskar 2008: 15).

The third position, which Bhaskar himself supports, is that of *transcendental realism,* which regards the objects of knowledge as the structures and mechanisms that generate phenomena and the knowledge that is produced as a result of the social activity of science. According to Bhaskar (2008: 15), 'these objects are neither phenomenon (empiricism) nor human constructs imposed upon the phenomena (idealism), but real structures which endure and operate independently of our knowledge, our experience and the conditions which allow us access to them'. This means that a constant conjunction of events is no more necessary than it is a sufficient condition for the assumption that a causal law operates. From this perspective science is not an epiphenomenon of nature, nor is nature a product of humankind;

> both knowledge and the world are structured, both are differentiated and changing; the latter exists independently of the former (though not of our knowledge of this fact); and experiences and the things and causal laws to which it affords us access are normally out of phase with one another.
>
> *(Bhaskar 2008: 15)*

Although moving in a significantly different direction, a focus on the importance of perception and ontology is also fundamental to phenomenology. For example, Heidegger (1962: 84) comments that:

> the environment is a structure which even biology as a positive science can never find and can never define, but must presuppose and constantly employ. Yet, even as an a priori condition … this structure itself can be explained philosophically only if it has been conceived beforehand as a structure of [consciously being-in-the-world].

9

As Heidegger (1982) commented, a narrowly instrumentalist view of human beings runs the risk of seeing nature as mere 'standing-reserve.' Similarly, Merleau-Ponty (2002) offers an alternative phenomenological account of the nature and the environment via ideas of 'embodiment' that stress the experiential dependence of humans with respect to physical being in the world.

Both transcendental realism and transcendental idealism reject the empiricist notion of science. Although they both agree that there could be no knowledge without the social activity of science, they differ over how nature is held. Transcendental realism suggests that the order discovered in nature exists independently of human activity. Transcendental idealism maintains that order is actually imposed by cognitive activity. The differences between the two approaches should be clear:

> According to transcendental realism, if there were no science there would still be a nature, and it is this nature which is investigated by science. Whatever is discovered in nature must be expressed in thought, but the structures and constitutions and causal laws discovered in nature do not depend upon thought.
>
> *(Bhaskar 2008: 17)*

There are clearly different ontological positions with respect to nature and the environment. These exist between and within sciences. For example, ecology is marked by a range of ontologies that provide different interpretations of the relationality between humans and the environment as well as epistemology and methodological approach. For ecology, and correspondingly studies of tourism and the environment, a key question is: 'Can an ecological entity be understood through an analysis of its biotic and abiotic components (reductionism), or must any ecological entity be explained by treating it as a unitary entry with unique characteristics (holism)?' (Keller and Golley 2000: 171). As Keller and Golley (2000) noted, the question is an epistemic one with ontological underpinnings (see also Stott 1998). Reductionists assert that the essence of an entity, such as an ecosystem, community or even the biosphere, is a function of the sum of its parts and therefore knowledge of the parts is adequate for understanding the whole. In contrast, holists assert that some entities have emergent properties that are not properties of the parts but of the whole instead, and therefore knowledge only of the parts does not constitute an understanding of the whole. Table 2.1 identifies five epistemic and ontological positions along the reductionism–holism continuum (Blitz 1992).

Ontological differences raise fundamental questions about how the environment can actually be understood, and the ethical relationships between humans and the environment, as well as criticism of environmental science. Acompora (2008) highlighted that concern about the reality and knowability of nature is significant for the ways in which animals are appreciated and understood, particularly as criticism of wildlife protection measures, such as the establishment and maintenance of zoological gardens and national parks, are sometimes mobilised by reference to authenticity. For example, there is substantial debate over the conduct of captive breeding programmes. Wuichet and Norton (1995: 239) suggest that 'a wild animal achieves a state of authentic well-being when it survives and reproduces offspring, based on its own genetic abilities and behavioural adaptations, in a truly natural (as opposed to [merely] naturalistic) environment'. In contrast, social constructionists dispute realist authenticators of animal nature,

> Once brought to human attention an animal is no longer an animal in itself – it can only be that away from human sight, experience and thought … the human experience of a [captive] creature destroys its authenticity (a quality which is linked to its independence) as a wild animal.
>
> *(Mullan and Marvin 1987: 3, 73)*

Table 2.1 Ontologies of ecology

Methodological Approach	Ontology	Epistemology
Reductionism	Properties of wholes are always found among the properties of their parts	Knowledge of the parts is both necessary and sufficient to understand the whole
Mechanism	Properties of wholes are of the same kind or type of those parts	Knowledge of the kind or type of the cause suffices to understand the type of kind of the effect
Emergentism	There is at least one property of some wholes not possessed by any of their parts. Parts can exist independently of the whole, and novel properties of wholes can be lost via submergence when a system is reduced to its parts	Knowledge of the parts and their relations is a necessary but not a sufficient condition to understand the whole.
Organicism	Recognise the existence of emergent properties of wholes. Once a whole has appeared, its parts cannot exist or be understood independently of a whole	Knowledge of the whole is a necessary condition to understand the parts and vice-versa
Holism	The emergent novel properties of the whole can be understood without further consideration of the parts and their relationships. The basic unit the whole – wholes are independent of parts	Knowledge of the parts is neither necessary nor sufficient to understand the whole

Source: After Blitz 1992: 175-178; Keller & Golley 2000.

Although it should be noted that Mullan and Marvin (1987: 3) moderate their anti?realism by noting that they are not suggesting that animals 'are not real physical entities living in a real physical world', but rather they are seeking to emphasise that 'they are also man-made in the sense that they are thought about by man, and it is the animal as it is thought about rather than the animal itself which is of significance'.

Issues regarding the authenticity of the wild are emblematic of a series of problems not only with the nature of wilderness and appropriate activities within it (Sax 1980; Krakoff 2003), but also the ontological status of nature itself. As Acompora (2008: 3) observes, 'Metaphysically speaking, many if not most environmentalists are naive naturalists in the sense that they believe in the "objective outdoors" – an external world existing beyond human edifice and mentality, upon which our buildings and theories are based'. Yet some commentators have rejected this approach in favour of a strong social constructionist stance (Fitzsimmons 1989; King 1990; Evernden 1992; Castree 2005), which has proven to be extremely influential in emphasising the anthropocentric values associated with the environment, nature and wilderness (Hall and Page 2006). Although stemming from a different ontological framework, such constructionist positions can provide a strong critique of natural science approaches and method by drawing attention to the significant institutional and social relations involved in producing scientific knowledge of the natural world and by challenging empiricist, positivist and realist epistemologies (Demeritt 2001a).

Geuss (1981) held that critical theories were fundamentally different from theories in the natural sciences, because whereas natural sciences claimed to be objective, critical theories are reflective. In addition, he noted that critical theories were also distinguished by the extent to which they provide guides for human action by being inherently emancipatory; having cognitive content; and being forms of knowledge in themselves. Habermas (1978) for example, placed great theoretical emphasis on what he termed cognitive or knowledge-constitutive interests, in order to explain the connections between knowledge and action. For Habermas (1978: 47), such interests arose out of human contact and participation with nature: 'From the level of pragmatic, everyday knowledge to modern natural science, the knowledge of nature derives from man's primary coming to grips with nature; at the same time it reacts back upon the system of social labor and stimulates its development'. Habermas did not subsequently develop a detailed analysis of the relationships between people and nature. Nevertheless, Habermas' critique of the relationship between theory and practice in modern science has been especially influential given that he believed that science had divorced itself from its social context (Unwin 1992). For Habermas (1978: 63), both material scientism and absolute idealism eliminate 'epistemology in favour of unchained universal "scientific knowledge"'.

One of the most significant difficulties in examining the implications of ontology for tourism research is that ontologies, epistemologies and methods are often conflated. Moreover, the material natural science ontology and its implications can be understood as an ideal type, which in practice may never be absolutely held by individuals, in exactly the same way that idealism is usually not fully held, yet such ontologies still influence environmental management, research and practice. The classic empirical realist account of natural science is strongly materialist, positivist, reductionist and mechanistic, as well as being strongly quantitative and instrumentalist (Keat and Urry 1975; Heidegger 1982). The hegemony of the long dominant positivist outlook that has 'fashioned our image of science' and 'usurped the title of science' (Bhaskar 2008: 1, 7) has been criticised from numerous standpoints, some of which are discussed further below, but these have done little to change the popular understanding of science and method.

As research on the history of science has indicated, institutions play an extremely important role in determining the trajectories of research. An institution represents a social order or pattern that has attained a certain state and helps establish the 'rules of the game' (Hotimsky *et al.* 2006: 41). Several reasons can be provided from an institutional perspective for the continued strength of the natural sciences in environmental research as well as the relative lack of standing for non-positivistic environmental studies. First, successive series of governments in many developed countries have been supporting a research and tertiary education agenda that is increasingly focused on supposedly apolitical economic and market-oriented research deliverables (Demeritt 2000). 'This is not to deny that much reflective research has indeed taken place, but it is to suggest that much logical positivist science, with its apparent capacity to explain, solve and predict, but most of all serve those in power, has not surprisingly continued to find favour' (Unwin 1992: 153). Second:

> At a time when individuals, departments and institutions are increasingly being assessed in terms of the levels of grants that they attract, there is much pressure to obtain grants for high cost research projects, which frequently reflect the technical interest of logical positivism to maintain the social and political order.
>
> *(Unwin 1992: 153)*

Third, the growth in the role of journal rankings as a means to not only measure the quality of research output but also influence academic hiring and rewards has favoured certain positivist approaches and methods as well as problem definition over others (Hall 2011a). Fourth, the combination of the above has served to institutionalise positivist science within universities and research institutions and structures as well as within environmental management processes and systems (Shrader-Frechette 1996; Bryant and Wilson 1998; Cashmore 2004; Hertin *et al.* 2009).

One of the best examples of the institutionalisation of instrumentalist science approaches to environmental issues is global climate and environmental change (Bryant 1998). The importance of integrating social and biophysical perspectives in environmental change research is widely recognised (Füssel and Klein 2006), along with an accompanying ontological shift (Turnpenny *et al.* 2010). In addition, research in the social sciences has demonstrated how knowledge is produced locally and globally in different forms (Slocum 2010), including with respect to the social dimensions of the scientific communities that study climate change and the roles of social science in climate change models and projections (Demeritt 2001a, 2001b, 2006; Yearley 2009). Demeritt's (2001a, 2001b) examination of the construction of climate change science and the politics of science is particularly informative (see also the response of Schneider 2001). Demeritt retraces the history of climate modelling and associated climate science to identify tacit social and epistemic communities that are characterised by the technocratic and reductionist inclinations of climate change science. Demeritt was not denying the existence of climate change, but rather focused on the way in which climate change science is constructed and how this leads into political issues and public trust concerns surrounding the dominant natural science-led formulation of the climate change problem. Unfortunately, as Demeritt (2001a: 309) notes:

> public representations of science seldom acknowledge the irreducibly social dimension of scientific knowledge and practice. As a result, disclosure of the social relations through which scientific knowledge is constructed and conceived has become grounds for discrediting both that knowledge and any public policy decisions based upon it.

Demeritt (2001a, 2001b, 2006) contends that global climate change has been constructed in narrowly technical and reductionist scientific terms by the IPCC and other international and national scientific bodies on climate change, and that this promotes certain kind of knowledge at the expense of others. 'For the most part, climate change model projections have been driven by highly simplistic business-as-usual scenarios of human population growth, resource consumption, and GHG emissions at highly aggregated geographic scales' (Demeritt 2001a: 312) that operate at a global scale, rather than framing the problem in terms of alternative, and no less relevant forms, such as the structural imperatives of the capitalist economy that drives emissions; the north–south gap in terms of emissions; or regionalised conceptions that focus on issues of poverty and deprivation. 'By treating the objective physical properties of [greenhouse gases] in isolation from the surrounding social relations serves to conceal, normalize, and thereby reproduce those unequal social relations' (Demeritt 2001a: 316). Similarly, Wainwright (2010) suggests that although climate scientists engage in debates about the meaning of their results, they rarely reopen the 'black boxes' that are taken for granted in their research, and provides an example of how carbon may be considered by physical and social scientists.

> Two physical scientists might engage in heady debate about the precise role of CO_2 or CH_4 in forcing a certain atmospheric process, but it is hard to imagine that carbon's basic qualities – its atomic number or weight, chemical properties, and so on – would be called into question. By contrast, two social scientists discussing, say, the hegemony of carbon emissions markets in climate policy discourse … would need to agree on the meaning of hegemony, markets, climate policy, discourse, and so on. This turns out to be no mean feat, because distinct interpretations of these and related concepts reflect different conceptions of the world … there is no metalanguage that lies outside of social life with which to objectively calibrate these concepts. Consequently, debates over the meaning of the building-block concepts for social thought are, by necessity, complex and interminable.
> *(Wainwright 2010: 984)*

13

Case study

The construction of the dominant scientific positions within the IPCC process has led to the physical reductionism of simulation modelling becoming the most authoritative method for studying the climate system (Demeritt 2001a, 2001b). Yet the appeals of formal quantitative evaluation methods are social and political as much as technical and scientific, particularly it also makes them more credible from a public perspective of natural science: 'insofar as adherence to rigidly uniform and impersonal and in that sense "procedurally objective" … rules limits the scope for individual bias or discretion and thereby guarantees the vigorous (self-)denial of personal perspective necessary to make knowledge seem universal, trustworthy and true' (Demeritt 2001a: 324).

Issues surrounding scientific construction of climate change research and its results are clearly significant for understanding the relationship between tourism and climate change and the debate surrounding that relationship. First, this helps explain why anthropogenic climate change has primarily been defined as an environmental rather than a political or economic problem (Gössling et al. 2010), or one that requires framing in terms of the imperatives of the capitalist economic system and its alternatives (Hall 2009, 2011c). Second, even though there has been a call for greater social science information to be brought into the climate change assessment process, this has primarily been assessed in terms of neo-classical economic contributions (e.g. Stern 2007), which have themselves been greatly influenced by natural science ontologies. Neo-classical economic accounts of climate change and the need for action to minimise the effects of climate change are also dominated by formal modelling (Dietz and Stern 2008). For example, Hamilton et al. (2005) was the only tourism-related paper cited in the Stern (2007) Report (Hall 2008b). Yet as Gössling and Hall (2006b, 2006c) indicate, there are numerous major weaknesses in such models with respect to predicting tourist response to climate change (Bigano et al. 2006; Gössling and Hall 2006b, 2006c; Scott 2008; for further discussion of these issues):

- Validity and structure of statistical databases;
- Temperature assumed to be the most important weather parameter;
- Importance of other weather parameters largely unknown (rain, storms, humidity, hours of sunshine, air pollution);
- Role of weather extremes unknown;
- Role of information in decision-making unclear;
- Role of non-climatic parameters unclear (e.g. social unrest, political instability, risk perceptions);
- Existence of fuzzy-variables problematic (terrorism, war, epidemics, natural disasters);
- Assumed linearity of change in behaviour unrealistic;
- Future costs of transport uncertain;
- Future levels of personal disposable income (economic budget) and availability of leisure time (time budget) that are allocated to travel uncertain.

Bigano et al. (2006) claim that the relationships between tourism and climate change are best studied through strategic cyclical scaling (Root and Schneider 1995), with small-scale, detailed case studies informing and being informed by large-scale, comprehensive statistical and simulation studies. The use of such an approach is undoubtedly widespread in research on environmental and other change (Gössling and Hall 2006a). However, such an approach has an implicit ontological position with respect to the relationship between the parts and the whole, which is only one of several potential positions with respect to knowledge of ecological entities – including the biosphere (see Table 2.1).

Just as significantly, the neo-classical economic belief that the social and economic value of things can be expressed in terms of aggregate individual willingness to pay, or in monetary terms at all, is debatable. As Demeritt and Rothman (1999: 404) noted, such a utilitarian view of value has been subjected to a number of different philosophical and moral critiques:

- it is anthropocentric and ignores intrinsic value (Leopold 1966);
- the world cannot be broken down into discrete and alienable entities to which monetary values might meaningfully be attached (Norgaard 1985);
- it confuses values and preferences (Sagoff 1988);
- its narrow decisionist framework artificially abstracts information about human values and preferences from an ongoing and multidimensional social process of (re)expressing them (Wynne 1997);
- money conceals a profound asymmetry in the apparent equality of the exchange relation (Harvey 1996).

Therefore, the choice of valuation procedure, like the definition of value itself as used by governments and supranational authorities such as the UNWTO, UNEP, WTTC, and the World Economic Forum in relation to tourism and the environment, is part of a mediated and embodied social construction of knowledge and is ultimately personal and political rather than objective and rational (Demeritt and Rothman 1999; Hall 2011c).

Conclusions

This chapter has outlined some of the basic elements of the natural science ontology of the environment and its criticisms. As noted, natural science and other ontologies have enormous implications not only for how the environment is seen but also for the conduct and acceptability of research, including major tourism research themes such as 'impacts' and climate and environmental change. The dominant material positivist ontology of natural science is, to many people, the discourse of 'normal science' because of the perceived authority of its empiricist and quantitative form, but it is also a position that often engenders mistrust and is open to critique. Demeritt (2001a: 309) suggests that instead of accepting an idealised vision of scientific truth and denying the socially situated and contingent nature of scientific knowledge, 'the proper response to it is to develop a more reflexive understanding of science as a situated and ongoing social practice, as the basis for a more balanced assessment'. Demeritt's observation is a further reinforcement of Feyerabend's (1993) critique of science:

> The success of "science" cannot be used as an argument for treating as yet unsolved problems in a standardized way … "non-scientific" procedures cannot be pushed aside by argument … the public can participate in the discussion without disturbing existing roads to success … in cases where the scientists' work affects the public it even *should* participate … a full democratisation of science (which includes the protection of minorities such as scientists) is not in conflict with science. It is in conflict with a philosophy, often called "Rationalism", that uses a frozen image of science to terrorize people unfamiliar with its practice. … *there can be many different kinds of science.*
>
> (Feyerabend 1993: 2)

Just as in any enterprise, there is valuable specialist expertise in the world of science. There is also a range of ontologies that frame different worldviews and methods, and that, sometimes unknowingly to their holders, favour certain interests and forms of knowledge. If a truly integrated approach to the environment is to be achieved in tourism, it therefore becomes vital to realise that there needs to be greater transparency and respect of the value of different knowledge (including lay knowledge) and methods as well as appreciation of the advantages and disadvantages of different ontological positions (Hall 2011b). Scientists (and tourism researchers) 'stand roughly in the same position with respect to the natural world as travel agents stand with regard to summer holidays … Their advice is the best available, but it does not constitute the final word' (Collins and Yearley 1992: 385).

References

Acompora, R.R. (2008) 'Animal constructs and natural reality: The import of environmental ontology for inter-species ethics', *Humana.Mente* 7 (October), 1–17.

Alm, L. and Burkhart, R. (2006) 'Differences that matter: Canada, the United States and environmental policymaking', *AmeriQuests* [Online], 3(1) (16 April). Available http://ejournals.library.vanderbilt.edu/ameriquests/viewarticle.php?id=57.

Balashov, Y. and Rosenberg, A. (eds) (2002) *Philosophy of Science: Contemporary Readings*. London: Routledge.

Bhaskar, R. (2008). *A Realist Theory of Science*, 2nd edn. Abingdon: Routledge.

Bigano, A., Hamilton, J.M., Maddison, D.J. and Tol, R.S.J. (2006) 'Predicting tourism flows under climate change. An editorial comment on Gössling and Hall (2006)', *Climatic Change* 79, 175–80.

Blitz, D. (1992) *Emergent Evolution: Qualitative Novelty and the Levels of Reality*. Boston, MA: Kluwer.

Bryant, R.L. (1998) 'Power, knowledge and political ecology in the third world: A review', *Progress in Physical Geography* 22, 79–94.

Bryant, R.L. and Wilson, G.A. (1998) 'Rethinking environmental management', *Progress in Human Geography* 22, 321–43.

Cashmore, M. (2004) 'The role of science in environmental impact assessment: process and procedure versus purpose in the development of theory', *Environmental Impact Assessment Review* 24(4), 403–26.

Castree, N. (2002) 'False antitheses? Marxism, nature and actor networks', *Antipode* 34, 111–46.

——(2005) *Nature*. London: Routledge.

Coles, T., Hall, C.M. and Duval, D. (2006) 'Tourism and post-disciplinary inquiry', *Current Issues in Tourism* 9, 293–319.

Collins, H.M. and Yearley, S. (1992) 'Journey into space', in A. Pickering (ed.) *Science as Culture and Practice*. Chicago, IL: University of Chicago Press.

Demeritt, D. (2000) 'The new social contract for Science: Accountability, relevance, and value in US and UK science and research policy', *Antipode* 32, 308–29.

——(2001a) 'The construction of global warming and the politics of science', *Annals of the Association of American Geographers* 91, 307–37.

——(2001b) 'Science and the understanding of science: A reply to Schneider', *Annals of the Association of American Geographers* 91, 345–8.

——(2006) 'Science studies, climate change and the prospects for constructivist critique', *Economy and Society* 35, 453–79.

Demeritt, D. and Rothman, D. (1999) 'Figuring the costs of climate change: An assessment and critique', *Environment and Planning A* 31, 389–408.

Dietz, S. and Stern, N. (2008) 'Why economic analysis supports strong action on climate change: A Response to the Stern Review's critics', *Review of Environmental Economics and Policy* 2, 94–113.

Evernden, N. (1992) *The Social Creation of Nature*. Baltimore, MD: John Hopkins University Press.

Farrell, B.H. and Twinning-Ward, L. (2004) 'Reconceptualizing tourism', *Annals of Tourism Research* 31, 274–95.

Feyerabend, P. (1993) *Against Method*, 3rd edn. London: Verso.

Fitzsimmons, M. (1989) 'The matter of nature', *Antipode* 21, 106–20.

Füssel, H.-M. and Klein, R.J.T. (2006) 'Climate change vulnerability assessments: An evolution of conceptual thinking', *Climatic Change* 75, 301–29.

Galison, P. and Stump, D. (eds) (1996) *The Disunity of Science: Boundaries, Contexts, and Power*. Stanford, CA: Stanford University Press.

Geuss, R. (1981). *The Idea of a Critical Theory: Habermas and the Frankfurt School*. Cambridge: Cambridge University Press.

Gössling, S., and Hall, C.M. (eds) (2006a) *Tourism and Global Environmental Change*. London: Routledge.

——(2006b) 'Uncertainties in predicting tourist flows under scenarios of climate change', *Climatic Change* 79(3–4), 163–73.

——(2006c) 'Uncertainties in predicting travel flows: common ground and research needs. A reply to Tol *et al.*', *Climatic Change* 79(3–4), 181–83.

Gössling, S., Hall, C.M., Peeters, P. and Scott, D. (2010) 'The future of tourism: A climate change mitigation perspective', *Tourism Recreation Research* 35(2), 119–30.

Greenberg, D.S. (1999) *The Politics of Pure Science*, 2nd edn. Chicago, IL: University of Chicago Press.

Gregory, D. (1978) *Ideology, Science and Human Geography*. New York: St. Martins.

Habermas, J. (1978) *Knowledge and Human Interests*, 2nd edn. London: Heinemann.

Hall, C.M. (2005) *Tourism: Rethinking the Social Science of Mobility*. London: Pearson.

——(2008a) *Tourism Planning*, 2nd edn. London: Prentice-Hall.

——(2008b) 'Tourism and climate change: Knowledge gaps and issues', *Tourism Recreation Research* 33, 339–50.

——(2009) 'Degrowing tourism: Décroissance, sustainable consumption and steady-state tourism', *Anatolia: An International Journal of Tourism and Hospitality Research* 20(1), 46–61.

——(2010) 'Tourism and biodiversity: More significant than climate change?' *Journal of Heritage Tourism* 5(4), 253–66.

——(2011a) 'Publish and perish: Bibliometric analysis, journal ranking and the assessment of research quality in tourism', *Tourism Management* 32, 16–27.

——(ed.) (2011b) *Fieldwork in Tourism*. London: Routledge.

——(2011c) 'Policy learning and policy failure in sustainable tourism governance: From first and second to third order change?' *Journal of Sustainable Tourism* 19(4–5), 649–671.

Hall, C.M. and Lew, A. (2009) *Understanding and Managing Tourism Impacts: An Integrated Approach*. London: Routledge.

Hall, C.M. and Page, S. (2006) *The Geography of Tourism and Recreation*, 3rd edn. London: Routledge.

Hall, C.M. and Saarinen, J. (eds) (2010) *Polar Tourism and Change: Climate, Environments and Experiences*. London: Routledge.

Hamilton, J.M., Maddison, D.J. and Tol, R.S.J. (2005) 'Climate change and international tourism: A simulation study', *Global Environmental Change* 15, 253–66.

Harvey, D. (1996). *Justice, Nature, and the Geography of Difference*. Oxford: Blackwell.

Head, L. (2007) 'Cultural ecology: The problematic human and the terms of engagement', *Progress in Human Geography* 31, 837–46.

——(2008) 'Is the concept of human impacts past its use-by date?' *The Holocene* 18, 373–7.

Heidegger, M. (1962) *Being and Time*, trans. J. Macqaurrie and E. Robinson. Malden: Blackwell.

——(1982) *The Question Concerning Technology, and Other Essays*, trans W. Lovitt. New York: Harper.

Henry, J. (2002) *The Scientific Revolution and the Origins of Modern Science*, 2nd edn. Basingstoke: Palgrave.

Hertin, J., Turnpenny, J., Jordan, A., Nilsson, M., Russel, D. and Nykvist, B. (2009) 'Rationalising the policy mess? Ex ante policy assessment and the utilisation of knowledge in the policy process', *Environment and Planning A* 41: 1185–200.

Hinchliffe, S. (2007) *Geographies of Nature: Societies, Environments, Ecologies*. London: Sage.

Hines, R. (1991) 'On valuing nature', *Accounting, Auditing and Accountability* 4(3), 27–9.

Holden, A. (2005) *Tourism Studies and the Social Sciences*. London: Routledge.

Hotimsky, S., Cobb, R. and Bond, A. (2006) 'Contracts or scripts? A critical review of the application of institutional theories to the study of environmental change', *Ecology and Society* 11(1), 41. Available at www.ecologyandsociety.org/vol11/iss1/art41/

Humphrey, M. (2000) 'Ontological determinism and deep ecology: Evading the moral questions', in E. Katz, A. Light and D. Rothenberg (eds), *Beneath the Surface: Critical Essays in the Philosophy of Deep Ecology*. Cambridge, MA: The MIT Press.

Jerneck, A., Olsson, L., Ness, B., Anderberg, S., Baier, M., Clark, E., Hickler, T., Hornborg, A., Kronsell, A., Lövbrand, E. and Persson, J. (2010) 'Structuring sustainability science', *Sustainability Science*, DOI: 10.1007/s11625-010-0117-x.

Keat, R. and Urry, J. (1975) *Social Theory as Science*. London: Routledge & Kegan Paul.

Keller, D.R. (2009) 'Toward a post-mechanistic philosophy of nature', *ISLE: Interdisciplinary Studies in Literature and Environment* 16, 709–25.

Keller, D.R. and Golley, F.B. (eds) (2000) *The Philosophy of Ecology. From Science to Synthesis*. Athens: University of Georgia Press.

King, R.J.H. (1990) 'How to construe nature: Environmental ethics and the interpretation of nature', *Between the Species*, 6(Summer), 101–8.

Krakoff, S. (2003) 'Mountains without handrails ... wilderness without cellphones', *Harvard Environmental Law Review* 27, 417–69.

Kuhn, T.S. (1970) *The Structure of Scientific Revolutions*, 2nd edn. Chicago, IL: University of Chicago Press.

——(1977) *The Essential Tension: Selected Studies in Scientific Tradition and Change*. Chicago, IL: University of Chicago Press.

Leopold. A. (1966) *A Sand County Almanac*. New York: Oxford University Press.

Mayr, E. (1982) *The Growth of Biological Thought: Diversity, Evolution, and Inheritance*. Cambridge, MA: The Belknap Press of Harvard University Press.

Merchant, C. (1980) *The Death of Nature: Women, Ecology and the Scientific Revolution*. San Francisco, CA: Harper & Row.

Merleau-Ponty, M. (2002) *Phenomenology of Perception*. London: Routledge.

Mullan, B. and Marvin, G. (1987) *Zoo Culture*. London: Weidenfeld & Nicolson.

Norgaard, R. (1985) 'Environmental economics: An evolutionary critique and a plea for pluralism', *Journal of Environmental Economics and Management* 12, 382–94.

Root, T.L. and Schneider, S.H. (1995) 'Ecology and climate: Research strategies and implications', *Science* 269(5222), 334–41.

Sagoff, M. (1988) *The Economy of the Earth: Philosophy, Law, and the Environment*. Cambridge: Cambridge University Press.

Sax, J. (1980) *Mountains Without Handrails: Reflections on the National Parks*. Ann Arbor: University of Michigan Press.

Schneider, S.H. (2001) 'A constructive deconstruction of deconstructionists: A response to Demeritt', *Annals of the Association of American Geographers* 91, 338–44.

Scott, D. (2008) 'Climate change and tourism: Time for critical reflection', *Tourism Recreation Research* 33, 356–60.

Shrader-Frechette, K. (1996) 'Throwing out the bathwater of positivism, keeping the baby of objectivity: Relativism and advocacy in Conservation Biology', *Conservation Biology* 10, 912–14.

Slocum, R. (2010) 'The sociology of climate change: Research priorities', in J. Hagel, T. Dietz and J. Broadbent (eds) *Workshop on Sociological Perspectives on Global Climate Change*. Arlington, TX: National Science Foundation.

Stables, A. (2010) 'Making meaning and using natural resources: education and sustainability', *Journal of Philosophy of Education* 44(1), 137–51.

Stern, N. (2007) *The Economics of Climate Change: The Stern Review*. Cambridge: Cambridge University Press.

Stott, P. (1998) 'Biogeography and ecology in crisis: The urgent need for a new metalanguage', *Journal of Biogeography* 25, 1–2.

Tribe, J. (ed.) (2009) *Philosophical Issues in Tourism*. Bristol: Channel View Publications.

Turnpenny, J., Jones, M. and Lorenzoni, I. (2010) 'Where now for post-normal science? A critical review of its development, definitions, and uses', *Science Technology Human Values*, DOI: 10.1177/0162243910385789.

Unwin, T. (1992) *The Place of Geography*. Harlow: Longman.

Wainwright, J. (2010) 'Climate change, capitalism, and the challenge of transdisciplinarity', *Annals of the Association of American Geographers* 100, 983–91.

Weston, A. (1999) *An Invitation to Environmental Philosophy*. New York: Oxford University Press.

Weyl, H. (2009) *Philosophy of Mathematics and Natural Science*, rev. edn. Princeton, NJ: Princeton University Press.

Worster, D. (1994) *Nature's Economy: A History of Ecological Ideas*. Cambridge: Cambridge University Press.

Wuichet, J. and Norton, B. (1995) 'Differing conceptions of animal welfare', in S. Norton, M. Hutchins, E.F. Stevens and T.L. Maple (eds), *Ethics on the Ark: Zoos, Animal Welfare, and Wildlife Conservation*. Washington, DC: Smithsonian Institution Press.

Wynne, B. (1997) 'Methodology and institutions: value as seen from the risk field', in J. Foster (ed.) *Valuing Nature: Economics, Ethics, and Environment*. London: Routledge.

Yearley, S. (2009) 'Sociology and climate change after Kyoto: What roles for social science in understanding climate change?', *Current Sociology* 57, 389–405.

3

Social science ontology of environment

Challenges to human exceptionalism

Bryan Grimwood

Introduction

The social science ontology of environment is one point of incision into the heart of theorising society and environment relations. Ontology refers to the branch of metaphysics concerned with the study and description of *being*, the general conditions of existence or the substance of reality. The tendency among social scientists to be concerned with ontology merely because it establishes disciplinary objects, relations or concepts has, in recent years, been complemented by an onto-logical 'turn' that entails incisive probing of everyday and disciplinary assumptions (Escobar 2010; Gregory *et al.* 2009). Such a project has been advanced by critical scholars concerned with environment, and especially those simultaneously burdened and ardent to illustrate the decep-tions of dualistic takes on reality. On the one hand, non-dualistic work is reactionary; it opens crucial space for social theory to dissent from excesses of determinism, reductionism, quantifi-cation and metanarratives. On the other, there are inventive and inter-disciplinary intentions at play that articulate environmental realities of inclusion, responsibility and emergence.

Philosophical resistance to human exceptionalism encapsulates these anxious, albeit creative, tensions. Following Haraway (2008), human exceptionalism refers to the fantasy that humanity alone is different from and superior to all other entities existing on Earth. It is manifest when we treat the world solely as a resource bounty for human well-being, or through 'save the world' campaigns that advocate humanity's return to an Eden-like nature. Human exceptionalism is also showcased in debates that emphasise objective or subjective extremes, as in naïve realism or strong versions of social construction. The uniting bond here is an ideology of human auton-omy rooted in binary logic and an absolute distinction between human society and non-human nature (Haraway 2008).

The objective of this chapter is to explain and analyse seminal constructs and paradigms in the social science ontology of environment. To distil this dense, nuanced, but relevant, theme, the chapter reviews four theoretical 'moments' that, in different ways, challenge the binary visions associated with human exceptionalism. Emulating Braun (2004), these moments should not be read as a linear evolution of academic thought, but instead, as inter-woven intellectual threads that intersect, reinforce, run parallel and diverge. The moments contained herein include critical realism, phenomenology of perception, social nature and ontological multiplicity. The chapter begins with a case study from the central Canadian Arctic, which is subsequently used to ground discussions of the ontological moments with research possibilities for nature-based tourism.

Two notes before proceeding. First, given the inter-disciplinary intentions of this text, I have opted to lean heavily on literatures from outside tourism studies. My objective is to participate in the encouragement of tourism research that explores beyond the field. Second, any author developing a critical synopsis has the challenge of balancing sufficient breadth and depth. The preparation of this chapter has been no exception. In addition to the literature reviewed and representational choices made for each ontological moment, readers will identify certain omissions, including substantial discussion of how complex systems, sociobiological, Marxist, feminist or Aboriginal thinkers have toiled with ontological questions. However, if only because of this chapter's relational emphasis, which has emerged as a prevalent orientation in social science, readers should recognise my attempts to be adequately inclusive and comprehensive.

Case study

The Thelon River is one of 41 rivers celebrated in Canada as a Heritage River for its natural, cultural and recreational values. With headwaters in the Northwest Territories, just east of the height of land that separates the Hudson Bay and Arctic Ocean watersheds, the Thelon stretches 900 km eastward across the central Canadian sub-Arctic and into Nunavut, before draining into Baker Lake west of Hudson Bay. As the river traverses Canadian jurisdictional boundaries, it also meanders among Dene First Nation, Métis and Inuit territories. The recognition of historical and contemporary human activity within the watershed has not altered the Thelon's appeal as northern wilderness. Such accolades are attributable to the watershed's remoteness from human settlements, unique combination of boreal and tundra ecosystems and abundant habitat for large mammals (wolves, grizzly bear, moose, caribou and muskoxen).

Cultural and recreational values associated with the Thelon are intimately tied to wildlife. For generations, Aboriginal hunters and their families have relied on barren-ground caribou as a primary source of food, clothing, shelter and tools. Hunting and trapping of muskoxen, Arctic fox, wolf and grizzly bear have also enabled local Aboriginal peoples to participate in wage economies. Euro-American travel and exploration within the Thelon basin was not prevalent until early in the twentieth century. Since 1962, recreational canoeists have accessed the Thelon by chartered aeroplane, and have travelled the length of the river in self-supported, multi-day expeditions (Morse 1987). Commercial tourism along the Thelon was first established in 1974 (Hall 2003), and a handful of companies currently guide and outfit Thelon expeditions as one component in their overall operation. Independent and commercial canoe, kayak and raft trips along northern Canadian rivers are an important sector in territorial economies. Often it is the lure of the northern wild, and especially the wildlife, that provides impetus for the scores of nature-based tourists visiting the Thelon and surrounding river systems each summer.

However, recent wildlife population estimates, field observations and local knowledge holders indicate drastic reductions to the size of barren-ground caribou herds, and shifting habitats of the other large mammals (BQCMB 2010; Hall 2003). These wildlife dynamics are supported by reports from Thelon canoeists who, in qualitative interviews, indicate that wildlife encounters are much fewer than anticipated based on their reading and research of the area. The wildlife spectacle along the Thelon River is, so it seems, no longer guaranteed, which is likely to have some bearing on tourism satisfaction rates and changing tourist demands.

Figure 3.1 is a photograph taken along one of the Thelon River's tributaries in June 2009. It shows a group of guided canoeists gazing on the landscape, taking photographs or searching for wildlife through binoculars. This image functions as a prompt for each of the forthcoming sections to bridge the ontological moments with suggestions for nature-based tourism research.

Critical realism

Critical realism is a philosophical position associated with the work of philosopher of science Roy Bhaskar (1978). Its influence in the social sciences has been profound among scholars in Europe, and clear attempts have been made to encourage its use among North American researchers (Frauley and Pearce 2007a).

Applications of critical realism have subtle and sizeable differences (Cruickshank 2004; Frauley and Pearce 2007b). However, its qualifying factor is a prescribed union of ontological realism and epistemological relativism. In other words, critical realists argue that independent reality exists beyond the scope of our knowledge, perceptions or actions, and that although our categories and concepts reflect some aspect of material referents, this knowledge never corresponds exactly to what exists. Knowledge is considered a fallible interpretation of reality and always open to criticism, refinement and further testing (Carolan 2005a; Frauley and Pearce 2007b). Thus, critical realism is set apart from other philosophies of science by the premise that establishes the primacy of ontology over epistemology. Bhaskar (1978: 30) reasons, 'it is not the character of science that imposes a determinate pattern or order on the world; but the order of the world that,

Figure 3.1 Touristic encounters within the Thelon River watershed

under certain determinate conditions, makes possible the cluster of activities we call "science"'. For the activities and accomplishments of science to exist as they do, an independent reality of a certain structure must also exist. Epistemology is therefore distinguishable from matters of ontology, and conflating the two – that is, reducing ontology to epistemology, or transposing questions about being into questions about knowing – warrants the charge of an *epistemic fallacy*, which Bhaskar (1978: 36–8) attributes to his empiricist and conventionalist predecessors.

From a critical realist perspective, material and social reality is understood as stratified, rooted and emergent (Sayer 1992; Carolan 2005a, 2005b; Bhaskar 1978). Social scientists concerned with 'environment', and its vernacular cousin 'nature', have found these concepts helpful for navigating debates between naïve realism and strong social constructivism (Carolan 2005a; Proctor 1998a; Dunlap 2010; Soper 1995). For example, stratification implies hierarchical differentiation between domains of existence, or ontological depth (Pearce 2007), meaning that inorganic nature provides the basis for organic nature, which, in turn, provides the basis for human society (Day 2007; 126). However, because the boundaries between strata are permeable, reality constitutes an open system characterised not by reduction and one-way causality, but by *rootedness* and *emergence* (Carolan 2005b). As these terms suggest, distinct socio-cultural and biophysical realms exert influences on one another (Carolan 2005b). The purpose of research then, is to highlight and understand the tendencies and contingent relations in a given circumstance, rather than determine causality (Gregory *et al.* 2009).

Applied to the case study, tourism researchers could use critical realism to position an investigation of the ecological impacts of tourist behaviour (wildlife photography and viewing), with the aim of identifying and understanding prevalent patterns and tendencies over time. One can imagine the extent to which the visual practices of Thelon tourists (i.e. observing, photographing or the ability to 'zoom in on'), and associated behaviours (e.g. establishing trails on the tundra to quality vantage points, approaching wildlife, distributing photographs), emerge from and exert influence on other domains. For example, how are viewing behaviours enabled or constrained by the habits and shifting habitats of wildlife? How is wildlife disturbance proliferated by touristic viewing, and can such impacts be offset by any increases to wilderness ambassadorship associated with tourism (Maher *et al.* 2003)? Attending to the specificity of individual species, tourism demographics or motivations, or the influence of local management policies and strategies would help flesh out the contingencies in these tourist–wildlife relationships.

In terms of methodology, critical realism is impartial and thus compatible with a range of strategies, including both quantitative and qualitative methods. Researchers could, therefore, incorporate a mixed methods approach to understand the relations between the picturing practices of tourists and wildlife. Such an approach would carry much relevance in managerial, operator or decision-making contexts.

Yet for all the promise of critical realism as a means for negotiating human exceptionalism, particularly in terms of how it softens the extremes of naïve realism and strong social construction, it seems limited on at least two fronts. First, critical realism tends to rely on analytical abstractions that implicitly detach subjects from embodied encounters that enable dwelling within the world (Ingold 2000). Second, underlining critical realism is the temptation of a unifying, metatheory to traverse disciplines and encompass the diversity of knowledge claims. These two issues are crucial in the moments discussed next.

Phenomenology of perception

Phenomenology is a Western philosophical tradition that prioritises descriptions of the *life-world*, the always-present world that precedes thoughts and knowledge, and is perceived through everyday actions, movements and encounters with meaningful things (Merleau-Ponty 1962: vii). Early thinkers such as Husserl, Heidegger, Satre and Merleau-Ponty, were concerned with how the 'objective facts' of science overshadowed the value of everyday, direct and spontaneous experience. They insisted that the activities of science be grounded in the understanding that all aspects of life happen only through our engagements of the world in which we dwell (Heidegger 2008) In short, our experience in and of the world is the *homeland* to our thoughts (Merleau-Ponty 1962: 24).

By calling attention to the life-world, phenomenology presents a direct and forceful challenge to the ontological assumptions lodged within Western systems of value by the influential philosophical work of Rene Descartes (Dillon 1988; Wylie 2007). Cartesian assumptions, which are closely associated with human exceptionalism, include the separation of reality into the human subject and the observable object, or the rational individual and the empirical world. Such assumptions translate into categories that order our lives – distinctions, for example, between mind and body, thought and reality, culture and nature or human and environment. Phenomenology intervenes in these dichotomies. It suggests that ontological tensions between phenomena as independently real (i.e. reality transcends human perspective) and as dependent on human experience (i.e. reality is equivalent to human cognition) can be negotiated, and indeed supplanted, by examining themes of subjectivity, knowledge and perception (Wylie 2007).

To refine my scope here, I will stay close to the work of Maurice Merleau-Ponty, for whom the life-world was understood as indelibly corporeal, a point that distinguishes his phenomenology of perception from Husserl and others. Merleau-Ponty's specific challenge to Cartesian distinctions occurs by placing mind, body and world in a state of perpetual consciousness. Bodies are not perceived as containers of consciousness, but rather bodies *are* consciousness (Carolan 2008). In Merleau-Ponty's (1962: 82) words, 'I am consciousness of my body *via* the world … and I am consciousness of the world through the medium of my body'. Thus, the crux of Merleau-Ponty's phenomenology is a shift from a separation of body and soul, of material object and subjective mind (both of which, he argues, distort the reality given to us in experience), to one of corporeal embodiment as the very basis of the perceptual world (Marshall 2008). The *body-subject*, as described by Merleau-Ponty, functions as the conduit of this worldly perception and knowledge (Abram 1996; Merleau-Ponty 2004). As an active, open and indeterminate form, the body-subject is in constant relation with other things and terrains of the world – exchanging, shifting, adapting, improvising and reciprocating. Space, or what we might refer to as environment, is configured through these situated encounters of things, terrains and bodies (Ingold 2000). This animate dance of receptivity and creativity in and of the world constitutes *perception* (Abram 1996), and is 'revealed to us by our senses and in everyday life' (Merleau-Ponty 2004: 31).

Shifting back to the Thelon River case study, phenomenology orients the researcher to a much different set of questions from the critical realist. For example, instead of trying to understand the inter-relationships and contingencies among impacts and tourist behaviour, with phenomenology we would be interested in understanding the meaning or essence of wildlife viewing and landscape photography for this group of travellers. Keeping with Merleau-Ponty's notion of perception, we might seek to describe that which is essential about the inter-subjective process of gazing, how tourists interpret their viewing experience, or how different bodies or entities performing as tourists interact with the world in this way. Moreover, immersion within the riverscape stimulates the senses in certain ways: skin is pricked by black flies, cooled by winds or hardened by the sun; walking up a hill to a lookout provides reprieve from the monotony of paddling, thus stretching the legs but also one's experience within, and awareness of, the landscape. Accordingly, we might also seek to understand the role that these sensations play in the meanings tourists' attribute to their lived-experience.

Given that the subject matter of phenomenology is what people experience and how they interpret the world, the most suitable methodologies are those that enable researchers to experience the phenomenon as directly as possible (Patton 2002). Qualitative research methods such as participant observation and in-depth interviewing are particularly appropriate and frequently employed. The rich and descriptive data gathered are often analysed and reported using thematic and narrative approaches (van Manen 2002).

Social nature

A third moment that contributes arguments against human exceptionalism includes a suite of orientations broadly referred to as the 'social construction of nature', or in geography circles as 'social nature' (Castree and Braun 2001; Demeritt 2002). For consistency, I use the latter term, and begin with general comments before moving to a refined focus on *discourse*.

According to Castree (2001), social nature constitutes a critical approach to society–nature relations that asserts 'nature' to be inescapably social. The argument here is that rather than an external or self-evident reality 'what counts as nature cannot preexist its construction; when we take nature to be self-evident, we simply mistake our discursive practices for the things they seek to describe' (Braun 2002: 17). In other words, nature is always an outcome of the conceptual and material activities of different societies.

The volume edited by William Cronon (1995a), has been influential to this line of thinking. Cronon's (1995b) essay, for example, has engendered extensive debate because of its assertion that wilderness, the archetype of an ontologically pure non-social environment, is a profound creation of particular human cultures at particular moments in time. Critics fear that Cronon's reasoning grants humans an unruly capacity to transform nature, undermining preservation and conservation efforts (Soulé and Lease 1995). In contrast, supporters identify the analytical and political possibilities for a radical environmentalism. They find social nature useful because it implies that humans have the capacity to improve current environmental circumstances by understanding, producing and practicing nature in more responsible and socially just ways (Castree and Braun 2001; Cronon 1995a).

As a general rule, adherents of social nature distance themselves from phenomenology's reification of human emotion, perception and embodiment. According to Marxist, feminist and poststructuralist thinkers, phenomenology ignores the ways in which the notion of the free, autonomous individual is shaped by social, economic, historical and political contexts (Wylie 2007). The humanistic hue of phenomenology is criticised by social nature theorists for holding out for an unmediated and essential experience of the world, one that implicitly values premodern environmental practices and relationships, and too easily conflates contemporary non-Western cultures with romanticised views of the past (Wylie 2007).

Social nature theorists are also united by an apprehension with universal categories and absolute distinctions, such as the one made by critical realists between ontology and epistemology. Braun (2002) asserts that 'nature' and 'environment' are as much epistemological conditions as they are ontological. Where critical realists allege an epistemic fallacy, social nature alleges 'our images and ideas of nature do not simply reflect a pre-existing reality, but, in important ways, constitute that reality for us' (Braun 2002: 14). Indeed, poststructuralism tends to treat language not as a reflection of reality, but as constitutive of it. In other words, the ontology of environment is viewed as an *effect* of culture. Accordingly, the nature of nature-based tourism along the Thelon River is (re)produced through various cultural texts (e.g. books, travel guides, websites containing canoe travel journals, territorial guiding license regulations) and culturally informed practices (e.g. proper canoe paddling techniques, manufacturing and marketing of outdoor equipment, aeroplane charter industry).

Much of the work in social nature is indebted to Michel Foucault and, in particular, his theoretical articulation of *discourse* (Foucault 1972, 1980). Although Foucault and others use the term in multiple and interchangeable ways (see, e.g., Castree 2005: 135–53), it is helpful here to understand discourse as 'a specific, collective series of representations, practices, and performances through which meanings give the world its particular shapes—their forms and norms. This implies that discourse is inherently productive, generative, and "object-constituting"' (Gregory 2001: 86). Discourses have rules and protocols about what is properly regarded as knowledge. They circulate through texts and are inscribed and naturalised through networks of individuals and institutions (Gregory 2001). Discourses are powerful precisely because they are productive: they produce subject-positions, bodies and objects. Here, it is important to recognise that, for Foucault, power is more than a repressive, hierarchical force possessed by a State, class or individual. Rather, in Foucault's (1980: 59) words, power 'produces effects … at the level of knowledge. Far from preventing knowledge, power produces it'. Power is thus 'positive' in that it influences and enables the formation of identities (Darier 1999).

Thus, unlike phenomenologists or critical realists who resort to some pre-given or essential reality (i.e. the body or an independent, external reality), Foucault and his followers argue that knowledge and truth are constituted by multiple, overlapping and conflicting discourses. And whereas Foucault's attention to environmental concerns was scant, others, such as Darier (1999), Braun (2002) and Haraway (1991), have extended his work into this sphere.

Social nature compels us to question the variety of self-evident categories we use to understand the world (e.g. 'tourism' or 'environment'). One way to do this is by investigating how power operates through discourse to normalise such categories. For example, in the Thelon River case we could explore how commercial discourses of wilderness tourism, which rely on touristic desires for untouched nature, contribute to the creation of the Arctic as a last remaining wilderness. Individuals, businesses and government agencies make money by selling the Thelon as wilderness, so to what extent is the practice of wildlife and landscape photography an effect produced by these wider political economies of tourism? A social nature approach might also consider how nature is framed in certain ways by tourists, which could relate to a desire to consume and collect the spaces represented elsewhere, or be intended to showcase to different audiences on the return home (Jenkins 2003). What becomes normalised through touristic photographs and what would be considered out-of-place? Important then from a social nature perspective, to expose how the touristic framing of nature silences, or makes absent, certain other ideas, practices or histories within the landscape (Rose 2007).

Given the breadth of social nature, a variety of methodological approaches are possible and appropriate. These include various qualitative methods oriented by semiotics, historical materialism, discourse analysis or actor-network theory (Castree and Braun 2001). However, an important feature distinguishing social nature research, especially from phenomenology, is its attention to the historical, cultural and political conditions that enable objects (e.g. the Thelon River) or identities (e.g. a canoeist) to attain legibility (Braun 2002). To reveal these kinds of conditions, researchers will often rely on textual analyses of archival and policy documents, photographs and popular magazines, or travel brochures, postcards and field guides (Waitt 2005).

Ontological multiplicity

Positive outcomes may result from ignoring social nature's theoretical challenge and insisting on the immutability of nature or environment, but as Quigley (1999) observes, these would be achieved through the use of authority rather than sound argument. This final section touches on ontological multiplicity, a perspective that draws on features of social nature to return to a more sophisticated realism. This relational understanding of ontology is gaining acceptance in a variety of intellectual spheres including the sociology of science, human geography, anthropology, political ecology and tourism studies (Braun 2009; Carolan 2004; Escobar 2010; Jóhannesson 2005).

A point of departure for thinking in terms of multiplicity is the notion that the world is constantly being made and remade. Although reality might seem to precede our occupation, Clark *et al.* (2008) remind us that the actions and inactions of individuals, cultures, nation-states, multinational institutions and non-human entities are always influencing the way the world is. Like it or not, we are all implicated in socio-material relations of the world, with all activities causing greater or lesser degrees of real-world effects (Clark *et al.* 2008). Certainly this is not meant to suggest that the world is a 'blank-slate' that imposes no demands upon us. Rather, as a multiplicity of space, reality is created through the co-existence of historical, changing and moving objects, stories or other socio-material phenomena (Massey 2005).

A principal concern for people thinking through multiplicity, such as those positioned around the theme of ontological politics, is to bring the materiality and agency of things back into consideration (Hinchliffe 2007; Law 2004; Mol 1999). The reasoning here builds on the seminal work of Latour (1993), who argued that research and theory prioritising discourse remains entrenched in the 'modern constitution' by presuming pure distinctions between nature and culture. This is inaccurate according to Latour because it leaves the 'things' of the world passive and mute, and to exist ultimately as epistemological terms (Hinchliffe 2007; Whatmore 2002). As such, ontological multiplicity relies on metaphors like intervention, performance and enactment, which speak to the many realities of an object crafted by various tools and practices that co-exist in the present (Mol 1999):

> reality does not precede the mundane practices in which we interact with it, but is rather shaped within these practices. So the term *politics* works to underline this active mode, this process of shaping, and the fact that its character is both open and contested.
>
> *(Mol 1999: 75)*

There are then options between multiple versions of reality, and the grounds for enacting a certain version of an object are debatable (Law 2004). Thus, as one derivative of multiplicity, ontological politics is concerned with understanding which options of a particular phenomenon are to be performed, where options are situated and what is at stake when a decision between alternative options is made (Mol 1999).

In terms of environment, an object like the Thelon River can be understood as simultaneously enacted through different material, conceptual or discursive practices. Such practices vary in time and space but overlap in many ways, so the reality of the river is open to negotiation. When it comes to the politics of the Thelon, the argument is that there is not just one reality to secure or protect against all other possible versions (Hinchliffe 2007). Instead, there are many possible rivers that may be enacted differently and with different implications.

Brief illustrations based on circumstances related to human–wildlife interactions within the Thelon River basin offer some grounding to these discussions.

The nature-based tourists in Figure 3.1 attempt to make wildlife present through practices associated with photography and gazing. Prior to the journey, these travellers would have studied the natural and human history of the area, purchased cameras and binoculars, and rehearsed how to use these technologies. On location, the travellers beached their canoes, climbed a hill to access a certain vantage point, and spread out for unobstructed views. The wildlife images they captured were brought home as symbols of their journey. It is the collection of these kinds of practices that perform the Thelon as a wilderness space and enact tourist identities.

Among the Inuit living in Baker Lake, Nunavut, shifting cultural practices have enabled hunters to make wildlife (particularly caribou) present to sustain livelihoods. Oral traditions and place names are passed between generations and used as navigational aids; elders share skills and knowledge about harvesting techniques, food preparation or the making of tools and clothing; technological changes, such as the use of snowmobiles, are accommodated when practical. These kinds of practices enable some Inuit to maintain subsistence lifestyles while shifting towards a wage economy. They perform the Thelon as cultural space, or homeland, and contribute to the enactment of Inuit identity.

The additional claim of multiplicity – that these different practices overlap in unpredictable ways and interfere with reality (Law 2004) – is equally apparent. For example, the canoe guide/ outfitter has supported his livelihood by travelling within the watershed for over 35 years. His guiding practices have made the Thelon into what can be referred to as his own backyard (Hall 2003). Moreover, a summer-long canoe expedition in 1999 involved Inuit, Dene First Nations and Germans travelling the length of the Thelon River (Gleeson 1999). The event emphasised cross-cultural learning, wilderness travel and living off the land, and was recorded in a feature-length documentary. The celebratory journey further troubles the distinction between wilderness and homeland. And, as a third example, many authors suggest that during an Inuit hunt, the animal offers its presence to a skilled hunter for his or her taking (Bennett and Rowley 2004; Mannick 1998). The agency of prey implies that human livelihoods and identities are crafted in part through the practices of another species.

An implication of ontological multiplicity is that what counts as 'environment' can be a kind of active experimentation (Braun 2009) where bodily senses and affective registers are prioritised, what counts as a research subject is extended, and knowledge and expertise is redistributed beyond the academy (Whatmore 2006). Accordingly, the options for tourism research methodology might best be left unbound, but also open to debate so that their effectiveness and positive contributions to the making of our world might be evaluated (Law 2004).

Conclusion

In a volume that considers new visions of nature, Proctor (2009) argues that persistent environmental problems result, in part, because we have not yet taken the risk to think deeply. When we do, it becomes clear that the notion of environment is astray, as are many of the sources of authority used to justify environmental concerns. Proctor speaks to the relevance of the social science ontology of environment. This chapter has provided another cut into this rich terrain. Specifically, I have drawn attention to various ontological positions that present possible alternatives to human exceptionalism, and, through this, attempted to identify possibilities for applying different ontologies in tourism research. A case study from a Canadian Arctic riverscape provided grounding for these discussions.

Three implications merit final comment. First, taking into account the issue of ontology might compel tourism and environment researchers towards consistency and precision in their methodological choices. Certainly some research methods are better suited to critical realists than phenomenologists. However, given the potential messiness of environmental ontologies, methods must also be engaged playfully, speculatively and reflexively so that innovative and inter-disciplinary approaches in tourism studies can thrive.

Second, tourism and environmental managers are tasked with making decisions in contexts of different, negotiable and fluid ideas about realities. Clarity and precision can be achieved by basing decisions in philosophical understandings of ontology, although care must be taken to avoid surrendering open philosophical discussion to uncompromising philosophical rigidity. The promises of adaptive co-management (see Chapter 48) seem ripe for addressing these kinds of challenges.

Finally, the social science ontology of environment and attempts to displace human exceptionalism call attention to ethics, a theme not lost on tourism researchers (Fennell 2006; Holden 2003; Smith and Duffy 2003). What we consider real and true about environment relates to how we act towards those things we consider part of the environment. Thus, different ontologies of environment provide different foundations for ethical consideration. For instance, when the self-evident category of nature is punctured from a social nature perspective, notions of intrinsic value, which laden environmental ethics, become tricky business (Proctor 1998b). Moreover, the metaphors of enactment and intervention that characterise multiplicity demands an ethics – towards environment, humans or non-humans, in research, or in tourism – that recoils from teleology (Haraway 2008; Latour 2004). When reality is understood as multiple, so too must be ethics. The political and environmental possibilities that result from this observation demand our best theoretical reflection and research practice.

Further reading

Bhaskar, R. (1978) *A realist theory of science.* Atlantic Highlands, NJ: Humanities Press Inc. (The philosophical kick start for critical realism.)

Castree, N. and Braun, B. (eds) (2001) *Social nature: Theory, practice, and politics.* Malden, MA: Blackwell Publishing Ltd. (Diverse theoretical perspectives and applications of social nature.)

Cronon, W. (ed.) (1995) *Uncommon ground: Toward reinventing nature.* New York: W.W. Norton and Co. (A foundational set of essays for understanding nature's social dimensions.)

Darier, É. (ed.) (1999) *Discourses of the environment.* Malden, MA: Blackwell Publishers Inc. (Foucault's thinking is applied to environmental contexts.)

Escobar, A. (2010) 'Postconstructivist political ecologies', in Redclift, M.R. and Woodgate, G. (eds) *The international handbook of environmental sociology*, 2nd edn. Northampton, MA: Edward Elgar Publishing. (A concise review of central threads and emerging trends in political ecology.)

Ingold, T. (2000) *The perception of the environment: Essays in livelihood, dwelling and skill.* New York: Routledge. (A classic anthropological account of perception that resonates significantly with Merleau-Ponty's phenomenology.)

Latour, B. (1993) *We have never been modern.* Cambridge, MA: Harvard University Press. (An important primer for ontological multiplicity and the politics of nature.)

Merleau-Ponty, M. (2004) *The world of perception.* London: Routledge and Kegan Paul. (Key ideas from Merleau-Ponty and reader friendly.)

Whatmore, S. (2002) *Hybrid geographies: Natures, cultures, spaces.* Thousand Oaks, CA: Sage. (A thorough examination and application of nature-cultures with important considerations for ethics.)

References

Abram, D. (1996) *The spell of the sensuous: Perception and language in a more-than-human world.* New York: Vintage Books.

Bennett, J. and Rowley, S. (eds) (2004) *Uqalurait: An oral history of Nunavut.* Montreal, QC, and Kingston, ON: McGill-Queen's University Press.

Bhaskar, R. (1978) *A realist theory of science.* Atlantic Highlands, NJ: Humanities Press Inc.

Braun, B. (2002) *The intemperate rainforest: Nature, culture, and power on Canada's west coast.* Minneapolis, MN: University of Minnesota Press.

——(2004) 'Nature and culture: On the career of a false problem', in Duncan, J.S., Johnson, N.C. and Schein, R.H. (eds) *A companion to cultural geography.* Malden, MA: Blackwell Publishing.

——(2009) 'Nature', in Castree, N., Demeritt, D., Liverman, D. and Rhoads, B. (eds) *A companion to environmental geography.* Malden, MA: Blackwell Publishing Inc.

BQCMB (2010) *Beverly and Qamanirjuaq Caribou Management Board 28th annual report 2009–2010.* www.arctic-caribou.com.

Carolan, M.S. (2004) Ontological politics: Mapping a complex environmental problem. *Environmental Values* 13, 497–522.

——(2005a) Realism with reductionism: Toward an ecologically embedded sociology. *Human Ecology Review* 12, 1–19.

——(2005b) Society, biology, and ecology: Bringing nature back into sociology's disciplinary narrative through critical realism. *Organization and Environment* 18, 393–421.

——(2008) More-than-representational knowledge/s of the countryside: How we think as bodies. *Sociologia Ruralis* 48, 408–421.

Castree, N. (2001) 'Socializing nature: Theory, practice, and politics', in Castree, N. and Braun, B. (eds) *Social Nature: Theory, Practice, and Politics*. Malden, MA: Blackwell Publishing Ltd.

——(2005) *Nature*. New York: Routledge.

Castree, N. and Braun, B. (eds) (2001) *Social nature: Theory, practice, and politics*. Malden, MA: Blackwell Publishing Ltd.

Clark, N., Massey, D., and Sarre, P. (eds) (2008) *Material geographies: A world in the making*. Thousand Oaks, CA: Sage.

Cronon, W. (ed.) (1995a) *Uncommon ground: Toward reinventing nature*. New York: W.W. Norton and Co.

——(1995b) 'The trouble with wilderness; or, getting back to the wrong nature', in Cronon, W. (ed.) *Uncommon ground: Rethinking the place in nature*. New York: W.W. Norton and Company.

Cruickshank, J. (2004) A tale of two ontologies: An immanent critique of critical realism. *The Sociological Review* 52, 567–85.

Darier, É. (ed.) (1999) *Discourses of the environment*, Malden, MA: Blackwell Publishers Inc.

Day, R. (2007) 'More than straw figures in straw houses: Toward a revaluation of critical realism's conception of post-structuralist theory', in Frauley, J. and Pearce, F. (eds) *Critical realism and the social sciences: Heterodox elaborations*. Toronto, ON: University of Toronto Press.

Demeritt, D. (2002) 'What is the 'social construction of nature'? A typology and sympathetic critique', *Progress in Human Geography* 26, 767–90.

Dillon, M. C. (1988) *Merleau-Ponty's ontology*. Indianapolis, IN: Indiana University Press.

Dunlap, R. E. (2010) 'The maturation and diversification of environmental sociology: From constructivism and realism to agnosticism and pragmatism', in Redclift, M.R. and Woodgate, G. (eds) *The international handbook of environmental sociology*, 2nd edn. Northampton, MA: Edward Elgar Publishing.

Escobar, A. (2010) 'Postconstructivist political ecologies', in Redclift, M.R. and Woodgate, G. (eds) *The international handbook of environmental sociology*, 2nd edn. Northampton, MA: Edward Elgar Publishing.

Fennell, D.A. (2006) *Tourism ethics*. Toronto, ON: Channel View Publications.

Foucault, M. (1972) *The archaeology of knowledge*. New York: Harper Colophon.

——(1980) *Power/knowledge: Selected interviews and other writings 1972–1977*. New York: Pantheon Books.

Frauley, J. and Pearce, F. (eds) (2007a) *Critical realism and the social sciences: Heterodox elaboration*. Toronto, ON: University of Toronto Press.

——(2007b) 'Critical realism and the social sciences: Methodological and epistemological preliminaries', in Frauley, J. and Pearce, F. (eds) *Critical realism and the social sciences: Heterodox elaborations*. Toronto, ON: University of Toronto Press.

Gleeson, R. (1999) *Canoeing across cultures: Eight-week canoe trip brings Germans, Dene and Inuit together*. Northern News Services, 14 June 1999. Accessed at www.nnsl.com/frames/newspapers/1999-06/jun14_99canoe.html.

Gregory, D. (2001) '(Post)colonialism and the production of nature', in Castree, N. and Braun, B. (eds) *Social nature: Theory, practice, and politics*. Malden, MA: Blackwell Publishing Ltd.

Gregory, D., Johnston, R., Pratt, G., Watts, M. J. and Whatmore, S. (2009) *The dictionary of human geography*. Malden, MA: Wiley-Blackwell.

Hall, A.M. (2003) *Discovering Eden: A lifetime of paddling Arctic rivers*. Toronto, ON: Key Porter Books.

Haraway, D.J. (1991) *Simians, cyborgs, and women: The reinvention of nature*. New York: Routledge.

——(2008) *When species meet*. Minneapolis, MN: University of Minnesota Press.

Heidegger, M. (2008) 'Building dwelling thinking', in Krell, D.F. (ed.) *Basic writings from Being and time (1927) and The task of thinking (1964)*. Toronto, ON: Harper Perennial.

Hinchliffe, S. (2007) *Geographies of nature: Societies, environments, ecologies*. Thousand Oaks, CA: Sage Publications.

Holden, A. (2003) In need of new environmental ethics for tourism. *Annals of Tourism Research* 30, 94–108.

Ingold, T. (2000) *The perception of the environment: Essays in livelihood, dwelling and skill*. New York: Routledge.

Jenkins, O.H. (2003) Photography and travel brochures: The circle of representation. *Tourism Geographies* 5, 305–28.

Jóhannesson, G.T. (2005) Tourism translations: Actor-network theory and tourism research. *Tourist Studies* 5, 133–50.

Latour, B. (1993) *We have never been modern*. Cambridge, MA: Harvard University Press.

——(2004) *Politics of nature: How to bring the sciences into democracy*. Cambridge, MA: Harvard University Press.

Law, J. (2004) *After method: Mess in social science research*. New York: Routledge.

Maher, P.T., Steel, G., and McIntosh, A. (2003) 'Antarctica: Tourism, wilderness, and "ambassadorship"', in Watson, A., and Sproull, J. (eds) *Science and stewardship to protect and sustain wilderness values: Seventh World Wilderness Congress symposium*. Ogden, UT: USDA Forest Service, pp. 204–9.

van Manen, M. (2002) Phenomenology Online. www.phenomenologyonline.com.

Mannick, H. (ed.) (1998) *Inuit Nunamiut: Inland Inuit*. Altona, MB: Friesen Corporation.

Marshall, G.J. (2008) *A guide to Merleau-Ponty's "Phenomenology of Perception"*. Milwaukee, WN: Marquette University Press.

Massey, D. (2005) *For space*. Thousand Oaks, CA: Sage.

Merleau-Ponty, M. (1962) *Phenomenology of perception*. London: Routledge and Kegan Paul.

——(2004) *The world of perception*. New York: Routledge.

Mol, A. (1999) 'Ontological politics. A word and some questions', in Law, J. and Hassard, J. (eds) *Actor-network theory and after*. Malden, MA: Blackwell Publishing.

Morse, E.W. (1987) *Freshwater saga: Memoirs of a lifetime of wilderness canoeing in Canada*. Toronto, ON: University of Toronto Press.

Patton, M.Q. (2002) *Qualitative research and evaluation methods*, 3rd edn. Thousand Oaks, CA: Sage.

Pearce, F. (2007) 'Bhaskar's critical realism: An appreciative introduction and a friendly critique', in Frauley, J. and Pearce, F. (eds) *Critical realism and the social sciences: Heterodox elaborations*. Toronto, ON: University of Toronto Press.

Proctor, J.D. (1998a) The social construction of nature: Relativist accusations, pragmatist and critical realist responses. *Annals of the Association of American Geographers* 88, 352–76.

——(1998b) Geography, paradox and environmental ethics. *Progress in Human Geography* 22, 234–55.

——(2009) 'Environment after nature: Time for a new vision', in Proctor, J.D. (ed.) *Envisioning nature, science, and religion*. West Coushohocken, PA: Templeton Foundation Press.

Quigley, P. (1999) 'Nature as dangerous space', in Darier, É. (ed.) *Discourses of the environment*. Malden, MA: Blackwell Publishers Inc.

Rose, G. (2007) *Visual methodologies: An introduction to the interpretation of visual materials*, 2nd edn. Thousand Oaks, CA: Sage Publications.

Sayer, A. (1992) *Method in social science: A realist approach*. London: Hutchinson.

Smith, M. and Duffy, R. (2003) *The ethics of tourism development*. New York: Routledge.

Soper, K. (1995) *What is nature? Culture, politics and the non-human*. Malden, MA: Blackwell Publishing Inc.

Soulé, M. and Lease, G. (eds) (1995) *Reinventing nature? Responses to postmodern deconstruction*. Washington, DC: Island Press.

Waitt, G. (2005) 'Doing discourse analysis', in Hay, I. (ed.), *Qualitative research methods in human geography*. Victoria: Oxford University Press, 163–91.

Whatmore, S. (2002) *Hybrid geographies: Natures, cultures, spaces*. Thousand Oaks: CA, Sage.

——(2006) Materialist returns: Practising cultural geography in and for a more-than-human world. *Cultural Geographies* 13, 600–9.

Wylie, J. (2007) *Landscape*. New York: Routledge.

4

Religious views of the environment

Sanctification of nature and implications for tourism

Dallen Timothy

Introduction

Since the beginning of human life on earth, people have found solace in the promise of the divine. This has been manifested in many ways, including a belief in a god or gods, the spiritual nature of inanimate objects, the divinity of self, or nature gods that controlled the elements and rewarded or punished people depending on their obedience or lack thereof. Several archaeological sites, some dating as far back as 10,000 years, are believed to have been built for religious purposes – sites of worship and spiritual transformation (Timothy 2010).

The natural environment and its component parts played a crucial role in ancient worship, for they were imbued with divine powers or inhabited by holy spirits. Much of this has stood the test of time and can still be found in many religious traditions and spiritualist movements. Most organised religions today accept the close connection between gods and nature, and many biotic and abiotic elements of ecosystems are sanctified as locations of godly interface with humankind, sites of miracles, or settings associated with religious leaders and their ministries. Contemporary spiritual communities still venerate nature, particularly topographic features and areas of energy flow, where earth's spirit is believed to be most profoundly exhibited. Sacred space in nature abounds in all parts of the world, with salient implications for religious tourism.

This chapter examines the primary interfaces between religion and nature, and spirituality and nature. It first examines religious views and treatments of the environment and the various components of natural landscapes that are most often revered. It then highlights non-organised religious perspectives on spirituality and how these inter-play with notions of nature and sacred space. Both of these perspectives are then brought into the realm of tourism by considering how spiritual and religious treatment of nature plays out in the tourism context.

Religion and nature

Most holy scriptures are replete with references to nature. The very creation of the earth in Judeo-Christian tradition details vividly the process by which God created the heavens, the earth, and all living and non-living things upon it. Some faith traditions believe in the spontaneous formation of the earth through natural processes. Regardless of the religious dogma associated with the earth's creation, nature and humankind's role in it are foundational elements of the story. According to the Bible, God created the earth as a habitat for humans. He gave humans dominion over the earth and its resources, to be stewards of his great creation, and to use the earth's resources wisely for their sustenance and comfort.

There are multitudinous references in the Bible, Book of Mormon, Bhagavad Gita, Quran, Talmud, Torah and Guru Granth Sahib to the importance of nature and the environment in the lives of humans and in their relationship with deity. Much sacred writ teaches of the inseparability of humans and the environment in which they live, and some believers see the earth as evidence of God's love and very existence (Alder 1991; Foltz 2003). It also re-affirms the eminence and omnipotence of god(s) in creating places of habitation for the human race.

Adherents to some religions, particularly a variety of Christian sects, have long interpreted the scriptural promise that the earth was made for the use of humankind to mean that it can be used in excess without forethought for its care (Dekker *et al.* 1997). In some fundamentalist Christian faiths there is a prevalent anti-conservation and anti-green ethos. According to several studies (e.g. Boyd 1999; Schultz *et al.* 2000; Sherkat and Ellison 2007), adherence to fundamentalist Christianity was a salient variable in predicting a lack of support for environmental causes. This is likely to be derived from Christians' belief in Jesus' eventual return to the earth to reign during the Millennium. Ancient prophets foretold that upon Jesus' return, the earth would be cleansed/destroyed by fire and then renewed. Thus, the depletion of resources and destruction of ecosystems is not seen as antithetical to the tenets of their religion. The oft-times general lack of support for environmentalism may be politically derived, in part at least, by suspicions of religious conservatives against the more environmentalist liberals (Eckberg and Blocker 1996; Greeley 1993).

Some environmental scientists, who are Christians, however, although believing in the Second Coming of Christ, also realise the godly commission to care for the earth as its stewards. In the words of Matthews (1972: 38), ' … the earth needs to be looked after and … man has the responsibility to dress, to keep, and to maintain the earth as a habitable place' where natural bounties should be used with good judgment, not in excess. Regarding earth as one of God's great creations, Alder (1991: 27) questioned, 'Can Heavenly Father be any less pleased with the willful destruction of nature than when we break the [commandments]? … It seems to me that part of our responsibility as caretakers for the earth is to … take advantage of opportunities to protect our world's resources'. Religious leaders outside of Christianity have also begun to support nature conservation because of its divine connotations (Sheikh 2006).

Other religions and spiritual traditions have long acknowledged the role of religion in protecting the environment. Many traditional spiritual practices valued the protection of landscapes, water bodies and forests through their religious beliefs, protection of sacred sites and certain hunting taboos, and in so doing have helped to preserve biodiversity (Xu *et al.* 2005). According to a study by Owen and Videras (2007), people who adhere to spiritual belief systems that are not part of organised religion, or who do not even possess a belief in God, but who none the less believe in the individual spirit, are more inclined to exhibit pro-conservation and pro-environmental attitudes. This derives primarily from their beliefs in the oneness of humans and the earth, that humankind is part of nature, not separate from it, and therefore a harmonious human–nature relationship must be nurtured. The Owen and Videras study concluded that environmental action is determined by a variety of socio-demographic traits, one of which is spiritual beliefs.

Whether a religion's leadership and membership view the earth as a resource to be consumed at will or as a blessing from God to be protected and utilised with caution, the majority of faith organisations have accepted certain ecosystems or natural features as sacred space, imbued with power and sanctity. The veneration of ecology (geopiety) derives from two primary sources. First, according to some creeds, features of the natural realm (e.g. rivers and forests) are intrinsically sacrosanct through their association with the earth's creation, human life, healing powers, habitat of spirits or abode of the gods. Second, ordinary landscapes or physical features are enshrouded with hallowed significance following a divine visitation, angelic ministry or mighty miracle. For example, the Jordan River, although a crucial water resource in an otherwise arid land for millennia, achieved religious significance for the Jews when, according to ancient scripture, the Lord temporarily dammed up the overflowing Jordan River so that Joshua, the successor of Moses, and the Israelites could return to Canaan and vanquish Jericho. It later gained additional importance for Christians as the location where Jesus was baptised by John the Baptist.

Sacrosanct environments

Believers have always sought environments and ecosystems that either exude a sense of spirit or that have been officially designated as holy places by faith organisations. This section highlights some of the most common sacrosanct components of the physical environment revered today as sacred space, including mountains, caves, rivers, forests and natural landscapes.

Mountains

Mountains and their environs are among the most sacred spaces on earth. Religions and spiritual philosophies of all sorts have venerated mountains for millennia. In many faith traditions and for many individuals, mountains are viewed as being literally and figuratively closer to deity than any other geomorphic features in the natural realm. Like the ancient Tower of Babel, constructed in the hope of ascending to heaven, the height of mountains was symbolic of reaching the sky, and by visiting them people could be 'within reach' of their Creator. Mountain scenery is likewise often revered as one of the world's most beautiful landscapes, where the very awe and inspiration of God can be seen and felt (Nicholson 1959, cited in Towner 1996: 142). In the words of one mountain scholar:

> As the highest and most impressive features of the landscape, mountains have an unusual power to awaken a sense of the sacred. Their soaring summits, the clouds and thunder that swirl about their peaks, the life-giving waters that flow from their heights, these and other characteristics imbue them with an aura of mystery and sanctity.
>
> *(Bernbaum 2006: 304)*

Buddhism, Taoism and Shintoism all accept mountains as sacred sites, and many mountains in Korea, Japan, China, Sri Lanka and other majority Buddhist countries are among the most important religious landscapes (Chen 1995; Guo 2006). The ancient Chinese believed mountains to be pillars separating earth from heaven and the abode of wise men and sages. The Tien Shan range has long been viewed not just as the abode of gods but the physical embodiment of gods, considered the holiest mountains in China for more than 2,000 years (Shackley 2001: 128). To the ancient Greeks, Mount Olympus was the domicile of the gods, seriously worshipped and feared.

The isolation of mountains has played a critical role in religion as well. For some groups, mountains served as protectors against evil or otherwise negative outside influences (Kay 1995). For others, their quietness and seclusion facilitated divine visitations. Mount Sinai was chosen by

God as a suitable location to bestow the Ten Commandments on Moses. St Katherine's Monastery rests near the spot thought to be the meeting place of Moses and God. Later, the Quran mentions Mount Sinai on several occasions as being a holy place, like Mecca. Several Islamic sacred sites, including mosques, have been erected on the mountain, and it has become an important pilgrimage destination for Muslims and Christians (Shackley 1998).

Many angelic visits have taken place on mountains and hills throughout the world and according to many faiths. In Medjugorje, Bosnia Herzegovina, the Virgin Mary appeared to three young Catholics in the early 1980s on Crnica Hill outside of town. The site has been officially recognised by the Roman Catholic Church and is one of the most popular pilgrimage destinations in Europe (Vukonić 2006). According to the history of the Church of Jesus Christ of Latter-day Saints, Joseph Smith was visited by an angel on the Hill Cumorah in upstate New York, where he received ancient engraved plates from which he translated the Book of Mormon.

Caves and grottos

Caves have been considered sacred space since the beginning of humanity. This comes largely from a sense that they are part of the womb of Mother Earth and represent birth, rebirth and regeneration. According to legend, the god Zeus was born in a cave on Mount Ida in Crete. Sacred caves exist all over the world and have yielded many informative archaeological sites. In various parts of the ancient world, holy men and prophets lived in caves for their protective properties, but also because of their concentration of spirit.

The Cave of Hira on Mount Hira, a few kilometres from Mecca, is one of Islam's holiest places. It is believed to be the location where Mohammed was visited by the angel Gabriel and received revelations from God, which then became the earliest portions of the Quran. Grottos are very important in Roman Catholicism, primarily because of Marian apparitions or sites of miracles. Likewise, there are many sacred caves and grottos in the Holy Land, including the location near Gethsemane where Jesus' apostles slept while he suffered in the garden. Many ancient homes and workshops in the Holy Land were located in caves and grottos, so today many sacred locales associated with Christianity and Judaism can be found in rock faces or in subterranean caves. The birthplace of Jesus in Bethlehem, shelters associated with the shepherds' field near Bethlehem, the Garden Tomb (the Protestant location of Jesus' tomb), the burial tomb of Mary, the birthplace of Mary, the Tomb of Lazarus, the place of the annunciation, the presumed workshop of Joseph in Nazareth and many more sacred places are all believed to have been in caves or grottos and have been marked as such.

In addition to being created naturally, caves have also been carved by Homo sapiens for millennia as burial sites, shelters, worship centres and homes for deity. Several cave churches in Turkey and Ethiopia have been inscribed on UNESCO's World Heritage List and are important cultural attractions. The cliff shores of Lake Prespa, in northern Greece, are home to several sacred caves enlarged by monks to house shrines. These are important pilgrimage destinations and cultural tourist attractions at the borders of Greece, Albania and Macedonia.

Rivers

Like mountains and caves, rivers have a long history of being sacrosanct, primarily for their healing powers and as divine origins of gods (Cooper 2009). Rivers are mentioned frequently in holy writ. The Jordan River, the Tigris and Euphrates, and the Nile are mentioned many times in the Bible and other Jewish scripture. Each of these is special in its own right in Christianity, Islam and Judaism. The Nile's historical association with Moses and the ancient Israelites' escape from Egyptian slavery is of particular interest to Jews and Christians.

Rivers have spiritual qualities of cleansing and healing. The Ganges River in India and Bangladesh is the holiest of all rivers for Hindus. It is worshipped as the Goddess Ganga and its waters are believed to have healing powers and an ability to purge a person's sins. For Hindus, a bath in the Ganges is a vital part of their spiritual life and a personal goal for many (Nyaupane and Budruk 2009; Singh 2006). Also from a forgiveness perspective, thousands of religious tourists are baptised each year in the Jordan River to demonstrate their devotion to God and to receive forgiveness for sin. Immersion in the river symbolises a rebirth, a clean slate and a recommitment to righteous living.

Forests

Forests have always radiated varying degrees of mystique. Throughout history people have revered forests and groves as spaces where spirits reside. Some people approached them with fear and trepidation, whereas others honoured their spiritual power. Sacred groves and forests can still be found in India. In certain parts of the country almost every village had its own sacred grove of varying sizes, which was the property of gods. Many of these groves still hold a spiritual significance and are used today as places of worship (Chadran and Hughes 1997; Shackley 2001). In West Africa, sacred groves are deemed to be the final resting places of tribal chiefs or homes of gods, and certain 'profane' behaviours, such as hunting reptiles, drumming, whistling or cutting trees are strictly forbidden (Shackley 2001). From a Christian perspective, the Church of Jesus Christ of Latter-day Saints also maintains a sacred grove in upstate New York, where Joseph Smith, the church's founder, witnessed a heavenly visit in the early nineteenth century (Hudman and Jackson 1992; Olsen 2006).

Forests have for many centuries been venerated as sacred in Europe and Asia. The forest conservation movement in Europe during the nineteenth and twentieth centuries, as well as protective legislation, was based largely on Europeans' view of forests as sacred space (Bürger-Arndt and Welzholz 2005). The same is true of many forests in India and other parts of Asia (Sinha and Sinha 2008). Japan's two primary religions, Buddhism and Shintoism, attribute spiritual and celestial attributes to trees, and many Shinto temples are set inside parks and gardens designed and landscaped with trees to symbolise eternal life and the divine attributes of forests (Albin and Berwick 2004: 565).

Implications for tourism

This intercourse between religion and the environment results in salient implications for tourism, including religious pilgrimage, cultural tourism, and the integration of geomantic design in tourist resorts and other settings.

Religious pilgrimage is one of the most salient types of contemporary tourism and one of the earliest forerunners to modern-day travel. Religious tourism, or pilgrimage, entails people travelling to hallowed sites for spiritual or religious purposes. Many pilgrims travel to seek forgiveness for sin, to be healed, to demonstrate devotion to God, to fulfil religious requirements, or to be uplifted and edified in other ways. The largest tourist gatherings in the world are religious in nature and comprise the most salient type of tourism for some countries and regions. From the beginning of time people have travelled in search of the sacred, visiting places deemed holy by religious associations and elevated individuals. For thousands of years Hindu and Buddhist pilgrims have sought access to holy rivers and mountain sites as a way of connecting with gods and Mother Earth. Many of the locales visited in ancient days are still important destinations for pilgrim tourists today in India, Nepal and Tibet. Soon after the crucifixion of Jesus Christ, converts to Christianity in Europe began to visit the Holy Land, as well as sites associated with the apostles. Greece, Turkey, Cyprus and Palestine were early pilgrim destinations and continue to be key stops on Christian tours of the eastern Mediterranean today.

Organised religion has varying degrees of obligation regarding pilgrimage. At one end of the spectrum, Islam requires devotees to undertake a pilgrimage to Mecca (the *hajj*) at least once in their lifetime, unless they are physically or financially unable (Timothy and Iverson 2006). At the other end are faiths that discourage travel for religious reasons; Sikhism is a good example of this. Although Sikhs are not prohibited from undertaking religious pilgrimage, they are commonly discouraged from it, because it is considered a waste of time and money, and may demonstrate a lack of humility. According to Guru teachings, travelling to sacred sites produces few spiritual benefits and is unnecessary, because adherents' faith is found within themselves rather than in any location or building (Jutla 2002). Between the two ends of the spectrum are varying levels of compulsion or freedom to participate in religious tourism. Common among nearly all pilgrimage patterns is the notion of visiting natural areas and features of the physical landscape that are considered sacred. As noted above, many of these include mountains, rivers, forests and caves.

The second perspective is non-believers visiting sacred sites to satisfy their curiosity rather than to exhibit devotion (Metreveli and Timothy 2010; Timothy 2011). Many of the world's sacrosanct places have become attractions simply because of their cultural importance and heritage value. Sailing on the Ganges, for example, to witness the unique architecture of Varanasi and to watch Hindus bathing and praying in the river is one of the most popular cultural attractions in northern India. The same can be said of many tourists' visits to Mount Sinai or sacred forests in Japan.

Finally, several of the East Asian religions have significantly influenced the design and development of tourism in various parts of the world. Feng Shui, a crucial element of Taoism, Confucianism and other popular religious traditions, has had relevant bearings on the planning, design and operation of hotels in the Asia–Pacific region (Guo 2006). Hobson (1994: 23) identified several ways in which Feng Shui influences the management of tourism establishments: location of the attraction or service; exterior design; interior design and layout; marketing to those who believe in Feng Shui; and managing workers who are believers in the power of Feng Shui. Many East Asian religionists believe that lighting, layout and form can affect people's health and luck. Poor design can be unlucky and curtail the flow of energy (Guo 2006).

Spiritualism, spirituality and nature

At this juncture, it is worth noting that spirituality and religiosity are not synonymous. Individuals may be religious but not spiritual, and there are millions of people in the world who claim to be spiritual but do not adhere to organised religion. Even atheists and agnostics are known to have spiritual experiences – when they feel a strong connection to nature or a sense that they are in fact only a small part of a greater transcendent and universal realm of existence. Beyond organised religion, there is a whole set of experiences and worldviews that can be classified as spiritual. Some of these are examined below.

Indigenous spirituality and nature

Native peoples throughout the world have for millennia venerated nature as an important element of life. Animism, or the belief that biotic and abiotic components of the environment possess souls or spirits, is one of the oldest spiritual philosophies. Topographic and weather-related features, including rivers, thunderstorms and mountains are seen to be living, breathing entities that, together with humans, comprise a single ecosystem. Most indigenous societies adhere to some degree of animistic beliefs, from which legends, literatures and livelihoods derive. Native Americans of the US southwest count the buttes and mesas of Arizona, Colorado, Utah and New Mexico among their most sacred spaces. The indigenous Australians revere Uluru (Ayers Rock) for its mystical powers and consider it one of the first creations, as well as the abode of spirits. There are thousands of examples, such as these, of aboriginal peoples revering unique outcrops, misshaped hills and mountains, unique vegetation, distinct canyons, and valleys, suggesting that their inimitability testifies of their spiritual origins or of earth's powers manifest within them (Brockman 1999).

New Ageism

One of the contemporary world's reactions to a growing dissatisfaction with organised religion was the establishment of a New Age spiritual philosophy during the mid-twentieth century. Increased disillusionment with traditional religion and a desire for a more wholesome lifestyle have led approximately 20 million people to adopt non-religious, yet spiritual, worldviews, largely in the developed countries of Europe, North America and Asia (Aldred 2000; Timothy and Conover 2006). This movement emphasises self-improvement for mind, body and soul through harmony of the universe, ancient spiritual traditions, the sanctity of nature, earth's powers, animism, extraterrestrial visitation, past-life regression, yoga and meditation, and self-deification (Timothy and Conover 2006).

New Agers glean elements of organised religions and non-religious movements to meet their own spiritual needs. The New Age movement can be seen in part as an amalgam of various nature religions, including neo-paganism, Wicca and Taoism. Adherents practice earth worship and nature reverence, and they see humans as being part of the environment, not apart from it. In most cases, New Ageism is a personal quest for spiritual enlightenment and embraces the one-ness of humanity, the environment and the universe. Most New Agers combine nature religion with self-religion (as opposed to god religion) and seek to find their own versions of truth in the cosmos. In addition, they each must find the 'god' within themselves through spiritual journeys in nature (O'Neil 2001). Goddess worship, or adulation of Gaia (Earth Mother), has become popular in recent years and is an obvious way of appeasing the spirit of the earth (Ivakhiv 2003). For devotees, nature promotes spiritual development and transcendence beyond the limitations of the physical world (Albanese 1990; Timothy and Conover 2006).

Secular spirituality and the environment

Secular spirituality exists in several forms. This is the least 'religious' of the trends discussed so far, but adulation and inward emotional stirrings are assuredly involved. Mass followings of pop culture icons are a good example. For instance, there is a significant segment of the population who adores Elvis Presley. His home and grave at Graceland (Tennessee, USA) have become a 'pilgrimage' destination for millions of Elvis fans (Alderman 2002). For many aficionados, a visit to his gravesite provokes emotional outbursts, tears, singing and prayer.

The same type of cult appeal is true for many Americans and Canadians regarding the countryside and natural areas of North America. There is a widespread nationalistic romanticism in the USA regarding what is often termed the 'countryside idyll', which glorifies rural living and traditional livelihoods (Ioannides and Timothy 2010; Timothy 2005). For many people, rurality is synonymous with wholesomeness, goodness, quality of life and honesty (Willits 1993).

The rural context includes natural areas and wilderness, which can evoke deep feelings of 'patriotism' or soul-stirring encounters with nature. Activities undertaken in natural settings can summon a sense of 'wonder, awe, wholeness, harmony, ecstasy, transcendence, and solitude' (Price 1996: 415, cited in Narayanan and Macbeth 2009). During the nineteenth century, wilderness areas in North America came to symbolise something unique, a national representation that distinguished 'the New World from the Old' (Towner 1996: 157). Towner (1996: 160) suggested that 'the concept of preserving the wilderness was, essentially an American innovation' as early as the 1820s. This early environmental movement was key in protecting large tracts of land that are now held in the highest regard as pristine territories where nature 'transcends the human' (Powici 2004: 78), creating, through the writings of John Muir and others, a 'virtual cult of the wilderness' in the USA that is preserved in America's national parks and forests (Knudsen and Greer 2008: 23). In the words of Louter (2003: 252, cited in Knudsen and Greer 2008),

> National parks are what we have made them, and nothing is more revealing than the way in which we have made them into wilderness. Perhaps one of the most powerful aspects of the wilderness ideal is that it advances an ideal of nature as a primeval landscape untouched by people. It is a place without history.

Knudsen and Greer (2008) suggest that the protected wilderness becomes 'enshrined' as a nationalist icon. Many countries have followed the lead of the USA and Canada in establishing an intricate global network of national parks and protected areas to enshrine natural landscapes as sacred ground that contributes to a sense of nationhood.

In the same way the rural and wilderness idyll dominates the USA, the desert emanates a sense of nationalism in Australia, where 'the vast expanses of red desert, interspersed with bush, shrub and wild grass symbolize the collective Australian psyche, and centrally occupy the Australian imagination' (Narayanan and Macbeth 2009: 372). The Outback is a place where Australians are humbled, inspired, learn their identity, renew themselves, get closer to nature, and 'reconnect with some idealized view of the "primitive"' (Narayanan and Macbeth 2009: 373). The desert wilderness sets people in their place in nature and causes them to realise the 'spiritual nature of human existence' (Narayanan and Macbeth 2009: 374).

Implications for tourism

These non-religious forms of spirituality and nature also have salient consequences for tourism. First, indigenous sacred sites have become tourist attractions for the masses. Shiprock, an igneous monolith in northwestern New Mexico (USA), has long been revered by the Navajos as the medium that brought their ancestors to the region. According to tradition, it was also the abode of early Navajos, who only left the mount to hunt and work the fields. Navajos do not climb the monolith because of its sacred connotations, but it is a popular attraction for tourists travelling several highways in the region. Devil's Tower (Wyoming, USA) is an even more salient tourist attraction that is deemed holy by Native Americans. This particular monolith is preserved and managed by the US National Park Service. Similarly, sacred Uluru is one of Australia's most prominent mass tourist attractions, which many tourists climb despite warning signs against it. The area has seen considerable controversy owing to conflict between the native peoples wishing to keep the monolith sacred and the tourists who want to scale it.

Second, New Age adherents comprise a huge tourist market. They love to travel, and many of the outward expressions of their spirituality require them to travel. Destinations that allow individuals to become spiritually tuned, where optimum earth energy flows, are the focus of most New Age tourism. This entails visiting locations that some religions (e.g. Buddhism, Judaism and Hinduism) consider sacred, but their most strategic foci are sacrosanct spots observed by indigenous beliefs and nature faiths. New Agers borrow heavily from druidism, neo-paganism, Wicca and other 'alternative religions', for these are seen to be closest to the earth's powers and the supremacy of the cosmos. Thus, locations that are esteemed by these spiritual philosophies comprise the principal destinations for New Age travellers (Ivakhiv 2003). The world's most popular New Age attractions include the Pyramids of Egypt, Machu Picchu, Avebury Circle, Stonehenge and thousands of natural features that were revered by indigenes and believed to possess tremendous Gaia powers (Timothy and Conover 2006).

Spiritual retreats attract millions of New Ager believers, but the two most central destinations are Glastonbury, England and Sedona, Arizona (Digance and Cusack 2002). Sedona, in fact, is dubbed by most adherents the 'New Age capital of the world', and the community has greatly capitalised on this unique competitive advantage. Sedona is located in the midst of plethoric mountains and canyons held sacred by Native Americans and believed to be endowed with the most intense earth powers, which are manifested in a series of 'vortexes'. The faithful also believe Sedona to be a chief transport hub for UFOs and other extraterrestrial encounters (Ivakhiv 1997; Timothy and Conover 2006).

Despite the New Age focus on deep ecology, ecofeminism, environmental conservation and nature adulation, the movement is one of the most environmentally controversial. Because the New Age practice is young, it has no holy sites of its own. As a result, it borrows sacred space and rituals from other faith traditions. Native peoples in various regions of the world have voiced their displeasure with the New Age use of their cultural heritage, suggesting that they misappropriate and profit from indigenous sites and sacred rituals. In addition, New Age pilgrims often build fires, construct sweat lodges and prayer wheels, and burn candles and incense to channel earth's energy. In the wake of their actions, sacred spaces and areas protected by national park or forest agencies are burned and scattered with 'ritual litter' (Blain and Wallis 2004; Ivakhiv 2003; Timothy 2011). Some of these spiritualists are avid collectors of stones, branches and pieces of built heritage as mementos of their sacred journeys, believing in the auspiciousness of possessing such souvenirs. Although many New Age influentials are beginning to discourage these types of behaviours, devotees are still seen as being among the most destructive tourists in both natural and cultural settings (McGivney and Archibald 1997; Powell 2003; Timothy and Conover 2006).

The third implication is that of secular tourism with a spiritual twist. There is significant demand for the natural realm among people who need to get away from the harried pace of life in the city. Visiting the countryside or wilderness areas provides solace and an opportunity to meditate and reflect on one's life trajectory. Many people describe their communion with nature as spiritual, transcendent and cathartic (Heintzman 2010; Ibrahim and Cordes 2008). In nature people find an inner peace and 'return to basics, and are in contact with *creation*, which is at the root of the word recreation' (Ibrahim and Cordes 2008: 29). Camping, hiking and other outdoor pursuits provide the ecological context where the spiritual entails a keen appreciation of nature and affinity with one's fellow creations and a harmonious universe (Meier and Mitchell 1993: 173, cited in Ibrahim and Cordes 2008).

For many people, visiting the majestic Alps of Europe, vast deserts of North Africa, the coral reefs of the sub-oceanic world, the ice caps and wildlife of Antarctica, and the rainforests and volcanoes of Central America is an experience of a lifetime that rouses within them a sense of wonder that extends beyond their everyday concerns. Growing demand for national parks in the USA and other countries attests to the importance of the sense of awe and appreciation experienced by visitors to highly valued natural areas.

Summary and conclusion

The crossover between religion, spirituality and the environment is multi-dimensional and complex. Some empirical studies suggest that ultra-conservative faiths have a somewhat less positive view of nature and environmental conservation than other many other faiths in general. For some, this might stem from a mistrust of the environmentalist political left, whereas for most it is likely a result in the belief that the earth was made for humankind not humankind for the earth and, among Christians, that Jesus will glorify the earth upon his triumphal return. Some Christian observers, though, take seriously the charge to care for God's creations.

Although numerous elements of nature may be seen as holy or divine, the most common in holy writ and doctrine are mountains, rivers, forests and caves. Such places are seen to possess godly powers and earth powers, or they are the abode of gods and spirits. These are the locales of miracles, divine visitations and ministering of angels. Many such landscape elements are very important tourist attractions and centres of pilgrimage, attracting not only religious tourists but also nature-based and heritage tourists.

Adherents to non-religious spiritual movements are also key elements of tourism and the environment. Besides organised religion, there are many spiritualist networks that revere or worship elements of nature and require various interactions between devotees and their environmental surrounds. Indigenous spirituality, the New Age movement and secular pilgrimage were described as being illustrative of this trend. Both religious and non-religious spirituality are significant motives for people undertaking pilgrimages or pilgrimage-like journeys to be renewed, forgiven for sin, to be healed or to fulfil religious convictions.

Clearly, nature is a crucial element of spiritual and religious tourism. Almost all faiths and spiritual philosophies venerate nature or elements thereof as sacred, transcendent and divine in one way or another. As long as organised religion and self-spirituality continue to exist, there will be demand for environmental encounters wherein the faithful will view nature with awe, inspiration and adulation.

References

Albanese, C.L. (1990) *Nature Religion in America: From the Algonkian Indians to the New Age*. Chicago, IL: University of Chicago Press.
Albin, N. and Berwick, C. (2004) 'Forests and religion in Japan—from a distinctive vision of trees to a particular type of forest management', *Revue Forestière Française* 56(6), 563–72.
Alder, G.M. (1991) 'Earth: a gift of gladness', *Ensign* 21(7), 27.
Alderman, D.H. (2002) 'Writing on the Graceland wall: on the importance of authorship in pilgrimage landscapes', *Tourism Recreation Research* 27(2), 27–33.
Aldred, L. (2000) 'Plastic Shamans and Astroturf sun dances: New Age commercialization of Native American spirituality', *American Indian Quarterly* 24(3), 329–52.
Bernbaum, E. (2006) 'Sacred mountains: themes and teachings', *Mountain Research and Development* 26(4), 304–9.
Blain, J. and Wallis, R.J. (2004) 'Sacred sites, contested rites/rights: Contemporary Pagan engagements with the past', *Journal of Material Culture* 9(3), 237–61.
Boyd, H.H. (1999) 'Christianity and the environment in the American public', *Journal for the Scientific Study of Religion* 38(1), 36–44.
Brockman, N.C. (1999) *Encyclopedia of Sacred Places*. Oxford: Oxford University Press.
Bürger-Arndt, R. and Welzholz, J.C. (2005) 'The history of protected forest areas in Europe—from holy groves to Natura 2000 sites', *News of Forest History* 36(1), 40–54.
Chadran, M. and Hughes, J.D. (1997) 'The sacred groves of South India: ecology, traditional communities and religious change', *Social Compass* 44(3), 413–27.
Chen, E.M. (1995) 'Taoism and ecology', *Dialogue and Alliance* 9(2), 5–15.
Cooper, M. (2009) 'River tourism in the South Asian Subcontinent', in B. Prideaux and M. Cooper (eds) *River Tourism*. Wallingford: CABI, 23–40.

Dekker, P., Ester, P. and Nas, M. (1997) 'Religion, culture and environmental concern: an empirical cross-national analysis', *Social Compass* 44(3), 443–58.

Digance, J. and Cusack, C. (2002) 'Glastonbury: a tourist town for all seasons', in G.M.S. Dann (ed.) *The Tourist as a Metaphor of the Social World*. Wallingford: CABI, 263–80.

Eckberg, D.L. and Blocker, T.J. (1996) 'Christianity, environmentalism and the theoretical problem of fundamentalism', *Journal for the Scientific Study of Religion* 35(4), 343–55.

Foltz, R.C. (ed.) (2003) *Worldviews, Religion, and the Environment: A Global Anthology*. Belmont, CA: Wadsworth.

Greeley, A. (1993) 'Religion and attitudes toward the environment', *Journal for the Scientific Study of Religion* 32(1), 19–28.

Guo, C. (2006) 'Tourism and the spiritual philosophies of the "Orient"', in D.J. Timothy and D.H. Olsen (eds) *Tourism, Religion and Spiritual Journeys*. London: Routledge, 121–38.

Heintzman, P. (2010) 'Nature-based recreation and spirituality: a complex relationship', *Leisure Sciences* 32(1), 72–89.

Hobson, P. (1994) 'Feng Shui: its impacts on the Asian hospitality industry', *International Journal of Contemporary Hospitality Management* 6(6), 21–26.

Hudman, L.E. and Jackson, R.E. (1992) 'Mormon pilgrimage and tourism', *Annals of Tourism Research* 19, 107–21.

Ibrahim, H. and Cordes, K.A. (2008) *Outdoor Recreation: Enrichment for a Lifetime*, 3rd edn. Champaign, IL: Sagamore.

Ioannides, D. and Timothy, D.J. (2010) *Tourism in the USA: A Spatial and Social Synthesis*. London: Routledge.

Ivakhiv, A. (1997) Red rocks, 'vortexes' and the selling of Sedona: environmental politics in the new age. *Social Compass* 44(3), 367–84.

——(2003) 'Nature and self in New Age pilgrimage', *Culture and Religion* 4(1), 93–118.

Jutla, R.S. (2002) 'Understanding Sikh pilgrimage', *Tourism Recreation Research* 27(2), 65–72.

Kay, J. (1995) 'Mormons and mountains', in W. Wyckoff and L.M. Dilsaver (eds) *The Mountainous West: Explorations in Historical Geography*. Lincoln: University of Nebraska Press, 368–95.

Knudsen, D.C. and Greer, C.E. (2008) 'Heritage tourism, heritage landscapes and wilderness preservation: the case of National Park Thy', *Journal of Heritage Tourism* 3(2), 18–35.

Louter, D. (2003) 'Nature as we see it: national parks and the wilderness ideal', *Ecological Restoration* 21(4), 251–3.

Matthews, R.J. (1972) 'What the scriptures say about ecology', *Ensign* 2(3), 38.

McGivney, A. and Archibald, T. (1997) 'Wizards of odd', *Backpacker* 25(8), 44–51.

Meier, J. and Mitchell, A.V. (1993) *Camp Counseling: Leadership and Programming for Organized Camp*. Dubuque, IA: William C. Brown.

Metreveli, M. and Timothy, D.J. (2010) 'Religious heritage and emerging tourism in the Republic of Georgia', *Journal of Heritage Tourism* 5(3), 237–44.

Narayanan, Y. and Macbeth, J. (2009) 'Deep in the desert: merging the desert and the spiritual through 4WD tourism', *Tourism Geographies* 11(3), 369–89.

Nicholson, M.H. (1959) *Mountain Gloom and Mountain Glory: The Development of the Aesthetics of the Infinite*. Ithaca, NY: Cornell University Press.

Nyaupane, G.P. and Budruk, M. (2009) 'South Asian heritage tourism: conflict, colonialism, and cooperation', in D.J. Timothy and G.P. Nyaupane (eds) *Cultural Heritage and Tourism in the Developing World: A Regional Perspective*. London: Routledge, 127–45.

Olsen, D.H. (2006) 'Tourism and informal pilgrimage among the Latter-day Saints', in D.J. Timothy and D.H. Olsen (eds) *Tourism, Religion and Spiritual Journeys*. London: Routledge, 254–70.

O'Neil, D.J. (2001) 'The New Age movement and its societal implications', *International Journal of Social Economics* 28(5), 456–75.

Owen, A.L. and Videras, J.R. (2007) 'Culture and public goods: the case of religion and voluntary provision of environmental quality', *Journal of Environmental Economics and Management* 54(2), 162–80.

Powell, E.A. (2003) 'Solstice at the stones', *Archaeology* 56(5), 36–41.

Powici, C. (2004) 'What is wilderness? John Muir and the question of the wild', *Scottish Studies Review* 5(1), 74–86.

Price, J. (1996) 'Naturalistic reactions', in P.H. van Ness (ed.) *Spirituality and the Secular Quest*. New York: Crossroad, 414–44.

Schultz, P.W., Zelezny, L. and Dalrymple, N.J. (2000) 'A multinational perspective on the relation between Judeo-Christian religious beliefs and attitudes of environmental concern', *Environment and Behavior* 32(4), 576–91.

Shackley, M. (1998) 'A golden calf in sacred space? The future of St Katherine's Monastery, Mount Sinai (Egypt)', *International Journal of Heritage Studies* 4(3/4), 123–34.

——(2001) *Managing Sacred Sites*. London: Continuum.

Sheikh, K.M. (2006) 'Involving religious leaders in conservation education in the western Karakorum, Pakistan', *Mountain Research and Development* 26(4), 319–22.

Sherkat, D.E. and Ellison, C.G. (2007) 'Structuring the religion-environment connection: identifying religious influences on environmental concern and activism', *Journal for the Scientific Study of Religion* 46 (1), 71–85.

Singh, R.P.B. (2006) 'Pilgrimage in Hinduism: historical context and modern perspectives', in D.J. Timothy and D.H. Olsen (eds) *Tourism, Religion and Spiritual Journeys*. London: Routledge, 220–36.

Sinha, B.C. and Sinha, S.P. (2008) Impact of religious tourism on Gir National Park, India. *Indian Forester* 134(5), 667–73.

Timothy, D.J. (2005) 'Rural tourism business: a North American overview', in D. Hall, I. Kirkpatrick and M. Mitchell (eds) *Rural Tourism and Sustainable Business*. Clevedon: Channel View Publications, 41–62.

——(2010) 'Foreword', in R.P.B. Singh (ed.) *Sacredscapes and Pilgrimage Landscapes*. New Delhi: Shubhi Publications, 1–4.

——(2011) *Cultural Heritage and Tourism: An Introduction*. Bristol: Channel View.

Timothy, D.J. and Conover, P.J. (2006) 'Nature religion, self-spirituality and New Age tourism', in D.J. Timothy and D.H. Olsen (eds) *Tourism, Religion and Spiritual Journeys*. London: Routledge, 139–55.

Timothy, D.J. and Iverson, T. (2006) 'Tourism and Islam: considerations of culture and duty', in D.J. Timothy and D.H. Olsen (eds) *Tourism, Religion and Spiritual Journeys*. London: Routledge, 186–205.

Towner, J. (1996) *An Historical Geography of Recreation and Tourism in the Western World, 1540–1940*. Chichester: Wiley.

Vukonić, B. (2006) 'Sacred placed and tourism in the Roman Catholic tradition', in D.J. Timothy and D.H. Olsen (eds) *Tourism, Religion and Spiritual Journeys*. London: Routledge, 237–53.

Willits, F.K. (1993) 'The rural mystique and tourism development: data from Pennsylvania', *Journal of the Community Development Society* 24(2), 159–74.

Xu, J.C., Ma, E.T., Tashi, D., Fu, Y.S., Lu, Z. and Melick, D. (2005) Integrating sacred knowledge for conservation: cultures and landscapes in southwest China. *Ecology and Society* 10(2), 151–75.

5

Tourism and Indigenous reverence

The possibilities for recovery of land and revitalisation of life

Keith Hollinshead

Introduction: tourism and Indigenity

Aim of the chapter: tourism and Indigenous cosmology

This broad aim of this chapter is to describe some of the important bonds that tie Indigenous populations to their lived environments, and to account for the role and function of tourism in both reinforcing those unities for Indigenous groups/communities themselves and in communicating those bonds and meanings for visiting non-Indigenous people. In order to cover these important psychic, symbolic, culture-sustaining matters, the chapter will be scaffolded in the following fashion:

- it will open by introducing (or reminding!) readers as to ways in which Indigenous populations are inclined to see their worlds, their environments, and tourism itself, today;
- it will explore these Indigenous ways of seeing the world (and the spaces and places in it) cosmologically, in terms of the ways in which some longstanding cum traditional outlooks and practices are conceivably surviving, but also of the ways in which other fresher cum transitional outlooks and practices have emerged to conceivably prosper;
- it will critique the fashion in which international tourism today has both culture-denying and culture-fortifying interface with Indigenous populations, notably with regard to the ways in which certain sorts of Western/Eurocentric/non-Indigenous orientation (in the opening decades of the twenty-first century) still dominate what is seen and valued through tourism; and,
- it will close by offering a critical assessment of the state of health of the critical awareness that currently exists in terms of Tourism Management/Tourism Studies in many of the cultural stewardship and environmental stewardship issues, which arise in the course of the chapter. To that end, it will call for an increase in the provision of postdisciplinary schooling in Tourism Management/Tourism Studies in order to help those who work in tourism within uncertain cross-cultural scenarios become more open to the worldviews of 'other', 'distant', 'Indigenous', populations on revered matters of culture and nature.

Focus: 'land' within the Indigenous worldview

In order to understand the intimacies that Aboriginal people have with their lived environment, it is necessary to appreciate the thought-world of Indigenous populations, and that is no simple task for non-Indigenous people to grasp. To perceive the thought-world of, for instance, Aboriginal people following a so-called traditional lifestyle, is to recognise a maze of relationships, and a myriad of networks of understandings that overlay other networks of knowing. Whereas Eurocentric knowledge tends to be based on the Western ideal of objective public knowledge, Indigenous knowledge (for traditional-following Aborigines in Australia) tends to be relational, and Aboriginals across the dry continent are vitally concerned with not only who owns the proper and received story through which the environment/the land is interpreted, but who has the right to hear (and know) that narrative. Thus, the environment to Indigenous populations is embodied as an element of and within Aboriginal thinking – that is, of patterned, relational thinking. The environment (the land) is not something that is separate from nature: the land is not distinct from people, from the heavens or from the longtime stories handed down from the past. In Stockton's (1995) basic introduction to Aboriginal spirituality, fundamental differences between Indigenous thinking and Western thinking are succinctly stated by David Mowaljarli, an Aboriginal from Derby in the north of Western Australia:

> Pattern thinking is Aboriginal thinking.
> There is no big boss.
> Patterns are about belonging. Nothing is separate from anything else.
> *The land is not separate from nature, people, the heavens, ancient stories.*
> Everything belongs in the pattern.
> There is no 'ownership' in pattern thinking. Only Belonging.
> Money cannot buy bits of a pattern.
> Power runs all through a pattern. It cannot be sold. It cannot be separate from the pattern.
> [But] Triangle thinking is Western culture thinking.
> There is always a big boss.
> There are other bosses who have power over people down the triangle.
> Triangles are about money and power …
> Triangle thinking separates everything into layers of power and administration.
> 'Ownership' is a triangle idea.
> 'Belonging' cannot fit into triangle thinking …
> Triangles are separate from each other, and separate from patterns.
>
> *(Mowaljarli in Stockton 1995: 42–3; emphasis added)*

Here, Mowaljarli sums up the essential difference between the Aboriginal and Western/Euro-centric reverence for land and life. To Mowaljarli in his own 'country' (i.e. in his own heartland and hearth-land), the environment cannot be separated from nature and nature cannot be se-parated from culture.

Whereas Western concepts of religion (and thereby the land and environment) contrast the sacred with the profane – or the supernatural with the natural (Stockton 1995) – there is no similar distinction within the Indigenous worldviews: everything is alive and connected, and therefore each thing is sacred. Accordingly, it is important for traditionally minded Aboriginal people to remain spiritually connected to the earth (to the land, to the environment) in order to continue living within that identity and thereby upholding those vitally inherited matters of being and becoming. In traditional society, groups and communities thereby conceive of themselves in terms of the sustained bond they have collectively with the earth (the land/the environment). The land is the generative font of existence: it is the spiritual point from and through which Aboriginal existence comes (Stockton 1995: 82). As Patrick Dodson – Chairman of the Australian Institute of Aboriginal and Torres Strait Islander Studies – reminds us:

> [The] land is a living place … not a thing, but a living entity. It belongs to me, belong to the land/rest in it/come from there. …
>
> [The] land provides for my physical needs and provides for my spiritual needs. It is a regeneration of stories.
>
> New stories are sung from contemplation of the land, stories are handed down from spirit men of the past who have deposited the riches of variant places – the sacred places.
>
> *(Dodson in Stockton 1995: 82)*

Indigenous cosmologies today: some critical caveats

Before attention is turned to the case study for this chapter (i.e. to a critique of the recent Melbourne University text *Blacklines*, which outlines the recent strong projection of intellectual vigour in local, national and international spheres by leading Indigenous commentators within and from Australia), a number of qualifying remarks need to be made about the manner in which Indigenous cosmologies are interpreted in Australia today. These observations will be given through the following sections:

- via caveats on the decipherability of *traditional* 'Aboriginality';
- via caveats on the decipherability of *transitional* 'Aboriginality';
- via caveats on the distinctiveness of Indigenous knowledge in general.

The interpretability of traditional Aboriginality

The processes by which Indigenous knowledges and practices are constructed are complex, as are the ways in which specific traditions are recognised and supported. The manner by which a cultural activity is deemed to be 'authentic' or 'correct', and the manner by which a natural setting or environmental feature is deemed to be 'proper' or 'appropriate' are – and have always been – influenced by prevailing power relations. Thus, received and popular notions in the modern-day world that traditions are static entities are as wide of the mark in Aboriginal settings as they are in European or other contexts (AlSayyad 2004). Thus, in recent years, those who have worked on matters of Indigenous traditionality in Australia have begun to develop not only richer insight into the political (or internal) struggles that have always surrounded definitions of legitimacy in the Aboriginal world, but have argued strongly 'for a deeper appreciation of the creativity inherent in Aboriginal and Torres Strait Islander social lives' (Taylor *et al.* 2005: xii).

The following example reveals how – in Australia – acts of social/cultural/political innovations are nowadays far from being automatically regarded as 'inauthentic endeavours'. In past decades, legal authorities in Australia have tended to work with over-restrictive interpretations of what constitutes an authentic tradition when questions of native title to land were examined. But the common law across the broader nation has lately begun to catch up with flexibilities of Aboriginal practice on the matter. Whereas etic judgements were made in the past that traditional activities and traditional activities were only those that were significant within pre-contact Indigenous society, it is now increasingly recognised that such external verdicts are overly prescriptive, and may even deny the given Aboriginal society its native right to allow its own traditions *to evolve ordinarily* (Strelein 2006: 66). Accordingly, it does not matter these days that traditional forms of fishing are now undertaken via modern dinghies powered by state-of-the-art outboard motors manufactured in factories in Hong Kong, Japan or Germany (as recognised in a number of like cases reported by Strelein).

The interpretability of transitional *Aboriginality*

It is increasingly the view of observers of contemporary Indigenous Studies across Australia that the concept of 'tradition' has been refined, and that – as Smith (2005: 203) reports, citing Sahlins (1999: xi) '[p]aradoxically, almost all of the "traditional" cultures studied by [early] anthropologists, and so described, were in fact neotraditional, already changed by Western expansion'. Indeed, a strong expectancy has ruled inspections by non-Indigenous agencies of Indigenous life over the last couple of centuries, something that has not only given rise to an underestimation of the different *transitional* systems of value and meaning that actually characterise Indigenous life, but that has also underappreciated the degree to which Aboriginal people have large *inter-cultural* and potent *inter-ethnic* dimensions to their practices in culture and in nature. The following example reveals much about the new transitional forms of behavioural practice that constitute the complex articulation of Indigenous being today. As Smith has shown in his studies of Aboriginality in the Central Cape York Peninsula of North Queensland, 'the socio-cultural heritage of hunter-gatherer society remains apparent in the lives of Aboriginal people across the region' (Smith 2005: 237), yet 'pastoralism, rather than hunting and gathering, has become the key economic mode and the foundation for the lived experience of regional landscape among the senior generation of Aboriginal families [there]' (Smith 2005: 237). Indeed Smith finds that too many active representatives of government and even of anthropology fail to recognise the dynamism of emergent forms of Aboriginal cultural practices, and miss the degree to which ambiguous characterisations of tradition do in fact resonate through all sorts of transitional use of space and mimetic activity. All too frequently, Aboriginal populations are expected to be traditional to be faithful to the 'true' culture in order (externally) to be deemed Aborigines. All too frequently they are expected (by such administrative outsiders) to be unequivocally traditional and to remain decidedly autonomous in their relationships with land, nature and the environment (Smith 2005: 230).

The differentiation of Aboriginality as a distinct and separate culture

The whole notion of Indigenous culture, *ipso facto*, has become something of a problem in the humanities in recent years. The pervasive notion in the humanities and the social sciences had been the view that global humanity could best be understood as a matrix of particular societies each of which were different, discreet and self-regulating, and that each of these significantly singular societies had their own significantly distinguishable cultures through which that society's institutions worked. In late decades, the neat seeming unity of distinct societies having distinct cultures has come into question. Certain social scientists (e.g. Warren (1998) working in Central America) have begun to reject the longstanding concept of *traditional knowledge* and of the visions of 'the simple', 'the savage', and 'the static' that came hand-in-glove with it, and now prefer to use the term *Indigenous knowledge*, instead, because in their view the latter term can more roundly cover the variety of dynamic ways in which supposedly distinct Indigenous societies variously conjoin the pursuit of longstanding practices with new and fresh adaptable mechanisms. The debate rages on. Although almost all applied anthropologists and development specialists are now keen to avoid the stereotypical connotations of the hackneyed term 'traditional knowledge', many are not convinced that the construction 'Indigenous knowledge' itself reasonably encapsulates the full context of *the lived experience* in which Indigenous populations engage. In lieu of this, Haverkart and Hiemstra (1996), for instance, prefer to talk of the *cosmovision* of Indigenous populations – a term that covers everything from a found population's land use/agricultural pursuits, its religious activity, its symbolic systems and its other local expertise. Although space limitations in this chapter do not permit a full critique of the language and other diffusive practices, and of the investigative issues of embedded ontologies and epistemologies with which this problematic concern is freighted, Rowse (2008) has provided a most useful baseline treatment of these issues of space and time. His main concern is the analysis of Indigenous people in Australia in terms of their uneven alignment with 'mainstream institutions and thoughtlines', but he is also tuned in to matters of Indigenous vulnerability and survival elsewhere around the globe.

It is therefore useful to pay homage to Rowse (2008) and take an illustration of and about these difficult matters of the categorisation of 'Indigenous knowledge' vis-á-vis 'Western knowledge' from the coverage of Indigenous culture he prepared for cultural analysts. In his coverage of supposedly bounded societies and of supposedly cultural authenticities, Rowse takes pain to remind us (citing Muellebach 2001) that the category 'Indigenous' is not one that can simply be claimed unilaterally, for there are always a large number of agents involved in such ratifications of being and identity, where some are internal to the group or community in question and some are external. Indeed, many have argued that even the word 'Aboriginal' is itself an external imposition on Indigenous populations, implying the existence of a unified across-the-nation collectivity – that is, of an unwavering people-dom. Such protestors maintain that the use of the term 'Aboriginal' in this fashion is indeed a colossal imposition: it constitutes nothing but 'an assumed other' as envisioned at distance 'from beyond', and in reality there is no secure totality or unified 'continental' or 'national-level' relationhood there to capture and so classify.

Case study: the rise of resistance literature

An introduction to the critical discourse of Blacklines

In order to provide for readers an up-to-date account of the cutting edge issues that confront the Aboriginal people of Australia in the representation and projection of their culture and its reverence for 'nature', a case study will now be offered focused on the recent *Blacklines* text produced by Melbourne University Press. This text (Grossman 2006) is a landmark work containing a collection of imaginative historical and personal commentaries, which would have been inconceivable even a couple of decades ago. Constituting a gathering in of the views of a range of the nation's foremost Indigenous intellectuals, *Blacklines* is a pungent articulation of and about concerns of history, being, becoming and projection. It stands as a cogent assembly of 'resistance literature' essays, which seek to explain and legitimate Indigenous worldviews, speaking collectively from the soul of 'Australian' Indigenity. Written with political, moral, ethical and pedagogical force, the Grossman publication is principally an assault on the sustained hegemony of institutionally blessed discourses of Aboriginality. To that end, 16 chapters of the aggregation are unified in the degree to which each commentator laments the limited extent to which Indigenous people have generally been able to define their own 'Aboriginality' from a, or any free, space. Thus, they are coherent in terms of the repeated demand within them that the Indigenous peoples of Australia must move to take repossession of themselves on their own terms, via their own perspectives. Hence, the Melbourne University Press commentators (in *Blacklines*) all appear to be drawn to the judgement that Aboriginality cannot be contained (as is often attempted from 'Western'/'mainstream' perspectives) within a single viewpoint or explanation. They are generally vehement that static representations of Indigenous being must be actively and performatively resisted so that Indigenous people can advance to become subjects and not just objects of the accounts of Aboriginality that are in common currency. In toto, *Blacklines* composes a critical and resistant storm of protest against the appropriation of 'Aboriginality' by, variously, 'white'/'euroAustralian'/'Western' interest groups and institutions. It serves as a pivotal account outlining the urgent need to develop a critical body of knowledge that addresses matters of Indigenous aesthetics and politics, whether it be composed by Aboriginal or non-Aboriginal people (see Langton 2006) in the specified areas of the arts, film, television and other media. Alas, the declarative role and function of tourism, *ipso facto*, is not often explicitly acknowledged in this respect in the Melbourne University text, but its looming articulative power is potently implicit.

Blacklines *and the call for re-imagined understandings*

Although the motley crew of established and emergent Indigenous intellectuals speak from a broad range of sides, standpoints and scenarios, a number of commonplace lines of protest and/or aspiration are discernable within *Blacklines*. The following perspectives appear to lie at the heart of what these Indigenous expositors state have been – and remain – the limitations of the 'whitefella' control over representations of Aboriginal history, identity and contemporaneity.

- *Aboriginality defined by 'the West'*
  All too commonly, Aboriginality has been defined by outsiders who operate within a racialised dialectics, which is centred on whiteness: Aboriginal people have thereby been repeatedly defined as a population that 'lacks', rather than a population that 'has'.
- *Self-regulation is essential*
  Indigenous 'Australians' are vitally concerned about who speaks for them in all settings and cultural processes, and demand a general and corrective shift towards self-representation.
- *Closed definitions debilitate*
  All too frequently, Aboriginal people are assumed (externally) to be one single population, and are contained with unitary or absolute definitions that inflexibly fail to recognise the constellation of different peoples and the multiverse of identities that exists.
- *Authenticities are externally determined*
  Indigenous 'Aboriginals' are regularly 'measured' in terms of Western textual interpretations of Indigenity, which became stale and hegemonic.
- *Non-traditional 'aboriginal' people are non-persons*
  All too commonly, even by anthropologists – and close contact government officials – authentic customary practice (and versions of it adjusted by outsiders/non-Indigenous institutions) is taken to be the critical or only yardstick to assess Aboriginal qualities of existence: consonantly, those who lead non-traditional lives tend to be grossly undervalued.
- *The underappreciated multiformity for art and cultural practice*
  The diversity of cultural practices (in general) and of art (specifically) is hugely under-regonised: outsiders in mainstream/Western society tend axiomatically but unwisely to search for the singular and unifying Aboriginal approach to such pursuits.
- *The casual and habitual appropriation of Aboriginal styles*
  All too frequently, Indigenous designs, expressions and narratives (and even identities) are fast-adopted by outsiders via a plethora of subtle and not-so-subtle strategies of 'Aboriginalism': not only are such non-Indigenous individuals and institutions not entitled to such styles and genres, but also they are regularly unaware of the precise meanings that sustain them.

- *The necessity for a complex repertoire of Indigenous responses*

  In order to protect Aboriginal values and virtues from the continuing caprice of outsider representations/misrepresentations and the calumnies of outsider appropriations, Indigenous populations need to deploy a complex repertoire of critical strategies and determinant articulations: manoeuvres for survival have to start from a multiplicity of Indigenous subject positions, and this litany of approaches will often appear to be inconsistent and contradicting.

- *The hybridisation of voice*

  In so many areas of life, Aboriginal people have to confront the densities of the 'settler presence', and it is often not thereby easy to determine whether an Indigenous person is thinking and speaking within or beyond 'colonial discourse': yet Aboriginal people must resist the defeatist assumption that they are axiomatically speaking from a marginalised perspective, wherever they stand on any felt concern.

- *Many Indigenous outlooks are not readily understandable, beyond*

  All too commonly, well-meaning or ignorant outsiders will venture into Indigenous settings claiming to be conversant with 'a' or 'the' Aboriginal truth: in verity, many aspects of Aboriginality are not readily understandable to non-Indigenous people, and cannot be acquired overnight. Some Aboriginal worldviews are not readily attainable by non-Indigenous people, no matter how 'deeply he/she/they dig' with the often grossly assumptive tools of mainstream/Western thought.

Blacklines and the call for engaged dialogue

It is common practice (when the future of Indigenous populations is discussed these days) for non-Indigenous interest groups and institutions that are sincerely concerned in advancing the conditions in which Indigenous peoples live (or with empowering them in some particular way), to maintain that the said Indigenous group or community must be accorded the right to self-determination, and must thereby be the body that always is given 'the stage' to speak on for all salient Indigenous matters of culture and nature (or 'culture-nature'). But the established and emerging Indigenous identities who have contributed to *Blacklines* do not support that view wholesale. The assembled commentators in the Grossman text do not call for the axiomatic right for Aboriginal people to control all of the Indigenous expressions of being and becoming that undergird Indigenous issues of identity, history and representation. Rather, and importantly, they call for an opening up of *the debate* on such matter (Moreton-Robinson 2006: 72) – that is between 'blacks' and 'whites', between Indigenous people and non-Indigenous people, between blackfella brothers and whitefella brothers, wherever.

Almost all of the commentators explicitly support the view that in so many contexts it is very difficult for most non-Aboriginal people in Australia to fast-understand the cosmology, the spirituality or the structured locative knowledge (i.e. the place-bound knowledge) by which (at least) traditional Aboriginal society works – or put more directly (by the Aboriginal poet Lionel Fogarty) when he states that whites 'can't catch my dreaming' (Huggins 2006: 62). But the contributors to *Blacklines* are generally in accord that as culture is a dynamic phenomenon (and a dynamic noumenon!), and as it is always everywhere created and defined *interactively*, it is nonsense now to enable only Aboriginal people themselves to speak up about Aboriginal issues (Perkins 2006: 98): Aboriginality is no fixed thing, but is a vitality or potency that arises *intersubjectively* between 'black and white *in dialogue*' (Langton 2006: 118). It can indeed be very trying and tiring for the particular lead Indigenous elder/community leader/group representative to have to regularly venture 'out' into non-Indigenous realms to speak on concerns of culture, cosmology or continuity (Sutton 2011: 5, 55, 172).

In this light, a number of the Indigenous intellectuals in *Blacklines* suggest that it is naive to maintain that Aboriginal people will make 'better' projections of and about Aboriginality simply because they have a 'greater' understanding of their own 'culture' and their own 'nature' (Langton 2006: 115), or their own 'culture-nature'. As Aboriginality is a process in dialogue and a product of dialogue time and time again, it is essential that the communicative forces at work in that dialogic space are recognised. Meaning of and about Aboriginality is created dynamically and dialogically, and it is simplistic to expect that only Aboriginal people can be communicatively effective in such inter-subjective 'territory'. The articulation put forward there, and the imagination cultivated there must thereby be substantively collective. What counts is whether – in that dynamic inter-subjective space – 'the Aboriginal' and 'the non-Aboriginal' are each treated in bone fide fashion as subjects not as objects. Clearly, the contributors to *Blacklines* do not think it is easy for most non-Aboriginal individuals to appreciate when they are addressing Indigenous issues from viewpoints supported by local Aboriginal groups and communities, for the most liberal and emancipated of non-Aboriginal speakers can soon falter to speak in stereotypical or ungrounded regard (Nakarta 2006: 132). Too many well-meaning 'Western experts' from each and every discipline can be closed to the baseless pretensions and the stultifying blindness of the standpoints they themselves operate from on and over 'culture' and 'nature' (Nakarta 2006: 133), or over 'culture-nature'.

Thus, what counts is the opening up of fuller/richer/more frequent communication between Indigenous and non-Indigenous people, and for the refinement of discursive space where dialogue is not denied but decidedly cultivated. Currently, too many non-Aboriginal scholars quote Indigenous writers or cite Aboriginal community views, but do not take the trouble to even engage with them (Morrissey 2006: 192).

Case study

Blacklines *and the call for engaged understanding about 'the environment'*

In order to appreciate the degree to which the call of the Indigenous intellectuals of *Blacklines* for dialogue readily pertains to matters of 'the environment', attention will now be turned to the specific 'Knowledge in Action' chapter in the book furnished by Fabienne Bayet-Charlton. Entitled *Overturning the Doctrine: Indigenous Peoples and Wilderness – Being Aboriginal in the Environmental Movement*, Bayet-Charlton (who lives in the Adelaide Hills of South Australia, and who has worked for the Native Title Unit and the Aboriginal Legal Movement, amongst other agencies) writes pointedly about the manner in which environmental policy so regularly works blindly but additively to dispossess Aboriginal people. As an environmentalist herself, she addresses the painful, identificatory difficulties involved in being 'black' and 'green' at the same time (Bayet-Charlton 2006: 171). In her view, many of the cultural clashes between Aboriginal ('black') and conservation ('green') interests are unthought ones. She appears not to be so much concerned where, for instance, Aboriginal groups and communities are perceived by environmentalists to be a direct threat to endangered species or to ecological diversity (Bayet-Charlton 2006: 175), but where those in the 'white'/'outside' environmental movement have only just begun to learn to listen to Aboriginal community voices about land and the environment, and where they have only just begun 'to learn to [cross-culturally] share' (Bayet-Charlton 2006: 179) with regard to land and nature. To her, the shared goal in terms of environmental care and use must not be merely for self-determination for Aboriginal people, but must provide 'realistic' and 'contemporary' self-determination. Although she acknowledges that some instances of successful alliances between (by implication) 'the black' and 'the green' do exist – such as the respective legislated agreements of 'Uluru-Kata Tjuta' and 'Kakadu' Natural Parks in the Northern Territory (where these two parks are located on Aboriginal land that has been leased to the Australian National Parks and Wildlife Service – Bayet-Charlton 2006: 176; see also Toyne and Johnson 1991)) – she maintains that insufficient cross-cultural listening has generally taken place.

It is useful to examine where the observations of Bayet-Charlton may be interpreted as a call for inter-cultural dialogue (or 'interlocution') about matters of land and life for Aboriginal people. For instance, at the end of her chapter, Bayet-Charlton considers specifically whether the new business of *ecotourism* can yield a new answer for Aboriginal groups and communities. In noting that the pressure for Aboriginal people to be involved in bandwagon ecotourism projects is becoming extreme, she suggests that the jury is still very much 'out' in terms of any conclusive cultural and psychic cost–benefit analysis conducted on them. In that light, Bayet-Charlton offers the following six penetrating questions about ecotourism today in Indigenous contexts:

- Is ecotourism sustainable on an Indigenous cultural basis?
- Is ecotourism yet another form of pressure on Aboriginal society and communities – this time as a form of duress on those least affected by the invasion and urbanisation of Australia?
- Will ecotourism continue to perpetuate the stereotype of the destitute and incapable non-urban Aboriginal?
- Will ecotourism perpetuate the stereotype of the wandering noble savage (i.e. of the quaint hunter–gatherer) as a sad or sorry remnant of the stone age – or is ecotourism in fact an appropriate and significant avenue of reconciliation between Aboriginal and non-Aboriginal people?
- Will ecotourism open avenues though which non-Aboriginal people can explore and freshly understand all sorts of different Aboriginal people, eventually venturing into improved cross-cultural relationships even with urban Aboriginals?
- Will ecotourism become yet another way by which non-Aboriginal interests continue to ignore urban Aboriginals for the sake of the supreme external vision of the 'traditional' Aboriginal – a longstanding stereotype that sells well in the marketplace of travel?

(Bayet-Charlton 2006: 178, adapted).

Perhaps, in her own view, it is the recent softening of (or the retrenchment of) native title legislation that has produced the largest frustration for Aboriginal people (or for Indigenous intellectuals)? Bayet-Charlton (2006: 180) covers the matter curtly:

[Eventually we will all] collectively realise that native title legislation has been so watered down from its original intentions, and acknowledge that those [Indigenous groups or communities] seeking to claim title to their land have so many provisos attached, so many hoops to jump through, so many hurdles to jump over, before a claim sees the light of say in the courts. These claims can then be rejected if records indicate that a non-Aboriginal person has so much as farted on that land. Native title has lost all but its simple and superficial meaning. This is a tragedy, considering all the good will and effort that went into the debating and formulating of the original legislation.

Such is the power of some of the direct feeling of the resistance commentators of *Blacklines* on matters of 'culture-nature'.

Tourism studies and Indigenous reverence for the environment

The call for open and engaged postdisciplinary knowing

This chapter has sought to present 'the environment' not as a discrete and singular thing as it is so often understood to be in the ' Western'/'urban-industrial'/'metropolitan' world, but (for the Indigenous people of Australia) as a connected 'cultural-natural-spiritual' force, which ought to be approached in terms of that broad and rich cosmological dimensionality. If the significances of the land, landscapes and myth, the importances of place, placescapes and revelation, and the criticalities of time, timescapes and reciprocity (as illustrated, for instance, in Hollinshead 1996) are to be decently and faithfully understood in terms of the cognitions, the hopes, the aspirations of Aboriginal people in Australia, it is vital that the environment is not just seen as limited matter of, for example, hills, rivers and rocks. It is vital that each such physical place and spiritual space is appreciated in a broader and postdisciplinary sense (Hollinshead 2012) in terms of its connected totemic potency for Aboriginal people whether that be translated today via the continued vibratory power of longstanding 'traditions', or via the fresh or the refreshed dynamism of new/emergent (but still cosmologically connected) 'transitions'.

Tourism is fast becoming the lead declarative industry for the world's cultural sites, spiritual spaces and natural settings. But are there many in Tourism Management/Tourism Studies who are currently geared up to catch *the said black dreaming?* Are there many in the twin fields of Tourism Management/Tourism Studies who are effectively ready to listen and to learn within and through *the sacred spirituality* (or rather, within and through the elements of 'the sacred' that are rendered cross-culturally 'accessible'), but also within and through *the everyday logic* of other populations? Or will that called-for dialogue about culture and nature (culture-nature) be a delayed event – a necessarily postponed feature of the 2030s and 2040s rather than being an immediate feature of the 2010s and the 2020s?

The catching of the cosmologies of others is a thoroughly demanding reflective, reflexive and reciprocal practice. Dialogic understandings about culture and nature cannot be won overnight. The sought understandings of and about culture-nature are not only generally deep-seated, they are frequently dynamic. Contextual perspectives always have to be gauged interpretively and contoured politically, even for and within Indigenous groups and communities. And perspectives on and about land, sea and the heavens can fast transmogrify. Thus, the cultural landscapes of the environment are no perpetually fixed objective 'thing': even Indigenous visions can effervesce, vaporise or hybridise at pace. In each place or any space, those who work in Tourism Management/Tourism Studies should therefore expect there to be not only many changing shades of 'green', but (in the light of the resistance Indigeneities discussed in this chapter) many changing shades of 'black'.

Acknowledgments

The author is deeply appreciative of the warm welcome given to him by the holders of traditional country in various parts of the Pilbara (in the north-west Western Australia) in the late 1970s, and later to the insights afforded to him by carriers of traditional country in the Western Desert/Border Country region of Western Australia/Northern Territory in the 1980s. He also acknowledges the help given to him by Milka Ivanova of Bulgaria and Bedfordshire, UK in support work for this chapter.

References

AlSayyad, N., (ed.) (2004) *The End of Tradition?* London: Routledge.
Bayet-Charlton, F. (2006) 'Overturning the Doctrine: Indigenous Peoples and Wilderness – Being Aboriginal in the Environmental Movement', in M. Grossman (ed.) *Blacklines: Contemporary Critical Writing by Indigenous Australians*, Carlton, Victoria: Melbourne University Press, 171–80.

Grossman, M., (ed.) (2006) *Blacklines: Contemporary Critical Writing by Indigenous Australians*. Carlton, Victoria: Melbourne University Press.

Haverkart, B., and Hiemstra, W. (1996) A Sequel to the Debate(5): COPASS: Intercultural Dialogue on Cosmovisions and Agricultural Development. *Indigenous Knowledge and Development Monitor*. www.nuffic.nl/ciran/ikdm/4–2/articles/agrawal.html.

Hollinshead, K. (1996) 'Marketing and Metaphysical Realism: The Disidentification of Aboriginal Life and Traditions through Tourism', in Butler, R. and Hinch, T. (eds) *Tourism and Indigenous Peoples*. London: International Thomson Business Press, 308–48.

Hollinshead, K. (2012) 'The Under-conceptualisation of Tourism Studies: The Case for Postdisciplinary Knowing', in Ateljevic, I., Pritchard, A and Morgan, N. (eds) *The Critical Turn in Tourism Studies: Creating an Academy of Hope*. London: Routledge, 55–72.

Huggins, J. (2006) 'Always Was Always Will Be', in Grossman, M. (ed.) *Blacklines: Contemporary Critical Writing by Indigenous Australians*, Carlton, Victoria: Melbourne University Press, 60–65.

Langton, M. (2006) 'Aboriginal Art and Film: The Politics of Representation', in Grossman, M. (ed.) *Blacklines: Contemporary Critical Writing by Indigenous Australians*, Carlton, Victoria: Melbourne University Press, 109–28.

Moreton-Robinson, A. (2006) 'Tiddas Talkin Up to The White Woman: When Huggins *et al.* Took on Bell', In M. Grossman (ed.) *Blacklines: Contemporary Critical Writing by Indigenous Australians*, Carlton, Victoria: Melbourne University Press, 66–80.

Morrissey, P. (2006) 'Moving, Remembering, Singing Our Place', In M. Grossman (ed.) *Blacklines: Contemporary Critical Writing by Indigenous Australians*. Carlton, Victoria: Melbourne University Press, 189–93.

Muellebach, A. (2001) ''Making Place' at the United Nations: Indigenous Cultural Politics and the UN Working Group on Indigenous Politics', *Cultural Anthropology*, 16 (3), 415–48.

Nakarta, M. (2006) 'Better', In M. Grossman (ed.) *Blacklines: Contemporary Critical Writing by Indigenous Australians*. Carlton, Victoria: Melbourne University Press, 132–44.

Perkins, H. (2006) 'Seeing and Seaming: Contemporary Aboriginal Art', in Grossman, M. (ed.) *Blacklines: Contemporary Critical Writing by Indigenous Australians*. Carlton, Victoria: Melbourne University Press, 97–103.

Rowse, T. (2008) 'Indigenous Culture: The Politics of Vulnerability and Survival', in Bennett, T. and J. Frow (eds) *The Sage Handbook of Cultural Analysis*, Los Angeles, CA: Sage, 406–26.

Sahlins, M. (1999) What is anthropological enlightenment? Some lessons of the twentieth century. *Annual Review of Anthropology*, 28, i–xxiii.

Smith, B.R. (2005) 'Culture, Change and the Ambiguous Resonance of Tradition in Central Cape York Peninsula', in Taylor, L. *et al.* (eds.) *The Power of Knowledge: The Resonance of Tradition*, Canberra: Aboriginal Studies Press, 223–35.

Stockton, E. (1995) *The Aboriginal Gift: Spirituality for a Nation*, Alexandria, NSW: Millennium Books.

Strelein, L. (2006) 'Culture and Commerce: The Use of Fishing Traditions to Prove Native Title', in Taylor, L., *et al.* (eds). *The Power of Knowledge: The Resonance of Tradition*. Canberra: Aboriginal Studies Press, 61–73.

Sutton, P. (2011) *The Politics of Suffering: Indigenous Australia and the End of Liberal Consensus*. Melbourne: Melbourne University Press.

Taylor, L., Wood, G.K., Henderson, G., Davis, R. and Wallis, A., (eds) (2005) *The Power of Knowledge: The Resonance of Tradition*. Canberra: Aboriginal Studies Press.

Toyne, P., and Johnson, R. (1991) 'Reconciliation, or The New Dispossession', *Habitat Australia*, 19(3) June, 8–10.

Warren, K.B. (1998) *Indigenous Movements and Their Critics: Pan-Maya Activism in Guatemala*, Princeton, NJ: Princeton University Press.

6

'Prophets of nature'

Romantic ideals of nature and their continuing relevance for tourism today

Diana Barsham and Michael Hitchcock

The idea that the natural environment provides a Romantic spectacle is so widely encountered in tourism that it is usually taken for granted. However, if you look back to the origins of this relatively modern industry it was not invariably the case. The forerunners of today's tourists, specifically those engaged in the seventeenth to early nineteenth century Grand Tour, usually regarded nature with some trepidation and even awe, and this is particularly evident in the way they regarded some of the landscapes that they passed through on their way to their favoured destinations: Italy, southern France and Greece. One of the major barriers that these early tourists had to surmount was the Alps, particularly the Swiss part of this mountain range, as its passes, notably the St Gotthard, provided some of the few access points to Italy from northern Europe. During the Romantic Era, the Alps were seen as both a geographical and a cultural demarcation zone.

Today the Swiss Alps are undoubtedly viewed 'romantically' by a wide variety of different cultures and this Romantic legacy is part of the marketing mix that drives one of Switzerland's most important earners of foreign income. In fact, so important is tourism as source of export revenue that it sits in third place behind the chemical industry (first) and the metal and machine industry (second) (Federal Department of Economic Affairs 2009). Switzerland's Romantic image is underpinned not only by Federal and Cantonal marketing, but is nurtured by a variety of popular sources, not least the Indian film industry, which often sets the love stories that are a staple of Bollywood's output in the Swiss Alps. It is perhaps not surprising that Indians and other Asians who consume Mumbai's movies represent a growing proportion of inbound tourism. In Lucerne, for example, which according to the 2010 *Rough Guide to Switzerland* (Teller 2010) is the prettiest Swiss town, Indians make up 3.5% of the visitor market, only a little behind the Chinese at 4% (Lucerne Tourism).

However, as Markus Marti of the University of Basel has documented in his exhaustive study of British and American visitors to Switzerland, this Romantic experience was not always foremost in the minds of those who crossed the forbidding barrier that comprised the Alps.[1] In fact, Adam of Usk, one of the first travellers to record his impressions of crossing the Gotthard in 1402, describes being blindfolded to avoid seeing the dangers of the pass (Wraight 1987: 101). This perspective hardly changes over the following centuries with subsequent visitors describing the hardships of traversing the Alps, providing little in the way of commentary on its attractions. By the early eighteenth century, however, this view had begun to soften. One writer who was influential in changing attitudes was the Swiss aristocrat, Albrecht von Haller whose long poem *Die Alpen* (1732) was highly regarded by its German and English readership alike. Combining botany with morality, von Haller represented the Alps as a symbolic domain, the home of Liberty and Virtue because of the simple, hard-working life style of its inhabitants and the exquisite beauty of its wild flowers, notably the blue gentian, later to become emblematic of German Romanticism as a whole. Gently politicising the landscape through his descriptive symbolism, von Haller's poem pointed the way for new interpretations of the Alps, one matched by the changing cartographic practices of the late eighteenth century, which developed new techniques of representing relief, contour and gradient in mountain areas.

The early eighteenth-century dramatist and journalist, Joseph Addison, also wrote enthusiastically of the visual and aesthetic aspects of alpine travel, claiming that he was ' … entertained with the prettiest variety of snow-prospects that you can imagine' from his vantage point on 'the highest mountain in Switzerland'. However, this view of the Alps as a pleasure-giving spectacle does not appear to have been a widely held one. After a traumatic crossing in 1739, Horace Walpole never wanted to see the Swiss Alps again!

Partly driven by the excavations in Herculaneum (1738) and Pompeii (1748), visitors to the Alps, especially from Britain, were becoming more numerous and by 1749 the first major guidebook to the Grand Tour had appeared, although the term 'Grand Tour' itself did not appear for another 11 years. What is today widely known as the Grand Tour flourished from the 1660s until the advent of the railways in the 1840s, and the denomination first appears in Richard Lassels' *Voyage of Italy* (1670), which was published in 1686. Primarily associated with the nobility of the British Isles, these travellers were also drawn from the largely Protestant lands of northern Europe. They were joined by small numbers of Americans and other nationalities from the mid-eighteenth century onwards. Despite the growing numbers of visitors, reactions to the Alps remained ambivalent. The demagogue John Wilkes (1725–97) describing them as horrible while at the same time being moved by the majesty of the conifers.

It is not until the advent of the Romantic era (1789–1837) that a consistent view of the Alps and other natural landscapes starts to appear. Care, of course, needs to be taken with the term 'natural landscape', because, as Jon Mathieu points out in his *History of the Alps* (2009), the appearance of the mountains have been extensively modified by centuries of human economic endeavour. Nevertheless, attitudes to these environments were profoundly altered by the writers, artists and philosophers collectively known as 'the Romantics'. Although we cannot attribute all such 'romantic' attitudes to this loosely designated group, they remain an important wellspring that has certainly fed into popular culture throughout the twentieth century and into the twenty-first. The verbal and visual art of the Romantics together constitutes a body of work that sheds light not only on the educated elite's attitude to the environment, but also provides insights into our enduring passion for nature and our view of its beneficial tendencies.

The best approach to Romantic ideals of nature is perhaps made through the figure of the traveller, a person of considerable diversity, which none the less provides one of the definitive tropes of European Romanticism. Either alone or with an intimate companion, it is the Romantic traveller whose imaginative gaze – whether rendered through poetry, prose or the developing vogue for landscape painting – gives a distinct visual organisation to the scenery. The sensibility of the Romantic traveller infuses meaning into what is seen, creating a particular kind of landscape. As the German philosopher, F.W.J. Schelling observed, 'landscape has only a reality in the eye of the beholder' (Koerner 2009: 90). It is precisely this shift of emphasis from the material objects of the existing scenery to the creative gaze of the traveller that distinguishes the

Romantic view of nature. It is impossible to separate Romantic ideals of nature from developments in landscape painting as the doctrines of Romanticism founded a new school of aesthetics. By 1843, John Ruskin was able to ground his championship of 'Modern Painting' on
the essentially Romantic assumption 'that the greatest thing a human soul ever does in this
world is to see something, and tell what it saw in a plain way. Hundreds of people can talk for
one who can think, but thousands can think for one who can see. To see clearly is poetry,
prophecy, and religion – all in one' (Warner and Hough 1983: 15).

Poetry, prophecy and religion were precisely the attributes that the eye of the Romantic
traveller directed towards natural scenery. The great Romantics saw themselves engaged in a
visual dialogue with the creative forces of nature itself. With an excitement comparable to that
generated in the late twentieth century by the Human Genome Project and the deciphering of
DNA, the Romantics believed that they had finally found an interpretive key to the great book
of nature's secrets. All that had seemed vague and mysterious in nature's aspects, her strange
weathers and material forms, her mists and clouds and shifting lights, could, when mediated
through the traveller's sensibility, become knowable symbols of a transcendent language that
embraced human life. Although the industrial revolution with its new understanding of the
principles of electro-magnetism began to harness the forces of the natural world, wealthy
landowners employed 'improvers' like Thomas Kent or 'Capability' Brown to enhance the
visual appearance of their estates, using dynamite to re-arrange views and re-situate water
courses. In response, the artists and writers of the Romantic period elevated nature into a new
cultural force, one capable of transforming as well as being transformed. Properly experienced,
nature was celebrated as a force able to guide, redirect and heal the emotional and spiritual
traumas of suffering humanity. According to William Wordsworth in *Lines composed a few miles
above Tintern Abbey, on revisiting the banks of the Wye during a tour, 13 July 1798*, one of many
poems written to illuminate his travels, 'nature never did betray the heart that loved her' but
remained the anchor, guide and guardian of his moral being (Wordsworth 1798: 110–125).

Collapsing the distinction between nature and art, the eye and interiority of the traveller literally
brought the Romantic landscape into being, infusing the scene with a passionate but particular
set of images and associations. So essential was this perspective that Casper David Friedrich, the
greatest artist of High Romanticism, was said to paint wearing nothing but a traveller's cloak.
Friedrich depicted spiritualised landscapes of Germanic forests and mountains, illuminating
ruined abbeys and alpine crosses with the dim lights and misty vapour of religious yearning. A
more secular combination of evocative scenery, famous names and scanty emotional underwear
enabled Lord Byron to transform his youthful travels through Europe into the best-selling poem
of the age, *Childe Harold's Pilgrimage (1812, 1816, 1818)*.[2] Illustrated by J.M. Turner a year after
completion and still colourful reading today, the four cantos of *Childe Harold* offer both a travel
guide to, and a history of, the great sites and political upheavals of European culture all interspersed with musings on Byron's own sense of blighted destiny. For Byron, the Alps were 'the
Palaces of nature', whose vast walls have 'throned Eternity in icy halls/of cold sublimity' (Byron
1816: Canto 3, v, 62) impervious to the heat and havoc of revolutionary politics.

Historians of the Grand Tour are invariably attracted to one particular alpine journey. In
1739, Horace Walpole, the son of the British prime minister and an early advocate for medieval
or 'Gothic' architecture, chose a poet, Thomas Gray, as his travelling companion. At Lyons,
Gray had rhapsodised the meeting of the two rivers, the Rhone and the Saone, as a love affair
of disparate temperaments. As the two friends set out for Geneva planning to visit the monastery of the Grande Chartreuse before crossing into Italy, their own disparity of viewpoint
quickly became apparent. Walpole's favourite spaniel, Tory, was trotting along beside their
carriage when a wolf suddenly sprang out of a thicket, seized the dog and promptly devoured it.

While Walpole screamed and wept, Gray provokingly transmuted the experience into a new awareness of the *other worldliness* of alpine landscape. It was an awareness that inevitably combined a sense of mortality with religious awe and transcendence: 'not a precipice, not a torrent, not a cliff', wrote Gray, 'but is pregnant with religion and poetry. There are certain scenes that would awe an atheist into belief … You have Death perpetually before your eyes, only so far removed as to compose the mind without frightening it' (Gosse 1882: 33). Gray, later to become famous for his *Elegy on an English Country Churchyard*, always travelled with 'a Claude Lorraine glass', a viewing device that transposed natural scenery into chiaroscuro landscapes after the manner of the great seventeenth-century painter of Arcadian scenes.

Gray later combined the figure of the inspired poet with a dramatic landscape in his other major work, *The Bard*, a poem made the subject of a celebrated painting by John Martin. Martin depicts the last surviving Celtic bard crouching over his harp on the summit of a Welsh mountain defying with prophetic song the conquering and colonising forces of the English King, Edward I. The poem illustrates how an interest in the wilder, farthest-flung regions of 'civilised' countries such as England was linked to a romantic sense of history and the idea of the native genius of a place or country. Across the countries of Northern Europe, Celtic myth provided the natural foundation stone for the emergence of national cultures. Gray, an early harbinger of Romanticism, finally turned his attention to the little known beauties of Cumberland and the Lake District, although his vision of the Alps remained an inspiration for later travellers such as the ubiquitous William Coxe in his 1789 *Travels in Switzerland in a Series of Letters to William Melmoth, Esq.*

When Wordsworth composed his autobiographical travelogue, *The Prelude*, the power of the poetic imagination had increased exponentially to match the size of what it contemplated and the great Romantic remembered how, in 1790, he had crossed the Alps at the Simplon Pass without even noticing. 'The home' of the Imagination, wrote Wordsworth grandly, is 'with infinitude, and only there' (Wordsworth 1805: Bk 6, ll 538–8). Without this power of active imagination, nature could only present 'soulless images to the eye' (Wordsworth 1805: Bk 6 l 525). On alpine excursions, poetic imagination also had to supply the deficiencies of late eighteenth-century cartography with its irregular use of *hachures*, or line tracings to indicate mountain slopes. It was not until the later nineteenth century that map makers agreed a coherent code for the representation of three-dimensional space in mountainous areas.[3]

A rural landscape imbued with passionate feeling and a numinous poetic presence (Klopstock) is the hallmark of Goethe's famous first novel, *The Sufferings of Young Werther* (1774). A prototype of the early Romantic traveller, whose flowing heart, artistic gaze and unseasonal suicide bind him to the fertile soils of the Fatherland, Werther's fictional grave became a site for generations of cultural pilgrims. As the character of Werther indicates, Romanticism flourished among such talented, ambitious, underemployed sons of the prosperous middle classes, frustrated by their lack of opportunity and denied entry into the exclusive circles of the Ancient regime. A victim of what Ruskin later designated as 'the pathetic fallacy', the Romantic belief that man and landscape shared the same emotional nature, Werther associates the torrential passions of his heart with the swollen rivers and refreshing rain of the German landscape. Cartoons of the period show other young men setting off on their travels wearing the politically progressive blue and buff of Werther's costume. Among this number was Napoleon himself. He took the novel with him on military campaigns and read it seven times, wondering if he could persuade Goethe to act as his biographer.

Of course, Romantic travel came in many forms and conveyances: from the sentimental journey of the dying Laurence Sterne to the solitary walker enjoying a space for reverie; from the laden baggage trains of the aristocratic milord completing his tour to the citizen armies of

Napoleon carrying their doctrine of revolution across the countries of Europe and beyond. With the cult of sensibility towards natural scenes, travel for its own sake also came into being: as a new art form with its own rules of 'taste'. The Protestantism of the north was influential in shaping a vogue for the Gothic, or medieval, style of architecture, a style seen as peculiarly reflective of the native genius of the land and its people, in contrast to the culture of Greece and Southern Italy. The great forests, ravines and mountains with their solemn light effects appeared to be the natural models for this ecclesiastic architecture of steep arches and aspiring lines.[4] The Swiss painter, J.H. Fuseli, celebrated the version of landscape painting often associated with this. Dismissive of 'that kind of landscape which is entirely occupied with the tame delineation of a given spot', he invoked a higher order of art in which light, of the sun and the artist's vision, was the centre. nature was a mysterious force revealed 'in the varied light of rising, meridian, setting suns; in twilight, night and dawn. Height, depth, solitude, strike, terrify, absorb, bewilder in their scenery' (Gregory 1992: 2). The Romantic affinity with vapour and vagueness of all kinds, with mist, fog, moonlight or Turner's 'rain, steam and speed', emphasised the veiled creativity of nature's ever-changing compositions. Where fog was said to have been God's assistant on the day of creation, moonlight, by contrast, was frequently associated with ideas of revolution.

As part of the new subjectivity of the time, the Romantic traveller often carried an interior burden of anxiety and unease. In the sensationally popular gothic fiction of the late eighteenth century, which drew heavily on scenic description, the hero is typically an estranged character adrift in a mountainous, danger-laden landscape of mystery and sensation. Valancourt, in Mrs Radcliffe's definitive gothic tale, *The Mysteries of Udolpho*, introduces himself as 'only a wanderer here' (Radcliffe 1794: ch. 3), and William Godwin's Fleetwood is described as 'contemplative, absent, enthusiastical, a worshipper of nature. His thoughts were full of rapture, elevation and poetry. His eyes now held commerce with the phenomena of the heavens, and now were bent to earth in silent contemplation and musing. There was nothing in them of the level and the horizontal' (Godwin 1805: ch. 3). Romantic selfhood was predicated on this impassioned interiority, which could move rapidly between inspired creativity and self-destructive depression. Such extremities found a natural correspondence in alpine scenery and the restless crossing of boundaries, whether geographical or cultural.

The Romantic traveller's encounter with nature was not all instinctual. It carried also an awareness of nearly a century of aesthetic debate, which had shaped responses to the natural world. Eighteenth-century writers had argued that a taste for nature was likely to refine sensibility and enhance 'benevolence' towards mankind. This view was shared by Romantic travellers like Goethe or Wordsworth, the brevity of whose stay in rural communities obviated the need to conform to their social hierarchies. A sympathetic response to unfamiliar scenes, especially when met by a generous hospitality, often warmed the feelings to acts of sudden intimacy. As Rousseau's *Confessions* repeatedly illustrated, travel was an erotic, as well as an artistic, pursuit for the Romantics. As Gray's Druid bard was to the mountains of Wales, so Jean Jacques Rousseau came to represent the *genius loci* of the alpine scenery of his native Switzerland. Although his books were later to be burned both in France and in his birthplace, Geneva, Rousseau's writings, which celebrated the inflammatory goodness of a secularised human nature, gave to the Alps their revolutionary associations. Crossing them became a rite of passage, a metaphor for this historic shift of perspective towards a new religion of humanity, daunting though Robespierre's 'Reign of Terror' quickly made that transition seem.

It was Rousseau, too, who, with his rapturous accounts of love affairs in beautiful locations, put the romance into Romanticism, creating a permanent confusion between two dissonant terms. 'I wanted', Rousseau wrote, 'an actual spot which might serve as a foundation, and create for me an illusion as to the reality of the inhabitants whom I intended to place there'. Deciding that a lake was 'an absolutely necessary' for the electric charge between his lovers, he chose the one for which he himself felt the strongest nostalgic associations, settling his protégés at Vevai (Vevey) (Rousseau 1781: Bk 9). In Canto 3 of *Childe Harold's Pilgrimage*, Byron celebrates Rousseau's ability to infuse a landscape with erotic promise. The setting for *La Nouvelle Heloise* becomes a shrine to its author, numinous with Rousseau's presence:

> Clarens! Sweet Clarens, birthplace of deep Love!
> Thine air is the young breath of passionate thought;
> Thy trees take root in Love; the snows above,
> The very Glaciers have his colours caught …
> All things are here of him …
>
> *(Canto 3, v 77 – 109)*

It was Rousseau's friend, the encyclopaedist, Denis Diderot, who helped to define the synergy between Romantic travel and contemporary landscape painting. Travel, Diderot argued in 1765, was a sign of that liberated energy, that cult of experience, which inspired his generation, an energy no longer to be constrained by church and state. Impervious to the will of God, the Romantic traveller struggled to control his own destiny, driven by the perversity of his own passions. This fierce but blind energy hidden in man's heart is, for Diderot, the explanation of the Romantic traveller's defining restlessness; his superabundant energy a hypergraphic sign of both loss and bereavement. To the man of settled life, he caustically observes: 'No one knows where the grave of the man of energy may be-yours is always under your feet' (Tollemache 1893: 71).

Diderot's advice to the painter, Hubert Robert, on how best to represent the Romantic traveller was to resonate throughout the following century. Before his involvement with the Louvre Gallery project, Robert had been a *catastrophe* painter whose ruins always included a crowd of on-lookers. 'Don't you feel', wrote Diderot in 1767, 'that you have far too many figures here, and that you should get rid of three-fourths of them … ? A solitary figure, with his arms crossed, and his head bowed, wandering in the gloom would have affected me far more' (Tollemache 1893: 76). Emphasising the particularising individuality, the essential solitariness of the Romantic encounter both with nature and with time, Diderot explains the importance of ruins and reflective solitude to this encounter:

> My path lies between two eternities … What is my ephemeral existence as compared to that of this work which crumbles away, or this valley which is being hollowed out, to this forest whose trees are fallings, to those shattered buildings above my head? … A torrent is carrying on the nations one after another to a common abyss; and shall I, I alone, expect to reach the shore … ?
>
> *(Tollemache 1893: 77).*

Romantic ideals of nature are often freighted with melancholy and nostalgia, a dug grave or potential scene of death grounding the beauty of the spectacle. In this way, the contemplation of nature could provide a healing catharsis, a release of emotional tension after the constraints of polite society. Discussing the 'domestication of terror in the picturesque', Robert Pogue Harrison revisits the evocative power of the Romantic ruin:

> One could say that, in its world forming capacity, architecture transforms geological time into human time, which is another way of saying it turns matter into meaning. That is why

the sight of ruins is such a reflexive and in some cases unsettling experience. Ruins in an advanced state of ruination represent, or better they literally embody, the dissolution of meaning into matter ... ruins have a way of recalling us to the very ground of our human worlds, namely the earth, whose foundations are so solid and so reliable that they presumably will outlast any edifices that we build on them.

(Pogue Harrison 2003: 3)

Two key terms relating to different types of the beautiful organised the discourse surrounding Romantic ideals of nature. The first of these, the Picturesque, developed the idea that natural scenery had inherently pictorial qualities, the principles of which could be recognised by an informed good taste. Theorised by John Gilpin in his *Three Essays: On Picturesque Beauty; On Picturesque Travel; and On Sketching Landscape: to which is added a Poem, On Landscape Painting*, published together in 1792, Gilpin's 'picturesque eye' educated the tourist to search for picturesque effects as part of the amusements of travel. A winding road, a flock of birds, a small herd of cattle standing in the shade on the edge of a dark hill were picturesque details that needed only to be harmonised into an aesthetic whole. The pursuit of picturesque beauty offered the educated traveller all the thrill of the chase, while remaining a more rational and moral amusement than the licentiousness of the age usually supplied. Gilpin wished to eradicate 'the vacant gaze' of the casual traveller and replace it with an appreciation of the pleasing irregularities of trees, rocks, broken grounds, woods, rivers, lakes, plains, valleys, mountains, lights and distances, which in the right combination were productive of picturesque beauty. This approach to landscape emphasised 'simplicity', the pleasures of the local scene rather than the visual extravagances of exotic travel; it valued emotional 'atmosphere' above scenic 'novelty'. Dorothy Wordsworth's *Grasmere Journal*, written under the sign of the picturesque, rendered the Lake District through a series of moonlit views, and her brother's poetry aligned the nurturing and restorative power of nature with the feeling heart and liberalised spirit.

The second key concept, outlined by Edmund Burke in his 1757 *Enquiry into the Sublime and Beautiful*, was even more far-reaching. Burke argued that the sublime derived its force from the dominant power that negative feelings, especially those of fear, self-preservation and a threatening sexuality, could exert over men. A sublime affect could be generated when sufficient distance from a source of danger permitted the conversion of terror into a sensation of awed enjoyment. Through a period of war and revolution, the masculine sublime, often linked to catastrophe, became a distinguishing feature of Romantic culture. Mapping landscapes of extremity that stretched human capacities to the limit, the alien spirit of the sublime presided over mountains, precipices, oceans, ice-floes, battlefields and deserts, generating sensations of beauty and terror in equal proportions. Where the picturesque invokes a place of order and tranquil belonging, the sublime stages a threatening otherness, that separation anxiety that is the origin of Romanticism.

If as Gilpin argued in his second essay, 'Beauty is best taught/By those, the favoured few, whom heaven has lent/The power to seize, select and reunite/Her loveliest features', then the proto-feminist, Mary Wollstonecraft, deserves to be recognised as one of the greatest educators of the era. Initially acting as a correspondent during the French Revolution, Wollstonecraft left Paris after witnessing the execution of Louis XVI, and set off alone on one of the most remarkable of Romantic journeys, travelling the unexplored regions of Scandinavia accompanied only by her baby daughter and her maid. She travelled to revive her love affair with the baby's father, Gilbert Imlay, an American entrepreneur who had lost a valuable cargo ship during the attempted blockage of the channel and wanted her to find it. Her account of her journey, *A Short Residence in Sweden, Norway and Denmark*, remains one of the classic texts of

Romantic travel, an inspiration to other Romantic writers, especially her own daughter, Mary Shelley, the author of *Frankenstein*. Entering uncharted regions of thought and feeling, Wollstonecraft's letters combine personal nostalgia with a sense of epic adventure, a journey away from all the known securities of her gender.

Interfusing descriptions of wild and beautiful scenery with political reflections on Sweden's liberal monarchy and the corruptions of mainstream Europe, the pioneering author of *A Vindication of the Rights of Women*, viewed everything she saw through the lens of her own revolutionary sympathies and the pain of her personal predicament. Herself the haunted, moonlit personification of Romanticism, 'Woman wailing for her demon lover', Wollstonecraft's travel writing is an object lesson in the artistry of the solitary Romantic gaze:

> With what ineffable pleasure have I not gazed – and gazed again, losing my breath through my eyes – my very soul diffusing itself in the scene … taking flight with fairy wing, to the misty mountains which bounded the prospect … more beautiful even than the lovely slopes on the winding shores before me. – I pause, again … to trace, with renewed delight, sentiments which entranced me, when, turning my humid eyes from the expanse below … my sight pierced the fleecy clouds that softened the azure brightness; and, imperceptibly recalling the reveries of childhood, I bowed before the awful throne of my Creator, while I rested on its footstool.
>
> *(Wollstonecraft 1796: 111)*

Experiencing herself as a picturesque fragment, 'a particle broken off from the mass of mankind' (Wollstonecraft: 69), Wollstonecraft recognises that the coast of Scandinavia is made of the same rudimentary stuff as her political aspirations: 'huge, dark rocks, that looked like the rude materials of creation'. 'Nature', she claims, 'is the nurse of sentiment, – the true source of taste; – yet what misery, as well as rapture, is produced by a quick perception of the beautiful and the sublime … how dangerous it is to foster these sentiments in such an imperfect state of existence' (Wollstonecraft: 99). Her faith in a more egalitarian future offset by the smell of roasted herrings, Wollstonecraft returned unhappily to England and threw herself into the Thames. Rescued by a passing boatman and those symbols of oppression, her voluminous petticoats, Wollstonecraft was to learn once again the re-integrative power of the picturesque when the philosopher, William Godwin, read her book and fell in love with its author.

It was left to their daughter, Mary Shelley, to articulate in *Frankenstein* (1818) the full demand for emotional recognition that the sublime Alpine landscape had bred in its admirers. At home in the Jura Mountains, invoking the brotherhood of man but cut off from all human contact, Frankenstein's monster is the apotheosis of the Romantic traveller, solitary, suffering and sublime. More insular than Shelley but just as persuasive, Jane Austen was also to speak of travel as the moving spirit of Romanticism. For her emotionally repressed heroines, a glimpse of the sea was both social privilege and sexual promise as the south coast replaced Bath as England's recuperative centre. Her last novel, *Persuasion* (1817), and the late fragment, *Sanditon*, both focus on the seaside resort as a symbol of economic growth and cultural change following the defeat of Napoleon.

Whatever their context, whether sublime or picturesque, the Romantics made their ideals of nature synonymous with a newly articulate self-consciousness. 'What we have loved/Others will love', proclaimed Wordsworth at the end of *The Prelude*, aware of his role as 'a Prophet of Nature' (Wordsworth 1805: Bk 12, 442–5) who was shaping the views and modelling the travel experiences of future generations. The emotional narratives these Romantic travellers inscribed on the landscape opened up new routes for cultural tourists determined to visit the grave of Young Werther or identify the exact spot where Jane Austen's Louisa Musgrave fell from the Cobb in Lyme Regis. Although the values of enlightenment selfhood were affirmed by these excursions to the great sites of Romantic creativity, the connotations of travel were modified for the later nineteenth century. By the 1830s, William Cobbett was able to redeploy the Romantic travel guide to highlight the plight of a peasantry for whom picturesque cottages and the simple life promised little more than starvation. On the same trajectory, Romantic walking groups and the later Rambling Associations eventually turned their 'right to roam' into a major political encounter with the landowning classes, establishing the traveller's footpath as a legal right of way into the future.

Given the scale and significance of Romanticism as a cultural force across Europe and in parts of America, it is unsurprising that so many of its perspectives are still discernible in contemporary tourism, especially where attitudes to the environment are concerned. What is less clear is why this outlook seems to have crossed cultural barriers with contemporary Asian tourists becoming as besotted as Europeans with 'natural' landscapes such as the Alps. However, if one considers that these more recent tourists are the representatives of Asia's growing middle classes, then it would be reasonable to assume that they have been influenced by similar consumerist pressures to their European counterparts, and have come to see landscapes through a similar prism.

Despite Byron's 1817 lament that '*we'll go no more a-roving*', tourism and Romanticism have become inseparable bedfellows, bound together at every level of popular appeal. Many of the major authors of the Romantic Period continue to be read and studied worldwide, and their stories provide subjects for that most international and easily accessible of art forms – film. The link between film and tourism is so well established that tourist agencies often promote the connection with dedicated websites targeting devotees, as is currently the case with Tourism Ireland. Romanticised landscapes have remained a stock in trade of the film industry, whether Hollywood or Bollywood, justifying the claims of the Romantics that they had discovered in nature the grammar of a universal language to which all travellers, whatever their origins, had access.

Case study: Jean-Jacques Rousseau

Born in Geneva on 28 June 1712, Jean-Jacques Rousseau was the son of a Protestant watchmaker whose wife was the daughter of a Calvinist preacher. Despite his artisan status, Rousseau's father was a well-educated music lover who taught his son to read and encouraged him to appreciate the countryside, a major solace for Rousseau in later life. Rousseau is widely recognised as a major philosopher influencing both the American and French Revolutions, and laying the foundations of modern political, sociological and educational inquiry.

His novel, *Julie, ou la nouvelle Héloïse* (1761) not only exerted a significant influence on the development of Romanticism in fiction, it also stimulated interest in the Swiss Alps. The book went into 70 editions and was one of the most successful novels of the eighteenth century. Rousseau's original title was *Letters by Two Lovers Living in a Small Villa at the Foot of the Alps* and the setting was the Montreux region, although he also refers to Chillon, Clarens and Lake Geneva. Inspired by this work, upscale travellers began to explore the places where the two fictional lovers met, among them Lord Byron who visited Chillon Castle in 1816.

A striking feature of Rousseau's work is his interest in walking, an interest he explored through autobiographical anecdotes, which combined sightseeing and botanising references with ongoing discussions of arguments published in earlier works. Entitled *Reveries of a (the) Solitary Walker* (1782), the book is divided into ten chapters or walks that were written between 1776 and 1778, although the last walk remained incomplete at Rousseau's death in 1778. A passionate traveller in more senses than one, Rousseau's epoch-making autobiography, *The Confessions*, published in 1781, gave a frank account of his remarkable life story and gift for misadventure.

Notes

1 Markus Marti's reading list at the University of Basel, entitled *British and American Visitors in Switzerland: History of Tourism in Switzerland*, provided us with a very useful overview. We are also grateful for his comments on our first draft.
2 The word 'Childe' used in Byron's title is a medieval term for 'knight'.
3 For an interesting discussion of Romantic cartography, see Carlson (2010).
4 Goethe wrote an influential essay on the Strasbourg cathedral in 1773 developing this connection between landscape and native genius.

Further reading

Kroeber, K. (1975) *Romantic Landscape Vision: Constable and Wordsworth*. Madison: University of Wisconsin Press.
Lucerne and the Tourist Industry *Salient Facts and Figures* (n.d.).
Page, F. (ed.) (1970) *Byron: Poetical Works*. Oxford: Oxford University Press.
Schama, S. (1996) *Landscape and Memory*, London: HarperCollins, Fontana Press.
Shleir, A. B. (1976) 'Albrecht von Haller's Botany and "Die Alpen". *Eighteenth Century Studies*, 10 (2): 169–84.
Wordsworth, D. (1971) *Journals (1798, 1800–1803)* Oxford: Oxford University Press.
Wu, D. (ed.) (1994, 2006) *Romanticism: An Anthology*, 3rd edn. Oxford: Blackwell Publishing.

References

Burke, E. (1757, 1998, 2004) *A Philosophic Enquiry into the Sublime and Beautiful*. Harmondsworth: Penguin Books.
Carlson, J.S. (2010) 'The Map at the Limit of his Paper: A Cartographic Reading of The Prelude, Book 6, 'Cambridge and the Alps'. *Studies in Romanticism*, 49 (3): 375 – 404.
Federal Department of Economic Affairs (2009) *Swiss Tourism in Figures*. Bern.
Godwin, W. (1805, 1832) *Fleetwood*, Standard Novels Edition, No 22. London: Richard Bentley.
Goethe, J.W.V. (1774, 1789, 1989) *The Sufferings of Young Werther*, trans. M. Hulse. Harmondsworth: Penguin.
Gosse, E. (1882, 1902, 1915), *Gray: English Men of Letters*. London: Macmillan & Co.
Gregory, M. (1992) *English Romantic Landscape*, Catalogue 60, Martyn Gregory Gallery.
Koerner, J.L. (1990, 2009) *Caspar David Friedrich and the Subject of Landscape*, 2nd edn. London: Reaktion Books.
Lassels, R. (1686) *The Voyage of Italy: or, a Compleat Journey through Italy*. London: printed for R.C. J.R. and A.C. and sold by Charles Shortgrave.
Mathieu, J. (2009) *History of the Alps, 1500–1900: Environment, Development, And Society*. Morgantown: West Virginia University Press.
Pogue Harrison, R.(2003) *The Dominion of the Dead*. Chicago, IL and London: University of Chicago Press.
Radcliffe, A. (1794, 1966) *The Mysteries of Udolpho*. Oxford: Oxford University Press.
Rousseau, J.-J. (1781, 1996) *The Confessions*. Herts: Wordsworths Classics.
Shelley, M. (1818, 1993) *Frankenstein*. Oxford: Oxford World Classics.
Teller, M. (2010) *Rough Guide to Switzerland*. London: Rough Guides Ltd.
Tollemache, B.L. (ed. and trans.) (1893), *Diderot's Thoughts on Art and Style*. London and Sydney: Remington & Co Ltd.

Warner, E. and Hough, G. (1983) *Strangeness and Beauty: An Anthology of Aesthetic Criticism, 1840–1910*, Vol. 1. Cambridge: Cambridge University Press.

Wollstonecraft, M. (1796, 1987) *A Short Residence in Sweden, Norway and Denmark*. Harmondsworth: Penguin Classics.

Wordsworth, W. (1805, 1933) *The Prelude*. Oxford: Oxford University Press.

Wraight, J. (1987) *The Swiss and the British*. Salisbury: Russell.

7

The importance of the aesthetic

Cain S. Todd

Conceptual issues

Any account of the importance of the aesthetic in tourism must begin by acknowledging some initial conceptual obstacles that make it particularly difficult to provide any definitive overview of this topic. First, the scope of the term 'aesthetic' is notoriously unclear and remains the subject of philosophical dispute. Pre-theoretically, it can be used to qualify virtually anything, including objects, values, attitudes, judgements and experiences. It is far from obvious what all of these phenomena have in common in virtue of which they are aesthetic. Indeed, clear and uncontroversial definitions and demarcations of 'aesthetic' have proved no less elusive than attempts to capture the essence of beauty.

Second, although beauty might be thought central to the nature of aesthetic appreciation, there is an indefinitely large range of aesthetic values (and disvalues), which includes, for instance, elegance, ugliness, prettiness, gracefulness, garishness, daintiness, harmony, the picturesque, the sublime and so on. Third, 'tourism' denotes a formidable array of different practices, attitudes, motivations and behaviours, often delimited by specific epithets, e.g. 'mass tourism', 'leisure tourism', 'agri-tourism', 'adventure tourism', 'package tourism', 'sustainable tourism', 'ethical tourism', 'cultural tourism' and so on. Fourth, the scope of the term 'natural environment' is equally vast and immensely varied, encompassing everything from pristine wilderness areas to urban parkland, gardens and environmental art; it embraces individual objects ranging from small pebbles to large elephants, and 'items' ranging from beaches to herds of wildebeest; it ranges through species of fauna and flora, from small to large ecosystems, and it incorporates objects, phenomena and forces that both conform to and elude all of our different senses.

It is thus evident that when all of these variables are combined, no short chapter can hope to do justice simply to *the* importance of the aesthetic, because there is no one way in which the aesthetic is important, even assuming we can usefully demarcate the relevant notion of 'aesthetic' at play in tourism.

In addition to these complexities, although some academic disciplines have, for some time now, taken tourism as a phenomenon seriously, few have written explicitly or comprehensively on tourism and aesthetic appreciation (see Tribe 2009: part 3). Rather, of the many potential values and attitudes that the phenomenon of tourism encompasses, the concentration has been on ethical, economic and social issues. (For examples and further discussion see Fennell 2006; Urry 2002.) Moreover, although philosophers have had much to say on the nature of aesthetic appreciation, and 'environmental aesthetics' has become a burgeoning sub-field within philosophical aesthetics, they have all but completely ignored the concept and phenomenon of tourism.

None the less, the aesthetic appreciation of natural environments is closely bound up with the nature of tourism, and philosophical reflection on the former can provide some important conceptual tools for understanding the latter, and their inter-connection. An examination of philosophical accounts of the aesthetic appreciation of nature, therefore, provides certain key concepts that can be employed to illuminate the role of aesthetic value and appreciation in tourism generally. In addition to standard aesthetic values such as the 'beautiful' or 'sublime', other prominent values that require examination are the 'trivial/serious', and the 'authentic/ inauthentic'.

Finally, we must highlight an important distinction that underpins the main topic of this chapter, namely that between a descriptive and normative way of understanding the role of the aesthetic in tourism. The descriptive dimension addresses the myriad ways in which tourists, and tourism in general, are *in fact* concerned with issues of aesthetic value, and might provide answers to questions such as: what sorts of *norms* govern the formation of aesthetic preferences and motivations in tourism? The normative dimension, in contrast, will treat questions that are less empirical in nature and philosophically more substantial, such as: should aesthetic considerations play a central role in shaping tourist preferences and environments? What role(s) should this be? Can reasons be given for preferring certain aesthetic values and preferences, and certain types of tourism that encourage them?

Although the descriptive issue is certainly not irrelevant to normative considerations, the discussion of this chapter, concerned as it is with fundamental values and types of appreciation, will concentrate primarily on normative questions, for two main reasons. First, the empirical data required to establish certain descriptive conclusions are simply lacking in many respects, and as just noted, the phenomena described are too complex and various to say anything substantial and informative about what importance the aesthetic *actually* has in tourism. Second, insofar as the aesthetic is a fundamentally normative notion, the normative questions about the role of aesthetic value in this area allow for greater theoretical treatment and reflection.

The aesthetic appreciation of nature

In order to understand the role and significance of the aesthetic in tourism, we need some grip on what makes a type of attitude, interest, experience or value an aesthetic one. Although this a hotly disputed philosophical area, there is a particular notion that has, since its formulation by Kant, remained central to most conceptions of the aesthetic; namely, that of *disinterestedness*. This concept is invoked in order to detach aesthetic interest and pleasure from everyday practical and personal interests and desires, comprising an interest or pleasure in an object (and its perceptual properties) 'for its own sake alone'; that is, not *instrumentally*, for the sake of satisfying some merely extraneous and self-interested desire or motive (Budd 2002).

The idea of 'disinterestedness' also serves, crucially, to demarcate the realm of aesthetic experience, pleasure, appreciation and judgement from the moral and cognitive realms. Beauty, it is often held, is completely distinct from truth and goodness: when appreciating the aesthetic value of something we are not thereby interested in its moral worth, nor in gaining knowledge, say, of what the object of our attention is, or how it functions. Instead, we are simply taking pleasure in its intrinsic value.

Although rather rough, and not uncontroversial, this conception of aesthetic interest does enable a first attempt to characterise its role in tourism by asking whether there is any form of tourism that does not have at its heart aesthetic interests and motivations, and the desire to experience aesthetic value. And it might at first glance appear not. Tourism is one of the main activities in which human beings engage – along with attending concerts, visiting art galleries or admiring landscapes – which seems to be motivated primarily by aesthetic considerations. After all, we visit places in order to see things, to experience unfamiliar, beautiful, and exotic sights and sounds, to experience the natural beauty as well as the art, architecture and culture of foreign shores.

However, equally common motivations for tourism surely exist in the aims of relaxation, escapism, romance and adventure, which by the criterion of disinterestedness might seem to be excluded from the realm of the aesthetic. For these activities are surely self-interested and self-directed, whereby our surroundings are chosen and enjoyed not solely for their intrinsic virtues but primarily instrumentally, as the means to satisfying our own particular desires and pleasures. Furthermore, many forms of tourism are clearly concerned with educational and ethical aims, such as learning about the geography or history of a place, or participating in conservation or welfare schemes to aid the local wildlife or population. It is questionable whether the various values at the heart of these different appreciative activities – the exotic, the curious, the difficult, the novel, the interesting, the relaxing, the romantic, the morally rewarding, the intellectually stimulating, etc. – are aesthetic values.

If this were right, then the aesthetic would be important only within certain quite narrowly defined types of tourism. Yet it seems undesirable to say that an aesthetic interest cannot be present in and mixed with other forms of tourist appreciation. After all, surely part of the reason we have chosen the Himalayas for our trekking and rafting adventure, or the shores of the Red Sea for our sunbathing and diving, will often, if not always, consist precisely in there being some sort of aesthetic value that we attach to such places and activities in the first place. Moreover, it is far from evident that intellectual or moral interests cannot be combined with aesthetic pleasures, or that the desire to escape the humdrum cannot be in part an aesthetic motivation. Unless we interpret the notion of disinterest/aesthetic interest broadly, therefore, we will be in danger of concluding, extremely counter-intuitively, that anywhere or anything visited as a tourist in order to satisfy some personal desire, or some moral or other *prima facie* non-aesthetic aim, will thereby be excluded from the realm of aesthetic value; and that is simply not plausible.

The natural response to these worries is to broaden and loosen the constraints on what counts as 'aesthetic', without blurring to the point of oblivion the differences between aesthetic and other values. It is fair to say that nobody has succeeded in doing a fool-proof job of this, but for the remainder of this chapter we can work profitably with a more or less intuitive notion of the aesthetic.

In addition to determining the boundaries and importance of the aesthetic vis-à-vis non-aesthetic dimensions of tourist appreciation, one might also be interested in determining which, among these, constitute *appropriate* types of aesthetic engagement. This concern has been at the heart of philosophical discussions of the aesthetic appreciation of nature, such as that revealed in the most comprehensive and influential philosophical framework developed in this area, Allen Carlson's *Natural Environmental Model* (Carlson 2000).

In order to appreciate nature appropriately, from an aesthetic point of view, claims Carlson, we need to appreciate it as it really is in itself – nature *qua* nature. The natural sciences – geology, biology, ecology – and their common-sense predecessors and analogues provide knowledge of nature *qua* nature, nature as it actually is, and hence aesthetic appreciation based on this will be appropriate and objectively valid (see also Stecker 1997; Saito 2004)

On this model, aesthetic appreciation thus involves an essentially cognitive component, for the perception of nature's aesthetic qualities requires conceptualising natural objects relative to the kinds of things they are. Moreover, different types of objects, such as different kinds of landscapes, will call for different ways of perceiving:

> we must survey a prairie environment, looking at the subtle contours of the land, feeling the wind blowing across the open space, and smelling the mix of prairie grasses and flowers. But such an act of aspection has little place in a dense forest environment. Here we must examine and scrutinize, inspecting the detail of the forest floor, listening carefully for the sounds of birds ...
>
> *(Carlson 2000: 50–51)*

Drawing on these elements, Carlson rejects other frameworks for appreciation, which he claims *falsify* and *trivialise* nature. Of particular relevance for our purpose is what he labels the 'landscape model', which promulgates the 'scenery cult'. Having its roots in eighteenth century aesthetic theories, practices and preferences, particularly a concern with the 'picturesque', this model treats nature as if it were a landscape painting or photograph. Focusing attention on colours and merely formal aesthetic qualities, 'flattening' nature into a static two-dimensional pictorial scene, the approach to appreciation it advocates is thus guilty of misrepresenting nature. Indeed, it involves regarding nature in some sense as if it were art (Carlson 2000: 34).

The main problem with this form of appreciation is that, by focusing exclusively on merely formal properties, on objects independently of the sorts of objects they are, it simply fails to accommodate the many other aesthetically salient properties that nature possesses. It neglects, for instance, the rich, multisensory, active mode of appreciation that the natural environment both encourages and allows. Instead, nature must be appreciated aesthetically also in terms of non-formal qualities such as expressive qualities – for example, the gracefulness of a gazelle, the serenity of the sea, the brooding-ness of the moors.

Other philosophers have also sought to preserve the normative dimension of aesthetic 'appropriateness' without, however, appealing to the centrality of scientific knowledge as such. Instead, they invoke the relevance of other ways of *understanding* nature, including for instance myth, religion, poetry, art and other types of 'fictional', imaginative narratives (e.g. Brady 2003; Eaton 2004; Foster 2004; Saito 1984). Also, according to such accounts, our aesthetic interest in nature should not reside merely in the 'uninterpreted' sensory, formal qualities that nature offers. Rather, we should seek to understand natural objects *qua* the objects that they are, understanding nature on its own terms, where this involves an element of conceptualisation. But such conceptualisation can, for instance, involve the imagination, where our present perception is imbued with imaginative thoughts and feelings; for example, seeing a falling autumn leaf *as* symbolising temporality and vulnerability.

Here is a widely quoted example from an influential article by Ronald Hepburn:

> Suppose I am walking over a wide expanse of sand and mud. The quality of the scene is perhaps that of wild, glad emptiness. But suppose I bring to bear upon the scene my knowledge that this is tidal basin, the tide being out. The realization is not aesthetically irrelevant. I see myself now as walking on what is for half the day sea-bed. The wild glad emptiness may be tempered by a disturbing weirdness.
>
> *(Hepburn 2004: 50)*

Such aesthetic appreciation widens the focus from merely formal properties to what might roughly be called the expressive properties possessed by nature, thereby enriching nature's aesthetic value and interest. More significantly, this enriched notion of the appreciation of nature 'on its own terms' is not arbitrary or merely subjective, but can be appropriate or inappropriate, allowing us to contrast a 'serious' aesthetic interest in nature, with a merely 'trivial' appreciation. These 'ways of seeing' are, it is held, no less 'true to nature' than scientific understanding.

The appreciation of both art and natural objects, Hepburn contends, can be more or less serious, where the latter means something like being 'hastily and unthinkingly perceived' (Hepburn 1995: 65). Perception can be 'attentive or inattentive, can be discriminating or undiscriminating, lively or lazy … The reflective component … can be feeble or stereotyped, individual, original or exploratory. It can be immature or confused' (ibid.: 68). Primarily, 'an aesthetic approach to nature is trivial to the extent that it distorts, ignores, suppresses truth about its objects, feels and thinks about them in ways that falsify how nature really is' (ibid.: 69).

Tourism and 'serious' appreciation

Clearly, these claims have significant repercussions for considering certain common tourist approaches to natural beauty, which manifest an overriding concern with the 'trivial', 'superficial' and 'picturesque'. Certain aspects taken to be definitive of the 'mass tourism' so despised by many writing in this area, readily lend themselves to such criticisms: the fleeting and detached modes of transport that fail to immerse subjects properly in their surroundings; the reliance on conventional vantage points and the aesthetic testimony of others; the overreliance on technological intermediaries – for example, cameras – to facilitate, capture and define their experiences; and so on.

The distinction between trivial and serious aesthetic appreciation thus offers some fundamental conceptual tools for assessing the relationship between tourism and the appreciation of nature. It serves to exclude as inappropriate any attitudes to nature that distort, falsify or neglect those properties accruing to them as natural. Thus, it also captures certain intuitions that some types of tourism – and the attitudes, experiences and behaviours associated with them – may be less aesthetically rewarding, rich or authentic than others.

These observations can, however, appear to be weak, misguided or even unwarrantedly elitist. Why should we care about misrepresenting nature or the authenticity of our aesthetic experiences of it? After all, if such experiences are held to be aesthetically valuable by the relevant appreciators themselves, the simple falsification of the object of the experience is irrelevant to the aesthetic value of the experience *per se*, however it is gained.

This issue highlights the difficulty in finding *aesthetic* fault with certain kinds of tourist experiences or attitudes, and suggests why many putative aesthetic criticisms of certain kinds of appreciation are (implicitly or explicitly) underpinned by consequentialist concerns, often of an ethical nature. For example, from an ethical-environmental perspective, it is easy to see how certain attitudes underpinning modern mass tourism, and the cheap travel that enables it, may involve a certain lack of awareness and respect for, say, the fragility or biodiversity of certain 'unscenic' natural environments. Moreover, they may even lead to the destruction of the very environments that tourists have come to see.

These kinds of concerns, coupled with practical policy-oriented environmental considerations, clearly motivate normative reflection on the importance of the aesthetic in tourism generally vis-à-vis other non-aesthetic (primarily moral or economic) evaluative considerations. The importance of the aesthetic may therefore be assessed in terms of its instrumental value in the service of these non-aesthetic ends. But does the trivial/serious distinction matter aesthetically as well as ethically?

There are, on reflection, genuine aesthetic reasons that count against certain forms of appreciation, and they appeal both to the state of the appreciator as well as the state of the appreciated, to aesthetic subject and object. For example, in respect of the latter, that mass tourism can come to destroy the very elements that gave rise to it in the first place is manifested not just in physical changes to a place's visual appearance, but in the damage to the aesthetic value of a place, the loss of valuable aesthetic qualities. The imposition of too many constructed viewpoints in an area of scenic beauty, for instance, replete with signs and walkways, and with the building of roads to access them, may result in the loss of the 'wild, glad emptiness' that drew visitors there initially.

There is additional reason, too, to think that certain aspects of tourism can have negative, impoverishing effects on the nature of the aesthetic experiences one might undergo. For instance, elements of mass tourism, such as the frequent speed and superficiality with which places are visited, may limit the time and physical engagement required fully to understand and aesthetically appreciate them. One may simply miss salient aesthetic properties available for appreciation, such as sounds and smells, that are integral to the surrounding environment. Similarly, as noted above, attention to conventional scenes and 'beauty spots' can limit our aesthetic experience and awareness of aesthetic properties because it leads to a focus primarily on formal 'scenic' properties at the expense of the many other types of properties and experiences that nature can offer. These might include expressive properties such as the eeriness of a moor, the solitude of a desert or the chaotic exuberance of a swamp.

Depending on context and whim, the notions of trivial and serious appreciation can be cashed out in any number of different ways, and in terms of any number of different values (and disvalues). A trivial view of nature might encompass a range of different faults and vices, such as simplification, falsification, sentimentality, inauthenticity, arbitrariness and romanticisation. One might, under the sway of a Disney upbringing, view all animals anthropomorphically, falsifying their behaviours and needs inappropriately, and indulging sentimental attitudes towards them. Or one might have a romanticised view of certain landscapes, desiring to conserve areas which are the way they are because in reality they are full of hardship and poverty (such as many of the pastoral landscapes of Europe).

Sentimentality, simplification, romanticisation and other purportedly problematic attitudes may in general be undesirable traits to encourage, but again it is difficult to say precisely what is intrinsically aesthetically wrong with them, as opposed to what is wrong them in terms of the (ethical) consequences to which they can lead. A sentimental view of animals, for example, may blind one to the need for harsh culling measures to help conserve a particular ecosystem. Yet all of these faults also potentially impose various undesirable limits on our aesthetic experiences of nature. A sentimental conception of animals may hinder one's aesthetic appreciation of their hunting movements, and of the savagery of nature 'raw in tooth and claw'; an overly developed romantic sense of natural beauty may hinder an aesthetic appreciation of parts of nature lacking in grandeur or obvious scenic appeal, such as a beehive or city park (Todd 2009).

Insofar as such modes of appreciation hinder or impoverish richer, deeper, more valuable aesthetic experiences of nature, they are to that extent aesthetically undesirable, and hence so too are the types of tourism that encourage them. There is thus good reason to think that there may well be aesthetic advantages to, and hence aesthetic (not just ethical) reasons for preferring some types of tourism (and the attitudes accompanying or manifested by them) in nature over others. Assuming the value of certain types of experiences, the aesthetic should no doubt be accorded a great deal of significance in tourist practices.

It is important, however, to acknowledge the limited scope of such claims. Various attitudes and forms of tourism *may* lead to inappropriate and impoverished aesthetic responses, yet it would appear to be impossible to show that such modes of appreciation *necessarily* entail such deleterious results; or, at best, that would be an empirical claim about individual (and perhaps collective) psychological states, which would be extremely difficult to verify.

It is also difficult to suggest practical measures for combating these aesthetically problematic responses. Any policy decisions taken in this respect would need to balance the relevant educational aims – for example, securing ecological knowledge, encouraging certain ways of perceiving and experiencing nature over others – with attention to preserving the natural environment itself from becoming merely an educational showpiece awash with instructional aims and bureaucratic lists. The failure to achieve such a balance may otherwise lead to, instead of from, the kinds of trivial and artificial encounters and attitudes to nature that we wish to avoid. Arguably, the most important part of any aesthetic tourist education will be to inculcate the attitudes of curiosity and wonder. This will be best achieved by encouraging, in our perceptions, the imagination of, for instance, vast natural forces and processes, depths of space and time, and the infinite variety of natural objects. The role of imagination here is thus crucial, both in the way in which a knowledge of natural history is brought to bear on the engagement with nature, and in the way in which an engagement with art and literature can inform our perceptions of nature. Many of the problematic attitudes towards nature discussed above can, it appears, be attributed to certain failures of, or inappropriate uses of, imagination.

Authenticity, well-being and the tourist gaze

Even granted some distinction between trivial and serious appreciation, the difficulty of drawing clear lines of demarcation between them in the hope of providing rule-like generalisations for assessing particular types of tourism and concomitant attitudes towards natural beauty should be evident. There is no one appreciative goal of tourism as such. Even if different general types of tourist attitudes can be roughly distinguished, in practice our attitudes towards nature, tourism and beauty are so varied, mixed, blurred and confused that it would be surprising if we were able to make anything other than rather crude generalisations and relatively cautious claims. Furthermore, these would ideally come packaged with the luxury of fine-grained qualifications that a modest book chapter cannot afford. In light of the previous discussion, however, there are a few crucial elements that must be considered in weighing up the aesthetic pros and cons of different types of tourism and tourist attitudes.

First, we must consider what we might call the 'mode of travel'. Given that a serious appreciation of nature is likely to be aided (although in extreme cases may no doubt be hindered) by time spent perceiving and contemplating it, slow tourism may encourage and afford the time required for deeper, more serious contemplation of and physical *engagement* with one's surroundings. Indeed, this should be unsurprising, for in all spheres of aesthetic interest, from wine tasting to artistic contemplation, the rewards of serious attention, interest and value accrue only with the great time and (perceptual and cognitive) effort often necessary to sustain them.

It follows from this that certain forms of tourism and travelling are likely to confer certain aesthetic advantages, namely, any that involve some enhanced and relatively prolonged degree of close physical engagement with one's natural surroundings. Concomitantly, it is easy to see the contribution that the quick and convenient nature of modern tourism can make to depleting the sense of wonder that forms one of the primary aesthetic values and motives for travel in the first place. Wonder lies partly in encountering the new and the strange, and in the sheer difficulty and effort often involved in doing so. Once a place becomes a tourist destination, however, this effort may no longer be required to experience the very attributes that drove tourists there initially, and those very attributes themselves are thereby endangered. Instead, more effort may now be spent in trying to maintain serious aesthetic appreciation in the face of all the detritus of modern tourism that has afflicted so many places of natural beauty. In these ways, tourism can be self-defeating and important aesthetic qualities of nature, such as wonder, awe, the sublime, seem particularly threatened by the impositions of certain modes of travel and tourist experience (Macfarlane 2003; Godlovitch 2004; Todd 2009).

One of the central values at stake here, and one of the most conceptually elusive, is that of authenticity. A frequent motivation for travel is underpinned by the desire to experience unfamiliar people and places, more or less unaffected by the various influences that govern the tourist's everyday reality. The search for the authentic is, as such, the search for the 'un-touristed'. Attributed to objects and places, authenticity thus implies the absence of any qualities grounded solely in, and directed at, merely touristic satisfactions. The problem that some have recognised, however, is that much of what passes for authenticity in tourist destinations may be designed to meet the tourists' expectations of authenticity, or will be at least partly determined by the tourist's own preconceptions (Lasua 2007: 282). Authenticity, that is, may often be either unattainable or illusory, as what the tourist construes as authentic (or what has been construed for them) will be in part a reflection of their own values. In other words, the tourist cannot, it might be thought, escape their own 'tourist gaze' (Urry 2002). Moreover, if authenticity – 'nature raw in tooth and claw' – fails in fact to please, then tourists may not in reality find themselves interested in the values they take themselves to be (Shiner 1994).

Second, insofar as a primary aesthetic goal of tourism, as such, is to visit and attempt to appreciate a place for its own sake, any tourism lacking this fundamental attitude is likely to lack the resources required to procure the available rich and rewarding aesthetic experiences. Moreover, as Alain de Botton (2002) has eloquently pointed out, the escapist pleasures that certain types of tourism are held to provide are easily tarnished and shown to be partly illusory by the constant, inescapable intrusions of banal reality. This problem, de Botton posits, stems fundamentally from the psychological difficulty of changing ourselves to match or reflect a change in place, and hence a tendency to colour the perception of our surroundings with our everyday cares and troubles.

As such, any tourism that aims above all at mere escapism is in danger of harbouring both disappointment and an impoverished appreciation of the surroundings of the natural environment for its own sake. Inspired by Pascal's thought that '[t]he sole cause of man's unhappiness is that he does not know how to stay quietly in his room' (de Botton 2002: 243), de Botton himself advocates a kind of local tourism, which involves taking a heightened aesthetic interest in our everyday, familiar surroundings, perceiving them in greater detail, with greater reflection, and experiencing the aesthetic rewards that any place, not merely the foreign and exotic, can yield up to proper aesthetic effort. In effect, de Botton suggests at least that we should broaden our idea of travel and tourism to incorporate such 'humdrum' aesthetic experiences. We should adopt the tourist gaze – a sub-species of the old concept of 'the aesthetic attitude' – towards potentially anything and everything.

This also offers us a salutary lesson concerning the potential pitfalls of 'serious' tourism where natural beauty is concerned. On the one hand, too much effort to engage with natural beauty, to appreciate nature on its own terms, may actually hinder us from enjoying it; either because of physical discomfort that may interrupt the contemplation necessary to aesthetic appreciation, or because our mere awareness of any (even potential) damage or disturbance to natural beauty may ruin all possible experiences of it for us. Too serious an attitude to tourism and natural beauty, that is to say, may indulge a certain preciousness in some ways akin to the kind of romantic or sentimental attitudes of which more trivial modes of appreciation stand accused.

Interestingly, these observations appear to enjoy some empirical support. Some studies in environmental psychology provide evidence that 'viewing natural scenes improves mental well-being including mental alertness, attention and better cognitive performance' (Kler 2009: 120). In particular, 'Attention Restoration Theory' posits that our preferences for natural environments are grounded in certain evolved basic human needs and concerns, and reflect the need for a balance between 'active' aesthetic attention and 'passive' enjoyment:

> Tourists are drawn to natural environments because those environments possess properties which help restore fatigued psychological faculties and provide relaxation. The specific psychological facility that is restored is directed attention and the specific properties of the environment are 'being away', 'extent', 'fascination', and 'compatibility'.
>
> *(Ibid.: 127)*

Aesthetic value is thus directly connected to well-being and human flourishing. Through appreciating the beauties of nature we learn more about our multifarious interests and pleasures, the nature of appreciation, and the meaningfulness and emotional expressivity that natural objects in the world can attain for us. And we become aware of our own powerful and subtle capacities for discriminating and evaluating. In learning all of this we are also cultivating and exercising the cognitive, perceptual and imaginative capacities that are central to our flourishing as human beings. The importance of the aesthetic in tourist motivations and experiences of the natural environment, therefore, cannot be underestimated.

References

de Botton, A. (2002) *The Art of Travel*. London: Penguin.

Brady, E. (2003) *Aesthetics of the Natural Environment*. Edinburgh: Edinburgh University Press.

Budd, M. (2002) *The Aesthetic Appreciation of Nature: Essays on the Aesthetics of Nature*. Oxford: Clarendon Press.

Carlson, A. (2000) *Aesthetics and the Environment: The Appreciation of Nature, Art and Architecture*. London: Routledge.

Eaton, M. (2004) 'Fact and Fiction in the Aesthetic Appreciation of Nature', in Carlson, A. and Berleant, A. (eds), 170–81.

Fennell, D. (2006) *Tourism Ethics*, Clevedon: Channel View Publications.

Foster, C. (2004) 'The Narrative and the Ambient in Environmental Aesthetics', in Carlson, A. and Berleant, A. (eds), 197–213.

Godlovitch, S. (2004) 'Icebreakers: Environmentalism and Natural Aesthetics', in Carlson, A. and Berleant, A. (eds), 108–26.

Hepburn, R. (1995) 'Trivial and serious in aesthetic appreciation of nature', in Kemal, S. and Gaskell, I. (eds), 65–80.

——(2004) 'Contemporary Aesthetics and the Neglect of Natural Beauty', in Carlson, A. and Berleant, A. (eds), 43–62.

Kler, B. (2009) 'Tourism and Restoration' in Tribe J. (ed.), 117–34.

Lasua, D. (2007) 'Eiffel Tower Key Chains and Other Pieces of Reality: the Philosophy of Souvenirs', *The Philosophical Forum*, 271–87.

Macfarlane, R. (2003) *Mountains of the Mind*. London: Granta.

Saito, Y. (1984) 'Is there a Correct Aesthetic Appreciation of Nature?', *Journal of Aesthetic Education* 18, 35–46.

——(1998) 'The Aesthetics of Unscenic Nature', *Journal of Aesthetics and Art Criticism* 56, 101–11.

——(2004) 'Appreciating Nature on Its Own Terms', in Carlson, A. and Berleant, A. (eds), pp. 141–55.

Shiner, L. (1994) ''Primitive Fakes', 'Tourist Art', and the Ideology of Authenticity', *Journal of Aesthetics and Art Criticism*, 52, 225–34.

Stecker, R. (1997) 'The Correct and the Appropriate in the Appreciation of Nature', *British Journal of Aesthetics* 37, 393–402.

Todd, C. (2009) 'Nature, Beauty and Tourism', in Tribe, J. (ed.), 154–70.

Tribe, J. (ed.) (2009) *Philosophical Issues in Tourism*. London: Channel View Press.

Urry, J. (2002) *The Tourist Gaze*. London: Sage.

Further reading

Berleant, A. (1995) 'The aesthetics of art and nature', in Kemal, S. and Gaskell, I. (eds), 228–43.

Carlson, A. and Berleant, A. (eds) (2004) *The Aesthetics of Natural Environments*. Ontario: Broadview Press.

Carroll, N. (1995), 'On being moved by nature: between religion and natural history', in Kemal, S. and Gaskell, I. (eds), 244–66.

Cooper, D. and Palmer, J. (eds) (n.d.) *The Environment in Question: Ethical and global issues*. London: Routledge.

Kaplan, R. and Kaplan, S. (1989) *The Experience of Nature. A Psychological Perspective*, Cambridge: CUP.

Kemal, S. and Gaskell, I. (eds) (1995) *Landscape, Natural Beauty and the Arts*, Cambridge: CUP.

Matthews, P. (2002) 'Scientific Knowledge and the Aesthetic Appreciation of Nature', *Journal of Aesthetics and Art Criticism* 60, 37–48.

Pearce, P. (2005) *Tourist Behaviour: Themes and Conceptual Schemes*. Clevedon: Channel View Press.

Saito, Y. (1998) 'The Aesthetics of Unscenic Nature', *Journal of Aesthetics and Art Criticism* 56, 101–11.

Stecker, R. (1997) 'The Correct and the Appropriate in the Appreciation of Nature', *British Journal of Aesthetics* 37, 393–402.

8

Viewing nature politically

Adrian Franklin

It is often imagined that tourism is a unique form of social space, distinguishable, broadly, from the everyday (MacCannell 1976), the world of work (Urry 1990) and the serious governmental and business concerns of the social centre (Shields 1990). Such 'touristic' places on the so-called social margin were deemed to be sociologically distinguishable as *ludic* places (Rojek 1993; Shields 1990), or as merely *ritual locations* of recreation, social reproduction and transition (see Franklin 2003 and 2009 for a discussion of this). Worse, some, have argued that tourism creates and transits through, many forms of non-*place*; of airports, aircraft, route ways, resorts etc., (Auge 1995) and 'spaces of travel' that are neither the social centre nor yet the social margin (Urry 2000).

All of this creates, and indeed maintains a view, commonly held outside scholarly circles, that tourism and its social-spatial contexts are somehow less important, less crucial, *less politically charged* than other activities and their social-spatial contexts. This is the only possible explanation for its relative obscurity in French intellectual life (Doquet and Evrard 2008), for example, or indeed why elsewhere it is confined to a substantive and operational form of *commerce* (Franklin and Crang 2001).

For some time there has been a strand of research that politicises tourism, particularly from the point of view of those host peoples, islands and localities who have been adversely affected by the arrival and operation of tourism in their localities or where the arrival of tourism has created a new politics and economy around tourism as a dominant economic industry (Smith 1989). Although significant, this has not spawned a more general concern to understand how tourism at a broader and more fundamental level is deeply politicised, deeply informed by political and ethical concerns of the mainstream and plays a role in the enactment of important social and political change in modern societies. If anything, such studies, laudable as they are, perpetuate the view of tourism on the social margin.

Taking the example of the curious history of our desire to visit, be among and in various ways consume nature, this chapter seeks to show how the tourism impulse and the anthropology of tourism has been deeply infected by major social and political currents in modernity, and how it has been, rather than an epiphenomenon of questionable intellectual importance, a central means of *enacting and realising* a range of important new projects of humanity. As Keith Thomas (1983) ably showed, the drive to experience 'nature' is neither an inevitable nor a universal characteristic of humanity, although we can agree with Raymond Williams (1992) when he alerts us to the very common way in which nature is appealed to as a source of inspiration and guidance for *social order*. Only in the absence of a rigorous survey of the anthropology of nature could anyone envisage *biophilia* as universal.

Given this, and its potential to deliver opposed and contested interpretations, the exact manner by which we comport ourselves before nature can drive a politics of nature tourism with very radical and wide-ranging consequences. This chapter aims to outline the main ways this politics has framed the development of nature tourism. The historic scope of this reaches back to formative ideas in early modern Europe, particularly in England, which is something of a cradle of tourism. It establishes the sense of social order that was formed around a religious idiom of nature, with both moral and social implications for behaviour and practice but also as a deeply embedded cultural space of belonging. The notion of travel to it was barely relevant to a largely rural society living cheek-by-jowl with the natural world, but it *did* lay the foundations for subsequent travel and visitation when that culture moved to the city and developed modern sensibilities that were seen to oppose an older natural order. This then situates the origins and arrival of Romanticism and its critique of modernity through, once again, the *idiom* of nature. Romanticism not only created a sense of pilgrimage and redemption around visits to nature, it also invoked a politics of protection and conservation, which sat awkwardly with the demo-cratising currents of an emerging tourism culture. Seen through the early twentieth-century form of tourism, dominated largely by a motorised middle class, the politics of Romanticism built an accommodation around a set of *national* institutions, the model of which was the National Trust. In this way, participation in nature was patriotic and also supportive of an apparatus of conservation. Through the mid-twentieth century this celebration of rural England enrolled more and more enthusiasts and as car ownership expanded, a new perception, of nature being overwhelmed by tourists, was added to a new politics of nature. This *environmental* view of nature framed around the critique of modernity as a toxic danger to something much wider and more abstract than a sacred temple of nature, the English countryside.

As a new political idiom of nature, *environment* detached English (as other) cultures from specific relationships with particular kinds of species, landscapes and ways of life, and rendered it into a global, universal and totalising entity, both bigger, more powerful and yet more remote from experience. Rather like the God figure of the Christian worldview, environment required mediation from ritual specialists, and environment empowered a newly politicised scientific fraternity to become, as Bauman (1992) astutely observes, 'legislators' – people who govern and order the world by virtue of their *expertise*. In turn, the expertise of scientists required an alli-ance with and mediation through those with economic and political power, and hence the clear sense of nation leadership and consensus around countryside was not really possible for envir-onment. Because poetical leaders required a policy objective to be distilled from the always-vague discourse of risk emanating from science (Furedi 2005), the notion of *sustainability* became the new objective that governed our primary relationship with nature. As Macnaghten and Urry (1998) argue, this created yet another politics built around a notion of nature as a *separate* domain from humanity, and one to be protected against the predations of humanity, generally.

From approximately the 1980s until the present a neo-liberal nature tourism can be discerned with the following qualities: an aesthetic of nature as delicate and facing multiple anthropogenic dangers and risks; a larger visiting public informed less from traditional nature associations or the benefits of nature to humanity than by information relating to the risks they pose to nature through their visitation; consistent with this, an increasing willingness to be separated from the nature they visit and submission to an escalating bureaucracy of regulation and other forms of external and self-discipline; a concomitant willingness to pay for more commodified forms of nature tourism where nature is packaged less as trails of discovery and more as ecotourism experiences or 'encounters' (highly packaged, circumscribed, regulated and controlled episodes of sustainable contact with increasing emphasis on ecological and environmental political objectives) (Dickens 2004; Bulbeck 2000; Desmond 1999).

Being with nature and the Christian worldview

I want to begin this section by re-examining how the Christian worldview of nature came to involve certain consequences for our relationship with it, but also, how its aesthetic, ethical and economic fields are still in operation (although in entirely unacknowledged, 'taken for granted' forms). It is a re-examination, mostly of Keith Thomas' (1983) masterful treatment of this subject, at least in the case of England from the late Middle Ages until the nineteenth century. Any anthropologist worth their salt will agree with Claude Levi-Strauss' (1962: 89) dictum that 'animal (and other natural forms) are good to think', by which he meant that it is a universal feature of our species to form basic understandings of themselves in relation to the natural world around them; not least drawing on an understanding of the natural world to determine what is properly human (Tester 1992). It follows then, that such understandings often lie at the centre of social and political change. As Thomas (1983: 17) himself remarks: 'The subject also has a great deal to offer historians, for it is impossible to disentangle what the people of the past thought about plants and animals from what they thought about themselves'.

The Christian worldview of nature as it manifested itself to thinkers and writers in Tudor and Stuart England was informed by Aristotle in that nature was understood to be a functional facility made largely for the sake of humankind. Nature's design was purposeful and directed to specific forms of use by humans and was executed by a talented higher authority in that it was economic and sparingly achieved through its use of resources and detail. This provided a framework with which the Bible might be interpreted and this gave way to what has become known as the design theory of creation but also in political and ethical terms the *Great Chain of Being*, as there was not only the question of design in nature but also of precedent and rights.

The Christian worldview of nature was also loosely mapped onto pagan beliefs and understandings, which, because of the directions given to Augustine, the first Christian missionary sent from Rome, were not discouraged or damned out of court. Rather, Augustine was told to try to insert Christianity into pre-existing forms of religion rather than replace them. This then accounts for the other tradition, at least in England, of a natural world that was *enchanted*: landscapes were animated by a variety of powers and agents, which provided a means of understanding not only the external world of non-humans but also much of what happened to humans. As with many other pre-modern cultures, the ethical, social and political world of humans was continuous with those of other species and forms, and there existed an overarching order that governed all life (Franklin 2002: 39–60). Something like that system of thought gave rise, again in the English tradition, to the *Mother Nature* figure as the spirit of nature itself, in addition to the many semi-autonomous powers belonging to individual species (hence a hare lip in a human was attributed to a hare crossing the path of a pregnant woman).

This enchanted world of humans in nature was a generous, social system rather than something to be feared, and, because of the required reciprocities between the elements, there were many human obligations to maintain and look after the world around them. An obvious example is the practice, still alive today although mostly misunderstood, of bringing elements of the forest into the home during the deepest and coldest period of winter. Logs and branches of trees were brought in the home to keep their spirits alive during the coldest periods (today called Yule Logs). The magical mistletoe, holly and ivy (that inexplicably fruits out of season) were also given shelter at this time and are still used to decorate the home at Christmas. The fact that these pagan practices were rolled into Christian rituals at Christmas shows the hybridity of English religious practices. However, the notion of responsibility for, and connection to, nature did not entirely die, nor did a multitude of other pagan beliefs and practices despite subsequently becoming the subject of religious oppression. The fact that it is possible to trace a continuous line of such folk practices and its welling up in literature, prose and poetry illustrates how it has continued to work into the present (Thomas 1983).

These antecedent themes to modern attitudes and practices toward nature provide the social base for a number of ways in which nature became aestheticised and thus desired as a place in which to visit or spend time. The most obvious one, which is often missed, is the *pastorale landscape*. In this aesthetic tradition, which has Greek, Roman and British forms, it is the balanced sense of *cohabitation* of human and non-human elements that is crucial. Here is the twin injunction on humans to live in balance and harmony with the benevolent and *giving* natural order, on the one hand, and on the other, not to stay too long in the city where this balance and healthiness is easily lost to other harmful impulses, like business and politics. In the early nineteenth century this is apparent in Jane Austen's *Pride and Prejudice* where the balance of nature and artifice in 'good' estates such as Pemberley are 'keys to the social virtue of their owners' (Bodenheimer 1981: 605). Keith Thomas (1983: 245–7) has assembled a procession of literary references to an association commonly held in Tudor England, that their towns were associated with vice and the countryside virtue. According to Thomas the 'classical convention that country dwellers were not just healthier, but morally more admirable than those who lived in the city, was a conspicuous literary theme in English literature of the seventeenth and eighteenth centuries' (Thomas 1983: 246).

In its English manifestation as 'countryside', the pastoral landscape seems to have had a continuous and sustained life as the aesthetic heart of the country. We know this for two reasons. It is unquestionable, for example, that the social elites of Tudor and Stuart England showed a distinct preference for living in the countryside, on their agricultural estates, and even when better transport made wintering in the cities possible, they always returned in the summer (ibid.: 247). Thus, even when the city-based intellectual elites of early modern England felt nature to be backward, unpleasant and even disgusting, a view that was generalised in Hobbes' view of the *State of Nature* as 'nasty, brutish and short', the balance of opinion at least across the educated classes was otherwise. For the uneducated rural peasantry there is only indirect evidence, albeit compelling. The first is the obvious despair that many felt when the countryside was cleared of their presence following the Enclosure Acts of the eighteenth and nineteenth centuries. A more poignant register of their values and aesthetics comes via the unusual route of housing research. According to Darnton, the nineteenth-century gardenless courts that were built for many rural migrants were common enough in mainland Europe, but, in England, builders and developers soon realised that renters had a distinct preference for the small villa style row cottages that boasted tiny front and rear garden spaces. Eventually, such was this preference that court building was largely abandoned and these small gardens of England eventually amounted to a space the size of Somerset. The gardens were very telling as they carried on the tradition of rural cottage gardens, and, in effect, became a means by which the country was taken into the city, at least as the most immediate space around most dwellings.

Thus, it seems that although we may talk about many shifts and changes in the aesthetic sensibilities that governed how we viewed and visited the natural world; it also makes some sense to take stock of important continuities. The arrival of the Romantic sensibility, for example, that introduced an aesthetic for wilderness spaces beyond the cultivated countryside, although important, may have been exaggerated in its appeal and cultural penetration beyond small, educated, artistic elites. Even for most people who had left the countryside for a life in industrial cities, it was true that most did not live far from the rural fringe and that these rural fringes were favoured spaces of leisure (Franklin 2002: 83–131). It was also true that extensive railway links provided the means to visit the countryside, often back to places of origin where the visitor still had relatives and friends. The travel posters issued by London Transport provide an important window on where Londoners travelled to for day trips and holidays. Not only is it the case that the southern countryside dominates these destinations of preference, but also that new areas of the city were first colonised as countryside commuter villages by London Underground (Green 1990).

Macnaghten and Urry (1998) have shown how in the twentieth century the notion of the English countryside was further entrenched politically as a largely 'endangered' entity of national significance, pointing up how it was thus socially constructed, but it was also true that for aesthetic, cultural and ethnic reasons, the English countryside was already embedded in the sensibilities and practices of a large number of English people, as well as in their literature and art.

The politics of Romanticism

Despite the foregoing it is probably acceptable to identify a tipping point in the aesthetic and political sensibilities of nature wrought by the Romantic Movement. The Romantic conception of nature and its connection to a moral and political order was, after all, extremely different. The key change was in identifying the principal mode of production as out of balance with aesthetic and traditional relationships between nature and society. Whereas prior to the capitalist mode of production, people lived on the land and had established a largely sustainable relationship with nature, the capitalist mode of agricultural production alongside an unquenchable demand for forest and other natural resources from industrial capitalism was clearly *unsustainable*, aesthetically moribund and destroying traditional relationships.

In many ways Romanticism represents a shift from the quasi-religious folk knowledge base at the heart of traditional relationships with nature and towards a more intellectualised means of knowing, principally through imagination, art and language. Much though the romantics cherished folk knowledges, folklore and traditional crafts, and much though they liked to see the presence of traditional forms of humanity on the landscape (dry-stone walls, hedges and cottages for example), they were not a traditional folk revival but an intellectual middle class elite, albeit influential and quirky.

To begin with, as Tester (1992) reminds us, the Romantics were a relatively small and singular circle of artistic and intellectual *outsiders*. Neither outcast by the formal cultural and political mainstream, nor descended from the cultural margins themselves, their outsider status derived mostly from a wish not to engage in politics directly but indirectly, through their artistic and creative works as well as by example, by identifying a new way to live with nature, outside the landscapes sullied by industry and industrial-styled agriculture. Walking, open-air sketching, nature study and climbing were all championed by Romantic enthusiasts.

By the late eighteenth century to the early nineteenth century, the English countryside had been massively changed through modernisation and expansion. The highly disturbing impact of steam technology, hitherto confined to despised factories in industrial towns, had found agricultural applications and the charming obscurity of its quiet backwaters had been opened up by the violating penetration of railway expansion – which the Romantics painted as a deranged monster destroying the world.

In this way, the spatial remoteness (and hence distinctiveness) of countryside was diminished as well as being aesthetically and morally sullied. By rejecting large swathes of countryside, the

Romantics were, in effect, identifying that the pastoral as a morally balanced entity had been compromised, and we begin to hear 'end of nature' tones in their creative projects.

As the pastoral landscapes abutted most towns and cities, we can sense the notion of proper nature having shifted to those places beyond their hinterlands and away from their influence. Given that any semblance of balance was now impossible between nature and modern agriculture, the former countryside slipped back from its aesthetic and moral centrality and was replaced by a very different conception of nature: that which was untouched and unsullied by mankind. Hence the notion of wilderness was, if not invented, upgraded and enshrined in an astonishing canon of literary and artistic works, new lifestyles and modes of comportment in natural areas. Now, the tension balance between nature and artifice was replaced by an aesthetic of nature in the raw, an untrammelled nature that was free to show a side rarely ever seen: a landscape devoid of human presence. Much of this 'human absence' was in itself a product of political, moral and legal processes in which former peasants, cottagers, crofters and others had been slowly removed or discouraged from staying in ancient upland and remote homelands, grouse moors, highland estates and mountain ranges. In colonial America, Australia and Africa, such wilderness areas, many enshrined as National Parks were predicated on the removal and relocation of indigenous peoples who once hunted and gathered there (Turnball 1972; Löfgren 1989; Cronon 1998; Franklin 2006).

New sensibilities such as these grew to appreciate not balance but overwhelming power; the push of nature as witnessed by storm, glacier, rapid and eruption. Nature shifted its location to the outer, remote and highland margins, to isolated and (if possible) dangerous coastal locations; to exotic colonial locations cleared of desert people, arctic hunters, mountain, island and forest people. In a sense, Romantics were lured into an aesthetic of nature without humanity, rather than alongside it, as it had always been, and this ushered in a sense of nature as privileged, deserving and *prior*, as well as being sacred.

When this sensibility was combined with the beginnings of 'risk society' in the 1960s, with the sense that mankind was destroying not just favoured landscapes but the environment itself, this idealised separation of nature from humanity became more entrenched and was translated into a more regulated and controlled humanity, particularly when visiting rare and endangered ecosystems protected across the globe. Nature was commodified into hived-off and themed visiting spaces as well as protected from direct *contact* and *impact* (Dickens 2004).

The new nature tourism was to create spaces for a visiting public that only minimally encroached on wildness and separateness. Such spaces grew considerably after 1980, when a new neo-liberal political sensibility upheld individual liberties to travel, the conservation ethic and the role of small businesses in the revitalisation of de-industrialised rural economies around the world. Neo-liberal views on nature travel and tourism were also shaped by a variant of conservational sentiments that Cartmill (1993) called 'Darwinian'. This belongs to that long tradition of hunting and outdoor movements that believed that human health and well-being was destroyed by office work and city lifestyles. The solution to modern living therefore is to spend a long time in nature, shooting, fishing, being self-sufficient and learning woodcrafts. It has a major social base in the USA and Canada, Scandinavia and other parts of Europe and Australia, and this too drives a form of tourism that is often very opposed to the politics of 'non-contact' with nature. It has been implicated in many fierce political battles over nature and natural areas, and counts on some very influential political backers and organisations (Franklin 1999).

Neo-liberal nature tourism

In the 1980s the arrival of neo-liberal politics, the free market, individualism and the decline of state-lead organisation and provision did not usher in an immediate shift in thinking about the politics of nature tourism. Being a child of conservative politics, neo-liberalism was intuitively conservative about nature herself. The conservative elites of the USA, the UK and Europe were, by inclination, an elite who had long usurped power and control over the countryside and had created very ample playgrounds from it, largely for their own purposes. Magazines like *The Field* continued in the 1980s to associate a social elite with the main forms of nature recreation, from riding, to hunting, fishing, walking, driving, tourism and gardening, as well as acquiring properties to live in or holiday in natural settings. Additionally, a powerful sub-set of the middle classes aspired to a similar lifestyle and together they had very specific interests to maintain by keeping such 'nature leisurescapes' intact.

Although many of the Romantic heroes were politically reclusive and inactive (and if anything, left wing) they, and their works, became championed by conservative culture. At the same time, the collapse of the left in post-1980s politics and the eventual political consensus around neo-liberal values (espoused by the Blair government in the UK and Clinton in the USA), saw a shift in political values away from what Inglehardt (1997) describes as the materialist politics of housing, income, food and consumables and towards a *postmaterialist* politics with concerns about the *quality of life* (human rights, sexuality, the quality of air, water and other environment issues). Hence, when environmentalism began to draw strength through the 1980s and into the 1990s, its support base was widely distributed. Nature and ecotourism were particularly important as they fulfilled duties to protect and conserve the countryside and wilderness fringes, but also because they delivered jobs and employment to the massively restructured industrial economy of the outer regional areas, now facing poverty.

Indeed, the politics of nature and ecotourism in neo-liberal times hinged on the relationship between the deepening poverty of rural and third world regions (and the affluence and mobilities of the hub nations) and the absence of strong regional policy (Bauman 1998; Urry 2000). Precisely because ecotourism could be delivered through countless thousands of new ecobusinesses, operating privately or in partnership with state or non-governmental organisations, nature tourism was quick to emerge and it emerged everywhere (Fennell 1999).

Increasingly, the state becomes less directly concerned with managing risk to nature directly and more involved as an information giver (Crook 1999), and also to partner private contractors in the nature tourism industry who thus became the disciplinary interface with tourists (Macnaghten and Urry 1998; Bulbeck 2000). This information is fed through to the individual who is required to make difficult decisions in the face of the confusing noise of conflicting claims, often from within science itself and this confusion is very evident in research on the nature tourist (Bulbeck 2000). Although nature maintained its therapeutic benefit to humanity in this period, the human benefits of travel to nature now took second place to the conservation ethic. In fact, the growth in tourism numbers meant that tourists were then interpreted as a *threat* to the true beneficiary of policy, nature herself. In addition to the self-disciplined individualism of informed choice, the tourist had to be disciplined by new social-spatial practices, designed to minimise damage and maintain spaces of separation; in effect, there was now a widespread apartheid in operation.

In order to fund this additional burden of human management and fulfil neo-liberal aims to reduce public spending, nature had to become more self-funding or commodified. Thus, although we saw an increasing regulation and control of human behaviour in natural areas, we also saw a proliferation of businesses that sell nature in this new controlled form, often with streams of funding making its way back to 'natural' or ecological 'subjects'. Even so, their combined effect and the variable quality of delivery caused Martha Honey (2002: 24) to question their value as a *human* industry: 'Because the stakeholders have various goals, profit not the least of them, ecotourism is not a panacea for developing countries who might want to take advantage of their natural resources – in some cases ecotourism is not much better than mining'.

Finally, and consistent with the above, in the past 30 years those spaces on the margins where human impact is minimal or minimised by enforced removal/resettlement have taken on increased value. In some nations where these so-called wilderness areas are more common, there has been a parallel tendency for areas with more human impact and interaction to *lose* their status as natural areas, and thus their desirability among tourists (Franklin 2006). This has had the unfortunate effect of pressuring wilderness areas with visitor demand while leaving very large areas of mixed natural habitat and farming devoid of interest (Franklin 2002). Paradoxically, these areas often contain the rarest and most endangered species and very high levels of biodiversity (Low 2002).

Conclusion

Sometimes it is extremely important to step outside the always-politicised nature of the present with the perspective of anthropology. Today, it might be considered inconceivable to imagine our world as anything other than divided into a past dominated by nature, when humanity was benign or relatively absent as a shaping force, and the present time of humanity, when nature is rapidly in decline and becoming itself disturbingly absent. Anthropology tempers such strong oppositions and reversal myths:

> To begin with humans modify the world around them on an enormous scale, and have done so through co-evolutionary interactions for many thousands of years. Effectively all landscapes with which humans routinely interact are therefore cultural: and our environment is every bit as much what is made socially as what is not. How strange, then, that in another version of the biological imagination (that of classical evolutionary taxonomy) domesticated animals and non-endemics are, somehow, *not* the real thing. The complexities of biological reality, enhanced by the insights of modern ecology and genetics, make drawing the boundary between what is cultural and what is natural, almost impossible.
>
> *(Ellen and Fukui 1996: 14–15)*

Not surprisingly, indigenous peoples around the world sense this, as did the ancestors of modern societies. This partly explains why the relationship between nature and culture was redolent with ethical and political implications because they were both implicated in a common economic and moral universe. For modern city-dwelling people (and Fennell 1999 reminds us that most ecotourists are affluent city-dwellers), the politics of nature tourism reflects this in that it describes a tension between, on the one hand, a drive to become re-embedded in nature (to be a part of it; to find one's true self, health, etc.) and, on the other, the drive to protect it (to act rationally and acknowledge that wild and human domains should be not be breached or compromised). In Bulbeck's (2000: 7) terms, this tension surfaces in animal-encounter tourism, where ecotourism guides demand strict separation and confront tourists' heartfelt desire to touch, feel, engage and relate. In many ways, exactly the same tension was acknowledged by Hobbes and Locke who saw the politics of nature in opposed ways (Macnaghten and Urry 1998). For Hobbes, wild nature was the absolute other, the opposite from what was properly human, whereas Locke saw nature as offering humanity a metaphor of civility, balance and justice.

Certainly some spaces of nature tourism that only a few years ago were seen as imperative to uphold and protect are in the process of being rethought. Wilderness, for example, is now considered an ecologically problematic and politically unfortunate concept, which, in turn, creates doubts and anxieties about the way other forms of contact, visitation and encounter proceed. Far from having identified an agreed-upon strategy and programme for the future, nature tourism is an illustration of nature's highly contested and fluid future.

References

Auge, M. (1995) *Non-Places: Introduction to an Anthropology of Supermodernity*. London: Verso.

Bauman, Z. (1992) *Intimations of Postmodernity*. London: Routledge.

——(1998) *Globalisation*. Cambridge: Polity.

Bodenheimer, R. (1981) 'Looking at the Landscape in Jane Austen', *Studies in English Literature, 1500–1900*, 21(4), Nineteenth Century (Autumn, 1981), 605–23.

Bulbeck, C. (2000) *Encountering the Wild*. London: Earthscan.

Cartmill, M. (1993) *A View to a Death in the Morning*. Cambridge, MA: Harvard University Press.

Cronon, W. (1998) 'The Trouble with Wilderness, or, Getting Back to the Wrong Nature.' in J.B. Caldicott, and M.P. Nelson (eds) *The Great New Wilderness Debate*. Athens: University of Georgia Press.

Crook, S. (1999). 'Ordering risks. *Risk and Sociocultural theory: new directions and perspectives.*' D. Lupton. Cambridge: Cambridge University Press.

Desmond, J.C. (1999) *Staging Tourism*. Chicago, IL: Chicago University Press.

Dickens, P. (2004) *Society and Nature*. Cambridge: Polity.

Doquet, A. and Evrard, O. (2008) 'An Interview with Jean-Didier Urbain', *Tourist Studies*, 8(2), 175–92.

Ellen R. and Fukui, K. (eds) (1996) *Redefining Nature*. Oxford: Berg.

Fennell, D.A. (1999) *Ecotourism*. London: Routledge.

Franklin, A.S. (1999) *Animals and Modern Cultures*. London: Sage.

——(2002) *Nature and Social Theory*. London: Sage.

——(2003) *Tourism*. London: Sage.

——(2004) 'Tourism as Ordering: Towards a New Ontology of Tourism', *Tourist Studies* 4(3), 645–57.

——(2006) 'The Humanity of the Wilderness Photo', *Australian Humanities Review*, 28, April: 1–16.

——(2009) 'The Sociology of Tourism', in Jamal T. and Robinson M. (eds) *Handbook of Tourism Studies*. London: Sage, pp. 65–82.

Franklin, A. S. and Crang, M. (2001) 'The trouble with tourism and travel theory?', *Tourist Studies* 1(1): 5–22.

Furedi, F. (2005) *Politics of Fear*. London: Pluto.

Green, O. (1990) *Underground Art*. London: Laurence King.

Honey, M. (2002) *Ecotourism and Sustainable Development*, 2nd edn. Who Owns Paradise? (2nd edn) Vancouver: Island Press.

Levi-Strauss, C. (1962) *La Pensee Sauvage*. Paris: Libraire Plon.

Löfgren, O. (1989) 'The Nationalization of Culture', *Ethnologia Europaea* XIX, 2–23.

Low, T. (2002) *The New Nature*. Melbourne: Penguin.

MacCannell, D. (1976). *The Tourist: A New Theory of the Leisure Class*. New York: Schocken Books.

Macnaghten, P. and Urry, J. (1998) *Contested Natures*. London: Sage.

Rojek, C. (1993) *Ways of Escape*. London: MacMillan.

Shields, R. (1990) *Places on the Margin*. London: Routledge.

Smith, V. (ed.) (1989) *Hosts and Guests*. Philadelphia: University of Pennsylvania Press.

Tester, K. (1992) *Animals and Society: The Humanity of Animal Rights*: London: Routledge.

Thomas, K. (1983) *Man and the Natural World: Changing Attitudes in England 1500–1800*. Harmondsworth: Penguin.

Turnbull, C. (1972) *The Mountain People*

Urry, J. (1990). *The Tourist Gaze*. London: Sage.

——(2000) *Sociology Beyond societies: Mobilities for the Twenty-first Century*. London: Routledge.

Williams, R. (1992) 'Ideas of Nature', in J. Benthal (ed.) *Ecology, The Shaping Enquiry*. London: Longman.

9

Using complexity theory to develop understanding of tourism and the environment

Nancy Stevenson

Introduction

An understanding of tourism and the environment requires an appreciation of the inter-connected and multiple relationships between humans and their surroundings. The inter-play between nature and society in a rapidly changing world creates problems that are highly complex, constantly evolving and ambiguous. These complex problems are not easily understood by traditional linear methods, and researchers in a wide range of disciplines are now exploring what complexity theory might offer to develop understanding of social/environmental interactions. Farrell and Twining-Ward (2004) perceive the problem in tourism thus:

> The central problem is that tourism researchers schooled in a tradition of linear, specialized, predictable, deterministic, cause-and-effect science, are working in an area of study that is largely nonlinear, integrative, generally unpredictable, qualitative and characterized by causes giving rise to multiple outcomes, quite out of proportion to initial input.
>
> *(Farrell and Twining-Ward 2004: 277)*

This chapter investigates and reviews approaches to, and applications of, complexity theory as a way of developing understanding the relationships between tourism and the environment. There is no unified version of complexity theory reflected in the diversity of applications and approaches that have been used in the tourism literature. These will be identified and briefly discussed under three main headings; chaos and complexity, ecological perspectives and social perspectives. Under each of the headings, specific applications of complexity theory in the tourism field will be identified.

The chapter illustrates and interrogates several complexity concepts referring to case study material and uses a hypothetical resort to explore interactions between its social and ecological aspects. Suggestions are made about how complexity theory might be developed to advance knowledge and understanding of tourism in a way that reflects the relationships between linked social and environmental worlds.

Complexity theory

Byrne defines complexity theory as:

> the interdisciplinary understanding of reality as composed of complex open systems with emergent properties and transformational potential.
>
> *(Byrne 2005: 95)*

Multiple approaches have been developed across different disciplinary fields as researchers have sought to understand various aspects of diverse systems within complex environments (Mitleton-Kelly 1998; Medd 2001a; Stevenson *et al.* 2009). Complexity theory has been developed across disciplines; initially natural sciences (e.g. Prigogine and Stengers 1984), physics (Gell Mann 1994), biology (Goodwin 1997), computer science (Traub and Werschultz 1998) and economics (Brian Arthur *et al.* 1997), and more recently education (Tosey 2002), management (Stacey 2003), spatial planning (Healey 2007) and sociology (Byrne 2001, 2005; Harvey 2001; Urry 2003, 2005a, 2005b). It is not possible to identify one complexity theory; however, there has been a degree of sharing and borrowing ideas across these different disciplines.

Complexity theory and tourism

A growing number of tourism studies make reference to concepts and ideas from complexity science. They draw from different strands and apply theories in widely varying ways and include a focus on the following: chaotic elements or events (McKercher 1999; Faulkner and Russell 1997); the roles, power and tensions between groups in the policy making process (Tyler and Dinan 2001; Stevenson *et al.* 2009; Zahra and Ryan 2007); entrepreneurs and destination development (Russell and Faulkner 1999, 2004); as a way of progressing sustainability research (Farrell and Twining-Ward 2004, 2005; McDonald 2009; Plummer and Fennel 2009); as a way of understanding the perceptions and behaviour of tourists (Lacitignola *et al.* 2010); and the inter-dependent networks involved in providing tourism services and preserving the ecology at a specific at a destination (Pavolvitch 2009).

Farrell and Twining-Ward (2005), Stevenson *et al.* (2009) and Zahra and Ryan (2007) identify the *complexity* of complexity science and some of the debates about method and approach. However, in tourism literature it is often difficult to ascertain the sources, boundaries and assumptions that underlie the complexity concepts as they are applied in the field. The next section will briefly consider three approaches to complexity in the tourism literature.

Chaos and complexity

Chaos and complexity theories have been used in the study of tourism phenomena, particularly incidents and aspects of which are perceived to be chaotic. For example, Russell and Faulkner (1999, 2004) draw from both theories to evaluate entrepreneurial activity on resort development on the Gold Coast in Australia. Faulkner and Russell (1997, 2001, 2003), McKercher (1999), and Russell and Faulkner (1999, 2004) use complexity theory to challenge models and methods that conceptualise tourism phenomena in a simplified, linear manner. They claim that these models ignore both the complexity and dynamism of those phenomena and the environments within which they operate. Their research plays an important role in developing studies that highlight the shortcomings of linear modelling and the potential contribution of both chaos and complexity theory to the understanding of tourism problems.

Ecological perspectives

McDonald (2009), Plummer and Fennel (2009), Ruiz-Ballesteros (2011) and Urry (2005a, 2005b) draw from complexity theory as a way of considering the relationships between the natural and social world. Farrell and Twining-Ward (2004, 2005) claim that although tourism research recognises the relationships between human and ecosystems, it has tended to treat them separately and has been dominated by approaches and interpretations from the social sciences. They call for an approach that draws from developments in ecosystem ecology and highlight research that involves futures modelling and stakeholder workshops to support adaptive systems thinking and scenario building (2005). They claim holistic understanding of the complex adaptive systems in which tourism activities take place might lead to a more sustainable approach. Farrell and Twining-Ward suggest a paradigm shift or 'reconceptualization of the structure of tourism study' (2004: 288) indicating that complexity theory surmounts or surpasses existing approaches. Other researchers are more cautious suggesting that 'room should be made for a diversification of perspectives' (Faulkner and Russell 2003: 216) and that complexity theory might involve 'reconstructing the tools and theories that we already have' (Byrne 2005: 98).

Social perspectives

A third strand of literature has emerged more recently, which has been used to understand the complexities underlying changes in organisation structures (Zahra and Ryan 2007), to understand networks and communications (Bramwell 2006) and the process of developing and enacting policy (Stevenson 2006; Stevenson *et al.* 2008, 2009). Stevenson's approach to understanding the policy process is developed from 'looser' (Van Uden 2005) interpretations of complexity and draws from the work of Byrne (2001, 2005), Fonseca (2002), Harvey (2001), Medd (2001a, b), Shaw (2002), Stacey (2003) and Tsoukas and Hatch (2001). These researchers reject traditional model building as a way of seeking to understand complex phenomena in society. Their concerns arise not just around the issues of reducing and simplifying complex phenomena in order to model them, but also around the mistaken assumption that the researcher can analyse the world in an objective-free way. They argue against the direct importation of scientific approaches to modelling complex social phenomena and for looser, nuanced, exploratory and more reflective approaches.

Exploring relationships between society and the environment

The particular interest in complexity theory in this chapter is its potential to explore relationships between what Urry (2005b) terms the physical, biological and social worlds. There is growing debate about the tensions that arise between the activities of humans and their impact on the environment. Some argue that increased interaction and mobility of people at the global scale has resulted in a profound change in the Earth's environment leading to climatic and ecological changes outside the 'normal' ranges exhibited over the past 500,000 years (Steffan and Tyson 2004). Some draw attention to the rapidly diminishing supplies of fossil fuels (which we rely on for heat, light and transport), and the changes that these are likely to engender in our lifestyles and consumption patterns (Jones 2010).

These debates are usually framed within a discussion of sustainability, an ambiguous concept that encompasses ideas about decision-making for the longer term and taking account of the wider economic, environmental and social implications of those decisions (Hjorth and Bagheri 2006). Although many governments have made a rhetorical commitment to sustainability, interpretations vary and it has been difficult to achieve in practice. This is in the context of a global economy that is predominantly market-led, with a high priority for economic growth and efficiency, and the externalisation of the social and environmental costs. Within this system, private and individual interests dominate tourism decision-making, for example the decision to develop hotels and attractions, to offer tourism services and the decision to travel. Tourism activities present apparently contradictory tensions and are characterised by their complexity, crossing social, environmental and economic spheres, normally with the latter dominating in decision-making.

Complexity concepts

The next section will explore several 'complexity' concepts and use them to explore the dynamic relationships between human and ecological systems in a hypothetical resort. Initially the term *complex adaptive system* will be explored considering the properties and nature of complex systems. Then several relevant concepts (*co-evolution, emergence, edge of chaos* and *positive and negative feedback*) will be discussed in respect to their contributions to understanding these dynamic relationships.

Complex adaptive systems

Complexity theory seeks to understand changes in *complex adaptive systems*. The term 'complex' is used to describe a system in which interaction is detailed, and where agents make choices about their individual actions. A complex system is adaptive in that it influences and is influenced by its environment (Stevenson *et al.* 2009).

A seaside resort can be conceptualised as a complex adaptive system, which is characterised by an inter-connected social-ecosystem. The resort includes man-made elements that serve tourists and the local community such as hotels, restaurants, a marina, houses, shops and roads. It also includes natural elements, for example the sea, beach, salt marsh, estuary, fish, birds, mammals and plants and microorganisms. These natural and man-made elements are influenced by a variety of evolving processes, which are inter-dependent.

Decisions are made about the development of the resort through a social process of negotiation. These decisions are made as people with different interests and responsibilities interact with one another. Negotiations between these groups are ongoing and are shaped by the power structures within the resort and wider society, formal relationships between the public, private and third sector organisations and informal personal factors. These negotiations might involve activities that impact on the environment, such as the building of a new hotel or visitor centre. There will be a continual tension around competing development and preservation interests, and decisions might be constrained by government regulation and policy aiming to preserve aspects of the environment. Each decision about the resort involves some interests winning and some losing. In this context the idea of a complex adaptive system can be used to draw attention to the way that people within the social system provide opportunities and are constrained by linkages to each other.

Social and ecological elements of the complex system are inter-related and adapt in response to one another. Elements such as the weather, tides and currents, and erosion will provide opportunities and threats to social and biological elements. Behaviour within the system is both 'patterned' and 'unpredictable' (Battram 1998; Stacey 2003), and relationships and processes are all constantly changing.

The resort has geographically defined boundaries but its social and ecological elements intersect and are *nested* within other complex social-ecosystems, which constantly adapt and change. So, for example, the salt marsh environment will be affected not only by local activities but also by changes in global systems such as rising sea levels arising from climate change. The relationships within these *nested* systems are not hierarchical. They are constantly evolving with power flowing in many directions and non-linear relationships between cause and effect creating an unpredictable dynamic (Byrne 2005; Urry 2005a).

Emergence and co-evolution

Co-evolution is the 'simultaneous evolution of entities and their environments' encompassing ideas of 'interdependency and mutual adaptation' (Porter 2006: 6) and 'the power of interrelationships' (Battram 1998: 183). It is based on the idea that the ability of any given entity to survive depends on the niche it is filling, other entities around it, the resources it can gather and its past history (Waldrop 1992). In our imaginary resort each element adapts, or co-evolves 'within an environment in which other similar agents are also adapting, so that changes in one agent may have consequences for the environment and thus the success of other agencies' (Gilbert 1995: 148, cited in Urry 2003: 80). The process is influenced by a combination of local and global factors and is two-way, with agents evolving in relation to their environment and vice versa (Porter 2006).

Co-evolution is a powerful force for *emergence*, which arises from multiple iterations or actions at the local level. Sometimes the collective behaviour of interacting agents results in a system or part of a system adapting and creating an emergent order (Stacey 2003). This emergent order arises through innovation and learning that occurs as the internal structure of systems evolves and changes (Battram 1998; Manson 2001). From a social perspective, *emergence* can be used to draw attention to the way that allegiances and groupings emerge within our resort and the way that people outside the formal system lobby and influence powerful decision-makers. However, the focus on social behaviours provides a partial picture as peoples' decisions are affected by the fragilities and possibilities of the physical resources of destinations. In this way, *emergence* can be seen to 'flow across the supposedly distinct and purified 'physical' and 'social' domains (Urry 2003: 77).

Emergence helps us to understand how the capacity of a complex system is greater than the sum of the constituent parts (Battram 1998; Manson 2001; Stacey 2003; Waldrop 1992) or is 'somehow different from its parts' (Urry 2003: 24). Consideration of *co-evolution* and *emergence* highlight that changes within a resort may be too complex for people to control in the way suggested by 'traditional' management or planning theory. Farrell and Twining-Ward (2005), Ohl *et al.* (2010), Ruiz-Ballesteros (2011), Schianetz *et al.* (2007) and Stevenson *et al.* (2009) suggest more adaptive, co-operative, inter-disciplinary approaches, with an emphasis on exploration and learning and developing resilience.

The edge of chaos

The dynamic of *emergence* pushes systems towards the *edge of chaos* (Battram 1998; Manson 2001; Tosey 2002). This phase is also termed the *zone of complexity* (Stacey *et al.* 2000) or *bounded instability* (Mitleton-Kelly 1998), and describes the transition phase in a complex system where ordered behaviour co-exists with disordered or turbulent behaviour (Battram 1998; Mitleton-Kelly 1998). It occupies the area between order and chaos, and is a place of intense learning, innovation and creativity where change can occur easily and spontaneously as the system breaks with the past and new systems of order emerge. At the *edge of chaos* there is a paradoxical dynamic where apparently conflicting elements appear to be operating at the same time (Lewin 1993; Battram 1998; Mitleton-Kelly 1998; Stacey *et al.* 2000; Stacey 2003; Tosey 2002).

In terms of understanding the dynamics in our resort, the *edge of chaos* challenges some of the traditional assumptions that have underpinned decision-making, that is the idea that for success contradictions and paradoxes must be resolved and the tension that they cause be relaxed. The traditional approach equates success with dynamics of stability, regularity and predictability. The *edge of chaos* opens up the possibility that contradictions and paradoxes can never be resolved. It highlights the dynamics of the resort in terms of continuing tension that generates patterns that are irregular, unstable and unpredictable (Stevenson *et al.* 2009). In our resort, a longstanding approach to sewage disposal might be deemed to be sustainable (i.e. the environment can adapt to this in a way that is considered acceptable). However, this relationship is not stable and an increase in temperature in the sea or in the estuary might lead to algae accumulating rapidly, leading to 'harmful algal bloom', which threatens both wildlife and the tourism industry. The *edge of chaos* concept can be used as a way of highlighting the relationships between people and the environment and our ability to control, preserve and protect the marine environments. Urry (2005a) claims that:

> Ecological systems are on the edge of chaos without a 'natural' tendency towards equilibrium, even if all humans were to depart forever from the scene. Indeed, many ecological systems themselves depend not upon stable relationships but upon massive intrusions. Of extraordinary flows of species from other parts of the globe and of fire, lightning, hurricanes, high winds, ice storm, flash floods, frosts, earthquakes and so on. The 'normal' state of nature is thus not one of balance and repose; the normal state is to be recovering from the last disaster.
>
> *(Urry 2005a: 6)*

Positive and negative feedback

Negative feedback is 'the process required to produce the dynamics of stability' (Stacey 2003: 33), with the assumption that links between cause and effect are clear-cut and that decisions will move systems towards equilibrium (Mitleton-Kelly 1998). So, for example, the policy process models discussed by Gunn (2002) and Veal (2002) are based on the assumption of *negative feedback*. They indicate a process that includes an explicit monitoring stage where the role of the policy maker is to take action to reduce the gap between the intended and the actual outcome.

Complexity theorists (including Brian Arthur *et al.* 1997; Waldrop 1992) argue that systems are subject to *positive feedback*, which means that actions may lead to unpredictable outcomes. *Positive feedback* is the term given to the progressive widening of the gap between the required and the actual results. Consideration of *negative* and *positive feedback* highlights how a policy response to a multifaceted problem in a complex environment can be successful at one level and unsuccessful at another (Battram 1998; Mitleton-Kelly 1998). For example, people in a destination that is perceived to offer low-quality service standards choose to develop a service training programme to improve the skills of its workers. This may result in 100 people being trained, and at one level be perceived to be a success. However, if those 100 people then use their training to gain better employment in competing destinations, or in other sectors, the overall outcome of that intervention may exacerbate the problem (Stevenson *et al.* 2009). In this case the concept of *positive feedback* draws attention to the implications of free will and human choice, which lead to a range of complex inter-relationships and interactions, which are non-linear and unpredictable.

Implications and applications

The complexity concepts identified in the previous section can be used to explore the inherent intricacies and inter-dependencies associated with interactions between social and ecological elements in complex adaptive systems. They provide a platform from which to critique thinking and modelling, which is based on notions of stability, universality, equilibrium and linear relationships between cause and effect. They emphasise continual evolution and the importance of interactions between elements as they adapt to one another rather than focusing on the individual elements. These interactions occur at different scales and time frames and can be both complementary and supportive and competitive and destructive at the same time.

Several studies have adopted complexity concepts as a way of developing understanding about socio-ecological systems and improving the learning capacity and resilience of these systems. Ohl *et al.* (2010) consider the tensions that arise during the interactions between ecological and human systems, which can result in changes in biological diversity in areas. They suggest a complex systems approach that can integrate natural and social science research as a way of understanding dilemmas that span natural and human systems. McDonald (2009) uses complex systems theory to underpin her investigation into tourism activities on the Swan River, Australia. She conceptualises the river as a complex system, recognising the relationships between human activity on the river and its foreshore and the ecology of the river. The tourism aspects of this system form just a small part of the wider system but are inter-connected with both the ecological and social parts of the wider system. Both of these studies identify the non-linearity of processes within complex adaptive systems and highlight the dilemma in trying to predict or envision the behaviour of a system from knowledge of what each component of a system does in isolation.

The complexity concepts identified above require a different approach to managing change. Zimmerman *et al.* (1998) claim that *'garbage can decision making'* is appropriate at the *edge of chaos*. This type of decision-making is intuitive and is characterised by muddling through, agenda building, brainstorming and dialectical enquiry. This is contrasted with the traditional management approaches required in an environment that is relatively stable and consensual. Farrell and Twining-Ward (2005) and Ruiz-Ballesteros (2011) claim that in the context of uncertainty and constant change it is necessary to developing our understanding of complex adaptive systems and developing their *resilience*. Schianetz *et al.* (2007) draw from literature on learning organisations and suggest that these ideas might be adopted in tourism destinations enabling them to learn and improve their capacity to identify opportunities and adapt to change in an environment characterised by change.

Complexity theory has the potential to develop understanding across disciplines; however, at present there are some divisions between the approaches advocated in the social and physical sciences (Byrne 2005, Farrell and Twining-Ward 2005; Healey 2007; Medd 2001a, 2001b). In the social sciences there are some concerns that complexity theory should not be applied literally, as a set of rules, methods and models when it is used to understand social phenomena. These researchers develop a 'softer' approach to the adoption of complexity theory seeing it as a way to encourage thought and learning as a 'frame of reference – a way of understanding what things are like, how they work, and how they might be made to work' (Byrne 2001: 7), rather than a set of methods.

Despite this apparent divergence in method and approach in the wider literature, it is possible to identify common concerns and themes across the complexity literature in tourism, particularly that which considers systems having both ecological and societal aspects. The main area of agreement is that if the tourism 'environment' is characterised by change and instability, it makes little sense to conceptualise it as a stable system and to develop models based on a notion of 'equilibrium'. Complexity theory challenges us to acknowledge that we can influence rather than control action within a complex environment (Tosey 2002). It highlights the need for approaches that are exploratory and intuitive (Stevenson *et al.* 2009; Zimmerman *et al.* 1998).

Suggested ways forward include adaptive approaches to manage resilience and to engender reciprocal social learning (Farrell and Twining-Ward 2005; Tosey 2002; Hjorth and Bagheri 2006), and comparative methods to engage with complex complexity (Byrne 2005).

Conclusion

This chapter provides an introduction to complexity theory, identifying several approaches that have been adopted in the tourism literature and some concepts that might be useful in developing our understanding of relationships and interactions between people and their environment. Complexity theory presents a plausible challenge to positivism, linear thinking and the notion that people can predict, control and shape complex environments. It helps us think about and develop our understanding of the nature of the relationship between the social world and the physical environment.

In this chapter several complexity concepts are identified and explored by considering a resort as a complex adaptive system. This highlights the complex dynamics that occur as social and ecosystems co-evolve within a geographically defined space. Complexity concepts are used to consider the non-linear and contradictory dynamics within the system, with *positive feedback* acting to exacerbate initial problems moving the elements within the resort further from equilibrium. The resort system is nested within wider systems, which means the dynamics within the system are affected by decisions made at the global level and in other places, and also that interactions in our resort may have significant effects on other places and other times.

Complexity theory helps us to recognise that society and the environment are inter-related and impact on one another. It challenges linear thinking and positivism and the emphasis of much research on the ordered, and more easily defined, aspects of systems. This encourages us to think holistically, considering problems at different scales and from different angles. Complexity theory does not provide a new 'truth' about the way the world works, but has a role in encouraging researchers to question their assumptions and broaden their thinking. It questions the stability and equilibrium that has traditionally underpinned the conceptualisation of the relationship between society and the environment. It provides a basis from which to explore the dynamics of these relationships in the context of 'real world' phenomena, taking account of turbulence and disequilibrium, *emergence* and *co-evolution*.

References

Battram, A. (1998) *Navigating Complexity*. London: The Industrial Society.

Bramwell, B. (2006) 'Actors, Power and Discourses of Growth Limits', *Annals of Tourism Research* 33(4) 957–78.

Brian Arthur, W., Durlauf, S. and Lane, D. (1997) *The Economy as an Evolving Complex System II*, Reading, MA: Addison-Wesley.

Byrne, D. (2001) *Complexity Science and Transformation in Social Policy in Social Issues* 1(2). www.whb.co.uk/socialissues/tb.htm (last accessed 24 November 2006).

——(2005) 'Complexity, Configurations and Cases *Theory Culture and Society* 22(5), 95–111.

Farrell, B. and Twining-Ward, L. (2004) 'Reconceptualizing Tourism', *Annals of Tourism Research* 31(2), 274–95.

——(2005) 'Seven Steps Towards Sustainability. *Journal of Sustainable Tourism* 13(2), 109–22.

Faulkner, B. and Russell, R. (1997) 'Chaos and Complexity in Tourism: In Search of a New Perspective', *Pacific Tourism Review* 1(1), 29–37.

——(2001) 'Turbulence, Chaos, Complexity in Tourism Systems: A Research Direction for the New Millennium', in Faulkner B. *et al. Tourism and the 21st Century: Reflections on Experience*. London: Continuum.

——(2003) 'Chaos and Complexity in Tourism: In Search of a New Perspective', in Faulkner, B., Fredline, L., Jago, L. Cooper, C. (eds) *Progressing Tourism Research*. Clevedon: Channel View Publications, 205–19.

Fonseca, J. (2002) *Complexity and Innovation in Organizations*. London: Routledge.

Gell Mann, M. (1994) *The Quark and the Jaguar: Adventures in the Simple and the Complex*. New York: Freeman and Company.

Goodwin, B, (1997) *How the Leopard changed its Spots: The Evolution of Complexity*. London: Phoenix.

Gunn, C. A. (2002) *Tourism Planning: Basics, Concepts, Cases.*, 4th edn. New York: Routledge.

Harvey, D. (2001) 'Chaos and Complexity: Their Bearing on Social Policy Research', *Social Issues* 1(2) www.whb.co.uk/socialissues/dh.htm (last accessed 24 November 2006).

Healey, P. (2007) *Urban Complexity and Spatial Strategies*. Abingdon: Routledge.

Hjorth, P. and Bagheri, A. (2006) 'Navigating towards sustainable development: A system dynamics approach', *Futures* 38: 74–92.

Jones, C. (2010) 'Beyond Economics: Managing the Impacts of Events and Festivals', Keynote Speech at *Global Events Congress IV: Events and Festivals Research: State of the Art*. Leeds. July 2010.

Lacitignola, D., Petrosillo, I. and Zurlini G. (2010) 'Time dependent regimes of a tourism-based social-ecological system: period-doubling route to chaos', *E:CO* 7(1), 44–54.

Lewin, R. (1993) *Life at the Edge of Chaos*. New York: Collier Books.

McDonald, J.R. (2009) 'Complexity science: an alternative world view for understanding sustainable tourism development', *Journal of Sustainable Tourism* 17(4), 455–71.

McKercher, B. (1999) 'A Chaos Approach to Tourism', *Tourism Management* 20(3), 425–34.

Manson, S. (2001) 'Simplifying complexity: A review of complexity theory', *Geoforum* 32 (3), 405–14.

Medd, W. (2001a) 'Complexity and the Policy Process', *Social Issues* 1(2) www.whb.co.uk/socialissues/wm.htm (last accessed 24 September 2006).

——(2001b) 'Critical Emergence: Complexity Science and Social Policy', *Social Issues* 1(2) www.whb.co.uk/socialissues/tb.htm (last accessed 24 September 2006).

Mitleton-Kelly, E. (1998) *Organizations as Complex Evolving Systems*. Oaces Conference Warwick.

Ohl, C., Johst, K., Meyerhoff, J., Beckenkamp, M., Grusgen, V. and Drechsler, M. (2010) 'Long-term socio-ecological research (LTSER) for biodiversity protection: A complex systems approach for the study of dynamic human–nature interactions', *Ecological Complexity* 7, 170–78

Pavolvitch, K. (2009) 'A Fractal Approach to Sustainable Networks', *E:CO* 11(3), 49–60.

Plummer, R. and Fennel, D.A. (2009) 'Managing protected areas for sustainable tourism: prospects for adaptive co-management', *Journal of Sustainable Tourism* 17(2), 149–68.

Porter, T. (2006) 'Coevolution as a Research Framework for Organizations and the Natural Environment', *Organization and Environment* 19(4), 479–504.

Prigogine, I. and Stengers, I. (1984) *Order out of Chaos: Man's New Dialogue with Nature*. New York: Bantam Books.

Ruiz-Ballesteros, E. (2011) 'Social-ecological resilience and community-based tourism. An approach from Agua Blanca, Ecuador', *Tourism Management* 32(3), 655–66

Russell, R. and Faulkner, B. (1999) 'Movers and Shakers: Chaos Makers in Tourism Development', *Tourism Management* 20(3), 411–23.

——(2004) 'Entrepreneurship, Chaos and the Tourism Area Life Cycle. *Annals of Tourism Research* 31(3), 556–79.

Schianetz, K., Kavanagh, L., and Lockington, D. (2007) 'The Learning Tourism Destination: The potential of a learning organization approach for improving the sustainability of tourism destinations', *Tourism Management* 28, 1485–96.

Shaw, P. (2002) *Changing Conversations in organizations: a complexity approach to change*. London: Routledge.

Stacey, R. (2003) *Strategic Management and Organizational Dynamics: The Challenge of Complexity*, 4th edn. Harlow: Prentice Hall.

Stacey, R. Griffen, D. and Shaw, P. (2000) *Complexity and Management: Fad or Radical Challenge to Systems Thinking*. London: Routledge.

Steffan W. and Tyson, P. (eds) (2004) *Global Change and the Earth System: A Planet Under Pressure*. Berlin: Springer IGBP series.

Stevenson (2006) 'Policy at the margins: Views from Leeds about local authority tourism policy activity.' Unpublished PhD research thesis. University of Surrey.

Stevenson, N. Airey, D. and Miller, G. (2008) 'Tourism Policy Making: The Policy Makers Perspectives', *Annals of Tourism Research* 35(3), 732–50.

——(2009) 'Complexity theory and tourism policy research', *International Journal of Tourism Policy* 2(3), 206–20.

Tosey, P. (2002) 'Teaching on the Edge of Chaos', *LTSN Generic Centre*.

Traub, J.F. and Werschulz, A.G. (1998) *Complexity and Information*. Cambridge: Cambridge University Press.

Tsoukas, H. and Hatch, M. (2001) 'Complex Thinking, Complex Practice: The case for a narrative approach to organizational complexity', *Human Relations* 54 (8), 979–1013.

Tyler, D. and Dinan, C. (2001) 'The Role of Interested Groups in England's Emerging Tourism Policy Network', *Current Issues in Tourism* 4 (2–4), 210–53.

Urry, J. (2003) *Global Complexity*. Cambridge: Polity Press.

——(2005a) 'The Complexity Turn', *Theory Culture and Society* 22 (5), 1–14.

——(2005b) 'The Complexities of the Global', *Theory Culture and Society* 22(5), 235–54

van Uden, J. (2005) 'Using complexity science in organization studies: A case for loose applications', *E:CO* 7 (1), 60–66.

Veal, A.J. (2002) *Leisure and Tourism Policy and Planning*, 2nd edn. Wallingford and New York: CABI.

Waldrop, M. (1992) *Complexity: The emerging science at the edge of order and chaos*. London: Penguin.

Zahra, A. and Ryan, C. (2007) 'From Chaos to cohesion–complexity in tourism structures: An analysis of New Zealand's regional tourism organizations', *Tourism Management* 28 (3), 854–62.

Zimmerman, B., Lindberg C., and Plsek (1998) 'Nine Emerging Connected Organiszational and Leadership Principles'. www.plexusinstitute.org/resource/collection/2361BA64-992E-4E4C-A2C2-47890A8 AC73E/Nine_Organizational_Principles_-_from_Edgeware__adapted_for_website.doc (last accessed on 19/12/12).

Further reading

Healey, P. (2007) *Urban Complexity and Spatial Strategies*. Abingdon: Routledge. (Develops a relational and institutionalist approach to policy and planning drawing from complexity concepts. Recommended reading for those interested in governance and tourism planning.)

Urry, J. (2003) *Global Complexity*. Cambridge: Polity Press. (Uses complexity concepts to explore global processes and argue against a conceptualisation of globalisation that is unambiguous and overly unified.)

10

Tourism and romantic myths of nature

The evolution of a discursive relationship

Tony Seaton

The late Raymond Williams once described nature as 'perhaps the most complex word in the English language'. (Williams 1976). It is also a concept that has profoundly influenced the evolution of tourism, and debate about its environmental effects. The varied meanings and ideologies associated with nature have influenced the development of tourism fashions for: sun bathing and seaside resorts; walking, hiking and backpacking; camping and caravanning; mountaineering; seeking out locations – with paintbrush, camera or video recorders – to turn into picture opportunities and collectible 'views'; and as places to stay. Ideas and beliefs about nature are embodied in many attitudes to tourism including: meeting the 'natives' or 'locals' on cultural tourism tours; seeking spiritual and emotional solace in 'unspoiled' spaces located among rivers, streams, woods and fields; and marvelling at the inanimate grandeur of wildernesses of desert, snow, ice or rock. And, increasingly, it is beliefs about the auratic importance of nature as a spiritual presence, and as a crucial, physical sustainer of life on the planet, that have produced passionate debate about environmental conservation, including critiques of tourism and its future directions.

Nature, although often seen as a self-evident 'given', has had many meanings. It has always been a construct, shaped by human intention and agency, under particular historical conditions, social and material. What we perceive as 'natural' in the physical world may be the result of decades, often centuries, of unseen human intervention and manipulation. One person's view of nature may differ from those of others living in different places and at different times.

This chapter sketches evolving notions of nature or Nature (the use of lower or upper case in naming it is part of the history of the concept) in Western culture, and its impact on leisure and tourism behaviour. Reflecting a broadly chronological treatment, the analysis traces how nature was understood in classical and pagan culture, in Western Christianity, and finally how social and ideological changes in the eighteenth and early nineteenth century, created the movement that became known as 'Romanticism'. Although both pagan classical and Christian notions of nature have had their legacy, it is Romanticism's revaluation of the concept that has had the most far-reaching impact on recreational tastes, tourist behaviour patterns and environmental assumptions that underpin modern tourism today.

Pagan and classical ideas of Nature

Greek and Roman culture approached the natural world, including speculation on the origin of life, through the lens of myth. Creation and its manifestations on land and sea, in woods and streams, above and below the earth, were peopled with, and explained by, a diversity of individual gods and goddesses. Among them were major players like Zeus, Jupiter and Saturn, supported by lesser figures, including a named, and nameless, collection of Nymphs and Dryads (Keightley 1890; Grant 1962: Ch. 3). These gods and goddesses were believed to control nature, and were beseeched, propitiated, praised or thanked in religious rituals by worshippers anxious to get them onside, to afford the natural conditions on which their survival and prosperity depended – fertile soil, rain for crops, good harvests, successful hunting, etc. These classical gods and goddesses inhabited the countryside, and poets celebrated an Arcadian world. Virgil did so realistically in his Eclogues and Georgics, which were almost do-it-yourself guides to best practices in agriculture. The Greek poets, Theocritus and Bion, celebrated rural life more fancifully, inventing a rural fairyland in which shepherd swains wooed pretty shepherdesses with pipes and song, and disported blissfully with them in grottoes, groves and fields.

One classical writer did more than devolve everything in nature to gods and goddesses. This was the Roman poet, Lucretius, whose work, 'De rerum Natura' ('On the nature of things'), includes an embryonic anticipation of scientific method. It was an attempt to anatomise and explain the cyclic patterns of growth, decline, death and re-birth in the natural world. It began by invoking 'increase-giving Venus', the goddess of love, as the 'sole mistress of nature' and the generative force behind all the components of the natural world – the winds, earth's fertility, the weather, etc. But after this fanciful introduction, Lucretius abandoned mythology and declared his aim to be more hard-edged and empirical, namely, 'to release the mind from the bond of religious scruples' (superstition, as he saw it) by seeking theoretical explanations of the workings of the natural world through observation (Adler and Gormon 1952). The late Susan Sontag viewed Lucretius's work as modern in its detachment, and proto-scientific advocacy of empirical evidence:

> Lucretius urged the natural sciences as a mode of ethical psychotherapy. Lucretius saw man as torn between the pleasures of sex and the pain of emotional loss, haunted by the fear of bodily decay and death. He recommended scientific knowledge, which teaches intelligent detachment, equanimity. Scientific knowledge is, for Lucretius, a mode of psychological gracefulness. It is a way of learning to let go.
>
> *(Sontag 1967: 72–3)*

Nature in medieval Christianity

The rise of Christianity in Europe and the West dismantled mythological accounts of nature, and revised the primary sense in which the word nature was understood. In medieval Christianity 'nature' did not designate the external, physical world (the word describing that was more likely to be 'Creation'), but the *human condition*. 'Nature' was the corrupt state into which all men and women were born through the legacy of original sin, brought into the world by the disobedience of Adam and Eve, and atoned for by Christ's sacrifice on the Cross. Nature was not an external world to observe and study, but an internal tendency to evil lurking in every human. Christianity proclaimed the necessity of resistance to the temptations of the flesh and the devil. In extreme forms it led to monastic ascetics living by rules of mortification that denied their bodies physical pleasures and comforts.

The physical environment that we now regard as 'Nature' with a capital N, was hardly celebrated in early Christianity. Religious painters of the Middle Ages rarely depicted what we would now call *landscape*, except as background to foregrounded Christian subjects (Christ, the Holy Family, disciples, saints and martyrs). Animals were mainly depicted in bestiaries for their allegorical significance. Reverence for the wonders of nature was discouraged by the early Christian Church, because they were tainted with pagan rituals and pantheism that the Church was anxious to stamp out among its heathen converts. The Church was more interested in taking over former sites of pagan worship, and adapting them to Christian uses:

> Fountains once inhabited by mother-goddesses, and stones on the moors haunted by fairies, became Christian ... The saints replaced the spirits of the mountains, valleys, and forests.
>
> *(Male 1984: 269)*

Later Christian attitudes to Nature and the external world modified. Instead of allowing only some small parts of it to assume religious significance, greater emphasis was put on the *whole* of the physical world as a *text* in which to *read* the shaping designs of God. This came about in the early sixteenth century as the spread of printing, and vernacular translations of the Bible and Prayer Books, previously only available as manuscripts in Latin or Greek, allowed larger populations to hear, or read, for themselves, in Genesis or the Psalms, celebrations of the bounteous plenty of the natural world created by God for mankind. This textual reading of nature continued in the seventeenth century, the century of scientific revolution, as a newly evolving scientific community, although empirically investigating the natural world, believed that in so doing they were revealing the details of God's work, an assumption that crashed for many in 1859 when Darwin published *Origin of Species*.

Nature and the seasons

Despite its early reluctance to celebrate the physical world too explicitly, there was one discursive aspect of Nature that the Church did include in its liturgical agendas, the calendar year and seasons. From the early Middle Ages it developed elaborate ritual structuring of the year for believers on a daily, weekly, monthly and seasonal basis (Tuve 1933; Pearsall and Salter 1973; Perez-Higuera 1998; Henisch 1999; Hourihane 2007). There were several reasons for organising the divisions of the year so exactly. The first was one we have already discussed, the necessity for re-branding existing pagan, seasonal festivals as Christian. Second, irrespective of what religious significance was attributed to them, seasonal changes in the natural world structured the *de facto* patterns of human work, play and perception in rural communities, which included nearly everybody in the Middle Ages (Webster 1938). Seasonal changes through the year were particularly visible in the temperate climates of Europe. Differentiation between seasons and months could be both dramatic and subtle, so that nature acted as a textured clock face on which rural communities observed the passages of the year. The Church was able to capitalise on these naturally occurring divisions of the year by overlaying them with religious meanings. This was done by naming days and weeks after religious festivals, saints and martyrs. Medieval breviaries, Missals, and Books of Hours included illustrations of biblical stories, saints and martyrs, alongside scenes illustrating the seasonal work associated with each month. Printed Bibles and Prayer Books later started with a 12-page calendar, one page for each month that allocated religious festivals, holy days and saints on a day-by-day basis.

The result was that the transformations in the world of nature, the world of work and play, and the world of Christian liturgy were combined in a way that put their faith at the centre of the daily life of Christians throughout the year.

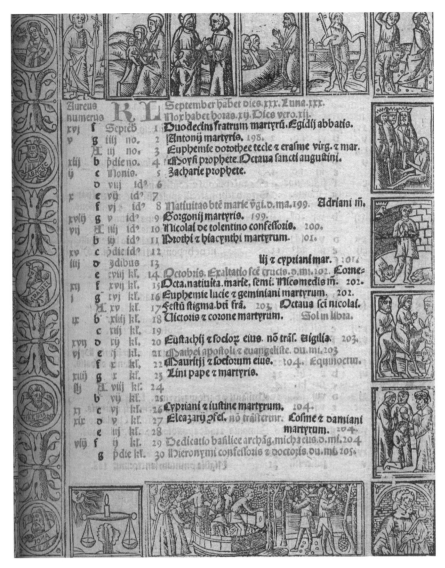

Figure 10.1 Medieval calendars and the seasons

The seasonal calendar also provided a fertile theatre of imagery and metaphor in both the literary and visual arts. Seasons in the natural world were compared with the stages of human life (Sears 1986). The 'springtime of life' and the 'seer and yellow leaf' are only two of the many analogic ways of describing human age in terms of an implicit equivalence with the seasons.

Romanticism and the re-valuation of Nature

Romanticism was a cultural movement that first swept Europe in the last decades of the eighteenth and the early nineteenth centuries, and revolutionised attitudes to nature. It comprised a number of inter-connected ideas articulated in literature, philosophy, music, art and social life.

Its dating, definition and meaning have been endlessly debated (Furst 1969; Christiansen 1988). But the one that concerns us here is Romanticism's intense and enduring preoccupation with nature that was to give it a privileged position within European culture. Romanticism's first impact on nature discourse was linguistic; the word's dominant meaning came to be the physical environment, pushing all other connotations into a subordinate place. The word became not just a noun, but an adjective. By the end of the century 'Nature poetry' was a recognised poetic genre, and 'Nature study' a widely taught subject in schools.

The three orientations to Nature

Three distinct discursive orientations to the world of nature may be discerned in the writings and practices of early Romantics: the rational-scientific; the transcendental-religious; and the aesthetic-consumable.

The *rational-scientific orientation* involved regarding nature as a vast data field for inquiry through methodologies of empirical observation and experiment. This paradigm, which partly resembled Lucretius' notion of detached observation of nature, had more recent roots in the 'Scientific Revolution' of the seventeenth century, spearheaded by canonical figures like Francis Bacon, Isaac Newton and Leibniz. It has become the basis of scientific procedures since. It primed tourists into amateur, quasi-scientific habits of nature observation and specimen collecting – geological specimens, shells, seaweed, birds eggs, pressed flowers, fossils and other natural objects – on trips to the countryside and seaside. Cartoonists sometimes cast doubt on the real motives for such collecting jaunts.

It led to the more grandiose presumptions of modern ecotourism, in which the affluent tourist is invited to adopt the prestigious persona of quasi-scientific pilgrim and inquirer after knowledge in remote environments, rich in exotic fauna and flora, and expensive beyond consideration for the many.

Figure 10.2 Nature study and romance at the seaside, 1860s

The *transcendental-religious* orientation embodied a more emotional relationship to Nature that imagined it to be a mystical presence that made contact with it an act of communion. The architects of this credo were poets and philosophers, whose secular ideas were implicitly influenced by models derived from monastic and hermit life, in believing that nature produced spiritual epiphanies and revelations in places far from the abode of men: by the lakes of Cumbria; on the high hills and mountain ranges of Switzerland, the Hartz in Germany and Scotland; in uninhabited islands on Swiss and Italian Lakes; among the rolling wolds of the English West Country.

These benefits came not just from the places themselves, but from contact with the indigenous peasantry and labouring classes who lived in them – farm workers, leech gathers, woodcutters – who were taken to have some of the uncorrupted natural goodness and, in some cases, warrior nobility of the 'noble savages' that Romantics imagined dwelt in the wilds of America and Oceania – and Scotland.

This Transcendental strain in the Romantic elevation of nature has been seen as a kind of secular religion that developed as Christian belief weakened in a modernising, industrialising world shaped by technology and science. Beach believed that nature was a stand-in for the spiritual isolation felt by moderns:

Figure 10.3 Scottish mountains, 1840s/1850s

Figure 10.4 The 'noble savages' of Scotland as seen by the French

> It provided philosophical bridges from faith to unfaith … It made possible without too great emotional strain a shift from medieval Christian faith to the scientific positivism which tends to dominate cultivated minds today … My general contention is that the metaphysical concept of nature is the joint construction of science, philosophy and religion, and is not dependent for its main force on Arcadian sentiment or on its supernaturalism.
>
> *(Beach 1936: 5–22)*

In relegating 'Arcadian sentiment' as a main force in the ideology of nature, Beach perhaps underestimated the long previous history of Arcadia, and also the fact that it was not, as he suggests, killed off by the march of science, but survives to this day in tourism behaviour, and also second home choices, which are frequently based on long-held fantasies of country living. His view that nature was a substitute, secular religion may be true for some, but not all. It fails to account for many Christians then and now who, although engaging in romantic nature discourses, still subscribe to the orthodox Christian doctrine that regards the diverse beauty of nature as evidence of God's hand.

Nature as aesthetic-consumable: the Sublime and Picturesque

The third orientation to Nature as aesthetic-consumable owed nothing to religion or science. It was a fashionable, new construct in the developing cult of taste and personal judgement that was influencing travel (Ousby 1990). Its central premise was that nature was an array of sensory effects to be differentiated, ranked and *consumed as forms of personal gratification*. The differentiation and ranking were decided on the basis of what Corbin has memorably called, 'the imperative aesthetics of natural attractions' (Corbin 1994: 137). These imperatives were the arbitrary codes constructed by tastemakers and aesthetic theorists, which established the criteria by which the sensory world of nature should be evaluated and ranked. Two of the most important Romantic 'imperative codes' were those of the Picturesque and the Sublime.

The Picturesque has received considerable, modern academic attention from Hussey's seminal study (Hussey 1927) to the more comprehensive work of Andrews (1989, 1994). It was a hierarchically ordered ideology of landscape in which places were rated on an aesthetic scale, according to their merit in offering vistas that were a suitable subject for a picture. Picturesque value was assessed on the basis of three features: content, arrangement and perspective. Content was predominantly rural landscape scenes – hills and mountains, rivers, streams, fields, cattle, dramatic skies, peasants at work or play, etc. These elements had to be carefully selected and arranged to conform to picturesque criteria. Winding streams were preferred to straight ones; gnarled trees to rows of neat, symmetrical ones; hills with irregular slopes to geometrically rounded ones; views down to views up; autumn to spring, because it produced more interesting tonal effects of light and shadow, etc. Lastly, the Picturesque vista normatively required a three-layered perspective comprising: a *foreground frame* made by some natural or man-made portal (a window frame, an arch or an overhanging branch), through which appeared a *middle ground* (where the principal subject scene was depicted), and beyond that a *background* that was a more distant feature, often a horizon.

The 'Search for Picturesque' (Andrews 1989) coincided with the development of water-colour painting in England that made the view a crucial feature for tourists (Clarke 1981). Picturesque views virtually created the attraction of some regions of Britain (Scotland, the Wye Valley, Northumberland, Durham and Cumbria) and even today, these regions still stage catalogue exhibitions of paintings that remind us of the fact (Anon 1982; Mitchell 2010).

The Sublime was a concept first discussed in the work of the Roman writer, Longinus. It had begun life as a rhetorical effect produced on audiences by the speeches of outstanding orators. It then became a more general characteristic of the work of men of genius (Nicolson 1959; Monk 1960). But the one that connects with discourses of Romantic Nature was that developed by Edmund Burke in 1757, which made it an aesthetic category for viewing the world of art and nature (Burke/Boulton 1958). For Burke, the Sublime was a quality of aesthetic pleasure that was different from beauty. If the beauty of a picture or scene pleased by its harmony and the calm contemplation it induced in observers, there were other kinds that pleased by their disturbing violence and power. The paradox that what induced terror and awe could be agreeable was Burke's theme. Sublimity was what induced awe and fear, and was a matter of quantitative and qualitative scale in the natural and man-made world: great seas, numberless battalions of troops; displays of pomp and conspicuous wealth; dark clouds driven by winds; the silence of a great cemetery at dusk. It was later theorised to have two different dimensions – one sacred and one profane. The sacred sublime were sights and experiences that elevated the mind with their transcendent power and offered intimations of the infinite – moving religious music, great paintings, holy mountains, a religious procession or a wonderful sunset. The profane or negative sublime were sights and experiences that tended to 'shock and awe' (a phrase perceptively used by the US military to describe its aerial assaults on Iraq), without elevating the mind – the clash of armies by night, the noise and glare of blackened factories, tortures and punishment, underground visions of dystopias and hell. Both kinds of sublimity became tourist attractions and part of Romantic nature. They included: crashing waterfalls, erupting volcanoes, vast mountain ranges, rushing torrents and dense forests.

Both the Picturesque and Sublime installed landscape – a concept that may be viewed as a 'place constructed in aesthetic discourse' – at the centre of the tourist experience to an extent never before envisaged, and never relinquished since. Increasingly, views had to awe or inspire with dramatic effects, or offer pretty pictures as subjects for watercolour sketches and in modern times, as photo opportunities. Without necessarily knowing much about the Picturesque or Sublime, millions of tourists joined the landscape chase, exemplifying how discourses become inscribed and activated in unconscious responses, and how the many may be enraptured in the present, by natural effects that have been historically theorised by a few.

Romanticism was articulated and theorised by many cultural figures – poets, novelists, essayists, artists, musicians, philosophers in Europe, particularly in England, France and Germany. Space does not allow discussion of many. We shall concentrate instead on one who was **the** seminal European influence in changing and advancing discourses about Nature.

Rousseau

Rousseau was a philosopher, novelist, botanist and musician. His views on nature were part of a much broader body of thought on human life and freedom and were initially conveyed in two novels that made him famous, *Julie, ou La Nouvelle Héloïse* (1761) and *Emile* (1762). His main contention was that humans were born good, but were corrupted by the effects of 'civilisation', which taught them greed, calculation and worldliness. Civilisation was, he argued, an urban disease. It was communion with nature in rural locations that brought peace and harmony in life:

> It is on the summits of mountains, in the depths of forests, on deserted islands that nature reveals her most potent charms.
>
> *(La Nouvelle Héloïse, Pt. 1v, letter 11)*

Rousseau's idealisation of rural life was not new. It had existed in Greek and Roman writers – Theocritus, Ovid, Virgil, Seneca and Cicero – who had advocated the simple life of Arcadia as an antidote to the pressures of the city. Romans, like modern Europeans with second homes, had country villas for periodic escapes. In Rousseau's time, rural innocence was also fondly imagined and mimicked at the French court. Inspired by classical literature and the paintings of Watteau and Boucher, courtiers dressed as peasants acted out pretty theatricals of Arcadian fantasy with their royal employees at picnics and fete champetres.

But Rousseau's version of Arcadia was different. His writings on nature transformed what had previously been recreational fancies for the privileged into ontology for everyman. In his eyes Nature was a kind of transcendental, feminised being in whose presence the solitary would find the nurturing consolations of teacher and mother. It was in Nature with a capital N, that people would realise their true natures with a lower case N (Christiansen 1988: 96–7).

Rousseau sought communion with nature in several ways. He was a frequent walker who, on one occasion, journeyed from France to Turin via the Alps on foot, as the poet, Wordsworth, was to do later. Rousseau used his walks as forms of spiritual exercise in which he cultivated habits of intense reflection. Late in life he wrote:

> My whole life has been little else than a long reverie divided into chapters by my daily walks.
> *(Rousseau 1782, 1989: 11)*

Figure 10.5 Jean-Jacques Rousseau or the Man of Nature, 1770s/1780s

'Reverie' was a key word in his philosophical vocabulary that was, he believed, the mechanism through which he apprehended nature. After one successful excursion on the Island of St. Pierre in Lake Brienne – a favourite retreat where he spent 2 months, but said he could have spent two centuries – he wrote:

> Such is the state which I often experienced on the Island of St Pierre in my solitary reveries. Whether I lay in a boat and drifted where the water carried me, or sat by the shore of the stormy lake, or elsewhere, on the banks of a lovely river or a stream murmuring over the stones.
>
> *(Rousseau 1782, 1989: 88–9)*

However, Rousseau's orientation to nature was not all transcendental reverie. It was combined with a more naturalistic-scientific interest, particularly in botany. He was a meticulous observer who wrote a textbook on the subject. He described how, during his observations he would first mark off a field in squares and then, with a magnifying glass and a botanical textbook at hand, begin a minute examination of each plant. The sexual organs of plants particularly fascinated him. He described the intensity of his absorption:

> They say a German once wrote a book about a lemon-skin: I could have written one about every grass in the meadows, every moss in the woods, every lichen covering the rocks – and I did not want to leave even one blade of grass or atom of vegetation without a full and detailed description.
>
> *(Rousseau 1782, 1989: 85)*

His combination of idiosyncratic mysticism and scientific inquiry towards nature, and other, more political beliefs about social justice and human freedom, attracted unwelcome attention from church and state. He was denounced as immoral by the church and for periods exiled from Paris and his birthplace, Geneva. It is not difficult to see why his ideas offended orthodox Christians. Where Christianity saw humans as corrupt at birth through Original Sin, Rousseau believed they were born good. Where Christianity preached reason and self-control, Rousseau valued and exhibited emotional display and feeling. Whereas Christianity cautioned against valuing the physical world too highly as a potential temptation to pagan worship, Rousseau seemed to regard nature as a benign goddess. Whereas Christianity encouraged collective worship and church membership, Rousseau preached solitary reverie.

Rousseau has also had his twentieth-century critics. He has been accused of paranoia and 'emotional misanthropy' (Babbitt 1919) in his desire for solitude, although one critic points out that he insisted that this state of isolation was 'alien to his nature and imposed on him by duress' (Green 1955: 362). Another charge is that his mystic philosophy was vague and facile, and, at worst, led to a bogus spirituality on the cheap – style, rather than substance:

> One of the reasons why pantheistic reverie has been so popular is that it seems to offer a painless substitute for genuine spiritual effort. In its extreme moments (it) amounts to a sort of ecstatic animality that sets up as divine illumination (and) encourages one to assume a tone of consecration in speaking of experiences that are aesthetic rather than truly religious.
>
> *(Babbitt 1919: 286)*

The same kind of criticism has been levied at modern youth cultures – influenced, knowingly or not, by Rousseau's philosophy – that tend to conflate nature, spirituality, reverie and walking.

They include hippy tourists trekking to India and Nepal in the name of religious enlightenment, and modern backpackers taking gap years in Vietnam and Australia. Babbitt viewed Rousseau's escape attempts as spiritual tourism, and the average follower of Rousseau as:

> .an aesthete who assumes an apocalyptic pose and gives forth as a profound philosophy what is at best only a holiday or weekend view of existence … There are times when we may properly seek solace and renewal in nature, when we may invite our souls and bodies to loaf. The error is to look on these moments of recreation and relief from concentration on some definite end as in themselves the consummation of wisdom. Rousseau … assumes that his art of mixing himself up with the landscape is identical with leisure; like innumerable disciples he confuses reverie with meditation.
>
> *(Babbitt 1936: 289, my italics)*

It has also been said that he did not fully practice what he preached in that, although advocating getting away into Nature, it was rarely remote wildernesses to which Rousseau escaped. Most of his daily walks were taken in the suburbs of Paris, and in Switzerland his favourite nature excursions were to the fields of a pretty island not far from Geneva. In these choices he was not unlike Thoreau, his most famous American disciple, whose rejection of civilisation for the backwoods joys of a rural wilderness in his celebrated book, 'Walden', was, in reality, taken in a home-made cabin in a local beauty spot, just off the main road into town, and less than a mile from his mother.

Whatever the criticisms made at the time or since, Rousseau's ideas were immensely influential in exporting a religion of Nature that still influences European thought and art. Thinkers and creators who have embraced Rousseau's ideas have included: in Germany, Goethe (like Rousseau a natural scientist, traveller and spiritual believer), Heine (a passionate walker in the Hartz mountains) and Caspar David Friedrich (mystical nature painter); in France, Chateaubriand (another walker and escapee to wild nature, including the remote, mountain monastery of La Grande Chartreuse); in the USA, Thoreau, Ralph Waldo Emerson and John Muir (all passionate, literary advocates, in philosophical works and/or memoirs, of their own encounters with Nature), as well as Ansell Adams (epic photographer of American landscape), and Walt Whitman (rhapsodic poet of nature and movement, whose poetry engendered the 'on the road' philosophy of Kerouac, and the Beats and made 'getting around' under open skies cool); and in England, Shelley (who combined dedication to poetry, with revolutionary political and religious agendas, as well as an interest in natural science that led him to keep scientific apparatus in his Oxford rooms); Coleridge (philosopher, poet and, like Rousseau, a pioneer influence on walking and mountaineering); and Hazlitt (essayist, biographer and art critic who affirmed that, in long-distance walking, the only possible company was oneself).

The tourism effects of romantic nature

Romanticism revolutionised social attitudes and behaviour towards nature to an extent that was unprecedented. Its impact can be seen not least in the development of tourism and the changing forms it took. Before the Romantic period aristocratic tourists on the Grand Tour, or travelling through Britain, rarely regarded nature as a prime attraction. Their main goal was classical and Renaissance culture in Italy. Mountains were regarded as an obstructive pain, not the spiritual 'high' they later became. The seaside was mainly a place to sail from, rather than vacation in. Nobody walked anywhere unless they had to. Peasants and 'primitive' communities, whom the young Wordsworth and Rousseau regarded as models of uncorrupted human nature, were of no interest to their social superiors, except as populations to manage or rule. The gentrified traveller did not look for encounters with rural labourers in regional costume. In Europe young, male Grand tourists mixed mainly in metropolitan capitals and great cities, with travelling companions and Europeans from their own class, apart from occasional comfort breaks in brothels and other venues where mixed company was kept (Hibbert 1987; Black 1992).

The myths of Romantic nature helped to change this tourism ethos, and led to a diverse repertoire of new scientific, aesthetic and physical tourism choices that were adopted by a wider, bourgeois audience. Some of the main ones will be briefly sketched.

The call of the sea – the fun of the seaside

Human relationships with the sea go back to earliest recorded history, but its tourism appeals are little more than 300 years old. There have been several good accounts of the development of seaside tastes and resort histories (Pimlott 1947; Walton 1983), but Corbin (1994) has provided the most suggestive, inter-disciplinary account of the changing discursive meanings of the sea in history, mythology and world cultures (Corbin 1994). His analysis traces how the sea went from being, in Biblical narrative and many world cultures, a 'great abyss' of unfathomable mysteries, engendering monsters and primeval floods, to pre-eminent status as multifaceted attraction. Its growing appeals evolved as: subject for picturesque representation; Romantic love object; fashion parade; and later, theatre of hedonistic spectacle. This rehabilitation was accomplished by developmental emphasis on the beach (Lencek and Bosker 1998), which started life as a functional space for sailors and fisherman, then became a base for bracing walks, bathing and enjoying the new taste for recreational swimming.

In elite French resorts the beach became a place for fashionable displays that Boudin captured in his impressionistic charivaris of the whirligig crinolines and parasols of Princess Eugenie's entourage promenading at Trouville and Deauville.

London. Publish May 12th 1810 by H. Humphrey. 27 St James's Street.   Etched by J. G.

A SQUALL.

New architectural styles sprang up in and around the beach. The apotheosis of these styles was the appearance, in major resorts, of the pier. Its gleaming, white painted spectacularity, obtruding from shore to sea, supported on arabesque or floriated ironwork, became the iconic trademark of resort hedonism. Like the beach, it offered the visitor the liminal promise of mystery and excitement in its marginality between land and sea, but without the impeding inconveniences of sand, and with the additional intoxication of a universe of micro-activities (funfair rides, slot machines, amusement arcades), and cheap and cheerful, retail opportunities (Lindley 1973; Adamson 1977).

The sea captivated all classes and transport progressively made it available to all but in different measure. For the middle classes a seaside visit might be a month's stay. Poorer people, with no holidays with pay in Britain until the late 1930s, took steam boats and excursion trains for a seaside day out.

Walking and rambling

Whoever would walk unless they had to? It was a question that must have been asked by the poor, who did nothing else but walk places, as they saw university-educated Romantics like Coleridge, Wordsworth, Heine and their acolytes striding through the countryside for pleasure. Walking is one of the most singular legacies of Romanticism (Marples 1959; Solnit 2001). Before the Romantics it had been rare, but not completely unknown among the genteel. After them, it became one of the most popular pastimes and resulted in the formation of local rambling groups and later, the national Ramblers' Association in the twentieth century. The Youth Hostel Association was formed partly to service walkers. Walking has been periodically rebranded as: 'hill walking', 'hiking' and 'backpacking'. Up to the Second World War, it also spawned a sub-genre of travel writing by gentlemen tramps, such as W.H. Davies and Stephen Graham, who took to the road to write about it.

Although Romantics had preached and practised walking alone, it became highly social, undertaken by parties who created crowd problems in popular places like the Lake District and eventually alarmed even prophets of nature like Wordsworth (who had actually written a guidebook to the area) and Ruskin, a great walker himself.

Mountaineering

Until the late eighteenth century, mountains were regarded as a 'horrid' and dangerous obstruction, particularly by Europeans going south into Italy. In crossing the Simplon Pass in the Alps, Grand tourists had to get out of their coach and walk. The coach was then dismantled and reloaded on to mules because the alpine paths were so narrow and bends so acute.

Mountains began to be revalued in the last decade of the eighteenth century and the first decades of the nineteenth, through the combined impact of: the Sublime as a fashionable quest; the high-level walks of Romantic opinion formers like Coleridge, Rousseau and Wordsworth; and the French writings of de Saussure. By the 1860s, mountaineering had become a competitive sport institutionalised by the foundation of the Alpine Club – a society whose members were predominantly university men who published their vacation accounts of climbs and scrambles in the Lake District, Scotland, the Alps and the Dolomites.

Women and family parties also engaged in less taxing climbs on the lower slopes of smaller mountains. By the end of the century Switzerland, Germany, Italy, France and Austria all had a mountaineering tourism base, to which was added a new past-time for the rich – skiing.

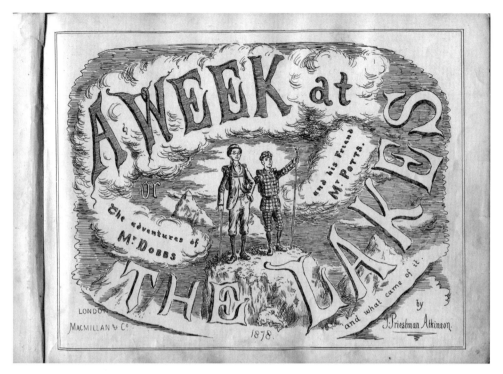

Figure 10.7 Mountain heights and heights of fashion in the Lake District, 1878

Camping and caravanning

Camping and caravanning were two other flirtations with outdoor living that one might suppose would be incongruous to affluent, middle-class people, after the human race had spent several thousand years evolving to fixed abode living. For the prosperous Victorian, the abode was a luxurious one, famously stuffed with every available mod con and knick-knack, produced by the most advanced mass production processes the world had ever seen. Why go back to live in a tent or caravan?

The answer is the immense impact of the myth of Romantic Nature. Camping and caravanning drew on different discursive branches of Romanticism. Camping became a leisure activity as a sort of recreational identification with Empire and Militarism, similar to the conception of the Boy Scout movement by Lord Robert Baden-Powell two decades later. It was well known that British soldiers lived under canvas in the outposts of Empire, particularly when engaged in the 'little wars' that were endemic through Victoria's reign. Camping combined the benefits of fresh air and patriotic preparation.

Caravanning drew on the myth of the freedom of gypsy life close to Nature, one that had fascinated English writers like George Borrow and Matthew Arnold. There was also a tinge of orientalism in the myth as caravans were associated with nomads trekking the Silk Roads and other exotic highways. Like camping, it started as a tourism fashion in the 1880s, and attracted public attention through a famous book by Gordon Stables, *The cruise of the land yacht Wanderer* (Stables 1886). This described a 2,000-mile trip round Britain in an expensive, 2-tonne caravan, pulled by horses, and equipped with every home comfort, including a servant!

THE WANDERER."

Figure 10.8 On the road 1880s

Throughout the book Stables proclaimed the joys of the simple, natural life and the freedom of the road, including a final section on how to follow his example. It neatly encapsulates the paradox of the simple joys of Romantic nature and the expensive, class resources that supported them.

All these new tourism fashions were reflected in travel writing over the period. Where earlier travellers like Bishop Burnet, Daniel Defoe and Celia Fiennes had described places they visited in political, religious and economic terms, post-Romantic diarists wrote more subjectively, recording their responses to picturesque landscape, sublime views and the novel charms of rural and seaside life. Newspapers and periodicals, including comic magazines, which multiplied from the 1830s onwards, covered the new fashions in nature escape in word and picture – the absurdities of beach wear and mixed bathing, the comic grind of mountaineering, the inconveniences of seasickness, the dangers of picturesque sketching (being chased by bulls, falling into lakes, etc.) and overcrowding in rural solitudes.

Summary

Despite the satirical comments, Romantic Nature travel burgeoned, and by the 1840s was normalised to such an extent that its appreciation was seen in some quarters as a test of moral, intellectual and aesthetic worth:

> An acquaintance with the country, and a love of its beauties and ever-varying scenes, are the foundation of a just appreciation of painting, poetry, and music. We judge of the merits of a picture according to its resemblance to Nature; of poetry, by the emotions it produces,

Figure 10.9 The perils of the Picturesque, 1860s

and the illustrations which it affords of all that is pleasing in earth, air, sea, or sky; of music, as it brings to our ears the sound of waters, the song of birds, or the rustling of the wind among trees and flowers … The quiet of country scenery is like a resting place for the mind; there is a tranquillity that draws the thoughts from the busy world, and makes us conscious that we live for nobler ends than to accumulate wealth.

(Miller 1837: vii)

Romanticism's Pagan and Christian survivals

Although mythic gods and goddesses had long been abandoned as explanatory influences on the natural world, they still populated art and literature and much of the 'cultural heritage' that has become a part of tourist consumption in galleries, palaces and aristocratic homes.

Nor did Medieval rural traditions and seasonal patterns completely die out. Even as industrialisation gradually eroded traditional work and leisure patterns, there were attempts to keep alive the rural past. A nostalgic literature celebrating seasonal traditions and folklore, that more and more people would never see, flourished. Hone (1824, 1825, 1832) and Chambers (1868) produced vast calendar compilations of information on archaic customs and festivals that were popular but could not halt the tide of modernity that was rendering them obsolete. But local customs and folklore were celebrated in Romantic poetry (e.g. Scott's Border Ballads) and were packaged as regional heritage traditions in tourism promotion in many parts of Britain.

Tourism also had its modern seasonal cycles. If medieval pilgrimages were undertaken in Chaucer's time in April, modern attractions open up around the same time today for Easter and the start of the tourism season, and in the USA students prepare for Spring breaks. May Day is a marketing opportunity for weekend breaks. Summer, as it was in Victorian times, is the high season when school and college vacations increase travel flows. Countries seeking to extend the season beyond summer run 'Autumn Gold' campaigns. From October to March come Christmas breaks and 'winter sun' escapes.

Romantic Nature and social change

Romanticism happened at a time of rapid economic and social change that continued throughout the nineteenth and twentieth centuries. Technology made travel easier and quicker. Canals had improved inland transport by the beginning of the century; steam boats had begun to make sea travel faster and safe a few decades later; railways were well advanced across Europe by mid-century; the car by the end of the century, and air travel common in twentieth century.

Over the period there developed a rapidly expanding, urban middle class, commercial and professional, in Europe with the time and money to travel. It was this class that adopted the new religion of Nature most fervently. Romanticism was the creation of a European intelligentsia – poets, philosophers and picturesque theorists in Germany, France and England. It is no coincidence that all three were the first great tourist nations, followed by the Americans.

Peasants and agricultural communities, who actually lived with Nature on a daily basis had little awareness of Romance in Nature. They were oblivious of picturesque views and sublime scenes, except in so far as some were able to earn a living as guides, porters and servants, servicing the needs of those tourists who came to see them. Similarly, indigenous mountain communities did not regard climbing with the same enraptured enthusiasm as Oxbridge undergraduates, young lawyers, vicars and civil servants who joined the Alpine Club in the 1860s, a point well made in a lecture delivered in Glasgow a hundred years later, with the intriguing title 'The influence of mountains upon intelligence':

> Men who were born among mountains … have left little trace of any awareness of mountains as entities, and none of seeking to climb them for pleasure … We feel no surprise, therefore, if no traces are left in mountainous countries, such as Scotland, Switzerland or Norway, of any abstract appreciation of local mountains.
>
> *(Young 1957: 5)*

The pursuit of Romantic Nature was thus originally a bourgeois taste, which spread down the social scale in the twentieth century, mainly because of a desire to escape from the increasing ugliness of the industrial cities.

But for nearly all escape was a social occasion, not a solitary one. The desire to be completely alone in spiritual reverie, in Britain at least, was, and still is, most commonly found, and then not very frequently, among academics, literary folk and others with an educated or professional need for isolation: Wittgenstein in rural Ireland; George Orwell in the Orkneys; the poet, Hugh Mcdiarmid in Whalsay in the Shetland Isles; more recently Will Self – all retreating writers on occasion.

Conclusion

This chapter has attempted to trace the impact of Romantic Nature myths on tourism. It began with a brief sketch of the concept of nature in classical and Christian societies, its radical re-valuation in the Romantic period and the transformations it produced in tourism tastes and habits.

Romanticism primed responsive populations of bourgeoisie with a seductive myth, that in Romantic Nature could be found *a,* if not *the,* meaning of life – an auratic ground of virtue, epiphany and self-realisation. This religiose dream spread more widely down the social grades and persists to this day. It is still the implicit force behind the desire for escape to, and encounter with, Nature. Tourism provides the bridge to these encounters, but inevitably the circumstances

LONDON: THE GRAPHOTYPING COMPANY, LIMITED, 7, GARRICK STREET, COVENT GARDEN.

Figure 10.10 Escaping from the city to seaside and countryside 1860s

in which they happen are very different from the ways the figures who created Romantic ideology told them. They were young writers with time on their hands and most of them did not have 'proper jobs', which is why Wordsworth could walk between 170,000 and 180,000 miles during his lifetime according to his friend, de Quincey (Solnit 2001: 104), and Shelley and Rousseau could spend months away studying nature and her ways. For modern, urban tourists with limited time, their brief encounters are less likely to be Rousseau–esque reveries, or pro-longed studies in one field, than speed dating with Nature, whose payoffs will be a walk round a garden open to the public, an afternoon trip down a canal on a hired narrow boat, and downloaded photo opportunities. And most of these things will happen with others, not in splendid isolation.

A different issue is whether Romantic myths of nature ever really worked in practice for many Romantics or their tourist disciples. Perhaps Romantic nature was always a literary trope, a form of creative self-intoxication that was difficult for many to actualise in real life. Some of its discursive assumptions seem questionable. If nature was really such a spiritual influence, then all peasants and rural populations must surely be morally superior to city-dwellers, and all sailors and fishermen who have spent their lives with the sea spiritually wiser than others.

Or perhaps these philosophical discourses about the spiritual benefits of contact with Nature were game rules, formulated by a sceptical but idealistic group of young intellectuals, hostile to industrialisation and then adopted by a growing bourgeoisie eager to show that, in addition to being richer and more successful than others, they were also capable of the finest feelings.

The survival power of Romantic Nature as an ideology may be its capacity to serve many audiences in many different ways, without demanding too much of any of them.

References

Adamson, S.H. (1977) *Seaside Piers*. London: B.T. Batsford Ltd.

Adler, M.J. and Gorman W. (1952) 'The Great Ideas. A synopticon of great books of the Western World'. 'Nature', two vols, *Encyclopaedia Britannica*, Chicago, London, Toronto and Geneva.

Andrews, M. (1989) *The search for the picturesque. Landscape aesthetics and tourism in Britain, 1760–1800*. Aldershot: Scolar Press.

——(ed.) (1994) *The Picturesque: Literary sources and documents*, three vols. East Sussex: Helm Information Ltd.

Anon (1982) *The picturesque tour in Northumberland and Durham c. 1720–1830*. Newcastle upon Tyne: Tyne and Wear County Council.

Babbitt, I. (1919) Rousseau and Romanticism. New York: Houghton Miflin.

Beach, J.W. (1936) *The concept of Nature in nineteenth century English poetry*. New York: Macmillan.

Black, J. (1992) *The Grand Tour in the eighteenth century*. Stroud: Alan Sutton.

Burke, E. (Boulton J.T., ed.) (1958) *A philosophical enquiry into the Origin of our Ideas of the Sublime and Beautiful*. London: Routledge and Kegan Paul.

Chambers, R. (1868) *The Book of Days. A miscellany of popular antiquities in connection with the calendar*, two vols. Edinburgh: W. and R. Chambers.

Christiansen, R. (1988) *Romantic affinities. Portraits from an age 1780–1830*. London: Cardinal, Sphere Books.

Clarke, M. (1981) *The tempting prospect. A social history of English watercolours*. London: British Museum.

Corbin, A. (1994) *The lure of the sea. The discovery of the seaside in the Western World 1750–1840*. Cambridge: Polity Press.

Furst, L.R. (1969) *Romanticism*. London: Methuen.

Grant, M. (1962) *Myths of the Greeks and Romans*. London: Weidenfeld and Nicholson.

Green, F.C. (1955) *Jean-Jacques Rousseau. A study of his life and writings*. Cambridge: Cambridge University Press.

Henisch, B.A. (1999) *The medieval calendar year*. University Park: Pennsylvania State University.

Hibbert, C. (1987) *The Grand Tour*. London: Thames Methuen.

Hone, W. (1826) *The Every-day book or Everlasting calendar of popular amusements, sports, pastimes, ceremonies, manners, customs, and events, incident to each of the three hundred and sixty-five days in past and present times forming a complete history of the year, months and seasons*, two vols. London: Hunt and Clarke.

——(1827) *The Table Book*, two vols. London: Hunt and Clarke.

——(1832) *The Year Book of daily recreation and information, concerning remarkable men and manners, times and seasons, solemnities and merry-makings, antiquities and novelties*. London: Thomas Tegg.

Hourihane, C. (2007) *Time in the Medieval World: Occupations of the Months and Signs of the Zodiac in the Index of Christian Art*. Princeton, NJ: Princeton University Press.

Hussey, C. (1927, reprint 1983) *The Picturesque*. London: Frank Cass.

Keightley, T. (1880) *The mythology of ancient Greece and Italy*, 4th edn. London: George Bell and Son.

Lencek, L. and Bosker G. (1998) *The Beach. The history of paradise on earth*. London: Secker and Warburg.

Lindley, K. (1973) *Seaside Architecture*. London: Hugh Evelyn.

Male, E. (1984) *Religious art in France. The thirteenth century*. Bollingen Series XC.2, Princeton, NJ: Princeton University Press.

Marples, M. (1959) *Shanks Pony a study of walking*. London: J. M. Dent and Sons Ltd.

Miller, T. (1837) *Beauties of the country or descriptions of Rural Customs, Objects, Scenery, and the Seasons*. London: John Van Voorst.

Mitchell, J. (2010) *The Wye Tour and its artists*. Herefordshire: Logaston Press.

Monk, S.H. (1960) *The Sublime. A study of critical theories in XVIII-century England*. Anne Arbor: The University of Michigan Press Paperbacks.

Nicolson, M.H. (1959) *Mountain gloom and mountain glory. The development of the aesthetics of the infinite*. New York: W.W. Norton and Co.

Ousby, I. (1990) *The Englishman's England. Taste, travel and the rise of tourism*. Cambridge: Cambridge University Press.

Pearsall, D. and Salter, E. (1973) *Landscapes and seasons of the medieval world*. London: Paul Elek.

Perez-Higuera, T. (1998) *Medieval Calendars*. London: Weidenfeld and Nicholson.

Pimlott, J.A.R. (1947) *The Englishman's holiday*. London: Faber and Faber.

Rousseau, J.-J. (1782, 1989, France, P. ed.) *Reveries of the solitary walker*. London: Penguin.

Sears, E. (1986) *The ages of man. Medieval interpretations of the life cycle*. Princeton, NJ: Princeton University Press.

Solnit, R. (2001) *Wanderlust. A history of walking*. London: Verso.

Sontag, S. (1967) *Against Interpretation*. London: Eyre and Spottiswood.

Stables, G. (1886) *The cruise of the yacht 'Wanderer' or thirteen hundred miles in my caravan*. London: Hodder and Stoughton.

Tuve, R. (1933) *Seasons and months. Studies in a tradition of Middle English poetry*. Paris: Librairie Universitaire, S. A.

Walton, J.K. (1983) *The English seaside resort. A social history 1750–1914*. Leicester: Leicester University Press.

Webster, J.C. (1938) *The labours of the months in antique and medieval art, to the end of the twelfth century*. Princeton, NJ: Princeton University Press.

Williams, R. (1976, 2nd edn 1983) *Keywords. A vocabulary of culture and society*. London: Fontana.

Young, G.W. (1957) *The influence of mountains upon the development of human intelligence*. Glasgow: Jackson, Son and Company.

Part 2
Ecosystems and impact issues

11

Introduction

David Fennell

The diversity of opportunities available to tourists occurs along a broad spectrum from settings that have been significantly modified or developed by human intervention, to those settings with little or no human modification. The importance of the natural environment to both developed and especially the undeveloped spaces cannot be underestimated. The search for the novel and exotic continues to propel tourists into unique environments that offer quite specific attractions. The type of setting is thus vitally important in generating the rather specific interests and motivations of tourists. Mountain systems – the plants and animals and people who inhabit these spaces – carry with them a certain type of character or romantic that offers a base of attractions far different from freshwater or marine systems. It is perhaps the inter-play between the natural and the social/cultural that generates touristic interest in all that these places have to offer in a general capacity, but it can also be an interest that is far more specific. Tourists seek different ecosystem types with quite specific interests in mind, and these can relate to adventure (e.g. climbing), nature (e.g. birding), culture (e.g. indigenous histories), and the list goes on.

The literature is replete with reference to the disconnect that urban–dwellers feel towards nature, and as the urban realm continues to grow and expand, that which is missing in urban life, that is wilderness and biodiversity, becomes highly valued for those who have the means, and of course the interest, to bring it back into their lives. The need for such is described in the following section by Mercer (biodiversity and tourism), Pickering and Ballantyne (charismatic megaflora) and Saarinen (wilderness and tourism). Mercer argues that although diversity in nature and culture has always been at the core of tourism, this is under threat because of an increasingly homogenised world. Singapore is used as an example with only 5 per cent of this region's lowland forest and mangrove forest still in existence, with upwards of 73 per cent of all native species now extinct. Biodiversity loss continues to escalate mainly through habitat loss. In 1700, only about 5 per cent of the world's wild biomes had been altered. By 2000 only 25 per cent of the planet could be classified as wild. Pickering and Ballantyne's work is included here as a manner by which to illustrate that when it comes to an interest in biodiversity for tourism purposes, charismatic mega*flora* can be just as attractive as mega*fauna*. People travel to orchid-focused conferences, orchid shows, orchid gardens and there is demand to see wild orchids not only as a by-product to some ecotourism products, also more specifically as the focus of some tours. Saarinen continues the discussion broached by Mercer, by suggesting that the heightened appreciation of wilderness environments has come packaged with many challenges for tourism operators and land managers. Many of the most highly regarded protected areas play host to millions of visitors per year, creating many carrying capacity issues of natural and sociological dimensions. Balancing this use is complicated. Perhaps most troubling in Saarinen's account is the belief that even the implementation of sustainable tourism practices may not be sufficient to save the wilderness areas because of human pressures.

This message, that is, that too much pleasure and accompanying pressure in an environment is bad for the ecology of an environment, is echoed by Dimmock *et al.* in reference to freshwater systems. These authors argue that the high demand for freshwater for recreational purposes is only going to increase in the future. Innovation is needed to regulate these activities, especially in places where the right to participate in an activity is challenged by private property. Good governance may include actions by proactive industry groups who may stem some of the problems through responsible action. Not surprisingly, the interest in the marine environment follows the same trend as freshwater environments in reference to recreational enjoyment. This is the message put forth by Orams and Luck, who also recognise and discuss various issues and impacts from overuse. Of relevance is the fact that there is a relationship between proximity to shore and level of use. That is, the closer the activity is to the shore and to human population, the greater is the number and diversity of use – in participants and activities. As observed by Dimmock *et al.* above, Orams and Luck argue that wise management is the key to mitigating problems, and marine protected areas and fisheries management are essential for improving the problems created by action, and further that these management approaches will not be successful in the absence of an ecological system and human system interface.

Pickering and Barros illustrate that mountain tourism supports a number of activities not restricted by time of year. Although snow-based activities like downhill skiing, cross-country skiing and snowmobiling are archetypal activities in the mountains, resorts also support a number of summer activities like fishing, hiking, birdwatching and camping. The building of resorts and the heightened use of trails and other high-impact areas create a range of problems from soil compaction to impacts on animal behaviour, as well as changes to hydrology of stream systems. On the other hand, benefits are numerous including employment and economic development. Mountain tourism provides employment for local people as guides, porters, cooks, cleaners and reception staff, as well as in provision of accommodation, transport and other services in areas adjacent to the mountains.

Finally, Baldacchino reveals why island environments are so attractive as places of residence and as tourist destinations. He partitions islands into two main categories. The first, cold water islands, are less populated, have shorter tourist seasons, more challenging weather conditions and there is less focus on a service industry. By contrast, the second category, warm water islands, have an extended tourist season and are geared more specifically to the tourist industry by virtue of their weather and infrastructure. Baldacchino identifies different models of island development, and his use of Malta as a case study provides a good example of how development has provided many opportunities, but also many problems. In particular, the accelerated rate of construction has compromised many of the cultural and ecological values that have been important in defining the island community.

12

Nature bites back

Impacts of the environment on tourism

Carl Cater

Environment as a hazardous resource?

As this volume has shown, the natural environment is a fundamental resource for tourism, and is often threatened by this activity from over- or inappropriate use. Furthermore, the relationship between tourism and the environment is complex and often confusing. This interaction may be described as a metaproblem (Hall 2008), in which these relationships are inherently messy. The sheer diversity of stakeholders; the deep cultural influences on tourism and our understanding of what constitutes nature (covered in Part 1); and the complexity of the environment itself, all contribute towards this mess. It is hoped that this collection contributes towards some understanding of the interaction of these myriad factors.

Some of this complexity has its origins through the gradual process of divorcing modern societies (especially Western ones) from the natural environment in which they were set. However, recent trends have shown that we are rediscovering a desire to be close to nature, explained in Edward Wilson's (1993) concept of 'Biophilia'. The growth of sectors such as ecotourism show that there is a strong touristic desire to connect to the natural environment. Of course one can only 'love' nature if one sees oneself as a discrete entity. Indeed, Franklin points out that the attractiveness of nature is at least partially culturally derived, being 'far from inevitable or 'natural' or even in leisure terms, stable' (Franklin 2003: 214). Nevertheless, it is important that there has been 'a shift from a pastoral approach to nature to a consumer approach ... this in itself is a huge and significant transition' (Wilson 1992: 24). However, the legacy of the Cartesian division between humans and their environment means that tourism only complicates things further. For example, as Stonehouse and Crosbie (1995) have illustrated, the desire for wilderness and 'treading where no human has done so before' is a particular problem in polar tourism, as it is itself an inherently unsustainable concept. Therefore, if we are to achieve greater sustainability in tourism, it is not only a case of examining how our practices may impact the environment, but also considering how the environment impacts tourists.

Another consequence of the split between humans and nature is that we often take a resource-based view that the environment has to 'provide' for many forms of tourism and recreation. This might include snow for skiing or waves for surfing, with an early travel commentator suggesting that 'mankinds' holiday tastes are as diverse as his business pursuits, but

Nature is a never failing storehouse' (Sinclair 1914). However, we do not always reflect that to some extent 'these activities involve pitting oneself against the elements of one's environment' (Lavoilette 2010: 2). This challenge does not always have to be active, in the sense of adventure tourism, for even the most psychocentric of tourists embark on some suspension of their normal environment.

Thus, the premise of this chapter is that often we are unprepared for the environments in which tourism takes place. Tourism, by its very desire for environments different to the every-day, embeds degrees of the unfamiliar at all levels. As a result, nature has the ability to 'bite back' and impact on tourists more frequently than in everyday situations. Indeed, as Wilks and Coory show, 'travel medicine research shows that tourists are most likely to be injured while in unfamiliar surroundings and engaged in unfamiliar activities' (Wilks and Coory 2002: 2). Fur-ther, 'injuries are the leading cause of travel-related mortality worldwide, accounting for up to 25 times more deaths than infectious disease' (ibid.). Although it is impossible to catalogue all of the incidences of where the environment impacts on tourism, we can give a variety of examples across all forms of tourism to illustrate this conflict. However, it is not the intention of this chapter to be sensationalist, and the statistics used in this chapter should be seen in context, recognising for example the much higher number of tourist injuries and fatalities caused by road traffic accidents (usually making up as much as 50% of all accidental tourist fatalities). Further, it should be recognised that it is never the 'fault' of the environment; it is only our lack of understanding, or indeed connection to the environment, in which tourism takes place. Thus it is the intention of this chapter to show some examples of where these connections have failed, and through this scope solutions that exemplify greater respect.

Different environments offer markedly different threats to tourists. For example, if we com-pare work on accidental overseas visitor fatalities in Australia and New Zealand, the former has a much higher proportion of water-related deaths (23.8% to 11.9%), the latter a higher pro-portion of accidental falls and object strikes (8.1% to 15%) (Wilks et al. 2002; Bentley et al. 2001). This reflects the differences in environments and activities encountered by visitors to the two countries, the former more aquatic, and the latter more mountainous. Thus in an investi-gation of environmental impacts on tourism it makes sense to look at these threats in a range of different environments in turn.

Polar hazards

Polar regions are perhaps the most readily identifiable of challenging environments, with 'a harsh climate and physical environment, the high degree of endemism among flora and fauna, and an extremely sensitive environment' (Hall and Johnston 1995: 6). It is certainly an environment in which tourist activity requires a high degree of technological intervention to survive. However, it is also a nature-based destination that has seen dramatic growth over the past two decades. This has brought with it an increasing incidence of tourist injuries. Building on a tradition of the 'race to the poles' there are a number of high latitude events such as the North Pole marathon (North Pole Marathon 2011) in existence. Competitors brave high winds, −37°C temperatures, blizzards and snowdrifts to complete the 42.2-km race. The growing interest in areas of the Arctic for adventure tourists has also brought them into contact with dangerous wildlife. On the Nor-wegian island of Svalbard there have been only four fatal polar bear attacks since the 1970s, although tourists were killed in two separate incidents in 1995 (IUCN 1998). However, in 2010 a kayaker was dragged by his head 130 ft from his tent before his companion was able to shoot the bear. Of course, many more bears are killed each year by humans when they are perceived as a threat (AFP 2008). Indeed, it is important not to undermine the very important work illustrating the unusual nature of any animal attack, despite their use by the media to foment scare stories (Dobson 2008), for example the frenzy following the Egyptian shark attacks in Sharm el Sheikh in December 2010 (BBC 2010).

Land-based visitors to the poles are in the minority due to the difficulties posed by this physical environment. Indeed, one of the earliest polar tourism disasters was the crash of an Air New Zealand DC10 sightseeing flight on 28 November 1979 on the northeast side of Mount Erebus, Antarctica, with the loss of all 257 lives on board. The loss of life here was attributed to bad visibility and consequent pilot error (Reich 1980). Although these flights resumed in 1994, they are of limited number annually. Instead, the vast majority of visitors to polar regions are 'ship-borne adventure travellers' (Stonehouse and Crosbie, 1995), and this proportion is increasing. Of the 36,881 tourists who visited Antarctica in 2009–10 (IAATO 2011), over 99% were ship-borne visitors, and some 41% were on cruises that did not land their passengers. However, IAATO has noted the increase in private sailing vessels visiting the continent, many without proper authorisation, where those 'not sufficiently prepared have encountered difficulties, caused damage to the natural environment and important historic sites, or ventured into specially protected areas that are off limits to visitors' (IAATO 2011: 1). In response, IAATO has launched a yacht education campaign to prepare these visitors more thoroughly.

Antarctic Tour operators typically run short cruises of between 10 and 20 days with perhaps 5–14 of these spent in Antarctic waters. The spectacular scenery and the relative proximity of the Antarctic Peninsula to South America means that the majority of cruises visit this portion of the continent, along with significant island groups in the region such as South Georgia. However, these trips have not been without incident, as in 2007 the *MS Explorer*, a boutique expedition cruise ship struck an iceberg 500 miles southeast of Ushuaia. Although all 154 passengers were rescued successfully and were taken to bases on King George island, the ship itself sank. In the same year, the *MV Alexy Maryshev* was on a 10-day sightseeing cruise in the Arctic around Svalbard when a glacier 'calved' an iceberg, creating large waves and littering the deck of the ship with slabs of ice. Sixteen passengers were injured, several seriously, suffering

Figure 12.1 The *MS Explorer* sinks off Antarctica in 2007 (Fiona Stewart/Oceans 8 Productions)

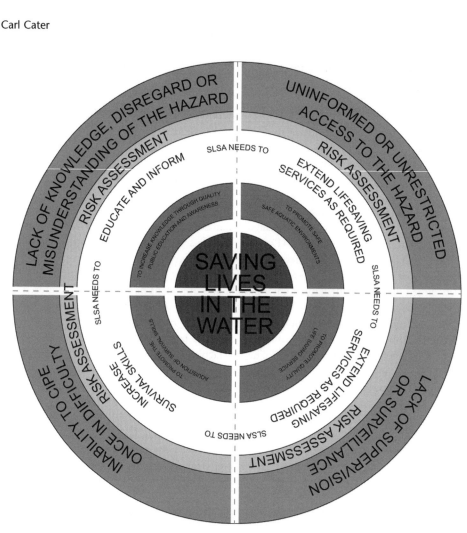

Figure 12.2 The four elements of the drowning chain in the marine environment (Surf Lifesaving Australia)

variously fractured ribs, clavicle and scapula, shoulder injuries, a fractured skull and life-threatening lung injuries, and are seeking damages from the tour operator (*Daily Mail* 2010).

Marine hazards

Apart from the injuries sustained on cruise ships detailed above, negative interactions between humans and the marine environment stem from the fact we evolved as land animals. As Cater and Cater suggest, in the oceans 'we cannot survive for very long without specialized equipment, and it is one of the few environments that still contain a significant number of other species that can kill us' (Cater and Cater 2007: 131). This was poignantly illustrated when American divers Thomas and Eileen Lonergan were accidentally left behind by a dive operator at St Crispin's Reef in Australia in January 1998. Although there were some theories at the time that their disappearance was faked, the coroner determined that, after being left afloat for two days, the couple became dehydrated and disoriented and in the end succumbed to the sea by drowning, or were eaten by sharks (BBC 1998). Indeed, the growing popularity of scuba diving – the Great Barrier

Reef hosts over one million dives per year (Wilks and Davis 2000) – has brought with it a number of extra environmental dangers. For example, for overseas tourists in Queensland, decompression illness was the second most frequent type of injury requiring hospitalisation, with 69 tourist cases being identified in a 12-month period (Wilks and Davis 2000). Although some marine creatures pose a threat to us, the sea itself poses the greatest threat to human life if not respected. The consistent link between tourist recreation and drowning is illustrated by both its significance in accidental visitor deaths (e.g. from 15% in the USA (Sniezek 1991), to 20% in Australia (Wilks *et al.* 2002)), and its higher incidence compared with resident groups.

Case study

Surf lifesaving and tourism

Despite the popularity of Australian water activities with international visitors, drowning is the second highest cause of accidental tourist deaths in the country (Wilks *et al.* 2002), with 140 tourist drownings between 1992 and 2000 (Mackie 1999; Wilks *et al.* 2002). Many tourist injuries happen in a marine environment that looks familiar, but poses challenges that are different to those at home. In particular the large waves and swell in Australia create rip and sweep currents that are rarely experienced by Europeans or Asians. In Mackie's (1999) study, 83 per cent of international tourist drownings were European or Asian. The link between international tourists and the higher incidence of getting into difficulty in the marine environment led lifesavers on Australia's Gold Coast to name two consistent rip currents the 'English Channel' and the 'Orient Express' to correspond with nationalities of tourists regularly caught in them. Between 1992 and 1997 international tourists made up almost a third of all Australian surf beach drownings (Mackie 1999). Consequently, surf lifesaving organisations in Australia recognise that 'tourists are a target group requiring special attention due to their unfamiliarity with ocean beaches and surfing activities, and in some cases having the additional challenge of poor swimming skills, language barriers, and disorientation in a foreign vacation environment' (Wilks *et al.* 2005: 121).

Surf Lifesaving Australia identifies four elements of the drowning chain related to the aquatic environment (Figure 12.2). Water safety at surf beaches has long been increased through the use of patrolled and flagged areas with lifesaving staff on duty. These areas are selected by lifesavers depending on conditions to mark the safest place to swim. Swimmers staying between the patrol flags who find themselves in need of assistance are most likely to be successfully rescued. For example, between 1999 and 2005 there were no beach drownings in Queensland between the flags (Wilks *et al.* 2007). However, these authors also show that there is an incorrect belief among swimmers that swimming in close proximity to the flags will provide the same levels of benefits if assistance is required. There were 54 deaths outside of the patrolled zone but within 1 km (70% of total drownings) in the same period (Wilks *et al.* 2007). Further, many international tourists did not necessarily know what the flags meant, with a 1991 study finding that over 90 per cent of overseas tourists were rescued in rips outside the patrol area and of these, 42% could not swim (Short *et al.* 1991).

Consequently, surf lifesaving organisations in Australia have implemented education campaigns to make tourists aware of the environmental risks and appropriate behaviour. For example, international airport arrivals are targeted with the message to 'swim between the flags' in baggage halls. This has included circulating over 10 million pamphlets with safety information to arriving tourists at the Gold Coast airport since 1988 (Wilks *et al.* 2007). In particular, 'identifying those visitor groups who are potentially 'at risk' assists health and tourism authorities to present appropriate safety information in the language of the target group, and to ensure this information is made available to visitors before they leave home' (Wilks *et al.* 2002: 555). The national *beachsafe* website is now available in 32 different languages to cater for different visitors. However, recognising that many beach visitors will still disregard the safety information, lifesaving organisations have also implemented strategies to provide broad patrol coverage beyond the flags. These include roving jetski patrols in resort areas to identify swimmers in trouble or take preventative action to prevent drownings arising. As 'Australia is a travel destination that promotes water-related activities, and the water is an unfamiliar environment with a history of injuries and fatalities involving overseas visitors, water safety is a priority area where education and prevention activities must continue' (Wilks *et al.* 2002: 555).

In sheer scale, natural disasters have the biggest impact on tourism activity, as they do not discriminate between residents and tourists. In the Boxing Day Tsunami of 2004, 227,898 people were killed or were missing and about 1.7 million people were displaced in 14 countries in South Asia and East Africa (USGS 2005). Of these, over 2,000 were tourists. Of course, the number of tourist dead was dwarfed by the residents of Indonesia and Thailand. Nevertheless, the impacts on tourism were dramatic as it 'impacted upon coastal tourism destinations in four countries, sweeping away beaches, infrastructure and superstructure, disrupting the services that tourism demands upon and severely depressing demand for affected resorts' (Cooper *et al.* 2008: 67). Tourism's status as the largest peacetime mass-migration of people, at its peak during the Christmas holiday period, meant that resorts were full, particularly with sun-seeking Scandinavians, and over 526 Swedish tourists died. Local populations, who depended so heavily on tourism, were those who had to live with the long-term consequences of the tsunami, as tourist numbers to Phuket and the Maldives fell to a third and halved, respectively, in the 6 months following the disaster. Concerns were expressed that it was particularly the informal tourist workers that suffered during the recovery phase (Ashley 2005).

Volcanoes, mountains and rivers

A less devastating, but no less disruptive, example of tectonic impact on tourism came with the eruption of the Eyjafjallajökull volcano in Iceland in April 2010. As the ash cloud from the eruption spread over Europe, and aircraft were grounded for safety fears, global air travel networks descended into chaos. Tens of thousands of Easter holidaymakers were stranded across the world, surpassing the travel impact of the 9/11 attacks on the USA in 2001 (Lund and Benediktsson 2011). Over 300 airports were closed across the continent, more than 100,000 flights were cancelled, and airlines' financial losses reached almost US$2 billion, forcing some into bankruptcy (Calleja-Crespo 2010). This was, of course, neither the first or last incidence of volcanic disruption to travel, as evidenced by the shorter closure of airspace in April 2011 from the Grímsvötn volcano. There is also much earlier evidence from the Laki volcanic eruption in 1783 when British travellers in Naples wrote that, 'the fogs continue, and are accompanied with so alarming an increase of obscurity that our bargemen do not dare venture on the waters without compass' (*The Morning Herald and Advertiser*, 9 August 1783, cited in Grattan and Brayshay 1995: 128). In 1980, the eruption of Mount St Helens in rural southern Washington, USA, was responsible for the deaths of 57 backpackers and campers (Diaz 2006). Nevertheless, in a case of any press is good press, since their recent activity Icelandic volcanoes have attracted an estimated 100,000 visitors in a boom of geotourism to the country (Heikkinen 2011).

The attraction of montane environments as a venue for tourism also has a long history, but once again there are challenging aspects to them that may not always be taken fully into account. Ironically, two tourists died in 2010 while visiting the Eyjafjallajökull volcano, not from extreme heat, but from hypothermia caused by extreme cold (Heikkinen 2011). Many climbers, skiers and hikers are injured while performing their recreational pursuits in these environments every year, and as more and more people voyage there, the numbers will only further increase. Several hundred climbers now attempt to climb Mount Everest every year for example (Hales 2007). Despite greater technology and knowledge of this environment, 'an analysis of the death rate on Mount Everest between 1980 and 2002 found it had not changed over the years, with about one death for every 10 successful ascents' (Sutherland 2006: 452). Although most deaths are put down to injury or exhaustion, Sutherland (2006) suggests that the environment itself is a major contributory factor. A significant number of deaths, and a major reason for admission to base camp medical facilities, are caused by high altitude cerebral oedema (HACE) and high altitude pulmonary oedema (HAPE–commonly lumped together as altitude sickness), which is why these high altitude areas are often called the 'death zone'. However, tourists do not have to be this extreme to suffer the ill effects of the mountain environment, as 77% of trekkers climbing Kilimanjaro in Tanzania suffered from acute mountain sickness (AMS) during their trek, in extreme cases leading to 16 altitude related tourist deaths between 1996 and 2003 (Davies *et al.* 2009).

These deaths have been partly blamed on the increasing commercialisation of adventure activity, requiring less skills and experience on the part of the tourist participant (Cater 2006). Indeed, the 1990s were particularly bad for tourist fatalities in mountain environments. As interest in pursuits such as whitewater rafting grew, with regulation and training in its infancy, the perils of this environment became clear. It was suggested that in the 1980s and 1990s approximately one fatality occurred a year in this activity in Queenstown, New Zealand (McLauhan 1995). The highest concentration of these was five deaths in an 18-month period in the mid-1990s, which sharply focused attention on safety standards in the industry. In June 1999, four British tourists drowned during a whitewater rafting trip in Austria (*The Times* 1999). Barely a month later, 21 people, many Australian and New Zealanders on a Kon Tiki tour were killed while canyoning in Switzerland when a torrential flash flood swept down the valley. The company running the trip, Adventure World, was severely criticised for ignoring storm warnings on the day of the trip (*The Guardian* 1999).

Desert and tropical environments

The extreme heat of desert environments is also likely to catch some travellers unawares. Australia, in particular, by virtue of its level of development coupled with extreme distances and high summer temperatures has struggled with tourist injuries in its desert environments. Despite frequent advice to travellers to remain with vehicles when broken down in the outback, many have sought to walk for help and perished in the process. In December 1998 an Austrian tourist, Caroline Grossmueller, and her companion became stranded in soft sand near Lake Eyre in temperatures over 40 degrees. Attempting to walk to the nearest settlement over 50 km away, Grossmueller was found dead with the word 'Help' scrawled in the red dirt several days later, half way to William Creek (Figure 12.3). Her companion was found alive with their four-wheel drive. Due to the high rate of tourist fatalities in the outback, since 2008 the South Australian Department for Environment and Heritage has closed the Simpson Desert Conservation Park during December and January each year.

Solar exposure is not limited to deserts, as is clear from its central place in the traditional 'Sun, Sand and Sea' (3S) holiday. It may be that developed countries are sitting on a cancer 'time-bomb' resulting from sun damage while on holiday. Statistics show that over the last 25 years, rates of

Figure 12.3 The environmental hazards of high temperature (Tiffany Cater)

malignant melanoma in Britain have risen faster than any of the other top ten cancers, and over 2,500 people die from skin cancer every year (Cancer Research UK 2008). Over 90% of these cancers are as a result of sun damage, which is often experienced while on 3S holidays. Cancer charities are alarmed by an increase in 'binge tanning' for younger tourists who may spend over five hours a day in the sun (Cancer Research UK 2008). The incidence of melanoma, unlike other cancers, is also highest in higher socio-economic groups, further underlining their link to exotic foreign holidays.

Thus, it is clear that to some degree that the relationship between tourists and their environment often results in uncomfortable experiences. In a study of tropical island tourists, Pearce (1981) showed how 'environmental shock' symptoms, such as stings, bites and sunburn, increased during the vacation, and by the end of their holiday, more than half of the tourists reported some of these symptoms. In Queensland, Australia, 38 per cent of overseas visitors admitted to hospital were for poisoning and injuries, whereas only 15 per cent of interstate visitors (who are more familiar with the environment) were for these causes (Nicol *et al.* 1996), again illustrating the link between environmental shock and tourism. In her discussion of how vaccinations help tourist bodies cope with the unfamiliar, Molz illustrates how 'making the body "global ready" produces the traveller's body as vulnerable and the world as risky' (Molz 2006: 10). One of her respondents likened developing country travel to 'center of the world's Petri dish of killer diseases' (ibid.: 11). However, this underlines an important consideration, that danger and difference in travel is a fundamental attraction as well as a challenge.

Respect and reconnection

As the democratisation of travel progresses, there is an increasing trend for tourists to turn from expert specialists to novice generalists (Duffus and Dearden 1990). To some extent, then, it is likely that the conflicts between humans on holiday and the environments in which they place themselves are only likely to increase. However, it is not the point of this chapter to somehow portray the environment as 'bad', rather that our awareness of the impacts of various environments on tourists is often lacking, and that this warrants greater attention. Similarly this is not a call for tourists to stay at home, as well-managed tourism can do much to contribute to the future of environments at home and abroad. Eassom contends 'what price a ripe old age in the sterilised bubble, when there is the temptation of adventure on the outside and a short sharp dose of Life?' (Eassom 1993: 27).

Rather, there are a number of lessons that can be learnt regarding the threat that environments pose to tourists. Awareness of the issue is important as 'it is important that destinations show consideration to environmental threats, as there is undoubtedly a greater contemporary concern from travelling tourists with their safety' (Wilks *et al.* 2002: 550). Probably the most crucial for destinations is that of education, for well-informed tourists are more able to adapt to the new environment in which they are placed. This may require preparation on behalf of hosts and tourists, for many of the incidences of tourist fatalities are down to being underprepared, or negligent of consequences. Regulation therefore also has its place in terms of closures or restrictions when there is an obvious danger. Lastly, destinations and the industry are increasingly recognising the importance of crisis management in coping with unforeseen environmental threats.

Through these strategies it is hoped that we might heal the rift between humans and their environments, and discover a global connection based on mutual respect. Contemporary circumstance requires that this will have to be different to past connections between the two as we have moved a long way beyond traditional societies. As discussed in the introduction of this volume, now 'issues of tourism and the natural environment are not only localised but transcend national boundaries that sometimes require both international and global responses'. Thus, the scale of our connections has to be much broader than before, so depth is a challenge. However, understanding global environmental threats does assist us with facing the environmental challenges of the current era. Indeed it is apparent that many of the tourist pursuits involving a high degree of environmental immersion and challenge also have a high degree of environmental concern (see, for example, Lavoilettes (2010) discussion of how the ethics of cliff jumpers in Cornwall are tied strongly to environmental concerns). All of these issues are connected at the end of the day, as perhaps the biggest environmental threats are those that are of our own making. Although their impact may be most obvious to us first through tourism, for example the disappearance of low-lying tropical islands such as the Maldives, it is at home that the long-term implications will be felt. It is only through greater respect and reconnection that sustainability can be realised.

References

AFP (2008) *Svalbard, where man and polar bears share the art of living.* 16 March.
Ashley, C. (2005) 'The Indian Ocean Tsunami and Tourism, *Opinions 33*. London: Overseas Development Institute.
BBC (1998) 'Missing divers 'unlawfully killed'. news.bbc.co.uk/1/hi/world/asia-pacific/190026.stm (accessed 23 June 2011).
——(2010) *Shark attack kills German tourist at resort in Egypt.* www.bbc.co.uk/news/world-middle-east-11922032 (accessed 19 July 2011).
Bentley, T., Page, S., Meyer, D., Chalmers, D., and Laird, I. (2001) 'How safe is adventure tourism in New Zealand? An exploratory analysis. *Applied Ergonomics*, 32, 327–38.

Calleja-Crespo, D. (2010) 'The EU's response to the ash crisis', Paper presented at the *Atlantic Conference on Eyjafjallajökull & Aviation*, Reykjavík, 15 September 2010. Available at en.keilir.net/static/files/conferences/eyjaaviation/intro/daniel-calleja-the-eu-s-response-to-the-ash-crisis.pdf (accessed 3 November 2010).

Cancer Research UK (2008) *Holiday 'binge tanning' increasing skin cancer risk for young brits*. Press Release 5 May 2008.

Cater, C. (2006) 'Playing with Risk? Participant perceptions of risk and management implications in adventure tourism', *Tourism Management* 27(2), 317–25. Oxford: Elsevier.

Cater, C. and Cater, E. (2007) *Marine Ecotourism*. Oxford: CABI.

Cooper, C., Fletcher, J., Fyall, A., Gilbert, D. and Wanhill, S. (2008) *Tourism: Principles and Practice* (4th edn). Hooper: Prentice Hall.

Daily Mail (2010) *Sixteen British cruise ship passengers sue luxury liner firm after iceberg crash*. www.dailymail.co.uk/news/article-1308704/Sixteen-British-cruise-ship-passengers-sue-luxury-liner-firm-iceberg-crash.html#ixzz1QZtztEJm (accessed 23 June 2011).

Davies A.J., Kalson N.S., Stokes S., Earl M.D., Whitehead A.G., Frost H., Tyrell-Marsh I. and Naylor J. (2009) 'Determinants of summiting success and acute mountain sickness on Mt Kilimanjaro (5895m)', *Wilderness & Environmental Medicine* 20, 311–17.

Diaz, J. (2006) 'Global Climate Changes, Natural Disasters, and Travel Health Risks', *Journal of Travel Medicine*, 13(6), 361–72.

Dobson, J. (2008) 'Shark! A New Frontier in Tourist Demand for Marine Wildlife', in Higham, J. and Luck M. (eds), *Marine Wildlife and Tourism Management*, Wallingford: CABI Publishing

Duffus, D. A. and Dearden, P. (1990) 'Non-consumptive wildlife-oriented recreation: a conceptual framework', *Biological Conservation*. 53: 213–31.

Eassom, S. (1993) 'Leisure, health and happiness: in praise of hedonism', in Brackenridge, C. (ed.) *Body Matters: Leisure images and lifestyles*. Leisure Studies Association publication 47 LSA, Brighton 32–49

Franklin, A. (2003) *Tourism: An Introduction*. London: Sage.

Grattan, J. and Brayshay, M. (1995) 'An Amazing and Portentous Summer: Environmental and Social Responses in Britain to the 1783 Eruption of an Iceland Volcano', *The Geographical Journal*, 161(2), 125–34.

The Guardian (1999) *Criticism grows of disaster gorge trip* (28 July).

Hales, R. (2007) 'Mountaineering', in Buckley R. *Adventure Tourism*. Oxford: CABI.

Hall, C.M. (2008) *Tourism Planning; policies, processes and relationships* (2nd edn). Essex: Prentice Hall.

Hall C. M. and Johnston, M.E. (eds) (1995) *Polar tourism: tourism in the Arctic and Antarctic regions*. Chichester: Wiley.

Heikkinen, J. (2011) *The Impact Of The Eyjafjallajökull-Eruption On The In-Bound Tourism In Iceland*. Unpublished Thesis Kajaani University of Applied Sciences School of Business, Spring 2011.

IAATO (2011) *Antarctica Tourism Fact Sheet 2010–2011*. http://image.zenn.net/REPLACE/CLIENT/1000037/1000115/application/pdf/IAATO_FactSheet_2010–11_3.pdf (accessed 24 June 2011).

IUCN (1998) *Polar bears: proceedings of the Twelfth Working Meeting of the IUCN/SSC Polar Bear Specialist Group*, 3–7 February 1997, Oslo, Norway.

Lavoilette, P. (2010) *Extreme Landscapes of Leisure; Not a Hap-Hazardous Sport*. Farnham: Ashgate.

Lund, K.A. and Benediktsson, K. (2011) Inhabiting a risky earth: The Eyjafjallajökull eruption in 2010 and its impacts. *Anthropology Today*, 27(1), 6–9.

Mackie, I.J. (1999) 'Patterns of drowning in Australia, 1992–97', *Medical Journal of Australia* 171, 587–90.

McLauhan, M. (1995) 'White water death: Why is the Shotover New Zealand's most lethal river?', *North and South* December, 70–81.

Molz, J. G. (2006) 'Cosmopolitan Bodies: Fit to Travel and Travelling to Fit', *Body & Society*, 12(3), 1–21.

Nicol, J., Wilks, J. and Wood, M. (1996) 'Tourists as inpatients in Queensland regional hospitals', *Australian Health Review*, 19(4), 55–72.

North Pole Marathon (2011) *North Pole Marathon: World's Coolest Marathon* www.npmarathon.com (accessed 19 July 2011).

Pearce, F. (1981) 'Environmental shock: a study of tourist reactions on two tropical islands', *Journal of Applied Social Psychology*, 11, 268–80.

Reich, R. J. (1980) 'The Development Of Antarctic Tourism', *Polar Record*, 20(126), 203–14

Short, A., May, A. and Hogan, C.L. (1991) 'A three year study into the circumstances behind surfbased rescues', *NSW Beach Safety Programme Report 91–1*. Sydney: Coastal Studies Unit, University of Sydney.

Sinclair, W.R. (1914) *A Guide to Wondrous Wakatipu*. Dunedin Expansion League, New Zealand

Sniezek, J.E. (1991) 'Injury mortality among non-US residents in the United States 1979–84', *International Journal of Epidemiology*, 1991

Stonehouse, B. and Crosbie, K. (1995) 'Tourist Impacts and Management in the Antarctic Peninsula Area', in Hall, C.M. and Johnston, M.E. (eds) *Polar tourism: tourism in the Arctic and Antarctic regions*. Chichester: Wiley.

Sutherland, A.I. (2006) 'Personal Views: Why are so many people dying on Everest?', *British Medical Journal*, 333(7565): 452.

The Times (1999) *Four Britons die in raft accident*, 8 June, p.1.

USGS (2005) *Earthquake hazards program. Magnitude 9.1 – off the west coast of northern Sumatra* 26 December 2004. http://earthquake.usgs.gov/earthquakes/eqinthenews/2004/us2004slav/#summary (accessed 19 June 2010).

Wilks, J. and Coory, M. (2002) 'Overseas visitor injuries in Queensland hospitals: 1996–2000', *Journal of Tourism Studies*, 13, 2–8.

Wilks, J. and Davis, R.J. (2000) 'Risk management for scuba diving operators on Australia's Great Barrier Reef', *Tourism Management*, 21(6), 591–99.

Wilks, J., Dawes, P., Pendergast, D. and Williamson, B. (2005) 'Tourists and Beach Safety in Queensland, Australia', *Tourism in Marine Environments* 2(1), 121–28.

Wilks, J., de Nardi, M. and Wodarski, R. (2007) 'Close is not Close Enough: Drowning and Rescues Outside Flagged Beach Patrol Areas in Australia', *Tourism in Marine Environments*, 4(1), 57–62

Wilks, J., Pendergast, D.L. and Wood, M.T. (2002) 'Overseas Visitor Deaths in Australia', *Current Issues in Tourism* 5(6).

Wilson, A. (1992) *The Culture of Nature*. Oxford: Blackwell

Wilson, E.O. (1993) 'Biophilia and the conservation ethic', in Kellert, S. and Wilson, E.O. (eds) *The Biophilia Hypothesis*. Washington, DC, and Covelo, CA: Island Press and Shearwater Books.

13

Biodiversity and tourism

David Mercer

According to Ghilarov (1996), the term 'biodiversity' first appeared (in his words, was 'invented') in the literature 16 years earlier in two separate publications authored, first by Lovejoy (1980), and second by Norse and McManus (1980). For Lovejoy the concept was a shorthand way of referring to species *totals*. For Norse and McManus, the main focus was on genetic and ecological *diversity*. A few years later the term was adopted as the title of Edward Wilson's (1988) landmark text. The concept is now synonymous with 'biological diversity' and defined in the 1992 United Nations Convention on Biological Diversity (CBD) as:

> The variability among living organisms from all sources ... and the ecological complexes of which they are a part; this includes diversity within species, between species and of eco-systems.

As a legally binding international treaty, the 1992 Convention – which initially was signed by some 50, mainly affluent, nations – came into force the following year because of growing alarm over species loss. This was especially the case in relation to forests and marine resources as well as the rapid expansion of commercial agriculture, large-scale tourism developments and urbanisation, and the negative consequences of the associated overconsumption of land and water resources for humans and planetary life-support systems.

The years immediately following the signing of the CBD saw a strong international focus on the relationship between tourism and biodiversity. In March 1997, this culminated in the publication of the *Berlin Declaration on Biological Diversity and Sustainable Tourism*, an aspirational document agreed to at an international conference of 18 environment ministers. *Inter alia*, this recommended:

- the promotion of tourist activities that directly or indirectly support the conservation of nature and biological diversity;
- the need to avoid additional tourism uses in areas that are already under stress;
- the need to protect the integrity of ecosystems and habitats (Vaughan 2000: 287).

Homogenisation

The rich diversity of the world's landscapes, ecosystems, flora and fauna, architecture, history and culture has long been at the core of tourism. But that diversity is under serious threat in an increasingly 'homogenised' world where languages (and the associated ecological wisdom) are disappearing almost as rapidly as species. Currently, nowhere is this process more apparent than in the largely untouched dry forest of the Chaco region in northern Paraguay. For centuries the 20,000-strong Ayoreo-Totobiegosode people lived in this largely untouched wilderness, home to native jaguars. But already, some 1 million hectares (10 per cent of the total area) have been cleared since 2007 in a largely Mennonite- and Brazilian-led land rush centred on livestock and biofuel crops for Western markets. As elsewhere, the associated road network attracts a growing tourist trade, something that is currently a particular focus of international concern in Africa with the Tanzanian government's plan for a road through the centre of Serengeti National Park and bisecting the main migration path for zebras and gazelles (Dobson *et al.* 2010).

Singapore provides another extreme, but quite different, example. As one of the most highly urbanised nations on earth, and a major international tourism hub, Singapore also ranks as one of the highest in terms of biodiversity extinction (Bradshaw *et al.* 2010). All but 5 per cent of that densely populated city state's native lowland forest and mangrove ecosystems are now gone, and it is believed that the overall extinction rate for plants, fish and mammals could be as high as 73 per cent (www.rri.org/singapore). But, as we shall see in the case of 'pristine' Antarctica, there are now no parts of the world that are untouched by humans either directly, or indirectly via a vast range of pollutants, alien organisms and species, transported by water or air.

Much of the literature on the relationship between biodiversity and tourism tends to focus on 'flagship' species such as elephants or the giant apes in tropical and sub-tropical countries (Kruger 2005). But at a quite different scale, a recent report from England on hedgerows has underscored the enormous significance of these micro-ecosystems both as a classic feature of the English landscape for overseas and domestic tourists, as well as being critical to that country's biodiversity. The Campaign to Protect Rural England (2010) study calculated that there are more than 400,000 km of hedgerows in the UK, some dating back hundreds of years. They provide important habitat and migration corridors for wildlife, yet the decade 1998–2007 witnessed a 6 per cent (26,000-km) reduction in overall length. This process is continuing, fuelled in part by technological changes in agricultural practices favouring large machinery and fields uninterrupted by vegetation.

The 2010 biodiversity target

Such was the momentum behind the global 'biodiversity movement' that by 2002, at the World Summit on Sustainable Development, held in South Africa, no less than 188 nations committed to the achievement, within 8 years, of 'a significant reduction of the current rate of biodiversity loss at the global, regional and national level' (UNEP 2002). Known as the 2010 Biodiversity Target, this also links strongly with the seventh of the eight Millenium Development Goals (MDG – 'ensure environmental sustainability'). There are 11 principal goals. Goal 1, for example, is to 'Promote the conservation of the biological diversity of ecosystems, habitats and biomes'; Goal 8 is to 'Maintain capacity of ecosystems to deliver goods and services and maintain livelihoods' and Goal 9 seeks to 'Maintain socio-cultural diversity of indigenous and local communities'. The most recent assessment is pessimistic about reaching many of the targets but – as with the parallel MDG process – argues that progress has been better in some parts of the world than in others (Secretariat of the Convention on Biological Diversity 2010).

The eighth edition of the *Living Planet Report* (WWF International 2010) reinforces these findings. It highlights a dramatic, 60 per cent overall *decline* in the Living Planet Index (LPI: a measure of biodiversity) in tropical regions between 1970 and 2007, but a 30 per cent *increase* in temperate areas. But even in the tropics there are some 'good news' stories. The declaration of the Los Amigos-Tambopata Conservation Corridor (LAT) is one of these. Over 500,000 acres in area, it connects Peru, Bolivia and Ecuador and provides a migratory corridor for jaguars and giant anteaters as well as ecotourism opportunities for local entrepreneurs. As well, until recently, Gabon had no conservation areas. But approximately 10 per cent of the country is now protected in 13 new national parks. As Vaughan (2000: 284) has argued more generally in his landmark paper on 'Tourism and biodiversity', 'the protected area system is vital, for it is realistically the only way most tour companies are able to promote nature tourism'. He also adds (Vaughan 2000: 285) a recent assessment by UNEP that, worldwide, nature tourism is worth US$260 billion annually.

Subsequently, the United Nations declared 2010 the International Year of Biodiversity. In October of that year, environment ministers from around the world attended a meeting in Nagoya, Japan, to negotiate the next round of the CBD and set new targets up to the year 2020. One outcome was the establishment of an equivalent body to the Intergovernmental Panel on Climate Change (IPCC), known as the Intergovernmental Science Policy Platform on Biodiversity and Ecosystem Services (IPBES). In the lead-up to the Nagoya conference, China, in particular, announced some significant reforms that will see around a quarter of the country protected in conservation areas. As well, US$4.5bn. has been allocated for 'rewards' to provincial districts that protect biodiversity (Watts 2010a).

Needless to say, in China as elsewhere, protected area status does not automatically guarantee species protection. In many countries the vast majority of critically endangered species are found outside protected areas (see, for example, Watson *et al.* 2011), and ongoing management requires substantial financial resourcing.

Evaluating biodiversity and ecosystem services

Those advocating the need for biodiversity conservation traditionally have done so by promoting one, or a combination of the following propositions: (i) all life on earth has intrinsic value and a 'right' to exist; (ii) it provides vital ecosystem services such as carbon storage or clean air and drinking water; (iii) there are substantial economic benefits to be derived from nature-based tourism; and (iv) medicinal/pharmaceutical breakthroughs often derive from recently discovered genes or species (Horwitz *et al.* 2001).

In some parts of the world experiences are on offer whereby indigenous people share their intimate knowledge of traditional medicinal plants and bush foods with Western tourists. Such enterprises can play an important role in keeping indigenous cultures alive and raising awareness of different spiritual traditions and the value of biodiversity. The 9-day, 80-km guided walk along the Lurujarri Dreaming Trail that takes place once a year, starting in Broome, Western Australia, is an outstanding example. Also, in Sri Lanka and India, a thriving tourist trade has built up over the years grounded in Ayurvedic herbal medicines and associated health practices.

A serious concern is that, until recently, the undoubted economic benefits of ecosystem services (the 'positive externalities') were largely invisible and unrecognised in dollar terms. This is changing, but slowly. The landmark synthesis study on this, by Robert Costanza and his colleagues, was first published in 1997. Aggregating upwards from the per-hectare level, they estimated the global economic value of 17 ecosystem services and 16 biomes (open ocean, forest, tundra, etc.) to be of the order of US$33 trillion per year. 'Recreation/tourism' is considered to be one of these services. Other examples are the regulation of: (i) climate; (ii) disturbance; and (iii) water, and nutrient cycling. More recently, Balmford *et al.* (2002: 950), including Costanza as one of the co-authors, have reconsidered and updated the original methodology, arguing that 'high local values of services such as tourism may not be maintained if extrapolated worldwide'.

Belatedly, the United Nations Environment Programme (UNEP) has recruited a team of international experts working on a project investigating the 'Economics of Ecosystems and Biodiversity' (TEEB; www.teebweb.org). Their recent estimate of the annual costs of forest degradation and loss, alone, ranges from US$2 trillion to US$4.5 trillion, but they calculate, optimistically, that this could be reversed by an annual injection of as little as US$45 billion (Secretariat of the Convention on Biological Diversity 2010).

Costa Rica provides a good example. Some 15 years ago, in order to discourage deforestation, the government decided to pay farmers who had forest on their land US$50 per hectare per year to preserve the trees. As a consequence, forest cover has expanded dramatically. In addition to the undoubted tourism-related benefits associated with biodiversity (one tree can host a thousand different life-forms), one of the positive outcomes has been much higher levels of reliable electricity generation from hydro-sources because dam water levels have risen substantially in protected catchments (ABC Radio 2010). This, in turn, has delivered clear benefits to tourism, a sector that is strongly reliant on a secure electricity supply, as well as on clean drinking water. Together with another Central American country – Belize – Costa Rica long ago recognised the commercial potential of biodiversity for the national benefit, not just from ecotourism, but also in the form of pharmaceutical products.

Marine protected areas (MPAs) provide another comparable example. Even though the rate of uptake for these has been slow by comparison with their terrestrial counterparts, there are now over 5,000 around the world covering almost 1 per cent of the oceans. In all parts of the world where they have been gazetted and policed, invariably there has been an explosion in the fish population both within and adjacent to the protected zones, generating substantial benefits for both the commercial fishing and tourism sectors. However, if MPAs are not appropriately managed and policed there can be serious ecological repercussions. This is happening in Hanifaru Bay, Baa Atoll, in the Maldives. This has been an MPA since 2009 but its 250 manta rays breeding in an area no larger than a football field are under serious threat from totally unregulated tourist visitation (Shelton 2010).

Australia now leads the world in terms of the total area of MPAs nationally, and the 344,000 sq km Great Barrier Reef Marine Park (GBRMP) is a clear case in point (Olsson *et al.* 2008). In 2004 re-zoning of the GBRMP resulted in the proportion of 'no-take' zones expanding in area from 4.5 per cent to 33.3 per cent. This has improved the health of the highly prized coral trout population, in particular, and a broader tourism-related fishing sector that now contributes more than A$150 million to the Queensland economy (Great Barrier Reef Marine Park Authority 2009). Needless to add, this has done little to change Australia's overall status with regard to its international standing on the number of threatened and extinct species. With a current total of 822 (including 95 fishes and 175 molluscs) threatened species, it has a far worse record than Cameroon, Tanzania or India. It also has the poorest record of all countries for the number of mammal species (22) that have become extinct over the last 200 years of European settlement (Johnson 2006).

Habitat loss and 'dead zones'

There are now 193 Parties to the CBD, but in many ways it is surprising, and disappointing, that it took so long to come to fruition. Interestingly, leading players in the early years included a number of countries with by far the highest rates of ecological change and species extinction. In the USA, for example, 126 major ecosystems covering most of the country have had their natural habitats reduced by 75 per cent or more over the centuries. For 30 of these the figure is 98 per cent, and for 58 of these 85 per cent (McDaniel and Gowdy 2000). The impact on wildlife has been dramatic. Common across North American grasslands prior to the nineteenth century, only two small populations of migratory bison now exist (Harris *et al.* 2009).

Further, to take but one of many possible recent cases, Stafford *et al.* (2010) report that the so-called Dead Zone of oxygen-starved waters in the northwestern Gulf of Mexico was initially identified as a serious problem in the early 1970s. But by the mid-1980s, fuelled by massive injections of nitrogen and other nutrients from heavy fertiliser application on US and Mexican farmland into rivers, and subsequently the marine environment, it had expanded to around 8,000 sq km and has more than doubled in size since then. Fish and crustaceans cannot survive in this ever-expanding toxic 'soup', and coastal communities formerly totally dependent on commercial fishing and tourism have suffered accordingly. The most recent UNEP *Year Book* reports that, globally, there are now around 400 'dead' marine zones and that they have been doubling in size approximately every decade over the last 50 years (UNEP 2010).

It is not uncommon in the affluent world for specific commercial interests like tourism to be compensated financially if livelihoods are decimated by serious oil pollution, as recently in the US states bordering the Gulf of Mexico, or by the legislated designation of 'no-take' fishing areas, as in Australia's Great Barrier Reef Marine Park (Macintosh *et al.* 2010). But commercial enterprises impacted by slow-onset environmental deterioration from multiple point-sources are rarely compensated in the same way.

Biologically 'dead zones' similar to the Gulf of Mexico example are now common around the world and serve as a stark reminder of the complex inter-play between ecosystems, governance systems and damaging practices associated with a variety of commercial activities. Stafford *et al.* (2010) point out that natural systems invariably demonstrate surprising resilience, but, when subjected to continued, cumulative stress from a process like nitrogen build-up, a crucial 'tipping-point' is reached beyond which restoration is difficult, if not impossible, to achieve.

Coral reef ecosystems are without doubt one of the single most important of all for the tourism sector. Coastal regions are now home to over half the world's population and a third of these live in close association with coral reefs. But reef ecosystems everywhere are under severe stress from mining (for construction materials and tourist souvenirs), dredging (for resort and marina developments), pollution and sedimentation, as well as from overfishing. Such activities weaken reef structures and make them especially vulnerable to extensive and often irreversible damage from sudden biological 'shocks' such as explosions in the population of the Crown-of-thorns Starfish (*Acanthaster planci*). This has occurred from time to time with devastating impact on the Great Barrier Reef and more recently (in 2009) on the UNESCO, World Heritage-listed Tubbataha Reefs in the Philippines' Sulu Sea.

Also, as became apparent following the 2004 Indian Ocean tsunami, intact coral reefs can act as a strong protective buffer against destructive waves. In Sri Lanka, for example, hotels along the densely settled south and eastern littoral that were guarded by largely unmodified reef, dune and mangrove ecosystems invariably escaped serious damage, whereas resort developments that had significantly altered these environments suffered either partial or total destruction. Unfortunately, there are signs that this lesson has already been forgotten, with major, resort-style tourist developments currently being promoted by the government and overseas commercial interests in significant mangrove and lagoon environments along the west and south coasts. In this, Sri Lanka is not alone. The Balmford *et al.* (2002) study, mentioned earlier, found that mangrove communities around the world are the most relentlessly eliminated of all biomes, at a far greater rate, for example, than tropical forests.

Levels of biological organisation

The CBD definition above highlights that there are different levels of biological organisation. From small-scale to large-scale, the four most commonly recognised are: genetic; species; community or ecosystem; and landscape or regional. As Noss (1995: 80) notes, 'Biodiversity is most commonly measured at the species level'. Yet, paradoxically, only a tiny proportion (around 1.9 million) of the world's estimated 10–100 million species have been scientifically classified. An ambitious, decade-long project – the Census of Marine Life – involving scientists from 80 nations, has recently concluded that biologists are aware of around 230,000 named marine species out of a likely total of anywhere between 1 million and 1.4 million (Carey 2010).

In short, there is still a remarkably high level of scientific ignorance about species, their interactions and ecosystem functioning and a serious paucity of evidence-based information to guide management decisions (Pullin and Salafsky 2010). The causes of Crown-of-thorns Starfish infestations on the Great Barrier Reef are a classic case. After years of generously funded, detailed research, there is still no certainty as to whether the intermittent plagues are 'natural' or human-induced, or indeed some combination of both. The costs of removal during an infestation can be as high as A$40 per starfish so this form of control has only ever been used for relatively small, intensively used tourist sites (Lawrence *et al.* 2002).

Definitional debates

Notwithstanding the rapid developments in international diplomacy related to the CBD, as in Ghilarov's (1996) paper and more recent contributions by Hamilton (2005), Mayer (2006) and Ridder (2008), there has been a vigorous, ongoing debate around rival definitions of 'biodiversity' and what these mean for ecosystem management and policy. Academic commentators from disciplines as diverse as anthropology, political science, economics and, of course, ecology, marine biology and genetics, have joined in sometimes heated argument about the origins, evolution and, indeed, ultimate utility of the concept. Diamond's (2005), best-selling book, *Collapse*, and the subsequent critique of that text by a number of writers in *Questioning Collapse* (McAnany and Yoffee 2009) provide a useful insight into the complexity of this trans-disciplinary issue. Since the early 1980s, a parallel debate has also centred around the related concept of 'ecosystem health'.

Ghilarov, in particular, is highly critical of the superficiality of the 'aeroplane rivets' metaphor that was so widely invoked in the 1990s and emphasises that biodiversity is not a 'thing', but a *process* involving constant change and evolution and sometimes massive disturbance through such media as flood, fire, tsunami or hurricane, etc. Thus, measurement always entails numerous complex issues revolving around precisely where the geographical borders are to be drawn with regard to any given system (the *scale* question), as well as the time-period involved (the *temporal* question). Mayer (2006), by contrast, argues that when viewed as a 'framework' for the variety of planetary life, biodiversity is not a measurable 'thing', but that, nevertheless, carefully specified features of biodiversity certainly can be calibrated.

Together with other scientific commentators, both Ghilarov and Ridder are adamant that management practices prioritising the protection of individual species (invariably 'world-wide flagship species, Kruger 2005) are quite different from those focusing on managing for diversity. Ghilarov (1996: 306) reminds us, for example, that:

> … the bear (*ursus arctos*) was a common species in forests just near Moscow up to the 17th century. Now, unfortunately, there are no more bears in the Moscow region, but the

forests continue to grow, consuming carbon dioxide and releasing oxygen in the same manner as they did centuries ago.

Further, in their critical commentary on the representation of biodiversity in the Western Pacific region in tourism promotion brochures and the publications of such bodies as the World Wide Fund for Nature (WWF) and Conservation International (CI), the anthropologists, Foale and Macintyre (2005: 13) comment that:

> We rarely see photographs of organisms of major ecological importance: the fungi in the soil, the symbiotic unicellular algae living within the tissues of corals, the thousands of drab little insects that perform vital pollination.

This view is shared by the zoologists, Zamin *et al.* (2010) in their recent overview of the poor state of National Red List (NRL) reporting around the world. They found that only 109 countries had such lists (less than 50 per cent in Africa, Oceania, Latin America and the Caribbean), and that there is an overwhelming emphasis on data collection for amphibians, birds and mammals rather than for plants or fungi, lichens and invertebrates. This again highlights the poor state of scientific knowledge for many parts of the developing world, in particular, that are often in a rush to embrace Western-style tourism-related infrastructure projects in the absence of crucial baseline data.

In terms of species numbers, invertebrates represent some 75 per cent of recorded global biodiversity and it is not uncommon for such organisms to be 'keystone species', performing a disproportionately pivotal role in ecosystem functioning and, indeed, collapse. A classic example is provided by the black sea urchin (*Diadema antillarum*) that plays such a key role in Caribbean coral reef ecosystem functioning and the tourism sector that is so dependent on the existence of healthy reefs. In 1983, a pathogen infected this sea urchin on a massive scale across 3.5 million sq km of the Caribbean in 'the most widespread epidemic ever documented for a species of marine invertebrate' (Lessios *et al.* 1984: 336). The impact on tourism-related dive and fishing enterprises in Jamaica has been profound. Live coral cover there declined from 52 per cent to 3 per cent between 1977 and 1993 (Carr and Heyman 2009).

Biodiversity and climate change

Since the early 1990s there has been growing scientific recognition and consensus regarding the crucial link between biodiversity (the 'ecosystem sector') and climate change, and the role that intact ecosystems can play in building resilience to climate change. Together, deforestation and agriculture, for example, contribute around 20 per cent of all greenhouse gas emissions, globally, whereas some 15 per cent of emissions are sequestered in tropical forests (van Oosterzee 2010).

Tourism, climate change and biodiversity are intimately connected at many different levels. The WTO/UNEP (2008) analysis, for example, identified five global 'hotspots' where climate change will almost certainly have major impacts on tourism destinations. In three of these – the Mediterranean region, and the Pacific Ocean and Indian Ocean Small Island Nations – both land and marine biodiversity decline on a large scale are anticipated, as is marine biodiversity in the other two hotspot regions, the Caribbean and Australia/New Zealand.

Potentially this has far-reaching negative consequences for tourism in the future, especially in countries like Antigua and Barbuda where coral reef ecosystems are the foundation for an economic sector contributing to 75 per cent of the nation's GDP (Carr and Heyman 2009). One controversial response that has been adopted by some airline companies is to encourage travellers to make a financial contribution towards voluntary carbon offsets for their flights. Effectively this is a modest carbon tax that can be used, for example, to fund afforestation projects to sequester carbon. A criticism of this approach is that it shifts the burden from *producer* to *customer* responsibility and, because of its voluntary nature, has had minimal impact (WTO/ UNEP 2008).

The growing dominance of anthromes

Mention has already been made of the extreme examples of biodiversity loss in Singapore, Australia and the USA. But these particular cases are part of the larger global picture of what many scientists believe to be the most recent of the world's six mass extinction phases characterised by a species destruction rate some 1,000 to 10,000 times higher than is 'natural' (iucn. org/what/tpas/biodiversity).

A recent study of the replacement of 'wild', terrestrial biomes by anthropogenic biomes (or anthromes) has painted a picture of relentless transformation of natural landscapes and ecosystems by humans, mapped for four specific time periods: 1700, 1800, 1900 and 2000 (Ellis *et al.* 2010). In pre-industrial 1700, around 5 per cent of the terrestrial biosphere was impacted to any significant degree by human activity. But by 2000, only 25 per cent could be classified as 'wild'. The early twentieth century marked the crucial 'tipping-point' for the transition of the world's ice-free lands from largely 'wild' to predominantly 'anthropogenic'. Interestingly, the research found that by far the most significant change in global land use occurred between 1800 and 2000. This was the sixfold increase in the area of pastures, or rangelands.

Tourism has contributed to biome transformation in many different ways, not least through the rapid growth in recent years in the popularity of golf and the massive expansion in the total area of golf courses around the world, even in arid countries like Egypt and Australia. Contemporary 36-hole golf courses typically have a coverage of around 300 hectares and frequently involve large-scale biodiversity depletion or loss of productive agricultural land. Heavy watering and fertiliser application regimes are also a common feature. The tropical island of Hainan in the South China Sea is one of the latest battlegrounds in the ongoing conflict between environmentalists and multinational golf resort interests. Catering largely for an affluent Chinese clientele, the island already has 30 golf courses but, with strong government support, there are plans to expand this number tenfold in anticipation of growing domestic demand, but also to compete with Hawaii for overseas tourists. Home to 300 endangered species, the biologically rich, Diaolou Mountains National Park is currently under serious threat from a proposed golf course development (Watts 2010b).

Habitat destruction and species loss

Since the signing of the CBD, 'biodiversity' has become a familiar term in the media and popular parlance, often being linked automatically with the words 'extinction', 'loss' or 'collapse' (Diamond 2005). However, it should not be forgotten that, through a process of selection, species disappear 'naturally' all the time. A commonly quoted statistic is that around 95 per cent of all species that have ever existed on earth are now extinct. Nevertheless, UN background documents regularly highlight the unprecedented historical changes to ecosystems that have taken place over the last 50 years, in particular, and the fact that the pace of destruction is accelerating. These processes and outcomes are elaborated on in the pathbreaking, 2005 *Millenium Ecosystem Assessment Report* (United Nations 2005), as well as in the annual *Red Lists of the World's Endangered Species*, produced by the International Union for the Conservation of Nature (IUCN).

Certain large mammals ('flagship species') are often iconic tourist attractions in their own right and – largely because of habitat destruction – many are on the verge of extinction. One of these is the rare Rothschild giraffe. Added to the *Red List* in 2010, there are now fewer than 700 of these alive in the wild, mainly in Uganda and Kenya, and largely restricted to small, isolated populations in predominantly agricultural landscapes and with limited capacity to range. Apart from rigid protection and captive breeding, one of the key strategies necessary for the survival of such species is to accommodate them in very large reserves or an inter-connected system of habitat corridors, often demanding international co-operation. Such an outcome has been successfully negotiated between Zimbabwe, Mozambique and South Africa in the form of the still-expanding Great Limpopo Transfrontier Peace Park, which incorporates the 19,000 sq km Kruger National Park, the largest conservation zone on the planet. Because of its sheer size, wild animals here have the freedom to make much-needed migrations over long distances in line with seasonal variations in rainfall and food resources.

Another worthwhile strategy, advocated for example by the Wildlife Conservation Society's (WCS) 'living landscapes' approach in Madagascar, is to engage in far-sighted consensus-building with government institutions and agricultural landholders to increase revenue generation at the local scale and facilitate land-use trade-offs (Erdmann 2010). So-called REDD (Reduced Emissions from Deforestation and Degradation) schemes also have potential. These pump millions of dollars into developing nations in return for forest protection. Norway has recently signed a $1-billion REDD deal with Indonesia, and Australia has committed A$70 million to the same country (Fogarty 2010). Positive ecotourism revenue increases over the long term are a hoped-for outcome.

The most recent of the *Red List* reports has underscored the often strong association between biodiversity 'hotspots', poverty and high numbers of threatened species (IUCN 2010). Ecuador, for example, tops the list with 2,227 threatened species (by comparison, highly developed Canada has only 68 and the UK 72); Indonesia (1,116) Malaysia (1,167) China (832) and Madagascar (641) also have large numbers of threatened species. In the latter country, all but 10 per cent of the original forest cover has been lost.

Consumptive and non-consumptive uses of wildlife

In such countries mammals, birds and plant associations are often a valuable tourist drawcard for specialist nature tours, catering especially for European and North American tourists. But, unfortunately, those same resources are frequently more highly valued domestically for environmentally destructive and/or illegal commercial ends such as logging, plantation establishment or the now lucrative and thriving international trade in endangered species. The latter is often run by well-organised crime syndicates serving Asian markets and can involve either live animals or body parts for medicinal and related purposes or – as in the case of elephant tusks – for highly valued ivory. Estimates now put the number of black and white rhinoceros in Africa, for example, at only 18,000, down from 65,000 in the 1970s. The black rhinoceros is critically endangered. In July 2010, poachers killed the last remaining rhinoceros cow in the 1500-hectare, Krugersdorp game reserve for its prized horn (*The Guardian* 2010). The reserve currently attracts over 200,000 visitors each year.

This highlights the important issue of significant and long-established cultural differences over the consumptive and non-consumptive use of wildlife – particularly between 'East' and 'West' (but also *within* such countries as Norway (Ris 1994) and the Azores (Neves 2010a, b)) – that so often bedevil the successful implementation of international conventions relating to the protection of wildlife and associated habitats. The ongoing conflict over Japanese whale-hunting in the Southern Ocean is a clear case in point.

It also should not be forgotten that until relatively recently hunting such animals as elephants, lions and tigers for 'sport' was widely considered an enjoyable and noble pursuit, especially on the part of male gentry in colonial nations. In Sri Lanka, according to official government statistics, over 5,000 elephants were killed in this way between 1845 and 1859, alone. The actual slaughter may have been much higher. This was a period that also witnessed the start of growing moral outrage in Britain with the formation of the Royal Society for the Prevention of Cruelty to Animals (Lorimer and Whatmore 2009).

Around the world, big game hunting has played a significant role in species depletion. Although far less 'respectable' today, it still continues, often illegally. A related issue is that in many countries tourists occasionally are killed by bears, crocodiles, dingoes, sharks, lions, etc., when confronted in their natural habitat. A not uncommon – and regrettable – reaction is to exact swift 'revenge' and fuel the stereotype of these animals as 'the enemy'. This happened on Fraser Island, a World Heritage site off the coast of Australia, after a fatal dingo attack on a 9-year-old boy in April 2001. Following extensive media coverage of the issue, the highly controversial management response was to identify *Canis lupus dingo* as 'the problem' on an island attracting some 300,000 visitors a year, and to cull 31 dingoes from their natural habitats regularly shared with tourists. Fraser island dingoes are an especially pure strain and the total population is only of the order of 150–200. The management problem, as articulated by Thompson *et al.* (2003: 46), is to determine 'if the animals are in our habitat or we in theirs'. Similar 'co-existence' issues apply to other forms of wildlife that are attractive to tourists.

Gorilla tourism in East Africa – at least on the surface – provides a positive example of how the attitudes of some locals and former poachers can be changed and species pulled back from the edge of extinction. Tourist interest in the estimated 786 surviving gorillas in contiguous national parks spanning Rwanda, Congo and Uganda now generates a respectable US$3 million a year for Rwanda alone, one of the world's poorest nations. At US$300 a time, visits in small groups and for only one hour to gorilla mountain habitat are expensive, but popular and generally well controlled. Thousands of related jobs have been generated and the most recent census has recorded an increase in the gorilla population in Rwanda from 380 to 480 between 2003 and 2010 (*The Age* (Melbourne) 2010). Nevertheless, the Rwandan experience does have its critics. Butynski and Kalina (2009), for example, argue that gorilla tourism has been allowed to grow too fast, based on an inadequate understanding of gorilla behaviour and the long-term impacts. They conclude that if protection of endangered populations is the ultimate aim there is a strong argument for using the well-established, conservation trust fund approach rather than following the tourism path. For these researchers tourism involves too many potential risks by comparison with the model of the US-funded Mgahinga and Bwindi-Impenetrable Forests Conservation Trust, started in 1994.

Even though there is evidence of gorillas and chimpanzees contracting respiratory diseases from tourists, by far the main dangers to their continued existence are from ongoing poaching and habitat destruction, especially associated with logging and mining. A recent collaboration between UNEP and INTERPOL (Nellemann *et al.* 2010) concluded that the combined threats are now so dire that gorillas may well disappear completely from much of central Africa by the mid-2020s.

Whale watching

The lucrative and rapidly growing tourism enterprise centred around whale-watching – currently valued at US$2.1 billion, and employing some 13,000 people in 119 countries (International Fund for Animal Welfare 2009) – clearly has a direct economic interest in the health of extremely small organisms as well as their much larger iconic prey and the extensive geographical zones within which they migrate. Minute phytoplankton are the food source for the invertebrate krill on which whales feed. But the total mass of Antarctic krill has declined dramatically in recent decades, almost certainly as a consequence of global and ocean warming. Extensive coral bleaching is a parallel response in tropical and sub-tropical waters. Plainly, if this process continues it will impact negatively on the number of tourists willing to pay for a whale watching experience (currently some 13 million a year), as well as on the potential of this economic sector for poorer maritime nations, in particular (Cisneros-Montemayor et al. 2010). Depending on the precise climate change scenario that unfolds we can anticipate significant poleward shifts in the migration of marine species – including whales. Indeed, there is already evidence that this is occurring (Last et al. 2011). Inevitably, this will have an impact on the changing geography of whale watching. Some coastal nations will benefit, whereas others will suffer.

Antarctica

Many commentators from the sub-discipline of invasive ecology have pointed out that one of the most serious threats to biodiversity comes from biological invasion. Tourism operations that have not adhered to strict biosecurity protocols have long been one of the main ways in which pathogens have been introduced into previously 'clean' environments. Of mounting concern over the last 25 years or so, for example, has been the impact of tourism in Antarctica and the sub-Antarctic islands, both from the growing number of cruise vessels themselves – their effluent, ballast water, contaminants, food refuse, etc. – but also from tourist landing parties at remote sites.

Unlike the Arctic, which is subject to the strict maritime laws of countries such as Canada and the USA, the Antarctic has no comparable regulatory regime for tourism operations. The Antarctic Treaty requires a unanimous vote of all member states for regulatory change but this has proven difficult to achieve even following environmental disasters such as the grounding of the Norwegian cruise ship, *MS Nordkapp*, at Deception island in January 2007 and the subsequent leakage of fuel into the sea. A related issue is that a number of the cruise ships visiting Antarctica are from non-treaty countries such as Cyprus.

The research of Navareen et al. (2001) documented a 425 per cent increase in landings from inflatable boats at 165 sites in the decade, 1989–99. As well, in the period 2000–07, there was a tripling of the number of cruise ship passengers to Antarctica, rising to close to 40,000 in the 2008/9 summer season (Eijgelaar et al. 2010). In 1996–97, the numbers were closer to 7,000. Around 20 different companies now operate cruises, with some ships now carrying between 1,000 and 3,000 passengers.

In addition to the upsurge in the intensity of tourism pressures, just discussed, in their exhaustive overview Frenot et al. (2005) identified three other significant trends in Antarctic tourism that are relevant to the spread of invasive species:

(1) high-diversity sites are the most vulnerable. Of the 85 sites most commonly visited by cruise ships, 23 per cent are categorised as having high-to-medium diversity. When combined, this relatively small number of sites attract around 50 per cent of all tourists to the region;
(2) there have been some changes in the popularity of the most visited sites, which means that the tourist 'load' is being spread more widely across Antarctica over time;
(3) there has been a tendency for cruises to become longer in duration and to take in a growing number of destinations. Kayaking and longer on-shore excursions are also becoming more commonplace, thus increasing the risk of species invasion.

Goudier Island provides a good example of a high-intensity destination. This has long been a popular site for viewing gentoo penguins (*Pygoscelis papua)*, with visitor numbers increasing from approximately 4,000 to 16,000 between 1996 and 2007. Of the ten breeding colonies on the island, all but four are regularly visited by tourists. A continuous, 12-year monitoring programme of all colonies has found that two of the visited sites demonstrate a steep decline in the number of breeding pairs but has concluded that there are many factors at play – including 'natural', inter-annual variability and 'scientific observer effects' in the experimental design – and that it is too premature to 'blame' tourism for this (Trathan *et al.* 2008).

Lewis *et al.* (2003) focused in some detail on the biological danger posed by marine organisms being transported into Antarctic waters from Tasmania. The island of South Georgia, which has an estimated 200 introduced alien species, is considered to be especially vulnerable because of its growing popularity as a tourism destination and also because of the changing environmental conditions associated with climate change. Already Macquarie Island has seen dramatic changes to its ecology caused by a worsening rabbit and mouse plague and this will have obvious impacts in the future on the attractiveness of this destination for cruise vessels.

Of the sub-Antarctic islands in general, Bargagli (2008: 222) concluded: 'As these regions have less extreme climatic and environmental conditions … they seem particularly at risk for environmental contamination as well as for the introduction of alien, pre-adapted organisms, including wildlife pathogens'. There have been repeated calls over the years for much stricter enforcement of biosecurity controls over tourists, ships – and, increasingly, aircraft – venturing into Antarctic territory. With the growing number of flights from South America, Australia and New Zealand, there is now the potential for the transport of alien organisms within a matter of hours.

'Captive' biodiversity and a new research frontier

In this chapter a number of case studies have been presented both of the positive impact carefully managed tourism can have on biodiversity preservation and the multiple benefits of biodiversity for tourism enterprises. Damaging relationships have also been identified. Biodiversity is synonymous with 'life' and 'richness', but paradoxically, 'dark tourism' (Lennon and Foley 2000) has a fascination with areas denuded or radically transformed by human activity and virtually devoid of life. The lunar-like landscapes around such mining towns as Queenstown, Coober Pedy or Broken Hill in Australia have long been tourist drawcards, as has the area around the crippled Chernobyl nuclear power plant in the Ukraine (Walker 2010). Unfortunately, the relentless process of biodiversity decline globally provides little cause for optimism. However, occasionally there are some signs of hope. Mention has been made of the most recent (2010) *Living Planet Report's* finding that there has been an estimated 30 per cent increase in biodiversity in temperate regions between 1970 and 2007. There are some surprising connections with tourism. A growing interest in 'culinary tourism', for example, has reportedly brought the critically endangered Basque pig back from the edge of extinction in southern France (Nolan 2010).

The case studies discussed have all focused on what might be described loosely as the natural world 'out there', or *in situ*. But to conclude, it is worth highlighting another growing trend in the form of usually privately owned and run free-range zoos and similar attractions in different countries, many of which have captive breeding programmes for critically endangered species. Australia's network of Earth Sanctuaries and the Healesville Sanctuary near Melbourne, as well as the Animal Park of Gramat in France and the Eden Project in the UK are outstanding examples of this genre. Opened in March 2001, in a disused quarry in Cornwall, the latter project consists of several spectacular, dome-shaped greenhouses (artificial biomes) that house thousands of plant species from all over the world (Bowker 2007). With some one-and-a-quarter million visitors a year, it is now one of the UK's most important tourist attractions in a formerly seriously economically depressed region and represents a new kind of biodiversity-related tourism, educational and architectural venture the likes of which may well become much more common in the future as natural ecosystems continue to be degraded.

A final point that needs to be emphasised is that recent years have seen the emergence of some interesting cutting-edge inter-disciplinary research on nature tourism that takes a highly critical and questioning stance coming largely from an animal welfare/animal beha-viour and human interactions perspective. The works of Katja Neves (2010a, 2010b) on whalewatching, Butynski and Kalina (2009) on gorilla tourism, Bargagli (2008) on Antarctic tourism and Thompson *et al.* (2003) on Australian dingoes have all been mentioned and are fine examples of this approach. It is to be hoped that the significant research findings of these and related researchers will, in time, be translated into much more strictly regulated industry practices grounded in rigorous longitudinal research on tourism impacts on animal behaviour.

References

ABC Radio (2010) 'Economic value of the environment', *The Science Show*, 21 August.

Balmford, A., Bruner, A., Cooper, P., Costanza, R., Farber, S., Green, R.E., Jenkins, M., Jefferiss, P., Jessamy, V., Madden, J., Munro, K., Myers, N., Naeem, S., Paavola, J., Rayment, M., Rosendo, S., Roughgarden, J., Trumper, K. and Turner, R.K. (2002) 'Economic reasons for conserving wild nature', *Science*, 297, 950–3.

Bargagli, R. (2008) 'Environmental contamination in Antarctic ecosystems', *Science of the Total Environment*, 400 (1–3), 212–26.

Bowker, R. (2007) 'Children's perceptions and learning about tropical rainforests: an analysis of their drawings', *Environmental Education Research*, 13(1), 75–96.

Bradshaw, C.J.A., Giam, X. and Sodhi, N.S. (2010) 'Evaluating the relative environmental impact of countries', *Plos ONE* 5(5), 1–16.

Butynski, T.M. and Kalina, J. (2009) 'Gorilla tourism: A critical look', in Milner-Gulland, E.J. and Mace, R. (eds), *Conservation of Biological Resources*. Chichester: Wiley-Blackwell, 294–313.

Campaign to Protect Rural England (2010) *England's Hedgerows: Don't Cut Them Out*. CPRE, London.

Carey, A. (2010) 'Sea census tallies untold number of species', *The Age* (Melbourne), August 4, 5.

Carr, L.M. and Heyman, W.D. (2009) 'Jamaica bound ? Marine resources and management at a crossroads in Antigua and Barbuda', *The Geographical Journal*, 175(1), 17–38.

Cisneros-Montemayor, A.M., Sumaila, U.R., Kaschner, K. and Pauly, D. (2010) 'The global potential for whale watching', *Marine Policy*, 34, 1273–8.

Costanza, R., d'Arge, R., de Groots, R., Farber, S., Grasso, M., Hannon, B., Limburg, K., Naeem, S., O'Neill, R.V., Paruelo, J., Raskins, R.G., Sutton, P. and van den Belt, M. (1997) 'The value of the world's ecosystem services and natural capital', *Nature*, 387, 253–60.

Diamond, J. (2005) *Collapse: How Societies Choose to Fail or Survive*. London: Allen Lane.

Dobson, A., Borner, M., Sinclair, T. and 24 others (2010) 'Road will ruin Serengeti', *Nature*, 467, 272–3.

Eijgelaar, E., Thaper, C. and Peeters, P. (2010) 'Antarctic cruise tourism: the paradoxes of ambassadorship, "last chance tourism" and greenhouse gas emissions', *Journal of Sustainable Tourism*, 18(3), 337–54.

Ellis, E.C., Goldewijk, K.K., Siebert, S., Lightman, D. and Ramankutty, N. (2010) 'Anthropogenic transformation of the biomes, 1700 to 2000', *Global Ecology and Biogeography*, 19, 589–606.

Erdmann, T.K. (2010) 'Eco-regional conservation and development in Madagascar: a review of USAID-funded efforts in two priority landscapes', *Development in Practice*, 20(3), 380–94.

Foale, S. and Macintyre, M. (2005) 'Green fantasies: Photographic representations of biodiversity and ecotourism in the Western Pacific', *Journal of Political Ecology*, 12, 1–22.

Fogarty, D. (2010) 'REDD project design method gets boost from auditors', *Planet Ark*, *World Environment News*, 17 August.

Frenot, Y., Chown, S.L., Whinam, J., Selkirk, P.M., Convey, P., Skotnicki, M. and Bergstrom, D.M. (2005) 'Biological invasions in the Antarctic: extent, impacts and implications', *Biological Reviews*, 80, 45–72.

Ghilarov, A. (1996) 'What does "biodiversity" mean – scientific problem or convenient myth?' *Trends in Ecology & Evolution*, 11(7), 304–6.

Great Barrier Reef Marine Park Authority (2009) *Great Barrier Reef Outlook Report*. Townsville, Australia.

Hamilton, A.J. (2005) 'Species diversity or biodiversity ?', *Journal of Environmental Management*, 75, 89–92.

Harris, G., Thirgood, S., Hopcraft, J.G.C., Cromsight, J.P.G.M. and Berger, J. (2009) 'Global decline in aggregated migrations of large terrestrial mammals', *Endangered Species Research*, 7, 55–76.

Horwitz, P., Lindsay, M. and O'Connor, M. (2001) 'Biodiversity, endemism, sense of place, and public health: Inter-relationships for Australian inland aquatic systems', *Ecosystem Health* 7(4), 253–65.

International Fund for Animal Welfare (2009) *Whale Watching Worldwide*, IFAW, Yarmouth.

IUCN (2010) *Red List of the World's Endangered Species for 2008*. Gland, Switzerland.

Johnson, C. (2006) *Australia's Mammal Extinctions: A 50,000 Year History*. Cambridge: Cambridge University Press.

Kruger, O. (2005) 'The role of ecotourism in conservation: panacea or Pandora's box?', *Biodiversity and Conservation* 14, 579–600.

Last, P.R., White, W.T., Gledhill, D.C., Hobday, A.J., Brown, R., Edgar, G.J. and Pecl, G. (2011) 'Long-term shifts in abundance and distribution of a temperate fish fauna: a response to climate change and fishing practices', *Global Ecology and Biogeography,* 19, 58–72.

Lawrence, D., Kenchington, R. and Woodley, S. (2002) *The Great Barrier Reef: Finding the Right Balance*, Melbourne: Melbourne University Press.

Lennon, J. and Foley, M. (2000) *Dark Tourism: The Attraction of Death and Disaster*. London: Continuum.

Lessios, H.A., Robertson, D.R. and Cubit, J.D. (1984) 'Spread of *Diadema* mass mortality through the Caribbean', *Science*, New Series, 226(4672), 335–37.

Lewis, P.N., Hewitt, C.L., Riddle, M. and McMinn, A. (2003) 'Marine introductions in the Southern Ocean: an unrecognised hazard to biodiversity', *Marine Pollution Bulletin*, 46, 213–23.

Lorimer, J. and Whatmore, S. (2009) 'After the "king of beasts": Samuel Baker and the embodied historical geographies of elephant hunting in mid-nineteenth-century Ceylon', *Journal of Historical Geography*, 35: 668–89.

Lovejoy, T.E. (1980) *The Global 2000 Report to the President* (Vol.2) (*The Technical Report*) (Barney, G.O., ed.): 327–32, New York: Penguin.

Macintosh, A., Bonyhady, T. and Wilkinson, D. (2010) 'Dealing with interests displaced by marine protected areas: A case study on the Great Barrier Reef Marine Park Structural Adjustment Package', *Ocean & Coastal Management* 53, 581–8.

Mayer, P. (2006) 'Biodiversity – the appreciation of different thought styles and values helps to clarify the term', *Restoration Ecology*, 14(1), 105–11.

McAnany, P.A. and Yoffee, N. (eds) (2009) *Questioning Collapse: Human Resilience, Ecological Vulnerability, and the Aftermath of Empire*. Cambridge: Cambridge University Press.

McDaniel, C.N. and Gowdy, J.M. (2000) *Paradise for Sale: A Parable of Nature*. Berkeley: University of California Press.

Navareen, R., Forrest, S.C., Dagit, R.G., Blight, L.K., Trivelpiece, W.Z. and Trivelpiece, S.G. (2001) 'Zodiac landings by tourist ships in the Antarctic Peninsula region, 1989–99'. *Polar Record*, 37, 121–32.

Nellemann, C., Redmond, I. and Refisch, J. (eds) (2010) *The Last Stand of the Gorilla. Environmental Crime and Conflict in the Congo Basin: A Rapid Response Assessment*. Nairobi: UNEP/INTERPOL, .

Neves, K. (2010a) 'Critical business and uncritical conservation: The invisibility of dissent in the world of marine ecotourism', *Current Conservation*, 3(3), 18–21.

——(2010b) 'Cashing in on cetourism: A critical eceological engagement with ominant E-NGO discourses on whaling, cetacean conservation and whale watching', *Antipode*, 42(3), 719–41.

Nolan, D. (2010) *A Food Lover's Pilgrimage to Santiago de Compostela*. Melbourne: Penguin.

Norse, E.A. and McManus, R.E. (1980) *Environmental Quality 1980: The Eleventh Annual Report of the Council on Environmental Quality. Washington, DC: Council on Environmental Quality.*

Noss, R.F. (1995) 'Biodiversity' in Paehlke R. (ed.), *Conservation and Environmentalism: An Encyclopedia*, New York: Garland.

Olsson, P., Folke, C. and Hughes, T.P. (2008) 'Navigating the transition to ecosystem-based management of the Great Barrier Reef, Australia'. *Proceedings of the National Academy of Sciences*, 105(28), 9489–94.

van Oosterzee, P. (2010) 'Carbon offsets, ecosystems, climate change and bad politics', *Ockhams's Razor*, ABC Radio National (Australia), 15 August.

Pullin, A.S. and Salafsky, N. (2010) 'Save the whales? Save the rainforest? Save the data!', *Conservation Biology*, 24(4), 915–17.

Ridder, B. (2008) 'Questioning the ecosystem services argument for biodiversity conservation', *Biodiversity Conservation* 17, 781–90.

Ris, M. (1994) 'Conflicting cultural values: whale tourism in northern Norway', in, Freeman, M.M.R. and Kreuter, U.P. (eds), *Elephants and Whales: Resources for Whom?*, Basel: Gordon and Breach.

Secretariat of the Convention on Biological Diversity (2010) *Global Biodiversity Outlook 3*, Montreal.

Shelton, E. (2010) Maldives 'tourism boom' putting manta rays at risk, *Ecologist*, 20 October.

Stafford, S.G. *et al.* (2010) 'Now is the time for action: Transitions and tipping points in complex environmental systems', *Environment* 52(1), 38–45.

The Age (Melbourne) (2010), 'Conservation effort for gorillas pays off ', 9 December.

The Guardian (2010) 'Poachers kill last female rhino in South African park for prized horn', London, 18 July.

Thompson, J., Shirreffs, L. and McPhail, I. (2003) 'Dingoes on Fraser Island – Tourism dream or management nightmare ?', *Human Dimensions of Wildlife*, 8, 37–47.

Trathan, P.N., Forcada, J., Atkinson, R., Downie, R.H. and Shears, J.R. (2008) 'Population assessments of gentoo penguins (*Pygoscelis papua*) breeding at an important Antarctic tourist site, Goudier Island, Port Lockroy, Palmer Archipelago, Antarctica', *Biological Conservation*, 141, 3019–28.

UNEP (United Nations Environment Programme) (2002) *Report on the Sixth Meeting of the Conference of the Parties to the Convention on Biological Diversity* (UNEP/CBD/COP/20/Part 2). Strategic Plan, decision VI/26. Convention on Biological Diversity, Montreal.

UNEP (United Nations Environment Programme) (2010) *UNEP Year Book. New Science and Developments in Our Changing Environment*. Nairobi: UNEP.

United Nations (2005) *Millenium Ecosystem Assessment Report*. New York: United Nations Environment Program.

UNWTO/UNEP (2008) *Climate Change and Tourism: Responding to Global Challenges*. Madrid, Spain

Vaughan, D. (2000) 'Tourism and biodiversity: a convergence of interests ?', *International Affairs*, 76(2), 283–97.

Walker, P. (2010) 'Chernobyl, tourist hot-spot', *The Age* (Melbourne), 15 December: 14.

Watson, J.E.M., Evans, M.C., Carwardine, J., Fuller, R.A., Joseph, L.N., Segan, D.B., Taylor, M.F.J., Fensham, R.J., and Possingham, H.P. (2011) 'The capacity of Australia's protected-area system to represent threatened species', *Conservation Biology*, 324–32.

Watts, J. (2010a) 'Beijing presents ambitious plan for protection of wildlife', *The Guardian Weekly*, October 22–8: 8.

Watts, J. (2010b) 'Passion for golf threatens rainforest', *The Guardian* (London), 31 May.

Wilson, E.O. (ed.) (1988) *Biodiversity*, Washington, DC: National Academy Press.

Zamin, T.J., Baillie, J.E.M., Miller, R.M., Rodriguez, J.P., Ardid, A. and Collen, B. (2010) 'National red listing beyond the 2010 target', *Conservation Biology*, 24(4), 1012–20.

14

'Tourism into the wild'

The limits of tourism in wilderness

Jarkko Saarinen

Wilderness areas are arguably the most sensitive physical resources for tourism.

Higham (1998: 27)

Introduction

Wilderness conjures up meanings and images referring to wild, remote, rough, free, empty and untrammelled natural areas. These kinds of landscapes are often considered to represent the last parts of 'true' nature, untouched by the modern world. In many respects, however, this is no longer true: wilderness areas have been explored and converted into administrative (conservation) management units. They are also often promoted as products or as sites of consumption, which is most clearly in evidence in connection with the tourism industry.

Wilderness and natural attractions, however, have not always been attraction elements for tourism. According to Short (1991: 6) 'fear of the wilderness was one of the strongest elements in European attitudes to wilderness up to the Nineteenth Century'. Thus, the history of wilderness as a tourist attraction is relatively short. In spite of this, wilderness environments presently attract millions of international and domestic tourists per year. The growing demand for tourists to experience 'the wild' is based on changed positive attitudes towards the environment in general, and the development of accessibility to remote wilderness environments has integrated peripheral areas more closely to global tourism markets (Hall and Page 2002: 273).

The increased attractiveness and numbers of visitors, along with diminishing wilderness areas, have caused challenges for the carrying capacity and management of these areas. The issue of carrying capacity has formed a particularly problematic task in wilderness management: wilderness areas are supposed to provide outstanding opportunities for solitude but, owing to the increased numbers of visitors, the possibilities for this are diminishing (Hendee *et al.* 1990: 401; Roggenbuck *et al.* 1993). Thus, there is a need for setting a limit to growth in wilderness tourism if the visitor numbers exceed an acceptable level. However, determining the maximum use levels is not a simple task (Lindberg *et al.* 1997) and this identification of the limits of acceptable change (LAC) is one of the main issues in recreation and tourism studies in wilderness settings (see Stankey *et al.* 1985). The LAC model originates from carrying capacity thinking and early debates in the 1960s and 1970s aiming to evaluate how much and what kind of recreation or tourism use would be too much in wilderness contexts (Lucas 1964; Wagar 1964, 1974). These kinds of questions are still valid and increasingly relevant. The solution models and frameworks, such as sustainable tourism, have changed (Saarinen 2006). However, the new frameworks have also turned out to be, and remained, problematic in determining the limits to growth in tourism in wilderness settings (Butler 1996, 2010).

This chapter discusses the relation of tourism and wilderness, and the challenges increasing and constantly changing tourism may create for wilderness environments. The purpose is not to describe the impacts of tourism in detail, covering ecological, social or managerial issues systematically, for example, but to focus on the increasing role of tourism in wilderness and the ideas aiming to limit the impacts of tourism in wilderness areas in the future.

Wilderness – a contested idea

In traditional societies the role and uses of wilderness may have not been problematic for people (Nash 1967), but, due to modernisation, increasing cultural contacts and the recent scale of globalisation, the meanings and uses of wilderness have turned into contested ideas and objects of various interests. As a result, different kinds of objectives, values and attitudes, often mutually contradictory ones, are connected with the meanings and uses of wilderness. Therefore, it is challenging to find a common ground for the idea of wilderness: what represents a wilderness for a Central European person may be a crowded space for a Canadian or Australian person, for example. However, several attempts have been made. The first wilderness legislation was prescribed in the USA in 1964. According to the US Wilderness Act (Public Law 1964: 1), wilderness is placed outside the organised society and culture: 'A wilderness, in contrast with those areas where man and his own works dominate the landscape, is hereby recognised as an area where the earth and its community of life are untrammelled by man, where man himself is a visitor who does not remain.'

The idea of the Act – man himself is a visitor, that is a tourist, who does not remain – is based on the historically constructed Anglo-American view on wild nature; Western (and masculine) frontier thinking, and preservation and conservation of natural areas (Short 1991). For example, the world's first large-scale wilderness preservation, the designation of the Yellowstone National Park in 1872, was based on the premise that the region was 'reserved and withdrawn from settlement, occupancy, or sale' (Nash 1967: 108), with a further emphasis on public use in tourism and recreation. This so-called Yellowstone or fortress model has dominated global conservation thinking and debate, but not without conflicts (see Spinage 1998). In the early days of legal conservation of wilderness environments, local views challenged the uninhabited wilderness and also the concept of wilderness as opposite to culture and organised society (Hall 1992; Hallikainen 1998; Saarinen 2005).

Presently, the polarisation of nature and culture is under increasing pressure. This is the case especially in developing countries aiming to use their remaining natural areas to attract tourism and create formal employment and foreign revenue through tourism development. In order to resolve tensions between the traditional uses and local benefits of wilderness and evolving tourism requiring an untouched 'pristine' wilderness, community-based natural resource management (CBNRM) models have been created (Nelson 2010; also Case study below). On its behalf in the developing countries contexts, the CBNRM also aims to answer to the increasing need of local involvement, which has been a relatively problematic issue in the traditional wilderness management processes (Hendee et al. 1990).

Case study

CBNRM: aiming to meet community needs in wilderness management in developing countries

CBNRM has become a popular policy tool that highlights the role of local communities and people in natural resource management. It represents a contrast to traditional wilderness conservation strategy that aims to separate human activities and impacts from nature by 'fencing out people' (Adams and Hulme 2001). As a strategy, CBNRM involves local communities in natural resource management by stating that communities are able to manage the resources on which they are dependent (Ostrom 1990) and they must have direct control over the uses and benefits of them (Nelson 2010). Many CBNRM programmes have a strong emphasis on tourism, as tourism activities are seen as providing economic relevance and a reason for both conservation and deeper community involvement in wilderness management. However, there are many challenges to involve the local communities both in natural resource management and tourism operations.

For example, Botswana adopted the CBNRM programme in 1989 when the Government and the United States Agency for International Development (USAID) embarked on a joint Natural Resource Management Programme (NRMP) (Gujadhar 2000). A formal institutional CBNRM policy was adopted in 2007 (Government of Botswana 2007). At present, Botswana's tourism policies and CBNRM programmes for the promotion of tourism are seen as a good strategy that can be used to attract visitors and capital to the country by utilising wilderness and wildlife in tourism: according to the revised National Tourism Policy's (UNWTO 2008) vision for 2020, Botswana should be globally renowned as the most authentic and exciting wilderness tourism destination in the world.

Botswana's current CBNRM programme sets a good example, but the success rate has been observed to differ greatly from one area and community to another (Arntzen et al. 2003). In general, CBNRM has promoted ecotourism development in the country and local communities have come together to form trusts that oversee such activities as photographic safaris from which they are able to realise benefits (employment and revenue) attributable to tourism (Chipfuva and Saarinen 2011; Mbaiwa 2004).

Based on the country's CBNRM programme, community conservation and tourism development activities are jointly carried out in Controlled Hunting Areas (CHAs), which are community concession areas, where communities collectively participate in tourism development and conservation (Mbaiwa 2004). Thus, in order to be effective, the CBNRM should be characterised by devolution of power from governmental institutions to local communities. However, local control can only follow the devolution if local institutions, which have a vested interest in natural resource conservation, are created (Chipfuva and Saarinen 2011). Devolution and decentralisation include a transfer of regulatory and executive powers, responsibility and authority in decision-making, institutional infrastructure and resources to the local communities (Ribot 1999). Also, Botswana's National Ecotourism strategy (DOT 2002) places emphasis on the involvement of the local people in wilderness-based ecotourism and further states the need to train local people to enable them to benefit from existing tourism opportunities and to create new possibilities in tourism.

However, this capacity building, which should also involve knowledge concerning the wilderness conservation goals, has been seen to be problematic in many cases and there is a growing concern over the relatively common situation that communities are not directly and actively involved in tourism operations (Chipfuva and Saarinen 2011). Instead they are passively participating in wilderness tourism through a leasing agreement of their wildlife (i.e. hunting) quota to a private tourism operator, who either uses it for non-consumptive or consumptive wildlife tourism (Mbaiwa 2004). In some countries, this kind of participation can also be based on land-leasing agreements without any further local involvement (Nelson 2010). However, for the community to fully benefit from tourism they should be actively involved with wilderness tourism operations. This would empower, benefit and build a capacity and an ownership to manage, guide and develop the operations, and also assist them to realise the value of wilderness conservation and management through tourism.

The CBNRM model is not an easy path to success in wilderness conservation with a tourism component. Local participation, empowerment and benefit sharing can be problematic (Adams and Hulme 2001; Ribot 1999), and have often caused drawbacks in the forms of resource overutilisation and poaching, for example. In addition, local communities do not necessarily have an intrinsic, that is traditional, knowledge of the impacts of the growing tourism activities they support or new technologies and tools they utilise on the environment. It is also important to note that even small natural resource-dependent communities may consist of different groups with different preferences with regard to the utilisation of wilderness and the role of tourism in wilderness. These challenges have turned some commentators against community-based conservation, which they see as neo-populist and misrepresentative of the success of the classical fortress model in wilderness conservation (Spinage 1998).

Despite different legal definitions and conservation models, the present wilderness uses, values and images are increasingly defined in seemingly distant global-scale processes such as the mass media. In these processes wilderness accommodates new meanings and values, and some previous ones may become relics, traces of the past with thinning connotations for new generations (Saarinen 2005). The tourism industry plays an important part in this transformation process.

Tourism in wilderness

The link between protected areas and tourism can be seen to be as old as the history of protected areas (Frost and Hall 2010; Hall 1992; Hall and Boyd 2005). Still, tourism represents perhaps the latest significant form of economy and mode of consumption using the wilderness areas, and several authors have emphasised the increasing attractiveness of wilderness in tourism (Hall and Page 2006; Saarinen 2005). Nowadays wild natural environments are 'universally regarded as a source of pleasure' (Wang 2000: 80) and in many peripheral destinations wilderness areas have turned into key attraction elements in tourism. As a result, the tourism industry has become a significant user, stakeholder and element of change in wilderness environments. Nowadays, many designated wilderness areas and national parks can face hundreds of thousands or even millions of visitors per year. For example the Grand Canyon National Park (USA) receives approximately five million visitors and Kruger National Park (South Africa) about 400,000 overnight visits per year (Grand Canyon National Park & Northern Arizona Tourism Study 2010; South African National Parks 2010).

These kinds of visitation levels are based mainly on packaged, that is organised tourism, but the growing trends of adventure tourism, ecotourism and other forms of alternative nature-based tourism are also important and influence socio-economic, cultural and ecological issues in wilderness areas (Buckley 1999; Saethorsdottir 2004). This is an essential perspective for the future of the wilderness areas and their tourism uses, as nature-based tourism and ecotourism in general are considered to be some of the fastest growing sectors of international tourism (Fennell 1999). Since the mid-1990s, new kinds of products of adventure tourism and activities such as snowmobile trekking, husky safaris and four-wheel drives have also become more visible forms of the new tourism activities in the wilderness environments, which may cause future conflicts and changes in wilderness experiences (Buckley 2006; Hall *et al.* 2009; Vail and Heldt 2004).

Wilderness tourism experiences

Tourism and its related consumption needs and attitudes construct and maintain new kinds of images of nature, which may affect the practices and uses related to distant wildernesses. This touristic wilderness is based on consumption, marketing and visualising natural environments, and staging wilderness settings for the purposes of the tourism industry. In advertising, positive images, such as the experience of freedom and naturalness are connected to the product to be marketed, and eventually become part of the identity of the consumer: the tourist. As such, touristic wilderness, with its related meanings, is a commodity and product based on the active production, reproduction and recycling of the images of wild, free, harsh and rugged nature (Saarinen 2005). Good examples of this are found in many Nordic countries, such as Iceland with its tourism marketing. According to Saethorsdottir (2010: 28), the Icelandic tourism industry uses marketing slogans referring to the wilderness characteristics of the country: for example 'Iceland naturally', 'Nature the Way Nature Made It' and 'Pure, Natural, Unspoiled'. These slogans are supported by the images of natural attractions and landscapes of the country. Based on this, it is not a surprise that a clear majority (76 per cent) of international tourists visit the country to experience nature, and about one-third of the tourists visit the Highlands, a large inland wilderness area in Iceland (Thorhallsdottir 2007).

There is a diverse scale of tourist experiences and motivations linked to visits in wilderness environments. Solitude is an acknowledged desirable state among wilderness visitors and a motive in many places (Hendee *et al.* 1990), and it is perhaps one of the most studied issues in research focusing on the wilderness experience (see Hammitt 1982; Roggenbuck *et al.* 1993). This is especially the case in the USA, where the Wilderness Act (Public Law 1964: 1) clearly emphasised that wilderness areas offer 'outstanding opportunities for solitude'. For public land managers that definition raised an obvious question: how many people and visitor encounters can a wilderness accommodate without jeopardising the opportunity to experience solitude by the visitors? This dilemma created a research programme focusing on crowding, encounter norms, visitor satisfaction and social carrying capacity that continues with changing emphases today (Lucas 1964; Williams *et al.* 1991; Roggenbuck *et al.* 1993; McCool and Lime 2001). However, these solitude-related motivational issues are complex in wilderness contexts as they are not created simply by the factual number of visitors or contacts between visitors. The encounter norms, that is standards individuals and groups use when evaluating contacts and activities as acceptable or unacceptable, vary depending on the contact numbers but also on group size, behaviour, activities, ethnicity and environmental and many other situational factors (Vaske *et al.* 1986; Patterson and Hammitt 1990).

In addition to solitude, primitive and unconfined recreational opportunities and remoteness, peace, challenges, escapism and being outside the modern organised society are characteristics of the wilderness experience (Hendee *et al.* 1990; Higham 1998). Many of these experiences clearly conflict with the increasing visitor numbers in wilderness and new kinds of visitor groups with different sets of motivations and understanding of what wilderness represents. In addition to the mentioned differences in group sizes, activities and behaviour, perceived differences in motives, attitudes and values among different types of visitors have also been reported to cause conflict in wilderness-user research (Vaske *et al.* 1986). Some tourist groups may value the provided structures, services and security backup by the area management, other groups may prefer the perceived solitude, freedom and unregulated settings, whereas some visitors actually expect relatively strict use limitations in order to feel that the touristic use of the wilderness environment is ethical and safeguarded for future visitors and generations. Thus, all wilderness tourists are not the same, and studies on different wilderness visitor groups and their experiences and motivations relate strongly to the management objectives and practices in those areas.

Although establishment and management of wilderness areas have created better possibilities for visiting them, the increasing use may also pose a threat to biological values of the wild, which can result in diminishing wilderness character of an area (Hendee *et al.* 1990). This, along with the increased and changed use, can conflict with wilderness experiences focusing on solitude and an unconfined type of recreation (Higham 1998). This resembles Hardin's (1968) tragedy of commons in which situations of unrestricted public access to a common resource will ultimately deplete the shared limited resource such as wilderness (experience). This situation has created a double dilemma for the management of tourism in and/of wilderness. As indicated by Nash (1967) and Hendee *et al.* (1990), wilderness management is a contradiction in terms as, in the dominating Anglo-American sense, wilderness refers to an environment that is not influenced or controlled by humans. Tourism as an activity is not usually linked with wilderness kinds of environments that provide solitude and have primitive levels of facilities.

Although, historically, tourism has clearly benefitted the conservation of many natural areas (Butler and Boyd 2000; Frost and Hall 2010), much of the currently increasing and changing tourism targets wilderness areas that are already conserved. Whether establishment of these areas was supported by tourism development or not, may not be a relevant point of departure, as the growing and transforming nature of tourism activities is currently changing the historically created and often relatively widely accepted balance between conservation and tourism in wilderness. This change can question the co-existence and future symbiosis of wilderness and tourism, but it definitely calls for greater sustainability and a revival of the limits to growth thinking in tourism in wilderness.

Wilderness tourism: an oxymoron?

The scale and nature of tourism in wilderness has changed dramatically in the past two decades. As Buckley (1999: 191) stated, there is an increase in the proportion of visitors as commercial rather than independent tourists, often labelled as hikers and trekkers. Buckley continues that this trend to commercial tourism is important for current and future wilderness management, because tourism is a large and politically influential activity, often representing the only viable industry in peripheral regions, where most of the remaining wilderness environments are located. This, along with the increasing physical and ecological impacts of tourism to wilderness, has created concerns about the capacity of managers to steer protected areas for conservation 'if management for tourism were given a higher priority' (Buckley 1999: 191).

There are active policies to steer tourism practices in an environmentally more sustainable direction. In this work, the idea of sustainable tourism has become hegemonic. UNWTO (2004) defined the concept as tourism that is ecologically sound, economically viable and socially acceptable by local communities in the long term. The idea of sustainable tourism has aroused criticism, which is widely discussed in existing tourism literature (see Butler 1999; Liu 2003; Sharpley 2000). As a result, there is an increasing need to understand the limits of growth and ethics in tourism (Fennell 2006; Holden 2003). In this respect, recent calls for the revival of carrying capacity approaches in tourism (Butler 2010; Cocossis and Mexa 2004) offer interesting and challenging, but also problematic, views on the discussion. The carrying capacity has been generally defined as the maximum number of people who can use a site without any unacceptable alteration in the physical environment and without any unacceptable decline in the quality of the experience gained by tourists (Getz 1983; Mathieson and Wall 1982: 21). Unlike sustainable tourism, the concept of carrying capacity does not rhetorically imply global intra-generational and inter-generational solutions (Saarinen 2006). Instead, it aims to offer more time-/space-specific answers at the local level. However, as a local-scale solution, carrying capacity could still have wide theoretical and practical dimensions in its relation to sustainable tourism development, planning and policies in wilderness settings (Butler 2010).

Carrying capacity has been occasionally interpreted as an application of sustainable tourism (Butler 1999: 9), implying that the two can co-exist and may both be useful frameworks for setting the limits for tourism development (Butler 1996; Cocossis and Mexa 2004). Indeed, there are similarities between the concepts and the idea of carrying capacity encountered some of the same problems in the past as the idea of sustainable tourism faces nowadays, for example providing unrealistic expectations of clear solutions and being conceptually vague (Lindberg *et al.* 1997; McCool and Lime 2001; Wall 1982).

In addition to practical and conceptual challenges, one of the major problems of using the carrying capacity model with the aim to set a strict limit on growth in tourism, is public acceptance of such decisions (Butler 2010: 58). As noted, tourism is an important and growing field of economy in many regions, which makes it difficult for natural resource managers, politicians and other decision-makers to support and agree on decisions aiming to limit the growth of tourism (Ryan 2002). Naturally, this would be extremely difficult for the industry. All this makes the usability of the carrying capacity concept challenging, but perhaps without setting clear and context-specific limits to growth, the wilderness character of a given area and the wilderness experiences may be lost due to the increasing flows of tourists and new activities. In that respect, tourism in wilderness is an unsolvable dilemma, and, rather than a win-win scenario, it represents a zero-sum game.

Conclusions and discussion

Modern tourism and increasingly diversified forms of nature-based tourism activities have been successful in using and commodifying the wilderness. Along with the general growth of global tourism, it is clear that tourism, especially nature-based tourism and its new forms, will increase in wilderness areas. At the same time, use patterns of wilderness-related tourism are likely to become more international and diversified. Increased tourism can make a positive contribution to environment, conservation and local communities that are dependent on natural resources and/ or tourism, but it can also have negative connotations. Therefore, the need to search for alternative and more environment-friendly practices in tourism development and management is crucial. Unfortunately, as many authors have critically expressed, the widespread acceptance of sustainable tourism has not provided a sufficient ethical backbone for protection of the environment in tourism development (Fennell 2006; Holden 2003). This has led some commentators to call for the revitalisation of the carrying capacity concept in tourism (Bramwell 2007; Butler 1996, 2010; Cocossis and Mexa 2004; Hunter 1995).

Whether or not the carrying capacity approach is still viable in tourism development and planning remains an open case. However, it is clear that present conceptualisations and practices of sustainable tourism may not save wilderness areas if the present scale of growth in tourism continues. Thus, instead of the current, popular and rather industry-oriented idea of sustainable tourism implying that all tourism and scales of tourism can be regarded as sustainable by appealing to certain codes of conduct (Clarke 1997), the relatively unfashionable carrying capacity thinking with strict limits to tourism growth in natural areas, if major problems occur, may be needed in future. However, as Butler (2010: 61) indicated, this requires academics to focus again on the concept and wilderness managers to implement carrying capacity thinking more effectively than previously. It is difficult to foresee if a revival of the carrying capacity model is realistic, but it is clear that, in order for wilderness and tourism to co-exist, further studies and strong management and planning models are needed to limit the growth of tourism if the ecological and socio-cultural elements of wilderness are endangered and the aim is for them to be conserved for the future.

References

Adams, W.M. and Hulme, D. (2001) 'If community conservation is the answer in Africa, what is the question?', *Oryx* 35, 193–200.

Arntzen, J.W., Molokomme, D.L., Terry, E.M., Moleele, N., Tshosa, O., Mazambani, D. (2003) *Main findings of the review of CBNRM in Botswana*. Gaborone: IUCN/Netherlands Development Organisation (SNV) CBNRM Support Programme.

Bramwell, B. (2007) 'Complexity, interdisciplinary and growth management: the case of Maltese resort tourism', in S. Agarwal and G. Shaw (eds) *Managing Coastal Tourism Resorts*, Clevedon: Channelview, 73–89.

Buckley, R. (1999) 'Wilderness in Australia', in S. McCool, D. Cole, B. Borrie and J. O'Loughlin (comps), *Wilderness science in a time of change conference, Vol. 2*, Ogden: U.S. Department of Agriculture, Forest Service, Rocky Mountain Research Station, 190–93.

——(2006) *Adventure tourism*. Oxford: CABI.

Butler R. (1996) 'The Concept of Carrying Capacity for Tourism Destinations: Dead or Merely Buried?', *Progress in Tourism and Hospitality Research* 2, 283–93.

——(1999) 'Sustainable Tourism: A State-of-the-Art Review', *Tourism Geographies* 1, 7–25.

——(2010) 'Carrying capacity in tourism', in D.G. Pearce and R. Butler (eds) *Tourism research: A 20–20 vision*, Oxford: Goodfellow Publishers, 53–64.

Butler, R. and Boyd, S. (eds) (2000) *Tourism and National Parks: Issues and implications*, Chichester: Wiley & Sons.

Chipfuva, T. and Saarinen, J. (2011) 'Community-Based Natural Resource Management and Tourism: Institutional Structures and Stakeholders in Botswana', in R. van der Duim, D. Meyer and J. Saarinen (eds) *Sustainable Tourism Development, Environmental Sustainability and Poverty Reduction: Cases from Eastern and Southern Africa*, Delft: Eburon.

Clarke, J. (1997) 'A framework of approaches to sustainable tourism', *Journal of Sustainable Tourism* 5, 224–33.

Cocossis, H. and Mexa, A. (2004) *The challenge of tourism carrying capacity assessment: theory and practice*. Aldershot: Ashgate.

DOT (2002) *Botswana National Ecotourism Strategy*. Gaborone: Department of Tourism.

Fennell, D. (1999) *Ecotourism: an introduction*. New York: Routledge.

——(2006) *Tourism ethics*. Clevedon: Channel view.

Frost, W. and Hall, C.M. (eds)(2010) *Tourism and National Parks*. London: Routledge.

Getz, D. (1983) 'Capacity to absorb tourism: concepts and implications for strategic planning', *Annals of Tourism Research* 10, 239–63.

Government of Botswana (2007) *Community-based natural resource management policy*. Gaborone: Government Printer.

Grand Canyon National Park & Northern Arizona Tourism Study (2010) *Executive Summary*. Available at www.nau.edu/hrm/ahrrc/reports/G_C_EXEC_SUMMARY.pdf#search=grandcanyon Accessed 29 November 2010.

Gujadhur, T.(2000) *Organisations and their approaches in community based natural resources management in Botswana, Namibia, Zambia and Zimbabwe*, Gaborone: IUCN/SNV CBNRM Support Programme.

Hall C.M. (1992) *Wasteland to World Heritage: Preserving Australia's Wilderness*. Melbourne: Melbourne University Press.

Hall, C.M and Boyd, S. (eds) (2005) *Nature-based Tourism in Peripheral Areas: Development or Disaster?* Clevedon: Channelview.

Hall, C.M. and Page, S.J. (2002) *The geography of tourism: environment, place and space*. London: Routledge.

Hall, C.M., Muller, D. and Saarinen, J. (2009) *Nordic tourism: Cases and Issues*. Clevedon: Channel view.

Hallikainen, V. (1998) 'The Finnish wilderness experience', *Metsäntutkimuslaitoksen tiedonantoja* 711, 1–288.

Hammitt, W.E. (1982) 'Cognitive dimensions of wilderness solitude', *Environment and Behaviour* 14, 478–93.

Hardin, G. (1968) 'Tragedy of the Commons', *Science* 162, 1243–48.

Hendee, J., Stankey, G. and Lucas, P. (1990) *Wilderness management*. Golden: Fulcrum.

Higham, J. (1998) 'Sustaining the physical and social dimensions of wilderness tourism: the perceptual approach to wilderness management in New Zealand', *Journal of Sustainable Tourism* 6, 26–51.

Holden, A. (2003) 'In need of new environmental ethics for tourism', *Annals of Tourism Research* 30, 94–108.

Hunter, C.J. (1995) 'On the need to re-conceptualise sustainable tourism development', *Journal of Sustainable Tourism* 3, 155–65.

Lindberg, K., McCool, S. and Stankey, G. (1997) 'Rethinking carrying capacity', *Annals of Tourism Research* 24, 461–65.

Liu, Z. (2003) 'Sustainable Tourism Development: A critique', *Journal of Sustainable Tourism* 11, 459–75.

Lucas, B. (1964) 'Wilderness perception and use: the example of the Boundary Waters Canoe area', *Natural Resource Journal* 3, 394–411.

Mathieson, A. and Wall, G. (1982) *Tourism: Economic, Physical and Social Impacts*, New York: Longman.

Mbaiwa, J.E. (2004) 'The Success and Sustainability of Community-Based Natural Resource Management in the Okavango Delta, Botswana', *South African Geographical Journal* 86, 44–53.

McCool, S. and Lime, D.W. (2001) 'Tourism carrying capacity: Tempting fantast or useful reality', *Journal of Sustainable Tourism* 9, 372–88.

Nash, R. (1967) *Wilderness and the American mind*. London: Yale University Press.

Nelson, F. (ed.) (2010) *Community rights, conservation and contested land*. London: Earthscan.

Ostrom, E. (1990) *Governing the Commons*, Cambridge: Cambridge University Press.

Patterson, M. and Hammitt, W. (1990) 'Backcountry encounter norms, actual reported encounters, and their relationship to wilderness solitude', *Journal of Leisure Research* 22, 259–75.

Public Law (1964) *Public Law 88–577*. 88th Congress, 3 September.

Ribot, J.C. (1999) 'Decentralization, Participation and Accountability in Sahelian Forestry: Legal Instruments of Political-Administrative Control', *Africa* 69, 23–65.

Roggenbuck, J., Williams, D. and Watson, A. (1993) 'Defining acceptable conditions in wilderness', *Environmental Management* 17, 187–97.

Ryan, C. (2002) 'Equity, management, power sharing and sustainability – issues in 'new tourism'', *Tourism Management* 23, 17–26.

Saarinen, J. (2005) 'Tourism in Northern Wildernesses: Nature-Based Tourism Development in Northern Finland', in Hall, C.M and Boyd, S. (eds) *Nature-based Tourism in Peripheral Areas: Development or Disaster?*, Clevedon: Channelview, 36–49

——(2006) 'Traditions of Sustainability in Tourism Studies', *Annals of Tourism Research* 33, 1121–40.

Saethorsdottir, A.D. (2004) 'Adapting to Change: Maintaining a Wilderness Experience in a Popular Tourist Destination', *Tourism Today* 4, 52–65.

——(2010) 'Planning Nature Tourism in Iceland based on Tourist Attitudes', *Tourism Geographies* 12, 25–52.

Sharpley, R. (2000) 'Tourism and sustainable development: exploring the theoretical divide', *Journal of Sustainable Tourism* 8, 1–19.

Short, J.R. (1991) *Imagined country: society, culture and environment*, London: Routledge.

South African National Parks (2010). *Annual Report 2009–10*. Available at www.sanparks.org/assets/docs/general/annual-report-2010.pdf, accessed 23 November 2010.

Spinage, C. (1998) 'Social change and conservation misrepresentation in Africa', *Oryx* 32, 265–76.

Stankey, G., Cole, D., Lucas, R., Petersen, M. and Frissell, S. (1985) 'The limits of acceptable change (LAC) system for wilderness planning', *USDA Forest Service General Technical Report*, INT-176. Ogden UT: Intermountain Forest and Experiment Station.

Thorhallsdottir T.E. (2007) 'Environment and energy in Iceland: A comparative analysis of values and impacts', *Environmental Impact Assessment Review* 27, 522–44.

UNWTO (2004) *Sustainable Development of Tourism Conceptual Definition*. Available at www.world-tourism.org/frameset/frame_sustainable.html, accessed 10 February 2006.

——(2008) *Policy for the Growth and Development of Tourism in Botswana*, Gaborone: UNWTO and Department of Tourism.

Vail, D. and Heldt, T. (2004) 'Governing snowmobilers in multiple-use landscapes: Swedish and Maine (USA) cases', *Ecological Economics* 48, 469–83.

Vaske, J.J., Shelby, B., Graefe, A. and Heberlein T. (1986) 'Backcountry encounter norms: theory, method and empirical evidence', *Journal of Leisure Research* 18, 137–53.

Wang, N. (2000) *Tourism and modernity*, Amsterdam: Pergamon.

Wagar, A. (1964) 'The carrying capacity of the wild lands for recreation', *Forest Science Monograph* 7, 1–24.

——(1974) 'Recreational carrying capacity reconsidered', *Journal of Forestry* 72, 274–78.

Williams, D., Roggenbuck, J. and Bange, S. (1991) 'The effect of norm-encounter compatibility on crowding perceptions, experience and behavior in river recreation settings', *Journal of Leisure Research* 23, 154–72.

Further reading

Frost, W. and Hall, C.M (eds) (2010) *Tourism and National Parks*. London: Routledge. (Explores the origins and multiple meanings of National Parks and their relationship to tourism in different national contexts.)

Hall, C.M. (1992) *Wasteland to World Heritage: Preserving Australia's Wilderness*. Melbourne: Melbourne University Press. (Provides an Australasian perspective on wilderness).

Hall, C.M. and Boyd, S. (eds) (2005). *Nature-based Tourism in Peripheral Areas: Development or Disaster?* Clevedon: Channelview. (Provides critical case studies on nature-based tourism in peripheries.)

Hendee, J., Stankey, S. and Lucas, P. (1990) *Wilderness management*. Golden: Fulcrum. (A good overview to wilderness resources, values, meanings, uses and management in the USA.)

Higham, J. (1998) 'Sustaining the physical and social dimensions of wilderness tourism: the perceptual approach to wilderness management in New Zealand', *Journal of Sustainable Tourism* 6, 26–51. (A treatment of wilderness resources, perceptions and experiences in tourism)

Wagar, A. (1964) The carrying capacity of the wild lands for recreation. *Forest Science Monograph* 7, 1–24. (Provides an early discussion and conceptualisation of recreational carrying capacity in wilderness settings)

15

Freshwater systems and tourism

Kay Dimmock, Jessica Taplin and John Jenkins

Introduction

Freshwater systems, which include rivers, streams, estuaries, lakes, sinkholes, underground reservoirs and caves, have long been popular recreational and tourist sites throughout the world, with areas such as Antarctica now also experiencing the impacts of human use and tourist visitation. Freshwater systems may be the sites of activities themselves (e.g. swimming and sailing), an ancillary support (e.g. snow making) or an aesthetic element (i.e. the scenic backdrop to the activity). Despite their significance as recreational and tourist resources, and although elements of their recreational management have long attracted attention, there has been little research into the economic, environmental and socio-political issues associated with recreational tourism and freshwater systems (Geering 1986; Wood and Hooy 1982; Hall and Stoffels 2006; Pigram 2006; Prideaux and Cooper 2009). This situation is in stark contrast to the body of research, which examines aspects of wider marine environments and tourism (e.g. see Orams 1999; Lück 2008; also see the journal *Tourism in Marine Environments*).

Freshwater systems support a wide range of recreational activities in diverse settings and contexts, with a variety of outcomes and impacts. According to Pigram (2003: 544)

> Water figures prominently in several aspects of outdoor recreation [and tourist activity]. The quantity and quality of available water can represent major constraints on the location, siting, design and operation of recreation facilities. As pressure grows on increasingly scarce water resources, the potential of areas, otherwise suitable for development, may be compromised by inadequate water supplies.

Management applications that fail to recognise the potential of multipurpose use, the need to ameliorate conflicts among different user groups, and the significance of risk may further limit recreational and tourism opportunity. Limits to recreational use are also presented in a variety of risks.

This chapter uses inter-disciplinary perspectives to review some of the key research trends and issues concerning tourism at freshwater locations. It draws on a model (Figure 15.1) the authors have adapted from Stolk's (2010) study of scuba diving on Australian artificial reefs. The

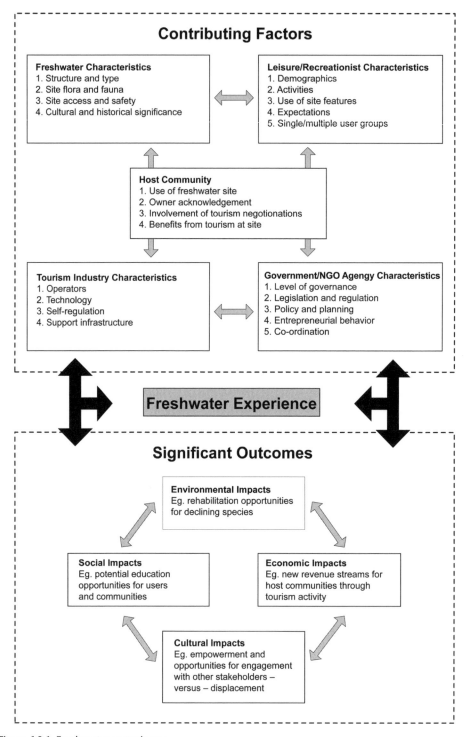

Figure 15.1 Freshwater experience

adapted model usefully highlights factors contributing to, and significant outcomes from, the development and use of freshwater systems for tourism. After a general introduction and brief discussion of necessarily selective contributing factors and outcomes presented in the model, we focus on case studies of two particular types of freshwater systems. The first case study examines recreational use of and access to streams in England and Wales, highlighting the complexity of freshwater management and ownership systems. The second case study focuses on recreational use of caves and sinkholes, highlighting the fragility of these sensitive ecosystems. The conclusion briefly summarises the chapter and describes opportunities for further research.

Freshwater systems as scarce and fragile recreational and tourist settings

Freshwater systems are popular sites in remote locations, such as Lake Argyle and the Ord River system in the Kimberley region of Western Australia, and in highly accessible locations within or in close proximity to urban centres, such as the Lakes District of the UK (McEvoy *et al.* 2008) or the Swan River, Perth, Australia (McDonald 2009). Almost 30 years ago, it was estimated that Lakes Burley Griffin and Ginninderra were the focus of more than 40 per cent of recreational activity in the Australian Capital Territory (ACT), in southeastern Australia (Hanrahan 1981). At first glance, it might seem that an extraordinarily large proportion of recreational activity in the ACT is water-based or water-related, but in fact the popularity of freshwater systems for outdoor recreation and tourism is well highlighted internationally by Cushman *et al.* (2005).

In their book focusing on free time and leisure participation in more than 15 countries, the work of Cushman *et al.* cites national and regional surveys and in its review highlights, among other things, the prominence of water-related and water-based activities, including swimming, fishing, sailing, boating, canoeing, kayaking, ice skating, ice hockey and downhill skiing. Cordell (2008) highlighted kayaking, visiting water (other than ocean beaches) and snowboarding as among the ten fastest growing outdoor recreation activities in the USA, with percentage changes in total number of days of participation between 2000 and 2007 being 29.4%, 28.1% and 23.9%, respectively. In the UK, the University of Brighton (2011: 15) revealed that 26% of the adult population in the UK spends some part of their leisure time 'in ways closely linked to coasts and inland waterways and watercourses', but noted that '[f]or most water-related recreation activities, participation rates are higher for men compared to women, younger age groups compared to older ones and wealthier … groups compared to the other socio-economic groups'.

Freshwater, however, is a scarce resource, representing only about 0.01% of the world's water (Dudgeon *et al.* 2006). Freshwater is in high demand and its major stores are often located in sparsely populated areas. The distribution of freshwater across the globe is remarkably uneven, and many people live in countries and regions that are water-deficient. Indeed, it is often these same freshwater-deficient countries or regions that also lack the resources and technology to harness water, to sanitise water to make it potable and to prevent deterioration in water quality (Pigram 2006).

Freshwater systems are highly fragile and intricate elements of natural and cultural landscapes, and these systems serve many purposes. Food production and irrigation (including aquaculture and agriculture), local council and municipal uses, generation of energy and hydroelectric power, gold mining and prospecting, water storage and sewage disposal, and outdoor recreation and tourism are among many potential, often competing, uses that require healthy freshwater resources.

In Australia, the National Irrigator's Council (NIC) estimates that agriculture uses between 65% and 70% of the water consumed in that country, and that about 90% of that water is distributed and used through irrigation, controlled by various licences and regulations, which vary between Australia's states and territories (National Irrigator's Council, NIC n.d.). According to the NIC:

> In 2007–8 irrigated land comprised less than 0.5 per cent of all agricultural land in Australia but produced 28 per cent of the total gross value of agricultural production. In 2007–8, vegetables contributed the highest value to total irrigated production of $2.9 billion, followed by fruit and nuts ($2.3 billion) and dairy production ($2.29 billion). These three commodities accounted for 61 per cent of the total gross value of irrigated agricultural product (GVIAP) in 2007–8.

Water for food production and irrigation is used not only in primary production, but also in the processing of foods and in other ways. In addition, some products involve far less water-intensive use and consumption than others. Cotton, for example, requires significant water allocations and consumption in Australia.

Freshwater systems are not only important for human-related uses; but also they are valuable elements of a nation's landscape and biodiversity, and are essential for migratory semi-aquatic and riparian species. The significance of some wetlands, for example, is highlighted by the fact that legislation is often used to protect them (e.g. the Macquarie Marshes of Australia are a Nature Reserve) (Jones 1994; Pigram 2006). Recognising the diverse and powerful threats to freshwater systems, Dudgeon *et al.* (2006) argued for the need for a new paradigm in the management and protection of freshwater ecosystems – 'reconciliation ecology'. Such a paradigm recognises that: (i) scientists, conservationists and others should turn their attentions not only to natural landscapes to preserve biodiversity but also to modified landscapes; and (ii) reconciling stakeholder demands with regard to freshwater systems (e.g. between those advocating biodiversity conservation and those advocating human use) is always going to be difficult.

Freshwater ecosystems are important and dynamic natural resources, which support high levels of biodiversity. We rely on freshwater to sustain us, but we use it in ways that draw down on it to such an extent that ecosystems are threatened. According to Dudgeon *et al.* (2006: 164), these 'may well be the most endangered ecosystems in the world', and they are especially vulnerable because of 'the disproportionate richness of inland waters as a habitat for plants and animals'. Dudgeon *et al.* (2006) go on to cite five major threats to freshwater biodiversity – overexploitation; flow modification; habitat degradation; water pollution; and species invasion.

Human development of, in and around many sites can impact on and dramatically reduce a location's biodiversity, and so sustainable approaches to planning and management are urgently needed (de Carlo and Bassano 2010; Viorosmarty *et al.* 2010). In many countries, strong debates about water rights, water access, water pricing and water flows to support freshwater ecosystems are being waged among primary producers, conservationists, recreational users and governments (Pigram 2006). The challenge presented is to improve understanding of water resources and freshwater ecosystems and the relationships between these and various forms of human use and consumption (e.g. Dudgeon *et al.* 2006), including recreational and tourist use. Buckley (2005, in Pigram and Jenkins 2006: 113), for example, has described the need for recreational ecology research 'to enhance the effectiveness of management of recreation impacts'. Reviews of research reporting recreation impacts on the biophysical environment in many settings, including freshwater environments, can nonetheless be found in Mathieson and Wall (1982), Hammitt and Cole (1998) and Liddle (1997).

European settlement in many countries has placed ever-growing demands on many freshwater systems, introducing more extractive and redistributive practices. For example, lakes and river systems are now accessed for irrigation and agriculture, transportation, fishing, recreational boating, swimming and diving (Prideaux and Cooper 2009). Freshwater sites have assumed greater recreational value because their physical amenity and attractiveness as sites for leisure have increased and have become even more popular as accommodation and transport infrastructure have developed around them (Naiman *et al.* 1995). The infrastructure that supported the Ord River Irrigation scheme at Lake Argyle in the Kimberley region of Western Australia, for example, has also supported the development of leisure and tourism. However, the expedition cruise industry established in the region generated unwelcome cultural and spiritual impacts at sites of Aboriginal significance as permission for access from traditional landowners was not sought and cultural protocols not followed. The lack of consultation, among other things, showed a lack of respect for the original inhabitants (Smith *et al.* 2009).

Smith *et al.* (2009) go on to argue that at freshwater locations environmentally and socially sustainable tourism needs to be managed in a way that is consistent with the natural and cultural values of the local communities. Major river systems like the Murray River in southeastern Australia, Lake Argyle and the Ord River in northwestern Australia, and Yellow Waters in Kakadu National Park have been central to the culture and lives of Aboriginal Australians who live on and near them (Barber and Rumley 2003; Braithwaite *et al.* 1996; Moore 1986). So, too, are the Amazon and Mekong rivers central features in the lives of indigenous people in South America and Asia. In short, indigenous peoples everywhere rely on freshwater systems to support their livelihoods, culture and heritage, and many such systems are under threat or have been negatively affected by various forms of economic development, including tourism development.

Tourism and recreation have been recognised by governments and industry in many developed and developing countries as means to restructure and diversify local economies. Tourism can contribute economically to rural and regional development at freshwater locations, and can be one way of diversifying a region's economy from dependence on traditional industries, such as agriculture, to an alternate economy and lifestyle choice in regional centres (e.g. Butler *et al.* 1998). Heritage and culture can also be maintained and restored (Moore 1986), and indeed agricultural and other industries can actually engage in the tourism industry through regional food networks (e.g. paddock to plate initiatives whereby local farm produce is used in local restaurants), on-farm accommodation (e.g. bed and breakfast), local sales direct to consumers (e.g. wine cellar door sales) and agri-tours. Nevertheless, tourism poses a significant threat to natural ecosystems, including freshwater ecosystems.

In the 1980s the potential for tourism to be a major industry in the Murray River Valley of Australia was identified and promotion of tourism to regional areas such as the Murray Valley gained momentum. In recent years, a figure of A\$1.6 billion has been quoted as the value of a healthy Murray River to tourism industries in three Australian states – New South Wales, Victoria and South Australia (Howard 2008). However, not all expenditures in regional economies stay in those regions. Hjerpe and Kim (2007), for example, reported that, in the Grand Canyon, USA, over 50% of tourist expenditures from river rafting leaked from the regional economy because of external investments and ownership, and that many of the jobs created were low-wage, low-skilled and seasonal. Kemper *et al.* (2008) found a similar situation at Beaver Lake in the USA.

Agricultural practices in southwestern China currently combine with unrelenting tourism development to threaten environmental quality, causing pollution and diminishing of the quality of natural resources. It has been argued that in China's Yunnan Great Rivers region, sustainable approaches are needed to reduce environmental and social impacts and protect the rich heritage that underpins tourism demand (Cater 2000). Ironically, although China's polluted lakes might not attract water-based tourism activities, those lakes do form part of the whole aesthetic gaze or scenic amenity of the landscape, which includes the built environment.

Indeed, Ryan *et al.* (2010) note that concerns about the low environmental quality of some freshwater systems might be a regarded as a Western perspective, and Arlt and Feng (2009) also suggest that ecological priorities might differ between Western and non-Western cultures.

In contrast to the situation in China, the high-quality landscape, flora and fauna that make up the waterways and wetland areas of Australia's Kakadu National Park have been recognised as a major tourist attraction in the Northern Territory for many decades (Braithwaite *et al.* 1996). Wildlife encounters, for example, have involved boat cruises on the beautiful Yellow Waters billabong and South Alligator River, but during the 1990s visitor experiences were diminished by boat noise, lack of comfort, crowding and lack of wildlife sightings. Ongoing visitation patterns of boat cruises were considered to have impacted on wildlife such that wildlife became *habituated* by the regularity of visitation (Braithwaite *et al.* 1996). Wildlife sightings were expected features of boat cruises, yet it is usually by disturbing animals that a wildlife *spectacle* actually occurs, thereby disrupting their feeding and breeding patterns and behaviour.

Naiman *et al.* (1995) make the point that ecological literacy is poor at best in many freshwater populations. One recommendation is for community co-operation to harness collective views while protecting biodiversity through ecotourism. Introducing environmental protection can bring way-of-life changes to host communities (Sithole 2005). Partnerships between local communities and governments and tourism organisations help to increase awareness and understanding of sustainable practices (Amunquandoh 2010). Nevertheless, many host communities are disempowered and perceptions of social displacement widespread. This is particularly emphasised in developing countries, where leisure is not a priority for host communities. Also often absent or weak is the ability of host communities to advocate on their own behalf. For example, Salmi and Salmi (2010) discuss recreational river fishing in Finland, where local river fishermen have commenced a social movement in an effort to restrict commercial salmon fishing in the open sea. Tourists are attracted to the area for river fishing and one view is that commercial salmon fishing is leading to a decline in fish stocks in the river and discouraging tourist visitation and tourism development.

Finally, developing an awareness of risk, and indeed risk analysis, planning and management, is a critical and increasingly common element in the establishment of guidelines and standards for water-related recreation. International *Guidelines for Safe Recreational Water Environments* were published by the World Health Organization (WHO) in separate volumes (1 and 2) in 2003 and 2006. The WHO has taken an active interest in 'the protection of human health from the use of recreational waters since the 1970s' (WHO 2003, Foreword p. ix). The second volume of the above mentioned guidelines, for example, presented a very detailed discussion of water-borne diseases arising from water-based recreation in a variety of environments, including marine and freshwater settings.

Standards for Recreational Water Quality (Kay and Fawell 2007) have been developed for the UK. In Australia and New Zealand, the Australian and New Zealand Environment and Conservation Council (ANZECC) has developed guidelines (published in 2000) for water quality with respect to different ecosystem types and water uses, including water used for recreational purposes (Australian and New Zealand Environment and Conservation Council 2000). Furthermore, in New Zealand 200 freshwater sites located in lakes and rivers used by recreationists are monitored by local and district councils during summer. The main focus of the monitoring is on the presence and levels of *Escherichia coli* (*E. coli*) bacteria, 'which do not necessarily cause human disease themselves but indicate the possible presence of other disease-causing organisms' (New Zealand Ministry for the Environment 2010). The guidelines were published by Australia's National Health and Medical Research Council (2008). The primary aim of the guidelines 'is to protect human health' (p. 11), an aim similar to that of the WHO (see above). The guidelines were designed to support local, state and territory authorities in the development 'of legislation and standards appropriate for local conditions and circumstances; and to encourage the adoption of a nationally harmonized approach to managing the quality of water used for recreational purposes' (ibid.).

Freshwater systems are complex, risk-prone and often highly contested areas, with much scope for innovative planning schemes as well as potential and actual conflict between competing uses and users (e.g. between supply of potable water, recreational use and energy generation; or between commercial fishing, recreational fishing and conservation), and indeed among recreationists and tourists themselves (e.g. among recreational fishers, motorised sports and swimmers). The two case studies that follow provide more detailed insights into many of the key issues described above.

Case study one

Recreational canoeists and anglers in England and Wales: access to freshwater streams

There are approximately 65,000 km of rivers and streams in England and Wales, with public and legal right of navigation to approximately 2,200 km. Based on these figures, the public can rightfully access less than 4 per cent of the two countries' inland waterways (The Rivers Access Campaign n.d., Church and Ravenscroft 2007). Most non-tidal inland waters are privately owned with no public right of navigation or access.

In 1998 an estimated 6 per cent of the UK's population enjoyed some form of freshwater recreation (Church *et al.* 2001). Canoeing is one of the most popular activities with up to two million people taking to the water in a canoe each year (Canoe England n.d.). Access to inland rivers can be difficult for canoeists. Where there is no public footpath or public access to the water's edge, permission must be negotiated with landowners to cross private land. To canoe on a river without permission constitutes as trespassing. Similar circumstances with regard to access to freshwater streams and rivers in the Australian countryside were described by Pigram (1981).

Angling is also a popular activity that uses freshwater resources. Contra to the situation for canoeists (and other freshwater recreationists like boaters and swimmers), anglers have a well-established process in which they are able to obtain legal rights to access freshwater for fishing, dating back to the nineteenth century. Anglers are required to purchase an access permit for fishing and a rod licence. They can buy access permits individually, from the landowner, or these can be arranged through membership of a club. Anglers also purchase rod licences from the government's Environment Agency, which generates £24 million annually and these fees are used to maintain fisheries (Church and Ravenscroft 2007: 179, Environment Agency n.d.). An estimated 1.4 million rod licences were sold in Britain in 2009 alone, reflecting a 27 per cent increase since 2000. It is an offence to catch freshwater fish and eels without a valid rod licence and fines of up to £2,500 can be imposed (Environment Agency n.d.).

Conflict can occur between recreational users sharing resources like freshwater streams (Pigram 1981; Pigram and Jenkins 2006), and the significance of social relationships in common property, environmental governance and sustainable development are being increasingly acknowledged (Plummer and FitzGibbon 2007: 55). For example, disparities in access rights to freshwater have led to conflict and tension between two very different user groups – canoeists and anglers (National Assembly for Wales 2009; Church *et al.* 2007). Church and Ravenscroft (2007) and Gilchrist and Ravenscroft (2008) explore difficulties in the relationship between canoeists and anglers in England and Wales. Church *et al.* (2007: 14) explain that the conflict can be understood as an 'argument of rights', the 'moral rights' of the canoeists and the 'legally enforceable rights' of the anglers. The canoeists take the position that they have a moral right to a fair share of the access to these fresh-water sites, whereas the anglers argue from their position as the legal rights holders.

Many anglers argue that canoeing, like angling, should be a regulated activity that involves licensing and financial payment (fishing licences are also required in countries such as Australia). Anglers further argue that canoeists and other boaters have a detrimental effect on fishing stocks (National Assembly for Wales 2009). However, it is noted that the environmental impacts of canoeing are not clear and are often disputed. Environmental impacts from freshwater recreation appear to be a contested topic with a need for further research to clarify claims and matters of debate and disagreement (e.g. Church *et al.* 2001). One issue raised by anglers is the risk of fish stocks being disturbed and salmon spawn lost if canoeists launch in certain areas at certain times. The Environment Agency asks paddlers to avoid launching in spawning areas to avoid disturbing fish. An open forum is seeking to determine how the Agency and paddlers can work together and improve ecologically sustainable practices (Environment Agency n.d.). If open access is granted, the issue of environmental impacts to freshwater sites could become an even more contentious issue (Church *et al.* 2001). In fact, Church and Ravenscroft (2007) consider the tensions between the user groups to have worsened in recent years. Campaigns have been launched and acts of conflict and hostility have included verbal abuse, physical threats, vandalism, protests and legal threats (Church and Ravenscroft 2007: 179, National Assembly for Wales 2009).

Advocating on behalf of many canoeists is the British Canoe Union (BCU), which had a 2009 membership in excess of 65,000 members and is increasing at 9 per cent annually (British Canoe Union 2009). In response to the inequality of freshwater access, the BCU embarked on the Rivers Access Campaign to lobby for legislation that opens up the inland water-ways to all members of the public (The Rivers Access Campaign n.d.). The strategy pursued by BCU encourages canoeists to seek voluntary agreements from landowners for access rights in the short term, while they pursue law reforms in the long term. The UK government has also encouraged canoeists to seek voluntary access agreements by negotiating with private landowners (Church and Ravenscroft 2007: 192).

Voluntary agreements involve sharing the water spaces and negotiating access. For example, agreements may include 'trading water' and allowing the canoeists to use certain stretches of water in exchange for not using other areas, or restricting access to certain times of the year (Church *et al.* 2007: 222–3). As a result of the political pressure, some landowners and anglers have been willing to engage in voluntary agreement negotiations with canoeists. Some of these agreements have been successful and in place for many years, but attempts to establish others have not been so fruitful. Issues of power have emerged with some 'voluntary agreements' because the rights owners are free 'to determine the nature of the agreement to an extent not available to the other party'. Mean-while, landowners and anglers are able to decide the restrictions and the conditions of the agreement (Church *et al.* 2007: 216).

There have also been instances when owners have retracted the rights of access they 'gifted' to the canoeists when canoeists did not adhere to the restrictive stipulations of an agreement (Church *et al.* 2007: 216, Gilchrist and Ravenscroft 2008: 133). An example of this occurred in Wales on the River Dee. Access to the river was 'gifted' by the Dee Fisheries Association; however, some canoeists were taking part in 'bandit runs' and ignoring the agreed access conditions. In response the Dee Fisheries Association retracted their offer of access. A protest was organised using the internet, and canoeists demonstrated in a street march. The actions uncovered the disparity being felt across the canoeing community in other locations. In support of the contribution canoeists make to local communities, during the Welsh 'Dee Day' protest, a number of retailers came out to show support 'in an acknowledgement of the impact of canoeing on the local economy' (Gilchrist and Ravenscroft 2008). There has been evidence of tension within the canoeing community itself as a result of acts and differences in opinion as to how to best manage the situation (Gilchrist and Ravenscroft 2008).

Canoeists and landholders have not resolved their differences in many instances, and the extent of the problem has been raised with the government agencies responsible for access, recreation and inland water. McDonald (2009) argues that conflict is necessary to promote creative processes and prevent stagnation. The websites of the respective government agencies offer advice and information to canoeists on how to seek voluntary access (British Canoe Union 2009; Environment Agency n.d.). The BCU also advises canoeists on legislation and access points about where to legally enter and exit the water. Membership of the BCU has reached record levels as a result of increased media and parliamentary awareness (British Canoe Union 2009). A division of BCU contends that canoeing has been voted the number one water sport for the seventh year in a row (www.canoe-england.co.uk).

Solutions to property rights and recreational access to and use of England's inland waterways have been variously described, and may rest in collaborative and communicative planning models and frameworks. A detailed discussion of possible governance and other models is not possible here, but it is worth noting that in recent studies exploring the complex property regimes for river corridors in Canada, Plummer (2006) highlighted the importance of communication and negotiation. Plummer suggested the concept of co-management captures and promotes among stakeholders 'the idea that rights and responsibilities should be shared among those with a claim to the environment or a natural resource' (Plummer 2009: 24). Building on the concept of co-management and his previous research, Plummer's later (2009) study concluded that the 'Adaptive co-management is receiving considerable attention as an innovative governance strategy to sustain social-ecological systems'. However, Church *et al.* (2007) have noted that conflict arises from the concept of resource 'sharing' and that in any system where rights are legally defined and ascribed, weaker parties actually have negligible power. Moreover, these authors suggested that by engaging in attempts to secure access, weaker parties (in their study these are canoe paddlers) may in fact be further 'legitimating the concentration and deployment of those rights in the hands of static land-based interests' (the anglers). The concept of sharing and expectations that rights will be voluntarily relinquished are common in debates about access to and use of freshwater systems worldwide. Where resolutions to conflicts over access rights and use are found, they very much rest on addressing peculiar local circumstances.

Case study two

Cave diving in Australia

Cave diving involves using SCUBA diving equipment to explore submerged caves that have been flooded from saltwater or freshwater systems. Cave diving is well developed in areas such as the Bahamas, Mexico, Brazil, the USA and Australia. Some inland locations offer access to freshwater-flooded caves. In Australia, much cave diving takes place within and around the Limestone Coast region of South Australia, where Mount Gambier is the regional centre and is well known to the cave diving community because its relatively unexplored underground sites hold much recreation and conservation appeal.

Groundwater in the underwater cave system is fed by the unconfined aquifer, which formed in the limestone layer beneath Mount Gambier. The aquifer flows southwards towards the coast and along the way, there are surfaces where sinkholes, caverns and caves have resulted from the dissolution of limestone and the collapse of the roof of water-filled caverns (Doolette and Prust 1999). Diving in these sinkholes and caves first began in the 1960s when some of the sinkholes were discovered by local farmers. Upon entering, divers were struck by the water clarity, which was dramatically different from diving in saltwater environments. By the 1970s, the 'new' freshwater caves had become known to the broader diving community (Wight 1994). Doolette and Prust (1999: 158) confirm that 'it was not unusual for up to 6 carloads of divers from Melbourne or Adelaide to be at any sinkhole on a weekend'.

Diver training and equipment at the time was rudimentary for the demands of the environment they entered. There were no reporting systems to co-ordinate demand and use, or organisations that trained people for the realities of the underground environment. Divers independently accessed sites – with no real knowledge of the depth or necessary equipment to guide them through the conditions they would confront. The social cost was evident in the period 1969–74, during which 11 divers' lives were lost (Doolette and Prust 1999). Access to the caves was subsequently denied by landowners, and some sites were locked. The legitimacy of the activity also came under question (Buzzacott and McDonald 2009). The cave diving community was motivated to resolve the situation and began to build an organisational base to enable the diving community to self-regulate and safely manage the activity. It was with these foci that the Cave Divers Association of Australia (CDAA) was conceived in 1973, when a group of divers met to elect the first committee, draw-up a constitution and set standards for cave diving in the Mount Gambier region (Buzzacott and McDonald 2009).

CDAA is now a strong and well-supported organisation, with a focus on ensuring the central aim remains on training and co-ordinating access to cave sites for its membership of almost 1,000 divers. Cave training certification is obligatory to access caves, and all caves have been rated to correspond with training levels to equip divers and signal the complexity demanded at each cave site. CDAA's role is crucial for the future of cave diving in Australia. Every five years a Landholder Liaison Meeting between stakeholder groups is held to reaffirm the detail of the partnership between landholders, CDAA and tourism organisations. There is a positive relationship between the organisations involved, which recognises the CDAA's attention to safety, site preservation and management. For example, access to sites is not guaranteed and is not year round so that sites are not overused. Caves are closed when there is a need to minimise deterioration from extensive physical impact and during fire bans. Every site has restrictions on the number of permits allocated at any one time to assist in managing to promote safety and minimise visitor impacts.

Because many sites are located on land owned or leased by farmers or government agencies, cave access often requires entering private land or land managed by an agency for a specific activity (e.g. forestry), and permission to dive involves obtaining a permit, presenting cave diving certification and membership of the CDAA. Maintaining ongoing access to about 40 key sites is so highly valued that within the CDAA National Committee a Site Officer is responsible for ensuring landowners' needs are understood and met, and for monitoring impacts at each site. Landholder relations can be jeopardised through misuse of access sites (e.g. littering, noise, cattle lost when a gate is left open). Within CDAA penalties are applied for misuse and inappropriate behaviour, and have been enforced. In extreme cases, memberships have been cancelled and prosecution has resulted (Buzzacott and McDonald 2009). There are benefits for landowners from the arrangement with CDAA, including: (i) a single point of contact (site manager); (ii) day-to-day access enquires are handled on the behalf of landholders; and (iii) the CDAA has agreed to install and maintain infrastructure such as steps, ladders and benches (Buzzacott and McDonald 2009).

There are well known and accessible sinkholes – Ewens Ponds and Piccaninnie Ponds – where snorkelling as well as diving are permitted, thus broadening the invitation to experience freshwater sites. Ewens Ponds Conservation Park includes three spring-fed inter-connected lakes reaching up to 10 m depth. Ewens Ponds is known for crystal-clear water and abundant aquatic fauna and flora. The main pond is 50 m in diameter and high water clarity means divers can easily see to the opposite side. Fauna in the ponds include black bream, Pygmy Perch and eels. Flora include many delicate plant species and communities.

In the 1980s, environmental decline (a dieback phenomenon) was reported in Ewens Ponds and led to its closure to divers. A much more recent report raised concerns about the decline in water quality, including a reduced water flow and a decline in aquatic life in the freshwater system. These impacts have led to calls for stricter environmental management. Responses have included limiting access to snorkelling only and the conduct of a review of the use of the underground water supply (Carmody, n.d.), especially as use degradation if not managed carefully, together with the potential impacts of climate change, could alter future access for divers.

Good buoyancy skills are required by divers to avoid disturbing algae and other flora (Wyschnja 1995). Guidelines in place are designed to minimise contact with flora and fauna. Instructions are to not to disturb, stand on or touch vegetation in the Ponds. Dive training or testing are not permitted. Piccaninnie Ponds Conservation Park is a wetlands habitat containing a series of sinkholes, which are another popular attraction for divers and snorkelers. Below Piccaninnie Ponds lies a chasm, leading to a large cavern called the Cathedral. Permits are limited to 1 hour and eight people at a time are required to enter the ponds. Divers must have completed the appropriate level of CDAA training to dive (Lenehan 1992).

Cave diving is a niche market and one on which regional communities do not rely heavily for economic development. However, cave diving is an evolving recreational and tourist market with a growing emphasis on environmental sustainability. It is perhaps unsurprising that cave divers are a small but important market. Tourism numbers reach up to 500,000 per annum in and around Mount Gambier but cave divers make up only about 2 per cent of this figure. Cave divers are perhaps more valued in the contribution they make towards the management of natural resources. For example, CDAA exploration dives involve mapping underwater ecosystems to continually expand knowledge of the systems. The information is often requested by government agencies to assist infrastructure and planning projects – like new roads. Similarly, water quality is monitored and reports are given to government departments about matters such as pollution. The invisibility of what lies underground often leads to ignorance about issues such as the importance of water quality (Todhunter 2010).

Conclusions and directions for future research

Freshwater systems are facing large-scale ecological threats from a variety of competing demands, which include recreational tourism development and use, and their management is becoming an increasingly complex concern for resource managers and other stakeholders. The above discussion and case studies reveal that freshwater systems are sites of high demand and conflict, circumstances that are likely to become more prevalent as demand for what is already an extremely scarce resource grows. Further research is needed on the impacts of tourism on freshwater systems in a variety of settings and contexts. Although the economic impacts of tourism are widely promoted and considered vital to local and regional economies, it is the environmental and socio-cultural impacts arenas where research is not only most urgent but also presents wonderfully rich opportunities for contributions to the conservation of ecosystems supporting enormous biodiversity.

It appears that regulatory means are necessary to minimise impacts of recreation and tourism at freshwater sites. The first case study revealed the importance of government regulations promoting access and accessibility, but the failure of individuals and groups of users to comply with use requirements led to contests between landowners and users, and between users themselves. Access rights and responsibilities in the UK have long attracted attention, but detailed knowledge of visitor behaviour in the countryside is lacking. The relationships between legislation and policy promoting access, visitor behaviour and landholders' attitudes to access are fertile grounds for more research. Moreover, comparisons among countries could be particularly informative.

In the second case study, the value of a proactive industry group, which set about forming an association championing the importance of moderate/regulated use, monitoring of impacts and contributing to knowledge of important ecosystems demonstrates, albeit not free of problems, the benefits of such an approach. It is important that innovative means of resolving conflicts that recognise resource sharing as a focus are pursued, but unfortunately too little attention has been given to their application in very few tourism-related industry sectors. That said, however, ideas concerning new paradigms for biodiversity conservation have also had little application to tourism. The notion or idea of 'reconciliation ecology', for example, might resonate with some researchers and resource managers and present a bridge or appropriate inter-disciplinary concept for formulating new ideas about the management of tourism in fragile environments such as freshwater systems.

References

Arlt, W.G. and Feng, G. (2009) 'The Yangzi River Tourism Zone' in *River Tourism*, B. Prideaux and M. Cooper (eds). Wallingford: CABI, 117–30.

Amunquandoh, F.E. (2010) 'Residents' Perceptions of the Environmental Impacts of Tourism in the Lake Bosomtwe Basin, Ghana', *Journal of Sustainable Tourism* 16(1), 101–121.

Australian and New Zealand Environment and Conservation Council (2000) *National Water Quality Management Strategy, An Introduction to the Australian and New Zealand Guidelines for Fresh and Marine Water Quality*, Australian and New Zealand Environment and Conservation Council and Agriculture and Resource Management Council of Australia and New Zealand. www.mincos.gov.au/~data/assets/pdf_file/0013/316120/anzwqg_intro.pdf Retrieved 18 February 2011.

Australian Government National Health and Medical Research Council (NHMRC) (2008) *Guidelines for Managing Risks in Recreational Water*. Australian Government, Canberra.

Barber, K. and Rumley, H. (2003) *Gunanurang: (Kumumurra) Big River Aboriginal Cultural Values of the Ord River and Wetlands*. Report prepared for the Waters and Rivers Commission.

Braithwaite, R.W., Reynolds, P.C., and Pongracz, G.B. (1996) *Wildlife Tourism at Yellow Waters: An analysis of the environmental, social and economic compromise options for sustainable operation of a tour boat venture in Kakadu National Park*. Final Report, CSIRO.

British Canoe Union (2009) *Thirtieth Annual Report of the BCU Board 2009*, www.bcu.org.uk/files/annual%20report%202009%20FINAL,%20V4,%20PO%20APPROVED%20-%20use%20this%20one.pdf. Viewed 5 October 2010.

Butler, R.W., Hall, C.M. and Jenkins, J.M. (eds) (1998) *Tourism and Recreation in Rural Areas*. New York: John Wiley and Sons.

Buzzacott, P. and McDonald, W. (2009) *The Cave Divers Association of Australia (CDAA) – Linking Landowners to End-Users*, Conference Proceedings, Australasian Cave and Karst Management Association Inc., 126–46.

Canoe England n.d. *Canoe England*, www.canoe-england.org.uk. Viewed 5 October 2010.

Carmody, G. n.d. 'Save Ewens Ponds!', *Australia New Guinea Fishers Association*, www.angfa.org.au/projec ts.html. Viewed 21 September 2010.

Cater, E.A. (2000) 'Tourism in the Yunnan Great Rivers National Parks System Project: prospects for sustainability', *Tourism Geographies* 2(4), 472–89.

Church, A. and Ravenscroft, N. (2007) 'Power Resource and Leisure Conflict' in *Tourism, Power and Space*, in A. Church and T. Coles (eds). Abindgon: Routledge, 171–96.

Church, A., Gilchrist, P. and Ravenscroft, N. (2007) 'Negotiating Recreational Access Under Asymmetrical Power Relations, The Case of Inland Waterways in England', *Society and Natural Resources* 20(3), 213–77.

Church, A., Ravenscroft, N., Curry, N., Burnside, N., Fish, P., Joyce, C., Hill, D., Smith, T., Scott, P., Markwell, S., Mobbs, B. and Grover, S. (2001) *Water-based sport and recreation: the facts Project Report.* DEFRA, London. Available at http://randd.defra.gov.uk/Document.aspx?Document=WC01001_1350 _FRP

Cordell, K. (2008) 'The Latest on Trends in Nature-Based Outdoor recreation', *Forest History Today.* Spring, 4–10.

Cushman, G., Veal, A.J., and Zuzanek, J. (2005) *Free Time and Leisure Participation: International Perspectives.* Wallingford: CABI.

De Carlo, F., and Bassano, A. (2010) 'Freshwater Ecosystems and Aquaculture Research', in F. De Carlo and A. Bassano (eds) *Freshwater Ecosystems and Aquaculture Research.* New York: Nova Science Publishers Inc, ix–xvi.

Doolette, D., and Prust, P. (1999) 'Cave Diving in Australia', *SPUMS Journal* 29(3), 158–61.

Dudgeon, D., Arthington, A.H., Gessner, M.O., Kawabata, Z.-I., Knowler, D.J., Leveque, C., Naiman, R.J., Prieur-Richard, A.-H., Soto, D., Stiassny, M.L.J. and Sullivan, C. (2006) 'Freshwater Biodiversity: Importance, Threats, Status and Conservation Challenges', *Biological Review* 81, 163–82.

Environment Agency (n.d.) *Fishing:* www.environment-agency.gov.uk/homeandleisure/recreation/fishing /default.aspx. Viewed 5 October 2010.

Geering, D. (1986) 'Recreational Management as the Basis for an Integrated Approach to Stream Management', *Proceedings of the Specialist Workshop on Instream Needs and Water Uses, Sydney,* 29–30 October, Teoh, C.-H. Paper 10.AGPS.

Gilchrist, P. and Ravenscroft, N. (2008) 'Power to the Paddlers? The internet, governance and discipline', *Leisure Studies* 27(2), 129–48.

Hall, C.M. and Stoffels, M. (2006) 'Lake Tourism in New Zealand: Sustainable Management Issues' in C.M. Hall and T. Harkonen (eds), *Lake Tourism: An Integrated Approach to Lacustrine Tourism Systems.* Clevedon: Channel View, 182–206.

Hammitt, W. and Cole, D.N. (1998) *Wildland Recreation: Ecology and Management.* New York: John Wiley and Sons.

Hanrahan, P. (1981) 'Trends in Riverside Recreation', *Australian Parks and Recreation* Nov., 46–51.

Hjerpe, E.E. and Kim, Y.-S. (2007) 'Regional Impacts of Grand Canyon river runners', *Journal of Environmental Management* 85,137–49.

Howard, J. (2008) 'The Future of the Murray River: Amenity Re-Considered', *Geographical Research* 46(3), 291–302.

Jones, A. (1994) 'Freshwater Ecosystems: Valuable, Vulnerable and Threatened by Human Population Increases', *Population 2040 Australia's Choice, Proceedings of the Symposium of the 1994 Annual General Meeting of the Australian Academy of Science,* Australian Academy of Science, 115–34.

Kay, D. and Fawell, J. (2007) *Standards for Recreational Water Quality, FR/G0005,* December, Foundation for Water Research, Marlow, Bucks, UK.

Kemper, N., Popp, J. and Miller, W. (2008) 'Regional growth and Beaver Lake: A study of recreation visitors', *Tourism Economics* 12(2), 409–26.

Lenehan, S. (1992) *Piccaninnie Ponds Conservation Park Management Plan,* National Parks and Wildlife Service, Department of Environment and Planning, South Australian Government.

Liddle, M. (1997) *Recreation Ecology.* London: Chapman and Hall.

Lück, M. (ed.) (2008) *Encyclopedia of Tourism and Recreation in Marine Environments.* London: Routledge.

Mathieson, A. and Wall, G. (1982) *Tourism: Economic, Physical and Social Impacts.* London: Longman.

Moore, P.J. (1986) *Recreation and Tourism in the South Australian River Murray Valley.* Magill: River Publications.

McDonald, J.R. (2009) 'Complexity Science: an alternative world view for understanding sustainable tourism development', *Journal of Sustainable Tourism* 17(4), 455–71.

McEvoy, D., Cavan, G., Handley, J., McMorrow, J. and Lindley, S. (2008) 'Changes to Climate and Visitor Behaviour: Implications for Vulnerable Landscapes in the North West Region of England', *Journal of Sustainable Tourism* 16(1), 101–21.

Naiman, R.J., Magnuson, J.J., McKnight, D.M., Stanford, J.A., and Karr, J.R. (1995) 'Freshwater Ecosystems and their Management: A National Initiative', *Science* 270(5236), 584–5.

National Assembly for Wales (2009) *Report of the Petition Committee's Short Inquiry into Access Along Inland Water, April 2009*, www.assemblywales.org/canoe_inquiry_report_with_cover_e_.pdf. Viewed 5 October 2010.

National Irrigator's Council (n.d.) *Food and Fibre for the Nation*, www.irrigators.org.au/?page=facts. Retrieved 18 February 2011.

New Zealand Ministry for the Environment (2010) *Monitoring of Freshwater Swimming Spots*. www.mfe. govt.nz/environmental-reporting/freshwater/recreational/monitoring.html Accessed on 19 February 2011.

Orams, M. (1999) *Marine Tourism: Development, Impacts and Management*. London: Routledge.

Pigram, J.J. (1981) 'Outdoor Recreation and Access to the countryside: A Focus on the Australian Experience', *Natural Resources Journal* 21(1), 107–23.

——(2003) 'Water-Based Recreation,' in J.M. Jenkins and J.J. Pigram (eds) *Encyclopedia of Leisure and Outdoor Recreation*. London: Routledge, pp. 543–6.

——(2006) *Australia's Water Resources: From Use to Management*. Collingwood: CSIRO Publishing.

Pigram, J.J., and Jenkins, J.M. (2006) *Outdoor Recreation Management*. London: Routledge.

Plummer, R. (2006) 'Sharing the management of a river corridor: A case study of the comanagement process,' *Society and Natural Resources* 19, 709–21.

——(2009) 'The adaptive co-management process: An initial synthesis of representative models and influential variables,' *Ecology and Society* 14(2), 24. www.ecologyandsociety.org/vol14/iss2/art24. Accessed on 22 December 2010.

Plummer, R. and FitzGibbon, J. (2007) 'Connecting Adaptive Co-Management, Social Learning, and Social Capital through Theory and Practice' in Armitage, D. (ed.) *Adaptive Co-Management: Collaboration, Learning, and Multi-Level Governance*. Vancouver: UBC Press.

Prideaux, B. and Cooper, M. (eds) (2009) *River Tourism*. Wallingford: CABI Publishing.

Ryan, C., Humin, G. and Chon, K. (2010) 'Tourism to polluted Lakes: Issues for Tourists and the Industry. An empirical analysis of four Chinese lakes', *Journal of Sustainable Tourism* 18 (5), 595–614.

Salmi, J. and Salmi, P. (2010) 'Fishing tourism, biodiversity protection and regional politics in the River Tornionjoki, Finland', *Fisheries Management and Ecology* 17, 192–8.

Sithole, E. (2005) 'Trans-boundary Environmental Actors: The Zambezi Society's Campaign for Sustainable Tourism Development in the Zambezi Bioregion', *Journal of Sustainable Tourism* 13(5), 486–503.

Smith, A.J, Scherrer, P. and Dowling, R. (2009) 'Impacts on Aboriginal spirituality and culture from tourism in the coastal waterways of the Kimberley region, North West Australia', *Journal of Ecotourism* 8 (2), 82–98.

Stolk, P. (2010) *If We Sink It, Will They Come? The Development and Management of Australia's Artificial Reefs as Resources for Sustainable Recreational Scuba Diving*, unpublished PhD Thesis, School of Tourism, Economics and Policy, The University of Newcastle, Callaghan, Australia.

The Rivers Access Campaign (n.d.) *The River Access Campaign*. www.riversaccess.org. Viewed 5 October 2010.

Todhunter, A. (2010) 'Deep Dark Secrets', *National Geographic* 218(2), 34–53.

University of Brighton (2011) *Enjoying Water – Strategic Water Priorities for Water Related Recreation in London and South East England*. www.brighton.ac.uk/waterrecreation/files/London-and-South-East.pdf. Viewed 2 March 2011.

Viorosmarty, C., McIntyre, P., Gessner, M., Dudgeon, D., Prusevick, A., Green, P., Glidden, S., Bunn, S., Sullivan, C., Reidy Liermann, C., and Davies, P. (2010) 'Global threats to human water security and river biodiversity', *Nature* 467, 555–61.

Wight, A. (1994) 'Bottomed Out', *Sportdiving* 42, February/March, 38–42.

Wood, J. and Hooy, T. (1982) 'Planning for Quality Sailing Experiences on Canberra's Lakes', *Australian Parks and Recreation* May, 14–21.

World Health Organization (2003) *Guidelines for safe recreational water environments. Vol. 1, Coastal and freshwaters*. Geneva, Switzerland: WHO.

——(2006) *Guidelines for safe recreational water environments. Vol. 2, Swimming pools and similar environments*. Geneva, Switzerland: WHO.

Wyschnja, A. (1995) 'Exploring Ewen's Ponds' *Sportdiving* 47, December 1994/January 1995, 82–85.

Further reading

Dudgeon, D., Arthington, A.H., Gessner, M.O., Kawabata, Z.-I., Knowler, D.J., Leveque, C., Naiman, R.J., Prieur-Richard, A.-H., Soto, D., Stiassny, M.L.J., and Sullivan, C. (2006). 'Freshwater Biodiversity: Importance, Threats, Status and Conservation Challenges', *Biological Review*, 81, 163–82.

Hjerpe, E.E. and Kim, Y.-S. (2007) 'Regional Impacts of Grand Canyon river runners', *Journal of Environmental Management* 85, 137–49.

Kemper, N., Popp, J. and Miller, W. (2008) 'Regional growth and Beaver Lake: A study of recreation visitors', *Tourism Economics*, 12(2), 409–26.

Pigram, J. (2003) 'Water-Based Recreation' in *Encyclopedia of Leisure and Outdoor Recreation*, J. Jenkins and J. Pigram. London: Routledge, 543–546.

Pigram, J.J. and Jenkins, J.M. (2006) *Outdoor Recreation Management*. London: Routledge.

Prideaux, B. and Cooper, M. (eds) (2009) *River Tourism*. Wallingford: CABI Publishing.

Ryan, C., Humin, G. and Chon, K. (2010) 'Tourism to polluted Lakes: Issues for Tourists and the Industry. An empirical analysis of four Chinese lakes', *Journal of Sustainable Tourism* 18(5), 595–614.

Salmi, J. and Salmi, P. (2010) 'Fishing tourism, biodiversity protection and regional politics in the River Tornionjoki, Finland', *Fisheries Management and Ecology* 17, 192–8.

Sithole, E. (2005) 'Trans-boundary Environmental Actors: The Zambezi Society's Campaign for Sustainable Tourism Development in the Zambezi Bioregion', *Journal of Sustainable Tourism* 13(5), 486–503.

Smith, A.J, Scherrer, P. and Dowling, R. (2009) 'Impacts on Aboriginal spirituality and culture from tourism in the coastal waterways of the Kimberley region, North West Australia', *Journal of Ecotourism* 8 (2), 82–98.

16

Marine systems and tourism

Mark Orams and Michael Lück

Introduction

The marine environment has always been an integral part of human activity. Throughout history, the sea has attracted people who have used it for a range of important functions including as a source of food, a means of transport, a receptacle for waste, a basis for exploration, discovery and settlement and as a location for recreation and leisure. Those areas of land that border the sea have also been attractive to people throughout the globe with coastal areas and islands playing a significant part in the geography of human settlement (Lück 2007). This historical trend has become even more significant throughout the twentieth century with coastal areas becoming highly desirable areas residential and industrial development. For example, in southeast Asia more than 350 million people now live within 50 km of the coast (Burke *et al.* 2002). Globally, around 70 per cent of the world's population lives within a day's walk of the coast (Brown *et al.* 2002) and the great majority of cities are located close to coasts (Crooks and Turner 1999).

Although Orams (1999) notes that there have been early records of the recreational use of marine environments, the growth of tourism and recreational activities based on the sea has primarily occurred over the past 100 years and the most dramatic growth has been since the 1970s (Higham and Lück 2007). Much of this recent growth has been facilitated by technological advances, which have allowed easier, safer and more affordable ways to access and utilise the sea (Orams 1999). Such developments include the invention of the self-contained underwater breathing apparatus (SCUBA), mass produced and marketed boats, kayaks, sailing vessels, surfboards and the like. In addition, the development of equipment that allows for safer and more comfortable use of the sea for recreation has had a major influence. Examples include the invention of wetsuits, drysuits and various clothing that has allowed for the use of colder water environments that were undesirable or unsafe for humans in the past. Furthermore, equipment such as GPS navigation systems, electronic chart plotters, more accurate and readily available weather and wave forecasting, and a variety of telecommunication systems suited for use on the sea have contributed to ease of access and use of marine environments for recreation.

Although marine tourism was initially viewed as a niche type of tourism (Jennings 2007), its rapid growth over the past four decades has led Hall (2001) and others to label ocean and marine tourism as one of the new frontiers. There is widespread evidence and agreement that this type of tourism is one of the fastest growing sectors of tourism and recreation (Hall and Page 2002; Orams 1999). A good illustration of this growth is in the activity of SCUBA diving. SCUBA was invented in the late 1950s but was not commercially available to the mass market until the mid-1970s. Its growth since that time has been massive. PADI, the world's largest diving organisation, estimates that every year about 600,000 new divers are being certified, a growth rate of 6 per cent (Garrod and Gössling, 2008). This is not a niche activity anymore. A further example is the phenomenal growth of the cruise-ship industry, which has been estimated at 7–10 per cent annually over the past two decades (Dowling 2006). Thus, marine recreation and tourism is a global phenomenon, which has become hugely influential for communities, both natural and human.

Marine systems and tourism

Marine ecosystems are complex and multifaceted natural systems that occur in a variety of contexts and settings (Alter 2008a). Categorising marine habitat types can be undertaken in two main ways. First, spatially and related to a habitat's distance from shore, zones are labelled as littoral, neritic and oceanic (Barnes and Hughes 1999). Second, habitats are labelled according to their types, utilising characteristics that influence or dominate their functioning. Examples include estuaries, sandy beaches, rocky shores, rocky reefs, coral reefs, kelp forests, inter-tidal areas, harbours, bays and inlets, sea-mounts, the continental shelf and open ocean (Tait and Dipper 1998).

Irrespective of how they are categorised, marine ecosystems are affected in terms of their biological functioning by a range of important variables including, light, depth, salinity, benthos/substrate, temperature, currents/tides, nutrients and up-welling (Barnes and Hughes 1999).

Traditionally, most oceanographic analyses of marine habitats and ecosystems tend to examine the natural processes that influence function, that is the biotic and abiotic variables that occur naturally in a particular location. However, it is clear that one of the most influential factors for any marine community is human activity. Irrespective of whether or not humans are physically present in a particular marine ecosystem, it is now accepted that the wider global influences of human activity do impact marine systems. Thus, there is an increasing recognition and inclusion of human influences in the study, understanding and management of marine resources.

Although the incorporation of human factors into oceanography is becoming more widely accepted and adopted, most of the emphasis has tended to be on human activities that are extractive (e.g. fisheries, mining, oil/gas exploration and extraction), dumping or discharges (e.g. sewage and storm-water runoff, sediment, litter and waste) and, most recently, human influences that are global in influence (climate change). Surprisingly, given their scale and spread, recreational and tourist uses and influences on marine ecosystems have received little attention in terms of their impacts and influences (negative and positive).

Defining marine tourism

Orams (1999) discusses the inherent challenges in defining 'marine tourism', and warns that too strict or too liberal definitions could become meaningless. For example, are people who are watching whales from shore actually marine tourists? Even more extreme, visitors to aquaria and maritime museums can be hundreds of miles away from the sea, but are exploring marine life (including human maritime history and heritage), and thus are focused on the marine environment. However, if definitions are based simply on human focus or interest in things marine, such as watching movies (e.g. *Finding Nemo*) or television documentaries (e.g. BBC's 'Seas of Life' in

The Blue Planet series), they would be too liberal to be meaningful. In order to find a useful understanding of what marine tourism includes, Orams (1999: 9) offers the following definition:

> Marine tourism includes those recreational activities that involve travel away from one's place of residence and which have as their host or focus the marine environment (where the marine environment is defined as those waters which are saline and tide-affected).

This definition has subsequently been adopted by other authors (Cater and Cater 2007; Hall 2001; Jennings 2007; Lück 2007). It is also worth noting that the terms 'tourism' and 'recreation' are used interchangeably in the context of this definition. This is due to the fact that all recreational users of marine environments are visitors who move from their place of residence to recreate on, in and under the sea. Although some might argue that those who reside on house-boats, live on yachts or other sea-based accommodation are not strictly marine tourists, in reality humans are not marine-based creatures. Thus, all are visitors to the marine environment, whether their actual place of residence is above or below the tidal high-water mark. Consequently, all who utilise the sea for recreational purposes are considered marine tourists.

The distribution and influences of marine tourism

Despite the rapid development of marine recreation and tourism and the increasing indepen-dence and safety of marine-based activities, the majority of recreational activities are still closely tied to the coast (Smith 2007), that is in the neritic province. This tendency is, however, complicated by a range of other influential variables. These include natural factors such as latitude, season, temperature, weather, sea-state, tides and the proximity of sheltered harbours, inlets and launching and retrieving areas. Human factors are also influential and include issues such as the availability and quality of ports, channels, docks, moorings, safety systems, navigational information and the socio-economic status of particular areas. In order to better understand the influences on tourist and recreational uses of marine environments, a model developed by Orams (1999) is helpful.

The Spectrum of Marine Recreation Opportunities (SMARO)

The Recreation Opportunity Spectrum (ROS) is as a tool for classifying differing recreational activities and the natural settings to which they are best suited (or in which they tend to occur) (Stankey 1985). This approach has been widely adopted as a planning and management tool for large terrestrial natural areas such as national parks, forests and mountain areas (Manning 1986). The underlying assumption on which the ROS is based is that diversity is a desired outcome with regard to managing recreation in natural settings. Furthermore, it explicitly recognises that particular settings are a prerequisite for certain recreational activities. For example, the remote wilderness experiences desired by some recreationists can only be found in pristine natural areas of significant size where there is little or no human influence (such as human-built structures, facilities and services). Conversely, recreationists who desire high levels of social interaction and who want or need access to a wide range of human-provided services (such as accommodation, retail facilities, electrical power, medical facilities and so on) need settings where these options and experiences are readily available. The ROS, therefore, is most often used in a land-use planning context, whereby inventories of resources and their spatial distribution are important information. Maps are typically used in combination with these inventories to designate particular ROS classes or zones, which are managed to meet the diverse needs of recreation user groups (Manning 1986).

A similar kind of approach to planning for, and managment of, marine recreation was proposed by Orams (1999). He termed this the Spectrum of Marine Recreation Opportunities (SMARO). Underlying the SMARO is the understanding that intensity of use is strongly influenced by distance from shore (i.e. it is inversely proportional). Furthermore, the intensity of recreational use of marine settings is also influenced by distance from areas of human habitation. Thus, the closer to shore and the closer to centres of human population (cities and urban areas) the greater the number and diversity of marine recreation participants and activities. The further offshore, and more distant from residential areas, the lower the level and diversity of recreational use (see Figure 16.1).

The SMARO (see Table 16.1) then provides a tool whereby general geographic patterns of use of marine systems for recreation and tourism can be understood. It uses a fivefold classification based on ease of access and intensity of use. Furthermore, the types of activities undertaken and the experiences of recreationists/tourists can also be overlaid or considered in terms of the model. Finally, the types and quality of the natural ecosystems that host each SMARO class can also be outlined in broad terms in the model.

SMARO Class 1 is dominated by coastal locations which are easily accessible, extremely popular and occur in close proximity to or on the shore. Experiences for participants are typically very social with large numbers of people, many activities, noise and crowding. Well known beaches and coastal parks are categorised in this class. Examples include beaches such as; Miami, Copacabana, Bondi and Waikiki.

SMARO Class 2 is typically a near-shore area that is relatively easy to access (from vehicle parking areas, docks, boat ramps and beaches). While such areas may be crowded at times, there are opportunities to find space to undertake recreational pursuits that are difficult or unsafe to conduct in SMARO Class 1 settings. Often people move from a base in a SMARO Class 1 location (such as a crowded urban beach) to a SMARO Class 2 location (50 metres offshore or a less crowded area along-shore) which permits recreational activities like small-boat sailing, windsurfing, fishing, snorkelling, kite flying and so on.

SMARO classes 3, 4 and 5 require increasing effort, experience, skill and often equipment for recreation. An offshore blue-water sailing voyage, for example, requires an ocean-going seaworthy vessel with suitable supplies, equipment and skilled crew to ensure safe passage. Some of

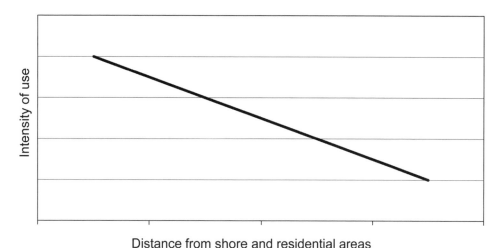

Figure 16.1 The Spectrum of Marine Recreation Opportunities (SMARO)

Table 16.1 The Spectrum of Marine Recreation Opportunities SMARO (after Orams, 1999)

Characteristics	Class 1 Easily Accessible	Class 2 Accessible	Class 3 Less Accessible	Class 4 Semi-remote	Class 5 Remote
Experiences	Much social interaction. High level of services. Usually crowded. Noisy. Lots of activity.	Frequent contact with others. Some spaces/ times to escape from others.	Some contact with others. Locations/times when no other people present. Quieter.	Infrequent contact with others. Peace and quiet. Close to nature.	Virtually no contact with others. Solitude. Tranquillity. Self-sufficiency.
Environment	Many human influences. Highly modified. Lower-quality natural environment.	Human structures and influences visible and close by. Environment quality variable.	Few human structures close by but some maybe visible. Higher environmental quality.	Limited evidence of human activity/ structures. High quality environment.	Isolated. Little to no evidence of human activity. Pristine environment.
Locations	Close to or in urban areas. Beaches, docks, piers, urban coastal parks and walkways/ cycleways. Close to road, parking and mass-transport options	Intertidal zone and areas up to 100 metres offshore. Often requires walk of several hundred metres from car parking, mass-transport.	100m to 1km offshore. More than 20km from major urban area. More remote beaches, islands and coastal areas. Often requires boat for access or walk in >500m.	1–50km offshore. Isolated coasts/ islands/reefs difficult to access. Boats or overnight hiking needed to access.	>50km offshore. Coastal areas >100km from any significant human habitation.
Examples of activities	Sunbathing/ baking. People-watching. Swimming. Playing games. Eating. Social gatherings. Sightseeing. Special events (e.g. concerts)	Swimming. Fishing. Boating. Surfing. Windsurfing/ kite-boarding.	Boating. Fishing. Snorkelling/ SCUBA. Nature-study. Surfing. Sailing. Sea-kayaking	Coastal sailing. Remote coast hiking and camping. Live-aboard vessels (fishing, diving, surfing etc.).	Offshore blue-water sailing. Live-aboard offshore vessels (for fishing, diving etc.). Remote coast/ reef sea-kayaking and surfing.

the attributes of Class 5 experiences are the wilderness, escapism and isolation and the challenges and satisfaction derived from independence and self-sufficiency.

While the SMARO model identifies general patterns of usage and typical experiences there are many activities which occur across all classes. Surfing, for example, occurs in crowded urban beach settings (Class 1) but also across all other SMARO classes including Class 5 when live-aboard offshore vessels explore remote islands and reefs for surf-breaks and surfing opportunities.

Similarly, sailing and fishing are also activities which occur across all classes. Thus, the model is one which seeks to provide a framework for understanding general patterns of use and experiences as opposed to a definitive tool for categorising all marine recreation and tourism activities and settings.

Additional factors which are universally influential with regard to marine recreation and tourism usage are weather and sea conditions. Particular activities are entirely dependent on this, for example, water-skiing and wake-boarding require relatively calm water-surface conditions, surfing however is entirely dependent on ocean swell conditions for surfable waves (which are also influenced by bottom type, wind and tidal state). While it may be self-evident that weather and sea conditions are significant variables affecting use (including seasonal influences), changes in weather forecasting accuracy and availability, and the invention and use of technologies (such as wet-suits, and more robust and sea-worthy vessels) have tended to mitigate the influence of weather, sea and temperature on marine recreation and tourism.

The distribution, intensity and types of marine tourism activities are, therefore, changing rapidly. Nevertheless, it is helpful, when analysing recreational activities available in a particular coastal and marine location, to simplify the wide range of opportunities so that the role of each is better understood. Consideration of where a particular marine tourism operation or activity lies in the SMARO clarifies the environmental characteristics and the experiences available for the wide variety of marine tourism enterprises.

Impacts on Marine Systems

The National Oceanic and Atmospheric Administration (NOAA) noted that '[c]lean water, healthy coastal habitats, and a safe, secure, and enjoyable environment are clearly fundamental to successful coastal tourism. Similarly, bountiful living marine resources (fish, shellfish, wetlands, coral reefs, etc.) are of critical importance to most recreational experiences' (National Oceanic and Atmospheric Administration 1997: 602). Thus, healthy, viable and resilient marine ecosystems are an important contributor to human recreational uses of those ecosystems. It is widely accepted that marine systems are under stress as a consequence of a wide range human induced changes (Earle 1995). Marine systems are subject to global phenomena such as climate change, to ocean-wide influences such as human produced sound and to regional and localised pressures from fishing, dredging, dumping, and point discharges. It is also worthwhile noting that many environmental pressures in near-shore marine ecosystems are a result of human land-based activities such as the urbanisation of catchments, sediment run off, coastal engineering works and the re-routing of water courses (Harriott 2004). An additional and growing impact is the influence of introduced 'alien' species. As the global movement of ships and other vessels has increased so has the transportation of species of plants and animals from one location to another. Many of these organisms are transferred inadvertently through attachment to vessel hulls (especially encrusting organisms such as barnacles and sponges as well as molluscs and crustaceans). In addition, the common practice of the deliberate ingress of sea-water into ballast tanks to help with the sea-worthiness of lightly loaded ships and the expelling of this ballast water at other locations when the ship needs to lighten to take on cargo has resulted in the introduction of many non-native species to marine ecosystems (Lavoie, Smith and Ruiz 1999; Lück 2010).

It is important to recognise that marine ecosystems differ from their terrestrial counterparts in an important way. Pristine and high-quality land-based resources such as forests, mountains, lakes and rivers are typically located away from major areas of urban development. In addition, there is now a century long tradition (and acceptance) of setting aside such areas for conservation purposes as national, regional and forest parks or other types of formal environment protection (Butler and Boyd 2000). Marine ecosystems however, do not have the same degree of protection (geographically or in terms of management regimes).

The most productive marine ecosystems are those close to shore and, in particular, those close to tidal areas (such as estuaries and wetlands), reefs, harbours, bays and areas of upwelling (Earle 1995). These locations have also historically been the most popular for human settlement. The great majority of coastal cities were established in bays, harbours and close to river mouths, estuaries and areas protected by reefs. Urban environments have the highest amounts of run-off, coastal 'reclamation', sediment, sewage discharge, shipping, dredging, dumping, litter and other forms of human activity. Thus, the most important and productive marine ecosystems are also the very locations that are subject to the most human influence. Furthermore, the protection of marine ecosystems (as marine protected areas) lags far behind the protection of terrestrial eco-systems (Orams 1993; Higham and Lück 2007).

Marine ecosystems are, therefore, under increasing pressure from human activity. Recreation and tourism uses of marine ecosystems are adding further pressure both in terms of their scale (intensity of use) and distribution (the increasing geographic spread of activities). The most sig-nificant of these influences has been the spread of housing and related infrastructural develop-ment along coasts. Much of this development has been driven by a desire to live in close proximity to the coast because of the recreational lifestyle it offers. In particular, the growing number of second or holiday homes built on the coast has resulted in a major change to the nature of beaches and near-shore hinterlands in the developed world. In New Zealand, for example, the widespread development of coastal land for holiday homes has become con-troversial (Peart 2009). In the developing world a related trend has been occurring with the development of coastal resorts where those from wealthier (primarily western) nations come for sea, sand and sun holidays.

A wide range of other impacts resulting from recreation and tourism activities has been occurring. These include: disturbance of wildlife (Newsome *et al.* 2005; Wilkes 1977), over-fishing (Ellis 2003), litter (Berghan 1998), damage to benthic organisms (eg. coral from anchors and trampling) (Rogers *et al.* 1990), noise pollution from vessels (Lusseau, 2007), vessel wake and wave action accelerating coastal erosion, dune and coastal plant trampling, souveniring (eg. shells, corals, driftwood etc.), waste water discharge from vessels (Lück 2010; Lumma and Gross 2009), sun-screen leaching and increased nutrient loads (from urine) at popular beaches, oil/fuel residue from recreational and cruise vessel exhausts and leaching of toxins from recreational vessel anti-fouling paints (Gray 2008; Klein 2002; Wang 2008).

Assessing impacts

One of the major challenges in assessing and managing impacts on natural ecosystems is differ-entiating between human induced change and change that occurs naturally. All ecosystems are dynamic and react to a wide range of influences. Examples include macro influences such as climatic events like the El Niño/La Nina oscillations, dramatic one off events such as hurricanes/cyclones and tsunamis, and localised influences such as floods/droughts, disease, and changes in predator/prey relationships. Because such changes are ongoing and hard to predict, understanding humans' role in influencing changes in marine systems is difficult. In addition, it is important to accept that human induced change is not necessarily detrimental to marine systems. All natural ecosystems have the ability to adapt to new influences. However, some ecosystems have a greater ability to withstand and accommodate change than others. It is these systems that can retain a healthy level of functioning that are of interest because the elimination of human influence is impossible. As a consequence, there has been a growing interest in better understanding and contributing to the concept of ecosystem resilience as a goal for management (Chapin *et al.* 2002; Walker *et al.* 2002).

The importance of ecosystem resilience

Resilience in the ecological context has been defined as 'the ability to absorb disturbances, to be changed and then to re-organise and still have the same identity (retain the same basic structure and ways of functioning)' (Resilience Alliance 2010). Ecosystems tend to be more resilient when:

- there are higher levels of biodiversity;
- there is greater complexity in food webs and trophic levels;
- there are higher levels of biomass and species abundance;
- when species exist within the main range of abiotic parameters appropriate for their existence (eg. temperature, sunlight, depth, nutrient levels). (Holling 1973).

Higher levels of adaptability are closely related to resilience. Thus, ecosystems that have the ability to re-organise and re-structure without a significant decline in fundamental ecological processes and functioning are more resilient (Hughes *et al.* 2005).

The concept of resilience has relevance to tourism because, unlike many other approaches to marine ecological system understanding and management, it specifically includes social systems in its consideration (Resilience Alliance 2010). The recognition that humans have a significant, important and legitimate role in ecological processes is long overdue. It is clear that a breaking down of the disciplinary boundaries between the biological sciences and social sciences has long been needed in attempting to better understand and manage human influences and impacts on ecosystems (Higham and Lück 2007). Thus, the socio-ecological approach of resilience is a useful framework to address issues associated with managing tourism in coastal and marine environments.

An Overview of Management Approaches

A wide range of approaches to managing human impacts on marine ecosystems have been developed and applied over the past five decades. Different locations, cultures and nations manage (or in some cases mismanage or do not actively manage at all) their marine resources in different ways. However, there are a number of approaches and principles that have become widely adopted internationally. These are briefly reviewed below.

The precautionary principle

While not a specific management tool, the precautionary principle is a guiding philosophy, which has been widely advocated as an essential basis for decision making when managing natural resources (including marine). It originated in the 1970s in Germany ('Vorsorgeprinzip') as a response to the growing recognition of the negative impacts on human health being caused by weak control of environmental pollution (Ebert 2003). In the absence of scientific proof of specific impacts, the precautionary principle suggests that management should adopt a conservative, precautionary approach, until reliable scientific data become available (Fennell 2006). Thus, a lack of scientific data or proof of potential detrimental impacts should not be used as a basis for permitting such activities (Cicin-Sain and Knecht 1998). In essence, the precautionary principle seeks to shift the burden of proof from an approach that allows actions if there is no current information or data showing negative impacts to a situation where actions are not permitted until there are conclusive data available demonstrating no negative effects. Thus, approval for actions should err on the side of caution, at least until scientific insights are available to support approval to proceed. According to VanderZwaag (1994: 7), the precautionary principle includes the following core elements:

- a willingness to take action (or no action) in advance of formal scientific proof;
- an assessment of the cost-effectiveness of action, that is, some consideration of proportionality of costs;
- providing ecological margins of error;
- consideration of the intrinsic value of non-human entities;
- a shift in the onus of proof to those who propose change;
- concern with future generations;
- paying for ecological debts through strict/absolute liability regimes.

While these elements are primarily focused on the natural environment, it should be noted that they can also be applied to potential social and cultural impacts. Since its inception in the 1970s, the precautionary principle has been adopted by more than 40 countries globally (Fennell 2006).

Adaptive management approaches

Adaptive management explicitly acknowledges the dynamic state of natural ecosystems and processes and the changing influences of human activities. It deliberately sets out to be a different management approach to those traditionally used which tend to focus on a 'problem identification – solution' style. Adaptive management focuses on understanding critical factors influencing the functioning of a system, identifying uncertainties and it deliberately includes human factors (such as the legal, political, economic and cultural context within which decisions are made) in the decision making framework. It has a particular emphasis on monitoring and understanding change and promoting flexibility in decision making systems to adapt to that change (Walters 1986).

Integrated Coastal Zone Management (ICZM)

ICZM explicitly recognizes that coastal areas are links between terrestrial or land based activities and those that occur in the near-shore sea. In addition, ICZM deliberately and explicitly includes human activities, desires and wants into a decision making process designed to ensure that human needs are balanced with essential ecological processes (both on land and in the sea) in an attempt to manage the area sustainably (Cicin-Sain and Knecht 1998; Thia-eng 1993). ICZM has become a recognised focus within university marine affairs and resource management schools and within management agencies with responsibilities for coastal and near-shore resources (Agardy 2010; Krishnamurthy *et al.* 2008). A number of nations and regions including Australia, the USA, England, Ireland and the European Commission have established or advocated for ICZM plans which seek to ensure the sustainable use of coastal ecosystems.

Marine Spatial Planning

Marine Spatial Planning uses processes developed to guide decision making on resources, which have been well established in terrestrial settings (Kidd *et al.* 2011). Typically these approaches utilise spatial zones to ensure that activities and development are compatible with settings and ecosystems in an attempt to ensure human activities and actions are sustainable. This type of approach has long been utilised by marine management agencies such as the Great Barrier Reef Marine Park Authority who have incorporated recreation and tourism management into their broader planning processes for the entire Great Barrier Reef area (Kenchington 1990).

Marine Protected Areas (MPAs)

Like their land-based counterparts (national parks, reserves and forests), MPAs seek to manage marine resources for conservation and recreation purposes (in some cases other purposes such as science and research, fisheries management and cultural significance are also included). Currently only a very small proportion of the seas globally are formally designated as MPAs (Alter 2008b; Hoyt 2005), however, there is strong advocacy, particularly from the environmental non-governmental agency sector, for increasing the number, size, type and distribution of MPAs. It is generally agreed that MPAs have proved beneficial for marine recreation and tourism, however, the restriction or prohibition of fishing in many MPAs has been controversial and, in some cases, has resulted in proposed MPAs being dropped.

Other management approaches

There are a wide range of other techniques utilised in managing marine resources. The most common of these is the regulatory approach. Governments and management agencies frequently utilise laws, by-laws, rules and regulations in order to control human activities on the sea. Such approaches are usually formal, written and backed up with punitive action (such as fines) or the threat of imprisonment or confiscation of assets for transgressors. A significant challenge with such approaches is the cost, resource and time needed for enforcement. Less common, but also widespread are the design and construction of specific barriers or facilities which seek to shape human activity and behaviour. Examples include the provision of mooring buoys, boardwalks, piers and docks, boat-ramps, fences and nets. A number of management agencies invest effort into educational approaches which seek to inform visitors and modify their behaviour. Examples include the provision of signs, brochures, advertising campaigns, visitor centers and educational staff. There are many other approaches where economic incentives/disincentives are deliberately used as a management tool and where indigenous communities use practices such as sacred areas, seasons, or activities to manage marine-based activities. There are, therefore, many management approaches which are applied in marine settings. Some of these approaches are formally recognised and have distinct parameters, training and a track record of application. Others are more arbitrary and variable in their use.

Utilising the SMARO as a basis for management planning

The SMARO provides a helpful tool for considering which management approaches are most appropriate. If it is accepted that one of the priority outcomes that management wishes to achieve is to provide for a range of settings and opportunities for different kinds of marine recreational experiences then the division of the marine system being managed into appropriate zones and SMARO classes is a useful starting point. Thus, the range of settings and their suitability for particular types of marine recreation activities and the diverse desires of visitors to marine systems can be considered under a framework which has as its basis, a desire to provide the widest range of opportunities possible.

Conclusion

It is clear that marine ecosystems provide enormous recreational opportunities and benefits for humankind. It is also clear that healthy marine ecosystems are fundamentally important to these activities. As human population grows, marine system degradation accelerates and challenges for marine life's long term viability accelerates. While the overall picture may appear bleak, it is important to recognise that there are a number of locations, species, habitats and ecosystems that have been improved through enlightened and wise management. The growing emphasis on marine protected areas, integrated coastal zone management, artificially enhanced natural ecosystems (as when artificial reefs are created) and more careful management of fisheries, coastal structures and near-shore catchments are all examples of marine ecosystems that have been improved as a consequence of human actions. These approaches, when they have been successful, have always been based on a sound understanding of the natural processes that occur in marine systems. Science and research have played an important role in this. However, probably even more important has been the recognition that no marine system exists in isolation from human activities. Thus, the traditional narrow approach of considering marine ecosystems in isolation, that is; by excluding a consideration of humans, their activities and influences, is being replaced. Marine systems and their management must include humans, because they are so influential. Consequently, the social sciences − economics, political science, anthropology, management, sociology, psychology − have a major contribution to make to the wise use and management of marine resources.

References

Agardy, T. (2010) *Ocean zoning: Making marine management more effective*. London: Earthscan.

Alter, S.E. (2008a) 'Marine ecosystem,' in M. Lück (ed.), *The encyclopedia of tourism and recreation in marine environments*. Wallingford: CABI, 287–88.

——(2008b) 'Marine protected area, ' in M. Lück (ed.), *The encyclopedia of tourism and recreation in marine environments*. Wallingford: CABI, 299–300.

Barnes, R.S.K. and Hughes, R.N. (1999) *An introduction to marine ecology*. Malden, MA: Blackwell Science.

Berghan, J. (1998) *Marine mammals of Northland*. Wellington: Department of Conservation.

Brown, K., Tompkins, E.L., and Adger, N. (2002) *Making waves: Integrating coastal conservation and development*. London: Earthscan Publications Limited.

Burke, L., Selig, L., and Spalding, M. (2002) *Reefs at risk in Southeast Asia* [webpage]. Accesed on 10.05.2002, http://www.wri.org/reefsatrisk/reefsatriskseaisa.html

Butler, R.W. and Boyd, S.W. (2000) 'Tourism and parks − a long but uneasy relationship' in R.W. Butler and S.W. Boyd (eds) *Tourism and national parks: Issues and implications*. Chichester: John Wiley & Sons, 3–11.

Cater, C. and Cater, E. (2007) *Marine ecotourism: Between the devil and the deep blue sea*. Wallingford: CAB International.

Chapin III, F.S., Kofinas, G.P. and Folke, C. (eds) (2009) *Principles of ecosystem stewardship. Resilience-based natural resource management in a changing world*. New York: Springer.

Cicin-Sain, B. and Knecht, R.W. (1998) *Integrated coastal and ocean management: Concepts and practices*. Washington, DC: Island Press.

Crooks, S. and Turner, R.K. (1999) 'Integrated coastal management: Sustaining estuarine natural resources,' *Advances in Ecological Research* 29, 241–89.

Dowling, R.K. (2006) 'The cruising industry, 'in R.K. Dowling (ed.), *Cruise ship tourism*. Wallingford: CABI, 3–17.

Earle, S. (1995) *Sea change. A message of the oceans*. New York: Random House.

Ebert, K.K. (2003) *Tourism and the precautionary principle: A survey of academic and government stakeholders*. (Unpublished Master of Arts thesis). Brock University, St. Catharines, ON, Canada.

Ellis, R. (2003) *The empty ocean*. Washington, DC: Island Press/Shearwater Books.

Fennell, D.A. (2006) *Tourism ethics*. Clevedon: Channel View Publications.

Garrod, B., and Gössling, S. (2008) 'Introduction', in B. Garrod and S. Gössling (ed.), *New frontiers in marine tourism: Diving experiences, sustainability, management*. Amsterdam: Elsevier, 3–28.

Gray, J. (2008) 'Two-cycle (two-stroke) pollution', in M. Lück (ed.), *The encyclopedia of tourism and recreation in marine environments*. Wallingford: CABI, 487–88.

Hall, C.M. (2001) 'Trends in ocean and coastal tourism: The end of the last frontier?', *Ocean and Coastal Management* 44(9/10), 601–18.

Hall, C.M., and Page, S. (2002) *The geography of tourism and recreation*. London: Routledge.

Harriott, V.J. (2004) 'Marine tourism impacts on the Great Barrier Reef,' *Tourism in Marine Environments* 1 (1), 29–40.

Higham, J., and Lück, M. (2007) 'Marine wildlife and tourism management: In search of scientific approaches to sustainability,' in J. Higham and M. Lück (eds), *Marine wildlife and tourism management: Insights from the natural and social sciences*. Wallingford: CAB International, 1–16.

Holling, C.S. (1973) 'Resilience and stability of ecological systems,' *Annual Review Ecological Systems* 4, 1–23.

Hoyt, E. (2005) *Marine protected areas for whales, dolphins and porpoises*. London: Earthscan Publications.

Hughes, T. P., Bellwooda, D. R., Folkeb, C., Steneck, R.S., and Wilson, J. (2005). 'New paradigms for supporting the resilience of marine ecosystems,' *Trends in Ecology & Evolution* 20(7), 380–86.

Jennings, G. (2007) 'Water-based tourism, sport, leisure, and recreation experiences,' in G. Jennings (ed.), *Water-based tourism, sport, leisure, and recreation experiences*. Amsterdam: Elsevier Butterworth-Heinemann, 1–20.

Kenchington, R.A. (1990) *Managing marine environments*. New York: Taylor and Francis.

Kidd, S., Plater, A., and Frid, C. (eds) (2011) *The ecosystem approach to marine planning and management*. London: Earthscan.

Klein, R. A. (2002) *Cruise ship blues: The underside of the cruise industry*. Gabriola Island, BC: New Society Publishers.

Krishnamurthy, R. R., Glavovic, B. C., Kannen, A., Green, D. R., Ramanathan, A. L., Han, Z., Tinti, S., and Agardy, T. (2008) *Integrated Coastal Zone Management. The global challenge*. Singapore: Research Publishing Services.

Lavoie, D.M., Smith, L.D., and Ruiz, G.M. (1999). The potential for intracoastal transfer of non-indigenous species in the ballast water of ships. *Estuarine, Coastal and Shelf Science* 48(5), 551–64.

Lück, M. (2007) 'Nautical tourism development: Opportunities and threats,' in M. Lück (ed.), *Nautical tourism: Concepts and issues*. Elmsford, NY: Cognizant Communication, 3–1.

Lück, M. (2010) 'Environmental Impacts of Polar Cruises,' in M. Lück, P. T. Maher and E. Stewart (eds) *Cruise tourism in the polar regions: Promoting environmental and social sustainability?* London: Earthscan, 109–31.

Lumma, K., and Gross, S. (2009). Ökologische auswirkungen von hochseekreuzfahrten. In H. Bastian, A. Dreyer and S. Gross (eds), *Tourismus 3.0: Fakten und perspektiven*. Hamburg: ITD Verlag, 197–226.

Lusseau, D. (2007) 'Understanding the impacts of noise on marine mammals,' in J.E.S. Higham and M. Lück (eds), *Marine wildlife and tourism management: Insights from the natural and social sciences*. Wallingford: CABI, 206–18.

Manning, R.E. (1986) *Studies in outdoor recreation*. Corvallis, OR: Oregon State University Press.

National Oceanic and Atmospheric Administration. (1997) *1998 year of the ocean-coastal tourism and recreation*. http://www.yoto98.noaa.gov/yoto/meeting/tour_rec_316.html, accessed on 10.12.2010.

Newsome, D., Dowling, R.K., and Moore, S.A. (2005) *Wildlife tourism*. Clevedon: Channel View Publications.

Orams, M. (1993) Towards a marine conservation ethic. Our marine protected areas can lead the way. *Trends* 30(2), 4–7.

Orams, M. (1999) *Marine tourism: Development, impacts and management*. London and New York: Routledge.

Peart, R. (2009) *Castles in the sand. What's happening to the New Zealand coast?* Nelson, New Zealand: Craig Potton Publishing.

Resilience Alliance (2010) *Key concepts*. http://www.resalliance.org/index.php/key_concepts. Accessed 21.12.2010.

Rogers, C.S., McLain, L.N. and Tobias, C.R. (1990) 'Damage to marine resources in Virgin Islands National Park: Often out of sight, but no longer out of mind,' in M.L. Miller and J. Auyong (eds) *Symposium conducted at the meeting of the 1990 Congress on Coastal and Marine Tourism: A symposium and workshop on balancing conservation and economic development*, Honolulu, HI. Abstract retrieved from G154.9/C67/1990/v.1

Smith, R.A. (2007) 'Anchoring tourism to the coast: Innovative spatial and community strategies,' in M. Lück (ed.) *Nautical tourism: Concepts and issues*. Elmsford, NY: Cognizant, 25–36.

Stankey, G. (1985) *Carrying capacity in recreational planning: An alternative approach*. USDA Forest Service.

Tait, R.V. and Dipper, F. (1998). *Elements of marine ecology*. Oxford: Butterworth Heinemann.

Thia-eng, C. (1993) 'Essential elements of Integrated Coastal Zone Management,' *Ocean and Coastal Management* 21, 81–108.

Walker, B., Carpenter, S., Anderies, J., Abel, N., Cumming, G., Janssen, M., Lebel, L., Norberg, J., Peterson, G.D. and Pritchard, R. (2002) 'Resilience management in social-ecological systems: A working hypothesis for a participatory approach,' *Conservation Ecology* 6(1), 14.

VanderZwaag, D. (1994) *CEPA and the precautionary principle/approach*. Hull, QC: Minister of Supply and Services.

Walters, C.J. (1986) *Adaptive management of renewable resources*. New York: McGraw Hill.

Wang, C. (2008) 'Anti-fouling systems,' in M. Lück (ed.), *The encyclopedia of tourism and recreation in marine environments*. Wallingford: CAB International, 22.

Wilkes, B. (1977) 'The myth of the non-consumptive user,' *The Canadian Field-Naturalist*, 91(4), 343–349.

17

Mountain environments and tourism

Catherine Pickering and Agustina Barros

Introduction

Mountain environments comprise approximately 27 per cent of the land surface, although the actual area of alpine vegetation is around 3 per cent (Blyth *et al.* 2002; Körner 2003). Mountains occur on all continents, as individual peaks or large mountain ranges that extend across several countries. Closer to the equator, alpine areas are restricted to areas above around 5,000 m altitudes on mountains such as Mt Wilhelm in New Guinea and Mt Kilimanjaro and Mt Kenya in Africa (Blyth *et al.* 2002; Körner 2003). The further from the equator the mountains are, the lower that altitude at which snow occurs, with the alpine areas of northern Europe merging into the tundra of the arctic (Körner 2003). Some of the most famous mountain ranges are the Andes in South America, the Rocky Mountains in North America, the Himalayas in Asia and the European Alps, but there are also important mountain ranges in New Zealand, Japan, Mexico and Australia.

Mountains are characterised by low temperatures, with an average decrease in temperature around 0.65°C per 100 m increase in altitude (Blyth *et al.* 2002). As a result, in many mountain regions there is snow on the ground for days, weeks, months or even permanently. Because of the variation in aspect and elevation in mountains they are also characterised by high variability, including in temperature and precipitation. This includes high rainfall/snowfall on the windward side of mountains, with less precipitation on the lee side (Blyth *et al.* 2002). Mountains also experience high levels of soil erosion due to strong winds, freezing and thawing cycles and the effects of runoff from rain and during the thaw. As a result, soils are often thin in mountains with rocks and scree common, particularly where there is no vegetation to protect the soils from erosion (Blyth *et al.* 2002; Körner 2003).

Mountains provide a wide range of ecosystems services. They supply 24 per cent of precipitation, act as the water towers of the world and support 22 per cent of the global population (Blyth *et al.* 2002). They are key sources of the worlds' major rivers playing a critical role in the water cycle by capturing moisture from air masses, storing snow until it melts in the spring and summer, and providing water for settlements, agriculture and industries downstream. Their unique biophysical characteristics have led to rich and diverse reservoirs of species and ecosystems (Blyth *et al.* 2002). They contain large numbers of endemic plants and animals driven by the isolated environments and small-scale habitat differentiation (Körner 2003). Vegetation cover in mountains ensures soil stability protecting communities and infrastructure against rock falls, landslides and avalanches (Blyth *et al.* 2002; Körner 2003).

Tourism in mountains

Mountains attract tourists with a diversity of motivations who undertake a variety of activities in a range of locations (Buckley *et al.* 2000; Scott and McBoyle 2007). Mountains are attractive to adventure tourists who desire challenges, danger and risk, novelty and excitement. They attract nature-based tourists who desire to experience natural environments and wildlife tourists who want to see wild animals such as mountain goats, snow leopards, condors or reindeer. It attracts religious tourists who travel individually or in groups for pilgrimage, to monasteries or specific religious ceremonies in mountains, such as seeing the start of the Ganges at Gaumakh in the Himalayan mountains or climbing the summit of Croagh Patrick in Ireland, in Mt Fuji in Japan (Hamilton and McMillan 2004). It also provides opportunities for mass tourism, with large numbers of people visiting ski resorts, monasteries, lakes, viewpoints or summits (Hamilton and McMillan 2004). The range and types of tourism will be determined by demand, opportunity and regulation, with large differences in the types of activities available, the origins, motivations and numbers of tourists among mountain regions.

A major component of mountain tourism is focused around snow, and snow-based activities (Buckley *et al.* 2000; Scott and McBoyle 2007). The most obvious example of this is ski resort tourism. These often highly modified environments provide a wide range of tourism infrastructure and cater for exclusive high end to mass tourism (Buckley *et al.* 2000; Scott and McBoyle 2007). Common tourism activities in ski resorts include downhill skiing and snowboarding, ice skiing, saunas and thermal pools, sightseeing, food and wine and relaxation-based activities in winter. At the adventure end of the distribution are riding mountain bikes with studs on snow, snow mobiling, heli-skiing, bobsledding and trick boarding (Buckley *et al.* 2000; Scott and McBoyle 2007).

As a result of the numbers of people involved and their often high expenditure, the value of ski resort tourism is high. The industry earns US$ 9,000 million annually in North America, Japan and Europe where there are large mountain ranges and well-developed resort facilities (Scott and McBoyle 2007). In the Southern Hemisphere there are often fewer/smaller ski resorts, but they are often a major focus for regional tourism including in New Zealand and Australia in Oceania and Chile and Argentina in South America. These often smaller scale destinations can still be valuable for the local tourism industry with the Australian ski fields worth an estimated US$ 1,000 million per year in 2005 (Pickering and Buckley 2010).

In addition to ski resorts, many people access mountain protected parks in winter to under-take snow-based tourism (Buckley *et al.* 2000). This includes back country skiing, often also referred to as cross-country or ski touring. Other activities are snow shoeing, winter ascents of mountains, ice climbing, glacier walking and snow cave camping. In some mountains, in or outside parks, it includes snowmobiles, ice fishing and hunting.

Mountain tourism is far from limited to snow-based activities. During winter in areas free of snow as well as for the rest of the year, there is greater diversity of tourism activities that often utilise a wider range of destinations (Buckley *et al.* 2000; Hamilton and McMillan 2004). Common tourism activities include fishing, camping, spas, mountain retreats, education courses, bird-watching, shorter walks and general sightseeing including from roads, gondolas, chairlifts and railways (Nepal and Chipeniuk 2005). More adventure-focused tourism includes mountaineering, trekking, rock climbing, rafting, kayaking, paragliding and base jumping (Nepal 2002; Buckley *et al.* 2000).

Religious tourism, defined as tourism exclusively or strongly motivated for religious purposes, is a common activity in mountain regions all around the world (Bernbaum 2006). Mountains have established a network of myths, beliefs and religious practices including pilgrimage, meditation and sacrifice (Bernbaum 2006). Places of sanctity and sacred sites in mountains with temples and monasteries are visited by thousands of individuals and groups (Bernbaum 2006).

In support of these different types of tourism is a range of tourism infrastructures, often provided by tourism operators and protected area managers (Buckley *et al.* 2000; Lockwood *et al.* 2006). Roads, tracks, railways, chairlifts, gondolas, ski lifts are just some of the infrastructures provided to allow tourists to access mountains and move around within them. Accommodation facilities range from major resorts, monasteries, hotels, guest houses, huts, permanent tents, snow caves and informal and formal campgrounds (Buckley *et al.* 2000, Pickering *et al.* 2003). In ski resorts, the natural landscape can be heavily modified for skiers including removing natural vegetation, rocks and other obstacles, landscaping slopes and constructing snowmaking infrastructure (Pickering and Hill 2003). Where there are high concentrations of facilities, basic infrastructure is often required such as power supplies, water storage and treatment, waste water treatment and garbage disposal: in effect all the requirements of a small to medium-size town.

Park agencies provide a wide range of support for tourism in mountain protected areas (Worboys and Hamilton 2004). This includes provision of information for tourists even before they arrive in the park. Paralleling other tourism destinations, mountain protected areas provide a wide range of information through websites and books including maps, flora and fauna, trip itineraries, regulations and booking services. Within the park, they provide similar information, including signs, maps, guided walks and talks. Some mountain parks have large visitor centres, which are an attraction in their own right, providing educational information, bookings services, food and cinemas.

Parks agencies construct, maintain, remove and rehabilitate a wide range of tourism facilities including walking and riding tracks, stock yards, jetties, picnic tables, car parks and even helipads for rescues (Lockwood *et al.* 2006). They regulate the types of activities permitted in the park including tourists and commercial operators. They also have to then police these regulations. They often provide rescue and medical services, which can put a high demand on park staff. They engage in hazard reduction for threats such as fires, avalanches and landslides. In many cases also have to deal with tourist waste including its removal, provide water for drinking and washing, provide firewood and lighting and test water quality for contaminants. They can monitor visitor numbers activities and locations, as well as monitoring the impacts and, in some cases, minimising impacts from tourism. All this is in addition to activities focused on the conservation of the natural environment, which is a major motivation for tourists to visit the destination (Newsome *et al.* 2002).

Impacts of tourism on mountain environments

Types of environmental impacts

Owing to the short growing season, often thin soils and steep topography, mountains are particularly susceptible to environmental damage from tourism use and slow to recover once damaged (Körner 2003; Pickering *et al.* 2003). Damage caused by the construction and use of ski resorts includes changes to the flora such as clearance of existing vegetation, deliberate and accidental introduction of non-native plants, introduction of plant pathogens, changes to soils and ground water that effect native flora and fauna in the resort and downstream (Buckley *et al.* 2000; Scherrer and Pickering 2010). Impacts on soils include soil compaction, erosion, changes in soil temperatures, sedimentation, changes to soil nutrients including from salting of roads and paths through to major alteration of the topography on ski slopes including remodelling of slopes

(Buckley *et al.* 2000; Pickering and Hill 2003). Impacts on animals include noise and light pollution, habitat clearance and fragmentation, increased risk of road-kill, introduction of diseases and increased number and diversity of feral animals (Liddle 1997; Buckley *et al.* 2000). Changes to the hydrology of the system include sedimentation and surface run off, changes to snow that alter its melt pattern, harvesting water for snow making, contamination of water ways with pollution including increased turbidity, nutrient enrichment and introduction of pathogens including from human waste into water ways (Buckley *et al.* 2000).

Away from resorts, winter-based tourism has a range of negative environmental impacts (Pickering *et al.* 2003). Winter back country activities including skiing on and off tracks, snowboarding, snow vehicles and ice climbing can result in compaction of the subnivial space that is used by animals to move around in winter, alteration to animal behaviour owing to noise and human activities, increased feral animal activity as they use tracks, modification of drainage patterns, contaminations of soil, visual pollution litter, human waste and noise pollution. Impacts from summer tourism include the same general types of impacts, although they may differ in intensities and location from winter tourism (Pickering *et al.* 2003). For example, the construction of facilities such as walking tracks, camp grounds and visitor centres also involves clearing native vegetation, but the locations are more diverse, and impacts are often linear compared with those concentrated in a single location in resorts (Buckley *et al.* 2000; Hill and Pickering 2006). Back country activities in snow-free areas such as walking on and off tracks, horse riding, mountain biking, rock climbing and fishing can result in vegetation clearance and disturbance, introduction of weeds, alteration of animal behaviour, soil erosion and compaction, soil nitrification and visual and noise pollution, as well as rubbish and human waste (Hammit and Cole 1998; Liddle 1997; Pickering *et al.* 2003, 2010a, 2010b).

Factors that affect the severity of impacts

The severity of the impacts from mountain tourism will vary with the intensity of use, the timing of use, activity and visitor behaviour, the way facilities are constructed including the types of materials used and the tolerance of the environment to use (Hammit and Cole 1998; Liddle 1997; Newsome *et al.* 2003; Leung and Marion 2000; Pickering 2010). A general pattern is that the greater the amount of use, the greater the environmental impact. However, it appears that in many, but not all plant communities, initial use causes more damage per person than repeated use (Cole 2004). As a result the impact of an activity such as trampling on vegetation shows a curvilinear relationship with the amount of damage per pass flattening out at higher use levels. Not all communities show this pattern, with some communities including in alpine regions, having a linear or sigmoidal pattern with increasing use (Hill and Pickering 2009; Pickering and Growcock 2009).

Ecosystems vary in their sensitivity to impacts, with vegetation types, soil properties and topography all affecting the nature and intensity of impacts (Liddle 1997; Monz *et al.* 2010). These can be measured using the resistance and resilience of the community to different levels and types of use (Liddle 1997). Resistance is the relative ability of plants to withstand disturbances before being damaged, and resilience is the capacity to recover after disturbance (Liddle 1997; Cole 2004; Pickering and Growcock 2009). The combination of recovery and resilience gives a measure of tolerance (Liddle 1997). Resistance and resilience can be affected by plant height, morphology and growth rates (Liddle 1997; Hill and Pickering 2009). In general, certain life forms appear to be more susceptible to trampling than others (Cole 2004; Hill and Pickering 2009). Forbs appear to be more sensitive than ferns, and ferns more sensitive than shrubs, which are more sensitive than grasses (Hill and Pickering 2009; Pickering 2010). Thus, community types dominated by more resistant growth forms, such as grasslands, are likely to be more resistant than other vegetation types dominated by forbs, ferns or mosses (Hill and Pickering 2009).

The timing of use affects the amount of damage. Obviously driving, riding or walking on unhardened tracks after high rainfall events can cause more damage than use of the same tracks when soils are dry (Liddle 1997; Newsome *et al.* 2003). Noise pollution from activities involving helicopters, trail bikes or quadbikes can cause greater disturbance when animals are calling, mating and nesting than at other times (Liddle 1997; Newsome *et al.* 2003). For mountains, the short time available for growth and reproduction for animals and plants increases the potential for impacts during the short snow-free period, which is often the time of peak use for some of these activities.

Recreational activities vary in their impacts (Liddle 1997; Newsome *et al.* 2003). Damage to vegetation, for example, varies among different types of use, with four-wheel drive causing greater impacts than horses, which cause greater impacts than hikers (Liddle 1997; Pickering 2010). There is often considerable controversy among user groups about their relative impacts. This includes among horse riders, mountain bike riders and hikers: all popular activity in mountain protected areas (Pickering *et al.* 2010a, 2010b). Unfortunately, a lack of experimental replicated studies quantifying the relative impacts of some activities such as mountain biking only contributes to the problem (Pickering *et al.* 2010a, 2010b).

Even for the same activity, the selection of different types of materials for facilities can affect the scale of impacts, for example, when the extent of vegetation clearance and presence of weeds can vary among different track types (gravel, paved, raised metal walkway and unhardened bare soil) (Hill and Pickering 2006). Unfortunately, limited funding often means that a greater emphasis is placed on immediate cost as opposed to long-term costs and impacts when selecting materials for tracks and other types of tourism infrastructure.

Weeds and human waste: important impacts from mountain tourism

Two impacts from tourism that are of particular concern in mountain protected areas are weeds and human waste. Owing to more limited human disturbance and naturally low biodiversity, there are often fewer species of weeds and lower weed cover in mountains compared with lower altitude sites (Johnston and Pickering 2001; Pickering *et al.* 2007). However, weeds are still a major threat to mountain environments, as they can displace native vegetation, alter fire regimes, soil nutrients and hydrology and habitats for native animals (Pickering *et al.* 2007). Once established, they are also expensive and hard to eradicate. Mountain tourism contributes to the spread of weeds intentionally and unintentionally. In resorts and other tourism facilities there are gardens of non-native plants, many of which have the potential to become major environmental weeds (Pickering *et al.* 2007). In addition, tourists can unintentionally spread weed seed including introducing new species into parks and spreading existing species further into mountain parks (Pickering and Mount 2010). Seed from over 750 species, of which 15 per cent were environmental weeds of concern internationally, have been collected from clothing, equipment, vehicles and horses (Pickering and Mount 2010). In experimental studies in the Snowy Mountains in Australia, large numbers of seed were collected on shoes, laces, socks and trouser legs after just 5 minutes walk on road sides (Mount and Pickering 2009). In addition to introducing weed propagules into parks and dispersing them within parks, trampling and other types of disturbance associated with tourism infrastructure and its use, favours weeds over native plants (Johnston and Pickering 2001; Pickering *et al.* 2007). As a result track and road verges and areas around buildings are often colonised by weeds that benefit from regular disturbance, compaction of soil and nutrient addition (Pickering and Hill 2007).

Human waste is a major issue in mountains, with different removal/disposal methods used depending on the remoteness of location, the amount of waste produced and the resources available to those dealing with the waste. Potential impacts from untreated human waste include increased nutrients in soils, presence of bacteria and pathogens in soil and water, pollution of water courses and glaciers, health hazards to humans and wildlife, and reduced amenity (Cilimburg *et al.* 2000; Kirkpatrick and Bridle 2005; AAC 2010). In remote mountain areas, methods of disposal and treatment range from surface deposition with no treatment, smearing on rocks, digging small holes and burying the waste (cat holes), carry out techniques, to more complex solutions such as composting toilets, dehydration or evaporation toilets, fly out systems and treatment plants (AAC 2010). The success of the systems varies with levels of compliance and maintenance, the level of residual impacts in cases in which the method is inadequate and ongoing costs (Liddle 1997; Kirkpatrick and Bridle 2005; AAC 2010).

Benefits of mountain tourism

A range of benefits arise from mountain tourism including economic development, employment and other income for local communities, cultural enrichment and enhanced human health (Hamilton and McMillan 2004). As mentioned, the economic value of mountain tourism can be large, particularly around ski resorts and other mass tourism destinations (Nepal 2002). Mountain tourism provides employment for local people as guides, porters, cooks, cleaners, reception staff, as well as in provision of accommodation, transport and other services in areas adjacent to the mountains (Hamilton and McMillan 2004; Nepal and Chipeniuk 2005). Also, locals are often employed in protected areas as park rangers and tour or interpretative guides. As mountain tourism tends to occur in rural areas where other job opportunities are limited, the contribution to the local economy is important. Cultural enrichment can also occur from exchanges between locals and tourists, adding to both groups' understanding and recognition of others (Butz 2006). However, interaction between tourists and locals can be complex or mainly negative, particularly for communities in remote mountain regions, which otherwise have limited interaction with other groups (Singh *et al.* 2004; Butz 2006). Mountain tourism contributes to human health and physical and mental well-being, with benefits arising from time spent in nature as well as exercises, cultural exchanges and socialising (Stolton and Dudley 2010).

Environmental benefits can arise from mountain tourism, including establishment and maintenance of protected areas to provide tourism opportunities. This limits the use of these areas for other more exploitive land uses such as logging and mining (Lockwood *et al.* 2006). However, the direct link between tourism and conservation is not as straightforward as is often claimed. Even where much of the income for parks agencies comes from tourism, this must be offset against the environmental impacts of tourism and the reallocation of protected area staff from conservation to tourism management. Further research is required to determine just how much tourism is actually a benefit for conservation in mountain regions.

Case study

Climate change and mountain tourism

Climate change is already affecting many mountain regions worldwide (IPCC 2007). Impacts include increased temperature in summer and winter, changes in precipitation, reduction in snow cover, melting of glaciers and increased extreme climatic events including flooding downstream as a result of the collapse of dams (IPCC 2007). Impacts of climate change on tourism include direct impacts from reduced snow cover and indirect impacts from changes in the marketing of tourism, the behaviour of tourists and synergies between climate change and some impacts from tourism such as the spread of weeds (Pickering 2007; Pickering and Buckley 2010).

For ski resorts, the immediate issue is reduction in natural snow cover (Scott *et al.* 2003; Scott and McBoyle 2007; Pickering and Buckley 2010). As a result, resorts are investing in infrastructure for snow making as a way of offsetting low natural snow (Scott and McBoyle 2007; Pickering and Buckley 2010; Pickering *et al.* 2010c). However, snow making, which requires large amounts of energy, is itself likely to contribute to greenhouse gas production, is expensive and, in some cases, limited by water availability (Hudson *et al.* 2004; Scott and McBoyle 2007; Pickering and Buckley 2010). Other responses by resorts are amalgamation and diversifying into year-round destinations (Scott and McBoyle 2007; Scott *et al.* 2008; Pickering and Buckley 2010). In some cases, resorts may benefit from increased temperatures in summer at lower altitude tourism destinations, which may result in mountains becoming more attractive as cool summer retreats (Scott and Jones 2006; Scott *et al.* 2007). The sale of properties in resorts and in surrounding areas is also being used as a way to diversify incomes. Change in usage of resorts, including a greater focus on summer activities such as mountain biking, hiking, horse riding and relaxation-based activities will have a range of impacts on mountain environments, as a result of differences in impacts from summer versus winter activities, and as summer-based tourism occurs in more diverse locations. Paralleling changes in tourism use are the risk of negative synergies between some tourism activities and existing impacts such as the spread of weeds. Increased summer usage is likely to increase the risk of the spread of weeds, whereas increased temperatures and decreased snow cover will also benefit many weed species. Therefore, weeds may benefit twice over from climate change in mountains (Pickering 2007; Pickering *et al.* 2007). More research is required into the direct effects of climate change on mountains, on mountain tourism and on the ways in which changes in the marketing of tourism in response to climate change may alter environmental impacts from tourism.

References

American Alpine Club [AAC] (2010) *Proceedings of the Exit Strategies Conference: Managing Human Waste in the Wild*. 31 July–1 August 2010. Boulder, CO: American Alpine Club.

Bernbaum, E. (2006) 'Sacred Mountains: Themes and Teachings,' *Mountain Research and Development* 26, 304–9.

Blyth, S., Groombridge, B, Lysenko, I., Miles, L. and Newton, A. (2002) *Mountain Watch: Environmental Change and Sustainable Development in Mountains*. Cambridge: UNEP World Conservation Monitoring Centre.

Buckley, R.C., Pickering, C.M. and Warnken, J. (2000) 'Environmental Management for Alpine Tourism and Resorts in Australia,' in P.M. Goode, M.F. Price and F.M. Zimmerman (eds), *Tourism and Development in Mountain Regions*. New York: CAB International, pp. 27–45.

Butz, D. (2006) 'Tourism and Portering: Labour Relations in Shimshal, Gojal Hunza,' in H. Kreutzmann (ed.) *Karakoram in Transition: Culture, Development and Ecology in the Hunza Valley*. Karachi: Oxford University Press, 394–403

Cilimburg, A., Monz, C. and Kehoe, S. (2000) 'Wildland Recreation and Human Waste: A Review of Problems, Practices and Concerns', *Journal of Environmental Management* 25, 587–98.

Cole, D.N. (2004). 'Impacts of Hiking and Camping on Soils and Vegetation: A Review' in R. Buckley (ed.) *Environmental Impacts of Ecotourism,* New York: CAB International, 41–60.

Hamilton, L. and McMillan, L. (2004) *Guidelines for Planning and Managing Mountain Protected Areas*. Gland: IUCN World Commission on Protected Areas.

Hammit, W.E. and Cole, D.H. (1998).' *Wildland Recreation: Ecology and Management*' Second Edition. New York: John Wiley and Sons.

Hill, R. and Pickering, C.M. (2009) 'Differences in the resistance of three subtropical vegetation types to experimental trampling', *Journal of Environmental Management* 90, 1305–12.

Hill, W. and Pickering, C.M. (2006) 'Vegetation Associated with Different Walking Track Types in the Kosciuszko Alpine Area, Australia', *Journal of Environmental Management* 78, 24–34.

Hudson, S., Ritchie, B. and Seldjan, T. (2004) 'Measuring Destination Competitiveness: an Empirical Study of Canadian Ski Resorts', *Tourism and Hospitality: Planning & Development* 1, 79–94.

Intergovernmental Panel on Climate Change [IPCC] (2007) *Climate Change 2007: The Physical Science Basis*, Geneva: Intergovernmental Panel on Climate Change.

Johnston, F.M. and Pickering, C.M. (2001) Alien plants in the Australian Alps. *Mountain Research and Development* 21, 284–91.

Kirkpatrick, J.B. and Bridle, K. (2005) *Impacts of Human Waste Disposal in the Backcountry Areas of Tasmania*, Gold Coast: Cooperative Research Centre for Sustainable Tourism.

Körner, C. (2003). *Alpine Plant Life: Functional Plant Ecology of High Mountain Ecosystems*. Berlin: Springer-Verlag

Leung, Y. and Marion, J.L. (2000) 'Recreation Impacts and Management in Wilderness: A State-of-knowledge Review', in D.N. Cole, S.F. McCool, W.T. Borrie and J. O'Loughlin (eds) *Wilderness Science in a Time of Change Conference, Vol. 5: Wilderness Ecosystems, Threats and Management*, Missoula, MT: US Department of Agriculture, 23–48.

Liddle, M.J. (1997) *Recreation Ecology*. London: Chapman and Hall.

Lockwood, M.L., Worboys, G.L. and Kothari, A. (2006) *Managing Protected Areas: A Global Guide*. London: Earthscan.

Monz, C.A., Cole, D.N., Leung, Y.F. and Marion, J.L. (2010) 'Sustaining Visitor Use in Protected Areas: Future Opportunities in Recreation Ecology Research Based on the USA Experience', *Journal of Environmental Management* 45, 551–62.

Mount, A. and Pickering, C.M. (2009) 'Testing the Capacity of Clothing to Act as Vector For Non-native Seed in Protected Areas', *Journal of Environmental Management* 91, 168–79.

Nepal, S.K. (2002) 'Mountain Ecotourism and Sustainable Development', *Mountain Research and Development* 22, 104–9.

Nepal, S.K. and Chipeniuk R. (2005) 'Mountain Tourism: Toward a Conceptual Framework', *Tourism Geographies* 7, 313–33.

Newsome, D., Moore, S.A., and Dowling, R.K. (2002) *Natural Area Tourism: Ecology, Impacts and Management*, Sydney: Channel View Publications.

Pickering, C.M. (2007) 'Climate Change and Other Threats in the Australian Alps', in M. Taylor and P. Figgis (eds) *Protected Areas: Buffering Nature Against Climate Change. Proceedings of a WWF and IUCN World Commission on Protected Areas Symposium*. Sydney: World Wildlife Fund, 28–34.

——(2010) 'Ten Factors That Affect The Severity of Visitor Impacts in Protected Areas', *Ambio* 39, 70–7.

Pickering, C.M. and Buckley, R. (2010) 'Climate response by Ski Resorts: The Shortcomings of Snow-making', *Ambio* 39, 430–8.

Pickering, C.M. and Growcock, A.J. (2009) 'Impacts of Experimental Trampling on Tall Alpine Herbfields and Subalpine Grasslands, Snowy Mountains, Australia', *Journal of Environmental Management* 91, 532–40.

Pickering, C.M. and Hill, W. (2003) 'Ecological change as a Result of Winter Tourism: Snow Manipulation in the Australian Alps', in R. Buckley, C.M. Pickering and D. Weaver (eds) *Nature-based Tourism, Environment and Land Management*. New York: CAB International, 137–49.

——(2007) 'Roadside Weeds of the Snowy Mountains, Australia', *Mountain Research and Development* 27, 359–67.

Pickering, C.M. and Mount, A. (2010) 'Do tourists disperse weed seed? A global review of unintentional human-mediated terrestrial seed dispersal on clothing, vehicles and horses', *Journal of Sustainable Tourism* 18, 239–56.

Pickering, C.M., Castley, C., Newsome, D. and Hill, W. (2010a) 'Environmental, safety and management issues of unauthorised trail technical features for mountain bicycling', *Landscape and Urban Planning* 97, 58–67.

Pickering, C.M., Castley, J.G. and Burtt, M. (2010c) 'Skiing Less Often in a Warmer World: Attitudes of Tourists to Climate Change in an Australian Ski Resort', *Geographical Research* 48, 137–47.

Pickering, C.M., Hill, W. and Bear, R. (2007) 'Indirect Impacts of Nature Based Tourism and Recreation: Association Between Infrastructure and Exotic Plants in Kosciuszko National Park', *Journal of Ecotourism* 6, 146–57.

Pickering, C.M., Hill, W., Newsome, D. and Leung Y.-L. (2010b). 'Comparing hiking, mountain biking and horse riding impacts in Australian and the United States of America,' *Journal of Environmental Management* 91, 551–62.

Pickering, C.M., Johnston, S., Green, K. and Enders, G. (2003) 'Impacts of Nature Tourism on the Mount Kosciusko Alpine Area, Australia', in R. Buckley, C.M. Pickering and D. Weaver (eds) *Nature-based Tourism, Environment and Land Management*. New York: CAB International, 123–35.

Scherrer, P. and Pickering, C.M. (2010) 'The Australian Alps: Opportunities and Challenges for Geo-tourism', in D. Newsome and R. Dowling (eds) *Geotourism: The Tourism of Geology and Landscape*. London: Goodfellow Publishers, 77–87.

Scott, D. and McBoyle, G. (2007) 'Climate Change Adaptation in the Ski Industry', *Mitigation, Adaptation Strategies to Global Change* 12, 1411–31.

Scott, D. and Jones, B. (2006) *Climate Change and Nature Based Tourism: Implications for Park Visitation in Canada*. Waterloo: Department of Geography, University of Waterloo. Available online at www.fes.uwater.ca/u/dj2scott.

Scott, D., Boyle, G. and Mills, B. (2003) 'Climate change and the skiing industry in southern Ontario (Canada): Exploring the importance of snowmaking as a technical adaptation', *Climate Research* 23, 171–81.

Scott, D., Dawson, J. and Jones, B. (2008) 'Climate change vulnerability of the US Northeast winter recreation – tourism sector', *Mitigation, Adaptation Strategies to Global Change* 13, 577–96.

Scott, D., Jones, B. and Konopek, J. (2007) 'Implications of climate and environmental change for nature-based tourism in the Canadian Rocky Mountains: A case study of Walterton Lakes National Park', *Tourism Management* 28, 570–9.

Singh, T.V., Chauhan, P. and Singh, S. (2004) 'Tourism Trespasses on the Himalayan Heritage: The Hermit Village, Malana,' in T.V. Singh (ed.) *New Horizons in Tourism: Stanger Experiences and Stranger Practices*. New York: CABI International, 49–61.

Stolton S. and Dudley N. (2010) *The Contribution of Protected Areas to Human Health Arguments for Protection of Vital Sites*. Geneva: World Wildlife Fund.

Worboys, G.L. and Hamilton, L.S. (2004) 'Managing Mountain Protected Areas in the 21st Century', in D. Harmon and G.L. Worboys (eds) *Managing Mountain Protected Areas: Challenges and Responses for the 21st Century*, Italy: Andromeda Editrice, 1–8.

18

Orchids

An example of charismatic megaflora tourism?

Catherine Pickering and Mark Ballantyne

Introduction

Seeing big game in southern and east Africa, gorillas in central Africa, whale watching in the Pacific and Atlantic and tiger tracking in India are well-recognised examples of wildlife tourism focused around 'charismatic mega-fauna' (Newsome *et al.* 2005). Tourism focused around birds is also a well-recognised specialised type of wildlife and nature-based tourism, with twitching a popular activity (Connell 2009; Newsome *et al.* 2005). There is less recognition that charismatic plants, such as orchids, can be such a focus of tourism (Kirby 2003). We illustrate how the desire to see wild and cultivated orchids has resulted in a diversity of types of tourism products ranging from mass conference tourism through nature-based tourism to specialised volunteer tourism (Figure 18.1). This typology is similar to that developed by Fennell (2001) to describe soft- and hard-path dimensions of ecotourism with nature-based orchid tourism similar to soft-path ecotourism, whereas orchid ecotourism and specialised volunteer tourism to conserve orchids would be examples of hard-path ecotourism in Fennell's typology (Fennell 2002).

Orchid tourism does not appear to have been characterised in the tourism literature as a particularly niche type of tourism, although a few examples of tourism operators and/or conservation organisations using or proposing to use orchids as an attraction have been described (Kirby 2003; Community Action, Global Impact 2006; Jalal *et al.* 2008; Piluek and Triboun 2008; Wei *et al.* 2009). Therefore there is a dearth of research on most aspects of orchid-focused tourism, whether examining social, environmental and/or economic aspects of the industry. As a topic for academic research, orchid-focused tourism should be as significant as birding and other well-recognised examples of wildlife tourism such as watching big game in southern and east Africa, gorillas in central Africa, whales in the Pacific and Atlantic or tiger tracking in India (Kirby 2003).

By documenting the range and importance of orchid-focused tourism, we hope to stimulate research interest in this type of tourism. Orchids could be used to test established theories and methods in conference tourism, nature-based tourism, ecotourism and volunteer tourism, as well as recreation ecology, as all can involve and effect orchids.

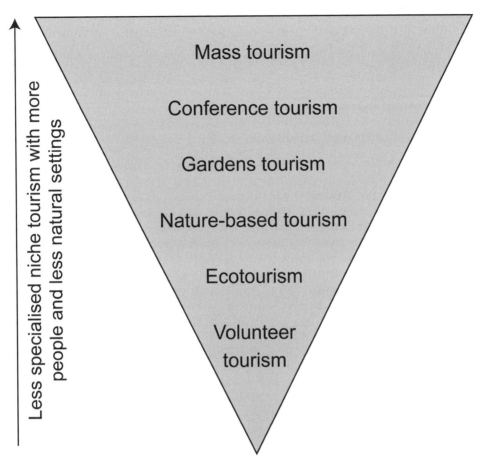

Figure 18.1 Hierarchy of types of tourism that can rely on orchids as part or all of the attraction (See Fennell 2002 for a similar figure outlining soft- to hard-path ecotourism)

Orchids

Orchids are the most diverse family of angiosperms accounting for around 10 per cent of earth's flowering plants (Cribb *et al.* 2003; Koopowitz *et al.* 2003). They have high conservation value owing to their diversity and because of their complex relationships with other species (Swarts and Dixon 2009). There is a long history of people collecting orchids from the wild and displaying them in glasshouses, gardens and shows (Koopowitz *et al.* 2003). From the beginning of the nineteenth century, orchid collecting increased and specially funded expeditions were conducted to bring back specimens of 'rare and exotic new genera' for the pleasure and status of wealthy Europeans and North Americans (Koopowitz *et al.* 2003; Swarts and Dixon 2009). Their beauty and extravagance was seen as a status symbol among the bourgeoisie of countries such as the UK, France, Germany and the USA.

Interest in seeing, talking about and collecting orchids has not declined today as reflected by the hundreds of orchid societies globally (Australian Orchid Society 2010; British Orchid Council 2010; Kirby 2003). The popularity of orchids extends beyond members of orchid societies into the wider community. Orchids are among the most popular types of plants, be it as cut flowers, plants sold by nurseries or plants on display in hotels and other tourism destinations (US Department of Agriculture 2009). As a result of the popularity of orchids, a range of orchid tourism products have been developed, each reflecting their continuing and increasing popularity.

Types of orchid tourism

Orchids as part of the marketing of mass tourism

Orchids are used in mass marketing by a wide diversity of tourism organisations because they are symbols of exoticism and luxury. At the national scale, this includes exploiting their status as floral symbols with Indonesia (Moon Orchid, *Phalaenopsis amabilis*), Colombia (Colombia Orchid, *Cattleya trianae*), Panama (Holy Ghost Orchid, *Peristeria elata*) and Singapore (the hybrid orchid – Vanda Miss Joaquim) all having orchids as their national flowers.

Orchids are also commonly used in names and logos for commercial companies involved in tourism even when the product itself has nothing directly to do with orchids. Potentially the best known, is the use of orchids in marketing by Thai Airways. Their 'Frequent Flyer Program' is called Royal Orchid Plus, they have separate Royal Orchid lounges in some airports and they offer Royal Orchid Tours. Orchids are also used in logos and names by tourism developments (Orchid Bay in Belize), spas (Halekulani Spa in Hawaii), tour operators (Orchid Travel and Tourism in Syria, Vientiane Orchidées in Laos), resorts (Orchid Resort in the USA, Koh Chang Grand Orchid Resort and Spa in Thailand, The Fiji Orchid Hideaway Resort), hotels (The Orchid Hotel in India, Chiang Mai Orchid Hotel and the Royal Orchid Park, Thailand), restaurants (Orchid Restaurant in the UAE, Blue Orchid Bistro in the USA, Orchid Restaurant and Bar in the UK, Thai Orchids chain of restaurants in the UK), charter airlines (Orchid Air Charters in Australia) and cruise ships (MS Orchid on the Nile in Egypt). In addition, orchids are common in many hotels, restaurants and resorts in tropical countries, in part because of their beauty, but also as symbols of luxury and warmth for international visitors who may be from colder climates, where such flowers are rare.

Orchid-focused conference and show tourism

The largest and most obvious example of mass orchid-focused tourism involves events run by orchid societies (Figure 18.1). These include large international orchid conferences that can attract local and international visitors. These conferences can include competitive displays of orchids by private individuals and nurseries, displays of products by commercial organisations, talks by scientist and other enthusiasts as well as a wide range of social events. They also regularly offer side trips to see orchids in gardens, nurseries and in the wild (Tan 2009). The major international orchid conference (World Orchid Conference) has been held every three years since 1954, with conferences held in the USA, France, Malaysia, Canada, Brazil, Scotland, New Zealand, Japan, South Africa, Thailand, Germany, Colombia, Australia, Singapore, England and Hawaii (Australian Orchid Society 2010). The Eighteenth World Orchid Conference held in Dijon, France in 2005 had displays, judging and exhibits from 30 nations and attracted 200,000 visitors. The 2008 conference in Miami, Florida had 100 exhibits, exhibitions and vendors from 20 countries and thousands of visitors (Nineteenth World Orchid Conference 2008). The twentieth conference is in Singapore in 2011 and it is anticipated will be even more popular. The conference will use the new 'Gardens by the Bay', a 101-ha tourism development that is currently under construction and includes large orchid displays (Australian Orchid Society 2010).

Even national orchid shows can be large events, with the Second Singapore Garden Festival and Orchid Show in 2008 having attracted 308,000 visitors and more than 30 exhibitors (Australian Orchid Society 2010). At a more local level, orchid societies continuously run shows, day trips, talks and other events. For example, the British Orchid Council listed 20 orchid shows or events in a three-month period spanning September to November in 2010 (British Orchid Council 2010). The popularity and diversity of these more local orchid events put them on par with birding festivals in the USA, which collectively attract large numbers of tourists (Lawton and Weaver 2010).

Research on orchid conferences and shows could assess social components including motivations and attitudes in similar ways to research into birding festivals (Lawton and Weaver 2010). It could look at the social and environmental issues associated with attending orchid conferences, as has been done for academic conferences (Hoyer and Noess 2001), or it could examine perceptions, attitudes and intended behaviour of attendees at orchid conferences in relation to environmentally sustainability as has been done for those attending citywide conventions in Washington, DC, in the USA (Park and Boo 2010).

Garden tourism

There are a wide range of tourism attractions focused around displays of orchid collections in gardens and nurseries. The most familiar examples of this are orchid houses in botanic gardens, where hundreds of local and cultivated orchids may be on display. One of the largest orchid displays in the world is in the Singapore Botanic Gardens in their National Orchid Garden, with over 1,000 species and 2,000 hybrids on display (Australian Orchid Society 2010; Tan 2009). The American Orchid Society runs its own visitor centre and 1.4-ha botanic gardens in Delray Beach, Florida, where they propagate and display orchids, as well as organise shows, workshops and educational events. In the Chiang Mai region of Thailand, there are five tourism orchid nurseries with mass displays of wild and hybrid/cultivated orchids, which also sell flowers and plants to tourists.

In other cases, the private orchid collections of individuals have been transformed into tourism destinations. An example of this is on the Pacific island of Viti Levu, Fiji, where there is an orchid garden named the 'Garden of the Sleeping Giant'. Visitors can spend up to a day visiting the private orchid collection of the late Raymond Burr as well as exploring the surrounding forests for wild orchids with guides.

Orchid-focused nature-based tourism

Nature-based tourism is a large component of the tourism industry, focused around natural destinations, which are often in protected areas (Newsome et al. 2002). Seeing orchids within a more general trip to a protected area can be a highlight for some tourists. There are also protected areas that have been explicitly declared to protect rare orchids. Examples include reserves to conserve the rare underground orchid Rhizanthella slatrii in Australia (Swarts and Dixon 2009), and the Yachang Orchid Nature Reserve in China, which was specifically established to preserve an area of high orchid diversity (Liu and Luo 2010; Liu et al. 2010).

The Gargano Peninsula National Park in Italy is a floral biodiversity hotspot containing herb-rich dry grassland, rocky valleys and pine forests. This area has one of the largest orchid floras in Europe, supporting around 56 species and five sub-species (Italian National Park Service 2010). The UK-based nature-tourism company, Naturetrek, runs eight-day holidays to the region twice a year, within which numerous day-trips seek to locate the many species of orchids that inhabit the region (Naturetrek 2010). The website advertises the trip using a day-by-day itinerary and the description of each day's activities includes reference to a variety of sought-after orchids. Orchids are also prominent in marketing other protected areas. Naturetrek provides 316 wildlife-based holidays worldwide, of which 96 have botanical elements and 14 use images of orchids or refer to them directly in their marketing on the web.

Iberian Wildlife Tours operate similar botanical trips to the Picos de Europa National Park in Spain (Iberian Wildlife Tours 2010). The itinerary describes the area as hosting 50 species of orchids, with the Black Vanilla-orchid (*Nigritella gabasiana*) used as the image for this tour. Other species are also listed as highlights of separate day-trips into the field. In addition to these general examples of nature based tourism with an orchid flavour, there is a sub-section of more specialised orchid-focused ecotourism tours on offer.

Orchid-focused ecotourism

Although there are a plethora of definitions of ecotourism, they commonly involve tourism to natural areas, conservation, culture, benefits to locals and education (Fennell 2001). Some types of orchid tourism may fit within these requirements for ecotourism where they: (i) involve travel to natural areas to see wild orchids; (ii) contribute to the conservation of nature including of orchids; (iii) involve education including about orchids; (iv) benefit locals through employment; and (v) may involve a greater cultural awareness among tourists, including the significance/meaning of orchids to local communities.

Searches on the web using terms such as 'orchid ecotourism' bring up a range of ecotourism trips and destinations in biodiversity hotspots such as Ecuador, Thailand, Malaysia, Costa Rica and Laos. These include one–10-day trips focused around seeing orchids in the wild, with local experts as guides. The importance of these types of ventures in promoting the conservation of orchids is recognised particularly for areas of high biodiversity including Costa Rica (Kirby 2003), India (Jalal *et al.* 2008), Borneo (Community Action, Global Impact 2006) and Thailand (Piluek and Triboun 2008).

An example of orchid ecotourism focused on conserving species in the wild are the orchid treks in Phu Khao Khoay National Biodiversity Conservation Area in Laos, offered by Vientiane Orchidées (Vientiane Orchidées 2007). With 5 per cent of the trip cost going to orchid conservation in the local area, the organisers arrange for local guides to lead the treks, and in doing so discourage illegal orchid harvesters in favour of employment as long-term orchid guides. They also provide funding for the protected area and for students studying botany at the National University of Laos. Orchids are sold to tourists and the international market, but done so in a sustainable manner through a joint partnership between villagers working as nursery maintenance staff with Vientiane Orchidées and the orchid sales department.

In addition to trips entirely focused on orchids, there are activities based around local ecotourism lodges or destinations, where, as a result of the expertise of one or more locals, orchid excursions are available. This includes Kumul Lodge in Papua New Guinea (Ballantyne pers. obs.), Bosque De Paz Biological Preserve, Central Volcanic Range, Costa Rica (Kirby 2003) and the Tetepare Island Ecolodge in the Solomon Islands. In some cases seeing orchids in the wild may be supplemented with viewing translocated orchids in cultivated gardens adjacent to the lodges (Ballantyne pers. obs., Kirby 2003).

More generally, some countries that specialise in ecotourism such as Bhutan and Costa Rica also have high orchid biodiversity, with orchids part of the natural attraction to tourists. Orchids benefit from the policies in these countries to promote ecotourism and, as a result of the income earned, the capacity to set aside natural areas for conservation is increased (Cribb *et al.* 2003).

In some ways parallels can be drawn between charismatic fauna-based ecotourism and orchid-based ecotourism activities and destinations. These trips, whether offered via orchid societies or others, may appeal to a select audience; generally middle-aged, affluent individuals, for example they may be similar to those who go bird watching (Jones and Buckley 2004). In some cases, the attraction is the diversity of orchids in an area, whereas in others it could be something iconic, such as a targeted species or group of species. The inherent fascination of humans with rarity makes rare species increasingly attractive; objects of desire and exoticism (Courchamp *et al.* 2006). It is this rarity that historically drove up the price of species of butterflies and orchids as their numbers declined, and that today is likely to influence the tourism motivations of enthusiasts (Courchamp *et al.* 2006).

An example of such rarity resulting in orchid ecotourism involves the Military Orchid (*Orchis militaris*), Monkey Orchid (*Orchis simia*) and Lady's-slipper Orchid (*Cypripedium calceolus*) in the UK (Kull and Hutchings 2005). These species are extremely rare and this has given rise to a micro-ecotourism industry during summer months when orchid enthusiasts regularly contact reserves in order to get details of impending flowering and consequently travel some distances to visit these iconic plants (Lancashire Wildlife Trust pers. comm.). These visitors will often stay in the local area for some time, contributing to the bed and breakfast industry as well as utilising local shops and other attractions.

Orchid-focused volunteer tourism

The most specialised type of orchid tourism described here is orchid volunteer tourism, which would fit into Fennell's (2002) typology of hard-path ecotourism (Figure 18.1). Volunteer tourism applies to tourists who volunteer in an organised way to undertake holidays that might involve restoration of certain environments or research into aspects of society or environment (Wearing 2001). Volunteer tourism is a sector of ecotourism that provides kinaesthetic learning experiences that can benefit both the tourists and the host communities (Guttentag 2009; Lyons and Wearing 2008). Being less consumptive and more experiential than mass tourism, such activities pose the question as to whether they constitute an alternative social phenomenon as opposed to the commodity-intensive fundamentals of mass tourism (Lyons and Wearing 2008). With an increased awareness of the need for conservation in the twenty-first century, orchids have become a prime candidate for volunteer tourism.

Several orchid societies, particularly those focused around native orchids, organise trips to protected areas or other sites where they contribute to orchid conservation and research. For example, the Australasian Native Orchid Society, Victorian Group is a foundation member of the Threatened Orchid Recovery Team along with state government organisations, universities, the Royal Botanic Gardens and Melbourne Zoo whose aim is to promote the recovery of 80 species of native orchids (Threatened Orchid Recovery Team 2006). Members of the orchid society cultivate these orchids and actively engage in community volunteer ventures such as surveying, fencing, weeding and other maintenance activities for populations of threatened orchids in Victoria (Threatened Orchid Recovery Team 2006). Although accessing some populations only involves day trips for volunteers, others require volunteers to travel for more than 100 km to sites and stay for several days (Australasian Native Orchid Society, Victoria Group 2010).

A species-specific example of orchid volunteer tourism in the UK is the Lady's-slipper Orchid (*Cypripedium calceolus*), which is an iconic species for national conservation. Collecting dramatically reduced this species in England (Cribb *et al.* 2003). The Sainsbury Orchid Project in collaboration with Natural England and the Royal Botanic Gardens Kew has overseen the re-introduction programme of this species to the northern counties of England (Natural England 2006). The sole remaining publicly accessible Lady's-slipper has become a botanical 'celebrity' among the British public. This has inspired a suite of volunteers, some devoted botanists, some just keen amateur naturalists, to give up their time to maintain a 'guard station' that overlooks the plant's location ensuring its safety. In the past, the plant had been vandalised on multiple occasions (most recently in 2009) and this has served to increase the determination of the local volunteers in preserving this plant in the wild (volunteers pers. comm. 2009).

Conclusion

We have described here, for the first time in literature, the diversity of tourism that involves orchids and hence demonstrated that this is an important, but under-researched tourism issue. Orchid-focused tourism ranges from the use of orchids in resort gardens as symbols of exoticism to specialist volunteer tourism. It includes activities organised and/or promoted by members of orchid societies, as well as more general nature-based tourism along with the massive popularity of international and national orchid shows and conferences. Further research is required to determine the economic, social and environmental significance of orchid-focused tourism.

Acknowledgements

We thank Ralf Buckley, David Weaver, Clare Morrison, an anonymous reviewer and, in particular, Campbell Ballantyne for their comments on this text. This chapter was one of the last things Campbell Ballantyne read before he suddenly passed away on 25 August 2010. His love of orchids inspired our interest in the topic.

References

Australasian Native Orchid Society, Victoria Group (2010) *Activities* www.anosvic.org.au/ANOS_Vic_Activities.html (accessed August 2010).
Australian Orchid Conference (2010) *Conference details* www.waorchids.iinet.net.au/19th_AOC_Conference.htm (accessed August 2010).
Australian Orchid Society (2010) *Orchids Australia* www.orchidsaustralia.com/oa_oz_societies.html (accessed August 2010).
British Orchid Council (2010) *Welcome to the British Orchid Council's Web Site.* www.british-orchid-council.info/ (accessed August 2010).
Community Action, Global Impact (2006) *The development of natural orchid ecotourism to strengthen community organisation in Sentarum lake,* West Kalimantan. Community Action, Global Impact. http://sgp.undp.org/web/projects/15704/the_development_of_natural_orchid_ecotourism_to_strengthen_community_organization_in_sentarum_lake_w.html (accessed August 2010).
Connell, J. (2009) 'Birdwatching, twitching and tourism: towards an Australian perspective', *Australian Geographer* 40, 203–17.
Courchamp, F., Angulo, E., Rivalan, P., Hall, R.J., Signoret, L., Bull, L. and Meinard, Y. (2006) 'Rarity value and species extinction: The anthropogenic allee effect', *Public Library of Science, Biology* 4, 2405–10.
Cribb, P.J., Kell, S.P., Dixon, K.W. and Barrett, R.L. (2003) 'Orchid Conservation: A Global Perspective', in K.W. Dixon, S.P. Kelly, R.L. Barrett and P.J. Cribb (eds) *Orchid Conservation.* Kota Kinabalu, Borno: Natural History Publications, 1–24.
Fennell, D.A. (2001) 'A content analysis of ecotourism definitions', *Current Issues in Tourism* 4, 403–21.
——(2002) 'The Canadian ecotourist in Costa Rica: ten years down the road', *International Journal of Sustainable Development* 5, 282–99.
Guttentag, D.A. (2009) 'The possible negative impacts of volunteer tourism', *International Journal of Tourism Research* 11, 537–51.

Hoyer, K.G. and Noess, P. (2001) 'Conference tourism: A problem for the environment as well as for research', *Journal of Sustainable Tourism* 9, 451–70.

Iberian Wildlife Tours (2010) *Iberian Wildlife Tours*. www.iberianwildlife.com/ (accessed August 2010).

Italian National Park Service (2010) *Parco Nazionale del Gargano*. www.parks.it/parco.nazionale.gargano/ Epar.php, (accessed August 2010).

Jalal, J.S., Rawat, G.S. and Kumar, P. (2008) 'An initiative to community based orchid conservation in the Gori Valley, Uttarakhand, Western Himalaya, India', *The McAllen International Orchid Society Journal* 9, 12–16.

Jones, D.N. and Buckley, R., (2004) *Bird watching tourism in Australia*. Gold Coast: Cooperative Research Centre for Sustainable Tourism, Griffith University.

Kirby, S. (2003) 'Neotropical orchid eco-tourism: educational experience of an orchid neophyte at the Boasque De Paz Biological Preserve, central volcanic range, Costa Rica', *Lankesteriana* 7, 121–24.

Koopowitz, H., Lavarack, P.S. and Dixon, K.W. (2003) 'The nature of threats to orchid conservation', in K.W. Dixon, S.P. Kelly, R.L. Barrett and P.J. Cribb (eds). *Orchid Conservation*, Kota Kinabalu, Broneo: Natural History Publications, 25–42.

Kull, T. and Hutchings, M.J. (2005) 'A comparative analysis of the decline in the distribution ranges of orchid species in Estonia and the United Kingdom', *Biological Conservation* 129, 31–9.

Lawton, L.J. and Weaver, D.B. (2010) 'Normative and innovative sustainable resource management at birding festivals', *Tourism Management* 31, 527–36.

Liu, H. and Luo, Y. (2010) 'Protecting orchids in nature reserves: research and restoration needs', *Botanical Review* 76, 137–9.

Liu, H., Feng, C., Luo, Y., Chen, B., Wang, Z. and Gu, H. (2010) 'Potential challenges of climate change to orchid conservation in a wild orchid hotspot in Southwestern China', *Botanical Review* 76, 174–92.

Lyons, K.D. and Wearing, S. (2008) *Journeys of Discovery in Volunteer Tourism*. London: CAB International Publishing.

Natural England (2006) *The Lady's-slipper Orchid in the Morecambe Bay Limestone Hills. Landscape Access Recreation and English Nature Leaflets*. London: Natural England Publications.

Naturetrek (2010) *Naturetrek* wildlife holidays. www.naturetrek.co.uk/ (accessed August 2010).

Newsome, D., Moore, S.A. and Dowling, R.K. (2002) Natural Area Tourism: Ecology, Impacts and Management. Sydney: Channel View Publications.

Newsome, D., Dowling, R. and Moore, S. (2005) *Wildlife Tourism*. Toronto: Channel View Publications.

Nineteenth World Orchid Conference (2008) *19th World Orchid Conference factsheet*. www.19woc.com/ news.htm (accessed August 2010).

Park, E. and Boo, S. (2010) 'An assessment of convention tourism's potential contribution to environmentally sustainable growth', *Journal of Sustainable Tourism* 18, 95–113.

Piluek, C. and Triboun, P. (2008) 'Wild orchids conservation for ecotourism in Thailand', *Acta Horticulture* 788, 69–76.

Swarts, N.D. and Dixon, K.W. (2009) 'Terrestrial orchid conservation in the age of extinction', *Annuals of Botany* 104, 543–56.

Tan, K. (2009) 'City in a Garden', *Orchid Digest*, July, August, Sept., 168–71.

Threatened Orchid Recovery Team (TORT) (2006) *Back from the brink: saving Victoria's threatened orchids*. Melbourne: Threatened Orchid Recovery Team. www.anosvic.org.au/Banksia_Awards_2006_Vic_Thr t_Orchid_Project.pdf (accessed August 2010).

United States Department of Agriculture (2009) Floriculture Crops 2008 Summary. Washington, DC: United States Department of Agriculture.

Vientiane Orchidées (2007) *Vientiane Orchids home page*. www.vientianeorchidees.com/ (accessed August 2010).

Wearing, S. (2001) *Volunteer Tourism: Experiences That Make a Difference*. New York: CABI Publishing.

Wei, N., Rong-hua, L., Wei, Z., and Wei-wei, W. (2009) 'Discussion on developing orchid cultural tourism in the city of Lanzi, Zhejiang', *Modern Landscape Architecture*. Doi CNKILSUN:NYYL.).)2009–08–006 (abstract in English).

19

Island tourism

Godfrey Baldacchino

Introduction: how 'the island' beckons

One comes across travel deals offering 'Island Escapes', but not 'Mainland Escapes'. One can buy an 'Islands' wall calendar, but asking for a 'mainland wall calendar' will surely cock an eyebrow or two. A widely distributed, recent full-page advert by Visa Inc. lists 'Visit an Uninhabited Island' as one of 23 '[T]hings to do while you're alive'. Googling the term 'mainland tourism' on 2 November 2010 delivered 11,200 hits; but googling 'island tourism' on the same day conjured up 717,000.

Tourism has become such an important industry for many island economies that 'small island tourist economies' represents one of three broad classes of development models postulated for island jurisdictions (*about which more below*). In such places, tourism is seen as a mechanism for generating jobs, foreign exchange and infrastructural enhancements, which connects readily with an often fine-tuned marketing strategy that seeks to tap a primordial allure for the exotic, the unexplored and, more recently, the green and pristine.

An enduring Western tradition, dating back at least to the Odyssey, has considered islands as special places of mystery, solace, danger or worship, first in the Mediterranean world and then beyond (Gillis 2004). With the onset of the European age of discovery, islands started being constructed as outposts of aberrant exoticism, peopled by innocent and exuberant natives (Lowenthal 1972: 14; Gillis and Lowenthal 2007). Later still, the island became the backdrop for the enactment of a male and heroic paean to colonialism, the subject of Robinsonnades that extend up to the present in the likes of Tom Hanks' movie *Castaway* or the TVB blockbuster series *Lost* (Loxley 1990). No wonder, with all this historical baggage, islands project themselves aggressively today as ideal destinations for the world's burgeoning travelling classes: whether for relaxation, adventure, frolic or self-discovery (Butler 1993). Indeed, as islands can also be bought, they also offer experiences of total control; you do not have to be a mad scientist to 'play God' on your own island (Wells 1896; Vladi Islands 2010; Island God 2010). This hedonistic drive goes hand in glove with the realisation by many developing island states and territories that they can 'sell' their natural capital to such visitors, by appealing to their constructed modern needs for travel and vacation, as much as for escaping stress, routine and responsibility. In this manner, such islands carve out for themselves what suggests itself as a beguilingly quick and easy route to development (e.g. Apostolopoulos and Gayle 2002; Löfgren 2002; Gössling and Wall 2007). Other island features can be added to the mix, enhancing the overall allure of the island tourism brand: physical separation, jurisdictional specificity, cultural difference, a sense of 'getting away from it all' and a possibility of claiming an understanding of the totality of the locale as trophy (Baum 1996). You can more easily conceive of 'doing' Barbados than Mexico; or doing Mauritius than Kenya.

The sum total of these forces at work is that islands are now, perhaps unwittingly, the objects of what may be the most lavish, global and consistent branding exercise in human history. They find themselves presented as locales of desire, as platforms of paradise, as habitual sites of fascination, emotional offloading or religious pilgrimage. The metaphoric deployment of 'island', with the associated attributes of small physical size and warm water, is possibly the central gripping metaphor within Western discourse (Hay 2006: 26). Expanding tourism development within various islands is today associated with rising income, in-migration of labour, higher literacy and longer life expectancy.

Island types

Aspects of remoteness, isolation and timelessness can be said to apply to most island spaces; but there are otherwise significant differences between 'warm water' and 'cold water' islands and their respective appeal to tourism. The warm water versions are typically densely populated. They generally include references to good food, fun and relaxation on emblematic sandy beaches in sunny and warm locations, and freer sex with friendly island inhabitants willing to tease and please … as their illustrated colour brochures make a point of describing (Gössling 2002). In contrast, located as they are beyond tropical latitudes, cold water islands have much shorter tourism seasons: strong cold winds and more challenging weather conditions effectively restrict the industry to a few weeks of activity every year. The sea is not for swimming, and there is a lower diversity of food, native plants and animals. Population density is low, and an unadulterated hinterland (typically pristine wilderness or rolling countryside) tends to dominate. Their inhabitants are less attuned to the service culture that global tourism has come to expect. If the Ss – sun, sea and sand (along with sex?) – characterise the first cluster, the second batch of islands are typified by the Is – ice, icebergs, isolation, indigenous people (Baldacchino 2006a).

Tourism penetration on islands

There are 36 small island states and territories, each with a resident population of less than one million and a land area of less than 5,000 km^2 (and for which reliable data is available for the start of the twenty-first century), which have the highest level of tourism penetration by jurisdiction in the world (McElroy 2006). All 36 are 'warm water' islands. The least developed tourist economies within this set are located primarily in the remote Indian and South Pacific Oceans and are characterised by small-scale facilities, absence of cruise traffic, longer average tourist stays and lower occupancy rates. Out of this set of 36, there are nine island jurisdictions, of which seven in the larger Caribbean region – the British Virgin Islands, US Virgin Islands, Dutch Sint Maarten, Aruba, Cayman Islands, Turks and Caicos, Bermuda, Malta and Guam – exhibit the 'most developed' and mature tourist economies of the cluster. They are not just very small and relatively crowded; they also manifest a high mean visitor density and high stock of tourist accommodation per km^2. When discounting for the particular footprint of cruise or yacht visitors, three island destinations stand out even more sharply with 63–75 tourist rooms per km^2: Dutch Sint Maarten (actually a half island) in the Caribbean, the UK Overseas Territory of

Bermuda in the northwest Atlantic, and the Mediterranean sovereign state of Malta. Indeed, Malta is the only sovereign state within this sub-set of nine.

Not surprisingly, these same locales are often cited in the literature for tourism-induced 'ecosystem damage, marine pollution, overcrowding, host tensions and declining vacation quality' (McElroy 2003: 237). These unwholesome effects impact even more heavily on island ecosystems with their low species diversity, small discrete species populations and a high level of biotic endemism that is closely adapted to specific environmental conditions and is thus highly vulnerable to external disturbance (MacArthur and Wilson 1967; Percy *et al.* 2007; Liew 1990). Tourism becomes the latest guise of a 'plantation island' economy model, where island milieux are radically transformed to accommodate a single, key cash crop (itself possibly an invasive species) or service: such as bananas, sugar, copra, cotton and tobacco (Warrington and Milne 2007; Watts 1993; Grove 1995) for the generation of rentier income from abroad. Tourism-related changes of the physical environments of islands include: migration and concomitant population growth, land conversion for infrastructure development, excessive use of (typically expensive) fresh water, high energy use, degradation of reefs and mangroves, and the pollution of coastal and near-shore marine habitats with sewage and garbage (e.g. Pearce 1989). Considerable and irreversible damage can also be caused to cultural and historic asserts through frequent tourist visitations. All this without factoring in the impact of global environmental change: sea-level rise may see considerable proportions of some island and coastal nations disappear under water; and rising salinity levels in the water table threaten islander livelihoods. Mass tourism may have contributed to the rise of an indigenous middle class and entrepreneurs on many island jurisdictions; but it has also swamped local culture, contributed to domestic inflation and damaged insular ecosystems, while not necessarily leaving much value-added to the local economy (Beller *et al.* 1990; Briguglio *et al.* 1996; Lanfant *et al.* 1995; WTO 2004, 2005).

Tourism and models of island development

One particular model of 'island development' has been highly influential since its formulation in 1985 and, within which, tourism is noticeable in its absence. This is the so-called MIRAB model, an acronym for migration, remittances, aid and bureaucracy. It describes a strategy for maximising welfare by individuals, households and governments, based significantly on two sets of flows from abroad: remittances from migrants, and aid (which is often more easily procured in small economies, especially from a former or vestigial colonial power), which allows states to support a waged civil service (Bertram and Watters 1985, 1986; Bertram 2006). Once set up, the MIRAB conditionalities tend to lock firmly into place and become hard to dislodge. There have been a number of suggested alterations to MIRAB that take on board the growing importance of tourism in many contemporary island economies (e.g. TouRAB by Guthunz and von Krosigk 1996; MIRTAB by Ogden 1993), possibly taking up the slack resulting from an offshore finance and banking industry that is now reeling from the considerable pressure being applied by such international organisations as the European Union, the G7 and the OECD. Current examples of MIRAB island economies would include Cape Verde, São Tomé e Príncipe and Kiribati.

Various small island states and territories fit this model of structural dependency; but there are other development paths and models that differ markedly from MIRAB. One such alternative is based on five capacities that characterise the creative political economies of another set of small-island societies. This is the PROFIT model, another acronym that stands for people considerations (affecting citizenship, rights of residence and employment), resource management, overseas engagement and recognition, finance and transportation. In contrast to MIRAB, these island societies are characterised by economically strategic migration policies, toughness in negotiating exploitation of local resources, control over viable means of transportation, and tax regimes designed to attract foreign investment, all of which are based on self-rule. The PROFIT model favours a more proactive policy orientation and a disposition towards carving out procedural and jurisdictional powers, with a smart use of jurisdiction and paradiplomacy to establish endogenous policy formulation (Baldacchino 2006b, 2010). Clear candidates for the PROFIT model are Malta, Mauritius and Singapore.

These models are dynamic and island jurisdictions do find themselves shifting from one type to another as their economic and political fortunes change. Greenland is moving decidedly from MIRAB to PROFIT (from the status of a poor and aid-dependent colony to a resource-rich and self-reliant independent state); whereas Nauru has gone from riches to rags and has been defined as a 'failed state' (Connell 2006): moving from PROFIT to MIRAB.

One needs to appraise the impact of tourism on both MIRAB and PROFIT economies. Tourism comes with 'genuine comparative advantages' for small island states and territories (Connell 1991: 265). Treadgold (1999) has argued that tourism has helped to break Norfolk Island, a previously classic MIRAB case, out of this structural mould, 'erasing' its MIRAB characteristics or rendering them insignificant. However, tourism is in itself a rent-accruing activity bearing its own 'geo-strategic' services; these hardly vest jurisdictional muscle in the provider. The industry remains fickle and vulnerable, mainly to economic uncertainty and both local and regional political instability; it is also a largely private-sector activity lying outside 'managed' external-relationships syndromes.

Small-island tourism economies (SITES) have originally been proposed as a new and distinct, third, small island development syndrome altogether (McElroy 2006), but more recently as a subspecies of the PROFIT syndrome (Oberst and McElroy 2007; Parry and McElroy 2009).

Tourism and infrastructure: a tale of two economic sectors

Even discreet tourism infrastructure on small islands can have considerable environmental impact. The opening of a new hotel, the extension of an airport runway, or the inauguration of a cruise liner terminal, in particular, can each significantly increase tourist visitations, and challenge the state of nature that was arguably the prime attraction (Newsome *et al.* 2000: 51–6). The expansion of tourism has been challenged on India's Andaman Islands (e.g. Earth Times 2010), but this is an exceptional case: the penguins on the Falklands, and the 'dragons' on Komodo, continue to act as tourism magnets. Even World Heritage Sites, like the Galápagos Islands (Ecuador) or Rapa Nui/Easter Island (Chile), can have, and have had, their (already fragile) locales and biota endangered.

On densely populated islands, tourist-driven infrastructure development can command considerable tracts of land. The building of airports (including landing strips/runways long enough to accommodate long-haul airplanes), seaports (including cruise ship terminals), roads, hotels, restaurants and other 'tourism product' sites (museums, fun rides, recreation parks …) provides a major injection of cash into the economy. Island tourism infrastructure and services can suffer from considerable economic leakages: food, furniture and equipment may have to be imported; and especially so where tourism is dominated by foreign-owned resort enclaves. Yet, other associated services can have compensatory domestic multiplier effects on demand: these include printing, transportation, communication, energy and various other trades and spinoffs. Such large-scale building activity may be indicative of the contribution that the construction and real estate industries may make to the island economy; possibly one as considerable as tourism. Indeed, whereas tourism is lauded for its significant contribution to island economics, the construction and real estate sectors are not usually accorded much, and certainly no equal, praise.

Unless such an appreciation is acknowledged and recognised, it may become hard to understand why so much construction activity goes on regardless of not just the environmental damage but also of the reduction of the basic attractive qualities of an island place to potential future visitors. As currently presented, neither MIRAB nor PROFIT island development models get close to this vital acknowledgement.

Case study

Malta

A 'monster' and an 'ugly conglomerate' block of apartments is rising at the seaside village of Marsascala, Malta, looming directly over the parish church (Inguanez 2010). A main tourist attraction in Malta's southeast, Marsascala is a 'popular, relatively laid back ... location; a fishing village since Roman times [with] a considerable number of good restaurants [and a] lovely seaside promenade' (Ta' Monita Residence 2010). This quaintness has become suspect of late: there are many more pleasure craft anchored in its sheltered bay than fishing boats. Even if the fantasy has survived so far, it is now being rudely challenged: covering 16,000 m^2, the Ta' Monita development is heralded as 'the first exclusive development' in the locality, towering over the parish church, and is targeting foreign purchasers (typically expatriate retirees or second home tourism).

A recent State of the Environment Report (MEPA 2006) has noted that there is in Malta ' ... [an] increasing tension between protective mechanisms and the desire of owners to redevelop their properties. This is resulting in loss of historic fabric, inappropriate design of new and restored buildings, and illegal excavations within archaeologically sensitive sites' (Camilleri *et al.* 2011; also Boissevain 2004).

The Maltese islands [Malta, the main island (population 380,000); Gozo (30,000) and Comino (barely inhabited)] are a set of arid, semi-desert, dry limestone blocks that today bear the full weight of a sovereign state with 410,000 residents and some 1.2 million annual visitors. Some 25 per cent of total land area is built up. Housing stock is running at some 20 per cent excess of supply over demand. Space is at a premium. When it acceded to the European Union in 2004, Malta obtained a permanent derogation, limiting foreigners from buying secondary residences on the islands.

Meanwhile, the Maltese must contend with a considerable stash of artefacts and cultural assets that jostle each other for priority conservation and management. A number of these – like Ġgantija, Ħaġar Qim and the Tarxien Megalithic Temple Complexes – are lucky enough to have made it on the list of UNESCO World Heritage Sites; the bulk, however, struggle to attract attention. Standing stones or giant's rocks survive surreptitiously between rows of houses. Perhaps, in some cases, these assets' best defence against the practices of appropriation for private use or vandalism is, simply and sadly, wanton abandon and benign neglect (Baldacchino 2007).

For those who look on 'from the outside in', it is easy to adopt a judgemental stance. The Maltese are not appreciative enough of their priceless heritage, they may say. In their enthusiasm to sample and experience the past, foreign observers may forget that Malta is *not* a living museum, and that its people are *not* just commodified quaint natives, but members of a society firmly wedded, for better or for worse, to the twenty-first century (e.g. Boissevain 1996: 235).

Indeed, an appreciation of personal property is absolutely fundamental to a more complete understanding of the Maltese socio-economic psyche. The construction industry has a huge multiplier effect on the local economy; there are also significant cost advantages involved in using globigerina limestone as construction material – it is one of the few, locally mined, natural resources.

Property assumes a towering importance as economic and cultural capital in Maltese society. In spite (or because) of the phenomenal cost of residences, many Maltese would undergo enormous sacrifices to purchase an owner-occupied dwelling. Owning a house is a major investment; an heirloom; a source of family pride; a fortress to protect its owners against an all-intrusive society where privacy comes at a premium. If there is money to spare and an own house is already available, a second summer house is a favourite acquisition. Housing is such a key rampant investment that no Maltese Government has yet mustered the courage of taxing it. As Margaret Mizzi has argued, the Maltese remain comfortably wedded to 'The *Stone* Age' (personal communication, November 2006). These insights collectively explain the glut of housing in space-starved Malta; and the continued tendency of appraising public space as potential private real estate. This also explains why, in the choice between construction for private gain and maintaining a cultural-historic asset for the common good, the choice for the former is, often, a foregone conclusion. Heritage (in its physical form) is tolerable and acceptable as long as it is functional; it is appreciated best if appropriated as a private good; but insufferable if it clashes with private and individual interests.

Thus, although crucial to the Maltese economy, tourism must rub shoulders with a construction industry that contributes even more significantly to the island country's gross domestic product. Between the census years of 1957 and 2005, the Maltese population has almost doubled, and yet the built-up area of the Maltese Islands has increased almost eight times in the same period: from 11 to 87 km^2 (MEPA, private correspondence, 2009). Coastal regions are under special threat. The long term challenge, for Marsascala as much as for Malta as a whole, is to avoid the 'Benidorm-isation' of the coastline, with hardly any control or regard for local culture, environment and landscape.

Conclusion

As long as islands continue to lure tourists, tourism will continue to lure island 'developers', maintaining its position as a strategic sector for many island societies, whether of MIRAB, PROFIT, SITE or any other mould (Clark 2009). The circumscribed nature of islandness, the inordinate impact of tourism, and the relative smallness of size and high population density, exacerbates the tensions surrounding heritage and landscape conservation, while making them visible and glaring.

References

Apostoulopoulos, Y. and Gayle, D.J. (eds). (2002) *Island Tourism and Sustainable Development: Caribbean, Pacific and Mediterranean Experiences*. Westport, CT: Praeger.

Baldacchino, G. (ed.) (2006a) *Extreme Tourism: Lessons from the World's Cold Water Islands*. Amsterdam: Elsevier.

——(2006b) 'Managing the Hinterland Beyond: Two, Ideal-Type Strategies of Economic Development for Small Island Territories', *Asia-Pacific Viewpoint* 47, 45–60.

——(2007) 'Jurisdictional Capacity and Landscape Heritage: A Case Study of Malta & Gozo', *Journal of Mediterranean Studies* 17, 95–114.

——(2010) *Island Enclaves: Offshoring Strategies, Creative Governance, and Subnational Island Jurisdictions*. Montreal and Kingston, Canada: McGill-Queen's University Press.

Baum, T.G. (1996) 'The Fascination of Islands: The Tourist Perspective', in D.G. Lockhart and D. Drakakis-Smith (eds). *Island Tourism: Problems and Perspectives*. London: Pinter, 21–35.

Beller, W., D'Ayala, P. and Hein, P.L. (eds) (1990) *Sustainable Development and Environmental Management of Small Islands*. Paris: UNESCO-Parthenon.

Bertram, G. (2006) 'Introduction: The MIRAB Model in the 21st Century', *Asia Pacific Viewpoint* 47, 1–13.

Bertram, G. and Watters, R.F. (1985) 'The MIRAB Economy in South Pacific Microstates', *Pacific Viewpoint* 26, 497–519.

——(1986) 'The MIRAB Process: Earlier Analysis in Context', *Pacific Viewpoint* 27, 47–59.

Boissevain, J. (2004) 'Hotels, Tuna Pens and Civil Society', in J. Boissevain and T. Selwyn (eds), *Contesting the Foreshore: Tourism, Society and Politics on the Coast*. Amsterdam: Amsterdam University Press, 233–60.

——(1996) 'But We Live Here! Perspectives on Cultural Tourism in Malta', in L. Briguglio, R. Butler, D. Harrison and W. Leal Filho (eds) *Sustainable Tourism in Islands and Small States – Vol. 2: Case Studies*. London: Pinter, 220–40.

Briguglio, L., Archer, B., Jafari, J. and Wall, G. (eds) (1996) *Sustainable Tourism in Islands and Small States – Vol. 1: Issues and Policies*. London: Pinter.

Butler, R.W. (1993) 'Tourism Development in Small Islands: Past Influences and Future Directions', in D. G. Lockhart, D. Drakakis-Smith and J.A. Schembri (eds), *The Development Process in Small Island States*. London: Routledge, 71–91.

Camilleri, M., Hili, M., Magro Conti, J., Attard, R., Stevens, D., Gambin, M.-T. and Galea, R. (2011) 'Managing Cultural and Natural Heritage in a Densely-Populated Island Jurisdiction: The Maltese Islands', in G. Baldacchino (ed.) *Extreme Heritage Management: Lessons from Densely Populated Islands*. New York: Berghahn Books, forthcoming.

Clark, E. (2009) 'Island Development', in R. Kitchin and N. Thrift (eds), *International Encyclopaedia of Human Geography*. Amsterdam: Elsevier, 607–10.

Connell, J. (1991) 'Island Microstates: The Mirage of Development', *Contemporary Pacific* 3, 251–87.

——(2006) 'Nauru: The first failed Pacific State?', *The Round Table: Commonwealth Journal of International Affairs* 95, 47–63.

Earth Times (2010) *Tourism danger lingers for tribes people in India's Andaman Islands*. 17 June. www.earthtimes.org/articles/news/329694,tourism-danger-lingers-for-tribes-people-in-indias-andaman-islands.html. Accessed 17 January 2011.

Gillis, J.R. (2004) *Islands of the Mind: How the Human Imagination Created the Atlantic World*. New York: Palgrave Macmillan.

Gillis, J.R. and Lowenthal, D. (2007) 'Introduction', *The Geographical Review* 97(2), iii–v.

Gössling, S. (2002) 'Human-Environmental Relations with Tourism', *Annals of Tourism Research* 29: 539–56.

Gossling, S and Wall, G. (2007) 'Island Tourism', in G. Baldacchino (ed.) *A World of Islands: An Island Studies Reader*. Luqa, Malta, and Charlottetown, Canada: Agenda Academic and Institute of Island Studies, 429–53.

Guthunz, U., and von Krosigk, F. (1996) 'Tourism in Small Island States: From MIRAB to TOURAB?', in L. Briguglio, B. Archer, J. Jafari, and G. Wall (eds), *Sustainable Tourism in Islands and Small States: Vol. 1 – Issues and Policies*. London: Pinter, 18–35.

Grove, R.H. (1995) *Green Imperialism: Colonial Expansion, Tropical Island Edens and the Origins of Environmentalism, 1600–1860*. Cambridge: Cambridge University Press.

Hay, P. (2006) 'A Phenomenology of Islands', *Island Studies Journal* 1, 19–42.

Inguanez, J. (2010) Posted Comments, *Times of Malta*. 25 May and 19 July. http://stocks.timesofmalta.com/articles/view/20100525/local/residents-try-to-steer-away-from-flyover-plan.

Island God (2010) *Be a God and Rule your Own Tribe*. www.facebook.com/apps/application.php?id=1253 18280856717. Accessed 17 January 2011.

Lanfant, M.F., Allcock, J.B. and Bruner, E.M. (1995) *International Tourism: Identity and Change*. London: Sage.

Liew, J. (1990) 'Sustainable Development and Environmental Management of Atolls', in W. Beller, P. D'Ayala, and P.L. Hein (eds), *Sustainable Development and Environmental Management of Small Islands*. Paris: UNESCO-Parthenon, 77–86.

Löfgren, O. (2002) *On Holiday: A History of Vacationing*. Berkeley, CA: University of California Press.

Lowenthal, D. (1972) *West Indian Societies*. London: Oxford University Press.

Loxley, D. (1990) *Problematic Shores: The Literature of Islands*. New York: St Martin's Press.

MacArthur, R.H. and Wilson, E.O. (1967) *The Theory of Island Biogeography*. Princeton, NJ: Princeton University Press.

MEPA (2006) *State of the Environment Report 2005. Sub-report 4: Land*. Floriana: Malta Environment and Planning Authority.

McElroy, J.L. (2006) 'Small Island Tourist Economies across the Lifecycle', *Asia Pacific Viewpoint* 47, 61–77.

——(2003) 'Tourism Development in Small Islands across the World.' *Geografiska Annaler* 85B, 231–42.

Newsome, D., Moore, S.A. and Dowling, R.K. (2000) *Natural Area Tourism: Ecology, Impacts, and Management*. Clevedon: Channel View Publications.

Oberst, A. and McElroy, J.L. (2007) 'Contrasting Socio-economic and Demographic Profiles of Two, Small Island, Economic Species: MIRAB versus PROFIT/SITE', *Island Studies Journal* 2, 164–76.

Ogden, R.M. (1993) 'Locating Technology in the Development Debate: From MIRAB to MIRTAB'. Chapter 6 in 'Islands on the Net: Technology and Development Futures in Pacific Island Microstates,' PhD thesis. Honolulu, HI: Department of Political Science, University of Hawai'i.

Parry, C.E. and McElroy, J.L. (2009) 'The Supply Determinants of Small Island Tourist Economies', *ARA: Journal of Tourism Research* 3, 13–22.

Pearce, D. (1989) *Tourist Development*. 2nd edn. New York: Wiley.

Percy, D.M., Blackmore, S. and Cronk, Q.C.B. (2007) 'Island Floras', in G. Baldacchino (ed.) *A World of Islands: An Island Studies Reader*. Luqa, Malta, and Charlottetown, Canada: Agenda Academic and Institute of Island Studies, pp. 175–98.

Ta' Monita Residence. www.tamonita.com. Accessed 13 December 2010.

Treadgold, M.L. (1999) 'Breaking out of the MIRAB Mould: Historical Evidence from Norfolk Island', *Asia Pacific Viewpoint* 40, 235–49.

Vladi Islands (2010) *Vladi Private Islands*. www.vladi-private-islands.de/islandsforsale.html Accessed 17 January 2011.

Warrington, E. and Milne, D. (2007) 'Island History and Governance', in G. Baldacchino (ed.) *A World of Islands: An Island Studies Reader*. Luqa, Malta, and Charlottetown, Canada: Agenda Academic and Institute of Island Studies, 379–427.

Watts, D. (1993) 'Long-term Environmental Influences on Development in the Islands of the Lesser Antilles', *Scottish Geographical Magazine* 109, 133–41.

Wells, H.G. (1896) *The Island of Doctor Moreau*. London: Heinemann, Stone & Kimball.

World Tourism Organization (2004) *Indicators of Sustainable Development for Tourism Destinations*. Madrid: World Tourism Organization.

——(2005) *Making Tourism Work for Small Island Developing States*. Madrid: World Tourism Organization.

Further reading

de Albuquerque, K. and McElroy, J. (1992) 'Caribbean small-island tourism styles and sustainable strategies', *Environmental Management* 16, 619–32. (An early foray into sustainable management practices, now a buzz, but rather empty, phrase.)

Apostolopoulos, Y. and Gayle, D.J. (eds) (2002) *Island Tourism and Sustainable Development: Caribbean, Pacific and Mediterranean Experiences*. Westport, CT: Praeger. (Treats the study of tourism from a sustainable development perspective.)

Archer, B.H. (1988) 'Tourism and island economies: impact analyses', in Cooper, C.P. and Lockwood, A. (eds) *Progress in Tourism, Recreation and Hospitality Management*. Vol. 1. Chichester: Wiley, 125–34. (An early contribution to a more scientific assessment of the impact of tourism on island economies.)

Baldacchino, G. (ed.) (2006) *Extreme Tourism: Lessons from the World's Cold Water Islands*. Amsterdam: Elsevier. (Proper treatment to the tourism appeal of cold islands.)

Bastin, R. (1984) 'Small island tourism: development or dependency?', *Development Policy Review* 2, 79–90. (A critical and perspicacious look at the dangers of large-scale tourism development in the Caribbean.)

Briguglio, L., Archer, B., Jafari, J. and Wall, G. (eds) (1996) *Sustainable Tourism in Islands and Small States – Vol. 1: Issues and Policies*. London: Pinter. (Reviews theories and concepts for sustainable tourism practice.)

Briguglio, L., Butler, R., Harrison, D. and Leal Filho, W. (eds) (1996) *Sustainable Tourism in Islands and Small States – Vol. 2: Case Studies*. London: Pinter. (Case studies in sustainable tourism practice and policy.)

Britton, R.A. (1977) 'Making Tourism More Supportive of Small State Development: The Case of St. Vincent', *Annals of Tourism Research* 6, 269–78. (Discusses indigenous and integrated island tourism, an early experiment in alternative tourism programmes.)

Britton, S.G. and Clarke, W. (eds) (1987) *Ambiguous Alternative: Tourism in Small Developing Countries*. Suva, Fiji: The University of the South Pacific. (One of the earliest edited comparative texts to critically consider tourism as the development route for small, mainly island, developing countries.)

Conlin, M.V. and Baum, T.G. (eds) (1995) *Island Tourism: Management Principles and Practice*. New York: Wiley. (Management approaches to island tourism.)

Gössling, S. (ed.) (2003) *Tourism and Development in Tropical Islands: Political Ecology Perspectives*. Cheltenham: Edward Elgar. (The interfacing of politics, development and the environment in island tourism.)

Harrison, D. (2001) 'Tourism in small islands and microstates', *Tourism Recreation Research* 26, 3–8.

Harrison, D. (2001) 'Islands, image and tourism', *Tourism Recreation Research* 26, 9–14. (These two, back-to-back journal articles are some of the earliest to discuss branding and marketing issues specifically in relation to island tourism.)

Ioannides, D., Apostolopoulos, Y. and Sonmez, S. (eds) (2001) *Mediterranean Islands and Sustainable Tourism Development: Practices, Management, and Policies*. London: Continuum Publishers. (A regional focus of management practices and policies in the Mediterranean Sea.)

Royle, S.A. (1989) 'A human geography of islands', Geography 74, 106–16. (A wonderful read, containing many seminal ideas that explain the island allure.)

Wilkinson, P.F. (1989) 'Strategies for tourism development in island microstates', *Annals of Tourism Research* 16, 153–77.

Wilkinson, P.F. (1987) 'Tourism in small island nations: a fragile dependency', *Leisure Studies* 6, 127–46. (In these two articles, Paul Wilkinson comes across as a then-rare critical voice, advising against rampant mass tourism as a development panacea.)

Part 3
Environmental policy, resource governance and management

20

Introduction

Andrew Holden

The progressive awareness of changes in our surroundings, often attributed to anthropogenic action has led to an increased emphasis on environmental policy, governance and management to mitigate negative effects and create symbiotically beneficial relationships. The focus of this section is to provide a holistic overview of relevant environmental policy, resource governance and management approaches to the tourism and environment relationship. A seminal work on the future of human and environment relationships is the Brundtland Report, which as Telfer comments, more than 20 years after its publication continues to have a far-reaching influence, including stakeholders in tourism. Telfer's chapter offers an in-depth analysis of the context and content of the Brundtland Report, highlighting the inherent ambiguities of the meaning of the term, critically referring to its differing cultural and social interpretations and subsequent contestations. He then proceeds to analyse the effects of the Brundtland Report on tourism, its significance and meaning and how it has manifested itself in different guises of tourism.

Alongside policy, there is also an evident requirement for rigorous management practice to achieve sustainable tourism (ST). Although environmental management practices are essential, business management techniques also have potential future use in achieving ST, a reflection and crossover that has had a limited audiencing to date. One aspect of management that has received surprisingly little attention to date is the demand management of tourism. In an economist-driven approach, Modica explains how price differentiation can be integrated into tourism strategy and utilised to overcome problems of seasonality, focusing on how the established concept of revenue management theory can be used by destinations to encounter environmental problems related to a high level of seasonality. In the context of the wider approach to environmental management, Clarke, Raffay and Wiltshier look at aspects of the role of education and knowledge management in sustainable tourism development.

The theme of management practices for ST is also developed in the collective chapters of Mason, McCool and Font. Utilising different case studies from around the world, Mason explores how zoning has been used in tourism areas. Alongside aiding environmental conservation, Mason highlights how the establishment of a tourism zone and specific tourism activities within a zone can help visitors make informed choices on the type of experience in which they desire to be involved. As a pioneer of the innovative approach of Limits of Acceptable Change (LAC), McCool analyses its application to tourism. As for many of the environmental management techniques in tourism, a key question relates to 'how many is too many?', or similarly in the context of global warming 'how hot is too hot?'. Notably, LAC permits a reflective process towards a goal of answering the question, or at least responding to it in a knowledge-based content, of 'what are the appropriate/acceptable conditions to achieve ST?'. In essence, LAC is designed to offer visitors the 'opportunities for a high quality experience and to limit the impacts of visitor behaviour and tourism development'.

Integrating the concepts of sustainable tourism and management, Font analyses the use of sustainable tourism certification in the context of the political difficulties of interpretation and against the extent it has delivered the benefits it promises. A key aspect of consideration relates to the extent that sustainability is recognised as a process or actual performance, the former interpretation being favoured by the industry and the latter by non-governmental organisations. The difficulties of achieving Global Sustainable Tourism Criteria are also problematic given the propensity for differing cultural interpretations of the concept, as Font refers to the 'multiple and contested meanings', which influence not only the interpretation of sustainable tourism but also the environment itself. Critically for the operation of certificate schemes that are designed to offer a simple comparative and consistent message to consumers in the market place, the why, what and how of measurement indicators may be contested territories.

The biggest challenge faced in the development of environmental policy and management of tourism is undoubtedly climate change. Beside agriculture, the global tourism industry is perhaps the most reliant on resources that require stable climatic conditions. Accepting global warming as fact, the tourism industry will need to have adaptive responses to climate change if livelihoods are to be sustained. The vulnerability of tourism to climate change is the theme of Scott and Lemieux's contribution to this volume. Utilising an innovative map to illustrate the incidence of effects of climate change on tourism on a global spatial scale, they provide a substantive overview of the pathways of how climate change will influence the competitiveness and sustainability of tourism businesses and destinations globally. This analysis indirectly refers to a systems approach to tourism, highlighting that climate change in the home or 'generating' areas of tourism will have a simultaneous effect on tourism to that of climate change in destinations.

Although destination and industry adaptability will be critical for the future of the tourism industry, tourism only has a context when placed in the frameworks of society. Subsequently, framework conventions for climate change have a direct relevance to society as much as they do to tourism. Utilising the 'meta discourses' of green governability, ecological modernisation and civic environmentalism as a framework for critiquing global governance, the crucial links between global and local scale of analysis of the tourism industry are highlighted by Hopkins and Higham in a highly illustrative analysis of governance and environmental management approaches in New Zealand.

21

The Brundtland Report (*Our Common Future*) and tourism

David Telfer

Introduction

More than 20 years after the World Commission on Environment and Development (WCED) published its report in 1987, *Our Common Future* continues to have far-reaching influence. It was in 1983 that the United Nations General Assembly created an independent commission to develop 'a global agenda for change' at a time when it was recognised that the development paths of industrialised nations were not sustainable and the environment was in increasing danger. Chair of the Commission, Mrs Gro Harlem Brundtland who was Prime Minister and leader of the Norwegian Labour Party, was charged with proposing long-term strategies for achieving sustainable development. The Brundtland Report, also published as *Our Common Future* by Oxford University Press (OUP), builds on previous work in the environmental movement such as the World Conservation Strategy in 1980, which highlighted the global nature of environmental problems (Gösling *et al.* 2009). Recognising the importance of global co-operation on environmental matters, the Brundtland Report acknowledged that "the 'environment' is where we all live; and 'development' is what we all do in attempting to improve our lot within that abode. The two are inseparable" (WCED 1987: xi). The Brundtland Report is widely known for setting out a definition of sustainable development that links economy and ecology, yet the definition has been both widely adopted and criticised. The definition reads as: 'Sustainable development is development that meets the needs of the present without compromising the ability of future generations to meet their own needs' (WCED 1987: 43). However, beyond just setting out a definition, the Report may be more important in firmly placing the concept of sustainable development into the political arena (Hardy *et al.* 2002) thereby influencing governments, international organisations, NGOs, industries, communities, individuals and academics, including those studying tourism. The discussion of sustainable development has moved forward considerably since the Brundtland Report serving as the basis for the 1992 Earth Summit in Rio de Janeiro, where Agenda 21, an action plan towards implementing sustainable development, was developed. Although only mentioning the word tourism once, *Our Common Future* has had significant impact on tourism. There is a sizeable and rapidly growing body of literature on tourism in the context of sustainable development (Butler 1999; Garrod 1998) as tourism has adopted the sustainable development paradigm. Many of the research articles in tourism employ the definition of sustainable development cited from *Our Common Future* as a stepping off platform before expanding on the debates on sustainable tourism development. Where initially the debates surrounded whether some specific types of tourism such as responsible tourism, ecotourism and community-based tourism were more sustainable than others, now the debate has moved towards making all forms of tourism more sustainable as government plans, codes of conduct, certifications and corporate social responsibility statements all claim to reflect sustainable development as outlined in the Brundtland Report. This chapter will begin by briefly examining the historical context for the WCED before exploring the 'Common Concerns', 'Challenges' and 'Endeavours' as laid out in the Report. The chapter will then turn to reflections on the impact of the Brundtland Report on tourism.

Historical context and mandate for the WCED

Setting the historical context for the WCED

Although the Brundtland Report is closely associated with raising the concept of sustainable development in recent scientific, political and popular debates, it is an enduring concept with a long history. It has been suggested that sustainable development is a reworking of longstanding philosophies on conservation and stewardship of resources for the future (Pigram and Wahab 1997) and it has been part of the resource conservation and management debate for almost 150 years (Gösling *et al.* 2009). The development of the WCED was an important step in the evolution of the environmental debate ongoing today. Increasing concern over the environment and development in the 1960s and 1970s saw the publication of a number of important documents all raising environmental awareness including 1962 *Silent Spring* (Carson 1962), 1968 *Tragedy of the Commons* (Hardin 1972) and 1972 *The Limits to Growth* (Meadows *et al.* 1972). Hardy *et al.* (2002) suggest that the rise of a conservation and community vision along with dissatisfaction with developmental economics all came together at the UN Conference on the Human Environment at Stockholm in 1972. The 1972 Conference gathered developed and developing countries together 'to delineate the "rights" of the human family to a healthy and productive environment' (WCED 1987: xi). The concept of sustainable development first came to public attention in the 1980 *World Conservation Strategy* published by the International Union for the Conservation of Nature and Natural Resources (IUCN 1980; Gösling *et al.* 2009). The *World Conservation Strategy* highlighted the global nature of environmental problems and recognised the North/South divide, a growing gap between the rich and poor nations of the world (Gösling *et al.* 2009). These reports and others all helped set the stage for the 1987 Brundtland Report.

The Commission and its mandate

The WCED was created out of General Assembly Resolution 38/161 from the 38th Session of the UN in 1983. The Commission was made up of 22 members, with the Chairman being Gro Harlem Brundtland from Norway and the Vice-Chairman being Mansour Khalid from Sudan. By design, the majority of members were from the developing world to reflect the makeup of the globe. It is interesting to note the changes that have occurred in the list of countries represented on the Commission as an indication as to the time that has passed since the Report was published in 1987. For example, the USSR has dissolved, as has Yugoslavia and the Berlin Wall has come down and now the Federal Republic of Germany is part of a unified Germany. The team assembled came from a range of backgrounds including foreign ministers, finance and planning officials, as well as those involved in policy making in agriculture, science and technology.

The idea was to generate an inter-disciplinary and integrated approach to global concerns (WCED 1987). In May of 1984 an organisational meeting was held, and in July a Secretariat was established in Geneva. In October the Commission held its first official meeting and at that meeting, the Commission selected the following eight key issues for analysis:

- Perspectives on Population, Environment and Sustainable Development
- Energy
- Industry
- Food Security, Agriculture, Forestry
- Human Settlements
- International Economic Relations
- Decision Support Systems for Environmental Management
- International Cooperation (WCED 1987: 358).

The Committee worked together for 3 years and part of the work involved open public hearings on five continents, where they heard from hundreds of organisations and individuals (WCED 1987). The Commission also appointed a group of Special Advisors on key issues as well as international Advisory Panels of experts who published reports under the titles of *Energy 2000*, *Industry 2000* and *Food 2000* (WCED 1987). A further group of international legal experts prepared a report on *Legal Principles for Environmental Protection and Sustainable Development* (WCED 1987). Finally, the Commission engaged experts, research institutes and academic centres of excellence to develop over 75 studies and reports on the eight main issues identified above (WCED 1987).

At the close of their final meeting on 27 February 1987 in Tokyo, the Commission issued the Tokyo Declaration. It called on 'all nations of the World, both jointly and individually to integrate sustainable development into their goals and to adopt the following principles to guide their policy actions' (WCED 1987: 363): (1) Revive Growth; (2) Change the Quality of Growth; (3) Conserve and Enhance the Resource Base; (4) Ensure a Sustainable Level of Population; (5) Reorient Technology and Manage Risks; (6) Integrate Environment and Economics in Decision Making; (7) Reform International Economic Relations and (8) Strengthen International Co-operation. The path that the Brundtland Report stresses to reduce poverty is a 'new era of economic growth, one that must be based on policies that sustain and expand the environmental resource base. And we believe such growth to be absolutely essential to relieve the great poverty that is deepening in much of the developing world' (WCED 1987: 1).

Common concerns, challenges and endeavours of the Brundtland Report

Although many studies in tourism research make note of the definition of sustainable development proposed in the Brundtland Report, few studies delve into the text beyond the definition. What this section will do is highlight some of the important issues and recommendations that were presented in the Report. Some of these issues will be considered in terms of tourism in the final section of the chapter. The Report was offered not to forecast the future, but rather as an urgent notice for decisions to be taken to secure resources to sustain for not only the current generation but also future generations (WCED 1987). Instead of offering a detailed blueprint, the authors hoped that the Report would offer a pathway so that the people of the world could enlarge their spheres of co-operation (WCED 1987: 2). The Report begins with a 'Foreword' by the Chairman and an 'Overview' followed by three main sections entitled *Common Concerns*, *Common Challenges* and *Common Endeavours*. These sections are examined below.

Common Concerns

The section on *Common Concerns* is divided into three chapters: (1) *A Threatened Future*; (2) *Towards Sustainable Development*; and (3) *The Role of the International Political Economy*. *Common Concerns* deals with problems and environmental stresses that the current generation has inherited and is experiencing now, and that future generations will experience in the years to come. The inter-generational nature of the Report is highlighted by the comment 'We borrow environmental capital from future generations with no intention or prospect of repaying' (WCED 1987: 8). Although progress has been made in many areas, the Brundtland Report deals in part with the so-called failures of development. The Report acknowledges that there are more people living in poverty than before, and there are fewer people that can read and write and fewer with safe water, safe homes and the fuel needed to cook and warm themselves. In addition, it acknowledges that the gap between rich and poor is widening and given present institutional arrangements, the prospect of that changing is remote (WCED 1987). These human concerns are coupled with serious environmental trends including water and air pollution, desertification, erosion, proliferation of hazardous chemicals and waste that has entered the food chain, acid precipitation, ozone depletion, depletion of groundwater, destruction of natural habitats, species extinction and burning of fossil fuels resulting in global warming causing shifting agricultural production areas, rising sea water and coastal city flooding (WCED 1987). The Report notes that poverty is a major cause and effect of global environmental problems, and it is impossible to separate economic development issues from environmental issues (WCED 1987). The crises are referred to as inter-locking crises in the Report and the viewpoint that human activities are compartmentalised within nations is no longer valid. 'Ecology and economy are becoming ever more interwoven – locally, regionally, nationally and globally into a seamless net of causes and effects' (WCED 1987: 5). Throughout the Report, the significant challenges facing the developing world are stressed.

Sustainable development

As a way forward, the Brundtland Report promotes sustainable development. Perhaps one of the most cited definitions in tourism articles on sustainability is that presented at the beginning of Chapter 2, which reads:

> Sustainable development is development that meets the needs of the present without compromising the ability of future generations to meet their own needs. It contains within it two key concepts:

> the concept of 'needs', in particular the essential needs of the world's poor, to which overriding priority should be given; and

> the idea of limitations imposed by the state of technology and social organisation on the environment's ability to meet present and future needs.

> *(WCED 1987: 43)*

Although stressing the need for economic growth, sustainable development requires that societies meet human needs by increasing productive potential and ensuring equitable opportunities for all

(WCED 1987). It must not endanger the natural systems supporting life, which include the atmosphere, water, soil and living beings (WCED 1987). The Report states that this all implies limits, but not absolute limits, limits determined by the present state of technology and social organisation and the ability of the biosphere to handle human activities (WCED 1987: 8). It is clear from the Report that sustainable development is an anthropocentric (human-centred) approach (Mitchell 1997). As a reflection of this, the Report goes on to state that 'technology and social organisation can be both managed and improved to make way for new era of economic growth' (WCED 1987: 8). Sustainable development requires that those with more must operate within the planet's ecological means and can only be pursued if population size and growth are in line with the potential of the ecosystem (WCED 1987). The Commission does not view sustainable development as a fixed state, but instead it is a process of change whereby the exploitation of resources, direction of investments and orientation of technological change are consistent for present and future needs (WCED 1987: 9). The Report calls for all nations to quickly design strategies to get on a more sustainable path. Key to moving towards the implementation of these strategies is to fix the many institutional challenges, such as highly fragmented environment organisations (WCED 1987). A call is made for a more comprehensive approach with effective international co-operation along with popular participation (WCED 1987). These strategies are all incorporated in the Tokyo Declaration outlined above. Table 21.1 includes a list of items that the Commission states is required in the pursuit of sustainable development. With respect to the role of the international political economy, the Report makes recommendations in the areas of enhancing the flow of resources to developing countries; linking trade, environment and development; ensuring responsibility in trans-national investment; and broadening the technological base (WCED 1987). Although the principles of sustainable development seem likely to be supported, the following case study illustrates that the concept is not without controversy.

Case study

Debates and paradoxes of sustainable development

One of the main problems with the definition of sustainable development is that it is so broad and generically applicable that its inherent vagueness leaves it inoperative and open to conflicting interpretations (Dovers and Handmer 1992). Others, however, suggest the vagueness and ambiguity allow for flexibility needed for specific places and times (Mitchell 2002). Proponents of the Report point out that it incorporates essential principles of intra-generational and inter-generation equity and it has persuaded many governments to endorse sustainability (Mowforth and Munt 2003). Detractors argue that the Brundtland Report contains inbuilt assumptions on the continued need for expansion of the global economy, and that it failed to stress radical changes in both lifestyles and society required for inherent problems in the Western model of development (Mowforth and Munt 2003). It is also argued that sustainable development is socially and culturally contested and open to different interpretations between cultures and interest groups (Fien and Tilbury 2002). Differences in interpretation surround questions such as those posed by Fien and Tilbury (2002): what time scales are involved (human generations or ecological time scales)? What development do we want sustained: social, cultural, political, spiritual and or economic (and are they separable)? What changes are required to achieve sustainability? Are there limits to economic growth in a sustainable society? Dovers and Handmer (1993) have noted the contradictions or paradoxes in sustainability described in Table 21.2 as outlined by Mitchell (2002). Readers can compare Table 21.2 with Table 21.3 later in the chapter in the second case study, which focuses on the weaknesses of sustainability in the context of tourism.

All the questions and paradoxes in Table 21.2 illustrate the variety of contesting ideologies and political debate about sustainable development futures (Fien and Tilbury 2002). They also then present challenges in examining sustainable development for tourism presented in the second case study later in this chapter.

Table 21.1 Required elements in the pursuit of sustainable development

- A political system that secures effective citizen participation in decision making,
- An economic system that is able to generate surpluses and technological knowledge on a self-reliant and sustained basis,
- A social system that provides solutions for the tensions arising from disharmonious development,
- A production system that respects the obligation to preserve the ecological base for development,
- A technological system that can search continuously for new solutions,
- An international system that fosters sustainable patterns of trade and finance, and
- An administrative system that is flexible and has the capacity for self correction (WCED 1987: 65).

Table 21.2 Contradictions or paradoxes in sustainability

Contradictions or Paradoxes in Sustainability	Key Concepts
paradox of technology	in many countries technology is used for resource-intensive growth solving many problems and causing environmental damage
humility or arrogance in the face of uncertainty	there is a need to be humble in the face of uncertainly but also arrogant enough to make decisions on resources in the face of inevitable ignorance
intergenerational versus intragenerational equity	how does a society chose how much to set aside for the future when many today do not have enough now
economic growth versus ecological limits	how to determine what type of growth is needed to meet human needs, how to sustain the growth and how to make sure it does not degrade the environment which is the base for growth
reconciliation of individual versus collective interest	some individual sovereignty may have to be constrained yet many societies place a premium on individual rights like private land and cars
balance between democracy and purposeful action	while there is a need for local empowerment it is too simplistic that all environmental problems can be resolved if delegated to the local level
adaptability versus resistance	some will adapt to change while others are resistant, seeking the status quo
optimization versus spare capacity	if resources are not used for humans they are not being used optimally however setting aside spare capacity allows for flexibility yet many today do not have their basic needs being met. (Dover and Handmer (1993) as outlined by Mitchell (2002))

Table 21.3 Weaknesses of sustainability in the context of tourism

- limited attention has been paid to the sustainability of tourism demand
- the focus on conservation & preservation of resources fails to incorporate the changing needs, preferences and technological capabilities of society
- intra-generational equity has not been addresses as often benefits of tourism are not shared fairly by the host community
- many view hosts should benefit from tourism but keep their culture however others argue tourism changes culture and any socio-cultural change needs to be avoided
- setting limits or thresholds on tourism development is difficult and using carrying capacity or indicators has met with limited success
- the new forms of tourism can not be relied upon as a way forward for a sustainable and growing tourism industry which is world wide (Liu 2003).

Common Challenges

Part two of the Report presents six chapters dealing with issues viewed as being highly connected. Incorporating detailed examples from around the world, the Report presents a list of recommendations in each chapter for a more sustainable path for the planet. Although it is beyond the scope of this chapter to present all of the recommendations due to space limitations, many of the key recommendations as they relate to the 'Policy Directions' section of the WCED (1987) 'Overview' are presented below under the six chapter headings. Each chapter heading below begins with a brief statement reflecting the nature of the problems the world is facing.

Population and human resources
   In many areas of the world available resources cannot sustain population growth:
   - steps must be taken to eliminate extreme rates of population growth to reduce mass poverty, assure more equitable resource access and by education better manage resources
   - provide people with facilities and education so they can chose family size thereby assuring (especially for women) right of self-determination
   - development of a broad health policy
   - develop human resource programmes to build technical knowledge and capabilities
   - Indigenous populations need special attention and they need a voice in determining resource use.
Food security: sustaining the potential
   - There is the potential to grow enough food for everyone but often the food is not available where it is needed:
   - developing nations need effective incentives to encourage production of food crops so terms of trade favour subsistence farmers, pastoralists and landless
   - developed nations must alter to cut surpluses, reduce unfair competition (i.e. subsidies) and promote ecological farming practices
   - take steps to facilitate distribution including land reforms to support subsistence farmers.
Species and ecosystems: resources for development
   - A growing scientific consensus indicates species are disappearing at alarming rates:
   - put disappearing species and threatened ecosystems on political agendas
   - prevent destruction of areas of biological diversity such as tropical forests

- increase protected areas for conservation
- develop, fund and implement International Species Convention.

Energy: choices for environment and development

- Safe and sustainable energy has not been found and energy demands are expected to increase raising warnings over global warming and acidification:
- develop and fund energy efficiency policies towards renewable sources
- place high priority on research for environmentally sound and ecologically viable alternatives to nuclear power and increase the safety of nuclear power
- need to develop 'low energy paths' that operate on renewable resources
- wood-poor nations must organise agricultural sectors to produce wood and plant fuels
- adopt 'conservation pricing' for energy.

Industry: producing more with less

- The consumption of manufactured goods will increase and manufacturing needs to incorporate new environmentally friendly technologies:
- nations have to bear costs of inappropriate industrialisation and developing nations may need assistance
- trans-national corporations have responsibility to help with industrialisation where they operate
- tighter controls on exports of hazardous and agricultural chemicals and dumping of hazardous wastes.

The urban challenge

- The twenty-first century will be highly urbanised and few cities have the resources, and ability to manage infrastructure, services and shelter:
- governments need to develop settlement strategies to reduce pressure off major urban areas
- city management needs decentralisation of funds, political power and personnel to local authorities
- tap into the skills of urban poor, neighbourhood groups and the informal sector (WCED 1987:11–17).

It is important to note that the only place in the entire Report (original Report and OUP edition) where tourism is mentioned is in Chapter 6 on Species and Ecosystems. In the discussion on causes of extinction it states 'Kenya has allocated 6 per cent of its territory as parks and reserves in order to protect its wildlife and to earn foreign exchange through tourism' (WCED 1987: 153). It then goes on to state that protected areas are under threat from a growing population and expanding farmland.

Common Endeavours

The final section of the report focuses on three chapters: (1) Managing the Commons; (2) Peace Security Development and the Environment; and (3) Towards Common Action: Proposals for Institutional and Legal Change. The Commons presents challenges to traditional forms of national sovereignty (WCED 1987). Specifically, the Report focused on the oceans, outer space and Antarctic. Focusing on oceans, the Report stresses that 'the effects of urban, industrial and agricultural growth are contained within no nation's Exclusive Economic Zone; they pass through currents of water and air from nation to nation, and through complex food chains from species to species, distributing the burdens of development, if not the benefits to both rich and poor' (WCED 1987: 262). The Report called for all nations to ratify the UN Law of the Sea,

Fisheries agreements to be strengthened to prevent overexploitation and conventions to be strengthened to regulate hazardous waste dumping (WCED 1987). The second area of the Commons is orbital space and concerns are raised over management of satellites and space debris as well as the possible orbiting weapons in space (WCED 1987). The final Common area addressed is the Antarctic managed under a 1959 Treaty; however, there are sovereignty disputes and pressures for resource development such as minerals. The Commission acknowledges the difficulties in developing international consensus on the continent but it must be done to maintain the area 'as a symbol of peaceful international co-operation and environmental protection' (WCED 1987: 286).

Peace and Security issues are discussed in two main ways. The first is that environmental stress can be a source of conflict, and the second, conflict as a cause of unsustainable development. The Commission notes that 'poverty, injustice environmental degradation, and conflict interact in complex and potent ways' (WCED 1987: 291). One of the environmental threats to security noted to be emerging at the time of the study was the consequence of global warming. It is interesting to note that climate change has now become one of the major environmental issues and is the focus of many tourism papers. In 1987 the greatest worry was nuclear war and the use of other weapons of mass destruction. In addition, concern was raised over military spending and, at the time, the over 40 unresolved disputes in the developing world (WCED 1987). In 2011, security issues still dominate after terrorist attacks such as those on 11 September, 2001, and the conflicts in Iraq, Afghanistan and the Middle East continue while new unrest in northern Africa has spread quickly. The broad principles presented in the Report in moving towards security included co-operative management, importance of early warning of environmental stresses and disarmament and security. The final section of *Common Endeavours* details many specific institutional and legal changes that are needed. Governments (all levels) and international organisations are called on to support development that is economically, and ecologically, sustainable (WCED 1987). Programmes such as reinforcing environmental agencies, developing programmes for assessing risk, strengthening environmental law and promoting investments towards sustainable development are all highlighted (WCED 1987).

Selected UN follow-up conferences from the Brundtland Report

Following the Brundtland Report, the UN adopted a resolution in 1988 to convene the UN Conference on Environment and Development (UNCED) in 1992 in Rio de Janeiro. Out of the Earth Summit, the Commission on Sustainable Development was created and *Agenda 21* was adopted, which is a blueprint for sustainable development. In addition, the legally binding instrument the *United Nations Framework Convention on Climate Change* was opened for signature (UN 2010). This led to the 1997 Kyoto Protocol on climate, which came into force in 2005. The *Rio Declaration* and Agenda 21 were reviewed in 1997 at a UN special session on the environment known as Rio+5 and a Rio+10 World Summit was held in Johannesburg in 2002. The next major Earth Summit is scheduled for 2012 in Rio de Janeiro, 25 years after the Brundtland Report and 20 years after the first Rio Earth Summit.

Influence of the Brundtland Report on tourism

The Brundtland Report was a major step in the evolution of the environmental debate. Subsequent international agreements, conventions, conferences have built on the work in the Report and have shifted towards developing ways to implement sustainable development, such as Agenda 21. Tourism also has closely followed the adoption of the sustainable development paradigm and has been struggling with implementation. Telfer and Sharpley (2008) suggest that over the past 15 years the concept of sustainable development has been the dominant issue in the study and practice of tourism, and this will be explored in the following sections.

The study of sustainable tourism

The Brundtland Report describes the *Common Concerns*, *Challenges* and *Endeavours* and these issues have been raised in the context of tourism. The failures of development from the *Common Concerns* have been mirrored in tourism in discussions on the negative impacts of tourism as well as using tourism as an agent of development. In discussing the historical context for the WCED, it was mentioned that through the 1960s and 1970s the alarm was being raised over the increasingly harmful effects of human action on the environment. These calls were also being raised over tourism development after many years of countries championing the industry as a strong foreign exchange earner. The growing concern was recognised through an increasing number of publications on the impacts of tourism (Mathieson and Wall 1982). Saarinen (2006) suggests that impact studies and the concept of carrying capacity were then replaced by the idea of sustainable tourism. In 1993 a journal even emerged devoted to the topic: *The Journal of Sustainable Tourism*. Tracing the evolution of tourism and development thought through time, Telfer (2002, 2009) noted five developmental paradigms: Modernisation, Dependency, Economic Neo-liberalism, Alternative Development and Beyond the Impasse: The search for a new paradigm (Telfer 2009). The shift towards integrating more of a sustainable approach in development thought was evident as the Alternative Development paradigm started to gain prominence and this was quickly picked up in tourism. Alternative Development is associated with basic needs; people-centred development; empowerment; women in development; and sustainable development (Telfer 2002, 2009). Just as sustainable development is offered as a way forward in the *Common Concerns* in the Brundtland Report, correspondingly in tourism, alternative forms of tourism were put forward as sustainable. Responsible, community-based, small-scale and ecotourism were put forward as arguably being more sustainable than those developed under the Modernisation or Economic Neo-liberalism paradigms, which were criticised for large-scale mass tourism. The arguments now, however, have moved on towards making all forms of tourism more sustainable. In addition to the different forms of tourism mentioned above, a range of tools and processes all aimed at incorporating the concepts of sustainable development into all forms of tourism have been promoted over time including sustainable tourism indicators and guidelines; local involvement in planning; empowerment of women through tourism; pro-poor tourism; fair trade in tourism; tourism certification and benchmarking; tourism codes of conduct; tourism ethics (Fennell 2006); measuring carbon footprints; impact on climate change; and corporate social responsibility in tourism (Telfer 2009).

Saarinen (2006) has identified three traditions of sustainability in tourism studies. The resource-based tradition looks at the limits of resources and the need to protect nature and local culture from the unacceptable changes caused by tourism. This has been linked to the work of carrying capacities focusing on local processes. The activity-based tradition reflects the needs of the industry as it aims to sustain the economic capital invested in tourism. It is suggested that this is the widely accepted hegemonic idea of sustainability that tourism can be a tool for development contributing to sustainability; however, this may in fact be the industry attempting to create a new legitimisation for itself (Mowforth and Munt 1998, cited in Saarinen 2006). Finally, the community-based tradition focuses on involvement and empowerment of various actors and especially the host community. Saarinen (2006) stresses that all the approaches have both advantages and limitations if utilised in the sustainable tourism process and that sustainability is both a global and local responsibility.

Under *Common Endeavours*, in the Brundtland Report, managing the commons and peace and security are highlighted. As Clarke (1997) suggested, sustainability can be linked to various kinds and scales of tourism and environments, including 'the Commons' (Holden 2009). Holden (2009) notes that 'common pool resources' used by tourism include oceans and seas, beaches, coral reefs, the atmosphere and mountains, and it is on these natural resources and ecosystems that impacts occur. In recent years, security has also become a major concern for the study of tourism industry including terrorism, biosecurity and the transmission of diseases through air travel.

Case study

Debates and paradoxes of sustainable development and tourism

In the first case study above, some of the challenges of the concept of sustainable development as presented in the Brundtland Report were explored. These all carry over then into the discussion on and implementation of sustainable development in the context of tourism. Butler (1999) raises the issue that sustainable tourism is not necessarily the same as tourism developed in line with the principles of sustainable development. The question then surrounds what is it the tourism industry has to sustain? Butler then notes that Wall (1996) suggests that focusing on a single sector such as tourism goes against the nature of sustainable development, which is meant to be holistic and multisectoral. Wheeler (1993) questions whether sustainable tourism development is appropriate, and if too many have accepted the notion without taking a critical look at it. Similarly, Garrod and Fyall (1998) argue the need to move beyond the rhetoric of sustainable tourism. Questions have also been posed as to whether there may be different levels or shades of sustainability. Weaver (2004) outlined the structural dimensions of ecotourism, which range from hard to soft ecotourism. Hard ecotourism has roots in the 1980s focusing on small-scale nature-based tourism with high environmental commitment, whereas soft ecotourism has a moderate or veneer commitment to environmental issues and can involve large numbers of more conventional tourists as part of a diversified experience. It is perhaps the soft ecotourism that can generate more money to help enhance the natural environment and managed into site-hardened more intensive zones (Weaver 2004). With the more recent rise in concern over climate change, questions have been raised about considering the entire person's trip including air travel and not just the impacts of tourism in the destination (Gössling *et al.* 2009). Therefore, ecotourism trips to remote areas of the globe may have a very large ecological footprint. More recently, authors in tourism have raised important questions asking us to re-evaluate how sustainability is incorporated in tourism. In raising the question of looking 'Beyond Sustainability?', Sharpley (2009) offers a destination capital model, whereas Hall (2010) argues for a change in paradigms from sustainable to steady state tourism, one that focuses on sufficiency rather than efficiency.

In the previous case study, Dovers and Handmer (1993) presented a number of paradoxes in sustainability as outlined in the Brundtland Report and these are summarised in Table 21.2. Similarly, Liu (2003) presents a list of weaknesses of sustainability in the context of tourism highlighted in Table 21.3.

Just as the Brundtland Report raised questions for sustainability, it has also raised questions and debates on what is sustainable tourism.

The practice of sustainable tourism

A variety of actors including international agencies, governments, conservation areas, NGOs and industry have all made efforts towards incorporating sustainable development in practice; however, questions remain as to whether 'green washing' is taking place. In 1995 *Agenda 21 for the Travel and Tourism Industry* was created by the World Travel and Tourism Council, the World Tourism Organisation and the Earth Council (Hardy *et al.* 2002). The UN World Tourism Organisation (WTO) has a section on the *Sustainable Development of Tourism*, in keeping with the shift towards poverty reduction as seen in the UN Millennium Development Goals. The WTO also established the *ST-EP Program*, which is *the Sustainable Tourism – Eliminating Poverty*. Our *Common Future* stresses the need for global poverty alleviation not just as an ethical objective, but also as a way to ameliorate pressures on the physical environment (Holden 2000). The WTO also established the *Global Code of Ethics for Tourism* calling for stakeholders in tourism development to safeguard the natural environment for continuous and sustainable economic growth (WTO 1999). The UN even declared 2002 as the *International Year of Ecotourism* and the IUCN published guidelines for sustainable tourism in protected areas (Eagles *et al.* 2002). An example of sustainable tourism planning efforts at a national level is the *New Zealand Tourism Strategy 2015*, which recognises that tourism must take a leading role in protecting and enhancing the environment (Connell *et al.* 2009). On the industry side, the World Travel and Tourism Council (WTTC 2003) published the *Blueprint for New Tourism* in 2003 (Gössling et al. 2009) and it also holds a competition for the *Tourism for Tomorrow Awards*, which are awarded for best practice in sustainable tourism. There are a growing number of ecolabels (Buckley 2002) and certifications for tourism products. The Blue Flag Programme operated by the non-profit Foundation for Environmental Education is a voluntary ecolabel award for sustainable development at beaches and marinas (FEE 2010), and the EarthCheck Benchmarking and Certification Programme is offered by EC3 Global, an international environmental management certification company (EarthCheck 2010). The development of corporate responsibility statements and 'green' initiatives in various tourism sectors (e.g. airlines, hotels) are becoming more widespread; however, questions remain on implementation. Concern has also been raised as to the extent to which sustainability is being widely adopted by the tourism industry (Weaver 2009).

The importance of climate change and the challenge it presents to sustainability has been widely debated. The Brundtland Report influenced the 1992 Earth Summit in Rio de Janeiro and that in turn resulted in the Climate Change Convention, which led to the Kyoto Protocol. More recent concern has been the impact of tourism on climate change (Hall and Higham 2005). Tourists themselves are being asked to purchase carbon credits, industries are facing pressures to reduce emissions and destinations are concerned over climate induced change. An interesting link back to The Brundtland Report is that Ms Brundtland was appointed as Special Envoy on Climate Change by Secretary General Ban Ki-moon (Baue 2007).

The 1987 Brundtland Report set the stage for an enhanced debate on the concepts and implementation of sustainable development. These debates and implementation challenges have been picked up both in the study and practice of tourism. A final comment from the Brundtland Report concludes this chapter applying not just to tourism, but to all forms of development, and that is 'In the final analysis, sustainable development must rest on political will' (WCED 1987: 9).

References

Baue, B. (2007) 'Brundtland Report Celebrates 20th Anniversary Since Coining Sustainable Development,' *Sustainability Investment News* June 2007. www.socialfunds.com/news/article.cgi/2308.html, accessed 17 June 2010.

Buckley, R. (2002) 'Tourism ecolabels', *Annals of Tourism Research* 29, 183–208.

Butler, R.W. (1999) 'Sustainable tourism: a state-of-art review', *Tourism Geographies* 1, 7–25.

Carson, R. (1962) *Silent Spring*. Greenwich: Fawcett.

Clark, J. (1997) 'A framework of Approaches to Sustainable Tourism', *Journal of Sustainable Tourism* 5, 224–33.

Connell, J., Page, S. and Bently, T. (2009) 'Towards sustainable tourism planning in New Zealand: Monitoring local government under the Resource Management Act', *Tourism Management* 20, 867–77.

Dovers, S. and Handmer, J. (1992) 'Uncertainty, sustainability and change', *Global Environmental Change* December, 262–76.

——(1993) 'Contradictions in sustainability', *Environmental Conservation* 20, 217–20.

Eagles, P., McCool, S. and Haynes, C. (2002) *Sustainable Tourism in Protected Areas*. Gland: IUCN.

EarthCheck (2010) *EarthCheck: Beyond Green*. www.earthcheck.org/en-us/about-us/default.aspx, accessed 15 September 2010.

Farrell, B. and Twining-Ward, L. (2005) 'Seven steps towards sustainability: Tourism in the context of new knowledge', *Journal of Sustainable Tourism* 13, 109–22.

FEE (2010) *Blue Flag Programme*. www.blueflag.org, accessed 15 September 2010.

Fennell, D. (2006) *Tourism Ethics*. Clevedon: Chanel View Publications.

Fien, J. and Tilbury, D. (2002). 'The global challenge of sustainability', in D. Tilbury, R. Stevenson, J. Fien and D. Schreuder (eds) *Education and Sustainability: Responding to the Global Challenge*. Cambridge: IUCN, 1–12.

Garrod, B. and Fyall, A. (1998) 'Beyond the rhetoric of sustainable tourism', *Tourism Management* 19, 199–212.

Gössling, S. Hall, C.M. and Weaver, D. (2009) 'Sustainable Tourism Futures Perspectives on Systems, Restructuring and Innovations', in S. Gössling, C.M. Hall, and D. Weaver (eds) *Sustainable Tourism Futures Perspectives on Systems, Restructuring and Innovations*. London: Routledge, 1–15.

Hall, C.M. (2010) 'Changing Paradigms and Global Change: From Sustainable to Steady State Tourism', *Tourism Recreation Research* 35, 131–45.

Hall, C. M. and Higham, J. (eds) (2005) *Tourism and Recreation and Climate Change*. Clevedon: Channel View Publication.

Hardin, G. (1968) 'Tragedy of the Commons', *Science* 162, 1243–48.

Hardy, A., Beeton, R. and Pearson, L. (2002) 'Sustainable Tourism: An Overview of the Concept and its Position in Relation to Conceptualisations of Tourism', *Journal of Sustainable Tourism* 10, 475–96.

Holden, A. (2000) *Environment and Tourism*. London: Routledge.

——(2009) 'Tourism and Natural Resources', in M. Robinson and T. Jamal (eds) *Handbook of Tourism Studies*. London: Sage Publications, 202–14.

International Union for the Conservation of Nature and Natural Resources (IUCN 1980) *World Conservation Strategy: Living Resource for Sustainable Development*. Gland, Switzerland: IUCN.

Liu, Z. (2003) 'Sustainable tourism development: A critique', *Journal of Sustainable Tourism* 11, 459–73.

Meadows, D.H., Meadows, D.L, Randers, J. and Behrens, W.W. (1972) *The Limits to Growth*. London: Earth Island.

Mathieson, A. and Wall, G. (1982) *Tourism: Economic, Physical and Social Impacts*. Harlow: Longman.

Mitchell, B. (1997) *Resource and Environmental Management*. Harlow: Longman.

——(2002) *Resource and Environmental Management Second Edition*. Harlow: Longman.

Mowforth, M. and Munt, I. (1998) *Tourism and Sustainability: A New Tourism in the Third World*. London: Routledge.

——(2003) *Tourism and Sustainability Development and New Tourism in the Third World Second Edition*. London: Routledge.

Pigram, J. and Wahab, S. (1997) 'Sustainable Tourism in a Changing World', in S. Wahab and J. Pigram (eds) *Tourism, Development and Growth*. London: Routledge, 17–32.

Saarinen, J. (2006) 'Traditions of Sustainability in Tourism Studies', *Annals of Tourism Research* 33, 1121–40.

Sharpley, R. (2009) *Tourism Development and the Environment: Beyond Sustainability?* London: EarthScan.

Telfer, D. J. (2002) 'The evolution of tourism and development theory', in D.J. Telfer and R. Sharpely (eds) *Tourism and Development Concepts and Issues*. Clevedon: Channel View Publications, 35–78.

——(2009) 'Development Studies and Tourism', in M. Robinson and T. Jamal (eds) *Handbook of Tourism Studies*. London: Sage Publications, 146–65.

Telfer, D. J. and Sharpley, R. (2008) *Tourism and Development in the Developing World*. London: Routledge.

Wall, G. (1996) 'Is ecotourism sustainable?' *Environmental Management* 2, 207–16.

Weaver, D. (2004) 'Manifestations of ecotourism in the Caribbean', in D. Duval (ed.) *Tourism in the Caribbean: Trends, Development, Prospects*. London: Routledge, 172–86.

——(2006) *Sustainable Tourism: Theory and Practice*. Oxford: Elsevier Butterworth-Heineman.

——(2009) 'Reflections on Sustainable Tourism and Paradigm Change', in S. Gössling, C.M. Hall, and D. Weaver (eds) *Sustainable Tourism Futures Perspectives on Systems, Restructuring and Innovations*. London: Routledge, 33–40.

Wheeler, B. (1993) 'Sustaining the ego', *Journal of Sustainable Tourism* 1, 121–9.

WCED (1987) *Our Common Future*. Oxford: Oxford University Press.

WTO (1987) *Global Code of Ethics for Tourism*. Madrid: WTO.

UN (2010) *United Nations Document Research Guide*. www.un.org/depts/dhl/resguide/specenv.htm, accessed 16 September 2010.

WTTC (2003) *Blueprint for New Tourism*. London: WTTC.

Further reading

Burnell, P. and Randall, V. (eds) (2005) *Politics in the Developing World*. Oxford: Oxford University Press. (A good edited book covering the challenges in the developing world.)

Sharpley, R. (2009) *Tourism Development and the Environment: Beyond Sustainability?* London: EarthScan. (A book that challenges us to re-examine the nature of tourism and sustainability.)

Weaver, D. (2006) *Sustainable Tourism: Theory and Practice*. Oxford: Elsevier Butterworth-Heinemann. (An excellent overview of sustainable tourism.)

22

Framework conventions for climate change

An analysis of global framework conventions with reference to resource governance and environmental management approaches in New Zealand

Debbie Hopkins and James Higham

Introduction

The global climate change discourse has identified a wide range of physical, social, economic and political issues (Solomon 2007; Giddens 2009; Stern and Treasury 2007; Adger *et al.* 2009a). Policy responses have emerged at a range of scales, from the United Nations Framework Convention on Climate Change (UNFCCC) at the global level, through to national and local government initiatives. These environmental policies have implicated many sectors including energy, agriculture and forestry, yet to date direct address to tourism has been limited. Holden (2009) states that this will change as tourism becomes increasingly constrained by environmental policy in due course. Tourism is an energy-intensive and natural resource-dependent industry (Becken and Hay 2007; Becken 2008a; Gössling *et al.* 2005) that both contributes to and is harmed by the effects of global climate change. This 'resource paradox' gives urgency to discussions surrounding the tourism–environment relationship (Williams and Ponsford 2009). Yet there is complexity in defining the boundaries of tourism, which in turn creates difficulty in allocating responsibility or calculating 'greenhouse gas intensity' (GHG emissions/economic value) (Perch-Nielsen *et al.* 2010). In this chapter we engage three 'metadiscourses': green governmentality, ecological modernisation and civic environmentalism to discuss and critically assess the field of tourism, environmental governance and climate change. In doing so, we also critique global governance frameworks specifically as they relate to national and regional/local scales of analysis, employing the New Zealand national context and the case of the regional winter/snow tourism industry in New Zealand.

Tourism, climate change and scale

Concerns surrounding unsustainable natural resource consumption have historically paled into insignificance alongside the economic and development goals of the tourism industry (Romeril 1989; Cater 1995). Tourism is dependent on finite resources, and often operates in delicate ecosystems such as small islands and alpine regions (Cohen 1978). The implications of climate change for tourism are serious and now widely documented (Parry *et al.* 2007). Yet the contributions of the tourism industry to greenhouse gas (GHG) emissions, primarily through air travel and energy usage continues to grow rapidly (Peeters *et al.* 2006). As a result the tourism industry will come under increasing pressure to act on climate change (Scott *et al.* 2008b). Although the tourism–environment relationship has been a subject of academic attention for over 30 years, the manner in which it affects and is affected by global scale environmental issues has only recently come to the fore (Gössling and Hall 2006). The impact of the tourism industry on climate change is now being addressed at a range of scales (Hall and Higham 2005). However, the affects of global and national governance policies and frameworks on the tourism industry have been limited. The UNFCCC, the Kyoto Protocol, and the tourism industry-specific Davos Declaration represent the current global governance regimes. They affect and are affected by national and regional/local policies, a point that is central to the discussions that follow.

Governance: the global–local nexus

Governance is defined by the Commission on Global Governance as 'the sum of the many ways individuals and institutions, public and private, manage their common affairs' (Carlsson *et al.* 1995: 2). Thus, global environmental governance incorporates varied actors and groups of actors engaged in managing the resources of the global commons. Global environmental governance has long been advocated as the route to environmental sustainability as well as part of the sustainable development rhetoric (e.g. 65th meeting in 2010 of the United Nations General Assembly). Ruggie (2004: 9) states that 'governance, at whatever level of social organisation it may take place, refers to conducting the public's business – to the constellation of authoritative rules, institutions, and practices by means of which any collectivity manages its affairs'. The physical and social complexity of global environmental resource governance has been addressed (Underdal 2010; Pahl-Wostl 2009), with environmental issues often characterised by vast temporal and spatial scales, along with scientific uncertainty (Rauschmayer *et al.* 2009; Meadowcroft 2007).

The human–environment relationship is formalised through environmental resource governance. However, the objective to prevent overuse and exhaustion of natural resources is no simple task. Modern society has prospered through unsustainable growth, with relentless mass consumption of natural resources triggering a range of chronic environmental issues (Carter 2007; Pelletier 2010). It has been argued that current governance regimes exclude societal dimensions through the political, scientific and technocratic focus. In response, Adger *et al.* (2009b) incorporate socio-cultural aspects to the resource governance definition, with governance engaging not only with the environment but also society. The human–environment relationship has been compounded by governance failures (Bäckstrand *et al.* 2010), and the increasingly complex landscape for resource governance and management in the wake of global climate change.

There are many different theories that can be engaged to examine and critique environmental governance across a range of spatial scales. We have selected the following three in part to highlight the progression of environmental resource governance over the past 30 years (and into the future into post-2012 (post-Kyoto) negotiations); green governmentality, ecological modernisation and civic environmentalism. These can be viewed as 'metadiscourses' in environmental governance (Bäckstrand and Lövbrand 2007), with the key climate change narratives translating from the wider environmental discourses, including the many dualisms that help perpetuate the problem; local versus global, North versus South, public versus private, decentralised versus centralised, economy versus environment (ibid.). Duit *et al.* (2010) note that, traditionally, social science perpetuates a linear and rational outlook, which neglects the complexities of current environmental problems, and thus adds to, rather than challenges, the climate change dilemma, through misinterpretation. Moreover, the systems in place to govern environmental resources (institutions, bureaucracies, etc.) are limited by conflicts, power, knowledge asymmetry and irrationality of actors (Pelletier 2010; Paavola 2007; Bäckstrand *et al.* 2010).

Green governmentality

Multilateralism and centralised global decision-making are key features of the green governmentality discourse. Green governmentality emerges from the Foucauldian concepts of 'bio-power' and 'governmentality' (Darier 1999), with Bäckstrand and Lövbrand (2006: 54) distinguishing a 'green twist', whereby governance moves beyond social structures to include the human–environment relationship. It is depicted as a top-down discourse, technocratic and expert-oriented, thus marginalising alternative understandings, favouring elites and perpetuating power asymmetries (Boehmer-Christiansen 2003). Further, it is characterised by global scale power, mega-science and prioritises big business (Bäckstrand and Lövbrand 2007). The discourse is seen to be promoting the role of science in monitoring and recording the environment, thus suggesting manageability and control, or human stewardship of the natural environment (Rutherford 1999; Bäckstrand and Lövbrand 2007). Moreover, Crutzen (2002) suggests that scientific mapping is presumed to guide the human–environment relationship to sustainability. This discourse dominated early environmental governance systems, and continues through to the present day's 'framework-protocol' approach.

Ecological modernisation

Capitalist ideology promotes private-level decision-making (as opposed to state intervention) and capital accumulation, which is central to the ecological modernisation discourse. Bäckstrand and Lövbrand (2007: 129) identify that 'the distinct feature of this discourse is the compatibility between economic growth and environmental protection, or more specifically between a liberal market order and sustainable development'. Hajer (1995) argues that capitalism has the ability to be environmentally friendly through the use of green regulations; thereby promoting it as the answer to environmental concerns. However, Bäckstrand (2004) questions whether institutions of modernity can resolve environmental problems, when modernity and its various developments have been the 'overarching cause of environmental destruction' (ibid.: 710). Further, it is argued that ecological modernisation neglects the social aspects of environmental degradation, which limits the role of the individual and neglects the call for wider participation in policy-making.

Christoff (1996) conceptualises a divergence between 'weak' and 'strong' ecological modernisation. The former is criticised for perpetuating centralised, top-down environmental governance, dominated by scientific elites, yet it is still identified as the 'predominant discourse in global policy rhetoric and practice' (Bäckstrand and Lövbrand 2007: 129). Strong ecological modernisation calls for the participation and inclusion of civil society. Ecological modernisation differs from green governmentality by challenging state-centric, science-based negotiations, promoting a decentralised liberal market order, which seeks business opportunities arising through 'green technologies'. However, it is argued that despite these differences current climate governance relies on both green governmentality and ecological modernisation concurrently (ibid.). Again, this is evident through the United Nations favoured 'framework-protocol' method, which has been exercised through a range of environmental discourses in the past three decades.

Civic environmentalism

Civic environmentalism emerges as a counter discourse critiquing the neo-liberal framing of the two former narratives as failing to prioritise the environment (Byrne *et al.* 2004). It argues that neo-liberalism commodifies the atmosphere and fails to challenge the rampant consumerism of the global North and has both radical and reform-oriented narratives. The 'radical resistance' faction is highly critical of current environmental governance regimes, emphasising asymmetric power relations, which are seen to perpetuate environmental degradation. Radical civic environmentalists advocate fundamental changes to current consumption driven lifestyles, with the environment taking priority over the economy (Bäckstrand and Lövbrand 2006). Methodologically, the reform-oriented account of civic environmentalism promotes multistakeholder participation to gain specialised, non-scientific expertise into environmental resource governance, proposing that this will raise public confidence in multilateral institutions, due to increased accountability and transparency. Moreover, Rauschmayer *et al.* (2009) highlight the benefits of participative methods to strengthen alternative voices. As adaptation to climate change is not an isolated political or financial process; it requires social action and therefore trust in the formal multilateral institutions. This metadiscourse is seen to challenge the many dualisms that confront global environmental politics by calling for 'cross-sectoral cooperation between market, state and civil society actors' (Bäckstrand and Lövbrand 2007: 124).

The distinctions between these metadiscourses are primarily analytical; there is a great deal of interaction and overlap between the three, with Bäckstrand and Lövbrand (2007) recognising that during climate negotiations, they 'competed for meaning'. Fogel (2004) identifies an increasingly reflexive version of green governmentality, where local actors are introduced to the global policy arena, acknowledging the local scale complexities, which can be overlooked by global governance systems. This draws parallels with reform-oriented civic environmentalism, perhaps responding to the critiques provided from this discourse to develop 'UN-induced "good governance"' (van der Heijden 2008). Reflexive green governmentality, strong ecological modernisation and the reformist civic environmentalism discourse all situate global climate change within the context of the metasustainable development narratives, with Tschakert and Olsson (2005) identifying the synergies between the Conventions on Climate Change, Biodiversity and Diversification.

Climate governance

The first conference at which governments began to address 'man-made' changes in climate was held in 1979 and represented the start of 30 years of negotiations, frameworks and policies. The responsibility of the tourism industry was, and continues to be, largely neglected due to the highly fragmented nature of the industry, national and local dependency on tourism revenue, and uncertainties relating to local vulnerability to climate change. However, recent progress in modelling and a growing response to calls for empirical research have served the need for better understandings of the tourism industry's role in climate change (Scott *et al.* 2005).

Within the climate change discourse, the global–local governance spectrum includes the UNFCCC, its Kyoto Protocol, the Davos Declaration, national government policies and tourism industry self-regulation. Although the focus to date has been largely on mitigation, this has expanded in recent years to incorporate adaptation (Parry *et al.* 2007). Climate governance is integrated within the wider environmental resource governance discourse due to the wide ranging risks associated with global climate change. Jagers and Stripple (2003: 385) identify climate governance as the 'purposeful mechanisms and measures aimed at steering systems towards preventing, mitigating or adapting to the risks posed by climate change'. The need for mitigative and adaptive action in the wake of these changes has prompted discussions into how, and indeed if, the climate can be governed. Governance of the climate is becoming increasingly complex, due to the global implications and the imbalance of causes and consequences. Furthermore, Hardin (1968: 1245) identifies that, 'the air and water surrounding us can not readily be fenced, and so the tragedy of the commons as a cesspool must be prevented by different means'. To date, a common agreement of what constitutes 'different means' remains elusive.

Climate change is not the first environmental issue to be addressed on a global scale, with the Stockholm Declaration in 1972 marking a defining moment in international politics. O'Riordan *et al.* (1998) offer a detailed examination of the sequential progression of environmental issues in the international politics arena, which include biodiversity, ozone depletion and desertification. Although recognising the unique situation of each environmental discourse, the green governmentality framework-protocol method was utilised in each, primarily differentiated by degrees of participation at national and regional scales. Moreover, each discourse displayed varying degrees of governance success, which has so far eluded global climate change.

Global governance frameworks

United Nations Framework Convention on Climate Change

The Intergovernmental Panel on Climate Change (IPCC) was established by the United Nations Environment Programme (UNEP) and the World Meteorological Organisation (WMO) in 1989. Its first assessment report published in 1990 informed the development of the 1992 UNFCCC. Subsequently, the second assessment (1995) contributed to the UNFCCC's Kyoto Protocol. The principle objective of the UNFCCC is 'to stabilise greenhouse gas concentrations in the atmosphere at a level that will prevent dangerous human interference with the climate system' (UNFCCC 1994; O'Riordan *et al.* 1998). There have since been two further IPCC assessments (2001, 2007) and various technical papers. Not until the fourth assessment (2007) did the IPCC directly address tourism due up to that point to the dearth of research (Scott and Becken 2010). Nevertheless, the fourth assessment saw regional chapters address national vulnerabilities including specific ecosystems including mountainous regions, thus providing the foundation for meaningful engagement with the risks posed to national and regional tourism industries (e.g. winter tourism activities). The latest assessments demonstrate a shift towards reflexive green governmentality, with the inclusion of a wider range of voices in vulnerability assessments.

As the first and only global framework, the UNFCCC signified the evolution of the climate change discourse into a state of maturity (Salinger 2010), which culminated in the ratification of its 1997 Kyoto Protocol. Salinger (2010) provides an interesting discussion of the progression of climate change science from the 1970s through to the present day 'midlife crisis', recognised by strengthening scepticism narratives. Thus, Salinger (2010) provides a time-series analysis to the understanding of the progression of governance processes. The progression towards reflexive green governmentality could be seen as a response to overcome the 'midlife crisis' and re-engage the public through increased transparency.

The role of global scale governance is to provide a cohesive framework for national scale action. The necessity of global co-operation for climate change is perceived to be self evident, due to the urgency and magnitude of the challenge to be confronted. Nevertheless, the methods utilised in UN-lead global governance have been heavily critiqued through the lens of civic environmentalism for science and expert dominated action, marginalising alternative voices. UN agencies underpin their policy making with extensive mapping and predicting with a presumption that science will direct the human–environment relationship back to a sustainable pathway (Crutzen 2002). Both the UNFCCC and its Kyoto Protocol are based on the substantial monitoring and modelling of the IPCC. Bäckstrand (2004: 701) argues that science has become 'increasingly professionalised and inaccessible to non-experts', and continues that 'the social and cultural 'embeddedness' of scientific knowledge of environmental risks needs to be highlighted' (ibid.). However, this could be addressed through greater communication between the science and policy communities (Bauer and Stringer 2009) with emphasis given to the cohesion between the environmental issue (in this case climate change) and the organisation(s) responsible for governance (in this case the UNWTO, WMO, etc.)

The reformist civic environmentalism discourse argues that participation is central to increasing public confidence, which is required in order to gain support for national government policy measures. Moreover, Oreskes (2004) discusses the promotion of 'scientific uncertainty' rhetoric among policy makers to avoid the drastic measures that will be required in order to achieve emissions reductions targets. It has been argued that the intense science focus associated with green governmentality can hinder the environmental decision-making process (Deere-Birkbeck 2009). Bäckstrand and Lövbrand (2006) note a 'discursive shift' in Conference of Parties (COP) negotiations, with the specific focus on global scale mitigation expanded to accommodate consideration of local and regional scale vulnerabilities. Hjerpe and Linnér (2010) point to the success of side events during international negotiations where groups of civil society actors are able to share practical information on adaptive strategies and coping capacities, thus using global climate negotiations to informally discuss local resource management. This could point to the function of civic environmentalism in the shadow of formal green governmentality systems. Lidskog and Elander (2010) concur, identifying two distinct factions in governance structures; formal institutions involving UN agencies and domestic government policy, and informal institutions consisting of social groups, voluntary organisations, private sector businesses and local governments. These participants are drawn together by 'policy proximity' (ibid.: 38), thereby establishing global networks.

Despite critiques of UN global climate governance through the lens of green governmentality and assumptions of the top-down nature of such governance, in reality the situation is far more complex. It is not only the bureaucratic nature of multilateralism that renders it 'top-down', but the national, regional and local governance systems that are operating in parallel. The convention-protocol approach to climate change adopted by the UN follows on the relative success of (among others) the response to ozone depletion. This is a compelling example of global scale co-operation to address an environmental issue (Clapp and Dauvergne 2008), from which understandings of global-local, top-down, bottom-up hybridity can be achieved.

The Kyoto Protocol

The adoption of the Kyoto Protocol in 1997 signified a milestone in global climate governance. Developed under the UNFCCC, the Kyoto Protocol represents the first legally binding international agreement, setting GHG emissions reduction targets for industrialised countries. It focuses on three market mechanisms: emissions trading, joint implementation and the clean development mechanism to reduce emissions by economic means (Breidenich *et al.* 1998; Grubb *et al.* 1999; Lövbrand *et al.* 2007). However, results to date have failed to impress (Nishiki and

Change 2009; Pearson 2007), thus providing support for critics of the weak ecological modernisation discourse. In keeping with the neo-liberal capitalist ideology, the Kyoto Protocol mechanisms encourage private-lead technical optimisation. The commodification of carbon through ecological modernisation constructs has encouraged a 'business as usual' approach, failing to address the mass consumption and carbon-intensive lifestyles at the root of the problem (Böhringer and Vogt 2003). Public and private institutions, as well as individuals, are now seeking carbon neutrality (Gössling 2009), perhaps in vain through carbon offsetting mechanisms rather than behavioural changes or clean technologies (Gössling et al. 2007).

Although the Kyoto Protocol did not specifically address the tourism industry, in order to achieve these targets (now most likely in a post-2012 agreement) a period of harsh austerity appears to await the tourism industry. Air travel contributes most to tourism GHG emissions (Becken 2002; Gössling et al. 2007; Scott 2006) and to date, this sector has been spared any direct or far-reaching policy.

The Davos Declaration

The United Nations World Tourism Organisation (UNWTO) Davos Declaration emerged in 2007 in response to the tourism industry's role in global climate change. The declaration identified four spheres for attention: mitigation of GHG emissions, adaptation to the affects of climate change, technological developments and financial support for the global South (Becken 2008b), thus bridging the three metadiscourses. Under a reformist civic environmentalism rhetoric, the Declaration calls for a wide range of actors to participate in mitigative and adaptive measures. These actors include governments, industry segments, research organisations and tourists, with specific tasks for each. Schwab (2008: 110) found that 'the stakeholder concept became the cornerstone of the Davos Declaration' and therefore the rhetoric is aligned with reformist civic environmentalism. However, despite identifying the stakeholders involved, Gössling (2009) questions whether these groups will engage with their charges. The Declaration (2007: 2) that 'there is a need to urgently adopt a range of policies which encourages truly sustainable tourism that reflects a "quadruple bottom line" of environmental, social, economic and climate responsiveness'. However, specific priorities and timelines are not indicated and once again, aviation is not explicitly addressed.

National/regional scale of analysis: the case of New Zealand

Tourism is of high economic value to New Zealand, with international tourists spending NZ$5.95 billion in 2008 (New Zealand Tourism Research), contributing 3.8 per cent to Gross Domestic Product and employing 94,600 full time equivalents (Statistics New Zealand 2009). Situated in the southwestern Pacific Ocean, New Zealand is geographically remote, and requires long haul air travel for all major tourism markets (with the exception of eastern seaboard Australia). As such, there is a paradox between the government's '100 per cent Pure' brand image, and the carbon-intensive travel required by visitors (Becken 2007). Under scenarios of climate change, New Zealand is in a delicate position; UNWTO/UNEP/WMO Tourism Vulnerability Hotspots (2008) identifies the key vulnerability to New Zealand's tourism industry as the increased travel costs resulting from climate change mitigation policies. Various research publications have addressed this vulnerability in terms of; technical innovations to achieve sustainability (Peeters et al. 2006), perceptions of tourists travelling to New Zealand (Higham and Cohen 2010), carbon offsetting of tourists travelling to and from New Zealand (Smith and Rodger 2009) and tourists' understanding and acceptance of possible policy measures (Becken 2007).

When New Zealand ratified the Kyoto Protocol in 2002 a number of measures were implemented by the government to achieve their obligations. The 2004 Resource Management (Energy and Climate Change) Amendment Act saw re-centralisation of climate change issues in decision-making, from the local government remit arguing that this would allow for cohesive and fair action (Connell *et al.* 2009). This may be viewed as a signal of green governmentality. New Zealand's main response has been the Emissions Trading Scheme (NZETS), which uses Kyoto Protocol mechanisms to provide a monetary incentive to reduce carbon emissions and increase carbon sinks through forestry projects, symbiotic of ecological modernisation.

New Zealand's 'Fifth National Communication' (2009) advocates two priorities: a medium-term responsibility target of 10–20 per cent reduction below 1990 levels by 2020, and a long-term target of a 50 per cent reduction in net GHG emissions from 1990 levels by 2050. Becken (2007: 351) identified three key policies addressing these reduction targets: voluntary initiatives, global air travel charge and per capital carbon budget; however, it was concluded that 'major societal change' (ibid., 351) is needed in order to reduce hyper-mobile tourists' air travel. Although it would be politically implausible for New Zealand to implement policies that would directly limit both inbound and outbound tourism, in a scenario where environmental resources were prioritised this would not be so unthinkable. Tourism industry climate change policies within New Zealand include initiatives to assist tourism businesses to measure and reduce carbon footprints; however, additional non-tourism-specific measures targeting overall consumption may also impact the tourism industry. It can be argued that these are not far-reaching, and are relying on ecological modernisation in the form of economically coercive behaviour, without addressing the societal transformation called for by civic environmentalism. Although climate change is often compared with the ozone depletion discourse, Lidskog and Elander (2010: 32) note the obvious point of distinction 'the causes of anthropogenically induced climate change are deeply embedded in the socio-economic fabric of modern technology'.

Deere-Birkbeck (2009) recognises that, although framed as a global issue, climate change mitigation and adaptation requires national and local level action, and thus the engagement of stakeholders through local level bottom-up environmental governance. In order for global frameworks to achieve their objectives, they need to be supported by domestic commitments and policies, so as to achieve a hybrid approach to promote agreements and outcomes – e.g. Vienna Convention for the Protection of the Ozone Layer and its Montreal Protocol (Eisner 2006: 217). Boehmer-Christiansen (2003) critiques highlights ineffective governance through green governmentality and ecological modernisation; however, Eisner (2006) states that there can be a successful midpoint for governance that combines top-down and bottom-down approaches.

Adaptation has occurred, and will continue to occur, on the national and local scale, as it is context- and location-specific, therefore addressing distinct vulnerabilities and coping capacities. Given that the adaptation process is essentially a governance issue (Adger *et al.* 2009b), there is a need to challenge governance failings and promote best practice. Although scale is a central topic in the social and environmental sciences, it has had a lack of attention within tourism literature (Hall 2007). Gössling (2002) identifies the role of tourism in global environmental concerns, with the sum of local level actions contributing to global scale climatic changes. Further, the tourism industry should actively participate in both mitigative and adaptive efforts, due to its obvious and inescapable engagement with the 'resource paradox'.

Smith (2007) argues that the global framing of climate change can act to reduce the perceived importance of local level contributions to the issue, stating that everyday mass consumption and unsustainable lifestyles need to be tackled. Paterson and Stripple (2007) discuss the local and individual actions taken as part of global climate governance through the form of action groups, personal carbon allowances and carbon offsetting. Effective local-level governance must involve policy making that will challenge current lifestyles, thus it is vital that individuals are engaged and prepared for the necessary adjustments. In New Zealand, environmental resource management includes minimising the effects of climate change and addressing the vulnerabilities of specific industries and locations, thus requiring the action of individuals. The Fifth National Communication (Ministry for the Environment 2009: 14) outlines a range of public awareness campaigns run by the national government between 2005 and 2008 to improve the collective understanding of climate change, and inspire action on a local scale. Further to this, in July 2009 the Minister for Climate Change Issues held a series of public meetings, which attracted over 1,600 attendees, in order to discuss the mid-term emissions reduction targets. Depending on the direction of communication (one way/two way), this behaviour could be viewed as an act of reformist civic environmentalism, whereby transparency is increased and a wider range of voices are included in the process. These actions are supported by Bäckstrand (2004), who suggests that the lack of consensus on climate change and GHG emissions calls for those affected by the problem to be involved in decision-making.

The question then remains, will local governments respond to local climate change vulnerabilities? Connell et al. (2009) report that New Zealand local governments struggle with inherent conflicts of interest (e.g. environment versus economy) when applying the Resource Management Act (1991). In practice, the ecological modernisation proposition for environmental protection can prove impractical. Nevertheless, as local level responses gather momentum, so too will their influence and impact on national and global environmental governance.

Local scale: ski industry regulation and policy

The ski industry as an example of a regional climate-reliant, natural resource-dependent tourism sub-sector. Global climate change has been identified as a particular threat to the sustainability of winter tourism (Scott 2006; Parry et al. 2007). Among other risks, it threatens natural snow availability, which is the *conditio sine qua non* of winter tourism activities (Gössling and Hall 2006). Research in this field to date has focused almost exclusively on North America (Scott et al. 2006, 2008b; Dawson and Scott 2007), Canada (Scott et al. 2003), Switzerland (Koenig and Abegg 1997; Elsasser and Bürki 2002), Austria (Wolfsegger et al. 2008) and Australia (Bicknell and McManus 2006; Hennessy et al. 2007). Scott et al. (2008a) identified a range of tourism-related risks as a result of climate change for Australia and New Zealand in particular, including warmer winters, increased extreme weather events and rising travel costs.

Although recognising the value of other international markets, the Ski Marketing Network (New Zealand) focuses on the Australian market. Eastern Australia is New Zealand's only medium haul international ski market (Higham and Cohen 2010). It has been suggested that, when considered alongside Australian ski areas, New Zealand's ski industry could benefit in relative terms from climate change-related effects (Wall and Badke 1994; Parry et al. 2007), thus potentially increasing New Zealand's attractiveness to the significant Australian ski market.

Although global frameworks and government policy often fail to explicitly address the resource consumption and carbon emissions resulting from the ski industry, unlike other industries (such as agriculture), these frameworks and policies will play a decisive role in adaptive options (Scott 2006). Through land, water and energy resource management, policy will influence the adaptive capacity of individual ski fields and the wider industry. Despite mitigative efforts, some degree of climate change is now inevitable (Parry et al. 2007), and it is therefore necessary to address the adaptive capabilities of tourism sectors. Scott (2006) identifies three categories of climate change response: hard technological developments, soft business practices, and government or industry policy. Hard and soft adaptations have received some attention (Bürki *et al.* 2007; Moen and Fredman 2007; Hennessy *et al.* 2007; Scott *et al.* 2008b). The latter includes environmental regulatory frameworks, government policies and ski industry climate change policy (Scott 2006). Ski industry self-regulation requires stakeholder recognition that they 'share and create common problems' (Dubois and Ceron 2006: 400). Although initiatives have emerged at an industry scale, the destination level has responsibility for both resource management at the micro scale and a contribution to the global climate change discourse and it is at this scale of analysis that responses to the climate change challenge have been largely absent.

Direct and indirect emissions resulting from tourism have been addressed (Becken 2002; Becken and Simmons 2002; Becken and Patterson 2006); however, it is a complex equation. With the majority of international arrivals for snow tourism originating from within Australasia, the impact on the snow tourism industry in particular is less clear. Viewing this industry in commercial or geographical isolation neglects the wider implications of global climate change as a result of anthropogenic carbon emissions. Furthermore, a successful manoeuvre towards radical civic environmentalism through socio-cultural responses towards low carbon lifestyles could show a shift away from international travel, or activities unavailable within the domestic context, thus having drastic implications for winter/snow tourism to New Zealand.

The ski industry does not operate in isolation, but is intrinsically connected to the national tourism and environmental resource policy, as well as being affected by international decision-making. Traditional 'command and control' regulations are avoided by governments, reluctant to constrain tax-generating tourism activities (Williams and Ponsford 2009). Thus, voluntary environmental programmes have emerged as a preferred governance structure. These are seen to promote perceptions of an industry-wide environmental ethic, thereby reducing calls for top-down regulations from pressure groups (King and Lenox 2000). An example of voluntary programmes can be found in the US ski industry through the Sustainable Slopes Charter (SSC) and 'Keep Winter Cool' campaigns. The US National Ski Area Association (NSAA) has produced a 'ski industry climate change policy', which acknowledges the vulnerability of the weather-dependent activities associated with winter tourism, and the resource consumption of the ski industry. Climate change adaptation has been neglected in this document; however, this could be attributed to the competitiveness of the market (Scott and McBoyle 2007). Nevertheless, the programme has been critiqued in terms of ambiguous standards, lack of third-party oversight and failing to sanction poor performance (Rivera and de Leon 2004). In New Zealand there is little evidence of cohesive industry-wide environmental resource management or climate change-related initiatives, with just three ski fields adopting the SSC. This could be attributed to the relatively optimistic short- to medium-term outlook within the Australasian context.

The success of industry-wide initiatives such as the NSAA's SSC, relies on individual operators accepting responsibility for their actions, and integrating the measures into their operational and strategic decision-making, which is currently not evident in New Zealand. Rivera (2004) suggest that working on a destination scale is optimal, as this can exert 'normative pressures', relying on peer pressures to conform. Further, the results of cohesive action can be far greater than those achieved individually, thus motivating operators who may perceive their own capacity to act as insignificant, with outcomes perceived to be ineffectual due to fragmentation. Understandings of neo-institutional theory can explain the requirement for stakeholder and social pressures to understand the success or failings of voluntary programmes (ibid.). Williams (2009) identify the benefits of destination scale governance to encourage integrated and co-ordinated action. Using the example of Whistler, Canada, they discuss the benefits of comprehensive destination-wide planning, using a civic environmentalism methodology to integrate multiple stakeholder knowledge and positioning to achieve social capital. This example may be used as a benchmark for other destinations, and this has not gone unnoticed in New Zealand, with

Queenstown (New Zealand) using this model to develop its own sustainability pathway. Nevertheless, on both a national, and specific destination scale, New Zealand is languishing behind the USA and Canada.

Conclusion

This chapter addresses the tourism–environment relationship within the context of climate governance, identifying the connections between global, national, regional and local scale actions. Three metadiscourses (green governmentality, ecological modernisation and civic environmentalism) provide a framework for critiquing global governance, highlighting the urgency of progression of climate change governance frameworks towards wider stakeholder participation. We have acknowledged the importance of patchwork policy making to both mitigate and adapt to global climate change, integrating top-down and bottom-up methods to facilitate hybrid actions. In association with governance efforts arises the need to curtail mass consumption lifestyles in order to adequately address sustainable resource governance and climate change concerns.

These metadiscourses also inform our review of the New Zealand national/regional context employing the case of New Zealand winter ski destinations to highlight the critical links between the global and local scales of analysis. 'Post-Kyoto' negotiations need to focus on widening the spectrum of participants, beyond governments and 'big business', to adopt a 'patchwork' approach to global climate governance, moving away from the rigid structures of the past to build a sustainable future. Greater transparency and engagement can invoke trust between individuals and the institutional structures, which, through civic environmentalism, may raise the discourse beyond the current 'midlife crisis'.

References

Adger, W., Dessai, S., Goulden, M., Hulme, M., Lorenzoni, I., Nelson, D., Naess, L., Wolf, J. and Wreford, A. (2009a) 'Are there social limits to adaptation to climate change?' *Climatic Change* 93, 335–54.

Adger, W.N., Lorenzone, I., O'Brien, K.L. (ed.) (2009b) *Adapting to Climate Change: Thresholds, Values, Governance.* Cambridge: Cambridge University Press.

Bäckstrand, K. (2004) 'Scientisation vs. civic expertise in environmental governance: eco-feminist, eco-modern and post-modern responses.' *Environmental Politics* 13, 695–714.

Bäckstrand, K. and Lövbrand, E. (2006) 'Planting trees to mitigate climate change: Contested discourses of ecological modernization, green governmentality and civic environmentalism.' *Global Environmental Politics* 6, 50–75.

——(2007) 'Climate Governance Beyond 2012: Competing Discourses of Green Governmentality, Ecological Modernisation and Civic Environmentalism,' in Pettenger, M.E., *The Social Construction of Climate Change. Power, Knowledge, Norms, Discourses.* Aldershot: Ashgate Publishing

Bäckstrand, K., Khan, J. and Kronsell, A. (2010) *Environmental Politics and Deliberative Democracy: Examining the Promise of New Modes of Governance.* Cheltenham: Edward Elgar Pub.

Bauer, S. and Stringer, L.C. (2009) 'The role of science in the global governance of desertification.' *Journal of Environment and Development* 18, 248–67.

Becken, S. (2002) 'Analysing international tourist flows to estimate energy use associated with air travel.' *Journal of Sustainable Tourism* 10, 114–31.

——(2007) 'Tourists' perception of international air travel's impact on the global climate and potential climate change policies.' *Journal of Sustainable Tourism* 15, 351–68.

——(2008a) 'Developing indicators for managing tourism in the face of peak oil.' *Tourism Management* 29, 695–705.

——(2008b) 'The UN climate change conference, Bali: What it means for tourism.' *Journal of Sustainable Tourism* 16, 246–8.

Becken, S. and Hay, J. (2007) *Tourism and climate change: risks and opportunities.* Clevedon: Multilingual Matters Ltd.

Becken, S. and Patterson, M. (2006) 'Measuring National Carbon Dioxide Emissions from Tourism as a Key Step Towards Achieving Sustainable Tourism.' *Journal of Sustainable Tourism* 14, 323–38.

Becken, S. and Simmons, D.G. (2002) 'Understanding energy consumption patterns of tourist attractions and activities in New Zealand.' *Tourism Management* 23, 343–54.

Bicknell, S. and Mcmanus, P. (2006) 'The canary in the coalmine: Australian ski resorts and their response to climate change.' *Geographical Research* 44, 386–400.

Boehmer-Christiansen, S. (2003) 'Science, equity, and the war against carbon.' *Science, Technology & Human Values* 28, 69.

Böhringer, C. and Vogt, C. (2003) 'Economic and environmental impacts of the Kyoto protocol.' *Canadian Journal of Economics/Revue canadienne d'économique* 36, 475–96.

Breidenich, C., Magraw, D., Rowley, A. and Rubin, J. (1998) 'The Kyoto Protocol to the United Nations Framework Convention on Climate Change.' *American Journal of International Law* 92, 315–31.

Bürki, R., Abegg, B. and Elsasser, H. (2007) *Climate Change and Tourism in the alpine regions of Switzerland*, in: Amelung, B., Blazejczul, B., and Matzarakis, A. *Climate change and tourism: assessment and coping strategies.* 165–172, Maastricht – Warsaw – Freiburg

Byrne, J., Glover, L., Inniss, V., Kulkarni, J., Mun, Y., Toly, N. and Wang, Y. (2004) 'Reclaiming the atmospheric commons: Beyond Kyoto', *Climate Change: Perspectives Five Years After Kyoto*. Plymouth: Science Publishers, 429–52.

Carlsson, I., Ramphal, S., Alatas, A. and Dahlgren, H. (1995) *Our global neighbourhood: The report of the commission on global governance.* Oxford: Oxford University Press.

Carter, N. (2007) *The politics of the environment: ideas, activism, policy.* Cambridge and New York: Cambridge Univ Press.

Cater, E. (1995) 'Environmental Contradictions in Sustainable Tourism,' *The Geographical Journal*, 161.

Christoff, P. (1996) 'Ecological modernisation, ecological modernities.' *Environmental Politics* 5, 476–500.

Clapp, J. and Dauvergne, P. (2008) *Paths to a Green World The Political Economy of the Global Environment.* Cambridge, MA: Academic Foundation.

Cohen, E. (1978) 'The impact of tourism on the physical environment.' *Annals of Tourism Research* 5, 215–37.

Connell, J., Page, S. and Bentley, T. (2009) 'Towards sustainable tourism planning in New Zealand: monitoring local government planning under the Resource Management Act.' *Tourism Management* 30, 867–77.

Crutzen, P. (2002) 'Geology of mankind.' *Nature* 415, 23.

Darier, E. (1999) *Discourses of the Environment.* Oxford: Wiley-Blackwell.

Dawson, J. and Scott, D. (2007) 'Climate change vulnerability of the Vermont ski tourism industry (USA).' *Annals of Leisure Research* 10, 550.

Deere-Birkbeck, C. (2009) 'Global governance in the context of climate change: The challenges of increasingly complex risk parameters.' *International Affairs* 85.

Dubois, G. and Ceron, J. (2006) 'Tourism and climate change: Proposals for a research agenda.' *Journal of Sustainable Tourism* 14, 399–415.

Duit, A., Galaz, V., Eckerberg, K. and Ebbesson, J. (2010) 'Governance, complexity, and resilience.' *Global Environmental Change.* Volume 20: 3, 363–368

Eisner, M. (2006) *Governing the environment: the transformation of environmental regulation*, Boulder, CO: Lynne Rienner Publishers.

Elsasser, H. and Bürki, R. (2002) 'Climate change as a threat to tourism in the Alps.' *Climate Research* 20, 253–7.

Fogel, C. (2004) 'The local, the global and the Kyoto Protocol.' *Earthly politics: Local and global in environmental governance*, 103–25.

Giddens, A. (2009) *The politics of climate change*, Cambridge: Polity Press.

Gössling, S. (2002) 'Global environmental consequences of tourism.' *Global Environmental Change* 12, 283–302.

——(2009) 'Carbon neutral destinations: A conceptual analysis.' *Journal of Sustainable Tourism* 17, 17–37.

Gössling, S. and Hall, C. (2006) *Tourism and global environmental change: Ecological, social, economic and political interrelationships.* London: Taylor & Francis.

Gössling, S., Broderick, J., Upham, P., Ceron, J., Dubois, G., Peeters, P. and Strasdas, W. (2007) 'Voluntary carbon offsetting schemes for aviation: efficiency, credibility and sustainable tourism.' *Journal of Sustainable Tourism* 15, 223–48.

Gössling, S., Peeters, P., Ceron, J., Dubois, G., Patterson, T. and Richardson, R. (2005) 'The eco-efficiency of tourism.' *Ecological Economics* 54, 417–34.

Grubb, M., Vrolijk, C. and Brack, D. (1999) *The Kyoto Protocol: a guide and assessment.* London: Earthscan Publications Ltd.

Hajer, M. (1995) *The politics of environmental discourse: ecological modernization and the policy process*. New York: Oxford University Press.

Hall, C. (2007) 'Scaling ecotourism: the role of scale in understanding the impacts of ecotourism.' In Higham, J. *Critical issues in ecotourism: understanding a complex tourism phenomenon*. Oxford: Butterworth-Heinemann

Hall, C. and Higham, J. (2005) *Tourism, recreation, and climate change*. Clevedon: Channel View Books.

Hardin, G. (1968) 'The tragedy of the commons. The population problem has no technical solution; it requires a fundamental extension in morality.' *Science* 162, 1243.

Hennessy, K., Whetton, P., Walsh, K., Smith, I., Bathols, J., Hutchinson, M. and Sharples, J. (2007) 'Climate change effects on snow conditions in mainland Australia and adaptation at ski resorts through snowmaking.' *Climate Research* 35, 255.

Higham, J. and Cohen, S. (2010) 'Canary in the coalmine: Norwegian attitudes towards climate change and extreme long-haul air travel to Aotearoa/New Zealand.' *Tourism Management*, Vol. 32:1, 98–105

Hjerpe, M. and Linnér, B.O. (2010) 'Functions of COP side-events in climate-change governance.' *Climate Policy* 10, 167–80.

Holden, A. (2009) 'The Environment-Tourism Nexus: Influence of Market Ethics.' *Annals of Tourism Research* 36, 373–89.

Jagers, S. and Stripple, J. (2003) 'Climate Governance beyond the State,' *Global Governance* 9, 385–400.

King, A. and Lenox, M. (2000) Industry self-regulation without sanctions: The chemical industry's responsible care program.' *Academy of Management Journal* 43, 698–716.

Koenig, U. and Abegg, B. (1997) 'Impacts of climate change on winter tourism in the Swiss Alps.' *Journal of Sustainable Tourism* 5, 46–58.

Lidskog, R. and Elander, I. (2010) 'Addressing climate change democratically. Multi-level governance, transnational networks and governmental structures.' *Sustainable Development* 18, 32–41.

Lövbrand, E., Nordqvist, J. and Rindefjäll, T. (2007) 'Everyone loves a winner–expectations and realisations in the emerging CDM market.' Presented at the Amsterdam Conference on the Human Dimensions of Global Environmental Change, May 2007.

Meadowcroft, J. (2007) 'Who is in Charge here? Governance for Sustainable Development in a Complex World.' *Journal of Environmental Policy & Planning* 9, 299–314.

Ministry for the Environment (2009) *New Zealand's Fifth National Communication*.

Moen, J. and Fredman, P. (2007) 'Effects of climate change on alpine skiing in Sweden.' *Journal of Sustainable Tourism* 15, 418–37.

Nishiki, M. (2009) *The Clean Development Mechanism and local sustainability*. Presented at the Amsterdam Conference on the Human Dimensions of Global Environmental Change, May 2007

O'Riordan, T., Cooper, C., Jordan, A., Rayner, S., Richards, K., Runci, P. and Yoffe, S. (1998) 'Institutional frameworks for political action,' in Rayner, S. and Malone, E.L. (eds) *Human choice and climate change*. Columbus, OH: Battelle Press.

Oreskes, N. (2004) 'Science and public policy: what's proof got to do with it?' *Environmental Science & Policy* 7, 369–83.

Paavola, J. (2007) 'Institutions and environmental governance: a reconceptualization.' *Ecological Economics* 63, 93–103.

Pahl-Wostl, C. (2009) 'A conceptual framework for analysing adaptive capacity and multi-level learning processes in resource governance regimes. *Global Environmental Change* 19, 354–65.

Parry, M., Canziani, O., Palutikof, J., Van Der Linden, P. and Hanson, C. (2007) *IPCC, 2007: climate change 2007: impacts, adaptation and vulnerability. Contribution of working group II to the fourth assessment report of the intergovernmental panel on climate change*. Cambridge: Cambridge University Press.

Paterson, M. and Stripple, J. (2007) 'Singing Climate Change into Existence: On the Territorialization of Climate Policymaking,' in Pettenger, M. E., *The Social Construction of Climate Change. Power, Knowledge, Norms, Discourses*. Aldershot: Ashgate Publishing Limited.

Pearson, B. (2007) 'Market Failure: why the Clean Development Mechanism won't promote clean development.' *Journal of Cleaner Production* 15, 247–52.

Peeters, P., Gossling, S. and Becken, S. (2006) 'Innovation towards tourism sustainability: climate change and aviation.' *International Journal of Innovation and Sustainable Development* 1, 184–200.

Pelletier, N. (2010) 'Of laws and limits: An ecological economic perspective on redressing the failure of contemporary global environmental governance.' *Global Environmental Change* 20:2, 220–228.

Perch-Nielsen, S., Sesartic, A. and Stucki, M. (2010) 'The greenhouse gas intensity of the tourism sector: The case of Switzerland.' *Environmental Science & Policy* 13:3, 131–140.

Rauschmayer, F., Van Den Hove, S. and Koetz, T. (2009) 'Participation in EU biodiversity governance: How far beyond rhetoric? *Environment and Planning C: Government and Policy* 27, 42–58.

Rivera, J. and De Leon, P. (2004) 'Is greener whiter? Voluntary environmental performance of western ski areas.' *Policy Studies Journal* 32, 417–37.

Romeril, M. (1989) 'Tourism and the environment–accord or discord?' *Tourism Management* 10, 204–8.

Ruggie, J.G. (2004) 'Reconstituting the global public domain – Issues, actors, and practices.' *European Journal of International Relations* 10, 499–531.

Rutherford, P. (1999) 'The entry of life into history.' *Discourses of the Environment*, 37–62.

Salinger, J. (2010) 'The climate journey over three decades: From childhood to maturity, innocence to knowing, from anthropocentrism to ecocentrism.' *Climatic Change* 100, 49–57.

Schwab, K. (2008) 'Global Corporate Citizenship-Working with Governments and Civil Society.' *Foreign Aff* 87, 107.

Scott, D. (ed.) (2006) 'US ski industry adaptation to climate change: hard, soft and policy strategies,' in Gossling, S. and Hall, C. M., *Tourism and Environmental Change: Ecological, Social, Economic and Political Interrelationships*. London and New York: Taylor & Francis.

Scott, D. and Becken, S. (2010) 'Adapting to climate change and climate policy: Progress, Problems and potentials.' *Journal of Sustainable Tourism* 18, 283–95.

Scott, D. and McBoyle, G. (2007) 'Climate change adaptation in the ski industry.' *Mitigation and adaptation strategies for global change* 12, 1411–31.

Scott, D., Amelung, B., Becken, S., Ceron, J., Dubois, G., Gossling, S., Peeters, P. and Simpson, M. (2008a) 'Climate change and tourism: Responding to global challenges.' *World Tourism Organization, Madrid*, 230.

Scott, D., Dawson, J. and Jones, B. (2008b) 'Climate change vulnerability of the US Northeast winter recreation–tourism sector.' *Mitigation and adaptation strategies for global change* 13, 577–96.

Scott, D., McBoyle, G. and Mills, B. (2003) 'Climate change and the skiing industry in southern Ontario (Canada): exploring the importance of snowmaking as a technical adaptation.' *Climate Research* 23, 171–81.

Scott, D., McBoyle, G., Minogue, A. and Mills, B. (2006) 'Climate change and the sustainability of ski-based tourism in eastern North America: A reassessment.' *Journal of Sustainable Tourism* 14, 376–98.

Scott, D., Wall, G. and McBoyle, G. (2005) 'Tracing the development of the climate change issue in the tourism sector,' in M.H.C. and J.H. (eds) *Tourism, Recreation and Climate Change*. Clevedon: Channel View Publications.

Smith, I. and Rodger, C. (2009) 'Carbon emission offsets for aviation-generated emissions due to international travel to and from New Zealand.' *Energy Policy* 37, 3438–47.

Smith, W.D. (2007) 'Presence of Mind as Working Climate Change Knowledge,' in Pettenger, M. (ed.) *The Social Construction of Climate Change*. Aldershot: Ashgate.

Solomon, S., Qin, D., Manning, M., Chen, Z., Marquis, M., Averyt, K.B., Tignor, M., Miller, H.L. (2007) *Climate Change 2007: the physical science basis: contribution of Working Group I to the Fourth Assessment Report of the Intergovernmental Panel on Climate Change.* Cambridge and New York: Cambridge University Press.

Statistics New Zealand (2009) *Tourism Satellite Account: 2009*. Wellington: Statistics New Zealand.

Stern, N. and Treasury, G. (2007) *The economics of climate change: the Stern review*. Cambridge: Cambridge University Press.

Tschakert, P. and Olsson, L. (2005) 'Post-2012 climate action in the broad framework of sustainable development policies: the role of the EU.' *Climate Policy* 5, 329–48.

Underdal, A. (2010) 'Complexity and challenges of long-term environmental governance.' *Global Environmental Change* 20, 386–93.

UNFCCC (1994) Article two. *UNFCCC 1994. Article two.* Available at www.unfccc.int [Accessed 1 September 2010].

United Nations World Tourism Organisation (2007) *Davos Declaration – Climate Change and Tourism: Responding to Global Challenges.*

van der Heijden, H. (2008) 'Green governmentality, ecological modernisation or civic environmentalism? Dealing with global environmental problems.' *Environmental Politics* 17, 835–39.

Wall, G. and Badke, C. (1994) 'Tourism and climate change: an international perspective.' *Journal of Sustainable Tourism* 2, 193–203.

Williams, P.W. and Ponsford, I.F. (2009) 'Confronting tourism's environmental paradox: Transitioning for sustainable tourism.' *Futures* 41, 396–404.

Wolfsegger, C., Gossling, S. and Scott, D. (2008) 'Climate change risk appraisal in the Austrian ski industry.' *Tourism Review International* 12, 13–23.

23

The vulnerability of tourism to climate change

Daniel Scott and Christopher Lemieux

Introduction

Scientific understanding and concern about climate change has increased worldwide over the past two decades and featured prominently in high-profile international policy debates. In the same year that the United Nations (UN) Intergovernmental Panel on Climate Change (IPCC) was awarded the Nobel Peace Prize (2007), its *Fourth Assessment Report* (AR4) concluded that the global climate has changed over the last 150 years and is anticipated to continue to change over the twenty-first century and beyond. The IPCC declared that 'warming of the climate system is unequivocal' and the observed increase in global average temperatures since the mid-twentieth century 'very likely' the result of human activities that are increasing greenhouse gas (GHG) concentrations in the atmosphere (Solomon *et al.* 2007). The conclusions of the IPCC have been reinforced by more recent studies on the state of the global climate system (e.g. NOAA 2010).

The IPCC also emphasised that human-induced climate change has only just begun and that the pace of climate change is 'very likely' to accelerate with continued GHG emissions at or above current rates, with the best estimate that global mean surface temperatures will increase by 1.8°C to 4.0°C by the end of the twenty-first century (Solomon *et al.* 2007). Even if GHG emission reduction commitments currently made by nations are successfully achieved, global average temperature increases will exceed +2°C by 2100, and it is increasingly recommended that society should be preparing to adapt to a +4°C increase (Rogelj *et al.* 2009).

Climate change represents much more than just increased temperatures. The IPCC *AR4* indicated that anthropogenic climate change is now implicated in a myriad of coincident environmental impacts: perturbations in regional temperature regimes and precipitation patterns; severe weather events; sea level rises; changes in ecosystem structure and function; and the extinction of species.

Climate change and associated environmental impacts will increasingly affect the lifestyles, economies, health and social well-being of populations around the world throughout the twenty-first century and beyond. Indeed, the IPCC concluded with 'very high confidence' that climate change would impede the ability of many nations to achieve sustainable development by mid-century (Yohe *et al.* 2007). Although the consequences of climate change will vary on a regional basis, all nations and economic sectors will have to contend with the challenges that climate change poses to sustainability through adaptation and mitigation.

With its close connections to the environment and climate itself, tourism will be no exception. The selected media headlines in Figure 23.1 illustrate the varied climate sensitivities in tourism supply (tourism destinations and tourism operators) and demand (tourism arrivals and travel patterns) around the world. Climate, the natural environment, personal safety, travel costs and accessibility are primary factors in travel decisions and the success of tourism, and each is anticipated to be profoundly impacted by global climate change and climate policy.

Scholarship on tourism and climate change now extends over a period of 25 years, with the engagement of the tourism sector (international and national tourism government agencies, non-governmental organisations) in climate change developing over the past decade. The state of knowledge of the potential implication of climate change and climate policy for tourism progressed slowly at first. Although the first research publications on the impacts of climate change on tourism appeared in the mid-1980s, tourism was not mentioned in the *First Assessment Report* of the IPCC in 1990. Wall's (1998: 68) review of the place of tourism in the IPCC *Second Assessment Report* (1995) five years later concluded that, '[w]hile it is encouraging that tourism is receiving greater attention in IPCC reports, it is also apparent that the likely consequences of climate change for tourism and recreation are not well understood'. At the turn of the millennium, in their closing summary to the high profile *International Tourism and Hospitality in the 21st Century* conference, Butler and Jones (2001: 300) similarly concluded that although, '(Climate change) could have greater effect on tomorrows world and tourism and hospitality in particular than anything else we've discussed ... The most worrying aspect is that ... to all intents and purposes the tourism and hospitality industries ... seem intent on ignoring what could be the major problem of the century'.

The volume of research on climate change and tourism began to grow rapidly in the early 2000s, with publications doubling between 1995–99 and 2000–04 and again between 2000–04 and 2005–09 (Scott 2011). The first high-level involvement of the tourism sector also occurred at this time, with the World Tourism Organization (UNWTO), World Meteorological Organization (WMO), United Nations Environment Programme (UNEP), United Nations Educational, Scientific and Cultural Organization (UNESCO) organizing the First International Conference on Climate Change and Tourism in Djerba, Tunisia in 2003. This event was a

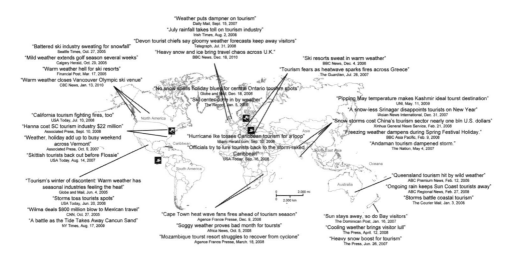

Figure 23.1 Recent media headlines of climate impacts on tourism

watershed in terms of developing awareness among government administrations, the tourism industry and other tourism stakeholders about the complex inter-linkages between the tourism sector and climate change and the need to collaborate with the international community in its respond. Building on the momentum created in Djerba, the UNWTO convened the Second International Conference on Climate Change and Tourism in Davos, Switzerland in 2007. The *Davos Declaration on Tourism and Climate Change* concluded that climate change ' … must be considered one of the greatest challenges to the sustainability of tourism in the 21st century' (UNWTO–UNEP–WMO 2008: 38). Two years later, leading up to the COP-15 conference in Copenhagen, Denmark, the World Travel and Tourism Council (2009) issued its first position paper on climate change, which specified 'aspirational' emissions reduction targets to cut carbon emissions 25–30 per cent by 2020 and 50 per cent by 2035 (from 2005 levels). These developments represented a very significant shift in the tourism sector's position on climate change in only five years.

This chapter is organised into four sections. The first provides a conceptual overview of the broad pathways by which climate change impacts will affect tourist decision-making and the competitiveness and sustainability of tourism businesses and destinations: (1) direct impacts of climatic change; (2) climate-induced environmental change; (3) climate-induced socio-economic change; and (4) climate change mitigation policy. Climate change mitigation is the focus of Chapter 22, therefore its implications for tourism demand and destinations will not be discussed here. Because the regional manifestations of climate change will generate both negative and positive impacts in the tourism sector and these impacts will vary substantially by market segment and geographic region, it is beyond the scope of this chapter to discuss the full range of potential climate change impacts on tourist decision-making and destinations. Readers are referred to recent synthesis works for a comprehensive summary of available scientific information on potential climate change impacts for destinations worldwide (Gössling and Hall 2006; Becken and Hay 2007; Scott *et al.* 2008, 2011). This section instead provides selected case studies (identified in Figure 23.1) to illustrate how climate change will affect the competitiveness and sustainability of major types of tourism destinations. The second section explores the comparative vulnerability of tourism regions, and the third examines the capacity of tourism stakeholders to adapt to climate change. Finally, the chapter concludes with consideration of how well prepared the tourism sector is for the risks and opportunities posed by climate change, including some thoughts on the needs for education and professional training.

The climate and tourism interface

The interface between climate and tourism is multifaceted and highly complex. In order to understand how climate change could affect the future prospects of global tourism and the relative competitiveness of tourism destinations, it is important to recognise that all of the major components of the global tourism system (tourists, source markets, transport systems, destinations) will be affected by four distinct impact pathways identified in Figure 23.2: (1) direct climatic changes (e.g. length and quality of tourism seasons, operating costs, increased infrastructure damage and business interruptions); (2) indirect climate-induced environmental changes (e.g. water availability, biodiversity loss, altered landscape aesthetic, increased natural hazards, coastal erosion and inundation, increasing incidence of vector-borne diseases); (3) indirect climate-induced social-economic changes (e.g. social unrest, political instability, decreased economic growth and discretionary wealth, altered environmental attitudes); and (4) climate change mitigation policy (e.g. increase in transport costs, routing-hubs altered by modal shifts, decreased accessibility to some destinations) – which is discussed in Chapter 22.

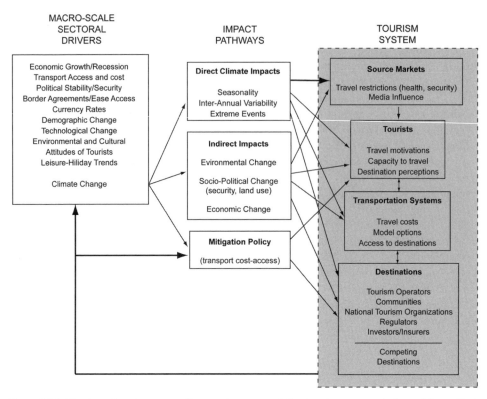

Figure 23.2 The interface between climate change and the tourism sector (adapted from Scott and Lemieux 2009)

Direct climate change impacts

For the tourism industry and tourists alike, climate represents both a resource to be exploited and an important constraint (Scott and Lemieux 2009). For tourism destinations and tourism operators, climate is a major determinant of tourism seasons as well as the patterns of demand. At the local scale, climate defines the length and quality of multibillion dollar tourism seasons (e.g. sun–sand–sea (3S) and ski holidays), whereas at the global scale, climate is a principal resource responsible for some of the largest international tourism flows (e.g. from Northern Europe to the Mediterranean and northern North America to the Gulf of Mexico and Caribbean). Climate directly affects many facets of tourism operations (e.g. water supply, heating and cooling costs, snowmaking requirements) that influence profitability, and is a central component of tourism marketing. Extreme events such as tropical cyclones, floods or extreme heat waves put tourism infrastructure at risk, cause major business disruptions, influence insurance and marketing costs, and are important deterrents to travel.

In addition to its salient supply-side influences, climate is also a central motivator for travel with seasonal patterns of domestic and international travel affected by climate conditions at both the point of origin and destinations. Climate and inter-annual climate variability have been found to influence destination choice and geographic patterns of travel (e.g. the relative proportion of domestic and international holidays and tourism expenditures). Weather conditions at destination have also been found to influence both tourism spending and holiday satisfaction.

With such strong influences of weather and climate, the implications of climatic change are anticipated to be far-reaching for some tourism segments and regions (Scott *et al.* 2011 for summary discussion). Changes in the length and quality of climate-dependent tourism seasons could have considerable implications for competitive relationships between destinations and therefore the profitability of tourism enterprises. Anticipated impacts include a gradual shift in climate resources suitable for tourism to destinations in higher latitudes and to higher elevations in mountainous areas during the summer months (Scott *et al.* 2004; Amelung *et al.* 2007). Tourists from temperate nations that currently represent major international tourism markets (e.g. central and northern Europe, northern USA, Japan and Canada) are projected to spend more holidays in their home country or nearby, adapting their travel patterns to take advantage of new climatic opportunities closer to home. As a result, the competitive position of some popular holiday areas is anticipated to decline (e.g. the Mediterranean in summer – see case study below), whereas other areas (e.g. southern England or southern Canada) are expected to improve (Hamilton *et al.* 2005; Berrittella *et al.* 2006; Bigano *et al.* 2006). This shift in travel patterns may have important implications, including proportionally more tourism spending in developed temperate climate nations and proportionally less spending in warmer nations (often developing countries) now frequented by tourists from temperate source markets.

Changes in the number and/or intensity of extreme weather events under climate change have important implications for tourism infrastructure damage, emergency preparedness requirements, higher operating expenses (e.g. insurance, backup water and power systems, and evacuations) and business interruptions. Yet, the affects of altered patterns of extreme events remain a crucial knowledge gap for the tourism sector.

Case study

Will the Mediterranean become 'too hot' for tourism?

The Mediterranean is the world's leading tourism destinations in terms of international arrivals. One of the principal reasons behind the popularity of the Mediterranean is demand for reliable sun, sand and sea tourism. With climate as one of the principal attractions of the Mediterranean region and projections that hotter and drier summer conditions will occur throughout most of the region in the decades ahead, with likely increases in the risk of heat waves, wildfires and drought, much speculation has occurred with regard to the implication for tourism.

A number of publications have surmised that climate change would push Mediterranean temperatures above the threshold for tourist comfort during the summer peak season, resulting in reduced arrivals during the summer months and perhaps overall (Maddison 2001; Perry 2006; Amelung and Viner 2006). Media stories have been far more bold, pronouncing that 'the likelihood [is] that Mediterranean summers may be too hot for tourists after 2020' (*The Guardian* – based on Amelung and Viner 2006), and 'by 2030, the traditional British package holiday to a Mediterranean beach resort may be consigned to the 'scrap-heap of history'' (BBC News – based on the Holiday 2030 report produced by Halifax Travel Insurance 2006). Although numerous media stories and travel writers have repeated this speculation, what is the scientific evidence for such statements?

Remarkably, studies that proclaim the Mediterranean will become too hot have never defined what is 'too hot' for tourists, nor sought to establish this climatic threshold with tourists.

Furthermore, the varied climate sensitivity of different tourism market segments (e.g. urban–cultural tourism versus 3S tourism) and the specific micro-climates of major destinations (e.g. urban heat islands, moderated coastal climate) were not considered. A more recent study utilising stated climate preferences of European tourists (Rutty and Scott 2010), found that the combined summer time average temperature and humidity of some Mediterranean urban (e.g. Athens and Istanbul) and beach destinations (e.g. Cyprus and Antalya) are already considered 'too hot' by the majority of respondents, but that even under the warmest climate change scenarios for the region, there is no evidence to support the contention that the Mediterranean region as a whole will become 'too hot' by the 2020s or 2030s. In fact, only those destinations that are already considered to be 'too hot' under existing summer conditions were projected to be 'too hot' in the next two decades. However, nine of 10 destinations examined were projected to become unacceptably hot by late century (2080s) under the warmest climate change scenario.

An important contrasting point is that at the same time there is a larger decrease in the number of months that are considered 'unacceptably cool' for both 3S and urban holidays and an increase in months that become 'ideal'. This is consistent with other studies that have projected that under climate change the months with suitable temperature conditions may shift to the Mediterranean's current shoulder seasons in spring and autumn (Maddison 2001; Bigano *et al.* 2006; Hamilton *et al.* 2005; Amelung and Viner 2006). Hence, overall visitation may not necessarily decline as a result of climate change, but rather see a shift in the timing of demand in the region by mid- to late century.

Other studies also suggest the assumption that higher temperatures in the Mediterranean region will result in a net loss of tourist arrivals needs further consideration. Moreno (2010) found that 72 per cent of survey respondents from the Netherlands and Belgium would still travel to the Mediterranean even if the 'ideal weather conditions' for beach tourism, as defined by the respondents, were to occur near their home in the future. This suggests the two destinations are not perfectly substitutable. This study also found that the potential influence of heat waves on Mediterranean holiday planning was ranked the lowest behind other potential climate change impacts, such as risk of disease, forest fires, water restrictions in hotel and reduced beach extension.

Additional research is needed to understand tourist perceptions and responses to the current climate variability and extremes, the importance of destination micro-climates, and relative importance of climate-induced environmental change on future travel patterns in Europe.

Indirect climate-induced environmental impacts

Many environmental resources that are critical attractions for tourism are sensitive to climate variability (e.g. biodiversity and wildlife abundance and migration patterns, water levels and water quality, snow conditions, glacial extent, coral reef bleaching) and extreme events (e.g. storm erosion of beach area). Climate also influences environmental conditions that can deter tourists, including infectious disease (e.g. malaria), wildfires, insect or water-borne pests (e.g. jellyfish and algae blooms).

The wide range of climate-induced environmental changes projected by the IPCC will have profound effects on tourism at the local and regional scale. Changes in water availability, biodiversity loss, reduced landscape aesthetic (e.g. glacial retreat, fire or disease-impacted forest landscape), altered agricultural production (e.g. wine tourism), increased natural hazards, coastal erosion and inundation, damage to infrastructure and the increasing incidence of vector-borne diseases will diminish the quality of the tourism product with implications for visitation and local economies. In contrast to the varied impacts of a changed climate on tourism, the indirect effects of climate-induced environmental change are anticipated to be largely negative and substantially greater under the warmest scenarios (see Gössling and Hall 2006; Becken and Hay 2007; Scott *et al.* 2008, 2011 for detailed discussions).

Paradoxically, these impacts of climate change have given rise to a new form of tourism, variously labelled, 'Last chance tourism', 'catastrophe tourism', 'doomsday tourism', 'extinction tourism' and 'disappearing destinations' (Eijgelaar *et al.* 2010; Lemelin *et al.* 2010). These terms have emerged in the popular press and more recently in the tourism industry and tourism studies to describe the phenomenon where destinations are identified or even market themselves as being at risk to climate change-induced environmental change or heritage losses. The attraction for tourists is to be among the *last* to view the attraction (a landscape, wildlife, heritage site or some combination thereof) before it has significantly degraded or disappeared.

Case study

Winter sports tourism and climate change

The winter sports tourism industry has been identified as highly vulnerable to global climate change by over 30 studies in more than 10 countries. This literature on the implications of climate change for the ski industry has consistently projected the following impacts to varying degrees: decreased reliability of natural snow cover, shortened and more variable ski seasons, increased snowmaking requirements and decreasing snowmaking opportunities, a contraction in the number of ski areas and decreased ski tourism demand.

A major limitation of many studies of the vulnerability of the ski tourism industry to climate change is that they not incorporate snowmaking; which is a common climate adaptation in many ski regions (see Scott *et al.* 2011 for a review). For example, the widely cited Organisation for Economic Co-operation and Development (2007) analysis that concluded the number of 'snow reliable' ski areas in the European Alps would decline from 609 under current climate conditions, to 404 under a +2°C warming scenario, and 202 under a +4°C warming scenario, did not account for snowmaking even though the report noted that over 50 per cent of skiable terrain in Austria, and somewhat lesser proportions in other nations currently utilise snowmaking. Consequently, this analysis does not reflect the current operating realities of many ski operators, let alone 25 years from now, when most ski area managers in the region plan to have enhanced snowmaking capabilities. In a survey of Austrian ski area managers, Wolfsegger *et al.* (2008) found that most ski area managers were highly aware of the risk posed by climate change, but also highly optimistic about their capacity to negate the impacts of future climate change. With further adaptation, primarily snowmaking, but including other business and technical options, 24 per cent believed that they could operate their businesses for another 30–45 years, and 44 per cent felt their businesses would be viable for at least another 75 years. When snowmaking was accounted for in studies in Eastern North America (Scott *et al.* 2003, 2007) and Austria (Steiger 2010) the vulnerability of ski areas was substantially lower than reported in earlier studies that did not include snowmaking. The performance of the ski industry during record warm winters, which serve as climate change analogue conditions, provide insight into the full range of supply- and demand-side adaptive responses (outlined in Figure 23.3) and also suggest that ski tourism has more adaptive capacity than some studies indicate (Scott 2005; Dawson *et al.* 2009; Steiger 2011). Incorporating a wider range of adaptations

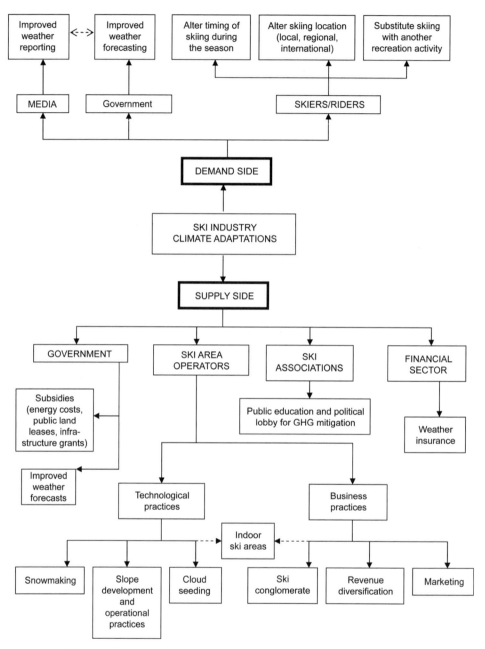

Figure 23.3 Climate change adaptation strategies in the ski industry (adapted from Scott and McBoyle 2007)

and evaluating their sustainability (e.g. snow production days, costs, water and energy usage) is essential for all future studies.

Fewer studies have examined the behavioural response of skier–tourists to marginal snow conditions or how the projected contraction in the number of ski areas might impact demand. A survey of Australian skiers (König 1998) found that 75 per cent would adapt their future skiing patterns if 'the next five winters would have very little natural snow'; 31 per cent would ski less often, 38 per cent would ski at another overseas location and 6 per cent would quit skiing altogether. A similar survey in Switzerland found that 70 per cent would adapt; 11 per cent would ski at the same location but less often, 28 per cent would ski at a more snow reliable resort at the same frequency, 21 per cent would ski at a higher resort less often and 4 per cent would give up skiing altogether (Behringer et al. 2000). A 2008 survey in Austria found that 68 per cent of ski tourists would give up their destination of choice for a destination with more reliable snow conditions, if several consecutive seasons were snow-deficient (Unbehaun et al. 2008). An additional 25 per cent stated that they would give up skiing altogether.

However, the observed impact of climate change analogue conditions (record warm winters) on ski tourism demand had been generally lower than these surveys suggest. In the record warm winter of 2001–02 in ski markets of Eastern Canada and the USA (a 2050s climate change analogue), Scott (2005) found that total skier visits declined between 7 and 11 per cent, but was concentrated in smaller, low-elevation ski areas. Steiger (2011) similarly found that the record warm winter of 2006–07 in the Tyrol region of the European Alps (Austria and Italy) reduced ski-lift transports by 11 per cent overall, but that the impact varied substantially with small-medium ski areas recording declines in lift ticket sales of -18 per cent to -39 per cent), whereas the largest ski areas and those at high elevation recorded sales increases (+1 per cent and +4 per cent respectively).

Case study

Sea level rise and coastal tourism in the Caribbean

Sea level rise (SLR) due to climate change is a serious and unidirectional global threat to coastal ecosystems and development, because even if GHG emissions were stabilised in the near future, sea levels would continue to rise for many centuries in response to a warmer atmosphere and oceans. The IPCC AR4 projected a global SLR of 18–59 cm by 2100 (Solomon et al. 2007), but these estimates have been criticised by a number of more recent studies as being very conservative because they do not account for the response of the Greenland and Antarctic ice sheets (Rahmstorf 2010). These more recent studies all project upper estimates of 1.4 m SLR or more by 2100, with central estimates typically exceeding 1 m.

Coastal tourism is thought to be the largest tourism market segment worldwide. The reliance on beach assets and the immediate proximity of much of coastal tourism infrastructure to the coast, make both highly vulnerable to inundation and erosion associated with SLR. Climate change research on coastal tourism is still in its very early stages. Recent works in the Caribbean have highlighted the response of tourists and tour operators to beach erosion (Uyarra et al. 2005; Buzinde et al. 2010) and assessed the vulnerability of coastal tourism infrastructure to SLR (Schleupner 2008). In the most wide-ranging study of the vulnerability of coastal tourism to SLR, it was found that infrastructure at 266 of 906 major tourism resorts in 19 Caribbean island nations were vulnerable to flooding by a 1 m SLR. A far greater proportion of these coastal resort properties (440 to 546) were projected to be vulnerable to coastal erosion anticipated to result from a 1 m SLR, with critical beach assets affected much earlier (Scott 2011). Such impacts would transform coastal tourism in the region, with implications for property values, insurance costs, destination competitiveness, marketing and wider issues of local social and economic well-being.

Similar assessments are required so that the considerable ongoing investment and future development plans for coastal tourism worldwide can begin to incorporate the long-term strategic implications of SLR. Adaptation to SLR through structural coastal protection has less potential for tourism developments because of the cost versus property value and because structural protection would result in loss of coastal tourism aesthetics (clear sight lines of beach and sea) and not prevent the 'drowning' of critical beach assets (both of which result in diminished tourism property values). Similarly, beach nourishment and other engineering interventions to restore beaches are considered temporary measures that will become less effective and more costly with increasing SLR.

Indirect climate-induced socio-economic impacts

The IPCC concluded with 'very high confidence' that climate change would impede the ability of many nations to achieve sustainable development by mid-century and become a security risk that would steadily intensify, particularly under greater warming scenarios (Yohe *et al.* 2007). *The Stern Review* (2006) on the *Economics of Climate Change* emphasised that the dangers of unabated climate change would be equivalent to at least 5 per cent of GDP each year and could be equivalent to 20 per cent of GDP or more when environmental factors (such as permafrost melting), the economic effects on human life and the environment, and approaches to modelling that take into account developing nations, are weighted appropriately.

Economic development is a central determinant of tourism. For example, as a result of the 2008–09 recession, international travel demand suffered a strong slowdown beginning in June 2008, with growth in international tourism arrivals worldwide falling to 2 per cent during the summer months (UNWTO 2009). This negative trend intensified during 2009, exacerbated in some countries due to the outbreak of the H1N1 influenza virus, resulting in a worldwide decline of 4 per cent in 2009 to 880 million international tourists arrivals, and an estimated 6 per cent decline in international tourism receipts (UNWTO 2009).

Although climatic change would most likely lead to a gradual shift in tourism demand toward destinations at higher latitudes and altitudes, the changes induced by climatic change are anticipated to be much smaller than those resulting from population and economic growth (Hamilton *et al.* 2005; Berrittella *et al.* 2006; Bigano *et al.* 2005).

UNWTO's Tourism 2020 Vision forecasts that international arrivals are expected to reach nearly 1.6 billion by the year 2020, with tremendous growth in China, India, Brazil and other developing countries. How climate change affects economic growth in these countries that are expected to become key tourism markets in the decades ahead will have critical implications for the future of global tourism. Moreover, climate change is considered a national and international security risk that will steadily intensify, particularly under greater warming scenarios (Barnett and Adger 2007). Climate change is argued to increasingly undermine human security by reducing access to, and the quality of, natural resources that are important to sustain livelihoods, which under certain circumstances may increase the risk of civil unrest and violent conflict (Barnett and Adger 2007; Smith and Vivekananda 2007). Climate change-associated security risks have been identified in a number of regions where tourism is highly important to local/national economies. For example, the consequences of climate change include a high risk of armed conflict in 46 countries with a total population of 2.7 billion people (e.g. India, Peru, Indonesia), and a high risk of political instability in a further 56 countries with a total population of 1.2 billion (e.g. Mexico, Brazil, Cuba, Jamaica) (Smith and Vivekananda 2007).

Contemporary evidence of tourism indicators following terrorism or the outbreak of war or social unrest illustrate very clearly that international tourists are averse to political instability

(Hall *et al.* 2004). As the World Business Council for Sustainable Development reminds us, 'business cannot succeed where societies fail'. Although the negative repercussions for tourism demand to countries that become climate change security hotspots is very obvious, no study has yet examined the economic consequences for these nations.

Comparative vulnerability of tourism regions

The integrated effects of the major types of climate change impacts identified in the previous section will generate both negative and positive impacts in the tourism sector and these impacts will vary substantially by market segment and geographic region. Because the implications of climate change for any tourism business or destination will also partially depend on the impacts on its competitors, a negative impact in one part of the tourism system may constitute an opportunity elsewhere. Consequently, there will be climate change 'winners and losers' at the business, destination and nation level (Scott *et al.* 2008).

A number of summary assessments have been done to identify the most vulnerable tourism regions worldwide, and these are compared in Table 23.1. Although our understanding of the impacts of climate change for various destination types has continued to improve over the last 5–7 years, both Scott *et al.* (2008) and Hall (2008) emphasise that there remain major regional gaps in our knowledge of how climate change will affect the natural and cultural resources critical for tourism in Africa, the Caribbean, South America, the Middle East and large parts of East Asia. Until systematic regional level assessments are conducted, a definitive statement on the net impacts of climate change on the tourism sector will not be possible.

(1) Impact criteria considered: climatic changes, regulatory burdens, substitution effects, adaptation possibilities. Data sources and indicators for these criteria were not identified.
(2) Many nations in the Middle East and Africa were 'not examined'; however, no rationale was provided regarding availability of information for selected nations.
(3) Impact criteria considered: land and marine biodiversity loss, urbanisation, water security, sea level rise, regime change, fuel costs, temperature changes, disease potential.
(4) Impact criteria considered: change in annual average temperature.

Table 23.1 Climate change vulnerability of tourism regions

Study	Timeframe Assessed	Vulnerability Categories	Most Vulnerable Regions
Deutsche Bank Research 2008	2030	Negatively Affected (slightly or strongly) (a)	South America, Caribbean/Mexico, Southeast Asia (including China and India), Middle East, Africa (b)
Gössling and Hall 2006, Hall 2008	Mid-21st century	Moderately to Strongly Negatively Impacted (c)	Africa, Asia, Latin America, Small Island Nations
Hamilton *et al.* 2005	2025, +4°C warming scenario	Negative Impact on Tourist Arrivals (d)	Caribbean/Mexico, South America (except Chile), Africa (except Zambia and Zimbabwe), Middle East, Southeast Asia (except China)
Scott *et al.* 2008	Mid-21st century	Vulnerability Hotspots (e)	Caribbean, Indian and Pacific Ocean Small Island Nations (f)

(5) Impact criteria considered: summer and winter climatic change, increases in extreme events, seal level rise, land and marine biodiversity loss, water scarcity, political destabilisation, health impacts/disease potential, transportation costs and relative importance of tourism to the economy.

(6) South America, Africa, Middle East, Southeast Asia were identified as potentially vulnerable, but not listed as 'hotspots' due to insufficient information on magnitude of potential impacts.

Climate change adaptation in the tourism sector

Accumulating evidence indicates that climate change, particularly high emission GHG scenarios, could transform key aspects of the global tourism sector (Scott *et al.* 2011). Adaptation to the integrated affects of climate change will be fundamental to the development of sustainable tourism systems in the decades ahead. Adaptation is defined by the IPCC as: adjustment in natural or human systems in response to actual or expected climate stimuli and their effects, which moderates harm or exploits beneficial opportunities.

Adaptation in the tourism sector can be pursued by tourists, tourism operators, tourism-dependent communities (destinations), national and international tourism organisations (government or industry), government agencies involved in tourism, tourism-focused NGOs, international development organisations and the financial sector (investors and insurers). As Figure 23.4 indicates, the adaptive capacity of tourism sector stakeholders varies substantially.

Tourists have the greatest capacity to adapt to the impacts of climate change, with freedom to avoid destinations impacted by climate change. It is the response of tourists to the complexity of destination impacts that will reshape consumer demand patterns and play a pivotal role in the eventual impacts on destinations. The perceptions of future climate, environmental or security conditions will influence destination image and will be central to the decision-making of tourists (Gössling and Hall 2006). Perceptions of climate change impacts in a region will be heavily influenced by the nature of media coverage. It is therefore critical to avoid the type of media speculation and misinformation that has occurred in the past, as it is likely to be more damaging to a tourism destination in the near-term than the actual impacts of climate change (Scott *et al.* 2008).

Climate change is slowly entering into decision-making of a range of tourism stakeholders. Studies that have examined the climate change risk appraisal of local tourism officials and operators have consistently found awareness of climate change, relatively low perceptions of risk and little evidence of long-term strategic planning in anticipation of future changes in climate (Scott *et al.* 2008). The tourism industry is very image-sensitive and is therefore very cautious about even acknowledging concerns about climate change risks for fear of adversely affecting their reputation as a destination or as a sustainable business. Consequently, we should not expect to hear much about climate change adaptation from tourism businesses, except where it may help portray a 'green' image for the company (Scott 2011). Where tourism companies see

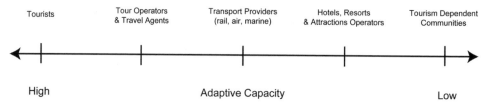

Figure 23.4 Relative adaptive capacity of the tourism sub-sectors

risk to their business or properties, they will not broadcast this vulnerability to guests, investors or insurers, but rather quietly adapt or divest high-risk assets. Similarly, where a company sees competitive advantage, they again will not broadcast this to competitors but use this insight like any other strategic business information to improve their position in the marketplace. Accordingly, climate change adaptation by private and public sector tourism-recreation operators is likely to remain reactive and consist mainly of incremental adjustments of existing climate adaptations (Scott and Becken 2010).

At the enterprise level, investments in climate change adaptation will primarily focus on preserving the sustainability of the tourism business. Government legislation (both existing and forthcoming) will strongly influence enterprise and community-level adaptation decisions, so that they are not divorced from broader sustainability considerations and maladaptation is avoided (Scott and Becken 2010). The influence of adaptation strategies by government and other economic sectors (particularly transportation and financial services – insurance and investors) will have important implications for adaptation by tourism operator, but these multisector interactions have not been explored for tourism (Scott 2011).

Destination communities possess the least adaptive capacity of major tourism stakeholders (Figure 23.3), because their economy can be greatly affected by the adaptation of other tourism stakeholders (e.g. the decision of tour operators to direct tourists to other destinations less affected by climate change or the decision of tourism operators or governments not to rebuild damaged or protect threatened tourism infrastructure) and the immobility of high-capital infrastructure. Adaptation will pose particular challenges in developing nations, which have lower adaptive capacity (Yohe *et al.* 2007), yet will have to undertake adaptations that will maintain environmental conditions and infrastructure to a sufficiently high quality to still attract international tourists (mainly from developed nations and with high expectations). The information requirements, policy changes and investments that are required for effective adaptation by tourism destinations will require decades in some cases, and therefore the process of adaptation needs to commence in the very near future for destinations anticipated to be among those impacted by mid-century (Scott *et al.* 2008).

Importantly, all major tourism businesses and destinations, regardless of whether they are potential 'winners' or 'losers' from climate change, will need to adapt to climate change. As the case studies in this chapter all illustrate, even for vulnerable tourism segments in vulnerable locations, it is not the entire tourism marketplace that is at risk, but specific tourism enterprises and destination communities. In a scenario where a proportion of competitors are eliminated by climate change and interactions with other business factors, and this competition is not immediately replaced in equal numbers (due to limited availability of suitable properties or other business conditions, such as insurability) and assuming tourism demand remains relatively stable or continues to grow as it is projected to by the UNWTO, those destinations and operators that remain viable will benefit from greater market share. Consequently, some destination communities will need to adapt to the loss of tourism jobs and income or develop alternate attractions and rebrand themselves. The destinations that are less vulnerable or can benefit from new opportunities arising from climate change will also need to adapt, but for different reasons (including congestion, development pressures, real estate speculation, resource conflicts).

The ability to implement adaptation measures in the tourism sector is a function of the capabilities, resources and institutions of this wide range of tourism stakeholders. Positively, based on the ability of the tourism sector as a whole to cope with a range of recent external shocks, including SARS and bird-flu pandemics, terrorism attacks, hurricane Katrina, or the Asian tsunami, it is thought to possess relatively high adaptive capacity (Scott *et al.* 2008).

Conclusion: how well is the tourism sector prepared for climate change?

The significance of climate change to tourism is not solely in some distant and remote future. Climate change is already affecting decision-making in the tourism sector and it will remain a pivotal issue affecting the medium- and long-term future of tourism development and management (Scott *et al.* 2008). Consequently, the *Davos Declaration on Tourism and Climate Change* urged a collective, expeditious and determined response by the tourism sector in four key directions (UNWTO–UNEP–WMO 2008):

- mitigate GHG emissions from the sector, derived especially from transport and accommodation activities;
- adapt tourism businesses and destinations to changing climate conditions;
- apply existing and new technologies to improve energy efficiency; and
- secure financial resources to assist regions and countries in need.

Despite visibly increased engagement of the tourism sector in the latter half of the 2000s, including the *Davos Declaration on Tourism and Climate Change* and WTTC's (2009) 'aspirational' CO_2 emission reduction targets for the sector, a critical question is how far has climate change discourse, and more importantly action, really penetrated the tourism sector? One answer comes from the business community itself. KPMG's (2008) assessment of the regulatory, physical, reputational and litigation risks posed to 18 major global economic sectors versus the level of preparedness, found tourism and aviation to be two of the six sectors in the 'danger zone'. Can tourism afford to continue to be one of the least prepared major global economic sectors? The task ahead for the tourism community to develop and implement a strategic response to climate change remains enormous and cannot be underestimated.

References

Amelung, B. and Viner, D. (2006) 'Mediterranean tourism: Exploring the future with the tourism climate index', *Journal of Sustainable Tourism* 14(4), 349–66.

Amelung, B., Nicholls, S. and Viner, D. (2007) 'Implications of Global Climate Change for Tourism Flows and Seasonality', *Journal of Travel Research* 45(3), 285–96.

Barnett, J. and Adger, W.N. (2007) 'Climate change, human security and violent conflict', *Political Geography* 26(6), 639–55.

Becken, S. and Hay, J. (2007) *Tourism and Climate Change – Risks and Opportunities.* Cleveland, OH: Channel View Publications.

Behringer, J., Bürki, R. and Fuhrer, J. (2000) 'Participatory integrated assessment of adaptation to climate change in alpine tourism and mountain agriculture', *Integrated Assessment* 1, 331–8.

Berrittella, M., Bigano, A., Roson, R. and Tol, R.S.J. (2006) 'A General Equilibrium Analysis of Climate Change Impacts on Tourism', *Tourism Management* 27, 913–24.

Bigano, A., Hamilton, J.M and Tol, R.S.J. (2006) 'The impact of climate on holiday destination choice', *Climatic Change* 76, 389–406.

Butler, R., Jones, P. (2001) 'Conclusions-problems, challenges and solutions', in A. Lockwood and S. Medlik (eds) *Tourism and hospitality in the 21st century.* Oxford: Butterworth-Heinemann, 296–309.

Buzinde, C.N., Manuel-Navarret, D., Yoo, E.E. and Morais, D. (2010) 'Tourists' perceptions in a climate of change: Eroding destinations', *Annals of Tourism Research* 37(2), 333–54.

Dawson, J., Scott, D. and McBoyle, G. (2009) 'Analogue Analysis of Climate Change Vulnerability in the US Northeast Ski Tourism', *Climate Research* 39(1), 1–9.

Eijgelaar, E., Thaper, C. and Peeters, P. (2010) 'Antarctic cruise tourism: the paradoxes of ambassadorship, 'last chance tourism' and greenhouse gas emissions', *Journal of Sustainable Tourism* 18, 337–54.

Gössling, S. and Hall, C. M. (2006) 'An Introduction to Tourism and Global Environmental Change', in S. Gössling and C.M. Hall (eds) *Tourism and Global Environmental Change.* London: Routledge, 1–34.

Halifax Travel Insurance. (2006) *Holiday 2030*. Available at www.hbosplc.com/media/pressreleases/articles /halifax/2006-09-01-05.asp?section=Halifax.

Hall, C.M. (2008) 'Tourism and climate change: Knowledge gaps and issues', *Tourism Recreation Research* 33, 339–50.

Hall, C.M., Timoth, D.J. and Duval, D.T. (2004) 'Security and Tourism: Towards a New Understanding?', *Journal of Travel and Tourism Marketing* 15(2/3), 1–18.

Hamilton, J.M., Maddison, D. and Tol, R.S. (2005) 'Effects of climate change on international tourism', *Climate Research* 29, 245–54.

KPMG. (2008) *Climate Changes Your Business*. Available at www.kpmg.nl/sustainability.

König, U. (1998) *Tourism in a warmer world: implications of climate change due to enhanced greenhouse effect for the ski industry in the Australian Alps*, Zurich: University of Zurich.

Lemelin, H., Dawson, J., Stewart, E.J., Maher, P. and Luck, M. (2010) 'Last chance tourism: the doom, the gloom, and the boom of visiting vanishing destinations', *Current Issues in Tourism* 13(5), 477–93.

Maddison, D. (2001) 'In search of warmer climates? The impact of climate change on flows of British tourists', *Climatic Change* 49(1/2), 193–208.

Moreno, A. (2010) *Climate change and tourism: impacts and vulnerability in coastal Europe*, PhD Dissertation, University of Maastricht, the Netherlands.

National Oceanic and Atmospheric Administration (NOAA) (2010) *2009 state of the climate report*, Washington, DC: Government of USA. Available at www.noaanews.noaa.gov/stories2010/20100728 stateoftheclimate.html.

Organisation for Economic Co-operation and Development. (2007) 'Climate Change Impacts and Adaptation in Winter Tourism', *Climate Change in the European Alps: Adapting Winter Tourism and Natural Hazards Management*. Paris: Organisation for Economic Co-operation and Development, 25–60.

Perry, A.H. (2006) 'Will Predicted Climate Change Compromise the Sustainability of Mediterranean Tourism?', *Journal of Sustainable Tourism* 14(4), 367–75.

Rahmstorf, S. (2010) 'A new view on sea level rise', *Nature Reports Climate Change,* doi:10.1038/climate.2010.29.

Rogelj, J., Hare, B., Nabel, J., Macey, K., Schaeffer, M., Markmann, K. and Meinshausen, M. (2009) 'Halfway to Copenhagen, no way to 2°C', *Nature Reports Climate Change* (0907), 81–3.

Rutty, M. and Scott, D. (2010) 'Will the Mediterranean become 'too hot' for tourism?: A reassessment', *Journal of Tourism Hospitality and Planning Development* 7(3), 267–81.

Schleupner, C. (2008) 'Evaluation of coastal squeeze and its consequences for the Caribbean island Martinique', *Ocean and Coastal Management* 51, 383–90.

Scott, D. (2005) 'Global environmental change and mountain tourism', in S. Gössling and C.M. Hall (eds) *Tourism and global environmental change: ecological, social, economic and political interrelationships*. London: Routledge, pp. 54–75.

Scott, D. (2011) 'Why Sustainable Tourism Must Address Climate Change', *Journal of Sustainable Tourism* 19(1), 17–34.

Scott, D., Becken, S. (2010) 'Adapting to climate change and climate policy: Progress, problems and potentials', *Journal of Sustainable Tourism* 18(3), 283–95.

Scott, D. and Lemieux, C.J. (2009) *Weather and Climate Information for Tourism*. Commissioned White Paper for the World Climate Conference 3, Geneva and Madrid: World Meteorological Organization and United Nations World Tourism Organization.

Scott, D. and McBoyle, G. (2007) 'Climate change adaptation in the ski industry', *Mitigation and Adaptation Strategies to Global Change* 12(8), 1411–31.

Scott, D., Amelung, B., Becken, S., Ceron, J.-P., Dubois, G., Gössling, S., Peeters, P. and Simpson, M. (2008) *Technical Report in Climate Change and Tourism: Responding to Global Challenges*, Madrid: United Nations World Tourism Organization; Paris: United Nations Environment Program; Geneva: World Meteorological Organization, 25–256.

Scott, D., Gössling, S. and Hall, C.M. (2011) *Climate Change and Tourism: Impacts, Adaptation and Mitigation*. London: Routledge.

Scott, D., McBoyle, G. and Mills, B. (2003) 'Climate change and the skiing industry in southern Ontario (Canada): exploring the importance of snowmaking as a technical adaptation', *Climate Research* 23, 171–81.

Scott, D., McBoyle, G. and Schwartzentruber, M. (2004) 'Climate change and the distribution of climatic resources for tourism in North America', *Climate Research* 27(2), 105–17.

Scott, D., McBoyle, G. and Minogue, A. (2007) 'The implications of climate change for the Québec ski industry', *Global Environmental Change* 17, 181–90.

255

Smith, D. and Vivekananda, J. (2007) *A Climate of Conflict.* London: International Alert, 1–48.

Solomon, S., Qin, D., Manning, M., Chen, Z., Marquis, M., Averyt, K.B., Tignor, M. and Miller, H.L. (eds) (2007) *Climate Change 2007: The Physical Science Basis. Contribution of Working Group I to the Fourth Assessment Report of the Intergovernmental Panel on Climate Change.* Cambridge and New York: Cambridge University Press.

Steiger, R. (2010) 'The impact of climate change on ski season length and snowmaking requirements in Tyrol, Austria', *Climate Research* 43(3), 251–62.

——(2011) 'The impact of snow scarcity on ski tourism. An analysis of the record warm season 2006/07 in Tyrol (Austria),' *Tourism Review* 66(3), 4–13.

Stern, N. (2006) *The Economics of Climate Change: The Stern Review.* Cambridge: Cambridge University Press.

Unbehaun, W., Probstl, U., Haider, W. (2008) 'Trends in winter sports tourism: challenges for the future', *Tourism Review* 63(1), 36–47.

United Nations World Tourism Organization, United Nations Environment Programme, World Meteorological Organization. (2008) *Climate Change and Tourism: Responding to Global Challenges,* Madrid: United Nations World Tourism Organization; Paris: United Nations Environment Program; Geneva: World Meteorological Organization.

United Nations World Tourism Organization (UNWTO). (2008) *World Tourism Barometer June 2009.* World Tourism Organization. Available at http://unwto.org/facts/eng/pdf/barometer/UNWTO_Barom09_2_en_excerpt.pdf.

Uyarra, M.C., Cote, I.M., Gill, J.A., Tinch, R.R.T., Viner, D. and Watkinson, A.R. (2005) 'Island-specific preferences of tourists for environmental features: implications of climate change for tourism-dependent states', *Environmental Conservation* 32(1), 11–19.

Wall, G. (1998) 'Climate change, tourism and the IPCC', *Tourism Recreation Review* 23(2), 65–8.

Wolfsegger, C., Gössling, S. and Scott, D. (2008) 'Climate Change Risk Appraisal in the Austrian Ski Industry', *Tourism Review International* 12(1), 13–23.

World Travel and Tourism Council. (2009) *Leading the challenge,* Available at www.wttc.org/bin/pdf/

Yohe, G.W., Lasco, R.D., Ahmad, Q.K., Arnell, N.W., Cohen, N.W., Hope, C., Janetos, A.C. and Perez, R.T. (2007) 'Perspectives on Climate Change and Sustainability', in M.L. Parry *et al.* (eds) *Climate Change 2007: Impacts, Adaptation and Vulnerability. Contribution of Working Group II to the Fourth Assessment Report of the IPCC.* Cambridge and New York: Cambridge University Press, 811–41.

Further reading

Gössling, S. (2010) *Carbon Management in Tourism: Mitigating the Impacts on Climate Change.* London: Routledge. (The first book devoted to carbon emission reductions and to showcase a wide range of practical mitigation options from the enterprise to sector scale.)

Gössling, S. and Hall, C. M. (2006) *Tourism and Global Environmental Change.* London: Routledge. (An early synthesis of the implications of climate change for tourism, with useful discussions for each major type of tourism environment (e.g. mountains, coasts, cities) and adaptive responses within the sector.)

Scott, D. (2011) 'Why Sustainable Tourism Must Address Climate Change,' *Journal of Sustainable Tourism* 19(1), 17–34. (Discussion of the place of climate change within sustainable tourism research and practice.)

Scott, D. and Lemieux, C. (2010) 'Weather and climate information for tourism,' *Proceedia Environmental Sciences* 1, 146–83. (A comprehensive overview of weather and climate information for the tourism sector. Commissioned by the World Meteorological Organization and World Tourism Organization.)

Scott, D., Amelung, B., Becken, S., Ceron, J.-P., Dubois, G., Gössling, S., Peeters, P., Simpson, M. (2008) *Technical Report in Climate Change and Tourism: Responding to Global Challenges.* Madrid: United Nations World Tourism Organization; Paris: United Nations Environment Program; Geneva: World Meteorological Organization, 25–256. (A comprehensive overview of the state of climate change and tourism knowledge and practice and served as the scientific foundation for the Davos Declaration of Tourism and Climate Change.)

Scott, D., de Freitas, C., Matzarakis, A. (2009) 'Adaptation in the Tourism and Recreation Sector,' in K. Ebi, I. Burton, and G. McGregor (eds) *Biometeorology for Adaptation to Climate Variability and Change,* 171–94. (A useful review on climate change adaptation in tourism and recreation.)

Scott, D., Gössling, S. and Hall, C.M. (2011) *Climate Change and Tourism: Impacts, Adaptation and Mitigation.* London: Routledge. (The most comprehensive overview of the field of climate change and tourism, including all aspects of research and policy. Provides a detailed chronology of the development of climate change research and policy, a critical review of each major area of research within the field and key knowledge gaps, discusses links between climate change and the future of tourism as international development mechanism.)

United Nations World Tourism Organization, United Nations Environment Programme and World Meteorological Organization (2008) *Climate Change and Tourism: Responding to Global Challenges.* Madrid: United Nations World Tourism Organization; Paris: United Nations Environment Program; Geneva: World Meteorological Organization. (Provides an overview of the positions of three UN agencies engaged in climate change and tourism initiatives and the full text of *Davos Declaration on Tourism and Climate Change.*)

Weaver, D. (2011) 'Can sustainable tourism survive climate change?' *Journal of Sustainable Tourism* 19(1), 5–15.

World Travel and Tourism Council. (2009). *Leading the challenge*. London: World Travel and Tourism Council. (Sets out the tourism industry position on climate change and a vision for greenhouse has emission reduction within the tourism sector.)

24

Demand management for the sustainability of tourism

Patrizia Modica

Introduction

This chapter explores how specific management practices can reduce the negative effects of tourism seasonality, which affect a number of destinations around the world. The phenomenon of seasonality creates high seasons accompanied with the arrival of masses of people in a determined time and space, and low seasons characterised by a limited number or lack of tourists. Both of these opposing situations – the excessive presence of tourists and a tendency towards an absence of tourist flows – can be highly significant for host countries, as regards environmental, economical and social consequences.

The management of tourist demand can play an important role in the sustainability of tourism at a destination level. Demand management is part of the wider system of revenue management or yield management. This system is regarded as a strategic approach in maximising revenues and profits, thus improving tourism industry performance.

Demand management applied to hospitality industries can encourage a balanced distribution of tourists throughout opening periods and additionally make the tourism season longer. Negative impacts produced by the irregular arrivals of visitors may also be reduced. There is also an opportunity to generate profits for tourism businesses and to identify how revenue management practices can be advantageous for the sustainability of tourism destinations.

Seasonality and tourism development

Seasonality is a characteristic of tourism in a variety of destinations and is defined, in the context of this study, as 'the tendency of tourist flows to become concentrated into relatively short periods of the year' (Allcock 1989: 387). Seasonality is a problematic issue of tourism worldwide and frequently persistent. In fact, natural causes, associated with the climatic characteristics of a territory, and institutionalised and social causes, associated with established behaviour in the pattern of tourism consumption, generate this phenomenon and contribute to its maintenance (Frechtling 2001). In the coastal regions of the Mediterranean, where tourism is frequently based around natural resources such as the sun and the sea, tourist flows are generally concentrated in the high season (summer). In the summer months (June, July, August and September), the number of arrivals increases rapidly. In the winter, arrivals decrease significantly until they are almost totally absent. In these areas the number of inhabitants of seaside destinations can multiply enormously in a short time in summer, with peak and off-peak periods during the year easily distinguishable. Tourism supply, local government and residents can all suffer from the negative effects caused by this seasonality and the significant fluctuation of tourist arrivals during the year. Tourism literature identifies three different sets of impacts: economic, environmental and socio-cultural (Andereck *et al.* 2005). Typical issues that characterise a seasonal model of tourism development include problems with public services, such as water scarcity and traffic congestion, a general condition of stress for residents, biodiversity modification and pollution, limited temporary employment and incomes, and the inefficient use of the capacity of hospitality industries.

Limiting seasonality and its negative effects implies a contribution to the development of a form of tourism consistent with the World Tourism Organization (WTO) principles for sustainable tourism development (WTO 2004). In other words, limiting seasonality means mitigating the obstacles to sustainable tourism development in a destination.

According to the WTO (2004), in order to avoid the negative effects of tourism activities, destinations should undertake a policy of sustainable tourism, using preventive or corrective measures. Literature and international tourism organisations suggest the use of public instruments to promote sustainable tourism, for example ecotaxes, user fees, zoning, quotas and ecoincentives (Eagles *et al.* 2002; Panayotou 1994). Literature and international, national and often sub-national organisations for the standardisation of environmental management systems also recommend voluntary managerial instruments for the sustainable management of organizations, for example ecolabels for managing processes and activities promoting environmental conservation. Codes of conduct and green branding are other examples of environmental management of tourist destinations (Font 2001; Holden 2008).

Literature also suggests strategies to reduce the effects of seasonality, including the variety of alternative services offered, niche products, the diversification of markets through price differentiation and the organisation of special events during the off-peak period (Commons and Page 2001; Goulding *et al.* 2004; Jang 2004).

In this study the effect of price differentiation on tourist demand is analysed, with specific reference to the strategies utilised in the hotel industry. It is known that in order to attract tourists in the off-peak period tourism enterprises offer their services at a lower price. In this way they can attract price-sensitive people who are more disposed to travel at unconventional times of the year. In this sense, the discrimination of price is a good strategic lever in order to reduce seasonality through the attraction of potential demand and the moving of tourists from high to low season. However, this strategy has two limits. First, some destinations are less attractive in the off-peak period, because of unappealing weather or the unavailability of services and attractions, with many people unwilling to visit at less popular times, despite the advantageous price. This is the case in the coastal Mediterranean area, where the climate makes extending the tourism season to the whole year more difficult. In similar circumstances tourism operators can expect to lengthen the opening period to 7/8 months, which can be considered a good result through the use of the lever of price.

Second, price differentiation does not always produce profitability in the tourism industry (Butler 2001). The unfounded price cut frequently reduces the net gain of destinations. Nevertheless, the opportune management of this strategic lever can maintain and increase profitability in the hospitality industry. The right price for appropriate services offered to different market segments is the core of the revenue management system.

Revenue management practices for sustainable tourism

Revenue management is considered a key managerial tool in the tourism sector. Its use is particularly prevalent in airlines, hotels and car rental firms and, less frequently, in other tourism businesses. Revenue management is a strategic approach that optimises the use of capacity and price, based on consumer behaviour prediction, with the objective of maximising revenues and profitability (Phillips 2005). A set of strategic levers are adopted to improve, manage and control the flow of customer demand, including knowledge of clientele segments, time of reservation, appropriate use of inventory units and a change in prices over time (Kimes and Chase 1998).

Elasticity of demand towards price is the economics of revenue management (Edgar 2000), and demand-based pricing permits the expansion and management of customer segments. Customers with a low willingness to pay are allowed to purchase at discounted rates at off-peak times with peak periods cleared for those customers who can pay the highest rates. A good knowledge of customer demand is necessary for the success of a revenue management programme (Anderson and Carroll 2007).

Revenue management has been widely researched in hospitality literature. Many definitions demonstrate the relationship between this managerial tool and an increase in profits (Cross 1997; Donaghy et al. 1995). An extensive number of case studies have been developed related to the hospitality industry and the effectiveness of revenue management practices in terms of revenues, profits and performance (Yeoman and McMahon-Beattie 2004; Sfodera 2006).

This study focuses on a new frontier of the revenue management theory. The observation of demand management applied to the hotel industry suggests that the method is worth considering in the development of sustainable tourism strategies. The capacity of revenue management in influencing tourist demand is not only seen in the improvement of profitability in the tourism industry, but also in directing tourist demand over time (Modica et al. 2009) and benefiting destinations in terms of the economy, the environment and the community, which all encounter the typical problems seen in areas with high levels of seasonality. The use of revenue management in the hotel industry can be promoted as a good practice for the sustainability of tourism in destinations. The strategic levers on which revenue management is based – *price, capacity, time, customer* – have a direct impact on hotel performance and an indirect impact on sustainable tourism destinations.

The adoption of appropriate *pricing policies* can capture those customers who are price-sensitive and are disposed to use the hotel rooms in slow periods, during which the prices of other tourism services, like transportation and car rental, can be greatly reduced with a general advantage for tourists. The lack of efficiency in the occupation of hotel capacity diminishes while ensuring the maximum price for the supply of the rooms in the off-peak periods. An increase in hotel customers and rooms sold generates a vitality in the utilisation of hotel services and requires the presence of staff during these less popular visiting times. There is an immediate effect on hotel profitability and on the occupation of workers during these times. The state of occupation and income derived from tourism activities is a crucial indicator in sustainable tourism development. Literature and international organisations indicate tourism seasonality as a reason for seasonal employment, and use different indicators, as shown in Table 24.1, in order to measure its effects on employment and the economy in destinations (WTO 2004; Miller 2001; Choi and Sirakaya 2006). The adoption of demand-based pricing policies can positively affect these economic indicators.

An appropriate use of hotel *capacity* through the adoption of revenue management practices can spread the presence of tourists along time. The hotel can avoid losing demand in the peak period when hotel capacity tends to be entirely occupied, and accommodate those clients in

Table 24.1 Indicators of tourism seasonality in destinations

Economic	Environmental and socio-cultural
Number and percentage of tourist industry jobs which are permanent or full-year	Number of tourists per square metre of the site
Percentage of tourist industry jobs which are for less than 6 months	Percentage of tourist overnight stays in peak period
Local unemployment rate in off-season	Number of tourists per resident in the peak period
Percentage of business establishments open all year	m^2 of beach area per tourist
Occupancy rates for licensed accommodation by month	Trend of waste water and solid wastes outflow per month and the trend of the consumption of resources during the year
Percentage of total tourism revenues earned in the peak period	Tourist arrivals by month or quarter (distribution throughout the year)

Sources: WTO (2004); Choi and Sirakaya (2006); Hughes (2002); Logar (2010)

convenient alternative periods. The positive effects are on both hotel profitability and the environment. Some indicators are able to note the intensity of tourist density and the excessive use of destinations in the peak period (see Table 24.1). For example, the WTO indicates the number of tourists per square metre of the site, and literature indicates the number of tourists per resident in the peak period (Logar 2010). The tourists' choice of an alternative period could modify these indicators and destinations could register an improvement in the local environmental condition and social welfare.

The management of *time* includes the consideration of the moment in which services are reserved and the time of consumption. Leisure clients tend to ask for services months before their utilisation to gain the best price at their preferred period. The leisure segment has a remarkable sensitivity to price, which generally exceeds the sensitivity to time. This is a strategic aspect in managing the presence of tourists in hotels, restaurants, spas, beaches, museums and more generally in destinations. The technique of using discounted prices during slow periods can change the time of the utilisation of services. Tourism activities suffering from seasonality have a more equal distribution of visitors and an increase in revenues in unfrequented fractions of opening periods, when usually there is a large part of the capacity unsold. The pressure caused by the concentration of tourists in destinations becomes lower and the incidence on seasonality indicators decreases. Specifically different indicators (Hughes 2002), for example, the trend of waste water and solid wastes outflow and the trend of the consumption of resources like water and electricity during the year, could tend to register a better distribution of tourists. The difficulties linked with an enormous mass of people concentrated in the peak period could be reduced. Beaches could be less crowded, people could make use of public services more easily and the risk of damage to the natural environment could diminished.

As regards the *customer*, the demand for hotel services is prevalently expressed making reservations and less frequently as walk-in clients. This demand needs to be segmented and forecaste through the knowledge of historical data, market data, booking patterns, cancellations and no-shows. Hotel managers apply price discrimination to meet different market segments and their approach to purchase. The scientific application of demand-based pricing permits hotels to open or close rate classes, encouraging or discouraging demand depending on its characteristics. Knowledge and management of customer demand influence the purchasing decision-making process of tourists for tourism services. Directing part of the demand with sensitivity to price to off-peak periods guarantees revenues for the hotel industry and positive effects on economic, environmental and social indicators of tourism seasonality.

The objective of the hotel industry in applying revenue management systems is to achieve high levels of occupancy year round, meet customers' desired time, desired price and opportune service, with a maximisation of profits. Revenue management ensures positive effects in the short to medium term. The system, with the systematic application of its set of strategies, promises good performances in an ample perspective of time. Other important factors may affect the hospitality industry performance, including location, quality of services, innovation, online visibility and customer care, which all can contribute, together with an effective revenue management system, to long-term success and profitability, and, equally important, to the sustainability of tourism, favouring environmental conservation, stability of employment and incomes, and reduced social stress on the resident population.

Case study

In order to investigate the effectiveness of revenue management in the hospitality industry in reducing seasonality and better distributing tourism demand during opening periods, a case study approach was used. The case study also explored the possibility of promoting this method at a destination level in hospitality businesses.

The study was conducted in Villasimius, a well-known Italian destination on the southeastern coast of Sardinia. The destination is characterised by a strong seasonality during the summer months, especially July and August. Economic, environmental and socio-cultural negative impacts are perceived by the residents and the local administration. During the peak period, residents complain of traffic congestion, pollution, crowded beaches and problems with the use of public services, and the municipality faces a serious problem with the management of public services. Negative consequences additionally concern the occupational status of local people and the private incomes generated by tourism. In fact, both of these aspects of the local economy are significantly penalised by the seasonality of tourism demand. The local administration and the regional government have been attempting to limit the negative effects of this seasonality, specifically on the environment, through the creation of the Protected Coastal Area (PCA) in 1998, which achieved important accreditations, the adoption of user fees for services provided by the PCA, ecotaxes applied only in 2008 and ecoincentives provided to enterprises located in the PCA territory. Nevertheless, the excessive seasonality of tourist flows continues to be present and to play a negative role in the management of the destination.

Complementary private and voluntary management practices in the tourism industry can be of help in improving sustainability at this destination. The effects of revenue management on hotel demand and revenues were considered through the analysis of two different indicators: the occupancy rate and the revenue per person. The first is an indicator of efficiency and emphasises the level of occupation of the structure. The second is an indicator of profitability and emphasises the average income generated by clients.

Data utilised in the case study refer to a local four-star hotel. The hotel started to use revenue management in 2006 and data registered after the introduction of revenue management were analysed in the case study. Through the comparison year by year, it is clear that the occupancy rate improved following the application of revenue management. Moreover, as Table 24.2 shows, the increase is more relevant in the months of the off-peak period, for example in April and in

October, than in the peak period. This implies that revenue management is able to extend the opening period and to better distribute tourism demand during the year.

The revenue per person, calculated per month of the opening period, has the same trend. It rises at the same time that the occupancy rate increases. This means that the growth of the hotel occupation is not generated by a reduction of prices through an indiscriminate discounted policy, but it is produced by an appropriate definition of the price level for the different market segments and for each time of the year. For example, in April, a traditionally off-peak month, the occupancy rate increases from 21 per cent in 2006 to 45 per cent in 2010. This growth is not generated by a general discounting policy, which only aims to improve the level of occupation of the hotel rooms, but is associated with the growth of the revenue per person, as Table 24.3 shows. This means that through the revenue management system hotel managers can define the right price and are able to increase the occupancy rate without negatively impacting on the hotel's economic performances.

The case study highlighted that the use of the revenue management method in the hotel produced more revenues, more efficient management of hotel capacity and the opportunity to employ permanent workers.

The possibility of promoting revenue management in Villasimius was also investigated. The town mayor believes that it is important that the method can benefit the tourism industry in terms of profitability, which can influence stakeholders to consider its adoption. The director of the local PCA thinks that the institution of an organisation with the competences to co-ordinate and manage the application of the method at a destination level is necessary. Hotel managers all consider it vital to adequately inform hospitality operators about the potential of the revenue management system in benefiting the area, allowing its application in Villasimius to be implemented and amplified.

Table 24.2 Occupancy rate trend after the introduction of revenue management

	2006	2007	2008	2009	2010	2006–10
	OR (%)	OR (%)	OR (%)	OR (%)	OR (%)	Δ (%)
April	21	29	34	46	45	114
May	35	30	33	48	46	31
June	70	69	85	80	84	20
July	80	79	90	88	92	15
August	89	88	92	95	98	10
September	75	79	78	83	89	19
October	40	42	44	59	61	53

Table 24.3 Revenue per person rate of change

	2006–07	2007–08	2008–09	2009–10	2006–10
	Δ revPP (%)	Δ revPP (%)	Δ revPP (%)	Δ revPP (%)	Δ revPP (%)
April	17	13	1	0	34
May	8	4	1	1	15
June	11	-3	1	9	19
July	6	2	7	26	45
August	11	1	1	17	33
September	5	5	4	5	20
October	12	10	4	4	33

Conclusion

The study emphasises the potential of revenue management in reducing the negative effects of seasonality on the economy of destinations. In addition, the application of this method could also help mitigate the environmental and socio-cultural impacts of tourism activities on destinations.

A better distribution of tourist demand through a generalised application of revenue management in hospitality businesses could allow more stable employment and consequently incomes, and favour less dramatic pressure of tourism on the environment and residents during the peak periods. The distribution of tourist demand through the months of the year is an important condition for sustainable tourism development. Destinations should develop public and private practices to adopt forms of sustainable tourism. Revenue management can represent one of these practices and contribute to reduced seasonality.

In the case study, revenue management, observed in a hotel context, reveals its potential in stimulating tourism demand. The analysis of the trend of the hotel occupancy rate demonstrates that since the application of the managerial system the number of tourists increased significantly in April and October. This indicates that the hotel demand increases remarkably in the off-peak period, with people likely to be attracted by the discounting policy of the hotel. The trend of the revenues per person emphasises that in no case did the application of new tariffs penalise the profits of the hotel. In fact, the revenues per person augmented year on year.

As the case study demonstrates, the management of demand can attract tourists in slow periods and more evenly distribute the flow of tourist arrivals. The direct consequence is a reduction of the anthropic pressure on destinations in the high season and the lengthening of opening periods. The positive effects on the economy, the environment and the quality of life of residents can be combined with the important results obtained through the adoption of recognised sustainable practices. However, the utilisation of the method should be spread through the hospitality industry as a whole. There is, therefore, a need for public and private stakeholders to join a co-ordinated action that stimulates and promotes the adoption of revenue management practices at a destination level.

References

Allcock, J.B. (1989) 'Seasonality', in Witt, S.F. and Moutinho, L. (eds), *Tourism Marketing and Management Handbook*. London: Prentice Hall, 387–92.

Andereck, K.L., Valentine, K.M., Knopf, R.C. and Vogt, C.A. (2005) 'Residents' perception of community tourism impacts', *Annals of Tourism Research* 4, 1056–76.

Anderson, C.K. and Carroll, B. (2007) 'Demand management: beyond revenue management', *Journal of Revenue and Pricing Management*, 6 (4), 260–63.

Butler, R.W. (2001) 'Seasonality in tourism: issue and implications', in Baum, T. and Lundtorp, S. (eds), *Seasonality in tourism*. Amsterdam: Pergamon, 6–21.

Choi, H.C. and Sirakaya, E. (2006) 'Sustainability indicators for managing community tourism', *Tourism Management* 27, 1274–89.

Commons, J. and Page, S. (2001) 'Managing seasonality in peripheral tourism regions: the case of Northland, New Zealand', in Baum T. and Lundtrop S. (eds), *Seasonality in tourism*. Amsterdam: Pergamon, 153–72.

Cross, R.G. (1997) 'Launching the revenue rocket: how revenue management can work for your business', *Cornell Hotel and Restaurant Administration Quarterly* 38 (2), 32–43.

Donaghy, K., MacMahon, U. and McDowell, D. (1995) 'Yield management – an overview', *International Journal of Hospitality Management*, 14, 139–50.

Edgar, D. A. (2000) 'Economic theory of pricing for the hospitality and tourism industry', in Ingold A., McMahon-Beattie, U. and Yeoman, I., *Yield management*. London: Thomson, 15–31.

Eagles, P.F.J., McCool, S.F. and Haynes, C.D. (2002) *Sustainable tourism in protected areas: guidelines for planning and management*. Cambridge: IUCN

Font, X. (2002) 'Environmental certification in tourism and hospitality: progress, process and prospects', *Tourism Management*, 23, 197–205.

Frechtling, D.C. (2001) *Forecasting Tourism Demand: Methods and Strategies*. Oxford: Butterworth-Heinemann.

Goulding, P.J., Baum, T.G. and Morrison, A.J. (2004) 'Seasonal trading and lifestyle motivation: experiences of small tourism businesses in Scotland', *Journal of Quality Assurance in Hospitality & Tourism* 5 (2, 3, 4), 209–38.

Holden, A. (2008) *Environment and tourism*, 2nd edn. London: Routledge.

Hughes G. (2002) ' Environmental indicators', *Annals of Tourism Research* 29 (2), 457–77

Jang, S.S. (2004) 'Mitigating tourism seasonality', *Annals of Tourism Research* 31 (4), 819–36.

Kimes, S. E. and Chase, R. B. (1998) 'The strategic levers of yield management', *Journal of Service Research*, 1 (2), 156–66.

Logar, I. (2010) 'Sustainable tourism management in Crikvenica, Croatia: An assessment of policy instruments', *Tourism Management* 31, 125–35.

Miller, G. (2001) 'The development of indicators for sustainable tourism: Results of a Delphi survey of tourism researchers', *Tourism Management* 22, 351–62.

Modica, P., Landis, C. and Pavan, A. (2009) 'Yield management and coastal hospitality industry demand', *Tiltai. Bridges. Brücken* 3, 53–66.

Panayotou, T. (1994) 'Economic instruments for environmental management and sustainable development', UNEP/EEU: Environmental Economics Series Paper no. 16. Online. Available: http://conservationfinance.org/Documents/CF_related_papers/panyouto_econ_instru.pdf.

Phillips, R.L. (2005) *Pricing and revenue optimization*. Stanford, CA: Stanford University Press.

Sfodera, F. (ed.) (2006) *The spread of yield management practices*. Heidelberg: Phisica-Verlag.

Yeoman, I. and McMahon-Beattie, U. (eds) (2004) *Revenue Management and Pricing: Case Studies and Applications*. London: Thomson.

World Tourism Organization (2004) *Indicators of sustainable development for tourism destinations: A guidebook*. Madrid: World Tourism Organization.

Further reading

Blancas, F.J., Gonzàles, M., Lozano-Oyola, M. and Pèrez, F. (2010) 'The assessment of sustainable tourism: Application to Spanish coastal', *Ecological Indicators* 10, 484–92. (An application of indicator system to evaluate sustainability in established coastal tourism destinations.)

Chiang, W., Chen, J. and Xu, X. (2007) 'An overview of research on revenue management: current issues and future research', *International Journal of Revenue Management* 1, 97–128. (About literature on revenue management in the last decades.)

Fernandez-Morales, A. (2003) 'Decomposing seasonal concentration', *Annals of Tourism Research* 30, 4, 942–56. (A statistical analysis about seasonality in three Mediterranean destinations.)

Jain, S. and Bowman, H.B. (2005) 'Measuring the gain attributable to revenue management', *Journal of Revenue & Pricing Management* 4, 83–94. (A method for measuring the benefits of revenue management systems.)

Koenig, N. and Bischoff, E.E. (2004) 'Analyzing seasonality in welsh room occupancy data', *Annals of Tourism Research* 31, 2, 374–92. (An analysis of the relationship between seasonality, occupancy rate and hotel characteristics.)

Lim C.C. and Cooper, C. (2009) 'Beyond sustainability: optimising island tourism development', *International Journal of Tourism Research* 11, 89–103. (Sustainable development of tourism in the islands.)

Nadal, J.R., Font, A.R. and Rossellò, A.S. (2004) 'The economic determinants of seasonal patterns', *Annals of Tourism Research* 31 (3), 697–711. (An analysis of the relationship between some economic variables and seasonality of tourism demand.)

Nagle, T.T. and Hogan, J.E. (2006) *The strategy and tactics of pricing*. Upper Saddle River, NJ: Pearson Education. (About effective pricing strategy.)

25

Zoning, land-use planning and tourism

Peter Mason

Introduction

Zoning is a geographical approach to land-use planning and has been used by national, regional and local governments in most developed countries and a number of developing countries. The term comes from the practice of designating permitted uses of land, based on mapped zones that separate one set of land-uses from another. Land-use zoning traditionally has been use-based, in which the uses to which land may be put is regulated, or zoning may regulate for example, building height or building lot coverage, or some combination of these.

In the UK, land-use planning dates back at least 2,000 years, with Roman planning being the first detailed recorded form of what was largely urban-based planning in the UK. Modern planning in terms of specific, detailed legislation is linked to several Town and Country Planning Acts (Mason 2008). These appeared in the early part of the twentieth century with the Housing and Town Planning Act of 1919, the Town Planning Act of 1925 and the Town and Country Planning Act of 1932. Legislation focusing on UK rural areas as well as urban locations appeared in 1947 with the Town and Country Planning Act of that year, followed by more recent legislation and is currently consolidated in the 1990 Town and Country Planning Act.

In federal countries such as the USA, Canada and Australia, state governments usually exercise rights over private property and special laws and regulations restrict the places where particular activities can take place. The legal framework for land-use zoning in Australia is established by the various States and Territories, hence each State or Territory has different zoning rules and land-use zones are generally defined at local government level. Zoning in France and Germany is regulated at the national or federal level and in Germany the contents of a zoning plan will be backed up by the legal procedure to enforce it. In New Zealand the planning system that establishes zones is embedded within the Resource Management Act of 1991.

Being largely urban-focused, much planning in nineteenth-century UK, Europe, the USA and Australasia was concerned to alleviate perceived and real problems connected with housing, industry and transport. It was often intended within planning to separate these differing land-uses (Mason 2008), particularly in the light of issues such as disease, housing deprivation and traffic congestion.

Tourism planning has tended to be more geographically focused on the countryside and has not normally been perceived by planners as issue-, or problem-based. In fact, tourism planning has been regarded by planners as largely unproblematic (Hall 2008). Also, urban planners in many developed countries have concentrated on public sector issues such as housing, health and education and have not given much attention to tourism, which has been viewed traditionally as a private sector activity (Mason 2008).

However, one of the most commonly used forms of tourism-related zoning used in the developed world is that of the establishment of National Parks (Mason 2008). Such areas are most frequently those that are regarded as having high landscape value, important natural heritage, significant cultural value or are in need of preservation because of, for example, certain rare or unusual animal or plant species.

In many parts of the world the development of human usage of the environment has taken place over a long period of time. In terms of zoning, this results in significant problems as it is almost impossible to establish zones that are exclusively of one use only. Instead zones are likely to have a number of different uses, but will tend to have one major, or a predominant, use. One of the few areas of the world where separate zones can be easily established is Antarctica. The continent is not owned by any one country and is managed by a unique system, known as the Antarctic Treaty System (ATS) in which all countries with a stake in Antarctica play a role (Stonehouse and Snyder 2010). Under the ATS, a number of activities including mining and most commercial land-uses are not allowed (Mason and Legg 1999) and there is little evidence of past human activity except the huts of explorers such as Scott, Mawson and Shackleton. Antarctica has a highly regulated and managed environment and the continent has been dedicated, since the establishment of the ATS, to the study of science, with tourism being one of a very few commercial activities actually allowed to take place, although in only a few locations. Hence, zoning is much easier here than almost anywhere else on Earth and Harris (1994, 2002) has suggested that there should be six separate zones: restricted, sensitive, scientific, historic, facilities and touristic. However, even in Antarctica with apparent separate zones, there is more than one use in some zones and the tourist zone there contains historic sites and scientific stations, as both are attractions for visitors to the continent.

Main aims of land-use zoning for tourism

A key aim of all land-use planning is to separate one form of usage from others. In terms of planning for tourism land-use, the general aim of land-use planning is echoed in relation to tourism. Once a tourism zone has been established, management of tourists/visitors is a key objective (Mason 2008). Visitor management involves a number of key processes including regulating usage of tourist attractions, managing visitor behaviour, modifying the resource for tourism and educating visitors (Mason 2005).

Zoning as part of the process of visitor management is likely to relate specifically to the types of activities that are permitted in particular zones, as well as delineating those activities that are not permitted. Rules and regulations, codes of conduct and actual laws may be applied in these zones and these forms of regulation may be supported by visitor education.

Hence, zoning will usually indicate areas in which specific types of tourism, depending on, for example, intensity of land-use and likely environmental impacts, can take place and where they are not permitted. In zones where tourism is permitted, it is commonly the case that other non-tourism activities, such as agriculture, forestry, mining and even military use also take place. It is, therefore, unlikely that tourism will be the only activity taking place in a zone, even if this is delineated as 'the tourism zone'. Although some of these differing activities may complement one another, such as tourism and forestry, it is often the case that the differing land-users are in competition. Even when tourism is viewed as being largely compatible with other countryside land-uses, such as farming, major problems may arise in specific contexts, with significant impacts on tourism. During the 2001 foot and mouth disease outbreak in the UK, large areas of the British countryside were closed to visitors from early spring to late summer, to prevent the spread of the disease among farm animals. As a result, large areas of previously accessible land were 'off limits' to both domestic and international tourists. The outbreak of foot and mouth disease severely affected farmers, but this also had a major negative impact on the tourism economy of rural Britain (Mason 2008). At the end of the outbreak, farmers were compensated, but those involved in tourism in affected areas were not. Hence, this particular example also indicates the political significance attached to one major land-use, that of farming, and its relatively greater importance when compared with tourism.

Criteria used in landscape zoning for tourism and resulting zonation systems

As stated above, zoning is often used in areas where tourism has been designated as the major land-use. For example, in national parks, zoning is a technique driven by ecological data in order to balance demands between protection and use (Wearing and Neil 2009). The major aim of this form of zoning is very similar to the key objective of all types of land zoning – to ensure that activities in one zone do not impinge on the planned activities of another (Buckley and Pannel 1990). Zoning may mean, in protected areas such as wilderness areas or national parks, that tourism, or any form of visitation is not permitted. Such zones are likely to be those that are highly sensitive or fragile.

One approach to zoning that shows the range of criteria that can be used when applied to tourism is that used in British Columbia, Canada. The Tourism Zonation System (TZS) is a land-use planning approach which allows tourism to be planned in an environmentally sensitive and economically viable way. Pioneered in British Columbia, the TZS uses a fourfold classification and maps the land base of the province into 'Urban', 'Frontcountry', 'Midcountry' and 'Backcountry' zones. The criteria used for this are:

- degree of naturalness (from urban to wilderness);
- type of outdoor tourism experience possible;
- environmental sensitivity;
- method of transport;
- intensity of use;
- scale of facilities.

(www.wilderness-tourism.bc.ca, accessed 9 August 2010)

Similar criteria to those used in British Columbia are deployed in other parts of the world and can result in similar types of zonation. In New Zealand, the government body, the Department of Conservation (DOC) uses the Resource Management Act of 1991 to manage large areas of rural land that have significant tourism usage. DOC uses the concepts of 'frontcountry' and 'backcountry' in relation to land management. The more remote mountain areas and some coastal margins are referred to as backcountry, and this is where much environment-focused tourism takes place (Mason 2008). However, the backcountry has few tourism facilities – this condition is as most New Zealanders' perceive the backcountry should be, and they do not wish such areas to have traditional tourism facilities as it would affect their visitor experience.

Although a protected site for its heritage significance rather than its environmental importance, and at a much smaller scale, being site-focused, the Angkor World Heritage Park in Cambodia is divided into five categories of protected zones, which show a number of similarities with the much larger scale regional zoning systems used in relation to environmental resources in British Columbia and New Zealand. Each of these zones has differing management objectives and are as follows.

> Zone 1: Monumental site. This zone is the core zone, monumental sites and protected archaeological reserves. It has the most significant archaeological features and the highest level of protection.
> Zone 2: Protected archaeological reserves. This zone acts as a buffer zone, around the monumental sites.
> Zone 3: Protected cultural landscapes. Areas preserved for their distinctive traditional physical and cultural features, including historic buildings and land-use practices.
> Zone 4: Sites of archaeological, anthropological or historic interest. This zone is of less significance than Zones 1 and 2, but requires protection for research, education and tourism.
> Zone 5: The socio-economic and cultural development zone. This zone is managed as a multiple-use area with an emphasis on economic and social development through sustainable natural resource use and cultural tourism.
>
> (http://portal.Unesco.org/en, accessed 12 August 2010)

A key similarity between the Angkor World Heritage Park zoning system and zoning in New Zealand and Canada is that there are specific zones where preservation/conservation is a key aim and certain activities are not permitted, whereas other zones allow a variety of uses. At the Angkor World Heritage Park, Zones 1 and 2 are the most restricted zones in terms of development, whereas Zone 5 has multiple uses.

Although traditional tourism activities frequently find themselves existing in zones alongside non-tourism activities, in the context of ecotourism, it is common for other land-uses, particularly more commercial ones, to be separated from ecotourism (Wearing and Neil 2009). This is because intensive land-uses such as industry, transport and residential use are generally seen as incompatible with ecotourism. Even traditional forms of tourism may be separated and restricted from areas important for ecotourism, particularly as many ecotourists want to be in a wilderness area and such visitors desire a landscape that is natural, wild, free and uncrowded (Cole 2000). This is usually achieved by limiting or not providing facilities that are expected within more traditional forms of tourism. As noted above, a similar situation is found in New Zealand's backcountry.

The WWF Guide to establishing ecotourism in protected environmental areas in developing countries (Ceballos–Lascurain 1996) provides guidance on criteria that should be used when creating zones and the nature of zones to be established, focusing specifically on protected areas. This guide indicates that zones should be established according to the natural and/or cultural values of an area and the particular fragility and carrying capacities within it, which will provide proper recognition of and protection for the area's resources. Zones indicate where physical development can and cannot be located. The zones proposed for each protected area are intended to be consistent with the objectives for which the area has been established. These zones, indicated below, show a number of similarities with those in use at the Angkor World Heritage Park:

- strict protection zones (sometimes called 'sanctuary' or 'reserve' zones), from which tourists are excluded;

- wilderness zones (also termed 'restricted use' zones) which tourists are permitted to enter, but only on foot;
- moderate tourism use zones where visitors are encouraged to carry out diverse activities compatible with the natural (and/or cultural) environment – these zones may have limited, low-impact tourist services (mainly of an interpretive nature) and contain representative samples of the park's important resources;
- development zones – areas of limited extent, in which facilities are concentrated (including facilities for tourism and park management and research).

In summary, the discussion above indicates that conservation of natural and/or cultural heritage as part of a visitor management strategy is a major criterion used in landscape zoning. The following case study discusses the criteria used to establish zones of landscape sensitivity in the very fragile environment of Iceland, which has seen a significant increase in tourist numbers over the past 20 years or so.

Case study: landscape sensitivity, zoning and tourism in Iceland

The northern periphery of the Northern hemisphere is characterised by particularly fragile ecosystems. In Iceland, the vegetation and soil cover are susceptible to pressure, both natural and human-induced. The major landscape problems of soil erosion and land degradation are a product of Iceland's climate and centuries of agricultural practice, but can be easily triggered by unsuitable forms of tourism. However, as with many parts of the world, there has been relatively little research into the environmental impacts of tourism on the landscape of Iceland.

Over the last 1,000 years, the landscape of Iceland has been greatly affected by the natural climatic conditions; frequent rain, and seasonal frost, ice and snow. Overgrazing of this fragile landscape, throughout this period, has made conditions worse. Soil erosion has affected 73 per cent of the land area, of which nearly one-fifth has suffered from severe or extremely severe erosion (Arnalds et al. 2001).

The landscape is made up of several vegetation systems of which the major types are: river and glacial systems, wetlands, grasslands and heathlands. These different vegetation types have varying levels of sensitivity to human activities, including tourism. Moss heath is the dominant plant in many of the most popular tourist sites in Iceland and Gísladóttir (2006) indicates that moss heath is the most susceptible to trampling. Trampling has contributed to major soil erosion problems. In addition to vegetation type, soil type and slope angle can contribute significantly to soil erosion and land degradation.

The study area that forms the basis for this case study borders the largest glacier in Iceland, Vatnajökull. As a result of global warming, the Vatnajökull ice cap and its outlet glaciers have retreated a great deal during the course of the last century. It seems very likely that the ice cap will continue to retreat over the coming decades. The result of glacial melting is the gradual exposing of land along the glacial margins. As newly exposed, this land is lacking in vegetation and is ultra-sensitive to physical and human impacts. Therefore, the location of land in relation to glacial margins is another important factor in indicating sensitivity.

The sensitivity of the landscape to tourism pressure can be estimated by analysing vegetation type in a given region in combination with soil type, slope angle and proximity to glacial margins. Combinations of these physical variables can provide a sensitivity range that can be categorised into several classes of sensitivity.

Using a Geographical Information System (GIS) – GIS is an electronic tool that is able to handle multiple spatial criteria and manipulate these, making it a powerful tool to aid decision-makers in planning tourism – these categories can be mapped and zones of sensitivity created. A typical GIS works by overlaying mapped information, which is usually in digital form, in this case derived from the variables of vegetation, soil type, slope angle and proximity to glacial margins. Through the GIS overlay that combines the information from these physical variables, a new information layer is created, which consists of accumulated sensitivity values from the individual sensitivity classes. The layers of information build up a digital map that combines the variables. In this way a map of sensitivity to tourism impacts can be created, manipulated, modified and interrogated. This enables the creation of a digital map in which all the physical variables are accumulated and levels of sensitivity can be shown. The map of the study area is divided into four zones: 'no sensitivity', low sensitivity', 'medium sensitivity' and 'high sensitivity'. Areas where the accumulated value equals 10 exhibited the highest sensitivity for the variables vegetation, soil type and slope gradient, and are additionally within 200 m of the glacier margin.

The research for this case study reveals that river and glacial systems have the least sensitivity to tourism impacts, wetlands with gravel soils on low angle slopes away from glacial margins have relatively low sensitivity to tourism impacts, and sandy soils on steep slopes with moss heath vegetation within 200 m of a glacial margin have very high sensitivity to tourism impacts.

(Adapted from Olafsdottir and Runnstrom 2009)

Coastal margins such as in Belize where mangrove swamps are the predominant vegetation have also been zoned in relation to their suitability for tourism, with a gradation from highly intensive recreational use, through to no recreational use at all. This zoning was done in an attempt to preserve the most fragile environments. It has also allowed tourism organisations to market their tourist experiences as being responsible and promoting sustainable tourism.

It is even possible to use the approach of zoning in non-land-based contexts. For example, the Great Barrier Reef to the east of Australia has a number of zones relating to recreational and tourism use and this is discussed in the following case study.

Case study

Zoning in a marine national park of the Great Barrier Reef, Australia

The Great Barrier Reef is one of the largest coral reefs in the world with over 600 islands, 300 cay islands and almost 300 submerged reefs. There are more than 15,000 species of fish, 4,000 mollusc species and 400 sponges, as well as over 350 different types of coral. The Great Barrier Reef remained relatively undeveloped for tourism until the mid-twentieth century because of its location off the eastern shore of Australia. From 1975 onwards, tourism developed rapidly. The number of traditional charter boats grew dramatically after this date and in the mid-1980s high-speed catamarans were introduced. Between 1982 and 1992 visitor numbers increased 35-fold and tourists were visiting four times as many sites (Williams 1998). By 1989 there were almost one million visitors, by 1996 this had reached two million and by 2004 over 2.5 million, with a significant proportion by this date being international visitors. The main activities in this period were snorkelling and scuba diving, as well as sightseeing from serum submersibles and glass-bottomed boats.

By the late 1990s there was evidence of significant environmental impacts, including physical destruction of reefs by anchors and divers' feet, and localised water pollution from sewage and fuel. There were also changes in fish behaviour, largely as a result of boat operator's crews feeding fish to entertain tourists. There was also the taking of souvenirs – visitors removing pieces of coral as well as fish specimens.

In 1975 the Great Barrier Reef Marine Park was established, largely in an attempt to provide a framework for dealing with the effects of increasing numbers of tourists. The main strategy within the Park management system is zoning. Three main categories of zoning were established:

- A general use zone (this accounted for approximately 80 per cent of the Park in the late 1990s), where almost all activities are permitted providing they are ecologically sustainable;
- National Park Zones that allow only activities that do not remove living species;
- Preservation Zones, which permit only scientific research.

Tourism was permitted in the first of these two zones, but not in the Preservation Zone. Nevertheless, permits were required for both the first and second zones. Factors considered in relation to the granting of permits at the time were the size, extent and location of usage, access conditions, likely effects on the environment in general and ecosystems in particular, and likely effects on resources and their conservation. A number of educational strategies including pictorial symbols, guides and codes of conduct were aimed at tourists and these were backed up with local controls and prohibitions depending on particular circumstances.

In 2004 the zones were revised and new zones introduced. Seven major zones were established:

- General Use Zone;
- Habitat Protection Zone;
- Conservation Park Zone;
- Buffer Zone;
- Scientific Research Zone;
- Marine National Park Zone;
- Preservation Zone.

In this new zoning scheme, the General Use Zone had the widest range of activities that was permitted, whereas the Preservation Zone was the most restricted in terms of usage. The permit system was maintained after 2004, as well as the targeting of visitors with a variety of educational strategies. Combined together, these are still the approaches being used to encourage responsible behaviour among tourists and to conserve the marine environment

(Adapted from Moscardo *et al.* 1997 and http://kurrawa.gbrmpa.gov.au, accessed 14 September 2010)

Issues with tourism zoning

To be effective, it is important that tourism zones are recognised and that there is awareness of their existence and purpose by tourists. However, the context of New Zealand indicates possible problems that can result. Here, even when zones are established and recognised, problems of interpretation of the nature of zones may occur. The great majority of New Zealanders hold the view that everyone should have free access to the countryside (Mason 2008). In particular, New Zealanders believe that they should have unrestricted access to the backcountry, which is generally remote from population centres. However, the New Zealand attitude of self-reliance also means that there has been opposition to improving visitor facilities in the backcountry. Nevertheless, with rising numbers of international visitors there is pressure to develop the backcountry for increased tourism and this will mean the development of more and better facilities in this zone. Such a move is likely to be opposed by many New Zealanders, who wish the backcountry zone to remain undeveloped.

In traditional tourism contexts, it is frequently the case that tourism is the major user, but not the only user, of a particular landscape zone. Although some other uses of a zone that has tourism as the predominant human activity may complement tourism, it is often the case that the different land-users are in competition, if not in direct conflict with each other. For example, in some relatively remote areas of Britain, such as Dartmoor and Salisbury Plain, which attract tourists because of their semi-natural environment, absence of urban development and perceived 'wildness', military usage is common. In these areas, tourists are unlikely to want to be confronted by military training events and in extreme situations will actually be prevented from entering designated military areas because of the perceived and real danger that may arise.

As landscape zones often have several uses in each zone, it can be difficult to establish where one zone ends and another begins and, again, this means that management can be a difficult task. However, as has been noted above, ecotourism is a specific form of tourism where other environmental uses tend not to exist in what has been defined as the tourism zone, as these uses are not seen as compatible with ecotourism. In relation to the designation of ecotourism zones, the concept of carrying capacity is frequently used. However, the term carrying capacity is problematic. It is often used as if solely a scientific term, usually refers to indicator plant and animal species and indicates a threshold beyond which these indicator species are not found or would be damaged if present. In this context, carrying capacity is viewed as something that can be accurately measured (Mason 2008). However, in a tourism context, the term can be used to denote the number of visitors to an area and often relates to efforts to designate a maximum level of visitation and measure crowding in an attempt to indicate whether a threshold has been passed and overcrowding has occurred. The use of the term here may appear to have a strict scientific basis, but as Doorne (2000) discussed, carrying capacity has a significant perceptual basis. In effect, crowding is 'in the eye of the beholder' (Mason 2008), and the way visitors perceive an environment depends on a variety of factors including age and nationality, as well as the actual context, including the time of day and season, in which the tourist experience occurs (Doorne 2000).

Zoning in a marine environment, such as the Great Barrier Reef, will be particularly difficult in terms of clearly demarcating specific zones, as the water-based environment is constantly moving and changing in very different ways to that of a terrestrial environment. However, even in a terrestrial zoning system demarcation problems can occur. Buckley and Pannel (1990) discuss the problems that can arise in a river catchment region. They indicate that if tourism activities take place in the upstream part of a catchment, this may adversely affect water quality in a lower part of the catchment, even if this area has no recreational or tourist activities. They suggest that there will be particularly negative consequences if this lower area has been designated a conservation area.

Monitoring of the use of tourism zones is an important process, particularly if certain activities are intended to be restricted or not allowed at all. However few countries have a sophisticated or efficient monitoring system for the use of specific zones. Size of zones, accessibility and the lack of an adequate 'police' force are common problems limiting the effectiveness of monitoring of activities within tourism zones. Even if accurate and detailed monitoring is possible, it is likely to be difficult to apply regulations and impose any penalties as the monitoring force may lack legal powers to enforce regulations. It is only in highly regulated tourism environments such as Antarctica, where there are relatively few visitors and these are concentrated in time and space, that accurate monitoring is possible and penalties can be applied if necessary. In less regulated environments than Antarctica, reliance on 'soft' management approaches such as interpretation, codes of conduct and education, rather than 'hard' management through laws and regulations, is likely to be the only feasible visitor management strategy.

The establishment of a tourism zone, or specific types of tourism activities within a zone, can help visitors to make informed choices on the type of experience in which they wish to be involved. They may, for example, be able to use zoning to assist in the selection of an ecotourism experience in preference to, say, a more traditional form of visitor activity. Also the use of zoning may enable tour operators to indicate that they are promoting appropriate tourism uses of a specific landscape area and to claim that they provide sustainable tourism experiences there. On the other hand, tourism zoning may be misused; unscrupulous operators can, through their use of 'greenwash' about the environment and tourism potential of a particular landscape zone, exploit visitor desire for sustainable tourism experiences.

Conclusion

Land-use zoning has a long history as part of both urban and rural planning. Much zoning involving designated tourism zones has been rural-focused and concerned with countryside-based activities. Although these countryside activities may complement each other, competition between different land-uses is common and conflict not unusual. Zoning of tourism land-usage is usually concerned with protecting fragile and sensitive environments from the negative consequences of visitor impact and is commonly part of a visitor management strategy. In extreme cases, in an attempt to preserve the environmental resource for long-term sustainability, visitors may be excluded, but areas allowing tourism are frequently multiple use zones. However, the boundaries of these multiple land-use zones are often blurred, making policing and hence management difficult, which can provide unscrupulous tour operators with an opportunity for greenwashing. The concept of carrying capacity may be used to help designate land-use zones, but using this supposedly scientific concept is problematic, particularly when it is accepted that it also has a perceptual dimension. However, despite a number of issues, land-use zoning is a very useful geographical approach that can assist in managing the environment for tourism purposes. The logic of zoning is generally easy for visitors to comprehend, can be visually represented through maps and is particularly suitable for use of electronic data handling and presentation through GIS, enabling it to be employed as a significant tourism management tool.

References

Arnalds, O., Gisladottir, F. and Sigurjonsson, H. (2001), 'Sandy Deserts of Iceland: an overview', *Journal of Arid Environments* 47, 359–71.

Buckley, R. and Pannel, J. (1990) 'Environmental impacts of tourism and recreation in national parks and conservation reserves', *Journal of Tourism Studies* 1 (1), 24–32.

Ceballos-Lascuráin, H. (1996) *Tourism, ecotourism, and protected areas.* Paris: IUCN

Cole, D. (2000) 'Natural, wild, uncrowded or free', *International Journal of Wilderness* 6 (2), 5–8.

Doorne, S. (2000) 'Caves, culture and crowds: carrying capacity meets consumer sovereignty', *Journal of Sustainable Tourism* 8 (4) 34–42.

Gísladóttir, G. (2006) 'The impact of tourist trampling on Icelandic Andosols', *Zeitschrift für Geomorphologie*, Supplement 143, 53–70.

Hall, M. (2008) *Tourism Planning*, 2nd edn. London: Pearson International.

Harris, C. (1994) 'Standardisation of zones within specially protected and managed areas under the Antarctic Environment Protocol', *Polar Record*, 30 (175) 283–6.

——(2002) *Standardisation of zones within specially protected and managed areas under the Madrid Protocol* (Unpublished) Colin Harris, 5 The Footpath, Grantchester Cambridge, UK.

Mason, P. (2005) 'Visitor Management in protected areas: from hard to soft approaches', *Current Issues in Tourism* 8 (2/3), 181–94.

——(2008) *Tourism Impacts Planning and Management*, 2nd edn. Oxford: Butterworth Heinemann.

Mason, P. and Legg, S. (1999) Antarctic tourism: activities, impacts, management issues and a proposed research agenda', *Pacific Tourism Review* 3, 71–84.

Moscardo, G., Woods, B. and Pearce, P. (1997) *Evaluating the effectiveness of pictorial symbols in reef visitor education*, CRC Reef Research Centre Technical Report No. 15. Townsville, Australia.

Olafsdottir, R. and Runnstrom, M. (2009) 'A GIS approach to evaluating ecological sensitivity for tourism development in fragile environments: a case study from SE Iceland', *Scandinavian Journal of Hospitality and Tourism* 9 (1), 22–38.

Stonehouse, B. and Snyder, J. (2010) *Polar Tourism: an Environmental Perspective*. Bristol: Channel View

Wearing, S. and Neil, J. (2009) *Ecotourism; Impacts, Potentials and Possibilities*. Oxford: Butterworth Heinemann.

Williams, S. (1998) *Tourism Geography*. London: Routledge.

26

Protected areas and tourism

Andrew Holden

A key aspect of the use of tourism in environmental policy and management is its relationship to protected areas, especially national parks. Tourism offers a potential economic rationale for nature conservation through the establishment of protected areas. However, in the absence of professional and committed environmental management it also has the potential to cause environmental degradation. Since the inception of the first national park in Yosemite in 1872, the balance between conservation and the use of nature for enjoyment by urban populations is one that has required close management. This chapter explores the relationship between tourism and protected areas, focusing on national parks and also tourism's relationship to World Heritage Sites.

Contemporary protected areas

The contemporary relationship between tourism and protected areas can be traced to the influence of the Romantic Movement on interpretation of landscape and reaction to the Industrial Revolution. During the time of rapid nineteenth-century industrialisation of Western economies, literary figures such as George Catlin in the United States and William Wordsworth in England, were instrumental to the construction of images that raised awareness of the value of landscape. The subsequent desire to visit culturally defined landscapes of 'beauty' and the need to conserve natural systems presents dilemmas of how to best deal with the interaction between tourism and conservation in protected areas. This dualism has been inherent since the creation of the first national park of Yosemite in 1872, which was established with an edict to act as a pleasure ground for the benefit and enjoyment of people (Eagles *et al.* 2002).

Protected areas are landscapes that are denoted as having special status. Many are developed in accordance with national legislation and systems that vary between countries, depending on national needs and priorities, and on differences in legislative, institutional and financial support. However, an oft-cited definition of what constitutes a protected area is the one given by the International Union for the Conservation of Nature (IUCN): 'A clearly defined geographical space, recognised, dedicated and managed, through legal or other effective means, to achieve the long-term conservation of nature with associated ecosystem services and cultural values' (www.iucn.org 2011).

Important aspects of this definition include the concepts of geographical space, recognition and dedication, management, conservation and cultural values. The emphasis on a long-term perspective is synonymous to the concept of sustainable development. There is then a requirement to integrate aspects of physical space and the conservation of nature and ecosystem services with cultural values. Typically protected areas are areas or combinations of areas of land, inland water or marine and coastal areas that have defined physical boundaries, transcending various environments and ecosystems that include mountains, seas and oceans, forests, deserts and lakes.

Recognition and dedication of protected areas are typically identified by the state based on international conventions. Typically, this would take the form of an Act of Parliament in the case of public land or by an act of covenant or conservation agreement in the case of private or indigenous land. This latter category can also consist of those declared by people, for example the Anindilyakwa Indigenous Protected Area (IPA) was self-declared by aboriginal communities of the Groote Eylandt peninsula in 2006, having its legal status recognised by the Australian government (Dudley 2008; www.environment.gov.au/indigenous/publications/fs-anindilyakwa.html 2011).

Inherent to the long-term existence of a protected area are management strategies and dedicated environmental management, requirements that demand consistent financial sourcing, either from state, private sector or non-governmental organisations (NGOs), or any combination of these stakeholder groups. Legal status is also critical to the recognition of protected areas, anointing the landscape with a special status for conservation and stricter planning regulations and enforcements than prevail elsewhere.

An emphasis on conservation may seem self-explicit in the context of protected areas, the IUCN interpretation of its constituents being: 'In the context of this definition conservation refers to the in-situ maintenance of ecosystems and natural and semi-natural habitats and of viable populations of species in their natural surroundings and, in the case of domesticated or cultivated species in the surroundings where they have developed their distinctive properties' (www.iucn.org 2011). Inherent to this explanation of the context of conservation is recognition that many landscapes have been culturally modified by human action during centuries of endeavour, which has impacted on and led to the establishment of modified ecosystems determined by anthropogenic activity. Similarly, in an attempt to clarify the concept of nature, the IUCN includes alongside biodiversity at genetic, species and ecosystem levels, the geodiversity of landforms and landscapes.

The recognition of cultural values is particularly important where indigenous peoples or communities live inside or alongside a protected area and are dependent on its resources for their livelihoods. Unfortunately, the establishment of protected areas has sometimes led to the displacement of local people, resulting in a denial of access to livelihood resources while fostering resentment to protected areas and the conservation of nature and wildlife. The recognition of cultural values and cultural economic practices that enhance conservation are important in the balance of using the resources of protected areas and providing livelihood opportunities, as is being enacted in the Indigenous Protected Area (IPA) of the Anindilyakwa.

Types of protected areas

Although the character of protected areas may vary between countries, the most common types of protected areas as defined by the IUCN and World Database on Protected Areas (WDPA) are as follows.

Category Ia: strict nature reserve

Category Ia are strictly protected areas set aside to protect biodiversity and also possibly geological/geomorphological features, where human visitation, use and impacts are strictly controlled and limited to ensure protection of the conservation values. Such protected areas can serve as indispensable reference areas for scientific research and monitoring.

Category Ib: wilderness area

Category Ib protected areas are usually large, unmodified or slightly modified areas, retaining their natural character and influence, without permanent or significant human habitation, which are protected and managed so as to preserve their natural condition.

Category II: national park

Category II protected areas are large natural or near-natural areas set aside to protect large-scale ecological processes, along with the complement of species and ecosystems characteristic of the area, which also provide a foundation for environmentally and culturally compatible spiritual, scientific, educational, recreational and visitor opportunities.

Category III: natural monument or feature

Category III protected areas are set aside to protect a specific natural monument, which can be a landform, sea mount, submarine cavern, geological feature such as a cave or even a living feature such as an ancient grove. They are generally quite small protected areas and often have high visitor value.

Category IV: habitat/species management area

Category IV protected areas aim to protect particular species or habitats and management reflects this priority. Many category IV protected areas will need regular, active interventions to address the requirements of particular species or to maintain habitats, but this is not a requirement of the category.

Category V: protected landscape/seascape

A protected area where the interaction of people and nature over time has produced an area of distinct character with significant ecological, biological, cultural and scenic value, and where safeguarding the integrity of this interaction is vital to protecting and sustaining the area and its associated nature conservation and other values.

Category VI: protected area with sustainable use of natural resources

Category VI protected areas conserve ecosystems and habitats, together with associated cultural values and traditional natural resource management systems. They are generally large, with most of the area in a natural condition, where a proportion is under sustainable natural resource management and where low-level non-industrial use of natural resources compatible with nature conservation is seen as one of the main aims of the area. (www.wdpa.org 2011)

The action of government is important to the establishment of protected areas, the prioritisation given to environmental protection and conservation reflecting its philosophy of the values of nature and economic challenges. As O'Riordan (1981) observes, concern over the natural environment is only likely to happen after national security and economic development has been achieved. Although there may have been a shift in international policy during the last four decades to recognise environmental value more widely, for the majority of countries both economic growth and development remain the inter-linked policy priorities. This is reflected in tourism development policy, which has traditionally emphasised macro-economic objectives, such as employment creation and regional development, while treating the environment in an instrumental fashion.

Although there now exists a higher level of awareness among policy makers over the need to pay more attention to natural resource management and conservation than previously, there still exists conflict over the extent to which stewardship of the environment should detract from economic growth. An allegation made by many developing countries against the Western world, which seemingly wishes to dictate environmental policy on a global level, is that the West has the luxury to be able to be concerned over the environment because it has largely fulfilled many of the national goals identified by O'Riordan. As Stone (1993: 42) comments: 'Joan Martin Brown, an official with UNEP [author's note: United Nations Environmental Programme], has remarked: "The Third World says you're telling us not to do what you did to achieve your high standard of living. What are you going to do for us?"'. It is therefore likely that the extent to which governments are willing to pursue policies where the conservation of the natural environment is made a priority will depend greatly on the ability of sustainable development to meet economic objectives. This will be reliant on the dissemination of knowledge based on models of good practice, advancement in environmentally benign technologies, and a revised market system based on a thorough practice in environmental economics that incorporates the costs of negative environmental externalities in the prices of goods and services. Subsequently, if tourism to protected areas can demonstrate an economic value and benefit to achieve wider development objectives, the argument for the conservation of natural resources and ecosystem services assumes an economic validity alongside an environmental one.

Protected areas and tourism

In the context of protected areas in which tourism is encouraged as part of a conservation strategy, it can offer a strong economic rationale for the conservation of natural resources, limited to variables of income and employment generation and the creation of livelihood opportunities. Sometimes, the economic argument for nature conservation through tourism may be prevalent against other development options. For example, in the case of the Mabira Forest Reserve in Uganda, the use of the forest for ecotourism was shown to provide a strong economic rationale for its conservation in the face of other development pressures. The area was given protected area status by the Ugandan government because of its rich biodiversity, including birdlife. However, its status was placed under intense pressure by the desire to remove a third of the forest for the growth of sugar cane for the production of biofuel. In the subsequent economic feasibility study it was found that the commercial value of ecotourism and carbon capture was US$316 million a year, whereas sugar cane production for biofuels was found to be worth less than US$20 million per annum (Smith 2007).

Tourism may also make a positive economic contribution to other uses in protected areas. For example, carefully regulated and managed tourism, such as small groups interested in scientific education, could help fund the research and protection of a scientific reserve, and tourism revenues have already directly aided the establishment of national parks especially in developing countries. Although traditionally national and local government agencies have provided the funding for protected areas, international policy directives, especially structural adjustment programmes to national economies based on neo-liberal principles have caused many governments to reduce their funding support to protected areas. Thus, tourism has become viewed as a mechanism to replace lost funding through a variety of methods, including: donations, entrance fees, rental fees and licences, taxing tourist retail purchases and from tax revenues from economic activity associated with tourism (Bushell and McCool 2007). There is an increasing pressure for protected areas to 'pay their way' and demonstrate their long-term economic value as conservation areas in the face of competing resource uses (Font *et al.* 2004). Nevertheless, the acceptance of pricing mechanisms based on entrance or user fees is evidently political contentious on the grounds of the equality of open access, and will depend on the context of the founding of the national park.

One of the most common protected area designations worldwide, and one in which tourism plays an important role, is the national park. The responsibility for passing legislation to establish a national park lies with governments. They are usually established with the objectives of protecting outstanding natural areas from overdevelopment and providing areas of access to nature for tourists and recreationists. The first national park in the world was created at Yosemite in America in 1872, and it is not an accident that its establishment coincided with the increasing urbanisation of America, in the latter half of the nineteenth century. The focus of the rationale for establishing Yosemite national park was not solely based on conservation but on the provision of nature for the enjoyment of urban-dwellers. The duality of conservation and use of national parks for the benefits of the community is then traceable to their origin. The extent of the expectation of community benefits that parks may provide now include: health benefits; cultural and spiritual sustenance; education; provision of ecosystem services, e.g. clean air and water; and poverty alleviation (Bushell *et al.* 2007).

National parks may also play a greater part in the national psyche than just purely being areas for nature conservation and recreation. Hall and Lew (1998) suggest that the development of the Yosemite National Park, and the need for a rapidly urbanising American population to stay in contact with nature, was to act as a reminder of the pioneer mentality that modern America had been built around as much as for recreational purposes. Instrumental to encouraging urbanised Americans to visit the mountains was John Muir, the founder of the Sierra Club in the USA, who advocated that visiting mountains was good for one's soul (Eagles *et al.* 2002). An interesting alternative perspective on why national parks were created is given by MacCannell (1992: 115):

> The great parks, even great urban parks, Golden Gate in San Francisco or Central in New York, but especially the National Parks, are symptomatic of guilt which accompanies the impulse to destroy nature. We destroy on an unprecedented scale, then in response to our wrongs, we create parks which re-stage the nature/society opposition now entirely framed by society.

In MacCannell's view, the creation of national parks is symptomatic of a release of collective guilt over the harm humans have caused to the non-human environment, during the process of industrial modernisation. The theme of guilt is also inherent to the American poet Catlin's avocation in the 1830s of the need to establish a nation's park in response to the destruction of Aboriginal cultures as a consequence of development (Eagles *et al.* 2002). By the end of the nineteenth century, national parks had been established in other countries including Banff National Park in Canada in 1887 and Tongariro National Park in New Zealand in 1894. Common features of the emerging national parks at the end of the nineteenth century was that they were created by government action; they consisted of large areas of natural environments; and they were available to all people (ibid.).

However, MacCannell (ibid.) suggests that although the creation of the parks represents a 'good deed' of industrial civilisation, their creation affirms the power of humans over nature. The collective conscious or subconscious guilt held by Western society over the way it has instrumentally used nature in the process of development, may also influence perceptions of tourism. The fact that tourism often takes place in relatively unspoilt environments helps us to imagine how nature and life may have been before industrialisation and development took place. It may therefore be difficult to perceive that tourism can be environmentally threatening, as many of the environments in which it takes place represent the antithesis of what is deemed to have gone wrong in developed societies.

Ironically, today, the biggest threat to some national parks in the developed world is tourism. For instance, the success of Yosemite in attracting tourists is without doubt, as Murphy commented nearly 30 years ago (1985: 41):

> In addition to serving the drive-through visitor, Yosemite accommodates those who wish to stop-over, providing campsites, cabins, and a hotel in Yosemite Village. At times the valley which contains this village and attracts most of the visitors becomes an off-shoot of Los Angeles, complete with traffic jams and smog conditions – the very conditions tourists are trying to escape.

Overpopularity is perhaps one of the greatest hidden dangers to the natural environment that the parks are trying to conserve, and by giving an area the status of a national park it automatically becomes an attractive place to visit. This can be especially problematic for park management in areas where national park status was given several decades ago, but the pace of technological change and transport development has meant that the spatial area has become easily accessible to large numbers of people for day-trips and vacations.

The creation of national parks is not restricted purely to terrestrial areas of the world's surface, for instance marine parks have also been established to protect coral reefs in places such as the Netherlands Antilles (Bonaire Marine Park) and the Seychelles (Saint Anne National Marine Parks). Ultimately, the type of national park or protected area that is established in a country is likely to be a reflection of a variety of different factors, including existing levels of economic development, population density and the extent of institutional and financial support from government.

In developing countries, the rationale for the establishment of national parks has been much more closely associated with the conservation of wildlife, supported by the revenues from tourism in some cases, rather than providing recreational opportunities for urban-dwellers. National parks act as important focal points for attracting international tourists, for example as in east and south Africa, Costa Rica, India, Nepal and Indonesia (World Tourism Organization 1992). Growth in domestic tourism numbers to national parks is also significant in many developing countries. However, sometimes the creation of national parks has adverse cultural impacts, including the displacement of indigenous peoples, leading to accusations of 'ecofascism'. Such criticisms of the establishment of national parks in developing countries have been made on the colonial and post-colonial practice of excluding indigenous communities, as Leech (2002: 78) comments:

> Though many of us crave sanctuaries away from the modern world, the idea of wilderness areas where tourists can sample nature, free of man, is a western romantic illusion. And

further, what is evident is that the preservation of these areas comes at a very high cost to local communities which are either removed from the land, have their lives regulated or are forced to play the role of theme park extras to satisfy the demands of ecotourism.

The removal of peoples from protected areas potentially can have a catastrophic effect on their livelihood security including access to opportunities to obtain natural resources. Criticisms can also be made of tourism development in national parks that fail to establish economic linkages with communities living on the peripheries of the protected areas, thereby denying them livelihood and human development opportunities.

Although national parks are very important for aiding conservation of the natural environment, their creation can result in costs besides benefits, as summarised in Table 26.1. The key to achieving success in national parks is the development and implementation of suitable management plans, which balance the use of natural resources, the needs of the local people and the expectations of the tourists.

Alongside national parks, a further type of protected area status with increased significance in the context of tourism is the World Heritage Site (WHS), a status confirmed by the United Nations Environment and Scientific Committee and Organisation (UNESCO).

World Heritage Sites

The catalyst to the concept of WHS was the construction of the Aswan High Dam in Egypt and the subsequent threat to the Abu Simbel temples from the flooding of the valley in 1959. After an appeal from the governments of Egypt and Sudan, UNESCO launched an international safeguarding appeal, with over half the campaign costs of US$80 million coming from other countries (UNESCO 2006a). The necessity to help protect sites containing significant cultural and natural heritage led UNESCO to establish the convention for World Heritage Sites in 1972. Central to the understanding of heritage is the linking together of natural and cultural environments as specified by UNESCO (2006b).

Today there are 830 designated WHS, of which 644 are classified as being cultural, 162 as natural and 24 as mixed (UNESCO 2006b). They are spatially diverse, being found in 138 nations, and vary from sites that are fairly remote from human habitation to ones that include living communities. However, the World Heritage Fund has less than US$4 million per annum

Table 26.1 Costs and benefits of tourism to national parks

Benefits	Costs
Designated protected areas for the conservation of nature, wildlife and eco-system services	Unless carefully managed, tourism and recreation can pose both a threat to landscape and wildlife that the park was established to protect
Provides a place for people to experience nature. Tourists can also provide revenues for park management, scientific research and conservation projects. It may also provide an economic rationale for conservation.	Granting of national park status focuses attention on the area. This may lead to the attraction of too many tourists and overcrowding of the area. The use of pricing mechanisms and entrance fees may discriminate against the less economically rich
Offers capacity building and employment opportunities for local people in conservation and tourism activities	Indigenous peoples can be excluded from their territory with a detrimental effect on their livelihood opportunities and security

to support these sites, meaning that alternative sources of income have to be found to support their management. One possible means of raising sources of income is tourism.

One outcome of the designation of a site on the World Heritage List, similar to the creation of a national park, is that it publicises it, emphasising that there is something worth visiting to. It consequently may become a focus for tourism, offering economic opportunities but also leading to problems of tourism management. The issue of balancing economic opportunity with the need for conservation has special relevance to iconic sites such as the Parthenon in Athens; Angkor in Cambodia; the Taj Mahal in India and Machu Pichu in Peru. There is a danger of such sites becoming items for tourists to tick off, 'been there ... done that', and a subsequent structuring of the operations of the site to cater for mass tourism, presenting a threat to its integrity and conservation. There is also a threat to sites in a much earlier phase of development, as the granting of WHS status may be significant in pushing a new site along the life-cycle of tourism development. A real danger is that such sites may be less equipped to respond to tourism than more iconic sites, which have traditions of dealing with visitors extending to well before their designation as WHS.

The economic benefits that WHS designation can bring to the area of a natural or cultural site are those generic to tourism. A variety of economic multiplier effects, including income and employment will be experienced as a consequence of tourism visitation. Other types of economic benefits include a macro-level contribution to the balance of payments and gross domestic product. For some communities, notably in the rural areas of developing countries, where development opportunities may be limited, tourism may be the most viable option for material advancement.

Pressures for overuse may exist, as there may be a temptation for countries to market WHS sites as iconic attractions for the reason of economic benefits. They may also arise because of the availability of increased information about a site and the easing of accessibility to it, through improved infrastructure. The influence of information and accessibility as factors of tourism demand is as relevant to WHS as it is to other types of tourism destinations. The propensity to visit these sites has been increased by the advent of cheap air travel and information technology, therefore placing even greater pressure on WHS that are located in close proximity to major tourism-generating zones. For example, Pompeii in Italy received 863,000 visitors in 1981, rising to two million by 2006. Inevitably, the advent of mass tourism to WHS, characterised by the involvement of tour operators and organised groups, leads to visitor management pressures.

Tourism that is not carefully planned may pose a threat not only to the physical and cultural entity of the WHS but also their continued designation. Along with problems of climate change, urbanisation and war, tourism is a potential problem. For example, in a report by the Centre for Future Studies (CFS), it is suggested that both WHS of Australia's Great Barrier Reef and Kathmandu could be unpopular by 2020, owing not only to climate change and urban development, respectively, but also the presence of too many tourists. The awareness of the problems that tourism may create led the World Heritage Committee to launch the World Heritage Sustainable Tourism programme in 2001. The programme covers different aspects as listed:

- building the capacity of site management in dealing with tourism, notably through the development of a sustainable tourism management plan;
- training local populations in tourism-related activities so that they can participate and receive benefits from tourism;
- helping to promote relevant local products at the local, national and international levels;
- raising public awareness and building public pride in the local communities through conservation outreach campaigns;
- attempting to use tourism-generated funds to supplement conservation and protection costs at the sites;

- sharing expertise and lessons learned with other sites and protected areas;
- building an increased understanding of the need to protect World Heritage, its values and policies within the tourism industry.

(UNESCO 2006b: 1)

Although there is an inherent emphasis on the relationship between economic benefits, conservation and community involvement, as would be expected in any strategy or plan purporting to sustainable principles, the problems of community support for a WHS may extend beyond purely its involvement or economic benefit. It can often be a question of how their heritage is being presented to tourists and who controls it. Alongside the problematic issue of how to define and identify a 'community' as referred to in the last chapter, issues of politics, power, representation and authenticity mean that how culture is presented is sometimes contentious. It is not necessarily the case that WHS designation will automatically have community support. For example, community dissent to the designation of World Heritage Status is a theme that is relevant in the context of the Wadden Sea in the Netherlands. Exploring local community reaction to the suggestion of the designation of the area as a World Heritage Site, there was found to be widespread opposition to the proposal (Bart *et al.* 2005). The main theme of the rationale for opposition was based on the perceived loss of control in local decision-making by the community as powers were transferred to UNESCO. Closely linked to this was a fear that the local area would be given global significance by this designation leading to increased pressures with little financial support to aid its management.

References

van der Aa, B.J.M., Groote, P.D. and Huigen, P.P.P. (2005) 'World Heritage as NIMBY? The Case of the Dutch Part of the Wadden Sea', in Harrison, D. and Hitchcock, M. (eds) *The Politics of World Heritage: Negotiating Tourism and Conservation.* Clevedon: Channel View Publications, 11–22.

Bushell, R. and McCool, S.F. (2007) 'Tourism as a Tool for Conservation and Support of Protected Areas: Setting the Agenda' in Bushell, R. and McCool, S.F. (eds) *Tourism and Protected Areas: Benefits Beyond Boundaries.* Wallingford: CABI, 12–26.

Bushell, R., Staiff, R. and Eagles, P.J. (2007) 'Tourism and Protected Areas: Benefits Beyond Boundaries' in Bushell, R. and McCool, S.F. (eds) *Tourism and Protected Areas: Benefits Beyond Boundaries.* Wallingford: CABI, 1–11.

Dudley, N. (ed.) (2008) *Guidelines for Applying Protected Area Management Categories.* Gland, Switzerland: International Union for Conservation.

Eagles, P.F.J., McCool, S.F. and Haynes, C.D. (2002) *Sustainable Tourism in Protected Areas: Guidelines for Planning and Management.* Cambridge: IUCN.

Font, X., Cochrane, J. and Tapper, R. (2004) *Tourism for Protected Area Financing: Understanding tourism revenues for effective management plans.* Leeds: Leeds Metropolitan University.

Hall, C. and Lew, A. (eds) (1998) *Sustainable Tourism: a Geographical Perspective.* Harlow: Addison Wesley Longman.

MacCannell, D. (1992) *Empty Meeting Grounds: the Tourist Papers.* London: Routledge.

Murphy, P. (1985) *Tourism: a Community Approach.* London: Routledge

O'Riordan, T. (1981) *Environmentalism,* 2nd edn. London: Pion.

Smith, L. (2007) 'Eco-tourists save forest 'jewels' from bulldozers', *The Times,* London, 29 October, p. 29.

Stone, C.D. (1993) *The Gnat Is Older than Man: Global Environment and Human Agenda,* Princeton, NJ: Princeton University Press.

UNESCO (2006a) *Partnerships for Conservation,* www.unesco.org

——(2006b) *Sustainable Tourism,* www.unesco.org

World Tourism Organization (1992) *Tourism Carrying Capacity: Report on the Senior-Level Expert Group Meeting held in Paris,* June 1990, Madrid: WTO. www.environment.gov.au/indigenous/publications/fs-anindilyakwa.html accessed 12 June 2011.

27

Limits of Acceptable Change and tourism

Stephen McCool

Introduction

How do managers sustain the values for which protected areas have been designated in the face of growing and diversifying societal expectations, changing climatic patterns, declining government support and accelerating tourism and visitation? This question dominates every manager's mind, drives thousands of public meetings annually, forms the basis for innumerable scientific studies, and challenges constituencies who not only want to preserve nature's heritage but also use it for their shelter and sustenance. Although no statistics exist on the global economic significance and use of protected areas for tourism, we do know that tourism is one of the largest industries – however fragmented it may be – in the world, that international travel is growing exponentially and that natural heritage protected areas host hundreds of millions of visitors annually.

At an individual level, managers grapple daily with the potential effects of tourism on the values preserved in a protected area. They struggle with how they can provide opportunities for high-quality visitor experiences that are the basis for a competitive tourism sector. They contend with communities in desperate need of economic opportunity, which see the protected area as a path out of poverty. And, they must integrate these demands into a coherent, effective plan that is resilient in the face of change, acceptable to protected area constituencies and one that is effectively implemented.

Addressing these tasks requires managers to 'work through' the complexities and nuances of tourism management, community relationships and impact mitigation. Tourism or visitor management frameworks provide the structure for this process by influencing what questions are asked and how. The Limits of Acceptable Change (LAC) planning framework (Stankey *et al.* 1985) is one such process. In this chapter, I provide a brief description of this planning framework. Prior to the description, I describe what is meant by a framework in this context. In the third major section of this chapter, I cover some of the significant issues and misunderstandings present in the tourism literature concerning this framework. A case study is briefly presented.

In providing this overview, the reader should note that I was involved as a facilitator, scientist and bureaucrat in the initial application of the LAC process. Over the years, I have worked with numerous protected area organisations, facilitated many educational workshops to help managers implement LAC and published a number of articles on it, its application, its relationship with the notion of recreation or tourism carrying capacity and how the framework can be strengthened. I thus hold a unique perspective in describing the framework and responding to some of the numerous issues identified in the literature.

What is a planning framework?

A framework may be defined as a process involving a sequence of steps that leads managers and planners to explicate, frame and understand a particular issue. A framework in this sense does not necessarily lead to formulation of *'the'* answer to an issue, but provides the conceptual basis and scaffolding through which it may be successfully resolved. Frameworks are structures that enable us to apply critical thinking skills to a complex problem; they are not processes or checklists that can be simply followed without understanding their underlying rationale and conceptual underpinnings. Frameworks allow us to gain insights and create deeper understanding of these issues by forcing us to explicate and 'work through' their various dimensions.

A tourism/visitor/recreation planning framework helps decision-makers gain insights about the particular issue confronting them and then provides some guidance on how to address the issue. Ideally, frameworks achieve these goals in ways that are conceptually sound, easily translated into practice, within the technical capacity of the organisation to implement the methodologies and actions proposed, and identify the distributional consequences of a decision (Brewer 1973). For example, reservation systems to allocate visitation discriminate against those who do not plan in advance; some protected area management policies marginalise the input of local residents; and other management actions may favour those with higher incomes. Finally, the framework must be pragmatic, that is it must be both efficient ('getting the biggest bang for the buck') and it must be effective, that is, simply put, it works.

The literature suggests a limited number of frameworks to assist protected area managers in making decisions about tourism and visitation exist. These include the Recreation Opportunity Spectrum, Visitor Impact Management, Visitor Experience and Resource Protection, Protected Area Visitor Impact Management, LAC and a few others (Nilsen and Tayler 1997; Newsome *et al.* 2002; and McCool *et al.* 2007 for comparative assessments of these frameworks). This chapter is focused on LAC both because of its widespread application and because of a number of issues have arisen with its use.

Brief description of the LAC framework

LAC was originally designed to address the failures of a 'carrying capacity' approach (see below) in managing visitor use in designated Wilderness in the USA. Since its initial application in the Bob Marshall Wilderness (Stankey *et al.* 1984), it has seen use in a variety of areas and in different ecosystems. It has been adapted to tourism (McCool 1994) and used in a number of nature-based situations. The underlying question that LAC focuses on (what are the appropriate and acceptable conditions for an area?) has been argued to be applicable to cultural heritage sites as well (McCool 2006).

LAC, as with other frameworks, can be embedded within planning processes that cover a broader scope of protected area decision-making, or can be used as a framework to assist decisions that are specific to visitor and tourism management. By using indicators and standards, it works within processes designed to assess management effectiveness (see, e.g. Hockings *et al.* 2006).

LAC has variously been described as a 'management by objectives' approach or an 'indicator-based' approach to management. It can be viewed as both a concept (e.g. one that focuses discourse on the appropriateness or acceptability of various conditions) and as a step-based framework to structure planning and decision-making. LAC is based on these propositions:

- any level of human use (e.g. tourism in this case) of a natural area results in some change to biophysical conditions and to visitor experiences;
- the character and amount of resulting change at some point become unacceptable to at least some constituencies;
- diversity in biophysical and social conditions exists and may be desirable;
- preservation of heritage and access (for visitation) are goals that are partly competing but partly overlapping;
- management is required to maintain human-induced impacts within a certain level of acceptability or appropriateness.

LAC as a planning framework incorporates these propositions (McCool (1996) later produced a set of principles underlying management of visitors in protected areas derived out of these propositions) into a series of steps with a particular order and rationale (see Figure 27.1 and Table

Figure 27.1 The Limits of Acceptable Change planning framework

27.1) that represent an adaptive management approach. Table 27.1 provides brief descriptions of each of the steps of the LAC planning framework. During the original application of LAC in the Bob Marshall Wilderness, public engagement was an integral component, and thus further applications in the USA generally proceeded with the proposition that consensus among constituencies was needed for implementation (McCool and Ashor 1984; Krumpe and McCool 1997; Stokes 1990).

Applicability of LAC to tourism management

A wide variety of authors have reported experience with use of LAC to manage various aspects of tourism, particularly in protected areas. Its initial application was to manage visitors in terrestrial designated Wilderness in the USA (Stankey *et al.* 1984; McCoy *et al.* 1995). Several authors report using LAC as a framework for managing snorkelling on reefs and in marine parks (Roman *et al.* 2007; Shafer and Inglis 2000; Schultz *et al.* 1999). Ahn *et al.* (2002) used LAC to examine resident attitudes to determine the applicability and usefulness of Tourism Development Zones at a county scale. McCool (1994) proposed modifications of the LAC framework for more direct applicability to regional tourism development. Brunson (1997) suggested using LAC in situations beyond designated Wilderness. Although use of visitor planning and management frameworks is relatively rare in Europe (Haider 2006), Erkkonen and Itkonen (2006) report use of LAC for a Finnish National Park. Although most applications in the past have occurred in the USA, LAC as a concept has been at the basis of many applications around the world.

Despite the wide variety of applications reported in literature that deal with nature-based tourism, LAC, either as a concept or as a planning framework, has received little attention in mainstream tourism journals (e.g. *Tourism Management, Annals of Tourism Research, Journal of Travel Research, Journal of Sustainable Tourism, Journal of Ecotourism*). Nor have many text authors given more than passing attention to LAC in books about environmental impacts of tourism (e.g. especially Mason 2003; Page 2009; Gunn and Var 2002; Telfer and Sharpley 2009; Singh 2008; Batta 2000) with many of these emphasising establishing a tourism carrying capacity as the solution to managing tourism's ecological and social consequences.[1]

LAC issues and questions

Those managers and planners that apply LAC to tourism development and management situations are often confronted by a number of issues and questions, not only in terms of application, but also in terms of critique. In this section, I examine a few of these issues in order to provide the reader with a more comprehensive background on what LAC does and what its limitations might be. Before moving on to that discussion, the reader should be aware that a number of assessments of LAC have been produced and are available in the literature. For example, McCool and Cole (1997b) organised a workshop to explicitly evaluate LAC and its first decade of use. Nilsen and Tayler (1997) in these proceedings developed a comparative analysis of several planning frameworks. Cole and Stankey (1997) also provided a review of the historical development of LAC, which is important in understanding the framework and the concept. Newsome *et al.* (2002) discuss LAC, its applicability and its limitations. This was followed by McCool *et al.*'s (2007) more comprehensive assessment of a number of recreation and visitor planning frameworks, providing descriptions of how each framework evolved and an evaluation of experience with each. McCool (1989) identified a number of issues and questions involved with application of LAC. A number of clarifications are presented below to complement this literature.

Table 27.1. Brief description of the steps involved in the LAC planning framework (adapted from Stankey *et al.* 1985)

LAC Step	Brief Description
(1) Identify area concerns and issues	Citizens and managers meet to identify what special values, features or qualities within the area require attention, what management problems or concerns have to be dealt with, what issues the public considers important in the area's management, and what role the area plays in both a regional and national context. Scientists also become involved because they may often hold information not readily available. The dialogue among scientists, managers and public helps unify agreement about important values and issues. This step encourages a better understanding of the natural resource base, such as the sensitivity of biodiversity to recreation use and tourism development, a general concept of how the resource could be managed, and a focus on principal management issues. LAC is very much an issue-driven process; issues identified here will be addressed later.
(2) Define and describe opportunity classes	Protected areas contain a diversity of biophysical features—waterfalls, canyons, valleys, beaches, reefs, forests, swamps, wetlands—with some evidence of human occupation and use. These features may vary significantly in terms of the amount and type of development. Likewise, social conditions, such as level and type of use, visitor density, and types of recreation experiences, vary from place to place. The type of management needed may vary throughout the area. Opportunity classes describe subdivisions or zones of the natural resource where different social, resource, or managerial conditions will be maintained (see in this Handbook for a more comprehensive review of zoning). For example, peripheral regions or easily accessible areas of parks may receive higher levels of use and may show evidence of greater levels of impacts. In some protected areas, isolated rest camps exist where the environment has been subject to significant modification. The classes that are developed in step 2 represent a way of defining a range of diverse conditions within the protected area setting. And, while diversity is the objective here, it is important to point out that the conditions found in all cases must be consistent with the objectives laid out in the area's organic legislation or decree. In this step, the number of classes are also defined as well as their general biophysical, social, and managerial conditions (the reader is referred to Stankey and Clark, 1979, for a discussion of the recreation opportunity spectrum which serves as the intellectual foundation for this step).
(3) Select indicators of resource and social conditions	Indicators are specific elements of the re- source or social setting selected to represent (or be "indicative of') the conditions deemed appropriate and acceptable in each opportunity class. Because it is impossible to measure the condition of and change in every biophysical feature or social condition within a protected setting, a few indicators are selected as measures of overall health, just as we relatively frequently monitor our blood pressure rather than more complete tests of blood chemistry. Indicators should be easy to measure quantitatively, relate to the conditions specified by the opportunity classes and reflect changes resulting from visitor use and tourism development. Indicators are an essential part of the LAC framework because their state reflects the overall condition found throughout an opportunity class. It is important to understand that an individual indicator might not adequately depict the condition of a particular area. It is the bundle of indicators that is used to monitor conditions.
(4) Inventory resource and social conditions	Inventories can be time-consuming and expensive components of planning; indeed they usually are. In the LAC process, the inventory is guided by the indicators selected in step 3. For example, level and type of development, use density, and human-induced impacts on biophysical attributes (e.g., soils, vegetation, coral) may be measured. Other variables, such as location of infrastructure (parking, roads, trails, trailheads, interpretive facilities, accommodation, picnic sites, shipwrecks, and docks) can also be inventoried to develop a better understanding of area constraints and opportunities.

Table 27.1. (continued)

LAC Step	Brief Description
	And, inventory information will be helpful later when evaluating the consequences of alternatives. Inventory data are mapped so both the condition and location of the indicators are known. The inventory also helps managers establish realistic and attainable standards. By placing the inventory as step 4, planners avoid unnecessary data collection.
(5) Specify standards for resource and social conditions	In this step, the range of conditions is identified for each indicator considered appropriate and acceptable for each opportunity class. By defining those conditions in measurable terms, the basis for establishing a distinctive and diverse range of settings is established. Standards serve to define the 'limits of acceptable change'. They are the maximum permissible change in conditions that will be allowed in a specific opportunity class. They are not necessarily objectives to be attained. The inventory data collected in step 4 play an important role in setting standards. The standards defining the range of acceptable conditions in each opportunity class should be realistic and attainable; they should not mimic existing (unacceptable) conditions.
(6) Identify alternative opportunity class allocations	Most protected area settings could be managed in several different ways. Protected areas often differ significantly in the amount of development, human density (both residents and visitors), and recreational opportunities available. In this step, we begin to identify some different types of alternatives. Using information from step 1 (area issues and concerns) and step 4 (inventory of existing conditions), managers and citizens can begin to jointly explore how well different opportunity class allocations address the various contending interests, concerns, and values.
(7) Identify management actions for each alternative	The alternative allocations proposed in step 6 are only the first step in the process of developing a preferred alternative. In addition to the kinds of conditions that would be achieved, both managers and citizens need to know what management actions will be required to achieve the desired conditions. In a sense, step 7 requires an analysis of the costs, broadly defined, that will be imposed by each alternative. For example, many people may find attractive the alternative to protect a specific area from any development, and restore to pristine condition any impacts that might exist. However, this alternative might require such a huge commitment of funds for acquisition and enforcement that the alternative might not seem as attractive.
(8) Evaluation and selection of a preferred alternative	With the various costs and benefits of the several alternatives before them, managers and citizens can proceed to the evaluation stage, and can select a preferred alternative. Evaluation must take into consideration many factors, but examples would include the responsiveness of each alternative to the issues identified in step 1, management requirements from step 7, and public preferences. It is important that the factors figuring into the evaluation process and their relative weight be made explicit and available for public review.
(9) Implement actions and monitor conditions	With an alternative finally selected, and articulated as policy by decision-makers, the necessary management actions are put into effect and a monitoring program instituted. Often, an implementation plan, detailing actions, costs, timetable, and responsibilities, will be needed to ensure timely implementation. The monitoring program focuses on the indicators selected in step 3, and compares their condition with those identified in the standards. This information can be used to evaluate the success of actions. If conditions are not improving, the intensity of the management effort might need to be increased or new actions implemented.

LAC as a change in tourism management paradigms

The LAC planning framework was designed to respond to the failures of using a carrying capacity approach to manage visitation – both its social and environmental consequences in designated Wilderness. The failures of a carrying capacity approach are well documented in the literature (e.g. McCool and Lime 2001; Buckley 1999; Washburne 1982; Wagar 1974). In their review of recreation planning frameworks, McCool *et al.* (2007) conclude:

> The experience of recreation carrying capacity in resolving the complex and often contentious issues associated with recreation and tourism development on public lands is uniformly a failure. Not only have intrinsic numerical carrying capacities failed to be identified, but policies limiting use (often portrayed as carrying capacities) often have been unsuccessful in resolving the issue instigating the search for a capacity. We come to this conclusion for three reasons: (1) carrying capacity is a misframing of the use-impact problem, (2) the theoretical foundation for recreation carrying capacity is invalid, and (3) practical implementation of carrying capacity in wildland settings is difficult.

An example might be the Saba Marine Park, located in the Netherlands Antilles and described in the Case study. That park avoided a carrying capacity approach by focusing on identifying acceptable conditions, indicators, zones, standards and management.

Case study

Saba Marine Park

The Saba Marine Park surrounds the island of Saba in the northeastern part of the Caribbean. Saba is part of the Netherlands Antilles. A small island, approximately 7 km in diameter, formed from a volcanic eruption, it is home to about 2,000 inhabitants. The Saba Marine Park was established in 1987 and encompasses about 1300 hectares of coral reef and sea floor from the high water tide mark on the island down to a depth of 60 m.

It is managed by the Saba Conservation Foundation under an agreement with the government of the Netherlands Antilles to protect the coral formations and fisheries within the boundary of the park. Because of the volcanic slopes, the park preserves a variety of coral and coral formations. Combined with clear water, these features make the Park an attractive destination for SCUBA diving.

The park is typical of many protected areas in the world: it is small, not particularly well resourced and intimately connected with the nearby community. At the time of the case study, it employed three people and maintained a small visitor centre. Divers were required to register and pay a dive fee.

SCUBA diving can lead to unacceptable impacts on coral and reefs, although the relationship between diving intensity and coral damage is not particularly deterministic. Poor buoyancy control, dive supervision and touching can lead to breakage and other damage of coral. In addition, visitor use densities and diver behaviour at some moorage points can result in lower quality visitor experiences. In the late 1990s, therefore, the Saba Conservation Foundation embarked on a planning process to protect coral and provide for high-quality visitor experiences using Limits of

Acceptable Change as the framework for planning (see Schultz *et al*. 1999 for the actual plan document).

The planning process involved a small group of Saba residents and the park manager working with a consultant, who resided on the island over a period of 4 months. The consultant facilitated the group in working through the nine steps of the LAC planning framework in this period. Planning proceeded based on the following propositions developed during the first step of the LAC:

- The marine environment forms the basis for all other values and benefits associated with the Saba Marine Park and its management.
- Recreational activities and fishing in the Park are dependent on maintenance of pristine conditions, yet provide substantial monetary and social benefits to participants, the local community and the Park administration.
- The Saba Marine Park and its management organisation exist to protect the values of the coral reef environment through active management of recreationists and provision of learning opportunities for the local community.
- The Saba Marine Park exists within a larger social and environmental context that requires active community involvement and understanding.

The LAC identified four prescriptive management zones displaying a continuum of biophysical, social and managerial conditions. Following this, the process identified several indicators. These indicators included turbidity, salinity, temperature and pollutants to measure water quality, sedimentation, diversity and abundance of fish stock, the amount of broken and abraded branching corals near mooring anchors, number of dive boats anchored at the same mooring point simultaneously and diving party group size. The process included a monitoring plan for each of the indicators.

Explicit standards could not be developed for several indicators because of the lack of available and credible scientific information. However, two examples of standards for the SMP are shown here to exemplify how they can be used.

For the amount of broken and abraded coral:

Zone 1: The proportion of damaged (broken and abraded) branching corals in high-use areas will not exceed 150 per cent of the proportion of damaged (broken and abraded) coral colonies in low-use areas at the same site.
Zones 2–4: The proportion of damaged (broken and abraded) branching corals in high-use areas will not exceed 200 per cent of the proportion of damaged (broken and abraded) coral colonies in low-use areas at the same site.

For the number of dive boats at a mooring buoy at once:

Zone 1: 90 per cent of the time only one dive boat will be present at each site.
Zones 2–4: 50 per cent of the time only one dive boat will be present at each site.

The plan then identifies a series of actions accompanied by a rationale. For example:

Action: The SMP will organise and schedule regular meetings with all the dive operators. These meetings will serve as a forum for addressing current issues and discussing special problems. The operators will also be able to provide feedback to Park management on areas that may need increased monitoring.

> *Rationale:* These actions are intended to modify the character of use by controlling where and when use occurs, as well as visitor behaviour.

LAC represents, if not a new paradigm of management, then a re-framing of the fundamental question driving management of visitors in nature-dominated settings from that of 'how many is too many?' to 'what are the appropriate/acceptable conditions?'. Focusing on identifying such conditions does not lead, as Cocossis (2004) argues in his treatise advocating use of tourism carrying capacities, to incremental and negative changes due to shifting social values. As Freimund and Cole (2001) note, the move from carrying capacity to LAC was a move from focusing on visitor numbers to emphasising setting quality. Even establishing a carrying capacity, if that were possible, would still reflect a debate about the relative importance of different goals and the trade-offs inherent in making decisions; such debates and trade-offs are a function of the social preferences underlying discourse about protected areas and tourism. LAC forces its users to explicitly consider such preferences, values and beliefs in making these decisions rather than having them hidden under an illusion of 'scientific objectivity'.

The difference between carrying capacity and use limit policies

LAC is focused first on identifying and securing agreement on the outcomes of management, then on translating those outcomes in quantified standards of acceptable change and finally on implementing management actions. Once the standards have been defined and implemented, then managers select from an array of tools to avoid standards being violated. One of those tools is a use limit policy. A use limit policy is a formalised statement of the maximum number of visitors permitted to enter a protected area during a specified time period. This statement occurs as policy and is enforced by management. These policies may also encompass limits on group size or length of stay and represent tools that are implemented to ensure that standards are not violated. For example, in the Saba Marine Park, group size limits are imposed primarily to achieve goals related to visitor experiences and avoid damage to corrals. Use limits are not the same as carrying capacities, which are often defined as the maximum amount of use that can occur before degradation of resources or experiences occurs (Wahab and Pigram 1997; Lubbe 2005).[2] In the carrying capacity approach, managers initially focus on identifying a capacity and then implement actions to achieve that capacity. A use limit policy differs in that it is designed to maintain, or not violate, accepted standards of change in conditions or outcomes, which are identified prior to choosing management actions. Managers implement use limit policies when other techniques and actions are either not maintaining conditions in a desired state or it is foreseen that standards will be violated.

LAC is not a method to identify carrying capacity

Some authors frame LAC as a method to identify an area's carrying capacity or as an approach to implementation of carrying capacity (Jensen and Guthrie 2006; Manning 2000, 2002). It is not. It is an alternative formulation of the objective of management and planning, which is to provide visitors with opportunities for high-quality experiences and to limit the impacts of visitor behaviour and tourism development.

Unfortunately, this perspective has led to a number of misunderstandings of the LAC process and similar planning frameworks. LAC was developed because of failures to identify quantitative carrying capacities, principally in US designated Wilderness, Wild and Scenic rivers and backcountry areas of national parks (see an early description of implication for tourism by McCool 1978). Although use limits (often called carrying capacities) were established, their efficacy in controlling, mitigating and reducing biophysical and social impacts of tourism use have rarely been evaluated.

LAC is not a process to establish a tourism carrying capacity. It is a process to help managers think through the complex challenges of integrating two often conflicting and yet frequently overlapping goals: that of providing access to protected areas while at the same time preserving the natural heritage values for which they were established (Cole 1995; McCool and Cole 1997a). Managers – working with their constituencies – identify which of these goals is most important, compromise the attainment of one (in order to achieve the other), but in so doing establish how much change (reflected in the compromise) is socially, politically and environmentally acceptable. Decisions about tourism in protected areas – what uses will be allowed where under what conditions – make these trade-offs, whether they are explicated in processes like LAC or they are hidden from purview like carrying capacity. LAC explicitly focuses on what conditions, for example natural heritage values or visitor experiences, are acceptable given the desire to have the areas accessible for tourism and visitation. Once those conditions are defined and agreed on, then tools are applied to ensure those conditions are achieved. In Saba, for example, no overall carrying capacities were established.

Public engagement and LAC

When LAC was in its developmental stages – in the early 1980s prior to publication of the process by Stankey *et al.* (1985) – there *was* initially little discussion of the role of public engagement. However, when LAC was first applied – and this application began before the Stankey *et al.* (1985) publication – public engagement was an explicit and important component. Engagement of the public in this initial application was deliberately and explicitly constructed using Friedmann's (1973) theory of transactive planning as the conceptual foundation.

The Bob Marshall LAC-based planning process used a task force consisting of managers, scientists, visitors and other constituencies to develop the plan. The task force, although now known by a different name, still holds annual meetings now 28 years after its initial formation. During the planning phase, the task force was engaged in discourse about how each of the nine LAC steps applies to the Bob Marshall Wilderness. Decisions about issues, zoning, indicators, standards, management actions and monitoring were all made in a public setting.

The role of the public in LAC processes has been extensively discussed in the literature (e.g. McCool and Ashor 1984; Stankey *et al.* 1984; Krumpe and McCool 1997; Stokes 1990; Eagles *et al.* 2002). It is succinctly represented in Figure 27.2. A better description of the relationship between the technical planning and public engagement processes would be to think of it as a double-helix with each process represented by a strand with connections between (see Chapter 48). Development of the Saba Marine Park plan involved a small group of local residents working with park management.

What is acceptable and what is preferred?

One point of confusion in application of LAC and other similar frameworks is the difference between what is acceptable and what is preferred. The standards that are set through the LAC planning framework are not conditions that are desired, they are conditions, given the goal of access for recreation or tourism, that are tolerated or accepted. Management seeks to avoid violating these standards just as management seeks to avoid violating water quality standards for

Figure 27.2 Effective planning – planning that can be implemented – in an era of complexity, change and uncertainty depends on integration of two factors

faecal coliform counts. Most people would prefer that standards describing limits of changes in conditions acceptable would be set at zero. However, given (1) the desire for visitor access and (2) that even small amounts of use result in some change, the LAC must be set at some level other than zero. So, protected area organisations seek to identify this limit of change deemed acceptable through the use of science, experiential knowledge, reference to law and policy and public engagement. This is a matter of making trade-offs between goals that are partly competing and partly overlapping.

This brings up the question of acceptable to whom? As many constituencies reflecting varying interests in protected areas exist, the question of whose values matter arises. Protected area tourism planning is very much a political process, where various constituencies vie, compete and collaborate in constructing, negotiating and pursuing their interests. The conditions acceptable to each constituency will vary. Ideally, managers would facilitate construction of standards that reflect the values of those constituencies involved in the initial designation of the area. Although this process is often termed 'balancing' various interests, the term 'integrating' or 'accommodating' interests would be more descriptive of what actually occurs. In this respect, McCool (2009) observes:

> Constructing and achieving such agreement [about goals and acceptable conditions] is a fundamental goal of protected area tourism planning … While there remain many such desired futures in pluralistic societies, partnerships can build a shared vision that is at least

acceptable, if not preferred, to a protected area's constituencies. Such shared vision is a prerequisite to allocation of resources, and indeed, often serves as a motivation itself for securing resources for implementation.

Conclusion

LAC is one of the most widely recognised concepts in protected area tourism planning. Used in a wide variety of situations, it was constructed as a response to failures of carrying capacity-based approaches to the issue of resolving conflicts between goals of preserving natural conditions and allowing access for visitation and tourism, goals commonly held among the globe's 140,000 or so nationally designated protected areas. LAC has three particularly noteworthy strengths: (1) focusing management on identifying desired conditions first, then identifying appropriate and effective management actions; (2) forcing the value judgements intrinsic to tourism management to be explicitly stated and therefore subject to discourse; and (3) its traditional use of engaging the public in development and implementation.

LAC is not designed to provide global or national level frameworks for tourism policy; it was never intended as such. LAC does not provide answers as such; its value is primarily in providing a structure for planners, managers and constituencies to work through the complexities of integrating preservation and access goals. Although it has been used in protected area settings, its use as a regional level planning tool for tourism development has been limited. This use should be tested so we can learn more about its utility.

Notes

1 An exception is Newsome *et al.* (2002) who provide good discussions of LAC and other similar visitor planning frameworks.
2 I note here that any level of use leads to some impact, which many would define as degradation, which leads to the ridiculous conclusion that the carrying capacity is zero.

References

Ahn, B.Y., Lee, B.K. and Shafer, C.S. (2002) 'Operationalizing sustainability in regional tourism planning: an application of the limits of acceptable change framework', *Tourism Management* 23(1), 1–15.
Batta, A. (2000) *Tourism and the environment: A quest for sustainability*. New Delhi: Indus Publ.
Brewer, G.D. (1973) *Politicians, bureaucrats, and the consultant: a critique of urban problem solving*. New York: Basic Books.
Brunson, M.W. (1997) 'Beyond wilderness: Broadening the applicability of limits of acceptable change?', in McCool, S.F. and Cole, D.N. (comps), *Proceedings—limits of acceptable change and related planning processes: progress and future directions*. Gen. Tech. Rep. INT-GTR-371. Ogden, UT: US Department of Agriculture, Forest Service, Rocky Mountain Research Station, 44–8.
Buckley, R. (1999) 'An ecological perspective on carrying capacity, *Annals of Tourism Research* 26 (3), 705–8.
Clark, R.N. and Stankey, G.H. (1979) *The recreation opportunity spectrum: A framework for planning, management, and research*. Gen. Tech. Report PNW-98. Portland OR. US Department of Agriculture, Forest Service, Pacific Northwest Research Station.
Cocossis, H. and Mexa, A. (2004) *The challenge of tourism carrying capacity assessment: theory and practice*, Aldershot: Ashgate Publ.
Cole, D.N. (1995) 'Defining fire and wilderness objectives: applying limits of acceptable change', in J.K. Brown, R.W. Mutch, C.W. Spoon and R.H. Wakimoto (eds), *Proceedings, symposium on fire in wilderness and park management*. Ogden, UT: USDA Forest Service, Intermountain Research Station, 42–7.
Cole, D.N. and Stankey, G.H. (1997) 'Historical development of limits of acceptable change: conceptual clarifications and possible extensions', in McCool, S.F. and Cole, D.N. (comps). *Proceedings—limits of*

acceptable change and related planning processes: progress and future directions. Gen. Tech. Rep. INTGTR- 371. Ogden, UT: US Department of Agriculture, Forest Service, Rocky Mountain Research Station, 5–9.

Eagles, P.F.J., McCool S.F. and Haynes, C.D. (2002) *Sustainable tourism in protected areas: Guidelines for planning and management*. Gland, Switzerland, International Union for the Conservation of Nature.

Erkkonen, J. and Itkonen, P.J. (2006) 'Monitoring sustainable nature tourism in practice – experiences from Pyha-Luosta National Park, Finland', in Siegrist, D., Clivaz, C., Hunziker, M. and Iten, S. (eds) *Exploring the Nature of Management. Proceedings of the Third International Conference on Monitoring and Management of Visitor Flows in Recreational and Protected Areas*. University of Applied Sciences Rapperswil, Switzerland, 13–17 September 2006. Rapperswil.

Freimund, W.A. and Cole, D.N. (2001) 'Use Density, Visitor Experience, and Limiting Recreational Use in Wilderness: Progress to Date and Research Needs', in Freimund, W.A. and Cole, D.N. (comps), *Visitor use density and wilderness experience: proceedings*, 1–3 June 2000, Missoula, MT. Proc. RMRS-P-20. Ogden, UT: US Department of Agriculture, Forest Service, Rocky Mountain Research Station.

Friedmann, J. (1973) *Retracking America*. New York: Anchor/Doubleday.

Haider, W. (2006) 'North American idols: Personal observations on visitor management frameworks and recreation research', in Siegrist, D., Clivaz, C., Hunziker, M. and Iten, S. (eds) *Exploring the Nature of Management. Proceedings of the Third International Conference on Monitoring and Management of Visitor Flows in Recreational and Protected Areas*. Rapperswil: University of Applied Sciences Rapperswil, Switzerland, 13–17 September 2006.

Gunn, C.A. and Var, T. (2002) *Tourism planning: basics, concepts, cases*. London: Psychology Press.

Hockings, M., Stolton, S., Levenington, F., Dudley, N. and Courrau, J. (2006) *Evaluating Effectiveness: A framework for assessing management effectiveness of protected areas*, 2nd edn. Gland, Switzerland and Cambridge: IUCN.

Jensen, C.R. and Guthrie, S. (2006) 'Outdoor recreation in America', *Human Kinetics*.

Krumpe, E. and McCool, S.F. (1997) 'Role of public involvement in the limits of acceptable change wilderness planning system', in McCool, S.F. and Cole, D.N. (comps), *Proceedings—limits of acceptable change and related planning processes: progress and future directions*. Gen. Tech. Rep. INT-GTR-371. Ogden, UT: US Department of Agriculture, Forest Service, Rocky Mountain Research Station, 16–20.

Lubbe, B. (2005) *Tourism management in South Africa*. Johannesburg: Pearson South Africa.

Mason, P. (2003) *Tourism impacts, planning and management*. Butterworth-Heineman.

Manning, R.E. (2002) 'How much is too much? Carrying capacity of national parks and protected areas', in A. Arnberger, C. Brandenburg, A. Muhar (eds) *Monitoring and Management of Visitor Flows in Recreational and Protected Areas Conference Proceedings*, Vienna: Bodenkulhs University Vienna, 206–313.

Manning, R. (2000) 'Crowding in Parks and Outdoor Recreation: A Theoretical, Empirical, and Managerial Analysis', *Journal of Park and Recreation Administration* 18(4), 57–72.

McCool, S.F. (1978) 'Recreation use limits and issues for the tourism industry', *Journal of Tourism Research* 17(2), 2–7.

——(1989) 'Limits of acceptable change: some principles towards serving visitors and managing our resources', in Graham, R. and Lawrence, R. (eds), *Proceedings of a North American workshop on visitor management in parks and protected areas*. Waterloo, ON: University of Waterloo, 194–200.

——(1994) Planning for sustainable nature dependent tourism development: The limits of acceptable change system, *Tourism Recreation Research* 19(2), 51–5.

——(1996) *Limits of acceptable change: A framework for managing national protected areas: Experiences from the United States*. Paper presented at Workshop on Impact Management in Marine Parks, Kuala Lumpur, Malaysia. 13–14 August 1996.

——(2006) *Framing the Question of Visitor Management at Cultural Heritage Sites: The Role of Planning and Related Methodologies From a Critical Perspective*. Paper presented at International Seminar on Tourism Planning at Major World Heritage Archaelogical Sites, The Alhambra, Granada, Spain, 19–23 February 2006.

——(2009) 'Constructing partnerships for protected area tourism planning in an era of change and messiness', *Journal of Sustainable Tourism* 17(2), 133–48.

McCool, S.F. and Ashor, J.J. (1984) *Politics and rivers: creating effective citizen involvement in management decisions in proceedings, national river recreation symposium*. Baton Rouge, LA: Louisiana State University, 136–51.

McCool, S.F. and Cole, D.N. (1997a) 'Experiencing limits of acceptable change: some thoughts after a decade of implementation', in McCool, S.F. and Cole, D.N. (comps), *Proceedings—limits of acceptable change and related planning processes: progress and future directions*. Gen. Tech. Rep. INT-GTR-371. Ogden, UT: US Department of Agriculture, Forest Service, Rocky Mountain Research Station, 72–8.

McCool, S.F. and Cole, D.N. (comps) (1997b) *Proceedings—limits of acceptable change and related planning processes: progress and future directions. Gen. Tech. Rep. INT-GTR-371.* Ogden, UT: US Department of Agriculture, Forest Service, Rocky Mountain Research Station.

McCool, S.F. and Lime, D.W. (2001) 'Tourism carrying capacity: Tempting fantasy or useful reality?', *Journal of Sustainable Tourism* 9(5), 372–88.

McCool, S.F., Clark, R.N. and Stankey, G.H. (2007) *An assessment of frameworks useful for public land recreation planning.* Gen. Tech. Report PNW-GTR-705. Portland, OR: US Department of Agriculture, Forest Service, Pacific Northwest Research Station.

McCoy, L., Krumpe, E.E. and Allen, S. (1995) 'Limits of Acceptable Change Planning-evaluating implementation by the US Forest Service', *International Journal of Wilderness* 1(2), 18–22.

Newsome, D.N., Moore, S.A. and Dowling, R.K. (2002) *Natural area tourism: ecology, impacts and management.* Buffalo, NY: Channel View Publications.

Nilsen, P. and Tayler, G. (1997) 'A comparative analysis of protected area planning and management frameworks', in McCool, S.F., Cole, D.N. (comps), *Proceedings—limits of acceptable change and related planning processes: progress and future directions. Gen. Tech. Rep. INT-GTR-371.* Ogden, UT: US Department of Agriculture, Forest Service, Rocky Mountain Research Station, 49–57.

Page, S.J. (2009) *Tourism management: Managing for change* (3rd edn). Butterworth-Heinemann.

Roman, G.S.J., Dearden, P. and Rollins, R. (2007) 'Application of zoning and limits of acceptable change to manage snorkeling tourism', *Environmental Management* 39, 819–30.

Schultz, E., McCool, S.F. and Kooistra, D. (1999) *Management plan, Saba Marine Park.* Saba Conservation Foundation, The Bottom, Saba Netherlands Antilles.

Shafer, C. and Inglis, G. (2000) 'Influence of social, biophysical, and managerial conditions on tourism experiences within the Great Barrier Reef World Heritage Area', *Environmental Management* 26(1), 73–87.

Singh, L.K. (2008) *Ecology, environment and tourism.* New Delhi: Gyan Publishing House.

Stankey, G.H., Cole, D.N., Lucas, R.C., Petersen, M.E. and Frissell, S.S., Jr (1985) *The limits of acceptable change (LAC) system for wilderness planning.* USDA Forest Service General Technical Report INT-176.

Stankey, G.H., McCool, S.F. and Stokes, G.L. (1984) Limits of acceptable change: a new framework for managing the Bob Marshall Wilderness Complex, *Western Wildlands* 10(3), 33–7.

Stokes, G.L. (1990) 'The evolution of wilderness management: The Bob Marshall Complex', *Journal of Forestry* 88(10), 15–20.

Telfer, D.J. and Sharpley, R. (2008) *Tourism and development in the developing world.* Abingdon: Taylor & Francis.

Wagar, J.A. (1974) 'Recreational carrying capacity reconsidered', *Journal of Forestry* 72(5), 274–8.

Wahab, S. and Pigram, J.J. (1997) *Tourism, development and growth: the challenge of sustainability.* London: Psychology Press,.

Washburne, R.F. (1982) 'Wilderness recreation carrying capacity: Are numbers necessary?', *Journal of Forestry* 80, 726–8.

Further reading

Cole, D.N. and McCool, S.F. (1997) 'Limits of acceptable change and natural resources planning: When is LAC useful, when is it not?', in McCool, S.F. and Cole, D.N. (comps), *Proceedings—limits of acceptable change and related planning processes: progress and future directions.* Gen. Tech. Rep. INT-GTR-371. Ogden, UT: US Department of Agriculture, Forest Service, Rocky Mountain Research Station, 69–71.

McCool, S.F. (2001) 'Limiting recreational use in wilderness: research issues and management challenges in appraising their effectiveness', in Freimund, W.A. and Cole, D.N. (comps), *Proceedings. RMRS-P-20.* Ogden, UT: US Department of Agriculture, Forest Service, Rocky Mountain Research Station, 49–55.

Stankey, G.H. and McCool S.F. (1984) 'Carrying capacity in recreational settings: Evolution, appraisal and application', *Leisure Sciences* 6(4), 453–73.

28

Sustainable tourism certification

Xavier Font

Introduction

Academics and practitioners have in the past been preoccupied with identifying practice that could represent the concepts of sustainability. Much case study work has been reported in the literature, and industry has promoted sustainability awards to showcase best practices. The further identification of best practices has led to setting lists of common characteristics of such businesses that can be identified, with a managerial aspiration to transfer best practices. The next logical step was that of setting criteria to assess sustainability, in the case of tourism either by non-governmental organisations, the public sector or a combination of both (WTO 2002).

These criteria need to be industry-relevant and achievable by a (small) proportion of the sector, achieved through benchmarking best practice, either qualitatively (through cases) or quantitatively (through the measurement of indicators such as water and energy consumption and waste production). Part of the process includes setting indicators that can credibly and effectively measure the standards across the range of applicants for which they are intended. Compliance with these indicators is verified by an assessor who has been deemed as competent for the task (involving skills and no conflict of interest). If the assessment is successful, the applicant is certified as meeting the standards. The certification body could be subject to a procedure of accreditation, guaranteeing that the certification body has undertaken its tasks correctly. The overall aim is that the label of this Sustainable Tourism Certification Program (STCP) will be recognised by consumers or distribution channels, and considered as added value that leads to its acceptance in the market place, to support the marketing of companies that meet standards.

Market-based instruments such as certification are appealing to both governments and industry because they are pro-active, enabling approaches to manage impacts. They encourage firms through economic incentives to uptake technologies and practices to reduce their environmental performance, while promoting longer term lower operational costs through ecosavings, and to encourage responsible purchasing by customers and intermediaries through showcasing environmental credentials at the point of purchase. The earlier writings in certification conceptualised the problems of sustainability around the lack of identification of firms, and as such have proposed certification as the instrument that will differentiate sustainable from unsustainable firms (Buckley 2002; Griffin and de Lacy 2002; most chapters in Honey 2002; Synergy 2000).

Although the number of labels has increased rapidly, this cannot be explained by their effectiveness or efficiency, as these are not often measured (UNEP 2005). Ten years ago the number of applicants for the great majority of labels was growing slowly, mainly due to geographical diversification, not market penetration (WTO 2002). There are no currently published figures on certified firms other than by reviewing one programme at a time – the largest scheme is currently the Green Tourism Business Scheme, operating primarily in the UK.

Certification redefines sustainability

The deceptive simplicity of conceptual sustainability definitions is the result of the contested nature of an ill-defined concept, that becomes obvious in attempting to operationalise the concept into metrics (Garrod and Fyall 1998). Without more robust definitions and shared understanding, we might have accepted some shortcuts that could compromise the integrity of both purpose and outcome. Three particular aspects of how certification redefines sustainability are reviewed: whether it is a process or an actual level of performance; the nature of the standards set (particularly whether they are environmental only, or also socio-economic); and the challenges in measuring sustainability.

The first aspect is considering whether sustainability is a process or an actual performance, and its implications. Non-governmental organisations tend to prefer *performance-based* standards over process ones wherever the first are available (Boström 2003), and have criticised process standards (mainly ISO 14001) based on the argument that process does not guarantee sustainability, that improvements could be too small to be meaningful and start from a low base (Krut and Gleckman 1998). Industry prefers to see sustainability in a *process-based*, incremental way (Mol 2000) because this allows firms to tackle one aspect at a time and prioritise. NGOs in tourism have criticised process standards influenced by a partisan analysis of Green Globe 21 by Synergy (2000) that studied breadth and not depth, and the subsequent attack on all process-based standards by Honey (Honey and Rome 2001; Honey and Stewart 2002).

It is here argued that Honey, as well as Synergy's analysis, were overly influenced by their political views on governance. They criticised both ISO and Green Globe not necessarily for encouraging process standards, but for being overly managerial, abstract and expensive global standards that do not involve civil society (see also Vivanco 2007). Their analysis is also too simplistic; looking at the criteria for 59 STCPs, around 40 per cent of the criteria refer to generic management actions (and therefore processes, not performance) such as developing a sustainability policy, and ensuring that procedures are in place for the identification and correction of impacts, combined with minimum threshold performance criteria, not as either/or (Font and Bendell 2002). The difficulties in measuring social standards also make their nature as process or performance a question of interpretation (Font and Harris 2004).

A particular aspect of interest is how the decisions over the criteria and priorities in tourism certification are socially constructed and politicised. This is because certification responds to society's demand for neatly packaged answers. Fennel and Malloy (2007a) suggest that teological codes (those that explain the consequences of behaviour) are more likely to be followed than deontological codes (those that rely on a sense of moral duty). However, the current 'holy grail' search in corporate social responsibility will mean that teological codes (and certification by extension) focus on 'doing good to do well' (Vogel 2005). Jamal et al. (2006) speak of this instrumentalist approach to both ecotourism and subsequently to certification.

Their view is that certification legitimises *egotourism* (Mowforth and Munt 1998) with '"positive" norms that appear neutral or morally appropriate because the discursive structures that deliver them deflect questioning the kind of experience, or the social behaviours and types of human ecological relationships being formed' (Jamal *et al.* 2006: 160). It is arguable that the larger scale the certification programme, the more compromises will be made to provide standardised answers driven by scientific ecological governmentality, further removed from the companies that need to apply them. Jamal *et al.* (2006) explain the reasons for poor social criteria in certification found by Font and Harris (2004) by arguing that the current instrumental form of ecotourism, and by extension ecotourism certification, is to use inhabitants as a means to an end of conservation. Local decision-making participation and social-cultural equity, they argue, should *really* be incorporated into ecotourism certification.

If we agree with the point above, the consequence is accepting that the meaning, practices and expectations of sustainability are culturally sensitive and specific to different types of firm (from an all-inclusive resort to a community ecolodge) – making the idea of Global Sustainable Tourism Criteria quite difficult. The meanings of sustainability need to be locally grounded, and the debate between stakeholders on the meaning of sustainability in a given locality is likely to be one of the richest (and most troublesome) episodes from certification.

Medina's ethnographic study suggests that sustainability criteria have 'multiple and contested meanings' (Medina 2005: 293), with different interpretations of key issues such as 'local' and 'participation' between the local stakeholders and certification efforts, backing up Yanow's (2000) point that policy development and analysis should be grounded in the views of those affected by it. Medina (2005) explained how national locals (as opposed to a growing number of expatriates owning ecolodges) are less able to contribute to the process of standard setting, and have fewer chances of meeting the standards set. Equally, Vivanco (2007) explains how indigenous voices are absent in the development of standards and certification programs, a situation already experienced 10 years earlier with reference to developing countries and ISO standards (Krut and Gleckman 1998).

This complexity in defining standards is, however, problematic for the operation of certification in the market place, because certification is meant to provide simple and consistent messages. The most common debate on the meaning of sustainability, between the environmental concerns of the North and the developmental needs of the South, can also be seen in certification. Hotel environmental efficiency certification started in Europe, measuring and improving water and energy consumption and waste production. Still, today, the majority of programmes focus exclusively on environmental aspects, which could be criticised as shallow environmentalism. In a study of five cases operating partly or wholly in developing countries, Font and Harris (2004) show how socio-economic (contribution to the local community and labour) standards are more complex.

A further point to be made in this section regards how measurement processes affect the working definition of sustainability. '"Environmental conscience" and "transformative" behaviour are not generally factored in ecotourism certification and management systems' (Jamal *et al.* 2006: 151), arguably because they are complex to measure. The argument put forward is that practicalities of the process of measurement take priority over the meaning of sustainability itself (Font and Bendell 2002), and therefore certification is 'a compromised product, and not necessarily an altruistic means of evaluating' (Sasidharan *et al.* 2002: 167), and as such 'independent verification' does not bring legitimacy in some cultural contexts (Vivanco 2007). In tourism, social criteria are much softer than environmental ones, and at the moment any programme certifying 'sustainability' basically focuses on the environment, with a sprinkling of socio-economic criteria (Font and Harris 2004). There are two reasons for this.

First, water, energy and waste are easily quantifiable and measurable. They are also favoured criteria because they lead to ecosavings with a relatively immediate return on investment, whereas social standards increase operating costs (echoing criticisms of current forms of EM as being too soft). This short-term cost-cutting mentality is also driving ISO 14001 compliance promoted by upstream supply chain demands (Smith and Crotty 2007), showing limited support for the argument that self-regulation will contribute to sustainable innovation (much as in the case of many Australian operators complying with EcoCert, Thwaites 2007).

Second, as social assessment methodologies are open to interpretation, most certifications demand examples of socio-economic aspects rather than surveying all practices, and there is more room for being 'understanding' as to why some measures are not implemented. If the alternative is approaching the measurement of sustainability through monetary valuation (Garrod and Fyall 1998), or by scoring points for criteria met (only in some certification programmes), this means criteria can be understood as being tradeable, and companies can make up poor performance on one issue by doing better on another (Korhonen 2003). The challenge ahead still remains how to measure with the same, or at least comparable, methodology such different elements of sustainability cost-effectively.

Certification not only changes the working definition of sustainability around what can be easily measured as earlier explained, but also gives ownership of this definition away from the companies practicing it. Speaking about Green Globe 21, Fennel and Malloy (2007b) say that 'there is something wrong about capitalising on intellectual assets' (2007b: 51). Ecolabels run by private firms or industry associations need transparency for trust (Fennell and Malloy 2007b; Mamic 2004). The moral high ground of certification means little is actually known about their finances other than to say they mainly rely on start-up funds for fixed costs and the income barely covers variable costs.

Benefits from certification

The second area of interest is the critical understanding of the benefits promoted and gained from certification, usually categorised as green *management* and *marketing* to differentiate certification from other governance tools that would only contribute to one of the two aspects. Certification stakeholders have developed, often overly enthusiastically, statements that environmental credentials sell and it is the limited market exposure arising from too many labels that lessen their impact. Since then, independent analyses started to question their environmental effectiveness and economic efficiency (OECD 2003), with corporate governance and pre-empting legislation being the major factors for Asian hotels to implement ISO 14001 (Chan and Wong 2006).

A recent study has found a strong myopic commitment justified through utilitarian discourses, based on levering additional funding for the environmental cause, even if there were concerns over the actual benefits of certification (Botterill and Nelson 2005). Green management benefits have not been achieved at the scale needed, because certification takes credit for the improved behaviour of the companies it portrays. It is arguable that many of the certified organisations have not improved their performance *thanks to* the process of certification, but they have used this new mechanism to promote past practice (Ayuso 2007). Equally, standards are created on the image of the early certification examples – often those firms that were 'good' before certification, without properly understanding how difficult it may well be for new lessexperienced firms to meet the standards.

However, green marketing is not doing any better. Ecolabels are meant to be useful marketing brands by translating complex issues into a simple, endorsed and meaningful message. But low consumer awareness, and for the majority of products low impact on decision-making or willingness to pay, have left most ecolabels without market traction (Jordan *et al.* 2004). Although 'commodity culture' consumption might have become the new activism and fuels purchases of products as varied as certified timber and a range of fair trade goods, certification cannot position itself as the vehicle to identify alternative forms of tourism consumption, and the equivalent political ecology narratives cannot be applied.

For those seeking this alternative, the products they find as certified are not meaningfully different to those they can find through other channels. Certification cannot reinforce Edenic values as in, for example, 'Save the Forest' campaigns linked to sustainable timber, because tourism is a high involvement purchase. There is little room for 'solidarity' or 'conservation' commodity cultures other than for a niche market, and when this will not affect the core enjoyment of the product. As the cost of monitoring is greater than the benefits accrued by the firm from visible compliance, limited funds are invested in monitoring (Fennell and Malloy 2007a).

Font and Epler Wood (2007) focused specifically on the ability of certification to deliver marketing-based competitive advantage to tourism firms, to challenge the discourses that promote sustainability as a competitive advantage tool, which are crucial to the acceptance of certification as a problem closure solution. They claim that most certification programmes had not collected evidence of consumer demand for certification, and only inferred from more general and often overly optimistic demand for sustainable products. Anecdotal information indicates that businesses may be able to position themselves more effectively in the market place if they follow sustainable practices. Certification may help to validate these practices in the market place, but this process will take between 8 and 15 years (Bien 2005).

The explanation behind this is that the limit to certification is the market itself. Market forces will inevitably focus on win–wins, the business case for responsible behaviour. Vogel (2005) says 'there is a place in the business system for responsible firms, but the market for virtue is not sufficiently important to make it in the interest of all firms to behave more responsibly' (Vogel 2005: 17). By extension, Vogel speaks about the unrealistic expectations placed on self-regulation, saying there is a time and a place for corporate and supplier certification, influenced by market forces and risk management. Using sustainability certification as part of the regulation toolbox will work for as long as government does not relinquish its responsibility to set minimum standards, and civil society understands the limits of corporate social responsibility.

Equity in access to certification

The argument put forward here is that there are inequities in accessing certification that short-term fundraising can only temporarily hide. Although it can be argued that participatory research, and community-based actions as their outcome, need to be biased in favour of the less powerful (Hall 2001; House 2005), the approach that lobbying and fundraising for certification has taken acts against this.

The point debated here is the extent of the benefits that firms should receive from certification, because tourism companies do not start from a level playing field that allows them access to be certified. Key preconditions for sustainable local economic development, such as local ownership, local sourcing and access to capital for the less-privileged sections of society have thus been compromised (Cleverdon and Kalisch 2000; Stonich 1998). The issue of whether Western European countries should have certification has not been questioned and not seen as a barrier to trade, but this is a key concern when thinking of developing countries (Font and Bendell 2002). Font (2005) argues that although sustainability-related policy interventions implicitly or explicitly aim to promote equity, certification is fundamentally fraud as a sustainability governance tool where it can promote, and legitimize, inequity. As put by Vivanco (2007), today certification is blamed as the tip of the iceberg for many injustices further below that it does not cause, but that it legitimises.

Equity was a factor in the work by Font and Bendell (2002) when examining the challenges for small firms and developing countries of setting a single global standard for sustainability. As the health and safety and quality assurance requirements part of supply chain management has limited access for small firms (Curtin and Busby 1999), more research is needed to understand if sustainability certification can be a facilitator or barrier to trade. The only data available are from a survey from 2000 where participation in the Costa Rican programme correlated highly with Chief Executive Officer's level of education and environmental expertise – but no differences were found between Costa Rican nationals and expatriates (Rivera and de Leon 2005).

Equitable access to certification is not just linked to nationality, and from Australia to Central America several studies point at it as key weakness (Ingram 2007; Medina 2005; Thwaites 2007; Vivanco 2007). This is, however, in an environment where neither the market nor the distribution channels have given preference to certified firms. As tour operators start to show interest in sustainability criteria for their supply chains, it will be important to conduct further research testing on whether certification is an effective mechanism to empower disadvantaged groups in the market place, or whether it legitimises inequities.

Font (2005) frames certification as a system whereby STCPs rely on government support, where none of these programmes are financially solvent and rely on subsidies, and with limited increase in numbers for the more established programmes. A firm's application fee only covers part of the costs of the service they receive (training and verification), but the services received are not sufficient to reduce their operating costs (through ecosavings) or to increase turnover (through marketing) to offset the price paid and time invested. This is only possible because programmes are government (or NGO) subsidised (although only for the start-up period), the main challenge being the long run.

With no evidence beyond anecdotes to back up the benefits of certification, it would be unwise to recommend that governments in developing countries should invest in certification at the cost of providing other services. The Australian programme, often praised as an example to follow, shows these challenges. Volunteer time was needed to keep prices low for small firms, and moving from self-assessment to audits was only possible through a grant, which takes place during the 3 years of being certified and not upfront, which has resulted in 45 per cent of audited firms having to make changes. In scaling-up benefits to attract more applicants, complex and sizeable applications are poorly completed by less committed firms, and more time is spent on educating and auditing applicants, which in turn means increased costs and affordability issues (Thwaites 2007).

Conclusion

This chapter has reviewed the current practices of environmental and sustainability certification as a market-based mechanism to promote sustainable production and consumption. It reviewed the consequences of the developments of certification as a movement, the expectations placed on this tool for both competitiveness through improved management and marketing. Two variations of certification, business to consumer and business to business, are included to show the increasing sophistication of certification as a tool in an environment where donor funding will decrease, companies will tighten their belts and ask for further benefits from their certification efforts, and customers may or may not pay attention to certification in their purchasing behaviour. The chapter has raised a number of critical questions to consider as the investment and the expectations on certification continue to grow.

References

Ayuso, S. (2007) 'Comparing Voluntary Policy Instruments for Sustainable Tourism: The Experience of the Spanish Hotel Sector', *Journal of Sustainable Tourism* 151, 44–59.

Bien, A. (2005) *Marketing strategy for sustainable & ecotourism certification Ecocurrents First Quarter 2005.* Washington, DC: The International Ecotourism Society.

Boström, M. (2003) 'Environmental organisations in new forms of political participation: ecological modernisation and the making of voluntary rules'. *Environmental Values* 121, 75–93.

Botterill, D. and Nelson, C. (2005) 'Researching the links between environmental quality kite marks and local tourism business performance: a discourse analysis of the Welsh rural beach quality 'Green Coast Award'', in D. Hall, I. Kirkpatrick, and M. Mitchell (eds), *Rural tourism and sustainable business*. Wallingford: CABI, 268–86.

Buckley, R. (2002) 'Tourism ecolabels'. *Annals of Tourism Research* 29 (1), 183–208.

Chan, E. and Wong, S. (2006) 'Motivations for ISO14001 in the hotel industry', *Tourism Management* 27, 481–92.

Cleverdon, R. and Kalisch, A. (2000) 'Fair trade in tourism', *International Journal of Tourism Research* 2 (3), 171–87.

Curtin, S. and Busby, G. (1999) 'Sustainable destination development: the tour operator perspective', *International Journal of Tourism Research* 11, 35–47.

Fennell, D. and Malloy, D. (2007a) *Codes of ethics in tourism: practice, theory, synthesis*. Bristol: Channel View Publications.

Fennell, D.A. and Malloy, D.C. (2007b) *Codes of Ethics in Tourism: Practice, Theory, Synthesis*. Bristol: Channel View Publications.

Font, X. (2005) 'Sustainable tourism standards in the global economy', in W. Theobald (ed.), *Global Tourism*. Oxford: Butterworth-Heinemann, 213–29.

Font, X. and Bendell, J. (2002) *Standards for sustainable tourism for the purpose of multilateral trade negotiations*. Madrid: World Tourism Organization.

Font, X. and Epler-Wood, M. (2007) 'Sustainable Tourism Certification Marketing and its Contribution to SME Market Access', in R. Black and A. Crabtree (eds), *Quality Assurance and Certification in Ecotourism*. Wallingford: CABI, 147–63.

Font, X. and Harris, C. (2004) 'Rethinking labels: from green to sustainable', *Annals of Tourism Research* 31 (4), 986–1007.

Garrod, B. and Fyall, A. (1998) 'Beyond the Rhetoric of Sustainable Tourism?', *Tourism Management* 19 (3), 199–212.

Griffin, T. and De Lacy, T. (2002) 'Green Globe: sustainability accreditation for tourism', in R. Harris, T. Griffin and P. Williams (eds), *Sustainable tourism: a global perspective* Oxford: Butterworth-Heinemann, pp. 58–88.

Hall, B.L. (2001) 'I wish this were a poem of practices of participatory research', in P. Reason and H. Bradbury (eds), *Handbook of action research: participative inquiry & practice*. London: SAGE, 171–8.

Honey, M. (2002) *Ecotourism & certification: setting standards in practice*. Washington, DC: Island Press.

Honey, M. and Rome, A. (2001) *Protecting Paradise: Certification Programs for Sustainable Tourism and Ecotourism*. Washington, DC: Institute for Policy Studies.

Honey, M. and Stewart, E. (2002) 'The evolution of green standards for tourism', in M. Honey (ed.), *Ecotourism & certification: setting standards in practice*. Washington, DC: Island Press, 33–72).

House, E. (2005) 'Qualitative evaluation and changing social policy', in N. Denzin and Y. Lincoln (eds), *The SAGE handbook of qualitative research, 3rd ed*. Thousand Oaks, CA: Sage, 1069–88.

Ingram, C. (2007) 'Certification in Protected Areas: a Western Australian Case Study', in R. Black and A. Crabtree (eds), *Quality Assurance and Certification on Ecotourism*. Wallingford: CABI, 266–98.

Jamal, T., Borges, M. and Stronza, A. (2006) 'The Institutionalisation of Ecotourism: Certification, Cultural Equity and Praxis', *Journal of Ecotourism* 5 (3), 145–75.

Jordan, A., Wurzel, R., Zito, A. and Brückner, L. (2004) 'Consumer responsibility-taking and national eco-labelling schemes in Europe', in M. Micheletti, A. Follesdal and D. Stolle (eds), *Politics, products and markets: exploring political consumerism*. Somerset, NJ: Transaction Publishers, 161–80.

Korhonen, J. (2003) 'Should we Measure Corporate Social Responsibility?', *Corporate Social Responsibility and Environmental Management* 10 (1), 25–39.

Krut, R. and Gleckman, H. (1998) *ISO 14001: a missed opportunity for sustainable global industrial development*. London: Earthscan.

Mamic, I. (2004) *Implementing Codes of Conduct: How Businesses Manage Social Performance in Global Supply Chains*. Sheffield: Greenleaf Publishing (UK).

Medina, L.K. (2005) 'Ecotourism and certification: confronting the principles and pragmatics of socially responsible tourism', *Journal of Sustainable Tourism* 13 (3), 281–95.

Mol, A. (2000) 'The environment movement in an era of ecological modernisation', *Geoforum* 31, 45–56.

Mowforth, M. and Munt, I. (1998) *Tourism and Sustainability: new tourism in the third world*. London: Routledge.

OECD (2003) *Voluntary approaches for environmental policy: effectiveness, efficiency, and usage in policy mixes*. Paris: OECD.

Rivera, J. and de Leon, P. (2005) 'Chief Executive Officers and voluntary environmental performance: Costa Rica's Certification for Sustainable Tourism', *Policy Sciences* 38 (2–3), 107–27.

Sasidharan, V., Sirakaya, E. and Kerstetter, D. (2002) 'Developing countries and tourism ecolabels', *Tourism Management* 23 (2), 161–74.

Smith, M. and Crotty, J. (2007) 'Environmental Regulation and Innovation: Driving Ecological Design in the UK Automotive Industry', *Business Strategy and the Environment* 17 (6), 341–9.

Stonich, S.C. (1998) 'Political ecology of tourism', *Annals of Tourism Research* 25 (1), 25–54.

Synergy (2000) *Tourism certification: an analysis of Green Globe 21 and other certification programs*. Godalming: World Wide Fund for Nature-UK.

Thwaites, R. (2007) 'The Australian EcoCertification Program (NEAP): Blazing a Trail for Ecotourism Certification, but Keeping on Track?', in R. Black and A. Crabtree (eds), *Quality Assurance and Certification in Ecotourism* Wallingford: CABI, pp. 435–63.

UNEP (2005) *The trade and environmental effects of ecolabels: assessment and response*. Paris: United Nations Environment Programme.

Vivanco, L.A. (2007) 'The Prospects and Dilemmas of Indigenous Tourism Standards and Certifications', in R. Black and A. Crabtree (eds), *Quality Assurance and Certification on Ecotourism*. Wallingford: CABI, 218–40.

Vogel, D. (2005) *The Market for Virtue: The Potential and Limits of Corporate Social Responsibility*. New York: Brookings Institution Press.

WTO (2002) *Voluntary Initiatives for Sustainable Tourism*. Madrid: World Tourism Organization.

Yanow, D. (2000) *Conducting interpretive policy analysis*. Thousand Oaks, CA: SAGE.

29

Lessons learned

Knowledge management and tourism development

Alan Clarke, Ágnes Raffay and Peter Wiltshier

Introduction

This chapter contains four sections, reviewing four issues that deserve our attention in developing and protecting sustainable tourism development projects. The research we present suggests the use and utility of a model (Figure 29.1) of knowledge-based development that is developed by the authors and demonstrated through two case studies. Our project work reviews public sector policy outputs that encourage Third Sector diversification and regeneration, supporting new ventures and encouraging Higher Education (HE) graduate entrepreneurship. Community stakeholders are expected to acquire vocational, transferable, cognitive and intellectual skills to meet contemporary socio-cultural, political, economic and more importantly, educational, expectations.

The first section reinforces the explicit need for public and private partners to agree the terms for collaborative approaches to development. References are made to past development projects that have successfully linked partners in consensual community tourism. We understand and recommend that analysis of the resources and disambiguation of key stakeholders' interests and expectations are made.

The next section focuses on the explicit and tacit knowledge outcomes from the projects discussed. From these outcomes we conclude that knowledge outputs and transfers must be managed as carefully, if not more carefully than other aspects of the project, as the project concept and implementation are often lost by somewhat careless repository activity over time.

The third section explores conceptual approaches to sustaining knowledge transfer of co-operation and collaboration through two key methodological approaches. Approach one is the building of systems thinking capacity within the destination (after Senge 2006). Approach two is the experiential theory of learning destinations (after Gibson 2006).

The final section tells the stories of two case studies that we have identified in knowledge management and consensual tourism development with a particular focus on the lessons to be learned about the embedded knowledge of actors, the processes and the project works completed. The first case study is English, the story of Wirksworth, a honeypot market town undergoing fairly comprehensive regeneration through an amalgam of development projects in

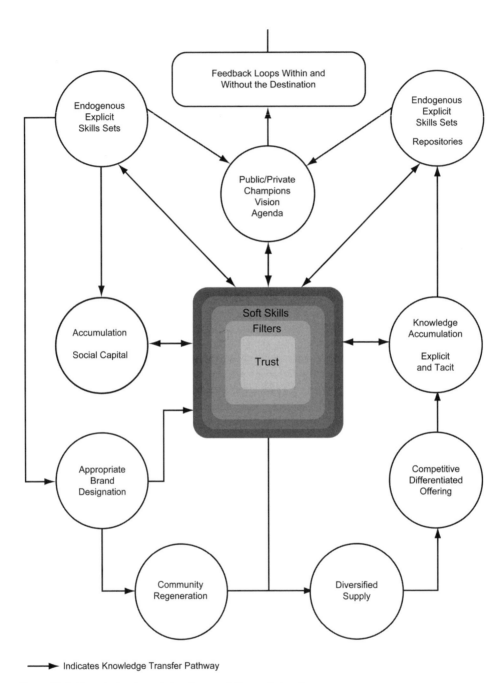

→ Indicates Knowledge Transfer Pathway

Figure 29.1 Knowledge-based development through tourism

tourism, trade, arts, education and heritage. The second case study is Hungarian and is considered notable in the greater scale of the project. Its location is the regional centre (in Hungarian it is recognised in the Hungarian classification actually as a de-centre) the historic medieval city of Veszprém.

Ultimately, it is essential that students and practitioners grasp the lessons in the processes and outcomes of tourism project work, review the shortfalls in sustaining effort to store and retrieve elements of good development and distil the characteristics of those successful projects by using our suggested proformer.

In a practical way this chapter can be read to produce a template to examine, measure and evaluate potential partnership opportunities. We welcome the chances to carry out project analysis and demonstrate the project knowledge management repository outcome.

Agreement to collaborate

The process of forming networks is an art, not a science. There may be certain legal standards and accounting procedures for business agreements, but getting people together and collectively identifying a common objective is a social skill or actually a complex set of social skills. Networks cannot flourish without trust, which in turn cannot develop without a social infrastructure that gives members a chance to interact (Rosenfeld 2001: 111). We take an agreement to reach consensus and some variation of joint decision-making as an integral element of and the central objective of collaboration (after Jamal and Getz 1995). This is in recognition that an abundance of skills is seldom discovered in organisations that independently embark on developing new and diversified products for an open tourism market. The decision to diversify into new businesses in tourism, by nature of the multiplicity of linked public and private partners, requires a highly attuned set of skills that can sift community social aspirations, manage demand from diverse and sophisticated tourists and make provision for return on the shared investment in what Burns would describe as triple-bottom line 'third way' capital (Burns 2004).

Such collaboration returns a social dividend as well as an economic return. This third way and social capital return on investment further legitimises collaboration and extends the building of community capital and the improvement of society. Ray's (1998) four-stage temporal model of community development through social capital is built on with declared and agreed collaboration and an outcome where a destination's identity is embraced, not artificially imposed by stakeholders on a destination community (Ray 1998). Granovetter (1983: 229) explored the significance of the differences between weak ties and strong ties in developing relationships and networks. Strong stakeholder collaboration is essential to creating networks, clusters and enduring innovations through funded regeneration projects, especially in the multidisciplinary field of tourism (Novelli *et al.* 2006).

The need for long-term development using tourism as a mechanism to build social, community and enterprise capital is not new. What is new is an understanding that systems-thinking and linear approaches need to build into the process model some fuzzy logic (McCool 2009) that recognises complex spatial and temporal relationships between key stakeholders, or partners, engaged in development and transactions at the destination (Svensson *et al.* 2005).

The complexity is caused by key stakeholders disputing and debating the best use of scarce capital and human resources, which could equally be deployed for tourism and other activities. Svensson *et al.* (2005) describe these resource dependencies as difficult to disentangle and re-create for the long-term benefit of the destination. The need for aggregation of data measuring outcomes becomes important as a result of competition for allocating these scarce resources not only between tourism and other sustainable projects, but also over time as other external and internal factors come into play. These may well be changing demographics, an ageing population or variable performance in a competitive global arena.

The need for inter-dependency of goals, competencies and skills between stakeholders and potential for conflict between competing aims and objectives has been recognised and is further documented in the chapter (Gray 1989).

Managing the knowledge and its transfer

Senge (2009) identifies that any innovation or development in modern society must necessarily be paralleled by innovation and development in education (Senge 2009). Therefore, we concur that to embed new knowledge, and its transfer, requires transformational thinking in both management and in education, where education is thought in its widest terms to include formal education and training.

> There are two dominant institutions in a modern society: business and education. While business is obviously the most powerful, schools are the 'power behind the throne' so to speak because they shape people in terms of skills, attitudes toward power and authority and expectations.
>
> *(Senge and Benedict 2010)*

The generic core skills required by regeneration professionals, identified by Egan (2004) are, with the exception of financial management, essentially inter-personal skills. For effective regeneration practice, Egan recognises that it is the people skills, underpinned by personal and inter-personal knowledge and behaviour sets, that are needed (Kagan 2010: 169).

Therefore, we can identify that successful tourism development project work defined as bringing community knowledge together, is predicated on using stocks of information from public, private and not-for-profit stakeholder engagement with development agendas and creating meaningful and purposive access to this knowledge. Knowledge transfer to build social, community and enterprise capital is well researched in the context of urban regeneration in areas of economic deprivation (Kagan 2010; Taylor 2006).

What Senge also identifies, and we also agree, is that to embrace a change culture requires communities, and therefore tourism destinations, to build larger collaborative networks and engage in significant leadership from social as well as business sectors and embed the partnerships between educators and business people (Senge 2009). A linear approach has evolved to enable collaboration in consensus implementation, monitoring and review with a wide range of stakeholders envisioned (Jamal and Getz 1995).

What is also important to identify is that the 'know what' explicit knowledge is as important as the 'know how to' or tacit knowledge that we emphasise can be lost in the development journeys taken (Davenport and Prusak 1998).

In the course of the authors' research activity, we have identified that key informants to projects developing sustainable tourism at enterprise and community levels are scarce resources in themselves. Moreover, these scarce informants, and we term them project workers, have no special intention to create repositories of successful projects and their narratives, for later retrieval and dispersal. This means destinations can frequently suffer from poor concept design and development due to inadequate reflection on prior projects. Worse still is an evident drain on the public purse in regional development or skills funding to pay for future developments (Parker 2005).

Publicly funded regeneration and tourism development projects are a matter of public record. The explicit knowledge will usually include the project background, scoping and external/

internal reflection and an implementation and review phase. What will be missing is the tacit knowledge that may overlook project time and funding shortfall and a consistent review of the process and systems used to justify the project and its outcomes. Not only do we consider the social and economic value of knowledge transfer, we also endorse the transformative social value to communities within tourism destinations (Hollinshead and Jamal 2007: 85). Higher education has a supplementary vital role to play in performing, underpinning and securing this transformative knowledge transfer and reviewing the social and economic capital value of sustaining development (Garrod *et al.* 2006: 118; Saxena 2006). The model developed identifies process outcomes that support the key links, and demystifies the conflicts, between economic, environmental and social dimensions of the development (Garrod *et al.* 2006: 118). Consensus building and 'path-dependent emergent phenomena' and relational compared with transactional value and change are important to understanding these development processes (Saxena 2005: 277).

Our model acknowledges the accumulation, interpretation and evaluation emerging intellectual (and/or social) capital (Cinca *et al.* 2003, cited in Williams 2007). A resource set can be brought into development by identifying best practices in joining and participating in networks and partnerships in third sector, (Shortall 2008: 451; Rosenfeld 2001). We have identified and confirmed the skills required to engage the learning community (Dredge 2006; Brennan and Luloff 2007) and highlighted the structures for knowledge transfer (Priestley and Samaddar 2007; von Friedrichs Grängsjö 2003).

Methodological issues: building systems thinking and the learning destination

As has been mentioned, sustainable approaches had been predicated on the earlier linear systems and enabling provided by stakeholder and collaboration theory (Jamal and Getz 1995).

Prior to the Rio Earth Summit 1992, poor collaborative pre-conditions and minimal synthesis process were negatives in addressing broader sustainability issues in tourism. The contemporary view of sustainability was fraught with dangers regarding fragmentation of approach, a narrow perspective on stakeholders' authority and distribution of power and all inequalities in decision support (Berno and Bricker 2001).

Non-linear socio-ecological component approaches with social and natural systems that are fuzzy and complex have since been elaborated (Farrell and Twining-Ward 2004). Sophisticated systems modelling, featuring collaboration, now used in teaching, became an emergent epistemology in systems thinking, creating teaching resources and employing a practice-based approach (Jamal *et al.* 2004). In moving on from these reductionist and linear approaches, we find adaptive approaches (Baggio 2008). Finally, natural issues surrounding capacity management yet incorporating collaboration theory and stakeholders are now implemented (see for an example, Jamal and Stronza 2009).

There are, conceptually, multiple methodological approaches to building sustainable tourism development knowledge because of the multi- and inter-disciplinarity of tourism, aside from the social as well as economic constructs and epistemologies that are available to the practitioner and to the student.

We have therefore identified two options for approaching problem-solving and these are broadly the episteme of systems theory and of the learning destination. Both of these approaches permit the fuzzy logic approach required to address complex interactions and inter-relationships within communities and tourism destinations. The approaches also encourage inductive, as well as deductive, methodologies to inform sustainable development, emphasising the active processes involved in constructing knowledge as a 'socially constructed context' (Smith 2003: 80) (method and process for work-based problem solving learning). We would also highlight the importance of networks 'integration theory' to empower actors within networks and partnerships (Sorensen and Torfing 2004: 14–16).

Soft systems methodologies can offer both a process and project-based approach to embedding tourist development knowledge in communities (Checkland and Scholes 1999; Carlsen 1999). As we identified, systems thinking capacity development can parallel this soft systems approach. The authors have adapted problem-based learning as the underpinning rationale to their methodology. Therefore, an effective combination of learning from problem-based learning and employing systems thinking underpins solutions to sustainable knowledge management.

Using the DETOUR model

The DETOUR model (Clarke and Dawson 2001) was originally elaborated within an EU-funded project looking at appropriate tourism development for six compact cities, based on the creation of stakeholder partnerships. Our case studies build from an articulation or expression by destinations of the definition of the problem at hand, an expression of the aim to resolve the problem or answer the questions posed by the destination. Senge (2010) identifies this is as a guiding idea and we take this as the starting point for further review of external and internal factors in demand and supply. We anticipate innovations in destination development by reviewing infrastructures, reviewing the existing tourism products and benchmarking against stakeholders' identified expectations and against a range of appropriate exemplar case studies.

Modelling best practice, having completed the review of resources, actors and policies, we emulate real world, *Weltanschauung*, situated issues. Specifically, we take the change-adaptability, skills and capabilities, beliefs and assumptions to identify possible changes at the next phase. Following Senge's building thinking capacity, the implementation phase reviews indicators of sustainable effective development, considers simultaneously the organisational action desired and reviews transformations. These are largely based on relational as opposed to transactional sustainable success measurements (Saxena 2005).

We concur with Gibson's (2006) model of inter-connected process, project and people in learning destinations. This model reflects endogenous development and consensual capacity building, knowledge transfer and later knowledge retrieval. The learning destinations model parallels Tonnies' (1887) paradigm of focusing on building stronger *gesellschaft* (society) and *gemeinschaft* (purposeful partnership), which are echoed in Ray's systemic approach to achieving consensus of identity and congruent shared values-based tourism development (Ray 1998; Gibson 2006; von Friedrichs Grängsjö 2003).

Significantly, there are multiple dimensions in this capacity building model. We defined tourism development as multi- and inter-disciplinary; the capacity building requires a review of implementation at varying stakeholder and product levels over time and stage (benchmarked to case studies of best-practice) and dimensions of sustainability according to life-cycle and return on investment. The latter ROI is considered according to social, economic and environmental constraints and enablers. This multiple dimensional aspect is complex but necessarily so, as key stakeholders resolve resource allocation conflicts as we will see in the two case studies.

Case study 1

Wirksworth, Derbyshire, England

The pretty post-industrial heritage town of Wirksworth is located on the southeast boundary of the Peak District National Park, which was established in 1951, and is now the busiest national park in Britain and second-most visited in the world. In the late 1970s, with the demise of quarrying and mining in the district, the local council bid for public funds to restore the fine Georgian architecture to ensure Wirksworth would become a great place to live and work. Wirksworth is a former mining town, population of 5,000, located 5 km south of the Peak District National Park. More than 22 million visitors enjoy the Park in an average year (PDNPA 2001, www.peakdistrict.gov.uk). In 2006 the town celebrated the 700th anniversary of the award of a market charter by royal decree in 1306. For the past 12 years, Wirksworth has been home to a local arts festival, the Wirksworth Festival, which is renowned nationally and internationally for the quality of performance and the arts and is regularly attended by in excess of 30,000 visitors over three weeks in September.

Therefore, we can see that Wirksworth is a case study of applied endogenous skills and social capital capacity building. Interventions since the 1980s have helped to smooth socio-economic disparities in this community and demonstrate the growth imperatives and environmental protection that form the policy platform in England's countryside (Gilg 2005).

Lead mining has been associated with Wirksworth since Roman times, and the town stands at what was once the core of the lead mining industry in England. The town is characterised by Georgian market-town vernacular architecture. Adjacent to the town is Richard Arkwright's Mill (1769) at Cromford. This area was the heart-land of the Industrial Revolution and the heritage of the Derwent Valley Mills World Heritage Site forms a large draw card to free, independent travellers. In addition to the Wirksworth Festival, visitor attractions include the Wirksworth Heritage Centre, the Ecclesbourne Valley Railway (EVR), the National Stone Centre and the Cromford to High Peak Trail, as well as Carsington Water, a reservoir owned and operated by Severn Trent Water. These attractions and the festival have the potential to deliver 100,000 visitors each year to the town and create further employment in related services.

Unfortunately, there are some related negative factors that emerged as the researcher engaged in dialogue with stakeholders. Power elites, nimbyism, low levels of cross-sectoral interest between organisations, disagreement over development agendas and competition for public funding, and finally the complete absence of any sector-specific or integrated implementation planning are notable but certainly not unique to Wirksworth.

Central to this regeneration is a community-led organisation, New Opportunities for Wirksworth (NOW!). NOW! is an organisation run by and for local people, under the name of The Wirksworth Regeneration Board. NOW! has articulated a tourism vision and mission statement that incorporates a strategy for tourism development, which, in its own words, is designed to be 'a framework for Tourism Development which can operate at strategic level, as a tool for funding applications and for ensuring clear aims and objectives for businesses and residents in Wirksworth' (NOW! 2006). In an attempt to redress the economic and social decline of Wirksworth, projects commenced in the 1980s to conserve the heritage architecture to retain the historic character of Wirksworth and focus on an improved local economy (Michell et al. 1989). In 2002, a further report (Davies 2002) was commissioned by the Town Council and funded through the East

Midlands Development Agency. This report identified that further research into developing tourism and retail, the arts and education would be desirable from the perspective of local solutions for local problems and the scoping of clusters to support regeneration was recommended. Over two decades a range of stakeholders from the arts, tourism, retail and services, initially through a Civic Trust umbrella and funded through local government grants, considered various pathways to regeneration. Initial work focused on community consultation, resource provision (usually defined in this context as experts and their advice) and tending towards the unofficial rather than official (Michell et al. 1989: 82).

As Foley and Martin (2000) observed governments have traditionally underestimated the practical problems at the local level – patchy support to endogenous policy creation, capacity concerns by the local community, effectiveness of disseminated experiences and lessons-learned and low skills levels and time resource provided by local and central government to the regeneration project.

The NOW! Project in Wirksworth amply demonstrates the potential to build co-operative ventures between different product silos. At the same time the NOW! Project alerted the various product champions to the potential of consensual development linking the arts, heritage, tourism and trade. The embedded tacit and explicit knowledge outcomes are to be stored by the university. The repository function has the potential to save £6 million of public sector investment in regeneration projects by avoiding unnecessary duplication of new project work including those in the voluntary sector (see Parker 2007 for examples). By storing and making such projects visible to the community, the university can inform product development and good practices for future modelling, and inform through skills development through various short and full-time courses.

Case study 2

Veszprém, Hungary

The need for collaboration had been apparent in Veszprém, a picturesque historical city close to the northern shores of Lake Balaton, for several years before the creation of the Veszprém Tourism Association (VTA), which we will focus on here. There had been numerous attempts to establish a forum with the earlier initiatives coming from the public sector with some private sector support (some businesses backed the idea). These proposals initially were limited to creating room for communication between the various actors within the tourism industry, but were mindful that they could later develop into a partnership with somewhat more ambitious objectives than simply communication. However, when the first enthusiasms faded these attempts always failed. One of the interviews conducted before the establishment of the VTA brought up the issue. The respondent, a restaurant owner, was rather sceptical about the attempts to bring the various actors together: 'There's no point in organising tourism forums until the people invited can actually have their voices heard.' Another respondent acknowledged that, although there are some key individuals who are trying to move tourism forward in the city, a city-level action is beyond any one individual's or a few individuals' capacities.

Collaborative capacity becomes an important issue and also makes sense in the terms of the analysis undertaken here. Traditionally, developing capacity has been seen as a broadening of the range of individuals and organisations that have the skills and knowledge to participate meaningfully in the project. This functional sense of capacity has to be reinforced with the capacity to recognise and be recognised in the discursive politics that inform and determine the context of the collaboration. Therefore, alongside the range of skills involved in urban tourism, the ability to construct positions within these discourses has to be recognised.

The VTA started to materialise primarily on the basis of personal links between owners and managers of tourism businesses, who thought extending relationships that had proved worthwhile in the past could benefit tourism in Veszprém and, in turn, their businesses.

The concrete invitation to start the discussions came from a young and energetic entrepreneur (not yet disillusioned by the failure of the previous attempts), who owns and runs one of the city centre hotels and is the founding father and organiser of one of the most prestigious cultural events in the city. In the first stage he approached businesses where he had informal links with the owners, then as the group widened he and his 'circle of friends' started talks with other tourism-related businesses. Here, we see a sense of community developed into a community of practice. Already, in these initial stages, they agreed to involve Tourinform Veszprém, a non-profit organisation run under the auspices of the city council. As the tourist information centre of the city, Tourinform Veszprém had established links with the tourism service providers, so they were considered an almost inevitable partner for the association. However, it must be noted that the manager of Tourinform was invited to these direction-setting discussions in her personal capacity, and not as a representative from Tourinform.

The entrepreneur built his informal discussions into a series of more formal gatherings, which subsequently became recognisable as the pre-association meetings. These became more frequent and with that the circle of the desirable partners was widening. By this phase, all accommodation providers were welcome to participate, and several restaurants, some cultural event organisers and attractions were getting invitations. Interestingly, the partners strongly expressed their wish not to invite the city council or any members thereof to be members in the VTA, although one of the key objectives of this body was to start talks with the local council regarding issues directly or indirectly involving tourism. The awkwardness of the situation heavily impacted, and still impacts, on the role of Tourinform, who are torn between the intention as well as obligation to help the tourism related businesses wherever possible and seeing the flaws in the operations of the city council that often set obstacles to the tourism businesses.

The aims of the VTA related to ensuring regular and institutionalised co-ordination between the players of tourism, primarily by establishing the appropriate channels of communication and the flow of information relevant for the tourism trade; representing the interests of the tourism sector and as a consulting partner becoming involved in the preparation of all tourism-related decisions; seeking funding opportunities to develop and implement projects in line with the joint interests of the members and which would contribute to the development of the sector; undertaking marketing activities, in particular presenting the city's tourism potential in brochures and the media as well as on the Internet and co-operating with national and local organisations to foster the development of the tourism offer of Veszprém and its surroundings (Veszprémi Turisztikai Egyesület Alapszabálya 2005).

The emphasis on the two-way communication between the public and private sectors was based on the impression that the council treated the businesses as 'cash-cows', that is they thought the council thought that the various businesses were fine so long as they paid the tourism tax, but their opinion was not needed (or even not welcome) when it came to making decisions directly aimed at or affecting tourism. The Association's basic proposition was that the private sector ought to be able to see how the tourism tax (which they regard as 'their money') was spent, and as a next step, they would have liked to be involved in decisions as to how to use the tax revenue generated by their businesses. To be able to achieve this, the Association wanted a place in the relevant committees of the city council, which they hoped would legitimise their involvement.

Conclusions

Our two case studies demonstrate that tourism developments are rarely based on recognising the needs of a learning destination. The developments take place despite, rather than because of, firmly grounded capacity building and knowledge sharing programmes. The cases identify a number of key points that are essential for the successful operation of partnerships, as can be seen in the model (Figure 29.1):

- involvement and engagement;
- inclusivity;
- trust;
- partnership champion;
- long-term (or at least not short-term) vision.

This impacts on both competency development and the ability to gather and share explicit and tacit knowledges in the destination. We see the dangers of compartmentalised (or specialist) knowledges operating to exclude participation as a real threat to successful sustainable developments. Using knowledges as a way to privilege positions deters open, inclusive engagement in tourism and denies individuals and groups the footholds they would need to become more closely involved. Co-operation and collaboration are important factors in understanding the dynamics of tourism development and help to move inclusive initiatives forward as our model suggests, with both systemic and experiential benefits flowing widely through and around the communities of practice and the local communities.

Observers and practitioners should note that tourism is just one of several commercial opportunities for resource allocation. It is not, as has been noted, a 'panacea for regional development policies' (Hall and Michael 2007: 7). Tourism can be considered as the mechanism for the learning destination to move forward, sharing a common identity and possessing explicit and agreed common goals.

References

Ateljevic, J. (2007) 'Small tourism firms and management practices in New Zealand: The Centre Stage Macro Region', *Tourism Management* 28, 307–16.
Baggio, R. (2008) 'Symptoms of Complexity in a Tourism System', *Tourism Analysis* 13, 1–20.
Baggio, R. and Cooper, C. (2009) 'Knowledge transfer in a tourism destination: the effects of a network structure', *The Service Industries Journal* 30 (8), 2010.
Berno, T. and Bricker, K. (2001) 'Sustainable Tourism Development: The Long Road from Theory to Practice', *International Journal of Economic Development* 3(3), 1–18.
Brennan, M.A. and Luloff, A.E. (2007) 'Exploring rural community agency differences in Ireland and Pennsylvania', *Journal of Rural Studies* 23(1), 52–61.
Burns, P. (2004) 'Tourism Planning; a Third Way', *Annals of Tourism Research* 31(1), 24–43.
Cardow, A. and Wiltshier, P. (2010) Indigenous tourism operators: the vanguard of economic recovery in the Chatham Islands', *International Journal of Entrepreneurship and Small Business* 10(4), 484–98.
Carlsen, J. (1999) 'A systems approach to island tourism destination management', *Journal of Systems Research & Behavioural Science* 16(4), 321–7.
Checkland, P. and Scholes, J. (1999) *Soft Systems methodology in action*. Chichester: John Wiley & Sons Ltd

Cinca, C.S., Molinerao, C.M. and Queiroz, A.B. (2003) 'The measurement of intangible assets in public sector using scaling techniques', *Journal of Intellectual Capital* 4 (2) 249–75, cited in Williams, J. (2007) *How does the effective measurement and management of intellectual capital affect the successful regeneration of Sheffield as an innovative and creative city* Unpublished Thesis, University of Sheffield.

Clarke, A. and Dawson, J. (2001) *Developing Strategy for Urban Tourism.* Derby: University of Derby.

Clarke, A, Raffay, A. and Wiltshier, P. (2009) 'Losing it: knowledge management in tourism development projects', *Tourismos* 4(3), 149–66.

Davenport, T.H. and Prusak, L. (1998) *Working Knowledge: how organizations manage what they know.* Boston, MA: Harvard Business School Press.

Davies, D. (2002) *Regeneration consultancy report. New Opportunities.* Wirksworth & University of Derby & Community Works. Unpublished report, University of Derby.

Dredge, D. (2006) 'Networks, Conflict and Collaborative Communities', *Journal of Sustainable Tourism* 14 (6), 562–81.

Egan, J (2004) *Skills for Sustainable Communities.* London: Office of the Deputy Prime Minister.

Farrell, B.H. and Twining-Ward, L. (2004) 'Reconceptualizing Tourism', *Annals of Tourism Research* 31(2), 274–95.

Foley P. and Martin S. (2000) 'Perceptions of community led regeneration: community and central government viewpoints', *Regional Studies* 34(8), 783–7.

von Friedrichs Grängsjö, Y. (2003) 'Destination networking: Co-opetition in peripheral surroundings', *International Journal of Physical Distribution & Logistics Management* 33(5), 427–48.

Gannon, C., Lynch, P. and Harrington, D. (2009) 'Dynamic Knowledge Management Capability for the Small Tourism Firm', in IAM Conference, Galway Mayo Institute of Technology, Galway, Ireland, 2–4 September.

Garrod, B., Wornell, R. and Youell, R. (2006) 'Re-conceptualising rural resources as countryside capital: The case of rural tourism', *Journal of Rural Studies* 22, 117–28.

Gibson, C. (2009) 'Geographies of tourism: critical research on capitalism and local livelihoods', *Progress in Human Geography* 33(4), 527–34.

Gibson, L. (2006) *Learning Destinations: The complexity of tourism development.* Doctoral thesis, Karlstad University.

Gilg, A.W. (2005) *Planning in Britain: understanding & evaluating the post war system.* London: Sage.

Granovetter, M. (1983) 'The strength of weak ties: a network theory revisited', *Sociological Theory* 1, 201–33.

Gray, B. (1989) *Collaborating: Finding Common Grounds For Multiparty Problems.* San Francisco, CA and London: Jossey-Bass.

Hall, C.M. and Michael, E.J. (2007) 'Issues in regional development', in Michael, E.J. (ed.) *Micro-clusters and networks: the growth of tourism.* Oxford: Elsevier, Chapter 2.

Hollinshead, K. and Jamal, T. (2007) 'Tourism and "The Third Ear": Further Prospects for Qualitative Inquiry', *Tourism Analysis* 12(1–2), 85–129.

Jamal, T. and Stronza, A. (2009) 'Collaboration theory and tourism practice in protected areas: stakeholders, structuring and sustainability', *Journal of Sustainable Tourism* 17(2), 169–89.

Jamal, T., Borges, M. and Figueiredo, R. (2004) 'Systems-based modeling for participatory tourism planning and destination management', *Tourism Analysis* 9, 77–89.

Jamal, T.B. and Getz, D. (1995) 'Collaboration theory and community tourism planning', *Annals of Tourism Research* 22 (1), 186–204.

Kagan, C. (2010) 'Interpersonal Skills and Reflection in Regeneration Practice', *Public Money & Management* 27 (3), 169–74.

McCool, S.F. (2009) 'Constructing partnerships for protected area tourism planning in an era of change and messiness', *Journal of Sustainable Tourism* 17 (2), 133–48.

Michell, G., Joyce, B. and Law, L. (1989) *The Wirksworth Story: New Life For An Old Town* (2nd edn). The Wirksworth Project, in Association with the Civic Trust. Wirksworth: Blackbear Press.

Novelli, M, Schmitz, B. and Spencer, T. (2006) 'Networks, clusters and innovation in tourism: a UK experience', *Tourism Management* 27, 1141–52.

Parker, K. (2005) *Rural Funding Programmes: A Case Study in the Peak District*, Peak District National Park Authority, Countryside Agency.

Priestley, J.L. and Samaddar, S. (2007) 'Multi-Organizational Networks: Three Antecedents of Knowledge Transfer', *International Journal of Knowledge Management* 3(1), 86–99.

Ray, C. (1998) 'Culture, Intellectual Property and Territorial Rural Development', *Sociologia Ruralis* 38(1), 3–20.

Rosenfeld, S. (2001) 'Advancing the Understanding of Clusters and Their Opportunities for Less Favored Regions, Less Advantaged Populations, and Small and Mid-Sized Enterprises' *Background paper prepared for Ford Foundation Cluster Study*. Carrboro, NC: Regional Technology Strategies Inc., November.

Saxena, G. (2005) 'Relationships, networks and the learning region: case evidence from the Peak District National Park', *Tourism Management* 26, 277–89.

——(2006) 'Beyond mistrust and competition: The role of personal and social bonding processes in sustaining livelihoods of rural tourism business: A case study of the Peak District National Park', *International Journal of Tourism Research* 8: 263–77.

Senge, P (2006). *The Fifth Discipline: Art and Practice of the Learning Organization*. London: Random House.

——(2009) 'Education for an Interdependent World: Developing Systems Citizens', *Second International Handbook of Educational Change Springer International Handbooks of Education*, 23(1), 131–51.

Senge, P. and Benedict, F. (2010) *Systems Thinking and Education for Sustainability: Educating systems citizens for the world we are living into A conversation with Peter Senge*. http://supportedu.org/webfm_send/576, accessed 10 October 2010.

Shortall, S. (2008) 'Are rural development programmes socially inclusive? Social inclusion, civic engagement, participation, and social capital: Exploring the differences', *Journal of Rural Studies* 24, 450–7.

Smith, P.J. (2003) 'Workplace Learning and Flexible Delivery', *Review of Educational Research* 73(1), 53–88.

Sorensen, E. and Torfing, J. (2004) *Making governance networks democratic*. Roskilde: Centre for Democratic Network Governance.

Svensson, B., Nordin, S. and Flagestad, A. (2005) 'A governance perspective on destination development – exploring partnerships, clusters and innovation systems', *Tourism Review* 60 (2), 32–7.

Taylor, M. (2002) *Public Policy in the Community*. Houndmills, Basingstoke: MacMillan.

——(2006) 'Communities in Partnership: Developing a Strategic Voice', *Social Policy and Society* 5(2), 269–79.

Tonnies, F. (1887) *Abhandlung des Communismus und des Socialismus als empirischer Culturformen* [Treatise on Communism and Socialism as Empirical Patterns of Culture].

Veszprémi Turisztikai Egyesület Alapszabálya (2005)

Wirksworth NOW! (2006) *How did NOW get to here?* New Opportunities Wirksworth.

Zografos, C. (2007) 'Rurality discourses and the role of the social enterprise in regenerating rural Scotland', *Journal of Rural Studies* 23, 38–51.

Part 4
Terminology and types of tourism

30

Introduction

David Fennell

Symptomatic of sustained growth in tourism over many years has been the development of a wide range of different tourism forms or types designed to represent the spectrum of attractions that tourists seek. Indeed, Boyd (1991) argued that upwards of 100 different types of tourism could be identified. For many, the need to develop and use new terms in tourism at the expense of others has complicated the landscape, especially in regards to those forms of tourism that rely on the natural environment as the foundation for the experience. This section presents a number of different forms of tourism all with direct ties to the natural world, and culminates with a meaningful treatise on tourism and romantic myths of nature, with the aim of providing clarity around the characteristics of each form.

Coghlan and Buckley argue that the nature-based tourism sector is 'broad, growing, and diversifying', and encompasses all forms of tourism that feature some aspect of nature. The sector is so diverse that theorists have argued that it occupies a scale of approximately US$1 trillion earned annually. The magnitude of the industry has meant that those who may fit under the nature-based tourism label are incredibly diverse in terms of their origins, interests, motivations and their actions while on trip. The authors provide a great deal of scope on the many shifts that have taken place in society that may have generated more enthusiasm for nature-based tourism, along with cross-cultural differences and similarities that continue to play heavily into values, motivations and behaviours. As a sub-set of nature-based tourism, Fennell observes that ecotourism has as its essential core a motivation for travel that has as its foundation a primary interest in the natural history of a destination. This is not travel for culture or adventure mainly, although these can certainly play a part, but rather plants, animals and any other features that may be used to understand and learn about the nature or essence of 'this place'. Sustainability, education and a nature-based affiliation are described as cornerstones of ecotourism, and, in a separate dimension, the ethics of marketing and management, low impact and non-consumptiveness, small-scale development and an affiliation with natural areas, are characteristics that are also described. A form of tourism closely aligned with ecotourism is wildlife tourism, and there has been a great deal of discussion over how these two forms differ (or not). Newsome and Rodger argue that although wildlife tourism can include both plants and animals – rendering it quite close to ecotourism – it is usually conceived as a form of tourism that focuses on just animals in their wild and captive forms. The similarity to ecotourism is represented in

David Fennell

the first of three different experiential categories: general nature-based tourism or ecotourism tours, wildlife tourism experience destinations like coral reefs and specialised wildlife tours that target specific species of, for example, birds or insects.

Moving from wilderness to the rural, Anthopoulou and Melissourgos argue that agri-tourism in both Western and lesser-developed contexts is an important vehicle for rural regeneration and farm diversification. The object of the tourist's gaze is actually a productive activity, and it is this that tourists come to admire and perhaps to reminisce in regards to days gone by (perhaps to show this lifestyle to their children?). As a new tourism practice, at least from the demand side of the equation, demanding a softer approach in line with symbolic values of what the countryside ought to be like (the authors use the example of pastoral landscapes, wholesome food, friendship and family ties, peace and quiet), there is the danger that increased consumption and the commoditisation of rural space may come packaged with the presentation of fictional landscapes associated with staged authenticity.

Another alternative to mass tourism is slow travel, which places emphasis on modes of transportation other than aeroplane and car, and on experiential aspects of the destination that are in line with the social and ecological objectives of the alternative tourism paradigm. Dickinson and Lumsdon argue that given the absence of a formal organising or driving structure behind this form of travel, those who travel as such might best be characterised as drifters or explorers. Although all destinations have the potential to be slow tourism venues, because of the principles that characterise this form of travel, some places, like Europe, have greater potential because of the travel infrastructure that is currently in place for short haul travel.

The experiential aspects in line with ecological and sociological objectives of slow travel can be transposed over to the responsible tourism agenda. Although the *modus operandi* of responsible tourism is not pace, as in above, there is the focus on a type of travel that is sensitive to the needs of the destination – all things considered. This is the message brought forward by Sharpley, who contends that it is all stakeholders who need to take responsibility for their actions in generating a type of tourism that is socially and environmentally sensitive. In the end, however, Sharpley feels that although tourists may state that they have every intention of trying to travel responsibly, the practice of such is fraught with many challenges – the reality of human nature creeping in to the equation; some impending doom or Sword of Damocles, as it were. A better approach would be to enlist those responsible for the planning and management of tourism to implement measures that would be designed to influence or control behaviour. The responsible tourism platform is seen in action in the chapter by Goodwin and Bah in reference to pro-poor tourism. Pro-poor tourism is a strategy that attempts to increase net benefits for the poor from tourism through the sale of goods and services. Furthermore, pro-poor strategies are designed to move control out of the hands of external forces alone, with initiatives intended to develop partnerships and empowerment for a more equitable distribution of decision-making and resources.

Reference

Boyd, S.J. (1991) 'Towards a typology of tourism: setting and experience', paper presented at the *Annual Meeting of the Association of American Geographers*, Ohio State University, Youngstown, Ohio, 1–2 November.

31

Ecotourism

David Fennell

Introduction

Ecotourism ('eco' as in ecological) is a type of tourism based on an interest in the natural history attractions of a destination. The term itself can be traced back to the work of Hetzer (1965), who used it to explain the intricate relationship between tourists and the environments and cultures in which they interact. Hetzer identified four fundamental pillars that need to be followed for a more responsible form of tourism: (1) minimum environmental impact; (2) minimum impact on – and maximum respect for – host cultures; (3) maximum economic benefits to the host country's grassroots; and (4) maximum 'recreational' satisfaction to participating tourists. In 2003 ecotourism earned US$25 billion globally, representing approximately 2–4 per cent of international tourism (Cater 2006). It is often referred to as the fastest growing segment of the tourism industry, and its reliance on parks and protected areas as a form of supply often diversifies marginalised economies in remote or peripheral areas.

The tenets of ecotourism

Figure 31.1 positions the various component parts of ecotourism according to three different dimensions. The first component, or basic ontology, characterises ecotourism, at its very essence, as travel with a primary interest in the natural history of a destination. Despite the prefix 'eco', natural history is used to frame ecotourism because of this concept's historical and present-day usages. Natural history, although scientific in nature, is a branch of science that is premised on observational rather than experimental practices. In this vein, Bartholomew (1996) wrote:

> A student of natural history, or a naturalist, studies the world by observing plants and animals directly. Because organisms are functionally inseparable from the environment in which they live and because their structure and function cannot be adequately interpreted without knowing some of their evolutionary history, the study of natural history embraces the study of fossils as well as physiographic and other aspects of the physical environment.

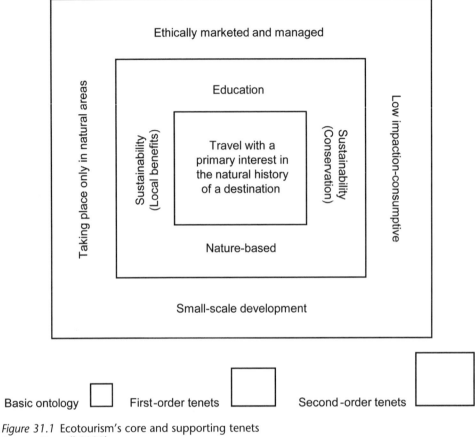

Figure 31.1 Ecotourism's core and supporting tenets
Source: Fennell 2002b.

Adding further scope to this definition, Lopez (1986) refers to natural history as the 'Patient interrogation of a landscape', whereas Wilcove and Eisner (2000) argue that natural history is 'The close observation of organisms—their origins, their evolution, their behavior, and their relationships with other species'.

Explained as such, ecotourists may be conceived as students of natural history. Some students strive to learn a great deal about natural history, but others rather less. They are motivated to pay close attention through observation of organisms, their role and function within the environment, and those of a more dedicated kind do this through patient observation. Furthermore, it would seem appropriate to characterise ecotourists as naturalists rather than ecologists, because of the observational tendencies of the former and the experimental practices of the latter. Natural history, and those who practice it, is taken to encompass the following areas in the broadest sense: botany, general biology, geology, palaeontology and zoology (see e.g. The Society for the History of Natural History, which publishes the *Archives of Natural History*, www.euppublishing.com/journal/anh, accessed 29 June 2011). It follows that the ecotourist, according to this manner of viewing ecotourism, would be interested in these types of attractions, and not just wildlife as in the case of wildlife tourism. For those theorists looking for a line of demarcation between ecotourism and wildlife tourism, the foregoing may be of use.

Building on the use of the term natural history in conceptualising ecotourism, some of the first organised tours of what we today refer to as ecotourism were presented by natural history societies. For example, the travel department of the American Museum of Natural History has conducted natural history tours since 1953. Participants on these tours are referred to as naturalists, and the term 'naturalist' is often used to describe a certain segment of the ecotourist market (see below). Some of the present day icons of ecotourism include the Monteverde Cloud Forest Reserve, Costa Rica, the Galapagos Islands of Ecuador, Iguaçu Falls, the Amazon basin, the Patagonian region of Argentina and Chile, Antarctica, hill tribe trekking in Southeast Asia, Ayers Rock, the Great Barrier Reef in Australia, the Milford Track in New Zealand, the Serengeti Plain, Kruger National Park in South Africa and polar bear watching in Churchill, Canada. Ecotourism thrives in all environments including rainforests, mountain regions, polar environments, islands and coasts, deserts and grasslands, and marine regions. Practices in these and other ecotourism destinations include the watching of specific animal groups like cetaceans, birds or bears.

Ecotourism has also branched out into the realm of culture (Indigenous practices) and adventure (kayaking and canoeing). Although this branching out has increased the market, there are serious issues surrounding the legitimacy of forms of tourism that are focused more on culture and adventure than on natural history and educational orientations. Connected to these problems is the level of intra-group variability in the ecotourism. The literature supports a number of studies that have endeavoured to establish typologies of the ecotourist on the basis of several different dimensions. At its most basic, ecotourists have been partitioned into two main groups: soft path and hard path ecotourists, with implications according to the types of programmes offered to these groups based on need. Figure 31.2 illustrates a number of factors or elements that might be used to differentiate between these two general categories – hard and soft.

Starting at the top of the inverted triangle in Figure 31.2, the base of interests and attractions represent the spectrum of attractions and activities available to the ecotourist while on vacation. The soft path ecotourist, the group that is representative of most ecotourists by number, would spend much more time engaged with interests and attractions that fall outside of the natural history attraction realm, that is many of the interests and attractions sought by the softest part of the soft path ecotourism segment would be spent on other attractions of the destination, including perhaps adventure, culture, shopping, theme parks and so on. Furthermore, the reliance on built or modified spaces and places would be more important to this part of the soft path segment, and there would be less specialisation, fewer natural history expectations and less time spent on these types of attractions. At the opposite end of the soft path continuum, that is, just above the hard path ecotourist part of the triangle, there would be a greater emphasis on specialisation, expectations and time spent, less reliance on modified spaces, and fewer numbers of tourists. The dashed line between the hard path group of ecotourists, as a very small number of the overall market, and the more dedicated soft path market is said to be less a matter of kind and more a matter of degree. Even within the hard path segment there is slight variation. But, in general, the hard path segment is far more specialised, with higher expectations and a great deal more time spent on attractions within the natural history attraction realm over the course of the vacation. Specialisation means a focus on specific species or groups of species, or it may include other natural history attractions as defined above. If the tour were inadequate in fulfilling the hard path ecotourists' expectations, there would exist a greater measure of dissatisfaction in comparison with the expectations of soft path ecotourists. As such, hard path ecotourists are motivated to find ecotour operators that provide the necessary dimensions of a trip to suit their needs, and often stick with these operators for subsequent ecotours (see, e.g. Quest Nature Tours, Toronto, Canada).

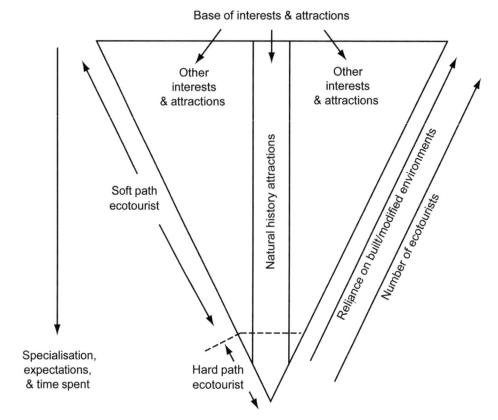

Figure 31.2 Soft and hard path dimensions of the ecotourist
Source: Fennell 2002b.

The second dimension of Figure 31.1, first-order tenets, outlines four concepts that are often at the heart of many definitions of ecotourism. These include sustainability (local benefits), sustainability (conservation),and a nature-based focus education. Sustainability is split into two different tenets here, local benefits and conservation, as a reflection of the ecotourism literature. However, if we are to accept that sustainable development can be defined as that form of development that 'meets the needs of the present without compromising the ability of future generations to meet their own needs', both local benefits and conservation should be subsumed under the SD label, especially for an activity like ecotourism.

Sustainable development: local benefits

Fennell (2002b) has argued that sustainable development, and indeed ecotourism, builds from the ecodevelopment literature of the 1970s, regarding the harmonisation of social and ecological objectives, wise management of environment, thresholds and the enhancement of people, communities and justice. During the latter part of the 1980s, these ideas were more formally crystallised through the sustainable development movement as a model for structural change within society. The application of sustainable development principles quickly entered into the tourism vernacular, with an expanding market of travellers clamouring to take advantage of new eco-based opportunities. The face of sustainable development in tourism emerged in the form of Alternative Tourism (AT) as a natural outgrowth of the dissatisfaction with the mass tourism industry, which by the 1980s had adversely transformed many of the world's most beautiful and sensitive regions at the expense of communities and the natural world. The philosophy behind AT – forms of tourism, like ecotourism, that advocate an approach opposite to mass conventional tourism – was to ensure that tourism policies no longer concentrate on economic and technical necessities alone, but rather emphasise the demand for an unspoilt environment, the needs of local people and the elimination of outside influences (e.g. external stakeholders) in winning back decision-making powers.

The ecotourism literature is replete with examples of how the introduction of tourism has led to the marginalisation of local people through the removal of control and rights. Pressure from outside investment often translates into inevitability about the pace and scale of development, and the perception of insignificance regarding the role of local people in development projects like ecotourism. Taken out of the hands of the people who live in the destination is the ability to control the effects that these large developments have on local resources, resulting in higher tourist impacts, the failure to put money into the hands of local people, with the unwillingness on the part of large firms to protect local ecological resources. A logical reaction to exogenous forces is to simply reject outside-funded tourism and ecotourism in order to fully control the tourism landscape. However, these efforts are constrained by: (1) the inability to organise to the point of political mobilisation; and (2) whether the mobilised unit can ever be strong enough to influence government policy, in the face of intense development interests from outside. The path of least resistance for cash-strapped governments, unfortunately, is often foreign investment.

Furthermore, it is important to recognise that just because a type of tourism provides local benefits, does not mean it is ecotourism. Ecotourism would be that form of development that contributes to local people and areas while nested in many of the broader tents discussed here.

Sustainable development: conservation

There are two main ways by which to examine how conservation has been associated with ecotourism. The first includes micro-scale involvement, whereas the second, although connected, includes larger scale initiatives. In regards to the former, theorists argue that for an activity to be viewed as ecotourism, there must be some type of conservation effort extended on behalf of the ecotourist and/or the service provider with which they are associated. This may come in the form of money contributed to parks and protected areas, local communities or specific projects that may be used to further these conservation objectives. It may also take the form of on-site involvement of ecotourists who directly assist in activities like species breeding programmes, rehabilitation of degraded sites, banding and so on. In regards to the latter, conservation is linked to ecotourism as a protraction of more broadly based conservation initiatives, whereby ecotourism may be a deliberate strategy to mesh and manage human and ecological processes according to various priorities. The following few cases serve to illustrate how ecotourism as a strategy links with broader conservation initiatives.

In Baja, Mexico, for example, poor fisheries conservation techniques led to a depletion of the in-shore fishery (López-Espinosa 2002). In an effort to bolster the local economy, whale watching ecotourism emerged as an option on extrinsic (profit) grounds only. As the whale watching industry evolved with the profit motive only in mind (in the absence of an ethical and well-managed approach to ecotourism), it has not been so lucrative as to alleviate the pressures on the in-shore fishery. As such, conflict over the right to use marine resources has only intensified as a result of ecotourism. In Mongolia, although local people have a strong conservation ethic, they were unwilling to discontinue grazing certain protected area regions without compensation. Parallel to this is the finding that a chief motivating factor for involvement in the ecotourism industry is a depleting natural resource base based on deforestation or over-grazing activities (Maroney 2006). This is also the case in Bohol, Philippines, where protected areas were established based on the effects of intensive deforestation, agricultural exploitation and quarrying. With the establishment of limits to traditional harvesting activities, local people accuse policy makers of ignoring their rights because of the top-down approach employed in the establishment of protected areas (Urich *et al.* 2001). This has led theorists to suggest that coexistence between local people, tourism and protected areas managers should be developed through adaptive governance models that are based on shared involvement and more inclusive objectives.

Nature-based

The focus of ecotourism as nature-based tourism, and later as part of a broader nature-based tourism landscape, has also been the focus of discussion. Early definitions of ecotourism demonstrate that there was little differentiation between what we today view as ecotourism and nature-based tourism. This started to change through the efforts of Laarman and Durst (1993), who identified a conceptual difference between ecotourism and nature tourism. Narrowly, nature-based tourism refers to operators running nature-oriented tours; however, broadly it applies to tourism's use of natural resources including beaches and country landscapes. Later work by Goodwin (1995) provides more of a differentiation between the two concepts. For Goodwin, nature-based tourism:

> encompasses all forms of tourism—mass tourism, adventure tourism, low-impact tourism, ecotourism—which use natural resources in a wild or undeveloped form—including species, habitat, landscape, scenery and salt and fresh-water features. Nature tourism is travel for the purpose of enjoying undeveloped natural areas or wildlife.

And conversely, *ecotourism* is:

> low impact nature tourism which contributes to the maintenance of species and habitats either directly through a contribution to conservation and/or indirectly by providing revenue to the local community sufficient for local people to value, and therefore protect, their wildlife heritage area as a source of income.

Ambiguity between ecotourism and nature-based tourism has led to the development of a number of certification schemes – programmes that provide a means of establishing the extent to which a business offering tourism experiences meets industry-nominated standards. Adherence to these standards, and the ability to advertise as such through ecologos, provide the organisation with the opportunity to be competitive. A good example of accreditation in action is the Nature and Ecotourism Accreditation Program (NEAP) of Australia, through which operators are given a core level of accreditation if they satisfy the programme's basic criteria. The system also encourages operators to implement measures beyond the standards of the core in earning advanced standing. An important aspect of NEAP is that programmes are accredited rather than operators. This means that although operators may run a number of programmes, only those that are worthy of ecotourism (over nature-based tourism) status get accredited (Buckley 2002).

Despite the advantages of these schemes, others argue that accreditation has become politicised because of the sheer number of these schemes in operation and the control over those which are most prominent (e.g. Green Globe 21). Just as important in the debate over the significance of such schemes is the basic question of whether accreditation is worth all of the time and energy. They may ultimately be less effective than simple government regulations and codes of ethics, but more research is required to answer this question. Other theorists argue that such schemes cannot do justice to the experiential aspects of ecotourism because there is simply too much of an emphasis on the institutionalisation of ecotourism through objective forms of evaluation, which serve to strengthen power structures rather than topple them. Consequently, accreditation schemes have turned more towards commodification of ecotourism, rather than well-being and participatory democracy – which is really what ecotourism ought to defend (Jamal *et al.* 2006).

Education

One of the key factors differentiating ecotourism from other forms of nature-based tourism or other more general forms of tourism is education. That is, the focus on learning about the natural history of a destination is one of the key features that sets ecotourists apart from other forms of tourism. In this sense, Fennell (2008) made use of Wilson's (1984) concept of biophilia to explain the intimate tie that exists between the learner and nature. Biophilia is 'the innate tendency to be attracted by other life forms and to affiliate with natural living systems' (Wilson 1984: 214). Learning about these other life forms, and the web of relationships in which they are immersed is foundational in this sense. An important but contentious issue surrounding education is the usefulness of this knowledge or information not at the destination, but rather over longer periods of time – the extent to which ecotourists apply this stewardship knowledge during their everyday existence back at home. Most of the literature points to the fact that there is a very weak relationship between education and the application of this new knowledge over the long term.

The third dimension of Figure 31.1, second-order tenets, includes another four characteristics that are often used to conceptualise ecotourism. This is not to say that these tenets are of lesser importance than first-order tenets, but rather that these exist as defining criteria beyond the four more central criteria assembled in the first order. It may be argued that these tenets are somewhat more inconsistent according to their frequency of appearance in ecotourism definitions. As such, they often take on a more transitory or supporting role in defining what is and what is not ecotourism. These four include ethically marketed and managed, low impact and consumptiveness, small-scale development and the link to natural areas.

Ethical marketing and management

The spectrum of nature-based tourism opportunities that may or may not be positioned as ecotourism is huge. As identified above, although some forms of ecotourism are ethically marketed and managed, others quite simply are not, and fall more in line with nature-based tourism or even further along the continuum to mass tourism.

This seems to be the case with places like SeaWorld, which are labeled and marketed as ecotourism, but without its philosophical foundation. Researchers argue that the capture and display of animals for touristic consumption should not be considered as *bona fide* ecotourism because it places the well-being of the animal at risk. As such, any form of tourism that places stress on the ecology of an area, including individuals and populations, should not be considered as ecotourism. This coincides with the extent to which other more consumptive forms of nature-based tourism have been considered as ecotourism. For example, moose hunting in

Sweden has been referred to as ecotourism if cultural and social aspects are taken into consideration (Gunnarsdotter 2006). In other cases, billfishing (sport fishing for marlin and sailfish) has been referred to as ecotourism because it directs economic assistance to the local community and has economic advantages over other uses. Theorists, however, argue that such an activity cannot be ecotourism because of: (1) the intention to catch the animal (ecotourism should be about minimum disturbance in all cases); (2) the pain and stress that results from catching the animal; (3) consumptiveness (catch-and-release practices still may be viewed as consumptive); and (4) values, such that ecotourists have a different set of values related to sport and the intrinsic/extrinsic motivations surrounding participation in these activities (Holland *et al.* 1998; Fennell 2000). The argument follows that the treatment of animals cannot be based on healthy populations (i.e. it is fine to catch animals because of the healthy state of the population), but rather that respect must be shown to individuals comprising these populations (Regan 1983). The development and use of weak ecotourism definitions has opened the door to a great deal of misrepresentation (and unethical marketing) and the prospect of more anthropocentric values superseding ecocentric ones. The rationale for including activities like hunting and fishing under the ecotourism umbrella is not clear. One hypothesis is that the ecotourism label offers these activities social acceptability in the face of declining memberships. Accordingly, the best way to increase participation is to make the activity more socially acceptable through normative measures hinged on sustainability and ethics (i.e. catch and release or contributions of meat, skins, bones and ivory to local people for commercial reasons).

The scale of development

Another issue that has come to the fore in ecotourism is the likelihood of infusing ecotourism's more responsible ethic into mass forms of tourism in making these other types somehow 'better'. Some ecotourism theorists argue that because scale does not matter in our efforts to be sustainable (i.e. small- and large-scale can either be good or bad), there is no reason to believe that ecotourism could not occur at a grander scale (Weaver 2002). The argument follows that because softer path ecotourists restrict their activities to frontcountry regions of protected areas, which are hardened sites that can absorb the impacts of numbers (with hard path ecotourists more likely to penetrate deeper into the sensitive back regions of these areas), this group has less of an impact. Furthermore, the softer path ecotourist is more likely to contribute to conservation financially through the revenue generated by larger numbers of tourists. An example of this 'ecotourism as mass tourism' model can be found in Thailand, where two of the region's oldest ecotour operators, Sea Canoe and Siam Safari, are said to uphold the principles of ecotourism even though they have structural connections to the package tourism industry that provides their main market. As such, ecotourism in Phuket has emerged not in opposition, but as a function of the mass tourism industry, where tourists typically stay in 4- to 5-star hotels, visit Phuket en route to other destinations or for short holidays, and book through travel agents and tour operators.

Other theorists, however, are not so keen to accept this mass scale linkage because of the belief that ecotourism loses its integrity along the way. The fact that some softer path ecotourists stay in more luxurious accommodations, as with Phuket above, means that their higher resource demands will contribute to a larger ecological footprint. The nature of this larger footprint often comes at the hand of the economic elite who gain considerable social capital by visiting exclusive softer path ecotourism resorts, even though they may not be very ecologically benevolent. The issue of impact is compounded by the fact that ecotourism involves long-haul travel and associated high usage of fossil fuels to satisfy hedonistic ends. The more that participate, the higher the fuel demand (Cater 2006).

Low impact and non-consumptive

Ecotourism is generally viewed as a non-consumptive form of tourism with relatively few impacts compared with other tourism forms (Duffus and Dearden 1990; Reynolds and Braithwaite 2001; Weaver 2001; Wilson and Tisdell 2001; Newsome, Dowling and Moore 2005; Fennell 2008; Lovelock 2008). Consumptiveness is used to separate activities that use the environment in different ways. By *consume* it is meant that, in the case of hunting, an animal is shot and removed from the environment altogether. Fishing can present itself as a form of consumptive recreation if anglers catch, kill and consume the fish itself, thus removing it from the environment. Fishing might also be viewed as a non-consumptive form of recreation, however, if anglers catch fish and release them back into the environment, stress and injury aside.

The following definition serves to illustrate the importance of use and supply in an understanding of consumptiveness in environmental and resource management contexts: 'Consumptive use is the use of a resource that reduces the supply (e.g., removing water from a source like a river, lake or aquifer without returning an equal amount)' (Mimi 2011). Non-consumptive use may be taken as use of a resource that does not reduce the supply of the target species or feature of the environment, that is there is no net loss to the environment as a result of our actions (Fennell 2012).

Tremblay (2001) argues that it is tempting to consider non-consumptive forms of tourism as being morally superior, because there is no evidence to suggest that non-consumptive experiences lead to increased education. Furthermore, profitability of the non-consumptive sector often means that higher numbers of individuals are required to match the economic gains realised through consumptive forms like hunting. Individual hunters contribute more to local economies than individual ecotourists, and the higher numbers of the latter contribute to crowding, habitat disruptions and the need for more infrastructure. Tremblay echoes the sentiments expressed by other theorists who would rather see consumptive and non-consumptive activities exist in a state of complementarity for commercial and environmental sustainability.

In a comprehensive overview of 166 documents containing original data, Boyle and Samson (1985) found that non-consumptive forms of outdoor recreation and tourism do in fact have significant impacts on fauna. The authors reported effects on fauna from hiking and camping (52 reports), boating (37), wildlife viewing and photography (27), ATV use (20), snowmobile use (12), shore recreation (8) and rock climbing (7). Birds were subjects affected most often (61 per cent), followed by mammals (42 per cent) and reptiles and amphibians (4 per cent). Specific examples reported include trampling of habitat; disturbance of large mammal movement patterns by hikers and campers; habituated animals more susceptible to poaching; tourist visits to waterfowl nests leading to nest and egg loss due to predation; and photographers being more disruptive to wildlife than recreationists who accidentally encounter wildlife, because the former are more frequent in their quest and stay for a longer period of time. The issue has been further compounded by the fact that newer forms of tourism like wildlife tourism encompass both consumptive (e.g. hunting) and non-consumptive (e.g. birdwatching) forms of wildlife use.

Taking place in natural areas only

There is a natural linkage between ecotourism and parks and protected areas, as noted above, by virtue of what parks serve to protect and represent: natural history (as defined above) in all its forms, and the wise management of this diversity for its own sake but also for the sake of human enjoyment. Having said this, those who step inside the boundaries of parks do not *automatically* become ecotourists. Ecotourism is both an attitude and an ethic, and protected areas may emphasise the types of attitudes seen as the proper ethic for convening with nature. However, other theorists argue that ecotourism may take place outside this conventional form of supply and take place in places like golf courses, and so on (Weaver 2001). Theorists have also gone so far as to argue that zoos are an appropriate venue for ecotourism because of proximity and education. However, Fennell (2012) argues that animals kept in captivity may be the most foreign concept imaginable as ecotourism because animals are not able to freely express their animal natures if kept behind bars. This follows from Acampora's (2005) concept of the 'carceral archipelago'. Zoos are very much like prisons where artificial space is created to impose occupancy, and in the case of zoos, demonstration. Both of these conditions, that is, occupancy and demonstration, violate animals' status as free living creatures, denying them the ability to express natural behaviours that would otherwise define their very being. No matter how dressed up zoos and aquaria get and how they change their themes and spaces, they remain morally objectionable because they keep animals as captives (Garner 2005).

Conclusion

The continued existence of ecotourism as a distinct form of nature-based tourism becomes important because of what it should represent: sustainability in terms of local benefits and conservation, education, ethical marketing and management, small-scale development, low impact and conservation, and a well-planned and well-managed relationship with parks and protected areas as the primary form of supply for ecotourism. However, perhaps most damning to ecotourism is the criticism that it is often planned and managed no differently than other more invasive forms of tourism through linear, instrumental modes of thinking that have made the marginalised morally unimportant in the face of industry efficiency. What also continues to limit ecotourism, apart from this inter-disciplinary void, is a disconnection between industry, local people, academics and government with respect to a collective vision for the future. It is indeed unfortunate that so many competing demands have sometimes disfigured ecotourism's most basic philosophical premise – the focus on natural history attractions within the destination first and foremost – because of more instrumental values.

References

Acampora, R.R. (2005) 'Zoos and eyes: contesting captivity and seeking successor practices', *Society & Animals* 13(1), 69–88.

Bartholomew, G.A. (1986) 'The role of natural history in contemporary biology', *Bioscience* 36, 324–9.

Boyle, S.A. and Samson, F.B. (1985) 'Effects of nonconsumptive recreation on wildlife: a review', *Wildlife Society Bulletin* 13(2), 110–16.

Buckley, R. (2002) 'Tourism ecocertification in the international year of ecotourism', *Journal of Ecotourism* 1(2–3), 197–203.

Cater, E. (2006) 'Ecotourism as a western construct', *Journal of Ecotourism* 5(1–2), 23–39.

Duffus, D.A. and Dearden, P. (1990) Non-consumptive wildlife-oriented recreation: A conceptual framework. *Biological Conservation* 53(3), 213–31.

Fennell, D.A. (2012) *Tourism and Animal Ethics*. London: Routledge.

——(2000) 'Ecotourism on trial: the case of billfishing as ecotourism', *Journal of Sustainable Tourism* 8(4), 341–5.

——(2002a) 'Ecotourism: where we've been and where we're going', *Journal of Ecotourism* 1(1), 1–6.

——(2002b) 'The Canadian ecotourism in Costa Rica: Ten years down the road', *The International journal of Sustainable Development* 5(3), 282–55.

——(2008) *Ecotourism: an introduction* (3rd edn). London: Routledge.

Garner, R. (2005) *The Political Theory of Animal Rights*. New York: Manchester University Press.

Goodwin, H. (1995) 'Tourism and environment', *Biologist* 42(3), 129–33.

Gunnarsdotter, Y. (2006) 'Hunting tourism as ecotourism: conflicts and opportunities', in S. Gössling and J. Hultman (eds). *Ecotourism in Scandinavia: Lessons in Theory and Practice*. Wallingford: CABI, 178–92.

Hetzer, N.D. (1965) 'Environment, tourism, culture', *LINKS* (July), reprinted in *Ecosphere* (1970) 1(2), 1–3.

Holland, S.M., Ditton, R.B. and Graefe, A.R. (1998) 'An ecotourism perspective on billfish industries', *Journal of Sustainable Tourism* 6(2), 97–116.

Jamal, T., Borges, M. and Stronza, A. (2006) 'The institutionalization of ecotourism: certification, cultural equity and praxis', *Journal of Ecotourism* 5(3), 145–75.

Laarman, J.G. and Durst, P.B. (1993) 'Nature tourism as a tool for economic development and conservation of natural resources', in J. Nenon and P.B. Durst (eds), *Nature Tourism in Asia: Opportunities and Constraints for Conservation and Economic Development*, Washington, DC: US Forest Service.

Lopez, B. (1986) *Arctic Dreams*. New York: Vintage.

López-Espinosa, R. (2002) 'Evaluating ecotourism in natural protected areas of La Paz Bay, Baja California Sur, Mexico: ecotourism or nature-based tourism?', *Biodiversity and Conservation* 11, 1539–50.

Lovelock, B. (2008) *Tourism and the Consumption of Wildlife*. London: Routledge.

Maroney, R.L. (2006) 'Community based wildlife management planning in protected areas: the case of Altai argali in Mongolia', *USDA Forest Proceedings RMRS-P-39*, pp. 37–49. Proceedings of the Conference on Transformation Issues and future Challenges, 27 January, Salt Lake City, UT.

Mimi (2011) 'Consumptive use', Environment. Online. Available at: http://en.mimi.hu/environment/index_environment.html (accessed 10 January 2011).

Newsome, D., Dowling, R.K. and Moore, S.A. (2005) *Wildlife Tourism*. Clevedon: Channel View.

Regan, T. (1983) *The Case for Animal Rights*. Berkeley: University of California Press.

Reynolds, P.C. and Braithwaite, D. (2001) 'Towards a conceptual framework for wildlife tourism', *Tourism Management* 22, 31–42.

Tremblay, P. (2001) 'Wildlife tourism consumption: consumptive or non-consumptive?', *International Journal of Tourism Research* 3, 81–6.

Urich, P.B., Day, M.J. and Lynagh, F. (2001) 'Policy and practice in karst landscape protection: Bohol, the Philippines', *The Geographical Journal* 167(4), 305–23.

Weaver, D.B. (2002) 'The evolving concept of ecotourism and its potential impacts', *International Journal of Sustainable Development* 5(3), 251–64.

——(2001) *The Encyclopedia of Ecotourism*. Wallingford: CAB International.

Wilcove, D.S. and Eisner, T. (2000) 'The impending extinction of natural history', *Chronicle of Higher Education* 15: B24.

Wilson, C. and Tisdell, C. (2001) 'Sea turtles as a non-consumptive tourism resource especially in Australia', *Tourism Management* 22, 279–88.

Wilson, E.O. (1984) *Biophilia*. Cambridge, MA: Harvard University Press.

32

Nature-based tourism

Alexandra Coghlan and Ralf Buckley

Introduction

This chapter reviews tourism activities, settings and providers, both private and public sector, which fall under the heading of nature-based tourism. The sector is broad, growing and diversifying. We examine the supply and demand for nature-based tourism; consider its social contexts and traditions; and discuss the various ways in which people, as tourists, experience relationships with nature and consume some of nature's goods and services. We argue that recognition of this complexity and diversity can lead to a more sophisticated understanding and management of nature-based tourism.

Supply: scope and scale of the sector

Nature-based tourism is simply tourism that features nature. It encompasses all forms of tourism where nature or the outdoors is the primary attraction or setting, particularly where nature is in an undisturbed or pristine state (Newsome *et al.* 2002; Buckley *et al.* 2003; Buckley 2009a). Nature-based tourism can thus include activities based on: passive enjoyment of scenery, geology, flora and fauna; outdoor recreation and adventure; consumptive uses such as hunting and fishing; and volunteer contributions to conservation or research (Benson 2005; Coghlan 2006, 2007). Indeed, commercial tour operators themselves generally describe their products principally in terms of specific activities, from abseiling adventures to wildlife watching. Nature-based is a tag used more in academia than commerce.

From a supply-side perspective, various sub-divisions have been proposed to recognise the variety in nature-based tourism products and enterprises. Early analysts such as Valentine (1992), for example, distinguished tour products for which nature is: (a) essential; (b) an enhancement; or (c) incidental to the tour. More recent academic literature reflects terminology used in the industry itself. Whereas Newsome *et al.* (2002) and Buckley *et al.* (2003) referred to natural-areas and nature-based tourism, respectively, authors such as Swarbrooke *et al.* (2003) and Buckley (2006, 2010a) refer to adventure tourism, and Shackley (1996) and Newsome *et al.* (2005) to wildlife tourism. Relevant research is also published in the fields of recreation ecology (Liddle 1997), wilderness science (Hendee and Dawson 2002) and protected area management (Lockwood *et al.* 2006).

There is also a large body of relevant literature under the heading of ecotourism, such as Fennell (2003), Weaver (2001, 2008) and Buckley (2003, 2004, 2009a, 2009b). Although academic and government definitions of ecotourism combine nature-based products, minimal-impact management, environmental education and contributions to conservation, some commercial tour operators and tourism industry associations advertise any form of nature-based tourism as ecotourism, irrespective of other criteria (Buckley 2000; Russell and Wallace 2004). Most recently, the term conservation tourism has been used to describe a limited sub-set of ecotourism, in itself a sub-set of nature-based tourism (Buckley 2010b).

Finally, as well as being sub-divisible, nature-based tourism overlaps with several related concepts and subsectors. Some authors have proposed aggregate product terms such as ACE – adventure, culture and ecotourism (Fennell 2003); NEAT – nature, eco- and adventure tourism (Buckley 2000); or ecocultural tourism (Russell and Wallace 2004). None of these acronyms, however, has been adopted to any significant degree either by industry or academia.

The estimated global economic scale of the nature-based tourism sector depends heavily on which specific components are included and how they are measured (Buckley 2009a,c). Most nature-based tourism takes place in protected areas, so the number of visitors to protected areas can be used as one surrogate measure of the size of the industry. Balmford *et al.* (2009) examined changes in visitor numbers in 280 protected areas in 20 countries over a 15-year period (1992–2006), and found that nature-based tourism was growing faster in developing countries than in developed countries.

Using visitation figures such as these, the social economic value of the nature-based tourism sector can be estimated using the costs of time, travel and equipment to visit parks and other outdoor destinations, as well as any direct access and activity fees and charges and the value of commercial tour products purchased. Using such approaches, the global economic scale of the nature-based sub-sector amounts to hundreds of billions of dollars annually (Buckley 2009a, 2009c). If the entire NEAT or outdoor tourism sector is included, then estimates of total economic scale range up to US$1 trillion p.a., again depending on what is included (Buckley 2009a, 2009c).

The size and scope of the nature-based tourism market has thus extended far beyond the labels of special interest or alternative tourism (Weiler and Hall 1992) or even what Weaver (2001) called mass ecotourism. To understand the nature-based tourism sector, therefore, it is first critical to recognise the diversity and variety among both the products supplied, and the customers who demand and buy them.

Demand: nature-based tourists

Just as nature-based tourism is a large and heterogeneous product sector, individual nature-based tourists are equally heterogeneous in origins, interests, motivations and behaviours. Most individuals who take part in nature-based tourism also have interests outside this specific sub-sector, and any realistic understanding of nature-based tourists must recognise these outside interests. In the same way that various analysts have segmented the supply-side spectrum of nature-based tourism products, other authors have segmented the demand-side spectrum of nature-based tourists, for example on the basis of their demographics, activities, motivations, values or psychographic characteristics (Silverberg *et al.* 1996; Strasdas 2006; Mehmetoglu 2007).

Two decades ago, Lindberg (1991) recognised four types of nature-based tourists: (1) *hard-core*, by which he meant scientific researchers or members of voluntary conservation tours; (2) *dedicated*, people who take trips to protected areas specifically in order to understand local, natural and cultural history; (3) *mainstream*, who visit well-known iconic nature destinations primarily so as to take an unusual trip; and, finally, (4) *casual*, who include nature-based components as part of a broader itinerary. The numbers of tourists in each of these categories differ greatly, from very few 'hard-core' to very many 'casual'. Fifteen years later, Strasdas (2006) proposed a similar typology, but with two further segments: those with 'cultural interests' who also include cultural elements in their nature-based tourism activities; and 'sports/adventure' and 'hunting/fishing' tourists, who see nature principally as a backdrop or setting for outdoor recreation.

A somewhat different approach was taken by Vespestad and Lindberg (2010), who argued that there are four ontological perspectives, that is ways of being, that dominate published research findings in nature-based tourists. In their view, these four perspectives provide: (1) *'genuine'* nature-based tourism experiences, where tourists seek out their 'true, authentic selves'; (2) nature-based experiences as *entertainment*, where nature becomes a setting for an activity or experience that has entertainment value; (3) nature-based experiences as a *state of being*, where the focus is on the rewards of a nature-based experience specifically to the individual concerned; and (4) *social* nature-based experiences that provide meaning and identity to group members.

Rather than segmenting nature-based tourists into discrete segments, some authors see these tourists as forming a continuum; although they do not always agree on the parameter or dimension that defines that continuum. Acott *et al.* (1998), Galloway (2002) and Weaver (2001) proposed continua from hard to soft, or deep to shallow. At the hard or deep end of the continuum are environmentally conscious visitors travelling in small groups on long, specialised trips including physically challenging, direct experiences with nature. At the soft or shallow end are tourists on short unspecialised tours, for example vacationers spending an all-inclusive holiday in a coastal resort, who are visiting a nearby protected area on a one-day excursion.

More recently, Arnegger *et al.* (2010) use a multidimensional matrix of travel behaviour and motivations to describe 'hybrid' tourists. This recognises that individual tourists may or may not be environmentally conscious, well informed or highly selective when choosing any particular nature-based tour; and that these three characteristics are not necessarily correlated. To understand the many variations of nature-based tourism, these authors developed a matrix of service arrangements and travel motivations. They recognised four types of service arrangement, namely independent, *à la carte*, customised and fully standardised. Similarly, they recognised four types of travel motivations, namely nature protection, nature experience, sports and adventure, and hedonism. The resulting 16-cell matrix provides a structured analytical framework, which none the less recognises the broad scope of nature-based tourism sector. This matrix approach leads to a 'pick and mix' conceptual view, where individual tourists can select very different levels of engagement with nature, which can also vary from tour to tour for the same individual.

Social context

The scale, popularity and diversity of the nature-based tourism sub-sector can best be understood as a consequence of changing social contexts. The relationships and attitudes that humans hold towards nature differ greatly between nations, peoples and socio-economic groups, and have changed greatly over time. In the Western developed world, for example, it is commonly suggested that until the late nineteenth century, the natural environment was often perceived, at least by urban residents and politicians, as something to be feared and/or tamed. In the West, the history of nature as a tourist attraction is relatively short, perhaps starting with the Romantic movement, with its landscape artists and visits to the countryside, and leading to the popular accounts of explorers of the late nineteenth century and early twentieth century, and the beginnings of armchair travellers with an interest in geography and natural history (Meyer-Arendt 2004).

In recent times, a number of authors have suggested that the popularity of nature-based tourism in the West arose as a result of the increasing urbanisation of Western societies, including alienation and separation from the natural environment. At the same time, images of the natural environment have become increasingly accessible through the mass media, even to those who have little personal contact with nature in their everyday lives (Buckley 1998a, 2000). This creates a market for nature-based tourism and recreation. In addition, most urban-dwellers have little time to learn the skills to live or travel in natural environments, or the equipment with which to do so. This creates opportunities for commercial nature-based tour operators to provide packaged adventure and nature tours.

There are a number of additional large-scale social trends that may have driven the development of nature-based tourism. Environmental activism has grown significantly over recent decades (Weaver 2001; Fennell 2003). Nature-based tourism has been promoted as a sustainable development opportunity, in rural or remote areas, sometimes as a substitute for declining agricultural and other rural activities (Rinne and Saastamoinen 2005). Tourism destinations that have experienced negative impacts from mass tourism may deliberately seek a change to alternative forms of tourism, including nature-based tourism (Fennell 2003).

At a broader societal level, Saarinen (2005) suggests that interest in nature-based tourism coincides with wider changes in consumption and economic production, and with a move towards post-Fordism. This is represented by a trend away from packaged multiclient mass tourism, towards individual travellers and products that cater to highly segmented markets. The post-Fordist approach to tourism thus favours flexibility, individuality, hybridity and activity. All of these match well, as outlined earlier, with trends actually observed in nature-based tourism products and their purchasers. In this way, Saarinen presents nature-based tourism as a challenge to mass tourism, away from standardised and institutionalised packaged tours. Saarinen (2005) suggested that this is associated with the rise of more discerning, educated and concerned travellers, who are more aware of their environmental and cultural impacts at tourism destinations. Post-Fordist patterns in product structures, however, are discernible irrespective of any possible change in travellers' attitudes.

Arnegger et al. (2010) extend this idea of a post-Fordist tourism experience to capture the diversity of nature-based tourists described in the previous section. They argue that although nature-based tourism suppliers developed their own packages and infrastructure in association with large tour operators that cater to mainstream 'soft' or 'casual' tourists, there is not necessarily any association between a tourist's degree of commitment towards nature protection (hard to soft) and the manner in which their trip was organised (packaged to independent traveller). That is, they argue that nature-based tourists are simply more diverse, not necessarily more aware of social and environmental issues and impacts. In addition, even travellers who do have high concerns for nature conservation may choose various different travel options. Some may travel as part of scientific or professional expeditions, whereas others with equal concerns may prefer highly packaged products such as commercial tours or volunteer tourism opportunities, where the logistics of the trip are organised by commercial intermediaries.

In addition to the different historical traditions and cultural contexts outlined above, there can be much larger differences between white nature-based tourists from Anglophone Western nations, and those from other continents, countries, linguistic traditions and ethnicities. Within the USA, for example, citizens of black or Hispanic descent may have different recreational preferences than those of Caucasian descent (Godbey et al. 2005; Lopez et al. 2005). The same applies for citizens of various different descent in countries such as South Africa or Fiji. Within Europe, traditions and practices relating to nature and outdoor recreation are very different in Scandinavia (Gössling and Hultman 2006) than Germany, Greece, Spain or France (Priskin and Sarrasin 2010).

There may be even greater cultural differences between the developed Western nations, and the large newly industrialised nations such as China, India and Brazil, each of which has a very large population, a very strong domestic tourism sector, and a rapidly growing outbound international sector. In China, for example, national parks are very powerful attractants for domestic tourists (Qiu 2006, cited in Ma *et al.* 2009). Preferred recreational activities, however, centre around the appreciation of landscape, culture and history (Su *et al.* 2007; Yan *et al.* 2007; Buckley *et al.* 2008); rely strongly on built infrastructure (Ma *et al.* 2009; Zhong *et al.* 2010); and typically focus on social rather than solitary outdoor activities. The Chinese domestic NEAT sector is developing rapidly, but along rather different lines to that in the West (Zhong *et al.* 2007; Buckley 2010b: 56–64).

In India, there is now a strong domestic nature-based tourism sector, which includes wildlife, adventure and cultural components (Buckley 2010b: 66–9). Most of this consists of independent family holiday travel, but there is also an increasing domestic market for upmarket wildlife watching lodges modelled on the southern African game safari sector. Popular parks can experience severe crowding, and this situation is likely to become exacerbated rather than alleviated as India's newly wealthy middle class continues to grow and to seek new leisure activities. Similar considerations apply in Brazil, where tourism is both a threat to endangered ecosystems such as coastal Atlantic forest, and also a potential protection against continued illegal logging inside protected areas (Buckley 2010b: 139–40; F. Pegas, pers. comm. 2011).

In these newly industrialised nations there is as yet very little research on the demographics, socio-economic status or cultural contexts of nature-based tourists, or on their attitudes and traditions towards nature, and their recreational preferences, motivations and behaviours. Yet these factors, both in the three largest countries mentioned above and in the many smaller nations of East and Southeast Asia, Central and South America, and the entire continent of Africa, will be critical to the development of nature-based tourism worldwide, and especially to its potential role in conservation of biodiversity hotspots.

Tourist experiences and welfare

In view of these post-Fordist trends towards individualised, pick and mix nature-based tourism products, how can we best interpret the experiences of individual nature-based tourists? Arguably, nature-based tourism has become part of the experience economy, in which space, time and human experiences come together in a system where individuals seek to perform a wide variety of new experiences, and:

> nature has become a product with certain qualities attached to particular places, which can be wildlife, untouched, untamed, scenic, beautiful, rough and so forth.
>
> *(Saarinen 2004: 440)*

The scope and growth of nature-based tourism indicates its appeal to a wide cross-section of the populations in both urbanised developed countries and newly industralised nations. It has even been suggested that nature 'is today universally regarded as a source of pleasure' (Wang 2000: 80). The desire to visit a natural attraction, however, does not necessarily indicate a willingness to protect nature (Sharpley 2006; Budeanu 2007). The natural environment is a strong attraction for holiday travellers, but there is little to indicate that these tourists act to protect biodiversity, or even to avoid the negative environmental effects of their travel behaviour (Sharpley 2006; Buckley 2009b).

One of the central issues in the study of nature-based tourism experiences is that nature cannot be controlled in the same way as many other attractions, and nature-based tourism experiences are therefore somewhat elusive. Commercial tour operators aim to manage tourism experiences closely, so as to control client satisfaction, impacts and hence profits. Although nature-based experiences provide powerful attractions on which tour operators can capitalise, they also bring high levels of uncertainty. Tour operators have only limited control over the key nature-based components of their clients' experiences. Although managing these as far as they can, therefore, they also focus on improving more easily manageable components such as infrastructure and comfort, and on managing client expectations so as to avoid disappointment.

In their studies of tourist satisfaction in parks, for example, Tonge and Moore (2007) have pointed out that the physical attributes of tourism, such as infrastructure in protected areas, are easier to manage and therefore dominate management efforts, even though these attributes are more commonly associated with minimising tourist dissatisfaction than increasing satisfaction. The elements that influence the actual experience, in contrast, are harder to measure and thus often overlooked. Tonge and Moore (2007), therefore, suggest a need for more concerted research attention on experiential satisfiers that focus on the less tangible aspects of nature-based tourism.

To do so requires new ways of understanding the tourist experience and satisfaction. In tourism settings that are relatively unstructured, and where tourist expectations are poorly defined, standard expectancy-(dis)confirmation paradigms are of limited value. New conceptual approaches and methodologies are therefore needed in order to understand and measure the experiences and satisfaction of nature-based tourists. Both affective and cognitive components are important in modelling consumer satisfaction (Bigne *et al.* 2005). This is particularly important in tourism services, where emotional involvement appears to play an important role in the tourist experience. A focus on the tourists' subjective experiences highlights the need to integrate cognitive and emotional concepts in order to explain tourist satisfaction (Zins 2002; Bigne *et al.* 2005). In particular, it appears that as urban residents become more alienated from nature during their day-to-day existence, nature-based tourism is valued increasingly for its ability to provide experiences that go beyond the passive and packaged to offer emotional, performative and even spiritual components (Meyer-Arendt 2004; Heintzman 2010; Vespestad and Lindberg 2010).

The health benefits of nature-based tourism have a well-established history. Meyer-Arendt (2004), for example, argued that the social context for nature-based tourism includes traditions that have built up around such diverse and long-established practices as spa and seaside tourism, religious and spiritual retreats, recreational school camps and inner-city urban parks. Heintzman (2010) reviewed research on the relationships between nature-based recreation and spirituality, and suggested that many visitors to parks and wilderness areas are seeking spiritual outcomes associated with senses of wonder, awe, amazement, peacefulness, calm, stillness and tranquillity. Health and wellness tourism rely heavily on the natural environment for marketing, albeit often with an element of hyperbole. This sub-sector sells the idea of being cared for in comfort and safety in a calming and peaceful environment, and enjoying the health benefits that nature has to offer (Erfurt-Cooper and Cooper 2009). Indeed, in countries such as the UK, the health benefits of sea air and salt-water bathing have been endorsed for many decades, and a recent resurgence is leading to new growth in beach and coastal tourism (Meyer-Arendt 2004).

Other social constructions of nature lead to so-called performative experiences (Cater and Cloke 2007), based on active adrenalin-based activities such as whitewater rafting, rock-climbing or surfing. Many of these aim to induce what Csikszentmihalyi (1990) has called flow. Activities that involve a balance of challenge and skill, motivation and expectation can create senses of heightened or optimal experience. The attraction of such experiences is that when a participant is completely involved in an activity requiring full attention, it can provide feelings of control and loss of anxiety and constraint, contrasting strongly with typical experiences at home and work.

Nature thus becomes a setting for a variety of very different activities linked to these traditions, each with its own way of constructing perceptions of nature and the benefits derived from being within it. These different constructions yield very different attitudes, behaviours and impacts on the natural environment. In addition, individual social constructions of nature influence how visitors respond to minimal-impact and conservation messages provided by parks and land management agencies. The four ontological perspectives of nature-based tourism proposed by Vespestad and Lindberg (2010), namely a search for self, a form of entertainment, a state of being and a form of social affiliation, could perhaps provide a future framework to analyse how partnerships to protect the landscape may or may not develop between land management agencies, tour operators and individual visitors or tourists.

This wide variety in the social constructions and contexts for nature-based tourism, the diversity of commercial tour products that have arisen to meet these differing interpretations of nature and the growth of the sector as a whole, provides an increasingly complex challenge for the owners and managers of lands and waters where nature-based tourism takes place (Buckley 2009a).

Managing nature for tourists

Maintaining natural landscapes, and their water and wildlife, should be important to nature-based tour operators as well as natural resource managers; but not necessarily for the same reasons, nor in the same way. The idea that nature-based tourism exposes visitors to the wonders of the natural world, and that this could engender support for conservation may be appealing; but because of the diversity in social constructions of nature, it is not necessarily correct. In fact, Beaumont (1998), Lee and Moscardo (2005) and Buckley (2009a, 2009b, 2009c) all note that there appears to be no actual test or evidence to show that a nature or ecotourism experience converts commercial clients to conservation lobbyists.

Indeed, it seems rather unlikely that tourists on the 'casual' or 'soft' ends of the nature-based tourism spectrum will be much transformed by their passing experience with nature. Their primary purposes for engaging in nature-based tourism may have little to do with being transformed by nature, or protecting it. Budeanu (2007) argued that environmental messages have little effect on most nature-based tourists, who are more likely to be influenced by their lifestyle and personal preferences. Powell *et al.* (2009), for instance, proposed a model to examine changes in the environmental dispositions of nature-based tourists based on interactions between sites, fellow travellers and management authorities.

Meanwhile, continuing growth in the number of visitors to national parks is forcing park management agencies to spend more on visitor infrastructure, management and education, so that they have less to spend on management of their natural resources for conservation (Buckley *et al.* 2003; Lockwood *et al.* 2006). Many protected area managers have a legal mandate to provide for public recreational use as well as conservation. Park managers may also see opportunities for environmental education, political support, and direct revenue from tourism and recreation in protected areas. At the same time, however, they are keenly aware of the environmental impacts and the additional costs and management efforts associated with increased park visitation and recreational activities.

Research on parks and visitor management tools and indicators thus aims to help protected area managers control the environmental impacts of visitors and tours so that they do not cause irretrievable damage to primary conservation values (Buckley 2004, 2009a, 2009c). Increasingly, such research now includes social components related to managing visitor satisfaction as well as the traditional tools of control and hardening (Buckley 1998b, 2009a). Fletcher and Fletcher (2003) called for identification of those aspects of outdoor recreation, which are both amenable to being managed, and have the strongest relationship to visitor satisfaction. Better under-standings of tourist experiences and satisfaction are especially relevant in the management of user conflicts (Buckley 2009a; Eagles *et al.* 2002, Manning 2011).

Because of the diversity of the nature-based tourism sector, its social contexts, and individual tourist preferences and social constructions of nature, management of visitor satisfaction within pro-tected areas and other natural environments is an unavoidably complex and difficult task. As noted by McCool (2009), for example, investments in environmental protection may not always lead to higher visitor satisfaction. In fact, it may be argued that within nature-based tourism, the onus is on commercial tour operators to devise means of boosting visitor satisfaction, whereas land managers focus on ways to screen and improve the environmental performance of tour operators.

Conclusions

Nature-based tourism is a very broadly defined catch-all term, which includes all forms of tourism where nature is the primary attraction or setting. This includes many different sub-sectors with very different histories and traditions, ranging from the predatory and consumptive to the spiritual and protective. This has led to a corresponding diversity in commercial nature-based tourism products. The nature-based tourism sector may now be seen as part of the experience economy, where individual tourists, most of them urban in origin, expect to be able to pick and mix components and activities to form customised rather than standardised holidays. This may be perceived as part of the so-called post-Fordist transformation of modern societies. Individual expectations of nature-based tourism depend heavily on social context and background, and on individual perceptual constructions of nature.

All of these very different tourists, however, still want to use nature as a place to play. This can generate conflicts both between different user groups, and between tour operators and land managers. Whereas some types of nature tourist, and corresponding tour providers, may indeed share the desire to protect nature, many do not. To some degree, these differences can be resolved by allocating different types of nature-based tourist operations into different land tenures, public or private. In other instances, the standard menu of visitor management tools used by parks agencies can suffice (Buckley 1998b). The idea that nature-based tourists neces-sarily care about nature, or have any concern to minimise their impacts, remains more wishful thinking than reality. The same applies for the idea that parks agencies can influence the atti-tudes and the behaviour of uncaring visitors simply through educational materials, or can exclude high-impact visitors through selective marketing campaigns.

Approaches that appeal to individual desires and satisfaction are commonly more successful than those that appeal to conscience and common good. Research on the factors that influence the satis-faction and dissatisfaction of nature-based tourists, the degree to which these factors are controllable either by land managers or by tour operators, and the ways in which these may influence individual behaviour and impacts, are thus increasingly important for the future of this large and growing component of the tourism industry. In particular, as much of the current growth in the nature-based tourism sector involves countries, languages and social traditions very different from the developed Western Anglophone nations that historically made up the bulk of this market sector, it is becoming increasingly important to extend and compare relevant research internationally.

References

Acott, T.G., La Trobe, H.L. and Howard, S.H. (1998) 'An evaluation of deep ecotourism and shallow ecotourism', *Journal of Sustainable Tourism* 6, 238–53.

Arnegger, J., Woltering, M. and Job, H. (2010) 'Towards a product-based typology for nature-based tourism: A conceptual framework', *Journal of Sustainable Tourism* 18, 915–28.

Balmford, A., Beresford, J., Green, J., Naidoo, R., Walpole, M. and Manica, A. (2009) 'A global perspective on trends in nature-based tourism', *PLoS Biology* 7, 1–6.

Beaumont, N. (1998) 'The conservation benefits of ecotourism: Does it produce pro-environmental attitudes or are ecotourists already converted to the cause?', in B. Faulkner, C. Tidswell and D. Weaver (eds) *Progress in Tourism and Hospitality Research*. Proceedings of the Eighth Australian Tourism and Hospitality Research Conference, Canberra: Bureau of Tourism Research, 273–5.

Benson, A. (2005) 'Research tourism: Professional travel for useful discoveries', in M. Novelli (ed.) *Niche Tourism: Contemporary Issues, Trends and Cases*. Oxford: Elsevier Butterworth-Heinemann, 133–42.

Bigne, J.E., Andreu, L. and Gnoth, J. (2005) 'The theme park experience: An analysis of pleasure arousal and satisfaction', *Tourism Management* 26, 833–44.

Buckley, R.C. (1998a) 'Ecotourism Megatrends', *Australian Review of Business*, December 52–5.

——(1998b) 'Tools and indicators for managing tourism in parks', *Annals of Tourism Research* 26, 207–10.

——(2000) 'NEAT trends: Current issues in nature, eco and adventure tourism', *International Journal of Tourism Research* 2, 437–44

——(2003) *Case Studies in Ecotourism*. Wallingford: CAB International.

——(ed.) (2004) *Environmental Impacts of Ecotourism*. Wallingford: CAB International.

——(2006) *Adventure Tourism*. Wallingford: CAB International.

——(2009a) *Ecotourism: Principles and Practices*. Wallingford: CAB International.

——(2009b) 'Evaluating the net effects of ecotourism on the environment: a framework, first assessment and future research', *Journal of Sustainable Tourism* 17, 643–72.

——(2009c) 'Parks and tourism', *PLoS Biol* 7, e1000143.

——(2010a) *Adventure Tourism Management*. Oxford: Elsevier.

——(2010b) *Conservation Tourism*. Wallingford: CAB International.

Buckley, R.C., Pickering, C.M. and Weaver, D. (eds) (2003) *Nature-based Tourism, Environment and Land Management*, Wallingford: CAB International.

Buckley, R., Zhong, L-S., Cater, C. and Chen, T. (2008) 'Shengtai luyou: Cross-cultural comparison in ecotourism', *Annals of Tourism Research* 35, 945–68.

Budeanu, A. (2007) 'Sustainable tourist behaviour – a discussion of opportunities for change', *International Journal of Tourism Studies* 31, 499–508.

Cater, C. and Cloke, P. (2007) 'Bodies in action: The performativity of adventure tourism', *Anthropology Today* 23, 13–16.

Coghlan, A. (2006) 'Volunteer tourism as an emerging trend or as expansion of ecotourism? A look at potential clients' perceptions of volunteer tourism organizations', *International Journal of Nonprofit Volunteer Sector Marketing* 11, 225–37.

——(2007) 'Towards an integrated typology of volunteer tourism organizations', *Journal of Sustainable Tourism* 15, 267–87.

Csikszentmihalyi, M. (1990) *Flow: The psychology of optimal experience*. New York: Harper & Row.

Eagles, P., McCool, S. and Haynes, C. (2002) *Sustainable Tourism in Protected Areas: Guidelines for Planning and Management*. Gland, Switzerland and Cambridge: IUCN.

Erfurt-Cooper, P. and Cooper, M. (2009) *Health and Wellness Tourism: Spas and Hot Springs*. Bristol: Channel View Publications.

Fennell, D. (2003) *Ecotourism* (2nd edn). London: Routledge.

Fletcher, D. and Fletcher, H. (2003) 'Manageable predictors of park visitor satisfaction: Maintenance and personnel', *Journal of Park and Recreation Administration* 21, 21–37.

Galloway, G. (2002) 'Psychographic segmentation of park visitor markets: Evidence for the utility of sensation seeking', *Tourism Management* 23, 581–96.

Godbey, G.C., Caldwell, L.L., Floyd, M. and Payne, L.L. (2005) 'Contributions of leisure studies and recreation and park management research to the Active Living agenda', *American Journal of Preventive Medicine* 28, 150–8.

Gössling, S. and Hultman, J. (2006) *Ecotourism in Scandinavia: Lessons in Theory and Practice*. Wallingford: CAB International.

Heintzman, P. (2010) 'Nature-based recreation and spirituality: A complex relationship', *Leisure Sciences* 32, 72–89.

Hendee, J.C. and Dawson, C.P. (2002) *Wilderness Management*, 3rd edn. Colorado: WILD Foundation and Fulcrum Publishing.

Lee, W.H. and Moscardo, G. (2005) 'Understanding the impact of ecotourism resort experiences on tourists' environmental attitudes and behavioural intentions', *Journal of Sustainable Tourism* 13, 546–65.

Liddle, M.J. (1997) *Recreation Ecology: The Ecological Impact of Outdoor Recreation*. Dordrecht: Kluwer Academic Publishers.

Lindberg, K. (1991) *Policies for Maximizing Nature Tourism's Ecological and Economic Benefits*. Washington, DC: World Resources Institute, pp. 1–37.

Lockwood, M., Worboys, G. and Kothari, A. (2006) *Managing Protected Areas: A Global Guide*. London: Earthscan.

Lopez, R., Lopez, A., Wilkins, R.N., Torres, C., Valdez, R., Teer, J. and Bowser, G. (2005) 'Changing Hispanic demographics: challenges in natural resource management', *Wildlife Society Bulletin* 33(2), 553–64.

Ma, X., Ryan, C. and Bao, J. (2009) 'Chinese national parks: Differences, resource use and tourism product portfolios', *Tourism Management* 30, 21–30.

Manning, R.E. (2011) *Studies in Outdoor Recreation: Search and Research for Satisfaction*. 3rd edn. Corvallis, OR: Oregon State University Press.

McCool, S.F. (2009) 'Constructing partnerships for protected area tourism planning in an era of change and messiness', *Journal of Sustainable Tourism* 17, 133–48.

Mehmetoglu, M. (2007) 'Nature-based tourism: A contrast to everyday life', *Journal of Ecotourism* 6, 111–26.

Meyer-Arendt, K. (2004) 'Tourism and the natural environment', in A. Lew, M. Hall and A. Williams (eds) *A Companion to Tourism*. Oxford: Blackwell Publishing, 425–37.

Newsome, D., Moore, S.A. and Dowling, R.K. (2002) *Natural Area Tourism: Ecology, Impacts and Management*. Clevedon: Channel View Publications.

Newsome, D., Dowling, R. and Moore, S. (2005) *Wildlife Tourism*. Clevedon: Channel View Publications.

Powell, R., Kellert, S. and Ham, S. (2009) 'Interactional theory and the sustainable nature-based tourism experience', *Society and Natural Resources* 22, 761–76.

Priskin, J. and Sarrasin, B. (2010) 'France and Francophone Nations', in R. Buckley (ed.) *Conservation Tourism*. Wallingford: CAB International, 110–24.

Rinne, P. and Saastamoinen, O. (2005) 'Local economic role of nature-based tourism in Kuhmo municipality, eastern Finland', *Scandinavian Journal of Hospitality and Tourism* 5, 89–101.

Russell, A. and Wallace, G. (2004) 'Editorial: Irresponsible ecotourism', *Anthropology Today* 20, 1–2.

Saarinen, J. (2004) 'Tourism and touristic representations of nature', in A. Lew, M. Hall and A. Williams (eds) *A Companion to Tourism*. Oxford: Blackwell Publishing.

——(2005) 'Tourism in the northern wildernesses: Wilderness discourses and the development of nature-based tourism in northern Finland', in C.M. Hall and S. Boyd (eds) *Nature-Based Tourism in Peripheral Areas – Development or Disaster?*, Clevedon: Channel View Publications, 36–49.

Shackley, M. (1996) *Wildlife tourism*. London: International Thomson Business Press.

Sharpley, R. (2006) 'Ecotourism: A consumption perspective', *Journal of Ecotourism* 5, 7–21.

Silverberg, K.E., Backman, S. and Backman, K. (1996) 'A Preliminary investigation into the psychographics of nature-based travelers to the Southeastern United States', *Journal of Travel Research* 35, 19–28.

Strasdas, W. (2006) 'The global market for nature-based tourism', in H. Job and J. Li (eds) *Natural Heritage, Ecotourism and Sustainable Development*. Kallmunz: Lassleben, 55–64.

Su, D., Wall, G. and Eagles, P. (2007) 'Emerging governance approaches for tourism in the protected areas of China', *Environmental Management* 39, 749–59.

Swarbrooke, J., Beard, C., Leckie, S. and Pomfret, G. (2003) *Adventure Tourism: The New Frontier*. London: Elsevier Butterworth-Heinemann.

Tonge, J. and Moore, S.A. (2007) 'Importance-satisfaction analysis for marine-park hinterlands: A Western Australian case study', *Tourism Management* 28, 768–76.

Valentine, P.S. (1992) 'Review. Nature-based tourism', in B. Weiler and C.M. Hall, (eds) *Special Interest Tourism*. London: Bellhaven Press, 105–27.

Vespestad, M. and Lindberg, F. (2010) 'Understanding nature-based tourist experiences: An ontological approach', *Current Issues in Tourism*, iFirst article: 1–18. DOI: 10.1080/13683500.2010.513730.

Wang, N. (2000) *Tourism and Modernity*. Amsterdam: Pergamon.

Weaver, D.B. (2001) 'Ecotourism as mass tourism: Contradiction or reality', *Cornell Hotel and Restaurant Administration Quarterly* 42, 520–38.

Weaver, D. (2008) *Ecotourism*, 2nd edn, Brisbane: John Wiley and Sons.

Weiler, B. and Hall, C.M. (1992) *Special Interest Tourism*. London: Belhaven Press.

Yan, J., Barkmann, J. and Marggraf, R. (2007) *Chinese tourist preferences for nature based destinations – a choice experiment analysis*. Available http://ideas.repec.org/p/zbw/daredp/0706.html.

Zhong, L.S., Buckley, R. and Xie, T. (2007) 'Chinese perspectives on tourism eco-certification', *Annals of Tourism Research* 34, 808–11.

Zhong, L.S., Qi, J. and Buckley, R.C. (2010) 'Ecotourism in China's west and east', in R. Buckley (ed.) *Conservation Tourism*. Wallingford: CAB International, 71–5.

Zins, A.H. (2002) 'Consumption emotions, experience quality and satisfaction: A structural analysis for complainers and non-complainers', *Journal of Travel and Tourism Marketing* 12, 3–18.

33

Wildlife tourism

David Newsome and Kate Rodger

Introduction

Wildlife human interactions play a significant and growing role in the tourism industry. In its broadest terms, wildlife tourism can incorporate both fauna and flora. Yet, in most cases wildlife tourism refers to the watching and interacting with animals and can include both free-ranging and captive wildlife (Newsome *et al.* 2005; UNEP/CMS 2006). However, for this chapter the focus will be on wildlife tourism where humans watch, and in some circumstances interact, with wildlife in their natural environment. This is similar to the US Fish & Wildlife Service, who include observing, photographing and feeding of wildlife in their definition of wildlife tourism (US Fish and Wildlife Service 2006).

The desire for people to interact with wildlife in the natural environment continues to grow in popularity. As a result, visitation to sites with wildlife is on the increase (Tisdell and Wilson 2004; Newsome *et al.* 2005; Rodger *et al.* 2007). In the United States alone, over 71 million people are reported to have participated in at least one wildlife tourism activity such as observing, photographing or feeding of wildlife. Globally, the market size of wildlife tourism has been estimated at 12 million trips annually with a growth rate of 10 per cent per year. It is estimated that the global wildlife market is now worth approximately £30 billion, with up to 3 million people each year taking a holiday to specifically view wildlife (Mintel 2008).

Correspondingly over the last several years, incremental growth has been seen in the type of wildlife tourism activities, different types of interactions and the number of businesses offering wildlife tourism worldwide (Curtin 2010). Recent research in Scotland found that wildlife tourism annually results in a net economic contribution of £65 million to Scotland's economy and creates the equivalent of 2,760 full-time jobs (Scottish Government 2010). Similarly, as in other forms of nature-based tourism, the growth in wildlife tourism has been accompanied by increasing concerns over negative impacts and its future sustainability (Higham and Luck 2008; Newsome *et al.* 2005; Stamation 2008; Rodger *et al.* 2010a). Due to the multidimensional nature of wildlife tourism, sustainable management can be difficult to achieve (Stamation 2008). The objective of this chapter, therefore, is to provide an overview of wildlife tourism by examining three areas that relate to its increasing popularity: the different types of wildlife tourists and activities, the role of marketing and visitor expectations, and the complexity of understanding negative impacts and the continuing sustainability of the industry.

Overview of wildlife tourism activities

Wildlife tourism is undertaken, delivered and experienced according to a vast range of species, destinations, viewing expectations and site management scenarios. Given the diversity of opportunities and conditions (Table 33.1; Newsome *et al.* 2005), wildlife tourism can be divided into three main experiential categories. First, there are general nature-based tourism tours that include a wildlife experience component. Second, wildlife experience destinations such as breeding colonies and aggregations of wildlife such as coral reefs, and third, specialised wildlife tours that target certain groups such as birds or certain species such as monkeys (e.g. Sulawesi Macaque, Indonesia) and apes (e.g. Mountain Gorilla, Rwanda). It is generally accepted that the core component of wildlife tourism involves observing animals in the wild (Newsome *et al.* 2005). Excluded from the categories described above, therefore, are semi-natural/captive animal encounters and incidental encounters that people may have while engaging in some other form of activity such as cycling or mountain trekking.

General nature-based tourism and ecotours

General nature-based tourism can involve guided, tour operator-led visits to natural areas and/or free independent travellers visiting a site with the intention of viewing wildlife as part of a package of natural experiences. Visitors may visit for just one day, or if camping opportunities and built accommodation are provided, may stay at the location for a number of days. Examples of this include, Santa Rosa National Park, Costa Rica; Kakadu National Park, Australia; and Khao Yai National Park in Thailand. Although wildlife may be important, other values are also sought such as scenery, natural soundscapes, walking in wild places, visiting waterfalls and other water-related features, appreciation of natural vegetation and solitude.

Rainforest tourism, as at sites such as Taman Negara National Park in Malaysia, focuses on a holistic nature tourism experience such as rainforest ecology as shown through forest structure, specific plant groups, plant–insect relationships, use of rainforests by aboriginal communities, bird observation and incidental sightings of mammals and reptiles. Wildlife can be experienced through un-guided and guided excursions along hiking trails, canopy walkways and from observation towers and hides. Taman Negara also offers boat trips, spotlighting excursions and the opportunity to stay overnight in a hide or to engage in a longer trek that involves camping in the forest for several days. Through this range of visitor access opportunities, various wildlife may be observed with mammals and birds being the most sought after sightings.

Ecotours can take many forms depending on how the word ecotour is interpreted by tourism policy makers, tourism providers and private tour guides. The whole concept of ecotourism, and how wildlife tourism fits within it, has been widely debated (Newsome *et al.* 2002, 2005) but most tour operators interpret and promote it to be environmentally/wildlife focused, educative, minimal impact and therefore sustainable. The Rottnest Island Eco-Adventure Tour in Western Australia comprises a boat-based tour that offers a cultural, heritage and wildlife-centred experience. The tour promotes seeing animals in their natural habitat and it is possible to see birds, whales, dolphins and Australian sea lions and to visit a breeding colony of New Zealand fur seals. Although not having a sole wildlife tourism focus, this tour, because of accessibility by boat and readily observable aggregations of species (birds, sea lions and fur seals), always delivers a successful wildlife tourism experience, which is strongly reinforced by a very effective commentary on the ecology and biology of observed species.

Table 33.1 Wildlife sighting opportunities and activities: some examples

Target species (selected examples)	Country location	Viewing conditions
Gorilla	Rwanda	Camping and trekking to locate habituated animals
	Uganda	
Orang utan	Sabah	Boat trip
Proboscis monkeys	Sabah	Boat trip
Polar bears	Canada	From all-terrain vehicle
Tiger	India	From vehicle
Sperm Whales	New Zealand	Helicopter
Minke Whales	Australia	Boat trip and swim with activity
Bottlenose dolphins	Australia	Shore based hand feeding and boat excursions
African savannah species	East and Southern Africa	Accommodation facilities located at artificially created waterholes
		Coach tour
		Private vehicle use
		Tour operator vehicles
		Guided walks and camping
		Hot air balloon trips
Nocturnal species:	Australia	Tour guide led spotlighting
Possums and gliders	Australia	Devil Kitchen (feeding site with observation hide)
Tasmanian devil		
Bird watching	New Zealand	Boat trips
	UK, USA, Europe and Australia	Independent visits to a number of sites
	Canada and Iceland	
	India, Costa Rica and Australia	Birding trails
	UK	Bird watching hot spot sites
	Bulgaria	Water bodies with access trails and hides
		Vulture feeding station
Turtles	Australia	Restricted area/guide led excursions to view egg laying
		Independent viewing of turtles emerging from sea to lay eggs
Chameleons	Madagascar	Guided walks
Whalesharks	Australia	Detection via spotter plane, boat trip and swim with interactions
Coral reef fish	Australia	Shore and boat based access to reef
	Sulawesi	Snorkelling and SCUBA diving
Great white sharks	South Africa	Boat trip, attraction with food and cage diving
Sting rays	Cayman Islands	Boat base access and feeding activity
Glow worms	Australia	Constructed viewing area
	New Zealand	Visit to cave habitats
Fireflies	Malaysia	Nocturnal boat trip

Wildlife experience destinations

Places where wildlife comes to breed (cliffs, islands, lakes, coastlines), congregates for the purposes of migration (monarch butterflies, wildebeest, caribou, frogs and birds), that represent specialised habitats (bat caves, glow worm caves) or simply reflect a rich diversity of species (African savannah in South Africa, Kenya and Tanzania, Kinabatangan Floodplain in Sabah, Pantanal Wetlands in Brazil, Great Barrier Reef, Australia), frequently become the focus of tourism activity and its related development. Such destinations need to be accessible (sometimes the only means of access is via a tour operator) and provide opportunities for the reliable viewing of wildlife. Sightings can be made while walking, from vehicles, from boats and aircraft and various combinations of these situations (Table 33.1). In some cases, wildlife observation can be made while riding other animals, as in the case of elephant rides in order to observe the Great Indian Rhinoceros in Chitwan National Park, Nepal.

Some sites are readily accessible by independent wildlife enthusiasts, as in the case of the RSPB Reserve at Bempton in England where people can arrive by private car and walk in to view various species of seabird (puffins, gannets and guillemots) that congregate on the cliffs to breed. Other situations may require several modes of transport and be highly dependent on tour operators for a successful trip, as in polar bear tourism and visits to off-shore locations such as the Galapagos Islands.

Various levels of development are associated with designated wildlife tourism destinations, ranging from simple (limited access/no hardened sites) to complex (entrance facilities, retail areas, viewing platforms). Facilities designed to facilitate access and wildlife sightings include road access, entrance gates/control points where fees are collected and information is disseminated, visitor centres and associated educational facilities, hardened pathways, observation hides, viewing platforms, feeding stations (vultures, hummingbirds), remote viewing technology (bats roosting in caves, raptor nests), microphones (whales, Tasmanian Devils) and audio playback devices (bird song to attract birds and confirm a sighting).

Higham (1998) documented the evolution of tourism development associated with an Albatross colony in New Zealand, where what at first comprised a specialist bird watching destination with no facilities subsequently evolved into a highly developed attraction with pathways, a visitor centre and an enclosed viewing area. The albatross viewing experience has become a significant tourism attraction with the construction of car parking areas in order to cater for organised tour bus arrivals. A similar evolution of visitor profile and management response to accommodate the increasing demands of tourism has occurred at Phillip Island in Australia. The island now has 3.5 million visitors per annum, with 650,000 people attending the 'Penguin Parade' each year. Over time, increasing demand for the viewing of Fairy Penguins, which emerge from the sea at night to locate their burrows, has resulted in a range of viewing opportunities being developed. There is a visitor centre, ranger-led excursions and talks, and an mp4 audio tour available in many languages. Viewing options include an elevated tier seated viewing stadium; an exclusive viewing platform and boardwalk limited to 170 people a day; the penguin skybox, which is a limited capacity elevated viewing tower supervised by a ranger; a ranger-led Private Penguin Parade Experience; and a ranger-led Ultimate Penguin Tour to a private beach, which is limited to 10 people a day. The idea behind this range of viewing opportunities is to cater for different visitor needs. Some visitors are more tolerant of larger groups and desire easy access, whereas others want more private, small-group experiences. The range of viewing options thus caters for organised coach tours and large groups through to small groups and individuals.

The African 'safari' is a long-standing wildlife tourism destination, but also the subject of specialised wildlife tours (see below). The Kruger National Park in South Africa, where up to

100 species of birds and more than 40 species of mammal can be seen in a four-to-seven day trip, can be visited by free independent travellers and tour groups alike. Visitors can utilise a number of wildlife viewing opportunities (Table 33.2), which they conduct on their own or alternatively under the guidance of park staff. The African wildlife experience has also lent itself to research/conservation-related tourism, where at some locations, such as Phinda in South Africa, visitors can arrange special tours with research staff who are capturing, tagging and measuring the health parameters of wildlife. Specialised wildlife tours, however, usually focus on seeing rare, charismatic and difficult to observe species under natural conditions.

Specialised wildlife tours

Despite the overlap with various wildlife experience destinations, as described above, wildlife tourism included in this category often involves focusing on a single species (e.g. tiger, gorilla) or groups of related species (e.g. whales, albatross). Viewing of such species can occur in settings developed for tourism (fireflies in Malaysia) or in larger protected areas such as national parks (e.g. Komodo Dragons in Indonesia; polar bears in Canada). The degree of attention paid to guarantee a sighting, ranges from no manipulation of conditions (penguin colonies in the sub-Antarctic) through to habituation of species to foster close contact (mountain gorillas in Rwanda and Uganda), food provisioning (vultures in Cambodia, dolphins at Shark Bay, Western Australia) and habitat modification (planting of shrubs and trees to attract birds, use of nest boxes).

Visitor activities, most of which will be under the guidance of a tour operator, park ranger, volunteer or docent, include searching for wildlife on foot, in vehicles and boats, observing species from hides, night spotting, use of binoculars and telescopes, hand feeding (Figure 33.1) and 'swim with' activities. Major swim with wildlife tourism operations in Australia involve manta rays, whalesharks, minke whales, dolphins, seals and sea lions. Such wildlife experiences are ostensibly confined to small groups, as in the case of many swim with operations (group size is limited to around 20 onboard boats), specialised bird watching tours or gorilla tourism (less than 10). Small-group wildlife observation activities allow a more 'personal and private' wildlife viewing experience, something that managers at Phillip Island (Australia) have tried to achieve

Table 33.2 Wildlife viewing opportunities in the Kruger National Park, South Africa

Rest camps	*Boundary fence line viewing of mammals foraging outside the rest camp and bird watching within campgrounds*
Self-drive during daylight hours	Majority of visitors arrive by private car and undertake wildlife viewing drives
Self-drive during daylight hours with opportunities to leave the vehicle while out on a drive	Wildlife viewing drive plus areas where the vehicle can be left in order to access a view point or fenced hide at a waterhole
Tour operator-led drive during daylight hours	Private tour operator vehicles and coach tours
Park management led nocturnal wildlife viewing drive	Ranger-led night drive. Tourists are allowed to use spotlights. Educational
Ranger-led guided walks for small groups	Supervised walk during the late afternoon with interpretation of animal tracks, spoor and signs during the late afternoon
Opportunities for longer ranger led walking excursions and overnight camping	Supervised walk and camping with interpretation of animal tracks, spoor and signs

Figure 33.1 Feeding parrots by hand
O'Reillys, Queensland Australia. This tourism facility is primarily a bird watching tourism provider comprising accommodation set in a natural sub-tropical rainforest setting (Lamington National Park). Wildlife tourism comprises guided and un-guided bird watching along a network of trails, a canopy walkway, observation tower and supervised bird feeding area. There is a second bird feeding activity where various species are fed as part of a guided bird walk. (Photo by D. Newsome)

given the demand for, and crowding, at the Penguin Parade (see above). However, maintenance of small-group viewing may be difficult to achieve in a number of cases due to separate smaller groups coming together to obtain a guaranteed sighting or where economic pressures may result in a 'creeping up' of loosely controlled group size limits.

The focus on particular species (large, spectacular, enigmatic, rare and dangerous species) that can provide rewarding experiences and significant must see and photograph values has grown in popularity in recent years. The public desire for such experiences has given rise to a wildlife tourist who can gain benefit and excitement form close contact and photographic opportunities with large species, as in the case of whaleshark swims (Mau 2008) and/or close observation of potentially dangerous carnivorous species such as polar bears and sharks (Lemelin 2006; Dobson 2008).

Lemelin (2006) explores the idea that photographs represent collectables and provide evidence of tourist accomplishments, with the risk of people becoming addicted to gaining photographic trophies of species, especially when the animal is potentially dangerous and enigmatic. Polar bears represent one such example; at Churchill, Manitoba in Canada, tourism has grown significantly over the last 20 years. Lemelin, (2006) cautions that wildlife tourism may degrade into a form of visual entertainment in the context of 'must see' and 'must photograph' and that it can become a 'quest for collectables in controlled, or worse, fabricated areas'. There is also the notion of experiencing a dangerous animal and the intensity of such an experience can be magnified by close contact. The relatively recent rise of great white shark tourism in Australia and South Africa and shark feeding operations that occur at various locations around the world signify this trend (Dobson 2008; Vignon *et al.* 2010). Both cases of shark tourism represent a form of manipulation of shark behaviour via food provisioning and represent the 'controlled/fabricated aspects of wildlife tourism', as raised by Lemelin (2006).

Understanding the wildlife tourist in terms of expectation, attitudes and the role of marketing

To better promote and manage wildlife tourism there is need to understand the visitor experience. This is because the encounter between the tourist and the wildlife is the core of the wildlife tourism activity (STCRC 2009). Visitor expectations, their behaviour and compliance with guidelines and regulations, along with satisfaction with their wildlife tourism experience, are linked together. Wildlife tourists can vary from the specialist through to the more generalist who is often influenced by promotion and marketing of wildlife tourism interactions and activities (Curtin 2010).

The expectation of tourists is in part determined by marketing and media representation of the wildlife tourism activity. Pictures of wildlife with and without people are frequently found in the travel media and environmental management agencies brochures. These virtual representations of wildlife–human interactions can influence pre-trip decision-making and expectations, environmental concern and awareness, and the actual experience and behaviour during the wildlife tourism activity (Bentrupperbaumer 2005). In some circumstances it is quite difficult for the actual wildlife tourism activity or interaction to meet visitor expectations developed from the marketing media. For example, many rainforest species are shy, cryptic, nocturnal and difficult to see in rainforest settings, and thus observations may be limited. Despite this, the principal marketing focus of many rainforest destinations is often on wildlife that is difficult to see, or rarely seen species. Setting up visitor expectations of successful wildlife observation in rainforests is, therefore, problematical in terms of ensuring visitor satisfaction. Another example is the dolphin feeding interactions at Monkey Mia in Western Australia. The majority of marketing material for this experience show people standing in the water feeding fish to dolphins resulting in an up close and personal encounter. However, in reality, at the appointed feeding times over 100 people can gather on the beach to be chosen to feed the dolphins, but only about six are given the opportunity (Figure 33.2). This can result in low visitor satisfaction for those who are not selected, as the wildlife interaction did not meet their expectation.

Media and media personalities can further influence public understanding of wildlife and wildlife tourism. The introduction of the 'Life on Earth' series on wildlife by David Attenborough in the late 1970s highlighted the influence the media can have on society's values. Coverage of wildlife in the media was seen to contribute to the shift in public values of wildlife from a utilitarian to a protectionist orientation (Champ 2002). In the 1990s Steve Irwin, known as the Crocodile Hunter, bought a different perspective to human–wildlife interactions into the public domain. Steve Irwin, described as a conservationist, was passionate about wildlife and took a very much hands on role invoking increased awareness on wildlife issues from the public. His up-close and hands-on interactions with wildlife also impacted on the way society viewed human wildlife interactions, with the possibility that an increasing number of tourists wanted to experience similar close interactions with wildlife. Such impressions may also give

Figure 33.2 Feeding dolphins by hand

false impressions as to how to behave when in contact with wildlife with visitors thinking that it is acceptable to touch, capture and hold animals. Such a desire for close contact and reliable sightings may also be magnified by the extreme close up filming now evident in most natural history documentaries. Such extensive media coverage of wildlife as presented in magazines, documentaries and BBC television series such as 'Trials of Life', 'Living Planet' and 'Life' may give the impression that wildlife is easy to see and photograph when in reality a 1–2 minute film segment may have taken weeks or even months to film.

Given the diversity of activities and interactions, the visitor expectation and experience can vary between sites and species. As Duffus and Dearden (1990) noted 'tourists cannot be considered a homogeneous population and this includes tourists that may primarily be motivated by the same stimulus, such as wildlife viewing' (Duffus and Dearden 1990: 222). Managers cannot assume that there is a one-dimensional profile for wildlife tourists (Lemelin and Smale 2006). However, according to Newsome *et al.* (2005), tourists can be segmented according to the sought after focal species and tourists' motivations. As in the case of general nature-based tourism, there are often common expectations and objectives of wildlife experience destinations and wildlife tours depending on the situation of the visit: (1) to gain a sighting; (2) to photograph the animal; (3) to obtain close contact; (4) to feed an animal; and (5) to attract and touch the animal. If these expectations are met, then visitor satisfaction is normally high.

Moscardo and Salzter (2005) found seeing wildlife in its natural environment, along with seeing wildlife behaving naturally and seeing rare, unique or unusual wildlife were three important features sought in a wildlife tourism experience. Valentine *et al.* (2004) found that swimming with minke whales and getting close to the whales was a significant factor in visitor satisfaction. Yet, recent research has shown that there is another aspect to wildlife tourism playing an important role in visitor satisfaction – interpretation. Interpretation has been found to contribute to visitor expectations being met and increased visitor satisfaction. Moscardo and Saltzer (2005) found a substantial correlation between the amount visitors thought they learnt about the wildlife during their experience and their overall satisfaction with the wildlife interaction. Therefore, more information and education could be developed for wildlife tourism activities and it would be likely to add value to visitor experience.

However, it must be said that there are still some wildlife tourism activities where this is not always the case. Wildlife visitors can have their expectations met resulting in high visitor satisfaction with little to no interpretation. This can be seen with a highly specialised form of wildlife tourism involving the viewing of and cage diving with great white sharks in South Africa. This type of tourism fits the criteria of large, charismatic, rare and dangerous wildlife. At Gaansbai in South Africa various tour operators offer cage diving excursions. A number of the tours are described as highly educational. The experience comprises travelling out to sea where tuna heads tied to a floating rope are thrown into the water to attract sharks. When sharks appear and initial photographs have been taken, groups of up to five clients enter the diving cage. The line is drawn close to the cage to maximise underwater photographic opportunities of sharks swimming in to feed on the floating meat (Figure 33.3). There may be five boats in the interaction area all at the same time and spaced only 100 m–200 m apart. There are concerns about the disruption of natural shark behaviour, habituation of sharks to humans, use of such species for this type of tourism activity and that the operation may be classed as wildlife tourism but exhibits more the characteristics of adventure tourism. Observers have also noted that the quality of interpretation onboard the boats is very poor and is counter to the defined characteristics of good wildlife tourism as described earlier (Dobson 2008).

Figure 33.3 Feeding dolphins from a boat
Cage diving tour Gaansbai, South Africa. The photograph illustrates a Great White Shark pursuing a baited rope. The rope is being pulled close to the cage so that clients can maximise photographic opportunities (Photo by D. Newsome)

The complexity of understanding negative impacts and the sustainability of wildlife tourism

In terms of understanding the impacts of wildlife tourism, Newsome *et al.* (2005) suggested a wildlife tourism paradigm in which visitor impacts could be examined in terms of accessing and locating wildlife, the activity of observing and photographing wildlife, feeding wildlife, touching and close interaction. Furthermore, the way wildlife responds to the presence of humans in the environment will vary greatly according to the specific responses (avoidance, habituation, attraction) of a particular species, the specifics of the situation, the mode of transport used to access wildlife, visitor expectations and information delivered during the sighting/interaction and the level of management employed designed to maximise a sighting, controls on human behaviour during a sighting/interaction and the management techniques employed to reduce disruption of a particular species' normal activities of daily living (Reynolds and Braithwaite 2001; Higginbottom 2004; Newsome *et al.* 2005; Higham and Luck 2008).

Exploring the impacts of tourism on wildlife according to an analysis of the disruption to the daily activities of an animal's life, provides a useful insight into how a particular species or groups of species could be impacted as a result of tourism (Table 33.3). It is also important to note that the degree of impact is likely to vary according to the number and frequency of visitors, behaviour of tourists, existing management, quality of tour guiding in terms of suitable information delivered, mode of access, seasonality and whether the wildlife is used to seeing people regularly or not. Gaining an understanding of tourism-related impacts on wildlife is compounded by external factors such as natural variability and non-tourism-related impacts. This is complicated further by the observation that some species may respond differently to a tourism situation when in different locations. This, and often unknown external factors, make it difficult to demonstrate tourism impact in any given situation.

In relation to managing the wildlife tourism visitor, there are direct and indirect approaches that are widely utilised within ecotourism in general. Newsome *et al.* (2002) describe a range of actions that are intended to restrict access, contain people and activities, allow controlled access and educate the public in terms of reducing their impact on the environment. Management actions specific to wildlife tourism situations are described by Newsome *et al.* (2005), and include the management of viewing through licensing tourism, codes of conduct, physical separation, viewing platforms and hides, setback distances, minimum approach distances, supervision of feeding, education and interpretation.

Sustainable wildlife tourism is therefore dependent on an understanding of the tourism situation in terms of visitor needs and aspirations for a sighting, an understanding of potential negative impacts and the quality and effectiveness of management.

An approach to overcome and deconstruct this complexity is to identify and simplify all of the factors potentially influencing the sustainability of a wildlife tourism operation. Rodger *et al.* (2010b) recently attempted to do this by the application of a wildlife sustainability framework to what has been considered best practice whaleshark tourism in Western Australia. The framework comprises a checklist approach to identifying sustainability issues and gaps in knowledge and understanding and uses ecological and environmental criteria and operational and social criteria (Table 33.4).

The ecological and operational part of the framework includes criteria relating to marine wildlife population and habitats where interactions with tourists take place. The operational criteria examined factors such as the types of interactions, general accessibility to the wildlife, rates of compliance by visitors and operators, along with any regulations and guidelines that are in place. The social assessment framework included visitor demographics and additional

Table 33.3 Potential negative impacts of tourism on the daily activities of wildlife

Normal Activity	Aspects of tourism impact	Wildlife groups potentially affected
Navigation and orientation	Migrating species may be target of tourism interest. Disturbance at resting and refuge sites	Birds Bats Cetaceans
Communication to attract mates, deter predators, show fear, keep in contact with others	Sight of humans Noise Smell of humans	Birds Whales Wildlife with a high dependence on olfaction for communication
Finding food	Disrupted feeding patterns/ hunting behaviours. Negative impacts on activity budget Food provisioning	Wide range of species especially birds and mammals Primates and bears at high risk of exhibiting attraction behaviours. Potential risk of tourists being bitten
Escaping from danger	Initiation of frequent flight responses resulting in stress and disruption to other normal activities	Wide range of species (some species more sensitive than others)
Social behaviour in relation to colonial breeding, concentrations of wildlife and interaction within family groups	Disturbance can cause increased intra-specific competition and aggression between species resulting in juvenile mortality in some species	Birds Primates
Courtship and mating	Disrupted courtship displays and egg laying	Birds Amphibians Insects
Breeding and rearing young	Disturbance that increases predation and mortality of young	Turtles Birds
Hibernation and aestivation	Disturbance (eg. bat caves) resulting in additional and expensive energy expenditure	Bats and some other mammals Amphibians and fish that are dug out of dry water bodies are at risk
Moulting behaviour	Birds need safe refuges to undergo plumage moults. Moulting reduces normal activities and increases susceptibility to impact	Birds

Source: Adapted from Newsome *et al.* (2005)

information on visitor experiences. Additional items covered availability of interpretation and the level of guide training (Rodger *et al.* 2010b).

To test the effectiveness of the framework Rodger *et al.* (2010b) applied the framework to the whaleshark tourism industry in Coral Bay, Western Australia. In recent years, whaleshark tourism in Ningaloo Marine Park has been showcased as a highly managed industry (Mau 2008; Moore and Rodger 2010). The application of the framework provided a useful summary of the whalesharks' status and known potentially negative impacts. In addition, the assessment also highlighted that information was lacking in population status and numbers of animals, along with their possible behavioural responses to tourists. For operational and social aspects, areas where the assessment framework highlighted that little knowledge is currently available

Table 33.4 Ecological, environmental, operational assessment framework

Ecological and environmental assessment criteria

1.	Species
2.	Threatened status
3.	Group dynamics
4.	Age of species
5.	Known behaviour
6.	Population
7.	Knowledge of species reproduction
8.	Knowledge of number of animals
9.	Knowledge of feeding behaviour
10.	Habitat where tourism takes place
11.	Have any potentially negative impacts from tourism been identified?
12.	Known behavioural response to tourism activity
13.	Are there other anthropogenic activities other than the tourism activity placing pressure on species? (*for example pollutants in water, sewerage, dredging...*)
14.	Is there consistent long-term research and/or monitoring taking place?

included: (1) total number of interactions; (2) the number of private recreationists interacting with whalesharks; (3) rates of compliance for tourists and operators; and (4) the types and focus of interpretation (for more detail see Rodger *et al*. 2010b, 2011).

The development of such a framework proves to be a useful tool for identifying and collating existing information on the wildlife of interest, and identifying knowledge gaps and areas of concern. The framework would be useful to wildlife managers and the wildlife tourism industry alike to: (1) assess proposed ventures, particularly to identify further information needed before a decision to proceed or otherwise is made; and (2) to gain preliminary understanding on how sustainable the venture might be. As a work in progress this framework offers great potential in helping advance the sustainable management of wildlife tourism. (Rodger *et al.* submitted 2011).

Conclusion

Human–wildlife interactions continue to increase worldwide and an understanding of these interactions is needed for sustainable management. Wildlife tourism is undertaken, delivered and experienced according to a vast range of species, destinations, viewing expectations and site management scenarios. This chapter examines three important dimensions that relate to its increasing popularity including the different types of wildlife tourists and activities, the role of marketing and visitor expectations, and the complexity of understanding negative impacts and the continuing sustainability of the industry.

Wildlife tourism offers a diverse range of opportunities and takes place under a variety of conditions. However, the encounter between the tourist and the wildlife is the core of the wildlife tourism activity. For this chapter, wildlife tourism was divided into three main experiential categories: nature-based tourism tours that include a wildlife experience component; wildlife experience destinations such as breeding colonies and aggregations of wildlife; and specialised wildlife tours that target certain groups such as birds or certain rare and enigmatic species.

Marketing and media representation of wildlife tourism activity play an important role in visitor expectations. To better promote and manage wildlife tourism there is need to understand the visitor experience as visitor expectations, visitor behaviour during a sighting and compliance along with overall satisfaction with the wildlife tourism experience. This is because a sustainable wildlife tourism industry is dependent on understanding the tourism situation in terms of visitor needs and aspirations for a sighting/interaction, an understanding of potential negative impacts and the quality and effectiveness of management. To detect effective management strategies, both ecological impacts and human dimensions including visitor attitudes and expectations need to be recognised.

References

Bentrupperbaumer, J. (2005) 'Human dimension of wildlife interactions', in Newsome, D., Dowling, R. and Moore, S.A. *Wildlife Tourism*. Clevedon: Channel View Publications.

Champ, J.G. (2002) 'A culturalist-qualitative investigation of wildlife media and value orientations', *Human Dimensions of Wildlife* 7, 273–86.

Curtin, S. (2010) 'Managing the wildlife tourism experience: the importance of tour leaders', *International Journal of Tourism Research* 12, 219–36.

Dobson, J. (2008) 'Shark! A new frontier in tourist demand for marine wildlife', in J. Higham and M. Lück *Marine Wildlife and Tourism Management*, Oxford: CABI.

Duffus, D.A. and Dearden, P. (1990) 'Non-consumptive wildlife orientated recreation: A conceptual framework', *Biological Conservation* 53(3), 213–31.

Higginbottom, K. (ed.) (2004) *Wildlife Tourism: Impacts, Management and Planning*. Altona, Victoria: Common Ground.

Higham, J.E.S. (1998) 'Tourists and albatrosses: the dynamics of tourism at the Northern Royal Albatross Colony, Taiaroa Head, New Zealand', *Tourism Management* 19(6), 521–31.

Higham, J. and Lück, M. (eds) (2008) *Marine Wildlife and Tourism Management*. Oxford: CABI.

Lemelin R.H. (2006) 'The gawk, the glance, and the gaze: ocular consumption and polar bear tourism in Churchill, Manitoba Canada', *Current Issues in Tourism* 9(6), 516–34.

Lemelin, R.H. and Smale, B. (2006) Effect of environmental context on the experience of polar bear viewers in Churchill, Manitoba' *Journal of Ecotourism* 5(3), 176–91.

Mau, R. (2008) 'Managing for conservation and recreation: The Ningaloo whale shark experience', *Journal of Ecotourism* 7 (2–3), 213–25.

Mintel (2008) *Wildlife Tourism International*. UK: Mintel International Group Ltd.

Moore, S.A. and Rodger, K. (2010) 'Wildlife Tourism as a common pool resource issue: enabling conditions for sustainability governance', *Journal of Sustainable Tourism* 18 (7), 831–44.

Moscardo, G. and Saltzer, R. (2004) *Understanding tourism wildlife interactions: Visitor market analysis*, Sustainable Tourism Cooperative Research Centre (STCRC), Gold Coast, Queensland, Australia.

Newsome, D., Dowling, R. and Moore, S.A. (2005) *Wildlife Tourism*. Clevedon: Channel View Publications.

Newsome, D., Moore, S. and Dowling, R. (2002) *Natural Area Tourism: Ecology, Impacts and Management*. Clevedon: Channel View Publications.

Reynolds, P.C. and Braithwaite, D. (2001) 'Towards a conceptual framework for wildlife tourism', *Tourism Management* 22, 31–42.

Rodger, K., Moore, S.A. and Newsome, D. (2007) 'Wildlife tourism in Australia: characteristics, the place of science and sustainable futures', *Journal of Sustainable Tourism* 15(2), 160–79.

Rodger, K., Moore, S.A. and Newsome, D. (2010a) 'Wildlife tourism science and scientists: barriers and opportunities', *Society and Natural Resources* 23, 1–16.

Rodger, K., Smith, A., Davis, C., Newsome, D. and Patterson, P. (2010b) *A framework to guide the sustainability of wildlife tourism operations: examples of marine wildlife tourism in Western Australia. Technical Report*. Cooperative Research Centre for Sustainable Tourism. The Gold Coast, Queensland, Australia.

Rodger, K., Smith, A., Newsome, D. and Moore, S.A. (submitted 2011) 'Developing and testing a rapid assessment framework to guide the sustainability of the marine wildlife tourism industry', *Journal of Ecotourism*.

Scottish Government Social Research (2010) *The Economic Impact of Wildlife Tourism In Scotland*. Available: www.scotland.gov.uk/socialresearch. Accessed 1 September 2010.

Stamation, K. (2008) 'Understanding human-whale interactions: a multidisciplinary approach', in Lunney, D., Munn, A. and Meikle, W. (eds) *Too close for comfort: contentious issues in human-wildlife encounters*. Mosman, NSW, Australia: Royal Zoological Society of New South Wales.

STCRC (2009) *Wildlife tourism: challenges, opportunities and managing the future*. The Gold Coast, Queensland: Cooperative Research Centre for Sustainable Tourism.

Tisdell, C. and Wilson, C. (2004) *Economics, wildlife tourism and conservation: three case studies*. The Gold Coast, Queensland: Cooperative Research Centre for Sustainable Tourism.

UNEP/CMS (2006) *Wildlife Watching and Tourism: A study on the benefits and risks of a fast growing tourism activity and its impact on species*. Bonn: Produced by UNEP/CMS Convention of Migratory Species and TUI. Available: www.cms.int/publications/pdf/cms_wildlifewatchingpdf. Accessed 1 September 2010.

US Fish and Wildlife Service (2006) *National Survey of Fishing, Hunting and Wildlife Associated Recreation*. Available: www.fws.gov/digitalmedia/cdm4/item_viewer.php?CISOROOT=/natdiglib&cisoptr=6535 &cisobox=1&rec=1. Accessed 1 September 2010.

Valentine, P.S., Birtles, A., Curnock, M., Arnold, P. and Dunstan, A. (2004) 'Getting closer to whales – passenger expectations and experiences, and the management of swim with dwarf minke whale interactions in the Great Barrier Reef', *Tourism Management* 25, 647–55.

Vignon, M., Sasal, P., Johnson, R.L. and Galzin, R. (2010) 'Impact of shark-feeding tourism on surrounding fish populations off Moorea Island (French Polynesia)', *Marine and Freshwater Research* 61, 163–9.

34

Agri-tourism

In between rural change, tourism restructuring and environmental imperatives

Theodosia Anthopoulou and Yorgos Melissourgos

Introduction

The term *agri-tourism* clearly denotes a relationship between tourism and agriculture. Of course, such a relationship is not something new, nor something inherently specific in this special form of tourism, not least because of agriculture having always been an important backward linkage for tourism services. Our current knowledge of agri-food chains and of the primary sector's supply side of tourism point to the importance of the multifacet connections between tourism and agriculture in terms of the ways food and drink are being delivered to tourists.

But what is essentially different here is a special relationship that distinguishes agri-tourism from other forms of soft tourism and practices of consumption. Undeniably, agri-tourism is nowadays considered to be an important type of tourism in both Western and less economically developed countries, providing new opportunities for rural regeneration. As a response to multiple assessments of the negative ecological, social and economic impacts that the productivist model had on rural areas, agri-tourism development increasingly attracted the interest of both academics and policy makers in the 1990s within debates on sustainable rural development and farm diversification. Emphasis has been placed on natural and cultural resource conservation as well as on social coherence.

It is the aim of this chapter to situate agri-tourism within a bilateral framework of understanding: processes of rural change *and* the restructuring of tourism. The former is best depicted within the concept of the multifunctional countryside; whereas the latter is about dealing with alternative forms vis-à-vis mass tourism. Overlapping this there is a major discussion concerning environmental preservation and sustainable rural development.

Defining agri-tourism

A variety of terms such as farm tourism, farm-based tourism, green tourism and rural tourism are often employed interchangeably to define agro-/agri-tourism (Phillip *et al.* 2010; Roberts and Hall 2001; Bazin and Roux 1997; Sharpley and Sharpley 1997). Actually these labels describe tourism activity in rural areas under the broader term of 'rural tourism' as an alternative form to 'traditional' mass tourism. Definitional clarification is nonetheless necessary, in order to place agri-tourism in its real dimensions. Key issues on definition approaches have been: the description of agri-tourism as a 'product' (types of accommodation, activities, produces, experiences); the scale and structure of the enterprise (localised small-scale activity, family-co-operative or community structure); the stakeholders involved (actors in local/rural communities, the state); and the impact on rural communities (territorial synergies, locally added values, supplementary incomes to rural holdings).

As Sharpley and Sharpley (1997: 9) mention, agri-tourism, more frequently, comprises tourism products that are 'directly connected with the agrarian environment, agrarian products or agrarian stays: staying on a farm, whether in rooms or camping, educational visits, meals, recreational activities, and the sale of farm produce or handicrafts'. Furthermore, they argue (ibid.) that agri-tourism is a broader concept than farm/farm-based tourism, as it also includes festivals, museums, craft shows and other cultural events and attractions. For many scholars, agri-tourism refers to tourism conducted on 'working farms', where working environment and potential participation in the activities of local people shape the picture from the perspective of the consumer. In other words, agri-tourism is directly linked to agriculture and its natural and human milieu.

Given the usual confusion that prevails in the literature on agri-tourism and related terms, Phillip *et al.* (2010) propose a framework of agri-tourism types built on three key areas of debate: whether or not the product is based on a 'working farm'; the nature of contact between the tourist and agricultural activity; and the degree of authenticity in the tourism experience. The authors propose the following taxonomy: (1) non-working farm agri-tourism; (2) working farm, passive contact agri-tourism; (3) working farm, indirect contact agri-tourism; (4) working farm, direct contact, staged agri-tourism; (5) working farm, direct contact, authentic agri-tourism (Phillip *et al.* 2010: 3). This typology provides a comprehensive framework that embraces the broad range of products and activities identified as agri-tourism. It thus permits bridging of the gap both between theory and practice and between highly differentiated practices (see Case study 1).

Case study 1

Farm tourism experiences in EU countries

Accurate statistics on agri-tourism, including numbers of agri-tourist units and of visitors to farms, are difficult to find. The same applies for the overall magnitude of the industry in different world rural areas. It is, however, expected that farm income deriving from tourism is much higher than agricultural income. But it is agriculture that makes up the scenery of nature, environment, landscape and heritage, which together constitute the core elements in the social construction of the rural idyll, and are therefore necessary in attracting tourists. A kind of territorial synergy between agriculture, tourism and environment preservation is thus established (see Case study 2). A look at web-publicity material of farm tourism associations in different European countries testifies the repackaging, by both textual and visual means, of the countryside and working farms so as to emphasise characteristics associated with popular images of farming and living close to the nature. Working farms possess a wide range of facilities, including accommodation, gastronomy, leisure and discovery activities, which appeal to different target groups.

France: Bienvenue à la ferme (www.bienvenue-a-la-ferme.com)

'Get to know *bienvenue à la ferme*: *Bienvenue à la ferme* brings you closer to country life. Set out to discover a different experience of country living: come and meet the 5,200 farmers'. One may specifically focus on accommodation: 'Choosing farm accommodation is to be certain to enjoy a natural and peaceful setting with your family or friends, far from the hustle and bustle of the city. According to your financial means and personal tastes, you may pitch your tent in the farm campsite, stay in a bed and breakfast for a single night or a whole week, or spend your holidays in a self-catering cottage'.

And as far as gastronomy is concerned: 'Whether you feel like a snack or a real meal at a *table d'hôte*, enjoy discovering the genuine tastes of local farm products (salted meats and charcuterie – assorted cooked pork meats –, fruit and vegetables, wines). The diversity of our regional food specialties will quite simply amaze you'.

Austria: Holidays on the Farm (www.urlaubambauernhof.at/)

The Holidays on the Farm network lists some 3,400 farms across Austria, including Holidays on an Organic Farm, on a Health & Wellness Farm, on a Baby- & Child-Friendly Farm, at the Winery, on the Cyclist-Friendly Farm, Farm Holidays with Riding Opportunities and Barrier-Free Vacations.

One may note, for example, about Holidays on a Baby- & Child Friendly Farm: 'Big Holidays for a Small Price … Life on the farm has a magical attraction for children: animals big and small, the farmers' tractors, working on the land and virtually boundless freedom are in synch with the kids' own personal needs. They are able to play here from early in the morning until evening sets in. They can feed and pet the animals. Their feet get dirty and their heads are full of silliness. It would appear that, here on the farm, their imaginations tend to walk around in wellingtons.'

United Kingdom: Farm Stay UK (www.farmstayuk.co.uk)

Farm Stay UK lists over 1,100 farms all across the UK. 'Why Choose Farm Stay. … The properties represent a unique choice of stylish country dwellings ranging from handsome farmhouses built centuries ago to picturesque holiday cottages with chickens in the orchard and roses round the door. Whatever you choose, comfort is guaranteed, as is a warm, truly genuine welcome … Stay on a working farm for a firsthand view of the farmers' world. Look out of your window over fields and orchards of ripening hops and fruit, visit the milking parlour or the newborn lambs and watch the plough etching its fresh furrows across the fields.'

This kind of typology could be helpful in countries where agri-tourism has relatively recently started to develop (such as in the Mediterranean Basin and Eastern Europe), and has been strongly supported by developmental policies for socio-economic and cultural regeneration in rural areas. Policy makers and territorial agencies have to carefully consider and design the content of agri-tourism products in order to satisfy tourists' expectations (i.e. to live in an authentic farming context) and to respond to sustainable development goals (in terms of local embedding and direct support of rural societies). Otherwise, a distorted agri-tourism development may undermine the very objectives of sustainability. In fact, previous case studies in Southern Europe (Bazin and Roux 1997; Anthopoulou 2000) have drawn attention to the fact that untargeted expansion of various and contestable forms of agri-tourism (such as simple accommodation in furnished studios in the countryside, as in the Greek case) and the absence of coherent agri-tourism planning at national or regional level could have negative socio-economic and environmental impacts. Spontaneous proliferation of agri-tourism may bring further tourism growth and spatial polarisation in already developed areas (e.g. coastal and mountainous destinations), while at the same time undermining the very maintenance of the farm holding. This means that challenges posed by rural restructuring, as well as potential threats to rural environment, require an understanding of agri-tourism in accordance with major principles of sustainable rural development.

Agri-tourism and rural change: towards sustainable rural development

It has been widely acknowledged that the significance of agriculture to rural development has decreased in recent years within the general context of farm crisis (questioning of the productivist regime), environmental and global climate change, and globalisation impacting on rural areas and family farms (market crisis). By the end of the Second World War, the dominant productivist model in agriculture had been characterised by intensification (including increasing use of agri-chemicals and machinery), land concentration and farm specialisation. Productivism, apart from fulfilling the basic objective of enhancing agricultural production, has had profound negative effects on rural societies, economies and environments: overproduction, socio-spatial disparities at the expense of smaller farmers and disadvantaged areas, and environmental degradation. These outcomes pushed, in the early 1990s, to a policy shift towards agri-environmental concerns, extensification and farm diversification. In this context, agriculture remains the principal land use and territorial marker, but loses its dominant position in relation to rural economy and local society and politics (Cloke 2006; Woods 2005). Farmers are increasingly in search of supplementary economic resources beyond the agricultural sector, given that primary production alone can no longer sustain rural households. These questions are more pressing in less favoured rural areas, where de-population and abandonment of farm activities would have irreversible negative effects on cultural heritage, as well as the physical environment (e.g. erosion, forest fires, etc.). The maintenance of local agri-productive systems is hence important in order to preserve socio-economic tissue in less favoured areas. Farmers are seen as 'gardeners of the nature' and are thus encouraged to enlarge the range of their activities.

In the late 1990s, rural development policies – as well as academic research – began to take into consideration the multifunctional character of agriculture and rural space, particularly the positive environmental services of agriculture. Policies were hence based on agriculture, which, except for its traditional productive function, was highly valued for its environmental and patrimonial services (non-commodity outputs) via the concepts of externalities and public property. Multifunctionality may be promoted though territorially connected activities, such as local traditional food produces and rural/agri-tourism. The inclusion of the 'multifunctionality of agriculture' in public policies (for example as in the EU's CAP, in 1999) provided public support for farming with a new legitimacy, given the social questioning of the agricultural sector that was due to productivism's negative environmental impacts (Mollard 2002; Aumand et al. 2006).

Economic diversification, commodification of the countryside and environmental protection initiatives within the rural multifunctionality concept are some of the responses to rural change processes (Woods 2005). Diverse forms of rural tourism have been promoted as important components of rural diversification. Agri-tourism, in particular, has been supported by rural development funds (e.g. the EU LEADER Program), as it has strong linkages to specific territorial resources such as natural and agricultural landscapes, traditional food products and gastronomies or cultural heritage. It may involve an alternative approach to agriculture and to rural development no longer through agricultural modernisation but rather via an emerging model of 'service-based agriculture' (Capt 1997; Perrin 2009).

On the other hand, agri-tourism responds to the increasing tourism and recreational demand towards place-based activities engaged with rural landscapes, environment, culture and lifestyles (see below). It is intuitively perceived as a safe way to 'create added values' in rural landscapes, environments and local produces. Agri-tourism, as a place-based tourism, is generally conceived as a suitable means to rural sustainability objectives as it has strong linkages to specific territorial resources and is able to mobilise social capital, local networks and traditional know-how; as a result, agri-tourism is able to drag on growth of other locally based economic sectors (small-scale food processing, direct sales by farmers and local producers, traditional handicrafts, thematic routes and museums). Given that notions of sustainable rural development embrace an integrated approach of socio-cultural, economic and environmental issues of rurality, policy makers, planners and local authorities have to take into consideration this holistic approach in every stage of design and implementation of agri-tourism projects. This is very crucial, due to an 'implementation gap' between the policy ideal and its application that is identified in rural areas. This reflects the fact that policy makers may regard rural (and agri-) tourism development in isolation from the other components, which together constitute the social, economic and ecological context for sustainable rural development processes (Roberts and Hall 2001: 55).

None the less, there are close connections between objectives of rural sustainability and agri-tourism as a soft/alternative form of tourism in rural areas. According to relevant literature (Lane 1994; Roberts and Hall 2001; Slee *et al.* 1997; Sharpley and Sharpley 1997; see also chapter on sustainable tourism), the development of agri-tourism with regard to rural sustainability faces a number of key challenges in three inter-connected fields. First, in the socio-economic field: to provide a source of supplementary income and employment for local people; to encourage retainment of population in remote rural areas or enable areas to be repopulated; to encourage collective community activity; to support social inclusion and reduce gender and other social power imbalances; and to create territorial synergies and added values, while providing opportunities for local initiative and control. Second, in the cultural field, agri-tourism is said to: respect local cultural traditions; maintain traditional agricultural practices, food processing and artisanal know-how; and enhance the sense of local pride, self-esteem and territorial identity. Third, in the physical (i.e. natural and built) environment, it should: contribute to conservation and protection; assist renovation of existing buildings and re-use of abandoned ones; and maintain semi-natural ecosystems associated with extensive, environmentally friendly farming vis-à-vis productivist agriculture. The Tuscan case (Case study 2) is illustrative of the complexities involved in the relationship between agri-tourism and rural sustainability.

Case study 2

The success of agri-tourism in Tuscany

Tuscany is the region where agri-tourism is now most developed in Italy. This is the result of early initiatives, to the presence of many beautiful ancient farmhouses and to a conductive institutional support. However, integration between agriculture and tourism, as well as the synergies that have been developed within the local milieu, are sometimes overestimated.

By the 1950s, Tuscan big landowners, who had been visiting the English or Austrian country-side, realised that the supply of touristic accommodation could be a new way to make money by renovating the numerous farmhouses, whose former tenants had left in order to work in the expanding urban industries. In this way, agri-tourism in Tuscany was first developed on large estates and for foreign clients (see Figure 34.1), and was initially limited to overnight or weekly accommodation provision and the sale of local products, primarily wine. Since the 1985 legislation reform, agri-tourism has spread on smaller farms and acquired specific characteristics, such as the attraction of more Italian and less wealthy customers, while incorporating shorter stays and also involving school camps and camp sites.

Today, the region of Tuscany seeks to promote the countryside, 'the other Tuscany', in reference to cities like Florence, Siena or Volterra, which are famous for their historic and art environments. But in most cases, agri-tourism still remains a simple form of accommodation for visiting these cities while escaping the summer urban heat. The time dedicated to the discovery of agriculture is often limited to a quick acquaintance with the local products.

Compared with tourism revenue, agriculture may appear unprofitable and become marginal. However, the farmer still has to prove the primacy of agricultural activity over tourism in order to continue to benefit from European subsidies and tax cuts. The 2003 regional law made it easier, as the farmer was given the ability to choose the method of calculation: by the working time, by the revenues or even by the costs incurred. Therefore, some farmers make a better living out of tourism than agriculture, but they point out that it is only the tourism revenues that allow them to maintain the cultural heritage that includes large farmhouses, dry stones terraces, extensive hydraulic system and (sometimes unprofitable) olive groves. This synergy between agriculture and tourism fosters

Figure 34.1 A restored villa at San Jacopo al Girona, Fiesole. Agricultural auxiliary buildings have been converted into cottages and small apartments. Photo: C. Perrin, 2006

sustainable rural development, because tourism helps preserve the environment and the cultivated landscapes, whereas agriculture itself contributes to the attractiveness of the territory.

Furthermore, some operators offer a real discovery of agriculture to tourists via tours in farms, vineyards and the processing operations (wineries, oil mills), and also through offering tasting experiences of farm products, thematic meetings on gastronomy or cultural excursions in the surrounding countryside. The 2006 national law also encouraged farmers to offer recreational, cultural and sporting activities, and recognised the latter as agri-tourism, even if these activities took place outside the farm. But not so many farmers are ready for this sort of diversification. And collaboration between farmers and other tourism local actors is often limited to Roads of Wine and olive oil.

Agri-tourism has thus been met with great success in the Tuscan countryside as an alternative form of tourist accommodation, but it is still marginal as a new tourist product based on agriculture and rural heritage. In addition, we may be talking of the success of agri-tourism, but most often the latter has not created strong ties with agricultural activity, except for direct on-farm sales.

(Case study report conducted by Coline Perrin, INRA, UMR Innovation, Montpellier, France)

These qualifications of agri-tourism reveal the difficult – if not utopian – aspect of sustainable development processes, which illustrate the complex relationship between economic growth (to the profit of rural societies) and the conservation of natural and patrimonial resources within ongoing rural restructuring. On the other hand, several of these positive factors of agri-tourism may be contested in specific rural contexts. For example, the construction and commodification of idyllic rustic images of the countryside may restrict rural identities in simplistic folklore, and family-based agri-tourist businesses that have been run by rural women may reinforce gendered roles in the household and the farm instead of contributing to women's social empowerment (Hall *et al.* 2003; Oldrup 1999; Little and Austin 1996). Yet, the notion of sustainability has been widely adopted in mainstream policy actions, whereas rural tourism is generally integrated in developmental projects as an essential feature of economic diversification in rural areas. Agri-tourism, regarded as a locally embedded development path, and also by being consistent with sustainability objectives, has an important role to play in the rural development arena.

Agri-tourism and tourism restructuring

Agri-tourism relates to the broader context of tourism restructuring in a number of ways. To begin with, agri-tourism may be considered as part of the 'new' tourism from a demand point of view. Actually there are a number of general and more specific demand-side features. The former relate to post-Fordist consumption, a key theme in tourism restructuring, and include: increasing market segmentation and product customisation, flexibility and differentiation of purchasing patterns. More tourism-specific features are cumulative travel experience, special interests and the will to differentiate oneself from mass consumption, rising demand levels for short-break holidays and active participation, a return-to-authenticity-and-nature mentality, a cultural and environmental as well as a quality-and-value consciousness, etc. (Urry 1990; Poon 1993). Agri-tourism appears to be fitting well into these categories (Hummelbrunner and Miglbauer 1994; Roberts and Hall 2001).

Similarly important is the rural idyll – the social construction of an idealised countryside – as a powerful rurality discourse within the contemporary tourist gaze (Little and Austin 1996; Bunce 2003). This shift in tourist demand reshapes the ways in which rural territories are themselves presented and marketed in line with tourists' prepossessions and expectations, where perceived rural identities and symbolic values of the countryside are central (pastoral landscapes, wholesome food, friendship and family ties, peace and quiet). It is no coincidence that rural localities are in a constant effort to highlight 'authentic' images, identities and values of a perceived old good time; they even transform themselves in anticipation of the 'tourist gaze', in order to take advantage of new tourism market niches.

Unsurprisingly, Kastenholz (2000) has demonstrated that ruralists exhibit varying degrees of 'tradition' and 'environment' attachment. Although agri-tourists are under-represented in this study, many features that are typically attributed to quality agri-tourism are highly valued by other segments as well. As there are neither fixed boundaries in demand groupings, nor a one-to-one relationship between specific demand and supply characteristics, these findings suggest that agri-tourism activities may well be encompassed within various sorts of 'new' tourism practices. Equally important is the perceived value not only of the farm and farming activities *per se*, but also of the rural landscape, that is the positive externalities that are intrinsic to rural environments (Fleischer and Tsur 2000; Carpio *et al.* 2008). However, one should also bear in mind that there is a dark side to the increased consumption role of rural space, which is the commodification of the countryside and the creation of 'fictional rural landscapes' (Woods 2005). In this respect, the making of a 'staged authenticity' (MacCannell 1976) contradicts the very qualities that are often attributed to agri-tourism. At the same time, the development of agri-tourism acts as an important vehicle for the realisation of such commodification.

On the other hand, supply-side changes also embrace agri-tourism. The restructuring thesis argues that there are a number of re-organisation forms that are applicable to the study of the tourism 'industry', for example product and labour reorganisation, spatial relocation and product transformation (Agarwal 2002). However, from a supply point of view, agri-tourism has mainly evolved within the farm diversification paradigm and the rapid transformations of rural economies. In other words, it is the farmers, not 'conventional' tourism providers, who are considered as the suppliers of agri-tourism; and it is the rural economy, not the (however loosely defined) tourism economy, that has been transformed so as to incorporate agri-tourism. In that sense, agri-tourism provision is about new players in tourism and, thus, differentiates itself from restructuring processes at the level of the tourism firm.

None the less, tourism restructuring is more relevant at the destination level, including the formation of sectoral and spatial policy. Although agri-tourism services may be considered as novel activities in remote rural areas, it is also important that a number of popular, mass tourism destinations have been attempting to diversify, including rural and farm tourism programmes. The rationale has been to tackle what are perceived as negative mass tourism outcomes, such as seasonality, non-local and 'industry' dependency, low spending power and destination substitutability, while at the same time contributing to resource utilisation and the spreading out of economic benefits at the local and regional scales (Bramwell 2004). Consequently, as the focus of analysis shifts from specific sectors and sub-sectors to local economies bearing their own path dependencies, the temporal and spatial positioning of agri-tourism within wider local economies is of crucial importance. First, we should consider that, within developed destinations, agri-tourism activities are considered marginal, meaning that their impact on local economies may be modest (Cavaco 1995). It is also difficult to distinguish whether it is such diversification strategies or the synergy of a variety of factors (including conventional ones like public investments, the general macro-economic conditions, export-oriented policies, etc.) that contribute to resort regeneration. It may also be the case that rural tourism is ineffective – empirical evidence suggests that the economic benefits are both below original expectations and unequally distributed among local communities. At the same time, rural tourism may act competitively to the traditional tourism sector for resources and markets, not least because in some cases it lacks the distinctive attributes that are normatively ascribed to it, therefore offering conventional and inauthentic tourism products (see above). Along the same line, the reported absence of local synergies, inadequacy of managerial skills, lack of co-operation in both backward linkages and marketing, constitute a powerful group of competitive disadvantages that may reproduce development lock-ins. Furthermore, agri-tourism activities, especially those that do not include lodging, may act complementarily to existing conventional chains of flexible tourism production (e.g. visiting farms on same-day trips within flexible packaged holidays). Therefore, it is possible that agri-tourism provision may not coincide with the niche market of agri-tourism and, conversely, augment existing reprehensible tourism supply structures. However, it is also important to note that such shortcomings are contingent both temporally and spatially, and that they relate to national frameworks of norms, state intervention and ways of doing business (Shaw and Williams 2004).

Agri-tourism and the environment: critical issues

Although a number of issues concerning the relationship between agri-tourism and the environment have already been discussed, there are some important aspects that need to be further explored. These aspects critically place agri-tourism within the wider tourism–environment debate from a geographical point of view and, in addition, shed some more light on our often normative view of alternative vis-à-vis mass types of tourism.

First of all, agri-tourism and its strong economic imperative, rural change, point to the importance of economic forces that have driven the convergence of tourism and agricultural activities in rural environments. In this way, we are principally dealing with major social changes occurring outside the tourism system *per se*. Thus, it is important to note that rural restructuring precedes critique on – and reorganisation of – mass tourism as a crucial factor conditioning the emergence of a special type of tourism. This element can be said to distinguish agri-tourism from other alternative types. Along the same line, an aspect that is relatively unique in agri-tourism is that what constitutes the object of the tourist gaze is actually a productive activity (i.e. farming in ideal-type agri-tourism) and, equally importantly, the overall agricultural environment. Both these features are conditioned on notions of authenticity and norms of entrepreneurship (as already stated above), but in any case their inter-connection – albeit highly differentiated across space – adds a special feature to Urry's (1990) spatial fixity of tourism services.

On the other hand, the extent to which agri-tourism fundamentally contrasts mass tourism can be questioned. Agri-tourism activities accounting for only a supplementary source of income mean that agri-tourism is substantially dependent on wider rural development trajectories. But this is not an agri-tourism feature exclusively. Some of its well-documented aspects, such as pluriactivity, are also a general feature of conventional, mass tourism labour markets in rural areas (Shaw and Williams, 2002). A similar point can be made concerning the supply structure of agri-tourism: SMEs and locally embedded networks are reported as having strong positive outcomes for rural development, because such forms of soft rural tourism demonstrate higher income and employment multipliers than hard ones (Sharpley and Sharpley 1997; Slee *et al.* 1997). However, this is true only in certain environments, given the management, marketing and collaboration structural inefficiencies reported in many cases where agri-tourism is a latecomer (Kizos and Iosifides 2007; Sharpley 2002). Both these strengths and weaknesses mean that agri-tourism resembles other conventional forms of tourism that exhibit the same characteristics. For example, a number of studies (Rodenburg 1980; Milne 1992; Andriotis 2002) have demonstrated that the small size of the (conventional) tourism firm corresponds to more positive impacts on local economic development. In addition, Buhalis and Cooper (1998) and Becton and Graetz (2001) have shown that structural inefficiencies constitute a major impediment in the development of SME-based tourism. But, crucially enough, agri-tourism and other forms of alternative tourism are facing much bigger challenges vis-à-vis mainstream forms of tourism, due not only to local and global competition, but also to the need for collectively creating a specialised destination, whose complementarities and positive externalities are a prerequisite for success. And it is this territorial-collective character of agri-tourism that, normatively, adds more to the sustainability perspective of local rural development.

Another theme of importance is the relationship between agri-tourism and the physical environment. The overall impact will depend on both the specific characteristics of the activity as well as on the characteristics of the destination. To begin with, agri-tourism relating to the radical departure from the productivist stage of intensive agriculture means that we are dealing with an important positive outcome: minimising the physical impact of agriculture. Of course this is not something that can be attributed to agri-tourism development; rather it should be seen as a consequence of rural restructuring, which in turn stimulates agri-tourism. On the other hand, policy stimuli for agri-tourism, especially in the EU, are part of a wider rural development strategy, in which agri-environmental measures play an important role. In this sense, the positive contribution of agri-tourism to minimising negative environmental impacts should be attributed as well to the overall rural development policy. In fact, the relative success of agri-environmental schemes, by having a direct impact on creating an 'ideal' rural environment, positively affects the specialisation of an agri-tourism destination in terms of providing for a *sine qua non* external resource.

Conclusion

Agri-tourism is still in the heart of interest of rural localities as it creates locally added values in existing explicit and tacit resources, and supplementary farm incomes in anticipation of negative impacts of ongoing rural change. Furthermore, the appeal of rural destinations transcends simple admission that conventional, mass tourism undermines physical and social environment. The pattern of agri-tourism benefits from rural diversification, as people seek more independent forms of travel and personalised contact with local societies and its natural and cultural heritage (Long and Lane 2000; Hall *et al.* 2003). In fact, agri-tourism responds to growing demand for place-based tourism directly connected with the agrarian milieu. Tourists are motivated by the desire to experience rural lifestyles and traditions as part of the increasing interest in heritage or as a nostalgia that represents social constructions of an idealised countryside. Therefore, accelerating pace of rural restructuring processes has caused significant economic, social and political change in rural areas, of which tourism has been both agent and subject (Roberts and Hall 2001: 47).

References

Agarwal, S. (2002) 'Restructuring Seaside Tourism: The Resort Lifecycle', *Annals of Tourism Research* 29 (1), 25–55.

Andriotis, K. (2002) 'Scale of Hospitality Firms and Local Economic Development – Evidence from Crete', *Tourism Management* 23 (4), 333–41.

Anthopoulou, Th. (2000) 'Agrotourism and the Rural Environment: Constraints and Opportunities in the Mediterranean Less-Favoured Areas', in H. Briassoulis and J. Van der Straaten (eds) *Tourism and the Environment: Regional, Economic, Cultural and Policy Issues.* Dordrecht, Boston, MA and London: Kluwer Academic Publishers, 357–73.

Aumand, A., Barthelemy D. and Caron, P. (2006) 'Definitions, References and Interpretations of the Concept of Multifunctionality in FRANCE', *European Series on Multifunctionality* 10, 5–39.

Bazin, G. and Roux, B. (1997) 'L'Agri-tourisme: un Atout pour les Zones Rurales Difficiles Méditerra-néennes?', in B. Roux and D. Guerraoui (eds) *Les Zones Défavorisées Méditerranéennes*. Paris: L'Harmattan, 339–61.

Becton, S. and B. Graetz (2001) 'Small Business – Small Minded? Training Attitudes and Needs of the Tourism and Hospitality Industry', *International Journal of Tourism Research* 3 (2), 105–13.

Bramwell, B. (2004) 'Mass Tourism, Diversification and Sustainability in Southern Europe's Coastal Regions', in Bramwell, B. (ed.) *Coastal Mass Tourism: Diversification and Sustainable Development in Southern Europe*. Clevedon: Channel View, 1–31.

Buhalis, D. and C. Cooper (1998) 'Competition or Co-Operation? Small and Medium Sized Tourism Enterprises at the Destination', in E. Laws, B. Faulkner and G. Moscardo (eds) *Embracing and Managing Change in Tourism: International Case Studies*. London: Routledge.

Bunce, M. (2003) 'Reproducing Rural Idylls', in P. Cloke and J. Little (eds) *Country Visions*. London: Pearson, 14–30.

Capt, D. (1997) 'Différenciation des Produits de Consommation Finale et Agriculture de Service', *Economie Rurale* 242, 36–52.

Carpio, C.E., Wohlgenant, M.K. and Boonsaeng, T. (2008) 'The Demand for Agri-tourism in the United States', *Journal of Agricultural and Resource Economics* 33 (2), 254–69.

Cavaco, C. (1995) 'Tourism in Portugal: Diversity, Diffusion, and Regional and Local Development', *Tijdschrift voor Economische en Sociale Geografie* 86 (1), 64–71.

Cloke, P. (2006) 'Conceptualizing Rurality', in P. Cloke, T. Marsden and P. Mooney (eds) *Handbook of Rural Studies*. London: Sage, 18–28.

Fleischer A. and Tsur, Y. (2000) 'Measuring the Recreational Value of Agricultural Landscape', *European Review of Agricultural Economics* 27(3), 385–98.

Hall, D., Mitchell, M. and Roberts, L. (2003) 'Tourism and the Countryside: Dynamic Relationships', in D. Hall, M. Mitchell and L. Roberts (eds) *New Directions in Rural Tourism*. London: Ashgate, pp. 3–16.

Hummelbrunner, R. and Miglbauer, E. (1994) 'Tourism Promotion and Potential in Peripheral Areas: The Austrian Case', *Journal of Sustainable Tourism* 2 (1–2), 41–50.

Kastenholz, E. (2000) 'The Market for Rural Tourism in North and Central Portugal: A Benefit Segmentation Approach', in D. Hall and G. Richards (eds) *Tourism and Sustainable Community Development*. London: Routledge, 268–84.

Kizos, Th. and Iosifides, Th. (2007) 'The Contradictions of Agrotourism Development in Greece: Evidence from Three Case Studies', *South European Society and Politics* 12 (1), 59–77.

Lane, B. (1994) 'What is Rural Tourism?' *Journal of Sustainable Tourism* 2 (1–2), 7–21.

Little, J. and Austin, P. (1996) 'Women and the Rural Idyll', *Journal of Rural Studies* 12 (2), 101–11.

Long, P., and Lane, B. (2000) 'Rural Tourism Development', in W. Gartner and D. Lime (eds) *Trends in Outdoor Recreation, Leisure and Tourism*. Wallingford: CABI, 299–308.

MacCannell, D. (1976) *The Tourist: a New Theory of the Leisure Class*. New York: Sulouker Books.

Milne, S. (1992) 'Tourism and Development in South Pacific Microstates', *Annals of Tourism Research* 19 (2), 191–212.

Mollard, A. (2002) 'Multifonctionnalité, Externalités et Territoires', *Les Cahiers de la Multifonctionnalité* 1, 37–56.

Oldrup, H. (1999) 'Women Working off the Farm: Reconstructing Gender Identity in Danish Agriculture', *Sociologia Ruralis* 39 (3), 343–58.

Perrin. C. (2009) '*Construire les Campagnes Méditerranéennes: Usages, Gestion et Valorisations du Foncier Agricole Périurbain en Provence et en Toscane (1950–2010)*', unpublished PhD thesis, Aix-Marseille Université (France) and Facoltà di Architettura di Firenze (Italy). Available http://tel.archives-ouvertes.fr/tel-0044 3001/fr/.

Phillip, S., Hunter, C. and Blackstock, K. (2010) 'A Typology for Defining Agri-tourism', *Tourism Management* 31 (6), 754–8.

Poon, A. (1993) *Tourism, Technology and Competitive Strategies*. Oxon: CAB International.

Roberts, L. and Hall, D. (2001) *Rural Tourism and Recreation: Principles to Practice*. Wallingford: CABI.

Rodenburg, E., (1980) 'The Effects of Scale in Economic Development: Tourism in Bali', *Annals of Tourism Research* 7 (2), 177–96.

Sharpley, R. (2002) 'Rural Tourism and the Challenge of Tourism Diversification: The Case of Cyprus', *Tourism Management* 23 (3), 233–44.

Sharpley, R. and Sharpley J. (1997) *Rural Tourism: An Introduction*. London and Boston, MA: International Thomson Business Press.

Shaw, G. and Williams, A.M. (2002) *Critical Issues in Tourism: A Geographical Perspective*, 2nd edn. Oxford: Blackwell.

——(2004) *Tourism and Tourism Spaces*. London: Sage.

Slee, W., Farr, H. and Snowdon, P. (1997) 'Sustainable Tourism and the Local Economy', in M.J. Stabler (ed.) *Tourism and Sustainability*. Wallingford: CAB International, 69–87.

Urry, J. (1990) *The Tourist Gaze: Leisure and Travel in Contemporary Societies*. London: Sage.

Woods, M. (2005) *Rural Geography*. London: Sage.

Further reading

Aumand, A., Barthelemy D. and Caron, P. (2006) 'Definitions, references and interpretations of the concept of multifunctionality in France', *European Series on Multifunctionality* 10, 5–39. (An extensive literature overview on concepts and research streams of multifunctionality of rural space, within which agritourism is placed.)

Cloke, P., Marsden, T. and Mooney, P. (eds) (2006) *Handbook of Rural Studies*, London: Sage. (An extensive treatment of the characteristics and processes of rural restructuring, commodification of the countryside and sustainability especially in Parts C: Sustainability, D: New Economies and F: New Consumerism.)

Lane, B. (1994) 'What is rural tourism?', *Journal of Sustainable Tourism* 2 (1–2), 7–21. (A landmark treatment of rural tourism.)

Roberts, L. and Hall, D. (2001) *Rural Tourism and Recreation. Principles to Practice*, Wallingford: CABI. (A comprehensive textbook on rural tourism and its different forms, including case studies of the European experience.)

Shaw, G. and Williams, A.M. (2004) *Tourism and Tourism Spaces*, London: Sage. (A critical introductory textbook to the political economy of tourism from a geography perspective.)

Woods, M. (2005) *Rural Geography*, London: Sage. (Textbook focusing on responses to rural change, including the commodification of the countryside and forms of rural tourism in chapter 12.)

35

Slow travel

Janet Dickinson and Les Lumsdon

Introduction

Slow travel has emerged over the last decade as an alternative to mass tourism. Slow travel strongly embraces experiential elements of travel, appeals to environmentally concerned tourists and embraces modes of transport other than air and car. Should it gain momentum as a new form of tourism, slow travel has the potential to address some of the environmental concerns posed by existing tourism structures, most specifically tourism's contribution to climate change. However, whether slow travel has the potential to make a significant contribution to low carbon tourism depends to a large extent on how it is defined. At the time of writing, although the term 'slow travel' has established a level of common usage in the media, on web communities and within academia, there are many different interpretations. Some interpretations are not so different to the consumptive forms of tourism that slow travel claims to replace.

This chapter begins with an analysis of the emerging idea of slow travel. It explores early usage of the term and its links to the wider slow movement. From this an eclectic picture emerges. The majority of material on slow travel focuses on tourism taking more time and enabling more meaningful engagement with people and place, but there is less consensus on the rejection of air and car travel thus, the potential for reduced environmental impact, although promoted, is not always clear. The chapter subsequently unpacks the core components of slow travel and analyses how it can make a contribution to low carbon tourism. Having set out the components of slow travel, the chapter explores how slow travel differs from mass tourism and other forms of tourism such as responsible and ecotourism. The chapter then considers the likely future directions that the development of slow travel might take. Will it become a niche market, will slow travel destinations emerge or will slow travel principles be applied to all tourism?

Finally, the chapter provides a case study that analyses the potential for slow travel based on a kayaking descent of the Ardèche Gorge in France. This case study analyses a number of issues surrounding both destination-based tourism and travel to destination areas. Although the Gorge descent by kayak provides a packaged, low carbon activity at the destination, with a strong physical engagement with place, currently most visitors arrive by car and this undermines the low carbon potential of the trip. The case study presents a structural analysis outlining the barriers that currently impede slow travel in tourism settings.

Although there are various explanations, our preferred explanation of slow travel suggests that it takes a holistic view of tourism, it is not just about travel or just about the destination. Travel is an essential, integral component of tourism, although it is often excluded from tourism analysis. Therefore, slow travel is about the whole tourist experience from home to destination and during the destination stay. It emphasises the significance of quality travel and destination-based experiences, taking time to enjoy the journey, as well as the destination, and engaging with the locations visited. It is also related to environmental consciousness, which the following early explanation emphasises:

> Holiday travel where air transport is rejected in favour of more environmentally benign forms of overland transport which generally take much longer and become incorporated as part of the holiday experience.
>
> *(Dickinson 2008: 2A1.1)*

The explanation discussed in this chapter excludes air and car travel, but within the varied use of slow travel these modes are not necessarily excluded. However, it is contended here that if slow travel is to usefully contribute to reducing the environmental impact of tourism then air and car travel should be excluded.

The emerging idea of slow travel

It is not clear when, or in what context, the term 'slow travel' was first used. A review of its usage by the media, web communities and in academia suggests that at least two reasonably distinct ideas about slow travel have emerged over the last 10 years. There is some synergy between these two ideas. Both strands of thinking about slow travel have strong links with the wider slow movement, which is based on three principles: doing things at the right speed, changing attitudes towards time and the use of it, and seeking quality over quantity (Peters 2006). The first perspective of slow travel has focused on facilitating longer stays in one place with tourists encouraged to explore that place in depth with little travel once in the destination area. This view of slow travel is destination-focused. Pauline Kenny was one of the first to present this perspective on the Slow Travel website (www.slowtrav.com) she founded in 2000. Slowtrav.com asks participants to:

> Spend a week in a vacation rental and see what is near you. Slow down, immerse yourself in the local culture and avoid the fast pace of rushing from one guidebook 'must-see' to the next.

This interpretation of slow travel therefore isolates the destination and largely ignores travel to the destination. Several web communities advertise long-haul destinations and access by air (e.g. www.slow-travel-for-women.com). This latter element is in direct conflict with the second version of slow travel.

The second strand of thinking about slow travel takes a more holistic view of tourism by considering the whole tourist experience from home to destination and at the destination. In this view, the journey can be as much the destination as a specific end point. As Dickinson *et al.*'s (2011) analysis of slow travellers describes:

> Slow travel was driven principally by travel experience, taking time to enjoy the journey, to engage with people (for good and bad) and to share a journey/destination and to explore destinations in a less superficial way.

This reflects Clawson and Knetsch's (1966) five-stage model of the outdoor recreation experience developed in the 1960s. This includes travel to the site of the recreation experience, on-site experiences and travel back, and additionally incorporates anticipation and recollection of the experience. Clawson and Knetsch understood that travel can be an integral part of the tourist experience and, in some instances, the main purpose.

The holistic view of slow travel also introduces a focus on reducing the environmental impact of tourism travel. It is evident that some tourists are choosing slow travel as it meets their lifestyle objective of low environmental impact, which is reflected in modal choice. On the other hand, by choosing modes of transport that facilitate an engaging travel experience, participants are avoiding air and car travel and thus minimising their environmental impact regardless of their level of environmental concern (Dickinson et al. 2011). In addition, by engaging more deeply with places visited and supporting local business, slow travellers further reduce the environmental impact by use of local goods and services.

Although the media and web communities draw on both strands of thinking about slow travel, attention in academia has focused on the potential of slow travel to reduce greenhouse gas (GHG) emissions (Ceron and Dubois 2007; Dubois and Ceron 2006; Gössling et al. 2008; Høyer 2000; Lumsdon and McGrath 2011; Simpson et al. 2008). In this context, the related terms 'slow tourism' and 'soft mobility' are also evident. There is also a growing body of literature on low carbon travel and tourism (e.g. Peeters et al. 2008), although this is focused on the carbon footprint and does not embrace the wider remit of slow travel.

There is some debate about the use of 'slow'. Slow travel does not necessarily take longer, inter-city high-speed trains being the prime example. Some argue that 'slow' has some negative connotations (Lumsdon and McGrath 2011), especially in a travel context where the emphasis is on speed, distance and time. However, studies have questioned the need to minimise travel time (Holley et al. 2008; Salomon and Mokhtarian 1998) and led to a review of transport policies. Slow travel is part of this re-evaluation of time as a travel cost to be minimised.

Slow travel and low-carbon tourism

In recent years many studies have drawn attention to the carbon footprint of tourism. Although estimates vary, the sector as a whole is responsible for between 4 per cent and 6 per cent of global GHG emissions (UNWTO 2007). In response, low-carbon tourism, that is, tourism with a low carbon impact through minimisation of GHG emissions (Peeters et al. 2008), has emerged. Climate change and low-carbon tourism has been analysed elsewhere in this book so is not repeated here. Suffice to say, analysis suggests that 50–90 per cent of tourism GHG emissions arise from transport (see, e.g. Simpson et al. 2008), and this is where slow travel may have a significant role in reducing the GHG emissions from tourism. The tourism sector's response to climate change involves mitigation, that is attempts to reduce the impact of tourism on climate change, and adaptation, that is attempts to adapt tourism to climate change.

Slow travel is primarily a mitigation strategy through its use of alternatives to air and car travel, a strategy, at least in part, endorsed by the UNWTO. In 2009 the UNWTO collaborated with the World Economic Forum to produce a report 'Travel and Tourism in a Low Carbon Economy', which was their contribution to the UN Climate Change Conference in Copenhagen in December 2009. This recognised the impact of GHG emissions from tourism and recommended a modal shift from car to public transport as part of the solution. Although not directly proposing a shift from air travel to other modes, the report recommended inclusion of aviation in international climate change agreements.

Given that tourism will also need to respond to national and international measures to cut GHG emissions, slow travel is also a potential adaptation strategy to response to governmental carbon management initiatives. The ability of tourism to move to a low-carbon economy through a slow travel strategy is very context-dependent. Within the tourism system, tourists generally have the best adaptation capacity as they can choose different destinations, change travel mode or increase the length of stay. Increasing the length of stay has the potential to improve the ecoefficiency of tourism as the GHG emissions from travel are averaged on a per day basis (Gössling *et al.* 2005), although destination-based impacts remain. Tour operators can make similarly adaptations should the need arise. Destinations on the other hand may have poor adaptive capacity depending on their geographical context (Bows *et al.* 2009), for example, distance from source markets or suitability of transport infrastructure.

In earlier work, low-carbon tourism was proposed as a core outcome of slow travel, while, at the same time, it can also be an incentive for slow travel fuelled by the desire of tourists' or tourism providers' to reduce GHG emissions (Dickinson and Lumsdon 2010). However, several studies show that although reduced environmental impact can be an important factor in tourist modal choice, it is not by any means a factor for all tourists (Dickinson *et al.* 2011; Guiver *et al.* 2007; Lumsdon and McGrath 2011). Further study of slow travellers is needed to clarify the role of environmental concerns as a core motivation. Given the present need for society to address GHG emissions, it is evident that some of the greatest potential for slow travel as an alternative to current tourism lies in its low-carbon outcome regardless of slow travellers' motivations.

The core components of slow travel: a conceptual framework

The various ideas about slow travel have increasingly coalesced into some level of shared consensus; however, there is also disagreement. This is no bad thing as Lumsdon and McGrath's (2011) analysis of experts' views suggest 'it is better to express the term slow travel as a group of associated ideas rather than a watertight definition'. Figure 35.1 represents a distillation of the ideas about slow travel into a conceptual diagram. This is by no means the final word on slow travel but an attempt to set out the core ingredients and their relationships into a framework for further development. The framework develops from the holistic strand of thinking, which views slow travel as the whole tourist experience including travel from home to destination, travel at the destination and the destination stay, activities, excursions, etc. The main argument for adopting this perspective lies in the low-carbon outcome of slow travel, which is less likely to be achieved if slow travel is viewed as a solely destination-based concept. This is not to ignore the considerable interest in slow travel as a destination-based concept and its potential as a destination development tool. However, its potential as a low carbon tourism strategy cannot be realised without considering the travel to the destination area.

The conceptual diagram (Figure 35.1) sets out the components of slow travel according to the context described above, ingredients and outcome. The term 'ingredients' is used to represent the core components of slow travel; however, it is considered that the ingredients might vary from individual to individual, by travel setting and from place to place. That is, the four main items, slowness, experience, locality and environment, may be more or less significant. Environment, under the umbrella of 'environmental consciousness', is separate to the other three, and it is evident from existing studies (Dickinson *et al.* 2011; Lumsdon and McGrath 2011) that sub-items such as 'carbon reduction' may be of little concern for some slow travellers. Three of the items (slowness, experience and locality) are linked under the umbrella of destination and travel experience. For some the journey will be the destination, whereas for others it remains a means to an end, but still one to be engaged with productively.

Context

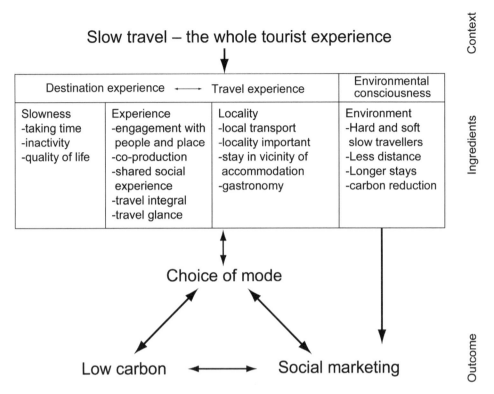

Ingredients

Outcome

Figure 35.1 Slow travel – the whole tourist experience

Choice of mode is purposely placed in an intermediate position in this framework between ingredients and outcome. Empirical data indicate that choice of mode can be a core ingredient for some slow travellers, as they have a commitment to specific modes such as coach, train or cycle tourism and base holiday choices around this (Dickinson *et al.* 2011). However, equally for others, it is an outcome of environmental concerns or fits with the travel experiences sought, such as spending time with family and friends and taking in the passing landscape, the travel glance (Larson 2001). Certain modes of transport are complementary to slow travel and, if the concept is to recognise its full potential as a low-carbon form of tourism, it is desirable that air travel is not a component. Although the carbon footprint of air travel is reducing through technological development, it is still large, and future technological developments have less potential to significantly reduce the impact while, at the same time, air travel is set to grow (Bows *et al.* 2009). There is some debate about the inclusion of car travel within slow travel (Lumsdon and McGrath 2011), some explanations include car travel (Macquarie Dictionary 2009; Mintel 2009). It is also evident that some of the core ingredients of slow travel, especially experiential elements, might be achieved through car travel. However, there is enough evidence of the environmental impact of car use at both a local destination (Dickinson and Lumsdon 2010) and global level (Holden 2007) to suggest that it should be excluded from any future development of slow travel where low-carbon travel is a fundamental outcome. There are also significant concerns about various forms of water-based transport, particularly cruise ships given their potential for high GHG emissions (Dickinson and Lumsdon 2010). It is anticipated that there will be ongoing debate about the inclusion of car travel and types of water-based transport into slow travel.

As described above, low-carbon tourism is an important outcome of slow travel regardless of the intention of the slow traveller concerned. Low-carbon tourism also features under the 'environmental consciousness' box in the ingredients section. The level of environmental concern and associated motivation of slow travellers is varied, therefore it is important that low-carbon tourism is recognised as an incidental outcome of slow travel related to experiential components as well as environmental concern. Social marketing is a further outcome of slow travel. Empirical data suggest that being a slow traveller can be a personal statement that is made to friends and family about an individual's environmental concerns (Dickinson *et al.* 2011). Through social contagion, this can lead others to re-evaluate how they take their holidays.

Slow travel, mass tourism and alternative forms of tourism

Although it is self-evident that tourism involves travelling to destinations, many forms of tourism essentially describe the destination element of tourism. Travel is, however, integral to slow travel and there is a much greater focus on travel both to and at destination. However, slow travel does not encourage travel *per se*; the focus is rather on travel over shorter distances and taking time to enjoy travel experiences. This is significantly different to mass tourism travel, which emphasises speed, increasing distance and less travel time. Under this model, tourism has expanded through the globe increasingly growing the distance between origin markets and destinations as transport technology has increased speeds, reduced travel time and costs. International tourism has developed in conjunction with transport infrastructure and increasingly been based around air transit routes and powerful mutual relationships between the airline industry and other key tourism actors (Høyer 2000). From a GHG emission perspective, the current tourism business model is heading in the wrong direction with increasing short trips of longer distance (Ceron and Dubois 2007). Slow travel is a move to reverse this trend by encouraging longer stays, less often and closer to home.

This is not to say that mass tourism is negative, it is likely to be the best development option in some situations (Sharpley 2009) and may be more sustainable than holiday options marketed on their green credentials. Over recent decades, a number of alternatives to mass tourism have evolved, such as ecotourism, responsible tourism and pro-poor tourism, which claim to have more positive social or environmental impact. Although slow travel might be allied with, and compatible with, these in some respects, it is a different concept. Most of the alternatives to mass tourism focus their impact analyses on the destination area and largely ignore travel to the destinations. For instance, given the economic development potential of tourism, pro-poor tourism developed to increase the equity benefits of tourism for poor communities in developing countries (Pro-Poor Tourism Partnership 2009). This has been used to justify long haul flights from developed countries to participate in tourism in the least developed countries and undermine arguments for increased costs of flights (Gössling 2008b). Analysis of pro-poor tourism suggests that there is some doubt about the economic benefits (Hall 2007; Zhao and Brent Ritchie 2007) and the dependence on long haul flights could further undermine the development potential should GHG emission impacts be taken into consideration (Nawjin *et al.* 2008). Ecotourism is another example focused on destination-based environmental issues, but largely overlooks travel to the destination. In an ecotourism context, such as Costa Rica, most travel is long haul producing significant GHG emissions.

Broadly speaking, alternatives to mass tourism come under the umbrella of sustainable tourism, which has emerged from the wider concept of sustainable development (see Chapter 21 this volume). Sustainable tourism tends to place an emphasis on economic development, whereas economic growth is typically not a goal, but a facilitator, of sustainable development

(Holden 2007). For example, the UNWTO ST-EP (Sustainable Tourism for Eliminating Poverty) scheme emphasises economic development and makes little reference to environmental concerns. Sharpley (2009), therefore, suggests that this might be an admission by the UNWTO that sustainable tourism is unachievable in some contexts. Many others have expressed doubts about the viability of sustainable tourism (e.g. Becken and Simmons 2002; Wheeller 1993), with transport impacts being a significant problem. Several researchers have explored the translation of sustainable development principles to transport more broadly (Holden 2007) and to transport for tourism (Høyer 2000; Hoyer and Aall 2005; Dubois and Ceron 2006). They suggest a shift is needed to rail, buses, walking and cycling, but also highlight significant travel inequalities, even within developed countries, and suggest that a more equitable share of travel is needed. For instance, analysis at a global scale shows that only around 2–3 per cent of the world's population enjoy international travel (Gössling *et al.* 2009). If tourism could be decoupled from high carbon-dependent forms of transport, such as through a slow travel model, then it might become a more sustainable development option (Dickinson and Lumsdon 2010). Slow travel is best suited to short to medium haul travel, and its climate change mitigation potential lies in this market. For tourism as a whole this would potentially free up carbon budgets for long haul markets, where the best economic development opportunities lie.

Future directions

Our earlier analysis of slow travel (Dickinson and Lumsdon 2010) suggested three possible scenarios for slow travel.

1   Slow travel as a niche market. This essentially represents the current situation where slow travel is chosen by predominantly middle class groups in developed countries, and also more socially deprived groups who have no alternative. Slow travel may remain a relatively small market segment alongside other forms of alternative tourism.
2   Slow travel destinations emerge. In this scenario slow travel becomes more mainstream through a destination development model based on slow travel. This would require a commitment by destinations to analyse their markets and travel infrastructure, and promote access to and around the destination by low-carbon modes. There is considerable potential for this development within Europe where there is good public transport infrastructure and most tourism is short haul.
3   Slow travel as a set of principles applied to all types of tourism. This scenario envisages more widespread adoption, with various factors, such as peak oil and growing recognition of climate change impacts, driving a transition to a low-carbon tourism system. Such a transition would require a significant shift in market behaviour and supplier production.

A fourth possible scenario is the development of slow travel transit regions, as there are regions and transit routes that are better able to develop slow travel modes. For instance, it is not particularly viable to develop slow travel from Europe to southern Africa due to poor infrastructure and political instability making overland travel not only time-consuming but difficult and dangerous. However, there are viable corridors for destinations such as Morocco in north Africa.

Although slow travellers can be segmented into categories of independent and organised tourists, slow travel is currently largely the prevail of independent travellers (Dickinson *et al.* 2011) who might be described as 'explorers' or, to a lesser extent, 'drifters' according to

Cohen's (1972) typology of tourist roles. In terms of Plog's (1974) model of tourism destination preference, they might be described as allocentric tourists, although slow travellers do not especially seek out undiscovered locations and there is an emerging role for tour operators to control less desirable aspects of slow travel (Dickinson and Lumsdon 2010).

Given the structural barriers to slow travel, there is a need for greater government intervention to facilitate overland travel, while tour operators need to improve integrated booking opportunities and develop slow travel packages. At the time of writing there is much talk of the growing Asian tourism market. Although slow travel might not be suitable for all Asian contexts, slow modes of travel are well established in some Asian markets, such as coach travel in China, and there is an opportunity to grow more sustainable tourism using slow travel in these contexts. It is a misunderstanding of slow travel to suggest that it could be viable in all settings. The focus should be on relatively close markets and destinations with well-developed overland transport infrastructure.

Case study

The Ardèche Gorge is located in southeast France in the Rhône-Alpes region. The Gorge, which includes the dramatic Pont d'Arc, a nature arch over the river Ardèche, provides a significant international tourist attraction. Although the Pont d'Arc can be accessed by road, the Gorge is largely inaccessible except on foot or river. As a result, kayak or canoe descent of the river Ardèche has become a popular tourism activity and numerous local businesses provide a trip package. Although canoes and kayaks differ, both are used in the Gorge, therefore they are collectively referred to as kayaks here. The trip, which can be anything from 6 km to 50 km depending on embarkation point, provides a transport as tourism experience (Rhoden and Lumsdon 2006). Guides are available to lead trips but many participants hire kayaks independently.

Much of the Gorge is protected by the Réserve Naturelle Gorges de l'Ardèche. Protection of the natural environment is of paramount importance and access is therefore controlled. Overnight camping is prohibited except by permit at two bivouac sites. Spaces are limited to 500 so advanced booking is required for busy weekends and the summer holidays (Syndicat de Gestion des Gorges de l'Ardèche 2010). Trips can last from half a day to several days. Boat access is prohibited after 6pm in the reserve area and the bivouac regulations are strictly enforced.

There is considerable potential for slow travel based on a kayaking descent of the Ardèche Gorge and a stay in one of the adjacent villages. The kayaking descent provides an intense destination and travel experience with a high level of self-reliance. The pace is limited by the natural flow of the river, participants co-produce the experience through their intense engagement with the natural environment and through sociable encounters during the trip. Given the nature reserve setting, it is likely to appeal to those with an interest and concern for the natural environment and has the potential to go hand in hand with environmentally aware tourism in a wider context. Although the Gorge descent by kayak provides a packaged, low-carbon activity at the destination, currently most visitors travel to the destination by car and this undermines the low carbon potential of the trip. The following analysis outlines the barriers that currently impede slow travel in tourism settings such as this. The analysis focuses on the two travel components in this context: access to the destination area and travel within the destination area.

The Gorge descent itself is a self-propelled activity that is carbon-neutral. Clearly, visitors need to return to their departure base and this is not feasible along the river because of strong currents.

Kayak hire is therefore integrated with return travel. This is organised co-operatively between a number of operators, which use a combination of coaches, minibuses and trailers to return tourists and kayaks. Transport is carefully allocated to maximise use of vehicle capacity for the 38-km return journey. Kayak hire operators are predominantly small businesses, often in co-operation with accommodation providers. Given the current dominance of car use by visitors to the area, a two-day kayak descent removes a car from the road for a similar period. At the same time, the trip is feasible for visitors without a car or access to their own kayak. Analysis of the destination-based trip alone illustrates a positive carbon outcome (Table 35.1).

Accommodation in the area is dominated by campsites, self-catering rentals and a few small hotels and bed and breakfasts. The main tourist market is from France, the Netherlands, Germany and the UK. The area is accessible via train to Montélimar then SNCF bus (Table 35.1 for GHG emission analysis). However, the dominance of camping accommodation, which involves transporting large volumes of equipment, means that car access dominates. Although train and coach are feasible, the connections can be poor requiring an extended wait at Montélimar. At Vallon Pont d'Arc, the main destination settlement, there is enough to amuse most people for a week but the tourist office advertises a wide range of attractions, most of which are not accessible without a car or considerable determination. Vallon Pont d'Arc is the bus terminus and the bus route is to Montélimar and several settlements to the north. This limits tourist mobility in the area without a car. Therefore, two issues are evident, car-dependent access to Vallon Pont d'Arc and car-dependent movement around the destination area. In order to potentially develop as a slow travel destination, the area would need a wider bus network during summer and a promotion strategy giving greater focus to tourist attractions within walking distance and on bus routes.

Table 35.1 Analysis of GHG emissions by mode of transport for trips to and within the Ardèche Gorge area

Destination example	Return trip Vallon Pont d'Arc to St Martin d'Ardèche		
	CO2 kg/passenger km[1]	Distance km	Kg of CO2 per passenger
Coach	0.027	76	2.1
Car	0.121	76	9.2

Origin to destination example	Return trip Paris to Vallon Pont D'Arc		
	CO2 kg/passenger km	Distance km	Kg of CO2 per passenger
Train	0.033	1024	33.8
Coach	0.027	116	3.1
			Total 36.9
Car	0.121	1140	137.9

Note: 1 Based on Dickinson et al. 2010

References

Becken, S. and Simmons, D.G. (2002) 'Understanding energy consumption patterns of tourist attractions and activities in New Zealand'. *Tourism Management* 23(4), 343–54.

Bows, A., Anderson, K. and Peeters, P. (2009) 'Air Transport, Climate Change and Tourism'. *Tourism and Hospitality Planning & Development* 6(1), 7–20.

Ceron, J.P. and Dubois, G. (2007) 'Limits to Tourism? A backcasting scenario for sustainable tourism mobility in 2050'. *Tourism and Hospitality Planning & Development* 4(3), 191–209.

Cohen, E. (1972) 'Toward a Sociology of International Tourism', *Social Research* 39(1), 164–82.

Clawson, M. and Knetsch, J.L. (1966) *Economics of Outdoor Education.* Baltimore, MD: The Johns Hopkins University Press.

Dickinson, J. (2008) 'Travelling slowly: an exploration of the discourse of holiday travel'. In *Proceedings of the Universities' Transport Studies Group Annual Conference.* 3–5 January, Portsmouth.

Dickinson, J. and Lumsdon, L. (2010) *Slow Travel and Tourism.* London: Earthscan.

Dickinson, J.E., Robbins, D. and Lumsdon, L. (2010) 'Holiday travel discourses and climate change'. *Journal of Transport Geography* 18, 482–9.

Dickinson, J.E., Lumsdon, L. and Robbins, D. (2011) 'Slow travel: Issues for tourism and climate change'. *Journal of Sustainable Tourism,* 19(3), 281–300.

Dubois, G. and Ceron, J.P. (2006) 'Tourism/Leisure Greenhouse Gas Emissions Forecasts for 2050: Factors for Change in France'. *Journal of Sustainable Tourism* 14(2), 172–91.

Gössling, S., Hall, M., Lane, B. and Weaver, D. (2008). 'Report: The Helsingborg Statement on Sustainable Tourism'. *Journal of Sustainable Tourism* 16(1), 122–4.

Gössling, S., Peeters, P., Ceron, J.P., Dubois, G., Patterson, T. and Richardson, R.B. (2005) 'The eco-efficiency of tourism'. *Ecological Economics* 54, 417–34.

Gössling, S., Peeters, P. and Scott, D. (2008b) 'Consequences of climate policy for international tourist arrivals in developing countries'. *Third World Quarterly* 29(5), 873–901.

Gössling, S., Ceron, J.P., Dubois, G. and Hall, M.C. (2009) 'Hypermobile travellers', in S. Gössling and P. Upham (eds) *Climate Change and Aviation: Issues, Challenges and Solutions.* London: Earthscan, 131–50.

Guiver, J., Lumsdon, L., Weston, R. and Ferguson, M. (2007) 'Do buses help to meet tourism objectives? The contribution and potential of scheduled buses in rural destination areas'. *Transport Policy* 14, 275–82.

Hall, C.M. (2007) 'Pro-poor tourism: do "tourism exchanges benefit primarily the countries of the South"?' *Current Issues in Tourism* 10(2/3), 111–18.

Holden, E. (2007) *Achieving Sustainable Mobility: Everyday and Leisure-time Travel in the EU.* Aldershot: Ashgate.

Holley, D., Jain, J. and Lyons, G. (2008) 'Understanding Business Travel Time and Its Place in the Working Day'. *Time Society* 17(1) 27–46.

Høyer, K.G. (2000) 'Sustainable tourism or sustainable mobility? The Norwegian case'. *Journal of Sustainable Tourism* 8(2), 147–60.

Høyer, K.G. and Aall, C. (2005) 'Sustainable mobility and sustainable tourism', in M.C. Hall and J. Higham (eds) *Tourism, Recreation And Climate Change.* Clevedon: Channel View Publications, 260–72.

Larson, J. (2001) 'Tourism mobilities and the travel glance: experiences of being on the move'. *Scandinavian Journal of Hospitality and Tourism* 1(2), 80–98.

Lumsdon, L. and McGrath, P. (2011) 'Developing a conceptual framework for slow travel: a grounded theory approach'. *Journal of Sustainable Tourism* 19(3), 265–79.

Macquarie Dictionary (2009) *Macquarie Dictionary: Australia's National Dictionary Online.* Available on: www.macquariedictionary.com.au/anonymous@9c98889861952/-/p/dict/index.html (accessed 23 June 2009).

Mintel (2009) *Slow Travel Special Report.* London: Mintel.

Nawijn, J., Peeters, P. and van der Sterren, J. (2008) 'The ST-EP programme and least developed countries: is tourism the best alternative?', in P.M. Burns and M. Novelli (eds) *Tourism Development: Growth, Myths and Inequalities.* Wallingford: CAB International, 1–10.

Peeters, P., Gössling, S. and Lane, B. (2008) 'Moving towards low-carbon tourism: New opportunities for destinations and tour operators', in S. Gössling, C.M. Hall and D.B. Weaver (eds) *Sustainable Tourism Futures: Perspectives on Systems, Restructuring and Innovations.* New York: Routledge, 240–57.

Peters, P. (2006) *Time, Innovation And Mobilities: Travel in Technological Cultures.* London: Taylor & Francis.

Plog, S.C. (1974) 'Why destination areas rise and fall in popularity'. *Cornell Hotel and Restaurant Administration Quarterly* 14(4), 55–8.

Pro-Poor Tourism Partnership (2009) *What is pro-poor tourism?* Available on: www.propoortourism.org.uk/what_is_ppt.html (accessed 22 September 2009).

Rhoden, S. and Lumsdon, L. (2006) 'A conceptual classification of the transport-tourist experience', in *Proceedings of Association for European Transport Conference.* Strasbourg.

Salomon, I. and Mokhtarian, P.L. (1998) 'What happens when mobility-inclined market segments face accessibility enhancing policies?' *Transportation Research D* 3(3), 129–40.

Sharpley, R. (2009) *Tourism Development and the Environment: Beyond Sustainability?* London: Earthscan.

Simpson, M.C., Gössling, S., Scott, D., Hall, C.M. and Gladin, E. (2008) *Climate Change Adaptation and Mitigation in the Tourism Sector: Frameworks, Tools and Practices*. Paris: UNEP, University of Oxford, UNWTO, WMO,

Syndicat de Gestion des Gorges de l'Ardèche (2010) *Environnment et Tourisme, un enjeu D'avenir*. Available at: www.gorgesdelardeche.fr/index2.php (17 August).

United Nations World Tourism Organization (UNWTO) (2007) *Davos Declaration: Climate change and tourism responding to global challenges*. Available on: www.unwto.org/pdf/pr071046.pdf (accessed 14 November 2007).

Wheeller, B. (1993) 'Sustaining the ego'. *Journal of Sustainable Tourism* 1(2), 121–9.

Zhao, W., and Brent Ritchie, J.R. (2007) 'Tourism and poverty alleviation: an integrative research framework'. *Current Issues in Tourism* 10(2/3), 119–43.

36

Responsible tourism

Whose responsibility?

Richard Sharpley

Introduction

The concept of responsible tourism is not new. More than 20 years ago, for example, Haywood (1988) was exploring the idea of 'responsible and responsive tourism planning' while Richter (1989: viii), in the preface to a book on the politics of tourism in Asia, made reference to a 'Centre for Responsible Tourism'. In fact, by the early 1990s, the term 'responsible tourism' had become synonymous with environmentally and socially appropriate forms of tourism in general and with alternative (to mass) forms of tourism in particular. In other words, as concern over the negative environmental and socio-cultural consequences of mass tourism became more widespread, responsible tourism became increasingly used by both proponents and critics as a collective descriptor of alternative forms of tourism (Cooper and Ozdil 1992; Harrison and Husbands 1996; Wheeller 1991). In short, responsible tourism was broadly synonymous with what, at that time, came to be referred to somewhat narrowly as sustainable tourism (Sharpley 2009).

More recently, however, it has been promoted as a conceptually distinctive approach to all forms of tourism that, although sharing the objectives of sustainable tourism, firmly places the emphasis on the needs of all stakeholders, including tourism businesses and tourists themselves, to take responsibility for their roles and actions in tourism (Goodwin 2009). At the same time, it has evolved as a tourism product or, more precisely, as a brand. In 2001, for example, www. responsibletravel.com was launched as the world's first dedicated online travel agent specialising in responsible holidays and now claims to offer 'the largest selection of responsible holidays anywhere on the web' (www.responsibletravel.com 2010a). Moreover, responsible tourism or, more specifically, responsible tourism business practice, has also become an objective for many tourism businesses, primarily in the UK but also elsewhere. Not only has the UK's Association of Independent Tour Operators (AITO) been committed to promoting responsible tourism since 2000 among its members (and, indeed, requiring adherence to its responsible tourism guidelines as a criterion of membership – AITO 2010), but also many tour operators, both independent and mainstream, have adopted the principles of responsible tourism (Table 36.1), in some cases explicitly through the appointment of a Responsible Tourism Manager. In short, responsible tourism has evolved into a tourism-specific manifestation of what is more broadly referred to as corporate social responsibility (CSR), the successful achievement of which by particular organisations and businesses is recognised by the annual Virgin Holidays Responsible Tourism Awards. Thus, responsible tourism, as a sustainable approach to the practice of tourism, appears to have achieved recognition and acceptance both by the tourism sector and also, as claimed by its proponents, among tourists themselves (Goodwin and Francis 2003). As a consequence, it could be argued that it represents a valid and effective means of not only mitigating tourism's negative environmental consequences, but also of enhancing the benefits of tourism to destinations, businesses and tourists alike.

Nevertheless, significant debate continues to surround the concept of responsible tourism with respect to both how it may be defined and, in particular, its specific focus on 'responsibility'. In turn, this suggests that the environmental credentials of responsible tourism as a sustainable approach to the practice of tourism may be questioned. The purpose of this chapter is to do just that. Specifically, it explores the extent to which stakeholders, in particular tourists, are amenable or responsive to messages of responsibility and, hence, the extent to which they seek out (as a niche product) or engage in (as a behavioural mode) responsible tourism for positive environmental reasons or concern. The first task, however, is to review briefly contemporary definitions of responsible tourism.

What is responsible tourism?

Responsible tourism may be variously defined. For example, Éveil, a French responsible tourism network, defines it as:

> a tourism or leisure activity implementing practices that are respectful of natural and cultural environment and which contributes in an ethical manner to the local economic development. It therefore favors the tourist awareness concerning his [sic] own impacts on the local territory and makes him an actor of his consumption.
>
> *(Éveil 2010)*

Thus, the emphasis here is very much on tourists being aware of their impacts and responding appropriately. A similar definition is provided by www.responsibletravel.org, although equal if not more emphasis is placed on the experience of tourists themselves – responsible travel is seen as means of self-fulfilment:

> Responsible travel is a new way of travelling for those who've had enough of mass tourism. It's about respecting and benefiting local people and the environment – but it's about far more than that. If you travel for relaxation, fulfilment, discovery, adventure and to learn – rather than simply to tick off 'places and things' – then responsible travel is for you.
>
> *(www.responsibletravel.com 2010b).*

In other words, responsible travel is primarily travel that cannot be labelled as 'mass tourism'; it is sold or promoted, effectively as a niche product, on the basis of the experience that responsible tourists desire or might expect, thus appealing to those who seek (whether for altruistic or more egotistical reasons) distinctive or non-mass produced holidays.

Conversely, Harold Goodwin, the leading proponent of the contemporary responsible tourism movement and a driving force behind its adoption in industry and policy circles (as well as the development of related research and education through the International Centre for Responsible Tourism), defines it more broadly. He suggests, somewhat vaguely, that responsible tourism is about making 'better places for people to live, and better places for people to visit' (Goodwin 2009: 12), although goes on to state more specifically that the realisation of these aspirations is dependent on 'all stakeholders taking responsibility for creating better forms of tourism'. Similarly, the Cape Town Declaration on Responsible Tourism (ICRT 2010), the only formal policy document concerned with defining responsible tourism, states that 'it is the responsibility of all stakeholders in tourism to achieve more sustainable forms of tourism'. The Declaration defines responsible tourism according to its characteristics, as shown in Table 36.1 below.

Two things are immediately evident from Table 36.1. First, responsible tourism is defined very much by its potential outcomes, not by the processes or procedures necessary to achieve those outcomes, although the Declaration does provide guidelines for economic, social and environmental responsibility. As can be seen from Table 36.2, however, these are not dissimilar from the principles or guidelines that have long been proposed for enhancing the environmental sustainability of tourism development more generally (see, for an early example, ETB 1991). Thus, it is not clear how responsible tourism or, more precisely, responsibility, might be achieved.

Second, and following on from this point, the characteristics of responsible tourism summarised in Table 36.1 may equally be thought of as the characteristics of sustainable tourism. In

Table 36.1 Characteristics of responsible tourism

Responsible tourism:
- minimises negative economic, environmental, and social impacts;
- generates greater economic benefits for local people and enhances the well-being of host communities, improves working conditions and access to the industry; involves local people in decisions that affect their lives and life chances;
- makes positive contributions to the conservation of natural and cultural heritage, to the maintenance of the world's diversity;
- provides more enjoyable experiences for tourists through more meaningful connections with local people, and a greater understanding of local cultural, social and environmental issues;
- provides access for physically challenged people; and
- is culturally sensitive, engenders respect between tourists and hosts, and builds local pride and confidence.

Source: ICRT (2010).

Table 36.2 Guiding principles for environmental responsibility

- Assess environmental impacts throughout the life cycle of tourist establishments and operations – including the planning and design phase – and ensure that negative impacts are reduced to the minimum and maximising positive ones.
- Use resources sustainably, and reduce waste and over-consumption.
- Manage natural diversity sustainably, and where appropriate restore it; and consider the volume and type of tourism that the environment can support, and respect the integrity of vulnerable ecosystems and protected areas.
- Promote education and awareness for sustainable development – for all stakeholders.
- Raise the capacity of all stakeholders and ensure that best practice is followed, for this purpose consult with environmental and conservation experts.

Source: ICRT (2010).

other words, the distinction between the two concepts is somewhat fuzzy, particularly as both share the same goal, namely, sustainable development (and, to further confuse the debate, contemporary approaches to sustainable tourism seek to affect change in all forms of tourism, including mass tourism, whereas some consider responsible tourism to be a solution – or at least an alternative – to mass tourism). It is claimed that the difference between the two lies, unsurprisingly, in the notion of responsibility: 'the major difference between the two is that, in responsible tourism, individuals, organisations and businesses are asked to take responsibility for their actions and the impacts of their actions' (Wikipedia 2010)[1], whereas, allegedly, progress towards the achievement of sustainable tourism has been hindered by an unwillingness of stakeholders to take responsibility for their own actions. That is, sustainability is seen to be someone else's problem. Whether this is the case or not remains debatable but what is certain is that responsible tourism, as defined by Goodwin, addresses what is widely considered to be the single greatest challenge to the achievement of sustainable tourism and sustainable development more generally, namely, a 'transformation in social values and lifestyles in general and the 'adoption' of responsible consumption in particular' (Sharpley 2009: 78; Porritt 2007).

As this chapter will go on to suggest, this ambition to encourage responsibility is, on the one hand, both logical and desirable; as the IUCN's (1991) document *Caring for the Earth* proposed, progress towards sustainable development is dependent on the adoption of more sustainable lifestyles for, as Ludwig *et al.* (1993) succinctly argue, 'resource problems are not really environmental problems; they are human problems'. On the other hand, it may be seen as idealistic to ignore the realities of contemporary production and consumption systems to seek such a fundamental shift in values. The point here, however, is that, conceptually, responsible tourism is not distinct *from* but a requirement *of* sustainable tourism development; moreover, as a term it is also used interchangeably with other manifestations of sustainable tourism. For example, The International Ecotourism Society defines ecotourism as 'Responsible travel to natural areas that conserves the environment and improves the well-being of local people' (TIES 2010), whereas others have suggested that 'true' ecotourism (however that may be defined) should in fact be redefined as responsible tourism in order to distinguish it from 'irresponsible ecotourism' (Russell and Wallace 2004). Similarly, in a special issue of the *Journal of Sustainable Tourism* in 2008, focusing on research perspectives on responsible tourism, papers addressed a variety of issues broadly related to sustainability and sustainable tourism, including sustainable supply chain management (Schwartz *et al.* 2008), justice tourism (Higgins-Desbiolles 2008) and ecotourism in Madagascar (Duffy 2008). In short, it is difficult, if not impossible, to distinguish responsible tourism from the concept of sustainable tourism more generally. Indeed, it is one of a number of words or terms that, as VisitBritain (the UK's national tourism body) observes, are 'used to describe what is essentially the same thing – tourism that seeks to minimise its negative impacts on the environment and society' (VisitBritain 2010). Accordingly, the organisation goes on to define responsible tourism as 'the closest definition to sustainable tourism; however, it tends to refer to the consumers' choice of destination and mode of transport based on their ethical, political and racial sensitivities as well as being concerned for the environment and local culture' (ibid. 2010).

Thus, the concept of responsible tourism remains problematic, not least because of definitional difficulties. In particular, however, it is value-laden. In other words, although it may be manifested in sets of guiding principles, such as those proposed in the 2002 Cape Town Declaration on Responsible Tourism (Table 36.2), or in operational guidelines and codes of conduct, in itself it does not represent a practical approach to developing and managing tourism within environmental parameters. Rather, it is, in a sense, a philosophy or, more precisely, a movement (Goodwin 2009: 13), the aim of which is to encourage responsible behaviour – or, to reveal its moralising foundation, to discourage irresponsible behaviour because, implicitly, to not engage with responsible tourism is to be an irresponsible tourist or tourism business (Butcher 2002). In other words, the objective of responsible tourism is, by definition, to change the ways in which tourists, businesses and other stakeholders behave, to encourage them to become 'responsible'. The question then to be addressed is, how likely is such a transformation in attitudes, values and behaviour, particularly among tourists themselves, likely to occur?

Responsibility in tourism

The promotion of responsible tourism is typically justified on the basis of two related arguments. First, it has long been suggested that the characteristics of the demand for tourism are undergoing a transformation; the conventional or 'old' tourist (Poon 1993), who was satisfied with a homogeneous, predictable, passive, sun–sea–sand type holiday experience, is allegedly being replaced by the 'new' tourist who is more experienced, independent and flexible, who seeks individual quality experiences that educate, are different and are environmentally benign. At the same time, according to Poon (1993: 145), the 'new' tourist also knows how to behave, how to consume tourism 'correctly' or responsibly – and if they do not, then advice has long been available on how to be a 'good' tourist (Wood and House 1991; more recently, Popescu 2008). Second, responsible tourism makes good business sense (Goodwin 2009). Not only does the alleged increase in demand for responsible holidays among enlightened 'new' tourists represent a significant market opportunity, but tourism businesses themselves have the potential to benefit from the widely claimed benefits of doing 'green business', such as cost-savings, competitive advantage, marketing and PR (that is, being seen to be responsible), as well as meeting CSR objectives and underpinning future business through contributing to the environmental and social sustainability of destinations.

There is undoubtedly evidence to support both arguments. For example, a number of organisations, such as the British Trust for Conservation Volunteers (BTCV), have long been popular among people wishing to engage in conservation and other charitable work while on holiday and nowadays volunteer tourism, or 'voluntourism' as it is now widely referred to, is a recognised and growing market sector (Mustonen 2005; Wearing 2001) – although the values and motivations of 'voluntourists' may vary significantly (Daldeniaz and Hampton 2010). Equally, demand for special interest, adventure, activity and, more generally, 'responsible' holidays is undoubtedly on the increase. For example, it has been reported that, in 2006, over one million responsible holidays were taken, with future annual growth of 25 per cent predicted (Goodwin 2007). Again, however, the values and motivations of such tourists are complex, varied and uncertain, and research has demonstrated that the onus may fall on destinations to encourage or ensure environmentally appropriate behaviour on the part of their visitors (Stanford 2008). Equally, there is also no doubt that numerous businesses and other organisations within the tourism sector are increasingly adopting responsible practices, whether in the context of day-to-day business operations or supporting development, education, health care and other projects at the destinational level. At the time of writing, for example, the 2010 Virgin Holidays Responsible Tourism Awards had received over 1,700 nominations from more than 600 organisations and, as referred to in the introduction to this chapter, many tour operators and other tourism businesses have explicitly adopted the principles of responsible tourism. Nevertheless, it must be stated, of course, that as impressive as these figures are with respect to the demand for responsible holidays and responsible business activity, they represent only a small proportion of total tourism activity. In 2009 UK residents made almost 59 million trips abroad. At the same time, there is also contradictory evidence with respect to tourism businesses' commitment to responsible practice; a recent survey found that only around one-third of travel agents and tour operators believe that 'the travel industry has a role to play in limiting global warming' (Taylor 2008).

However, of particular relevance to this chapter is the extent to which the alleged emergence of the 'new', environmentally aware tourist is manifested in reality. In other words, it may be argued that the success of responsible tourism, or the achievement of environmentally benign or sustainable tourism practices, is largely dependent on tourists adapting or modifying their behaviour according to genuine environmental values rather than for other reasons, such as guilt-avoidance or ego-enhancement (Munt 1994). That is, the consumption of a 'responsible holiday' may not be motivated by strong environmental values, nor may it be characterised by responsible behaviour on the part of tourists while at the destination.

For example, and as explored in more detail elsewhere (Sharpley 2006), the relatively limited research into the motivations and benefits sought by ecotourists (that is, people participating in touristic activities that conform to definitions of ecotourism) reveals that the 'true' ecotourist is less numerous than might be assumed. Blamey and Braithwaite's (1997) research, for instance, concluded that the majority of potential ecotourists do not hold particularly green values, and Palacio and McCool (1997) found that, according to their criteria, less than 20 per cent of a sample of tourists in Belize, renowned as an ecotourism destination, could be considered ecotourists. Other research has similarly demonstrated that there exist wide-ranging preferences and behaviour among ecotourists but that, generally, the natural environment and opportunities for active rather than passive participation are fundamental factors in the demand for and satisfaction with ecotourism experiences (Holden and Sparrowhawk 2002; Wight 1996). In other words, eco-tourists seek the personal benefits of the enjoyment of nature; conversely, there is little or no evidence that they are motivated by or behave according to environmental or responsible values.

Of course, the outcomes of research into ecotourism, as a specific market segment, are not necessarily representative of responsible tourism more generally, whereas the environmental credentials of many ecotourism products are questioned in many quarters. Indeed, as is now discussed, proponents of responsible tourism draw on research into consumers' environmental attitudes in general and tourists environmental/ethical values in particular as evidence of increasing responsibility inherent in tourist-consumer behaviour.

The responsible tourist?

Since the early 1990s, successive surveys in the UK have identified an increasing incidence of green or responsible attitudes on the part of consumers. For example, it was found that increasing numbers of people considered themselves to be either 'dark green' (that is, 'always or as far as possible buy environmentally friendly products') or 'pale green' (that is, 'buy if I see them') consumers (Mintel 1994). A subsequent survey by the same organisation (Mintel 2007) found that green consumerism was continuing to become more widespread, although consumers are more likely to buy environmentally friendly products to feel good about themselves rather than for altruistic reasons. Interestingly, a more recent study revealed that people who are exposed to green products, such as looking at them on a website, subsequently behave more altruistically than those who actually buy the products. The implication of this study was that the act of purchasing may make people feel that they have 'done their good deed' and thus may act less altruistically when presented with other ethical dilemmas (Mazar and Zhong 2010). Importantly, in the context of tourism, this may imply, of course, that the act of buying a responsible holiday may absolve tourists from any sense of responsibility while actually on holiday, a point that has long been made: 'Responsible tourism is a so-called solution that keeps everyone happy. It appeases the guilt of the 'thinking tourist' while simultaneously providing the holiday experience they or we want' (Wheeller 1991: 96).

With respect to research that specifically explores the ethical dimension of tourism consumption, surveys again suggest that tourists may favour tour operators or other businesses with strong environmental or ethical credentials. A survey by the charity Tearfund, for example, found that although affordability, good weather and a good hotel were key attributes that were accorded highest importance in buying a holiday, significant importance was attached to the fact that the holiday was designed to minimise environmental impacts and that a company had ethical policies. Moreover, 59 per cent of respondents stated that they would be happy to pay more for their holidays if the extra money were to contribute to higher local wages, environmental conservation and so on (Goodwin and Francis 2003). Similarly, other research has revealed that 64 per cent of UK tourists believe that tourism causes some degree of damage to the environment and that, generally, they would be willing to pay more for an environmentally appropriate tourism product (Diamantis 1999).

Conversely, other research has consistently demonstrated that tourism is relatively immune to environmental concerns (or that 'responsible' tourist behaviour is motivated by factors other than environmental concern). For example, in a recent poll, just 1 per cent of tourists stated that their carbon footprint was an important factor when deciding on a holiday purchase, whereas cost is the most important consideration for 43 per cent of tourists (Skidmore 2008). Even despite the growing awareness of climate change, research has shown that this is having little or no impact on travel behaviour. For example, one study found that the few people who expected to fly less frequently in the future would do so as a result of a change in personal circumstances rather than because of concerns over the environmental impacts of aviation (CAA 2008: 49). Thus, despite the long-held belief that tourists are demanding 'greener' holidays, the evidence suggests that environmental concern remains low on their list of priorities when actually purchasing holiday or travel experiences.

Underpinning these more negative findings is widespread recognition of what might be termed the value–action or intention–action gap. That is, a distinction frequently exists between aspiration (what consumers say they would do) and what they actually do in practice. Research has increasingly demonstrated that the link between general environmental awareness (which itself may be diminishing in importance compared with other issues, such as terrorism and security) and green consumerism in particular is tenuous. Not only is the widespread adherence to green purchasing behaviour, as suggested in surveys, rarely witnessed in practice, but there is a lack of clarity over the meaning of green consumerism or how it may be manifested (Peattie 1999). Consumers address environmental issues in complex and ambivalent ways (Macnaghten and Urry 1998) and, as a result, their consumer behaviour is frequently contradictory and compromises may be made between ethical values, product performance, cost and so on. In the case of tourism, given its high economic value and its significance as a form of consumption, such compromises may well be made and, overall, there is little concrete evidence to suggest that the demand for responsible tourism and other forms of alternative or appropriate tourism can be related directly to increased environmental concern.

In addition, consideration must also be given to both the motivation for participation in tourism and its meaning as a form of consumption when addressing tourists' potential responsiveness to the 'responsibility' message. Indeed, applying knowledge and understanding of tourism motivation and consumption may go some way to explaining the ambivalence of tourists towards environmental concerns or why 'relatively few tourists seem to make decisions based on environmental concerns' (Swarbrooke and Horner 1999: 204). It is not possible to explore these issues here in detail but two points are of fundamental relevance to the arguments in this chapter. First, tourist motivation is complex, dynamic and potentially determined by a variety of person-specific psychological factors and extrinsic social forces. That is, a number of different pressures and influences may shape the needs and wants of tourists at any one time. Nevertheless, most commentators suggest that tourists are motivated primarily by, on the one hand, a desire to escape – as van Rekom (1994) suggests, 'a central need which has been revealed time and time again in empirical research is the "escape" notion' – and, on the other hand, by the potential rewards of participating in tourism. Such rewards may be personal, interpersonal, psychological or physical and, collectively described as 'ego-enhancement'. In other words, tourism represents a form of self-reward or self-indulgence.

Second, people consume tourism in a variety of ways; that is, as a specific form of consumption, tourism embraces a number of different meanings, principal among which is the creation of self-identity (Sharpley 2008). Other means of consumption include 'play' (that is, the opportunity to experience tourism with other tourists, perhaps in liminal contexts) and, reflecting the contemporary significance of tourism, as relaxation, fun and hedonism. Undoubtedly, tourists may also attempt to integrate themselves with the object of consumption (that is, behave in a manner appropriate to destination environment and communities), although, as already demonstrated, this is likely to be the exception rather than the rule. Indeed, as has long been argued (Wheeller 1991, 1993), the consumption of responsible tourism may be driven more by 'ego' than eco-concerns, while, more generally, by succumbing to green-washing, so-called responsible tourists may in fact be contributing to the continued spread of mass tourism.

Conclusion

What are the implications then, for the potential success of viability of responsible tourism as a means enhancing tourism's contribution to sustainable development generally, and its environmental sustainability in particular? As noted earlier in the chapter, the encouragement of responsibility in the practice of tourism (both production and consumption) is both logical and desirable, not least because, as is widely accepted, sustainability in general is dependent on the adoption of sustainable (that is, responsible) lifestyles. However, as research consistently shows, stated intentions of responsible consumer behaviour are rarely reflected in practice whereas the motivation for and significance of tourism as a specific form of consumption suggest that the promotion of responsibility faces major challenges. To put it simply, to be a responsible tourist requires 'working' at tourism, which contradicts, for most tourists, its fundamental purpose. Thus, to conclude, efforts may be better directed at those people and organisations involved in the planning, management and, indeed, legislation of tourism; in general, sound or responsible environmental practice results more often than not from control and legislation. In other words, to expect widespread adoption of responsible behaviour among tourists is, perhaps, to ignore the realities of tourist consumption.

Note

1 Although entries on Wikipedia are anonymous and not subject to validation or peer review, this reference provides a concise and accurate definition and explanation of responsible tourism.

References

AITO (2010) *Sustainable Tourism*. Association of Independent Tour Operators. Available on: www.aito.co.uk/corporate_Responsible-Tourism.asp (accessed 12 October 2010).

Blamey, R. and Braithwaite, V. (1997) 'A social values segmentation of the potential ecotourism market', *Journal of Sustainable Tourism* 5(1), 29–44.

Butcher, J. (2002) *The Moralisation of Tourism: Sun, Sand and … Saving the World*. London: Routledge.

CAA (2008) *Recent Trends in Growth of UK Air Passenger Demand*. London: Civil Aviation Authority. Available on www.caa.co.uk/docs/589/erg_recent_trends_final_v2.pdf (accessed 21 September 2009).

Cooper, C. and Ozdil, I. (1992) From mass to responsible tourism: The Turkish experience. *Tourism Management* 13(4), 377–86.

Daldeniaz, B. and Hampton, M. (2010) *Charity-based Voluntourism versus 'Lifestyle' Voluntourism: Evidence from Nicaragua and Malaysia*. Working paper No.211. Kent Business School. Available on: www.kent.ac. uk/kbs/documents/research/working-papers/2010/211-daldeniz-hampton.pdf (accessed 15 October 2010).

Diamantis, D. (1999) 'Green strategies for tourism worldwide', *Travel & Tourism Analyst* 4, 89–112.

Duffy, R. (2008) Neoliberalising nature: Global networks and ecotourism development in Madagascar', *Journal of Sustainable Tourism* 16(3), 327–44.

ETB (1991) *Tourism and the Environment: Maintaining the Balance*. London: English Tourist Board.

Éveil (2010) *Responsible Tourism: Definition*. Éveil. Available at: www.eveil-tourisme-responsable.org/uk/responsible-tourism-definition.php (accessed 12 October 2010).

Goodwin, H.(2007) *Advances in Responsible Tourism*. ICRT Occasional Paper No.8. Leeds Metropolitan University: International Centre for Responsible Tourism.

——(2009) *Taking Responsibility for Tourism: The Inaugural Lecture of Professor Harold Goodwin*. ICRT Occasional Paper No.12. Leeds Metropolitan University: International Centre for Responsible Tourism.

Goodwin, H. and Francis, J. (2003) 'Ethical and responsible tourism: Consumer trends in the UK', *Journal of Vacation Marketing* 9(3), 271–84.

Harrison, L. and Husbands, W. (1996) *Practising Responsible Tourism: International Case Studies in Tourism Planning, Policy and Development*. Chichester: John Wiley & Sons.

Haywood, K. (1988) Responsible and responsive tourism planning in the community. *Tourism Management* 9(2), 105–18.

Higgins-Desbiolles, F. (2008) 'Justice tourism and alternative globalisation', *Journal of Sustainable Tourism* 16(3), 345–64.

Holden, A. and Sparrowhawk, J. (2002) 'Understanding the motivations of ecotourists: the case of trekkers in Annapurna, Nepal', *International Journal of Tourism Research* 4(6), 435–46.

ICRT (2010) *Cape Town Declaration*. International Centre for Responsible Tourism. Available on: www.icrtourism.org/capetown.shtml (accessed 13 October 2010).

IUCN (1991) *Caring for the Earth: A Strategy for Sustainable Living*. Gland, Switzerland: World Conservation Union.

Ludwig, D., Hilborn, R. and Walters, C. (1993) 'Uncertainty, resource exploitation, and conservation: Lessons from history', *Science* 269 (5104), 17, 36.

Macnaghten, P. and Urry, J. (1998) *Contested Natures*. London: Sage Publications.

Mazar, N. and Zhong, C. (2010) 'Do green products make us better people?', *Psychological Science* (online). Available at: http://pss.sagepub.com/content/early/2010/03/01/0956797610363538 (accessed 15 October 2010).

Mintel (1994) *The Green Consumer I: The Green Conscience*. London: Mintel International.

——(2007) *Green and Ethical Consumers*. London: Mintel International.

Mustonen, P. (2005) 'Volunteer tourism: modern pilgrimage?', *Journal of Tourism and Cultural Change* 3(3), 160–77.

Munt, I. (1994) 'Eco-tourism or ego-tourism? *Race & Class* 36(1), 49–60.

Palacio, V. and McCool, S. (1997) 'Identifying ecotourists in Belize through benefit segmentation: A preliminary analysis', *Journal of Sustainable Tourism* 5(3), 234–43.

Peattie, K. (1999) 'Rethinking marketing: Shifting to a greener paradigm', in M. Charter and M. Polonsky (eds) *Greener Marketing: A Global Perspective on Greening Marketing Practice*. Sheffield: Greenleaf Publishing, 57–70.

Poon, A. (1993) *Tourism, Technology and Competitive Strategies*. Wallingford: CABI.

Popescu, L. (2008) *The Good Tourist: An Ethical Traveller's Guide*. London: Arcadia Books.

Porritt, J. (2007) *Capitalism As If The World Matters*. London: Earthscan.

van Rekom, J. (1994) 'Adding psychological value to tourism products', in J. Crotts and W. van Raaij (eds) *Economic Psychology of Travel and Tourism*. New York: Haworth Press, 21–36.

www.responsibletravel.com (2010a) *About Us*. Available on: www.responsibletravel.com/Copy/Copy100427.htm (accessed 12 October 2010).

www.responsibletravel.com (2010b) *Responsible travel and responsible tourism*. Available on: www.responsibl etravel.com/Copy/Copy100259.htm (accessed 13 October 2010)

Richter, L.(ed.) (1989) *The Politics of Tourism in Asia*. Honolulu: University of Hawaii Press.

Russell, A. and Wallace, G. (2004) 'Editorial: Irresponsible ecotourism. *Anthropology Today* 20(3), 1–2.

Schwartz, K., Tapper, R. and Font, X. (2008) 'A sustainable supply chain management framework for tour operators', *Journal of Sustainable Tourism* 16(3), 298–314.

Sharpley, R. (2006) 'Ecotourism: a consumption perspective', *Journal of Ecotourism* 5(1+2), 7–22.

——(2008) *Tourism, Tourists & Society*, 4th Edition. Huntingdon: Elm Publications

——(2009) *Tourism, Development and the Environment: Beyond Sustainability*. London: Earthscan.

Skidmore, J. (2008) 'Britons: More mean than green', *Daily Telegraph, Telegraph Travel* 14 June, T4.

Stanford, D. (2008) 'Exceptional visitors': dimensions of tourist responsibility in the context of New Zealand', *Journal of Sustainable Tourism* 16(3), 258–75.

Swarbrooke, J. and Horner, S. (1999) *Consumer Behaviour in Tourism*. Oxford: Butterworth Heinemann.

Taylor, I. (2008) 'Trade out of step on climate, study finds', *Travel Weekly*, July 4, p.3.

TIES (2010) *What is ecotourism? The definition*. International Ecotourism Society. Available on: www.ecoto urism.org/site/c.orLQKXPCLmF/b.4835303/k.BEB9/What_is_Ecotourism – The_International_Ecot ourism_Society.htm (accessed 15 October 2010).

VisitBritain (2010) *Sustainable Tourism: Glossary of Terms*. Available on: www2.visitbritain.com/en/campaig ns/green/glossary.aspx (accessed 15 October 2010).

Wearing, S. (2001) *Volunteer Tourism: Experiences That Make A Difference*. Wallingford: CABI.

Wheeller, B. (1991) 'Tourism's troubled times: responsible tourism is not the answer', *Tourism Management* 12(2), 91–6.

——(1993) 'Sustaining the ego. *Journal of Sustainable Tourism* 1(2), 121–9.

Wight, P. (1996) 'North American ecotourism markets: Motivations, preferences and destinations', *Journal of Travel Research* 35(1), 3–10.

Wikipedia (2010) *Responsible tourism*. Available on: http://en.wikipedia.org/wiki/Responsible_Tourism (accessed 8 October 2010).

Wood, K. and House, S. (1991) *The Good Tourist: A Worldwide Guide for the Green Traveller*. London: Mandarin.

37

Pro-poor tourism and local economic development

Harold Goodwin and Adama Bah

The election of the Labour government in 1997 and the creation of the Department for International Development (DFID), with a seat at the cabinet table occupied by Clare Short, coincided with the development within the United Nations of the Millennium Development Goals, which seek to reduce poverty. In 1998, DFID commissioned a working paper on *Sustainable Tourism and Poverty Elimination* for discussion through a multistakeholder process; note the radicalism of poverty elimination. In the late 1990s, UK citizens were collectively the fourth-largest purchaser of international tourism. The discussion paper addressed the question: 'What contributions can [tourism] make to the development of sustainable tourism and poverty elimination?'. The focus of the discussion paper was on how 'existing tourism to developing countries' could be improved and 'new tourism developments planned, so as to maximise their contribution to local sustainable economic development and poverty elimination' (Goodwin 1998: 1). 'Pro-poor tourism' (PPT) was coined in the subsequent report commissioned from Deloitte and Touche (Oliver Bennett) with the International Institute for Environment and Development (Dilys Roe) and the Overseas Development Institute (Caroline Ashley) (Bennett 1999).

The conceptualisation of PPT grew out of DFID's interest in whether tourism could contribute to poverty reduction and how this could be achieved. The focus of the United Nations and the development agencies of the Organisation for Economic Co-operation and Development (OECD) countries on the poverty reduction targets in the Millennium Development Goals (MDGs) shifted the focus from growth and the trickledown of economic benefits to a more explicit focus on poverty reduction. The MDGs recognised that poverty is multidimensional, that there are issues of income; access to food and other natural resources; and health, education and gender equity; and that poverty is a consequence of inequality. MDG Goal 1 is to halve the proportion of people whose income is less than one dollar per day; there are a number of other targets including universal education, gender equality, child and maternal health, HIV/AIDS and environmental sustainability. Where tourism creates wealth that can be taxed and the revenues used to alleviate hunger and poverty, or to improve access to health and education, tourism businesses contribute, as do the taxes paid by other businesses and their employees, to achieving the MDGs. Tourism creates employment but it does not necessarily benefit the poor, it is often easier for businesses to attract skilled and semi-skilled labour into the area rather than to train local people who are new to tourism and to create progression opportunities for them within the business. The issue is not whether tourism contributes to economic growth but rather can it contribute to poverty reduction, and if it can, how can those contributions be maximised? Tourism has the potential to contribute to poverty reduction, where the economically poor gain from it. Like many other forms of economic activity it can contribute to poverty reduction through employment, the generation of livelihood opportunities in the supply chain, taxation and infrastructure improvements generated through tourism. Tourism can also stimulate philanthropic engagement. The causes of poverty are generally deep-seated. Tourism is no more, or less, of a band aid solution than any other form of economic activity.

The international focus on the MDGs and the commitment of the new Labour government in the UK to a more active engagement in international development and poverty reduction produced a favourable context in which to review the potential of tourism for poverty reduction. The language of PPT reflected the debates about pro-poor growth. As Klassen has argued, although widely used the term is not well defined, the use of the term suggests a form of growth that results in significant reductions in poverty and provides the poor with more access to economic opportunities. However, it is not clear what the policy implications are, nor how pro-poor growth might be measured. Klassen argued that pro-poor growth requires that the poor benefit 'disproportionately more from growth than the non-poor' and greater weight should be given to the poorest of the poor' (Klassen 2003: 3–4). Bennett *et al.* (1998) were less ambitious for tourism. They defined PPT as 'tourism that generates net benefits to the poor. Economic benefits are only one (although a very important) component of this, as social, environmental and cultural costs and benefits also need to be taken into account' (Bennett *et al.* 1998: 6). From the outset, those who argued the case for poverty reduction through tourism recognised that it can have serious negative consequences for local communities where, for example, there is a loss of access to conserved land, for fodder, thatching and game, or beaches and the sea for fishing.

The Pro-Poor Tourism Partnership of Ashley, Goodwin and Roe worked with this definition on a series of desk studies funded by DFID. PPT developed as an approach to tourism development, used to refer to 'interventions [which] aim to increase the net benefits for the poor from tourism, and ensure that tourism growth contributes to poverty reduction'. The objective was to 'unlock opportunities for the poor – whether for economic gain, other livelihood benefits, or participation in decision-making'. Poverty is the core focus of PPT, 'rather than one element of (mainly environmental) sustainability' (Ashley *et al.* 2001: viii). PPT was not envisaged as a product, it developed as an approach that sought to use tourism, all forms of tourism, to generate benefits for the poor, through sales of goods and services to tourists and tourism businesses, through other livelihood benefits, for example potable water, clinics or roads, and broader and more challenging, empowerment and partnership outcomes.

From the first paper in 1998 there was a clear understanding that engagement with the mainstream industry was essential if there was to be a significant contribution to poverty reduction, location matters, 'PPT works best where the wider destination is developing well' (Ashley *et al.* 2001: vix). The economically poor and marginalised rarely have access to, or control over, the kinds of resources that may attract tourists. Where they did, as in some areas gazetted as national parks, they are generally excluded and disinherited. PPT works best in destinations where there are sufficient numbers of tourists to provide a market. However, in some remote areas relatively few tourists can make a major contribution to local livelihoods, particularly where tourism is the only source of monetary income (Saville 2001).

The PPT Partnership differentiated PPT from the other forms of alternative tourism, recognising that 'there is a welcome overlap between many sustainable tourism and PPT approaches', but asserting that 'there are differences in the core focus'. Most of the sustainable tourism initiatives post-Rio had focused on environmental sustainability (Ashley *et al.* 2001: 2). The PPT Partnership differentiated PPT from ecotourism because its focus is on delivering net benefits to the poor, its primary purpose; whereas conservation of habitat and species was, and is, the primary focus of ecotourism. Community-based tourism initiatives aim to increase local people's involvement in tourism, PPT focuses on measurable poverty reduction. PPT drew on earlier work on tourism and rural livelihoods (Ashley 2000; Ashley *et al.* 2000) and advocated a holistic livelihoods approach focusing 'simply on cash or jobs is inadequate', the PPT Partnership insisted that 'the range of livelihood concerns of the poor – economic, social and environmental, short-term and long-term – need to be recognised' (Ashley *et al.* 2001: 50).

DFID's interest in tourism had also been triggered by the agenda for the 1999 Commission on Sustainable Development (CSD7), which was to discuss tourism in the context of the post-Rio Earth Summit work on Environment and Development. DFID (1999) in its briefing document for CSD7 argued that tourism was already contributing to growth in poor countries and that initiatives were required in order to maximise its contribution to poverty elimination and that PPT strategies generate 'net benefits for the poor (i.e. benefits are greater than costs)'. The concept of net benefit was important because 'social, environmental and cultural costs and benefits also need to be taken into account'. PPT strategies are concerned with impacts on poor people, although it was recognised that the 'non-poor may also benefit' (DFID 1999: 1). From the outset it was recognised that tourism could have both positive and negative impacts on the poor, it may exclude the poor from access to natural resources, to beaches and protected areas, it may result in the loss of agricultural land and in social and environmental costs, hence the emphasis was on net benefits. At the Rio Earth Summit in 1992 it was recognised that the challenge was sustainable development, Rio was about environment and development. It was about finding ways in which the developing world could achieve development, and significant reductions in poverty, without undermining the earth's environment. PPT was one effort to square the circle, to overcome the oxymoron of sustainable development. At CSD7 governments were urged, among a host of other things, to 'maximize the potential of tourism for eradicating poverty' (CSD7 1999: 2), the importance of addressing economic development for the poor alongside caring for the environment was asserted.

Few interventions have been written up and published along with data on the outcomes, the donors have rarely required it and those implementing have not considered it necessary. Understandably neither the donors nor the implementers have sought to be held to account for the outcomes and impacts of their interventions. The Dutch development agency SNV and the ST-EP Foundation have both implemented major programmes but the results have not yet been published. There is therefore surprisingly little evidence that the poor have benefited. There are, however, a number of published studies that suggest that the benefits are locally significant and the ODI have published a series of studies demonstrating at the destination level the benefits to the economically poor (Mitchell and Ashley 2010).

Reports on particular interventions have demonstrated what can be achieved by a targeted intervention. In West Humla, in Nepal, an agricultural development and local capacity building project secured additional livelihood opportunities for local communities on a remote pilgrimage trekking route, demonstrating that even a small number of tourists can provide a market capable, in a subsistence economy, of making a significant contribution to livelihoods. By following an import substitution strategy, providing goods and services locally that had previously to be imported into the valley, significant livelihood gains were demonstrated (Saville 2001). The environmental impact was at least neutral.

In Tanzania, Harro Boekold enhanced the livelihoods of economically poor coffee farmers by working with their coffee co-operative and the outbound tourism industry in the

Netherlands to include a visit to a coffee farm in a scheduled tour itinerary. The visit was added to an existing itinerary; on arrival in Kenya the tour groups enjoyed lunch and a coffee farm tour on their first afternoon. The initiative has provided additional livelihoods for the farmers and their wives, provided communal income and encouraged the farmers to plant new coffee bushes; again the environmental impact is probably slightly positive (Goodwin 2007; Goodwin and Boekold 2010). In Don Det Tok, in Laos, recent tourism development has brought demonstrable livelihood benefits to the villagers. Whereas for 65 per cent of sampled households agriculture was still their main source of income, 38 per cent of households surveyed had at least one adult working in tourism. For 22 per cent of households tourism was their main source of income, and for a further 11 per cent it was their second-most important source of income (Harrison and Schipani 2007: 219).

In the Gambia, Bah and Goodwin worked with the informal sector to identify the barriers to access that restricted their ability to engage with the tourism industry. The Gambia, in West Africa, on both sides of the River Gambia, is surrounded by Senegal. Less than 30 per cent of the Gambia's land is arable, it supports a population of around 1.6 m, more than 50 per cent of which is urbanised. The Gambia is 168th out of the 182 countries for which UNDP has data, on the Human Development Index (UNDP 2009). The World Travel and Tourism Council estimates that travel and tourism contributed 12.3 per cent of GDP, 9.9 per cent of total employment and 33.6 per cent of exports in 2010. They estimate that 27,000 people are directly employed in tourism (WTTC 2010: 5–6). Tourism plays an important role in the economic development of the Gambia, a country that is heavily dependent on subsistence agriculture and with few alternative export opportunities.

The Gambia faces robust competition in the winter sun, sand and sea market from northern Europe and recently some operators have switched flights to Cape Verde. There is little prospect of the Gambia significantly increasing its international arrivals in a highly competitive market and it is endeavouring to become a year-round destination. There is scope to increase the yield from existing tourism to the Gambia with slightly positive environmental impacts. The intervention with the informal sector in 2000–02 (the DFID project) was designed to increase the earnings of the informal sector from existing tourism to the Gambia – the impact on the environment was broadly neutral, although there was a small increase in wood carving sales, which contributes to tree felling. The 'Gambia is Good' project, described here at greater length, had a positive environmental impact in that it continues to improve agricultural practices and reduces the transport impacts of importing fruit and vegetables.

Through a multistakeholder process, the issues and barriers to access that made it difficult for informal sector traders to engage in the tourism sector were identified and addressed. There were a series of changes in badging, service, craft quality and diversity, and the traders were organised to reduce hassle; relationships within the informal sector and between the formal sector and the informal sector were renegotiated and codes of conduct were established enforced through the informal sector trade associations and backed by the Gambian Tourism Authority. There was no increase in the number of visitors between the two seasons, but year on year the average earnings of the fruit sellers increased by 50 per cent and the juice pressers by 121 per cent. At Kotu Beach the weekly incomes of licensed guides increased by 33 per cent and at Senegambia by 18 per cent. Employment and earnings increased in the Koto Beach and Senegambia craft markets (Bah and Goodwin 2003). The yield from tourism was increased and the beneficiaries of the intervention were from the informal sector.

The Gambia is Good case study secured revenues from the tourism sector in two different ways, both identified as opportunities during the DFID project. In reviewing with the hotels opportunities for greater engagement with the economically poor, fruit and vegetable production emerged as a promising opportunity. The hotels expressed a preference to purchase fresh local produce, but there was no wholesale market that would enable them reliably to secure the volume of fruit and vegetables they require for their kitchens. The issues of quality, volume, continuity of supply and stable pricing are major challenges that need to be addressed if the economically poor in the informal sector are to be enabled to sell successfully to formal sector tourism businesses, supply is generally a bigger challenge than the market when supplying tourism business (Ashley *et al.* 2001: 31).

Gambia is Good

The Gambia is Good initiative is a simple idea, but complex in delivery. Established in 2004, it works to connect economically poor farmers, in Western and North Bank Regions remote from the Tourism Development Area on the coast, with the tourism industry, a market that can be used to raise incomes in rural areas and create small enterprise opportunities. One of the challenges of tourism is to retain value in the destination, to encourage the recirculation of tourism spend in the local economy in order to maximise local economic linkages and to increase the multiplier. The Gambia is Good initiative, which goes by the eloquent and highly marketable acronym of GiG, has very successfully substituted locally grown vegetables for imported ones. The vision was ambitious: 'a catalyst to stimulate a vibrant Gambian fresh produce market that develops local livelihoods, inspires entrepreneurship, and reduces the environmental and social cost of imported produce'. The plan was to achieve this by establishing best practice and to ensure the take up of low coast and appropriate packaging, storing, grading and transportation of fresh produce and to leverage 'technical excellence in horticulture' to improve the livelihoods of the rural poor (Ebrahim *et al.* 2008: 2).

GiG is the result of collaboration between Concern Universal, an international development NGO, and Haygrove a leading UK horticultural business, which seeks by creating an example of a successful small to medium-sized enterprise in the developed world to stimulate progress in the developing world. Initially supported by the UK Department for International Development Business Linkages Challenge Fund, it received £197,000 between June 2003 and June 2006. GiG has also received support from the Travel Foundation. GiG was conceived as a not-for-profit marketing company, a social enterprise designed to assist economically poor famers to engage in commercial horticulture for the hotel and restaurant market in the Tourism Development Area. GiG guarantees to purchase the fruit and vegetables grown to the quality and schedule it provides for the growers at an agreed price, and it takes the risk of market price fluctuations and the costs of transporting the produce to the market. Concern Universal already had a SMILE, Smallholder Irrigation for Livelihood Enhancement, initiative under way. GiG capitalised on this and added to improved irrigation, technical support with seeds and cultivation, the grading of harvests, distribution and marketing.

At the outset it was assumed that the major challenge would be to secure a market. However, as the following tables show, the bigger challenge was supply. Table 37.1 presents data on the sales of fruit and vegetables by weight since 2006 and Table 37.2 by value. These tables show that GiG had to become an importer in order to ensure that it could meet the demand of its customers, 40 hotels and restaurants. GiG supplies 14 of the 25 major hotels, it has ceased to supply two hotels because they were unreliable in paying their invoices. Engagement with the Travel Foundation brought engagement from tour operators who were able to encourage the hoteliers to buy from GiG.

Farmers in the Gambia face many challenges, they have limited access to seeds, fertiliser and irrigation, a tropical climate with a long rainy season, poor access to training and information,

Table 37.1 GiG Produce: Sources by weight in Kg

	GiG Farm produce	Local Farmers	Imports	Imports %	Total
2006	10,162	39,589	67,585	57.6	117,336
2007	23,013	85,083	97,794	47.5	205,890
2008	16,816	90,108	76,156	41.6	183,080
2009	13,606	93,889	84,159	43.9	191,654
2010 to 30 April	4,024	51,216	38,319	41.0	93,559
Total to Date	67,621	359,885	364,013	46.0	791,519

Table 37.2 GiG Produce: Sources by value in dalasi

	GiG Farm produce	Local Farmers	Imports	Imports %	Total
2006	136,565	698,593	1,456,831	63.6	2,291,989
2007	364,448	1,465,728	1,620,592	47.0	3,450,768
2008	285,137	1,787,733	1,373,475	39.9	3,446,345
2009	235,316	2,175,061	2,312,234	49.0	4,722,611
2010 to 30 April	68,817	1,088,158	1,167,384	50.2	2,324,359
Total to Date	1,090,283	7,215,273	7,930,516	48.8	16,236,072

labour-intensive water management, which results in low yields, poor quality and considerable wastage between the farm and the market, which is in any case difficult to access. In the North Bank Region GiG works with mostly male growers who have individual gardens of between 0.5 and 1 hectare, and in the Western Region with community gardens, which will have between 50 and 300 women farmers in each garden.

Given that GiG imports fruit and vegetables to meet peaks of demand or to ensure supplies when production is below the demand of the hotels, it is to be expected that the value of imports is 48.8 per cent of total sales. In 2009 43.9 per cent of sales by weight were imported and 49 per cent by value. As GiG has developed, only those fruit and vegetables that cannot be grown in the Gambia and those that are seasonally unavailable are imported.

GiG has since 2004 worked with more than a thousand small-scale, largely subsistence, farmers, and estimates that it has indirectly benefited 5,000 people in the households engaged in the programme. By working with subsistence farmers and enabling them to grow crops for sale to the hotels, GiG has facilitated their transition to commercial farming on a small scale and without curtailing their household subsistence farming. Ninety per cent of the farmers are women. The earnings from commercial fruit and vegetable production have added to household incomes so that earnings from tourism are providing additional livelihood opportunities. In most rural communities the women farmers have virtually no cash income. Over the last three years GiG producers have increased their earnings fivefold, some are now earning as much as £150 per month in the peak season (Mbaye 2006: 110; World Bank 2007).

Between 2004 and April 2010 GiG has spent 7 million dalasi, approximately £175,000, on 500 tonnes of produce purchased from local farmers. The purchase of locally produced fruit and vegetables benefits economically poor Gambian farmers enabling people living on the north bank of the river to benefit from the tourism economy, which is on the coast on the south bank.

The GiG initiative should not only be evaluated in terms of its contribution to the national economy through import substitution or to the rural economy and poverty reduction, the initiative also affects the lives of those empowered by it:

With CU's help, year round production became a reality. This contributed to an increase of our incomes through more crops but also better prices during rainy season whereby vegetable cropping was considered impossible before. In particular, nursery issues are now a thing of the past thanks to the permanent training carried out in our garden.

(Fatou Manneh, Ndmeban Japichum community garden, Western Division, The Gambia)

Despite my age and my legs, which sometimes give me a hard time, I used to grow local varieties of vegetables in the rainy season for the family. But then I heard through GiG about a new cabbage variety and got hold of some seeds. I decided to nurse those seeds, transplant the seedlings the way I was taught in my small compound garden, and take care of them by myself. Two months later, I harvested three bags of big and beautiful cabbage heads. I sold the product to the Gambia is Good project for a total price of 2,800 Dalasi [£58]. I was really impressed by these results, as before I could not expect to earn so much money. One of the plants I left for my family consumption continued to grow, finally becoming taller than I am; then it flowered and is currently producing seeds that I hope to use in my next production. Next year, I also plan to try out a new sweet pepper variety!

(Jonsoba, 65-year-old lady, Kambong village, Western Division, The Gambia)[1]

Research carried out during the research phase of the informal sector intervention in the Gambia in 2001 found that 62 per cent of tourists interviewed in the tourist hotels would like the opportunity to see crops being grown and agricultural activity. This was not offered in the Gambia, and the existing ground handers were unconvinced of demand for day visit activities featuring visits to farms and the fields.

In 2005 GiG partnered with The Travel Foundation to launch their own farmyard, which is used to train and demonstrate best horticultural practices and to generate additional revenue for GiG through production of the farm, important in ensuring continuity of supply, developing the quality and range of produce and securing an additional income through tourism visits. Since the tourism excursion was introduced in 2006, the farm has had over 3,000 visitors and collected over £10,000 in income (GiG farm records).

GiG has not yet become self-sufficient, it is not yet able to reinvest in itself and has not achieved sustainability as a business. There are potential opportunities to commercially produce juices and dried foods, herbs and preserves, cosmetics, beeswax products and mango rum for direct and indirect sales to tourists.

Neither DFID nor the PPT Partnership was unaware of the negative impacts of tourism, the emphasis was 'less on expanding the overall size of tourism, and more on unlocking opportunities' for the poor. However, PPT had to be integrated with general tourism development because mainstream tourism and tourism planning needed to be influenced by the principles of PPT in order for it to be successful and to have scalable impact; and because the success of PPT depends on a thriving destination: 'pro-poor tourism cannot succeed without successful development of the whole tourism destination' (DFID 1999: 1). From the outset PPT engaged with mainstream tourism and in that it differed markedly from community-based tourism (CBT) and ecotourism (Goodwin 2008a, 2008b; Harrison 2008) PPT is best understood as a potential dimension of all forms of tourism where there is poverty, and there is poverty, a relative concept, in most destinations. PPT is likely to be most successful where engaged with successful destinations and private sector businesses, where addressing local poverty becomes a dimension of master plans, government economic development strategies and private sector initiatives. The sustainability of PPT initiatives is dependent on the success of the sector in particular places and the beneficiary focus.

PPT was not predicated on any assumption that growth in tourism was either desirable or undesirable, PPT sought to unlock opportunities for the poor in, and through, tourism, where tourism was already occurring. Tourism exists and is growing rapidly; the focus of PPT was on yield and net benefits to the poor rather than on growth in arrivals. PPT emphasised that all forms of tourism could be pro-poor and sought to avoid the ghettos of ecotourism and CBT, and the trap of turning to tourism as a development strategy of last resort for the lack of any alternative. PPT can only work where there are tourists (Goodwin 2009). Tourists in destinations are an additional local market for goods and services produced by the economically poor, either directly or indirectly through tourism businesses. The principle of additionality is important to PPT interventions; the fundamental idea was to add a livelihood opportunity to benefit the economically poor, dependency would only result if at the household level other livelihood strategies were abandoned or if tourism development removed livelihood opportunities, for example foraging in a national park, access to marine resources or loss of agricultural land. PPT focused on improving livelihood opportunities, any losses had to be deducted from gains to determine net benefit. There have been many initiatives, only a few have reported on their impacts. There is still a lot to learn about how to increase the yield from existing tourism and to ensure that more of the benefits reach the poor.

Note

1 www.concernuniversal.org/index.php?/gambia_is_good/what_is_being_said_about_gig (accessed 14 September 2010).

References

Ashley, C. (2000) *The Impacts of Tourism on Rural Livelihoods: Namibia's Experience*. Sustainable Livelihoods. Working Paper No. 128. London: ODI.

Ashley, C., Boyd, C. and Goodwin, H. (2000) *Pro-poor Tourism: Putting Poverty at the Heart of the Tourism Agenda*. Natural Resource Perspectives No. 51. London: ODI.

Ashley, C., Roe, D. and Goodwin, H. (2001) *Pro-poor Tourism Strategies: Making Tourism Work for the Poor*. London: ODI, CfRT, IIED, PPTP.

Bah, A. and Goodwin, H. (2003) *Improving Access for the Informal Sector to Tourism in The Gambia* Working Paper 15. London: PPT.

Bennett, O., Roe, D. and Ashley, C. (1999) *Sustainable Tourism and Poverty Elimination Study* London: Deloitte & Touche, IIED and ODI for DFID.

CSD7 (1999) 'Economic sector/major groups: Tourism', *Tourism and Sustainable Development* – (United Nations E/CN.17/1999/L.6).

Department for International Development (DFID) (1999) *Tourism and poverty elimination: untapped potential* London: DFID.

Ebrahim, Z., Hartman, M., Quinn, M. and Schlagenhauf, J. (2008) *Harnessing the potential in The Gambia to foster development through sustainable business*, unpublished.

Goodwin, H. (1998) *Sustainable Tourism and Poverty Elimination, A Discussion Paper for the Department for the Environment*, Faversham: Transport and the Regions and the Department for International Development.

——(2007) 'Measuring and Reporting the Impact of Tourism on Poverty', in Airey, D. and Tribe, J. (eds), *Tourism Research: New Directions, Challenges and Applications*. Elsevier, 63–75.

——(2008a) 'Pro-poor Tourism: a response', *Third World Quarterly* 29 (5), 869–71.

——(2008b) 'Tourism, local economic development, and poverty reduction', *Applied Research in Economic Development* 5 (3) December 2008, 55–64.

——(2009) 'Reflections on 10 years of Pro-Poor Tourism', *Journal of Policy Research in Tourism, Leisure and Events* 1 (1) March 2009, 90–4.

Goodwin, H. and Boekold, H. (2010) 'Beyond Fair Trade – enhancing the livelihoods of coffee farmers in Tanzania', in Jolliffe L. *Coffee Culture, Destinations and Tourism*. Clevedon: Channel View Publications, Chap 12, 181–96.

Harrison, D (2008) 'Pro-poor Tourism: a critique', *Third World Quarterly* 29 (5), 851–68.

Harrison, D. and Schipani, S. (2007) 'Lao Tourism and Poverty Alleviation: Community-Based Tourism and the Private Sector', *Current Issues in Tourism* 10 (2&3), 194–230.

Klassen, S. (2003) *In Search of the Holy Grail: How to Achieve Pro-Poor Growth?* Discussion Paper 96 Ibero-America Institute for Economic Research, Goettingen, Germany.

Mbaye, C.T. (2006) *Contribution à l'étude d'impact du projet maraîcher 'Gambia is Good' sur le revenu des agriculteurs: diagnostic agraire dans la zone centre du North Bank Division en Gambie.* INRA Montpellier https://web.supagro.inra.fr/pmb/opac_css/index.php?lvl=categ_see&id=7426.

Mitchell, J. and Ashley, C. (2010) *Tourism and Poverty Reduction: Pathways to Prosperity.* London: Earthscan.

Saville, N. (2001) *Practical Strategies for Pro-Poor Tourism: Case Study of Pro-Poor Tourism and Snv in Humla Distict, West Nepal,* PPT Working Paper 3, London.

United Nations Development Programme (UNDP) (2009) *The Human Development Index* http://hdrstats.undp.org.

World Bank (2007) *Diagnostic Trade Integration Study for the Integrated Framework for Trade-related Technical Assistance to Least Developed Countries THE GAMBIA: From Entrepôt to Exporter and Eco-tourism.* Washington DC: World Bank.

World Travel and Tourism Council (WTTC) (2010) *Travel & Tourism Economic Impact Gambia,* London: WTTC.

Web resources

www.concern-universal.org

www.haygrove.co.uk/haygrove-development/gambia-is-good/?language=eng

Millennium Development Goals www.un.org/millenniumgoals.

Part 5
Contemporary and future issues

38

Introduction

David Fennell

The aim of this section is to analyse the contemporary and future issues that are of importance to the tourism–environment relationship. From this perspective, tourism scholars have over the past decade begun to delve into important inter-disciplinary themes for the purpose of examining more deeply the entrenched problems that exist in practice. This lateral shift will continue to be important in efforts to better understand very dynamic issues in a richly complex world. The issues have become that much more important because of many imminent global challenges that have a direct effect on the tourism industry. But it is not just these issues that impact tourism. Tourism, because of its magnitude and distribution, contributes its fair share to the global environmental dilemma with which we are now faced.

The first two chapters deal specifically with the issue of climate change. Burns and Bibbings identify many of the fundamental issues related to global warming and the tourism industry. It is here that the reader can gain a full appreciation of the impact of global warming on tourism, as well as the impact of tourism on global warming. Building from this base, Gössling identifies a range of policy directives and decisions that have been formulated to address the climate change problem. Policies discussed include aviation, including emission reduction targets and suggested action in aviation, international shipping, regional climate policy and national climate policy, as well as organisational climate policies. This is followed by climate mitigation strategies in addition to speculation on where we are going in the future.

Hadjikakou, Chenoweth and Miller illustrate the extent to which tourism is a major user of water, and how such use contributes to the impairment of water systems and to water scarcity. In some island states such as Cyprus, tourism is responsible for almost 17 per cent of domestic water use. Water use in many of these tourist destinations is seasonal, with heightened pressure on reserves during peak periods. The authors argue that any figures on water use often mask this reality. As the industry continues to expand, many destinations will experience increased stress if appropriate measures are not taken to make extraction more sustainable. The same can be said of waste in general, and this is the message taken forward by Brown in his chapter on tourism's wasteful ways – a topic that demands a much greater degree of investigation in tourism studies. After providing a conceptual framework for the understanding of waste in tourism, Brown discusses consumption/disposal practices of tourists; waste and tourist behaviour; the policy, regulatory and administrative environment(s) in which the tourism occurs; and the waste management infrastructure that is in place in a given jurisdiction. One of the most sobering conclusions drawn by Brown is the belief that the tourism sector, overall, has been dismal in the planning and management of waste.

Farrelly employs the use of social capital in her work on social entrepreneurship among indigenous communities. In this approach, strategies are developed for the purpose of allowing indigenous people to interact with the global economy on their own terms. In achieving this aim, both indigenous and non-indigenous entrepreneurial value systems are required for socio-ecological as well as financial imperatives. Ecotourism is the type of tourism utilised as the vehicle by which to satisfy these imperatives.

Another form of tourism utilised here as a contemporary issue in tourism, is fair trade in tourism. Kalisch, having been instrumental in the development of this concept in theory and practice, argues that an approach was needed in tourism that focused on the 'equitable partnerships between the industry and local communities, transparency and accountability, equitable negotiation, fair distribution of tourism benefits, such as fair price, support of the local economy, and sustainable use of natural resources'. What is important in this is the testing of the market in regards to consumer confidence of fair trade products. Although fair trade can never fully approach the depth needed to address entrenched human rights and injustice issues, there is the belief that the concept has symbolic value in building confidence in the many stakeholders associated with the tourism industry.

The field of environmental management has in the past decade made a series of innovative strides forward that provide enhanced inter-disciplinary knowledge and understanding on the nature of social and ecological processes and how these are intertwined. Three important concepts in this new knowledge are resiliency, uncertainty and adaptive management. Jamal combines the first two, resiliency and uncertainty, and applies these to many of the most important issues and themes in tourism. As an example, tourism has long been recognised as a resilient industry based on recovery, and Jamal emphasises this through a discussion of climate change, other environmental crises, natural hazards, security and safety, infectious diseases and social inequity. Reducing tourism's vulnerability to various environmental shocks, will require adaptation, mitigation and future-focused management of uncertainty. Plummer, Stone-Jovicich and Bohensky carry this discussion forward through their work on adaptive co-management, a concept that moves away from government to governance and emphasises dynamism, trial and error, self-organisation, a reliance on networks and cross-scale synthesis in novel ways that re-define the manner by which groups work together for common benefit. The authors apply adaptive co-management to the Great Barrier Reef, Australia, for the purposes of investigating and mitigating the many ecological, social, cultural and economic challenges facing this popular resource.

Reference to environmental security and safety briefly addressed by Jamal in this section, is expanded on in Hannam's chapter on environmental security in tourism. Hannam argues that, despite recent attempts, the concept of security is vastly undertheorised in tourism studies. He writes that existing geopolitical systems that have been used for resource exploitation are too dated and will lead not to environmental security and stability, but rather to insecurity and greater international instability. Hannam discusses the challenges of environmental security through a review of the BP oil spill in the Gulf of Mexico. Beyond the significant cost to the environment, the economic impact of the oil spill on tourism in the Gulf region amounts to several billion dollars for a region that relies so heavily on tourism revenue.

The chapters by Buckley and de Vasconcellos Pegas and de Groisbois deal with the concept of corporate social responsibility (CSR). Buckley and de Vasconcellos Pegas argue that, although the literature in the area of CSR is voluminous, in practice CSR is relatively weak within the mainstream tourism industry. Tourism companies level their CSR responsibilities down to the lowest common factor, and some fail to even comply with the most basic standards. This wide-ranging chapter examines many different entities that ought to employ CSR policies and guidelines, including the hotel and transport sector, communities, the ecotourism sector and commercial tourism in protected areas, in addition to social welfare programmes in developing countries, and codes of ethics and certification schemes, all of which may be subsumed under the CSR label. As a complement to this chapter, de Grosbois's work focuses more on the measurement of corporate social performance in tourism. Like Buckley and de Vasconcellos Pegas, de Grosbois argues that tourism companies find it difficult to put into operation CSR initiatives and, just as disturbing, is their inability to fully understand and evaluate the impact of these initiatives.

39

Climate change and tourism

Peter Burns and Lyn Bibbings

Introduction

This chapter will give some insights into global warming, its anthropogenic links, the complexities of media communications, and the relationship between global warming and tourism. It examines the significance of global warming for humankind and highlights the differences between global warming, temperature and weather. In particular, it provides insights into human behaviour aspects that are necessary to translate scientific findings into acts that contribute to resolving the problems being faced by living in a warming world.

Global warming

Global warming in its balanced state is a natural occurrence by which solar energy, in the form of sunrays, strikes planet Earth. Some of this solar energy is reflected and scatters back into space, but about 70 per cent remains and is absorbed into the atmosphere, at the molecular level, by the so-called greenhouse gases (GHG – explained in further detail below). The absorbing and emitting energy creates sufficient warmth on the Earth's surface and in the lower atmosphere to sustain life, that is the 'greenhouse effect'.

The main GHGs are: carbon dioxide (CO_2), nitrous oxide (N_2O), methane (CH_4) and ozone (O_3), although there are others including water (H_2O). As solar energy strikes planet Earth, some of it evaporates water from the oceans, adding the most important GHG, water in its gaseous form (water vapour), which creates clouds, storms and rain. Although GHGs only make up about 1 per cent of Earth's total atmosphere, their capacity to absorb and release energy makes them spectacularly important. Not all GHGs have the same warming effect, nor do they share the same length of time they spend in the atmosphere acting as warming agents (cf. Gillenwater (2010) and Weart (2009) for a historical and technical background).

The greenhouse effect

In understanding global warming it is important to unpick the most commonly used metaphor in these discussions: that of a greenhouse. Warmth or energy from outside enters the garden greenhouse and becomes trapped by the glass panes. The result is a gradual increase in the temperature inside the greenhouse. In particularly cold winters, gardeners cannot rely on energy from the atmosphere, so they have to install heaters (most often electric or kerosene) to raise the temperature. Gardeners who live in a climate with moderate to severe winters understand the value of a greenhouse in providing a warm atmosphere for plants to grow and prosper. Without the artificially warmed atmosphere of the greenhouse, the plants would not survive the winter. Although not perfect, the metaphor works quite well because it is about human intervention in nature: the greenhouse is a result of human action. The greenhouse effect is the metaphor used to describe the way the GHGs regulate the Earth's temperature. The Earth reflects the light and heat received from the sun back into space. Part of the outgoing energy is absorbed by GHGs and re-irradiated back to the Earth, creating the warm atmosphere that sustains life.

The greenhouse effect creates warmth sufficient for biological life, as we know it, to exist. Without it, the Earth's average temperature would be some 30°C colder: too cold to support life. Although most GHGs are natural, since the beginnings of industrialisation and population growth, anthropogenic activity has significantly increased their presence in the atmosphere. It is worth noting at this stage that the twentieth century saw average global temperature increase by about 0.6°C; computer climate models estimate that by 2100 the average global temperature will increase by 1.4°C to 5.8°C (IPCC AR4 2007). The projection was arrived at through a system of scientific scenario planning undertaken by the Intergovernmental Panel on Climate Change (IPCC) called the Special Report on Emissions Scenarios (SRES). The IPCC introduce and describe SRES in the following terms:

> Future greenhouse gas (GHG) emissions are the product of very complex dynamic systems, determined by driving forces such as demographic development, socio-economic development, and technological change. Their future evolution is highly uncertain. Scenarios are alternative images of how the future might unfold and are an appropriate tool with which to analyze how driving forces may influence future emission outcomes and to assess the associated uncertainties. They assist in climate change analysis, including climate modeling and the assessment of impacts, adaptation, and mitigation. The possibility that any single emissions path will occur as described in scenarios is highly uncertain.
>
> (GRID-Arendal n.d.)

Given that these naturally occurring and anthropogenically produced GHGs absorb the sun's energy, higher concentrations of GHGs mean increased absorptive capacity of the atmosphere and thus increased, accelerated global warming, possibly, according to the IPCC, to the extent that patterns of habitation on Earth will be severely disrupted.

At the planetary scale, the increased rate of global warming (as opposed to the entirely natural variations in surface and lower atmosphere temperatures up until the industrial revolution) is cause for concern because the increasing concentrations of GHG in the atmosphere (Ledley *et al.* 1999) are causing the 'global greenhouse' to be too effective. Not enough solar energy is being released back into space but the increased amount of GHG in the atmosphere, due to human activity, especially the reliance on fossil fuels and deforestation, means that increased amounts of solar energy are being absorbed by GHG molecules, in particular CO_2. This is by no means a new idea: 'The increased warming of the Earth's atmosphere due to increased levels of carbon dioxide and other atmospheric gases that, like the glass panels of a greenhouse, let heat in but prevent some of it from going back out' (Schneider 1990: 13).

CO_2 accounts for about 60 per cent of the increased greenhouse effect caused by GHGs (IPCC AR4 2007). Moreover, the level of CO_2 in the atmosphere is increasing by more than

10 per cent every 20 years. If these CO_2 emissions rates are extrapolated, there will be a doubling of CO_2 in the atmosphere from pre-industrial levels by 2100 (ibid.).

As the critical mass of scientists contributing to IPCC increases, and climate changes remain in the spotlight, more sources of GHGs are being uncovered or seen to be more significant than at first thought. For example:

- although aviation emissions are widely discussed, which has resulted in the aviation industry accelerating efforts through technology and handling to reduce emissions, shipping has had a much lower profile and almost escaped criticism. The International Maritime Organization, in their second report on GHG emissions and shipping (2009) estimates that 'ships engaged in international trade in 2007 contributed about 2.7 per cent of the world's anthropogenic CO_2 emissions' (IMO 2009);
- in 2000, scientists in Germany discovered a new GHG called trifluoromethyl sulphur pentafluoride (SF_5CF_3) produced as a by-product in the manufacture of fluorochemicals, mainly oils, greases and waxes), which has been described as 'the most potent GHG measured to date' (Environment News Service 2000);
- a report published in the *New Scientist* describes soot particles (black carbon particulates caused by, inter alia, wood and biomass burning), although fairly easy to control, as being worse for the environment than CO_2 (Hecht 2003).

In an article called 'Climate warning as Siberia melts', Pearce (2005) reported Russian scientists claiming an 'ecological landslide that is probably irreversible and is undoubtedly connected to climatic warming … the entire western Siberian sub-Arctic region has begun to melt [which has] all happened in the last three or four years'. Pearce goes on to claim that 'The sudden melting of a bog the size of France and Germany combined could unleash billions of tonnes of methane, a potent greenhouse gas [which, he says, is 20 times as potent at CO_2], into the atmosphere'.

The increasing greenhouse effect is a real and present danger caused by human intervention through fossil fuel usage, and it is threatening the balance of the atmosphere to an extent that human life and habitats may be altered beyond description. However, rapid and sustained action at both local and global levels together with political will can make inroads: accelerated, unbalanced global warming is not inevitable but is a manageable process requiring courage and willingness to reduce anthropogenic sources of GHG.

Anthropogenic contribution to global warming

Accelerated global warming, of the type identified by the IPCC as problematic, is highly likely to be caused by increases in GHGs attributed to pollution through human activity, especially the burning of fossil fuels. In addition to naturally occurring GHGs, some anthropogenic GHGs have been added to the atmosphere (cf. Gillenwater 2010).

Ledley *et al.* (1999) were among many to identify the industrial era as being the tipping point for the acceleration of heat-trapping emissions thus placing anthropogenic emissions generating activity in the limelight (cf. Donnellan 2005: 4). Stern (2006: 2) indicates that the problem is worsening 'the annual flow of emissions is accelerating, as fast-growing economies invest in high-carbon infrastructures and as demand for energy and transport increases around the world'. Such factors and activities include:

- burning natural gas, coal and oil (including maritime bunker fuel), internal combustion engines emitting CO_2, soot particles and other pollutants;

- intensive livestock farming, especially cattle farming, adds methane (CH_4), which is released as a normal part of the livestock digestive process;
- industrial gases from factories, a problem that started in the industrialised developed world (the 'global north') but which has now been transferred to the transitional industrialising countries of the global south and China;
- deforestation and land disturbance including the destruction of wetlands, tundra, heaths and bogs. Deforestation of virgin rainforest for agriculture (intensive monocrops, cattle ranching) or living space for increasing populations disturbs the equilibrium. Deforestation also disrupts water cycles. Moreover, the rotting or burning of felled trees releases the CO_2 locked in them (through photosynthesis) back into the atmosphere so that forests turn from a carbon sink (i.e. absorbing CO_2) into a GHG pollutant;
- population growth and urbanisation produces such intensive pressure on the natural environment that one school of thought describes birth control on a massive global scale as the most effective way of reducing emissions (cf. Webster 2009).

The consequences of accelerated global warming

Global warming is what enables biological life to exist on Earth and warming and cooling cycles are natural to the planet. What has changed in the twenty-first century is, first, that we are becoming aware that 'something is wrong'. Second, that there is a general willingness to accept that increased GHGs have an anthropogenic cause and, third, there is a recognition that 'something must be done' to reduce the impact of the effects this has on climate, sea levels, availability of fresh water and temperature rises that may make some parts of the world uninhabitable. The 4th Assessment Report of the IPCC (IPCC AR4 2007) noted that by 2100 global average surface temperatures will rise by between 1.1°C and 6.4°C. Although confidence levels about the mechanisms for these projections have increased, uncertainties remain. The level of future emissions and GHGs, their net warming effect in the atmosphere, and the way in which the Earth's climate system responds still requires caution. Even so, IPCC AR4 specifically stated that the Earth's average surface temperature is likely to increase by 1.1–6.4°C by the end of the twenty-first century relative to 1980–90, with a best estimate of 1.8–4.0°C. The average rate of warming over each inhabited continent is very likely to be at least twice as large as that experienced during the twentieth century. Moreover, IPCC AR4 concluded that warming would not be evenly distributed around the globe because, for example, water's ability to store heat means that land areas will warm more than oceans. Africa, Europe, northern and central parts of Asia, Central and South America, and the whole of North America are likely to experience more than the global average growth in warmth.

IPCC AR4 suggest that the warming will be close to the global average in southern Asia, Australia and New Zealand, and southern South America. Seasonal differences in warming will occur, with winters warming more than summers in most areas. However, even small increases in global average temperatures lead to significant climate and weather perturbations including cloud cover, precipitation and wind patterns, the frequency and intensity of storms, and established seasonal weather patterns.

The IPCC AR4 identifies a number of other direct and indirect consequences that may occur from global warming:

- disruption of traditional agricultural methods, as water ecosystems can no longer rely on seasonal runoff from glaciers and mountain because snow-caps have reduced in size. This makes communities who depend on a nomadic pattern, or subsistence farming particularly vulnerable;

- increased vulnerability of coastal and small island systems as the polar ice caps melt. Sea levels have risen about 17 cm in the twentieth century and may continue to rise from between 18 and 59 cm. Sea level rises have the effect of altering water tables and reducing availability of fresh water – already a stress problem in many areas of the world;
- more exceptional weather events such as droughts, heat waves, floods and severe storms with regional precipitation increases and decreases of typically 5–20 per cent of annual average rainfall;
- increased vulnerability of agricultural ecosystems as weather and seasonal changes impact on agricultural practices and confound local knowledge;
- coral reef bleaching caused by acidifying oceans, which creates stress on marine ecosystems and breeding and feeding grounds;
- vector-borne infectious diseases like malaria may become more widespread and expand their range northward as temperatures increase;
- increased stress and potential extinction of vulnerable species as natural habitats change in response to a changing climate.

Beyond 2100, if global warming is not stabilised, it will become more likely that major changes in the climate system will occur, such as alteration of North Atlantic Circulation system or collapse of the West Antarctic Ice Sheet (IPCC 2001b). A recently identified phenomenon (discovered, *inter alia*, by Beate Liepert in 2005) is 'global dimming', which is linked to Atmospheric Brown Clouds (ABCs) and solar radiation (Ramanathan 2007). The increased presence of aerosol particles (i.e. the suspension of fine solid particles or liquid droplets in a gas) in the atmosphere (via ABCs) is said to be bouncing sunlight back into space giving rise to regionally concentrated surface dimming and atmospheric solar heating (ibid.). This reflection of sunlight could severely disrupt global climate through effects such as delay of the Indian monsoons (Wetter-Klimawandel 2007).

With this complex array of information sources, emerging data, new climate phenomena, contradictory political messages and obscure science, clarity in communicating the climate change and global warming messages is of fundamental importance in improving responses needed to alleviate and mitigate causes and effects of anthropogenic behaviour.

Communicating global warming and climate change messages

Alarmist media stories about catastrophic scenarios in relation to global warming seem to have completely contradictory effects. On the one hand citizens and governments feel compelled to take action, and yet, on the other, the problem seems so ubiquitous, so immense that there seems little to be done apart from hand-wringing, denial or feeling angst. There is little idea of what actions may be taken as policy options appear unacceptable to citizens, which may include, for example, challenging the consensus on twenty-first century capitalist modes of production and consumption.

This highlights a further challenge for both scientists and governments: to create a clear understanding of global warming and to communicate unambiguous messages that do not produce alarmist responses. Longitudinal climate observations, both proxy and measured, when compared chronologically against economic history, and in particular the industrial revolution, support the conclusion that accelerated global warming is caused, as already mentioned, by human action. Page (2005: 6) argues that anthropogenic climate change has a long history citing John Tyndall, who wrote: 'In 1863 … first posited the possibility that small changes in the atmospheric concentration of CO_2 due to industrial activities could cause global temperatures to increase'. However, it is only relatively recently that the general public have been able to observe for themselves repeated, unusual and dramatic weather events such as hurricanes, flooding and record hot summers, which has raised their awareness and given tangible evidence of climate change.

The scientific discourse on global warming and climate change, especially IPCC AR4 (2007) has generated an avalanche of information. However, confusion rather than consistency was created in the public mind about the significance of global warming. One reason for this has been the muddling of terminology used by the print, broadcast and electronic media. Three things need to be made clear about the official discourse and terminology. First, that global warming is not the same as climate change. Second, climate and temperature is not the same thing, and, third, as alluded to above, climate and weather mean different things. Page's analysis (2005) indicates inappropriate merging of global warming and climate change terminology.

Climate change refers to long-term changes in climate and average temperature, and is a particular facet of global warming. Temperature is a 'state of atmosphere in a given place at a given time … for a specific area of the Earth's surface', whereas climate describes 'the prevailing condition of the atmosphere deduced from long periods of observation' (Gomez Martin 2005: 572). The IPCC (2001a) argues that the term 'climate' is more general and addresses a longer time interval, whereas 'weather' describes a particular period of time. As the time scale plays a significant role in the determination between both expressions, Page, in discussing the work of Stehr and von Storch (1995), notes that weather 'influences decisions and actions on a daily basis [whereas climate] does not influence society with anything close to the same immediacy' (Page 2005: 6).

This confusion in the significance of different terminology in the global warming debate leads to misunderstanding and misperceptions about the impact of climate change. The differentiation between climate and temperature is of enormous importance in understanding the severity of the core problem. The rhetoric of technical terms like global warming, greenhouse effect and climate change, are sometimes problematic in that they can be associated with 'warm is good', 'greenhouses grow beautiful plants' and 'change is good'. In order to drive the message home, Page (2005: 9) suggests that terms like 'human climate disruption' would be more effective to use in climate terminology and discourse.

The role of the media

Effective communication of scientific findings and discourse can contribute to beneficial behavioural changes by individuals, communities and other group responses to climate change issues. Generally speaking, it is not scientists or politicians who will influence individual behaviour directly, but rather newspapers, television, radio and the internet, including social networking. In this sense, scientists, politicians and the public are all, in different ways, dependent on the media to generate discussion and response. However, the range of information is not only very diverse in terms of tone and rhetoric, from sombre to strident to dismissive, but, more problematically, inconsistent.

Boykoff and Boykoff (2007) undertook a content analysis of climate change media coverage of the principal US newspaper articles and television between 1989 and 2004. Their study revealed that journalistic norms were repeatedly violated. Scientific findings, usually expressed in probabilities, were downplayed or dramatised in order to reinforce the established position of the news outlet, thus creating misunderstanding and confusion. Boykoff and Boykoff's (2007) work highlights the power of media in the social construction of climate change perceptions.

Ereaut and Segnit (2007: 6) undertook similar research, using similar methods, in the UK. They also found an 'uncertain and contrary field of climate change', and further identified major players who influence the public domain. By categorising media into major groups, Ereaut and Segnit (2007: 20) analysed how communication of climate change, between March and July 2007, could be improved and how language could be utilised in order to change public behaviour in relation to climate change. According to their research, information from serious sources, such as the IPCC, did not gain sufficiently nuanced attention from the media because their findings were expressed in 'dry' scientific language not considered media-friendly. Ereaut and Segnit (2007) reported a shift towards rhetorical consensus on climate change resulting from a reinvestment in language, more serious rhetoric and a move away from hyperbolic alarmism. Measured discussion in the media about the problems of global warming is helpful as it encourages people to take action and control rather than generating despair and helplessness. However, this fragile and apparent consensus of sensible discourse was temporarily disrupted by the 'Climategate' affair when leaked emails from the University of East Anglia seemed, at first glance, to indicate that scientists were compromising their data to reinforce their pro-climate change stance.

Page's (2005) investigation into the social construction of global warming highlights the need for specific rhetorical approaches by the media in order to involve people in climate change actions. He claims that using the right social construction 'even for large issues such as global warming, might be a simple and possible indirect process utilizing the correct rhetoric at the correct time to trigger specific collective response in the social world' (Page 2005: 5). Moreover, he identifies how behavioural changes that act against global warming can be encouraged. His main finding was that resistance to change is directly linked to differences in an individual's values, attitudes and behaviour. So, if media rhetoric can demonstrate that certain consumptive behaviours are out of line with the values and attitudes of social responsible and caring individuals then cognitive dissonance can be generated. Then individuals can be helped to resolve this dissonance by the media giving guidance on behaviours coherent with those values and attitudes that are most likely to result in mitigating climate change problems. Unfortunately, this process has also been subjected to some corruption by a lack of information on appropriate coherent behaviour in the media and by companies promoting the use of carbon offsets as a simple way of 'paying' your way out of having to change behaviour.

It can be seen that the complex field of climate change is vulnerable to confusion; therefore, a clear and consistent communication structure can help minimise misconceptions.

Ereaut and Segnit (2007) argue that 'by harnessing the latent power of locality, interested organisations could begin to close the gap between the official consensus on climate change and the public's willingness to do something about it'. In a small group the feeling of having the power to act and to achieve changes becomes more accessible and achievements are rather visible, therefore acting physically in a community can have a major impact on a behavioural change. The implications of the relationship between media and climate change are captured in Figure 39.1

Impact of global warming on tourism

Tourism comprises a set of industries that heavily rely on natural resources as part of the core product. Tourists are mobilised from their home environments to destinations, in effect the flows and 'scapes of tourism, where they consume local resources. Global warming has caused tourism's future to come under scrutiny, with the World Travel and Tourism Council and UNWTO both suggesting continued global growth in tourism (although both organisations recognise the need for an emergent carbon-neutral approach). Dubois and Ceron (2006: 18) suggest that transportation presents the most significant contributor of tourism's GHG emissions. Viner and Agnew

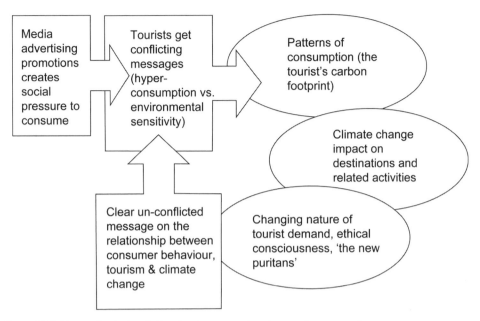

Figure 39.1 Dynamic circle of climate change on tourism and consumption

(1999: 1) argue that there are direct impacts on tourism, such as a shift away from destinations because of increased humidity or mean temperature, and indirect impacts like, for example, the reduction of air quality because of photochemical smog, which will threaten tourism activities. Modern mobility, freedom of choice and rapid spread of information through digital and terrestrial platforms make destinations particularly vulnerable: tourists will simply go elsewhere.

The UNWTO (2007a: 13) reiterate the rather obvious but important point that tourism is largely reliant on dependent, predictable weather patterns and climate, 'With its close connections to the environment and climate itself, tourism is considered to be a highly climate-sensitive economic sector'. Thus, if climate at destinations does not fulfil the expected conditions, tourist demand will simply shift or disappear completely. Burns and Bibbings (2007: 8) highlight Frangialli's point (2005: 19) that 'Favourable climatic conditions at destinations are key attractions for tourists. It is especially true for beach destinations and conventional sun-and-sea segment, which is still the dominating form of tourism'. Stern (2006: 14) on the other hand reveals that an increase of temperature might have quite positive benefits for tourism in destinations at higher latitude regions. These used to be the actual generating regions that may then shift towards becoming new attractive destinations with short winters and pleasant weather conditions. The close relationship between tourism and climate change can therefore be noticeable in both directions, an increase in temperature can thus either downsize tourist arrivals or attract them depending on the destination. The perception on the dependency between tourism and climate change is a precondition in order to adapt demand patterns and achieve changes. Tourism, as a globally significant multisectored industry, is intricately dependant on climate and the environment (Viner and Agnew 1999: 1). As changes in climate caused by global warming occur, with IPCC predicting severe impacts, tourism itself is likely to be obliged to change in response. This response is, however, inter-twined with consumer attitudes and corporate responsibility. Anable *et al.* (2006: 9) note that 'knowledge and attitudes about climate change or environmental issues often fail to be translated into changes in travel behaviour to mitigate its effects'. She calls it the 'attitude-behaviour gap' and argues that if changes in travel behaviour are to be achieved then attitudes and behaviour need to converge.

Climate – in the form of daily weather, extreme events or gradual changes – impacts on tourism both directly and indirectly. Directly, climate variability and changing weather patterns can affect the planning of tourism programmes and daily operations. Changing weather patterns at tourist destinations and in tourism-generating countries can largely affect tourists' comfort, their decisions on trips and, eventually, the tourist flow. For example, a warmer summer in Europe can reduce the motivations of tourists in northern countries to visit the Mediterranean coasts, which can be excessively hot in summertime, and destinations closer to their homes can become more attractive. Adverse conditions may not only impact on tourists' experience, but also on their health and safety. Extreme climatic events, such as cyclones and hurricanes, or flooding can damage physically the tourism infrastructure and pose a great risk for the safety of both tourists and host communities. Tourist destinations affected by major climate-related hazards can greatly suffer from secondary effects, such as economic impacts at local businesses, or negative image in the media.

Indirectly, climate change can have a significant impact on tourism activities by altering the natural environment that represents both a key attraction and basic resources for tourism. Examples of negative impacts are coastal erosion, damage to coral reefs and other sensitive and biodiversity-rich ecosystems, or insufficient snow coverage at winter sports destinations in mountain areas. Problems with water supply affect a wide range of destinations, especially considering that in many of them the high tourist season and increased demand for water coincides with dry periods and reduced water supply capacities.

Changing climatic conditions might negatively impact certain tourism activities and destinations, but climate change might also bring some opportunities, and it can induce the re-structuring of both tourism demand and supply patterns. For example, extremely hot temperatures in the main seasons of seaside tourism destinations might reduce tourist motivation to travel, but could increase visitations in shoulder seasons, or in warmer winter periods. This could also divert tourists to more inland and higher altitude coastal areas with cooler temperatures. In mountain regions, it seems very probable that demand for winter tourism activities will be affected, due to changing snow conditions (diminishing precipitation and snow-reliability, especially at lower altitudes). The season will probably shorten, opportunities for beginners to learn the sports on lower-lying slopes will diminish and demand pressures on high-altitude resorts will increase, which in turn could raise environmental pressures and cause further damage. Summer seasons in mountain regions, meanwhile, could lengthen and generate increased demand, although this could bring further environmental impacts. The balance of costs and benefits can be illustrated by the situation in the Arctic, where a longer summer season might benefit cruise tourism and activities such as whale watching, but shorter winters could reduce the range of Arctic fauna and flora, which attracts some visitors.

Whatever the environmental outcome, tourism cannot be seen in isolation. Major changes in the pattern of demand will lead to wider impacts on many areas of economic and social policy – such as, for example, in employment and labour demand and in regional policy issues such as housing, transport and social infrastructure. Knock-on effects could influence other sectors, such as agriculture supplying tourism demand, handicraft industries, local small business networks and so on.

Climatic conditions are dynamically changing, posing new risks to tourism operations, and the tourism sector needs to develop its capacity to adapt in order to maintain its viability, to continue generating the socio-economic benefits for the host communities and to provide quality experiences for tourists.

Climate change will lead to major impacts on biodiversity and ecosystem services, which has already been recorded on every continent (UNWTO 2007b), on economic activities and on human health and welfare, including the loss of life and forced migration, with associated implications for international equity. Watkiss *et al.* (2005) mention effects on energy use due to the increase in temperature, including heating and cooling as well as effects on agriculture. In addition, effects to human health from changes in cold and heat-related effects, as well as from the disease burden will occur. Water resources, water supply and water quality are threatened, too, and therefore also have to be considered in the context of tourism consumption as tourists consume far more water than local residents in tourism destinations, as stated in the Djerba Declaration (UNWTO 2003). Furthermore, resulting water stress is likely to arise within areas that already suffer from inherent water shortages. Moreover, Watkiss *et al.* (2005) suggest that global warming effects are likely to be greatest at high latitudes and most evident in the autumn and winter seasons, although the equatorial regions will also experience noticeable warming. In general, wetter weather is to be expected in the mid-latitudes, with drier weather in the sub-tropics, thus challenging long-established patterns of weather-dependent tourism and seasonal activities.

Most of the effects mentioned above are inter-related. Negative impacts on unique or threatened systems and risks from extreme climate events occur with a temperature change of 1°C, and these impacts and risks are projected to become significant for changes of 2–3°C. Above a 2°C global temperature increase, the majority of market impacts are predicted to be negative and most regions will suffer adverse affects from climate change. Risks from large-scale discontinuities become significant above a temperature change of 3°C (Watkiss *et al.* 2005). Changes to the tourism potential of destinations can occur, as tourism is very climate-sensitive (Viner 2005).

Impact of tourism on global warming

Over the past decade or so, the big change for tourism has been the shift from how economists have traditionally seen it (an activity dependent on disposable income) to a far more nuanced description of tourism being embedded in twenty-first century society as a cross-cutting societal theme shaping society at large (Franklin 2003). Moreover, global warming and climate change cannot simply be read as scientific phenomena that have scientific solutions: the problems are social and so are the solutions. In the case of tourism, the potent mix of politics, culture and questions of social identity raises important, if somewhat understated issues for the present volume and its concern with a rapidly changing world. Just like globalisation, tourism is a set of cultural, economic and political phenomena, its meanings and applications loaded with ambiguities and uncertainties (Franklin and Crang 2001). For the developing world, it is equally embedded in the economies of most of the less developed countries where it is the primary source of foreign exchange earnings in 46 of the 49 Least Developed Countries. Another fuzzy aspect to tourism is that it is characterised by considerable fragmentation and dominance of small and medium-sized enterprises (SMEs) and micro-enterprises. It is further characterised by a high number of sub-sectors including transportation (airlines, shipping, rail, motor vehicles), accommodation of various sorts and sizes, hospitality services ranging from laundries to bars, travel agents, tour operators, attractions and events, casinos, tourist-oriented retail services and entities that may not even recognise that they are in the tourist business such as sporting events, museums and galleries. Capturing data for such a large number of sub-sectors, especially when they slip between easy categorisation in national industrial databases, is extremely difficult and has led to a lack of reliable overarching data about the tourism 'industry' as a whole.

However, one major attempt was made by UNWTO and UNEP to calculate tourism's direct impact on global emissions using 2005 as the base year.

It can be seen then that tourism's role in global warming is complex from scientific, social and sector viewpoints. In trying to attain some clarity, the UNWTO (2007: 4) notes that 'the tourism sector is a non-negligible contributor to climate change through GHG emissions derived especially from the transport and accommodation of tourists'. The organisation furthermore argues that 'tourism emissions from three main sub-sectors (transportation, accommodation and attractions) are estimated to represent between 4.0% and 6.0% of global emissions in 2005' and reveals 'that in 2005 transport generated the largest proportion of CO_2 emissions (75%) from global tourism, with approximately 40% of the total being caused by air transport alone' (UNWTO 2007: 13). More specifically, in discussing the UNWTO/UNEP (2008) data sets from the 2005 baseline, they went on to explain:

> The analysis also showed that emissions can vary greatly per tourist trip, between a few kilograms of CO_2 up to 9t CO_2 for long-distance, cruise-based journeys. A globally averaged tourist journey is estimated to generate 0.25t of CO_2 emissions. A small share of tourist trips, however, emits much more than this: while the aviation based trips account for 17% of all tourism trips, they cause about 40% of CO_2 emissions from tourism. Long-haul travel by air between the five UNWTO world tourism regions represents only 2.2% of all tourist trips, but contributes 16% to global tourism-related CO_2 emissions. In contrast, international tourist trips (i.e., overnight tourist trips) by coach and rail, which account for an estimated 16% of international tourist trips, stand only for 1% of CO_2 emissions generated by all international tourist trips (transport emissions only).
>
> (UNWTO/UNEP 2008: 34)

However, this only profiles direct responsibility for emissions. If the same calculations are used to profile emissions by the size of the tourism economy, that is the mechanisms used by UNWTO and WTTC to arrive at the conclusion that tourism is the world's largest industry (as used in the heavily promoted tourism satellite accounts system), then tourism's contribution should be counted as at least double the 4–6 per cent range claimed by industry proponents. Hall and Higham (2005: 9), in a brief summary of these claims, note that 'the travel and tourism economy is expected to total 10.4% of the world economy and total 73.7 million jobs or 2.8% of total

Table 39.1 Estimated emissions from global tourism (including same-day visitors), 2005(a)

Source	Metric Tonne CO_2 equivalent	% From Tourism
Air Transport	515	39.6
Car	420	32.3
Other Transport	45	3.5
Accommodation	274	21.0
Activities	45	3.5
TOTAL	1,302	100
Total world emissions	26,400	
Tourism's share of global total		4.95

Note: (a) Estimates include international and domestic tourist trips, as well as same-day visitors (base year 2005).
Source: adapted from UNWTO/ UNEP (2008: 34)

employment'. The discrepancy between the economic and social necessity of tourism, and the required change in global travel behaviour has created a particularly difficult contradiction.

Conclusions

The principle of 'the polluter pays' gives rise to an understanding that further efforts should be devoted to environmentally sustainable tourism by all concerned, and especially by the tourism industry itself. Although concerns about tourism's polluting effects cover all aspects of a tourist's activity, the primary issue concerning climate change factors relates the GHG emissions generated through travellers' consumption of transport services, notably road and air transport, and energy consumption in tourism establishments from air conditioning, heating and lighting. In the wider area of sustainability, tourism's high per capita consumption of water, energy, waste generation and the effects that tourism has on flora and fauna should be considered. The tourism sector has a responsibility to minimise harmful emissions by encouraging sustainable, carbon-neutral transport solutions, improving the efficiency of the use of natural resources, in particular, water, and contributing to the conservation of natural areas. Minimising environmental impacts of tourism on natural areas can enhance the resilience of ecosystems, which serve as natural protective barriers to climate impacts, for example reefs and mangroves protect coasts from waves, and storm surges.

Given that destination stability is a non-negotiable foundation for successful tourism, however, global warming and the resultant climate change is having an impact on political stability and food and water security. Climate change is also changing the way in which tourism is organised through companies, managed at destinations and consumed by tourists. These changes are shaping global politics, influencing economies and altering everyday lives.

The model of carbon-intensive tourism growth, consumption and production developed during the post-war period of relatively cheap oil is now under the microscope. The consequence of tourism continuing with the 'business-as-usual' scenario envisaged by the IPCC is an unacceptable increase in contributions to carbon emissions by all sectors along the tourism supply chain, making global reduction targets harder to achieve. The drive must now be to decouple growth from increased GHG emissions.

Increased awareness about environmental issues is also a driver for industry change as consumers become increasingly conscious of the need to shift their lifestyle towards low-carbon living. Burns and Bibbings (2007: 18), argue that 'The making and consuming of tourism takes place within a complex social milieu whereby culture and people become part of the commercial product'. As tourism is embedded in society and cannot be removed or decoupled from it, ways must be found for tourism to reduce its threat to the environment. This can, however, only happen when attitudes, behaviour and patterns of reporting, producing and consuming travel, and tourism goods and services in the light of global warming are changed.

The fragmented and global nature of the sector, comprising some 80 per cent SMEs and micro-enterprises, means that the main challenge for tourism lies in generating a cohesive response to the challenges of living and working in a low-carbon economy. In particular, the size and nature of the sector put it into the spotlight for criticism by the media and some environmental and green consumer groups.

Favourable climatic conditions at destinations are key attractions for tourists. It is especially true for beach destinations and the conventional sun-and-sea segment, which is still the dominant form of tourism. For example, tourists are attracted to the Mediterranean coast and to tropical islands by ample sunshine, warm temperatures and little precipitation, escaping from harsher weather conditions and seasons in their home countries. Other forms of tourism, such as mountain tourism and winter sports are also highly dependent on favourable climate and weather conditions, such as adequate precipitation and snow levels. In general, for all forms of tourism activities taking place outdoors, accurate climate and weather information is key for the planning and carrying out of trips and programmes. Tourism forms, as mentioned above, the backbone of the economy in many local communities worldwide, and inadequate climatic conditions can seriously harm tourism operations and the host communities that depend on them.

However, there remain areas of concern. The most significant of these is air transport, which, if dramatically reduced in response to mitigation demands in the developed world will have equally dramatic changes in the tourist-dependent economies of the global south and thus potentially have a direct negative impact on the livelihoods of the bottom billion.

In a sense, what happens if the 'stop flying' agenda comes to fruition is a question of such magnitude that it becomes the elephant in the room: a problem too big to deal with and almost too complex to comprehend. Either way, it is the poor who will pay through decreased resilience and increased vulnerability through lost livelihoods presently created by direct, indirect and induced tourist expenditure.

The reality of global warming, however, is that the bundle of benefits brought about by established patterns of sun, sand and sea can readily be substituted by destinations nearer to the main tourist-generating conurbations (more or less 'old' Europe, North America and developed Asia) – especially if touristic destinations in the north (with limited weather seasons at present) become warmer. Emerging travel patterns from BRIC countries are, as yet, unclear, although some evidence seems to indicate that the Chinese, for example, want to follow familiar leisure tourism patterns established through conventional Western capitalism (even if the travel routes and flows may differ). Incidentally, there is much more to be said about the sheer magnitude of Chinese outbound growth patterns (especially when linked to unfulfilled, latent demand from other BRIC countries) impacting the entire twentieth-century tourism paradigm that still dominates world travel. However, such a discussion, although needing to be flagged up as an issue at this stage, needs time and space to develop outside the parameters of the present chapter.

Acknowledgement

Sincere thanks to Tanja Keim for assisting with the literature review as part of her Masters thesis at the Centre for Tourism Policy Studies, University of Brighton.

References

Anable, J., Lane, B. and Kelay, T. (2006) *Review of public attitudes to climate change and transport: Summary report*. The Department of Transport.

Boykoff, M.T. and Boykoff, J.M. (2007) 'Climate change and journalistic norms: A case-study of US mass-media coverage'. *Geoforum* 38(6), 1190–204.

Burns, P. and Bibbings, L. (2007) 'Policy Dialogue on Tourism Transport and Climate Change: Stakeholders meet Researchers,' *Paper published for the E-CLAT Technical Seminar*. Paris: Oxford Brookes University.

Donnellan, C. (ed.) (2005) *The Climate Crisis*. Cambridge: Independance.

Dubois, G. and Ceron, J.-P. (2006) 'Tourism and Climate Change: Proposal for a Research Agenda'. *Journal of Sustainable Tourism* 14(4), 2006.

Environment News Service (2000) 'Potent New Greenhouse Gas Discovered', available at: www.ens-newswire.com/ens/jul2000/2000-07-31-02.asp.

Ereaut, G. and Segnit, N. (2007) 'Warm Words II: How the climate story is evolving and the lessons we can learn for encouraging public action'. London. Available at: www.ippr.org/publicationsandreports/publication.asp?id=561 (accessed 26 April 2008).

Franklin, A. (2003) *Tourism: an introduction*. Sage: London.

Franklin A. and Crang M. (2001) 'The trouble with tourism and travel theory?' *Tourist Studies* 1(1), 5–22.

Frangialli, F. (2005) 'Secretary General, UN World Tourism Organisation at the technical conference of climate as a resource for tourism (Beijing 1–2 November)', in Burns, P. and Bibbings, L. 'The End of Tourism' unpublished paper for E-Clat.

Gillenwater, M. (2010) *What are Greenhouse Gases? Greenhouse Gas Management Institute.* Available at: http://ghginstitute.org/2010/06/15/what-are-greenhouse-gases/ (accessed 21 September 2010).

Gomez Martin, M.B. (2005) 'Weather, Climate and Tourism: A geographical Perspective'. *Annals of Tourism* 32(3), 571–91.

GRID-Arendal (n.d.) 'What are scenarios and what is their purpose?', *IPCC Special Reports on Climate Change – Complete online versions*. www.grida.no/publications/other/ipcc_sr/?src=/climate/ipcc/emission/

Hall, C.M. and Higham, J. (eds) (2005) *Tourism, Recreation and Climate Change.* Clevedon: Channel View Publications.

Hecht, J. (2003) *Soot Worse for Global Warming than Thought. New Scientist* www.newscientist.com/article/dn4508-soot-worse-for-global-warming-than-thought.html.

IPCC (2001a) 'Introduction to the Climate System'. Cambridge and New York. Available at: www.ipcc.ch/ipccreports/tar/wg1/039.htm#111 (accessed 6 January 2010).

——(2001b) '*Climate Change 2001: Impacts, Adaptation and Vulnerability*'. Geneva: United Nations Intergovernmental Panel on Climate Change

IPCC AR4 (2007) *Climate Change 2007 Synthesis Report.* Geneva: IPCC www.ipcc.ch/publications_and_data/publications_ipcc_fourth_assessment_report_synthesis_report.htm (accessed 9 February 2010).

International Maritime Organization (2009) 'Second IMO GHG Study 2009'. www.imo.org/ourwork/environment/pollutionprevention/airpollution/documents/ghgstudyfinal.pdf.

Ledley, T.S., Sundquist, E.T., Schwartz, S.E., Hall, D.K., Fellows, J.D. and Killeen, T.L. (1999) 'Climate Change and Greenhouse Gases'. *Eos* 80(39), 453.

Page, M. (2005) 'Shall We Call It Global Warming, Climate Variability or Human Climate Disruption?' Berlin. Available at: http://web.fu-berlin.de/ffu/akumwelt/bc2005/papers/page_bc2005.pdf (accessed 5 January 2008).

Pearce, F. (2005) 'Climate warning as Siberia melts'. *New Scientist* 2512. www.newscientist.com/article/mg18725124.500 (accessed 24 September 2010).

Ramanathan, V. (2007) 'Global Dimming by Air Pollution and Global Warming by Greenhouse Gases: Global and Regional Perspectives', *Nucleation and Atmospheric Aerosols* Part V, 273–483.

Schneider, S.H. (1990) *Global Warming: Are we entering the Greenhouse Century?* Cambridge: The Lutterworth Press.

Stehr, N. and von Storch, H. (1995) 'Climate Research' 5, 99–105, in Page, M. (2005) 'Shall We Call It Global Warming, Climate Variability or Human Climate Disruption?' Berlin. Available at: http://web.fu-berlin.de/ffu/akumwelt/bc2005/papers/page_bc2005.pdf (accessed 5 January 2008).

Stern, N. (2006). *The Economics of Climate Change: The Stern Review.* Cambridge: Cambridge University Press.

Tourism Concern (2008). *Homepage.* Available at: www.tourismconcern.org.uk/ (accessed 4 May 2008).

UNWTO (2003). 'Djerba Declaration on Tourism and Climate Change' Djerba. Available at: www.unwto.org/sustainable/climate/decdjerba-eng.pdf (accessed 29 March 2009).

——(2007a) 'Second International Conference on Climate Change and Tourism – Davos Declaration'. Switzerland. Available at: www.unwto.org/pdf/pr071046.pdf (accessed 29 March 2008).

——(2007b) 'Climate Change and Tourism – Responding to Global Challenges. Advanced Summary'. Switzerland. Available at: www.unwto.org/media/news/en/pdf/davos_rep_advan_summ_26_09.pdf (accessed 30 October 2010).

UNWTO/UNEP (2008) 'Climate Change and Tourism: Responding to Global Challenges'. Madrid and Paris: UNWTO and UNEP joint publication.

Viner, D. (2005) ECLAT – das wissenschaftliche Netzwerk rund um Klimawandel, Umwelt und Tourismus'. *Integra* 2/05, 9–10.

Viner, D. and Agnew, M. (1999) 'Climate Change and Its Impacts on Tourism' Norwich. Available at: www.wwf.org.uk/filelibrary/pdf/tourism_and_cc_full.pdf (accessed 1 March 2009).

Watkiss, P., Downing, T., Handley, C. and Butterfield, R. (2005) 'The impacts and costs of climate change'. Oxford. Available at: http://ec.europa.eu/environment /climat/pdf/final_report2.pdf (accessed 10 December 2007).

Weart, S. (2009) *The Discovery of Global Warming' American Institute for Physics.* Available at: www.aip.org/history/climate/co2.htm (accessed 21 September 2010).

Webster, B. (2009) 'Birth Control: the most effective way of reducing greenhouse gas emissions'. *The Times*. www.timesonline.co.uk/tol/news/environment/article6922245.ece (accessed 23 September 2010).

Wetter-Klimawandel (2007) 'Global Dimming – Die globale Verdunkelung'. Available at: www.wetter-klimawandel.de/global-dimming.php (accessed 24 February 2008).

Further reading

DWD (Deutscher Wetterdienst) (2007) 'Wärmster Winter aller Zeiten'. Press release 27 February 2007. Germany. Available at: www.dwd.de (accessed 28 March 2008).

Etscheid, G. (2006) 'Hightech gegen Klimawandel'. *Der Spiegel*. 21 November.

IPCC (2007) 'Intergovernmental Panel on Climate Change'. Switzerland. Available at: www.ipcc.ch/ (accessed 2 February 2010).

Schwarb, M. and Kundzewicz, Z.W. (2004) 'Alpine snow cover and winter tourism in the warming climate'. *Papers on Global Change* 11, 59–72.

40

Climate policy and tourism

Stefan Gössling

Climate change and tourism

Global environmental and socio-economic risks associated with the magnitude of climate change projected for the end of the century have been outlined in various reports (IPCC 2007; Stern 2006; Global Humanitarian Forum 2009) and are the focus of international policy negotiations including the Conference of Parties (COP) in Copenhagen in December 2009 (COP-15), and COP-16 in Cancun, Mexico, in December 2010. The Intergovernmental Panel on Climate Change (2007) concluded with very high confidence that climate change beyond certain threshold levels will impede the ability of many nations to make progress on sustainable development and become a growing security risk. The Stern Review (Stern 2006) concluded that the costs of reducing greenhouse gas (GHG) emissions now would be much smaller than the costs of economic disruption resulting from inaction, a view now apparently shared by many business organisations (Ernst and Young 2010; PricewaterhouseCoopers 2010; UN Global Compact 2010; WEF 2009).

Although additional warming from present levels cannot be avoided, future temperature increases will heavily depend on global emission pathways (IPCC 2007). To avoid 'dangerous interference with the climate system', defined as average global warming exceeding 2°C by 2100 (cf. UNFCCC 2010a, 2010b), action needs to be taken swiftly: if current emission trends continue, or even if emission reduction commitments as currently made by nations are successfully achieved, temperature increases are likely to be greater than 2°C (Anderson and Bows 2008; Hansen *et al.* 2006; Meinshausen *et al.* 2009; Parry *et al.* 2008; Rogelj *et al.* 2009). The Copenhagen Diagnosis (2009) consequently concludes that there is a very high probability (>90 per cent) that warming will exceed 2°C by 2100, unless global emissions peak soon and start to decline rapidly. Notably, warming rates will accelerate if positive carbon feedbacks significantly diminish the efficiency of land and oceans to absorb CO_2. At the high end of business-as-usual emission scenarios, global mean warming is estimated to reach 4–7°C by 2100 (Copenhagen Diagnosis 2009: 51).

To stay within 'safe' limits of climate change, the German Advisory Council on Global Change (WBGU 2009) suggests that cumulative CO_2 emissions in the period 2010–50 are limited to 750 Gt, resulting in a 67 per cent probability of limiting global warming within 2°C.

Based on this approach, there is thus an overall 'cap' on the emissions that can be emitted up to 2050, which in turn allows for calculation of the amount of emissions that can be emitted every year. Depending on when emissions peak, this will demand a flatter (peak earlier in time) or steeper (peak later) decline in emissions over time.

As outlined by the German Advisory Council on Global Change (WBGU 2009), if emissions peaked in 2011, sustainable emissions would need to decline to 4 Gt CO_2 in the year 2050, or less than half a ton CO_2 per capita per year at a projected world population of 9 billion (Copenhagen Diagnosis 2009). This value can be compared with current average global per capita emissions of about 4.2 t CO_2 per year (IPCC 2007). The challenge to reduce emissions will consequently be greatest in countries with already high per capita emission levels. These countries have often committed to considerable reduction targets (-5 per cent to -40 per cent by 2020 compared with 1990), representing absolute emission reduction values exceeding 4 t CO_2 per capita per year in some countries within the next 10 years to 2020 (e.g. for Germany under its own climate policy 40 per cent mitigation goal). In this context it is important to acknowledge that the challenge will be far greater in the most heavily emitting countries, such as the USA and Canada, which have per capita emissions exceeding 25 t CO_2-eq per year, followed by Japan, Australia and New Zealand, with per capita emissions of 15 t CO_2-eq per year. In the European Union, emissions are in the order of 11t CO_2-eq per year (IPCC 2007).

The relevance of these figures for tourism lies in the fact that emissions from a single long haul flight can exceed sustainable annual per capita emissions: for instance, a typical return flight from Germany to New Zealand will lead to emissions of more than 4 t CO_2. Adding accommodation and activities, a two-week holiday can thus exceed sustainable averaged per capita per year emissions. Mobility, and thus tourism, is usually the main factor driving up emissions and explaining per capita differences in emissions, with highly mobile travellers causing emissions exceeding 50 t CO_2 per year (Gössling et al. 2009).

Tourism as a contributor to GHG emissions

Tourism has grown rapidly over the past 60 years. From 1950 to 2005, international arrivals have grown by 6.5 per cent per year, from an estimated 25 million in 1950 to 806 million in 2005 (UNWTO 2001, 2010a). Between 2005 and 2008, international arrivals increased by another 100 million to a total of 920 million. Even though the global financial crisis stopped the strong growth trend, with arrivals declining by 4 per cent in 2009 to an estimated 880 million (UNWTO 2010b), the UN World Tourism Organization (UNWTO 2010b) projects that the world economic system will stabilise and growth will resume to reach 1.6 billion over the coming decade as projected in its 2020 vision (UNWTO 2001).

Tourism-related emissions include all domestic and international leisure and business travel, and are usually calculated for three sub-sectors, that is transports to and from the destination, accommodation and activities (UNWTO-UNEP-WMO 2008). Together, their contribution to global anthropogenic CO_2 emissions has been quantified at about 5 per cent in the year 2005 (UNWTO-UNEP-WMO 2008). Most CO_2 emissions are associated with transport, with aviation accounting for 40 per cent of tourism's overall carbon footprint, followed by cars (32 per cent) and accommodation (21 per cent) (Table 40.1). Cruise ships are included in 'other transport', and account with an estimated 19.17 Mt CO_2 for around 1.5 per cent of global tourism emissions (see also Eijgelaar et al. 2010).

All calculations in UNWTO-UNEP-WMO (2008) represent energy throughput. As the construction of hotels, cars, airports and other infrastructure all consume considerable amounts

Table 40.1 Contribution of tourism to CO_2 emissions and radiative forcing, 2005

	Mt CO_2	%	RF (excluding AIC), W/m²	RF (with average AIC), W/m²	RF (with maximum AIC), W/m²
Air transport	515	40%	0.0452	0.1080	0.1829
Car transport	420	32%	0.0204	0.0204	0.0204
Other transport	45	3%	0.0022	0.0022	0.0022
Accommodation	275	21%	0.0133	0.0133	0.0133
Activities	48	4%	0.0023	0.0023	0.0023
Total tourism	1 304*	100%	0.0835	0.1462	0.2211
Total world	26 400		1.6	1.678	1.771
Share (%)	4.94		5.22	8.72	12.49

Note: * = rounded
Source: UNWTO-UNEP-WMO 2008, Scott *et al.* 2010.

of energy, a lifecycle perspective accounting for the energy embodied in the tourism system would lead to higher estimates. Furthermore, tourism also leads to emissions in associated sectors, including tour operators and their offices or the commuting of employees to work (e.g. Gössling *et al.* 2009). Finally, in particular aviation is not only relevant as a contributor to emissions of CO_2, but other GHGs as well, which can be measured as radiative forcing, that is the change in global average temperature caused by all emissions of GHGs in a given year, relative to the year 1750 (for further details see, e.g. Lee *et al.* 2009). A recent estimate presented by Scott *et al.* (2010) assessed the contribution made by tourism to climate change in terms of radiative forcing and found the sector to contribute to 5.2–12.5 per cent of all anthropogenic forcing in 2005.

Based on a business–as–usual scenario for 2035, which considers changes in travel frequency, length of stay, travel distance and technological efficiency gains, UNWTO-UNEP-WMO (2008) calculate that CO_2 emissions from tourism may grow considerably in the coming 25 years. The scenario shows that emissions will increase by 135 per cent compared with 2005 (UNWTO-UNEP-WMO 2008), reaching 3,059 Mt CO_2 by 2035. A similar projection for emission growth has been presented by the World Economic Forum (WEF 2009), which suggests emissions of 3,164 Mt CO_2 by 2035.

As a result, if travel and tourism remain on a business–as–usual pathway, they will become important sources of GHG emissions in the medium–term future. Figure 40.1 shows this for a world economy embarked on an absolute emission reductions pathway (Scott *et al.* 2010). Lines A and B in Figure 40.1 represent emission pathways for the global economy under a -3 per cent per year (A) and -6 per cent per year (B) emission reduction scenario, with emissions peaking in 2015 (A) and 2025 (B) respectively. Both scenarios are based on the objective of avoiding a +2°C warming threshold by 2100 (for details see Scott *et al.* 2010). As indicated, a business–as–usual scenario in tourism, considering current trends in energy efficiency gains, would lead to rapid growth in emissions from the sector (line C). By 2060, the tourism sector would account for emissions exceeding the emissions budget for the entire global economy (intersection of line C with line A or B).

These results emphasise the importance of emission reductions in the tourism sector on a global scale, as continued growth in GHG emissions will be in conflict with emission reduction needs as outlined by the Intergovernmental Panel on Climate Change (IPCC 2007) and existing climate policy objectives of the international community.

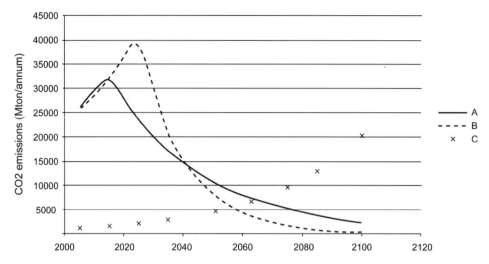

Figure 40.1 Global CO$_2$ emission pathways versus unrestricted tourism emissions growth.
Source: Scott *et al.* 2010.

Climate policy for tourism

Global climate policy

As a response to a growing understanding of the consequences of climate change for ecosystems and socio-economic development, a range of conferences have been held since 1992, when the United Nations Conference on Environment and Development (UNCED) took place in Rio de Janeiro (Brazil). One of the outcomes of UNCED was the United Nations Framework Convention on Climate Change (UNFCCC), a treaty with the objective to stabilise GHG concentrations in the atmosphere to prevent 'dangerous interference with the climate system'.

The Kyoto Protocol to the UNFCCC was adopted in 1997 in Kyoto, Japan, at the Third Session of the Conference of the Parties (COP-3) and entered into force on 16 February 2005. The Kyoto Protocol ascribes differentiated responsibilities to countries to reduce GHG emissions, depending on their economic development and emission levels. Under the protocol, 37 industrialised countries and the European Community have committed to reduce their emissions by an average of 5 per cent of 1990 emissions in the period 2008–12 (UNFCCC 2010c).

Further emissions cuts have to be achieved to not exceed the 2°C warming target by 2100, as defined in the Copenhagen Accord, and negotiations for either a binding post-Kyoto climate policy framework or non-binding voluntary emission reductions as outlined in the Copenhagen Accord (UNFCCC 2010d) and during the Conference of Parties 16 (COP-16) in Mexico in December 2010. Notably, emissions from aviation and cruise-ships and other sea-borne transport are not covered by the Kyoto protocol and not specifically mentioned in the Copenhagen Accord. Responsibility for emission reductions in these sectors lies with the international aviation and shipping organisations the International Civil Aviation Organization (ICAO) and International Maritime Organization (IMO). Both constitute rapidly growing emission sectors.

Aviation

Civil aviation has grown constantly since the 1960s. The sector was responsible for emissions of about 700 Mt of CO_2 in 2004, that is 2.6 per cent of total anthropogenic CO_2 emissions in that year, or 1.3–14.0 per cent of radiative forcing (90 per cent likelihood range) (Lee *et al.* 2009). As outlined by UNWTO-UNEP-WMO (2008), about 80 per cent of this share can be attributed to tourism, the remainder primarily being airfreight. Article 2 of the Kyoto Protocol states that the responsibility for limiting and reducing GHG emissions from international aviation is the responsibility of the ICAO, whereas emissions from domestic flights are included in national GHG inventories and part of national emission reduction targets. However, for almost one and a half decades, ICAO has made no progress on reducing emissions from aviation. Because of continued strong growth, CO_2 emissions are expected to increase 2.0–3.6-fold over 2000 levels by 2050 (Owens *et al.* 2010). More recently, ICAO has formed the Group on International Aviation and Climate Change (GIACC). The Group recommends an 'aspirational' global fuel efficiency target of 2 per cent per annum from 2021 to 2050 (ICAO 2009). Even if this target is reached, absolute emission growth from the sector will thus continue, given observed and expected growth rates in passenger traffic of about 4 per cent per year.

The ICAO, International Air Travel Association (IATA) and Aviation Global Deal (AGD) groups have formulated various commitments to reduce emissions from aviation. Both ICAO and IATA envisage absolute emission reductions in aviation by -50 per cent over 2005 by 2050 (Table 40.2). Whereas ICAO foresees stabilisation of emissions by 2030, IATA anticipates stabilisation by 2020. 'Stabilisation' refers in both cases to no further growth in net emissions. The AGD group (including Air France-KLM, BAA, British Airways, Cathay Pacific Airways, Finnair, Qatar Airways, Virgin Atlantic and the Climate Group) is more ambitious, foreseeing emission reductions by -50 per cent to -80 per cent by 2050 and up to a -20 per cent emission reduction by 2020. However, as outlined, it is highly unlikely that there will be absolute emission reductions in aviation by 2020 due to high growth rates in passenger volumes, and measures as suggested by the organisations (Table 40.2) are unlikely to be sufficient. Rather, the sector is likely to 'offset' emissions through the purchase of permits from other sectors in the case of airlines participating in the EU ETS, whereas airlines not affected by the EU ETS will simply grow in emissions. Notably, non-CO_2 emissions from aviation are not even addressed in current policy frameworks.

Table 40.2 Emission reduction targets and suggested action in aviation

	International Civil Aviation Organisation (ICAO)	International Air Transport Association (IATA)	Aviation Global Deal Group (AGD group)
Emission reduction goal	-50% until 2050, stabilisation by 2030 (base year 2005)	-50% until 2050, stabilisation by 2020 (base year 2005)	-50% to -80% by 2050, up to -20% by 2020
GHG considered	CO_2	CO_2	CO_2
Suggested measures	Energy efficiency measures Air traffic management Biofuels Open and unlimited emission trading with other sectors	Energy efficiency measures Air traffic management Biofuels Open and unlimited emission trading with other sectors	Energy efficiency measures Air traffic management Biofuels Open and unlimited emission trading with other sectors

Source: ICAO 2009;, IATA 2009a; AGD group 2009.

International shipping

Emissions from shipping are estimated to have been in the order of 1,046 Mt CO_2 in 2007, which corresponds to 3.3 per cent of global CO_2 emissions in that year (IMO 2009a), about half of this from tourism (cf. UNWTO-UNEP-WMO 2008; WEF 2009). The IMO (IMO 2009a, 2009b) anticipates that, in the absence of mitigation policies, emissions from shipping will grow by 1.9–2.7 per cent per year until 2050, leading to overall growth by 150–250 per cent in the period 2007–50. As reported by Eijgelaar et al. (2010), tourism is an important component in this growth: worldwide cruise demand has grown steadily at an average annual rate of 7.4 per cent since 1990 (CLIA 2009), and emission growth from this sector has consequently been faster than from shipping more generally. For the year 2007, IMO estimates the global fuel use of all passenger ferries and cruise ships at 31.3 Mt, corresponding to 96 Mt CO_2 (IMO 2009a). The sector is thus less important in contributing to overall global emissions of CO_2, but it should be noted that cruise ships have carried only 16 million passengers in 2007 (Mintel 2008): on a per tourist per day basis, it is the most energy intense form of mass tourism. As is the case with aviation, efforts to reduce absolute CO_2 emission levels from international shipping have been unsuccessful (Haites 2009), and neither binding targets nor measures to reduce emissions have been adopted by IMO.

Regional climate policy

The European Union (EU) is the only region in the world with a legally binding target for emission reductions, imposed on the largest polluters. Current legislation foresees emission reductions by 20 per cent by 2020, compared with the base year 1990, but a recent call by ministers in France, Germany and the UK has been to adopt a 30 per cent reduction target (OECD 2010a). Discussions are ongoing of how to control emissions from consumption not currently covered by the EU ETS, which may lead to the introduction of carbon taxes in the EU in the future (Euractiv 2009). Moreover, the EU ETS will set a tighter cap on emissions year-on-year, and is likely to affect the consumption of energy-intense products and services, including tourism.

The EU will also include shipping and aviation in an open emission trading scheme from 2012 onwards (European Parliament and Council 2009). Emissions from aviation will be capped at 97 per cent of their average 2004–06 levels by 2012. This cap will decline to 95 per cent from 2013 onwards, although this percentage may be reviewed as part of the general review of the Emissions Trading Directive. EU policy will include all flights originating from or ending in the European Union with 27 member states (EU 27), irrespective of the country of origin of airlines and/or aircraft. Although the EU approach is the only regional policy initiative for aviation worldwide, it is not likely to significantly change tourism flows or to reduce absolute emissions from the aviation sector (Mayor and Tol 2009; Gössling et al. 2008; Scott et al. 2010).

With regard to tourism more generally, the EU has recently presented its new EU Tourism policy framework, which mentions as strategic objectives promotion of continuous sustainable development of EU tourism, and enhancement of Europe's image as home to sustainable and high-quality destinations (CEC 2010). However, the document makes mention of climate change only once, with regard to facilitating 'a better identification of the risks linked to climate change by the European tourism industry in order to avoid unsuccessful investments and to explore opportunities to develop alternative tourist offers'.

National climate policy for tourism

In 2010, the Organisation for Economic Co-operation and Development (OECD) and the United Nations Environment Programme (UNEP) Secretariats conducted a survey on 'Climate

Change and Tourism' to understand how well countries are prepared to deal with the climate change challenge for tourism. The Secretariat received 16 replies from the following countries: Austria, Australia, Egypt, Estonia, Germany, Hungary, Ireland, Israel, Japan, Mexico, Netherlands, New Zealand, Poland, Slovak Republic, Slovenia and South Africa. OECD and UNEP (2010) note that the development of tourism-related mitigation policy in OECD and selected other countries has hardly begun. As shown in Table 40.3, only one-third of countries have identified tourism-related mitigation strategies, and only six countries have already implemented policies, that is excluding the EU ETS as a policy framework for aviation. Although there are a considerable number of potential strategies, including energy-efficiency gains in buildings, the use of biofuels, carbon offsetting, GHG disclosure, educational programmes and awareness building, energy-efficiency measures, incentives, investments, information technology to facilitate low-carbon choices, low-carbon mobility, mobility management, public transport, development of renewable energies, strategic assessment of emissions to identify mitigation options, sewage treatment, spatial planning, solid waste management, taxation and the enforced use of low-carbon technology, no country has presented a comprehensive strategy to achieve measurable and monitorable emission reductions in tourism.

Organisations

Tourism organisations have postulated various goals regarding mitigation, with the World Tourism and Travel Council (WTTC) setting out a vision to cut by half carbon emission levels of 2005 by 2035. There is also an interim target of achieving a 30 per cent reduction by 2020 in the presence of an international agreement or 25 per cent reduction in the absence of such an agreement (WTTC 2009, 2010). To this end, the WTTC (2010: 7) suggests producing 'an internationally agreed framework of standards to measure progress against GHG emission targets', that is to monitor emissions development in tourism. WTTC (2010) also suggests a wide range of other measures.

The WEF initiated a taskforce in collaboration with UNWTO, ICAO, UNEP and travel and tourism business leaders, which produced the *Towards a Low Carbon Travel and Tourism Sector* report (WEF 2009). Even though no goals are formulated, the WEF suggests as mechanisms to achieve emission reductions: (1) a carbon tax on non-renewable fuels; (2) economic incentives for low-carbon technologies; (3) a cap-and-trade system for developing and developed countries; and (4) the further development of carbon trading markets.

Other organisations, including UNEP do not provide perspectives on emission reduction goals, but have developed documents to enable mitigation (UNEP-Oxford University-UNWTO 2008), and the development of biofuels (UNEP 2009). The International Energy Agency (IEA) and OECD suggest in a review of transport energy use and emissions that climate policy should focus on: (1) land-use planning to increase population density and mixed-use development; (2) promote teleworking and other information-based substitutes for travel; (3) parking supply (limiting parking space, car free zones) and pricing (cash out schemes); (4) car sharing; (5) road pricing; (6) improved bus transit systems; and (7) encouragement of cycling and walking (IEA and OECD 2009). Finally, the UNWTO adopted the Davos Declaration in October 2007, specifying that the tourism sector must rapidly respond to climate change, within the evolving UN framework, and progressively reduce its GHG contribution. UNWTO outlines that this will require action by the sector *inter alia* to 'mitigate its GHG emissions, derived especially from transport and accommodation activities'.

Climate mitigation in tourism: road to nowhere?

There appears to be consensus among tourism stakeholders that average global warming should not exceed 2°C by 2100, and that the tourism system should de-carbonise in line with other

Table 40.3 Mitigation action in selected OECD member and non-member countries*

Country	Mitigation strategies identified	Policy in place	Perception as threat/opportunity
Anguilla	E, EE, RE, I	Under development	Marketing opportunities
Australia	ETS, RE, EE, CO	D, RE, EE, CO	-
Austria	TE, BIO, MM, E, EE, PT, T, I, SP	Under development (EU ETS)	Increasing costs, marketing opportunities
Bahamas	-	-	-
Belgium	-	(EU ETS)	-
Brazil	-	-	-
Canada	T**, ETS	-	-
Chile	-	-	-
Costa Rica	-	-	-
Czech Republic	-	(EU ETS)	-
Denmark	-	(EU ETS)	-
Egypt	EE, SW, SEW, TE	-	Financial constraints Limited potentials (aviation) Possibility for fund raising
Estonia	RE, BIO	I, EE (EU ETS)	Increases long-term competitiveness
Finland	-	-	-
France	B, CO, EI, I, INV, PT, RE	EI, I, INV	-
Germany	EE, RE, TE, BIO, T, E, SW	(EU ETS)	-
Greece	B, E, EE, INV, RE, TE	(EU ETS), INV	-
Hungary	-	(EU ETS)	Transport costs Investment necessary (accommodation) New marketing opportunities Competitive advantage
Iceland	-	-	-
India	-	-	-
Indonesia	-	-	-
Ireland	D, SA, E	T, D, BIO, E, I, EE (EU ETS)	Reduced costs
Israel	-	-	-
Italy	-	(EU ETS)	-
Japan	-	-	-
Korea	-	-	-
Luxembourg	-	(EU ETS)	-
Mexico	EE, D, SA, RE, E	Under review	Additional investment costs Marketing opportunity
Netherlands	E	(EU ETS)	-
New Zealand	-	EE, D, ETS	Competitiveness of aviation
Norway	ETS, T	-	-
People's Republic of China	-	-	-

Table 40.3 (continued)

Country	Mitigation strategies identified	Policy in place	Perception as threat/opportunity
Poland	EE	(EU ETS)	-
Portugal	-	(EU ETS)	-
Romania	-	(EU ETS)	-
Russian Federation	-	-	-
Slovak Republic	LCM	(EU ETS)	Emission reductions pose challenge
Republic of Slovenia	EE, RE, SW, PT, IT	(EU ETS)	Higher operational costs
South Africa	EE, RE, BIO	T, I, under further development	Increased costs for travel Costs for energy efficiency programmes Reduced arrivals Technology transfer
Spain	-	(EU ETS)	-
Sweden	TE	(EU ETS)	-
Switzerland	-	-	-
Turkey	-	-	-
United Kingdom	-	(EU ETS)	-
USA	-	-	-

Source: OECD and UNEP 2010
Notes: * Directly or indirectly relevant for tourism; ** in some states or parts of the country.
Abbreviations:
B: Buildings
BIO: Biofuels;
CO: Carbon offsetting;
D: Disclosure, i.e. audit of emissions;
E: Educational programmes and awareness building
EE: Energy Efficiency measures;
ETS: Emission Trading Scheme;
I: Incentives;
INV: Investments;
IT: Information Technology to facilitate low-carbon choices;
LCM: Low Carbon Mobility, such as cycling or walking;
MM: Mobility Management;
PT: Public Transport;
RE: development of renewable energies;
SA: Strategic Assessment of emissions to identify mitigation options;
SEW: Sewage treatment;
SP: Spatial Planning,
SW: Solid Waste Management;
T: Taxes;
TE: introduction of Technology;
EU ETS: European Union Emission Trading Scheme, relevant for aviation from 2012.

economic sectors. This would require the global tourism system to reduce absolute emission levels by about 20 per cent by 2020, compared with 1990. However, plans or ongoing efforts to identify mitigation options for tourism appear to exist in only a very limited number of countries. Moreover, most strategies as currently presented are generic in character ('energy-efficiency achievements', 'use of biofuels') and not connected to or based on quantified or quantifiable emission reduction goals and the monitoring of progress. To the contrary, tourism is identified as a growth area for emissions by some governments, and policy in many countries is even contradictory to climate policy goals, as exemplified by plans in, for example, many European countries to develop long haul markets. With the exception of a few countries, there are thus no discernable efforts to curb emissions from tourism in a systematic, co-ordinated and controlled way.

This situation is even worse with regard to aviation, the most important emissions sub-sector, because of the lack of action by ICAO to address mitigation. The EU is currently the only region in the world with an ambition to reduce emissions from the sector. However, because an open trading approach has been chosen, this may mean that aviation will grow in emissions by purchasing comparably cheap carbon credits from other sectors. As trading is focusing on CO_2 and ignoring the non-CO_2 impacts of the sector, this may mean that the overall impact from aviation will grow (cf. Sausen and Lee 2000), possibly leading to CO_2 emissions 2.0–3.6 times higher by 2050 than in 2000 (Owens *et al.* 2010) and associated growth in radiative forcing.

If tourism is to play the role in global efforts to curb emissions that supranational and national governments, business organisations and others advocate, fundamental changes have to be achieved in the tourism system. First of all, in order to be effective, tourism-related climate policy needs to focus on significant emission sub-sectors, both with regard to current and future emissions. Together, aviation, car travel and accommodation account for 93 per cent of CO_2 emissions. Considering non-CO_2 GHG on the basis of radiative forcing, aviation is the single most important emissions sector, responsible for 54–83 per cent of global warming. Measures reducing growth rates in air travel and structural change towards low-carbon mobility thus appear unavoidable (Peeters and Dubois 2010; Scott *et al.* 2010; UNWTO-UNEP-WMO 2008). The following section discusses the innovation needed to achieve a low-carbon tourism system.

Towards a low-carbon tourism system

One of the most fundamental obstacles to re-structuring the global tourism system appears to be the lack of knowledge and awareness among key stakeholders. One way of generating this awareness may be to introduce mandatory carbon auditing. Several global assessments now exist of the contribution made by tourism to climate change (UNWTO-UNEP-WMO 2008; WEF 2009), but only few countries and businesses assess and monitor their tourism-related energy use and emissions. National tourism emission inventories as well as policy demanding companies to assess their energy use and related emissions, would both create a better knowledge base for decision-making and raise awareness among stakeholders. Moreover, only on the basis of such databases can progress be made to reduce emissions, involving regular monitoring.

In this context, energy use and emissions have to reflect their environmental costs. Through mandatory carbon audits, businesses will understand their contribution to global climate change, and their role in affecting the lives of millions of people (e.g. Global Humanitarian Forum 2009) as well as the fact that climate change is affecting the very basis of tourism (e.g. UNWTO-UNEP-WMO 2008). This will help to implement the most important measure in curbing emissions, that is taxation. From a policy perspective, emissions of GHGs represent a market failure. The absence of a price on emissions encourages pollution, prevents innovation and creates a market situation where there is little incentive to use innovations (OECD 2010b). Although governments have a wide range of environmental policy tools at their disposal to address this problem, the fairest and most efficient way of reducing emissions is to increase fuel prices, that is to introduce a tax on fuel or emissions (e.g. Sterner 2007; Mayor and Tol 2007, 2008, 2009, 2010a, 2010b; Johansson 2000, see also OECD 2009, 2010b; Tol 2007; WEF 2009; PricewaterhouseCoopers 2010). It is important for these economic instruments to significantly increase the costs of fossil fuels and emissions. Price levels also need to be stable (not declining below a given level), progressive (increasing at a significant rate per year) and foreseeable (be implemented over longer time periods), to allow companies to integrate energy costs in long-term planning and decision-making. Perverse subsidies, such as the non-taxation of kerosene or the financial support of fossil fuel consumption also need to be addressed: IEA (2010) even sees 'eliminating fossil fuel subsidies as the single most effective measure to cut energy demand in countries where they persist'. Energy taxes need to be proportional to emissions, and be harmonised between countries to avoid 'fuel tourism'. Notably, there appears to be broad support for such policy intervention (OECD 2010a; PricewaterhouseCoopers 2010; WEF 2009).

Although carbon pricing is the most efficient tool to stimulate behavioural change and changes in production, market failures justify additional policy intervention. Energy-intense forms of tourism and transport as well as behavioural change difficult to steer through rising energy costs also need to be addressed through other measures, such as speed limits, or bans of jet skis, quads or other motorised transport at the destination level. Moreover, regulation could include building codes and other minimum standards to reduce emissions. Actual enforcement of existing environmental regulations needs to be ensured.

Carbon taxes may be feasible for accommodation, car transport and other situations where tourism activities cause environmental problems, but they are more difficult to implement in aviation because of a range of bilateral agreements under the Chicago Convention. For aviation, national fees increasing mobility costs proportional to energy use, for instance in the form of a structured, fuel-use related departure tax, may thus be the most efficient in the current situation, and could be implemented by governments in co-ordination with concerned ministries.

As taxes are usually less acceptable by businesses, market-based instruments can be combined with incentive structures to support the introduction of low-carbon technologies and to increase the speed of innovation, also because such measures appear to be more acceptable by business organisations (e.g. WTTC 2010). This could include tax breaks, credits or grants to businesses, the re-distribution of tax burdens through internalisation of environmental costs or their re-distribution between high-level and low-level polluters, as exemplified by bonus-malus systems.

Finally, biofuels may be one of the few options to make a contribution to emission reductions in the aviation sector, and their rapid introduction would be meaningful once regulation, demand management and efficiency measures have contributed to a reduction in overall energy demand for aviation. However, the production of biofuels faces considerable technical, social, economic and environmental difficulties, including potential competition with food production and impact on biodiversity and water use.

To move towards low-carbon tourism will demand fundamental changes in the global tourism system. Although these ultimately require behavioural change, there are also clear economic arguments to pursue low-carbon tourism strategies: tourism is highly wasteful of energy, and significant emission reductions could be made by simply realising efficiency and innovation potentials.

References

Aviation Global Deal (AGD) Group (2009) *A sectoral approach to addressing international aviation emissions. Discussion Note 2.0 09 June 2009.* Available at: www.agdgroup.org/pdfs/090609_AGD_Discussion_Note_2.0.pdf.

Anderson, K. and Bows, A. (2008) 'Reframing the climate change challenge in light of post-2000 emission trends', *Philosophical Transactions of the Royal Society* 366 (1882), 3863–82.

CEC (Commission of the European Communities) (2010) *Europe, the World's No. 1 Tourist Destination – A New Political Framework for Tourism in Europe.* European Commission, Brussels, http://ec.europa.eu/enterprise/sectors/tourism/files/communications/communication2010_en.pdf.

CLIA. (2009) *2009 CLIA cruise market overview: statistical cruise industry data through 2008*: Cruise Lines International Association.

Copenhagen Diagnosis (2009) *Updating the World on the Latest Climate Science*. I. Allison, N.L. Bindoff, R. A. Bindschadler, P.M. Cox, N. de Noblet, M.H. England, J.E. Francis, N. Gruber, A.M. Haywood, D. J. Karoly, G. Kaser, C. Le Quéré, T.M. Lenton, M.E.

Eijgelaar, E., Thaper, C. and Peeters, P. (2010) 'Antarctic cruise tourism: the paradoxes of ambassadorship, last chance tourism' and greenhouse gas emissions', *Journal of Sustainable Tourism* 18 (3), 337–54.

Ernst & Young (2010) *Action amid uncertainty: the business response to climate change*. Available at: www.ey. com/Publication/vwLUAssets/Action_amid_uncertainty:_the_business_response_to_climate_change/$F ILE/Action_amid_uncertainty.pdf.

Euractiv (2009) *EU carbon tax on new Commission's agenda early next year*. Available at: www.euractiv.com/ en/climate-change/eu-carbon-tax-new-commission-agenda-early-year/article-187029 (accessed 25 February 2010).

European Parliament and Council (2009) 'Directive 2008/101/EC of the European Parliament and of the Council of 19 November 2008 amending Directive 2003/87/EC so as to include aviation activities in the scheme for greenhouse gas emission allowance trading within the Community', *Official Journal of the European Union*, 13 January 2009.

Global Humanitarian Forum (2009) *The Anatomy of a Silent Crisis*. London: Global Humanitarian Forum.

Gössling, S., Ceron, J.-P., Dubois, G. and Hall, C.M. (2009) Hypermobile travellers, in Gössling, S. and Upham, P. (eds) *Climate Change and Aviation*. London: Earthscan, 131–48.

Gössling, S., Peeters, P., and Scott, D. (2008) 'Consequences of climate policy for international tourist arrivals in developing countries', *Third World Quarterly* 29(5), 873–901.

Haites, E. (2009) 'Linking emissions trading schemes for international aviation and shipping emissions', *Climate Policy* 9, 415–30.

Hansen, J., Sato, M., Ruedy, R., Kharecha, P., Lacis, A., Miller, R., Nazarenko, L., Lo, K., Schmidt, G. A. and Russell, G. (2006) 'Dangerous human-made interference with climate: A GISS modelE study', *Atmospheric Chemistry and Physics* 7, 2287–312.

Intergovernmental Panel on Climate Change (IPCC) (2007) *Fourth Assessment Report: Climate Change 2007*. Cambridge: Cambridge University Press.

International Civil Aviation Organization (ICAO) (2009) *Group on International Aviation and Climate Change (GIACC). Report*. 1 June 2009. Available at: www.icao.int/env/meetings/GiaccReport_Final_en.pdf.

International Energy Agency (IEA) (2010) *Press release World Energy Outlook 2010*. Available at: www. worldenergyoutlook.org/docs/weo2010/press_release.pdf.

International Energy Agency and Organization for Economic Co-operation and Development (IEA & OECD) (2009) *Transport, Energy and CO_2. Moving Toward Sustainability*. Paris: IEA.

International Maritime Organization (IMO) (2009a) *Prevention of Air Pollution from Ships*. Second IMO GHG Study 2009. Available at: www.imo.org/includes/blastDataOnly.asp/data_id%3D26047/INF-10. pdf.

——(2009b) *Climate change: A challenge for IMO too!* Available at: www.imo.org/includes/blastDataOnly. asp/data_id%3D26316/backgroundE.pdf.

Johansson, B. (2000) *The Carbon Tax in Sweden*, in Organisation for Economic Co-operation and Development (OECD) Innovation and the Environment. Paris: OECD Proceedings.

Lee, D.S., Fahey, D.W., Forster, P.M., Newton, P.J., Wit, R.C.N., Lim, L.L., Owen, B. and Sausen, R. (2009) 'Aviation and Global Climate Change in the 21st Century', *Atmospheric Environment* 43, 3520–37.

Mayor, K. and Tol, R.S.J. (2007) 'The impact of the UK aviation tax on carbon dioxide emissions and visitor numbers. *Transport Policy* 14, 507–13.

——(2008) 'The impact of the EU-US Open Skies agreement on international travel and carbon dioxide emissions', *Journal of Air Transport Management* 14, 1–7.

——(2009) 'Aviation and the environment in the context of the EU-US Open Skies agreement', *Journal of Air Transport Management* 15, 90–5.

——(2010a) 'Scenarios of carbon dioxide emissions from aviation', *Global Environmental Change* 20, 65–73.

——(2010b) 'The impact of European climate change regulations on international tourist markets. *Transportation Research Part D* 15, 26–36.

Meinshausen, M., Meinshausen, N., Hare, W., Raper, S.C.B., Frieler, K., Knutti, R., Frame, D.J. and Allen, M.R. (2009) 'Greenhouse-gas emission targets for limiting global warming to 2°C', *Nature* 458 (7242), 1158–62.

Mintel 2008. *Cruises International – June 2008*. Mintel Oxygen.

Organisation of Economic Co-operation and Development (OECD) (2009) *The Economics of Climate Change Mitigation*. Paris: OECD.

——(2010a) *OECD Tourism Trends and Policies 2010*. Paris: OECD.

——(2010b) *Taxation, Innovation and the Environment*. Paris: OECD.

OECD and UNEP (2011) *Climate Change and Tourism Policy in OECD Countries*. Organization of Economic Co-operation and Development (OECD) and United Nations Environment Programme (UNEP). Paris: OECD.

Owens, B., Lee, D.S. and Lim, L. (2010) 'Flying into the Future: Aviation Emissions Scenarios to 2050', *Environ Sci Technol* 44, 2255–60.

Parry, M., Lowe, J. and Hanson, C. (2008) *The consequences of delayed action on climate change*. Available at: www3.imperial.ac.uk/pls/portallive/docs/1/53345696.PDF.

Peeters, P.M. and Dubois, G. (2010) 'Exploring tourism travel under climate change mitigation constraints', *Journal of Transport Geography* 18, 447–57.

PricewaterhouseCoopers (2010) *Appetite for Change. Global business perspectives on tax and regulation for a low carbon economy*. Available at: www.pwc.com/appetiteforchange.

Rogelj, J., Hare, B., Nabel, J., Macey, K., Schaeffer, M., Markmann, K. and Meinshausen, M. (2009) 'Halfway to Copenhagen, no way to 2°C', *Nature Reports Climate Change* (0907), 81–83.

Sausen, R. and Lee, D.S. (2000) 'New Directions. Assessing the real impact of CO_2 emissions trading by the aviation industry', *Atmospheric Environment* 34, 5337–8.

Scott, D., Peeters, P. and Gössling, S. (2010) 'Can Tourism 'Seal the Deal' of its Mitigation Commitments? The Challenge of Achieving 'Aspirational' Emission Reduction Targets', *Journal of Sustainable Tourism* 18(3), 393–408.

Stern, N. 2006. *The economics of climate change: The Stern review*. Cambridge: Cambridge University Press.

Sterner, T. (2007) 'Fuel taxes: An important instrument for climate policy', *Energy Policy* 35, 3194–202.

Tol, R.S.J. (2007) 'The impact of a carbon tax on international tourism', *Transportation Research Part D* 12, 129–42.

UNEP (2009) *Towards Sustainable Production and Use of Resources: Assessing Biofuels*. Paris: United Nations Environment Programme. www.unep.fr/shared/publications/pdf/WEBx0149xPA-AssessingBiofuelsSummary.pdf

United Nations Environment Programme (UNEP), University of Oxford, United Nations World Tourism Organization (UNWTO), World Meteorological Organization (WMO) (2008) *Climate Change Adaptation and Mitigation in the Tourism Sector: Frameworks, Tools and Practice*. Paris: UNEP, Oxford University, UNWTO, WMO.

United Nations Framework Convention on Climate Change (UNFCCC) (2010a) *Article 2: Objective*. Available at: http://unfccc.int/essential_background/convention/background/items/1353.php.

——(2010b) *Report of the Conference of the Parties on its fifteenth session*, 7–19 December 2009, Copenhagen. Available at: http://unfccc.int/resource/docs/2009/cop15/eng/11a01.pdf.

——(2010c) *Fact sheet: the Kyoto Protocol*. Available at: http://unfccc.int/files/press/backgrounders/application/pdf/fact_sheet_the_kyoto_protocol.pdf.

——(2010d) *Report of the Conference of the Parties on its fifteenth session*, 7–19 December 2009, Copenhagen. Available at: http://unfccc.int/resource/docs/2009/cop15/eng/11a01.pdf.

United Nations Global Compact (2010) *259 Investors Representing $15 Trillion Call for International Action on Climate Change*. Available at www.unglobalcompact.org/news/83-11-16-2010.

United Nations World Tourism Organization (UNWTO) (2001) *Tourism 2020 vision*. Volume 7. Global forecasts and profiles of market segments. Madrid: World Tourism Organisation (WTO).

——(2010a) *Historical perspective of world tourism*. Available at: www.unwto.org/facts/eng/historical.htm (accessed 24 February 2010).

——(2010b) *UNWTO World Tourism Barometer* 8 (1), January 2010. Available at: www.unwto.org/facts/eng/pdf/barometer/UNWTO_Barom10_1_en_excerpt.pdf.

United Nations World Tourism Organization, United Nations Environment Programme, World Meteorological Organization (UNWTO-UNEP-WMO) (2008) *Climate Change and Tourism: Responding to Global Challenges*. Madrid, Spain: UNWTO.

WBGU – German Advisory Council on Global Change (2009) *Solving the climate dilemma: The budget approach*. Berlin: WBGU.

World Economic Forum (WEF) (2009) *Climate Policies: From Kyoto to Copenhagen*. Available at: www.weforum.org/en/knowledge/Themes/Enviroment/ClimateChange/KN_SESS_SUMM_28001?url=en/knowledge/Themes/Enviroment/ClimateChange/KN_SESS_SUMM_28001.

World Tourism and Travel Council (WTTC) (2009) *Leading the Challenge on Climate Change*. London: World Travel& Tourism Council. Available at: www.wttc.org/bin/pdf/original_pdf_file/climate_change_final.pdf.

——(2010) *Climate change – a joint approach to addressing the challenge*. Available at: www.wttc.org/bin/pdf/original_pdf_file/climate_change – a_joint_appro.pdf.

41

Water and tourism

Michalis Hadjikakou, Jonathan Chenoweth and Graham Miller

Introduction

This chapter examines the use of water in the tourism sector with the aim of highlighting how relevant the issue of water scarcity is to the sector. It should be obvious to tourism scholars that tourism development requires a reliable supply of good-quality water. What is less obvious is the extent to which tourism development is a major user of water and can contribute to water scarcity and water-quality impairment, with serious social, economic and environmental repercussions. In order to devise measures that can be used to promote the prudent use of water in the tourism sector, research is needed to further understand the scale and nature of the problem. Despite heightened academic and media interest in sustainable tourism in recent years, this has mostly concentrated on the contribution of carbon emissions from travel and accommodation to climate change, with the result that water use in the tourism sector remains a seriously understudied area (Gössling 2005).

This chapter offers a review of the literature on water use in the tourism sector, but also draws heavily on studies outside tourism to explain issues of general water scarcity and sustainable water use. First, the chapter looks at the consequences of current water use by the tourism sector and how these are having an impact on local water resources. The section that follows looks at how the future development and growth of the sector along with impacts of climate change could induce changes in the way water is managed in tourism destinations, especially those likely to face increased water shortages. Finally, the chapter examines measures that have been effectively employed to encourage sustainable use of water in tourist destinations and also emphasise how a better understanding of the nature of the problem could eventually lead to possible solutions.

Global water scarcity – current and future outlook

Having access to a clean supply of water constitutes one of the fundamental pillars for any civilisation. Water is a vital necessity for everyday needs such as drinking, washing and cooking and is also, most importantly, required for growing the food we depend on for survival and for economic development (Chenoweth 2008). In most of the developed world, where we have become accustomed to readily available water through our taps, water is a resource that the majority of us take for granted. However, with nearly 1.2 billion people around the world still lacking guaranteed access to water and more than 2.6 billion without adequate sanitation, many countries find themselves in the midst of a global water crisis, which seriously threatens the pursuit of goals such as development and poverty reduction (Jacobson and Tropp 2010). It would appear that, at present, there is enough water on a global scale to satisfy human needs, as withdrawals only currently account for less than 10 per cent of the available renewable fresh water resources (Oki and Kanae 2006). Nevertheless, global water resources are unequally distributed in space and time (Postel *et al.* 1996). Some parts of the globe are naturally blessed with abundant water, whereas others are located in arid or semi-arid zones of the world. Moreover, the precipitation regime in many places is characterised by a short rainy season followed by a long dry season. Another limiting factor to exploiting all available water resources is that not all the water is fit for human purposes due to pollution from human activities, which compromises the quality of the water available downstream.

Water scarcity is, however, not only the result of water shortage in the physical sense. In many developing countries, lack of access to water is compounded by insufficient funds, inadequate infrastructure, poor governance, corruption and an inability to provide water of decent quality. In most cases, water scarcity is a combination of first order (physical) scarcity and second order scarcity (implying poor water management) (Ohlsson and Turton 1999). Furthermore, it is often extremely difficult to assess whether water scarcity is caused by insufficient supply or excess demand (Rijsberman 2006). Similar to the supply of water, which varies in space and time around the globe, human demand for water also varies in different places, as it is a factor of societal values and human behaviour (Molle and Mollinga 2003). Although scarcity often arises due to a combination of different causes, most societies facing water scarcity have options available to them in order to address their problems (UN-Water 2006). What are often lacking, however, are the resources and appropriate incentives to implement these options.

The water situation is likely to become even worse in the future. Ongoing climatic change will, most certainly, have a severe impact on water supplies in many parts of the world. Climate change is expected to threaten the reliability of both the quantity and quality of water supplies by stretching the current variability in the climate, through an intensification of extremes such as droughts and floods (World Water Assessment Programme 2009). According to the latest Intergovernmental Panel on Climate Change (IPCC) report, it is in the areas already suffering from water scarcity where precipitation is expected to decrease and evaporation to increase the most (Kundzewicz *et al.* 2007). Furthermore, as depicted in Figure 41.1, there is a complex interconnectedness between processes such as climate, land-use, demand for food and water

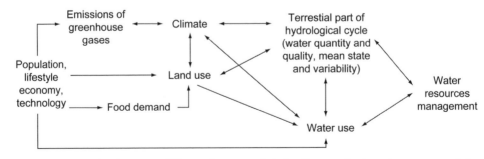

Figure 41.1 Inter-play between different factors and their effect on fresh water resources (after Oki 2005 in Kundzewicz *et al.* 2007)

resources. This means that non-climatic drivers such as population growth, economic development, technological advances and lifestyle changes are also likely to have a huge impact on water withdrawals and the way in which we manage this resource (Sophocleous 2004; UN-Water 2010), possibly to an even greater extent compared to climatic changes (Vorosmarty *et al.* 2000). Over the past one hundred 100 years population has quadrupled, whereas water use has increased sevenfold, indicating a general trend according to which a wealthier world has also become thirstier (UNDP 2006). The strategies for mitigating against or adapting to the continuous increase in the demand for fresh water will play an important part in domestic and international politics in the coming years and will also affect our choices as individuals (Black *et al.* 2010).

Fresh water use is usually divided into three main sectors of the economy: domestic, industrial and agricultural. Globally, agriculture is by far the largest user with a 70 per cent share of all water withdrawals, whereas industry accounts for 19 per cent with the remaining 11 per cent coming from household use (FAO 2011). As global averages, these figures tend to be biased towards countries with high water withdrawals and hide significant differences between countries. They do, however, point to the fact that a huge amount of the water abstracted is used in the production of food. The volume of water required to grow, produce and package agricultural commodities has been given the name 'virtual water' (Allan 1996). Most of this virtual water is not even present in the final version of a product as it has been evaporated during production. This concept has been used to establish the notion of a 'water footprint' (Hoekstra 2003), which, similar to the concept of carbon footprint, has been used to calculate water use on an international (Chapagain and Hoekstra 2004; Hoekstra and Chapagain 2007) or corporate scale (Ercin *et al.* 2011) and to suggest potential ways in which water savings could be achieved. Diets rich in meat and dairy products, for example, are associated with much higher water footprints because of the large amounts of feed crops, drinking water and service water required by the animals, but this also varies from place to place depending on climate and agricultural efficiency (Hoekstra and Chapagain 2008). The water footprint concept has highlighted the fact that an overwhelming majority of global water use takes place in the agricultural stages and this, in turn, has highlighted the fact that consumers and manufacturers will need to become more engaged in the agricultural stages of production (Ridoutt *et al.* 2009).

For regions already suffering from some form of water scarcity, the additional consumption of water from tourism development can lead to severe water stress. However, the extent of this stress is not always evident from official water use statistics. Hence, the water footprint concept offers a very useful way to consider both the quantity and nature of water use in the tourism sector. The annual water footprint of a consumer or industry is defined as the sum of the virtual water content of all the products consumed (supply-chain footprint) and the additional water directly consumed for drinking, washing, cooking (operational footprint) (Hoekstra *et al.* 2009). Similarly to any business or economic sector, tourism consumes significant volumes of water and has both supply-chain and operational footprints, drawing water directly from the domestic water (used in hotels and other accommodation facilities) and indirectly from the agricultural sector (through food and beverage consumption). The indirect component of water use in the tourism sector has yet to be considered in any detail in either policy or academic research.

Water demand from tourism – impacts on local water resources

According to Gössling (2002), the lack of research on water and tourism may be due to a lack of available data, which means academics and policy makers cannot make reliable calculations of water consumption from tourism. Another reason why this may be the case is that the overall impact of tourism on a global scale appears to be unworthy of further serious consideration, as water use by tourism only amounts to 0.04 per cent of the total water withdrawals (Gössling 2005). Compared with the aforementioned figures for agriculture, industry and domestic water use, these figures can appear to be negligible. Nevertheless, these figures do not capture differences between tourist destinations. Tourism can be responsible for up to 16.9 per cent of domestic water use in island states like Cyprus (Gössling 2006), which corresponds to 5 per cent of the total mean annual water use (Savvides *et al.* 2001). Furthermore, what is important to consider in this overall consumption is that the use of water by the tourist sector may be very seasonal in nature, meaning that the annual figures mask the actual stress exerted from the tourist sector on local water resources. Conflict over water resources during the peak tourism period is not uncommon, especially in drought years when local residents and farmers have restricted access to water while the supply to tourist establishments remains unaffected (Holden 2000). As a high-value user of water where a single day of insufficient water supply could severely affect the public image and reputation of any tourist destination, tourism commonly takes priority over other uses.

Part of the reason why tourist use of water resources can create stress and conflict is proven by studies that have calculated average daily per capita consumption in tourist accommodation. These have shown that tourists tend to use considerably more water on average compared with the domestic population (Essex *et al.* 2004; Gössling 2005; Emmanuel and Spence 2009). Estimates of tourist water use in the Mediterranean range from 300 to 850 l/capita/day (de Stefano 2004). As a means of comparison, the global average in domestic water consumption is around 161 l/capita/day, but this varies widely between countries and also tends to vary seasonally (FAO 2009). Especially in developing countries where the national per capita use is low, the difference between local and tourist consumption can be large. A study by Gössling (2001) showed that average per capita daily water use in hotels in Zanzibar corresponds to around 15 times the daily per capita demand from the local population. This understandably raises issues of inequity as tourism, being a higher-value user than the local population, is given priority over water resources. Added to this is the fact that most of the tourists come from developed temperate countries where water is abundant. They, therefore, often have little appreciation of how their water use compares with that of the local population. When in 'holiday mode' and in the absence of financial incentives to promote more prudent use, pro-environmental behaviour can be rare (Miller *et al.* 2010).

However, these averaged figures detract from the fact that water used by tourism also varies enormously depending on the accommodation and the recreation facilities pursued. Despite the general consensus that tourists use more water compared with local residents, it is also apparent that the tourism sector is extremely diverse in terms of both the amounts and the specific uses of water demand (Kotios *et al.* 2009; Rico-Amoros *et al.* 2009). The general pattern would appear to be that increased luxury leads to increased water consumption in hotels and other types of accommodation, both as a result of the facilities offered but also the density of the accommodation. Mass tourism, so often associated with its negative aesthetic impact on the landscape, actually registers much lower consumptions per capita compared with so-called quality tourism, due, mainly, to inherent efficiencies in the distribution systems of densely constructed apartment and hotel complexes, which remain in operation for most of the year (Rico-Amoros *et al.* 2009). Gössling (2001) reports an exponential growth in water use with increasing hotel size due, mainly, to larger pools and larger gardens that require extensive irrigation. This is supported by a study of the hotel sector in Barbados, where annual consumption showed a strong positive correlation with the number of employees working for a hotel and reflects both the absolute size and the service level of the hotel (Charara *et al.* 2010). Gardens, water parks, swimming pools and golf courses are all popular tourist attractions but are also extremely water-intensive. The presence of a swimming pool on the premises of a hotel can lead to an average increase in per capita guest consumption of around 60 l/capita/day (Kotios *et al.* 2009), whereas a golf course is estimated to use around 1 million cubic metres per year, which corresponds to the water consumption of a city with 12,000 inhabitants (WWF Spain 2003, cited in de Stefano 2004).

As previously mentioned, water use in tourism is highly seasonal, with many destinations experiencing extremely high water demand during the summer holiday period. In the Mediterranean region, which is the world's leading holiday destination and where most countries suffer from some form of water scarcity, the climate is characterised by marked seasonality in precipitation with the majority of the rainfall falling during the winter months (Kent *et al.* 2002), as this is the only period where the polar jet stream penetrates into the sub-tropical zone creating unstable conditions. The summer period is dominated by anti-cyclonic (high pressure) conditions that create stable conditions in the atmosphere and give rise to sunny weather. At the same time, tourists are attracted to Mediterranean resorts largely because of the warm and sunny climate (Holden 2008), with summer months being the most popular. Statistics from different areas of the Mediterranean such as the Provence-Côte d'Azur region in France, the Cyclades island group in Greece and the Costa Brava in Spain show that the population in tourist resorts can increase more than tenfold at certain times of the year (de Stefano 2004). As a result, water demand often surpasses water availability during the summer months (Gikas and Angelakis 2009). As tourism on a global level tends to shift water consumption from water-rich to water-poor areas (Gössling 2006), it is the added stress on water resources at the destination that really matters, as the water saved in the source regions cannot compensate for overuse of local water resources in the destination regions.

Summer resorts are, therefore, usually forced to rely on groundwater, surface water stored in dams or transported from more humid parts of the island or country as well as non-conventional, energy-hungry resources such as desalination and, to a lesser extent, treated wastewater. Added to the temporal aspect of the problem, there is also the fact that tourism tends to concentrate in coastal areas, which adds further stress to local water supplies. Within small islands, coastal regions often have comparatively low precipitation totals compared with areas at higher altitude (Kent *et al.* 2002). The problem is even worse in places where local residents also tend to live along the coast. This is very common in Caribbean islands such as Jamaica and Barbados (Goodwin and Walters 2007). Although water demand from the tourist industry is characteristically seasonal in nature, tourism can often lead to a permanent increase in water demand for facilities and leisure structures (Iglesias *et al.* 2007).

Where unsustainable pumping of groundwater takes place, this can create water quality problems due to saltwater intrusion (where saline water from the sea is drawn into the aquifer). The main cause for this phenomenon is groundwater over-abstraction for public water supply (Nixon *et al.* 2003), a large proportion of which comes from tourism in certain areas. This can be a problem in islands with very permeable geology, where groundwater is the only conventional source of water (Kent *et al.* 2002; Sapiano 2008; Manoli *et al.* 2004). Water quality impairment of groundwater and surface water also results from significant increases in sewage effluents due to the very high population densities. Contamination of rivers and estuaries are common problems, particularly where sewage receives no treatment, with severe impacts for the ecology. Pollution of aquifers and coastal waters from fertilisers and herbicides used on golf courses and hotel gardens is another frequent problem (Holden 2000; Shaalan 2005).

As explained in the previous section, although tourism has a direct impact on water consumption through the water used in accommodation facilities and activities such as swimming pools and golf courses, growth in tourism is often associated with a water demand multiplier effect as tourism has close linkages to other sectors of the economy (Emmanuel and Spence 2009). Approximately one-third of all tourist expenditure is used to buy food (Torres 2003;

Gössling *et al.* 2010a), meaning that the summer increases in population in certain resorts significantly increase the demand for food, which is either produced locally or has to be imported. Depending on the products required and their associated water requirements, local resources could suffer even more as a result of tourism. What makes the situation even more complicated is that, due to the manner in which water resources are currently managed, an increase in water demand only usually appears to be associated with the domestic and agricultural sectors, with no indication of the demand from tourism. Yet, creating linkages between tourism and agriculture provides an opportunity to enhance the benefits of tourism to the local community if the food is produced locally (Telfer and Wall 1996). Any attempts to boost local production and reduce economic leakage could, nevertheless, create water shortages if too much pressure is put on local water resources.

Future tourism development and climate change

There is no doubt that tourism is already having significant impacts on water resources in water scarce areas, with climate change and further tourist development expected to exacerbate the problem even further in the not-so-distant future. Promoting prudent water use thus becomes a prerequisite if tourism is to become environmentally sustainable. It is also required to enable projected growth of the tourist sector as environmental changes could ultimately diminish the attractiveness of certain destinations (Gössling 2002). Tourism arrivals worldwide are expected to increase by an annual growth rate of 3 per cent over the period 1995–2020 (Becken and Hay 2007). Currently, over 70 per cent of international arrivals originate from Europe and North America (UNWTO 2010), but an increased number of travellers from emerging economies such as China and India is likely to add further stress to resources in existing popular destinations and potentially open up new destinations. Perry (2005) sees endemic water scarcity as a very likely future scenario in many popular tourist destinations, which could lead to rising tension between local people and tourist authorities. Increased stress from both tourism and climate change could eventually make certain destinations extremely water stressed, to the extent that further growth in their tourist industries will not be possible (Becken and Hay 2007). This is unless the tourist industry in these places invests heavily in the development of non-conventional water resources such as desalination and treated wastewater. This is not possible everywhere due to a lack of resources and proximity to the sea and also has significant implications for carbon emissions associated to tourism, which are increasingly becoming the focus in academic research (Chenoweth 2009; Gössling *et al.* 2010b).

Although making accurate long-term regional projections of tourist arrivals is fraught with uncertainty (due, mainly, to an inability to model future political stability and tourist preferences), some regions emerge as consistently robust with regards to the potential impacts of both climate change and future tourism development. Figure 41.2 shows the regions identified as hotspots (areas likely to face the most severe consequences as a result of climate change) by the World Tourism Organization (Scott *et al.* 2008). Water scarcity is likely to be an important issue in all five hotspot areas and could become one of the limiting factors for further tourism development, with severe economic consequences in formerly popular destinations (Gössling 2006; Essex *et al.* 2004), such as the Caribbean and the Mediterranean. Nevertheless, it remains extremely hard to predict how climate change is likely to influence the relationship between tourist numbers and water availability at a given location, due to the inter-play of several possible feedback loops. Areas such as the Mediterranean could become unpopular during the summer months as temperatures will not allow tourists (especially those from northern European countries who are not accustomed to such high temperatures) to venture outside safely (Perry

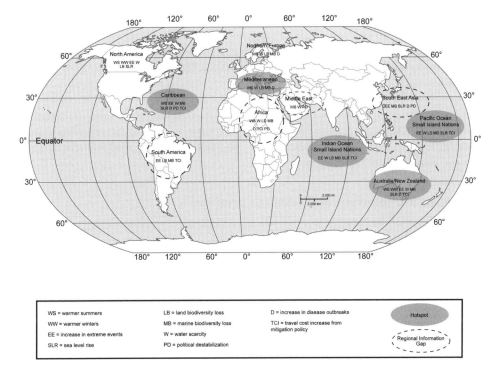

Figure 41.2 Tourism destinations identified as hotspots.
It is evident that water scarcity is likely to pose serious problems in popular tourist regions such as the Mediterranean and the Caribbean (Scott *et al.* 2008).

2005, 2006). A smaller number of tourist arrivals in the height of summer may be positive with regards to water consumption, but there could still be less water available overall if precipitation decreases significantly. Furthermore, a reduction in summer arrivals does not necessarily equate to a decrease in mean annual tourist numbers as it could be compensated by increased tourist arrivals during the rest of the year. On the other hand, climate change in the home countries of tourists should also be considered in any modelling exercise that attempts to look at possible future changes in tourist arrivals. More favourable conditions at home coupled with increasing awareness of the environmental impacts of flying or travelling long distances could lead to tourists opting to stay in their home countries during their holidays, or amending their travel behaviour when they do travel.

Decisions to diversify or expand the tourist product offered at a destination are also likely to dictate future water demand from the sector. The propensity for golf course development, which is apparent in Morocco, Tunisia, Libya, Egypt, Turkey, Greece, Italy and Cyprus forms part of a strategy to diversify tourism facilities and attract higher spending customers (Tourism Concern 2011). Yet, higher spending tourists tend to be associated with higher per capita tourist water use. This implies that an overall reduction in tourist numbers does not necessarily mean that water demand will also decrease. The fact that diversification and upgrading of the tourist product is actually encouraged as a means of climate change adaptation is indicative of the serious information and knowledge gap on the topic of water use in the tourist sector (Hof and Schmitt 2011). Another ongoing trend in the Mediterranean is an increase in the number of second homes, which have long been recognised as an important extra form of stress for water demand that is, however, extremely hard to quantify and often eludes official statistics

(Statzu and Strazzera 2011; Hof and Schmitt 2011). This occurs because as private dwellings second homes are not classified as tourist accommodation. Even a decision to invest in agro-tourism can have important repercussions for water use. An example of a country that has invested heavily in agro-tourism in recent years is Jamaica. Large papaya and banana plantations, rum distilleries and coffee plantations are all heavily promoted as places of interest for tourists to visit (Lew *et al.* 2008). This implies that agricultural water management is a crucial aspect of water use efficiency in the tourism sector in this case. Any decision to diversify or expand the tourist product offered at a destination must consider future economic gains in relation to the effects on local water resources. This includes considering environmental impacts as well as economic impacts for other water users.

Possible future solutions and research priorities

Even in terms of consideration given to sustainability issues, research on water and tourism could not be considered to have a high priority. Yet, within a weak sustainability paradigm of tourism businesses trying to make the existing business more sustainable, without resorting to fundamental change of the business itself, there is arguably more that tourism businesses can do to address their water impact than their climate change impact. As examples of industry action, in 2009, the UNWTO became a member of UN-Water (estabiluded in 2003 in order to promote interest and co-operation in water-related issues). Spain has also recently become the first country to explicitly consider the use of the water footprint as a means of promoting sustainable tourism (Llamas *et al.* 2010). Furthermore, in the UK, charities such as the 'Travel Foundation' and 'Tourism Concern' are both trying to promote responsible water management as part of sustainable tourism initiatives in different countries. As with water scarcity in general, demand management represents potentially the most effective method of reducing water scarcity. By making tourism less water-intensive, significant water savings could potentially be realised. This can only be achieved through a combination of changes in policy and legislation, financial incentives such as taxation, behavioural changes and technological innovations. Before implementing any measures, there is still considerable work to be done in order to improve our knowledge of what is an under-researched topic, both at academic and policy levels.

Accurate knowledge is very much dependent on information and this requires a lot more research and collection of data in order to allow for more reliable estimates of the use of water in the tourist sector. The water footprint concept is a potentially useful way of highlighting both the direct and indirect (in the form of virtual water) use of water in the tourist sector. Especially where food consumed by tourists is grown locally, the water used in the production must be explicitly accounted for. Eurostat has suggested the need to reclassify golf under the tourism sector in order to facilitate control over the source and quantity of water it consumes (Tourism Concern 2011). A common problem is that despite the fact that water use statistics for different sectors of the economy are already collected by most water authorities, these rarely explicitly indicate water use by the tourist sector. A recent study in the Mediterranean highlights the importance of having a sound knowledge of the quantitative impact of tourism on water resources, which can then be used to correctly inform local authorities and tourism companies (Lootvoet and Roddier-Quefelec 2009). With such information, separate tariffs for use of water by the tourist sector can be introduced, as in Tunisia (Lootvoet and Roddier-Quefelec 2009).

Improved knowledge would eventually lead to governments, tour operators and destination managers being more aware of the extent to which tourism impacts water resources both directly and indirectly. This could then lead to the appropriate legislation and incentives, which as a first step should aim to address the direct use of water in the industry. In the case of hotel managers and tour operators it is also important to make it clear that there are also strong financial incentives to conserving water (Deng and Burnett 2002). Beyond the direct savings possible, conserving water leads to the preservation of the visual attraction of the environment, on which tourism depends (Mouliérac and Thivet 2009). Small-scale infrastructure improvements such as water-saving devices in showers and irrigation equipment (Simpson *et al.* 2008) must be encouraged through studies showing how these investments pay-back for themselves through saving in bills. This ultimately comes back to the need for a better knowledge of both the quantitative and qualitative impacts of water use by the tourist industry in specific destinations, which in turn, depends on collecting and combining the right data.

An excellent example is the Hilton LightStay Programme launched across Hilton hotels worldwide to support the sustainability commitments of the company. The results from 2009 showed that properties using LightStay achieved a reduced energy use of 5 percent and a reduced water use of 2.4 percent compared with 2008, which translates into savings of more than 29 million dollars (Hilton Worldwide 2011). The Hilton example also highlights the potential in linking water savings to energy savings. In terms of outdoor water use, studies have shown this to make up a huge part of the total water demand in tourist facilities, use of plant species better adapted to the local climate as well as use of pool covers and more extensive water reuse in swimming pools should be encouraged through appropriate legislation and economic incentives (Hof and Schmitt 2011). However, it is also important to realise that water saving devices can only achieve their purpose if they are used alongside behavioural changes.

Any attempt to promote prudent water use in tourism will also have to involve raising public awareness on the issue of water scarcity, especially at destinations already suffering from water shortage. Guest education is as important as employee education. Increased public awareness could also lead to bottom-up pressure, whereby tourists themselves pursue environmentally sustainable activities and demand that tour operators offer sustainable options. Nevertheless, it is important that awareness is based on sound knowledge of water issues. Research shows a weak public understanding of how tourist activities relate to the environment (Miller *et al.* 2010). This highlights that there is still a lot of work to be done in getting tourists to understand how their actions are affecting local water resources.

Summary

This chapter has looked at the importance of considering water issues as part of a broader attempt to promote sustainable tourism practices in existing and emerging holiday destinations. Water scarcity is already a significant environmental problem and current trends suggest that the situation is likely to get worse in the future due to the combined pressures from population growth, economic development and climate change. Despite the fact that water use in the tourism sector may appear to be dwarfed by use in other sectors such as agriculture when looking at average figures, the spatial and temporal concentration of water use by tourism implies that unsustainable use can still lead to severe depletion of local resources and conflict between tourist facilities, other industrial sectors and local residents. Furthermore, with tourism's anticipated continued expansion, some destinations are likely to experience increased water stress if measures are not taken to make tourism's water consumption more sustainable. Understanding the extent and nature of the problem is the first step towards devising solutions to address it. The development of the climate change debate will be instructive in helping the water debate to advance more quickly. Yet, improvements in the water use efficiency of the tourism industry may prove to be an area where the tourism industry can make more significant progress than with reducing greenhouse gas emissions, and so demonstrate industry commitment to helping achieve greater sustainability.

References

Allan, J.A. (1996) 'Water use and development in arid regions: environment, economic development and water resource politics and policy', *Review of European Community & International Environmental Law* 5(2), 107–15.

Becken, S. and Hay, J.E. (2007) *Tourism and climate change: risks and opportunities.* Clevedon: Channel View Publications.

Black, E., Mithen, S., Hoskins, B. and Cornforth, R. (2010) 'Water and society: past, present and future', *Philosophical Transactions of the Royal Society A* 368, 5107–10.

Chapagain, A.K. and Hoekstra, A.Y. (2004) *Water footprints of nations.* Delft, Netherlands: UNESCO-IHE.

Charara, N., Cashman, A., Bonnell, R. and Gehr, R. (2010) 'Water use efficiency in the hotel sector of Barbados', *Journal of Sustainable Tourism* 19(2), 231–45.

Chenoweth, J. (2008) 'A re-assessment of indicators of national water security', *Water International* 33(1), 5–18.

——(2009), 'Is tourism with a low impact on climate possible?', *Worldwide Hospitality and Tourism Themes* 1 (3), 274–87.

de Stefano, L. (2004), *Freshwater and Tourism in the Mediterranean.* Rome: WWF Mediterranean Programme.

Deng, S.M. and Burnett, J. (2002) 'Water use in hotels in Hong Kong', *International Journal of Hospitality Management* 21(1), 57–66.

Emmanuel, K. and Spence, B. (2009) 'Climate change implications for water resource management in Caribbean tourism', *Worldwide Hospitality and Tourism Themes* 1(3), 252–68.

Ercin, A.E., Aldaya, M.M. and Hoekstra, A.Y. (2011) 'Corporate Water Footprint Accounting and Impact Assessment: The Case of the Water Footprint of a Sugar-Containing Carbonated Beverage', *Water Resources Management* 25(2), 721–41.

Essex, S., Kent, M. and Newnham, R. (2004) 'Tourism Development in Mallorca: Is Water Supply a Constraint?', *Journal of Sustainable Tourism* 12(1), 4–28.

Food and Agriculture Organization (FAO) (2009) *Aquastat: FAO's Information System on Water and Agriculture, Land and Water Development Division, Food and Agriculture Organization.* Available at: www.fao.org/nr/water/ aquastat/data/query/index.html (accessed 28 March 2011).

——(2011) *AQUASTAT – Water use,* (14 February 2011, last update). Available at: www.fao.org/nr/water/aquastat/water_use/index.stm (accessed 28 March 2011).

Gikas, P. and Angelakis, A.N. (2009) 'Water resources management in Crete and in the Aegean Islands, with emphasis on the utilization of non-conventional water sources', *Desalination* 248(1–3), 1049–64.

Goodwin, H. and Walters, K. (2007) *World Travel Market 'No water, no future' report 2007.* World Travel Market.

Gössling, S. (2001) 'The consequences of tourism for sustainable water use on a tropical island: Zanzibar, Tanzania', *Journal of Environmental Management* 61(2), 179–91.

——(2002) 'Global environmental consequences of tourism', *Global Environmental Change* 12(4), 283–302.

——(2005) 'Tourism's contribution to global environmental change: space, energy, disease, and water' in C.M. Hall and J.E.S. Higham (eds) *Tourism, recreation, and climate change.* Clevedon: Channel View Books, pp. 286–300.

——(2006) 'Tourism and water', in Gössling, S. and Hall, C.M. (eds), *Global Environmental Change, Ecological, Social, Economic and political interrelationships.* Abingdon: Routledge, pp. 180–94.

Gössling, S., Garrod, B., Aall, C., Hille, J. and Peeters, P. (2010a) 'Food management in tourism: Reducing tourism's carbon footprint', *Tourism Management* 32, 534–43.

Gössling, S., Hall, C.M., Peeters, P. and Scott, D. (2010b) 'The future of tourism: Can tourism growth and climate policy be reconciled? A climate change mitigation perspective', *Tourism Recreation Research* 35(2), 119–30.

Hilton Worldwide (2011) *Lightstay* (Homepage of Hilton Hotels). Available at: www.hiltondevelopment.com/sustainability/ lightstay (accessed 29 March 2011).

Hoekstra, A.Y. (2003) *Virtual water trade.* Delft, Netherlands: IHE Delft.

Hoekstra, A.Y. and Chapagain, A.K. (2007) 'Water footprints of nations: water use by people as a function of their consumption pattern', *Integrated Assessment of Water Resources and Global Change,* 35–48.

——(2008) *Globalization of water: sharing the planet's freshwater resources.* Oxford: Blackwell Publishing.

Hoekstra, A.Y., Chapagain, A.K., Aldaya, M.M. and Mekonnen, M.M. (2009) *Water footprint manual.* Enschede, Netherlands: Water Footprint Network.

Hof, A. and Schmitt, T. (2011) 'Urban and tourist land use patterns and water consumption: Evidence from Mallorca, Balearic Islands'. *Land Use Policy,* doi:10.1016/j.landusepol.2011.01.007

Holden, A. (2000) *Environment and tourism.* London: Taylor & Francis.

——(2008) *Environment and tourism*, 2nd edn. Abingdon: Routledge.

Iglesias, A., Garrote, L., Flores, F. and Moneo, M. (2007) 'Challenges to manage the risk of water scarcity and climate change in the Mediterranean', *Water Resources Management* 21(5), 775–88.

Jacobson, M. and Tropp, H. (2010) 'Addressing corruption in climate change water adaptation', *Reviews in Environmental Science and Biotechnology* 9, 81–6.

Kent, M., Newnham, R. and Essex, S. (2002) 'Tourism and sustainable water supply in Mallorca: a geographical analysis', *Applied Geography* 22(4), 351–74.

Kotios, A., Plageras, P., Galanos, G., Koutoulakis, M. and Saratsis, Y. (2009) *The Impact of Tourism on Water Demand and Wetlands: Searching for a Sustainable Coexistence*, University of Thessaly, Department of Planning and Regional Development, Volos, Greece.

Kundzewicz, Z.W., Mata, L.J., Arnell, N.W., Döll, P., Kabat, P., Jiménez, B., Miller, K.A., Oki, T., Sen, Z. and Shiklomanov, I.A. (2007) 'Freshwater resources and their management' in M.L. Parry, O.F. Canziani, J.P. Palutikof, van der Linden, P. J. & C.E. Hanson (eds), *Climate Change 2007: impacts, adaptation and vulnerability: contribution of Working Group II to the fourth assessment report of the Intergovernmental Panel on Climate Change*. Cambridge: Cambridge University Press, 173–210.

Lew, A.A., Hall, C.M. and Timothy, D.J. (2008) *World geography of travel and tourism: a regional approach*. Oxford: Elsevier.

Llamas, M.R., Aldaya, M.M., Garrido, A. and Lopez-Gunn, E. (2010) *Lessons learnt by applying the water-footprint to the Spanish water policy*, Water Footprint and Public Policy Seminar, Stockholm World Water Week, 7 September 2010.

Lootvoet M. and Roddier-Quefelec C. (2009) *MEDSTAT II: 'Water and Tourism' pilot study*. Luxembourg: Eurostat, European Commission.

Manoli, E., Assimacopoulos, D. and Karavitis, C.A. (2004) 'Water supply management approaches using US on the island of Rhodes, Greece', *Desalination* 161(2), 179–89.

Miller, G., Rathouse, K., Scarles, C., Holmes, K. and Tribe, J. (2010) 'Public understanding of sustainable tourism', *Annals of Tourism Research* 37(3), 627–45.

Molle, F. and Mollinga, P. (2003) 'Water poverty indicators: conceptual problems and policy issues', *Water Policy* 5(5), 529–44.

Mouliérac, A. and Thivet, G. (2009) *L'eau dans le secteur touristique*, Plan Bleu unpublished report (obtained through personal correspondence). Marseille: Plan Bleu.

Nixon, S., Trent, Z., Marcuello, C. and Lallana, C. (2003) *Europe's water: An indicator-based assessment. Topic report 1/2003*. Copenhagen: European Environment Agency (EEA).

Ohlsson, L. and Turton, A.R. (1999) *The turning of screw: social resource scarcity the bottle-neck in adaptation to water scarcity*. London: SOAS Occasional Paper.

Oki, T. and Kanae, S. (2006) 'Global hydrological cycles and world water resources', *Science* 313(5790), 1068.

Perry, A. 2005, 'The Mediterranean: how can the world's most popular and successful tourist destination adapt to a changing climate?', in C.M. Hall and J.E.S. Higham (eds) *Tourism, recreation, and climate change*. Clevedon: Channel View Books, 86–96.

——(2006) 'Will Predicted Climate Change Compromise the Sustainability of Mediterranean Tourism?', *Journal of Sustainable Tourism* 14(4), 367–75.

Postel, S.L., Daily, G.C. and Ehrlich, P.R. (1996) 'Human appropriation of renewable fresh water', *Science* 271(5250), 785.

Rico-Amoros, A.M., Olcina-Cantos, J. and Sauri, D. (2009) 'Tourist land use patterns and water demand: Evidence from the Western Mediterranean', *Land Use Policy*, 26(2), 493–501.

Ridoutt, B.G., Eady, S.J., Sellahewa, J., Simons, L. and Bektash, R. (2009) 'Water footprinting at the product brand level: case study and future challenges', *Journal of Cleaner Production* 17(13), 1228–35.

Rijsberman, F.R. (2006) 'Water scarcity: Fact or fiction?', *Agricultural Water Management* 80(1–3), 5–22.

Sapiano, M. (2008) 'Measures for facing Water Scarcity and Drought in Malta', *European Water* 23/24, 79–86.

Savvides, L., Dörflinger, G. and Alexandrou, K. (2001) *The assessment of water demand of Cyprus*. FAO Land and Water Development Division.

Scott, D., Amelung, B., Becken, S., Ceron, J.P., Dubois, G., Gossling, S., Peeters, P. and Simpson, M. (2008) *Climate change and tourism: Responding to global challenges*. Madrid: World Tourism Organization (UNWTO).

Shaalan, I.M. (2005) 'Sustainable tourism development in the Red Sea of Egypt threats and opportunities', *Journal of Cleaner Production* 13(2), 83–7.

Simpson, M.C., Gössling, S., Scott, D., Hall, C.M. and Gladin, E. (2008) *Climate change adaptation and mitigation in the tourism sector: frameworks, tools and practices*. Paris: UNEP, University of Oxford, UNWTO, WMO.

Sophocleous, M. (2004) 'Global and regional water availability and demand: prospects for the future', *Natural Resources Research* 13(2), 61–75.

Statzu, V. and Strazzera, E. (2011) 'A panel data analysis of residential water demand in a Mediterranean tourist region' in F. Cerina, A. Markandya and M. McAleer (eds) *Economics of Sustainable Tourism*. Abingdon: Routledge, 58–75.

Telfer, D.J. and Wall, G. (1996) 'Linkages between tourism and food production', *Annals of Tourism Research* 23(3), 635–53.

Torres, R. (2003) 'Linkages between tourism and agriculture in Mexico', *Annals of Tourism Research* 30(3), 546–66.

Tourism Concern (2011) *Tourism: a thirsty business*. Available at: www.tourismconcern.org.uk (accessed 19 February 2011).

UNDP (2006) *Human Development Report 2006: Beyond scarcity*. New York: Palgrave Macmillan.

UN-Water (2006) *Coping With Water Scarcity: a strategic issue and priority for system-wide action*, United Nations. Available at: www.unwater.org/downloads/waterscarcity.pdf.

——(2010) *Climate Change Adaptation: The Pivotal Role of Water*, United Nations. Available at: www. unwater.org/downloads/unw_ccpol_web.pdf.

UNWTO (2010) *UNWTO Tourism Highlights*, World Tourism Organization (UNWTO). Available at: www.unwto.org/facts/eng/highlights.htm.

Vorosmarty, C.J., Green, P., Salisbury, J. and Lammers, R.B. (2000) 'Global water resources: vulnerability from climate change and population growth', *Science* 289(5477), 284.

World Water Assessment Programme (2009) *The United Nations World Water Development Report 3: Water in a Changing World*. London: Earthscan.

42

Community-based ecotourism as indigenous social entrepreneurship

Trisia Farrelly

Introduction

> The vanua ... which refers to the connection of people with the land through their ancestors and guardian spirits ... could serve as a powerful mechanism promoting the linkage between biodiversity conservation and tourism management.
>
> *(Sinha and Bushell 2002: 35)*

Indigenous community-based ecotourism (ICBE) can only benefit from the insights of indigenous social entrepreneurship (ISE) literature when human–environment relationships such as the Fijian vanua are recognised. ISE is a newly defined subject area, which originates in business studies literature. One example of ISE is CBE. ISE may be explained as an indigenous group's endeavours to address or create broadly defined social value through entrepreneurship (Anderson *et al.* 2006a). It implies local agency and this is reflected in the strategies many indigenous communities develop to interact with the global economy on their own terms (Anderson *et al.* 2006b). ISE also emphasises the role of social capital in development. Social capital has been explored by many theorists (including Bourdieu 1986; Putnam 2000; and Fukuyama 1999). Putnam (2000) defines social capital as 'features of social organization such as networks, norms, and social trust that facilitate coordination and cooperation for mutual benefit' (Putnam 2000: 36), and believes that it can be measured by the amount of trust and reciprocity in a community or between individuals. For Putnam, social capital refers to the collective value of all 'social networks' (who people know) and 'norms of reciprocity' (the inclinations that arise from these networks to do things for each other) (Putnam 2000: 20, 135). Granovetter (1985) recognises the value of sociality to economic activities in his notion of 'social embeddedness'. Sociality, he argues, drives and informs economic activity. This realisation of social embeddedness in economic activity is also taken up by Cahn (2008) who states that entrepreneurship 'is dependent on non-economic institutions and activities including culture, social networks, politics, and religion' (Cahn 2008: 1). Here, I argue that economic activity is not just socially embedded. In indigenous contexts at least, economic activities such as community-based ecotourism are also ecologically embedded.

The ISE literature goes some way to addressing the lack of attention applied to the cultural values in entrepreneurship literature to date. However, one weakness I identify in much of the

ISE literature, is its inadequate attention to the complex ways many indigenous cultures relate to their environments and how these human–environment relationships shape examples of ISE (such as ICBE). This chapter, then, will illustrate the need to incorporate culturally contingent human–environment relationships in community-based ecotourism planning and management policies and strategies.

The Boumā National Heritage Park (BNHP), Fiji, is presented as an example of ICBE. The indigenous Boumā community living within the Park understands their relationship with their natural, social and cosmological environment as holistic, relational and inter-connected. A high failure rate of ICBEs and ecotourism initiatives in general (Epler Wood 2003)[1] may be attributed to 'outsider stakeholders' lack of attention to the human–environment relationships and associated cultural values constituting these endeavours. Conversely, indigenous communities that create new ICBE initiatives by embedding these enterprises into pre-existing ecosocial relationships may have a higher chance of meeting local needs. After situating ISE within the broader literature, I present an indigenous Fijian ICBE case study as an example of ISE. The case study will illustrate why ISE literature must more adequately address indigenous human–environment relationships if we are to fully understand local engagement in ICBEs.

Indigenous ecotourism and human–environment relationships

Recently, a number of books and articles have been written that explore ecotourism as indigenous entrepreneurship, for example, Zeppel (2006). Some of these publications present indigenous ecotourism as a social enterprise emphasising cultural values (e.g. Berkes and Adhikari 2006), whereas others have highlighted a set of cultural characteristics or traits necessary for engagement in successful ecotourism enterprise (Hinch 2001). Some have emphasised the centrality of site-specific human–environment relationships in the management of ecotourism enterprise (Higgins-Desbiolles 2009), whereas others are sceptical (Fennell 2008). Other writers/researchers have found that social entrepreneurship literature can contribute to a deeper understanding of indigenous communities' relationships with their environment and how these relationships determine the local interpretations and outcomes of ecotourism initiatives (Campbell-Hunt et al. 2010). This chapter will argue, however, that if social entrepreneurship is to provide answers that will illuminate questions surrounding the sustainability of indigenous ecotourism, a greater attention to socio-ecological relationships must first be embedded within the literature.

Social entrepreneurship and indigenous entrepreneurship

Anderson et al. (2006b: 57) suggest that ISE can operate at the intersection of social entrepreneurship and indigenous entrepreneurship. There is almost no agreement as to the definition of entrepreneurship and many definitions are vague. Most models of entrepreneurship have been developed following Eurocentric models. For example, McClelland (1961) lists some of the psychological factors that contribute to successful entrepreneurship in different cultures. These cultural characteristics are representative of those found in the West and include achieved rather than ascribed status; anti-traditionalism; the belief that all citizens are born equal; and self-orientation rather than collectivism.

Although all entrepreneurship involves social and economic components, the difference between social entrepreneurship and other forms of entrepreneurship is that social entrepreneurship prioritises social over economic goals (Christie and Honig 2006). Anderson et al. (2006b) define social entrepreneurship as 'organizations combining resources toward the delivery of goods and services that provide social improvements and change' (2006b: 62). Another definition offered by Peredo and McLean (2006) suggests that the entrepreneur can be an individual or a group as long as the goal is the creation of social value.

> Where some person or group aims either exclusively or in some prominent way to create social value of some kind, and pursue that goal through some combination of (1) recognizing and exploiting opportunities to create this value, (2) employing innovation, (3) tolerating risk, and (4) declining to accept limitations in available resources.
>
> *(Peredo and McLean 2006: 56)*

Hindle and Landsdowne identify indigenous entrepreneurship as an 'explicit globally relevant research paradigm' (Hindle and Landsdowne 2007: 8). They also present indigenous entrepreneurship as one of the most likely solutions to dependency caused by international hand outs. The indigenous entrepreneurship paradigm, they say, is based on a 'theory of values' rather than on a Eurocentric economic 'values theory'. If we are to understand how indigenous peoples negotiate modernity, we must understand the different values they attribute to the world around them. This theory of values has profound implications for the recognition of the diverse ways in which indigenous peoples value their environment, and, therefore, examples of ISE.

Indigenous entrepreneurship may be distinguished from other forms of entrepreneurship by the fact that it is only managed by indigenous peoples who share a common worldview. For those who have maintained links with their communities and their value systems, that common worldview includes a close attachment to ancestral territories and the natural territories within them (Anderson *et al.* 2006b: 59).

Te Ahukaramu Charles Royal's 'indigenous' includes 'those cultures whose world views place special significance on the idea of the unification of the humans with the natural world' (cited in Cunningham and Stanley 2003: 403).

> The indigenous worldview sees God in the world, particularly in the natural world of the forest, the desert, the sea and so on. Human identity is explainable by reference to the natural phenomena of the world … Hence, indigenous worldviews give rise to a unique set of values and behaviours which seek to foster this sense of oneness and unity with the world.
>
> *(Royal 2002: 4)*

This is not to say that all indigenous entrepreneurship involves collective effort built on traditional values. Peredo *et al.* (2004) offer the possibility of a broad spectrum of indigenous entrepreneurship including individual enterprises that share similar values to non-indigenous entrepreneurship described above. However, as the focus of this chapter is how ISE literature can contribute to ICBE theory and practice, it is the collective expressions of indigenous entrepreneurship that are most relevant here. I also argue that those indigenous groups that retain a collective function are more likely to retain a worldview that they are 'a part' of the environment rather than 'apart' from the environment.

Indigenous social entrepreneurship (ISE)

Peredo *et al.* (2004) distinguish ISE from other forms of indigenous entrepreneurship in its emphasis on social development over economic development. ISE consists not only of economic prosperity in a Western sense, but also includes collective cultural and social identity and well-being (more closely aligned with indigenous notions of 'prosperity'):

... [and may be defined as] a community acting corporately as both entrepreneur and enterprise in pursuit of the common good ... to create and operate a new enterprise embedded in its existing social structure. [These are also intended to] yield sustainable individual and group benefits over the long and the short term.

(Peredo et al. 2004: 15–16).

Therefore, ISE is more likely to emphasise collectivity and community-based goals than the broader category of indigenous entrepreneurship.

ISE's propensity toward collective endeavours is what other researchers have referred to as 'tribal entrepreneurship' (e.g. Ingram 1990; de Bruin and Mataira 2003). Those who use this term suggest that it is possible to incorporate tribal values and ethics into the running of a business. Like ISE, the primary objectives of tribal entrepreneurship are self-determination and community-control (de Bruin and Mataira 2003: 173). In addition, Ingram (1990) notes that, 'unlike the Western entrepreneur, [the] informal sector [indigenous] entrepreneur may not view the maximisation of profit as the primary motivation of success' (Ingram 1990: 66). She suggests, instead, for example, that an indigenous Pacific form of entrepreneurship may be realised through 'subsistence entrepreneurship' in which economic activities are developed 'while maintaining a unique and preferred way of life' (ibid.). Cahn (2008) also notes that those who live their lives fa'a Samoa (i.e. according to indigenous Samoan values) 'choose to trade off potential economic business success in order to ensure their family's status is not harmed in any way' (Cahn 2008: 8). Consequently, social and cultural capital is maintained and enhanced.

Fijian veiwekani (kinship ties) as social networks in Fiji can benefit ISE as they may encourage collectivity in environmental and entrepreneurial endeavours. Veiwekani can also mean that access to land for ISE is made available to kin through customary land systems while excluding those who do not share the same system of values (i.e. non-indigenous).[2] Veiwekani can provide a system of gate-keeping that prevents foreign investors from purchasing, or signing long-term leases for, indigenous tenured land, thus ensuring local autonomy. For example, in 1996, one kin group in Boumā wished to allow an American to sign a 99-year lease on a plot of land. Land and the natural resources within plots of land are scarce in Boumā. At that time, the appeal to the chief for the long-term lease was denied because the resource needs of the next generation would have been sacrificed through such an agreement. Edward Hviding's work in Morovo Lagoon is another example of the ways in which traditional social structures have contributed to the politics of access to indigenous land (1993).

One weakness in ICBE and ISE literature is its tendency to ignore a prior pre-colonial existence or a tendency toward 'an unreflective plenitude in which tradition is hegemonic and simply reproduced' (Ewing 1997: 20). A greater attention to cultural hybridity would bring to light the dynamic and 'porous' nature of culture, and thereby counter the treatment of indigenous communities as homogeneous, passive and harmonious. Cultural hybridity entails 'discovering the new, while changing, adapting and preserving the best of the old' (Kao et al. 2002: 44). For example, Foley (2008) writes, 'Maori entrepreneurs within the tourism industry are indeed modern yet maintaining cultural sustainability; a complex and multifaceted phenomenon' (Foley 2008: 94).

With new environmental and social impacts come changes in human–environment relationships. We can see plenty of examples of this in the complex ways indigenous peoples continue to organise themselves and negotiate new knowledge, skills and dynamic natural environments. Examples include climate change (Crate and Nuttall 2009), the introduction of new environmental and economic values and practices constituting 'conservation' (e.g. Adams 2004) and 'sustainability' (e.g. the Indigenous Peoples' Plan of Implementation on Sustainable

Development 2002), and the cash economy (see plenty of examples of this in Parry and Bloch's 1989 *Money and the Morality of Exchange*). ISE can only be successful when a community is empowered to make choices (given time and through trial and error) when confronted with new knowledge, values and practices. These choices include how contemporarily meaningful cultural values and expressions may be incorporated into community endeavours in a way that will most likely increase socio-ecological well-being. Choices also include rejection and resistance.

Moore and de Bruin go some way to suggesting how local cultural values and ethics may be inter-woven into ISE:

> … [A] collective vision for tribal prosperity, tribal tradition and customary lore, the collective understanding of living in harmony with the nature, the spiritual and the inner-self, which in turn … [are] … dynamically being reshaped by other influences such as global capitalism and neo-tribalism.
>
> *(Moore and de Bruin 2003: 44)*

Despite this reference to nature, human–environmental objectives and relationships are commonly 'glossed over' or left out in the way writers distinguish between indigenous and non-indigenous entrepreneurship, as well as social and indigenous entrepreneurship. Often, the reader can only assume that culturally contingent human–environment relationships exist somewhere within the mingling of social, cultural, environmental and economic objectives. In addition, the significance or the complexity of the inter-connectedness of indigenous entrepreneurship and diverse social and natural environments is not always clear. The reason for this may be found in the differences between rational and objective Western versus inter-subjective indigenous perceptions and interpretations of 'environment' (Farrelly 2010).

A number of writers have advocated against the 'intellectual colonisation' (Weaver 1998: 16) of indigenous peoples by preaching universal, homogeneous 'expert' scientific epistemologies and ontologies. Positivist, rational, objective and instrumental approaches to human–environment relationships in ISE research have the potential to alienate indigenous peoples from their own cultures (Dwyer 1994, cited in Weaver 1998: 12). Weaver (1998) posits that there is a danger of implying that indigenous peoples can '"save" their environment and make money [e.g. through community-based ecotourism] if they convert to a standard of rationality that sees nature as "other"' (Weaver 1998: 14). This does not suggest that biology is redundant (in ICBE), but that it can be meaningfully applied 'to a point' (ibid.).

As a response to these concerns, there have been recent calls for new ecologies that re-imagine human–environment relationships as 'holistic, connective, and relational'. These new ecologies (Biersack 2009) provide researchers, policy makers and consultants with a more useful lens through which they may better understand ICBE. The most profound difference between these ecological perspectives and many previous ones include a new emphasis on the dissolution of culture–nature dichotomies. Their more holistic and cross-culturally inclusive approach better encapsulates indigenous human–environment relationships such as the Fijian vanua. The case study shows how the vanua cannot be understood when the social is separated from the environmental and how ICBE management is negotiated alongside the vanua.

A positive contribution of ISE literature to ICBE is its promotion of indigenous self-determination and sustainability in the face of global economic forces. In the event that indigenous communities choose to engage with the global economy, the literature emphasises that indigenous peoples define and carry out development 'on their own terms'. ISE may also provide insights into indigenous attitudes and motivations for ICBE enterprise.

Those of us who research and write within the academic fields of ISE and ICBE must ensure that we do not reinforce neo-colonial constructs 'that continue to subjugate indigenous people [sic]' (Marchetti 2006; Smith 1999, cited in Foley 2009: 607). Hindle and Landsdowne caution that it is 'Indigenous people themselves [who] must create the paradigm of indigenous entrepreneurship. It cannot be thrust upon them by non-indigenous scholars as just one more imposition of the dominant culture' (Hindle and Landsdowne 2007: 11).

Although ISE can valuably contribute to ICBE, it must first adequately address the complex human–environment relationships that exist in indigenous contexts in their lack of reference to environmental stewardship and sustainability. These are two major motivating factors driving the establishment of ICBE. The natural environment is considered an important element in ICBE literature, particularly in its frequent reference to traditional ecological knowledge (TEK) or traditional indigenous knowledge (TIK) and ecological sustainability. Conversely, the broader ISE literature makes only general statements surrounding land tenure in terms of control of natural resources. However, neither body of work adequately addresses the cultural complexities of the environment in unique indigenous contexts. Certainly, neither subject area describes the relationships indigenous peoples have with their environment as inter-subjective, cosmological or relational in quite the same way that their participants may experience them. This is almost certainly as a result of the dominance of dualistic ontologies found in environmental science, tourism and entrepreneurship discourse constituting ISE literature.

ICBE as ISE

Indigenous communities around the world have suffered various forms of disempowerment and dislocation as a result of colonial expansion, neo-colonial modes of development, global economic forces and different technologies. It is often argued that involvement in ICBE is one way that indigenous peoples may benefit socially and financially from involvement in the global economy while at the same time maintaining local control of natural resources and socio-cultural values (Berkes and Davidson-Hunt 2010).

The UN Commission on Sustainable Development (2002) highlights the role indigenous peoples have played in their contribution to the conservation of global biodiversity.

> Indigenous peoples consist five per cent of the world's population but embody 80% of the world's cultural diversity. They are estimated to occupy 20% of the world's land surface but nurture 80% of the world's biodiversity on ancestral lands and territories. Rainforests of the Amazon, Central Africa, Asia and Melanesia is home to over half of the total global spectrum of indigenous peoples and at the same time contain some of the highest species biodiversity in the world.
>
> *(cited in Zeppel 2006: 6)*

The Indigenous Peoples' Biodiversity Network in 1997 declared indigenous peoples as the 'creators and conservers of biodiversity' (ibid.), and the UN Convention on Biological Diversity in 1992 emphasised the ecological guardianship and traditional dependence of many indigenous peoples on their natural resources (Prance 1998, cited in ibid.). Therefore, an emphasis on how indigenous peoples understand their natural resources is a vital task in ICBE research and implementation.

Many indigenous communities have made the choice to engage with the global economy to improve livelihoods and alleviate poverty by establishing community-based ecotourism enterprises. ICBE, according to Drumm (1998: 198, cited in Zeppel 2006: 10) involves 'ecotourism programs which take place under the control and active participation of the people who inhabit a natural [tourist] attraction'. The twin primary objectives of ICBE have been noted in the literature as nature conservation and income generation (e.g. Sproule 1996, cited in Zeppel 2006: 11). By its very nature, ICBE is dedicated to sustainable entrepreneurship: 'a form of managed economic growth that occurs within the context of sound environmental stewardship' (Harris and Lieper 1995: xx).

Zeppel's (2007) summary of the differences in perceptions between the ecotourism industry and indigenous ecotourism emphasises the socio-ecological as a vital bottom-line (Zeppel 2007: 325). Her summary shows indigenous ecotourism as offering local control compared with a potentially exploitative ecotourism industry alternative. In addition, for Zeppel (2006), indigenous ecotourism emphasises social goals of collective participation and self-determination over economic goals. Indigenous ecotourism is also presented as 'based on indigenous knowledge *systems* and *values*' [my emphases] (ibid.: 12). These systems and values are embedded within integrated socio-ecological relationships. One example of these relationships is the Fijian vanua.

Vanua as indigenous human–environment relationship

Vanua, whenua and fonua are some Pacific concepts that have been inadequately equated to 'land' when applied to community-based ecotourism as an indigenous form of entrepreneurship. Vanua, for example, not only refers to land. It also encompasses 'the Fijian worldview, ethos, cosmos, all living and non-living things together as one' (Helu-Thaman 1997: 14). Vanua has also been described as 'identity, territorial root, habitat' and 'a sacred sociological point of reference' (Olutimayin 2002: 6).

Fijian theologian I.S. Tuwere (2002) emphasises the connection between people and place in terms of the vanua.

> The vanua is a 'social fact' which for the Fijian people holds life together and gives it meaning. To be cast out from one's vanua is to be cut off from one's source of life: one's mother as it were. In many Pacific languages, the world for land is related or identical with the word for womb or placenta.[3] The best examples are: fanua (Samoan), fonua (Tongan), fenua (Maohi Nui or Tahitian), and whenua (Maori). They have parallel meanings with the Fijian vanua, referring as it does to the basis of life on earth. The connection between place and person is physical. Not only is this demonstrated in one's tract of land for gardening, but it can also be shown by a father planting, for example, a coconut tree on the same spot where the wa ni vicovico (umbilical cord) of his newborn child has been buried.
> *(Tuwere 2002: 36, cited in Daye 2009: 116)*

Vanua prioritises the collective over the individual, and social capital over economic capital. Here, Ravuvu (1983) highlights social values in the definition of vanua concept.

> It does not mean only the land area one is identified with, and the vegetation, animal life and other objects on it, but it also includes the social and cultural system – the people, their traditions and customs, beliefs and values, and the various other institutions established for the sake of achieving harmony, solidarity and prosperity within a particular social context.
> *(Ravuvu 1983: 70)*

The vanua also acts as a guiding set of principles for living life the right way. As the people, the land and everything in it are understood as inter-connected, caring and sharing with each other, and living life for the good of the whole community rather than for the self is vital for social, economic, and environmental sustainability. Although a commitment to the vanua and its meaning for the Fijian people is becoming somewhat diluted, its revitalisation could be crucial if indigenous entrepreneurial endeavours are to be socially and environmentally sustainable. For example, Sinha and Bushell (2002) suggest that the vanua may be instrumental in 'regulat[ing] the consumptive and tourism uses of local biodiversity' (Sinha and Bushell 2002: 1). Similarly, Batibasaqa et al. argue that the vanua offers 'an alternative set of values, based in the past but aware of the present, that can act as an effective counter to dominant ideologies of resource development and exploitation' (Batibasaqa et al. 1999: 106).

The notion of the vanua contrasts with the dominant non-indigenous epistemological approach of treating humans as independent of other cosmological and physical environmental elements and as humans positioned against the landscape (see, e.g. Ingold 2000). The Boumā National Heritage Park is one example of a Fijian people's endeavours to culturally hybridise the vanua with entrepreneurship to create a locally meaningful form of ICBE for the well-being of its people. The Boumā people call this hybrid 'business va'avanua'. The ideal form of business va'avanua involves respect for the chiefly leadership in guiding the community to adhering to the laws of the vanua. This includes working for the good of the community rather than working for the self.

However, as the case study shows, those originating outside Boumā society will not realise the potentially regulatory value of the vanua to the impacts of ecotourism unless the complexities of this human–environment relationship are fully appreciated. Boumā's Waitabu Marine Reserve as ICBE is not only socially embedded, but also ecologically and cosmologically embedded. This is because these three realms are inextricably linked in indigenous Fijian human–environment relationships. It follows that these complex human–environment relationships are central to fully understanding their implications for, and impacts on, ICBE planning and management.

Case study

Boumā National Heritage Park

In Fiji, a province, district, or even a single clan can have traditional ownership rights over a marine area (qoliqoli). Within that marine area are dedicated areas (kanakanas) within which specific clans can subsistence fish. The Waitabu village and their Waitabu Marine Reserve and Campground ICBE are located within the Boumā National Heritage Park. A tabu (locally managed no fishing zone) was set aside as a marine protected area (MPA) in 1998 within their qoliqoli, and in March 2001, the first paying tourists were provided with a snorkelling experience in the marine reserve.

In Fiji, the yavusa or sub-tribe is named after the yavu (ancestral site or house mound) of the yavutū (settlement) and the vū (ancestor/one originator) of that yavusa. The yavusa, as the descendents of the same vū, recognise one kalou-vū (originating spirit). The kalou-vū is normally the father of the vū, and one totem or set of totems (i cavuti), may be inherited from the kalou-vū. A sense of place and identity is strengthened by the totems, spirits and ancestors to which both the land and the people belong. In 1941, Capell and Lester reported that the introduction of Christianity meant that a declining number of Fijians were observant of the prohibitions and respect traditionally accorded their totems. However, there is still plenty of contemporary literature written about how modern day Fijians acknowledge and respect their totems, regardless of widespread

Christianity. Totems perform the role of ensuring the adherence of the values of the vanua and environmental sustainability because they determine linkages between different yavusa and between the yavusa and the land. Consequently, they contribute to the integrity of the tribe. Through the symbolic nature of totems, the Kalou vū, vū, and/or the Christian God governs by rewarding and punishing for observing or failing to observe the vanua laws and protocols and for the correct or incorrect treatment of the environment.

Adherence to vanua values including loving one another, helping one another and observing tabu is rewarded by the Christian God and vū with tribe-specific symbols from the natural environment: tribe-specific because each tribe has its uniquely recognisable signs. The reward is a contribution toward sautu (peace and prosperity), which may be revealed in the abundance of harvests from crops or fishing, the health of the people and animals and, more recently, the ongoing success of community-based enterprises.

Totems can reinvigorate vanua integrity when their distribution is conducted strategically. The community members were very careful in the distribution of their totem fish[4] when I observed the totem ritual harvest in Waitabu Village in 2004. The yavusa ensured that the Vunisā (Head Chief) received the first of the harvest, and then that all in the tribe received their share. In its gathering and careful distribution, there was a palpable sense of love of, and respect for, community and reverence for the totem. From my perspective, in the current climate of uncertainty as to the integrity of the Boumā tribe, the harvest could not have come at a better time. The harvest appeared to reinvigorate a sense of unity between the various sub-clans that made up the Boumā tribe in the Park. It also seemed to bolster hope for the future of the tribe as at that time social cohesion had begun to 'unravel'.[5] Many Waitabu villagers interpreted the abundance of their harvest in 2004 as directly related to the Waitabu Marine Reserve. The implication was that the ICBE project was 'right' and 'just'. Therefore, the majority of the community felt reassured by their totems (ancestors) and their God that they were doing the right thing in continuing to manage the project as they had been. Ultimately, their abundant harvest was a symbol of sautu. However, the impact of ICBE was not always positive and symbols manifest themselves in other ways. If tourism in Boumā was carried out outside vanua laws and protocols, the communities constituting Boumā would receive punishment from vū and God. Punishment may be manifested as crop diseases, reduced fish stocks and illness among other things.

Conclusion

The Boumā case study illustrates that the cosmological links with the social and ecological profoundly impact on notions of 'stewardship', and 'sustainability' central to Western indicators of 'successful' or 'unsuccessful' environmental/ecotourism management. The vanua requires a broader treatment of the of the word 'environment' than that defined by rational and instrumental sciences assumed in much of the ISE literature.

A characteristic of many indigenous knowledge systems, illustrated in this case study, includes cosmological or spiritual dimensions. Despite attempts to deal sensitively with indigenous cultural issues, the literature is written from a predominantly Eurocentric worldview. This is revealed in its propensity to dissect the social and the political from the environmental while dismissing the spiritual. Morgan (2007) notes that debate over resource management and economic development seldom include the spiritual significance of elements of the environment. This is despite much literature written about the Pacific that identifies the fundamental spiritual connection of people and place to economic relationships. For example Mauss (1990), recognising the relationship between spiritual elements and economy states:

all kinds of institutions are given expression at one and the same time—religious, juridical, and moral, which relate to both politics and the family; likewise economic ones ... as if there were a constant exchange of spiritual matter, including things and men, between clans and individuals, distributed between social ranks, the sexes, and the generations.

(Mauss 1990, cited in Morgan 2007: 61)

The spiritual connection between indigenous peoples and their natural environment has received growing attention by ecologists and anthropologists. Evidence of this can be found in Fikret Berkes' 'sacred ecology' and Leslie Sponsel's 'spiritual ecology'. Fijian ethnographers Ravuvu (1983) and Tuwere (2002) reaffirm the importance of including a spiritual component in discussions and debates involving economic development and resource management.

The case study also shows that social networks and reciprocity can strengthen the collective efforts toward ICBE as ISE. By protecting the environment, there is a greater likelihood for a greater flow of marine resources through the community circulating back to a strengthening of social networks through a greater potential for reciprocity.

If the ISE literature is to positively contribute to ICBE, it must go beyond Western notions of the 'social' as clearly demarcated from the 'environmental' to consider alternative integrated relationships between humans and non-humans within a culturally contingent landscape. In the indigenous Fijian context, Timoci Waqaisavou (2001) calls for 'future research [needs] to be undertaken to fully understand the synergy between the vanua and the impact of tourism on native land' (Timoci Waqaisavou 2001: 11). This research, he says, should be carried out while adopting 'a Pacific approach of sensitivity to traditional values within a predominantly westernised industry, that of tourism' (ibid.).

The Fijian vanua and other indigenous and integrated human–environment relationships can be considered motivating factors and mechanisms for enhancing and supporting entrepreneurial activities rather than hindering them. These relationships increase the likelihood of resilience and reduce vulnerability when social and cultural capital are developed as a product of appropriately and socially embedded economic activity. Successful examples of ICBE are those that blend traditional culture with entrepreneurship. However, it must be remembered that cultures have never been static. Therefore, the way these approaches are blended must meet the indigenous human–environment relationships that suit the present day.

Notes

1 A French study cited by Epler Wood (2003) found that as many as 90 per cent of ecotourism projects fail.
2 This can also mean that those outside landowning groups may be excluded when their membership is deemed damaging to contemporary and collective cultural values.
3 Margaret Jolly provides more evidence of the human–environment relationship inherent in the term stating that, 'in many Austronesian languages, the word for land (*whenua, fanua, vanua*) is the same as that for placenta, and a person's attachment to place is secured by the planting of the placenta soon after birth' (Jolly 2007: 515).
4 Out of respect for Naisaqai and their totem fish, I will not record its name here.
5 This was largely due to historical and micro-political conflict.

References

Adams, M. (2004) 'Negotiating Nature: Collaboration and Conflict between Aboriginal and Conservation Interests in New South Wales, Australia', *Australian Journal of Environmental Education* 201, 3–11.
Anderson, R.B., Dana, L.P. and Dana, T.E. (2006a) 'Indigenous Land Rights, Entrepreneurship, and Economic Development in Canada: 'Opting-In' To the Global Economy', *Journal of World Business* 411, 45–55.

Anderson, R., Honig, B., Anderson, R.B. and Peredo, A.M. (2006b) 'Communities in the Global Economy: Where Social and Indigenous Entrepreneurship Meet,' in C. Steyaert and D. Hjorth (eds) *Entrepreneurship as Social Change: A Third Movements in Entrepreneurship Book*. Cheltenham and Northampton, MA: Edward Elgar, 56–78.

Batibasaqa, K., Overton, J. and Horsley, P. (1999) 'Vanua: Land, People, and Culture in Fiji', in J. Overton and R. Scheyens (eds) *Strategies for Sustainable Development: Experiences from the Pacific*. London: Zed Books, 100–8.

Berkes, F. and Adhikari, T. (2006) 'Development and Conservation: Indigenous Businesses and the UNDP Equator Initiative', *International Journal of Entrepreneurship and Small Business* 36, 671–90.

Berkes, F. and Davidson-Hunt, J. (2010) 'Innovation through Commons Use: Community-Based Enterprises (Editorial)', *International Journal of the Commons* 41.

Biersack, A. (2009) 'From the New Ecology to the New Ecologies', *American Anthropologist* 1011, 5–18.

Bourdieu, P. (1986) 'The Forms of Capital', in J.G. Richardson (ed.) *Handbook of Theory and Research in the Sociology of Education*. New York: Greenwood, 241–58.

de Bruin, A. and Mataira, P. (2003) 'Indigenous Entrepreneurship', in A. de Bruin and A. Dupuis (eds) *Entrepreneurship: New Perspectives in a Global Age*. Aldershot, Hampshire: Ashgate Publishing Ltd, 169–84.

Cahn, M. (2008) 'Indigenous Entrepreneurship, Culture and Micro-Enterprise in the Pacific Islands: Case Studies from Samoa', *Entrepreneurship & Regional Development: An International Journal* 201, 1–18.

Campbell-Hunt, D., Freeman, C. and Dickinson, K.J.M. (2010) 'Community-Based Entrepreneurship and Wildlife Sanctuaries: Case Studies from New Zealand', *International Journal of Innovation and Regional Development* 21, 4–21.

Christie, M. and Honig, B. (2006) 'Social Entrepreneurship: New Research Findings', *Journal of World Business* 411, 1–5.

Crate, S.A. and Nuttall, M. (eds) (2009) *Anthropology and Climate Change: From Encounters to Actions*. Walnut Creek, CA: Left Coast Press.

Cunningham, C. and Stanley, F. (2003) 'Indigenous by Definition, Experience, or World View', *BMJ* 327, 403–4.

Daye, R. (2009) 'Poverty, Race Relations and the Practices of International Business: A Study of Fiji', *Journal of Business Ethics* 892, 115–27.

Epler Wood, M. (2003) 'The Ecoclub Interview', *International Ecotourism Monthly* 554.

Ewing, K. (ed.) (1997) *Arguing Sainthood: Modernity, Psychoanalysis and Islam*. Durham, NC: Duke University Press.

Farrelly, T. (2010) 'Reimagining 'Environment' in Sustainable Development', *Massey University Development Studies Working Paper Series*. Palmerston North, New Zealand Institute of Development Studies, Massey University, 1–13.

Fennell, D. (2008) 'Ecotourism and the Myth of Indigenous Stewardship', *Journal of Sustainable Tourism* 162, 129–49.

Foley, D. (2008) 'What Determines the Bottom Line for Maori Tourism Smes?', *Small Enterprise Research: The Journal of SEAANZ* 161, 86–97.

——(2009) 'Are Maori Entrepreneurs within the Aotearoa Tourism Industry Sustainable? Are They Driven by Economic Needs or Cultural Values?', *6th Annual Australian Graduate School of Entrepreneurship (AGSE) Conference*. Adelaide, SA.

Fukuyama, F. (1999) *Social Capital and Civil Society*, IMF Conference on Second Generation Reforms.

Granovetter, M. (1985) 'Economic Action and Social Structure: The Problem of Embeddedness', *American Journal of Sociology* 91, 481–510.

Hagen, E.E. (ed.) (1962) *On the Theory of Social Change: How Economic Growth Begins*. Homewood, IL: The Dorsey Press Inc.

Harris, R. and Leiper, N. (eds) (1995) *Sustainable Tourism: An Australian Perspective*. Chatswood, NSW: Elsevier Butterworth-Heinemann.

Helu-Thaman, K. (1997) 'Invited Address: Of Daffodils and Heilala: Understanding Cultural Contexts in Pacific Literature', *Multi-Ethnic Literature Society of America (MELUS) Conference*. Honolulu, Hawai'i.

Higgins-Desbiolles, F. (2009) 'Indigenous Ecotourism's Role in Transforming Ecological Consciousness', *Journal of Ecotourism* 82, 144–60.

Hinch, T. (2001) 'Indigenous Territories', *The encyclopedia of ecotourism*, 345–57.

Hindle, K. and Lansdowne, M. (2007) 'Brave spirits on new paths: Globally relevant paradigm of indigenous entrepreneurship research', in L.P. Dana and R.B. Anderson (eds), *International Handbook of Research on Indigenous Entrepreneurship*. Cheltenham: Edward Elgar Publishing, 8–19.

Hviding, E. (1993) 'Indigenous Essentialism? 'Simplifying' Customary Land Ownership in New Georgia, Solomon Islands', *Bijdragen tot de Taal-, Land-en Volkenkunde* 1494, 802–24.

Indigenous Peoples' Plan of Implementation on Sustainable Development (2002) *United Nations World Summit on Sustainable Development*, Johannesburg, South Africa.

Ingold, T. (ed.) (2000) *The Perception of the Environment: Essays in Livelihood, Dwelling and Skill*. London and New York: Routledge.

Ingram, P.T. (1990) *Indigenous entrepreneurship and tourism development in the Cook Islands and Fiji*. Massey University, New Zealand, Doctoral thesis.

Jolly, M. (2007) 'Imagining Oceania: Indigenous and Foreign Representations of a Sea of Islands', *Contemporary Pacific* 192, 508–45.

Kao, R.W.Y., Kao, K.R. and Kao, R.R. (2002) *Entrepreneurism for the Market Economy*. London: Imperial College Press.

Marchetti, E. (2006) 'The Deep Colonising Practices of the Australian Royal Commission into Aboriginal Deaths in Custody', *Journal of Law and Society* 33(3), 451–74.

McClelland, D.C. (ed.) (1961) *The achieving society*. Princeton: D. Van Nostrand.

Moore, C. and de Bruin, A. (2003) 'Ethical Entrepreneurship', in A. de Bruin and A. Dupuis (eds) *Entrepreneurship: New Perspectives in a Global Age*. Aldershot and Burlington, VT: Ashgate Publishing Ltd., 43–56.

Morgan, C.R. (2007) 'Property of Spirits: Hereditary and Global Value of Sea Turtles in Fiji', *Human Organization* 661, 60–8.

Olutimayin, J. (2002) 'Adopting Modern Information Technology in the South Pacific: A Process of Development, Preservation, or Underdevelopment of the Culture?', *The Electronic Journal of Information Systems in Developing Countries* 9, 1–12. Available at: www.is.cityu.edu.hk/research/ejisdc/vol9/v9r3.pdf.

Parry, J. and Bloch, M. (1989) *Money and the Morality of Exchange*. Cambridge: Cambridge University Press.

Peredo, A.M., Anderson, R.B., Galbraith, C.S., *et al.* (2004) 'Towards a Theory of Indigenous Entrepreneurship', *International Journal of Entrepreneurship and Small Business* 11–12, 1–20.

Peredo, A.M. and McLean, M. (2006) 'Social Entrepreneurship: A Critical Review of the Concept', *Journal of World Business* 411, 56–65.

Putnam, R.D. (ed.) (2000) *Bowling Alone: The Collapse and Revival of American Community*. New York: Simon & Schuster.

Ravuvu, A. (ed.) (1983) *Vaka I Taukei: The Fijian Way of Life*. Suva: University of the South Pacific.

Royal, T.A.C. (2002) *Indigenous Worldviews: A Comparative Study*. Wellington, New Zealand Te Wanaga-o-Raukawa.

Sinha, C.C. and Bushell, R. (2002) 'Understanding the Linkages between Biodiversity and Tourism: A Study of Ecotourism in a Coastal Village in Fiji', *Pacific Tourism Review* 6, 35–50.

Tuwere, I.S. (ed.) (2002) *Vanua: Towards a Fijian Theology of Place*. Suva, Fiji: University of the South Pacific.

Waqaisavou, T. (2001) *Native Landowners, Tourism, Attitude, Leases, Fiji*, Pacific Rim Real Estate Society Annual Conference: Tourism in Fiji: Native Land Owner Attitude and Involvement, Adelaide.

Weaver, S. (1998) 'Co-Existence and Cultural Difference: Postcolonial Ecology in the Contemporary Pacific', *Pacific Conservation Biology* 4, 11–20.

Zeppel, H. (2006) *Indigenous Ecotourism: Sustainable Development and Management*, Wallingford: CABI.

——(2007) 'Indigenous Ecotourism: Conservation and Resource Rights', in J. Higham (ed.) *Critical Issues in Ecotourism: Confronting the Challenges*. Oxford: Elsevier, 308–48.

Further reading

Blaser, M. (2004) 'Life Projects: Indigenous People's Agency and Development', in M. Blaser, H. A. Feit and G. McRae (eds) *In the Way of Development: Indigenous Peoples, Life Projects, and Globalization*, London and New York: Zed, 26–44. (Explores the complex negotiations that occur when indigenous peoples are faced with free-market capitalism.)

Dana, L.P. and Anderson, R.B. (eds) (2007) *International Handbook of Research on Indigenous Entrepreneurship*. Edward Elgar Publishing.

Drucker, P.F. (ed.) (1985) *Innovation and Entrepreneurship: Practice and Principles*. New York: Harper.

Farrelly, T. (2009) 'Business Va'avanua: Cultural Hybridisation and Indigenous Entrepreneurship in the Bouma National Heritage Park', *Social Anthropology* Palmerston North Massey University PhD. (The author's PhD thesis providing an extended analysis of indigenous social entrepreneurship in the Boumā National Heritage Park.)

Fuller, D., Buultjens, J. and Cummings, E. (2005) 'Ecotourism and Indigenous Micro-Enterprise Formation in Northern Australia Opportunities and Constraints', *Tourism Management* 266, 891–904.

Hindle, K. and Lansdowne, M. (2005) 'Brave Spirits on New Paths: Toward a Globally Relevant Paradigm of Indigenous Entrepreneurship Research', *Journal of Small Business and Entrepreneurship* 182, 131–42.

Hoselitz, B.F. (1963) 'Entrepreneurship and Traditional Elites', *Economic development and cultural change* 2 (Fall), 36–49.

Maiava, S. and King, T. (2007) 'Pacific Indigenous Development and Post-Intentional Realities,' in A. Ziai (ed.) *Exploring Post-Development: Theory and Practice, Problems and Perspectives*, London and New York: Routledge, pp. 83–98. (Further treatment of indigenous development in the South Pacific.)

Mataira, P.J. (2000) *Nga Kai Arahi Tuitui Maori: Maori Entrepreneurship: The Articulation of Leadership and the Dual Constituency Arrangements Associated with Maori*. Unpublished doctoral thesis: Massey University, Auckland. (Specifically deals with Maori entrepreneurship from an insider perspective.)

Plumwood, V. (2002) *Environmental Culture: The Ecological Crisis of Reason*. London: Routledge. (Explains ecological humanities.)

Roth, G.K. (ed.) (1973) *Fijian Way of Life*. Melbourne, Australia: Oxford University Press.

Veitayaki, J. (2002) 'Taking Advantage of Indigenous Knowledge: The Fiji Case,' *International Social Science Journal* 543, 395–402. (A traditional knowledge focus from an indigenous Fijian perspective.)

Zimmerman, M. (1996) 'The Postmodern Challenge to Environmentalism', *Terra Nova* 12, 131–40. (Explains an integrated or 'integral' approach to ecology and environmentalisms.)

43

Tourism's wasteful ways

David T. Brown

Thar bi men segget a uorbisne:
'Dahet habbe that ilke best
That fuleth his owe nest.'★
      Nicholas de Guilford, fl. 1250, 'Disputation of Ane Hule and a Niʒtingale',
             a.k.a 'The Owl and the Nightingale'

Human endeavour on any scale brings with it the generation of waste products, be they the unwanted by-products of production, consumption and combustion, or the metabolic wastes of humans themselves. And as the thirteenth-century Middle English quote from *The Owl and the Nightingale* implies, concern about waste management is not new. Concentrations of people, be they transitory or permanent, tourist or resident, bring with them concentrations of waste, and dealing with waste has always been a necessary preoccupation of human societies.

What *have* changed are the scale, magnitude, nature and distribution of waste products, as well as our understanding of the term 'waste' – particularly in light of our improved understanding of ecosystem process and function, and of the cycling of materials in the natural environment.

Throughout much of recorded history, we have behaved as if waste management problems could be solved in isolation from their ecosystem context. Until the late twentieth century, emphasis was on the so-called disposal of waste materials, rather than on more environmentally responsible notions of recycling, reuse or source reduction. However, the late twentieth century brought the realisation that, at least from an ecosystem perspective, it is impossible to actually throw anything away … there *is* no 'away'. We now realise – in principle, if not always in policy and practice – that dealing with waste is of course just one element of the sustainability equation, and it cannot be decoupled from other environmental, social and economic criteria.

Tourism's wasteful ways

Whether stationary or mobile, active or sedentary, solitary or in groups, all tourists produce waste – often at a rate greater than the assimilative capacity of the destinations they are visiting, and often in greater quantity than they do in their home context, due to elevated levels of consumption, increased mobility and higher spending associated with tourist activity. When this happens, we have a waste management problem.

Third-world activist and tourism critic Anita Pleumarom pointedly summarised many of the wasteful practices of tourists with the following quote:

> Tourists have a 'use and throw' mindset. They have no investment in the community. They pollute the environment. It is a lifestyle issue: the tourist would like to travel light. Therefore the use of disposables – more plastics, more waste, no recycling. The local communities have to become either waste absorbers or waste managers. New forms of tourism, such as medical tourism, and disaster tourism even increase the generation of toxic waste.
>
> *(Pleumarom 2004)*

Although Pleumarom's pointed comments might appear to profile the worst species of tourist, they contain some essential and undeniable truths about virtually all travellers. In tourism, all of the ordinary challenges of waste management in other economic sectors are there, but are further complicated by the fact that tourists are inherently mobile, transient, active across multiple jurisdictions (often in the same day) and frequently difficult to hold accountable for their actions. They may also act in ways uncharacteristic or unrepresentative of their normal modes of behaviour because they are out of their usual element, indulging themselves and overconsuming while enjoying their vacations. Every international tourist in Europe generates at least 1 kg of solid waste per day (IFEN 1999), and tourists from developed countries probably produce even more (up to 2 kg/person/day for the US EPA, UNEP/Infoterra). The tourism industry must come to meaningful terms with these unattractive realities if it is serious about sustainable tourism.

Chronologically, concern about tourism waste has roughly paralleled general societal concerns about waste management. Initial research identified and qualitatively assessed the problems of waste disposal. Focused quantitative analyses of waste generation (waste audits, life cycle analyses) followed, and have been useful to inform strategic decision-making and management practices. But narrowly technical approaches to waste management are only a part of a much broader arsenal of necessary tools and approaches. By the mid-1990s, waste management issues in the tourism industry were being addressed as part of best practice environmental management (Pilgrim 1996), and rising awareness of the paradigms of sustainability soon led to a much more holistic understanding of waste – not only in the context of ecosystem process and function, but also in the context of socio-political and economic realities. Today, responsible operators in the tourism industry recognise that they must consider waste management issues within the much broader environmental, social, political and economic context of their operations as they work towards the goals of sustainable tourism. Given the enormous diversity, jurisdictional fragmentation and myriad complexities of the tourism industry, this is not a trivial undertaking.

The goal of this chapter is to provide at least a conceptual understanding of the many interrelated factors that influence the production and impacts of wastes by tourists, and to briefly examine some of the generic methods by which waste can be identified and recycled, reused, reduced or eliminated altogether.

The main factors which influence the production and impacts of tourism wastes are: (1) consumption and disposal practices of tourists; (2) the tourism context in which the tourist is immersed; (3) the policy, regulatory and administrative environment(s) where the tourism occurs; and (4) the waste management infrastructure that is in place in a given jurisdiction. We will explore these factors later in this chapter, after outlining some fundamental definitions and principles of waste generation and management.

David T. Brown

What is waste?

Despite its very tangible and often destructive presence, waste is as much an abstract definition as it is a concrete entity (Brown 1993). It is overtly a human construct in both a physical and a semantic sense, defined by the personal proclivities and economic wealth of individuals, the waste management infrastructures of individual jurisdictions, the material prosperity of societies, and the local and global availability of resources.

In undisturbed natural ecosystems, the concept of 'waste' is quite meaningless, as the material residues and breakdown products of one natural system are the raw materials for another, joined in an enormously complex assemblage of inter-related biogeochemical cycles. These cycles work in dynamic equilibrium and on different time scales (e.g. the cycling time of decaying organic matter is typically a lot faster than the cycling time of rocks and minerals), but eventually virtually all naturally occurring materials in the ecosphere are incorporated into some biogeochemical process or other.

Humans, however, have tended to adopt a rather more narrow and self-centred perspective on the cycling of materials and the flow of energy in the ecosphere. Historically, we have rushed to take advantage of those parts of the system that are of direct economic or practical utility to us, extracting the resources we want and de-emphasising, dismissing, or ignoring those processes, functions and ecological perturbations that are not of immediate and obvious relevance to our proximate needs. In the late nineteenth and much of the twentieth centuries, cheap, abundant and accessible energy supplies like fossil fuels and hydroelectricity exacerbated the process, allowing us to find, extract and mobilise material resources in unprecedented quantities, and at an unprecedented rate. Many of our common manufacturing, use and disposal practices are thus inconsistent with the dynamics of natural cycles, and – as we continue to discover, to our chagrin – can result in potentially dangerous perturbations to ecosystem process and function.

Some of our wastes (e.g. food wastes, paper) are readily biodegradable under the right ecological conditions, and, when properly handled in reasonable volumes, can be assimilated quite easily into sustainable waste management systems. Other waste materials (e.g. metals, plastics, glass) are persistent and refined, and represent both proximate materials handling challenges and very significant life cycle impacts in energy use and collateral waste generation. Still other wastes (certain natural or synthetic substances, their derivatives and their breakdown products) are extremely persistent, toxic or both. In our quest to locate, extract, process and consume economically useful materials and energy, we generate many other materials that are not economically useful, which we define as 'waste' and attempt to 'throw away'.

Unfortunately, as stated earlier, there *is* no 'away', as Annie Leonard's wonderful little pop-culture web cartoon *The Story of Stuff* pointed out so simply and eloquently when it went viral in 2007–08 (Leonard 2007). When humans perturb the natural cycles of breakdown and re-assimilation that are in dynamic equilibrium in an intact ecosystem, or when we introduce materials from extraneous sources that are ecologically unmanageable in composition, volume or toxicity, the result is a waste management problem.

We identify and classify our wastes in many ways: by *material* or *composition* (e.g. plastic wastes, wood waste, wastepaper), by *origin* (e.g. pulp mill waste, kitchen waste, mine tailings), by *management* (e.g. industrial waste, municipal solid waste), by *toxicity* (hazardous waste, radioactive waste) or by *economic value* (i.e. anything surplus to our needs that we want to dispose of can be considered waste).

But waste is a complex, subjective and often controversial issue. There are many ways to define, describe and measure it, and making comparisons between different sources of data is often very difficult (UNEP 2004). This data discord has many profound planning and policy implications, causing confusion, allowing for accidental or intentional obfuscation, and slowing down meaningful progress towards responsible, sustainable integrated waste management strategies.

In common parlance, we use several words interchangeably for stuff we do not want: *garbage, trash, refuse* and *rubbish* are used synonymously in everyday speech for solid wastes, but in fact have been ascribed more precise meanings (which arguably may add to the confusion, rather than alleviating it). Rathje (1992) defined *rubbish* as a fairly inclusive term referring to all unwanted solid materials, including construction and demolition debris. *Refuse* has been described as a combination of wet and dry wastes, including *trash* (dry discards like newspapers, boxes, cans, etc.) and *garbage* (soggy discards like food remains, yard waste and offal). To simplify matters, I will refer collectively to all of the above, plus sewage and undesired or unintended gaseous emissions, as *waste*.

This chapter will be concerned with:

1. wastes associated with production and consumption of material goods and food. This category is by far the largest and most diverse source of materials in the waste stream. Resource extraction, processing, manufacturing, packaging, distribution, sales, use and ultimate disposal of the bewildering array of products available to the modern consumer produces a wide range of waste materials at every step and on all branches of the extraction–production–distribution–use–collection–disposal continuum;
2. organic wastes of biological metabolism (urine and faeces). Throughout much of the so-called developed world, these solid, liquid and gaseous wastes are synonymous with *sewage* – a waterborne slurry of faeces and urine, supplemented by paper products, plastics, latex rubber, an array of other wastes and chemicals of domestic, industrial or agricultural origin. In the 'developed' world, these wastes are flushed through the plumbing to wastewater treatment facilities some distance away, or discharged untreated into local water bodies. In the 'developing' world (and some notable examples in the developed world – see footnote), discharge of untreated sewage tends to be the norm, often in close proximity to where it is generated. Untreated discharge is also the case for certain cities in industrialised nations,[1] and for many modern cruise ships travelling in international waters. Whatever the origin or destination, when these wastes are generated and discharged at a rate that exceeds the assimilative capacity of the ecosystem that receives them, problems arise.

Dealing with sewage and wastewater

UNEP (2003) summarised common sources of wastewater in tourism facilities (Table 43.1), as well as outlining the most common means of wastewater treatment (Table 43.2).

In a few rare cases, faeces and urine are dealt with effectively *in situ*, either through agrarian practices that recycle biological wastes back into the soil as fertilisers (e.g. the 'night soil' of rural China), or through in-vessel decomposition processes, which reduce the pathogenicity and the volume of human waste material by converting it to relatively benign compost for disposal on land (e.g. the Clivus Multrum composting toilet). *In situ* treatment of modest volumes of graywater (wastewater from sinks, showers and galleys – see Table 43.1) can also be accomplished effectively in carefully managed surface or sub-surface wastewater treatment facilities (UNEP 2003) or in well-designed constructed wetlands (Anderson *et al.* 2002; UNEP 2003). When these processes are properly managed and maintained in dynamic equilibrium with their surrounding ecological context, they represent a viable and sustainable way of dealing with organic wastes.

These two major waste streams frequently converge; for example, waterborne organic wastes of food processing operations or industrial wastes from manufacturing operations may find their way into municipal or industrial wastewater systems. Similarly, solidified dewatered sewage slurries may be disposed of with solid wastes in landfills or on agricultural lands.

David T. Brown

Table 43.1 Common sources of wastewater at a typical tourism facility (UNEP 2003).

Source of Wastewater	Possible Contaminants
Kitchen/restaurant	food scraps, tissue paper, detergents and other cleansing agents
Toilets and washroom	fecal matter, soap and detergents, tissue paper, etc.
Laundry	detergents and cleaning chemicals
Grounds	organic materials, suspended and dissolved solids and other substances picked up as water travels on the ground

Table 43.2 Unit Processes and operations in wastewater reclamation (UNEP 2003)

Solid/Liquid Separation

Process	Applications
• Sedimentation	Removal of particles from wastewater larger than 30µm. – typically used as a primary treatment approach
• Filtration	removal of particles from wastewater larger than 3µm. – typically used downstream of sedimentation (conventional treatment) of following coagulation/flocculation
• oil and grease removal	removal of oil and grease from wastewater – flotation process may also be used

Biological treatment

Process	Applications
• Aerobic treatment	Removal of dissolved and suspended organic matter from wastewater
• Oxidation pond	reduction of suspended solids, BOD, pathogenic bacteria and ammonia from wastewater
• Nutrient removal	Reduction of nutrient content of reclaimed wastewater
• Disinfection	Protection of public health by removal of pathogenic organisms

Advance treatment

Process	Applications
• Activated carbon	Removal of organic compounds
• Air stripping	Removal of ammonia nitrogen and some volatile organics from wastewater

Chemical Coagulation and Precipitation

Process	Application
• Lime treatment	use if lime to precipitate cations and metals from solution
• Membrane filtration	Removal of colloids and micro-suspended impurities
• Reverse osmosis	Removal of dissolved salts and minerals from water – also effective for pathogen removal

Although extremely important in tourism or any other context, and critical to the pursuit of sustainable tourism practices, a third category – wastes associated with energy transformation (transportation, space heating, space cooling and electrical power generation) – will not be considered in this chapter. These wastes generally consist of unwanted gaseous hydrocarbons like CO_2 and related atmospheric emissions, but may also comprise liquids (e.g. petrochemical residues) or solids (e.g. combustion residues like coal slag and wood ash).

Tourism, waste generation and affluence

As a general rule, people with greater disposable incomes tend to travel more and spend more on tourism activities (Ryan 2003: 29). Waste generation is also positively correlated with economic and material prosperity (Beigl *et al.* 2004). Rekacewicz (2004) demonstrated, using OECD data, that there is a positive correlation between GDP and municipal waste generation. The wealthier the individual, the higher the quantity of waste produced (UNEP 2004: 22; Medina 2008: 40). The consumption and disposal of non-biodegradables is particularly true for affluent people – the rich throw away more non-biodegradables than the poor (UNEP 2004; Medina 2008: 41; Milea 2009). High-income countries lead in terms of per capita garbage generation, but middle-income countries such as India and China are quickly catching up as a result of the emergence of a strong middle class and changing patterns of consumption in these rapidly growing economies (Medina 2008: 40). In 2004, China overtook the USA as the top trash-producing nation in the world. By 2007, India was producing more than 105 million tons of municipal waste per year (Medina 2007: 199). Unsurprisingly, the Asia-Pacific region is the acknowledged motor behind the global tourism growth, with China and India representing the fastest-growing markets (Pleumarom 2007).

Some have proposed that wealthier and better educated individuals produce less waste, but the evidence to support this is quite tenuous. Mazzanti *et al.* (2008) tested whether per capita waste generation would drop at the higher end of the income curve, using data for 103 provinces in Italy. They found some evidence to support this, but the turning point at which waste generation began to decrease with income was at a very high income level, reached by only a few of the provinces. Also, instead of a decline, they found a stabilisation in waste generation in some of the richest areas (Mazzanti *et al.* 2008: 63). So as a general rule, greater affluence brings greater tourism activity, and bigger waste management problems.

Concentrations of people generate concentrations of wastes. Pleumarom (2007) observed, 'Like other big industries, tourism is characterised by unhealthy mass concentrations of people, mass production, and mass activities. Today, it is common for people to criss-cross the globe to search for an exotic paradise … *En route*, the travelling consumers can satisfy their needs and desires in the same fast food chains, supermarkets and designer brand shops like at home'. Concentrations of tourists in popular resorts, heavily visited holiday destinations, or on large conveyances like airliners or cruise ships undeniably do produce concentrated waste streams, which may overload the local capacity to collect, manage and dispose of them.

Because tourists travel to (or through) locations foreign to their own domestic contexts, they may have no knowledge of local waste management practices, and their behaviour pertaining to consumption, waste generation and waste disposal may be inappropriate.

Identifying, categorising and quantifying waste

There are no universally agreed classification schemes for solid wastes (Adapa *et al.* 2006; Gawaikar and Deshpande 2006). Waste taxonomies that have been adopted by researchers to date are quite variable and keyed to the context of the analysis. Adapa *et al.* (2006) state that municipal solid waste is heterogeneous, consisting of residues from nearly all materials used. The content varies with location, lifestyle, season, trends in packaging, local recycling schemes, and the collection policies and data collection protocols of the local waste management authorities.

However, within certain economic sectors or political jurisdictions, some semi-standardised waste classification schemes have evolved over time. Municipal solid waste in North American and European cities is classified into a few relatively standard broad categories: organics, recyclables, non-recyclables and hazardous waste. Sub-categories of these broad categories may be adopted depending on their relevance to the local waste management infrastructure: in one jurisdiction, recyclables might simply consist of metals, glass and paper; in another jurisdiction with more sophisticated recycling infrastructure, they might include various types of plastics, organics and hazardous wastes.

More comprehensive schema such as the European Waste Catalogue List of Waste have been widely adopted in the European Union and the UK for municipal, industrial and hazardous wastes (EUR-Lex Europa 2010), and specialised waste streams such as biomedical waste may have their own classification schemes (e.g. the WHO HCW (Health Care Waste) classification and management scheme (WHO 2010a), which classifies health care wastes into 10 main categories (WHO 2010b)).

Specialised waste generators may adopt waste classification schemes tailored to their operations. A meat packing plant is likely to use a very different waste classification taxonomy from an electronics factory, a hotel or an office building. Such classifications may be shared among groups of similar industries. For example, industries in NAFTA nations use the North American Industry Classification System (NAICS) (Statistics Canada 2010). Similarly classified industries often employ sector-specific waste classification schemes for purposes of economic analysis and statistical comparison.

Producers of highly toxic or hazardous wastes are usually legally mandated to classify, track and monitor their hazwastes much more rigorously than non-hazardous wastes. Attempts have been made to harmonise definitions across Canada and between Canada and the USA, and to remain consistent with Canada's commitments under the Basel Convention and the Organisation for Economic Co-operation and Development (OECD) decision regarding the transboundary movement of hazardous waste (Environment Canada 2010). In Canada, hazardous wastes fall under both federal legislation (notably the Canadian Environmental Protection Act) and an array of differing provincial and territorial waste management statutes (Environment Canada 2010). Even cursory analysis shows that the classification and regulation of waste within and across jurisdictions can be bewilderingly complex, providing yet another obstacle to responsible waste management.

Tourists purchase, consume and dispose of a wide range of products while moving about through different tourism contexts. For example, wastes generated and disposed of as part of the in-flight consumption on an airliner will be different from wastes generated while sightseeing in a city, taking a bus tour, backpacking in a national park, visiting a market or relaxing on a beach – all activities that could easily occur on a single trip. A large, mobile tourism facility like a cruise ship is often of such a massive scale that its waste stream is effectively analogous to that of a city, necessitating similarly broad and comprehensive classification and analysis schemes. Also, travellers and their conveyances may cross several political jurisdictions and waste management regimes in the course of a single trip (this happens routinely for aircraft and cruise ships).

Fortunately for researchers and policy makers, though, certain tourism *sectors* tend to produce somewhat predictable waste streams (see the third part of this chapter for some examples). Sector-by-sector analyses of per-capita waste generation in a given tourism context tend to be more useful and productive than attempting to determine the waste generation impacts of a given individual tourist.

If waste generation profiles for individual tourists are desired, one must examine waste generation in all the specific tourism contexts the tourists will encounter, and extrapolate additively based on their itineraries, activities and specific travel plans. Such analyses may be useful for calculating (and minimising) aggregate waste generation impacts for tourists following predetermined, package-tour itineraries, which incorporate multiple destinations, contexts and jurisdictions.

Managing waste

There are unfortunately no magic formulae or tourism-specific shortcuts for waste management in the tourism industry. The now well-known hierarchical 'three Rs' approach to waste reduction (Reduce, Reuse, Recycle), first proposed in the 1980s, still appears to be the most logical and promising framework for a waste management strategy, and has been explicitly adopted by policy makers worldwide.

There is a definite and logical hierarchy to the three Rs, reflecting the effectiveness of each approach at controlling waste generation. Reduction at source is the most straightforward and effective of the approaches. If a waste is not created in the first place, the waste control problem is not created. Examples of waste reduction include downsizing or eliminating packaging, substituting reusable items for disposables and developing more durable, repairable items. Source reduction emerged as the top solid waste management priority worldwide more than two decades ago (Brown 1993), but numerous cultural, economic and practical barriers continue to stand in the way of widespread source reduction. Virgin raw materials are still often priced so cheaply that reducing their use carries no significant economic advantage, particularly in industries with large capital investments in equipment where the costs of developing more efficient manufacturing processes would outweigh any materials savings. All the while raw materials are plentiful and disposal options for waste materials are inexpensive, there is little incentive for industries to reduce waste generation. And overstated rhetoric about the effectiveness of recycling has drawn affluent consumers into complacency about the importance of reduction at source.

In industrial nations, resource consumption and waste production have been virtually synonymous with material prosperity, and self-imposed austerity runs contrary to the contemporary ethos in developed and developing nations. Thus, once obvious excesses and blatantly superfluous consumption are eliminated from the waste stream, source reduction becomes much more challenging. Cultural norms, economic prosperity and aspirations tied to income very much dictate what is a 'necessity' and what is a 'luxury' in a given society. Ethical limits to consumption and resource use, engrained in the social fabric of a people, change quite slowly.

Also, when waste reduction entails a perceived drop in the quality of life, voluntary source reduction at the individual level becomes an altruistic process, and is thus unlikely to be adopted without strong ideological imperatives (Brown 1993). This is particularly relevant in tourism – with the possible exception of ideologically motivated 'green tourists', many people on vacation wish to indulge themselves and to forget about the constraints and strictures of everyday life.

Reuse simply means using objects or materials again. After source reduction, reusing existing material resources is the next best way to control energy use and waste generation. Well-known examples include reusable shipping crates, pallets or storage containers, reusable crockery and cutlery, and refillable bottles.

Reusing a serviceable item or device instead of committing resources for the manufacture of a new one may be a highly effective way of reducing inputs to the waste stream. It is also a strategy over which tourism operators have a considerable degree of control, particularly in the accommodation sector and in packaged tours or inclusive resorts. A common and widely promoted example of reuse in the tourism industry is the option of reusing towels in hotel rooms, which saves energy and reduces waste associated with energy production and detergent manufacture, as well as reducing water use and wastewater generation.

In general, reuse is sensible if an object or substance may be used again without requiring excessive energy- and materials-intensive processing or shipping. A good example is the provision of reusable cutlery and dinnerware instead of disposables. Reusing plates and cutlery in place of disposable paper or plastic food service items almost always saves resources and reduces waste generation in the long term.

However, the benefits of reuse versus other options are not always absolutely clear-cut or problem-free: food-service operations that serve food on reusable dinnerware may have to use energy-consuming dishwashers, large quantities of water and harsh chemical detergents to clean dishes to acceptable hygienic standards. Is it possible that a low-mass, recyclable, single-use food-service container would have lower net impact than the apparently more environmentally friendly option of reusing regular dishes? Or do the resource extraction and manufacturing processes used to create the single-use packages entail greater costs, risks and hazards? This is clearly a context-determined, systems-dependent question. If the impacts of cleaning, reconditioning or redistributing a potentially reusable object exceed the costs or impacts of manufacturing a disposable alternative, then reuse may ultimately be more detrimental. The economic and environmental cost-accounting for such comparisons is quite complex, and impartial assessment is required on a case-by-case basis.

Recycling means using 'waste' material in place of virgin material to manufacture new products. The best recyclable materials can theoretically be used over and over again without any significant loss in quality or quantity. An example would be aluminium – after initial smelting, metallic aluminium may be used in one product, remelted and remanufactured into a new product of identical quality, theoretically a limitless number of times, and with energy savings of some 90 per cent over the initial smelting and refining process. Other substances are limited in their recyclability due to degradation in quality or physical characteristics, a phenomenon known as 'downcycling' or the 'cascade effect'. Downcycling is delayed disposal, creating a product of lesser value or in some way compromising the integrity of the material through the reclamation process; downcycled materials cannot be used again in making the original product. For example, paper can only be recycled a limited number of times due to the weakening and breakage of the cellulose fibres that give the paper its strength and durability. Each successive recycling attempt degrades the quality of the paper until it is no longer useful for its original intended purpose. Plastics are susceptible to an analogous cascade effect, where polymer degradation results in loss of desirable properties and reduced resin quality.

Nevertheless, recycling offers significant opportunities for waste reduction. Recycling conserves both materials and energy, and provides a comparatively simple way to make substantial reductions in the overall volume of wastes. Source separation programmes, such as the now-commonplace curbside blue-box programmes introduced throughout North America, have been enthusiastically adopted by the populace. Despite volatility in markets for certain recyclable commodities (notably glass and newspaper), more and more municipalities are adopting recycling programmes. In developing economies, the informal sector may play a very significant role in recycling, although sometimes at the expense of the health and safety of informal-sector workers and of the local environment (Brown and Chalermwat 1999; Medina 2007).

Recycling is not a substitute for source reduction. Although individuals and institutions may rightfully feel that they are performing an environmentally appropriate action by recycling wastes, conspicuous consumption of any commodities, recyclable or not, exacerbates the problems of waste management and increases energy use. Gluts of recyclable materials on the markets keep prices artificially low, and may provide cheap sources of recycled raw materials to manufacturers of non-essential or frivolous manufactured goods, exacerbating the cycle of consumption. Downcycled items require additional energy and chemicals to facilitate the recycling process, increasing their net impacts. Recycling cannot and should not be viewed as a palliative for the conscience of conspicuous consumers. It is instead an important but limited component in an overall integrated waste management programme.

Composting, a form of biologically mediated recycling that breaks down organic wastes to fertiliser and soil conditioner through the action of aerobic microorganisms, has long been practiced in developing nations, and is growing in importance in industrialised nations. In developed nations, organic food and yard wastes comprise about one-third by weight of the municipal waste stream, and proportions are higher in other jurisdictions. Municipal composting programmes divert wastes away from the landfill, and create a marketable end product (compost) that is a beneficial soil amendment. As food wastes comprise a large proportion of the waste stream in certain tourism sectors, composting may play an important role as a waste management strategy.

Motivation to adopt the three Rs in tourism is still largely economic – the costs of environmentally responsible waste management are high. Environmentalists have always been correctly preoccupied with the destruction of natural systems, the waste of resources and the production of pollutants, but a deeper appreciation of the intrinsic worth of natural systems and their link to human economic and social activity has begun to filter into the popular conscience. Ecotourism, responsible tourism and other ethically accountable modes of tourism have prompted a re-evaluation of the practices of the industry. Outrage over the destructive practices of conventional tourism has provided added ideological impetus to the search for responsible waste management alternatives, impetus that is being translated into public policy, legislation and economic reality.

Waste disposal

Even if the three Rs have been rigorously applied to tourism initiatives, there will almost always be waste materials to deal with. Organic materials can be separated out and composted, and residual hazwaste can be diverted for specialised handling and disposal at licensed facilities – but for the solid wastes that remain, there are only three basic methods of waste disposal, which have been used since antiquity: dumping, burning and burial. Variations on these three basic themes abound: dumping on the land surface, at sea or in inland waters or wetlands; burning in open fires, controlled incineration devices or sophisticated refuse-to-energy incineration facilities; and burial in excavated pits or engineered sanitary landfills (Brown 1993).

Variants on the basic disposal techniques have fallen in and out of favour over the decades, fluctuating with economic, social, political, technological and environmental conditions, and moderated by the regulatory climate in a given jurisdiction. Controversy abounds in the tourism literature as it does in the general waste management literature about the appropriateness of such disposal procedures as incineration, landfilling or dumping of organic wastes in the sea.

Generation of waste in tourism

Activities that generate waste in tourism include travel, accommodation and food service, most of which are contracted for commercially and provided by third parties. The baseline needs of eating, drinking, sleeping and bathing are catered to in a context removed from home, and possibly on the move (e.g. cruise ship or bus tour), which may generate more waste than is typical in the home context.[2] In addition, the included or optional daily activities undertaken by the tourist as part of a package tour (e.g. bus tour, jet boat ride, theme park visit) and discretionary ancillary consumption (souvenirs, optional side trips, snacks, travel 'necessities' and apparel, etc.) will influence the total amount of waste produced.

The main factors influencing waste generation in tourism are: (1) tourist behaviour (notably consumption and disposal practices); (2) the tourism context in which the tourist is immersed;

and (3) the policy, regulatory and administrative environment(s) where the tourism occurs. The intersection of these three factors at a given moment will determine the proximate waste generation by the tourist The overall sustainability of the tourism enterprise from a waste management standpoint is constrained by the assimilative capacity (ecological, economic and sociopolitical) of the system where the waste generation occurs.

Tourist behaviour

Tourists are not in their usual element. Compared with their everyday lives, tourists are generally exploring new locations, experiencing new environments, sampling novel foods, and purchasing new products and services (including souvenirs and duty-free items). To reach holiday destinations, they may travel longer distances than their usual workaday commute. If on a road trip, cruise or bus tour, they may also move about much more on a daily basis than they do when at home.

Deep-seated personal, social and cultural proclivities may influence the waste generating behaviour of tourists. For example, well-intentioned but ill-informed affluent Western tourists may assume that the same recycling and disposal infrastructures are in place in their travel destination as at home, and continue to consume and dispose accordingly. Others may simply consume irresponsibly and excessively while on vacation. In a study of bed and breakfast establishments in the Niagara region, Canada, van Haastert and de Grosbois (2010) noted that although customers generally have positive attitudes to environmental efforts, they also often are wasteful or not willing to compromise on the quality of their experience. Cultures in which waste generation and littering are not strongly socially condemned, where informal-sector trash collection activity provides a degree of waste diversion, or where individuals do not feel that their actions have any significant effect on waste generation or management (Milea 2009; van Haastert and de Grosbois 2010), may continue to consume and dispose according to their domestic norms.

Butler (1998) reported some scepticism about the public's willingness to incur additional costs and sacrifices involved with more sustainable modes of consumption by tourists. Tourism operators implementing more sustainable tourism practices have commented on differences in the response between passengers of different nationalities, with European tourists being more likely to take an interest in sustainability issues than tourists from other regions (Johnson 2006).

Some tourists view their vacation time as a reward for hard work and a break from their workaday routine, and may spend and consume with uncharacteristic extravagance (Boissevain 1996: 4). This may manifest as a form of context-induced irresponsibility, where perceived freedom from everyday behavioural constraints may result in excesses of behaviour (including excessive consumption of food and material goods and a temporary abandonment of accountability for waste generation and disposal – the 'use-and-throw' mentality referred to by Pleumarom (2004)). On the other hand, so-called hard core green tourists (Barrow 2006) or 'responsible' tourists may make a concerted effort to choose goods and services very carefully, attempting to limit the extent of the sociological and environmental impacts (including waste generation) that their travel may cause (Beech and Chadwick 2005). However, these committed and enlightened travellers seem to be in the significant minority.

Tourism context

Tourism context is the aggregate of factors (discretionary and mandatory) pertaining to accommodation, food service, daily activities and material consumption with which a given tourist is faced. Tourism context is not homogeneous throughout a trip; it may change significantly within the course of a given vacation, or indeed even within the course of a given day (compare the dramatically changing contexts of the cruise ship passenger debarking from the luxurious and well-provisioned surroundings of an ocean liner for a day trip and shore excursion in Haiti).

Certain types of tourism experiences inherently generate more waste than others: for example, tourists at the buffet table on an all-inclusive cruise will almost certainly generate more food waste per capita than tourists on a self-catered bus trip or hikers packing their own foodstuffs on a wilderness excursion. Aggregate impacts and overall waste generation will be different on long-distance travel days than on stationary days, and waste generation may be influenced considerably by discretionary one-off activities (e.g. an optional day-trip with a catered boxed lunch).

Enlightened and responsible tourists may attempt to minimise the waste they generate, but even responsible tourists are constrained at multiple levels by the availability of appropriate choices, as dictated by the tourism context they are in. For example, if the number of beds in less impacting accommodations (such as low-impact hostels, B&Bs or locally managed agritourism facilities) is limited, then the number of tourists that spend their holiday in a less sustainable type of accommodation will be necessarily higher (Sala and Castellani 2009). Similarly, if the range of available choices for food at a given tour destination is limited to multinational corporate franchises distributing fast food with excessive packaging waste, the choice for responsible tourists is reduced to either generating waste or not eating.

Despite the variance from patterns of behaviour and consumption in everyday life, the typical behaviour of groups of tourists *within a particular tourism context* is somewhat predictable, and is actively influenced by the marketing forces and implicit expectations within a given tourist experience. For example, cruises are legendary for providing passengers with large quantities and an enormous diversity of food, and cruise ships predictably produce prodigious quantities of food and other organic wastes. Knowing the components of a given tourist experience – the tourism context – can help us to understand the nature, composition and quantity of wastes that are generated, and to identify opportunities for waste minimisation.

Waste generation for a given tourist is the sum of waste generated across all of the tourism contexts encountered. However, it is difficult, costly and time-consuming to try to measure the individual waste generation of a given tourist on a given trip. Also, unless we are examining standardised trip plans or packaged itineraries, the myriad possibilities for changing contexts makes a life cycle approach for individual tourist experiences of limited practical utility.

Infrastructure

Proper waste management requires appropriate physical infrastructure to facilitate reuse, recycling and composting, as well as the collection, transport, processing and disposal of unwanted materials. Clearly, in the absence of appropriate infrastructure, processing of wastes is sub-optimal: a recyclable container remains garbage if recycling facilities do not exist, and materials that are illegally dumped in inappropriate places exacerbate waste management problems. For example, a 2003 study in Jamaica found that only about two-thirds of the island's municipal solid waste is actually transported to the island's one main landfill (Riverton); the remainder was illegally dumped elsewhere throughout the island and surrounding sea (Faucette and Ediger 2003). Tourist facilities often generate disproportionately high proportions of the total waste stream, and can easily overwhelm local infrastructure. About one-third of the waste generated in the Mayan Riviera is of tourist origin (GTZ 2010), and some 80 per cent of annual waste generated in certain Himalayan trekking destinations is the result of tourist activity (Kuniyal 2005).

As mentioned earlier, the informal sector – entrepreneurial waste pickers, itinerant recyclers and so-called scavengers – can have a significant effect on the diversion of reusable and recyclable materials from the waste stream, and can achieve diversion rates that are better than formal municipal recycling programmes (Brown and Chalermwat 1999). However, their efficiency is tied directly to the market value of the commodities they collect. They also operate opportunistically, with little or no true infrastructure, so the long-term effectiveness of the otherwise valuable contributions of this sector to waste management remains somewhat unpredictable.

Regulatory, policy and administrative context

A tourist's geographical and jurisdictional location can have a profound influence on waste generation and disposal options. For example, a tourist making souvenir purchases in a boutique in Ireland will not automatically be furnished with plastic shopping bags, which have been taxed since 2002 (Rosenthal 2008), whereas the same tourist making similar purchases in the USA may be plied with plastic shoppers with every transaction. Policy, regulatory and administrative factors at all levels can dramatically influence waste generation, from overarching national laws and regulations like the Irish PlasTax right down to policy decisions made by individual businesses.

Local jurisdictional realities pertaining to solid waste, sewage and wastewater can strongly influence the degree to which tourist-generated wastes impact the surrounding environment. In many cases, tourists at a destination far outnumber local residents. However, the local solid waste and sewage infrastructures may be designed to service the population of local residents, and funded by their limited tax dollars.

Equally important is the degree of *enforcement* of proactive policy or legislation. Keeping with the plastic shopper example, China also implemented a plastic bag ban for thin plastic bags in June 2008. However, the effectiveness of the law is dubious, and it is routinely flouted throughout the country; government-mandated fees for thicker plastic bags are too low to be effective, and their use continues to proliferate (Wang 2009). Infrastructure plays a role as well; almost all of Ireland's shops and markets are chain stores with computerised cash registers that already collect government's value-added tax (VAT). That meant minimal re-programming to add the bag tax, and also left little room for evasion – which would be much more of a problem in the small markets in the developing world (Rosenthal 2008). Equally problematic are large affluent jurisdictions where proactive legislation like plastic bag bans have not gained traction, as in all of the USA except for the Californian cities of San Francisco, Malibu, Palo Alto and Fairfax, and North Carolina's environmentally sensitive Outer Banks beach tourist destination (Jones 2010).

Because tourists are highly mobile, they and their well-equipped conveyances frequently move *across* jurisdictional and administrative boundaries, which are highly variable in waste management legislation and enforcement. Often, this mobility is used strategically to increase profits and simplify disposal: waste is discarded as cheaply and quickly as possible, legally or otherwise, in the least stringent jurisdiction and in the most expedient manner, with little regard for the impacts. A telling example of this phenomenon is the checkered waste management record of the cruise industry, which routinely takes advantage of jurisdictional boundaries to dispose of organic and inorganic wastes at sea, and which has been repeatedly charged and fined for ocean dumping transgressions over recent decades (see *Cruise ship wastes*, below).

Responsibility for waste generation in tourism exists at all levels. There are numerous stakeholders in the decision-making process: local administrators play an important role in spatial planning, selecting building areas and giving permissions for the building of hospitality structures and facilities; entrepreneurs (directly or indirectly involved in tourism activities) determine the type of tourist services available for tourists, influencing their possibility for making sustainable consumption choices; tourists make consumption choices that are limited by the effective availability of sustainable products and services and are determined by their environmental consciousness (Sala and Castellani 2009). Shared responsibility and meaningful accountability are necessary components in successful tourism waste management strategies.

Measuring waste and its impacts

A range of methods, tools and approaches can be employed to gain insight into waste generation in various contexts. Most of these methods are generic – they can be applied across a wide array of waste generation situations, or adapted to individual specialised contexts. Common analytical approaches to waste management include identification, classification and quantification of materials in the waste stream in order to gain insight about strategic policy changes to improve prospects for sustainability. It must be remembered that such narrowly focused technical approaches to understanding waste generation are but a part of the overall picture; the trend in assessing sustainability performance has been away from narrow-focus indicators toward those derived from a number of multidisciplinary inputs (Barrow 2006: 338). Nevertheless, the tried-and-true techniques of waste auditing, life cycle analysis and other empirical approaches to understanding materials cycling, provide reliable and meaningful data to inform strategic planning and decision-making for sustainability.

Waste audits

Waste audits are systemic and process-oriented analyses that examine the origin, distribution and ultimate disposal of materials within a given institutional, industrial or jurisdictional context. Waste audits identify the locations, systems and processes that generate waste in a given institution, facility or operation, and lead to recommendations about source reduction. In simple terms, a waste audit is a study of the quantity, distribution and composition of waste that a given process, activity or facility generates. An audit tells you how much waste is produced, what kinds of waste are generated, and helps identify the sources and causes of waste. Performing a waste audit also helps to identify priority wastes – those high-volume, toxic or hazardous substances that should be eliminated from the waste stream for environmental, economic or safety reasons. Auditing also helps operations comply with new and existing environmental laws and regulations, and to meet the standards required for international certification (e.g. ISO 14000 environmental certification).

In principle, a waste audit consists of a few simple steps:

- review the operations of the facility, process or activity;
- identify the wastes produced;
- plan the audit;
- conduct the audit (describing the nature, quantity and distribution of wastes);
- analyse the data; and
- report and implement the findings.

Both quantitative and qualitative waste auditing methodologies can be applied. Visual estimate approaches (usually volume-based) are a quick way to estimate the overall waste production for a given operation, whereas quantitative approaches (usually weight-based) give a more accurate picture of the quantities of waste produced at each stage of a given operation, but usually require more time, effort, labour and expense.

In 2003 the United Nations Environment Programme released *A Manual for Water and Waste Management: What the Tourism Industry Can Do to Improve Its Performance* (UNEP 2003). The manual presented a practical overview of both the wastewater and solid waste management processes in the context of small to medium-sized tourism operations, illustrated liberally with tourism case studies. Using generic methods and approaches (solid waste auditing to identify the sources of the problem, followed by development of a management plan based on source reduction, green purchasing, waste reuse and recycling, waste recovery and waste disposal), the manual assists tourism operators to develop a solid waste management plan comprising operational structures and procedures, phasing process, budgeting, staff training and involvement, and follow-up monitoring (Figure 43.1).

Waste generation can be modelled in certain contexts. For example, municipal solid waste models have been used to predict the amount of waste produced in towns and cities for planning purposes. Similar approaches can theoretically be applied to waste generation in large-scale tourism contexts, such as cruise ships, resorts or airliners.

Life cycle analysis

Waste audits are useful for determining patterns of waste generation in a given circumscribed context. However, we get an incomplete picture of the volume and impacts of waste produced if we simply look at the waste materials generated in a given process, activity or facility, or discarded at the end of a product's useful life. To fully appreciate all the impacts, it is necessary to undertake a much more comprehensive *life cycle analysis* (Day 1981; OECD 2004), also known as *life cycle assessment, ecobalance* or *cradle-to-grave analysis*) (ISO 14040: 2006). This includes raw material extraction and processing, manufacture, packaging, distribution, use and ultimate disposal, including all intervening transportation steps. The sum of the waste and toxins produced and the energy consumed in all those steps represent the life cycle impacts of the product. Life cycle analysis consists of compiling an inventory of relevant inputs and outputs, evaluating the potential environmental impacts associated with those inputs and outputs and interpreting the results of the inventory and impact phases in relation to the objectives of the study (Environmental Management standard *ISO 14040: 2006 – Life Cycle Assessment – Principles and Guidelines*).

For example, the ubiquitous and persistent plastic water bottle produces significantly more waste throughout its life cycle than we see when the empty bottle is discarded or recycled, and consumes more energy than is represented by the energy content of the bottle itself. Impacts include the waste materials produced and energy consumed when: (1) the raw material, petroleum, is extracted and refined (which, in turn, can vary enormously depending on the source of

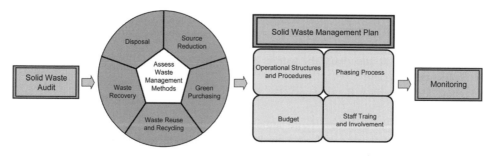

Figure 43.1 A conceptual overview of the solid waste management process as applicable to tourism operations (UNEP 2003)

petroleum, from conventional wells to oil sands extraction); (2) when the polyethylene feedstock is produced using industrial polymer production techniques; (3) when the parison (bottle form) is injection-moulded, and the bottle is blow-moulded; (4) when the bottle is transported to the filling line, filled, capped and labelled; (5) when the filled bottle is packaged and distributed to the vendor, possibly refrigerated, and then sold to the consumer, possibly in a plastic or paper shopping bag; (6) when the empty bottle is discarded by the consumer to a trash receptacle or recycling bin; and (7) when the empty bottle is picked up and delivered to landfill, materials recovery facility or an incineration facility (all separate pathways in their own right) (Foolmaun and Ramjeawon 2008). All of these stages consume energy, produce emissions and generate material waste. An accessible, entertaining, accurate and very unflattering overview of the life cycle of the plastic water bottle is presented in Annie Leonard's (2010) *The Story of Bottled Water*.

Lewis and Demmers (1996) stated, 'In its early days [life cycle analysis] was primarily used for product comparisons, for example to compare the environmental impacts of disposable and reusable products. Today its applications include government policy, strategic planning, marketing, consumer education, process improvement and product design. It is also used as the basis of eco-labelling and consumer education programs throughout the world'.

Another well-known form of life cycle analysis comes from tourism. Like most products, destinations also have a life cycle. Butler (1980) proposed the Tourism Area Life Cycle (TALC) model, a widely accepted model of the life cycle of a tourist destination, which has had considerable follow-up in the tourism literature (e.g. Martin and Uysal 1990; Tooman 1997; Baum 1998; Butler 2004).

There has undoubtedly been progress in our understanding of waste generation in the past two decades, but our theoretical and practical approaches remain out of phase. As Beigl (2007) stated with regard to modelling municipal solid waste generation:

> To date, policies promoting greater sustainability in waste management have not been followed by equal efforts to boost adequate knowledge about waste generation. Climbing up the waste management hierarchy from landfilling, energy recovery, and material recycling up to waste minimisation will lead to increasing data complexity, thus requiring more detailed information on waste generation and composition … In spite of the fact that decision–support orientated waste management models, such as cost benefit analyses, life cycle analyses and multicriteria decision analyses, have been established over the last decades, waste generation models, which deal with the underlying, indispensable planning fundamentals, are lagging behind and are far from reaching general modelling standards.

More sophisticated analytical approaches such as life cycle analysis (Day 1981; Castellani and Sala 2008), environmental impact assessment (Barrow 2006), ecological footprint analysis (Wackernagel and Rees 1998; Gössling *et al.* 2002; Monfreda *et al.* 2004, Barrow 2006) and sustainable consumption (Hertwich 2005) attempt to place waste generation within a broader context of energy use and materials cycling in the ecosystem, and to use this understanding in policy and practice. Gössling *et al.* (2002) explored ecological footprint analysis as a tool to assess tourism in the Seychelles.

In recent years, ever more integrative approaches have been proposed in a tourism and hospitality context, bringing life cycle assessment, ecological footprint and sustainable production and consumption strategies together to improve consciousness and responsibility of organisations that provide goods and services and of consumers (Sala and Castellani 2010). Such approaches, although interesting in theory and promising in principle, may attempt to be so all-inclusive and integrative as to be unmanageable in a practical everyday sense.

Case studies of tourism waste

To a large degree, waste management strategies and systems in tourism are extrapolations or applications of generic waste management strategies applied in other contexts, collated and combined in a systemic manner to reflect the constraints, requirements, infrastructure and jurisdictional realities of the tourism context in question. However, certain tourism contexts provide particularly interesting case studies for the application of these waste management principles, illustrating both the complexity of the problems and the utility of generic waste management approaches.

Rural tourism wastes

Communities in rural areas worldwide attract tourists interested in local culture, arts, crafts, cuisine, wildlife, and other natural and cultural attributes. Influxes of tourists result in higher overall waste generation, and in the production of new waste streams aligned with tourist consumption patterns. Appropriate waste management is a common challenge faced by rural tourism destinations, not only to ensure the success of tourism but also to enhance the quality of life of inhabitants in terms of sanitation and public health.

One representative example of an initiative to manage waste more sustainably in rural tourism destinations is aligned with India's Endogenous Tourism Project (ETP). In collaboration with the Government of India, NGOs and *panchayats* (local village governance councils), the UNDP is implementing the ETP in selected villages spread over 20 states across the country, in a bid to provide sustainable livelihoods to communities in rural areas through tourism based on art, craft, and natural endowment. A *Handbook on Waste Management in Rural Areas* (Nair and Jayakumar 2008) has been produced to 'help NGOs and local governments to assist communities to manage discards in the ETP sites, and to develop a plan to deal with sustainable management of waste so that it will not distract visitors or deny them the special experiences of the unique sites in rural India'. The handbook emphasises Zero Waste principles, consultation and involvement of local stakeholders, and the establishment of local waste management infrastructure to address problems of waste in rural tourism destinations. Although basically an assemblage of well-known waste management principles, analytical tools and approaches, the manual is significant in that it presents these approaches in a simple and practical manner in the specific context of rural tourism.

Cruise ship wastes

The massive size and sophisticated facilities of modern ocean liners are indeed impressive. Royal Caribbean Cruise Lines' largest Oasis-class cruise ships exceed 360 m in length and carry upwards of 6,200 passengers and crew (Royal Caribbean 2010), and offer all the amenities of modern life to their pampered passengers. They also consume energy and produce waste on the scale of a small city, consisting of sewage; graywater (wastewater from sinks, showers and galleys); hazardous wastes; solid waste; oily bilge water; ballast water; and air pollution (Copeland 2008). However, unlike cities, cruise ships are mobile, and can take advantage of their ever-changing geographical and jurisdictional locations to minimise the costs and maximise the ease of waste disposal, particularly on the open ocean.

Ocean dumping has been recognised as an environmental problem for decades. The waste generation problems associated with cruise tourism are well summarised by Copeland (2008).

> Solid waste generated on a ship includes glass, paper, cardboard, aluminum and steel cans, and plastics. It can be either non-hazardous or hazardous in nature. Solid waste that enters

the ocean may become marine debris, and it can then pose a threat to marine organisms, humans, coastal communities, and industries that utilize marine waters. Cruise ships typically manage solid waste by a combination of source reduction, waste minimization, and recycling. However, as much as 75% of solid waste is incinerated on board, and the ash typically is discharged at sea, although some is landed ashore for disposal or recycling. Marine mammals, fish, sea turtles, and birds can be injured or killed from entanglement with plastics and other solid waste that may be released or disposed off of cruise ships. With large cruise ships carrying several thousand passengers, the amount of waste generated in a day can be massive. For a large cruise ship, about 8 tons (823 kg) of solid waste are generated during a one-week cruise. It has been estimated that 24% of the solid waste generated by vessels worldwide (by weight) comes from cruise ships. Most cruise ship garbage is treated on board (incinerated, pulped, or ground up) for discharge overboard. When garbage must be off-loaded (for example, because glass and aluminum cannot be incinerated), cruise ships can put a strain on port reception facilities, which are rarely adequate to the task of serving a large passenger vessel especially at non-North American ports). Cruise ships produce hazardous wastes from a number of on-board activities and processes, including photo processing, dry-cleaning, and equipment cleaning. Types of waste include discarded and expired chemicals, medical waste, batteries, fluorescent lights, and spent paints and thinners, among others. These materials contain a wide range of substances such as hydrocarbons, chlorinated hydrocarbons, heavy metals, paint waste, solvents, fluorescent and mercury vapor light bulbs, various types of batteries, and unused or outdated pharmaceuticals. Although the quantities of hazardous waste generated on cruise ships are small, their toxicity to sensitive marine organisms can be significant. Without careful management, these wastes can find their way into graywater, bilge water, or the solid waste stream.

Cruise ship wastes are governed by a number of protocols in international waters, and by domestic laws, regulations and standards within specific national jurisdictions (e.g. the Clean Water Act and the Act to Prevent Pollution from Ships in the USA), but there is no single law or rule in effect across the board, and there are regulatory overlaps in some areas and gaps in others (Copeland 2008).

International concern about irresponsible waste disposal practices at sea resulted in the drafting of the 1973 MARPOL convention, which regulates the pollution of marine waters by oceangoing vessels. MARPOL was updated in 1978, but was not implemented until 1983.

Some cruise ship waste streams appear to be well regulated under MARPOL, such as bilge water and solid wastes (particularly plastics). Annex V (Prevention of Pollution by Garbage from Ships) of MARPOL came into force on 31 December 1988. It specifies the distances from land and the manner in which solid waste may be disposed of, and features a complete ban on ocean dumping of all forms of plastic.

A number of other, quite variable, regulatory regimes are, in effect, in different jurisdictions. Some protocols, like Alaska's waste disposal regulations for cruise ships, are relatively stringent, requiring high standards of wastewater and sewage treatment (Copeland 2008). Other laws, like Canada's regulations to control discharges from cruise vessels operating in Canadian waters (Transport Canada 2010), are more lenient, allowing ocean dumping of macerated but otherwise untreated raw sewage and garbage 12 miles offshore. Cruise discharge protocols in the State of Washington, although reasonably stringent, are set out in a voluntary Memorandum of Understanding between the state, the Port of Seattle and the Northwest Cruise Ship Association. Instead of abiding by Alaskan regulatory standards or the voluntary standards in the State of

Washington, most cruise ships simply wait and dump their waste – legally – in Canadian waters, taking advantage of the more lenient regulatory climate (van der Voo 2010).

But because a waste is *regulated* does not necessarily mean that it is being adequately minimised or responsibly managed. Per capita waste generation levels by cruise tourists remain very high by world standards, and 'disposal' of many cruise ship wastes simply consists of dilution in seawater.

On average, each cruise ship passenger generates at least 2 lbs (0.91 kg) of non-hazardous solid waste per day, and disposes of two bottles and two cans (Sweeting and Wayne 2006). Although cruise ships are barred from dumping plastics anywhere at sea and floatable garbage within 25 miles (40 km) of shore, they are permitted to dump macerated garbage ground into pieces smaller than 2.5 cm when they are 3 miles (4.8 km) from shore, and unground garbage when they are at least 12 miles (19 km) from shore (Oceana 2003).

A cruise ship with 3,000 persons aboard generates about 113,500 litres of human waste and 965,000 litres of graywater every day (Oceana 2003). Cruise ships are required to have onboard sewage treatment systems, known as marine sanitation devices (MSDs), which chemically treat sewage to reduce bacteria levels and dissolve solids. Discharge from MSDs must be logged, but the industry is not required to monitor the quality of the waters into which they routinely dump their waste (Oceana 2003). With the exception of Alaskan waters and a relatively small number of coastal marine 'no discharge zones' (NDZs) (US EPA 2010), cruise ships are allowed to release MSD-*treated* sewage into the sea almost anywhere they sail. And raw sewage can simply be stored onboard and legally dumped *outside* the regulated areas: with few exceptions, cruise ships can lawfully release *un*treated sewage anywhere beyond 4.8 km from the shore. Some wastes, such as graywater and ballast water, go largely unregulated in marine environments (Copeland 2008). Cruise ships are permitted to release *un*treated graywater anywhere they sail (Oceana 2003).

Despite efforts to clean up their act and their reputation, the cruise industry still enjoys little credibility with regard to self-regulation or environmental responsibility, largely as a result of its own ongoing practices, aggressive legal challenges to environmental legislation, industry lobbying and long record of environmental infractions. Between 1993 and 1998 there were 87 confirmed illegal discharge cases from foreign-flagged cruise ships in US waters (New Zealand Parliamentary Commissioner for the Environment 2003). Fines paid by cruise lines for illegally dumping oily wastewater and destroying coral reefs between 1995 and 1999 amounted to US $50 million (Bluewater Network 2006). In 1998 and 1999, Royal Caribbean Cruises pleaded guilty to 30 charges and was fined US$27 million for a fleetwide conspiracy to dump oily bilge wastewater into US waters by deliberately bypassing environmental control devices (Klein 2009; Sweeting and Wayne 2006; animated overview presented online at USA Today 2002).

The cruise industry (Royal Caribbean, Carnival Corporation and the International Council of Cruise Lines) has engaged in high-stakes lobbying of US Congress, spending a total of US $904.5 million on lobbying efforts between 1997 and 2004 alone (Bluewater Network 2006) – and apparently with some success, as the proposed Federal Clean Cruise Ship Act of 2009 (S.1820) (GovTrack 2010a) and its antecedents (reintroduced six times since 2003) have died in Congress every time (GovTrack 2010b), and the current incarnation of the Act has not progressed beyond referral to committee.

Cruise industry associations have aggressively negotiated memoranda of understanding (MOU) with certain states (e.g. Washington, Florida and Hawaii) to fend off regulatory action. Unlike laws and regulations, MOUs are not legally binding, do not carry any penalties, do not apply to all cruise ships and may be cancelled with only a few month's notice (Oceana 2003). They also contain loopholes that allow cruise ships to opt for less stringent local regulations over MOU provisions (e.g. pertaining to sewage discharge in Florida coastal waters) (Oceana 2003).

Cruise ships, like many other oceangoing vessels, routinely fly a 'flag of convenience', registering in countries like Panama, Liberia and the Bahamas. These countries have weak environmental regulations, lax labour laws and low taxes (Oceana 2003), and are ineffective in following up on reports of MARPOL or other international infractions (Copeland 2008). Royal Caribbean actually argued in US federal court that because its ships are registered outside the USA, they are not subject to US environmental laws – even when operating in US waters. Their plea was (appropriately) unsuccessful. Royal Caribbean eventually pleaded guilty, and the courts assessed them an $18 million fine (Oceana 2003).

In response to its atrocious track record, some authors claim that the cruise industry is now making a concerted and legitimate effort to clean up its act and rehabilitate its image. Sweeting and Wayne (2006) reported on the creation of the 2003 Ocean Conservation and Tourism Alliance, an industry-sponsored initiative aimed at minimising environmental impacts and protecting marine biodiversity at cruise destinations. And Conservation International, an environmental NGO largely supported by industry stakeholders, produced a comprehensive 2006 publication entitled *From Ship to Shore – Sustainable Stewardship in Cruise Destinations*, which outlines a range of sustainability initiatives by and among cruise lines, governments, civil society and shore operators (Conservation International 2006).

Airline industry wastes

According to the National Resource Defense Council (NRDC) (Aiken *et al.* 2006), the US airline industry alone discards almost 67,000 kg of aluminium cans each year (enough to build 58 Boeing 747 airplanes), 8,164,000 kg of plastic in 2004, and enough newspapers and magazines to fill a football field to a depth of more than 70 metres (see Table 43.3 for a summary). The report states, 'the airline industry has a dismal record when it comes to grappling with the amount of waste it generates each year. Although airports are responsible for a huge amount of trash ... most of the trash discarded at airports is sent to landfills and incinerators. At this rate of waste generation, the 30 largest airports in the USA generate an amount of waste equal to that of a city the size of Miami'.

The NRDC study provides a detailed overview of the methods used and survey instruments used to collect data on waste generation in US airports. The report claims that the implementation of recycling programmes at airports throughout the USA would save not only resources, but also money. Specific proposals to the industry (Aiken *et al.* 2006) included:

(1) recycling efforts must begin with airport infrastructure. In-flight waste is recycled only if there is a system on the ground that allows it to happen. Airlines can influence the development of recycling infrastructure at the airports to which they fly;

(2) airports should increase aluminium recovery to maximise energy savings and emissions reductions. Although aluminium accounts for only 1 per cent of the air travel industry's waste stream, the energy and emissions reduction benefits of recycling this material are disproportionately larger. For example, the energy benefits of recycling 1 tonne of aluminium are 11 times that of recycling 1 tonne of newspaper and eight times that of recycling the same amount of PET plastic;

(3) airports should also focus on recovery of wastepaper to maximise environmental benefits. Paper is the largest single category of waste generated by the airline industry (about 40 per cent). Focusing on paper recovery can divert the greatest amount of tonnage away from landfills and incinerators;

Table 43.3 Common wastes associated with air travel (Aikin *et al.* 2006)

Source	Category of waste	Constituents
Airliners	Airline waste	Waste from passenger airplanes, ticketing counters, gate areas, and airline offices. Accounts for about half of the passenger related waste handled at airports. Typically includes food and drink containers, uneaten food, newspapers, magazines, computer printouts, and other paper generated at ticketing counters. Characteristics and quantities of waste generated on an airplane vary by length of flight and by carrier.
Airport terminals	Terminal waste	1. Terminal public areas and the airport authority's administrative offices ("terminal public area waste"): food and drink containers, food scraps, newspapers, magazines, plastic wrappers, restroom trash, and other trash generated in the public areas of the passenger terminal. In addition, this category includes the copier paper, toner cartridges, and discarded office supplies used in airport authority offices. Terminal public area waste does not include restaurant waste or waste produced at airline passenger gate areas. 2. Terminal retail and restaurant concession tenants (referred to as "terminal tenant waste"): cardboard boxes, paper and plastic packaging, food scraps, and food wrappers disposed of in shops, restaurant kitchens, and airport dining areas. Also includes aluminum, plastic, and glass containers.
Airport maintenance and support	Other airport waste	Waste: a) from catering operations and flight kitchens; b) from cargo operations, maintenance areas, and hangars; and c) from landscaping, construction, and demolition. Each of these areas creates distinct waste streams, making it more complicated to ascertain the per-capita waste generation impacts or establish an airport-wide waste reduction or recycling programs.

(4) airport recycling programmes should target the sectors that generate the most waste – airlines and retail and restaurant tenants. These two sectors combined account for nearly 90 per cent of the waste generated at a typical airport.

Hotel and resort waste

Although the plight of environmentally sensitive areas with poor tourist infrastructure is well known, waste management issues also threaten the long-term viability of well-established small regional hotels and resorts as well as those in heavily exploited mass tourism destinations.

A comprehensive overview of solid waste and wastewater management issues in small to medium-sized tourism facilities was provided in UNEP (2003). Figure 43.2 provides an overview of the main inputs and outputs of a typical tourism operation.

Many studies have investigated sustainability practices adopted in the tourism and hospitality industries (Carlsen *et al.* 2001; Vernon *et al.* 2003; Schaper and Carlsen 2004; Manaktola and Jauhari 2007). UNEP (2003) developed a practical solid waste and wastewater management manual for small to medium-sized tourism facilities, and presented an overview of applied management techniques. Although often reactive and tardy, some of the rearguard initiatives undertaken to address the problems in this sector offer instructive insights about how to proceed in similar contexts worldwide.

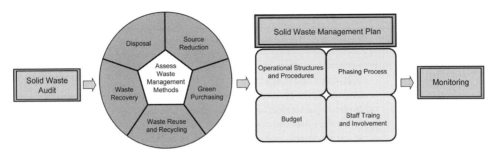

Figure 43.2 Sources of solid waste and wastewater in a typical tourism operation (UNEP 2003)

Collectively, small hotels constitute a significant solid waste management (SWM) problem (Radawan *et al.* 2010), and improvements in these establishments can have a significant aggregate effect. UNEP (2003) produced a table of common solid wastes and their sources in tourism facilities (Table 43.4a), and Hoang (2005) undertook an audit of waste management patterns in small-scale hotels in Vietnam, producing a list of common wastes that is representative of similar establishments in the region and beyond (Table 43.4b). A composting trial using hotel waste was also implemented. After 60 days of composting and maturing, about 60 kg of fine compost was produced from the input of 702 kg of compostables. Recommendations were made regarding waste separation at source, seasonal effects and compost application for improving the implementation of composting in HaLong City.

Van Haastert and de Grosbois (2010) investigated the implementation of environmentally responsible practices in bed and breakfast establishments (which are among the smallest firms in the hospitality industry) in the Niagara Region of Canada. The study addressed issues including motivations, scope of environmental initiatives (including waste management) and challenges faced during their implementation. The research indicated that environmental initiatives at bed and breakfast establishments were quite limited, and the majority were economically, not environmentally, motivated. Systemic waste management initiatives include recycling and composting (both of which were supported by curbside municipal programmes in the study area), reducing or recycling packaging, buying in bulk and using recycled timber while building. Other waste management initiatives included use of soap dispensers, reusing paper towels when possible, reusing garbage bags, reusing plastic containers or cardboard boxes, fertilising the garden with compost and installing worm farms for vegetable waste. The three major barriers to adoption of environmental practices by these tourism micro-businesses are budgetary constraints, lack of knowledge and conflict with customer attitudes and expectations. The study highlighted a significant lack of understanding of the terminology of sustainability, very low awareness of the impacts of business activities on the environment by the owners of bed and breakfast establishments, and called for additional education and training on sustainability for small business owners.

Radwan *et al.* (2010) focused on the SWM practices of small hotels in a local authority in Wales, and examined the role of the public sector in helping small hotels manage their solid waste effectively. Only a minority of the small hotels were considering the adoption of sustainable SWM practices, either because hoteliers felt negatively about sustainable SWM alternatives or were concerned about perceived challenges (the public sector provided only very modest services to enhance SWM practices). The researchers proposed a best practice model for the public sector to encourage small hotels to manage their solid waste effectively, and pointed out the importance of the support of local waste management authorities to make waste management hierarchy options more accessible to small hotels.

Table 43.4a Typical solid wastes generated by tourism facilities (UNEP 2003)

Accomodation Sector (hotels, guesthouses)
Accomodation facilities generate various types of solid waste: • newspapers and magazines • cleansing agent containers used by housekeeping and laundry services • flowers in guestrooms and public areas • plastic shampoo and cosmetic soap bottles • old towels, linens, bed sheets and furniture • paint and varnishes, used fittings, fixtures and plumbing supplies, refrigerators and other bulk items Food and Beverage Services Most restaurants or restaurant/bar sections of hotels, guesthouses or golf courses dispose of large quantities of solid waste including: • empty cans, bottles, tins and glass • food • small non-refillable product containers (sugar, salt, pepper, flour and cream) • paper serviettes, coasters, straws, toothpicks and cocktail napkins • used aprons, kitchen towels and napkins Open Spaces and Grounds Landscaping and gardening activities at golf courses and many hotels generate ground related solid waste including: • plant trimmings • empty pesticide/insecticide bottles and fertilizer packs, pesticides, insecticides and fertilizer products (chich are often hazardous) Administrative and Office Functions A facility's main office, front desk and shipping/receiveing areas create solid waste including: • paper and envelopes • travel pamphlets and brochures which are often quickly discarded by tourist

One large-scale initiative involving the hotel and resort sector is the project on 'sustainable waste management' in the Mexican Caribbean, commissioned by the German Federal Ministry for Economic Cooperation and Development (BMZ). In October 2008, the Swiss tour operator Kuoni Travel Holding, the non-governmental organisation Amigos de Sian Ka'an (funded by Travel Foundation Netherlands) and the state of Quintana Roo's Ministries for the Environment (SEDUMA) and Tourism (SEDETUR) began a public–private partnership to promote integrated waste management in the region (GTZ 2010).

Tourism is booming in the region, with more than 7 million visitors to Cancún, Cozumel and the Riviera Maya, Mexico, in 2007. About half of the tourism traffic is in the Riviera. Tourism in the area accounts for around one-third of the region's total waste generation of approximately 400 tonnes of waste per day. Improper waste disposal causes soil and groundwater pollution, leachate migration through porous karst soils, and damage to exceptionally sensitive underground watercourses and nearby coral reefs (GTZ 2010).

State ministries SEDUMA and SEDETUR created the legal and regulatory environment for introducing waste management plans in the tourism sector. Legal prerequisites for standardised waste management plans in the hotels of the Mexican Caribbean were established, paving the way for widespread introduction of these changes. Travel Foundation Netherland financed campaigns conducted by Amigos de Sian Ka'a to raise awareness about waste management among tourists, hoteliers and hotel employees. In addition, market analysis was conducted to

Table 43.4b Hotel wastes in HaLong City, Vietnam (Hoang 2005)

Source	Category of waste	Constituents
Waste from Guest Room	Compostables	Leftover food; Fruit waste; Flower waste
	Recyclables	Metal (aluminum cans); Glass (drink bottles, drinking glasses); Recyclable plastics (bottles, clear bags); Recyclable paper (tissues, cardboard, print paper, newspaper)
	Miscellaneous	Non-recyclable plastics (plastics bags, hard plastics); other miscellaneous materials (sand, dust, rubber, cloth)
Kitchens and Restaurants	Compostables	Leftover food and food wastes (fruits, vegetables, meats, seafood, bones, egg shells, etc.)
	Recyclables	Recyclable paper (tissues, cardboard, fine paper, newspaper); Metal (aluminum cans), Glass (drink bottles, drinking glasses); Recyclable plastics (bottles, clear bags); Recyclable paper (tissues, cardboard, print paper, newspaper)
	Miscellaneous	Non-recyclable paper (damp napkins, tissues); Non-recyclable plastics (plastics bags, hard plastics); Other non-recyclables (dirt, sand, cloth, rubber)
Waste from Gardens and Grounds	Compostables	Leaves, pine needles, brush, tree trimmings, grass clippings
	Miscellaneous	Dirt, sand, rubber, cloth, foam

identify the potential for recycling activities at the state level. Incentive-based strategies and recommendations were developed by the state to encourage greater private sector involvement in waste management. The state is now attempting to integrate these strategies and recommendations into the national environmental policy (GTZ 2010).

Waste in mountain trekking and expeditions

Kuniyal (2005) examined the waste generation patterns in two popular trekking and expedition destinations in the Indian Himalayas, the Valley of Flowers and the Pindari Valley in Uttaranchal State. Mountain ecotourism trekkers and adventure tourism mountaineers are increasing the burden of solid waste being deposited in the ecologically sensitive and topographically fragile areas of the Himalayas (Table 43.5). No proper facilities exist for waste collection or disposal in these high mountain communities, leading to littering and disposal in the landscape.

More than 140,000 tourists visited the two areas during the four month tourist season, each generating 0.2–0.288 kg of waste per day. Tourist wastes (Table 43.5) accounted for more than 80 per cent of the total waste generated annually at both of these sites.

Non-biodegradable waste dominated biodegradable waste at 66.4 per cent for expedition and 84.5 per cent for trekking areas. Sustainable solid waste management options recommended included source reduction (e.g. of disposable packaging and water bottles), reuse, recycling and biocomposting. The study showed how visitors, host communities and government could reduce waste generation and earn income from waste in various ways from materials that are usually considered valueless and useless by local people, trekkers and mountaineers.

Table 43.5 Mountain trekking and expedition wastes (Kunial 2005)

Source	Category of waste	Constituents
Trekking and expeditions	Readily biodegradable	Food: Vegetables, Fruits, Beverages, Plant residues, Fine organic matter
	Biodegradable	Fruit seeds/shells; Paper; Clothes/rags; Wooden matter; other miscellaneous biodegradable substances; bones/eggshells
	Non-biodegradable	Polythene; 'tin' cans; glass (bottles); candles; synthetic cloth; batteries; crockery, paints; hairs; candy wrappers; processed leather; mattresses; stone and bricks; ash and fine earth; plastic; rubber; metal; glass(broken); medical waste

There is no definitive figure on how much trash has been left on world-renowned Mount Everest, but the debris of 50 years of climbing has given Everest the name of the world's highest dump. Irresponsible waste disposal from earlier mountain expeditions still remains an issue. In April 2010 a team of 20 Sherpas left for Mount Everest to collect rubbish left behind by climbers and retrieve bodies of victims of the mountain's 'death zone' above 8,000 metres (AFP 2010). The team had set up two camps at 6,065 m and 6,500 m to collect rubbish that was brought down and put on display at base camp.

The 2010 Clean Up Everest initiative collected more than 1,800 kg of garbage from the mountain, as well as the remains of several of the 300 climbers who have died in expeditions over the years. As well as oxygen canisters, the detritus includes food containers, discarded tents, ropes and backpacks – all of which were put on display in an exhibition at Everest base camp (Extreme Everest blog 2010).

In 2009 an expedition lead by Dawa Steven Sherpa from Asian trekking paid Sherpas a bounty to bring down trash through a 'cash for trash' programme. They brought 6,000 kg of garbage down to base camp for proper disposal, as well as wreckage of an Italian Army helicopter that crashed in 1973 at the edge of the Khumbu Icefall (Arnette 2010).

Waste in parks and wilderness areas

In addition to concerns about visitor numbers, erosion, wildlife habitat disturbance and access issues, problems of solid waste and human waste management continue to plague parks and wilderness areas worldwide.

Responses have included programmes such as the US Department of Agriculture Forest Service's 'leave no trace' initiative, formally conceived by the USDA Forest Service in the 1960s (www.lnt.org). Initially targeting human and solid waste concerns, the programme has expanded into a broader code of visitor conduct, encompassing planning and preparation of wilderness visits, camping and travel guidelines to minimise trail erosion and soil compaction, appropriate solid waste and human waste disposal procedures, non-interference with natural attributes, minimising campfire impacts, respect for wildlife and consideration for fellow travellers (Leave No Trace Canada 2010). Allied programmes include the now-global 'Pack it in – Pack it out' programme, where visitors to parks and wilderness areas are exhorted to carry out absolutely everything they carry in, leaving no waste or other physical evidence of their passage.

Collection and disposal of solid waste in parks and wilderness areas has long been an area of concern. Interactions between waste and wildlife have always been problematic, leading to behavioural and dietary disturbances, troublesome or dangerous human–wildlife interactions, and expensive relocation or removal programmes for so-called problem animals (!) like scavenging bears. Ironically, the garbage dump at Churchill, Manitoba, spawned a mini-tourism industry of its own from the 1960s until its closure in 2004, having been identified as one of the best places in the world to view polar bears, which were drawn from the tundra to scavenge at the town dump (Eliasson 2004).

Responses have included widespread development of park waste disposal guidelines, education programmes, and the purchase of expensive animal-proof waste receptacles, adding millions of dollars to the cost of operation for parks such as Yosemite (see Williams 2002 for a popular review of US national parks).

In some heavily visited North American national parks such as Banff, Jasper, Yellowstone, Yosemite and the Grand Canyon, solid waste management infrastructure rivals that of small cities, and involve millions of dollars in annual expenditures. The budget for bear-proof trash receptacles alone in Yosemite National Park was over US$2 million between 1998 and 2001, with an additional US$500,000 annually for night-time animal patrols, education campaigns and research.

Affluent tourists generate waste in quantity even in so-called wilderness contexts, and in Western nations, management of these wastes often involves private–public partnerships. For example, the Xanterra Park and Resort consortium manages a relatively sophisticated waste management infrastructure at its resort concessions in Yellowstone National Park, which includes extensive composting, recycling, reuse and reduction initiatives to minimise the amount of waste going to landfill (Xanterra Parks and Resorts 2010). However, only a small minority of wilderness areas and parks worldwide have the infrastructure, expertise, financial resources or regulatory incentives and pressures to adopt such wide-ranging waste management programmes for their visitors.

A number of solutions have been proposed for human waste management in wilderness areas. An early, comprehensive and still very relevant treatise on the personal management of human waste by tourists in wilderness areas is found in Kathleen Meyer's wryly titled book 'How to Shit in the Woods' (1989, 1994 (2nd edn)). Even in cases where human wastes do not pose a significant environmental threat (Hercock 1999; Bridle and Kirkpatrick 2003), the aesthetic aspects of open disposal of human faeces have a negative impact on the amenity value of wilderness destinations, a factor very important to the visitors of natural areas (Moore and Polley 2007).

Symposia on the subject have proposed a broad range of solutions, from ecologically compatible on-site composting toilet facilities through to 'pack-it-out' solutions (Australian Alps Liaison Committee 2000). Later variants on the 'leave no trace' programme explicitly extend the 'pack-it-out' directive to human waste, recommending the use of so-called 'poo[p] tubes', transport bags or other sealed devices, for the collection and removal of human faeces and sanitary products from wilderness areas (Bath and Byrne 2000). These may be commercial products (e.g. WAG Bags – Phillips Environmental 2010) or home-built devices (e.g. Schroeder's (2003) poop tube for kayakers, or a similar device (wikiHow 2010) for mountaineers). Despite a somewhat facetious literature approach to the topic, these devices represent a very serious and significant future trend in human waste management in heavily used and fragile wilderness areas (see Grand Canyon National Park human waste pilot program cover letter (US National Parks Service 2010b)).

Tourism waste in polar environments

Polar tourism is now a significant reality in both the Arctic and the Antarctic. According to UNEP (2007), Arctic tourism has grown so much over the past 200 years that tourists have become the single largest human presence in many Arctic regions, greatly exceeding their host population at many popular destinations. Arctic communities are increasingly reliant on the jobs, income and business revenues generated by tourism, and many indigenous communities view tourism as a more sustainable economic opportunity than their historical dependence on unreliable subsistence or resource extraction economies (UNEP 2007).

In Antarctica, ship-borne and land-based tourists have increased dramatically in recent years. Over 20 years ago, the number of tourists in Antarctica eclipsed the number of scientists conducting research there, and the disparity between numbers of tourists and scientists has steadily increased since then.

Intensive promotion and popular appeal, improvements in transportation, increasing wealth and leisure time, and a moderating climate are all contributing to the growth of tourism in the polar regions. With this growth has come a range of environmental problems, including waste management issues.

First the Arctic and then the Antarctic have been subjected to a multitude of poor waste management and disposal practices over the years, including widespread open dumps, landfills and burning, as well as the practice of 'sea-icing' – dumping garbage onto the sea ice during winter to float away and sink during the summer. Sewage has been routinely discharged with little or no treatment straight into the sea, or has been burned. Some areas around towns, industrial settlements, research stations and field camps have become contaminated from dump and landfill leachate, oil and fuel spills, and chemical spills.

Garbage, waste and pollution remain significant problems for many tourism operations in polar regions, both from previous human activity and from tourism itself. Decomposition is slow and waste remains visible atop the permafrost in many Arctic areas. For understandable economic and logistical reasons, land-based facilities for sewage treatment and waste management are frequently not up to the demand of high peak tourist populations. UNEP (2007) states, 'The cost of building, operating, and maintaining tourism infrastructure is a huge economic burden for Arctic communities and governments. Support facilities and services of all types are built and maintained to serve relatively large numbers of persons that exceed the resident population … [W]ater and wastewater utilities and waste collection and disposal incur capital and operating costs, require advanced work force skills, spare parts, and need specialized supplies in order to sustain their functions. Tourism normally occurs for a few months of the year, but the infrastructure must be maintained under adverse conditions for the entire year'.

Jurisdictional realities are also quite complex in the Arctic. A long history of international competition over sovereignty, access, resource ownership, military and strategic control and navigation rights has resulted in fragmented ownership of Arctic land and resources, and these disputes affect the policy and legislative regimes under which tourism operates. Denmark, Norway, Canada, Russia, the USA, Iceland, Finland, Sweden and a number of Arctic indigenous peoples, each with their own laws, policies, procedures and infrastructure requirements for waste management and environmental protection, continue to dispute borders and ownership of various parts of the northern polar regions (Ice News 2010). As a result, policies and procedures pertaining to tourism and waste management are quite heterogeneous, and the weakest provisions often prevail. For example, some Arctic jurisdictions (e.g. Alaska) have invoked quite stringent controls on tourist activities and cruise ship discharge in Alaskan territorial waters, but these legislative constraints disappear immediately outside the Alaskan jurisdictional boundaries. Cruise ship operators are known to routinely wait until such boundaries are crossed before discharging their stored-up sewage and waste burdens into less stringently regulated waters of Canada and other jurisdictions (van der Voo 2010).

However, there has been some progress despite the regulatory heterogeneity. One of the most successful management techniques for conserving Arctic resources and directly influencing lawful visitor behaviour is guide licensing, which has expanded well beyond hunting and fishing. Guide licensing programmes have been established by relevant management agencies in all Arctic nations. Licensing requirements vary considerably among Arctic nations, but common requirements include proven knowledge of specific locations, technical skills, safe and efficient recreation delivery systems, and emergency response systems, as well as specific skills pertaining to waste removal (UNEP 2007).

The Antarctic was explored and settled later than the Arctic, and therefore is nominally afforded the protection of more consistent international accords controlling access, exploration, resource exploitation and waste management, primarily under the complex of multilateral agreements of the Antarctic Treaty System, in particular the 1959 Antarctic Treaty itself. As part of a comprehensive commitment to protect the Antarctic environment, Annex 3 of the Madrid Protocol (1991) obliges all countries to apply responsible waste management principles and to develop waste management plans. Certain hazardous materials, including polystyrene beads, PCBs and radioactive materials, are prohibited from import to Antarctica, and specific guidelines are in place for the management and disposal of solid waste, including cleanup of pre-existing wastes in research sites.

However, the Protocol is still quite limited in its power over land- or ice-based tourist camps and over organic discharge from cruise ships. Annex 3 does not specifically preclude the disposal of raw sewage into Antarctic waters from Antarctic settlements. Also, the gradual discharge of raw sewage and of ground-up food wastes of less than 2.5 cm in size into Antarctic seas is also permitted from ships moving at speeds of 4 knots or more, at distances of more than 12 nautical miles from land and ice shelves (Annex 4). Vessels carrying 10 or fewer passengers are not subject to these constraints. There also appears to be no absolute limit on the cumulative amount of such wastes that can be dumped into the sea. Also, control of ocean dumping of organic and other wastes immediately outside the Antarctic treaty area is treated only vaguely under Article 8 of the Protocol (i.e. 'due consideration shall be given to the need to avoid detrimental effects on dependent and associated ecosystems, outside the Antarctic Treaty area').

Dumping of wastes in international waters is constrained only by the relatively weak provisions of MARPOL 73/78 (the International Convention for the Prevention of Pollution from Ships 1973, as amended by the Protocol of 1978). Most pointedly, the continent of Antarctica derives absolutely no economic benefits from tourism, but can suffer environmental and heritage resource costs. As UNEP (2007) summarises:

> Unlike most parts of the world, there are no indigenous people to benefit from tourism in Antarctica and thus tourism is not an alternative to local unsustainable economics activities. This blunt fact is a serious consideration for anyone motivated to propose tourism management practices on the southern continent. There is no continuous stream of money devoted to tourism management, environmental monitoring, emergency services, waste collection and disposal, the design and implementation of risk minimization or mitigation programmes, or any other 'best practices' normally associated with reasonably managed tourism.

Clearly, if the trend of increasing tourism traffic to the Antarctic continues, existing regulatory provisions may not be stringent enough to protect the long-term ecological integrity of Antarctic ecosystems.

The future

As practical experience, literature reports and industry practice all demonstrate, there are no simple solutions for waste management problems in the tourist industry. Waste management is but one part of the broader quest for sustainable tourism, and waste management strategies must be contextualised with other environmental parameters, and ultimately reconciled with the other environmental, economic and socio-political components of sustainability.

The cornerstone empirical techniques of waste auditing and life cycle analysis will continue to be important in assessing and managing tourism wastes. Integrative approaches based on environmental management systems have been around for almost two decades (e.g. Kirk 1996; Tribe et al. 2000; Buckley et al. 2000; Barrow 2006). Although there are indeed some hopeful initiatives and positive approaches to waste management on the horizon, the overall record of the tourism sector has been, quite frankly, dismal. Despite the hopeful strident rhetoric and genuine progress of international agencies like the UNWTO, the equally strident rhetoric of tourism's detractors contains just as much truth, and must be heeded.

The tourism industry is a classic complex system, comprising mutually inter-dependent inter-related factors, which are not easily addressed individually. There are very few simple cause-and-effect mechanisms, and therefore very few simple prescriptive solutions. Like most challenges of sustainability, waste management in tourism is a systemic problem that must be addressed on a systems level, employing all of the best techniques of proactive planning and adaptive management. Realistically, if progress is to be made in making waste management more sustainable in tourism, it is likely to be as a result of the aggregate of many small incremental positive changes. However, this approach is threatened by the high rate of degradation of intact ecosystems relative to the slow pace of human innovation.

Ultimately, natural and cultural resources must be used sustainably in a way that will safeguard human needs in the future (Redcliffe 1987; WCED 1987; Spangenberg 2005; Saarinen 2006). Regardless of the degree of sophistication of analytical techniques or the technical excellence of waste management technologies, sustainability should be connected primarily with the integrity of natural systems and the needs of people – not the needs of any specific industry like tourism.

Notes

* Roughly translated from Middle English: 'There are men who quote the proverb: Misfortune comes to the beast which fouleth its own nest'.
1 Somewhat surprisingly, direct discharge of untreated municipal sewage into the sea still occurs in affluent developed nations. For example, although most Canadian cities have respectable sewage treatment facilities, a number of municipalities continue to dump raw sewage into the sea, a practice that Eco-justice Canada calls a 'national disgrace'. Unlike the European Union and the USA, Canada has no national standards for municipal sewage treatment. The highest-profile offender is British Columbia's capital city of Victoria, which dumps its raw sewage directly into the Strait of Juan de Fuca, an arm of the Pacific Ocean. Montreal pumps 900 billion litres of sewage annually into the St. Lawrence River, most of which receives primary treatment (i.e. settling and straining out the lumps), but 3.6 billion litres of that total enters the river as untreated raw sewage. Other Canadian cities cited for their dismal record include Halifax and St. John's. Public outcry and imposed legislation are slowly correcting this situation, however – Halifax and St. John's have recently introduced improved wastewater treatment facilities, and high-profile offender Victoria has been mandated by the province of British Columbia to site and construct a sewage treatment plant, which is slated to open by 2016 (Macqueen 2009).
2 This is not *necessarily* so. Although we tend to consider tourist activity as highly consumptive and energy-intensive, baseline patterns of everyday consumption in affluent Western consumer societies may not be different. In some cultures, particularly North American car-dependent suburban culture, the carbon footprint can be very large, and everyday reliance on takeaway food and drive-through restaurants can generate enormous quantities of container and packaging waste on an ongoing basis. Aggregate long-distance commuter activity in car-dependent commuter societies may in fact eclipse tourism travel for the same time period. Consider the case of a long-distance car commuter living in Grimsby, Ontario, Canada, and commuting by mid-sized SUV (e.g. Chevrolet Equinox) to a job in downtown Toronto, a (depressingly commonplace) daily commute of 200 km. Carbon emissions total approximately 0.31 tonnes per week. Add to this a hypothetical propensity for the time-stressed

commuter to stop at drive-through restaurants and purchase takeaway foods, generating considerable food-service packaging waste.

Contrast this same individual taking a two-week vacation at an inclusive resort in Cuba. Total carbon emissions for a return flight from Toronto to Varadero are (flight = 0.51 tonnes) + (return commute to airport = 0.06 tonnes) = 0.57 tonnes. By staying in one place at an inclusive resort, the carbon impacts of travel are actually slightly lower than the carbon impacts of a daily commute to the workplace (0.57 tonnes versus 0.62 tonnes) over the 2-week period. The use of disposable food service products is also likely to be significantly lower in a Cuban all-inclusive resort.

Although obviously not an exoneration of the environmental impacts of tourism, the above scenario points out the underlying societal patterns that contribute to a profoundly unsustainable consumptive lifestyle that can be the norm in many affluent industrialised nations.

References

Adapa, P.K., Tabil, L.G. and Schoenau, G.J. (2006) *Municipal Solid Waste – A Review of Classification System (sic)*. American Society of Agricultural and Biological Engineers paper number MBSK 06–209, ASABE/ CSBE North Central Intersectional Meeting. http://asae.frymulti.com/abstract.asp?aid=22368&t=2.

AFP (2010) *Everest clean-up team makes grisly discovery*. www.google.com/hostednews/afp/article/ALeqM5i _FKJcpu98EFlvMpFG-VGC2ziqAQ.

Anderson, J.L., Axler, R., Christopherson, S., and Gustafson, D.M. (2002) *Constructed Wetlands. Innovative Onsite Sewage Treatment Systems*. www.extension.umn.edu/distribution/naturalresources/DD7671.html.

Arnette, A. (2010) *Everest Clean-up above 8000 m*. www.alanarnette.com/news/2010/01/21/everest-clean-up-above-8000m.

Atkin, P., Hershkowitz, A. and Hoover, D. (2006) *Trash Landings: How Airlines and Airports Can Clean Up Their Recycling Programs*. National Resource Defense Council, New York. www.nrdc.org/cities/recyclin g/airline/airline.pdf.

Australian Alps Liaison Committee (2002) *Human Waste Management Best Practices – Workshop Papers and Presentations*. Compiled by Karen Civil, Environment ACT and Brett McNamara, Australian Alps National Parks. 222 pp. www.australianalps.environment.gov.au/publications/research-reports/pubs/ human-waste.pdf.

Barrow, C.J. (2006) *Environmental Management for Sustainable Development* (2nd Edn). London: Routledge.

Baum, T. (1998) Taking the Exit Route: Extending the Tourism Area Life Cycle Model. *Current Issues in Tourism* 1, 167–75.

Beigl, P.E., Lebersorger, S. and S. Salhofer (2007) Modelling municipal solid waste generation: A review. *Waste Management* 28 (2008) 200–214.

Beigl, P., Wassermann, G., Schneider, F. and Salhofer, S. (2004) *Forecasting Municipal Solid Waste Generation in Major European Cities*. Proceedings of the International Environmental Modelling and Software Society International Conference (iEMSs 2004) on Complexity and Integrated Resources Management, 14–17 June 2004 University of Osnabrück, Germany. www.iemss.org/iemss2004/pdf/regional/beigfore.pdf.

Beech, J. and Chadwick, S. (eds) (2005) *The Business of Tourism Management*. Harlow: Prentice Hall.

Bluewater Network (2006) *Cruise Ships: More Ships, More Passengers, More Pollution*. Bluewater Network/ Friends of the Earth. www.bluewaternetwork.org/reports/cv/Cruiseship_MiniReport_06.pdf.

Boissevain, J. (ed.) (1996) *Coping with Tourists: European Reactions to Mass Tourism*. Providence, RI: Berghahn Books. www.questia.com/read/2968585?title=Introduction.

Buckley, R.C., Pickering, C.M. and Warnken, J. (2000) Environmental Management for Alpine Tourism and Resorts in Australia, in Godde, P.M., Price, M.F. and Zimmermann, F.M. *Tourism and development in mountain regions*. Wallingford, Oxon, UK, New York: CABI Publishers, 27–46.

Butler, R. (1980) The concept of a tourist area cycle of evolution: Implications for management of resources. *Canadian Geographer / Le Géographe canadien* 24, 5–12. http://onlinelibrary.wiley.com/doi/ 10.1111/j.1541–0064.1980.tb00970.x/abstract

——(1998) Sustainable tourism – looking backwards in order to progress?, in C. Hall and A. Lew (eds). *Sustainable Tourism: A Geographical Perspective*. Essex: Longman, 25–34.

——(2004) The Tourism Area Life Cycle in the Twenty-First Century, in A. Lew, M. Hall and A. Williams (eds). *A Companion to Tourism*, Oxford: Blackwell, 159–69.

Bridle, K.L. and Kirkpatrick, J.B. (2003) Impact of nutrient additions and digging for human waste disposal in natural environments, Tasmania, Australia. *J Environ Manage* 69, 299–306.

Brown, D.T. (1993) The Legacy of the Landfill: Perspectives on the Solid Waste Crisis, in Mustafa, N. (ed.) *Plastics Waste Management – Disposal, Recycling and Reuse*. New York: Marcel Dekker, Inc., Chapter 1: 1–35.

Brown, D.T. and Chalermwat, K. (1999) *Solid Waste Collection and Management in Laem Chabang*. www.brocku.ca/epi/ciet/existing.htm.

Byrne, N. (2000) 'Poo tubes protect the bush', in: Civil, K. and B. McNamara (2002) *Best Practice Human Waste Management Workshop: Workshop Proceedings and Papers*, Canberra and Jindabyne, 32–36. http://www.australianalps.environment.gov.au/publications/research-reports/pubs/human-waste.pdf

Carlsen, J., Getz, D. and Ali-Knight, J. (2001) The environmental attitudes and practices of family businesses in rural tourism and hospitality sectors. *Journal of Sustainable Tourism* 9(4), 281–97.

Castellani V. and Sala, S. (2008) *Ecological Footprint: a way to assess impact of tourists' choices at local scale*. Proceedings of Sustainable Tourism 2008, 3–5 September, Malta.

Conservation International (2006) *From Ship to Shore: Sustainable Stewardship in Cruise Destinations*. www.conservation.org/Documents/CI_ecotourism_from_ship_to_shore_eng.pdf.

Copeland, C. (2008) *Cruise Ship Pollution: Background, Laws and Regulations, and Key Issues*. Congress Research Service (CRS) Report for Congress, 6 February. Order Code RL32450. Available online through the National Council for Science and the Environment CRS Reports, www.ncseonline.org/nle/crsreports/07dec/rl32450.pdf.

Day, G. (1981) 'The Product Life Cycle: Analyses and Applications Issues', *Journal of Marketing* 45, 60–7.

Eliasson, K. (2004) *Goodbye Churchill Dump*. Hudson Bay Post, Churchill, Manitoba – May. Archival copy online at www.polarbearalley.com/churchill-dump.html.

Environment Canada (2010) *Pollution and waste: Guide to Classification*. www.ec.gc.ca/gdd-mw/default.asp?lang=En&n=A8D9E099–1&offset=1&toc=show.

EUR-Lex Europa (2010) *European Waste Catalogue List of Waste* available online at http://eur-lex.europa.eu/LexUriServ/LexUriServ.do?uri=CONSLEG:2000D0532:20020101

Extreme Everest (2010) *Extreme Everest Expedition 2010 blog*. http://extremeeverest.wordpress.com/.

Faucette, B. and Ediger, L. (2003) Jamaica: Composting boosts tourism and coffee production. *Biocycle* December, 59–62.

Foolmaun, R.K. and Ramjeawon, T. (2008) 'Life Cycle Assessment (LCA) of PET bottles and comparative LCA of three disposal options in Mauritius', *International Journal of Environment and Waste Management* 2(1/2), 125–38. http://inderscience.metapress.com/link.asp?id=ek3qh61h7tw10110

Gawaikar, V. and Deshpande, V.P. (2006) *Source Specific Quantification and Characterization of Municipal Solid Waste – a Review*. Waste to Energy Research and Technology Council working paper. www.seas.columbia.edu/earth/wtert/sofos/Gawaikar_Source%20Specific%20Quantification%20and%20Characterization%20of%20MSW.pdf.

Gössling, S., Borgström-Hansson, C., Hörstmeier, O. and S. Saggel (2002) 'Ecological footprint analysis as a tool to assess tourism sustainability', *Ecological Economics* 43(2–3):192–211.

GovTrack (2010a) *S. 1820: Clean Cruise Ship Act of 2009*. www.govtrack.us/congress/bill.xpd?bill=s111–1820.

——(2010b) *S. 1820: Clean Cruise Ship Act of 2009 (Related Legislation)*. www.govtrack.us/congress/bill.xpd?bill=s111–1820&tab=related.

GTZ (Deutsche Gesellschaft für Technische Zusammenarbeit GmbH) (2010) *Sustainable waste management in the tourism sector of the Mexican Caribbean*. Project summary available online at www.gtz.de/en/weltweit/lateinamerika-karibik/mexiko/27811.htm.

de Guilford, N. (1250) *'Disputation of Ane Hule and a Niʒtingale', a.k.a 'The Owl and the Nightingale'*. Excerpted from pp. 403–4 of Cochrane, J.G. (1837) On Proverbs and Popular Sayings. *Cochrane's Foreign Quarterly Review* No.II, Article V, pp. 381–404. http://books.google.ca/books?id=cPoEAAAAQAAJ& lpg = PA403& ots = ZjAaYbsFs3& dq = fouleth%20his%20own%20nest& pg = PA403#v = snippet& q = Contents%20Of%20No.%20II& f = false.

van Haastert, M. and de Grosbois, D. (2010) 'Environmental Initiatives in Bed and Breakfast Establishments in Canada: Scope and Major Challenges with Implementation', *Tourism and Hospitality Planning & Development* 7(2), 179–93.

Hercock, M. (1999) 'The impacts of recreation and tourism in the remote North Kimberley region of Western Australia', *Environmentalist* 19, 259–75.

Hertwich E.G. (2005) 'Life Cycle Approaches to Sustainable Consumption: A critical review', *Environmental Science and Technology* 39(13), 4673–84.

Hoang, P.C. (2005) *Audit of solid wastes from hotels and composting trial in Halong City, Vietnam*. Master of Engineering Thesis, Department of Civil Engineering, University of Toronto. 94 pp. www.utoronto.ca/waste-econ/HoangPhuongChi.pdf.

IceNews (2010) *Arctic nations in summit rift.* Article posted 31 March 2010. www.icenews.is/index.php/2010/03/31/arctic-nations-in-summit-rift/.

Johnson, D. (2006) Providing Ecotourism Excursions for Cruise Passengers. *Journal of Sustainable Tourism* 14 (1), 43–54.

Jones, B. (ed.) (2010) 'California rejects ban on plastic shopping bags', *GreenHouse (USA Today)*, 1 September. Available at: http://content.usatoday.com/communities/greenhouse/post/2010/09/california-rejects-plastic-bag-ban/1.

Kirk, D. (1996) *Environmental management for hotels: A student's handbook.* Oxford and Boston, MA: Butterworth Heinemann.

Klein, R.A. (2009) *Getting a Grip on Cruise Ship Pollution. Friends of the Earth.* Available at: www.foe.org/sites/default/files/CruiseShipReport_Klein.pdf.

Kuniyal, J.C. (2005) 'Solid Waste Management in the Himalayan Trails and Expedition Summits', *Journal of Sustainable Tourism* 13(4), 391–410.

Leave No Trace Canada (2010) www.leavenotrace.ca/principles.

Leonard, A. (2007) *The Story of Stuff.* (Web video). http://storyofstuff.org/.

——(2010) *The Story of Bottled Water.* (Web video). http://storyofstuff.org/bottledwater/.

Lewis, H. and Demmers, M. (1996) 'Life Cycle Assessment and Environmental Impact', *Australian Journal of Environmental Management* 3(2), June 1996.

Macqueen, K. (2009) 'Many cities still dump raw sewage: Halifax is dumping raw waste again, after a new plant failed', *Maclean's*, Thursday, 30 April, available at: www2.macleans.ca/2009/04/30/many-cities-still-dump-raw-sewage/.

Madrid Protocol (1991) *Protocol on Environmental Protection to the Antarctic Treaty.* www.antarctica.gov.au/antarctic-law-and-treaty/the-madrid-protocol.

——Annex 3: Waste Disposal and Waste Management. www.antarctica.gov.au/antarctic-law-and-treaty/the-madrid-protocol/annex-iii-waste-disposal-and-waste-management.

——Annex 4: Prevention of Marine Pollution: www.antarctica.gov.au/antarctic-law-and-treaty/the-madrid-protocol/annex-iv-prevention-of-marine-pollution.

Manaktola, K. and Jauhari, V. (2007) Exploring consumer attitude and behaviour towards green practices in the lodging industry in India. *International Journal of Contemporary Hospitality Management* 19(5): 364–77.

MARPOL (1973/78) *International Convention for the Prevention of Pollution From Ships, 1973 as modified by the Protocol of 1978.* www.imo.org/About/Conventions/ListOfConventions/Pages/International-Convention-for-the-Prevention-of-Pollution-from-Ships-(MARPOL).aspx.

Martin, B.S., and Uysal, M. (1990) 'An Examination of Relationship Between Carrying Capacity and the Tourism Life Cycle: Management and Policy Implications', *Journal of Environmental Management* 31, 327–33.

Mazzanti, M., Montini, A. and Zoboli, R. (2008) 'Municipal Waste Generation and Socioeconomic Drivers: Evidence from Comparing Northern and Southern Italy' *Journal of Environment and Development* 17, 51–69.

Medina, M. (2007) *The World's Scavengers. Salvaging for Sustainable Consumption and Production.* Plymouth: AltaMira Press. http://books.google.co.in/books?hl=en&id=daCm1Eck0pkC&dq=Martin+Medina&-printsec=frontcover&source=web&ots=ZIooTzaCJ5&sig=5gyKIRjnZSy_4GUniLcRi7eUU-4&sa=X&-oi=book_result&resnum=1&ct=result, retrieved on 10 November 2008.

——2008. Let's Talk Trash, Prime Numbers. *Foreign Policy*, September-October.

Meyer, K. (1994) *How to Shit in the Woods: An Environmentally Sound Approach to a Lost Art.* 2nd edn. Berkeley, CA: Ten Speed Press.

Milea, A. (2009). *Waste as a Social Dilemma: Issues of Social and Environmental Justice and the Role of Residents in Municipal Solid Waste Management*, Delhi, India. Master of International Development and Management thesis, Lund University, May. Available at: www.lumid.lu.se/thesis_Adriana.pdf.

Monfreda, C., Wackernagel, M. and Deumling, D. (2004) 'Establishing national natural capital accounts based on detailed ecological footprint and biological capacity accounts', *Land Use Policy* 21, 231–46.

Moore, S.A. and Polley, A. (2007) 'Defining indicators and standards for tourism impacts in protected areas: Cape Range National Park, Australia', *Environ Manage* 39, 291–300.

Nair, S.K. and Jayakumar, C. (2008) *A Handbook for Waste Management in Rural Tourism Areas – A Zero Waste Approach.* Ministry of Tourism, Government of India / United Nations Development Programme. Full report available at: www.no-burn.org/downloads/Thanal_UNDP_Handbook-Low-Res.pdf.

New Zealand Parliamentary Commissioner for the Environment. 2003. *Just cruising? Environmental effects of cruise ships.* Wellington: Parliamentary Commissioner for the Environment. 56 pp.

Oceana (2003) *Protect Our Oceans: Stop Cruise Ship Pollution – Cruise Ship Waste——U.S. Laws and Regulations.* 3 pp. http://na.oceana.org/sites/default/files/o/uploads/cruiseshipwaste_uslawsandregulations.pdf.

OECD (Organization for Economic Cooperation and Development) (2004) 'Environment and the OECD Guidelines for Multinational Enterprises: Corporate Tools and Approaches' http://www.oecd.org/dataoecd/12/1/34992954.pdf

Phillips Environmental (2010) *The WAG Bag Waste Disposal* Kit. www.thepett.ca/products/wag.html.

Pilgrim, J.J. (1996) *Best Practice Environmental Management and the Tourism Industry*, in Page, S. and Connell, J. (eds) (2008) Sustainable Tourism – Critical Concepts in the Social Sciences. Volume III: Destinations: Progress and application of principles. New York: Routledge, Ch. 53: 143–59.

Pleumarom, A. (2004) 'Preparations of tourism-related events for the World Social Forum 2004 – The Dark Side of Tourism', briefing document, www.twnside.org.sg/title2/ttcd/TA-02.doc.

——(2007) Does tourism benefit the Third World? *Third World Resurgence* #207/208 (Nov/Dec 2007). Available at: www.twnside.org.sg/title2/resurgence/twr207–8.htm.

Radwan, Hatem R.I. , Jones, Eleri and Minoli, Dino. 2010. 'Managing solid waste in small hotels', *Journal of Sustainable Tourism*, 18(2): 175–190.

Rathje, W. and Murphy, C. (1992) *Rubbish! The Archaeology of Garbage*. New York: HarperCollins Publishers.

Rekacewicz, P. (2004) 'The richer we get, the more we discard (OECD, 1999)'. Captioned figure, p. 22, in: UNEP (United Nations Environment Program) (2004) *Vital Waste Graphics.Produced by the Basel Convention Secretariat and in partnership with the Division of Environmental Conventions (DEC) of UNEP, Grid-Arendal and the Division of Early Warning Assessment-Europe of UNEP for the seventh meeting of the Conference to the Parties of the Basel Convention (COP7).* Available online at http://www.grida.no/_res/site/file/publications/vital-waste/wastereport-full.pdf

Rosenthal, E. (2008) 'By 'bagging it,' Ireland rids itself of a plastic nuisance', *New York Times*, Thursday, 31 January. Available at: www.nytimes.com/2008/01/31/world/europe/31iht-bags.4.9650382.html.

Royal Caribbean (2010) *Oasis of the Seas*. www.royalcaribbean.com/findacruise/ships/class/ship/home.do?shipCode=OA.

Ryan, C. (2003) *Recreational tourism: demand and impacts.* Clevendon: Channel View Publications. http://books.google.ca/books?id=OifwDs6PcM4C& source = gbs_navlinks_s.

Sala, S. and Castellani, V. (2009) *A proposal for integration between Life Cycle Assessment and other instruments and indicators as a way to promote Sustainable Production and Consumption strategies.* http://boa.unimib.it/bitstream/10281/7557/1/Castellani-Sala_SETAC%20LCA_extended_abstract.pdf.

Schaper, M. and Carlsen, J. (2004) 'Overcoming the green gap: improving the environmental performance of small tourism firms in Western Australia', in R. Thomas (ed.) *Small firms in tourism: international perspectives.* New York: Elsevier, 197–214.

Schroeder, J.R. (2003) *The Kayaker's 'Poop Tube'.* www.fastq.com/~jrschroeder/poop.htm.

Statistics Canada (2012) *North American Industry Classification System (NAICS) Canada 2012.* http://www.statcan.gc.ca/pub/12-501-x/12-501-x2012001-eng.pdf

Sweeting, J.E.N. and Wayne, S.L. (2006) 'A Shifting Tide: Environmental Challenges and Cruise Industry Responses', in Dowling, R.K. (ed.) *Cruise Ship Tourism.* Oxford: CABI Publishing, Ch. 30: 327–37.

Tooman, L. (1997) Applications of the Life-Cycle Model in Tourism. *Annals of Tourism Research* 24, 214–34.

Transport Canada (2010) *Regulations to control discharges from cruise vessels operating in Canadian waters.* www.tc.gc.ca/eng/mediaroom/backgrounders-b02-m018–2230.htm.

Tribe, J., Font, X., Grittis, N., Vickery, R. and Yale, K. (2000) *Environmental Management for Rural Tourism and Recreation.* London: Cassell.

UNEP (United Nations Environment Programme) (2003) *A Manual for Water and Waste Management: What the Tourism Industry Can Do to Improve Its Performance.* Joint initiative of UNEP's Global Programme of Action (GPA) and UNEP's Division of Technology, Industry and Economics (DTIE), with financial support from the German Agency for Technical Cooperation – Regional Division for Asia, Pacific, Latin America and the Caribbean (GTZ). www.unep.fr/pc/tourism/library/waste_manual.htm.

——(2004) *Vital Waste Graphics.* Produced by the Basel Convention Secretariat and in partnership with the Division of Environmental Conventions (DEC) of UNEP, Grid-Arendal and the Division of Early Warning Assessment-Europe of UNEP for the seventh meeting of the Conference to the Parties of the Basel Convention (COP7). Available at: www.grida.no/_res/site/file/publications/vital-waste/wastereport-full.pdf.

——(2007) *Tourism in The Polar Regions – the Sustainability Challenge.* www.unep.fr/scp/publications/details.asp?id=DTI/0938/PA. PDF version at www.unep.fr/shared/publications/pdf/DTIx0938xPA-PolarTourismEN.pdf.

US EPA (United States Environmental Protection Agency) (2010) 'Marine Sanitation Devices (MSDs): Proposed Regulation To Establish a No Discharge Zone (NDZ) for California State Marine Waters', http://edocket.access.gpo.gov/2010/pdf/2010-21950.pdf

US National Parks Service (2010a) *Grand Canyon National Park – Backcountry Waste Management*. www.nps. gov/grca/planyourvisit/waste-mgmt.htm.

——(2010b) *Grand Canyon National Park human waste pilot program cover letter*. www.nps.gov/grca/planyourvisit/upload/Waste_Mgmt_Pilot_letter.pdf.

USA Today (2002) 'Breaking environmental laws: How one cruise liner illegally dumped waste', Graphic by Brennen Lucas, Jerry Mosemak and George Petras, *USA Today*, 2011–11–08. http://www.usatoday.com/travel/_graphics/gcruisedumping/flash.htm

van der Voo, L. (2010) 'Green Cruising? Cruise lines dodge states' tougher rules by dumping in Canadian waters', *InvestigateWest*, 15 August 2010. http://invw.org/green_cruising.

Vernon, J., Essex, S., Pinder, D. and Curry, K. (2003) 'The 'greening' of tourism micro-businesses: outcomes of focus group investigations in South East Cornwall', *Business Strategy and the Environment* 12(1), 49–69.

Wackernagel M. and Rees, W. (1998) *Our Ecological Footprint: reducing human Impact on the Earth*. Gabriola Island, BC: New Society Publishers.

Wang, T. (2009) 'Effectiveness of plastic bag ban policy is questionable – researcher', *InterFax China*, Wed, 12 February 2009. Available at: www.interfax.cn/news/11996.

WHO (World Health Organization) (2010a) *Healthcare Waste Management: Introduction*. www.healthcarewaste.org/en/115_overview.html.

——(2010b) *Healthcare Waste Management: Classification – The 10 Categories of HCRW*. www.healthcarewaste.org/en/128_hcw_categ.html.

wikiHow (2010) *How to make a poop tube.* (various authors). www.wikihow.com/Make-a-Poop-Tube.

Williams, D. (2002) *Conspicuous consumption*. National Parks, April–May 2002, pp. 40–45. Available at: http://books.google.ca/books?id=oT6SNqlB05AC&lpg=PA40&ots=O7WZCr01Rn&dq=animal20-proof%20garbage%20waste%20containers%20national%20park&pg=PA41#v=onepage&q&f= false.

Xanterra Parks and Resorts (2010) *Solid Waste Management & Recycling at Yellowstone National Park*. www.yellowstonenationalparklodges.com/solid-waste-management-recycling-8054.html.

44

Fair Trade in tourism

Critical shifts and perspectives

Angela Kalisch

Background

The General Agreement on Trade in Services (GATS), launched in 1995, firmly embedded tourism as a trade export on the agenda of international trade negotiations in the context of liberalisation and free market access. However, the Agreement was severely critiqued for potentially reinforcing environmental degradation, poverty and inequality in developing countries through liberalisation in tourism and other related sectors, such as water and health (Kalisch 2001, 2010). This provided the context in 1996 for the launch of an investigation by the UK based non-governmental organization (NGO) Tourism Concern into the feasibility of Fair Trade in Tourism, modelled on the success of Fair Trade in primary commodities, such as coffee, tea and bananas (Badger *et al.* 1996; Cleverdon and Kalisch 2000; Kalisch 2001, 2010).

The Fair Trade paradigm, initially applied to primary commodities, was used as a basis for developing a new vision on equitable trade in tourism as part of the service sector. Yet, there was no experience of Fair Trade in services. The only models of ethical trade in services in the UK at the time were in the banking and financial investment sectors, such as the Co-operative Bank, and a new ethical investment organisation, called Triodos. Moreover, in their 1996 analysis of the GATS and its implications for tourism in developing countries, Tourism Concern saw the need for a 'macro-economic critique' of liberalisation and free market access in countries affected by Structural Adjustment policies (Badger *et al.* 1996: 25). However, developing a Fair Trade label for tourism would have largely addressed an elite niche market at micro-level; initially, at least. This was hardly an appropriate response to a 'macro-economic critique'.

Thus, in 1999, Tourism Concern, together with an international multistakeholder Network, proceeded on the one hand to raise awareness on the impacts of the GATS in tourism, and on the other to develop criteria for Fair Trade tourism (FTT) policy and practice to be implemented by governments, NGOs and tour operators in the context of Corporate Social Responsibility (Kalisch 2001, 2002, 2010). The Network identified 'root causes of inequality', such as lack of access to capital, ownership of resources, control of marketing and representation, transparency of tourism operations and unequal distribution of benefits (Cleverdon and Kalisch 2000). Therefore, FTT criteria focused on equitable partnerships between the industry and local communities, transparency and accountability, equitable negotiation, fair distribution of tourism benefits, such as fair price, support of the local economy and sustainable use of natural resources (Kalisch 2001). The development of a label was unfeasible at the time, beyond the organisation's brief and capacity. The criteria were considered work in progress as network members required time to discuss them within their various organisations. In addition, there was concern that the implementation of a certification process was complex, costly and controversial (Kalisch 2001). Only one initiative in South Africa (Fair Trade in Tourism South Africa, FTTSA) developed specific certification criteria from this work. The Network's last international conference in 2002, held in the Gambia, proposed the formation of South-South networks, starting with Africa. Yet, financial and logistical challenges thwarted the realisation of this venture. Nevertheless, the criteria and the consultation process of the International Network influenced many tourism policies and projects around the world to incorporate social justice, human rights issues and corporate social responsibility into debates on sustainability in tourism. However, resolving the relationship between trade and inequality in tourism still requires further empirical investigation.

This chapter explores the complexities of applying the concept of Fair Trade labelling to tourism and attempts to provide some perspectives for the way forward, using the case study of FTTSA.

The Fair Trade concept

The Fair Trade concept was developed in the 1960s by international citizens' movements from the message 'trade not aid'. It embraces an alliance between consumers and NGOs in Europe and North America, and small producer organisations in less economically developed countries. This alternative vision of international trade thrives on socially conscious business practice, partnership, co-operation and transparency, enshrined in the accreditation of high-quality standards as a consumer guarantee, such as fair price, and promoted by skilful marketing.

The focus on marginalised producers in less developed countries has its roots in an analysis of the development paradigm and the 'core-periphery' dependency relationship, which emerged as a critique of modernisation in the 1960s (Barratt Brown 1993; Sharpley and Telfer 2002; Holden 2005; Telfer and Sharpley 2008).

Fair Trade aims to shift the historic power and trade imbalance, caused by mercantilist and colonial domination, in favour of small producers in predominantly agricultural economies.

Consumers in Europe, America and Australasia have seized this opportunity with enthusiasm. Fair Trade is one of the fastest growing markets in the world. By 2005, Fair Trade sales in Europe had been growing at an average 20 per cent per year since 2000 (Krier 2006) and in 2008, despite the recession, global sales of Fair Trade products grew by 22 per cent (Fairtrade Foundation 2009).

Such success has attracted the attention of large corporations. Since 2005, Fair Trade-certified coffee and chocolate have been adopted by Starbucks and Nestlé. The award of the label to companies, controversial for their human rights practices, has caused consternation and vigorous debates within the Fair Trade movement (Jaffee 2007). This development exposes the contradictions of addressing structural trade inequalities, caused by neo-liberal capitalist free market ideology, by seeking access to those very same markets. Jaffee (2007: 199) discusses this 'paradox' in his excellent work on 'Brewing Justice' in the context of 'dancing with the devil'. As Schmelzer (2006: 4) notes:

> Fair Trade can be analyzed as a complex and multilayered process of social defence against destructive effects of unrestricted market forces that tries to re-embed the economy. As such it is a site of contestation, conflict and negotiation between different actors that brings about multiple and partly contradictory effects on different levels.

Fair Trade in tourism – challenges and contradictions

International tourism has been analysed in the context of dependency theory and exploitation and critiqued for promoting uncontrolled economic growth and neo-liberal expansion. From this perspective it seems feasible to investigate the use of the Fair Trade concept as an ideological basis for more equitable trade in tourism.

However, FTT is just as (if not more) vulnerable to the vagaries of neo-liberal market philosophy as Fair Trade primary commodities. The complexities and contradictions in the Fair Trade process, noted by Schmelzer (2006) and Jaffee (2007), are intensified in the tourism trade, due to the complexity of the tourism production process as a service export and the political and socio-economic tensions resulting from its vigorous international promotion (Cleverdon and Kalisch 2000).

The following section analyses some of these complexities and contradictions in relation to some of the core elements that would need to be part of a FTT certification process: the product, the producers/providers, the purchasers and consumers.

The tourism product

Compared with primary commodities, which exist with or without Fair Trade, a FTT product would have to be created, materialised from the enormous diversity of tourism products and experiences that exist on the market. These are constantly being increased, reinvented and modified to suit changing cultural trends, consumer expectations and technological innovations. The creation of a FTT product would be a seriously challenging prospect, because in the competitive global market environment, tourism as a product is elusive and contested; elusive because the definition of precisely what constitutes the tourism product can vary according to different analytical approaches: is it the destination or the destination 'concept' (Cooper and Hall 2008)? Does it consist of the supply, commodity or value chain (Clancy 1998; FIAS and OECD 2006; Steck *et al.* 2010)? Does it embrace the whole of the tourism system, including outbound and inbound operators and the transition stage? Or is it all or aspects of the entire tourist experience that should be addressed (Judd 2006)? A tourist experience comprises both tangible (accommodation, flight) and intangible parts (climate, weather, views). Moreover, tourism is inter-connected with other sectors, such as transport, construction and finance. It relies on appropriate governance in destinations. This dependency results in a lack of strategic and quality control over the product. Measuring such a complex product, or bargaining on the basis of fair price would be extremely difficult (Beyer 2007). In New Zealand, for example, research on community benchmarking for Green Globe certification highlights the challenges of measuring tangible environmental indicators, which embrace aspects that are not entirely specific to tourism activity (McNicol *et al.* 2004).

It is contested due to the ethical implications of packaging, marketing and selling people, cultures, heritage and natural resources as raw material of a product; a product to which value is added on the one hand through the mechanisms of the tourism distribution system, owned and controlled largely by foreign companies, and on the other hand by the fashions and trends of the markets.

The producers/providers

Linked to the diversity of the tourism product is the diversity of tourism producers, or rather service providers. Who would be the key stakeholders involved in the certification process, and who would be the beneficiaries?

The definition of Fair Trade in Tourism, developed by Tourism Concern's International Network on Fair Trade in Tourism, contains a focus on 'local small-scale destination stakeholders' and 'indigenous host communities'. Beneficiaries would be employees in the formal and informal sectors and groups in the destination that are ready to engage with domestic and international markets but need technical and organisational support (Kalisch 2001: 11). Community-based tourism enterprises were considered at the time to 'provide consumers with fair trade alternatives for their holidays and tour operators with products to develop their fair trade practice' as they were deemed to demonstrate practical evidence of benefiting the poorest communities through tourism (Kalisch 2001: 30).

However, Kalisch suggests that certain requirements need to be in place before community-based tourism can be viable and 'bring the development of a fair trade product within the realm of possibility' (Kalisch 2001: 30). Such requirements would crucially include the availability of a good-quality tourism product that is attractive to relevant tourism markets. Additionally, communities need to provide stability and continuity, strong leadership, efficiency and realism in business dealings, combined with fund raising skills, equity in terms of gender equality, transparency and democracy, and economic self-sufficiency (Kalisch 2001). Yet, such attributes are usually hard to find. Experience has shown that communities are rarely harmonious, homogeneous units and community-based tourism schemes generally tend to suffer from lack of occupancy, poor market access and poor governance (Goodwin and Santilli 2009). Community-based tourism enterprises (CBTEs), questioned for a feasibility study on a FTT label commissioned by Fair Trade Labelling Organisations International (FLO), were reticent about becoming involved with a complex certification process, because of their struggle with operational deficiencies and economic viability (Font 2008). Commodity producers of coffee, tea or bananas who have started to diversify into eco-or agri-tourism have also been considered for Fair Trade certification. Yet, according to Font (2008), these are equally cautious about becoming involved, due to lack of experience of the tourism sector and the need for additional investment in infrastructure, catering for Western tourists' expectations under FTT criteria.

In contrast to the FLO study, a consultancy report on fair pricing, commissioned by the German NGO Tourism Watch, recommends an exclusive focus on mainstream tourism and package tours. They reason that CBTEs play a minor niche market role in the tourism system and would substantially limit the impact of any FTT label (Beyer 2007). Beyer's report concludes that a 'model calculation' of individual service components of a package offer, based on products in existing tourism markets, would be the only practicable method to address the issue of fair pricing. This should be undertaken in co-operation with large operators or market leaders and should start with hotel businesses in terms of 'overnight stays' (Beyer 2007: 17). Such a calculation would then enable evaluation of other core components at destination level linked to the tourism experience (ibid.).

The purchasers

Fair Trade primary commodities were initially promoted in the UK through NGO collaboration, setting up non-profit making trading functions to trade with and to market primary producers (Cleverdon and Kalisch 2000). Their marketing policies incorporated not just selling points but, more importantly, elements of awareness raising and public education on development issues, combined with real life stories about the producers. There is scant potential of such a model in tourism. UK NGOs have had neither the power nor the capacity to develop a viable FTT product and the mechanisms required for its certification (Kalisch 2001).

Without a model of NGOs as trading partners in tourism, the focus for developing FTT purchasing mechanisms must be on existing industry structures, possibly collaborating with relevant NGOs. Whether this is a realistic expectation remains to be seen. There are some indicators that the tourism industry has begun to embrace the concepts of sustainable tourism, pro-poor tourism and responsible tourism, even beyond mere rhetoric and promotional mission statements. There is some uncertainty, however, as to whether they would be prepared to take on the challenge of developing and promoting a FTT label.

Since 2000, www.responsibletravel.com (RT.com), the online worldwide travel agent, based in the UK, with a newly created sister site in the USA (www.responsiblevacation.com), represents the hub of a new generation, using electronic marketing to pioneer a more ethical approach to travel. It markets only holidays and tour operators that have undergone a transparent screening process based on a set of minimum responsible travel criteria created by the company. It then requires customers to provide feedback on whether those criteria have been met. In addition, it campaigns for change in the tourism industry and leads debates on controversial issues, such as climate change, carbon offsetting and human rights (www.responsibletravel.com 2010a).

Far removed from the rigorous verification procedures embodied by Fair Trade certification, this presents a compromise that frankly acknowledges the problems of developing and verifying universally agreed criteria that suit every aspect of this complex industry.

Indeed, RT.com, in conjunction with the International Centre for Responsible Tourism (ICRT) firmly reject efforts at certification and accreditation, as, for example, embodied by the Partnership for Global Sustainable Tourism Criteria, which has created minimum sustainable tourism standards for the industry in response to the challenge of the Millennium Development Goals. RT.com reason that there 'is no evidence that the criteria will bring market advantage' and reject the 'one size fits all' approach to responsible tourism, given the differences in sustainability issues at destinations (www.responsibletravel.com 2010b).

Critics could argue that customer monitoring provides merely anecdotal evidence of compliance with RT criteria, as holidaymakers lack the time and objective expertise normally required for independent monitoring and verification. On the other hand, if Fair Trade in Tourism is about creating market access for small stakeholders, responsible marketing and representation of destination partners, and creating consumer demand for more ethical tourism, the company has certainly generated an important momentum in the drive towards Fairer Trade in Tourism.

Large package tour operators in the UK, collaborating since 2002 under the auspices of the charitable trust The Travel Foundation, have created the Travelife Sustainability Store. This is a system created for European tour operators to support suppliers of holiday components, such as hotels, excursions and transportation, with the implementation of sustainability criteria. These include fair wages for employees, use of local produce and energy efficiency. Handbooks, checklists and audits serve as a basis for offering an 'internationally recognised award' in the form of a 'Travelife logo' for top performers (ABTA 2008; Travelife 2010).

In terms of Fair Trade, further research is required to reveal to what extent the Travelife logo helps to empower small producers/providers and local communities in developing countries. The logo promotes sustainability criteria construed by powerful corporations in tourism-generating countries. In view of many of the smaller suppliers in tourism-receiving countries struggling with economic viability in the face of the overwhelming bargaining power of those very same foreign corporations (Bastakis *et al.* 2004), there is a risk of reinforcing such power imbalances.

An interesting example of business and NGO collaboration is the Ethical Tour Operators Group. Co-ordinated by the NGO Tourism Concern, the group includes around 18 small and medium-sized UK-based tour operators, actively committed to Fair Trade. This group could potentially form the locus of a FTT labelling mechanism in the UK in conjunction with Tourism Concern. However, additional resources would need to be galvanised to support the research and development work essential for such a project.

The consumers

Consumers are the core element of fairtrade labelling. Although the success of Fair Trade primary commodities in the more developed world is quantifiable and measurable, the evidence of consumer demand for potential FTT products is difficult to assess without a comparable product to test market demand. Even FTTSA, who have been certifying tourism businesses since 2004 under Fair Trade criteria, to date only have anecdotal evidence of consumer demand for FTT. They believe that, at this point, the label generates more demand within the value chain, that is when promoting products to tour operators (email communication, 15 December 2010).

Experience suggests that consumer demand for responsible tourism exists in the form of added value and intrinsic quality of the product/service rather than as an objective in its own right (Goodwin and Francis 2003).

Mintel market research on RT in 2007, found that although awareness and interest in local employment and best practice is strong among tourism consumers, only a minority actively seek a holiday with an ethical code of practice, and even fewer would change their holiday plans because of responsible tourism. They conclude that consumers may be feeling confused and helpless, and the availability of tangible consumer options, such as a Fair Trade holiday, accredited by a recognised authority, might increase their willingness to make pro-active ethical choices, even paying an extra premium. Although research indicates that existing tourism certification schemes are failing to attract sufficient consumer demand, the well-known Fair Trade brand could provide that credibility.

Rather than using terms such as 'responsible' and 'ethical', which may seem too serious and virtuous to an escape-seeking public, there may instead be ways of focusing on Fair Trade criteria as an intrinsic element of product quality, making FTT 'cool' and enjoyable (Kalisch 2003). For poorer people in developing countries, Fair Trade is a matter of survival. For tourism consumers, travel is a matter of life style and well-being. There must be a mutually beneficial way of bringing together the well-being of tourists with the well-being of their 'hosts'. Perhaps such an approach could be a more political extension of the increasing consumer need for self-actualisation through charitable giving.

Travel philanthropy is thriving. A report by ICRT commissioned for the 2009 World Travel Market Responsible Tourism Day, identifies a figure of £160,000,000 raised in the UK alone by travel companies through charitable donations by corporations and individuals (Goodwin *et al.* 2009). Demand for charity challenges and volunteer tourism (or Voluntourism) has grown to a total of 1.6 million volunteer tourists a year since 1990 (Tourism Research and Marketing 2008). These two markets are controversial in their impact on communities. Nevertheless, their growth indicates an increased need by travellers to link recreational activity with personal challenge, benefiting local communities at home or abroad, in the context of social learning, consciousness-raising and personal fulfilment. Volunteer tourism is deemed to promote responsible citizenship, duty and fairness (Sin 2009). McGehee and Santos (2005: 774) emphasise the powerful role of network ties and increased social consciousness developed during volunteer tourism experiences in creating 'social movement participation'. Verbeek and Mommas (2008) surmise that 'citizen-consumers' returning from sustainable holidays may even become 'active change agents' (Verbeek and Mommas 2008: 639) and political consumers in relation to campaigning for ethical corporate practice in tourism. Connolly and Shaw (2006) emphasise the 'self-symbolic role of fair trade consumption' and social identity as being the 'antecedent to the purchase of fair trade products' (Connolly and Shaw 2006: 361). Quoting Renard (2003), they highlight the power of Fair Trade as the power of social capital in the sense that it creates solidarity not only with disadvantaged communities in remote corners of the globe but also among an imagined community of like-minded people at home. The Fair Trade label thus becomes 'symbolic capital' and buying it a 'symbolic action'.

The question is whether the enthusiasm for social and financial generosity and self-actualisation through ethical consumption will reach the extra mile to pay for a Fair Trade holiday; particularly as a holiday requires a stronger financial commitment than the weekly or monthly purchase of coffee, tea or bananas. Moreover, charitable and volunteer tourism are a double-edged sword. Depending on the motives of the tourists and the management of the operation, they can be either a fulfilling experience for all parties involved, or simply a selfish and superficial act, creating more poverty than they were intended to alleviate (Sin 2009).

Yet, although Volunteer tourism may be organised in an 'apolitical manner' (Sin 2009: 497), Fair Trade, in conjunction with the campaigns of a Fair Trade movement, has the potential to be a more political, educational tool, albeit capturing possibly exclusively a niche market. Nevertheless, even if a certified FTT product may not embrace a price-sensitive mass market, it could still have the potential to influence responsible policy and practice within the mass tourism industry, which would be strengthened by independent verification and possibly legislation.

Case study

FTTSA

In 1999, IUCN (the International Union for Conservation of Nature), a global membership organisation, based in Geneva, launched a Fair Trade in Tourism Initiative in South Africa with financial support from Switzerland. The initiative was part of a participative action research and pilot project to assess the feasibility of a FTT label (Kalisch 2001) in the context of post-apartheid growth and socio-economic transformation (Mahoney 2007; Seif and Spenceley 2007). Such development was focused on affirmative action to re-dress the legacy of structural socio-economic inequality resulting from the apartheid era (Mahoney 2007).

The project took two years for consultation on the feasibility structure of a FTT label and one year operating as a pilot project before initiating the certification process.

In 2004, it became an independent non-profit company (Seif and Spenceley 2007), awarding the world's only tourism label based on FTT criteria. The criteria are embodied in a set of 16 standards, including labour standards, employment equity, ownership and control, community benefits and environmental management.

The abundance of standards, each broken down into individual indicators, reflects the complexity of the sustainability requirements in tourism. Application of the standards needs to be adapted according to the nature of the business, that is an excursion will have different requirements from a hospitality business. This enables a complicated but rigorous award system, combined with assistance for continuous improvement for companies.

By 2011, it had certified over 70 products, including mostly accommodation establishments, but also adventure activities, attractions and, since 2011, voluntourism programmes.

FTTSA measures its success against the level of media exposure, website visits, the number of tour operators, particularly international operators using FTTSA-certified businesses, and recognition by the tourism industry. To date, there is no available research on how the label influences consumer demand for FTTSA-marked products. Development benefits and gains in human rights as a result of the certification are difficult to measure as it has not been possible for FTTSA to conduct any Social Impact Assessments, due to lack of funding. The industry is currently considered the main beneficiary in relation to ethical credibility, networking, public relations exposure, enhanced staff morale and technology and knowledge transfer. In addition to awarding the FTTSA mark, the company is involved with active advocacy work for the implementation of a code of practice against child sex exploitation in travel and tourism, providing technical assistance and capacity building on responsible tourism, and assisting local communities and farmers with the development and management of appropriate tourism products. Other countries in southern Africa, such as Mozambique, are now exploring the feasibility of replicating the FTTSA model (Fair Trade in Tourism South Africa 2009).

In 2010, FTTSA launched another innovatory pilot initiative aimed at certifying Fair Trade Travel packages as part of the tourism value chain, in collaboration with Swiss NGOs, tour operators and the Swiss State Secretariat for Economic Affairs (SECO). The pilot is endorsed by Fair Trade Labelling Organizations International (FLO). It includes at least two Swiss outbound tour operators who have committed themselves to pay their South African partners fair prices, which cover the costs of production, living wages for the staff and address environmental sustainability. Suppliers will be paid on arrival of the guests, instead of months after the event, and a Fair Trade premium of 5 per cent will be added to the price paid to local service providers. The premium will be used to pay for social development in the destination. This new pilot addresses key areas of concern for suppliers in tourist-receiving countries and will be an important landmark for equalising power relationships between outbound and inbound tourism organisations. Using the 'root causes of inequality' identified by the International Network on Fair Trade in Tourism as indicators for the development benefits of both the FTTSA and FTT mark, it could be asserted that they are all being addressed by both marks in some way. It remains to be seen to what extent this system could be extended to operators in other countries, considering the commitment to transparency involved, and the amount of preparation and negotiation required for successful implementation.

Conclusion

FTTSA has provided valuable experience in respect to creating a tangible Fair Trade holiday product with the potential to make a step change towards improved living conditions and greater equality for the most disadvantaged groups in South Africa. This now needs to be tested in other policy environments in different countries, to assert whether there is sufficient potential for a global FTT standard. It cannot be assumed that one pilot project in one country could provide the answers for all other countries, or all other types of tourism products. FTTSA was developed on fertile policy ground. The government was focused on creating equitable and responsible development policies, recognising that tourism provided an ideal opportunity to showcase such policies. South Africa's reconstruction was supported European development programmes. In that context, FTTSA received assistance from Swiss government agencies and NGOs, such as IUCN, and Arbeitskreis Tourismus und Entwicklung (akte), who campaign on trade justice in tourism.

As research in the UK suggests, a great deal of development work still has to take place to convince the tourism industry and consumers of the economic and social benefits of certification in general. Testing consumer demand for a FTT label is imperative to generate public confidence. Only then can speculation turn into certainty about the value of FTT labelling to more equitable socio-economic trading conditions in less developed countries. FTTSA's Fair Trade Travel package, tested in Swiss markets, will provide crucial evidence in this respect, even though different markets vary in their preferences. Due to the diversity of policy and socio-economic contexts in different destinations, a FTT label would need to incorporate the flexibility of being tailored to local contexts within the overall framework of a global standard. Consultation, research, consumer awareness raising and capacity building for small businesses are crucial prerequisites for developing a tourism label. Funding and knowledge transfer need to be available to enable this process. Political, financial and operational support from industry and governments would need to be harnessed. To this end, the establishment of an institutional mechanism specifically oriented towards creating and marketing FTT, separate from but linked to a global Fair Trade organisation, is crucial (Kalisch 2010).

Testing consumer demand is all the more important, as global tourism flows are shifting. With an increasingly affluent customer base in India and China expecting to travel the world, the predominant long haul flows of environment-friendly, socially conscious tourists from the northern to the southern hemisphere can no longer be taken for granted. Moreover, the importance of regional tourism far outweighs the impact of international tourism (Ghimire 2001). A FTT label not only has to appeal to European or American markets, but also to global markets, with their differing cultural perceptions of what fair trade and ethics mean.

Global power shifts also put in question the historic roots of fair trade in dependency theory. The classic North/South core-periphery analysis needs to be re-evaluated to account for the changing, more complex trends in contemporary economic and political globalisation.

Trade injustice and human rights issues in tourism will never be addressed by a FTT label alone. However, in tandem with other policy instruments addressing structural imbalances at political and socio-economic levels, globally and locally, it could embody symbolic value by providing tangible and workable evidence of the social and economic benefits of equitable negotiation, respect, trust and transparency in international trading. This might instil consumer confidence, especially in these times of capitalist crisis and diminishing public trust, and present a catalyst for a more systematic approach to ethical trading in tourism.

References

ABTA (2008) *The Travelife Sustainability System Rolled Out To ABTA Members*. www.abta.com/resources/news/view/66 (accessed 3 January 2011).

Badger, A., Barnett, P., Corbyn, L. and Keefe, J. (eds) (1996) *Trading Places: Tourism as Trade*. London: Tourism Concern.

Barratt Brown, M. (1993) *Fair Trade*. London: Zed Books.

Beyer/mas/contour (2007) *Fair Trade Certification in Tourism: Challenges, Conditions, and First Recommendations regarding Fair Pricing in the Tourism Branch*. Bonn: Evangelischer Entwicklungsdienst.

Bastakis, C., Buhalis, D. and Butler, R. (2004) 'The perception of small and medium sized tourism accommodation providers on the impacts of tour operators' power in Eastern Mediterranean', *Tourism Management* 25, 151–70.

Clancy, M. (1998) 'Commodity chains, service and development: theory and preliminary evidence from the tourism industry', *Review of International Political Economy* 5(1), 122–48.

Cleverdon, R. and Kalisch, A. (2000) 'Fair Trade in Tourism', *International Journal of Tourism Research* 2, 171–87.

Connolly, J. and Shaw, D. (2006) 'Identifying fair trade in consumption choice', *Journal of Strategic Marketing* 14, 353–68.

Cooper, C. and Hall, M. (2008) *Contemporary Tourism – an international approach*. Oxford: Elsevier Butterworth-Heinemann.

Fairtrade Foundation (2009) *Global Fairtrade sales increase by 22%*, www.fairtrade.org.uk/press_office/ press_releases_and_statements/jun_2009/global_fairtrade_sales_increase_by_22.aspx?printversion=true (accessed 18 January 2011).

Font, X. (2008) *Potential for a Fair Trade Label in Tourism: Feasibility Study*, ESRC Seminar Series 1: Tourism, Inequality and Social Justice Fairly Traded Tourism, Centre for Leisure, Tourism and Society, UWE, Bristol.

Fair Trade in Tourism South Africa (2009) *Annual Report 2008/09.*

FIAS and OECD (2006) *The Tourism Sector in Mozambique: A Value Chain Analysis*, Vol. 1, International Finance Corporation, World Bank Group

Ghimire, K. (2001) 'Regional Tourism and South-South Cooperation', *The Geographical Journal* 167(2), 99–110.

Goodwin, H. and Santilli, R. (2009) *Community-based Tourism: a success?* Responsible Tourism and GTZ, ICRT Occasional Paper 11.

Goodwin, H., McCombes, L. and Eckardt, C. (2009) *Advances in Travel philanthropy*, WTM Responsible Tourism Day Report 2.

Goodwin, H. and Francis, J. (2003) 'Ethical and Responsible Tourism: Consumer Trends in the UK', Practitioner Papers, *Journal of Vacation Marketing* 9(3).

Holden, A. (2005) *Tourism Studies and the Social Sciences*. London: Routledge.

International Finance Corporation (2006) *The tourism sector in Mozambique: a value chain analysis*, Vol. 1, Foreign Investment Advisory Centre and OECD Development Centre.

Jaffee, D. (2007) *Brewing Justice – Fair Trade Coffee, Sustainability, and Survival*, Berkeley: University of California Press.

Judd, (2006) 'Commentary: Tracing the Commodity Chain of Global Tourism', *Tourism Geographies* 8(4), 323–36.

Kalisch. A. (2001) *Tourism as Fair trade: NGO Perspectives*. London: Tourism Concern.

——(2002) *Corporate Futures: Social responsibility in the tourism industry*. London: Tourism Concern.

——(2003) 'Getting Consumers on Board', *Integra* (Institut fuer Integrativen Tourismus und Entwicklung), Vol. 1.

——(2010) 'Fair Trade in Tourism: a marketing tool for transformation?', in Cole, S. and Morgan, N. *Tourism and Inequality*. Wallingford: CABI

Krier, J.-M. (2006) *Fair Trade in Europe 2005, Facts and Figures on Fair Trade in 25 European countries*. Brussels: FLO, IFAT, NEWS! And EFTA.

Mahoney, K. (2007) 'Certification in the South African Tourism Industry', *Development Southern Africa* 24(3).

McGehee, N.G. and Santos, C.A. (2005) 'Social change, discourse and volunteer tourism', *Annals of Tourism Research* 32(3), 760–79.

McNicol, J., Shone, M. and Horn, C. (2004) *Benchmarking the performance of the tourism community in Kaikoura*. www.landcareresearch.co.uk (accessed 10 November 2010).

Mintel Oxygen (2007) *Holiday Lifestyles – Responsible Tourism – UK* – January 2007.

Responsibletravel.com (2010a) *Our Responsibility Report: our social, environmental and economic impacts* 1 July 2009 – 30 June 2010.

——(2010b) *Global Sustainable Tourism Criteria Debate*. www.responsibletravel.com/copy/global-sustainable -tourism-criteria-debate (accessed 19 January 2011).

Schmelzer, M. (2006) *In or Against the Market – Is Fair Trade a neoliberal solution to market failures or a practical challenge to neoliberal trade and the free market regime in general?* UC Berkeley, Research Paper for Sociology 190; Peter Evans: Globalization; Spring 2006.

Seif, J. and Spenceley, A. (2007) 'Assuring Community Benefit through Certification', in Black, R. and Crabtree, A. *Quality Assurance and Certification in Tourism*. Wallingford: CABI.

Sharpley, R. and Telfer, D. (2002) *Tourism and Development: Concepts and Issues*. Clevedon: Channel View Publications.

Sin, H.L. (2009) 'Volunteer Tourism – "Involve me and I will learn"?', *Annals of Tourism Research* 36(3), 480–501.

Steck, B., Wood, K. and Bishop, J. (2010) *Tourism: more value for Zanzibar*. Summary Report, SNV, VSDO, ZATI, 3 February.

Telfer, D. and Sharpley, R. (2008) *Tourism and Development in the Developing World*. London: Routledge.

Tourism Research and Marketing (2008) *Volunteer tourism: A global analysis*, www.atlas-webshop.org/ epages/61492534.sf/en_GB/?ObjectPath=/Shops/61492534/Products/ATL_00073 (accessed 2 January 2011).

Travelife (2010), www.travelifecollection.com/awards (accessed 3 January 2010).

Verbeek, D. and Mommas, H. (2008) 'Transitions to Sustainable Tourism Mobility: The Social Practice Approach', *Journal of Sustainable Tourism* 16(6), 629–44.

Further reading

Beddoe, C. (2004) *Labour standards, social responsibility and tourism*. London: Tourism Concern. (Useful case studies from around the world on working conditions of tourism workers.)

Erikkson, J, Noble, R., Pattullo, P. and Barnett, T. (2009) *Putting Tourism to Rights – A challenge to human rights abuses in the tourism industry*. London: Tourism Concern. (Exposes the many violations of human rights that occur as a direct result of tourism.)

Fennell, D. (2006) *Tourism Ethics*. Clevedon: Channel View Publications. (Introduces ethical theories and moral concepts into the study of tourism through a wide selection of readings, anecdotes and case studies.)

Khor, M. (2001) *Rethinking Globalization*. London: Zed Books. (Sets out concrete proposals for developing countries' governments to benefit from trade liberalisation.)

Litvinoff, M. and Madeley, J. (2007) *50 Reasons to Buy Fair Trade*. London: Pluto Press. (A guide analysing the benefits of Fair Trade consumption, including travel.)

Mowforth, M. and Munt, I. (2009) *Tourism and Sustainability: Development, Globalization and New Tourism in the Third World*. London: Routledge. (Critiques uneven development in tourism through globalisation and explores new tourism forms to create greater equality.)

Plüss, C. and Hochuli, M. (2005) *Perspectives on Tourism: Tourism and GATS*. Hong Kong: Ecumenical Coalition on Tourism. (Activist perspectives on the impacts of the GATS in tourism in developing countries.)

Stieglitz, J.E. and Charlton, A. (2005) *Fair Trade for All – How Trade can promote Development*. Oxford: Oxford University Press. (Presents an alternative economic model that makes trade work for developing countries.)

Tallontire, A., Rentsendorj, E. and Blowfield, M. (2001) *Ethical consumers and ethical trade: a review of current literature*. Policy Series 12, Wallingford: Natural Resources Institute, University of Greenwich. (Policy analysis of ethical and Fair Trade consumerism.)

Zadek, S. (2000) *Ethical Trade Futures*. London: New Economics Foundation. (A report on critical issues of governance, accountability and ethical trade in the context of globalisation.)

45

Resiliency and uncertainty in tourism

Tazim Jamal

Discourses of resilience and uncertainty are associated with a number of concepts such as vulnerability, recovery, mitigation, adaptation, risk perceptions, resiliency planning and uncertainty management. The chapter addresses these in the context of tourism and the environment, commencing with a look at one of the major uncertainties facing tourism, climate change, and then goes on to address other dimensions. This is followed by a brief look at some institutional efforts to increase resiliency through sustainable (tourism) development and related initiatives. A short case example addressing the issue of collaborative governance and behaviour change is discussed in the latter part of the chapter.

A couple of terms are useful to clarify before commencing. 'Environment' in this chapter refers broadly to the biophysical world and human relations with it. While 'resiliency' and 'resilience' are often used synonymously, the term 'resilience' is well situated in ecosystem science. Resilience has been defined as 'the capacity of a system to absorb disturbance and reorganize while undergoing change so as to still retain essentially the same function, structure, identity, and feedbacks' (Walker *et al.* 2004: 1). Tyrrell and Johnston (2008: 16) define resiliency in a tourism context as the 'ability of social, economic or ecological systems to recover from tourism induced stress'. They acknowledge that while concepts of environmental resilience are often couched in terms of ecological models and measurable impacts, other approaches are possible, like approaching sustainability goals in terms of the relationships between environmental and cultural resilience (ibid.). Theories of resilience include 'analyzing the factors which cause vulnerability in systems and, by extension, the factors which can enhance their capacity to absorb disturbance' (Cochrane 2009: 7). An early conceptual discussion of resilience in tourism is provided by Farrell and Twining-Ward (2004), who forward the notion of a 'Complex Adaptive Tourism System' (CATS). It is surprising, as Cochrane (2009) says, that resilience is not widely used in tourism; tourism's dependency on natural resources, its cross-cultural characteristics and its international linkages are indicative of complex social-ecological systems.

Key resiliencies, major challenges

Resiliencies and uncertainties in tourism span a range of topics and events. The tourism industry has demonstrated resiliency in relation to the recent economic crisis, with relatively robust recovery in international travel (driven by emerging economies), although international receipts appear to be recovering more slowly (UNWTO 2010a). International tourist arrivals totalled 421 million during the first 6 months of 2010, up 7 per cent on 2009, but still 2 per cent below that of the record year of 2008 (428 million arrivals in the same period). As stated in the UNWTO report, these results 'follow one of the toughest years for the tourism sector with international tourist arrivals declining by 4.2% in 2009 to 880 million and international tourism receipts reaching US$852 billion (€611 billion), a decrease in real terms of 5.7%'. The report notes furthermore that as in previous occasions, such as the Asian financial and economic crisis (1997–8), the SARS outbreak (2003) and the Indian Ocean tsunami (2004), Asia has once again shown a strong capacity for recovery – it is currently the second-most visited region in the world. Domestic and regional travel is also showing increased strength as travellers tend to travel closer to home in times of economic downturn. Worldwide, domestic arrivals are expected to exceed four times the number of international arrivals (ibid.). This has helped the resiliency of the tourism industry. However, potential future shocks (e.g. economic, oil, infectious disease), political instabilities and acts of terrorism, and the uncertainties associated with environmental hazards, biodiversity loss, climate change and resource depletion present potential risk and significant uncertainty to the well-being of the local-global tourism industry. Globalisation has made world tourism more vulnerable to crises, with greater economic and financial inter-dependence and integration as well as cultural, social and technologically driven mobilities (UNWTO 2009a).

In 2009, the Tourism Resiliency Committee of the UNWTO developed The Roadmap for Recovery, a set of strategic guidelines based on three inter-locking action areas: Resilience–Stimulus–Green Economy, to support the global economy and the Tourism sector. The Roadmap emphasised the nexus between tourism and the transition to the green economy, noting that the upcoming challenges of climate change and other environmental issues will not make the transition to a green economy a choice but rather an obligation (UNWTO 2009b). With only 5 per cent of CO_2 emissions totally, tourism was perceived to be well positioned and committed to progressively reducing its carbon emissions and contributing to the transformation towards a Green Economy (ibid.). Climate change and global warming, however, constitute strong uncertainties in tourism-environment relations and futures, presenting significant challenges as well as some opportunities for adaptive tourism stakeholders (Becken 2010).

Climate change and global warming

The Intergovernmental Panel on Climate Change (IPCC) in its Fourth Assessment Report warned that warming of the climate system is 'unequivocal' and most of the global average warming over the past 50 years is 'very likely due to anthropogenic GHG increases' (IPCC 2007: 72). Critiques of their work notwithstanding, a wide body of research and publications support the need for urgent action at the global and local level. The United Nations Climate Change Conference, also known as the Conferences of the Parties 15, took place in Copenhagen, 2009. The implications for tourism were stark and clear, as Scott and Becken (2010) note: 'The Davos Declaration on Climate Change and Tourism prioritised climate change as the greatest challenge to the tourism's sustainability in the twenty-first century' (see also Becken 2010).

The CO_2 emissions from international tourism, including all forms of transportation, accounted for just under 5 per cent of the world total or 1,307 million tonnes in 2005. Of this, transport accounted for 75 per cent of all emissions by the tourism sector, with aviation making up about 40 per cent of all tourism emissions, road transport 32 per cent and other forms of transportation 3 per cent. Accommodation represented about 21 per cent of total tourism sector emissions. Emissions from tourism are predicted to grow rapidly, with an increase of 152 per cent predicted between the years 2005 and 2035 unless concrete action is not taken to reduce them (UNWTO 2007).

In addition to policy response, technological change and concerted societal response, adaptation and mitigation in managing the risks associated with enhanced greenhouse gas effects will be required (Tompkins and Adger 2005). As described in UNWTO-UNEP (2008: 34), climate change mitigation 'relates to technological, economic and sociocultural changes that can lead to reductions in greenhouse gas emissions'. This UNWTO-UNEP report outlines a number of mitigation policies and measures that can lead to reduction of greenhouse gas emissions, and recommends that mitigation should be combined with different strategies (e.g. voluntary, economic and regulatory instruments), and targeted at various stakeholder groups including tourists, tour operators, airlines, car manufacturers, destination managers, tour operators, accommodation providers, airlines, etc. Four major mitigation strategies for addressing greenhouse gas emissions mentioned in their report are: (1) reducing energy use; (2) improving energy efficiency; (3) increasing the use of renewable energy; and (4) sequestering carbon through sinks.

It should be noted that adaptation and mitigation address different aspects of future climate-related risk: 'Mitigation reduces the number and magnitude of potential climate hazards, reducing the most severe changes first. Adaptation increases the ability to cope with climate hazards by reducing system sensitivity or by reducing the consequent level of harm' (Jones et al. 2007: 685). Reducing emissions and aiming for stabilisation of greenhouse gases in the atmosphere, mitigation strategies such as mentioned in the UNWTO-UNEP (2008) report aim to manage risk at the more extreme range of potential climate change (hence often need global aggregation of action and information); adaptation is more suited to work at the local level with changes of less magnitude and conditions of sufficient adaptive capacity (Jones et al. 2007).

Economic costs

The economic costs of climate change (i.e. the 'costs of inaction') are important to gauge in order to identify areas of uncertainty and concern, and to inform policy debate, adaptive planning and mitigation. While biophysical impacts have been the subject of much study, fewer attempts have been made to address economic impacts, particularly on a global or regional scale (see, for example, the study by Bigano et al. 2008 of the economic implications of two specific consequences of climate change: sea-level rise and change in tourism flows). Mishev and Mochurova (2008) summarise some climate change-related impacts predicted by the Hamburg Tourism Model (version 1.2) on tourism in Europe (including mountain resorts, Nordic regions and coastal Mediterranean areas), and call for more research on the economic costs of climate change and also the cost of adaptations at the organisational, local and regional level. New policy frameworks at the regional plus local level are also needed.

Similarly, study of the flow-on economic impacts of climate change on five Australian destinations by Pham et al. (2010: 449) shows that there could be significant impact for the Australian economy as a whole. Their study points to the importance of conducting regional/destination analyses as a basis of scenario examination for policy development. Coghlan and Prideaux (2009) examined the relation between weather conditions and snorkelling/diving-related reef experiences to understand the role of weather in reef tourism resilience, and noted the potentially adverse economic implications of poor weather to reef-centred tourism industry. Reef degradation poses a serious risk to the industry, as coral reefs are under threat globally from climate change, destructive fishing practices, overfishing, coastal development, land and marine-based pollution, etc. (www.iucnredlist.org, accessed 8 October 2010).

Environmental crises, natural hazards and social equity

A number of environmental changes, crises and natural disasters are being increasingly connected to climate change. One consequence of increasing temperatures, lack of rainfall and storm activity is seen to be the rising occurrences and severity of wildfires, such as experienced during the 2003 Australian Alps bushfires (Sanders *et al.* 2008). As these authors state: Australia's alpine areas have a lot to lose from a decline in tourism that is related to climate change from an economic point of view, but also from a socio-cultural perspective as visitors benefit from environmental education and experience (Sanders *et al.* 2008: 4).

Climate change impacts are expected to impact the livelihoods and well-being of up to 2.7 billion people who live on US$2 per day or less, and tend to be exacerbated in poorer places, which often lack necessary resources to mitigate and manage the impacts (Smith 2006). Reduction of greenhouse gas emissions, provisions to aid developing countries on adaptation and mitigation (assisted by climate justice and the polluter pay principle for countries that contributed to the problem), and focused attention on poverty reduction, sustainable development and social equity are integral considerations. Integrating these into natural resource management and disaster risk-reduction initiatives provides for a synergistic strategy for managing these complex social ecological systems. Technologies facilitating low-emission development and resource conservation are considered essential to achieving these goals (Smith 2006).

Inclusion and social equity are especially important considerations as health, habitation and livelihoods of vulnerable groups, especially the poor, women, children, elderly and indigenous populations in rural and coastal communities, are at risk of being disproportionately affected (Dulal *et al.* 2009). Priority areas identified by Dulal *et al.* (2009: 363) in implementing climate change adaptation policies in the Small Island Developing States of the Caribbean included 'increasing community participation, local initiatives and filling critical socioeconomic and livelihood data gaps, which policy makers need to focus on and incorporate in their climate change adaptation plans in order to ensure effective and equitable climate change adaptation'.

Resiliency planning and management

Planning and managing to enhance resilience and reduce uncertainty in relation to tourism and the environment requires institutional response and multistakeholder collaboration to assess vulnerability (environmental, social and economic), risk, etc., and to develop adaptation and mitigation strategies (see Hystad and Keller 2008, in relation to disaster-related recovery planning). In addition to mitigation and adaptive planning, resiliency planning and recovery planning, plus scenario planning under conditions of uncertainty has been usefully applied (Cochrane 2009; Page *et al.* 2010). Disaster planning, vulnerability assessments, hazard mitigation and response are especially important considerations in areas vulnerable to natural hazards, such as cyclones, hurricanes, typhoons, earthquakes, tsunamis, floods, volcanic eruptions, drought, bush fires, etc. (Faulkner 2001; Johnston *et al.* 2007; Larsen *et al.* 2008; Ritchie 2009).

An important goal of resiliency planning as applied to climate change is developing the physical and social structures that can reduce vulnerability and proactively tackle human and non-human impacts of climate change (Gurran *et al.* 2008). Gurran *et al.*'s study of coastal amenity communities vulnerable to 'sea change' in Australia included a social vulnerability model to identify communities requiring most assistance, and recommendations for climate change mitigation and adaptation. Planning approaches across five themes relevant to climate change were reviewed in this report: environment, community well-being, economy and tourism, infrastructure and governance. A number of principles for leading practice in climate change mitigation and adaptive planning were identified, such as the need to uphold the principles of ecologically sustainable development in designing adaptation and mitigation approaches, including environmental integrity, social equity and participation, economic viability and the precautionary principle (Gurran *et al.* 2008: 5). As the authors noted, this is 'critical for coastal amenity communities whose populations include higher proportions of lower income and socially disadvantaged groups' (ibid.: 5). Aging populations and destination visitors also require consideration during crises management, hazard recovery and contingency planning.

Cochrane's (2009) report on vulnerability and resilience in Sri Lankan tourism also offers useful insights for resilience planning and disaster recovery (the report addressed tsunami-affected areas plus two inland sites believed to enhance understanding). The post-tsunami tourism context in Sri Lanka represents a particular type of Complex Adaptive Tourism System (Farrell and Twining-Ward 2004), as Cochrane states. The study's conceptual framework was informed by: (1) concepts of vulnerability and resilience (noted as becoming increasingly prominent in recent understandings of human-ecological systems; see Adger 2000; Folke 2006; Holling 1973); (2) policies of natural resource management and adaptive co-management, and flexible, collaborative management; and (3) crises and disaster management. Turner *et al.*'s (2003) vulnerability framework was used here, of which resilience is an important component. As Cochrane (2009) explains, although determining the causes of vulnerability is helpful, the notion of resilience enables seeking the factors that might facilitate renewal of a damaged or disrupted system (see Walker *et al.*'s 2004 definition of resilience; see also Calgaro and Cochrane 2009).

Adaptive capacity and stakeholder involvement

Adger *et al.*'s (2005) study of resilience in coastal areas (inhabited by the majority of the world's populations) was also applied in the above research by Cochrane (2009). It showed that the effects of disasters could be mitigated by enhancing the adaptive capacity of social systems through the use of 'collective institutions, robust governance systems, and a diversity of livelihood choices' (Adger *et al.* 2005, cited in Cochrane 2009: 8). Adger *et al.* (2005) also recognised the importance of national and international action as well as local action for enhancing resilience. 'Climate change adaptation is a process whereby governments, business, and civil society aim to moderate, cope with, and benefit from the consequences of climate change in order to manage risk and reduce vulnerability' (Jopp *et al.* 2010: 591; see also Becken and Hay 2007). The ability or potential of a tourism system to respond successfully to climate variability and change, that is adaptive capacity, can also refer to multiple tourism stakeholders, including tourists, tourism businesses, attractions or destinations (ibid.).

Jopp *et al.* (2010) propose a holistic adaptation model to increase resilience and resistance to climate change through various adaptation strategies to reduce vulnerability and increase opportunity-seeking readiness; a decrease in long haul flights from the UK to Australia, for instance, may be offset by increases in domestic travel). Following Scott *et al.* (2006), they note that climate adaptation cannot be undertaken effectively by discrete actor groups, but requires a sustainability-oriented approach in which co-operation among diverse stakeholders and multiple adaptation strategies may be needed.

A number of tourism sectors are now preparing for climate change, or implementing adaptation, co-operative or co-management strategies, as information becomes available in various sectors and regions (e.g. Gurran *et al.* 2008; UNWTO 2009). For example, concern about potential rising sea levels and atmospheric disturbances has stimulated the Florida lodging and resort sector to undertake a number of mitigation and adaptation approaches. The Florida

Green Lodging Program created by the Florida Department of Environmental Protection (FDEP) provides principles and criteria related to: communication, water conservation, energy efficiency, waste reduction and clean air practices (FDEP 2007). Richins and Scarinci (2009) observe commitment to be strong, with programme membership growing from 21 resorts in 2007 to 170 resorts with first level certification in 2008 (there were 680 designated Florida *Green Lodging* properties as of 23 June, 2011, www.dep.state.fl.us/greenlodging).

Risk perceptions and information communication

Discussing the notion of perceived risk and local government capacity to respond to such risk, Burton and Dredge (2007) point out that climate change risk management is not seen as a physical–environmental problem to be solved by technological fixes, but rather as human–environment problem where risks and hazards may be addressed via combinations of social change and technology (Haque and Etkin 2007). Understanding the risk perceptions of tourism managers and other stakeholders, as well as community awareness and preparedness for handling hazard-related emergencies, are important to effective mitigation, planning and management. A recent study by Marshall *et al.* (2010) in the Red Sea indicated apparent changes in dive tourists' perceptions and awareness of climate change, but dive operators have tended to discount the data. These authors note that such a 'perception gap' can increase the vulnerability of dive operators (ibid.).

Méheux and Parker's (2006) research of resort owners and managers in the small island of Tanna in the South Pacific showed that their perception of natural hazards can influence implementation of appropriate mitigation and preparedness measures to decrease vulnerability to such hazards. However, the study also indicated that accurate perceptions do not appear to guarantee that adequate mitigation and preparedness measures are adopted. The authors recommend a strategy of persuasive communication and developing awareness raising measures (e.g. interactive workshops and museum/information centres to inform and educate residents and visitors on natural hazards. As these authors note, scientific data can be used to educate participants, but it should be presented in an understandable manner. Past research indicates that scientific understanding is not essential for the adoption of positive adaptive actions (Mileti 1999, cited in Méheux and Parker 2006).

Drastic alterations in the Arctic and sub-Arctic have spurred indigenous communities whose livelihoods and existence are being threatened to share information about the effects of climate change. Examples provided by Grossman (2008) include: (1) large community discussions that were held by one Inuit community in Nunavut and a video produced; and (2) interviews with hunters and fishers from twenty-six Inuit and Cree communities around Hudson Bay resulted in a co-operatively produced educational book. Inter-generational involvement of elders and youth is vital in such discussions and in gathering of field data and observations as Aleut leader Larry Merculieff said: 'As species go down, the levels of connection between older and younger go down along with that' (Rosen 2004, cited in Grossman 2008: 10).

Protected areas: co-managing complex social systems

Strickland-Munro *et al.* (2010) argue that traditional assessment methods and the use of sustainability indicators do not offer effective understanding of impacts of tourism in protected areas. As they indicate, research in systems thinking and resilience suggest greater challenges and uncertainties, hence the need for new approaches as 'future conditions may be different, more extreme and rapidly changing than previously experienced' (ibid.: 499). These authors investigate the impacts of protected area tourism on communities by framing them as a complex socio-ecological system. The resiliency adoption measures they used in their system to address community-related impacts related to four phases: (1) system definition; (2) factors affecting the system; (3) key people in the system and understanding their institutions; and (4) system development and thresholds. Systems thresholds are important to identify, they point out. For example, joint management arrangements between park authorities and traditional Aboriginal custodians initiated in Australia's protected areas, such as Kakadu National Park, 'provide evidence of system behavioral change following the reaching of a tolerance threshold' (Strickland-Munro *et al.* 2010: 514).

Natural resource conservation and issues of rights, obligations and self-determination of indigenous people have coincided positively in co-managed protected areas. For instance, British Columbia's Gwaii Haanas National Park Reserve is co-managed between the Haida Nation and Parks Canada (a federal agency). Kakadu National Park in the Northern Territory of Australia (noted above) is jointly managed by the Kakadu National Park (KNP) Traditional Owners and the federal Australian Nature Conservation Agency. The report on the 2008 Climate Change Symposium held by KNP included views of its Traditional Owners on climate change, plus sections of the Kakadu Plan of Management (2007–14) related to climate change, which also involved extensive consultation with Traditional Owners (Winderlich 2010a). Uncertainty as to what climate change actually is and what it means for local people, changes in weather, seasons, fruiting/flowering, fire frequency or intensity over the previous 30 years, and the need for expert information, plus communicating information to the Bininj (Aboriginal people), talking with people living on the land who have experienced change, looking at old stories (not many were left, it was noted), were among some of the views gathered from the Traditional Owners (Winderlich 2010b; see also Green *et al.* 2010 for additional information on Aboriginal knowledge and relationships with the ecosystems that provided food, shelter and cultural meaning). As the case example also indicates, collaborative governance and multistakeholder involvement in resiliency planning, adaptation and mitigation will be needed to manage the increasing challenges, hazards and uncertainties faced by tourism and the environment.

Case study

Local collaboration and climate change action

The mountain community of Canmore, Canada, is located at the foot of the Canadian Rockies, approximately 100 km west of Calgary, Alberta (Canada), just outside Banff National Park. Prolonged conflict and local concern over rapid population growth driven by resort and tourism development, as well as amenity migration since the 1980s (over 30 per cent of the town's current population of 17,970 is made up non-permanent residents), has resulted in numerous initiatives to address the resulting environmental and social impacts. Over the past decade, climate change concerns have also contributed to involve the government, tourism industry, non-profit organisations and local residents in collaborative governance and local action. The Natural Step is a Swedish-based programme that was introduced to the mountain community of Canmore, Alberta (Canada), through the Canmore-based Biosphere Institute, a non-profit society registered in 1997 and awarded charitable status in 2003 (www.biosphereinstitute.org, accessed on 5 July 2009). The programme aims

Figure 45.1 View from town: main street and front ranges

to help communities, organisations and individuals to understand, design and implement sustainability-oriented practices and behaviours. After a 2-day workshop and site visit by the Natural Step programme organisers who were setting up in Canada then (Canmore was among its first projects), a $300,000 programme was initiated (grant fundraising commenced in 2002, and a 2-year programme commenced by 2004). Municipal staff and early adopters were trained in this programme, including Tourism Canmore, the local destination management organisation. For more on this Swedish-based programme, see: www.biosphereinstitute.org/?q=p-natural-step, accessed 5 July 2009. Note the 16-page case study posted on the website.

The Natural Step to a Sustainable Canmore provides a collaborative framework for learning, discussion and action among multiple stakeholders in this mountain destination. It has generated multiple outcomes in addition to collective sustainability education among the network of participating stakeholders. All town employees are introduced to the Natural Step process where it is used as a tool for decision-making. The town has also identified completed, current and future Natural

Step initiatives by department, and the Natural Step system conditions are used in capital budget justifications. In addition, the Town of Canmore has implemented several policies based on its involvement with the Natural Step. One of these policies is the Town's Sustainability Screening Report Process required for each new development project. Through this process, developers are now asked what the net benefit is from their project for the community of Canmore and what their project will do to help to sustain Canmore into the future.

The Biosphere Institute has also actively engaged school children, parents, taxi drivers and others to undertake responsible actions towards a sustainable future (see www.biosphereinstitute.org/?q=p-sustain-home). Specific programmes have been implemented, oriented towards resource use and conservation, as well as climate change, such as the Mountain Air Program (see above website) and Social Action Canmore Program, an innovative effort in community social marketing (see Jamal and Watt 2011). Furthermore, the Biosphere Institute facilitated the Climate Kids Program, a pedagogic program that enabled school children in developing dialogic film and videos to explore, communicate and teach others about climate change and impact management strategies (www.biosphereinstitute.org/?q=p-climatekids, accessed 8 October 2010). NGO-mediated programmes like The Natural Step, participatory films and direct involvement of youth and adults in learning, teaching and behaviour change through social marketing offer potential gains to facilitated sustainability-oriented local action and climate change pedagogy at the community level.

Sustainable (tourism) development

The case and discussion thus far suggests that tourism resiliency and uncertainty management may be facilitated through policy changes and participatory planning. Implementing programmes for resident involvement and tourist education can contribute towards adaptation and mitigation of climate change impacts, as well as risk management, crisis and disaster planning (see Becken and Hay 2007). Scott (2011) argues for greater reflection on 'sustainable tourism' and the future of tourism development in a carbon-constrained global economy, and states unequivocally that 'how tourism responds to climate change is absolutely critical to sustainability of tourism … ' (Scott 2011: 28). He also calls for longer time-horizons in preparing for a +4°C world that entails great risks for tourism globally and locally.

Biodiversity conservation, ecosystem health and a resilient tourism industry thus far are closely inter-woven in complex relationships ranging from complementary to inimical and uncertain (Budowski 1976; Holden 2005); these complex socio-ecological systems will require multi-scalar collaborative action over long-term planning and policy horizons. At the global level, for instance, subsequent to the Brundtland Commission's report on sustainable development (WCED 1987), the 1992 United Nations Conference on Environment and Development held in Rio de Janeiro (the Rio Summit) established Agenda 21 to implement sustainable development. Local Agenda 21, with a procedural goal of encouraging local participation in sustainability-related planning and decision-making was launched subsequently. In addition to natural heritage and biodiversity conservation, the World Tourism Organization's (UNWTO) approach to sustainable tourism also acknowledges the importance of tackling socio-economic issues and, especially, poverty alleviation (UNWTO 2010b). Informed participation by stakeholders (e.g. raising tourist awareness and their involvement in sustainability practices) is considered essential.

Various forms of community-based conservation programmes, ecotourism, as well as pro-poor tourism and sustainable rural tourism, have arisen to address environmental concerns and local livelihoods (Buckley 2009; Fennell and Weaver 2005; Lane 2009; Mbaiwa and Stronza

2009; Scheyvens 2002). 'Green' certification and indicator, carbon offset programs, as well as local-global initiatives such as the Global Sustainable Tourism Criteria (www.sustainabletourism criteria.org, accessed 5 October 2010) and the Sustainable Cities Programme (www.unhabitat. org/categories.asp?catid=540, accessed 10 October 2010) have been launched with multi-stakeholder involvement including civil society organisations and community groups (Font and Harris 2004; Font *et al.* 2003; Honey 2002; Linstroth and Bell 2007; UNWTO 2004). Multi-level networks that contribute to global environmental governance have also emerged, such as the Cities for Climate Protection (Betsill and Bulkeley 2006). They illustrate that collaboration between experts, tourists and local inhabitants is crucial to bring scientific knowledge, indigenous knowledge and local knowledge (including citizen science) to bear on issues related to resource conservation, climate change, social equity and poverty alleviation (Agrawal 1995; Rettie *et al.* 2009).

Yet, biodiversity continues to decline, despite increasing worldwide conservation efforts and widespread political recognition, and growing regional, national and international policy mechanisms, as well as a large number of local, national and regional non-governmental organisations and community groups (Rands *et al.* 2010). The UN Convention on Biological Diversity (CBD) agreed on at the 1992 UN Conference on Environment and Development is widely ratified, and since 2002, 193 parties to the CBD have committed themselves to substantially reducing rates of biodiversity loss by 2010 (ibid.). Rands *et al.*'s review also notes that this goal was later endorsed by the World Summit on Sustainable Development and incorporated into the UN Millennium Development Goals in 2005. Mechanisms like REDD+ that provide revenue streams through direct payments for conservation or payments for ecosystems services offer potential for joint gains, reducing emissions from deforestation, forest degradation and other activities affecting forest carbon stocks, and contributing to local incomes and livelihood gains (ibid.; see also Verweij *et al.* 2009).

Sustainable tourism and the pro-poor agenda

All aspects of global environmental change are inter-related and inter-acting, and tourism plays a two-way role here, being affected by it, but also driving some of these processes (Gössling 2005). In addition to its significant role in transportation-related impacts on climate change, it influences global shifts in water consumption and contributes to the spread of infectious diseases (ibid.). Its role in the pro-poor agenda appears to follow similar bi-dimensional characteristics, offering potential for poverty alleviation and yet also exacerbating equity and socio-economic well-being (UNWTO 2010b). Use and conservation conflicts arise in relation to scarce natural resources in developing regions, such as equity in water usage by tourists and local residents in the Honduras (Stonich 1998).

Political ecology studies have shown that the crucial factor underlying environmental degradation and human poverty in developing countries is institutionalised inequalities in access to, and use of, resources. Inequitable distribution of environmental benefits and costs among low-income groups, and minority populations, including indigenous people, is a focal concern of environmental justice. It raises issues around distributive and participatory justice, environmental equity, environmental racism and environmental discrimination (Lee and Jamal 2008). One might expect that all forms of responsible tourism, sustainable tourism, ecotourism have, by now, clearly defined indicators and parameters for addressing these aspects, especially with respect to the biophysical environment and human–environmental relationships. Yet, tourism researchers have generally paid scant attention to the environmental justice literature in relation to low income, marginalised and diverse populations in natural area destinations. Greater policy focus on poverty alleviation, and much greater research and planning attention is needed to aspects such as climate justice and the pro-poor agenda.

Aimed towards balancing economic (business) and environmental use for *sustainable development*, the Brundtland Commission's influential report *Our Common Future* (WCED 1997) directed attention to incorporating equity into the sustainability agenda. Primarily spurred by evidence of global biodiversity loss and fragmentation, degradation of fisheries and oceans, loss of forest and soil cover due to development, depletion of natural resources, and increasing demands for energy and goods by emerging economies and an expanding global population, the report acknowledged the need to address inter-dependent social issues, such as the socio-economic disparities between the 'North' and the 'South' and the co-dependent impacts of impoverished populations on biodiversity and resource conservation. Of note in this respect is the 'Climate Justice and Tourism' side event held on 10 December 2009 at the Copenhagen Climate Conference, which included participants from NGOs, academics, national tourism official and UNWTO. Organised by the Ecumenical Coalition on Tourism, it focused on emission reductions, adaptation and issues of equity and justice and tourism's role in developing countries – and concluded that structural and behavioural changes were needed in addition to technological changes (Scott and Becken 2010). This will require better understanding of human–environmental relationships, that is our ethnic and cultural relations with the biophysical world.

Ryan *et al.*'s (2010) study of tourism to four polluted lakes in China, for example, briefly mentions the issue of how cultural conceptions of nature (e.g. through classical literature) may influence tourist relations with these lakes; their study also raises the need for 'realistic appraisals' and assessment of corrective measures to deal with environmental degradation for the long-term sustainability of tourism in such settings. Macnaghten and Urry's (1987: 242) in-depth study similarly reveals 'differing and different conceptions of nature, by contrast with the global and unified conceptions of nature and the local and rational conceptions of action, which are articulated within the official discourses of sustainability'. However, what nature is being represented, how it is communicated to visitors, or addressed in tourism and environmental certification schemes and policy making, is rarely addressed. Social relations with, and social constructions of, 'nature' are deeply embedded in geopolitical and cultural influences, symbolic meanings and myths, and narratives of science, economics/business that privilege discourse of ecological modernisation (ibid.; Jamal *et al.* 2003). Future action will need to contend with the complex uncertainties of neo-liberal agenda on a global stage.

Facing the future

Environmental sustainability and climate change, terrorism, natural disasters and infectious diseases (with potential new viruses), are among the many uncertainties facing tourism. New crises can be anticipated, further economic crises and environmental hazards, food security and safety, water scarcity, loss of forestry, fisheries and agricultural livelihoods, resource depletion in fragile democracies, etc. Climate refugees, economic migrants and population mobilities will add further pressure on social ecological systems, and concerted societal and policy response to address social inequity, health and poverty alleviation will be needed. Conflicts over land and natural resources, and sustainability trade-offs will require closer examination of 'public interest', public involvement, and impacts on low-income and diverse groups and indigenous populations (Dredge and Thomas 2009; Lane and Williams 2008).

At the same time, it is important to recognize the ongoing resiliency of travel and tourism, through crises such as the SARS epidemic and Indian Ocean tsunami, other disasters related to tsunamis, hurricanes, earthquakes, cyclones and wildfires, as well as global oil and economic shocks. Reducing tourism's vulnerability to environmentally related shocks and crises, and working towards future resiliency will also require active adaptation, mitigation and management of uncertainty. Various factors have been discussed in this chapter, and a few strategic directions are summarised here:

(1) addressing consumer and industry willingness to pay for conservation, climate change adaptation and mitigation, historic sites and climate change, and 'green' technologies (especially assisting developing countries and populations at risk);
(2) facilitating corporate social responsibility and transparency in evaluating organisational practices and accounting (e.g. via sustainability reporting, environmental footprint calculations, adoption of relevant sustainability monitoring and criteria (e.g. GSTC);
(3) revising certification programmes and indicators to include human–environmental relationships, environmental and (eco)cultural justice, and participatory processes for including traditional/indigenous and local knowledge, in addition to 'expert' knowledge (scientific/managerialist discourses especially);
(4) ensuring inter-generational and multistakeholder involvement in resiliency planning, including the risk perceptions and participation of those who stand to be impacted most by climate change (see case study above);
(5) enhancing tourism's resiliency and ability to manage future risks through joint learning and active tourism pedagogy, collaborative governance and collective action on adaptation and mitigation, as well as multilevel policy and programmes.

Among future actions, greater effort will be needed to enable tourism's pedagogic role in interpretive learning and understanding of environmental challenges, risks and uncertainties in tourism – enabling counter-discourses and an informed citizenry that can participate in destination governance. Knowledge gaps such as the paucity of research on tourist demand responses in relation to climate change and management also merit attention (Gössling *et al.* 2012). It should be noted here that, as McKercher *et al.*'s (2010) research (among others) concludes, awareness alone is inadequate to engender change in tourist behaviour – governmental intervention may be needed to enable meaningful behaviour change in travel patterns, to reduce carbon footprint, for instance. This means, of course, contending with neo-liberalism both in the global (tourism) commons, and in the public–private sector (Telfer 2009), and arguing for enhancing self-regulation and voluntary schemes with measured government intervention. The urgencies of climate change and resource conservation call for collaborative governance, public–private partnerships and informed resident as well as tourist participation in various aspects of resiliency planning and uncertainty management.

Reference

Adger, W.N. (2000) 'Social and Ecological Resilience: Are They Related?,' *Progress in Human Geography*, 24: 347–364.

Adger, W.N. Hughes, T.P., Folke, C., Carpenter, S.R. and Rockstrom, J. (2005) 'Social-Ecological Resilience To Coastal Disasters', *Science* 309, 1036-1039.

Agrawal, A. (1995) 'Bridging Research and Policy Dismantling the Divide Between Indigenous and Scientific Knowledge,' *Development and Change*, 26(3), 413–439.

Becken, S. (2010) 'The Importance of Climate and Weather for Tourism,' Literature Review. Canterbury, New Zealand: LEAP Research Centre, Lincoln University.

Becken, S. and Hay, J.E. (2007) *Tourism and Climate Change: Risks and Opportunities*. Clevedon: Channel View. (Authoritative examination of climate change and tourism.)

Betsill, M. and Bulkeley, H. (2006) 'Cities and the Multilevel Governance of Global Climate Change,' *Global Governance*, 12, 141–159.

Bigano, A., Bosello, F., Roson, R. and Tol, R.S.J. (2008) 'Economy-Wide Impacts of Climate Change: A Joint Analysis for Sea Level Rise and Tourism,' *Mitig Adapt Strateg Glob Change*, 13, 765–791.

Buckley, R. (2009) *Ecotourism Principles and Practices*, Wallingford: CABI.

Budowski, G. (1976) 'Tourism and Environmental Conservation: Conflict, Coexistence, or Symbiosis?,' *Environmental Conservation*, 3(1), 27–31.

Burton, D. and Dredge, D. (2007) 'Framing Climate: Issues for Local Government,' *Queensland Planner*, 47(3), 23–15.

Calgaro, E. and Cochrane, J. (2009) Comparative Destination Vulnerability Assessment for Thailand and Sri Lanka, Stockholm: Stockholm Environment Institute, Project Report - 2009. Report available on: http://sei-international.org/mediam.0assessment.pdf

Cochrane, J. (2009). *Resilience and Recovery: Tourism in Sri Lanka after the Asian Tsunami*. Stockholm: Stockholm Environment Institute, Project Report. (Wide range of planning issues related to disaster recovery and post-tsunami tourism.)

Coghlan, A. and Prideaux, B. (2009) 'Welcome to the Wet Tropics: The Importance of Weather in Reef Tourism Resilience,' *Current Issues in Tourism*, 12(2), 89–104.

Dredge, D., & Thomas, P. (2009) 'Mongrel management, public interest and protected areas management in the Victorian Alps, Australia', *Journal of Sustainable Tourism*, 17(2), 249–267.

Dulal, H.B., Shah, K.U. and Ahmad, N. (2009) 'Social Equity Considerations in the Implementation of Caribbean Climate Change Adaptation Policies,' *Sustainability*, 1, 363–383.

Farrell, B. and Twining Ward, L. (2004) 'Reconceptualizing Tourism,' *Annals of Tourism Research* 31(2), 274–95.

Faulkner, B. (2001) 'Towards a Framework for Tourism Disaster Management,' *Tourism Management*, 22 (2), 135–147.

Fennell, D. and Weaver, D. (2005) 'The Ecotourism Concept and Tourism-Conservation Symbiosis,' *Journal of Sustainable Tourism*, 13(4), 373–390.

Florida Department of Environmental Protection (FDEP) (2007) *Florida Green Lodging Certification Program*, Tallahassee, FDEP.

Folke, C. (2006) 'Resilience: The Emergence of a Perspective for Social–Ecological Systems Analyses,' *Global Environmental Change*, 16, 253–267.

Font, X. and Harris, C. (2004) 'Rethinking Standards from Green to Sustainable,' *Annals of Tourism Research*, 31(4): 986–1007.

Font, X., Sanabria, R. and Skinner, E. (2003) 'Sustainable Tourism and Ecotourism Certification: Raising Standards and Benefits,' *Journal of Ecotourism*, 2(3), 213–218.

Gössling, S. (2005) 'Tourism's Contribution to Global Environmental Change: Space. Energy, Disease, Water.' In *Tourism, Recreation and Climate Change*, Clevedon: Channel View, 286-300.

Gössling, S., Scott, D., Hall, C.M., Ceron, J-P., Dubois, G. (2012) Consumer behaviour and demand response of tourists to climate change,' *Annals of Tourism Research* 39(1), 36-58.

Green, D., Jack, B. and Tapim, A. (2010) 'Indigenous Australians' Knowledge of Weather and Climate,' *Climatic Change*, 100: 337–354.

Grossman, Z. (2008) 'Indigenous Nations' Responses to Climate Change,' *American Indian Culture and Research Journal*, 32(3), 5–27.

Gurran, N., Hamin, E. and Norman, B. (2008) *Planning for Climate Change: Leading Practice Principles and Models for Sea Change Communities in Coastal Australia*. Report prepared for the National Sea Change Task Force, July, 2008. Sydney, Australia: Faculty of Architecture, The University of Sydney.

Haque, C. and Etkin, D. (2007) 'People and Community as Constituent Part of Hazards: The Significance of Societal Dimensions in Hazards Analysis,' *Natural Hazards*, 41(2), 271–282.

Holden, A. (2005) 'Achieving a Sustainable Relationship between Common Pool Resources and Tourism: The Role of Environmental Ethics,' *Journal of Sustainable Tourism*, 13(4), 339–353.

Holling, C.S. (1973) 'Resilience and Stability of Ecological Systems,' *Annual Review of Ecology and Systematics*, 4, 1–23.

Honey, M. (ed.) (2002) *Ecotourism & Certification: Setting Standards in Practice*, Washington, DC: Island Press.

Hystad, P.W. and Keller, P.C. (2008) 'Towards a Destination Tourism Disaster Management Framework: Long-Term Lessons from a Forest Fire Disaster', *Tourism Management* 29, 151–62.

IPCC (2007) 'Climate Change 2007: Synthesis Report', Contribution of Working Groups I, II and III to the Fourth Assessment Report of the Intergovernmental Panel on Climate Change, Geneva,

Switzerland: WMO and UNEP. Report online at: http://www.ipcc.ch/publications_and_data/publications_ipcc_fourth_assessment_report_synthesis_report.htm

Jamal, T. and Watt, E.M. (2011) 'Climate change pedagogy and performative action: Towards community-based destination governance,' *Journal of Sustainable Tourism*, 19(4-5), 571-588.

Jamal, T., Everett, J. and Dann, G.M. (2003) 'Ecological Rationalization and Performative Resistance in Natural Area Destinations,' *Tourist Studies*, 3(2), 143-169.

Johnston, D., Gregg, C., Houghton, B. Paton, D. Leonard, G. and Garside, R. Gregg, C., Houghton, B. Paton, D. Leonard, G. and Garside, R. (2007) 'Developing warning and disaster response capacity in the tourism sector in coastal Washington, DC,' *Disaster Prevention and Management* 16(2), 210-216.

Jones, R.N., Dettmann, P., Park, G., Rogers, M. and White, T. (2007) 'The Relationship Between Adaptation and Mitigation in Managing Climate Change Risks: A Regional Response from North Central Victoria, Australia,' *Mitig Adapt Strat Glob Change*, 12, 685-712.

Jopp, R., DeLacy, T. and Mair, J. (2010) 'Developing a Framework for Regional Destination Adaptation to Climate Change,' *Current Issues in Tourism*, 13(6), 591-605.

Lane, B. 2009 'Rural Tourism: An Overview,' in T. Jamal and M. Robinson (eds.) *The SAGE Handbook of Tourism Studies*, London: SAGE, 354-370.

Lane, M. B. and Williams, L.J. (2008) 'Color Blind: Indigenous Peoples and Regional Environmental Management,' *Journal of Planning Education and Research* 28: 38

Larsen, R.M. Calgaro, E. and Thomalla, F. (2011) 'Governing resilience building in Thailand's tourism-dependent coastal communities: Conceptualising stakeholder agency in social–ecological systems,' *Global Environmental Change*, 21(2), 481–491

Lee, S. and Jamal, T. (2008) 'Environmental Justice and Environmental Equity in Tourism: Missing Links to Sustainability,' *Journal of Ecotourism*, 7(1), 44–67.

Linstroth, T. and Bell, R. (2007) *Local Action: The New Paradigm in Climate Change Policy*, Lebanon, NH: University Press of New England.

Macnaghten, P. and Urry, J. (1998) *Contested Natures*, London: SAGE.

Marshall, N.A., Marshall, P.A., Abdulla, A., Rouphael, T. and Ali, A. (2010) 'Preparing for Climate Change: Recognising its Early Impacts through the Perceptions of Dive Tourists and Dive Operators in the Egyptian Red Sea,' *Current Issues in Tourism*, iFirst article: 1–12.

Mbaiwa, J.E. and Stronza, M.L. (2009) 'The Challenges and Prospects for Sustainable Tourism and Eco-tourism in Developing Countries,' in T. Jamal and M. Robinson (eds.) *The SAGE Handbook of Tourism Studies*, London: SAGE, 333–353.

McKercher, B., Prideaux, B., Cheung, C. and Law, R. (2010) 'Achieving Voluntary Reductions in the Carbon Footprint of Tourism and Climate Change,' *Journal of Sustainable Tourism*, 18(3), 297–317.

Méheux, K. and Parker, E. (2006) 'Tourist sector perceptions of natural hazards in Vanuatu and the implications for a small island developing state,' *Tourism Management* 27, 69–85.

Mileti, D.S. (1999) *Disasters by Design: A Reassessment of Natural Hazards in the United States*, Washington, DC: Joseph Henry Press.

Mishev, P. and Mochurova, M. (2008) 'Impacts of Climate Change on Tourism,' in V. Alexandrov, M.F. Gajdusek, C.G. Knight and A. Yotova (eds.) *Global Environmental Change: Challenges to Science and Society in Southeastern Europe*. Selected Papers presented in the International Conference held 19–21 May in Sofia Bulgaria, London: Springer.

Page, S.J., Yeoman, I., Connell, J. and Greenwood, C. (2010) 'Scenario Planning as a Tool to Understand Uncertainty in Tourism: The Example of Transport and Tourism in Scotland in 2025,' *Current Issues in Tourism*, 13(2), 99–137.

Pham, T.D., Simmons, D.G. and Spurr, R. (2010) 'Climate Change-Induced Economic Impacts on Tourism Destinations: The Case of Australia,' *Journal of Sustainable Tourism*, 18(3), 449–473.

Rands, M.R.W. plus 11 co-authors (2010) 'Biodiversity Conservation: Challenges Beyond 2010.' *Science* 329(5997), 1298–1303.

Rettie, K., Clevenger, A.P. and Ford, A. (2009) 'Innovative Approaches for Managing Conservation and Use Challenges in the National Parks: Insights from Canada,' in T. Jamal and M. Robinson (eds.) *The SAGE Handbook of Tourism Studies*, London: SAGE, 396–415.

Richins, H. and Scarinci, J. (2009) 'Climate Change and Sustainable Practices: A Case Study of the Resort Industry in Florida,' *Tourismos: An International Multidisciplinary Journal of Tourism*, 4(2), 107–128.

Ritchie, B.W. (2009) *Crisis and Disaster Management for Tourism*. Bristol: Channel View Publications.

Rosen, Y. (2004) 'Warming Climate Disrupts Alaska Natives' Lives,' Reuters, April 20. Available at http://omega.twoday.net/20040420 (accessed March 1, 2008).

Ryan, C., Huimin, G. and Chon, K. (2010) 'Tourism to Polluted Lakes: Issues for Tourists and the Industry. An Empirical Analysis of Four Chinese Lakes,' *Journal of Sustainable Tourism*, 18(5), 595–614.

Sanders, D., Laing, J. and Houghton, M. (2008) *Impact of Bushfires on Tourism and Visitation in Alpine National Parks*, Queensland, Australia: Sustainable Tourism Cooperative Research Centre.

Scheyvens, R. (2002) *Tourism for Development: Empowering Communities*, London: Prentice Hall.

Scott, D. (2011) 'Why sustainable tourism must address climate change,' *Journal of Sustainable Tourism*, 19 (1), 17–34.

Scott, D. and Becken, S. (2010) 'Adapting to Climate Change and Climate Policy: Progress, Problems and Potentials,' *Journal of Sustainable Tourism*, 18(3), 283–295.

Scott, D., de Freitas, C.R. and Matzarakis, A. (2006) 'Adaptation in the Tourism and Recreation Sector,' in K.L. Ebi, I. Burton and P. Hoeppe (eds), *Biometeorology for Adaptation to Climate Variability and Change*, Dordrecht, Netherlands: Springer.

Smith, D.M. (2006) *Just One Planet: Poverty, Justice and Climate Change*, Warwickshire: Intermediate Technology Publications Ltd.

Stonich, S.C. (1998) 'Political ecology of tourism,' *Annals of Tourism Research*, 25(1), 25–54.

Strickland-Munro, J.K., Allison, H.E. and Moore, S.A. (2010) 'Using Resilience Concepts to Investigate the Impacts of Protected Area Tourism on Communities', *Annals of Tourism Research* 37(2), 499–519.

Telfer, D. (2009) 'Development Studies and Tourism' in T. Jamal and M. Robinson (eds.) *The SAGE Handbook of Tourism Studies*, London: SAGE, 146–165.

Tompkins, E.L. and Adger, W.N. (2005) 'Defining Response Capacity to Enhance Climate Change Policy,' *Environmental Science & Policy*, 8, 562–571.

Turner, B. L., Kasperson, R. E., Matson, P. A., Mccarthy, J. J., Corell, R., Christensen, L., Eckley, N., Kasperson, J. X., Luers, A., Martello, M. L., Polsky, C., Pulsipher, A. and Schiller, A. (2003) 'A Framework For Vulnerability Analysis In Sustainability Science,' *Proceedings Of The National Academy Of Sciences Of The United States* 100(14), 8074–8079.

Tyrrell, T.J. and Johnston, R.J. (2008) 'Tourism sustainability, resiliency and dynamics: Towards a more comprehensive perspective,' *Tourism and Hospitality Research*, 8(1), 14–24.

UNWTO (2004) *Indicators of Sustainable Development for Tourism Destinations*, Madrid: World Tourism Organization.

——(2007) 'Tourism & Climate Change: Confronting the Common Challenges—UNWTO Preliminary Considerations', October 2007, Madrid: World Tourism Organization.

——(2009a). *Global Economic and Financial Crisis: What are the Implications for World Tourism?*, Madrid: World Tourism Organization.

——(2009b) *Report of the Third Meeting of the UNWTO Tourism Resilience Committee*—Astana, Kazakhstan, 8 October 2009. Madrid: World Tourism Organization. (Institutional response towards a green economy in tourism.)

——(2010a) 'International Tourist Arrivals up 7% in the First Half of 2010: Asia Leads Growth,' August Interim Update, September 2. Available at http://www.unwto.org/media/news/en/press_det.php?id=6561&idioma=E (accessed October 13, 2010).

——(2010b) 'Sustainable Tourism – Eliminating Poverty,' http://www.unwto.org/step/news/en/news.php (accessed February 28, 2011).

UNWTO-UNEP (2008) Climate Change and Tourism—Responding to Global Challenges, Madrid and Paris: World Tourism Organization and United Nations Environment Programme.

Verweij, P., Schouten, M., van Beukering, P., Triana, J., van der Leeuwen, K. and Hess, S. (2009) *Keeping the Amazon Forests Standing: A Matter of Values*, Zeist: WWF Netherlands.

Walker, B., Holling, C.S., Carpenter, S.R. and Kinzig, A. (2004) 'Resilience, Adaptability and Transformability in Social–Ecological Systems,' *Ecology and Society*, 9(2), 5.

WCED (World Commission on Environment and Development) (1987) *Our Common Future*, New York: Oxford University Press.

Winderlich, S. (2010b) 'The View of Kakadu National Park's Traditional Owners on Climate Change,' in Kakadu National Park Landscape Symposia Series 2007–2009. Symposium 4: Climate change, 6–7 August 2008, Gagudju Crocodile Holiday Inn Kakadu National Park. Internal Report 567, January, Supervising Scientist, Darwin, 3–9.

——(ed.) (2010a) *Kakadu National Park Landscape Symposia Series 2007–2009*. Symposium 4: Climate Change, 6–7 August 2008, Gagudju Crocodile Holiday Inn Kakadu National Park. Internal Report 567, January, Darwin, Australia: Supervising Scientist.

Further Readings

Brody, S. D. (2003) 'Are We Learning to Make Better Plans?: A Longitudinal Analysis of Plan Quality Associated with Natural Hazards,' *Journal of Planning Education and Research* 23, 191. (US study of changes in the ability of local plans to mitigate natural hazards).

Coombes, E.G. and Jones, A. P. (2010) 'Assessing the impact of climate change on visitor behaviour and habitat use at the coast: A UK case study.' *Global Environmental Change* 20, 303-313. (Examines biodiversity impacts arising from different coastal users, plus changes likely under a modified climate.)

Fennell, D.A. and Rowling R.K. (eds) (2008) *Ecotourism Policy and Planning*. CABI Publishing. (International contributions on ecotourism policy, economic and social impacts, ethics, institutional stakeholders, planning and governance)

Gössling, S. and Hall, C.M. (eds.) (2006) *Tourism and Global Environmental Change: Ecological, Social, Economic and Political Interrelationships*, New York: Routledge, 54–75. (Wide range of environmental issues and challenges for tourism discussed.)

Gössling, S. Peeters, P., Hall, C.M., Ceron, J.-P., Dubois, G., Lehmann, L.V., Scott, D. (2012) Tourism and water use: Supply, demand, and security. An international review. *Tourism Management* 33, 1-15. (Current water demand of the tourism sector and management challenges).

Henson, R. (2011) *The Rough Guide to Climate Change: The Symptoms, The Science, The Solutions*, London: Rough Guides Ltd. (Concise account of the symptoms, science, debates, and possible solutions related to climate change.)

Lambert, E., Hunter, C. Pierce, G.J. and MacLeod, C.D. (2010) 'Sustainable whale-watching tourism and climate change: towards a framework of resilience,' *Journal of Sustainable Tourism* 18(3), 409–427. (Interdisciplinary framework evaluating resilience of whale watching to changes in species occurrence – see also other articles in this special issue.)

Lane, M.B. and Hibbard, M. (2005) Doing It for Themselves : Transformative Planning by Indigenous Peoples', *Journal of Planning Education and Research* 25, 172 (Potential practices of transformative planning by indigenous people to address natural resource conflicts, enhance indigenous capacity and manage custodial lands.)

Owen, A.L. and Videras, J. (2008). Trust, cooperation, and implementation of sustainability programs: The case of Local Agenda 21. *Ecological Economics*, 68(1–2), 259–272. (Issues related to *Local Agenda 21* and sustainability program implementation)

Plummer, R. and Fennell, D.A. (2009) 'Managing protected areas for sustainable tourism: prospects for adaptive co-management' Journal of Sustainable Tourism 17 (2), 149–168. (Uncertainty and complex systems governance through cooperative and adaptive approaches to protected areas management.)

46

Tourism and CSR

Ralf Buckley and Fernanda de Vasconcellos Pegas

Introduction

Corporate social and environmental responsibilities (CSR) are a significant concern throughout the tourism industry, but only sometimes under that name. Some mainstream hotel chains do refer specifically to CSR. Some tourism companies operate social benefit programmes and foundations, but without calling them CSR. There are community tourism enterprises where social benefit is the main aim of the business. In highly impoverished areas, tourism is promoted as a poverty alleviation mechanism, with associated broad-scale social benefits. A variety of organisations run social and environmental awards and certification programmes for tourism enterprises, which may fall within the scope of industry self-regulation as a form of CSR, and in many countries, commercial tourism development interests continually press for access to public conservation reserves and protected areas, using CSR rhetoric as a lobbying tool.

The research literature on CSR presents two main perspectives: either as something that companies actually do; or as something they only pretend to do. Actions that corporations do in fact carry out may have either commercial or philanthropic motivations. Actions they only pretend to carry out are generally politically motivated. As political manoeuvres commonly aim to improve commercial competitive positions, the various goals are not mutually exclusive. A wide range of business cases have been put forward for CSR (Crane *et al.* 2008). Different cases consider customers, staff and legal frameworks. Some of these suggestions have been tested, but not all, and only under limited circumstances. There is thus no general cross-sector CSR model that can be applied ready-made in tourism.

As an industry sector, tourism has several critical features: (1) the tourism industry must deliver its customers to its products rather than the reverse; (2) these products cannot be stored, but must be consumed as they are produced; (3) these products consist of bundles of goods and services, typically assembled from sources around the world, with highly distributed social and environmental impacts; and (4) most of these goods are not produced solely for tourism, and it is not until the final assembly that they become tourism products; so CSR in tourism necessarily involves consideration of extended supply chains.

CSR components of commercial tourism operations can be considered at two levels. Base-level CSR simply involves compliance with commercial, environmental and industrial-relations laws, for example in relation to fair dealings with clients, suppliers, staff and lessors. This includes staff working conditions, truth in advertising and customer service. Relevant laws and practices differ considerably between countries, so assessing compliance is rarely straightforward. The relevant laws are largely those of destination countries, many of them in the developing world.

Higher-level CSR reflects external social pressures beyond the strict requirements of the law or the market place. Social expectations include both those of local residents in destination areas, and those of international clients from countries of origin. Often these expectations may be very different. They may include contributions to conservation, cultures or community well-being.

Depending on the country of operations, expectations may include pressures to: minimise social impacts associated with differences in wealth or culture; provide employment and entrepreneurial opportunities for local residents; train staff and customers in cultural sensitivity; contribute directly to local community health and education; encourage philanthropy in cases where rich tourists visit poor communities; and negotiate and uphold fair leases and contracts with community landowners. In addition, there are pressures for tourism corporations to: minimise, manage, monitor and offset their impacts on natural environments; contribute to conservation of biodiversity and ecosystem services; and contribute to climate change mitigation measures. All of these differ between countries and market sectors.

Mainstream hotels and transport

Mainstream tourism means: large-scale hotels and resorts; high-volume passenger transport operations by air, land or water; and high-volume purpose-built urban tourist attractions and activities. All of these components are commonplace in both developed and developing nations worldwide. For the mainstream accommodation sector, the principal CSR issues are staff employment conditions and environmental management technologies. For the air transport sector, atmospheric emission and contributions to climate change are critical. For passenger ships, discharges to rivers, lakes or the ocean are most significant, as well as employment conditions for crews on contract. For land transport, the local impacts of road or rail access corridors and vehicle noise can be critical in some instances. Exhausts and emissions from engines of various types contribute to air pollution locally and to climate change at a global level.

There is extensive academic literature on sustainable tourism, but with rather little quantitative information on any of the critical aspects of CSR identified above. There is a key distinction between corporate social and environmental marketing, management and performance, that is what they claim, what they do and what they achieve.

According to Rodriguez and Cruz (2007), improved social and environmental performance boosts the mean profitability of Spanish hotels by 2 per cent, but management or marketing alone have no detectable effects. Buckley and Araujo (1997) found that many of the mainstream tourist accommodation venues in a large-scale beach and theme-park destination in Queensland, Australia, had adopted at least some practices and technologies intended to conserve energy, water and resources, but that very few had done so systematically or sufficiently to yield any significant effect.

Dalton et al. (2007) found that tourism accommodation venues in Queensland only adopted renewable energy sources where they do not have access to grid power. Ayuso (2007), Kasim (2007), Kim and Miller (2008) and Pedreira and Souza (2008) found that CSR practices for hotels in Spain, Malaysia, Korea and Brazil are all relatively weak.

Owen and O'Dwyer (2008) found that only the larger tourism corporations report their CSR practices, and that their reports are unreliable. Holcomb et al. (2007) found that for the 10 largest hotel chains in the USA, even the CSR claims in their own marketing materials were remarkably weak, with the main focus on vaguely defined vision statements, or equal employment opportunities, which are in any event mandated by law.

In Europe, Blanco *et al.* (2009) reported five previous studies, mostly from Spain, covering around 400 hotels in total. Their own analysis, however, was merely theoretical. They also reported one study of 164 hotels in Costa Rica. There are a number of additional descriptions of CSR-related activities by individual corporations for example in Indonesia (Ross and Wall 1999), Canada (Speck 2002), Australia (Buckley 2003: 194–8) and South Africa (Ashley and Haysom 2008).

In Brazil, the three main hotel groups in the coastal resort town of Costa do Sauipe all make claims of CSR, but only one has >50 per cent local staff, and other efforts were minimal (Neto 2003; Cardoso 2005; Oliveira 2007). In Praio do Forte, the principal resort supported a school with over 500 students (Cardoso 2005; Pegas 2009; Pegas and Stronza 2010), but was bought out by a Portuguese hotel chain, which ceased support despite continuing to advertise it. Of 33 hotels in Santa Catarina, 60 per cent had some form of energy conservation measures, but only 46 per cent had installed adequate treatment facilities for liquid wastes, which they promoted as CSR initiatives even though they were legally required (Moratelli 2005). Elsewhere in Brazil, Bogo and Dreher (2007) and Pedreira and Souza (2008) found that tourism industry representatives have extremely vague and general views of CSR, ranging from paying taxes, complying with legal requirements, and providing adequate working conditions for staff, to small-scale assistance for external organisations.

A number of large airlines and cruise ship lines have also established social and environmental programmes, or at least adopted relevant labels and applied for awards, notably the 'World Savers' award run by the magazine *Conde Nast Traveler* (Anon 2009). Qantas contributes funds to The Fred Hollows Foundation (2010) in its efforts to improve eyesight among Indigenous communities in Australia and elsewhere. In Brazil, the regional airline Gol (2009) has historically supported youth programmes aimed at health, nutrition, education and leadership. P&O Cruises (2011) has recently released its first 'sustainability report'.

To the extent that these few reports allow, it does indeed appear that mainstream tourism corporations follow practices in other industries (Crane *et al.* 2008) in that: (1) they treat CSR largely as a public-relations exercise to distract attention from the impacts of their core businesses; and (2) they boost CSR visibility as a strategic tool in negotiating with government, either to gain development approvals in environmentally sensitive locations, or in reaction to social or environmental legislation.

Social benefits programmes and foundations in developing countries

Social welfare concerns are both more widespread, and less well-funded in developing compared with developed nations. In developed nations, social welfare requirements such as health, education and aged care are provided through private providers and purchases, through private or public insurance schemes, or through tax-funded government programmes. The detailed design and funding mechanisms are an endless topic of political debate. Most of the population in developed nations, however, does have access to welfare services through one means or another.

In developing nations, both the level of funding for social welfare programmes, and their technical quality, are considerably lower. In addition, much higher proportions of their populations lack access to large-scale schemes, and rely instead on local-scale extended-family or other traditional social support systems. In such circumstances, there are strong social and political expectations that private-enterprise employers, including those in tourism, will make significant contributions to the health and education of staff, their families and other members of local communities. This has historical antecedents in countries that are now developed. In addition, national tourism policies in many developing countries refer explicitly to the role of tourism in so-called community upliftment: and the UN World Tourism Organization states that one of the goals of global tourism is to alleviate poverty.

In practical terms, this means that fixed-site tourism operations in rural areas in developing nations are commonly seen by local residents, as well as direct employees, as nodes of wealth and expertise that can be relied on for help. Such help may include: occasional transport for medical emergencies; the supply of nutritional supplements for sale; provision of condoms and arrangements for routine HIV testing; and the establishment of schools and health clinics. There are many examples of such programmes for hotels and lodges in Africa (Buckley 2003, 2006, 2010a; Lutalo 2007; Livingstone Tourism HIV/AIDS Partnership 2008) and Latin America (Ribeiro and Lacorte 2003; Oliveira 2007; Pegas 2009; TAMAR 2010).

The companies concerned may establish such programmes directly, or provide funds and technical assistance to relevant local community organisations to deliver the same services. They may provide funds either from their own (pre-tax) profits, or by establishing trusts and foundations to which their clients and other philanthropists may elect to make voluntary donations, generally tax-deductible. Irrespective of the mechanism, there are many reported programmes with successful outcomes, albeit mostly on small scales.

Community tourism

Community tourism provides an alternative model to harness the economic opportunities of tourism to contribute to local social welfare. Instead of relying on the philanthropy of private enterprise, or applying political pressure, a local community can choose to operate commercial tourism ventures directly. There are many barriers to this, relating especially to: legal rights over land, water and wildlife; expertise in hospitality and marketing; local community dynamics; and larger-scale political patronage (Mbaiwa 2005; Southgate 2006; Groom and Harris 2008; Spenceley 2008; Stronza and Durham 2008; Nelson 2010). In many cases, therefore, communities may opt for a middle road where they take control of tourism assets, but then lease these assets to private tourism enterprises under legal contractual arrangements of various types.

There are now many examples of community tourism in Asia (Pathak and Kothari 2003; ACAP 2008; Buckley 2010a), South America (Stronza and Gordillo 2008; Pegas and Stronza 2010) and sub-Saharan Africa (Mbaiwa 2005; Honey 2009; Castley 2010), but with mixed success.

Responsible tourism and ecotourism

The specialist tourism sub-sectors known as ecotourism and responsible tourism have particular interests in social and environmental responsibility (Spenceley 2008; Buckley 2008, 2009a). The term responsible tourism originated in South Africa (Goodwin, pers. comm. 28 Jan 2011), and has a strong focus on employment opportunities and economic returns to local communities (Spenceley 2008; Castley 2010). Ecotourism focuses principally on the natural environment, but does also include community issues (Weaver and Lawton 2007; Weaver 2008; Buckley 2009a, 2009b). Relevant components may include technologies and management measures to reduce energy and water consumption and to treat or recycle wastes (Buckley 2004), and contributions to conservation and community development (Buckley 2010a).

There are now a number of meta-analyses and case study compilations in ecotourism and responsible tourism (Buckley 2003, 2009a, 2009b; Kruger 2005; Gössling and Hultman 2006; Zeppel 2006; Spenceley 2008; Stronza and Durham 2008; Saarinen et al. 2009). These meta-analyses have reached three main conclusions: (1) many enterprises use eco- or responsibility branding purely for marketing purposes; (2) some enterprises do contribute to conservation, principally by providing economic and political support for private and community reserves; and (3) some enterprises do contribute to local communities, by providing direct funding, community welfare services, markets for local businesses and new jobs that include training and good promotion prospects. Wages and working conditions for staff, including opportunities for employees from local communities to rise to senior management positions, have been a key concern for private lodges in sub-Saharan Africa (Castley 2010). Many of these lodges also provide organised mechanisms for their guests to make philanthropic donations to local community initiatives, especially in education.

Contributions to conservation and communities, as under (2) and (3) above, may be characterised as follows: (1) they are as yet relatively small in scale; (2) they are largely disconnected from business travel, urban tourism and mainstream resort sectors; (3) they are highly sensitive to global economic conditions; (4) they are largely confined to developing nations; and (5) they are particularly small in the large newly industrialised nations of India and China, in comparison with the massive and rapid growth of mainstream domestic tourism in those countries (Buckley 2003, 2006, 2010a).

Overall, therefore, CSR in the ecotourism and responsible tourism sub-sectors may be summarised as follows: (1) a large proportion of enterprises that use these terms in marketing may not adopt their principles to any significant extent in practice; (2) a small number of enterprises have indeed successfully adopted those principles, can justifiably claim a positive triple bottom line and meet all or most of the various criteria proposed for corporate responsibility; (3) most of these are in developing nations, and they make up a significant proportion of the tourism industry as a whole only in less wealthy nations with strong reliance on international inbound tourism; (4) these enterprises are indeed growing in number and in some cases also in scale, and to some degree they are linking in to the large and growing international adventure tourism sector and to improved environmental management in mainstream tourism; and (5) on a global scale, they remain a very small proportion of the tourism sector overall, especially in large newly wealthy nations.

Codes and certification schemes

The most powerful of the seven types of CSR in the classification put forward by Auld *et al.* (2008) is the type they refer to as non-governmental soft law. In the context of CSR, this phrase refers to rules developed, accepted, monitored and enforced by the private sector, not by governments. As with public-sector legislation, such rules may range from vague, brief statements of intent with no clear criteria or effective mechanism for enforcement; to detailed and practical sets of instructions, supported by institutions that have sufficient resources and support to ensure that they are followed frequently enough to influence real-world outcomes.

Such rules can be important for several reasons: (1) if they are widely followed, they provide a level playing field; (2) competing corporations can all adopt a particular CSR practice or practices, without any of them suffering commercial disadvantage; (3) if they are advertised publicly, they provide an accepted guideline as to what particular corporate activities are considered as socially responsible; (4) a company that follows them can thus make a clear claim, which is valuable in bolstering its reputation; (5) within an individual corporation, these rules can form part of the corporate culture and staff performance management systems; and (6) where such rules are established by professional or industry associations, they provide a mechanism for peer scrutiny.

If rules of this type become generally endorsed and accepted by the industry sub-sector concerned, they may later be adopted into hard law through various forms of government recognition. Codes of conduct may be seen as descriptions of standard industry practice, which can be referred to in actions under common law. Governments may provide explicit legal recognition to certification programmes operated by professional industry associations, such as wilderness medicine and river rescue; sometimes, rules developed by private corporations may be written directly into government legislation and regulations.

Many different organisations have compiled codes of practice covering either social or environmental issues in tourism (Buykx 2001; Buckley 2002; Lorimer 2006). Garrod and Fennell (2004), for example, identified 58 different codes for whale watching tours. Many of these are regulations requiring legal compliance, but even so, many operators ignore them (Scarpaci and Dayanthi 2003; Waayers *et al.* 2006).

There are numerous privately- run eco-certification programmes (Font and Buckley 2001; Black and Crabtree 2007). Most of these are checklist-based approaches, which refer only to the presence or absence of particular technologies or practices, although a few do prescribe quantitative thresholds. They are thus similar to codes of conduct, but with third-party certification of compliance. Such systems contain innate incentives for abuse (Gunningham and Grabowsky 1998; Nunez 2007).

There are also customer-feedback approaches such as those trialled by tour packager Touristik Union International or booking agency World Hotel-Link, but these are less effective than blog sites such as TripAdvisor. Within the CSR typology proposed by Auld *et al.* (2008), these are information-based approaches that rely purely on public reporting to provide pressures for corporate responsibility.

Some tourism operators have internal codes of practice, which are significantly more stringent than third-party systems. Staff are more likely than external auditors to detect breaches, and companies have immediate sanctions against any employee who breaches the code. There are also codes of practice developed by syndicates of tourism enterprises offering similar products in the same region, where each can observe behaviour by the others; as, for example, at Madikwe private game reserve in South Africa (Castley 2010).

Individual enterprises are more likely to follow syndicated codes if four conditions are met: (1) they were involved in drafting them; (2) everyone who uses the resource also subscribes to the code, so there are no spoilers or freeriders; (3) breaches of the code are readily observable, and can be attributed unambiguously to particular individual enterprises; and (4) there is an accepted and practically implemented mechanism to apply realistic penalties to any enterprises that do breach the code.

Boat-based tourism in the Antarctic offers a good test of syndicated codes, as individual nations have no direct legal jurisdiction there. Most relevant tour operators are members of the International Association of Antarctic Tour Operators (IAATO), which developed a code of practice for expedition cruise vessels. This code has deficiencies (Buckley 2010a), but it does address key issues such as passenger landings at wildlife sites, and sets quantitative rules for key parameters such as minimum approach distances to nesting seabirds. Difficulties arose when much larger conventional cruise ships also began visiting the Antarctic. Two large US-based cruise ship companies were apparently reluctant to subscribe to the IAATO code. As one large ship can create as much environmental impact as many smaller ones, this threatens the entire function and stability of IAATO as a self-regulatory organisation.

Commercial tourism in public protected areas

The appropriate role and regulation of commercial tourism operations in national parks and other public protected areas can provide a powerful test of CSR in tourism. Most countries have public protected area systems and management agencies, although levels of funding, legal protection and enforcement differ greatly between nations. Most parks allow limited recreational use, and parks agencies use well-established tools to manage visitors and impacts (Buckley 1998, 2009c; Butler and Boyd 2000; Manning 2000; McCool and Moisey 2001; Lockwood *et al.* 2006). Commercial tourism operations in public protected areas, however, are much more contentious.

Small-scale, low-impact mobile tour operators are permitted by many parks agencies. These guide small groups of clients to undertake the same activities as are permissible for independent visitors, and must commonly comply with the same rules regarding access, activities, fees, group sizes, bookings etc. These operators must usually obtain permits from the parks agency, covering issues such as insurances, indemnities, safety equipment and guide skills. Complications can arise when commercial tour operators ask for special privileges, such as: exclusive access to particular areas; pre-assigned quotas or special booking rights; permission to carry out particular activities not otherwise permitted; or exemptions from particular restrictions, for example on maximum group sizes, or the opportunity to use packstock or motorised vehicles to transport baggage. Permissions such as these, however, can be reversed by the parks agency should the need arise. The agency does not surrender control, and thus does not rely on CSR (Buckley 2010b).

Once privately funded infrastructure or accommodation is constructed within a public protected area, in contrast, it is effectively impossible to remove, either for legal or political reasons or both. Such developments thus provide a further test of self-regulation within the tourism industry. Tourism industry associations lobby continually for access and development rights, using a wide range of political and legal manoeuvres (Buckley 2010b). Private tourism developments inside public protected areas gain a number of commercial advantages, including: exclusive access to highly desirable attractions; publicly subsidised infrastructure and marketing; and immediate access to a stream of potential clients. Only rarely, however, is there any net environmental, social or even economic gain for the public parks agencies (Buckley 2010a, 2010b; Castley 2010). Claims of CSR by tourism industry lobbyists thus fall largely in the political rather than the practical category, as distinguished earlier.

Conclusions

The academic literature of CSR provides a useful framework to analyse the social and environmental aspects of corporate behaviour in the tourism industry. The CSR perspective is valuable not because tourism corporations are necessarily responsible, but because the broader literature in this field can provide insights into the behaviour of individual enterprises and industry associations alike. Relevant perspectives cover political lobbying, advertising and marketing, adoption of environmental management technologies and practices, philanthropy, and organisational culture and dynamics.

CSR in the mainstream tourism industry is very weak. Few companies do significantly more than the minimum required by law. Many do not even comply with legal minimal standards. Those that do, often advertise compliance with taxation, industrial relations or planning and pollution control law as CSR. Voluntary initiatives that go beyond compliance are miniscule in comparison with the overall scale of corporate core business, in tourism as in other sectors. Even these initiatives can be co-opted as political tools to gain permits for high-impact commercial developments. Similarly, the widespread use of ecolabels in tourism seems to be principally political in nature.

In rural areas in developing nations, tourism operations can provide significant sources of local employment, social welfare and community benefits. There are considerable complexities, however, where private tourism enterprises are established on land under communal ownership, whether through modern or traditional tenure systems. In such cases, responsibility may not be easy to define.

For tourism in protected areas, including marine as well as terrestrial parks, regulations and minimal-impact codes are commonly more stringent and detailed than elsewhere. For mobile tourism enterprises operating under permit, these define legally mandated responsibility. There are many good examples worldwide. There are also good examples of syndicated common-property resource management in the nature-based tourism sector, including Antarctic regions outside the jurisdiction of individual nations.

In a number of nations worldwide, tourism property developers have lobbied intensively for increased opportunities to build and run private tourism accommodation and facilities inside public protected areas. These lobbying efforts have employed a variety of arguments, many of them spurious. From an analytical perspective this is a typical use of CSR rhetoric for financial gain through political processes.

From a research perspective, CSR claims and practices have been analysed in much more depth in other sectors than in tourism. There are thus excellent opportunities to apply CSR approaches to analyse a range of real-life practices, pressures and organisational behaviours within the tourism sector, including government as well as private-sector components.

References

ACAP (2008) *Annapurna Conservation Area Project*. Available at: www.visitnepal.com/acap/ (accessed 12 October 2010).

Anon (2009) *Preservation: 2009 World Savers Awards*. Available at: www.concierge.com/cntraveler/articles/501472 (accessed 14 January 2011).

Ashley, C. and Haysom, G. (2008) 'The development impacts of tourism supply chains: Increasing impact on poverty and decreasing our ignorance', in A. Spenceley (ed.) *Responsible Tourism*. London: Earthscan. pp. 129–56.

Auld, G., Bernstein, S. and Cashore, B. (2008) 'The new corporate social responsibility', *Annual Review of Environment and Resources* 33, 413–35.

Ayuso, S. (2007) 'Comparing voluntary policy instruments for sustainable tourism: The experience of the Spanish hotel sector', *Journal of Sustainable Tourism* 15, 144–59.

Black, R. and Crabtree, A. (2007) *Quality Assurance and Certification in Ecotourism*. Wallingford: CAB International.

Blanco, E., Rey-Maquieira, J. and Lozano, J. (2009) 'Economic incentives for tourism firms to undertake voluntary environmental management', *Tourism Management* 30, 112–22.

Bogo, C. and Dreher, M. (2007) 'Responsabilidade social empresarial: o emprego da agenda 21 nas empresas turisticas da regiao da AMMVI', *Dynamia Revista Techno-cientifica* 13, 70–81.

Buckley, R.C. (1998) 'Tools and indicators for managing tourism in parks', *Annals of Tourism Research* 26, 207–10.

——(2002) 'Minimal impact guidelines for mountain ecotours', *Tourism Recreation Research* 27, 35–40.

——(2003) *Case Studies in Ecotourism*. Wallingford: CAB International.

——(2004) *Environmental Impacts of Ecotourism*. Wallingford: CAB International.

——(2006) *Adventure Tourism*. Wallingford: CAB International.

——(2008) 'Testing take-up of academic concepts in an influential commercial tourism publication', *Tourism Management* 29, 721–9.

——(2009a) *Ecotourism: Principles and Practices*. Wallingford: CAB International.

——(2009b) 'Evaluating the net effects of ecotourism on the environment: A framework, first assessment and future research', *Journal of Sustainable Tourism* 17, 643–72.

——(2009c) Parks and tourism. *PLoS Biol*, 7:e1000143.

——(2010a) *Conservation Tourism*. Wallingford: CAB International.

——(2010b) 'Private tourism in public parks' in Hsu, Yi-Chung (ed.) *Issues Confronting the Management of the World's National Parks*. National Dong Hua University, Taipei. Proceedings of the Conference held on 2–3 August 2010, Taiwan.

Buckley, R.C. and Araujo, G. (1997) 'Environmental Management Performance in Tourism Accommodation', *Annals of Tourism Research* 24, 465–9.

Butler, R.W. and Boyd, S.W. (2000) (eds) *Tourism and National Parks: Issues and Implications*. Chichester: John Wiley & Sons.

Buykx, C. (2001) *The Responsible Travel Guide Book*. World Expeditions, Sydney. Available www.worlde xpeditions.com.au/index.php?section=about_us&id=322 (accessed 1 February 2011).

Cardoso, R. (2005) *Dimensões sociais do turismo sustentável: Estudo sobre a contribuição dos resorts de praia para o desenvolvimento das comunidades locais*. Fundação Getúlio Vargas – Escola de Administração de Empresas de São Paulo. Doctoral Dissertation

Castley J.G. (2010) 'Africa' in R. Buckley *Conservation Tourism*. CAB International, Wallingford, 145–75.

Crane, A., McWilliams, A., Matten, D., Moon, J. and Siegel, D.S. (eds) (2008) *The Oxford Handbook of Corporate Social Responsibility*. Oxford: Oxford University Press.

Dalton, G.J., Lockington, D.A. and Baldock, T.E. (2007) 'A survey of tourist operator attitudes to renewable energy supply in Queensland, Australia', *Renewable Energy* 32, 567–86.

Font, X and Buckley, R.C. (eds) (2001) *Tourism Ecolabelling*. Wallingford: CAB International.

Garrod, B. and Fennell, D.A. (2004) 'An analysis of whalewatching codes of conduct', *Annals of Tourism Research* 31, 334–52.

Gol (2009) *Voar com responsabilidade social*. Available http://mobileri.voegol.com.br/gol2009/web/arquivos /GOL_RelatRespSocial_port.pdf (accessed 12 January 2011).

Gössling, S. and Hultman, J. (2006) *Ecotourism in Scandinavia: Lessons in Theory and Practice*. Wallingford: CAB International.

Groom, R. and Harris, S. (2008) 'Conservation on community lands: The importance of equitable revenue sharing', *Environmental Conservation* 35, 242–51.

Gunningham, N. and Grabowsky, P. (1998) *Smart Regulation*. Oxford: Clarendon.

Holcomb, J.L., Upchurch, R.S. and Okumus, F. (2007) 'Corporate social responsibility: What are top hotel companies reporting?', *International Journal of Contemporary Hospitality Management* 19, 461–75.

Honey, M. (2009) 'Community conservation and early ecotourism: Experiments in Kenya', *Environment: Science and Policy for Sustainable Development* 51, 46–56.

Kasim, A. (2007) 'Corporate environmentalism in the hotel sector: Evidence of drivers and barriers in Penang, Malaysia', *Journal of Sustainable Tourism* 15, 680–99.

Kim, N. and Miller, G. (2008) 'Perceptions of the ethical climate in the Korean tourism industry', *Journal of Business Ethics* 82, 941–54.

Kruger, O. (2005) 'The role of ecotourism in conservation: Panacea or Pandora's box?', *Biodiversity and Conservation* 14, 579–600.

Livingstone Tourism HIV/AIDS Partnership (LTHP) (2008) *Promoting HIV Prevention through Zambia's Tourism Industry*. Available www.pepfar.gov/c23652.htm (accessed on 12 October 2010).

Lockwood, M., Worboys, G. and Kothari, A. (2006) *Managing Protected Areas: A Global Guide*. London: Earthscan. 802 pp.

Lorimer, K. (2006) *Code Green*. Melbourne: Lonely Planet.

Lutalo, M. (2007) *The Wellness Program of Serena Hotels, Kenya – A Case Study*. World Bank Global HIV/ AIDS Program. Available http://gametlibrary.worldbank.org/FILES/1145_Getting_results_Kenya_Sere na_hotel.pdf (accessed on 12 October 2010).

McCool, S. and Moisey, R. (2001) *Tourism, Recreation and Sustainability: Linking Culture and the Environment*. New York: CAB International.

Manning, R. (2000) 'Visitor experience and resource protection: A framework for managing the carrying capacity of national parks', *Journal of Park and Recreation Administration* 19, 93–10.

Mbaiwa, J. (2005) 'Enclave tourism and its socio-economic impacts in the Okavango Delta, Botswana', *Tourism Management* 26, 157–72.

Moratelli, R. (2005) 'Estudo sobre a responsabilidade social no setor hoteleiro de Santa Catarina', Masters Thesis, Universidade do Vale do Itajai.

Nelson, F. (2010) *Community Rights, Conservation and Contested Land: The Politics of Natural Resource Governance in Africa*. London: Earthscan.

Neto, A. (2003) 'A responsabilidade socioambiental da indústria do turismo e do lazer: O empreendimento Costa do Sauípe', Masters Thesis, Universidade de Brasília – Centro de Desenvolvimento Sustentável.

Nunez, J. (2007) 'Can self regulation work?: A story of corruption, impunity and cover-up', *Journal of Regulatory Economics* 31, 209–33.

Oliveira, E. (2007) 'Impactos socioambientais e econômicos do turismo e as suas repercussões no desenvolvimento local: caso do município de Itacaré – Bahia', *Revista Internacional de Desenvolvimento Local* 8, 193–202.

Owen, D.L. and O'Dwyer, B. (2008) 'Corporate social responsibility. The reporting and assurance dimension', in A. Crane, A. McWilliams, D. Matten, J. Moon, D.S. Siegel (eds) *The Oxford Handbook of Corporate Social Responsibility*. Oxford: Oxford University Press, 384–409.

P& o Cruises (2011) *This is How to Holiday*. Available at: www.pocruises.com.au/aboutus/pages/sustainability.aspx (accessed 1 February 2011).

Pathak, N. and Kothari, A. (2003) 'Community-conserved biodiverse areas: Lessons from South Asia', in D. Harmon and A. Putney (eds) *The Full Value of Parks*. Lanham, MD: Rowman and Littlefield Publishers, pp. 211–26.

Pedreira, I. and Souza, M. (2008) *A responsabilidade social no turismo de Blumenau (SC) sob a ótica de seus dirigentes*. V Seminário de Pesquisa em Turismo do MERCOSUL – SeminTUR.

Pegas, F. (2009) 'Twenty-five years of sea turtle protection in Brazil: Evaluating local effects', Doctoral Dissertation, Texas A&M University.

Pegas, F. and Stronza, A. (2010) 'Ecotourism and sea turtle harvesting in a fishing village of Bahia, Brazil', *Conservation and Society* 8, 15–25.

Ribeiro, M. and Lacorte, G. (2003) *Gestão social do turismo*. Ministério do Turismo/Fundação Getúlio Vargas.

Rodriguez, F.J.G. and Cruz, Y.M.A. (2007) 'Relation between social-environmental responsibility and performance in hotel firms', *International Journal of Hospitality Management* 26, 824–39.

Ross, S. and Wall, G. (1999). 'Evaluating ecotourism: The case of North Sulawesi, Indonesia', *Tourism Management* 20, 673–82.

Saarinen, J., Becker, F., Manwa, H. and Wilson, D. (eds) (2009) *Sustainable Tourism in Southern Africa: Local Communities and Natural Resources in Transition*. Bristol: Channel View Publications.

Scarpaci, C. and Dayanthi, N. (2003) 'Compliance with regulations by swim-with-dolphins: Operations in Port Phillip Bay, Victoria, Australia', *Environmental Management* 31, 342–7.

Southgate, C.R.J. (2006) 'Ecotourism in Kenya: The vulnerability of communities', *Journal of Ecotourism* 5, 80–96.

Speck, E. (2002) 'The Fairmont Chateau Whistler Resort: Moving towards sustainability', in R. Harris, T. Griffin and P. Williams (eds) *Sustainable Tourism: A Global Perspective*. Oxford: Butterworth, pp. 269–83.

Spenceley, A. (2008) *Responsible Tourism: Critical Issues for Conservation and Development*. London: Earthscan.

Stronza, A. and Durham, W.H. (eds) (2008) *Ecotourism and Conservation in the Americas*. Wallingford: CAB International.

Stronza, A., and Gordillo, J. (2008) 'Community views of ecotourism: Redefining benefits', *Annals of Tourism Research* 35, 444–68.

TAMAR. (2010) *Comunidades: Primeiro desafio*. Available: www.tamar.org.br/interna.php?cod=163 (accessed on 8 November 2010).

The Fred Hollows Foundation (2010) *The Fred Hollows Foundation*. Available http://www.hollows.org.au/ (accessed 23 December 2010).

Waayers, D., Newsome, D. and Lee, D. (2006) 'Observations of non-compliance behaviour by tourists to a voluntary code of conduct: A pilot study of turtle tourism in the Exmouth region, Western Australia', *Journal of Ecotourism* 5, 211–22.

Weaver, D. (2008) *Ecotourism*. Milton: Wiley.

Weaver, D.B. and Lawton, L.J. (2007) 'Twenty years on: the state of contemporary ecotourism research', *Tourism Management* 28, 1168–79.

Zeppel, H. (2006) *Indigenous Ecotourism: Sustainable Development and Management*. Wallingford: CAB International.

47

Environmental security and tourism

Kevin Hannam

Introduction

The concept of security has been rather undertheorised in tourism studies despite recent attempts to do so. For example, in the introduction to their edited text, *Tourism, Security and Safety*, Pizam and Mansfeld (2006) attempt to develop a threefold typology of tourism security concepts and variables: tourism-related security incidents and crises; impacts of security incidents; and reaction to tourism crises by stakeholders. Despite the laudable aims, however, Pizam and Mansfeld fail to develop any in-depth conceptual discussion of the notion of security itself. Hall *et al.* (2003) in the introduction to their edited collection entitled *Safety and Security in Tourism*, do develop arguments that suggest that the concept of security has been transformed from one of collective security to one of common security through the work of the United Nations. They note that tourism is 'irrevocably bound up with the concept of security' (Hall *et al.* 2003: 2) but also acknowledge that tourism organisations have had little influence on security agendas. Nevertheless, they persist with a view of tourism as a potentially emancipatory project that may ward off potential future global insecurities. More recently a number of researchers have analysed the impacts of a range of environmental crises and disasters (Hannam 2004). It has been recognised that it is not just the initial crisis or disaster itself that has an impact on tourism but also the longer lasting image of the management of that event (Cassedy 1991). As Young and Montgomery (1998: 4) have noted: 'a crisis has the potential to be detrimental to the marketability of any tourist destination, particularly if it is dramatised and distorted through rumours and the media'.

In his seminal paper Bill Faulkner (2001: 136) developed an initial framework for tourism disaster management. He noted that few tourism destinations have developed adequate disaster management plans and relatively little systematic and theoretically informed research hitherto has been carried out on disaster phenomena in tourism. 'Whether the incidence of disasters is increasing, or it is simply a matter of each disaster having more devastating effects … it is apparent we live in an increasingly complex world and this has contributed to making us more crisis or disaster prone'. Moreover, 'the increased volume of global tourism activity has combined with the attractiveness of high-risk exotic locations to expose tourists to greater levels of risk'. The critical role of the media in disaster situations is also noted by Faulkner (2001: 142): 'the impacts of disasters on the market are often out of proportion with their actual disruptive effects because of exaggeration by the media'.

Similarly, environmental instability has also created increasing uncertainty for the tourism industry and thus tourism marketing (Drabek 1995). The impact of the 2001 foot and mouth disease (FMD) outbreak in Britain and elsewhere in Europe had greater implications for rural tourism development than for agriculture. Initial estimates placed the total national loss of revenue from tourism in the UK at £2–3 billion, although the full impact has yet to be assessed (Countryside Agency 2001). In their analysis of the impact of FMD in the UK, Miller and Ritchie (2003) have argued that recovery in this instance was limited due to the lack of planning and preparation for such an event, the length of time of the disease outbreak, the speed and severity of international media coverage and problematic dissemination of government information. Furthermore, the environmental and tourism impact of the 2004 tsunami in South and South-East Asia has been widely documented (Leopold 2008; Lebel and Khrutmuang 2006; Henderson 2007; Calgaro and Lloyd 2008).

From the perspective of the new mobilities paradigm, meanwhile, the significance of environmental security issues have been recognised. Indeed, Hannam *et al.* (2006: 1) have argued that:

> Fears of illicit mobilities and their attendant security risks increasingly determine logics of governance and liability protection within both the public and private sectors. From SARS and avian influenza to train crashes, from airport expansion controversies to controlling global warming, from urban congestion charging to networked global terrorism, from emergency management in the onslaught of tsunamis and hurricanes to oil wars in the Middle East, issues of 'mobility' are centre-stage. Many public, private and not-for-profit organizations are seeking to understand, monitor, manage and transform aspects of these multiple mobilities, and of the new 'immobilities', social exclusions and security threats that may be associated with them.

Moreover, the social and environmental impact of the 2010 Icelandic ash cloud on such mobilities has also been recently investigated from a security perspective. Indeed, Adey and Anderson (2011: 12) have explored 'how the aerial mobilities disrupted by the ash cloud were remarkably contingent upon a series of systems and technologies of anticipation and speculation that sit within wider nested logics of governance and security'. Moreover, the recent 2011 multiple environmental impacts of the tsunami on Japan have yet to be researched.

Nevertheless, the concept of environmental security in relation to tourism in this context has not been sufficiently engaged with. This chapter seeks to re-dress this by providing a more in-depth examination of the concept of environmental security *per se*. In particular, this chapter draws on the theoretical work of Simon Dalby who has developed the concept of environmental security in his analysis of contemporary geopolitical discourses on the environment. The chapter then examines a case study of the impacts of the recent BP oil spill on tourism and the environment. Furthermore, it is argued that the BP oil spill has also led to significant geopolitical debates over national and international environmental security. The chapter, therefore, concludes by discussing the relationship between tourism and contemporary notions of environmental security in terms of geopolitical discourses. First, however, I discuss conceptualisations of the notion of security itself.

Conceptualising security

Soroos (1997: 236) defines security as 'the assurance people have that they will continue to enjoy those things that are most important to their survival and well-being'. Beyond this simple definition, Dalby (2002: 163–4) usefully summarises that:

Security is about the future or fears of the future. It is about contemporary dangers but also thwarting potential future dangers. It is about control, certainty, and predictability in an uncertain world, and, in an attempt to forestall chance and change, it is frequently a violent practice. It is about maintaining certain collective identities, certain senses of who we are, of who we intend to remain, more than who we intend to become. Security provides narratives of danger as the stimulus to collective action but is much less useful in proposing desirable futures. … Security discourses specify the endangered entity. But these are multiply coded and embedded in cultural contexts.

During the Cold War, definitions of security, however, were widely used to justify political action and/or inaction, that is providing protection from threats to social order and tied to notions of international law. Realist approaches to politics, at this time, argued that states develop notions of security as a response to possible external violations of their territory (such as a military invasion of some kind). In 1987, the term security was still intimately connected with military issues (Page and Redclift 2002). The Cold War emphasised military and technological national security ideas based on the gathering of intelligence and the prevention of nuclear war through the division of the world into a system of 'blocs'. Security here meant maintaining the geopolitical status quo; of stasis. As a result many serious abuses of human rights were rationalised as being necessary for the maintenance of national security and to maintain governmental power. Klein (1998) has shown how these practices of security were an effective part of the US policy machinery, which led to US political hegemony during the Cold War.

Much of the US media on security in the 1990s, meanwhile, initially emphasised a sense of post-Cold War insecurity and uncertainty that ensued as nation-states grappled with the application of what were essentially *national* security discourses to global political and environmental changes. Most of this painted a rather depressing picture of the future where anarchy would reign instead of the previous stability and order under the Cold War (e.g. Homer-Dixon 1991; Kaplan 1995). Indeed, this paralleled dominant representations in the US media of much of the rest of the world, but particularly Africa, as being violent, hostile and out of control. Significantly, these discourses positioned Africa as a place of political instability, which could threaten Western affluence and thus needed 'containment'. Moreover, many of these analyses had a significant effect on actual US foreign policies such as President Clinton's in relation to the Balkans. More popularly, this also still pervades much of Hollywood thinking as films such as *Independence Day* and *Armageddon* testify with their emphasis on the world being saved by US forces (Dalby 2002).

Since the early 1990s environmental concerns have become an essential part of discussions of global security by nation-states and supra-national organisations. Dalby (2002) has argued that there is a need to reconceptualise the term security in terms of its assumption of national territorial solutions to problems of resource exploitation. In short, he has argued, that there is a need to reformulate the concept of security to take ecology much more seriously, in part because of the potential for war and conflict over access to key scarce resources. Climate change, ozone depletion and biodiversity impacts, as well as environmental catastrophes, have all highlighted the significance of environmental (and indeed human) security following the United Nations Conference on Environment and Development (UNCED) in 1992 (Barnett 2003). Although non-governmental organizations (NGOs) and environmental activists have sought to subvert the idea of national security by developing international linkages, it is now accepted – even in the USA – that maintaining the existing system of resource exploitation will lead to environmental insecurity and greater international instability.

Hence, in the twenty-first century, the notion of the nation-state as the arbiter of geopolitics is no longer tenable as the United Nations and NGOs with their focus on human and environmental concerns have challenged the traditional notions of security that stemmed from the Cold War. The United Nations Human Development Report (1994) was the first to articulate the concept of human security as having four essential aspects. First, the notion that human security was a *universal* concern to people everywhere regardless of their residence in a particular nation-state. Second, that human security emphasised the *inter-dependence* of nation-states. Third, that human security can only be ensued through *early* intervention. And, fourth, that the focus of security should shift from nation-states to *people* themselves. Thus, human security is then defined as: 'first, safety from such chronic threats as hunger, disease and repression. And second, it means protection from sudden and hurtful disruptions in the patterns of daily life' (UNDP 1994 cited in Dalby 2002: 8). The United Nations Development Programme (UNDP) thus considered six human security threats: unchecked population growth; disparities in economic disparities; excessive international migration; environmental degradation; drug production and trafficking; and international terrorism. Furthermore, terms such as 'common security' have been put forward to focus attention on the mutual vulnerability of *all* societies in the face of numerous environmental challenges. This has then been extended to the notion of 'comprehensive security' encompassing environmental concerns as well as human rights and feminist issues.

Rothschild (1995) usefully summarises the extension of traditional security concerns in terms of four key themes. First, 'downwards' – extending security from nations to groups and individuals. Second, 'upwards' – extending security from nations to international organisations. Third, 'horizontally' – extending security from military concerns to broader economic, social and environmental concerns (as in human security). Fourth, 'universally' – extending the political responsibility for ensuring security in all directions. Much of these discussions of security though are more political aspirations rather than actual reality and, indeed, much of the work of the United Nations has been critiqued for just this reason, particularly as the political elites in smaller, weaker and poorer nation-states still see national security primarily in military terms (Dalby 2002).

The concept of security also assumes that there is something that has to be secured: 'What is to be secured, how and by what means are questions conventionally answered by focusing on the state. But when environment is added into the consideration of security, it may well be that the state is no longer the obvious referent object of security' (Dalby 2002: xxii). Thus, the question of securing the global environment challenges nation-states' claims to sovereignty. However, security can also be conceptualised as something dangerous, both for the nation-state and for the individual who loses control in the face of international environmental issues. Thus, the notion of security raises fundamental questions about the identities of nations and political actors. This then takes us into the realm of geopolitics: 'Geopolitical reasoning, that is, using geographical categories as part of the practices of representation among foreign policy makers and politicians, specifies the world in particular ways that have political effects' (Dalby 2002: xxiv). Such geopolitical reasoning has a tendency to reduce complex geographical realities to simple strategic action or even inaction. For example, Dodds (1997) has charted the changing geopolitical rivalries over Antarctica from national security scares during the Cold War to more recent various international treaty negotiations and international scientific research collaborations that monitor environmental change. The geopolitical significance of Antarctica has thus changed in the face of new discourses of the environment as constructed by various governmental and non-governmental institutions (Dodds 2002).

Importantly, and parallel to Western military security concerns during the Cold War, many Western states in the 1970s also developed *social security* programmes that provided health and education services for their populations. Similarly, some form of economic security was also provided through various income support payments. Thus, the notion that the state would provide security was, in a sense, all pervasive. However, Klein (1998) has also demonstrated the privatisation of security in recent years has developed apace since the 1990s, with a growing number of private security firms involved in 'managing' both political and environmental conflicts as well as the increasing phenomenon of 'gated communities' with their own systems of security as part of wider systems of surveillance. Many trans-national firms, meanwhile, use private security firms to maintain their investment interests in countries that they perceive to be unstable – particularly in firms involved in mineral extraction including oil. Moreover, we can see similar discourses at work in the increasing role of private organisations involved in policing and the management of prison populations, as well as advertising agencies playing on personal insecurities in diverse economic realms from car ownership to insurance and health.

The increasing privatisation of security further undermines the role of nation-states as the locus of security provision and also raises further questions about the scope of global environmental management. However, although the geopolitical discourses of international environmental security have very laudable aims, evidence suggests that notions of national security in relation to the environment still remain as is illustrated below in the discussion of the recent British Petroleum (BP) oil spill disaster in the Gulf of Mexico.

Case study

BP and the oil spill in the Gulf of Mexico

The Deepwater Horizon oil spill (also referred to as the BP oil spill) was a significant environmental disaster in the Gulf of Mexico, which resulted from the 20 April 2010 Deepwater Horizon drilling rig explosion that killed 11 platform workers and injured 17 others. As a result, oil flowed from the ocean floor into the Gulf of Mexico from April to July 2010. It has recently been recognised as the largest accidental marine oil spill in the history of the petroleum industry (Robertson and Krauss 2010).

On 15 July 2010, the oil leak was effectively stopped by capping the gushing wellhead after it had released approximately 5 million barrels of crude oil into the Gulf of Mexico. On 19 September 2010, the relief well process was successfully completed and the US federal government declared the well 'effectively dead' (Whitehouse 2010). The US Government named BP as the main responsible party, and US government officials have committed to holding the company accountable for all clean-up costs and other damages. After its own internal investigations, BP admitted that it had made mistakes that led to the Gulf of Mexico oil spill. The oil spill has caused extensive damage to marine and wildlife habitats as well as the Gulf's fishing and tourism industries (Tangley 2010), and the impact of the spill has continued since the well was capped.

BP's Initial Exploration Plan for the extraction of deepwater oil from the Gulf of Mexico, dated 10 March 2009, argued that 'it is unlikely that an accidental spill would occur' and 'no adverse activities are anticipated' to fisheries or fish habitat (Griffitt 2009). Nevertheless, a significant environmental impact ensued. In terms of this environmental impact, the oil spill threatened environmental disaster due to factors such as petroleum toxicity, oxygen depletion and the use of chemical dispersants. Eight US national parks were threatened, with more than 400 species living in the Gulf islands and marshlands being put at risk, including many endangered species of turtle, as well as many non-endangered species of fish, crustaceans, dolphins and bird life (NPCA 2010).

At the end of April 2010, the Louisiana Governor, Bobby Jindal, declared a state of emergency in Louisiana after weather forecasts predicted that the oil slick would reach the Louisiana coast. This led to an emergency shrimping season being opened so that a catch could be brought in before the oil advanced too far (BBC 2010a). In May 2010, the US National Oceanic and Atmospheric Administration closed commercial and recreational fishing in affected federal waters between the mouth of the Mississippi River and Pensacola Bay and the US federal government declared a fisheries disaster for the states of Alabama, Mississippi and Louisiana (Alpert 2010). Initial cost estimates to the fishing industry of the oil spill are estimated at around US$2.5 billion (Walsh 2010).

In terms of the tourism impacts of the oil spill, although many people cancelled their vacations in the region affected, hotels close to the coasts of the US states of Louisiana, Mississippi and Alabama all initially reported increases in business during the first half of May 2010. However, significantly, this increase was deemed likely to be due to an influx of people who had come to work on oil removal efforts rather than due to an increase in holiday makers (Reed 2010). Jim Hutchinson, the then-assistant secretary for the Louisiana Office of Tourism, called the occupancy numbers misleading, but not surprising. 'Because of the oil slick, the hotels are completely full of people dealing with that problem … They're certainly not coming here as tourists. People aren't sport fishing, they aren't buying fuel at the marinas, they aren't staying at the little hotels on the coast and eating at the restaurants' (Reed 2010).

BP subsequently gave Florida US$25 million to promote their beaches for tourism and the company has planned to give US$15 million each to the US states of Alabama, Louisiana and Mississippi. Hotels in these states cut rates, offered special deals such as free golf, changed cancellation policies and offered refunds to many tourists who had been affected. Overall, a report on the potential impact of the oil spill for the US Travel Association estimated that the economic impact of the oil spill on tourism across the Gulf Coast over a three-year period could exceed approximately US$23 billion, in a region that supports over 400,000 travel industry jobs generating US$34 billion in revenue annually (Oxford Economics 2010). This report also pointed out that: 'A review of disasters affecting tourism destinations reveals that the impact endures beyond the resolution of the crisis itself due to brand damage and ongoing traveller misperceptions' (Oxford Economics 2010: 2).

In terms of the overall economic impact of the oil spill, in July 2010 BP reported that its own expenditures on the oil spill had reached US$3.12 billion, including the cost of the spill response, containment, relief well drilling, grants to the affected US states, claims paid and federal costs (Peterson 2010). Although the United States Oil Pollution Act of 1990 limited BP's liability for non-clean-up costs to US$75 million unless gross negligence is proven, BP admitted that it would pay for all clean-up and remediation regardless of this statutory liability cap. Nevertheless, some US politicians have sought to pass legislation that would increase the liability limit to US$10 billion. By the end of June 2010, BP's stock market value reached a new low, with the company's total lost value since the oil spill standing at some US$105 billion. At that time, BP reported a second-quarter loss of US$17 billion, its first loss in 18 years. This included a one-time US$32.2 billion charge, including US$20 billion for the fund created for reparations and US$2.9 billion in actual costs (Tharp 2010).

However, conversely, local officials in Louisiana expressed concerns that the offshore drilling moratorium imposed in response to the spill by the US federal government would further harm the economies of the coastal communities affected. The oil industry directly employs about 58,000 Louisiana residents and has indirectly created another 260,000 oil-related jobs, accounting for about 17 per cent of all Louisiana jobs (Sasser 2010). Furthermore, BP – at the time of the incident, the UK's largest corporation and a major business in the UK investment world – came under intense popular, media and political pressure to cancel its 2010 dividends in their entirety (Armitstead *et al.* 2010). Indeed, media reports stated that BP is of such a size and significance in the UK, that 'one pound in every seven' of investment and pension fund income in the UK is derived from BP (BBC 2010b).

A geopolitical confrontation

Beyond the environmental, economic and social impacts of the oil spill, what was significant was the playing out of discourses of environmental security by politicians on both sides of the Atlantic. In terms of the geopolitical impact of the oil spill, thus, the disaster was seen as placing stress on US–UK geopolitical relationships, insofar as BP was popularly perceived in the US as a British rather than as a trans-national company. In the US, BP gas stations, the majority of which the company does not actually own, reported a downturn in sales of between 10 per cent and 40 per cent due to a consumer backlash against the company. Indeed, some BP station owners in the USA that lost sales argued that the BP brand name should change back to Amoco. Rather than notions of common, international environmental security being espoused, it was quickly evident that the more traditional conceptualisations of national security were dominant as the US cartoon in Figure 47.1 below illustrates.

President Obama's initially aggressive tone, his decision to ignore the role of US firms in the oil spill and his comparisons of the event with 9/11, all inflamed political and popular opinion in both the UK and the US. In an interview, President Obama stated that: 'In the same way that our view of our vulnerabilities and our foreign policy was shaped profoundly by 9/11', he said, 'I think this disaster is going to shape how we think about the environment and energy for many years to come'. The British Prime Minister, David Cameron, was similarly criticised in the UK media for not defending BP sufficiently (Bates 2010). The Organization for International Investment, a Washington-based advocate for overseas investment in the USA, warned in

Figure 47.1 The true cost of oil. Copyright Mike Luckovish. Reprinted by permission.

early July 2010 that the political rhetoric surrounding the disaster was potentially damaging for the reputation of all British companies with operations in the USA and had sparked a wave of US protectionism that has restricted British firms from winning government contracts, making political donations and lobbying (Teather 2010; Mason 2010).

Indeed, the British MP Andrew Rosindell, was forced to point out that, 'It is not the British government or the British people who are to blame. It's a multinational company and it is up to them to fix this' (Alfano 2010). Both Obama and Cameron were subsequently under considerable pressure to comment politically on the matter (Kirkup 2010), and did so. The US Department of State was forced to issue a statement that the issue would not affect US–UK relationships, calling the UK its 'closest ally'. David Cameron went on to state that a 'sensible dialogue' was needed and BP would require certainty over its liability for compensation. Obama was later reported to have said that 'his frustration over the mammoth oil spill in the Gulf of Mexico is not an attack on Britain' and that he had 'no interest in undermining BP's value', as the two leaders tried to soothe trans-Atlantic tensions over the disaster and re-forge a sense of 'common security' (Armitstead 2010).

Conclusions

In this chapter we have seen how the concept of security has been rather undertheorised in tourism studies, despite recent attempts to do so. This chapter has sought to re-dress this by providing a more in-depth examination of the concept of environmental security. The chapter has examined the impacts of the recent BP oil spill on tourism and the environment. Moreover, the BP oil spill has also led to significant geopolitical debates over national and international environmental security. In this conclusion, it is, perhaps, worth repeating President Obama's statement that: 'In the same way that our view of our vulnerabilities and our foreign policy was shaped profoundly by 9/11', he said, 'I think this disaster is going to shape how we think about the environment and energy for many years to come'. Leaving the comparison with 9/11 to one side, this is an extremely bold statement for President Obama to make and it remains to be seen whether the oil spill will really be the watershed for global reliance on oil. Moreover, other recent environmental disasters have highlighted the ways in which tourism mobilities have significant environmental security impacts – most importantly the 2011 tsunami that has affected Japan and the global nuclear industry.

Further reading

Adey, P. and Anderson, B. (2011) 'Anticipation, Materiality, Event: The Icelandic Ash Cloud Disruption and the Security of Mobility', *Mobilities* 6(1), 11–20.
Dalby, S. (2002) *Environmental Security*. London: University of Minneapolis Press.

References

Adey, P. and Anderson, B. (2011) 'Anticipation, Materiality, Event: The Icelandic Ash Cloud Disruption and the Security of Mobility', *Mobilities* 6(1), 11–20.
Alfano, S. (2010) *BP oil spill not our fault, British government official says, calls criticism extreme and unhelpful.* Available online: www.nydailynews.com/news/world/2010/06/05/2010–06–05_bp_oil_spill_not_our_fault_british_government_official_says_calls_criticism_extr.html.
Alpert, B. (2010) *The feds declare fisheries disaster in La., Miss., Ala.* Available online: www.nola.com/news/t-p/capital/index.ssf?/base/news-8/1274769077181360.xml&coll=1.
Armitstead, L., Butterworth, M., and Jamieson, A. (2010) 'BP oil spill: shares plummet as US warns it will 'take action' to stop dividend', *The Daily Telegraph.* Available online: www.telegraph.co.uk/finance/newsbysector/energy/oilandgas/7816593/BP-oil-spill-shares-plummet-as-US-warns-it-will-take-action-to-stop-dividend.html.

Barnett, J. (2003) 'Security and climate change', *Global Environmental Change* 13, 7–17.

Bates, D. (2010) '9/11 families' fury as Obama compares BP oil spill to Twin Towers attack', *The Daily Mail*. Available online: www.dailymail.co.uk/news/worldnews/article-1286245/BP-OIL-SPILL-Fury-Obama-compares-Gulf-leak-9-11-attacks.html#ixzz12XE5TMs9.

BBC (2010a) *Oil 'reaches' US Gulf Coast from spill*. Available online: http://news.bbc.co.uk/1/hi/world/americas/8653162.stm.

——(2010b) *BP crisis: The impact on your savings and investments*. Available online: www.bbc.co.uk/news/10293829.

Calgaro, E. and Lloyd, K. (2008) 'Sun, sea, sand and tsunami: examining disaster vulnerability in the tourism community of Khao Lak, Thailand', *Singapore Journal of Tropical Geography* 29(3), 288–306.

Cassedy, K. (1991) *Crisis management planning in the travel and tourism industry*. San Francisco, CA: PATA.

Countryside Agency (2001) *Foot and mouth disease: The state of the countryside report*. Available at: www.countryside.gov.uk/stateofthecountryside/past.htm (accessed 2 July 2003).

Dalby, S. (2002) *Environmental Security*. London: University of Minneapolis Press.

Dodds, K. (1997) *Geopolitics in Antarctica: Views from the Southern Oceanic Rim*. Chichester: Wiley.

——(2002) *Pink Ice: Britain and the South Atlantic Empire*. London: Tauris.

Drabek, T. (1995) 'Disaster responses within the tourism industry', *International Journal of Mass Emergencies and Disasters* 13(1), 7–23.

Faulkner, B. (2001) 'Towards a framework for disaster management', *Tourism Management* 22, 135–47.

Griffitt, M. (2009) 'Initial Exploration Plan Mississippi Canyon Block 252 OCS-G 32306', *BP Exploration and Production*, New Orleans, LA: Minerals Management Service.

Hall, C. M., Timothy, D. and Duval, D. (2003) 'Security and tourism: Towards a new understanding?', in Hall, C. M., Timothy, D. and Duval, D. (eds) *Safety and Security in Tourism: Relationships, Management and Marketing*. New York: The Haworth Press.

Hannam, K. (2004) 'Tourism and Development II: Marketing destinations, experiences and crises', *Progress in Development Studies* 4(3), 1–8.

Hannam, K., Sheller, M., and Urry, J. (2006) 'Editorial: Mobilities, immobilities and moorings', *Mobilities* 1(1), 1–32.

Henderson, J. (2007) 'Corporate social responsibility and tourism: Hotel companies in Phuket, Thailand, after the Indian Ocean tsunami', *International Journal of Hospitality Management* 26 (1), 228–39.

Homer-Dixon, T. (1991) 'On the Threshold: Environmental Changes As Causes of Acute Conflict', *International Security* 16(2), 76–116.

Kaplan, R. (1995) *The Coming Anarchy and the Nation-State Under Siege*. Peaceworks, Number 4, United States Institute of Peace, 5–12.

Kirkup, J. (2010) 'Oil spill: David Cameron confronts Barack Obama in battle to protect BP', *The Daily Telegraph*. Available online: www.telegraph.co.uk/finance/newsbysector/energy/oilandgas/7834242/Oil-spill-David-Cameron-confronts-Barack-Obama-in-battle-to-protect-BP.html.

Klein, B. (1998) 'Politics by design: remapping security landscapes', *European Journal of International Relations* 4(3), 327–45.

Lebel, L. and Khrutmuang, S. (2006) 'Tales from the margins: small fishers in post-tsunami Thailand', *Disaster Prevention and Management* 15(1), 124–134.

Leopold, T. (2008) *The Construction of a Disaster Destination: Rebuilding Koh Phi Phi, Thailand*. PhD Thesis. Denedin: University of Otago.

Mason, R. (2010) 'UK firms suffer after BP oil spill', *Daily Telegraph*. Available at: www.telegraph.co.uk/finance/newsbysector/energy/oilandgas/7883303/UK-firms-suffer-after-BP-oil-spill.html.

Miller, G. and Ritchie, B. (2003) 'A farming crisis or a tourism disaster? An analysis of the Foot and Mouth Disease in the UK', *Current Issues in Tourism* 6(2), 150–71.

NPCA (2010) *Gulf Oil Spill Response*. Available online: www.npca.org/oilspill/.

Oxford Economics (2010) *Potential Impact of the gulf Oil Spill on Tourism. Report prepared for the US Travel Association*. Available online: www.mpiweb.org/ … /Gulf_Oil_Spill_Analysis_Oxford_Economics_710.pdf.

Page, E. and Redclift, M. (2002) 'Introduction: Human security and the environment at the new millennium', in Page, E. and Redclift, M. (eds) *Human Security and the Environment*. Cheltenham: Edward Elgar.

Peterson, K. (2010) 'US Stocks Futures Lose Gains After GDP Estimate Revised Down', *The Wall Street Journal*. Available online: http://online.wsj.com/article/BT-CO-20100625–704980.html.

Pizam, A. and Mansfeld, Y. (2006) 'Toward a theory of tourism security', in Mansfeld, Y. and Pizam, A. (eds) *Tourism, Security and Safety: From theory to practice*. Amsterdam: Elsevier.

Reed, T. (2010) *Spill hasn't yet emptied hotels on Gulf Coast*. Available online: www.thesunnews.com/2010/05/27/1497705/spill-hasnt-yet-emptied-hotels.html?story_link=email_msg.

Robertson, C. and Krauss, C. (2010) 'Gulf Spill Is the Largest of Its Kind, Scientists Say', *The New York Times*. Available at: www.nytimes.com/2010/08/03/us/03spill.html?_r=1&fta=y.

Rothschild, R. (1995) 'What is Security?', *Daedalus* 124(3), 53–98.

Sasser, B. (2010) *Despite BP oil spill, Louisiana still loves Big Oil*. Available online: www.csmonitor.com/USA/2010/0524/Despite-BP-oil-spill-Louisiana-still-loves-Big-Oil.

Soroos, M. (1997) *The Endangered Atmosphere: Preserving a global commons*. Columbia: University of South Carolina Press.

Tangley, L. (2010) 'Bird Habitats Threatened by Oil Spill', *National Wildlife*. Available at: www.nwf.org/News-and-Magazines/National-Wildlife/Birds/Archives/2010/Oil-Spill-Birds.aspx.

Teather, D. (2010) 'British companies' reputation in the US is under threat, warns Washington overseas investment group', *The Guardian*. Available at: www.guardian.co.uk/business/2010/jul/14/british-companies-reputation-threat-us.

Tharp, P. (2010) *Stormy weather: BP's stock hits new low*. Available online: www.nypost.com/p/news/business/stormy_weather_bp_stock_hits_new_R9j0pMVMYMpgrQodvaymOP.

United Nations (1994) *Human Development Report*. Oxford: Oxford University Press.

Walsh, B. (2010) *With Oil Spill (and Blame) Spreading, Obama Will Visit Gulf*. Available online: www.time.com/time/health/article/0,8599,1986323,00.html.

White House (2010) *BP Oil Well Effectively Dead*. Available at: www.wwltv.com/news/Blown-out-BP-oil-well-finally-killed–103237684.html.

Young, W. and Montgomery, R. (1998) 'Crisis management and its impact on destination marketing', *Journal of Convention and Exhibition Management* 1(1), 3–18.

48

Adaptive co-management

A new frontier for nature-based tourism

Ryan Plummer, Samantha Stone-Jovicich and Erin Bohensky

Introduction

A re-orientation is under way in how environmental challenges should be approached and understood. Prompting this shift is the proliferation of environmental challenges, severity of ecosystem changes and widespread realisation of the limitations associated with conventional command and control approaches. Although these past approaches were relatively successful at addressing definable or point sources of issues such as pollution, there are increasing concerns about compliance and enforcement, growing conflicts pertaining to regulatory policies, and ineffectiveness in addressing 'wicked' problems characterised by complexity and uncertainty (Holling and Meffe 1996; Kettl 2002).

The shift from 'government' to 'governance' is a phenomenon under way in various spheres of social life (e.g. nation-states, corporate spaces, policy making with international donors), and essentially concerns critical questions about the roles and relationships of actors in steering or guiding societal aims (Jessop 1998; Stoker 1998). Environmental governance is a more specific form that typically has the normative dimension of sustainability (Hempel 1996) and 'refers to the set of regulatory processes, mechanisms and organizations through which political actors influence environmental actions and outcomes' (Lemos and Agrawal 2006: 298). Common key ideas present in the environmental governance literature include: the facilitation of collective action via novel institutions and incentives; the imperative of involving non–state actors and different types of knowledge; and, the way in which it occurs in complex contexts and links across scales (de Loë *et al.* 2010).

The manner in which the environment is understood, as well as our relationship to it, is also being understood in new ways. The nature evolving worldview highlights: unpredictable and abrupt dynamics; self organisation and emergence; and discontinuities and surprises from non-linear relationships (Levin 1999; Holling *et al.* 2002; Berkes *et al.* 2003). Complex systems theory juxtaposes the mechanistic and linear machine metaphor with that of an organism responding to feedback (Capra 1982; Innes and Booher 1999). The applicability of complex systems theory to natural and social systems, as well as the dynamic inter-relationship between them, has resulted in considerable attention being directed at understanding transformative changes in adaptive systems from an integrative perspective. Emphasis has also been put on the coupled integrated concept of social-ecological systems and social-ecological linkages (Berkes *et al.* 2003). In this context of social-ecological systems, resilience involves the amount of change a system can undergo, the extent to which it is capable of self-organisation and the capacity to learn and adapt (Folke 2006). Sustainability, consequently, is re-oriented as a dynamic ongoing process that requires adaptive capacity to address change (Berkes *et al.* 2003; Gunderson *et al.* 2002).

Set against this backdrop, the idealised models of environmental governance (e.g. state, community, market) are giving way to hybridisation such as co-management, public–private partnerships, and private–social partnerships (Lemos and Agrawal 2006). At the same time, the complex systems perspective necessitates governance to be adaptive and multilevel (Folke *et al.* 2002; Duit and Galaz 2008). Adaptive co-management is gaining considerable attention as a multilevel governance strategy that explicitly embraces the spirit of adaptive management. In this chapter we describe adaptive co-management, appraise its potential application in tourism and explore how it could be applied to the iconic nature tourism destination of the Great Barrier Reef, Australia.

What is adaptive co-management?

The precise origins of the term adaptive co-management (synonym adaptive collaborative management) are unclear, as it appears to have materialised independently in two places; the term appeared in a project initiated in 1997 by the Center for International Forestry Research (CIFOR) to emphasise the social context of adaptive management as well as more broadly in the co-management scholarship to signal new directions in line with complex systems thinking and social-ecological resilience (Plummer and Armitage 2007a). In responding to the transitions concerning governance and complex systems thinking outlined in the introductory section, adaptive co-management specifically brings together the collaborative management and adaptive management narratives (Berkes *et al.* 2007; Plummer and Armitage 2007a; Armitage *et al.* 2009). As a result of combining and building upon these narratives, a distinct approach emerges that 'creates an "adaptive dance"' between resilience and change with the potential to sustain complex social-ecological systems (Olsson *et al.* 2004: 87).

In one of the initial CIFOR publications on the subject, Ruitenbeek and Cartier (2001) strongly cautioned that it contravenes the spirit of adaptive co-management to seek a single definition via reductionism. With this caveat, adaptive co-management is described as a 'process by which institutional arrangements and ecological knowledge are tested and revised in a dynamic, ongoing, self-organized process of trial and error' (Folke *et al.* 2002: 20). It is depicted as a governance system consisting of a network of heterogeneous actors who interact across scale (Folke *et al.* 2002; Olsson *et al.* 2004; Fabricius *et al.* 2007; Plummer 2009). Unlike conventional approaches, 'adaptive co-management systems are flexible community-based systems of resource management tailored to specific places and situations and supported by, and working with, various organizations at different levels' (Olsson *et al.* 2004: 75).

As adaptive co-management is unique from either collaborative management or adaptive management, its nuances are usefully clarified by illuminating its attributes or features. Plummer and Fennell (2009) recently synthesised these from the adaptive co-management literature broadly and by drawing extensively from the Plummer and Armitage (2007a) Delphi study and workshop that aimed to assess how the quickly developing concept of adaptive co-management was being understood. Attributes of adaptive co-management include:

- pluralism and communication. Actors from diverse spheres of society (and at multiple levels) and who have varying principal interests enter into a process to generate shared understanding of an issue or problem. This process is grounded in communication and negotiation. Conflict is viewed as an opportunity;

- shared decision-making and authority. Transactive decision-making is employed as a basis for achieving decisions. Multiple sources of knowledge are acknowledged. Authority (power) is shared in some configuration among the actors involved;
- linkages, levels and autonomy. Actors are connected or linked both within levels (i.e. a community) and across scales (i.e. community, provincial, national). Despite shared interests and commitments, actor autonomy is appropriate at multiple levels. Institutional arrangements therefore encompass multiple levels as well as retain flexibility;
- learning and adaptation. Actions and policies are considered experiments. Feedback provides opportunities for social learning in which outcomes are collectively reflected on and modifications to future initiatives are based. Learning may concern routines, values and policies, and/or critical questions of the underlying governance systems; referred to as multiple-loop learning. Capacity to change and adapt develops as trust and knowledge accumulates in the collective social memory (Plummer and Fennell 2009: 6–7).

The intense interest in adaptive co-management has led to a proliferation of literature on the topic. In many instances these are descriptive accounts of applying adaptive co-management to a resource or environmental issues (e.g. fisheries, forestry, wetlands, climate change, protected areas) or to a particular location. As the adaptive co-management scholarship matures, associated investigations are probing new boundaries. Armitage *et al.* (2009) recently described these as five thematic areas: institutions, incentives and governance; learning through complexity; power asymmetries; assessment; and linking to policy. Plummer (2009) has synthesised associated literature regarding analytical and causal models to gain insights into understanding of the adaptive co-management process as well as the influential exogenous and endogenous variables. Within the adaptive co-management literature, particular attention and effort appears to be directed at the issues of: learning and knowledge (e.g. Armitage *et al.* 2008; Berkes 2009; Cundill and Fabricius 2009); social networks and bridging (e.g. Bodin *et al.* 2006; Olsson *et al.* 2007; Hahn *et al.* 2008); power, ethics and culture (e.g. Marschke and Nong 2003; Nadasdy 2007; Fennell Plummer and Marschke 2008); and evaluation and monitoring (e.g. Plummer and Armitage 2007b; Cundill and Fabricius 2010).

The potential for adaptive co-management in tourism?

The re-orientations outlined in the introductory remarks are gaining traction in tourism. Shifting towards novel governance arrangements in tourism is partially a response to limited or declining capabilities/budgets by governments (Hall 2000), but also to the possible strategic advances they offer, such as pooling resources and realising competitive advantages (Jamal and Getz 1995; Bramwell and Lane 2000a; Brinkerhoff 2002; Plummer and Fennell 2009). The concept of 'working together', inclusive of partnerships, collaboration, co-management, is being increasingly put forward with regards to nature-based and/or sustainable tourism (e.g. Bramwell and Lane 2000a; Plummer *et al.* 2006). Although to a much lesser extent, there is some evidence of interest among tourism researchers to apply complex adaptive systems thinking (Fennell 2004; Farrell and Twining-Ward 2004, 2005; Lemelin 2005). Farrell and Twining-Ward (2004: 274) argue that complex studies 'is of great interest and relevance to contemporary tourism studies'.

Movement in the tourism field in the aforementioned directions prompted Plummer and Fennell (2009) to explore the prospects for adaptive co-management in a special issue of the *Journal of Sustainable Tourism* on tourism and protected area partnerships. The following appraisal is from their work as it represents the only attempt we are aware of thus far to explore the potential for adaptive co-management in tourism. Their assessment employs the policy appraisal framework by Brewer (1973) and Lee (1999) and draws attention to conceptual, technical, ethical and pragmatic aspects. The following points summarise their appraisal along these key aspects.

- *Conceptual.* Adaptive co-management is conceptually consistent with the transitions towards governance and complex systems thinking as set forth in the introduction. As established above, the shift toward collaborative forms of governance is well established and interest in complex adaptive systems is nascent in nature-oriented tourism. Therefore, adaptive co-management appears to be a sound and sensible idea. For example, Jamal's work (Jamal 2004; Jamal *et al.* 2002) in Banff National Park, Canada, is closely conceptually aligned with adaptive co-management. However, caution should be exercised that tourism may be reticent as much of the discourse in sustainable tourism has occurred in isolation and has resulted in an overly simplistic and inflexible paradigm (Hunter 1997).

- *Technical.* Translating adaptive co-management into policy and practice, or making it actionable, is identified as a general challenge by Berkes (2007). An ongoing challenge in tourism specifically is co-ordinating policy at multiple scales and with competing interests (Fennell 2004; Dredge 2006). Forging horizontal and vertical linkages and establishing routine interactions are anticipated obstacles. Learning from early experiences in environmental management offers guidance as adaptive co-management can be fostered or enabled by: having rewards for pluralistic participation; creating opportunities for multilevel learning; creating incentives for flexible institutional arrangements; and providing space for experimentation (Berkes *et al.* 2007; Armitage *et al.* 2009).

- *Ethical.* Although the integrity of adaptive co-management is often implicitly aligned with the principles of good governance (see Folke *et al.* 2005; Lebel *et al.* 2006), early evidence suggests that it is not exempt from institutional and individual power struggles (Gunderson 2003) as well as larger socio-political interests (Nadasdy 2007). Fennell *et al.* (2008) have argued that ethical probing is thus necessary and exploration of this question using the case of Cambodia, revealed potential pitfalls and possibilities for it to be a governance strategy that is good, right and authentic.

- *Pragmatic.* Adaptive co-management is a relatively new idea and its explicit application in the context of tourism is nascent. Preliminary experiences are accruing in several social-ecological systems (e.g. fishery, forestry, wetlands and rivers) and when combined with conceptual inquires offer insights into whether adaptive co-management actually works. It is receiving considerable attention for its potential to foster resilience, build adaptive capacity and pursue sustainable trajectories. Armitage *et al.* (2009) suggest ten conditions for success including: well-defined resource systems; small-scale resource use contexts; reasonably clear property rights; and key leaders. It is also clear that 'adaptive co-management is not a governance panacea, and will not be appropriate in all cases' (Armitage *et al.* 2008: 100). Some resource dilemmas will overwhelm such novel institutional arrangements, for example situations where resource stocks are not fixed to a particular place (Armitage *et al.* 2009). Other examples of barriers include: an unwillingness to share power, insufficient resources and capacities, and entrenched social dynamics (Plummer and Armitage 2007a). Contemplating success presupposes that it is discernable, measurable and agreed-on by those involved. These presumptions are being challenged and the need for better evaluative metrics is identified in the tourism context concerning collaboration (see Bramwell and Lane 2000b), as well as specifically in the adaptive co-management literature (e.g. Plummer and Armitage 2007b; Cundill and Fabricius 2010).

Probing the possible application of adaptive co-management to the Great Barrier Reef

Australia's Great Barrier Reef (GBR) is a nationally and internationally significant area with outstanding natural, social, cultural and economic values. Declared a Marine Park in 1975 and listed as a World Heritage Area in 1981, the GBR is a major tourist attraction. Despite its protected status, it faces considerable pressures including overharvesting of marine resources, water quality decline from land-use in adjacent coastal catchments and climate change (Hughes *et al.* 2007; Johnson and Marshall 2007; GBRMPA 2009a). As the biggest commercial user of the Marine Park, the tourism industry has long been recognised as a critical partner in helping protect the GBR (Chadwick 2004a, 2004b, 2005). Since the 1980s, the government agency overseeing the management of the Marine Park, the Great Barrier Reef Marine Park Authority (GBRMPA), has aimed to develop a strong partnership with the tourism industry to promote ecologically sustainable tourism and to assist in the collaborative management of the Marine Park. As this partnership has evolved, so has its governance structure, from one largely led by GBRMPA to a more inclusive and heterogeneous network of stakeholders. In the case study we explore the possible application of adaptive co-management in sustainable tourism in the GBR as a means to achieve more desirable outcomes for the Marine Park. The case is undertaken as a desktop exercise to generate some preliminary reflections. Plummer and Fennell's (2009) schema (Figure 48.1) is used to guide the exploration. It is important to acknowledge that adaptive co-management in 'reality' is a participatory process of joint analysis and collective problem-solving. Therefore, as a desktop study, limited insights are offered in particular to the latter steps of the schema.

The potential for adaptive co-management in sustainable tourism in the GBR

1. Defining the GBR socio-ecological system

The GBR Marine Park (348,000 km^2) extends some 2,300 km along the coast of Queensland in Australia (see Figure 48.2). It is home to one of the largest and most diverse coral reef ecosystems in the world. As a federal multiple-use marine park, it is co-managed by a partnership between the Australian government (GBRMPA) and the Queensland government (Queensland Parks and Wildlife Services – QPWS). Tourism and recreational use of the Marine Park is one of four critical issues managed by GBRMPA (GBRMPA 2011a).

The tourism industry in the GBR has a long history with cruises to Green Island, off the coast of Cairns, first organised in the 1890s (GBRMPA 2009a). Since then, tourism has grown to become the largest commercial activity in the Marine Park, contributing over A$6 billion to the national economy (Oxford Economics 2009) and supporting approximately 50,000 jobs (Access Economics 2008). Each year, roughly 1.9 million people visit the Reef as tourists. However, geographically, over 85 per cent of tourists go to the offshore Cairns/Port Douglas and Whitsunday areas, which, combined, comprise an area of approximately 7 per cent of the Marine Park (Harriott 2002). In early 2009, there were approximately 700 tourist operators and 1,500 tour vessels (including small sailing vessels, super-yachts, large catamarans and cruise ships) and aircraft permitted to operate in the Marine Park (GBRMPA 2009b). The 10 largest operations serviced 35 per cent of tourists in 2008 (GBRMPA 2009b).

2. Mapping management tasks and problems to be solved

The principal focus of management of the GBR Marine Park, and GBRMPA, is balancing conservation and multiple uses for recreational and commercial purposes, as set out by the *Great*

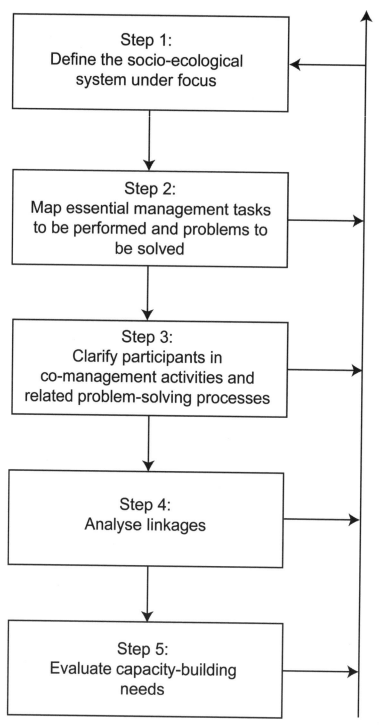

Figure 48.1 The sustainable tourism co-management process (Plummer and Fennell 2009: 10)

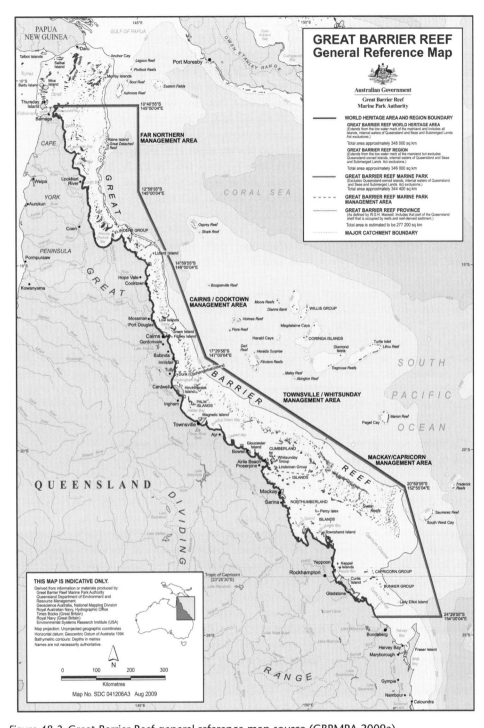

Figure 48.2 Great Barrier Reef general reference map source (GBRMPA 2009a)

Barrier Reef Marine Park Act (1975). In the case of tourism in the GBR, this entails providing a range of tourism and other recreational opportunities while minimising environmental impacts (GBRMPA 2011a). Under the 1975 Act, a Zoning Plan provides the broad framework within which all management decisions and tasks are defined. These have to meet the management objectives for each of the seven zone types (which range from preservation to 'general use'). For intensively used, or particularly vulnerable, Marine Park areas more detailed site-specific plans of management are required (Hassal *et al.* 2006). GBRMPA is the principal agency responsible for developing and implementing all management decisions. Users of the Marine Park, including the tourism industry, are regularly consulted and provide input into management decisions.

A myriad of biophysical and socio-economic pressures face the GBR. Among the most significant biophysical threats is climate change and its impacts on the coral reef ecosystem, as well as on habitats such as mangroves and islands (Marshall and Schuttenberg 2006; Marshall and Johnson 2007; Johnson and Marshall 2007). One specific problem, viewed as threatening key tourism sites on the Reef, has been outbreaks of the crown-of-thorns starfish. Other problems and threats facing the GRB include overfishing, declining water quality, cyclones, shipping impacts, and downstream effects from coastal development and urban growth (Hassal *et al.* 2006; Hughes *et al.* 2007; GBRMPA 2009a).

Ecological impacts from the tourism industry on the Marine Park are considered, overall, to be low (Harriott 2002; GBRMPA 2009a). In the highly visited areas of the Cairns/Port and Whitsundays regions, however, there are concerns regarding the potential negative impacts of tourism operations. These include coastal tourism development; island-based tourism infrastructure (marinas, sewage discharge, construction); marine-based tourism infrastructure (pontoons, moorings, fish feeding); boat-induced damage (anchoring, ship grounding, litter, waste discharge); and damage incurred from water-based activities (diving, snorkelling, reef walking, fishing) (Kenchington 1991; Harriott 2002; GBRMPA 2009a).

3. Clarifying participants in co-management activities and related problem-solving processes

The tourism industry has limited capacity to influence, much less solve, the majority of the problems threatening the Marine Park. None the less, it is considered by GBRMPA to be one of the key collaborators in helping ensure a 'healthy reef' (GBRMPA 2011a). The management arrangement between GBRMPA and the tourism industry combines a strong industry–government partnership with a comprehensive set of policies, statutory plans and guidelines (Hassal *et al.* 2006). Responsibilities, rights and roles are defined within a set of management tools and processes developed by GBRMPA, in conjunction with QPWS (GBRMPA 2011a). All levels of the tourism industry, including operators, sector associations and the peak marine tourism body (the Association of Marine Park Tourism Operators – AMPTO) are regularly consulted by GBRMPA on tourism management issues (Kenchington 1991; GBRMPA 2011a). In addition, GBRMPA set up in 2000 the Tourism and Recreation Reef Advisory Committee (TRRAC) and in 2006 the Tourism Climate Change Action Group (TCCAG), both of which serve as advisory committees to GBRMPA.

The tourism industry's contribution to tourism-related management decisions in the Marine Park ranges greatly. On the one hand, all tourist programmes and operations in the Marine Park require permits, which are administered by GBRMPA. This permit system provides a mechanism for the government to control and limit tourism activities, particularly in highly visited tourist sites (Kenchington 1991). On the other hand, the tourism industry is actively involved, in partnership with GBRMPA, in the development of major tourism activities (for example, see the online handbook *Onboard: The Tourism Operator's Handbook for the Great Barrier Reef)* (Chadwick 2005; GBRMPA 2011b). Tourism operators also work with GBRMPA as 'reef stewards' by participating in volunteer reef monitoring programmes, including monitoring compliance with the 'no-take' zones. With financial assistance from the government, tourist operators also assist in controlling crown-of-thorns starfish outbreaks at major tourism sites. Another way the tourism industry contributes to the management of the Marine Park is through the Environmental Management Charge, a fee of A$4.50 per day/per tourist, which in 2004/2005 contributed to 20 per cent of the budget of GBRMPA (Hassal *et al.* 2006).

The partnership between GBRMPA and the tourism industry has evolved and expanded over time. In 2006, the Tourism Climate Change Action Group (TCCAG) was formed. The TCCAG, hosted by GBRMPA, acts as a forum to discuss and provide guidance on climate change-related actions the tourism industry can take to help protect and improve the health and resilience of the Reef. GBRMPA and TCCAG have drafted a Climate Change Strategy (GBRMPA 2009b) intended to be a living document, adjusted as strategies are implemented. In addition, since 2008, GBRMPA has been working with Aboriginal and Torres Strait Islander Traditional Owners to manage 'sea country' (i.e. the Marine Park). Administered by GBRMPA, the five-year $10 million Reef Rescue Indigenous Land and Sea Country Partnership Program includes tourism activities undertaken by Traditional Owners (GBRMPA 2011c).

4. Analysing linkages

Although decision-making remains relatively centralised at the government level, GBRMPA has aimed to build and sustain a collaborative and adaptive approach to sustainable tourism management (Chadwick 2005). Public forums and discussions, and formal partnerships (e.g. TRRAC and TCCAG), provide the vertical ties between the tourism industry and government agencies (in particular, GBRMPA's Tourism and Recreation Group). These formal structures and processes also connect a wide range of tourism organisations, businesses and individuals operating at different scales. This includes national- and state-level operators and industry associations (e.g. Ecotourism Australia, Association of Marine Park Tourism Operators and the Queensland Tourism Industry Council), small local operators and Traditional Owners engaged in tourism initiatives.

These horizontal and vertical networks have been very effective for information sharing, reflection and feedback, and conflict resolution. Although the tourism industry can provide suggestions on proposed changes to legislation, regulations and policies, such as the Zoning Plan, which define which areas of the reef are accessible for use by tourism operators, the final decision rests with the legislature. This is to protect the Act (1975) from being changed by executive government or by the influence of powerful interest groups (Kenchington 1991). There is more room for joint problem-solving and decision-making at the level of site-specific management plans, guidelines, codes of best practice, and strategies to address critical problems such as climate change and crown-of-thorns starfish outbreaks. For example, site-specific reef use management plans, which outline what tourism activities and infrastructure can be developed in specific Marine Park sites, can be amended to reflect changing management arrangements as long as they are consistent with the Zoning Plan (Hassal *et al.* 2006; GBRMPA 2009a). However, they can be reviewed and altered by GBRMPA at any time (Hassal *et al.* 2006).

5. Evaluating capacity-building needs

It is challenging to identify and evaluate capacity-building needs *a priori* because these requirements emerge through the iterative and participatory process of adaptive co-management.

However, GBRMPA recognises the need for proper alignment and co-ordination of projects, programmes and actions proposed by government, research institutions and tourism industry partners as a means to maximise investments and ensure positive outcomes for both the reef and tourism operators. This requires careful consideration of both formal and informal structures and processes for bridging these different groups' interests and capacities and for co-ordinating actions. In addition, zoning and plans of management are viewed by the tourism industry as resource-intensive to prepare and amend, poorly understood and difficult to administer (TRRAC 2002). A 'Co-operative Framework', proposed by TRRAC, could provide a guideline for identifying capacity-building needs in this area. Moreover, GBRMPA has been working towards supporting a diversity of tourism operators and activities, including culturally sensitive tourism products with Traditional Owners (Chadwick 2005). Some considerable challenges are immediately apparent with working with smaller operators, who vary considerably in their capacity to effectively engage with GBRMPA in the negotiation and implementation of co-management agreements. Language, concepts, rules and procedures are all elements of capacity that require careful consideration. Conversely, time and effort needs to be expended on educating government officials about the perspectives, values, knowledge and needs of Traditional Owners and other small tourism operators.

6. Prescribing remedies

In Plummer and Fennell's (2009) schema, the final step involves communicating results of the iterative and participatory process of adaptive co-management to enhance policy making and resolve problems. Given the explorative nature of this case, in this final section we highlight some key considerations illuminated through the desktop review for the possibility of applying adaptive co-management.

Issues related to linkages, levels and autonomy, and to pluralism and communication

Although climate change, overfishing and other problems facing the GBR Marine Park manifest themselves at the 'local' scale (i.e. the Marine Park), they are the result of multi- and cross-scale pressures, processes and actions. This highlights the need for considering management tasks, and supporting governance arrangements, that span multiple scales and multiple actors, of which the tourism industry is just one. This presents a highly complex challenge pragmatically, politically and ethically. A diversity of actors have an interest or stake in the GBR and its resources, from commercial enterprises to recreational fishers and Traditional Owners. Some operate at the international scale, others at a local scale; some have a longstanding cultural attachment to the GBR, whereas others have a significant economic stake in specific resources; and some have the capacity and resources to effectively engage with GBRMPA, whereas others are constrained. Thus, the various pressures on the Marine Park impact these groups in different ways and may require a range of distinct co-management strategies. Pressures on the Marine Park, and relevant actors, will inevitably shift and change over time highlighting the need to also develop structures and processes that allow for regularly updating information, shared reflection and adjustment of co-management arrangements.

Issues related to shared decision-making and authority

Given the extensive geographical scale of the Marine Park, it is important to have matching institutions and decision-making processes (i.e. a large governance structure such as GBRMPA)

(Bohensky and Lynam 2005). One challenge facing GBRMPA is ensuring the proper implementation of the 1975 Act and associated regulations, while at the same time opening up spaces for joint problem-solving, decision-making and learning with the tourism industry and other stakeholders. This fine-tuned blend of top-down and bottom-up management is critical. Experiences in other parts of the world have shown that co-management set out on government terms and conditions led to resistance and conflict (Stevenson 2006). Given the relative lack of flexibility in the 1975 Act and associated policies and regulations, aiming for co-management arrangements at finer scales of management (both formal arrangements, such as site-specific management plans and guidelines and informal agreements and working relationships) may be more appropriate and achievable, at least in the short term.

Issues related to learning and adaptation

As in the case of most government organisations, GBRMPA is a large and complex institution with legal and political responsibilities to ensure the protection of a highly valued marine ecosystem. As such, experimenting with, learning from and adapting co-management strategies is not an easy task. None the less, GBRMPA has in the past achieved significant transformations in its governance focus and structure through internal reorganisation and management innovation (Olsson *et al.* 2008).

Conclusions

Adaptive co-management is a novel governance strategy, which incorporates collaboration, multilevel linkages, institutional flexibility, and experimentation and learning. Ultimately, it strives to foster sustainability – understood as an ongoing process in which the social-ecological resilience is paramount. Knowledge and experiences associated with adaptive co-management are accumulating quickly and, as presented in the second part of this chapter, are coalescing in several aspects. At the same time, it is important to re-iterate that adaptive co-management is not a governance panacea and is confronted with several challenges.

Reflecting on the prospects of adaptive co-management for tourism offered by Plummer and Fennell (2009), these promises and pitfalls are illuminated. Nature-based or sustainable tourism is characterised as a complex problem domain in which collaboration is being pursued as a logical course. In some circumstances adaptive co-management may provide an area to embrace uncertainty and coincide with the principles of good governance, whereas in others it may further power imbalances. Although experience in tourism is nascent, it appears much can be learned with regards to enabling conditions and barriers from the social-ecological systems literature.

In the GBR, adaptive co-management involving the tourism industry has potential as a governance arrangement for helping protect the ecological, social, cultural and economic values of the GBR. However, the processes of assessing, designing, implementing and adapting a co-management arrangement would need to take into consideration a number of important factors. First, given the diversity within the tourism industry as well as among the broader range of groups with a stake or interest in the Marine Park, co-management strategies must be sensitive to and be able to balance the needs of multiple stakeholders. Second, co-management arrangements must be flexible enough to deal with the volatility of the tourism industry, resulting from pressures and shocks at multiple scales such as cyclones and the global financial crisis (Biggs 2011) that affect tourist perceptions and demand. The historical ability of the GBRMPA to navigate governance transformations positions it well to realise future opportunities from adaptive co-management strategies.

References

Access Economics (2008) *Economic Contribution of the Great Barrier Reef Marine Park 2006–07*. Canberra: Access Economics Pty Limited.

Armitage, D., Marschke, M. and Plummer, R. (2008) 'Adaptive Co-Management and the Paradox of Learning', *Global Environmental Change* 18(1), 86–98.

Armitage, D.R., Plummer, R., Berkes, F., Arthur, R.I., Charles, A.T., Davidson-Hunt, I., Diduck, A.P., Doubleday, N.C., Johnson, D.S., Marschke, M., McConney, P., Pinkerton, E.W. and Wollenberg, E. K. (2009) 'Adaptive Co-Management for Social–Ecological Complexity', *Frontiers in Ecology and the Environment* 7(2), 95–102.

Berkes, F. (2007) 'Adaptive Co-Management and Complexity: Exploring the Many Faces of Co-Management' in D. Armitage, F. Berkes and N. Doubleday (eds) *Adaptive Co-Management: Collaboration, Learning and Multi-level Governance*. Vancouver: UBC Press, 19–38.

——(2009) 'Evolution of Co-Management: Role of Knowledge Generation, Bridging Organizations and Social Learning', *Journal of Environmental Management* 90(5), 1692–702.

Berkes, F., Armitage, D. and Doubleday, N. (2007) 'Synthesis: Adapting, Innovating, Evolving' in D. Armitage, F. Berkes and N. Doubleday (eds) *Adaptive Co-Management. Collaboration, Learning, and Multi-Level Governance*. Vancouver: University of British Columbia Press, 308–27.

Berkes, F., Colding, J. and Folke, C. (2003) 'Introduction', in F. Berkes, J. Colding and C. Folke (eds) *Navigating Social-Ecological Systems*. Cambridge: Cambridge University Press, 1–30.

Biggs, D. (2011) 'Understanding Resilience in a Vulnerable Industry: The Case of Reef Tourism in Australia', *Ecology and Society* 16(1), 30. Available at: www.ecologyandsociety.org/vol16/iss1/art30/ (accessed 3 February 2011).

Bodin, Ö., Crona, B. and Ernstson, H. (2006) 'Social Networks in Natural Resource Management: What is There to Learn From a Structural Perspective?', *Ecology and Society* 11(2), 2. Available at: www.ecologyandsociety.org/vol11/iss2/resp2/ (accessed 17 August 2010).

Bohensky, E. and Lynam, T. (2005) 'Evaluating Responses in Complex Adaptive Systems: Insights on Water Management From the Southern African Millennium Ecosystem Assessment (SAfMA)', *Ecology and Society* 10(1). Available at: www.ecologyandsociety.org/vol10/iss1/art11/ (accessed 3 August 2010).

Bramwell, B. and Lane, B. (2000a) 'Collaboration and Partnerships in Tourism Planning', in B. Bramwell and B. Lane (eds) *Tourism Collaboration and Partnerships: Politics, Practice and Sustainability*. Clevedon: Channel View Publications, 1–19.

——(2000b) 'Collaborative Tourism Planning: Issues and Future Directions', in B. Bramwell and B. Lane (eds) *Tourism Collaboration and Partnerships: Politics, Practice and Sustainability*. Clevedon: Channel View Publications, 333–41.

Brewer, G.D. (1973) *Politicians, Bureaucrats, and the Consultant. A Critique of Urban Problem Solving*. New York: Basic Books.

Brinkerhoff, J. (2002) 'Government-Nonprofit Partnership: A Defining Framework', *Public Administration Development* 22, 19–30.

Capra, F. (1982) *The Turning Point*. Toronto: Bantam Books.

Chadwick, V. (2004a) 'Tourism: A Key partner in the Great Barrier Reef's Future', *Paper Presented 12th National Ecotourism Australia Conference*, Leura, Blue Mountains, NSW, 8–12 November 2004.

——(2004b) 'The Value of Tourism to the Great Barrier Reef's Future', *Paper presented at the Third National Conference on Tourism Futures: Wealth Creating Growth Sustaining*, Townsville, Queensland, 4–7 August 2004.

——(2005) 'Keeping the Great Barrier Reef Great: Ensuring a Sustainable Tourism Industry on the Great Barrier Reef', *Paper Presented at the 13th National Ecotourism Australia Conference*, Hobart, Tasmania, 28 November – 2 December 2005.

Cundill, G. and Fabricius, C. (2009) 'Monitoring in Adaptive Co-Management: Toward a Learning Based Approach', *Journal of Environmental Management* 90(11), 3205–11.

——(2010) 'Monitoring the Governance Dimension of Natural Resource Co-management,' *Ecology and Society* 15(1), n.p. Available at: www.ecologyandsociety.org/vol15/iss1/art15/ (accessed 2 August 2010).

Dredge, D. (2006) 'Networks, Conflict and Collaborative Communities', *Journal of Sustainable Tourism* 14 (6), 562–81.

Duit, A. and Galaz, V. (2008) 'Governing Complexity: Insights and Emerging Challenges', *Governance* 21, 311–35.

Fabricius, C., Folke, C., Cundill, G. and Schultz, L. (2007) 'Powerless Spectators, Coping Actors, and Adaptive Co-Managers: A Synthesis of the Role of Communities in Ecosystem Management', *Ecology and Society* 12(1), 29. Available at: www.ecologyandsociety.org/vol12/iss1/art29/ (accessed 7 July 2010).

Farrell, B. and Twining-Ward, L. (2005) 'Seven Steps Towards Sustainability: Tourism in the Context of New Knowledge', *Journal of Sustainable Tourism* 13(2), 109–22.

Farrell, B.H. and Twining-Ward, L. (2004) 'Reconceptualizing Tourism', *Annals of Tourism Research* 31(2), 274–95.

Fennell, D.A. (2004) Towards Interdisciplinarity in Tourism: Making a Case Through Complexity and Shared Knowledge', *Recent Advances and Research Updates* 5(1), 99–110.

Fennell, D., Plummer, R. and Marschke, M. (2008) 'Is Adaptive Co-Management Ethical?', *Journal of Environmental Management* 88(1), 62–75.

Folke, C. (2006) 'Resilience: The Emergence of a Perspective for Social–Ecological Systems Analyses', *Global Environmental Change* 16(3), 253–67.

Folke, C., Carpenter, S., Elmqvist, T., Gunderson, L., Holling, C.S., Walker, B., Bengtsson, J., Berkes, F., Colding, J., Danell, K., Falkenmark, M., Moberg, M., Gordon, L., Kaspersson, R., Kautsky, N., Kinzig, A., Levin, S. A., Mäler, K.-G., Ohlsson, L., Olsson, P., Ostrom, E., Reid, W., Rockstöm, J., Savenije, S. and Svedin, U. (2002). 'Resilience and Sustainable Development: Building Adaptive Capacity in a World of Transformations', *Report for the Swedish Environmental Advisory Council 2002*, Stockholm, Sweden: Ministry of the Environment.

Folke, C., Hahn, T., Olsson, P. and Norberg, J. (2005) 'Adaptive Governance of Social–Ecological Systems', *Annual Review of Environment and Resources* 30, 8.1–8.33.

GBRMPA (2009a) 'Great Barrier Reef Outlook Report 2009', *GBRMPA*, Townsville, Australia. Available at: www.gbrmpa.gov.au/−data/assets/pdf_file/0005/41198/OutlookReportFull.pdf (accessed 18 February 2011).

——(2009b) 'Great Barrier Reef Tourism: Climate Change Action Strategy 2009–12', *GBRMPA*, Townsville, Australia. Available at: www.gbrmpa.gov.au/−data/assets/pdf_file/0018/41085/GBRMPA_ CCActionStrategy_Full_web_version_FINAL.pdf (accessed 19 February 2011).

——(2011a) 'Tourism and Recreation Management', *GBRMPA website*. Available at: www.gbrmpa.gov. au/corp_site/key_issues/tourism/management (accessed 16 February 2011).

——(2011b) 'Onboard: The Tourism Operator's Handbook for the Great Barrier Reef,' *GBRMPA website*. Available at: www.gbrmpa.gov.au/onboard (accessed 16 February 2011).

——(2011c) 'Indigenous Partnerships in the Great Barrier Reef,' *GBRMPA website*. Available at: www. gbrmpa.gov.au/corp_site/key_issues/conservation/indigenous_partnerships (accessed 17 February 2011).

Great Barrier Reef Marine Park Act (1975) *Office of Legislative Drafting and Publishing, Attorney-General's Department*. Canberra, Australia. Available at: www.comlaw.gov.au/Details/C2010C00166/Download (accessed 20 March 2011).

Gunderson, L. (2003) 'Adaptive Dancing: Interactions Between Social Resilience and Ecological Crises', in F. Berkes, J. Colding and C. Folke (eds) *Navigating Social-Ecological Systems*. Cambridge: Cambridge University Press, 33–52.

Gunderson, L.H., Holling, C.S. and Peterson, G.D. (2002) 'Surprises and Sustainability', in L.H. Gunderson and C.S. Holling (eds) *Panarchy*. Washington, DC: Island Press, 315–33.

Hahn, T., Schultz, L., Folke, C. and Olsson, P. (2008) 'Social Networks as Sources of Resilience in Social-Ecological Systems', in J. Norberg and G.S. Cumming (eds) *Complexity Theory for a Sustainable Future*. New York: Columbia University Press, 119–48.

Hall, C.M. (2000) 'Tourism, National Parks and Aboriginal Peoples', in R.W. Butler and S.W. Boyd (eds) *Tourism and National Parks: Issues and Implications*. New York: John Wiley and Sons, 57–71.

Harriot, V.J. (2002) 'Marine Tourism Impacts and Their Management on the Great Barrier Reef', *CRC Reef Research Centre Technical Report No 46*. Townsville, CRC Reef Research Centre. Available at: www.reef.crc.org.au/publications/techreport/pdf/Harriott46.pdf (accessed 29 February 2011).

Hassal, J., Skeat, H., Smith, A. and Mulqueeny, L. (2006) 'Framework and Partnerships: Ensuring Sustainable Marine Tourism in the Great Barrier Reef', Paper Presented at the Coast to Coast 2006, Melbourne, Victoria, 22–25 May 2006.

Hempel, L.C. (1996) *Environmental Governance: the Global Challenge*. Washington, DC: Island Press.

Holling, C.S., Gunderson, L.H. and Peterson, G.D. (2002) 'Sustainability and Panarchies', in L.H. Gunderson and C.S. Holling (eds) *Panarchy*. Washington, DC: Island Press, 63–102.

Holling, C.S. and Meffe, G.K. (1996) 'Command and Control and the Pathology of Natural Resource Management', *Conservation Biology* 10(2), 328–37.

Hughes, T., Rodrigues, M.J., Bellwood, D.R., Ceccarelli, D., Hoegh-Guldberg, O., McCook, L., Moltschaniwskyj, N., Pratchett, M.S., Steneck, R.S. and Willis, B. (2007) 'Phase Shifts, Herbivory, and the Resilience of Coral Reefs to Climate Change', *Current Biology* 17, 360–5.

Hunter, C. (1997) 'Sustainable Tourism as an Adaptive Paradigm', *Annals of Tourism Research* 24(4), 850–67.

Innes, J.E. and Booher, D.E. (1999) 'Consensus Building and Complex Adaptive Systems,' *American Planning Association Journal* 65(4), 412–23.

Jamal. T. (2004) 'Conflict in Natural Areas Destinations: A Critique of Representation and 'Interest' in Participatory Processes', *Tourism Geographies* 6(3), 352–79.

Jamal, T., Stein, S.M. and Harper, T.L. (2002) 'Beyond Labels: Pragmatic Planning in Multi-Stakeholder Tourism-Environmental Conflicts', *Journal of Planning Education and Research* 22, 164–77.

Jamal, T.B. and Getz, D. (1995) 'Collaboration Theory and Community Tourism Planning', *Annals of Tourism Research* 22 (1), 186–204.

Jessop, B. (1998) 'The Rise of Governance and the Risks of Failure: The Case of Economic Development', *International Social Science Journal* 50(155), 29–45.

Johnson, J.E. and Marshall, P.A. (eds) (2007) 'Climate Change and the Great Barrier Reef: A Vulnerability Assessment', *Great Barrier Reef Marine Park Authority (GBRMPA) and Australian Green House Office,* Australia. Available at: www.gbrmpa.gov.au/corp_site/info_services/publications/misc_pub/climate_change_vulnerability_assessment/climate_change_vulnerability_assessment (accessed 3 February 2011).

Kenchington, R. (1991) 'Tourism Development in the Great Barrier Reef Marine Park', *Ocean and Shoreline Management* 15, 57–78.

Kettl, D.F. (2002) *Environmental Governance: A Report on the Next Generation of Environmental Policy.* Washington, DC: Brookings Institution Press.

Lebel, L., Anderies, J., Campbell, B., Folke, C., Hatfield-Dodds, S., Hughes, T.P. and Wilson, J. (2006) 'Governance and the Capacity to Manage Resilience in Regional Social-Ecological Systems,' *Ecology and Society* 11(1), 19. Available at: www.ecologyandsociety.org/vol11/iss1/art9/ (accessed 1 August 2010).

Lee, K.N. (1999) 'Appraising Adaptive Management', *Conservation Ecology* 3(2), 3. Available at: www.consecol.org/vol3/iss2/art3/ (accessed 28 June 2010).

Lemelin, H.R. (2005) 'Wildlife Tourism at the Edge of Chaos: Complex Interactions Between Humans and Polar Bears in Churchill, Manitoba', in F. Berkes, R. Huebert, H. Fast, M. Manseau and A. Diduck (eds) *Breaking Ice: Renewable Resource and Ocean Management in the Canadian North.* Calgary: University of Calgary Press, 183–202.

Lemos, M. C. and Agrawal, A. (2006) 'Environmental Governance', *Annual Review of Environment and Resources* 31, 297–325.

Levin, S. (1999) *Fragile Dominion.* Cambridge: Perseus Publishing.

de Loë, R.C., Armitage, D., Plummer, R., Davidson, S. and Moraru, L. (2009) 'From Government to Governance: A State-of-the-Art Review of Environmental Governance', *Final Report. Prepared for Alberta Environment, Environmental Stewardship, Environmental Relations,* Guelph, ON: Rob de Loë Consulting Services.

Marschke, M. and Nong, K. (2003) 'Adaptive Co-Management: Lessons from Coastal Cambodia', *Canadian Journal of Development Studies* 24(3), 369–83.

Marshall, P.A. and Johnson, J. (2007) 'The Great Barrier Reef and Climate Change: Vulnerability and Management Implications', *Great Barrier Reef Marine Park Authority (GBRMPA) and Australian Greenhouse Office,* Australia.

Marshall, P. A. and Schuttenberg, H. (2006) 'Reef Managers Guide to Coral Bleaching', *GBRMPA,* Townsville, Australia.

Nadasdy, P. (2007) 'Adaptive Co-Management and the Gospel of Resilience', in D. Armitage, F. Berkes and N. Doubleday (eds) *Adaptive Co-Management: Collaboration, Learning and Multilevel Governance.* Vancouver: UBC Press, 208–27.

Olsson, P., Folke, C. and Berkes, F. (2004) 'Adaptive Co-Management for Building Resilience in Social–Ecological Systems', *Environmental Management* 34, 75–90.

Olsson, P., Folke, C., Galaz, V., Hahn, T. and Schultz,L. (2007) 'Enhancing the Fit Through Adaptive Co-Management: Creating and Maintaining Bridging Functions for Matching Scales in the Kristianstads Vattenrike Biosphere Reserve Sweden', *Ecology and Society* 12(1), 28. Available at: www.ecologyandsociety.org/vol12/iss1/art28/ (accessed 1 August 2010).

Olsson, P., Folke, C. and Hughes, T.P. (2008) 'Navigating the Transition to Ecosystem-Based Management of the Great Barrier Reef, Australia', *PNAS* 105(28), 9489–94. Available at: www.pnas.org/content/105/28/9489.full.pdf+html (accessed 10 February 2011).

Oxford Economics (2009) 'Valuing the effects of Great Barrier Reef Bleaching', *Great Barrier Reef Foundation,* Newstead, Queensland, Australia. Available at: www.oxfordeconomics.com/samples/gbrfoxford.pdf (accessed 20 March 2011).

Plummer, R. (2009) 'The Adaptive Co-Management Process: An Initial Synthesis of Representative Models and Influential Variables', *Ecology and Society* 14(2), 24. Available at: www.ecologyandsociety.org/vol14/iss2/art24/ (accessed 18 June 2010).

Plummer, R. and Armitage, D.R. (2007a) 'Charting the New Territory of Adaptive Co-Management: A Delphi Study', *Ecology and Society* 12(2), 10. Available at: www.ecologyandsociety.org/vol12/iss2/art10/ (accessed 26 June 2010).

Plummer, R., and Armitage, D. (2007b) 'A Resilience-Based Framework for Evaluating Adaptive Co-Management: Linking Ecology, Economics and Society in a Complex World', *Ecological Economics* 61, 62–74.

Plummer, R. and Fennell, D. (2009) 'Managing Protected Areas for Sustainable Tourism: Prospects for Adaptive Co-Management', *Journal of Sustainable Tourism* 17(2), 149–68.

Plummer, R., Kulczycki, C. and Stacey, C. (2006) 'How are We Working Together? A Framework to Assess Collaborative Arrangements in Nature-Based Tourism', *Current Issues in Tourism* 9(6), 499–515.

Ruitenbeek, J. and Cartier, C. (2001) 'The Invisible Wand: Adaptive Co-Management as an Emergent Strategy in Complex Bio-Economic Systems', *Center for International Forestry Research Occasional Paper* 34. Available at: www.cifor.cigar.org (accessed 10 June 2010).

Stevenson, M.G. (2006) 'The Possibility of Difference: Rethinking Co-Management', *Human Organization* 65(2), 167–80.

Stoker, G. (1998) 'Governance as Theory: Five Propositions', *International Social Science Journal* 50(155), 17–28.

TRRAC (Tourism and Recreation Reef Advisory Committee) (2002) *A Co-operative Framework for the Sustainable Use and Management of Tourism and Recreation Opportunities in the Great Barrier Reef Marine Park. Proposal prepared by TRRAC for GBRMPA.* Available at: www.gbrmpa.gov.au/__data/assets/pdf_file/0020/7616/rac_tourism_framework.pdf.

49

Measurement of corporate social performance in tourism

Danuta de Grosbois

Introduction

It is widely agreed that private sector businesses are important and indispensable partners in contributing to sustainable development (Carroll and Shabana 2010). Over decades, the concept of corporate social responsibility (CSR), which captures the corporate contribution to sustainability, has evolved and grown in importance. Companies in many sectors are increasingly implementing diverse CSR practices and communicating their progress to the public and other stakeholders. However, despite significant progress made in recent years in adoption of CSR practices by business, many companies still find it difficult to choose appropriate initiatives, and even more difficult to evaluate the contribution these efforts have made. Better understanding and measurement of corporate social performance (CSP) is increasingly recognised as important both from a company's perspective and from the stakeholders' perspective. Companies are interested in finding effective ways to assess the effectiveness of their CSR initiatives in order to better manage them, improve decisions about resource allocation, and to communicate the achieved results to stakeholders in order to improve their corporate image and get recognition for their efforts. On the other hand, stakeholders increasingly want to find out about the corporations behind the brands and products they purchase, and are looking for greater transparency and accountability on their part (Lewis 2001).

A growing number of organisations, governments, academics and practitioners strongly encourage companies to develop appropriate measures and to report their environmental and social performance as an important part of their commitment to sustainable development. New standards and guidelines for non-financial reporting have been developed, such as the Global Reporting Initiative and the UN Global Compact. Governments and international organisations are undertaking efforts aimed at facilitating or, in some cases, mandating CSR disclosure, such as regulations under the European Modernization Directive. At the same time, the pressure for inter-firm comparison of environmental and social performance is gaining momentum due to market forces and direct regulation (Hooper and Greendall 2005). Given this environment, measurement of CSP is now widely recognised as a necessary element of an effective sustainability management system or CSR programme. However, despite the agreement regarding the need for and importance (both internally and externally) of measuring CSP, there is still lack of a widely agreed methodology on how to achieve it. As Carroll (2000) pointed out, CSP should be measured, because it is an important topic to business and to society; however, the real question is whether valid and reliable measures can be developed.

A number of different frameworks and recommendations have been proposed in order to facilitate CSP assessment by companies and their stakeholders. They range from measures focusing on individual impacts such as air pollution, energy consumption, waste generation or water use to comprehensive measures and frameworks addressing the overall sustainability of the company. Some of these frameworks include, among others, the Global Reporting Initiative Framework, the Measuring Impacts Framework developed by the World Business Council for Sustainable Development (WBCSD), ecological footprint, carbon footprint, sustainability indices, or diverse certification schemes and awards. The objective of this chapter is to review, compare and evaluate different measures and tools that are currently available for the tourism industry and its stakeholders for measuring CSP. The advantages and disadvantages of different assessment methods will be discussed, as well as their popularity and the difficulties with application. Finally, the chapter will highlight the current trends and challenges in measuring CSP and will provide recommendations for the tourism sector.

CSP construct

When talking about measurement of CSP or sustainability performance, it is important first to define the concept to be measured. CSR, corporate citizenship and corporate sustainability are only a few of many terms used to describe the ethical and sustainable behaviour of a company towards society and the environment. The concept itself has been defined by numerous authors and evolved significantly over the years. In the early 1960s CSR was typically seen as synonymous with a company's voluntary and philanthropic acts aiming to alleviate social ills or benefit a disadvantaged group above and beyond economic and legal obligations. This model implied that companies conduct their business unaffected by the social and environmental concerns and then make charitable donations to selected causes. Over time, CSR started to be seen as a core business activity that would transform the company's business model and its operations.

One of the most widely adopted definitions of CSR was proposed by the WBCSD at the Stakeholder Dialogue on CSR held in 1999. It states that 'CSR is the continuing commitment by businesses to behave ethically and contribute to economic development while improving the quality of life of the workforce and their families as well as the local community and society at large' (WBCSD 1999). The WBCSD further specified that CSR is an integral part of sustainable development and encompasses business contributions to its achievement. Although there are many different definitions of sustainable development in academic and industry literature, the most widely accepted is that proposed in the Brundtland Report: 'Development that meets the needs of the present without compromising the ability of future generations to meet their own needs'. Sustainable development is usually conceptualised as having three main dimensions: environment, economy and society. Consistent with this view, CSR is also often conceptualised as having the same three dimensions. In the light of the above definitions, it can be stated that CSP captures corporate contributions to sustainability, that is contributions that private companies can make to sustainable development, including economic, social and ecological dimensions. However, the question remains: what components constitute the construct of 'corporate contributions to sustainable development' and how can we measure them?

It is widely recognised that the constructs of CSR and CSP are multidimensional. One of the first conceptual models of CSP was proposed by Carroll (1979). He identified four domains of CSR: economic responsibility (companies should fulfil the institutional role of resource conversion), legal responsibility (companies should obey the law), ethical responsibility (companies should obey society's ethical guidelines) and discretionary responsibility. Carroll's model was updated by Wartick and Cochran (1985) and later by Wood (1991). Wood's model of CSP recognised three elements: principles of social responsibility (legitimacy, public responsibility and managerial discretion), processes of social responsiveness (environmental scanning, stakeholder management and issues management) and outcomes and impacts of performance (effects on people and organisations, effects on the natural and physical environments, effects on social systems and institutions). As Carroll (2000) argues, CSP should be a comprehensive assessment of a firm's social performance and not assessment of a firm's performance with respect to only one social issue (e.g. environment, minority relations, corporate giving, product safety) or one stakeholder. He recommended that CSP needs to encompass performance with respect to at least four to five stakeholder groups, that is employees, consumers, owners, community and the environment.

A number of empirical studies have attempted to adapt and operationalise different conceptual models of CSP. As a result, numerous different dimensions of CSR and CSP have been proposed in different studies. For example, Esrock and Leichty (1998) identified 13 CSR areas: fair business practices, worker health and safety, product safety, cultural diversity, environment, charity, children, education, health, volunteerism, support of the arts, civic involvement and quality of work life. Maignan and Ralston (2002) distinguished between CSR processes and stakeholder issues. The CSR processes included: philanthropic programmes, sponsorships, volunteerism, code of ethics, quality programmes, health and safety programmes and management of environmental impacts. Stakeholder issues, on the other hand, included: community (arts and culture, education, quality of life, safety, protection of the environment), customers (quality, safety), employees (equal opportunity, health and safety), shareholders (involvement in governance) and suppliers (equal opportunities and supplier safety).

In the tourism context, Holcomb et al. (2007) focused on hotels and evaluated 16 social responsibility aspects grouped into five broad themes: community (worldwide and local communities and charities; jobs for handicapped and disadvantaged; aid policy; employee volunteer), environment (environment; architectural integration of cultural heritage; guidelines for sustainability development), market place (business partner and supplier diversity; responsible gaming), vision and values (vision/mission statement; code of conduct/ethics; board conducted CSR review; independent verification), and workforce (employee diversity, family services and employee welfare programmes; child care). In another tourism-related study, Cowper-Smith and de Grosbois (2010) evaluated airlines' CSP reporting against 11 themes of CSR: emissions, waste, energy, water, biodiversity, noise, other environmental, employee well-being and engagement, diversity and social equity, community well-being, and economic prosperity. The themes were selected based on the content of the CSR reports published by companies, as well as the principles of sustainability and CSR drawn from the Global Reporting Initiative (GRI 2006) and United Nations Environmental Programme and World Tourism Organization (UNEP and WTO 2005). What the above examples show is that despite some overlap in categories between the different studies, there is a lack of an agreed list of dimensions and subdimensions of CSR and CSP. As a result, studies by different authors or in different industries are not easily comparable.

Measurement of CSP

Although there is little agreement with respect to dimensions of CSP, significant effort has been dedicated to its measurement none the less, based on different conceptual frameworks. Four major groups of methods and approaches to measurement of CSP can be identified, although it is important to note that they are related to each other and often use the same data. They include:

- *sustainability accounting frameworks and methodologies* that can be used internally by companies to measure their performance;
- *measurement-based on analysis of corporate disclosure,* which encompasses different methods of evaluating CSP based on the corporate disclosure of sustainability-related information;
- *voluntary certification schemes*, including environmental standards, ecolabels or sustainability awards;
- *composite indices* of corporate sustainability, which provide rankings of companies based on reputation evaluation or on disclosed information.

Sustainability accounting frameworks

Corporations are increasingly addressing the concept of sustainability in their accounting and reporting practice (Wiedmann *et al.* 2009). There are a number of different methodologies proposed in the accounting domain in order to assess sustainability performance of companies, including triple-bottom line, life cycle analysis, input–output analysis, footprint analysis, etc. An in-depth overview of sustainability accounting methods is provided by, among others, Lamberton (2005). The advancements in accounting frameworks for corporate sustainability are closely followed by development of reporting frameworks and regulations. However, it is important to distinguish between these two aspects, because there is often a gap between what information companies collect and assess for their use and the information they report to the general public.

One of the possible ways for companies to capture their sustainability performance is triple-bottom line (TBL) accounting. The TBL concept was derived from the definition of the sustainable development in the Brundtland Report and it requires that companies evaluate and report their performance in all three aspects of sustainability: economic, social and environmental. TBL accounting encompasses a number of different indicators from each of the three pillars of sustainability. Some versions of TBL use monetary units to measure economic, social and environmental performance, whereas others recommend a number of indicators to measure sustainability performance. The second approach is adopted, most notably, by the GRI in its sustainability reporting guidelines.

The latest version of the *GRI Sustainability Reporting Guidelines*, released in 2006, provides a comprehensive framework for the application of TBL accounting and reporting. The guidelines propose a series of performance indicators to measure economic, environmental and social dimensions, as well as a set of integrated indicators capturing multiple dimensions. Additionally, these guidelines suggest using both absolute and relative (or normalised) indicators that enable comparisons among companies (GRI 2006). An important contribution from the GRI guidelines is the development of social performance indicators covering employees, consumer and human rights, corruption and bribery.

When using traditional indicators to measure the corporate environmental and social impacts or performance, an additional challenge was identified. Although the direct impacts from a company's operations may be insignificant (low CO_2 emissions, low energy use, etc.), at the same time the company's operations may be a cause of significant impacts generated by its suppliers. In order to address this issue, businesses started to adopt a life cycle perspective. A life cycle assessment captures impacts and performance through the entire supply chain of a business and takes into account the direct impacts of the on-site processes, as well as indirect impacts embodied in the supply chains of a company. The life cycle assessment is conducted with the use of 'footprint' indicators, which capture a company's wider environmental impacts. There are three major corporate footprint indicators: the ecological footprint, the carbon footprint and the water footprint. The carbon and water footprint assessments have especially gained popularity in the recent years, although their adoption by the tourism industry is still low. The ecological footprint (Holland 2003; Barrett and Scott 2001) has also been proposed for business. The common theme of the footprint calculations is that not only on-site impacts should be considered, but also indirect impacts from upstream supply chain activities and downstream impacts (caused by the use and disposal of the product). Efforts have been undertaken to develop standards for these assessments, such as the methodologies for the carbon footprint proposed in the Greenhouse Gas (GHG) Protocol (WRI and WBCSD 2004), or the Carbon Trust standard.

The life cycle approach of footprint indicators allows for more accurate comparisons of performance by incorporating all possible indirect impacts and therefore avoiding problems related to the choice of boundaries. At the same time, however, another challenge emerges: it is necessary to assign responsibility for these indirect impacts to different organisations in a supply chain, as all of them are involved in their creation and reporting on them must avoid double-counting. A number of authors call for accounting practices that are free of boundary problems and of double-counting stating this is critical to enable comparisons and rankings of CSP in a robust and reproducible way (Wiedmann *et al.* 2009; Krajnc and Glavic 2005). The life cycle analysis and the footprint analysis have for a long time been limited to only environmental impacts and performance of companies. However, new comprehensive tools for measuring sustainability performance of organisations have also been proposed, such as the Measuring Impacts Framework developed by WBCSD.

Measurement based on analysis of the corporate disclosure

Triple-bottom line accounting, life cycle analysis and footprint analysis are all important developments in accounting practice, and improve assessment and management of CSP by companies. Companies are increasingly using them within their sustainability or environmental management systems in order to collect and process CSR data. Although companies have access to all of these data internally, in most cases they can choose how much of it to report to their stakeholders. A number of researchers and other third-party organisations have undertaken efforts to assess CSP based on information disclosed by the companies.

There has been a growth in corporate social disclosure in business over the past few decades. Interested stakeholders can learn about corporate efforts from a number of sources, including the companies themselves (through corporate websites, sustainability reports) and third-party organisations (media, NGOs, government, investment organisations). Recent research indicates that, although a growing number of companies increasingly report implementation of different sustainability-related initiatives, they are lagging when it comes to reporting their CSP. Different measures are used by different companies, the scope of the measures often changes from year to year, and many areas of impacts are not measured at all, making it hard, if not impossible, to compare performance of different companies.

Part of the problem is that there are no globally accepted international standards or regulations regarding CSR disclosure, as is the case in financial disclosure. In the USA and the EU, CSR reporting has so far been a voluntary activity, although over the last 10 years a number of countries in the EU have been experiencing a move towards non-financial mandatory disclosures. In 2003, the EU activated the European Modernization Directive, requiring all member countries to create legislation obliging companies to publish a 'balanced and comprehensive' analysis of their development and performance during the financial year. This information should include not only key financial performance indicators but also, where appropriate, non-financial indicators, including information relating to environmental and employee matters. As a result, an increasing number of member countries of the EU (such as France in 2001, Spain in 2005, Germany in 2005, Greece in 2006, Italy in 2007 and Denmark in 2009, among others) have made it mandatory for different types of companies to issue CSR-related information to the public.

Changes in legislation, growing pressure from stakeholders and realisation of the benefits that can be derived through CSR disclosure (e.g. improved company image, customer satisfaction), have resulted in a notable growth in CSR communication activities over the past 10 years as well as in the volume of research devoted to CSR reporting. The range of CSR information reported by companies has been evaluated in a number of academic studies; many focused on different tourism sectors. A number of authors have attempted to analyse the reported information in order to determine CSP scores based on the quality and extent of sustainability disclosure.

Despite the progress made with respect to CSP reporting, there is a concern about the quality and usability of the reported information. Additionally, as Igalens and Gond (2005) pointed out, assessments based on data produced and disclosed by companies themselves can be strongly biased. Researchers point out that currently available corporate environmental information is difficult to use for external evaluation and comparison (Synnestvedt 2001; Hooper and Greenall 2005) and call for disclosure standards and auditing procedures that would improve the quality and comparability of the reported information. Although a growing number of companies have third-party audit of sustainability reports, their number is still very small and the majority of reports have not been verified by any external parties. Finally, it is important not to forget that analysis of annual reports or websites will always involve more of a measurement of social 'discourse' than of CSP *per se* (Ullman 1985).

An issue that makes comparison of performance difficult is the previously mentioned lack of a universally accepted list of dimensions of CSP that should be used in such an assessment. In the majority of papers evaluating CSR reporting, a subjective list of CSR activities, policies and practices is identified, and then for each issue the companies are assigned scores of 0 if they did not address the issue or 1 if they addressed the issue (e.g. Esrock and Leichty 1998; Maignan and Ralston 2002; Mak *et al.* 2007, Holcomb *et al.* 2007). Although this approach gives the researcher and the reader some insight into the CSR reporting practice, it does not take into account that there might be many varying degrees of addressing an issue, ranging from simply stating commitment to it, to reporting performance and relevant initiatives. As a result, the extent of performance reporting by tourism industry and other sectors, is to a large extent unknown. Several recent papers have explicitly focused on performance reporting (e.g. Cowper-Smith and de Grosbois 2010; Mak *et al.* 2007).

One of the major critiques of reports as a way of assessing CSP has been the diversity of report contents and measurement methods applied by different companies. In order to overcome this challenge, reporting guidelines have been developed, aiming to provide a standard reporting framework that would make it possible to compare the performance of different companies. This approach, that is the GRI *Sustainability Reporting Guidelines*, were developed explicitly with the aim of assisting companies and their stakeholders in articulating and understanding companies' contributions to sustainable development (GRI 2002). The GRI is the result of a project of the Coalition for Environmentally Responsible Economies with the United Nations Environmental Programme, which published the first sustainability reporting guidelines in 2000 and then the second version in 2002 with the aim of assisting 'reporting organizations and their stakeholders in articulating and understanding contributions of the reporting organization to sustainable development' (GRI 2002). The GRI lists a number of areas and performance indicators that should be reported by companies. Although the GRI guidelines are highly valued and increasingly adopted across different industries, they have also been criticised for a number of shortcomings (Moneva *et al.* 2006; Wiedmann *et al.* 2009). These issues include: the socially biased focus of GRI, with over 50 per cent of performance indicators included in social category; the absence of proposals for integrated indicators; the lack of full cost accounting models; and inconsistencies and issues with the so-called boundary problem. Current reporting practices have been criticised for a lack of clear definition of entity boundaries, the lack of integrated indicators and lack of independent verification statements

Several authors investigated CSR and environmental reports published by tourism companies in order to identify CSR performance measures used and reported by these companies. For example, Hooper and Greenall (2005) focused on environmental performance indicators (EPIs) reported in the airline industry. They found that despite a wide range of indicators reported by airlines, there was a very low degree of overlap in their use: of the 118 EPIs identified, only 14 were utilised by five or more airlines. Comparability of the performance data reported by different airlines was questioned due to a number of issues: some airlines included subsidiaries in their calculations whereas others did not, different airlines used different measurement units and there were differences in the reporting time frames adopted by different airlines. Other authors focused on developing a recommended set of indicators to evaluate environmental sustainability, for example Upham and Mills (2005) proposed a measurement framework to capture environmental performance of airports.

Voluntary certification programmes and awards

Another group of methods to assess CSP encompass voluntary certification programmes and related sustainability awards. The notion of certifying a business, product or operation has been popular for several decades, initially focusing mostly on health, safety, quality and cost. According to Honey and Stewart (2002), the American Automobile Association introduced one of the first rating systems to certify overall quality and comfort of restaurants and hotels in Europe. With the growing demand for CSR, the certification schemes had expanded by the 1990s to address environmental and social issues as well (Honey and Stewart 2002). Although a number of different definitions can be found, certification process is usually defined as a process that evaluates a product, process or company for conformance against predetermined set of criteria (Toth 2002) and provides a marketable logo to companies that exceed (or claim to exceed) a specific standard (Synergy 2000). The logo allows certified businesses to demonstrate their performance to consumers. In the context of CSR, the logo should (in theory) enable customers to identify companies that have sustainable or environmentally responsible operations or a desired level of environmental and/or social performance. Certification of a business or a product is therefore often perceived and marketed as assurance of a certain desired level of environmental or sustainability performance of that company or product. In addition, a number of other benefits of certifications have been established, including: encouraging tourism enterprises to attain high environmental standards and educating tourists regarding the impacts of their tourism-related activities. Despite those benefits, a number of authors identified several concerns that may hinder the role of certification schemes in providing objective evaluation or assurance of corporate social or environmental performance. First of all, there are many different types of certification schemes that can lead to confusion and lack of understanding among customers, therefore leading to general mistrust.

According to Synergy (2000), certification programmes include ecolabelling programmes, programmes for which membership criteria are set and a membership fee is paid in return for use of a logo, self-assessed accreditation programmes, and third-party audited and externally verified accreditation programmes. In addition, there are a number of other related initiatives, such as environmental or social awards. Award schemes are not generally considered to be ecolabels, because an ecolabel is available to any applicant who meets predefined criteria, whereas an award is only available to a smaller number of applicants, selected by a competitive ranking (Buckley 2001a).

A number of studies have been devoted to tourism certification schemes, ecolabels and awards (UNEP 1998; Synergy 2000; WTO 2002; Spittler and Haak 2001). Although they showed increased popularity of these schemes (Font 2002; Buckley 2001b), they also identified a number of still unresolved challenges. The research focused on the range of programmes promoted, criteria, costs, stakeholders involved and the system through which compliance is assessed.

Despite the growth in their popularity, certification programmes have also been widely criticised as a method for assuring the desired level of CSP. The Synergy (2000) report argues that certification schemes can be misleading for the public who may not realise the distinction between commitment, process- or performance-based certification. Process-based certification focuses on implementation of management systems and policies, whereas performance-based certification focuses on using an environmental, and sometimes social and economic criteria to set goals or targets that must be achieved to receive certification (Honey and Stewart 2002).

For example, the authors identify ISO 14001 and Green Globe 21 as process-based certification schemes. What this means is that a company may achieve certification against the international ISO 14001 environmental management standard by establishing an environmental management system following the steps set out by the ISO 14001 standard. At the same time, as companies set their own targets for improvement, there is no requirement to achieve any specific environmental *performance* objectives. In practice, ISO 14001 certification indicates the presence of a management system, but does not mean that a company is sustainable or that it has better performance than another, non-certified company. Similarly, the Green Globe 21 ecolabel allows its logo to be used as soon as a company commits to undertaking the certification programme before any specific levels of performance are established. In general, in process-based schemes companies get certified once they have developed an environmental policy and set up an environmental management system, although they may still operate in an unsustainable way and their performance may be poor.

A number of authors provide a series of recommendations that could further improve certification schemes and make them more useful in assessing CSP. Their recommendations call for: certifications and awards that are given only for achievement in excess of best practice performance standards rather than for commitment to improvement (Synergy 2000); certification of sustainable (not only environmental) performance (Synergy 2000); and a potentially centralised umbrella accreditation body that oversees the creation of universal standards and increases comparability among schemes (Synergy 2000). Current efforts of this nature are undertaken, among others, by the Global Sustainable Tourism Council, which works on developing common understanding of sustainability in the tourism industry and on accreditation of certification bodies.

Synergy (2000) argues that 'only where universal *performance* levels and targets that tackle sustainability (environmental, social and economic) are specified within and by a standard, and where criteria making their attainment a prerequisite are present, can something akin to sustainability be promised by certification'. However, development of such standards is challenging, as it is extremely hard to define those universal performance targets that would have international applicability. While these approaches are being developed, it is important in the meantime for consumers and businesses to clearly understand the difference between process and performance certification.

Composite sustainability indices

There is a growing popularity of different aggregate indicators or indices of sustainability that can capture CSP of companies. They are usually based on multiple criteria for evaluation of CSP, either coming from company disclosure or from third parties (stakeholders, suppliers, etc.) Some of the most widely used indices are corporate reputation indices. They can be based on perceptions of the general public, businesspeople, students, suppliers or other stakeholders. An example of a corporate reputation index is *Fortune* magazine's reputation index rating a corporation's 'responsibility to the community and environment' (Wokutch and McKinney 1991). It is based on subjective measurement derived from surveys of people external to a company who assess the company on a 10-point scale based on eight Corporate Reputation attributes. An aggregate score is next calculated based on these eight assessments to form the overall corporate reputation score. As a measurement based on perceptual assessment, it has been criticised due to its significant subjectivity and halo effect risks (Fryxell and Wang 1994; Igalens and Gond 2005).

The second group of sustainability or environmental indices is based on more objective data, either coming from companies or from third-party organisations. Several indices have been developed for the tourism industry or specific tourism sectors, such as, for example, the Atmosfair Airline Index (Atmosfair 2011). It compares 130 of the biggest passenger airlines in the world based on their climate efficiency when transporting passengers and freight (payload). It is based on CO_2 emissions per payload kilometre, averaged over all city pairs of an airline. It uses independent and internationally established data sources, for example the International Civil Aviation Organization (ICAO).

Constructing and using composite indices requires a number of choices to be made. The aspects (dimensions) that will be considered part of the index have to be identified, indicators that are going to be included have to be chosen, a weighting scheme has to be determined (in cases when some of the dimensions are considered more important than other) and the method of aggregating data into a single index has to be developed. Composite indicators are often criticised due to the high degree of subjectivity in these required choices.

Conclusions

This chapter has provided an overview of different methods that have been applied to evaluation of CSP in business in general or in the context of the tourism industry. It is not an all-encompassing list: the methods are evolving and new ones are added continuously. An extensive review of CSP measurement methods is also provided in Wood (2010), although it does not address the tourism context. Currently, research on adoption of the different methods and their effectiveness in the tourism industry is scarce. The majority of existing studies focus only on some aspects of CSR or small samples of companies.

As new methods for assessing CSP are developed, there is a growing body of literature investigating their properties and limitations. The most challenging of these limitations that need to be overcome in order to move the field forward, include, among others, the lack of explicit definition and conceptualisation of the construct of CSR; focusing on outcomes while ignoring the process; and dealing with networks of companies. For example, with respect to focusing on outcomes and not process, Agle and Kelley (2001) and Iglens and Gond (2005) pointed out that a situation can arise when a high level of output (i.e. large donations) is achieved, but through practices that do not agree with sustainability principles, such as coercion of donors. The authors call for a comprehensive measurement of CSP that would take into account not only the outputs but also the processes that led to them. Another challenge that has to be addressed, refers to the distinction between a company and a network of companies (Korhonen 2003). Product flows, material and energy flows and the environmental and social impacts of a product change during its life cycle as it moves across the supply chain, crossing organisational and often national borders. However, it is not clear how to attribute costs and benefits to different players. These limitations still need to be overcome to develop comparable and meaningful assessments of CSP in tourism or in business in general.

References

Agle, B.R. and Kelley, P.C. (2001) 'Ensuring validity in the measurement of corporate social performance: Lessons from corporate United Way and PAC campaigns', *Journal of Business Ethics* 31, 271–84.

Atmosfair (2011) *Atmosfair Airline Index 2011. Documentation of the methodology.* Atmosfair: Berlin.

Barrett, J., and Scott, A. (2001) 'The ecological footprint: A metric for corporate sustainability', *Corporate Environmental Strategy* 8 (4), 316–25.

Buckley, R. (2001a) 'Major Issues in Tourism Ecolabelling', in X. Font and R.C. Buckley (eds). *Tourism Ecolabelling: Certification and promotion of sustainable management.* Oxford and New York: CABI Publishing.

——(2001b) 'Turnover and Trends in Tourism Ecolabels', in X. Font and R.C. Buckley (eds). *Tourism Ecolabelling: Certification and promotion of sustainable management.* Oxford and New York: CABI Publishing.

Carroll, A.B. (1979) 'A three-dimensional conceptual model of corporate social performance', *Academy of Management Review* 4, 497–505.

——(2000) 'A commentary and an overview of key questions on corporate social performance measurement', *Business & Society* 39 (4), 466–78.

Carroll, A.B., and Shabana, K.M. (2010) 'The business case for corporate social responsibility: A review of concepts, research and practice', *International Journal of Management Reviews* 12(1), 85–105.

Cowper-Smith, A., and de Grosbois, D. (2010) 'The adoption of corporate social responsibility practices in the airline industry', *Journal of Sustainable Tourism*, 1–19.

Esrock, S. and Leichty, G. (1998) 'Social responsibility and corporate web pages: self-presentation or agenda-setting? *Public Relations Review* 24 (3), 305–26.

Font, X. (2002) 'Environmental certification in tourism and hospitality: progress, process and prospects', *Tourism Management* 23, 197–205.

Fryxell, G.E., and Wang, J. (1994) 'The Fortune corporate 'reputation' index: reputation for what?', *Journal of Management* 20 (1), 1–14.

GRI (2006) *Sustainability reporting guidelines.* Global Reporting Initiative.

Holcomb, J.L., Upchurch, R.S., and Okumus, F. (2007) 'Corporate social responsibility: What are top hotel companies reporting?', *International Journal of Contemporary Hospitality Management* 19, 461–75.

Holland, L. (2003) 'Can the principle of the ecological footprint be applied to measure the environmental sustainability of business?', *Corporate Social Responsibility and Environmental Management* 10, 224–32.

Honey, M. and Stewart, E. (2002) 'The Evolution of 'Green' Standards for Tourism', in M. Honey (ed.). *Ecotourism & Certification: Setting standards in practice.* Washington, DC: Island Press.

Hooper, P.D., and Greenall, A. (2005) 'Exploring the potential for environmental performance benchmarking in the airline sector', *Benchmarking* 12, 151–65.

Igalens, J., and Gond, J.P. (2005) 'Measuring corporate social performance in France: A critical and empirical analysis of ARESE Data', *Journal of Business Ethics* 56 (2), 131–48.

Krajnc, D., and Glavic, P. (2005) 'How to compare companies on relevant dimensions of sustainability', *Ecological Economics*, 55 (4) 551–63.

Korhonen, J. (2003) 'Should we measure corporate social responsibility?', *Corporate Social Responsibility and Environmental Management* 10, 25–39.

Lamberton, G. (2005) 'Sustainability accounting: A brief history and conceptual framework', *Accounting Forum* 29 (1), 7–26.

Lewis, S. (2001) 'Measuring corporate reputation. *Corporate Communication: An International Journal*, 6(1), 31–35.

Maignan, I. and Ralston, D.A. (2002) 'Corporate Social Responsibility in Europe and the U.S.: Insights from Businesses' Self-Presentations'. *Journal of International Business Studies* 33(3), 497–514.

Mak, B., Chan, W., Wong, K., and Zheng, C. (2007) 'Comparative studies of standalone environmental reports – European and Asian airlines', *Transportation Research Part D* 12, 45–52.

Moneva, J.M., Archel, P., and Correa, C. (2006) 'GRI and the camouflaging of corporate unsustainability', *Accounting Forum* 30, 121–37.

Spittler, R. and Haak, U. (2001) 'Quality Analysis of Tourism Ecolabels', in X. Font and R.C. Buckley (eds). *Tourism Ecolabelling: Certification and promotion of sustainable management*. Oxford and New York: CABI Publishing.

Synergy. (2000) *Tourism Certification*. WWF-UK.

Synnestvedt, T. (2001) 'Debates over environmental information to stakeholders as a policy instrument', *Eco-Management and Auditing* 8, 165–78.

Toth, R. (2002) 'Exploring the Concepts Underlying Certification', in M. Honey (ed.). *Ecotourism & Certification: Setting standards in practice*. Washington, DC: Island Press.

Ullman, A. (1985) 'Data in search of theory: a critical examination of the relationship among social performance, social disclosure and economic performance of US firms', *Academy of Management Review* 10, 540–57.

UNEP and WTO (2005) *Making tourism more sustainable: A guide for policy makers*. United Nations Environmental Programme & World Tourism Organization.

UNEP (1998) *Ecolabels in the tourism industry*. Paris: United Nations Environmental Programme.

Upham, P.J., and Mills, J.N. (2005) 'Environmental and operational sustainability of airports: Core indicators and stakeholder communication', *Benchmarking: An International Journal* 12 (2), 166–79.

Wartick, S.L. and Cochran, P.L. (1985) 'The evolution of the corporate social performance model', *Academy of Management Review* 10, 758–69.

WBCSD (1999) *Corporate social responsibility: Meeting changing expectations*, World Business Council for Sustainable Development.

Wiedmann, T.O., Lenzen, M., and Barrett, J.R. (2009) 'Companies on the scale: Comparing and benchmarking the sustainability performance of businesses', *Journal of Industrial Ecology* 13 (3), 361–83.

Wokutch, R.E., and McKinney, E.W. (1991) 'Behavioral and perceptual measures of corporate social performance', in J.E. Post (ed.), *Research in Corporate Social Performance and Policy* 12, 309–30.

Wood, D.J. (1991) 'Corporate social performance revisited', *Academy of Management Review* 16, 691–718.

——(2010) 'Measuring corporate social performance: A review', *International Journal of Management Reviews* 50–84.

WRI and WBCSD (2004) *The greenhouse gas protocol: A corporate accounting and reporting standard, revised edition*. World Resources Institute and World Business Council for Sustainable Development.

WTO (2002) *Voluntary Initiatives for Sustainable Tourism*. Madrid: UN World Tourism Organization.

Index

van der Aa, B.J.M., Groote, P.D. and Huigen, P.P.
    P. 284
ABC Radio 133
Aboriginality: Aboriginal styles, casual and habitual
    appropriation of 48; defined by 'West' 48;
    differentiation as distinct and separate culture 46–
    47; process of 50; spirituality and 44–45;
    traditional Aboriginality, interpretability of
    45–46, 49; transitional Aboriginality,
    interpretability of 46
Abram, D. 23
ABTA 498
ACAP 524
accelerated global warming, consequences of
    409–10
acceptable change, limits of 285–96; acceptability
    294–96
Access Economics 545
accreditation in ecotourism 328–29
Acompora, R.R. 10, 11, 332
Acott, T.G., La Trobe, H.L. and Howard, S.H. 336
acute mountain sickness (AMS) 125
Adam of Usk 54
Adams, Ansell 104
Adams, M. 450–51
Adams, W.M. and Hulme, D. 147, 148
Adamson, S.H. 106
Adapa, P.K., Tabil, L.G. and Schoenau, G.J. 465
adaptation: adaptive capacity and stakeholder
    involvement 509–10; adaptive management of
    marine systems 178; climate change and 234; and
    investment in, vulnerability of tourism to climate
    change and 252, 253
adaptive co-management, nature-based tourism and
    541–51; actionability 544; adaptive
    co-management, definition of 542–43, 551;
    Association of Marine Park Tourism Operators
    (AMPTO) 548, 549; attributes of adaptive
    co-management 542–43; Center for
    International Forestry Research (CIFOR) 542;
    conceptual consistency 544; environmental
    understanding 541–42; ethical integrity 544;
    'governance,' phenomenon of shift from
    'government' to 541; Great Barrier Reef,

probing possible application of adaptive co-
    management to
    545–50, 551; idealised models of environmental
    governance 542; learning and adaptation, issues
    related to 551; linkages, levels and autonomy,
    issues related to 550; *Onboard: The Tourism
    Operators' Handbook for the Great Barrier Reef*
    (online) 549; pluralism and communication,
    issues related to 550; potential for adaptive
    co-management in tourism 543–44; pragmatism
    544; Queensland Tourism Industry Council 549;
    shared decision-making and authority, issues
    related to 550–51; sustainable tourism
    co-management process 546; Tourism and
    Recreation Reef Advisory Committee
    (TRRAC) 548, 549, 550; Tourism Climate
    Change Action Group (TCCAG) 548, 549
Addison, Joseph 55
Adey, P. and Anderson, B. 532
Adger, W. *et al.* 227, 228, 509
Adger, W.N. 509
Adger, W.N., Lorenzone, I. and O'Brein, K.L. 234
Adler, M.J. and Gormon, W. 95
adventure tourism 334
aesthetics, importance of 65–74; aesthetic
    appreciation of natural environments 65–66;
    aesthetic appreciation of nature 66–69; aesthetic
    'appropriateness' 68; aesthetic-consumable
    orientation to Nature 100–101; aesthetic
    engagement. 67; aesthetic interest, conception of
    67; aesthetic sensibilities, shifts and changes in
    78–79; aesthetic values 65, 73; aesthetically
    problematic responses 70–71; 'Attention
    Restoration Theory' 72–73; authenticity, well-
    being and tourist gaze 71–73; conceptual issues
    65–66; 'disinterestedness,' idea of 66; escapism
    72; further reading 74; 'mode of travel' 71–72;
    motivations for tourism 67; natural beauty,
    pitfalls of 'serious' tourism and 72–73; *Natural
    Environmental Model* (Carlson, A.) 67–68;
    perception of nature's aesthetic qualities 67–68;
    role of the aesthetic in tourism 66; romantic
    ideals of Nature, aesthetic debate on 58;
    romanticisation 70; sentimentality 70;

567